"Value-packed... comprehensive

"Unbeatable...

—*The Washington Post*

Let's Go
ALASKA &
THE PACIFIC NORTHWEST

is the best book for anyone traveling on a budget. Here's why:

■ No other guidebook has as many budget listings.

Take Vancouver, for example. We list 7 hotels and hostels where you can stay for under $35 a night. We tell you how to get there the cheapest way, whether by bus, plane, or bike, and where to get an inexpensive and satisfying meal once you've arrived. We give hundreds of money-saving tips that anyone can use, plus invaluable advice on discounts and deals for students, children, families, and senior travelers.

■ Let's Go researchers have to make it on their own.

Our Harvard-Radcliffe researcher-writers travel on budgets as tight as your own—no expense accounts, no free hotel rooms.

■ Let's Go is completely revised each year.

We don't just update the prices, we go back to the place. If a charming café has become an overpriced tourist trap, we'll replace the listing with a new and better one.

■ No other guidebook includes all this:

Honest, engaging coverage of both the cities and the countryside; up-to-the-minute prices, directions, addresses, phone numbers, and opening hours; in-depth essays on local culture, history, and politics; comprehensive listings on transportation between and within regions and cities; straight advice on work and study, budget accommodations, sights, nightlife, and food; detailed city and regional maps; and much more.

■ Let's Go is for anyone who wants to see Alaska and the Pacific Northwest on a budget.

Books by Let's Go, Inc.

EUROPE

Let's Go: Europe

Let's Go: Austria

Let's Go: Britain & Ireland

Let's Go: France

Let's Go: Germany & Switzerland

Let's Go: Greece & Turkey

Let's Go: Ireland

Let's Go: Italy

Let's Go: London

Let's Go: Paris

Let's Go: Rome

Let's Go: Spain & Portugal

NORTH & CENTRAL AMERICA

Let's Go: USA & Canada

Let's Go: Alaska & The Pacific Northwest

Let's Go: California & Hawaii

Let's Go: New York City

Let's Go: Washington, D.C.

Let's Go: Mexico

MIDDLE EAST & ASIA

Let's Go: Israel & Egypt

Let's Go: Thailand

Let's Go

The Budget Guide to

ALASKA & THE PACIFIC NORTHWEST

1994

Mira M. Kothari
Editor

Benjamin Peskoe
Assistant Editor

Written by
Let's Go, Inc.
A subsidiary of
Harvard Student Agencies, Inc.

M
Macmillan Reference

HELPING LET'S GO

If you have suggestions or corrections, or just want to share your discoveries, drop us a line. We read every piece of correspondence, whether a 10-page letter, a velveteen Elvis postcard, or, as in one case, a collage. All suggestions are passed along to our researcher-writers. Please note that mail received after May 5, 1994 will probably be too late for the 1995 book, but will be retained for the following edition. Address mail to:

Let's Go: Alaska & The Pacific Northwest
Let's Go, Inc.
1 Story Street
Cambridge, MA 02138
USA

In addition to the invaluable travel advice our readers share with us, many are kind enough to offer their services as researchers or editors. Unfortunately, the charter of Let's Go, Inc. and Harvard Student Agencies, Inc. enables us to employ only currently enrolled Harvard students.

Published in Great Britain 1994 by Pan Macmillan Ltd., Cavaye Place, London SW10 9PG.

10 9 8 7 6 5 4 3 2 1

Maps by David Lindroth, copyright © 1994, 1993, 1992, 1991, 1990, 1988 by St. Martin's Press, Inc.

Published in the United States of America by St. Martin's Press, Inc.

ISBN: 0 333 61161 6

Let's Go: Alaska & The Pacific Northwest is written by the Publishing Division of Let's Go, Inc., 1 Story Street, Cambridge, MA 02138.

Let's Go® is a registered trademark of Let's Go, Inc.
Printed in the U.S.A. on recycled paper with biodegradable soy ink.

Acknowledgments

Researcher-Writers

Sergio Camacho grappled with a trunk load of camera equipment and a mother lode of work for two *Let's Go* guides. Sergio's divine ability to transform his frank responses into insightful writing never left him, not even in Hell's Canyon.

Jen Etter completed a colossal and exhausting itinerary across Washington and Oregon without losing the relaxed outlook of a true native. We just hope we left her enough time to dip her toe into the waters at the Oregon shoreline.

Seth Harkness was a flawless researcher who sent back flawless prose that made us feel superfluous. He packed the guide with astute observations, intriguing history, and magnificent meals which appealed to the glutton and the miser in all of us.

Matthew Heid trekked north until he could go no farther. He trekked west until he could go no farther. He covered Historic Chicken. Never has one researcher covered such a vast expanse of land (and covered it so damn well). Let's Go Travel *Incorporated*. Word.

Liz Potter's difficult start may have forced her into discovering the joy's of public transportation, but it never slowed her down. Her enthusiasm and hard work benefitted both the guide and our spirits back at 1 Story.

A special *gracias* goes to **Thomas Lauderdale** for his uncanny knowledge of Portland and under-Portland. *Muy bueno!* Great thanks to **Alaska Pass** and **Greyhound Canada,** whose generosity made our researchers' lives much easier.

Vicariously traveling through Alaska inspired me during the entire production of this guide. But, inspiration would not have brought me to the final frontier without Ben's intelligence, organization, diligence, and sharp wit. Ben was a stellar co-editor whose work I admired all summer. Dov's help and support were critical, especially as the nights got longer, and longer. Peter deserves congratulations for being a great Managing Editor. Dan and Maia, you helped pull it all together.

Thanks to: Lynne for synchronous spirit; JT for unfaltering brilliance; Andorra room for my kind of delirium; Moody for the free spree; UGH+Lindy+Amy, for teaching me not to like spinning restaurant/bars; Ed and Mark for inimitable efficiency; Sid for reminding me about lunch; Justin for being here more; Thailand for being here after. PH for actually going; Alyssa, Lisa, Laurie, AmyB, and Sabina for understanding; Lori for *Miralor*; Suzy for being there from the start; Mummy, Papa, Priti, and Shefali for my life's core.   **MMK**

Mira put much of her time and still more of herself into this book, and it shows—she did a wonderful job. To Dov, Daniel, Ben, and David, many thanks and much respect. Thanks also to Pete Keith for his steady guidance through our twelve-step summer, and especially for helping to pull us through in the final days; to Mike Balagur for leaving us such a fine book to work with; to Ed Owen for being so competent and capable; to Marc and Jahan, friendly tenants of benhostel; to Maia for always offering her help; to Mike and Sarthak in Mexico; to Mimi, Peter, Amy, Lynne, Alex, JT, Alexis, Justin, Moody, John, Liz, Brian, Dave, and all of the other great people in this office. Finally, thanks and love to my family. Nick—I AM HAVING FUN (Direct Quote).   **BRP**

Contents

■ Maps

About Let's Go

Back in 1960, a few students at Harvard got together to produce a 20-page pamphlet offering a collection of tips on budget travel in Europe. For three years, Harvard Student Agencies, a student-run nonprofit corporation, had been doing a brisk business booking charter flights to Europe; this modest, mimeographed packet was offered to passengers as an extra. The following year, students traveling to Europe researched the first full-fledged edition of *Let's Go: Europe*, a pocket-sized book featuring advice on shoestring travel, irreverent write-ups of sights, and a decidedly youthful slant.

Throughout the 60s, the guides reflected the times: one section of the 1968 *Let's Go: Europe* talked about "Street Singing in Europe on No Dollars a Day." During the 70s, *Let's Go* gradually became a large-scale operation, adding regional European guides and expanding coverage into North Africa and Asia. The 80s saw the arrival of *Let's Go: USA & Canada* and *Let's Go: Mexico*, as well as regional North American guides; in the 90s we introduced five in-depth city guides to Paris, London, Rome, New York, and Washington, DC.

This year we're proud to announce three new guides: *Let's Go: Austria* (including Prague and Budapest), *Let's Go: Ireland*, and *Let's Go: Thailand* (including Honolulu, Tokyo, and Singapore), bringing our total number of titles up to twenty.

We've seen a lot in thirty-four years. *Let's Go: Europe* is now the world's #1 best selling international guide, translated into seven languages. And our guides are still researched, written, and produced entirely by students who know firsthand how to see the world on the cheap.

Every spring, we recruit nearly 100 researchers and an editorial team of 50 to write our books anew. Come summertime, after several months of training, researchers hit the road for seven weeks of exploration, from Bangkok to Budapest, Anchorage to Ankara. With pen and notebook in hand, a few changes of underwear stuffed in our backpacks, and a budget as tight as yours, we visit every *pensione*, *palapa*, pizzeria, café, club, campground, or castle we can find to make sure you'll get the most out of *your* trip.

We've put the best of our discoveries into the book you're now holding. A brand-new edition of each guide hits the shelves every year, only months after it was researched, so you know you're getting the most reliable, up-to-date, and comprehensive information available. And even as you read this, work on next year's editions is well underway.

At *Let's Go*, we think of budget travel not only as a means of cutting down on costs, but as a way of breaking down a few walls as well. Living cheap and simple on the road brings you closer to the real people and places you've been saving up to visit. This book will ease your anxieties and answer your questions about the basics—to help *you* get off the beaten track and explore. We encourage you to put *Let's Go* away now and then and strike out on your own. As any seasoned traveler will tell you, the best discoveries are often those you make yourself. If you find something worth sharing, drop us a line and let us know. We're at Let's Go, Inc., 1 Story Street, Cambridge, MA, 02138, USA.

Happy travels!

How To Use This Book

Let's Go: Alaska & The Pacific Northwest is written especially for the budget traveler. The **Essentials** section provides information that you will need to know *before*
you leave. **Planning Your Trip** lets you know where to write for information about
the region; what to do about customs, visas, and the bureaucratic blah; how to stay
safe and healthy; what to do if you'd like to work and/or study on your sojourn; and
how to pack. **Getting There and Getting Around** sorts out the various modes of
transportation to and around the region. **Once There** helps you to find the cheapest and the cleanest in Accommodations and provides detailed information on
Camping and the Outdoors. The **Appendix** is a quick reference for information on
telephones, time zones, holidays, and metric conversions.

The main body of the guide is divided into two parts: Alaska and the Pacific Northwest. **Alaska** opens with coverage of Anchorage and the southcentral part of the
state. The second chapter discusses the voyage up the Panhandle and the third section heads toward Fairbanks and the Interior. Alaskan wilderness is discussed at
length in the fourth chapter entitled The Bush. The **Pacific Northwest** regions
include: British Columbia, the Yukon Territory, Alberta, Washington, and Oregon.
The coverage of each of these areas, excluding the Yukon, begins with a major metropolitan area. Keep in mind that these exciting cities also provide gateways into
the surrounding parks and wilderness areas. The Yukon follows British Columbia in
order to best serve readers driving to Alaska. However, many of the Yukon's towns
border Alaska and can be cross-referenced from Alaska when needed.

For each specific area, the guide lists **Practical and Orientation Information,
Accommodations, Food,** and **Sights.** A discussion of hiking and paddling in the
Outdoors follows Sights when appropriate. It may be useful to flip through a few
sections to familiarize yourself with the book; understanding its structure will help
you make the most of the wealth of information we offer.

A NOTE TO OUR READERS

The information for this book is gathered by *Let's Go*'s researchers during
the late spring and summer months. Each listing is derived from the assigned
researcher's opinion based upon his or her visit at a particular time. The
opinions are expressed in a candid and forthright manner. Other travelers
might disagree. Those traveling at a different time may have different experiences since prices, dates, hours, and conditions are always subject to
change. You are urged to check beforehand to avoid inconvenience and sur-
prises. Travel always involves a certain degree of risk, especially in low-cost
areas. When traveling, especially on a budget, you should always take particular care to ensure your safety.

ESSENTIALS

▩ Planning Your Trip

Planning ahead is one of the keys to an enjoyable vacation. Spend the time now rather than later getting in touch with travel resources in Alaska and the Pacific Northwest, and figuring out how to handle the basic issues: when to go, how to have enough money on hand, how to remain in good health, and a variety of other concerns small and large. Set aside a few hours well before your trip begins to make calls and write letters to organizations with useful information, and to compile lists of things to consider and bring along. It'll save you time and frustration once you hit the road and will help you take crises and unforeseen circumstances in stride.

As you plan your itinerary, it's a good idea to consult the *Let's Go* listings for the specific destinations you intend to include. Tourist Bureaus and Chambers of Commerce can send you information in advance that can help you to plan (see addresses listed below, and also check the Practical Information sections within cities and regions themselves). For other organizations catering to travelers with specific interests or needs, see the section on Specific Concerns below.

■■■ WHEN TO GO

Traveling is like comedy —timing is everything. In the Pacific Northwest, your rival concerns will be the tourist season and the weather. In general, summer (June-Aug.) is high season; during those months, you can expect to share the warm weather with crowds of fellow tourists. If you prefer to experience the region as its human and animal residents do, go during the off-season when crowds are smaller and rates are lower. Beware the disadvantages of winter travel in certain parts, however— slush, icy roads, and prohibitively cold weather (especially in Northern Canada and Alaska) will constrain your movement and your desire to be outdoors. All things considered, May and September may be the best times to travel in the Northwest.

■■■ USEFUL ORGANIZATIONS AND PUBLICATIONS

■ Tourist Bureaus

Each state and province has its own travel bureau (listed below), which can refer you to other useful organizations, send you travel brochures and maps, and answer your specific questions about the region. One good general resource worth writing to is the **U.S. Government Printing Office,** Superintendent of Documents, U.S. Government Printing Office, Washington, DC 20402 (202-783-3238). Among the government's many publications are a wide selection of travel and recreation guides. *Let's Go* lists many of the most useful, but you can call or write for complete bibliographies. Bibliography #17 deals with outdoor activities in general, and #302 with travel to particular regions. The pamphlet *Travel and Tourism* covers travel within the U.S.

Alaska Division of Tourism, P.O. Box 110801, Juneau, AK 99811 (907-465-2010).

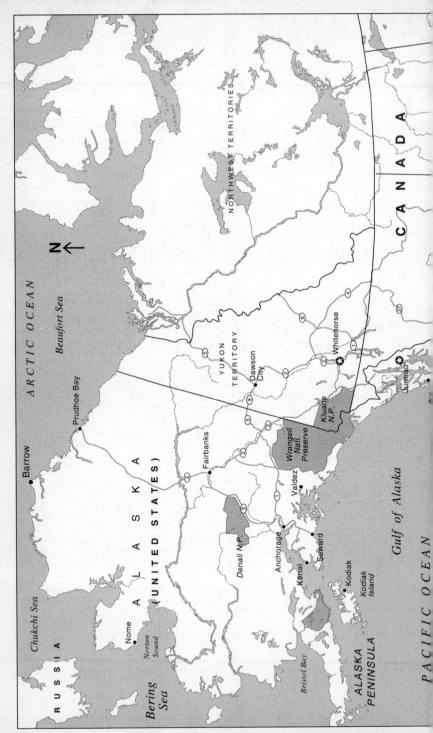

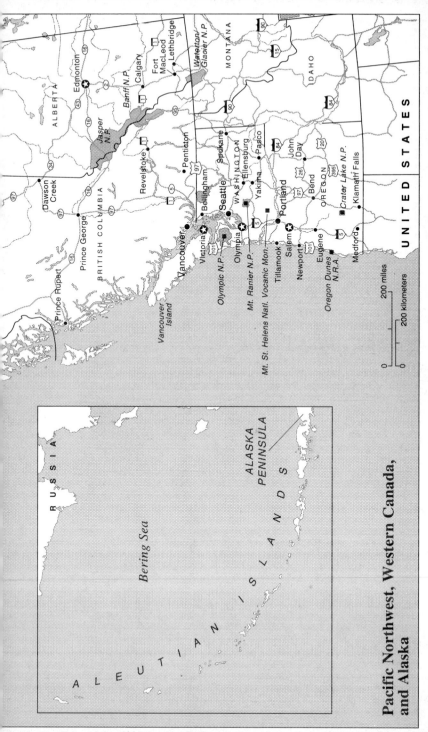

Pacific Northwest, Western Canada, and Alaska

Alberta Tourism, City Centre Building, 10155 102nd St., Edmonton, AB T5J 4L6 (800-222-6501; 800-661-8888 outside Alberta).

Tourism British Columbia, 1117 Wharf St., Victoria, BC V8W 2Z2 (604-387-1428 or 800-663-6000).

Oregon Tourism Division, Dept. of Trade and Economic Development, 775 Summer St. NE, Salem, OR 97310 (800-543-8838; 800-547-7842 outside Oregon).

Washington Tourism Division, Dept. of Trade and Economic Development, 101 General Administration Bldg., Olympia, WA 98504-0613 (800-544-1800 for free travel booklet; 206-586-2088 for general information).

Yukon Department of Tourism, P.O. Box 2703, Whitehorse, YT Y1A 2C6 (403-667-5340).

U.S. Travel and Tourism Administration (USTTA), Department of Commerce, 14th St. and Constitution Ave. NW, Washington, DC 20230 (202-482-4003 or 202-482-3811). USTTA has branches in Australia, Belgium, Canada, France, Germany, Japan, Mexico, and the United Kingdom; contact the Washington office for information about the branch in your country. Provides information for those planning to travel to the U.S.

■ Budget Travel Services

Council on International Educational Exchange (CIEE/Council Travel/Council Charter): Provides low-cost travel arrangements, books (including *Let's Go* and *Where to Stay U.S.A.)* and gear. CIEE affiliates can charter airline tickets, arrange homestays, sell international student ID cards, travel literature, travel insurance, and hostel cards. Operates 43 offices throughout the U.S., including those listed below and branches in Boston, MA; Dallas, TX; Chicago, IL; and San Diego, CA. **Los Angeles,** 1093 Broxton Ave. #220, CA 90024 (310-208-3551). **New York,** 205 E. 42nd St., NY 10017 (212-661-1450; 800-223-7402 for charter flights only). **Portland,** 715 S.W. Morrison #600, OR 97205 (503-228-1900). **San Francisco,** 919 Irving St. #102, CA 94122 (415-566-6222). **Seattle,** 1314 N.E. 43rd St. #210, WA 98105 (206-632-2448). **London,** 28A Poland St., England W1V 3DB (tel. (071) 437 7767). CIEE also helps students secure work visas and find employment through its **work-exchange programs.**

CIEE International Affiliates: Canada: Travel CUTS (Canadian University Travel Services Limited), 187 College St., Toronto, Ont. M5T 1P7 (416-979-2406). In Britain, 295-A Regent St., London W1R 7YA (tel. (071) 637 31 61). **Australia: SSA Swap Program,** P.O. Box 399 (1st Floor), 220 Faraday St., Carlton South, Melbourne, Victoria 3053 (tel. (03) 348 1777). **United Kingdom: London Student Travel,** 52 Grosvenor Gardens, London WC1 (tel. (071) 730 34 02). For other international affiliates, contact CIEE's main office in New York (see address above) or the International Student Travel Confederation (see address below).

STA Travel, 17 E. 45th St., New York, NY 10017 (800-777-0112 or 212-986-9470) Worldwide youth travel organization which offers discount airfares for travelers under 26 and full-time students under 32. Also offers railpasses, accommodations, tours, insurance, and ISICs. Operates 10 offices in the U.S. and more than 100 offices around the world. **Los Angeles,** 7202 Melrose Ave., CA 90046 (213-934-8722). **New York,** 48 E. 11th St., NY 10003 (212-477-7166). **San Francisco,** 51 Grant Ave., CA 94108 (415-391-8407). In the **United Kingdom,** STA's main offices are at 86 Old Brompton Rd., London SW7 3LQ England and 117 Euston Rd., London NW1 2SX (tel. (071) 937 99 71). In **New Zealand** they're at 10 High St., Auckland (tel. (09) 309 9995).

International Student Travel Confederation (ISTC), Store Kongensgade 40H, 1264 Copenhagen K, Denmark (tel. 45 33 93 93 03). Affiliated with travel agencies throughout the world which arrange charter flights and discount air fares, provide travel insurance, issue International Student Identity Cards, and sponsor the Student Air Travel Association for European students.

American Automobile Association (AAA), 1000 AAA Drive (mail stop 100), Heathrow, FL 32746-5080 (407-444-7883), and **Canadian Automobile Association (CAA),** 60 Commerce Valley Drive East, Thornhill, Ont. L3T 7P9 (416-771-3111). Permits such as the **International Driver's Permit (IDP)** are available if needed, but check with the car rental agency before you purchase one—they may not require it. The permit, valid for 1 year, is available from any AAA or CAA affiliate. For more information on AAA and CAA, see Getting There and Getting Around: By Car; for more information on the IDP, see Documents and Formalities.

Educational Travel Centre (ETC), 438 North Frances St., Madison, WI 53703 (608-256-5551). Flight information, HI/AYH cards, Eurail and regional rail passes. Write for their free pamphlet *Taking Off.*

Campus Travel, 52 Grosvenor Gardens, London SW1W 0AG (tel. (071) 730 8832; fax (071) 730 5739). Budget travel service offering discount fares, IDs, insurance, maps, and guides.

International Student Exchange Flights (ISE), 5010 East Shea Blvd., #A104, Scottsdale, AZ 85254 (602-951-1177). Budget student flights, BritRail and Eurail passes, traveler's checks, and travel guides. Free catalog.

Let's Go Travel, Harvard Student Agencies, 53a Church St., Cambridge, MA 02138 (617-495-9649 or 800-553-8746).

USIT Ltd., Aston Quay, O'Connell Bridge, Dublin 2 (tel. (01) 679 8833; fax (01) 677 8843).

■ Useful Publications

Animal and Plant Health Inspection Service, U.S. Department of Agriculture, 6505 Belcrest Road, Hyattsville, MD 20782-2058. Provides information about restrictions in the wildlife trade, as well as a pamphlet titled *Travelers' Tips on Bringing Food, Plant, and Animal Products into the United States.*

Forsyth Travel Library, P.O. Box 2975, Shawnee Mission, KS 66201 (800-367-7984). Call or write for their catalog of maps, guides, railpasses and timetables.

Hippocrene Books, Inc., 171 Madison Ave., New York, NY 10016 (212-685-4371; orders 718-454-2360; fax 718-454-1391). Free catalog. Publishes travel reference books, travel guides, maps, and foreign language dictionaries.

Rand McNally publishes one of the most comprehensive road atlases of the U.S. and Canada, available in most bookstores for US$8.

Travelling Books, PO Box 77114, Seattle, WA 98177, publishes a comprehensive catalogue of travel guides.

Wide World Books and Maps, 1911 N. 45th St., Seattle, WA 98103 (206-634-3453). A good selection of hard-to-find maps. Open Mon.-Fri. 10am-7pm, Sat. 10am-6pm, Sun. noon-5pm.

■■■ DOCUMENTS AND FORMALITIES

Be sure to file all applications several weeks or (better) months in advance of your planned departure date. Applications can take a considerable amount of time to process. Moreover, the agency might deem your applications inadequate and return them to you, so you should allow time for resubmission. Most offices suggest that you apply in the winter off-season (Aug.-Dec.) for speedier service.

When you travel, *always carry on your person two or more forms of identification, including at least one photo ID.* A passport combined with a driver's license or birth certificate usually serves as adequate proof of your identity and citizenship. Many establishments, especially banks, require several IDs before cashing traveler's checks. Never carry your passport, travel ticket, identification documents, money, traveler's checks, insurance, and credit cards all together; one instance of absent-mindedness or thievery could leave you bereft of IDs and funds. It is wise to carry a few extra passport-size photos that you can attach to the sundry IDs you will eventually acquire. If you plan an extended stay, you might want to register your passport with the nearest embassy or consulate.

■ Entrance Requirements

International visitors to the United States and Canada are required to have a **passport, visitor's visa,** and **proof of intent to leave** (for example, an exiting plane ticket). To visit Canada, you must be healthy and law-abiding, and demonstrate ability to support yourself financially during your stay. To work or study in the U.S. or Canada, you must obtain special documents (see Work and Study, below).

U.S. or Canadian citizens who are adults may cross the **U.S.-Canadian border** with only proof of citizenship (passport, birth certificate, or voter registration card) while those under 18 need the written consent of a parent or guardian. At the U.S.-Canadian border, persons who are not citizens of either country will need a visa to cross in either direction (citizens of Greenland excepted). See the Visas section below for further exceptions and restrictions. Naturalized citizens should have their naturalization papers with them; occasionally officials will ask to see them.

Canada places severe limits on what **firearms** may be brought into the country. Contact a Canadian consulate with questions. Canadian customs officials are equally stringent in regard to **crafts and other souvenirs** made with the skins or bones of wild animals. Ivory is one example of a substance which may be transported from Alaska into the Continental U.S., but which may not be transported through Canada without permission. Seal, sea-lion, and whale products are other restricted items.

Mexican citizens may cross into the U.S. with an I-186 form. Mexican border crossing cards (non-immigrant visas) prohibit you from staying more than 72 hours in the U.S., or traveling more than 25 mi. from the border.

■ Passports

As a precaution in case your passport is lost or stolen, be sure *before you leave* to photocopy the page of your passport that contains your photograph and identifying information. Especially important is your passport number. Carry this photocopy in a safe place apart from your passport, perhaps with a traveling companion, and leave another copy at home. Better yet, carry a photocopy of all the pages of the passport, including all visa stamps, apart from your actual passport, and leave a duplicate copy with a relative or friend. These measures will help prove your citizenship and facilitate the issuing of a new passport. Consulates also recommend that you carry an expired passport or an *official* copy of your birth certificate (not the one issued at birth, of course) in a part of your baggage separate from other documents. You can request a duplicate birth certificate from the appropriate piece of your home country's bureaucratic pie.

Losing your passport can be a nightmare. It may take weeks to process a replacement, and your new passport may be valid only for a limited time. In addition, any visas stamped in your old passport will be irretrievably lost. If it is lost or stolen, immediately notify the local police and the nearest embassy or consulate of your home government. To expedite the replacement of your passport, you will need to know all the information that you had previously recorded and photocopied and to show identification and proof of citizenship.

Applying for a passport is complicated, so make sure your questions are answered in advance; you don't want to wait two hours in a passport office just to be told you'll have to return tomorrow because your application is insufficient.

British citizens are required to obtain a full passport for entrance into the U.S. or Canada. Full passports are valid for 10 years (5 yr. if under 16); apply in person or by mail to the London Passport Office or to an office located in Liverpool, Newport, Peterborough, Glasgow, or Belfast. The fee is £18. Children under 16 may be included on a parent's passport. Processing usually takes four to six weeks. The London office offers same-day walk-in rush service; arrive early.

Irish citizens can apply for a passport by mail to one of the following two passport offices: Department of Foreign Affairs, Passport Office, Setanta Centre, Molesworth St., Dublin 2 (tel. (01) 671 1633), or Passport Office, 1A South Mall, Cork (tel. 021 272 525). You can obtain an application form at a local Garda station or request one from a passport office. Passports cost £45 and are valid for 10 years. Citizens younger than 18 and older than 65 can request a 3 year passport that costs £10.

Australian citizens must apply for a passport in person at a local post office, a passport office, or an Australian diplomatic mission overseas. An appointment may be necessary at all three. Passport offices are located in Adelaide, Brisbane, Canberra, Darwin, Hobart, Melbourne, Newcastle, Perth, and Sydney. Application fees are adjusted every three months; call the toll free information service for current details (tel. 13-12-32).

Applicants for **New Zealand passports** must contact their local Link Centre, travel agent, or New Zealand Representative for an application form, which they must complete and mail to the New Zealand Passport Office, Documents of National Identity Division, Department of Internal Affairs, Box 10-526, Wellington (tel. (04) 474 81 00). Overseas citizens should send the passport application to the nearest embassy, high commission, or consulate that is authorized to issue passports.

South African citizens can apply for a passport at a Home Affairs Office. Two photos, either a birth certificate or an identity book, and the R30 fee must accompany an application. For more information, contact the nearest Home Affairs Office.

■ Visas

A visa is an endorsement that a foreign government stamps into a passport; it allows the bearer to stay in that country for a specified purpose and period of time. Most visas cost US$10-30 and allow you to spend about a month in a country, within six months to a year from the date of issue.

To acquire a visa for entrance to the **U.S.,** you will need your passport and proof of intent to leave. Contact the nearest U.S. consulate to obtain your visa.

Visitors from certain nations may enter the U.S. without visas through the **Visa Waiver Pilot Program.** Travelers qualify as long as they are traveling for business or pleasure, are staying for 90 days or less, have proof of intent to leave and a completed form I-94W, and enter aboard particular air or sea carriers. Participating countries are Andorra, Austria, Belgium, Denmark, Finland, France, Germany, Iceland, Italy, Japan, Liechtenstein, Luxembourg, Monaco, the Netherlands, New Zealand, Norway, San Marino, Spain, Sweden, Switzerland, and the U.K. Contact the nearest U.S. consulate for more information.

To acquire a visa for entrance to the **Canada,** you will need your passport and proof of intent to leave. Contact the nearest Canadian consulate to obtain your visa.

Visitors from certain nations may enter Canada without visas. Travelers qualify if they are staying for 90 days or less, have proof of intent to leave, and are citizens of Australia, the Bahamas, Barbados, Costa Rica, Dominica, the E.C., Singapore, Swaziland, the U.K., the U.S., Venezuela, Western Samoa, or Zimbabwe. Contact the nearest Canadian consulate for more information.

If you want to stay longer, apply for a visa at a U.S. or Canadian embassy or consulate in your home country well before your departure. Unless you are a student, extending your stay once you are abroad is more difficult. You must contact the country's immigration officials or local police well before your time is up. You must show sound proof of financial resources (see Entrance Requirements).

For more information, get the U.S. government pamphlet *Foreign Visa Requirements*. Mail a check for 50¢ to Consumer Information Center, Dept. 454V, Pueblo, CO 81009 (719-948-3334). One way to circumvent an often baffling bureaucracy is to contact **Visa Center, Inc.,** 507 Fifth Ave. #904, New York, NY 10017 (212-986-0924). This company secures visas for travel to and from all possible countries. The service charge varies; the average cost for a U.S. citizen is US$15-20 per visa.

■ Customs

Unless you plan to import something as exotic as a BMW or a barnyard beast, you will probably pass right over the customs barrier with minimal ado. The many rules and regulations of customs and duties hardly pose a threat to the budget traveler. Most countries prohibit or restrict the importation of firearms, explosives, ammunition, fireworks, controlled drugs, most plants and animals, lottery tickets, and obscene literature and films. To avoid problems when you transport **prescription drugs,** ensure that the bottles are clearly marked, and carry a copy of the prescription to show the customs officer.

Upon returning home, you must declare all articles acquired abroad and pay a duty on the value of those articles that exceeds your country's established allowance. Holding onto receipts for purchases made abroad will help establish values when you return. It is wise to *make a list*, including serial numbers, of any valuables that you carry from home; register this list with customs before your departure and have an official stamp it, and you will avoid import duty charges and ensure an easy passage upon return. Be especially careful to document items manufactured abroad.

Keep in mind that goods and gifts purchased at duty-free shops abroad are not exempt from duty or sales tax at your point of return; you must declare these items along with other purchases. **"Duty-free"** merely means that you need not pay a tax in the country of purchase.

United States citizens returning home face a variety of restrictions. For more information, consult the brochure *Know Before You Go*, available from R. Woods, Consumer Information Center, Pueblo, CO 81009 (item 477Y). You can direct other questions to the U.S. Customs Service, P.O. Box 7407, Washington, DC 20044 (202-927-6724). Foreign nationals living in the U.S. are subject to different regulations; refer the leaflet *Customs Hints for Visitors (Nonresidents)*. **Canadian citizens** should contact External Affairs, Communications Branch, Mackenzie Ave., Ottawa, Ontario, K1A 0L5 (613-957-0275). **British citizens** should contact Her Majesty's Customs and Excise, Custom House, Heathrow Airport North, Hounslow, Middlesex, TW6 2LA (tel. (081) 750 16 03; fax (081) 750 15 49). *HM Customs & Excise Notice 1* explains the allowances for people traveling to the U.K. both from within and without the European Community. **Irish citizens** should contact The Revenue Commissioners, Dublin Castle (tel. (01) 679 2777; fax (01) 671 2021).

Australian citizens may import AUS$400 (under 18 AUS$200) of goods duty-free, including 250 cigarettes, 250g tobacco, and 1L alcohol. You must be over 18 to import either. For information, contact the Australian Customs Service, 5 Constitution Ave., Canberra, ACT 2601. **New Zealand citizens** should consult the *New Zealand Customs Guide for Travelers,* available from customs offices, or contact New Zealand Customs, 50 Anzac Avenue, Box 29, Auckland (tel. (09) 377 3520; fax (09) 309 2978). **South African citizens** should address their inquiries to: The Commissioner for Customs and Excise, Private Bag X47, Pretoria, 0001. This agency distributes the pamphlet, *South African Customs Information,* for visitors and residents who travel abroad. South Africans residing in the U.S. should contact: South African Mission, 3201 New Mexico Ave. NW, Suite 390, Washington, DC 20016 (202-234-4400; fax 202-364-6008).

■ Hostel Membership

Hostelling International (HI) is the new and universal trademark name adopted by the International Youth Hostel Federation (IYHF). The 6000 official youth hostels worldwide will normally display the new HI logo (a blue triangle) alongside the symbol of one of the 70 national hostel associations.

A one-year Hostelling International (HI) membership permits you to stay at youth hostels all over the U.S. and Canada at unbeatable prices. And, despite the name, you need not be a youth; travelers over 25 pay only a slight surcharge for a bed. You can save yourself potential trouble by procuring a membership card before you leave home. Some hostels do not sell them on the spot, and it may even be cheaper (or more expensive) depending on currency exchange rates. For more details on youth hostels, see Accommodations: Hostels below.

One-year hostel membership cards are available from some travel agencies, including Council Travel and STA (see Useful Addresses: Budget Travel Services above), and from the hostelling organization of your home country.

Independent hostels vary widely in quality and service. Many neither require nor offer membership. Many fine hostels are not HI-affiliated.

Hostelling International (trademark name of the International Youth Hostel Federation), Headquarters, 9 Guessens Rd., Welwyn Garden City, Herts AL8 6QW England (tel. (44) 0707 33 24 87). An umbrella organization for more than 200 hostels in the U.S. and more than 6000 worldwide. Publishes *Hostelling North America,* which gives addresses and descriptions of all affiliated hostels on the continent. Most of these organizations vend ISICs, arrange student and charter flights, and sell travel equipment and literature on budget travel. Contact your national association first.

U.S.: American Youth Hostels (AYH), 733 15th St. NW #840, Washington, DC 20005 (202-783-6161). Also dozens of regional offices across the U.S.; 1-year membership fee $25, under 18 $10, over 54 $15.

Canada: Hostelling International-Canada (HI-C), Suite 608, 1600 James Naismith Dr., 6th Floor, Gloucester, Ottawa, Ont. K1B 5N4 (613-748-5638); 1-year membership fee CDN$26.75, under 18 CDN$12.84, 2-year CDN$37.45.

United Kingdom: Youth Hostels Association of England and Wales (YHA), Trevelyan House, 8 St. Stephens Hill, St. Albans, Hertz AL1 2DY (tel. (44) 727 8552 15); fee £9, under 18 £3.

Ireland: An Oíge (Irish Youth Hostel Association), 61 Mountjoy Sq., Dublin 7, Ireland (tel. (01) 304555; fax (01) 305808); fee £9, under 18 £3.

Australia: Australian Youth Hostels Association (AYHA), Level 3, 10 Mallet St., Camperdown, NSW 2050 (tel. (61) 2 565 1699; fax 565 1235); fee AUS40 when purchased by Australians for use overseas.

New Zealand: Youth Hostels Association of New Zealand (YHANZ), P.O. Box 436, Christchurch 1, New Zealand (tel. (64) 3 379-99 70; fax 365-44 76); fee NZ$24.

Rucksackers North America (trademark name of the American Association of Independent Hostels), P.O. Box 28038, Washington, DC 28038. Send a self-addressed stamped envelope, and they'll send you a free guide to RNA hostels.

■ Youth and Student Identification

In the world of budget travel, youth has its privileges. Two main forms of student and youth identification are accepted worldwide; they are extremely useful, especially for the insurance packages that accompany them.

The **International Student Identity Card (ISIC)** is the most widely accepted form of student identification. Some one million plus students flash it every year. Carrying this card can garner you discounts for sights, theaters, museums, accommodations, train, ferry, and airplane travel, and other services throughout the U.S. and Canada (although in neither of these countries are discounts nearly so common as in Europe). Present the card wherever you go, and ask about discounts even when none are advertised. It also provides accident insurance of up to US$3000 as well as US$100 per day of in-hospital care for up to 60 days. In addition, cardholders have access to a toll-free Traveler's Assistance hotline whose multilingual staff can provide help in medical, legal, and financial emergencies overseas. In many cases, establishments will also honor a student ID from your college for student discounts.

Many student travel offices issue ISICs, including Council Travel, Let's Go Travel, and Student Travel Network in the U.S.; Travel CUTS in Canada; and any of the organizations under the auspices of the International Student Travel Confederation (ISTC) around the world (see Useful Addresses: Budget Travel Services above). When applying for the card, procure a copy of the *International Student Identity Card Handbook,* which lists by country some of the available discounts. You can also write to CIEE for a copy (see addresses above).

Applicants must be at least 12 years old and must be a student at a secondary or post-secondary school. The fee is US$15, and the card is valid from September 1 of one year to the end of the following year. Because of the proliferation of improperly issued ISIC cards, many airlines and some other services now require double proof of student identity. It is wise to have a signed letter from the registrar attesting to your student status and stamped with the school seal, or to carry your school ID.

The new, US$16 **International Teacher Identity Card (ITIC)** offers identical discounts, in theory, but because of its recent introduction many establishments are reluctant to honor it. **Federation of International Youth Travel Organizations (FIYTO)** issues its own discount card to travelers who are not students but are under 26. Known as the **International Youth Discount Travel Card** or the **GO 25 Card,** this one-year card offers many of the same benefits as the ISIC, and most organizations that sell the ISIC also sell the Go 25 Card. A brochure that lists discounts is free when you purchase the card. The fee is US$10, CDN$12, and £4. For more information, contact FIYTO at Bredgage 25H, DK-1260, Copenhagen K, Denmark (tel. 45 33 33 96 00; fax 45 33 93 96 76).

■ International Driver's License

Unless you have a valid driver's license from the U.S. or Canada, a foreigner who drives in either country is required to have an International Driving Permit (IDP). Most car rental agencies do not require the permit; thus, some drivers risk driving without one. Also, a valid driver's license from your home country must always accompany the IDP.

Most credit cards cover standard insurance. If you drive your own car or rent or borrow one, you will need a **green card,** or **International Insurance Certificate,** to prove that you have liability insurance. The application forms are available at any AAA or CAA office. Or, you can get one through the car rental agency; most of them include coverage in their prices. Verify whether your auto insurance applies abroad; even if it does, you will still need a green card to certify this to foreign officials.

■■■ MONEY

Money will always cause you trouble—even when you have it. Plan a budget with a projection of how much you will spend, and expect overruns. (This may be the only thing the budget traveler and the United States federal government have in common.) If you stay in hostels and prepare your own food, expect to spend any-where from US$25-50 per day, depending on local cost of living and your needs. A variety of surcharges will inflate your expenses on the road as well.

No matter how low your budget, if you plan to travel for more than a couple of days you will need to keep handy a much larger amount of cash than usual. Carrying it around, even in a money belt, is risky; personal checks from home may not be acceptable no matter how many forms of ID you carry (even banks may shy away).

■ Currency and Exchange

CDN$1 = US$0.76	**US$1 = CDN$1.31**
UK£1 = US$1.52	**US$1 = UK£0.66**
IR£1 = US$1.40	**US$1 = IR£0.72**
AUS$1 = US$0.67	**US$ = AUS$1.49**
NZ$1 = US$0.56	**US$1 = NZ$1.80**

U.S. currency uses a decimal system based on the **dollar ($).** Paper money ("bills") comes in six denominations, all the same size, shape, and dull green color. The bills now issued are $1, $5, $10, $20, $50 and $100. You may occasionally see denominations of $2 and $500, which are no longer printed but are still acceptable as cur-rency. Some restaurants and retail stores may not accept $50 bills and higher. The dollar divides into 100 **cents (¢);** fractions such as 35 cents can be represented as 35¢ or $0.35. The penny (1¢), the nickel (5¢), the dime (10¢), and the quarter (25¢) are the most common coins. The half-dollar (50¢) and the one-dollar coins (which come in two sizes) are rare but valid currency.

It is nearly impossible to use **foreign currency** in the U.S., although in some regions near the Canadian border, shops may accept Canadian money at a very unfa-vorable rate of exchange. In some parts of the country you may even have trouble **exchanging your currency** for U.S. dollars. Convert your currency infrequently and in large amounts to minimize fees. Buy U.S. traveler's checks, which can be used in lieu of cash (when an establishment specifies "no checks accepted" this usually refers to checks drawn on a bank account). **Personal checks** can be very difficult to cash in the U.S.; most banks require that you have an account with them to cash one. You may want to bring a U.S.-affiliated credit card such as Interbank (Master-Card) or American Express. For more information see Banking and Credit Cards below.

In both the U.S. and Canada, public telephones and most laundromats take coins and not tokens, and drivers of local buses generally do not give change for dollar bills. Keep this in mind and make sure to carry coins with you.

The main unit of currency in **Canada** is the Canadian **dollar,** which is identical to the U.S. dollar in name only. You will need to exchange your currency when you go over the border. As in the U.S., Canadian currency uses a decimal system, with the dollar divided into 100 **cents (¢);** fractions are represented in the same way: 35¢ or $0.35. Paper money comes in denominations of $2, $5, $10, $20, $50, and $100, which are all the same size but color-coded by denomination. Several years ago, the Canadian government phased out the $1 bill and replaced it with a **$1 coin,** known as the loony for the loon which graces its reverse.

Many Canadian shops, as well as vending machines and parking meters, accept U.S. coins at face value (which is a loss for you). Many stores will even convert the price of your purchase for you, but they are under no legal obligation to offer you a fair exchange. Banks provide a reasonable exchange rate, but often charge a han-dling fee and shave off several percentage points; **ATM Cirrus** and **Plus** networks

CURRENCY AND EXCHANGE

Don't forget to write.

Now that you've said, "Let's go," it's time to say
"Let's get American Express® Travelers Cheques." If they are lost or
stolen, you can get a fast and full refund virtually anywhere you
travel. So before you leave be sure and write.

allow you to draw Canadian currency from American or British bank accounts at the official exchange rate. Exchange houses have the best rates and hours, with most open on weekends when banks close. During the past several years, the Canadian dollar has been worth 15 to 20% less than the U.S. dollar; the **exchange rate** hovers around 18%. All prices in the Canada section of this book are listed in Canadian dollars unless otherwise noted.

■ Traveler's Checks

Traveler's checks are the safest way to carry large sums of money. Most tourist establishments will accept them and almost any bank will cash them. Usually banks sell traveler's checks for a 1% commission, although your own bank may waive the surcharge if you have a large enough balance or a certain type of account. In addition, certain travel organizations, such as the American Automobile Association (AAA), offer commission-free traveler's checks to their members. Try to purchase traveler's checks in small denominations ($20 is best, never larger than $50)—otherwise, after having made a small-to-medium purchase, you'll find yourself carrying a large amount of change. If the bank doesn't have small denominations available, try a larger institution or come back another day.

Always keep the receipts from the purchase of your traveler's checks, a list of their serial numbers, and a record of which ones you've cashed. Keep these in a separate pocket or pouch from the checks themselves, since they contain the information you will need to replace your checks if they are stolen. It's also a good idea to leave the serial numbers with someone at home as a back-up in case of luggage loss. Larger firms like American Express can provide immediate refunds at their branch offices. Call any of the toll-free numbers below to find out the advantages of a particular type of check and the name of a bank near you that sells them.

American Express: 800-221-7282 in U.S and Canada. From elsewhere, call collect at 800-964-6665, or contact the U.K. office at (0800) 52 13 13 and ask for the *Traveler's Companion,* which gives full addresses for all their travel offices. Their traveler's cheques are perhaps the most widely recognized in the world, and the easiest to replace if lost or stolen—just contact the nearest AmEx Travel office or call the (800) number. The *Checque for Two* option allows two people traveling together to share one set of checks.

Citicorp sells Visa traveler's checks. Call 800-645-6556 in the U.S. and Canada; 071 982 4040 in London; from elsewhere call collect 813-623-1709. Commission is 1-2% on check purchases. Check holders automatically enrolled in **Travel Assist Hotline** (800-523-1199) for 45 days after checks are bought. This service provides travelers with an English-speaking doctor, lawyer, and interpreter referrals as well as traveler's check refund assistance. Citicorp also has a World Courier Service which guarantees hand-delivery of traveler's checks anywhere in the world.

Mastercard International: 800-223-9920 in the U.S. and Canada; from abroad, call collect 609-987-7300. Issued only in US$. Free from Mastercard, though bank commissions may run 1-2%.

Thomas Cook: call 800-223-7373 from the U.S. to report loss or theft, 800-223-4030 for orders. From elsewhere call collect 212-974-5696. Thomas Cook and Mastercard International have formed a "global alliance;" Thomas Cook now distributes traveler's checks which bear both the Mastercard and Thomas Cook names. Some Thomas Cook Currency Services offices (located in major cities around the globe) do not charge any fee for purchase of checks, while some charge a 1-2% commission.

Visa: 800-227-6811 in U.S. and Canada; from abroad, call (71) 937 80 91 (London) or call New York collect 212-858-8500.

■ Credit Cards

With a major credit card you can rent cars, make reservations, obtain cash advances at most banks, and make large purchases without depleting your cash on hand. But many places mentioned in *Let's Go* will not honor major credit cards. This is just as well—if you rely on them too much, your trip will no longer be "budget travel."

Mastercard (800-999-0454) and **Visa** (800-336-8472) credit cards are sold by individual banks, and each bank offers different services in conjunction with the card. Visa and MasterCard are accepted in more establishments than other credit cards, and they are also the most useful for getting an instant cash advance. Visa holders can generally obtain an advance up to the amount of the credit line remaining on the card, while Mastercard imposes a daily limit. Be sure to consult the bank that issues your card, however, since it may impose its own rules and restrictions. Note that the British **"Access"** is equivalent to Mastercard. You can often reduce conversion fees by charging a purchase instead of changing traveler's checks. At a bank, you should be able to obtain cash from a teller, who will essentially "charge" you as if you had made a purchase. Remember, not all ATMs will honor your credit card; those that do require you to enter your personal access code. Expect a service charge for electronic cash advances.

American Express (800-528-4800) has a hefty annual fee ($55), but offers a number of services to cardholders. Local AmEx offices will cash personal checks up to $1000 for Green Card holders ($200 in cash, $800 in traveler's checks). You can do this once every seven days—note that the money is drawn from your personal checking account, not your AmEx account. Green Card holders can also get money from ATMs, if enrolled in Express Cash Service. Cash advances are available in certain places to Gold Card holders. At some major airports, American Express also operates machines from which you can purchase traveler's checks with your card. Cardholders can take advantage of the American Express Travel Service. Benefits include assistance in changing airline, hotel, and car rental reservations, sending mailgrams and international cables, and holding your mail (if you contact them well in advance; see Keeping in Touch below), as well as **Global Assist** (800-333-2639), a 24-hour helpline that provides legal and medical assistance. You can pick up a copy of the *Traveler's Companion,* a list of full-service offices throughout the world at any American Express Travel Service office. For more information, contact the American Express Travel Service office or affiliate nearest you.

If you're a **student** or your income level is low, you may have difficulty acquiring a recognized credit card. American Express, as well as some of the larger, national banks have credit card offers geared especially toward students, even those who bank elsewhere. Otherwise, you may have to find someone older and more established (such as a parent) to co-sign your application. If someone in your family already has a card, they can usually ask for another card in your name (this encourages travel economy, as they will see the bill before you do). When using your credit card, keep in mind that there is no free lunch—in addition to the annual fee that AmEx and many Visa and Mastercard accounts charge, beware the hefty interest rate if you do not pay your balance each month.

■ Electronic Banking

Automatic Teller Machines (frequently abbreviated as ATMs; operated by bank cards) offer 24-hour service in banks, groceries, gas stations, and even in telephone booths across the U.S. You will find that most banks in the larger cities are connected to an international money network, usually **PLUS** (800-THE-PLUS/ 843-7587) or **CIRRUS** (800-4-CIRRUS/ 424-7787). Depending on the system that your bank at home uses, you will probably be able to access your own personal bank account whenever you're in need of funds. Do this whenever possible, because ATM machines get the wholesale exchange rate, which is generally 5% better than the retail rate most banks use.

■ Sending Money

If you run out of money on the road, you can have more mailed to you in the form of **traveler's checks** bought in your name, a **certified check,** or through **postal money orders,** available at post offices (orders under $25, 75¢ fee; $700 limit per order; cash only). Certified checks are redeemable at any bank, while postal money orders can be cashed at post offices upon display of two IDs (1 of which must be photo). Keep receipts since money orders are refundable if lost.

Money can be **wired** directly from bank to bank for about $30 for amounts less than $1000, plus the commission charged by your home bank. Once you've found a bank that will accept a wire, write or telegram your home bank with your account number, the name and address of the bank to receive the wire, and a routing number. Also notify the bank of the form of ID that the second bank should accept before paying the money. **Bank drafts** or **international money orders** are cheaper but slower. You pay a commission of $15-20 on the draft, plus the cost of sending it registered air mail. As a *last, last* resort, **consulates** will wire home for you and deduct the cost from the money you receive. But they won't be very happy about it.

Another alternative is **cabling money.** Through **Bank of America** (800-346-7693), money can be sent to any affiliated bank. Have someone bring cash, a credit card, or a cashier's check to the sending bank—you need not have an account. You can pick up the money one to three working days later with ID, and it will be paid out to you in U.S. currency. If you do not have a Bank of America account, there is a $40 fee for domestic cabling, $45 for international. Other fees apply depending on the bank at which you receive the money. **American Express' Moneygram** service (800-543-4080) will cable up to $10,000 to you within 30 minutes. It costs $36 for the first $1000 sent domestically and $70 for the first $1000 sent abroad (subsequent thousands cost less). Non-cardholders may use this service for no extra charge, but money can only be sent from England, Germany, and some locations in France—other European and Australian AmEx offices can only receive Moneygrams. Some offices may require the first $200 to be received in cash and the rest as a money transfer check which may be cashed at a bank; others will allow the entire sum to be received as a money transfer check.

To take advantage of a classic, time-honored, and expensive service, use **Western Union** (800-325-6000). You or someone else can phone in a credit card number, or else someone can bring cash to a Western Union office. As always, you need ID to pick up your money. Their charge is $50 for $500, $60 for $1000. Money sent from Europe to the U.S. will usually be available within two working days, but there is an additional surcharge.

■ Sales Tax

Sales tax is the **U.S.** equivalent of the Value Added Tax. Expect to pay 5 to 10% depending on the item and place. See the state introductions for information on local taxes. Some areas charge a hotel tax; ask in advance.

Prices in general tend to be higher in **Canada** than in the U.S., as are taxes; you'll quickly notice the 7% **goods and services tax (GST)** and an additional **sales tax** in some provinces. See the provincial introductions for information on local taxes. Oddly enough, you will often find yourself being taxed on taxes; in Quebec, for example, provincial sales tax is 8%, so that the total tax will be 15.56%. Visitors to Canada can claim a rebate of the GST they pay on accommodations of less than one month and on most goods they buy and take home, so be sure to save your receipts and pick up a GST rebate form while in Canada. The total claim must be at least CDN$7 of GST and must be made within one year of the date on which you purchased the goods and/or accommodations for which you are claiming your rebate. A brochure detailing numerous other restrictions is available from local tourist info booths or by contacting Revenue Canada, Customs and Excise Visitor's Rebate Program, Ottawa, Canada K1A 1J5 (800-668-4748 in Canada, 613-991-3346 outside Canada). Some provinces offer refunds of provincial sales tax as well; contact the Provincial Tourist Information Centres for details (see Practical Information listing of each province).

■ Tipping

Waiters, taxi drivers, and many others providing services in the U.S. and Canada will expect you to add a **tip** to the bill: 15% is the general rule. Bellboys and airport porters expect about a dollar per piece of luggage.

■■■ HEALTH

For **medical emergencies** in the U.S. and Canada, dial **911.** This number works in most places. If it does not, dial 0 for the operator and request to be connected with an ambulance service or hospital.

■ Before You Go

For minor health problems on the road, a compact **first-aid kit** should suffice. Some hardware stores carry ready-made kits, but it's just as easy to assemble your own. Items you might want to include are bandages, aspirin, antiseptic soap or antibiotic cream, a thermometer in a sturdy case, a Swiss Army knife with tweezers, moleskin, a decongestant (to clear your ears if you fly with a cold), motion sickness remedy, medicine for diarrhea and stomach problems, sunscreen, insect repellent, burn ointment, and an elastic bandage.

Any traveler with a medical condition that cannot be easily recognized (i.e. diabetes, epilepsy, heart conditions, allergies to antibiotics) may want to obtain a **Medic Alert Identification Tag.** In an emergency, their internationally recognized tag indicates the nature of the bearer's problem and provides the number of Medic Alert's 24-hour hotline. Lifetime membership (tag, annually updated wallet card, and 24-hr. hotline access) begins at US$35. Contact Medic Alert Foundation, P.O. Box 1009, Turlock, CA 95381-1009 (800-432-5378). The **American Diabetes Association,** 1660 Duke St., Alexandria, VA 22314 (800-232-3472), provides copies of an article "Travel and Diabetes" and diabetic ID cards—messages in 18 languages on the carrier's diabetic status. Contact your local ADA office for information.

All travelers should be concerned about **Acquired Immune Deficiency Syndrome (AIDS),** transmitted through the exchange of body fluids with an infected individual (HIV-positive). Remember that there is no assurance that someone is not infected: HIV tests only show antibodies after a six-month lapse. Do not have sex without using a condom and do not share intravenous needles with anyone. Neither the U.S. nor Canada require a medical exam for those visiting their countries, meaning that HIV-infected individuals may enter. The Center for Disease Control's **AIDS Hotline** provides information on AIDS in the U.S. and can refer you to other organizations with information on Canada (800-342-2437; Spanish 800-344-7432; TTD 800-243-7889). Call the **U.S. State Department** for country-specific restrictions for HIV-positive travelers (202-647-1488; fax 202-647-3000; modem-users may consult the electronic bulletin board at 202-647-9225), or write Bureau of Consular Affairs, Rm. 5807, Dept. of State, Washington D.C. 20520). The **World Health Organization** (202-861-3200) provides written material on AIDS internationally.

Reliable **contraception** may sometimes be difficult to come by while traveling. Women on the pill should bring enough to allow for possible loss or extended stays. **Condoms** are increasingly available from drugstores and pharmacies throughout the U.S. and Canada. They are the most commonly used form of protection against AIDS and unwanted pregnancies in these countries.

For additional information before you go, you may wish to contact the **International Association for Medical Assistance to Travelers (IAMAT).** IAMAT provides several brochures on health for travelers, an ID card, a chart detailing advisable immunizations for 200 countries and territories, and a worldwide directory of English-speaking physicians who have had medical training in Europe or North America. Membership to the organization is free (although donations are welcome) and doctors are on call 24 hour for IAMAT members. Contact chapters in the **U.S.,** 417 Center St., Lewiston, NY, 14092, (716-754-4883); in **Canada,** 40 Regal Rd., Guelph, Ontario, N1K 1B5 (519-836-0102), and 1287 St. Clair Ave. West, Toronto M6E 1B8 (416-652-0137); in **New Zealand,** P.O. Box 5049, 438 Pananui Rd., Christchurch 5 (tel. 03 352 9053; fax 03 352 4630).

Complete health information for travelers is available from a variety of published sources. Consult your local bookstore for books on staying healthy at home or one the road or write the **Superintendent of Documents,** U.S. Government Printing Office, Washington D.C. 20402 (202-783-3238). Try their publication *Health Information for International Travel* ($5) detailing immunization requirements and other health precautions for travelers.

■ Medical Attention On the Road

While you travel, pay attention to the signals of pain and discomfort that your body may send you. This may be due to a new climate, diet, water quality, or pace when you first arrive or even after a couple of weeks. Once you get going, some of the milder symptoms that you may safely ignore at home may be signs of something more serious on the road; your increased exertion may wear you out and make you more susceptible to illness. The following paragraphs list some health problems you may encounter but should not be your only information source on these common ailments. Check with the publications and organizations listed above for more complete information or send for the **American Red Cross** *First-Aid and Safety Handbook* ($15), available by writing to your local office or to American Red Cross, 99 Brookline Ave., Boston MA, 02215. If you are interested in taking one of the many first-aid and CPR courses that the American Red Cross offers before leaving on your trip, contact your local office—courses are well-taught and relatively inexpensive.

Extreme cold brings risks of hypothermia and frostbite. **Hypothermia** is a result of exposure to cold and can occur even in the middle of the summer, especially in rainy or windy conditions. The signs are easy to detect: body temperature drops rapidly, resulting in the failure to produce body heat. Other possible symptoms are uncontrollable shivering, poor coordination, and exhaustion followed by slurred speech, sleepiness, hallucinations, and amnesia. *Do not* let victims fall asleep if they are in advanced stages—if they lose consciousness, they might die. To avoid hypothermia, always keep dry. Wear wool, *especially* in soggy weather—it retains its insulating properties even when wet. Dress in layers, and stay out of the wind, which carries heat away from the body. Remember that most loss of body heat is through your head, so always carry a wool hat with you. **Frostbite** occurs in freezing temperatures. The affected skin will turn white, then waxy and cold. To counteract the problem, the victim should drink warm beverages, stay or get dry, and gently and slowly warm the frostbitten are in dry fabric or with steady body contact. NEVER *rub* frostbite—the skin is easily damaged. Take serious cases to a doctor or medic as soon as possible.

Travelers in **high altitudes** should allow their body a couple of days to adjust to the lower atmospheric oxygen levels before engaging in any strenuous activity. This particularly applies to those intent on setting out on long alpine hikes. Those new to high-altitude areas may feel drowsy and get headaches, and one alcoholic beverage may have the same effect as three at a lower altitude.

If you plan to **romp in the forest,** try to learn of any regional hazards. Know that any three-leaved plant might be poison ivy, poison oak, or poison sumac—pernicious plants whose oily surface causes insufferable itchiness if touched. (As Marge Simpson tells Bart and Lisa before they leave for camp, "Leaves of three, let it be; leaves of four, eat some more.") Look before you leap into any wilderness area, even if it is simply the side of the highway; many areas have their own local snakes, spi-

MEDICAL ATTENTION ON THE ROAD

ders, insects and creepy-crawlies. See the Wilderness Concerns section of Camping & the Outdoors below for more thorough information on safety concerns while in the wilds.

Food poisoning can spoil any trip. Some of the cheapest and most convenient eating options are also most prone: street vendors, tap water, and carrying perishable food such as mayonnaise for hours in a hot backpack. Fried or greasy foods, especially prevalent in the U.S., may weigh you down or cause indigestion (especially for those not used to eating them).

One of the most common symptoms associated with eating and drinking in another country is **diarrhea.** Known variously as *turista, Montezuma's revenge,* and "what a way to spend my vacation," diarrhea has unmistakable symptoms but also, thankfully, some means of relief. Many people take with them over-the-counter remedies (such as Pepto-Bismol). Since dehydration is the most common side effect of diarrhea, those suffering should drink plenty of fruit juice and pure water. The simplest anti-dehydration formula is still the most effective: 8oz. of water with a ½ tsp. of sugar or honey and a pinch of salt. Down several of these a day.

■■■ INSURANCE

Beware of unnecessary coverage—your current policies might well extend to many travel-related accidents. **Medical insurance** (especially university policies) often cover costs incurred abroad. **Medicare's** foreign travel coverage is limited but is valid in Canada. Canadians are protected by their home province's health insurance plan: check with the provincial Ministry of Health or Health Plan Headquarters.

Buying an **ISIC,** International Teacher ID or Student Card in the U.S. provides US$3000 worth of accident and illness insurance and US$100 per day up to 60 days of hospitalization while the card is valid. **CIEE** offers the inexpensive Trip-Safe plan with options covering medical treatment and hospitalization, accidents, baggage loss and even charter flights missed due to illness; **STA** offers a more expensive, more comprehensive plan. **American Express** cardholders receive automatic car-rental and flight insurance on purchases made with the card. (For addresses for CIEE and STA, see Useful Addresses: Budget Travel Services, above.)

Always carry policy numbers and proof of insurance. Note that some of the plans listed below offer cash advances or guaranteed bills. Check with each insurance carrier for specific restrictions. If your coverage doesn't include on-the-spot payments or cash transferals, budget for emergencies.

Access America, Inc., 6600 West Broad St., P. O. Box 11188, Richmond, VA 23230 (800-284-8300). Covers trip cancellation/interruption, on-the-spot hospital admittance costs, emergency medical evacuation. 24-hr. hotline.

ARM Coverage, Inc./Carefree Travel Insurance, P. O. Box 310, Mineola, NY 11501 (800-323-3149 or 516-294-0220). Offers two comprehensive packages including coverage for trip delay, accident and sickness, medical, baggage loss, bag delay, accidental death and dismemberment, travel supplier insolvency. Trip cancellation/interruption may be purchased separately at a rate of $5.50 per $100 of coverage. 24-hr. hotline.

Globalcare Travel Insurance, 220 Broadway, Lynnfield, MA 01940 (800-821-2488; fax 617-592-7720). Complete medical, legal, emergency, and travel-related services. On-the-spot payments and special student programs.

Traveler's Aid International, 918 16th St., NW, Washington DC 20006 (202-659-9468; fax 202-659-2910). Provides help for theft, car failure, illness, and other "mobility-related problems." No fee, but you are expected to reimburse the organization for expenses.

Travel Assistance International, 1133 15th St., NW, Washington DC 20005 (202-821-2828; fax 202-331-1609). Provides on-the-spot medical coverage ranging from US$15,000 to US$90,000 and unlimited medical evacuation insurance, 24-hr. emergency multilingual assistance hotline and worldwide local presence.

Optional forms of coverage such as trip cancellation/interruption, baggage and accidental death and dismemberment insurance are also offered. Short-term and long-term plans available.

■■■ SAFETY AND SECURITY

For emergencies in the U.S. and Canada, dial 911. This number works in most places. If it does not, dial 0 for the operator and request to be connected with the appropriate emergency service (i.e., police, fire, ambulance, etc.).

■ Staying Safe

Tourists are particularly vulnerable to crime for two reasons: they often carry large amounts of cash and they are not as savvy as locals. To avoid such unwanted attention, the best tactic is to blend in as much as possible: the gawking camera-toter is much easier prey than the casual local look-alike. Muggings are more often impromptu than planned; walking with nervous, over-the-shoulder glances can be a tip that you have something valuable to protect. Carry all your valuables (including your passport, railpass, traveler's checks and airline ticket) either in a **money belt** or **neckpouch** stashed securely inside your clothing. These will protect you from skilled thieves who use razors to slash open backpacks and fanny packs (particular favorites of skilled bag-snatchers). Making **photocopies** of important documents will allow you to recover them in case they are lost or filched. Carry one copy separate from the documents and leave another copy at home. Keep some money separate from the rest, to use in an emergency or in case of theft. Label every piece of luggage both inside and out.

When exploring a new **city,** extra vigilance may be wise, but no city should force you to turn precautions into panic. When you get to a place where you'll be spending some time, find out about unsafe areas from tourist information, from the manager of your hotel or hostel, or from a local whom you trust. Both men and women may want to carry a small **whistle** to scare off attackers or attract attention, and it's not a bad idea to jot down the number of the police if you'll be in town for a couple days. When walking at night, you should turn day-time precautions into mandates. In particular, stay near crowded and well-lit areas and do not attempt to cross through parks, parking lots or any other large, deserted areas.

Among the more colorful aspects of large cities are the **con artists.** Although less prevalent in the U.S. and Canada than in Europe, these hucksters use tricks which are many and adaptable. Be aware of certain classics: sob stories that require money, rolls of bills "found" on the street, mustard spilled (or saliva spit) onto your shoulder distracting you for enough time to snatch your bag. Always put on a bag so that the strap passes over your head and runs diagonally across your torso.

If you choose to sleep in a **car,** be aware that this is one of the most dangerous ways to get your rest—when you lock other people out, you also lock yourself in; if you are going to do it anyway, it is advisable to park in a well-lit area as close to a police station or 24-hour service station as possible. Sleeping outside can be even more dangerous—camping is recommendable only in official, supervised campsites or in wilderness backcountry.

There is no sure-fire set of precautions that will protect you from all situations you might encounter when you travel. A good self-defense course will give you more concrete ways to react to different types of aggression but it might cost you more money than your trip. **Model Mugging** (East Coast 617-232-2900; Midwest 312-338-4545; West Coast 415-592-7300), a national organization with offices in several major cities, teaches a very effective, comprehensive course on self-defense.

(Course prices vary from $400-500. Women's and men's courses offered.) Community colleges frequently offer self-defense courses at more affordable prices.

For official **Department of State** travel advisories on the U.S. and/or Canada, including crime and security, call their 24-hr. hotline at 202-647-5225. Also available: pamphlets on traveling to specific areas. More complete information on safety while traveling may be found in *Travel Safety: Security and Safeguards at Home and Abroad,* from **Hippocrene Books, Inc.,** 171 Madison Ave., New York, NY 10016 (212-685-4371; orders 718-454-2360; fax 718-454-1391).

■ Drugs and Alcohol

In Oregon, Washington, and Alaska, the drinking age is 21 years of age and is strictly enforced. British Columbia and the Yukon Territory prohibit drinking below the age of 19, while in Alberta you can drink at 18. In both the U.S. and Canada, the law is strictly enforced. Particularly in the U.S., be prepared to show a photo ID (preferably some government document—driver's license or passport) if you look under 30. Some areas of the country are still "dry," meaning they do not permit the sale of alcohol at all, while other places do not allow it to be sold on Sundays.

Drugs and traveling are not a good combination. If you carry **prescription drugs** while your travel, it is vital to have a copy of the prescriptions themselves readily accessible at country borders. As far as **illegal drugs** are concerned, possession of marijuana no longer constitutes a misdemeanor in a state's reckoning, but it is a U.S. federal offense subject to imprisonment. At the Canadian border, if you are found in possession of drugs, you will be subject to an automatic seven-year jail term, regardless of how small an amount you are found with, and if you are a foreigner, you will be permanently barred from entering the country—and that's just the beginning. Police attitudes towards drugs vary widely across the region. In some cities, police tend to ignore pot smokers who mind their own business. But don't be fooled by their seeming lack of interest; arrests are not uncommon. And while private use of marijuana used to be legal in **Alaska,** the law was recently repealed, and possession of the drug, even on private property, is now a punishable offense.

Officials at both the United States and Canadian borders also take **drunk driving** very seriously. No matter what kind of transportation you use for entry, if the customs guards discover a drunk driving conviction, you will be denied access.

■■■ WORK AND STUDY

■ Working

Finding a job far from home is usually a matter of luck and timing. Your best leads in the job hunt often come from local residents, hostels, employment offices and Chambers of Commerce. Temporary agencies often hire for non-secretarial placement as well as for standard typing assignments. Marketable skills (e.g. touch-typing, dictation, computer knowledge, and experience with children) will prove very helpful, if not necessary, in your search for a temporary job. Consult local newspapers and bulletin boards on local college campuses.

VISA REQUIREMENTS FOR NON-RESIDENTS

Working in the **U.S.** while carrying only a B-2 tourist visa is grounds for deportation. Before an appropriate visa can be issued to you, you must—depending on the visa category you are seeking—join a USIA-authorized Exchange Visitor Program (J-1 visa) or locate an employer who will sponsor you (usually an H-2B visa) and file the necessary paperwork with the Immigration and Naturalization Service (INS) in the United Sates on your behalf. In order to apply to the U.S. Embassy or Consulate for a J-1 visa you must obtain an IAP-66 eligibility form, issued by a U.S. academic institution or a private organization involved in U.S. exchanges. The H-2 visa is difficult to obtain, as your employer must prove that there are no other American or foreign permanent residents already residing in the U.S. with your job skills. For more specific information on visa categories and requirements, contact your nearest U.S. Embassy or Consulate and Educational Advisory Service of the Fulbright Commission (a U.S. embassy-affiliated organization).

If you intend to work in **Canada,** you will need an **Employment Authorization,** which must be obtained before you enter the country; visitors ordinarily are not allowed to change status once they have arrived. The processing fee is CDN$100. Employment authorizations are only issued after it has been determined that qualified Canadian citizens and residents will not be adversely affected by the admission of a foreign worker. Your potential employer must contact the nearest **Canadian Employment Centre (CEC)** for approval of the employment offer. For more information, contact the consulate or embassy in your home country. Residents of the U.S., Greenland, St. Pierre, or Miquelon only may apply for employment authorization at the point of entry.

PAID EMPLOYMENT

Finding work in Alaska or the Pacific Northwest depends largely on pure persistence. The once-rapid expansion in industries such as construction, fishing, lumber, and oil has slowed somewhat, and as more people head to the region each year in search of employment, jobs become harder to find. Summer is the best season for job hunting, as warm weather and long daylight hours are put to good use before winter closes many industries down.

Paid employment can occasionally be found through the **USDA Forest Service;** in **Alaska,** write USDA Forest Service, 1675 C St., Anchorage 99501-5198 (907-271-4126); to find employment in the **Pacific Northwest** write the USDA Forest Service, Pacific Northwest Region, P.O. Box 3623, Portland, OR 97208-3623 (503-326-3816). The Pacific Northwest Region, consisting of Oregon and Washington, has 19 forests with 102 ranger districts and 4 job corps.

Agriculture in the Northwest generates a huge variety of temporary unskilled jobs, but expect low wages and poor conditions. **Fruit pickers** are always needed in Oregon, Washington, and BC's Okanagan Valley, since shortages of workers cause tons of fruit to spoil each year.

Cannery and **fish processing** jobs are currently the most popular forms of summer employment in Alaska. Many processing plants in the southeast, on Kodiak Island, and in the Aleutians have long waiting lists, and nearly two-thirds of their employees are hired through company offices in Washington, Oregon, or California. However, canneries that need help often have jobs available on short notice. You can obtain a list of processing plants from the **Alaska Department of Fish and Game,** Commercial Fisheries Management and Development Division, P.O. Box 25526, Juneau, AK 99802-5526 (907-465-4210; open Mon.-Fri. 8am-4:30pm). Inquiries about the current employment outlook should be addressed to the **Alaska Department of Labor,** P.O. Box 1149, Juneau 99811 (465-4839; open Mon.-Fri. 8am-4:30pm), or check with job service agencies in the towns where you wish to work. The major fish seasons are in July, August, and September.

To some, the continued popularity of **cannery** work is baffling. The work (gutting fish by hand) is difficult, boring, and unpleasant. Strenuous 16- to 18-hour days are often demanded (sometimes non-stop for up to 45 days). This will bring you tons of money, especially since all overtime pays time-and-a-half, and you're almost guaranteed to save what you earn since you'll probably be too tired to spend it.

As a crew member on an Alaskan **fishing boat,** you can make over $2000 per week baiting halibut hooks. However, the work is dangerous, and you can expect to sleep less than four hours per night. Also, you will be paid with a percentage of the profits, so if it is a bad season for halibut, it will be a bad season for you. In short, do not work with fish in Alaska unless you can roll with a few punches. You may be able to find more stable seasonal work at resorts in the region or with companies

WORKING

that organize hiking, climbing, and boat trips. For more information on these tamer jobs, as well as information on Fairbanks and the Interior, call and sign up with Alaska's **Private Industry Council,** 500 First Ave., Fairbanks 99701 (907-456-5189; open Mon.-Thurs. 9am-noon and 1-5pm).

VOLUNTEERING

Volunteer jobs are readily available throughout the Pacific Northwest and Alaska. Some jobs provide room and board in exchange for labor. Write to **CIEE** (see Budget Travel Agencies under Useful Addresses above) for *Volunteer! The Comprehensive Guide to Voluntary service in the U.S. and Abroad* ($11, postage $1.50). CIEE also administers the **International Voluntary Service Program**, an international work-camp program which places young people interested in short-term voluntary service with organizations conducting projects worldwide, including the United States. Projects include restoring historical sights, working with children or the elderly, constructing low-income housing, and taking part in nature conservation. Room and board are provided. For more information, write to CIEE. The **USDA Forest Service** invites everyone to volunteer as hosts to visitors to the greener woods of the U.S. Contact the USDA Forest Service, Human Resource Program Office, P.O. Box 96090, Washington, D.C. 20090-6090.

WORK EXCHANGE PROGRAMS

Many student travel organizations arrange work-exchange programs. Both CIEE and YMCA place students as summer camp counselors in the U.S. In some areas you may be able to work a desk job at an AYH Hostel in exchange for a bed. Check at hostels in the area you in which you are interested for opportunities. Foreign university-level students can get on-the-job technical training in fields such as engineering, computer science, agriculture, and natural and physical sciences from the **Association for International Practical Training,** which is the U.S. member of the **International Association for the Exchange of Students for Technical Experience (IAESTE).** You must apply through the IAESTE office in your home country; application deadlines vary. For more information, contact the local IAESTE committee— try universities or colleges in your area —or write to IAESTE, c/o AIPT, 10 Corporate Center, Suite 250, 10400 Little Patuxent Pkwy., Columbia, MD (410-997-2200). If you are interested in staying with an American family and learning firsthand, check out World Learning's **Homestay/USA,** formerly The Experiment in International Living. Programs are available to international visitors of all ages for stays from several days to several months in urban, suburban, and rural areas, in volunteer hosts' homes. For more information, contact Homestay/USA at 25 Bay State Rd., Boston, MA 02215 (800-327-4678 or 617-247-0350). Other organizations to contact are:

Central Bureau for Educational Visits and Exchanges, Seymour Mews House, Seymour Mews, London W1H 9PE, England (tel. 071 486 5101; fax 071 935 5741). Publishes *Working Holidays* (£10.45), an annual guide to short-term paid and voluntary work opportunities in Britain and around the world; *Volunteer Work* (£9.49), a guide to organizations recruiting people, usually with skills and experience, for long-term voluntary service worldwide; and *Teach Abroad* (£10.49), a guide to organizations who recruit qualified teachers to work overseas, whether on a paid or voluntary basis. All prices include postage. These publications are also available from the **Institute of International Education** (see Enrolling in a U.S. or Canadian College or University below).

SCI—International Voluntary Service, Route 2, Box 506B, Crozet, VA 22932 (804-823-1826). Established after WWI as a means to promote peace and international understanding, SCI arranges placement in workcamps in Europe and the US for people over 18 and 16, respectively. Registration fees range from $40 (US) to $200 (former USSR).

■ Studying

VISA REQUIREMENTS FOR NON-RESIDENTS

International students who wish to study in the **U.S.** must apply for either a J-1 visa (for exchange students) or a F-1 visas (for full-time students enrolled in an academic or language program). To obtain a J-1, you must fill out an IAP 66 eligibility form, issued by the program in which you will enroll. Neither the F-1 nor the J-1 visa specifies any expiration date; instead they are both valid for the duration of stay, which includes the length of your particular program and a brief grace period thereafter. In order to extend a student visa, fill out an I-538 form. Requests to extend a visa must be submitted 15 to 60 days before the original departure date.

To study in **Canada** you will need a Student Authorization in addition to any entry visa you may need (see Documents and Formalities above). To obtain one, contact the nearest Canadian Consulate or Embassy. Be sure to apply well ahead of time; it can take up to six months, and there is a fee of $75. You will also need to prove to the Canadian government that you are able to support yourself financially. A student authorization is good for one year. If you plan to stay longer, it is extremely important that you do not let it expire before you apply for renewal.

LANGUAGE EDUCATION PROGRAMS

If you are interested in studying in the **U.S.,** there are a number of different paths you can take. One possibility is to enroll in a language education program, particularly if you are interested in a short-term stay. Contact **World Learning, Inc.**, which runs the **International Students of English** program, offering intensive language courses at select U.S. campuses. The price of a four-week program averages US$1800. For more information, write to World Learning, PO Box 676, Brattleboro, VT 05302-0676 (802-257-7751).

ENROLLING IN A U.S. OR CANADIAN COLLEGE OR UNIVERSITY

If you would rather live the life of an American or Canadian college student, you might consider a visiting student program lasting either a semester or a full year. Contact colleges and universities in your country to see what kind of exchanges they administer. Many colleges in the Pacific Northwest welcome visiting students. The colleges and universities listed below all offer summer terms (3-11 weeks). Direct all correspondence to the **Director of Admissions** unless otherwise noted.

University of Alaska, Fairbanks, 102 Signers Hall, Fairbanks, AK 99775-0060 (907-474-7521).

University of Alaska, Anchorage, 3211 Providence Dr., Anchorage, AK 99508 (907-786-1480).

Lewis & Clark College, 0615 SW Palatine Hill Rd., Portland, OR 97219 (503-768-7040 or 800-444-4111).

Reed College, 3203 SE Woodstock Blvd., Portland, OR 97202 (503-777-7511 or 800-547-4750).

University of Oregon, 240 Oregon Hall, Eugene, OR 97403 (503-346-3201).

Oregon State University, Administrative Services S-104, Corvallis, OR 97331-2106 (503-737-4411).

University of Washington, Smith Hall, 1400 NE Campus Pkwy., Seattle, WA 98195 (206-543-9686).

Washington State University, 342 French Administration Bldg., Pullman, WA 99164-1036 (509-335-5586).

University of Alberta, 120 Administration Bldg., Edmonton, AB T6G 2M7 (403-492-3113).

University of Calgary, 2500 University Dr. NW, Calgary, AB T2N 1N4 (403-220-6640).

Simon Fraser University, Burnaby, BC V5A 1S6 (604-291-3224).

University of British Columbia, Office of the Registrar, Brock Hall, 2016-1874 East Mall, Vancouver, BC V6T 1Z1 (604-822-3159; fax 822-5945).
University of Victoria, P.O. Box 3025, Victoria, BC V8W 3P2 (604-721-8111).

Most U.S. and Canadian colleges have offices that give advice and information on studying in the U.S. To help you choose the college which suits you, seek out one or all of the following annually revised reference books which provide summaries and evaluations of various colleges, describing their general atmosphere, fields of study, tuition, and enrollment data. Among the most useful are *The Insider's Guide to the Colleges* (St. Martin's Press, $20), the *Fiske Guide to Colleges* by Edward Fiske (N.Y. Times Books, $16), and *Barron's Profiles of American Colleges* ($19).

If English is not your native language, you will generally be required to pass the **Test of English as a Foreign Language and Test of Spoken English (TOEFL/ TSE),** administered in many countries. For more information, contact the TOEFL/ TSE Application office, P.O. Box 6155, Princeton, NJ 08541-6155 (609-951-1100).

One excellent source of information on studying in the U.S. and Canada is the **Institute of International Education (IIE),** which administers many exchange programs in the US and abroad. IIE publishes *Academic Year Abroad*, which describes over 2,100 semester and academic-year programs offered in the US and Canada ($43 plus $4 shipping); *Vacation Study Abroad*, with information on 1,500 short term programs in the US and Canada ($37, shipping $4); and *English Language and Orientation Programs*, detailing language and cultural programs, (1993/4 edition $43, plus $4 shipping). Many **Central Bureau** books (see Work-Exchange programs above) are also available from IIE. Contact IIE Books, Institute for International Education, 809 United Nations Plaza, New York, NY 10017-3580 (212-883-8200)

■■■ PACKING

■ What to Pack

Pack light. Set out everything you think you need, then pack only half of it. And leave room for gifts. Traveling light will make your life easier in a number of ways.

Your first decision is what kind of luggage you need. If you'll be biking or hiking a great deal, a **backpack** is in order (see Tent Camping, Hiking, and Climbing below). If you plan to stay in one city or town for a while, you might prefer a light suitcase. Large shoulder bags or duffels are good for stuffing into lockers, crowded baggage compartments, and all-purpose lugging. Whatever your main piece of baggage, be sure to have a daypack for carrying a day's worth of food, camera, first-aid essentials, and valuables and documents.

In the Northwest, be prepared for a wide range of weather conditions no matter what time of year you travel. To cover the most bases, stick with the "layer concept": start with several T-shirts, over which you can wear a sweatshirt or sweater in cold or wet weather. It is a good idea to have at least one layer that will insulate while wet, such as polypropylene, polarfleece, or wool. For winter, and depending on which regions you visit, you may want a few heavier layers as well, and a winter coat with a breathable, waterproof shell. Natural fibers and lightweight cottons are the best materials for hot weather, although they may not be appropriate for the cold and wet of the Northwest. A rain poncho, which will cover both you and your pack, and can double as a groundcover for a night outdoors. And, of course, never go anywhere without your **towel.**

Shoes are very important whether you'll be doing serious hiking or not. Break your shoes in before you leave. Don't be caught without some type of rainproof footwear, from slipover rubbers to hiking boots, depending on your needs.

Other **odds and ends** to consider bringing: sleeping bag, sleep sack (required at many hostels—see Accommodations below), flashlight, pens and paper, travel alarm, plastic canteen or water bottle, padlock, plastic garbage bags (for isolating damp or dirty clothing), sewing kit, safety pins, pocketknife, earplugs for noisy hostels, waterproof matches, clothespins and a length of cord, sunglasses, and assorted toiletries, including toilet paper and mild, *biosafe* liquid soap (Dr. Bronner's and Mountain Suds are two popular brands) for campers. A rubber squash ball can be a sink stopper; soap or shampoo should do for handwashing clothes.

Pack light! (It's worth repeating.) A convenient method of keeping organized is to pack items in different colored stuff sacks (found at camp stores)—shirts in one, underwear in another, etc. Wrap sharper items in clothing so they won't stab you or puncture your luggage, and pack heavy items along the inside wall if you're carrying a backpack. Carry your luggage around the block a few times to simulate real travel—if beads of sweat start trickling down your brow, take some things out.

■ Electricity

Electricity is only 100V AC in the U.S. and Canada, only half as much as that of most European countries. Visit a hardware store for an adapter (which changes the shape of the plug) and a converter (which changes the voltage). Do not make the mistake of using only an adapter, or you'll have problems. Travelers who heat-disinfect their **contact lenses** should consider switching to a chemical disinfection system.

■ Photography

At every turn in the Northwest, you'll want to photograph your breathtaking surroundings. You will need to carefully consider before you leave, though, how much equipment you absolutely *need:* camera gear is heavy, fragile, and costly to replace. Buy film before you leave, or in the big cities as you go. Often large discount department stores have the best deals. The sensitivity of film to light is measured by the **ASA/ISO number:** 100 is good for normal outdoor or indoor flash photography, 3200 is necessary for night photography. Consult a photo store for advice about the right film for special types of photography.

Although most tourists visit Alaska during the period of its endless summer light, residents maintain that their land is most beautiful in the winter. One reward for the intrepid winter traveler is the *aurora borealis,* or "northern lights." Shimmering spectrums of color dance like smoke, visible whenever the sky is dark. The brightest displays occur in fall and spring when the earth's tilt toward the sun accentuates their light most. To photograph the Northern Lights, you'll need 10 to 30 second exposures on a tripod-based 35mm camera with a locking cable release. For 400 ASA film, use the following scale as a guide: f 1.2 for 2 seconds; f 1.4 for 3 seconds; f 2 for 10 seconds; f 2.8 for 20 seconds; and f 3.5 for 30 seconds.

Even the greatest photographs cannot do the scenery perfect justice, so don't let the need to snap the perfect photo fill your every waking hour. To preserve some of the grandeur, shoot slides instead of prints—they're also cheaper to process.

Process your film after you return home; you will save money, and it's much simpler to carry rolls of film as you travel, rather than easily damaged boxes of slides or packages of prints and negatives. Protect exposed film from extreme heat and the sun. Despite disclaimers, **airport X-ray equipment** can fog film; the more sensitive the film, the more susceptible to damage: anything over ASA 1600 should not be X-rayed. Ask security personnel to inspect your camera and film by hand. Serious photographers should purchase a lead-lined pouch for storing film.

WOMEN AND TRAVEL

■■■ SPECIFIC CONCERNS

■ Women and Travel

Women exploring any area on their own inevitably face additional **safety concerns**. In all situations it is best to trust your instincts: if you'd feel better somewhere else, don't hesitate to move on. You may want to consider staying in hostels which offer single rooms which lock from the inside or religious organizations which offer rooms for women only. Stick to centrally-located accommodations and avoid late-night treks or metro rides. Remember that **hitching** is *never* safe for lone women, or even for two women traveling together. Choose train compartments occupied by other women or couples. In some parts of the world, women (foreign or local) are frequently beset by unwanted and tenacious followers. To escape unwanted attention, follow the example of local women; in many cases, the less you look like a tourist, the better off you'll be. In general, dress conservatively, especially in more rural areas. If you spend time in cities, you may be harassed no matter how you're dressed. Look as if you know where you're going (even when you don't) and ask women or couples for directions if you're lost or if you feel uncomfortable. In crowds, you may be pinched or squeezed by oversexed slimeballs; wearing a conspicuous **wedding band** may help prevent such incidents. Don't hesitate to seek out a police officer or a passerby if you are being harassed. Always carry change for the phone and enough extra money for a bus or taxi.

A **Model Mugging** course (see Safety and Security: Staying Safe above) will not only prepare you for a potential mugging, but will also raise your level of awareness of your surroundings as well as your confidence. Offices exist in 14 U.S. states, as well as in Quebec and Zurich. All of these warnings and suggestions should not discourage women from traveling alone.

A series of recent **travelogues** by women outline their sojourns; check a good library or bookstore for these and other books: *Nothing to Declare: Memoirs of a Woman Traveling Alone* (Penguin Books; $9) and *Wall to Wall: From Beijing to Berlin by Rail* (Penguin Books; $10) by Mary Morris; *One Dry Season* (Knopf) by Caroline Alexander; *Tracks* (Pantheon) by Robin Davidson; *The Road Through Miyama* (Random House/Vintage) by Leila Philips; and anything by Isak Dinesen, especially *Out of Africa* (Random House). For additional tips and suggestions, consult *The Handbook for Women Travelers* (£8) by Maggie and Gemma Moss, published by Piatkus Books, 5 Windmill St., London W1P 1HF England (tel. 44 071 631 0710). Also consult **Women Going Places** ($14), a new women's travel and resource guide emphasizing women-owned enterprises. The guide is geared towards lesbians, but offers advice appropriate for all women. Available from Inland Book Company, P.O. Box 120261, East Haven, CT 06512 (203-467-4257).

■ Bisexual, Gay, and Lesbian Travelers

Generally, in the larger cities of the Pacific Northwest, you need not compromise your freedom to enjoy your trip. Be warned, however, that smaller communities may not be so receptive to openly gay and lesbian travelers. Wherever possible, *Let's Go* lists local gay and lesbian information lines and community centers.

Ferrari Publications, P.O. Box 37887, Phoenix, AZ 85069 (602-863-2408). Publishes *Ferrari's Places of Interest* ($15), *Ferrari's Places for Men* ($14), *Ferrari's Places for Women* ($12), and *Inn Places: US A and Worldwide Gay Accommodations* ($15). Also available from Giovanni's Room (see below).

Gay's the Word, 66 Marchmont St., London WC1N 1AB, England (tel. 071 278 7654). Tube: Russel Sq. Open Mon.-Fri. 11am-7pm, Sat. 10-6, Sun. and holidays 2-6pm. Information for gay and lesbian travelers. Mail order service available.

Gayellow Pages (U.S./Canada edition $12) is available through Renaissance House. For further details, send a self-addressed, stamped envelope to Box 292, Village Station, New York NY 10014-0292 (212-674-0120).

Giovanni's Room, 345 S. 12th St., Philadelphia, PA 19107 (215-923-2960; fax 215-923-0813). International feminist, lesbian and gay bookstore with mail-order.

Spartac International Gay Guide, ($30). Order from 100 East Biddle St., Baltimore, MD 21202 (410-727-5677) or c/o Bruno Lützowstraße, P.O. Box 301345, D-1000 Berlin 30, Germany (tel. 49 30 25 49 82 00); also available from Giovanni's Room (see above) and from Renaissance House, P.O. Box 292 Village Station, New York, NY 10014 (212-674-0120). Extensive list of gay bars, restaurants, hotels, bookstores and hotlines throughout the world. Very specifically for men.

Women Going Places, a new women's travel and resource guide emphasizing women-owned enterprises. Geared towards lesbians, but offers advice appropriate for all women. $14. Available from Inland Book Company, P.O. Box 120261, East Haven, CT 06512 (203-467-4257).

■ Older Travelers and Senior Citizens

Senior citizens are eligible for a wide range of discounts on transportation, museums, movies, theater, concerts, restaurants, and accommodations. Proof of age is usually required (e.g., a driver's license, Medicare card, or membership card from a recognized society of retired persons).

Hostelling International (HI) sells membership cards at a discount to those over 54 ($15). Write the **American Youth Hostel (HI/AYH)** National Headquarters, P.O. Box 37613, Washington DC 20013-7613 (202-783-6161). See Hostels in the Accommodations section below for more information. To explore the outdoors, seniors 62 and over can buy a **Golden Age Passport** (free), allowing free entry into all national parks and a 50% discount on recreational activities. See Parks & Forests in the Camping & the Outdoors section below for more information. Also consult the following organizations for information on discounts and special services:

AARP (American Association of Retired Persons), 601 E St. NW, Washington, DC 20049 (202-434-2277 or 800-927-0111). U.S. residents over 50 and their spouses receive benefits which include travel programs and discounts for groups and individuals, as well as discounts on lodging, car and RV rental, air arrangements and sight-seeing. $8 annual fee.

Elderhostel, 75 Federal St., 3rd floor, Boston, MA 02110. You must be 60 or over, and may bring a spouse who is over 50. Programs at colleges and universities in over 40 countries focus on varied subjects and generally last one week.

Gateway Books, P.O. Box 10244, San Rafael, CA 94912 (800-669-0773). Publishes Gene and Adele Malott's *Get Up and Go: A Guide for the Mature Traveler* ($11, postage $1.90). Offers recommendations for the budget-conscious senior.

National Council of Senior Citizens, 1331 F St. NW, Washington, DC 20004 (202-347-8800). For $12 a year, an individual or couple of any age can receive hotel and auto rental discounts, a senior citizen newspaper, use of a discount travel agency and supplemental Medicare insurance (if you're over 65).

Pilot Books, 103 Cooper St., Babylon, NY 11702 (516-422-2225). Publishes *The International Health Guide for Senior Citizens* ($5, postage $1) and *The Senior Citizens' Guide to Budget Travel in the United States and Canada* ($6 postpaid).

■ Travelers with Disabilities

Countries vary in their general accessibility to travelers with disabilities. Some national and regional tourist boards provide directories on the accessibility of various accommodations and transportation services. If these services are not available, contact institutions of interest directly rather than relying upon travel agents. The amount of information for travelers with disabilities is still quite small; if you find additional publications or other information, please let us know.

Arrange transportation well in advance. **Hertz, Avis,** and **National** have hand-controlled vehicles at some locations (see By Car in the Getting There and Getting Around section below). **Amtrak** and all **airlines** can better serve passengers with disabilities if notified in advance; tell the ticket agent when making reservations which services you'll need. Both **Greyhound** and Canada's **VIA Rail** allow a person with disabilities and a companion to ride for the price of a single fare with a doctor's statement confirming that a companion is necessary. Wheelchairs, seeing-eye dogs, and oxygen tanks are not counted against your luggage allowance. If you are without a fellow-traveler, call Greyhound (800-231-2222) at least 48 hours before you plan to travel so that they can make arrangements to assist you. Many **ferries** that run up and down the Pacific coast can also accommodate travelers who are disabled; consult the companies listed under By Ferry in the Getting There and Getting Around section below.

American Foundation for the Blind, 15 W. 16th St., New York, NY 10011 (212-620-2147). ID cards ($10); write for an application, or call the Product Center (800-829-0500). Also call this number to order AFB catalogs in braille, print, or on cassette or disk.

Directions Unlimited, 720 North Bedford Rd., Bedford Hills, NY 10507 (800-533-5343 or 914-241-1700). Specializes in arranging individual and group vacations, tours and cruises for those with disabilities. Organizes tours for individuals.

Evergreen Travel Service, 4114 198th St. SW, Suite #13, Lynnwood, WA 98036 (800-435-2288 or 206-776-1184). Arranges wheelchair-accessible tours and individual travel worldwide. Other services include tours for the blind, the deaf and tours for those not wanting a fast-paced itinerary.

Mobility International, USA (MIUSA), P.O. Box 3551, Eugene, OR 97403 (503-343-1284 voice and TDD). International headquarters in Britain, 228 Borough High St., London SE1 1JX (tel. 44 071 403 5688). Contacts in 30 countries. Information on travel programs, international work camps, accommodations, access guides, and organized tours. Membership costs $20 per year, newsletter $10. Sells updated and expanded *A World of Options: A Guide to International Educational Exchange, Community Service, and Travel for Persons with Disabilities* ($14 for members, $16 for non-members, postpaid).

Society for the Advancement of Travel for the Handicapped, 347 Fifth Ave. #610, New York, NY 10016 (212-447-7284; fax 212-725-8253). Publishes quarterly travel newsletter *SATH News* and information booklets (free for members, $3 each for non-members). Advice on trip planning for people with disabilities. Annual membership is $45, students and seniors $25.

Twin Peaks Press, P.O. Box 129, Vancouver, WA 98666 (206-694-2462, orders only 800-637-2256). *Travel for the Disabled* lists tips and resources for disabled travelers ($20). Also available are the *Directory for Travel Agencies of the Disabled* ($20) and *Wheelchair Vagabond* ($15). Postage $2 per book.

■ Travelers with Children

If you're planning a family vacation with the kids, you'll need to adapt your travel pace to their needs. There are plenty of attractions in the Pacific Northwest to keep both you and your kids entertained, possibly at the same time. Consult local newspapers or travel bureaus to find out about events that might be of special interest for young children, such as the Cannon Beach Sandcastle Festival in Oregon or the annual Magicazam magic show that visits Portland in the summer. Most national parks offer **Junior Ranger** programs, which introduce kids ages 8-12 to nature in half- or full-day trips (see Parks & Forests in the Camping & the Outdoors section).

Many fares, admission prices, and fees are lower for children and/or families. Some lodgings, such as the **Days Inn,** offer special rates for rooms with kitchenettes (see Accommodations below). **Amtrak** and many airlines also offer discounts for children (see Getting There and Getting Around, below), but it's often easier to travel by car than by other forms of transportation. With a car, you have the freedom to make frequent stops, and children have more room to spread out.

Children require additional health and safety considerations while on the road. If you're renting a car, be sure that the company supplies a child safety seat for children under five years old. Before forging into the wilderness, consider picking up one of the following publications:

Lonely Planet Publications, Embarcadero West, 112 Linden St., Oakland, CA 94607 (510-893-8555 or 800-275-8555); also P.O. Box 617, Hawthorn, Victoria 3122, Australia. Publishes Maureen Wheeler's *Travel with Children* ($11, postage $1.50 in the U.S.).

John Muir Publications, P.O. Box 613, Santa Fe, NM 87504 (800-888-7504). The *Kidding Around* series ($10 each; $4.25 shipping) are illustrated books intended for children, depicting mostly U.S. destinations.

Wilderness Press, 2440 Bancroft Way, Berkeley, CA 94704-1676 (800-443-7227 or 510-543-8080). Publishes *Backpacking with Babies and Small Children* ($10) and *Sharing Nature with Children* ($9).

■ Traveling Alone

Single accommodations are usually much more costly per person than doubles. In addition, if you do travel alone, you should be extremely careful about where you sleep: outdoor locations make the lone traveler an easy target.

Even if you're alone, chances are you won't be hurting for company along the way. If you carry your copy of *Let's Go,* you might be noticed by others doing the same (sympathetically, we hope—although they may ask you things like "What's a nice person like you doing with an ugly book like that?"). Another trick for finding people with whom you may have some connection is to wear a baseball cap or T-shirt from your home state or college.

■ Kosher and Vegetarian Travelers

The Northwest heaps blessings on vegetarian and kosher travelers alike. Fresh fish, fruits, and vegetables abound in both the larger cities and smaller towns of the region. Delicious apples and Chinook salmon are just a couple of the area's indigenous treats. Vegetarian travelers can obtain *The Vegetarian Travel Guide* and *Vegetarian Times Guide to Natural Foods Restaurants in the U.S. and Canada* (each costs $16 plus $2 postage) from the **North American Vegetarian Society,** P.O. Box 72, Dolgeville, NY 13329 (518-568-7970).

Kosher travelers should contact synagogues in Seattle, Portland, Vancouver, Edmonton, and Calgary for information about kosher restaurants in those cities; your own synagogue or college Hillel should have access to lists of Jewish institutions across the continent. *The Jewish Travel Guide* ($12 plus $1.75 postage) from **Sepher-Hermon Press,** 1265 46th St., Brooklyn, NY 11219 (718-972-9010), lists Jewish institutions, synagogues, and kosher restaurants in over 80 countries.

■ Minority Travelers

We have been hard-pressed to find any resources that advise members of visible minorities on specific travel concerns; if our readers have knowledge of any such information, please write to and let us know.

In terms of safety, we don't have any easy answers. Traveling in groups and taking a taxi whenever you are uncomfortable are always good ideas; your personal safety should always be your first priority. Keep abreast of the particular cultural attitudes of the countries you're planning to visit. But above all, keep in mind that your own ethnicity or religion will not necessarily be problematic; you very well may find your vacation trouble-free and your hosts open-minded.

Getting There and Getting Around

■■■ BY AIR

■ Commercial Airlines

When dealing with any commercial airline, buying in advance is always the best bet. The commercial carriers' lowest regular offer is the **APEX** (Advanced Purchase Excursion Fare); specials advertised in newspapers may be cheaper, but have correspondingly more restrictions and fewer available seats. APEX fares provide you with confirmed reservations and often allow "open-jaw" tickets (landing and returning from different cities). APEX tickets must usually be purchased two to three weeks ahead of the departure date. Be sure to inquire about any restrictions on length of stay (the minimum is most often 7 days, the maximum 2 months; shorter or longer stays usually mean more money).

To obtain the cheapest fare, buy a round-trip ticket and stay over at least one Saturday; traveling on off-peak days (Mon.-Thurs. morning) is usually $30-40 cheaper than traveling on the weekends. You will need to pay for the ticket within 24 hours of booking the flight, and tickets are entirely non-refundable. Any change in plans incurs a fee of between $25 (for some domestic flights) and $150 (for many international flights), even if only to change the date of departure or return. Since travel peaks between June and August and around holidays, reserve a seat several months in advance for these times.

In the last few years the major U.S. carriers have taken to waging **price wars** (sometimes including two-for-one specials) in the spring and early summer months. Because there is no way to tell when (if at all) such sales will occur, advance purchase may not always guarantee the lowest fare. It will guarantee a seat, though, which has its advantages.

Last-minute travelers should also ask about **"red-eye"** (all-night) flights which are common on popular business routes. It is not wise to buy "free" tickets (i.e. **"frequent-flyer" coupons** given by airlines allowing the passenger named on them to fly a stated number of miles) from others—it is standard policy on most commercial airlines to check a photo I.D., and you could find yourself paying for a new, full-fare ticket. Whenever and however you fly, call the airline the day before your departure to reconfirm your flight reservation, and get to the airport early to ensure you have a seat; airlines often overbook. (On the other hand, being "bumped" from a flight does not spell doom if your travel plans are flexible—you will probably leave on the next flight and receive either a free ticket or a cash bonus. You might even want to bump yourself when the airline asks for volunteers.) Chances of receiving discount fares increase on competitive routes; flying smaller airlines instead of the national giants can also save money. Most airlines allow children under two to fly free (on the lap of an adult), but discounts for older children and seniors are rare.

Be sure to check with your travel agent for system-wide air passes and excursion fares, especially since these generally have fewer advance-purchase requirements than standard tickets. Consider **discount travel agencies** such as **Travel Avenue,** 180 N. Desplains St., Chicago, IL, 60661 (800-333-3335), which rebates 7% on the price of all domestic airline tickets minus a $10 ticketing fee, and rebates an average 5% to 17% on international airline tickets minus a $25 ticketing fee. Student-oriented agencies such as **CIEE, Travel CUTS,** and **STA Travel** (see Useful Organizations: Budget Travel Services above) sometimes have special deals that regular travel agents can't offer. The weekend travel sections of major newspapers (especially *The New York Times*) are good places to seek out bargain fares from a variety of carriers. If you're looking to bypass travel agents altogether, consult the *Official Airline Guide (OAG)*, 2000 Clearwater Dr., Oakbrook IL 60521 (800-323-3537), which publishes both North American and worldwide editions. The *OAG* is published twice a month and lists every flight and connection on nearly every carrier; the guide also lists toll-free phone numbers for all the airlines which allow you to call in your reservations directly. Since schedules change frequently and the guides are updated twice a month, a far better idea than purchasing the guides is to look at copies in a library reference room.

A total **smoking** ban is in effect on all scheduled service flights within and between the 48 contiguous U.S. states, within Hawaii and Alaska, and to and from Hawaii and Alaska if the flight is under six hours. This ban applies to both U.S. and international carriers operating within these areas. Flights touching a point outside the U.S. are not affected.

The Canadian policy is still more stringent: a total smoking ban is in effect on all aircraft registered in Canada. This includes service within and between points in Canada as well as all international service (except flights to and from Japan).

WITHIN NORTH AMERICA

International travelers should realize that given the long distances between points within the United States and Canada, North Americans rely on buses and trains for travel much less than everyone else in the world. Buses and trains take considerably longer, and, especially over larger distances, do not always confer a savings equal to the added trouble (a cross-country trip will take 3 or 4 days, compared with 6 hours by plane). Expect, then, to use these forms of transportation less than you would at home. The major carriers serving Alaska and the Pacific Northwest are listed below, together with some sample fares:

Air Canada, P.O. Box 14000, St. Laurent, Quebec H4Y 1H4 Canada (800-776-3000). Ask about special discounts for youths ages 12-24 on stand-by tickets for flights within Canada. Discounts can be substantial, although youth tickets can sometimes be more expensive than advance purchase fares. In summer 1993, regular fares included Montreal to Seattle $486; Toronto to Anchorage $600; Montreal to Vancouver $524. All quoted prices 14-day advance purchase with a max. stay of 1 year.

Alaska Airlines, P.O. Box 68900, Seattle, WA 98168 USA (800-426-03333). In summer 1993, round-trip fares included LA to Anchorage $542; Seattle to Anchorage $430 (although specials are sometimes offered); Montreal to Anchorage $628; Anchorage to Fairbanks $214. Quoted prices are 14-day advance purchase for a mid-week flight with a Saturday stop-over.

Northwest, P.O. Box 249, Fort Smith, NWT X0E 0P0, Canada (800-225-2525). In summer 1993, round-trip fares included LA to Seattle $200-340 with max. stay of 30 days, and $380-470 for max. stay of 1 year; NYC to Anchorage $672 with max. stay of 30 days, and $732 with max. stay of 1 year; Toronto to Anchorage $558 with max. stay of 1 year.

Other airlines to consider when flying into Alaska and the Pacific Northwest include **United,** P.O. Box 66100, Chicago, IL 60666 USA (800-241-6522); **USAir,** Crystal Park Four Dr., Arlington, VA 22227 USA (800-428-4322); and **Continental,** 2929 Allen Parkway, Houston, TX 77210 USA (800-525-0280).

Many major U.S. airlines offer special **"Visit USA"** air passes and fares to international travelers. You must purchase these passes outside the U.S., paying one price for a certain number of "flight coupons." Each coupon is good for one flight segment on an airline's domestic system within a certain time period; typically, all travel must be completed within 30-60 days. Some cross-country trips may require two segments. The point of departure and the destination must be specified for each coupon at the time of purchase, and once in the States any change in route will incur a fee of between $50 and $75. Dates of travel may be changed once travel has begun at no charge. **United** offers three vouchers for $305, and additional vouchers (up to 5 more) sell for $97 apiece. **USAir** offers three vouchers for $409 from July through mid-September, and for $349 off-season. Additional vouchers (up to 5 more) run $80 apiece year-round. **Continental, Delta** (800-221-1212), and **TWA** (800-892-4141) all offer programs as well.

   Mexican residents who live more than 100 mi. from the border may be eligible for "Visit USA" discount flight passes on some carriers. Otherwise, because flying in the U.S. is expensive, it may be cheaper to fly on a Mexican airline to one of the border towns, and then to travel by train or bus from there. Contact **AeroMexico** (800-237-6639) for more information.

   In recent years **American Express** has run promotions whereby students are offered a pre-approved green card along with vouchers for inexpensive domestic flights. Of course, you have to pay the $55 annual fee for the card, but the savings on longer flights can be substantial. Be sure to read the fine print about black-out dates and other restrictions. See Money: Credit Cards above for more information.

   If all you need is a short flight, scout **local airfields** for prospective rides on private, non-commercial planes. Some airfields have ride boards. If not, a good place to begin is the operations counter, where pilots file their flight plans. Ask where they are headed and if they'd like a passenger. Remember that propeller planes have a much higher accident rate than their larger commercial counterparts; if the pilots seem even slightly concerned about the weather, think about staying earthbound.

FROM EUROPE

Travelers from Europe will experience the least competition for inexpensive seats during the off-season. Peak season rates generally take effect on either May 15 or June 1 and run until about September 15. You can take advantage of cheap off-season flights within Europe to reach an advantageous point of departure for North America. (London is a major connecting point for budget flights to the U.S.; New York City is often the destination.) Once in the States, you can catch a coast-to-coast flight to make your way out West; see Within North America above for details.

   If you decide to fly with a commercial airline rather than through a charter agency or ticket consolidator (see below), you'll be purchasing greater reliability, security, and flexibility. Many major airlines offer reduced-fare options, such as three-day advance purchase fares: these tickets can only be purchased within 72 hours of the time of the departure, and are restricted to youths under a certain age (often 24). Check with a travel agent for availability. **TWA** (800-892-4141) and **British Airways** (800-247-9297) both offer these fares on a variety of international flights. Seat availability is known only a few days before the flight, although airlines will sometimes issue predictions. The worst crunch leaving Europe takes place from mid-June to early July, while August is uniformly tight for returning flights; at no time can you count on getting a seat right away.

   Another reduced-fare option is the **APEX,** described at the beginning of the Commercial Airlines section. For summer travel, book APEX fares early; by June you may have difficulty getting the departure date you want. **American,** 15 Berkeley St., London, W1A 6ND (800-624-6262), often has good fares from London: 1993 rates included London to NYC $593 peak-season, and $357 off-season, with a maximum stay of one year. Tickets must be purchased 21 days in advance, and flights leave mid-week. **British Airways,** P.O. Box 10, Heathrow Airport (London), Hounslow TW6 2JA, England (800-247-9297) has extensive service from London to North America. 1993 round-trip fares included London to NYC $609 peak-season, and $395 off-season; London to Seattle $736 peak, and $517 off-season. All fares are 14-day advance purchase, leaving mid-week with a Saturday stop-over. For three-day advance purchase tickets, the maximum stay is one year with an open return, and you must be under 25. A three-day advance purchase ticket from London to NYC runs $876 peak-season.

Smaller, budget airlines often undercut major carriers by offering bargain fares on regularly scheduled flights. Competition for seats on these smaller carriers during peak season is fierce—book early. Discount trans-Atlantic airlines include **Virgin Atlantic Airways** (800-862-8621 daily 7am-11pm) and **Icelandair** (800-223-5500). Virgin Atlantic's fares from London to NYC range between $430-$645, depending on the season, and prices to Boston, MA are equivalent. Tickets require a 21-day advance purchase with mid-week travel and a Saturday stop-over. Icelandair flies heavily out of Luxembourg; all trans-Atlantic flights connect through Iceland.

FROM AUSTRALIA, NEW ZEALAND, ASIA, AND SOUTH AFRICA

Whereas European travelers may choose from a variety of regular reduced fares, their counterparts in Asia, Australia, and South Africa must rely on APEX. A good place to start searching for tickets is the local branch of one of the budget travel agencies listed above, near the beginning of the Commercial Airlines section. **STA Travel** is probably the largest international agency you will find: they have offices in Sydney, Melbourne, and Auckland. For more information on STA, see Useful Organizations: Budget Travel Services above.

Qantas (800-227-4500), **Air New Zealand** (800-663-5494), **United,** and **Northwest** fly between Australia or New Zealand and the United States, and both **Canadian Pacific Airlines** and **Northwest** fly to Canada. Prices are roughly equivalent among the five (American carriers tend to be a bit less), but the cities they serve differ. A typical fare from Sydney to Los Angeles ranges $1250-1400 peak-season, and $1000-1200 off-season. A typical fare from Sydney to Toronto ranges $100-150 more. Advance purchase fares from Australia have extremely tough restrictions. If you are uncertain about your plans, pay extra for an advance purchase ticket that has only a 50% penalty for cancellation. Many travelers from Australia and New Zealand reportedly take Singapore Air or other Far-East based carriers during the initial leg of their trip. Check with STA or another budget agency for more comprehensive information.

From Japan, U.S. airlines such as **Northwest** (800-225-2525) and **United Airlines** (800-538-2929) offer rates slightly higher than those of **Japan Airlines** (800-525-3663). Expect to pay between $2000 and $2500 in the summer months for a round-trip ticket from Tokyo to Los Angeles, and between $1100 and $1700 off-season. From Hong Kong, fares on these airlines generally run $300-400 less than from Tokyo for round-trip tickets.

British Airways (800-247-9297), **American** (800-624-6262), and **South African Airways** (800-722-9675) all connect South Africa with North America. Round-trip fares for the 16½-hour flight between Johannesberg and New York City range from $1400 to $2200 peak-season, and from $1150 to $2000 off-season.

■ Charter Flights

Those wishing to bypass the larger commercial airlines should consider booking through a charter company or through a ticket consolidator. **Charter flights** can save you a lot of money. They are roughly equivalent to flying a commercial airline: your reservation guarantees you a seat on the plane, and you can be certain that if you don't get on the flight someone (other than you) is to blame. Many charters book passengers up to the last minute—some will not even sell tickets more than 30 days in advance. However, many flights fill up well before their departure date. You must choose your departure and return dates when you book, and you will lose all or most of your money if you cancel your ticket. Charter companies themselves reserve the right to change the dates of your flight or even cancel the flight a mere 48 hours in advance. Delays are not uncommon. To be safe, get your ticket as early as possible, and arrive at the airport several hours before departure time. Many of the smaller charter companies work by contracting service with commercial airlines, and the length of your stay is often limited by the length of the company's contract. Prices and destinations can change (sometimes markedly) from season to season, so be sure to contact as many organizations as possible in order to get the best deal. For more information, contact the charter companies listed below:

CIEE Travel Services, 205 E. 42nd St., New York, NY 10017 (800-800-8222 or 212-661-03111; fax 212-972-0194). A variety of flights from Europe to the U.S., although none originating from London. Rates are higher in peak-season, which runs mid-June to mid-Sept. In summer 1993, Paris to New York City (NYC) was $608 peak season, and $478 off-season. Brussels to NYC $669 peak, and $569 off-season. All prices for round-trip tickets. Phones open Mon.-Fri. 8am-8pm, Sat. 9am-5pm. (For more information on CIEE, see Useful Organizations above.)

Travel CUTS, 187 College St., Toronto, Ont. M5T 1P7 (416-979-2406; fax 416-979-8167). The Canadian equivalent to CIEE. One program, open to all Canadians, flies direct into major Canadian destinations from the larger European cities; peak season (and rates) run May-Oct. A second program for students and youths (under 26) is similar to the first, except that all European flights connect through London and the fares are somewhat less. Student/Youth tickets have a min. stay of 1 week, and a max. stay of 6 months. Student/Youth fares from London to Toronto $530-650 mid-June to mid-Sept., and $430-540 off-season. Both programs also feature discount rates on domestic charters within Canada. Student/Youth fares from Toronto to Vancouver $330-$430 for a round-trip ticket. Phones open Mon.-Fri. 9am-5pm. (For more information on Travel CUTS, see Useful Organizations above.)

Unitravel, 1177 N. Warson Rd., St. Louis, MO 63132 (800-325-2222; fax 314-569-2503). Specializes in trans-continental and long distance flights within the U.S. 1993 fares included NYC to Seattle $422; NYC to L.A. $414; Chicago to L.A. $342. All prices round-trip; 6-day advance purchase with a Saturday stop-over required. Max. stay varies with the carrier involved. All payments will be held in a bank escrow until the completion of your trip. Phones open Mon.-Fri. 8am-8pm, Sat. 8am-4pm.

Also try **DER Tours,** 9501 West Devon Ave. Ste. 400, Rosemont, IL 60018 (800-782-2424), Mon.-Fri. 8am-8pm central time; fax 800-282-7474), and **Travel Charter,** 1120 East Longlake Rd., Troy, MI 48098 (800-521-5267 or 313-528-3500; fax 313-528-0743), both of which offer charter flights to a more limited range of cities.

■ Ticket Consolidators

Ticket Consolidators are companies which sell unbooked commercial and charter airline seats; tickets gained through them are both less expensive and more risky than those on charter flights. Companies work on a space-available basis which does not guarantee a seat; you get priority over those flying stand-by but below that of regularly-booked passengers. Although Consolidators which originate flights in Europe, Australia, or Asia are scarce, the market for flights within North America is a good one, and growing. Consolidators tend to be reliable on these domestic flights, both in getting you on the flight and in getting you exactly where you want to go. Flexibility is often necessary, but all companies guarantee that they will put you on a flight or refund your money. On the day of the flight, the earlier you arrive at the airport the better, since ticket agents seat passengers in the order that they've checked them in. Now Voyager and Airhitch are currently the largest and least-expensive consolidators. **Now Voyager,** 74 Varick St. #307, New York, NY 10013 (212-431-1616), boasts reliability which rivals that of most charter companies (97% of customers get on their flights the first time), while its prices are still considerably less. NYC to LA runs $125 each way; and NYC to Chicago $75 each way. Flights run exclusively out of and into NYC. (Phones open Mon.-Fri. 10am-5:30pm and Sat. noon-4:30pm, EST.)

Airhitch, 2790 Broadway #100, New York, NY 10025 (212-864-2000 on the East Coast; 310-394-0550 on the West Coast), works through more cities and to a greater number of destinations, although their prices are slightly higher and flights are less destination-specific (meaning that often you must list, in order of priority, two or three cities within a given region which you are willing to fly to; Airhitch guarantees only that you will get to one of these cities). For most flights you must give a range of three to five days within which you are willing to travel. Be sure to read *all* the fine print (especially since payment occurs well in advance of the actual flight), and to check all flight times and departure sites directly with the carrier. The aptly named "Calhitch" program connects NYC with L.A. and San Francisco for $129. All fares are one-way in either direction. (East Coast phone lines open Mon.-Fri. 10am-6pm, Sat. 11am-4pm; off-season open Mon.-Fri. 10am-4pm, Sat. 11am-1pm.)

■■■ BY CAR

■ Getting Revved Up

If you'll be relying heavily on car travel, you would do well to join an automobile club. For $15-70 per year (depending on where you live and how many benefits you choose) the **American Automobile Association (AAA),** 100 AAA Drive, Heathrow, FL 32746-5080 (800-AAA-HELP/ 800-222-4357 or check your local yellow pages), offers free trip-planning services, roadmaps and guidebooks, discounts on car rentals (in association with Hertz), emergency road service anywhere in the U.S., free towing (although the number of miles varies with your regional association and can sometimes be as few as 3), the International Driver's License (see Documents and Formalities, above), and commission-free AmEx traveler's cheques. Your membership card doubles as a $5000 bail bond (if you find yourself in jail) or a $1000 arrest bond certificate (which you can use in lieu of being arrested for any motor vehicle offense except drunk driving, driving without a valid license, or failure to appear in court on a prior motor-vehicle arrest). If someone in your household already owns a membership, you may be added on as an associate with full benefits for a cost of about $20-25 per year. Many clubs also have an "AAA Plus" membership program, often costing about $20 more than basic membership, which provides more extensive emergency road service, insurance protection, and 100 mi. of free towing (this is not as far as it seems in rural areas, where AAA-affiliated garages can be few and far between). AAA has reciprocal agreements with the auto associations of many other countries which often provide you with full benefits while in the U.S.

Other automobile travel service organizations are affiliated with oil companies or other large corporations. These include:

AMOCO Motor Club, P.O Box 9041, Des Moines, IA 50368 (800-334-3300). $50 annual membership enrolls you, your spouse, and your car. Services include 24-hr. towing (5 mi. free or free back to the tower's garage) and emergency road service. Premier membership ($75) brings 50 mi. free towing.

Mobil Auto Club, 200 N. Martingale Rd., Schaumburg, IL 60174 (800-621-5581). $45 annual membership covers you and one other person of your choice. Benefits include locksmith, free towing (up to 10 mi.) and other roadside services, as well as car-rental discounts with Hertz, Avis, and National.

If you'll be driving during your trip, make sure that your **insurance** is up-to-date and that you are completely covered. Car rental companies often offer additional insurance coverage, as does American Express if you use them to rent the car. *In Canada, automobile insurance with coverage of CDN$200,000 is mandatory.* If you are involved in a car accident and you don't have insurance, the stiff fine will not improve the experience, and your car may be impounded to boot. U.S. motorists are advised to carry some form proving that they have insurance, the most effective of which is the **Canadian Non-Resident Inter-Provincial Motor Vehicle Liability Card.** The cards are available through U.S. insurers. For more information on insurance issues within Canada, contact The Insurance Bureau of Canada, 181 University Ave., Toronto, Ont. M5H 3M7. For information on the **International Driver's License,** see Documents and Formalities above.

Let's Go lists U.S. highways in the following format: "I" (as in "I-90") refers to Interstate highways, "U.S." (as in "U.S. 1") to United States Highways, and "Rte." (as in "Rte. 7") to state and local highways.

■ On The Road

Learn a bit about minor automobile maintenance and repair before you leave, and pack an easy-to-read manual—it may at the very least help you keep your car alive long enough to reach a reputable garage. If you've never done it before, practice changing your tire once or twice without help, and spend an afternoon discovering what's under the hood. Your trunk should at least contain the following **bare necessities:** a spare tire and jack, jumper cables, extra oil, flares, a blanket (several, if you're traveling in winter), extra water (if you're traveling in summer or through the desert), and a flashlight. If there's a chance you may be stranded in a remote area, bring an emergency food and water supply. Always have plenty of gas and check road conditions ahead of time when possible, particularly during the winter. (*Let's Go* provides road condition hotline numbers where available.) Carry a good map with you at all times. **Rand McNally** publishes the most comprehensive road atlas of the U.S. and Canada, available in bookstores for around $8.

Gas is generally cheaper in towns than at interstate service stops. When planning your budget, remember that the enormous travel distances of the Pacific Northwest and Alaska will require you to spend more on gas than you might expect. Burn less money by burning less fuel. Tune up the car, make sure the tires are in good repair and properly aligned and inflated, check the oil frequently, and avoid running the air conditioner unnecessarily. Don't use roof luggage racks—they cause air drag, and if you need one, you've probably over-packed. Check college campus ride boards, bulletin boards, and the classified ads (particularly those in newspapers geared to students) to find traveling companions who will split gasoline costs. Those in Alaska should **gas up whenever possible.** Filling stations can be few and far between. And it's also a good idea to carry and emergency supply of cash, since many filling stations in the more remote areas don't accept credit cards.

If you take a car into a major city, try not to leave valuable **possessions**—such as radios or luggage—in it while you're away from the car. Radios are especially tempting; if your tape deck or radio is removable, hide it in the trunk or take it with you. If it isn't detachable, at least conceal it under some junk. Similarly, hide baggage in the trunk—although some savvy thieves can tell if a car is heavily loaded by the way it is settled on its tires. (Solution: travel light; see Packing above.) Park your vehicle in a garage or well-traveled area. Sleeping in a car or van parked in the city is extremely dangerous—even the most dedicated budget traveler should not consider it an option.

Be sure to **buckle up**—it's the law in Washington, British Columbia, and Alberta. Before you hit the road, check rental cars to make sure that the seatbelts work properly. In general, the speed limit in the U.S. is 55mph, but rural sections of major interstates may well be 65mph (when posted). Heed the limit; not only does it save gas, but most local police forces and state troopers make frequent use of radar to catch speed demons.

In the 1950s, President Dwight D. Eisenhower envisioned an **interstate system,** a federally funded network of highways designed primarily to increase military mobility and subsidize American commerce. Eisenhower's asphalt dream gradually has been realized, although Toyotas far outnumber tanks on the federally funded roads. Believe it or not, there is actually an easily comprehensible, consistent system for numbering interstates. Even-numbered interstates run east-west and odd ones run north-south, decreasing in number the further north or west they are. If the interstate has a three-digit number, it is a branch of another interstate (i.e., I-285 is a branch of I-85), often a bypass skirting around a large city. An *even* digit in the *hundred's* place means the branch will eventually return to the main interstate; an *odd* digit means it won't. North-south routes begin on the West Coast with I-5 and end with I-95 on the East Coast. The southernmost east-west route is I-4 in Florida. The northernmost east-west route is I-94, stretching from Montana to Wisconsin.

The greatest difficulty posed by interstates is not the state troopers, the other drivers, or even bad road conditions (although these can be imposing)—it's the sheer **boredom.** For a normally active brain, license plate games only stave off the soporific monotony for so long. To prevent "frozen vision," don't keep your eyes glued to the road. If you feel drowsy, pull off the road to take a break, even if there are no official rest areas in the vicinity. To avoid over-exhaustion, start driving in the wee hours of the morning and stop early in the afternoon (this way, you'll also have more time to find accommodations). When you're driving with companions, insist that one of them is awake at all times, and keep talking. If you can't pull over, try listening to an aggravating radio talk show (music can be as lulling as silence). A thermos of coffee is also helpful. And remember that turning up the heat too high in the car can also make you sleepy.

Never drive if you've had anything alcoholic to drink or if you've used drugs or any potentially impairing substance. Don't believe the myth that a cup of hot coffee or a cold shower can sober you up; the only remedy for a buzz is time, preferably spent doing some sort of activity (it burns off the alcohol faster), but several hours' sleep should do. Also, avoid the open road on weekend nights and holidays, when more drivers are likely to be drunk.

■ Driving in Alaska

Juneau, the only state capital in the nation that cannot be reached by automobile, is symbolic of Alaska's inaccessibility. In fact, roads reach only a quarter of the state's area. In 1942—under pressure to create wartime supply routes for Alaska's far-flung military bases—the U.S. Army Corps of Engineers built a 1500-mi. road from British Columbia to Fairbanks in an astonishingly quick eight months. The **Alaska Hwy.,** as it is now called, runs from Dawson Creek, BC, to Fairbanks. The Canadian stretch of the road is poorly maintained, causing the entire drive to take three to five days. Only hardsiders should attempt this trip; lodgings en route are hard to come by. Winter and summer travelers alike are advised to let a friend or relative know of their position along the highway several times in the course of the trip.

The **Haines Hwy.** connects Haines with the Alaska Hwy. at Haines Junction. Similarly, **Route 2** connects Skagway with the Alaska Hwy. in Whitehorse. In Fairbanks, the Alaska Hwy. merges into the **Dalton Hwy.,** which runs all the way north to Prudhoe Bay. Running south from the Alaska Hwy., the **George Parks Hwy.** goes to Denali and Anchorage from Fairbanks; the **Richardson Hwy.** goes to Glennallen from Delta Junction and continues on to Valdez; and the **Tok Cut Off** goes to Glennallen from Tok and merges into the **Glenn Hwy.,** which continues to Anchorage. From Anchorage, the **Seward Hwy.** goes to Seward, and the **Sterling Hwy.** splits off to go to Homer. The highways that traverse the southern part of the state are narrow, often gravelly ribbons extending from town to town with few services in between.

Many major roads in Alaska are still in **desperately bad shape.** Dust and flying rocks are major hazards in the summer, as are the road construction crews, which interrupt long-distance trips with miserable 10- to 30-mi. patches of gravel as they repave the road. Many of the worst roads in Alaska (such as the Dalton Hwy. from Fairbanks to Prudhoe Bay) have been treated with calcium chloride to minimize the dust flying up from the road. Calcium chloride can be very hard on your car's paint, though, and you should take every opportunity to wash your car. And *drive* *slowly*— it will not make the trip much easier on your own car, it will also keep dust from flying into the windshields of those behind you. Melting and contracting permafrost in the north causes "frost heaves," creating dips and Daliesque twists on the road. Radiators and headlights should be protected from flying rocks and swarming bugs with a **wire screen;** plastic **headlight covers** can protect your lights; good **shocks** and a functional **spare tire** are absolutely essential. Wintertime snow cover can actually smooth your ride a bit: the packed surface and the thinned traffic it brings permit easy driving without the summer's mechanical troubles (although the dangers of avalanches and driving on ice offer a different set of concerns). Check road conditions before traveling; in Anchorage call 243-7675 (winter only) or tune in to local radio stations.

As a final precaution, keep in your car at all times the following in case of emergency or break-down: flares, a good set of tools and wrenches, a good jack, electrician's tape, and a fan belt.

Two valuable guides which include maps, detailed, mile-by-mile car routes and general travel information are available from **Vernon Publications, Inc.,** 3000 Northup Way, Suite 200, Bellevue, WA (800-726-4707). *The MILEPOST* is an exceptional guide to Alaska and northwestern Canada ($19), and, for off-the-road travel in Alaska, *The Alaska Wilderness Guide* covers bush communities and remote national parks, monuments, wilderness areas, and refuges ($17).

■ Driving in the Northwest

Unlike the more densely populated regions of the continent, the Northwest does not have an extensive system of quality secondary roads. Older highways predominate; they merge with the main street of each town in their path, and are slower to drive—but far more rewarding—than most interstate freeways. Venture down unpaved roads for some unforgettable vistas, but be sure to have plenty of gas and a healthy driving machine. And before you hit the road, particularly during the winter, check out the **road conditions.**

Several major interstate highways provide connections between cities in the Northwest. Running north-south through Oregon and Washington are **I-5** and **US 101.** I-5 connects Portland and Seattle and is the fastest route through the region, while 101 hugs the coast and is known for its scenery. **I-84,** running east-west, connects with I-5 near Portland and runs along the Oregon/Washington border before dipping southeast toward Boise, Idaho and Salt Lake City, Utah. **I-90** runs east from its junction with I-5 near Seattle through Spokane and then into northern Idaho and Montana.

The **Trans Canada Hwy.** (Hwy. 1) is Canada's major east-west artery and connects Calgary and Vancouver. The **Mackenzie Hwy.** (Hwy. 2) runs north-south through Alberta and connects Calgary and Edmonton. Hwy. 97, the **Cariboo Hwy.,** joins southern and northern BC, including the towns of Prince George and Dawson Creek. For those continuing north from Dawson Creek, it's the 2647-km-long **Alaskan Hwy.,** which goes through the Yukon Territory and into northeastern Alaska, ending in Fairbanks (see Driving in Alaska, below). To more easily picture the roads listed above, see the map to the Yukon Territory and Alaska.

■ Renting

Although the cost of renting a car for long distances is often prohibitive, renting for local trips may be reasonable. **Auto rental agencies** fall into two categories: national companies with thousands of branches, and local agencies that serve only one city or region. The former usually allow cars to be picked up in one city and dropped off in another (for a hefty charge). By calling a toll-free number you can reserve a reliable car anywhere in the country. Drawbacks include steep prices and high minimum ages for rentals (usually 25). If you're 21 or older and have a major credit card in your name, you may be able to rent where the minimum age would otherwise rule you out. Student discounts are occasionally available. Try **Alamo** (800-327-9633), **Avis** (800-331-1212), **Budget** (800-527-0700), **Dollar** (800-800-4000), **Hertz** (800-654-3131), **National** (800-328-4567), or **Thrifty** (800-367-2277). Dollar, Thrifty, and Alamo rent to those 21 to 25; expect to pay an additional charge of $10-20 per day, even when renting for a week or more.

Local companies are often more flexible and cheaper than major companies, but you'll generally have to return the car to its point of origin. Some local companies will accept a cash deposit ($50-100) or simply proof of employment (e.g., check stubs) in lieu of a credit card. Companies such as **Rent-A-Wreck** (800-421-7253) supply cars that are long past their prime. Sporting dents and purely decorative radios, the cars sometimes get very poor mileage, but they run and they're cheap. *Let's Go* lists the addresses and phone numbers of local rental agencies in most towns.

When dealing with any car rental company, make certain the price includes **insurance** against theft and collision. This may be an additional charge (commonly $12 per day), though **American Express** automatically insures any car rented with the card. If using AmEx to rent over a long period, you must enter a new contract with the rental company every 15 days for the card to continue its coverage; call AmEx's car rental, loss, and damage division (800-338-1670) for more information. **Rates** change on a day-to-day basis without notice, so be sure to call for information. Basic rental charges for a compact car run $17-45 per day and $85-250 per week (bills are commonly the same for 5 days as for 7), but most companies offer specials. Standard shift cars are usually a few dollars cheaper than automatics. Most packages allow you a certain number of miles free before the usual charge of 30 to 40 cents a mile takes effect; if you'll be driving a long distance (a few hundred miles or more), ask for an unlimited-mileage package. For rentals longer than a week, look into **automobile leasing,** which costs less than renting. Make sure, however, that your car is covered by a service plan to avoid the risk of outrageous repair bills.

■ Auto Transport Companies

Automobile transport companies match drivers with car owners who need cars moved from one city to another. Would-be travelers give the company their desired destination; the company finds the car. The only expenses are gas, food, tolls, and lodging. The company's insurance covers any breakdowns or damage. You must be at least 21, have a valid license, and agree to drive about 400 mi. per day on a fairly direct route. Companies regularly inspect current and past job references, take your fingerprints, and require a cash bond. Cars are available between most points, although it's easiest to find cars for traveling from coast to coast; New York and Los Angeles are popular transfer points.

If offered a car, look it over first. Think twice about accepting a gas guzzler since you'll be paying for the gas. With the company's approval, however, you may be able to share the cost with several companions. For more information, contact **Auto Driveaway,** 310 S. Michigan Ave., Chicago, IL 60604 (800-346-2277). Also try **A Anthony's Driveaway,** P.O. Box 502, 62 Railroad Ave., East Rutherford, NJ 07073 (201-935-8030; fax 201-935-2567).

■■■ BY TRAIN

Locomotion is still one of the cheapest and most comfortable ways to tour the Northwest. You can walk from car to car to stretch your legs, buy overpriced edibles in the snack bar, and shut out the sun to sleep in a reclining chair (the budget traveler should avoid paying unnecessarily for a roomette or bedroom). It is essential to travel light; not all stations will check your baggage and not all trains carry large amounts (though most long-distance ones do).

BY TRAIN

Amtrak, 60 Massachusetts Ave. NE, Washington, DC 20002 (800-872-7245), offers a discount **All-Aboard America** fare which divides the Continental U.S. into three regions—Eastern, Central, and Western. Amtrak charges the same rate for both one-way and round-trip travel, with three stopovers permitted and a maximum trip duration of 45 days. During the summer, rates are $199 if you travel within one region, $299 to travel within and between two regions, and $399 among three (from late-Aug. to Dec. 17 and early-Jan. to late-May, rates are $179, $229, and $259). Drawing a line from Chicago south roughly divides the first region from the second; drawing a north-south line through Denver roughly divides regions two and three. Your itinerary, including both cities and dates, must be set at the time the passes are purchased; the route may not be changed once travel has begun, although times and dates may be changed at no cost. Amtrak recommends reserving two to three months in advance for summer travel.

Another discount option, available only to those who aren't citizens of North America, is the **USA Rail Pass** which allows unlimited travel and unlimited stops over a period of either 15 or 30 days. As with the All-Aboard America program, the cost of this pass depends on the number of regions within which you wish to travel. The pass allowing 30 days of travel nationwide sells for $389 peak season, and $308 off-season; the 15-day nationwide pass sells for $309 peak season, and $208 off-season. The 30-day pass which limits travel to the western region only (as far east as Denver) sells for $229 peak season, and $178 off-season; the 15-day pass for the western region sells for $178 peak season, and $158 off-season.

Full fares vary according to time, day, and destination: Amtrak seldom places advance purchase requirements on its fares, although the number of seats sold at discount prices is often limited. These discount tickets are naturally the first to sell, so it's best to plan in advance and reserve early. One-way fares don't vary with the season, but round-trip tickets can be significantly cheaper if traveling between late August and late May, excepting Christmastime. Several routes, such as the *Coast Starlight* between Seattle and L.A., cross stunning countryside; round-trip tickets sell for $189 peak-season, and $164 off-season.

Amtrak offers several **discounts** from its full fares: children ages two to 15 accompanied by a parent (half-fare); children under age two (free on the lap of an adult); senior citizens (15% off for travel Mon.-Thurs.) and travelers with disabilities (25% off); current members of the U.S. armed forces and active-duty veterans (25% discount) and their dependents (12.5% discount). Circle trips and special holiday packages can save you money as well. Keep in mind that discounted air travel, particularly for longer distances, may be cheaper than train travel. For up-to-date information and reservations, contact your local Amtrak office or call. Travelers with hearing impairments may use a teletypewriter (800-523-6590; 800-562-6960 in PA).

VIA Rail, Place Ville Marie, Lobby Level, Montreal, Quebec H3B 2G6 (800-561-7860), is Amtrak's Canadian analogue, and makes British Columbia, Alberta, and the Yukon accessible to the Northwestern traveler. Routes are as scenic as Amtrak's and the fares are often more affordable. If you'll be traveling by train a great deal or across the rest of Canada as well you may save money with the **Canrail Pass,** which allows travel on 12 days within a 30-day period; distance traveled is unlimited. Between early June and late September, passes cost CDN$489, and, for senior citizens and youths under 24, CDN$439. Off-season passes cost CDN$329, and CDN$299 for youths and senior citizens.

Remember in pricing tickets that round-trip tickets are simply double the price of a one-way fare, and that off-season rates are 40% off peak rates, which are in effect between mid-June and early September. During the peak season, a one-way ticket from Toronto to Vancouver sells for CDN$474 in either direction.

A number of **discounts** apply on full-fare tickets: children ages two to 11 accompanied by an adult (half-fare); children under two (free on the lap of an adult); students and senior citizens (10% discount); passengers with disabilities and their companions together are charged a single fare, although a letter from a physician stating the companion is necessary for travel is required (see Special Concerns, above).

For Alaskans in the most isolated regions, the **Alaskan Railroad** may be the only link to civilization. North America's northernmost railroad covers 470 mi. of land—connecting Seward and Whittier in the south with Anchorage, Fairbanks, and Denali National Park farther north—much of which is inaccessible by road or boat. In 1984, the railroad, one of the last nationally-owned railroads in the country, was sold into private hands, changing its name to the **Alaska Railroad Company (ARRC),** P.O. Box 107500, Anchorage, AK 99510 (800-544-0552 or 907-265-2623). ARRC runs daily between Anchorage and Fairbanks (with a stop in Denali National Park) for $130 one-way and $260 round-trip; and between Anchorage and Seward (summer only) for $40 one-way and $70 round-trip. Given advance notice in the winter, the engineer will drop cargo or passengers along the way. The train is the only overland route to Whittier (round-trip $16 from Portage; add bus fare from Anchorage to Portage), and the 30-minute ride runs from Portage several times per day to coincide with the schedule of the ferry *M.V. Bartlett.* Advance reservations are required for all except Portage-Whittier trips.

On the Panhandle, the 90-year-old **White Pass and Yukon Route** carries passengers over an old Klondike Gold Rush trail from Skagway to Bennet, BC ($72). Motorcoach service continues on from there to Whitehorse in the Yukon Territory. For more information, contact the White Pass and Yukon Route, P.O. Box 435, Skagway 99840 (800-343-7373 or 983-2217).

■■■ BY BUS

Buses generally offer the most frequent and complete service between the cities and towns of the Pacific Northwest. Often they are the only way to reach smaller locales without a car. The exceptions are some rural areas and more open spaces, particularly in Alaska and the Yukon, where bus lines are sparse. Your biggest challenge when you travel by bus is scheduling. *Russell's Official National Motor Coach Guide* ($12.80 including postage) is an indispensable tool for constructing an itinerary. Updated each month, *Russell's Guide* contains schedules of literally every bus route (except Greyhound) between any two towns in the United States and Canada. Russell's also publishes a semiannual *Supplement,* which includes a Directory of Bus Lines, Bus Stations, and Route Maps ($5 each). To order any of the above, write Russell's Guides, Inc., P.O. Box 278, Cedar Rapids, IA 52406 (319-364-6138). Since schedules change frequently and the guide is updated monthly, a far better idea than purchasing the guide is to look at a copy in a library reference room.

Greyhound, P.O. Box 660362, Dallas TX 75266-0362 (800-231-2222 in the U.S.), operates the largest number of routes in both the U.S. and Canada. Within specific regions, other bus companies may provide more exhaustive services. Greyhound can get you both to and around the Northwest. As for Western Canada and Alaska, Greyhound doesn't run beyond Whitehorse, YT, but scheduled bus service connects British Columbia, Whitehorse, Skagway, and Haines with central Alaska, including Anchorage.

A number of **discounts** are available on Greyhound's standard-fare tickets (restrictions apply): senior citizens (Mon.-Thurs. 10%, Fri.-Sat. 5% off); children ages two to 11 (50% off); children under age two travel free (if they'll sit on your lap); travelers with disabilities and their companions together ride for the price of one.

Greyhound allows passengers to carry two pieces of luggage (up to 45 lbs. total) and to check two pieces of luggage (up to 100 lbs.). Whatever you stow in compartments underneath the bus should be clearly marked; get a claim check for it, and watch to make sure your luggage is on the same bus as you. Take a jacket, too; surprisingly efficient air-conditioning brings the temperature down to arctic levels.

If you plan to tour a great deal by bus within the U.S., you may save money with the **Ameripass,** which entitles you to unlimited travel for seven days ($250), 15 days ($350), or 30 days ($450); extensions for the seven- and 15-day passes cost $15 per day. The pass takes effect the first day used, so make sure you have a pretty good idea of your itinerary before you start. Before you purchase an Ameripass, total up the separate bus fares between towns to make sure that the pass is indeed more economical, or at least worth the unlimited flexibility it provides. TNM&D Coaches and Vermont Transit are actually Greyhound subsidiaries, and as such will honor Ameripasses. Check with the companies for specifics.

Greyhound also offers an **International Ameripass** for those from outside North America. These are primarily peddled in foreign countries, but they can also be purchased in either of Greyhound's International Offices, located in New York City (212-971-0492) and Los Angeles (213-629-840). A seven-day pass sells for $175, a 15-day pass for $250, and a 30-day pass for $325.

Greyhound schedule information can be obtained from any Greyhound terminal, or from the reservation center at the new toll-free number (800-231-2222). Greyhound is implementing a reservation system much like the airlines, which will allow you to call and reserve a seat or purchase a ticket by mail. If you call seven or more days in advance and want to purchase your ticket with a credit card, reservations can be made and the ticket mailed to you. Otherwise, you may make a reservation up to 24 hours in advance. You can also buy your ticket at the terminal, but arrive early. If you are boarding at a remote "flag stop," be sure you know exactly where the bus stops. It's a good idea to call the nearest agency and let them know you'll be waiting at the flag-stop for the bus and at what time.

Greyhound is a useful organization for the budget traveler; its fares are cheap, and its tendrils poke into virtually every corner of America. Be sure, however, to allow plenty of time for connections, and be prepared for possibly unsavory traveling companions. By all means avoid spending the night in a bus station. Though generally guarded, bus stations can be hangouts for dangerous or at least frightening characters. Try to arrange your arrivals for reasonable day or evening times. This will also make it easier for you to find accommodations for the night.

For a more unusual and social trip, consider **Green Tortoise,** P.O. Box 24459, San Francisco, CA 94124 (800-227-4766, in CA 415-821-0803). These funky "hostels on wheels" are remodeled diesel buses done up with foam mattresses, sofa seats, stereos, and dinettes; meals are prepared communally. Bus drivers operate in teams so that one can drive and the other can point out sites and chat with passengers. Prices include transportation, sleeping space on the bus, and tours of the regions through which you pass. Deposits ($100 most trips) are generally required since space is tight and economy is important for the group.

Green Tortoise can get you to San Francisco from Boston or New York in 10 to 14 days for $299-349 (plus $75-85 for food); from Seattle for $69; or from Los Angeles for $30. A "commuter" line runs between Seattle and Los Angeles; hop on at any point. For the vacation-oriented, Green Tortoise also operates a series of round-trip "loops" which start and finish in San Francisco and travel to Yosemite National Park, Northern California, Baja California, the Grand Canyon, and Alaska. The Alaska trip includes a ferry ride through the Inside Passage and forays into the Canadian Rockies (35 days, $1700, plus $250 for food). Much of Green Tortoise's charm lies in its low price and the departure it offers from the impersonality of standard bus service. Beyond San Francisco, there are regional agents in Los Angeles, Vancouver, Seattle, Portland, and Eugene, OR. To be assured of a reservation, book one to two months in advance; however, many trips have space available at departure.

Alaskon Express, 745 W. 4th Ave., Anchorage 99501 (907-277-5581), a subsidiary of **Gray Lines of Alaska** (800-544-2206; open Mon.-Fri. 8am-5pm, Sat. 9am-1pm), based in Anchorage, runs four buses per week to a variety of cities in Alaska and the Yukon, including Whitehorse ($179 one-way for a two-day trip, meaning you'll need to pay for 1 night's lodging), Tok ($99 one-way) and Skagway ($199 one-way for a two-day trip). Several enterprising van owners run small operations from

Haines to Anchorage, synchronized with the ferry. Fares can be as low as $115, but service is sometimes unreliable.

Two small, affordable bus lines operate out of Anchorage. Throughout summer, **Caribou Express** (278-5776) makes daily runs from Anchorage to Fairbanks ($75; other routes available). **Homer and Seward Bus Lines** (278-0800) runs to Seward ($30) and Homer ($35) on the Kenai Peninsula.

Try to use the **local bus systems** to travel within a town. The largest cities also have subways and commuter train lines. In most areas, however, mass public transport remains limited; local buses, while often cheap (fares 25¢-$1.35), are sparse. Call city transit information numbers and track down a public transport map with schedules. *Let's Go* helps you find this information wherever possible.

■■■ BY FERRY

Along the Pacific coast, ferries are an exhilarating and occasionally unavoidable way to travel. Some Alaskan towns can only be reached by water or air—Juneau, the state capital, for example. In addition to basic transportation, the ferry system gives travelers the chance to enjoy the beauty of the water and the coast, one of the Northwest's finest outdoor experiences. Ferry travel, however, can become quite expensive when you bring a car along with you. Ferries traveling along the coast serve the area between Seattle, Vancouver Island, and the northern coast of British Columbia. Contact these companies for further information:

BC Ferries, 1112 Fort St., Victoria, BC V8V 4V2 (604-669-1211). Operates *Queen of the North* between Port Hardy and Prince Rupert year-round; during the summer, northbound and southbound sailings on alternate days. Special facilities for passengers with disabilities.

Black Ball Transport, Inc., 430 Bellevue St., Victoria, B.C. V8V 1W9 (604-386-2202); Foot of Laurel, Port Angeles 98362 (206-457-4491). Ferries daily between Port Angeles and Victoria, with a crossing time of 90 min. Fare for an adult around $6 each way; for car and driver, around $25 each way; for a motorcycle and driver, $15.50 each way. Bicycles $3 extra. All prices in U.S. funds.

Washington State Ferries 801 Alaskan Way, Seattle, WA 98104 (206-464-6400). Ferries between Anacortes, WA and Sidney, BC, and from Anacortes to San Juan Islands. Ferries between Seattle and points on the Kitsap Peninsula.

The **Alaska Northwest Travel Service, Inc.,** 130 2nd Ave. S., Edmonds, WA 98020 (206-775-4504), is an agent for Alaska and British Columbia ferries as well as a full service travel agency specializing in Alaska; they can book ferries and offer advice on itineraries. Ferry scheduling information can also be found in *The Milepost,* published by Vernon Publications; see By Car above for information on how to obtain a copy.

Information about fares, reservations, vehicles, and schedules varies greatly during the various times of the year. *Let's Go* provides more information in this book's sections on Seattle, southwestern BC, and Alaska. Be sure to consult each ferry company to clear up any questions when putting together your itinerary.

■ Alaska Marine Highway

The Alaska Marine Highway consists of two completely unconnected ferry systems administered by one bureaucracy. The **southeast** system runs from Bellingham, WA up the coast to Skagway, stopping in Juneau, Ketchikan, Haines, and other towns. The **southcentral** network serves Kodiak Island, Seward, Homer, Prince William Sound, and, occasionally, the Aleutian Islands. For both systems, the ferry schedule is a function of tides and other navigational exigencies. **Stopovers** are encouraged. There is no additional charge for stopovers if they are reserved at the same time as the rest of your itinerary. Once your itinerary is reserved, you may still add stopovers at the port-to-port rate, which may result in a slightly higher fare. Write ahead; for all schedules, rates, and information, contact Alaska Marine Highway, P.O. Box 25535, Juneau 99802-5535 (800-642-0666 from the U.S. except 800-585-8445 from WA state; 800-665-6444 from Canada; 907-465-3941; fax 907-277-4829).

SOUTHEAST

Practically none of southeast Alaska (the Panhandle) is accessible by road; most of this area can be reached only by plane or on the Marine Highway ferry from Bellingham, WA. Connections can also be made from most towns via **Alaska Airlines,** or overland from Haines and Skagway. (See **Alaskon Express** under Bus Travel above).

The full trip from Bellingham to Skagway takes three days—an adventure in itself, peppered with whales, bald eagles, and the majesty of the Inside Passage. (The *Love Boat's* notorious Alaskan voyages took this same route.) All southeast ferries have free showers, cafes, lectures on history and ecology, and a heated top-deck "solarium" where cabinless passengers can sleep (bring a sleeping bag). Ferries depart Friday evenings; departure times are dictated by the tides.

The fare from **Bellingham to Skagway** is $236 (Bellingham to Haines $230). Senior citizens travel for $5 from Ketchikan to Skagway from October to April with a pass, available with proof of age at port of embarkation; those taking advantage of this deal must book 30 days in advance and are confined to standby status. The same deal is available to travelers with disabilities. Children ages 6-11 travel for about half price; children under age 6 travel free. Pets travel for $10 extra; a health certificate is required. The waiting list for standby passengers opens at 8:30am on the Monday before Friday's departure from Bellingham. Walk-ons have a decent chance for a ride if they sign up on Thursday. Call the Bellingham terminal at 206-676-8445 for standby information. **Vehicles** up to 70 ft. can be taken aboard (vehicles up to 10 ft. $262, up to 15 ft. $564; driver NOT included). Spaces for vehicles are very limited; reservations are crucial and often necessary six months in advance for summer trips. Reserved vehicles must check in at the Bellingham terminal three hours prior to departure. For more information, see Bellingham: Practical Information and Orientation in the Washington section, above.

A different Marine Highway ferry travels from **Prince Rupert, BC to Skagway** for $118 (half the price of the Bellingham-Skagway route). The ferry from Bellingham to Skagway does not stop in Prince Rupert; to get there, you must travel overland through British Columbia or fly. (See Prince Rupert: Practical Information in the British Columbia section, above.)

SOUTHCENTRAL

The ferries in southcentral Alaska are more expensive and less swish than those in the southeast. The boats are older, the food is worse, and the solariums are smaller. They also ride the open sea, where navies of seasickness bugs love to rock your vessel to and fro. For information on schedules and rates in the southcentral, see individual entries in the Practical Information sections of Whittier, Valdez, Cordova, Homer, Seward, Kodiak, and the Aleutian Islands.

■■■ BY MOTORCYCLE

It's cheaper than driving a car, but the physical and emotional wear and tear of motorcycling may negate any financial gain. Fatigue and the small gas tank conspire to force the motorcyclist to stop more often on long trips; experienced riders are seldom on the road more than six hours per day. Lack of luggage space can also be a serious limitation. If you must carry a load, keep it low and forward where it won't distort the cycle's center of gravity. Fasten it either to the seat or over the rear axle in saddle or tank bags.

Annoyances, though, are secondary to risks. Despite their superior maneuverability, motorcycles are incredibly vulnerable to crosswinds, drunk drivers, and the blind spots of cars and trucks. *Always ride defensively.* The dangers skyrocket at night; travel only in the daytime. Half of all cyclists have an accident within their first month of riding. Always wear the best **helmet** you can get your hands on. For information on motorcycle emergencies, ask your State Department of Motor Vehicles for a motorcycle operator's manual.

■ ■ ■ BY BICYCLE

Travel by bicycle is about the cheapest way to go. You move much more slowly for much more effort, but that doesn't mean you'll be ill-rewarded. The leisurely pace gives you a chance to take in the view. In addition, cycling is pollution-free and a good way to exercise.

Get in touch with a local biking club if you don't know a great deal about bicycle equipment and repair. When you shop around, compare knowledgeable local retailers to mail-order firms. If the disparity in price is modest, buy locally. Otherwise, order by phone or mail and make sure you have a local reference with which to consult. Make your first investment in an issue of *Bicycling* magazine (published by Rodale Press; see below), which advertises low sale prices. **Bike Nashbar,** 4111 Simon Rd., Youngstown, OH 44512 (800-627-4227; fax 216-782-2856), is the leading mail-order catalog for cycling equipment and accessories. They will beat any nationally advertised price by 5¢. The regularly ship anywhere in the U.S. and Canada, and to overseas military addresses. Their own line of products, including complete bicycles, is the best value. They also have a **technical telephone line** (216-788-6464) to answer questions about repairs and maintenance. Another exceptional mail-order firm which specializes in mountain bikes is **Bikecology,** P.O. Box 3900, Santa Monica, CA 90403 (800-326-2453).

Safe and secure cycling requires a quality helmet and lock. A **Bell** or **Tourlite** helmet costs about $40—much cheaper than critical head surgery or a well-appointed funeral. **U**-shaped **Kryptonite** or **Citadel locks** start at around $30, with insurance against theft for one or two years if your bike is registered with the police.

Long-distance cyclists should contact **Bikecentennial,** P.O. Box 8308-P, Missoula, MT 59807 (406-721-1776), a national, non-profit organization that researches and maps long-distance routes and organizes bike tours for members. Their 4450-mi. TransAmerican Trail has become the core of a 19,000-mi. route network of cycling-specific North American maps. Bikecentennial also offers members maps, guidebooks (including the *Cyclists' Yellow Pages*), nine issues of *Bike Report,* the organization's bicycle touring magazine, and a catalog describing their extensive organized tour program. Annual fees in the U.S. are $22 per person (students $19) and $25 per family. In Canada and Mexico, they are US$30 per person and $35 for families. (Phones open Mon.-Fri. 8am-5pm). American Youth Hostels and the Sierra Club also help plan bike tours. **Rocky Mountain Cycle Tours,** Box 1978, Canmore, AB T0L 0M0 (403-678-6770 or 800-661-2463), organizes tours in Alberta and British Columbia.

There are also a number of good books about bicycle touring and repair in general. **Rodale Press,** 33 E. Minor St., Emmaus, PA 18908 (215-967-5171), publishes *Mountain Biking Skills* and *Basic Maintenance and Repair* (US$7 apiece) and other general publications on prepping yourself and your bike for an excursion. *Bike Touring* (US$11, Sierra Club) and *Bicycle Touring* in the 90s (US$7, Rodale Press) both discuss how to equip and plan a bicycle trip. *Bicycle Gearing: A Practical Guide* (US$9) is available from **The Mountaineers Books,** 1011 SW Klickitat Way #107, Seattle, WA 98134 (800-553-4453), and discusses in lay-terms how bicycle gears work, covering everything you need to know in order to shift properly and get the maximum propulsion from the minimum exertion. *The Bike Bag Book*

(US$5 plus $2.50 shipping), available from **10-Speed Press,** Box 7123, Berkeley, CA 94707 (800-841-2665 or 415-845-8414), is a bite-sized manual with broad utility.

Information about cycling in the Northwest is available from tourist bureaus, which often distribute free maps. You can obtain the *Oregon Bicycling Guide* and *Oregon Coast Bike Route Map* from the Bikeway Program Manager, Oregon Department of Transportation, Salem, OR 97310 (503-378-3432). Mountaineers Books publishes a series about bicycling through Washington and Oregon. Two good guides are *Bicycling the Pacific Coast,* by Tom Kirkendall and Vicky Spring ($13, Mountaineers Books), and *Bicycling the Oregon Coast,* by Robin Cody ($11), published by The Mountaineers' subsidiary Umbrella Books, 18821 64th st. NE, Seattle, WA 98155 (206-485-6822).

Bikers should keep in mind that the Northwest possesses fewer well-paved backroads than other regions of the U.S. When traveling the coast and the mountains, bikers should also be wary of strong winds from the northwest. It's not easy, but you can transport your bike with you as you travel by bus, train, or air—check with each carrier about weight limits, packing requirements, insurance, and fees.

■■■ BY THUMB

> *Let's Go* urges you to consider the risks and disadvantages of hitchhiking before deciding whether to use your thumb as a means of transport. We do not recommend hitchhiking, especially for women.

If you feel you have no other alternative, you *insist* on ignoring our warnings, and decide to hitchhike anyway, there are many precautions that must be taken. First, assess the risks and your chances of getting a ride. **Women** traveling alone should never, ever, *ever* hitch in the United States. It's too big of a risk. Don't believe assurances to the contrary. For single men, it is slightly less dangerous, but also much more difficult to get a ride. A woman and a man is perhaps the best compromise between safety and utility. Two men will have a hard time getting rides and if they do, it will probably be in extremely uncomfortable circumstances. Three men won't be picked up.

Next, don't take any chances with drivers. Choosy beggars might not get where they're going the fastest, but at least they'll get there alive. Experienced hitchers won't get in the car if they don't know where the driver is going. Hitchers never get into the back seat of a two-door car, or into a car whose passenger door doesn't open from the inside. Beware of cars that have electric door locks which lock you in against your will. Women especially should turn down a ride when the driver opens the door quickly and offers to drive anywhere. Never put yourself in a position from which you can't exit quickly, never let your belongings out of your reach, and *never* hesitate to refuse a ride if you will feel at all uncomfortable alone with the driver.

Experienced hitchers talk with the driver—even idle chatter informs hitchers about their driver—but never divulge any information that they would not want a stranger to know. They also won't stay in the car if the driver starts making sexual innuendoes. It may be harmless joking, but it's best not to find out. If at all threatened or intimidated, experienced hitchers ask to be let out no matter how uncompromising the road looks, and they know *in advance* where to go if stranded and what to do in emergencies.

People who travel by thumb often consider hitchhiking in the Pacific Northwest—and Alaska in particular—as generally safer than in other areas of the U.S. and Canada (see Hitching in Alaska below). However, they still take care to observe the many precautions that lower the dangers inherent in hitchhiking.

All states prohibit hitchhiking while standing on the roadway itself or behind a posted freeway entrance sign; hitchers more commonly find rides on stretches near major intersections where many cars converge. Hitchhiking in the United States is a

BAD idea. Don't toy with your life, and don't ever compromise your safety. Plan ahead, and never get yourself into a situation in which hitchhiking is necessary.

■ Hitching in Alaska

To reiterate, *Let's Go* does not recommend hitchhiking as a means of transportation. The information provided below is not intended to do so.

Many people hitchhike instead of depending on buses in Alaska. In fact, Alaska state law prohibits moving vehicles from *not* picking up stranded motorists, as the extreme weather conditions can be life-endangering. However, hitchhiking backpackers may only legally thumb for rides on the on-and-off ramps of major highways—not on the highways themselves. (Sticking to the ramps makes sense anyway; motorists need space to slow down and stop.) Hitchhikers keep their placement in mind even on smaller thoroughfares and beware of being stranded on lightly traveled stretches of road. A wait of a day or two between rides is not unusual on certain stretches of the Alaska Hwy., especially in Canada. Luckily, Alaskans are generally a friendly and cooperative group, and most rides last at least a day. Campgrounds and service stations make the best bases for hitching, providing an opportunity for mutual inspection of both driver and hitchhiker before a long journey.

Women should never hitchhike alone. It is safer for them to travel in pairs or with men. Drivers will often pick up females and then proceed to warn them sternly against hitching alone.

Carrying a large cardboard sign clearly marked with your destination can improve your chances of getting a ride. Drivers may not want to stop if they don't know where you're going. When it gets particularly tough, hitchers add "SHARE GAS" to their signs.

Catching a ride from Canada into Alaska on the Alaska Hwy. involves passing the **Alaska-Yukon "border" check,** which is a series of routine questions about citizenship, residency, insurance, contraband, and finances, followed by an auto inspection. In the event that a hitchhiker is turned back, it is the driver's responsibility to return the hitchhiker to the "border." Hitchers should walk across the border to avoid hassles, and obviously **never attempt to carry illegal drugs across the border.**

A popular alternative to hitching the entire length of the Alaska Hwy. is to take the **Marine Highway** (see By Ferry above) to Haines and hitch a ride with cars coming off the ferry. Often the competition for rides in summer is heavy; it may be easier to remain on the ferry to Skagway, take a bus or train to Whitehorse in the Yukon, and hitch the Alaska Hwy. from there. Always carry extra money, food, and warm sleeping gear. The next town or ride could be days away.

Once There

■■■ ACCOMMODATIONS

Before you set out, try to locate places to stay along your route and make reservations, especially if you plan to travel during peak tourist seasons. Even if you find yourself in dire straits, don't spend the night under the stars in an unsupervised campground; it's often uncomfortable, unsafe, and sometimes illegal, even in national parks and forest areas. The local crisis center hotline may have a list of persons or groups who will house you in an emergency.

■ Youth Hostels

Youth hostels offer unbeatable deals on indoor lodging, and they are great places to meet traveling companions from all over the world; many hostels even have **ride boards** to help you hook up with other hostelers going your way. As a rule, hostels are dorm-style accommodations where the sexes sleep apart, often in large rooms with bunk beds. (Some hostels allow families and couples to have private rooms.) You must bring or rent your own sleep sack (two sheets sewn together will suffice); sleeping bags are often not allowed. Hostels frequently have kitchens and utensils available, and some have storage areas and laundry facilities. Many also require you to perform a communal chore daily, usually lasting no more than 15 minutes.

Hostelling International/American Youth Hostels (HI/AYH), P.O. Box 37613, Washington, D.C. 20013-7613 (202-783-6161), maintains over 300 hostels in the U.S. Hostelling International is the newly-adopted trademark name of the International Youth Hostel Federation; rates and services remain the same. HI memberships (and IYHF memberships that have not yet expired) are valid at all HI/AYH hostels. Basic HI/AYH rules (with some local variation): check-in between 5 and 8pm, check-out by 9:30am, maximum stay three days, no pets or alcohol allowed on the premises. All ages are welcome. Fees range from $7-14 per night. Hostels are graded according to the number of facilities they offer and their overall level of quality—consult *Let's Go* evaluations for each town. Reservations may be necessary or advisable at some hostels, so check ahead of time. HI/AYH membership is annual: $25, $15 for ages over 54, $10 for ages under 18, $35 for a family. Non-members who wish to stay at an HI/AYH hostel usually pay $3 extra, which can be applied toward membership. Regional AYH Councils schedule recreational activities and trips for members, ranging from afternoon bike rides to extended trips. Councils within Alaska and the Pacific Northwest include: **Alaska Council,** 700 H St., Anchorage, AK 99501 (907-562-772); **Washington State Council,** 419 Queen Anne Ave. North #101, Seattle, WA 98109 (206-281-7306); and **Oregon Council,** 1520 S.E. 37th Ave., Portland, OR 97214 (503-235-9493).

Hostelling International-Canada (HI-C), 1600 James Naismith Dr., Gloucester, Ont. K1B 5N4 (613-748-5638, or 800-663-5777 in Canada), a newly-assumed trademark name for the Canadian Hostelling Association (CHA), was founded in 1933, and maintains over 80 hostels throughout the country. Graded "basic," "simple," "standard," or "superior," hostels (CDN$8-15 per night) usually have kitchens, laundries, and often meal service. Open to members and non-members, most hostels allow a maximum stay of three nights. For hostels in busy locations, reservations are recommended. As with U.S. hostels, most Canadian hostels require that you have a "sleepsheet"—two sheets sewn together will do; rentals are usually available for CDN$1. Sleeping bags are sometimes acceptable, but often they are not. Most Canadian hostels have full-day access, and quiet hours are generally between 11pm and 7am. Otherwise, regulations are generally the same as in U.S. hostels. Annual membership costs CDN$25, under 18 CDN$12.

HI has recently instituted an **International Booking Network.** To reserve space in high season, obtain an International Booking Voucher from any national youth hostel association (in your home country or the one you will visit) and send it to a participating hostel four to eight weeks in advance of your stay, along with US$2 in local currency. Locations are listed in the Accommodation sections of the particular cities or regions. If your plans are firm enough to allow it, pre-booking is wise. Note that effective use of this pre-application is how populous school groups always manage to get dibs on rooms.

There are also a number of non-HI/AYH affiliated hostels across the country. A number of these are members of **Rucksackers North America,** PO Box 28038, Washington, DC 28038, formerly the American Association of Independent Hostels. For only the cost of a self-addressed stamped envelope, they'll send you a free guidebook to RNA hostels. If you send an additional $5, they will include a validation sticker, good for the life-span of the annual guidebook, entitling you to a dollar discount on the first night at any participating RNA Hostel.

■ Hotels and Motels

Those interested in bypassing hostels and moving up to mid-range hotels should consider joining **Discount Travel International,** 114 Forrest Ave. #203, Narberth, PA 19072 (215-668-7184). For an annual membership fee of $45, you and your household gain access to a clearing-house of discounts on organized trips, car rentals (with National, Alamo, and Hertz), and unsold hotel rooms.

Many budget motels preserve single digits in their names (e.g. Motel 6), but the cellar-level price of a single has matured to just under $30. Nevertheless, budget chain motels still cost significantly less than the chains catering to the next-pricier market, such as Holiday Inn. Chains usually adhere more consistently to a level of cleanliness and comfort than locally operated budget competitors; some budget motels even feature heated pools and cable TV. In bigger cities, budget motels are

normally just off the highway, often inconveniently far from the downtown area; so, if you don't have a car, you may well spend the difference between a budget motel and one downtown on transportation. Contact these chains for free directories:

Motel 6, 3391 S. Blvd., Rio Rancho, NM 87124 (505-891-6161).
Super 8 Motels, Inc., 1910 8th Ave. NE, P.O. Box 4090, Aberdeen, SD 57402-4090 (800-800-8000).
Choice Hotels International, 10750 Columbia Pike, Silver Springs, MD 20901-4494 (800-453-4511).
Best Western, P.O. Box 10203, Phoenix, AZ 85064-0203 (800-528-1234).

It is fortunate that the **Canadian hostel system** is somewhat more extensive than that of the U.S., because the country's dearth of budget motel chains puts most Canadian hotels and motels beyond the means of most budget travelers.

■ Bed and Breakfasts

As alternatives to impersonal hotel rooms, bed and breakfasts (private homes with spare rooms available to travelers, abbreviated B&Bs) range from the acceptable to the sublime. B&Bs may provide an excellent way to explore an area with the help of a host who knows it well, and some go out of their way to be accommodating—accepting travelers with pets or giving personalized tours. Often the best part of your stay will be a home-cooked breakfast (and occasionally dinner). However, many B&Bs do not provide phones or TVs, and showers must sometimes be shared with other guests.

Prices vary widely. B&Bs in major cities are usually more expensive than those in out-of-the-way places. Doubles can cost anywhere from $20-300 per night; most are in the $30 to $50 range. Some homes give special discounts to families or senior citizens. Reservations are almost always necessary, although in the off-season (if the B&B is open), you can frequently find a room on short notice.

For information on B&Bs, contact **Pacific Bed and Breakfast,** 701 NW 60th St., Seattle, WA 98107 (206-784-0539), or consult CIEE's *Where to Stay USA* ($14) which includes listings for hostels, YMCAs and dorms, along with B&Bs with singles under $30 and doubles under $35. Two useful guidebooks on the subject are *Bed & Breakfast, USA* ($14), by Betty R. Rundback and Nancy Kramer, available in bookstores or through Tourist House Associates, Inc., RD 2, Box 355-A, Greentown, PA 18426 (717-676-3222); and *The Complete Guide to Bed and Breakfasts, Inns and Guesthouses in the U.S. and Canada,* by Pamela Lanier, from Ten Speed Press, Box 7123, Berkeley, CA 94707 (800-841-2665 or 415-845-8414). If you're interested in "delightful" or "charming" accommodations at slightly less than charming prices, you might want to look at *America's Wonderful Little Hotels and Inns* ($20), by Sandra W. Soule, St. Martin's Press. In addition, check local phone books, visitors' bureaus, and information at bus and train stations.

Most every city in **Canada** offers at least one B&B to give rest to the needy who aren't so needy that they have to stay in hostels (rooms generally run $25-70 per night for a double room). You might want to check out the *The Complete Guide to Bed and Breakfasts, Inns, and Guesthouses in the U.S. and Canada* (information necessary for ordering is given above). And, as was suggested for B&Bs in the U.S., seek out information in phone books, at visitors' bureaus, and at bus and train stations.

■ YMCAs and YWCAs

Not all Young Men's Christian Associations (YMCAs), 224 East 47th St., New York, NY 10017 (212-308-2899; fax 212-308-3161), offer lodging; those that do are often located in urban downtowns, which can be convenient though a little gritty. Rates in YMCAs are usually lower than a hotel but higher than the local hostel, normally $20-45 per night depending on the size of the city and whether you want a single or a double room. Renting a room often allows you use of the showers (usually communal), library, pool, and other facilities. Economy packages (3-8 days; $116-$368), which include lodging, some meals, and excursions are available in a few of the larger cities. The maximum stay is most often 28 days. Reservations (strongly recommended) cost an additional $3 in the US and Canada, except Hawaii ($5), and key deposits are $5. Payment for reservations must be made in advance, with a traveler's check (signed top and bottom), US money order, certified check, Visa, or Mastercard; personal checks are not accepted. To obtain information and make reservations, write the Y's Way to Travel at the above address. Send a self-addressed envelope with a 65¢ stamp for a free catalogue.

Most **Young Women's Christian Associations (YWCAs),** 726 Broadway, New York, NY 10003 (212-614-2700), accommodate only women. Non-members are usually required to join when renting a room. For more information, write YWCA of the USA at the above address.

The network of YMCAs and YWCAs extends to many larger **Canadian** cities. You will generally find the same types clean and affordable rooms as those offered in the States, mostly in downtown areas. For further information, and to make reservations at YMCAs around Canada, contact the YMCA in Montreal at 1450 Stanley St., Montreal, PQ H3A 2W6 (514-849-8393; fax 514-849-5863), or the YW/YMCA in Ottawa at 180 Argyle St., Ottawa, Ont. K2P 1B7 (613-237-1320; fax 613-233-3096).

■ Alternative Accommodations

Many **colleges** and **universities** in the U.S. and Canada open their residence halls to travelers when school is not in session—some do so even during term-time. No general policy covers all of these institutions, but rates tend to be low, and some schools require that you express at least a vague interest in attending their institution. Since college dorms are popular with many travelers, you should call or write ahead for reservations.

Students traveling through a college or university town while school is in session might try introducing themselves to friendly looking local students. At worst travelers will receive a cold reception: at best, a good conversation might lead to an offer of a place to crash. International visitors may have especially good luck here (flex your accent if you've got one). In general, college campuses are some of the best sources for information on things to do, places to stay, and possible rides out of town. In addition, dining halls often serve reasonably priced, reasonably edible all-you-can-stomach meals. To contact colleges and universities in Alaska and the Pacific Northwest, make use of the addresses and phone numbers given in the Work and Study section above.

If you wish to stay in a U.S. home during your vacation, try **Servas,** run by the U.S. Servas Committee, 11 John St. #407, New York, NY 10038 (212-267-0252). Servas is an international cooperative system which matches hosts and travelers in about 100 countries. Stays are limited to two to three nights, unless your host invites you to stay longer; guests must complete arrangements with hosts in advance of their stay. Travelers pay a $55 fee per year to Servas, plus a $25 refundable deposit for up to five host lists which provide a short description of each host member. No money is exchanged between travelers and hosts—rather, they share conversation and ideas. Travelers must submit an application, provide two letters of reference, and arrange for an interview at least one month before the trip. Contact the above address for information.

The World Learning's **Homestay/USA,** formerly The Experiment in International Living, coordinates homestay programs for international visitors over 14 wishing to join a U.S. family for three to four weeks. Homestays are arranged for all times of the year. For the appropriate address to contact in your country, see the Work and Study section above. The **Institute of International Education (IIE)** publishes a "Homestay Information Sheet" listing homestay programs for foreign visitors. For a more thorough description and a contact address, see Work and Study above. **CIEE** can also help arrange homestays.

■■■ CAMPING AND THE OUTDOORS

■ Useful Publications

For information about camping, hiking, and biking, write or call the publishers listed below to receive a free catalog.

Sierra Club Books, 730 Polk St., San Francisco, CA 94109 (415-923-5500). Books on many national parks, as well as *The Best About Backpacking* ($11), *Cooking for Camp and Trail* ($12), *Learning to Rock Climb* ($14), and *Wildwater* ($12). For information on Alaska in particular, consult *Adventuring in Alaska* ($12), by Peggy Wayburn.

The Mountaineers Books, 1011 Klickitat Way #107, Seattle, WA 98134 (800-553-4453 or 206-223-6303). Numerous titles on hiking (the *100 Hikes* series), biking, mountaineering, natural history, and environmental conservation.

Wilderness Press, 2440 Bancroft Way, Berkeley, CA 94704-1676 (800-443-7227 or 510-543-8080). Specializes in hiking guides and topographic maps for the Western U.S. Also publishes *Backpacking Basics* ($9) and *Backpacking with Babies and Small Children* ($10).

Woodall Publishing Company, P.O. Box 5000, 28167 N. Keith Dr., Lake Forest, IL 60045-5000 (800-323-9076 or 708-362-6700). Publishes *Woodall's Campground Directory* in many regional editions (Western edition US$11 or CDN$13; shipping $2.75). Also useful is *Woodall's Plan-It, Pack-It, Go...!: Great Places to Tent, Fun Things to Do* (North American edition, US$12 or CDN$14; shipping $3.25).

For **topographical maps,** write the **U.S. Geological Survey,** Map Distribution, Box 25286, Denver, CO, 80225 (303-236-7477) or the **Canada Map Office,** 615 Booth St., Ottawa, Ont., K1A 0E9 (613-952-7000), which distributes geographical and topographical maps as well as aeronautical charts.

■ Parks and Forests

At the turn of the century it may have seemed unnecessary to set aside parts of the vast American and Canadian wilderness for conservation, but today that act is recognized as a stroke of genius. **National parks** protect some of America and Canada's most spectacular scenery. Alaska's crowning Denali (Mt. McKinley), Oregon's stone-still Crater Lake, and Alberta's Banff and Jasper are treasures that will remain intact for generations. Though their primary purpose is preservation, the parks also make room for recreational activities such as ranger talks, guided hikes, skiing, and snowshoe expeditions. Most national parks have backcountry camping and developed tent camping; others welcome RVs, and a few offer opulent living in grand lodges. Internal road systems allow you to reach the interior and major sights even if you are not a long-distance hiker.

Write to one or all of the following addresses for information on camping, accommodations, and regulations: for **Washington** and **Oregon** contact Forest Service/National Park Service, Outdoor Recreation Information Center, 915 2nd Ave. #442, Seattle, WA 98174 (206-220-7450); for **Alberta** and **British Columbia** contact Canadian Parks Service #520, 220 4th Ave., Calgary, AB T2P 3H8 (403-292-4401); for the **Yukon Territory** and **Northwest Territories** contact Canadian Parks Service, Prairie and Northern Region Information Office, 4th floor, 457 Main St., Winnipeg, Manitoba R3B 3E8 (204-983-2290; 204-983-0551 for the hearing impaired; fax 204-984-2240); and for **Alaska** contact -Alaska Public Lands Information Center, 605 W. 4th Ave., #105, Anchorage, AK 99501 (907-271-2737).

Entry fees vary from park to park. The larger and more popular national parks charge a $3-5 entry fee for vehicles and sometimes a nominal one for pedestrians and cyclists. Most national parks offer **discounts** such as the annual **Golden Eagle Passport** ($25), which allows the bearer and family free entry into all parks. Visitors ages 62 and over qualify for the **Golden Age Passport,** entitling them to free entry and a 50% discount on recreational fees; travelers with disabilities enjoy the same privileges with the **Golden Access Passport.** Both the Golden Age and Golden Access Passports are free, and both are also valid at national monuments. For more information, visitors centers at parks offer excellent free literature and information, and the U.S. Government Printing Office, 732 N. Capitol NW, Washington, DC 20401 (202-512-0000), publishes two useful pamphlets: *National Parks: Camping Guide* ($3.50) and *National Parks: Lesser-Known Areas* ($1.50). The Winnipeg office of the Canadian Parks Service (see address above) distributes free of charge *Parks West,* a thorough and beautiful book about all the national parks and historic sites of western and northern Canada.

Many states and provinces have parks of their own, which are often smaller than the national parks but offer some of the best camping around—handsome surroundings, elaborate facilities, and plenty of space. In contrast to national parks, the primary function of **state and provincial parks** is recreation. Prices for camping at public sites are almost always better than those at private campgrounds. Don't let swarming visitors dissuade you from seeing the large parks—these places are huge, and even at their most crowded they offer many opportunities for quiet and solitude. Reservations are absolutely essential at the more popular parks in the Pacific Northwest; make them through MISTIX (800-365-2267). U.S. states will also have a State Division of Parks which you can contact for information and brochures; find their addresses and phone numbers listed in the Practical Information sections following the introductions to the respective states. Lodges and indoor accommodations are generally in the shortest supply and should be reserved months in advance.

However, most campgrounds are strictly first-come, first-camped. Arrive early: many campgrounds, public and private, fill u̦ʲ by late morning.

If the national parks are too developed for your tastes, **national forests** provide a purist's alternative. While some have recreation facilities, most are equipped only for primitive camping—pit toilets and no running water are the rule. Fees are nominal or nonexistent. Forests are generally less accessible than the parks, but less crowded as a consequence. Backpackers can take advantage of specially designated **wilderness areas,** which are even less accessible due to regulations barring all vehicles. **Wilderness permits,** required for backcountry hiking, can usually be obtained (sometimes for a fee) at parks; check ahead. Adventurers who plan to explore some real wilderness should always check in at a USDA Forest Service (see phone number below) field office before heading out. Many of the wilderness areas are difficult to find, so write ahead for detailed, accurate maps.

The **USDA Forest Service** oversees more than 200 scenic and well-maintained wilderness **log cabins** for public use, scattered throughout the southern and central regions of the Alaska. User permits are required along with a fee of $20 per party (of any size) per night. Reservations are usually necessary several months in advance. Most cabins have seven-day use limits (hike-in cabins have a 3-day limit May-Aug.), and are usually accessible only by air, boat, or hiking trail. Cabin sizes vary, and facilities at these sites rarely include more than a wood stove and pit toilets, but some cabins provide skiffs. For maps or further information write to the USDA Forest Service (see Visitors Information). For general information, contact the Forest Service's regional office in the **Pacific Northwest** (503-326-3816) or **Alaska** (907-271-4126) (for addresses see Working: Paid Employment above).

The **U.S. Fish and Wildlife Service,** 1011 E. Tudor Rd., Anchorage 99503 (786-3486), maintains numerous campgrounds within the National Wildlife Refuges of the Alaska, including the Kenai National Refuge (907-262-7021; 15 campgrounds with sites from $5 and a max. stay of either 3 or 14 days depending on the campground).

Believe it or not, the U.S. Department of the Interior does more than grant public lands to oil companies for exploitative development. Its **Bureau of Land Management (BLM),** Public Affairs, Washington D.C., 20240 (202-208-5717), offers a wide variety of outdoor recreation opportunities—including camping, hiking, mountain biking, rock climbing, river rafting and wildlife viewing—on the 270 million acres it oversees in ten Western states and Alaska. These lands also contain hundreds of archaeological artifacts and historic sites like ghost towns. The BLM's many **campgrounds** include 20 sprinkled throughout Alaska, all free (except for the Delta BLM campground on the Alaska Hwy.).

The **Pacific Crest Trail,** which stretches 2620 mi. from the Mexico-California border into Canada, is particularly attractive for one- or two-week hiking trips along its shorter segments. Heated cabins and some running tap water along the trails add convenience. Consult BLM or an area tourism bureau for maps of the trail; another valuable source is *The Pacific Crest Trail, Vol. 2* (Wilderness Press, $25), which covers Oregon and Washington.

■ Tent Camping and Hiking

EQUIPMENT

Whether buying or renting, finding sturdy yet inexpensive equipment is a must. Spend some time examining catalogs and talking to knowledgeable salespeople. Mail-order firms are for the most part reputable and cheap—order from them if you can't do as well locally. Look for prices on the previous year's line of equipment to decline precipitously (sometimes by as much as 50%) when the new year's line starts to sell, usually sometime in the fall.

At the core of your equipment is the **sleeping bag.** What kind you should buy depends on the climate of the area you'll be camping in and climbing through.

Sleeping bags are rated according to the lowest outdoor temperature at which they will still keep you warm. Bags are sometimes rated by season rather than temperature: keep in mind that "summer" translates to a rating of 30-40°F, "three-season" can be anywhere from 5-30°F, and "four-season" means below 0°F. Sleeping bags are made either of down (warmer and lighter) or of synthetic material (cheaper, heavier, more durable, and warmer when wet). When choosing your bag, get the most specific temperature rating you can. The following prices are reasonable for good bags: $60-70 for a summer synthetic, $150 for a three-season synthetic, $150-180 for a three-season down bag, and upwards of $250-300 for a down sleeping bag you can use in the winter. If you're using a sleeping bag for serious camping, you should also have either a foam pad ($13 and up for closed-cell foam, $25 and up for open-cell foam) or an air mattress (up to $50) to cushion your back and neck. Another good alternative is the **Therm-A-Rest,** which is part foam and part air-mattress and inflates to full padding when you unroll it (from $50-80).

When you select a **tent,** your major considerations should be shape and size. A-frame tents are the best all-around. When pitched their internal space is almost entirely usable, which means little unnecessary bulk. One drawback to keep in mind: if you're caught in the rain and have to spend a day or two holed up inside your tent, A-frames can be cramped and claustrophobic. Dome and umbrella shapes offer more spacious living, but tend to be bulkier to carry. As for size, two people *can* fit in a two-person tent but will find life more pleasant in a four-person tent. If you're traveling by car, go for the bigger tent; if you're hiking, stick with a smaller tent that weighs no more than 3.5 lbs./1.5kg. For especially small and lightweight models, contact **Sierra Design,** 2039 4th St., Berkeley, CA 94710, which sells a two-person tent that weighs less than 1.4kg (3 lbs.) Be sure your tent has a rain fly. Good two-person tents start at about $100; $150 for a four-person. You can, however, often find last year's version for half the price.

If you intend to do a lot of hiking or biking, you should have a **frame backpack.** Buy a backpack with an internal frame if you'll be hiking on difficult trails that require a lot of bending and maneuvering—internal-frame packs mould better to your back, keep a lower center of gravity, and can flex adequately to follow you through a variety of movements. An internal-frame backpack is also good as an all-around travel pack, something you can carry by hand when you return to civilization. External-frame packs are more comfortable for long hikes over even terrain since they keep the weight higher and distribute it more evenly. The size of a backpack is measured in cubic inches (cu. in.). Any serious backpacking requires at least 3300 of them, while longer trips require around 4000. Tack on an additional 500 cu. in. for internal-frame packs, since you'll have to pack your sleeping bag inside, rather than strap it on the outside as you do with an external-frame pack. Backpacks with many compartments generally turn a large space into many unusable small spaces. Packs that load from the front rather than the top allow you access to your gear more easily (see Packing above for more hints). Sturdy backpacks start anywhere from $75-125. This is one area where it doesn't pay to economize—cheaper packs may be less comfortable, and the straps are more likely to fray or rip quickly. Test-drive a backpack for comfort before you buy it.

Other necessities include: **battery-operated lantern** (gas is inconvenient and dangerous), **plastic groundcloth** for the floor of your tent, **nylon tarp** for general purposes, and a **"stuff sack"** or plastic bag to keep your sleeping bag dry. Don't go anywhere without a **canteen** or water bottle. Plastic models keep water cooler in the hot sun than metal ones do, although metal canteens are a bit sturdier and leak less. If you'll be car-camping at sites with no showers, bring **water sacks** and/or a **solar shower,** a small black sack with an attachable shower head (backpackers may find these items unnecessary or cumbersome). Although most campgrounds provide campfire sites, you may want to bring a small **metal grate** of your own, and even a grill. For those places that forbid fires or the gathering of firewood, you'll need a **camp stove** (Coleman, the classic, starts at $30). Make sure you have **waterproof matches,** or your stove may do you no good.

Shop around locally before turning to mail-order firms; this allows you to get an idea of what the different items actually look like (and weigh), so that if you later decide to order by mail you'll have a more exact idea of what it is you're getting. The mail-order firms listed below offer lower prices than those you're likely to find in stores, and they can also help you determine which item is the one you need. Call or write for a free catalog:

Cabela's, 812 13th Ave., Sidney, NE 69160 (800-237-4444). Offers great prices on quality outdoor equipment.

Campmor, 810 Rte. 17N, P.O. Box 997-H, Paramus, NJ 07653 (800-526-4784). Has a monstrous selection of equipment at low prices.

L.L. Bean, Freeport, ME 04033-0001 (800-341-4341). Open 24 hours a day, 365 days a year.

Recreational Equipment, Inc. (REI), Sumner, WA 98352-0001 (800-426-4840). Stocks a wide range of the latest in camping gear and holds great seasonal sales.

Cheaper equipment can also be obtained on the used market, but, as with anything used, know what you're buying. Consult publications like the want-ads and student bulletin boards. Retail outlets like **L.L. Bean** may save you money, but remember that with camping gear you usually get what you pay for. Spending a little more money up front may save money down the line.

A good initial source of information on **recreational vehicles (RVs)** is the **Recreational Vehicle Industry Association,** P.O. Box 2999, 1896 Preston White Dr., Reston, VA 22090-0999 (703-620-6003). For a free catalog that lists RV camping publications and state campground associations, send a self-addressed, stamped envelope to the **Go Camping America Committee,** P.O. Box 2669, Reston, VA 22090-0669 (703-620-6003).

WILDERNESS CONCERNS

The first thing to preserve in the wilderness is you—health, safety, and food should be your primary concerns when you camp. See Health above for information about basic medical concerns and first-aid. A comprehensive guide to outdoor survival is *How to Stay Alive in the Woods* ($8), by Bradford Angier; to order, write or call Macmillan Publishing Co., Front and Brown St., Riverside, NJ 08075 (800-257-5755). Many rivers, streams, and lakes are contaminated with bacteria such as *giardia,* which causes gas, cramps, loss of appetite, and violent diarrhea. To protect yourself from the effects of this invisible trip-wrecker, always boil your water vigorously for at least five minutes before drinking, or use a purification tablet or solution made from iodine. Filters do not remove all bacteria, but they can be useful when drawing water from small streams withered by drought. *Never go camping or hiking by yourself for any significant time or distance*. If you're going into an area that is not well-traveled or well-marked, let someone know where you're hiking and how long you intend to be out. If you fail to return on schedule or if someone needs to reach you, searchers will at least know where to look.

The second thing to protect while outdoors is the wilderness. The thousands of would-be woodspeople who pour into the parks every year threaten to slowly stamp it out. Because firewood is scarce in popular parks, campers are asked to make small fires using only dead branches or brush. Using a campstove is the more cautious way to cook; check ahead to see if the park prohibits **campfires** altogether. Travelers in Alaska and the Yukon are asked not to build campfires on the Arctic Tundra. To avoid letting rain swamp your tent, pitch it on high, dry ground. Don't cut vegetation, and don't clear campsites. If there are no toilet facilities, bury human waste at least 4 in. deep and 100 ft. or more from any water supplies and campsites. Avoid using toilet paper—use a rock or the rounded surface of a stick if possible, use leaves only if certain they're free of noxious oils. **Biosafe soap** or detergents may be used in streams or lakes. Otherwise, don't use soaps in or near bodies of water. Always pack up your trash in a plastic bag and carry it with you until you reach the next trash can; burning and burying pollute the environment. In more civilized camping circumstances, it's important to respect fellow campers. Keep light and noise to a minimum, particularly if you arrive after dark.

BEAR NECESSITIES

No matter how tame a bear appears, don't be fooled—they're dangerous and unpredictable animals who are simply not impressed or intimidated by humans. As a basic rule, if you're close enough for a bear to be observing you, you're too close. To avoid a grizzly experience, never feed a bear or tempt it with such delectables as open trash cans. They may even come back for seconds. Keep your camp clean, and don't cook near where you sleep. Do not leave trash or food lying around camp.

When sleeping, don't even consider leaving food or other scented items (trash, toiletries) near your tent. The best way to keep your toothpaste from becoming a condiment is to **bear-bag.** This amounts to hanging your edibles from a tree, out of reach of hungry paws. Ask a salesperson at a wilderness store to show you how. In order to do it properly, you'll need heavy nylon strapping, thin nylon rope, and caribiners, as well as a bit of instruction. Food and waste should be sealed in airtight plastic bags, all of which should be placed in duffel bags and hung in a tree 10 ft. from the ground and 5 ft. from the trunk.

Also avoid indulging in greasy foods, especially bacon and ham. Grease gets on everything, including your clothes and sleeping bag, and bears find it an alluring dressing for whatever or whomever is wearing it. Bears are attracted to perfume smells; do without cologne, scented soap, and hairspray while camping. Park rangers can tell you how to identify bear trails (don't camp on them!). *Leave your packs empty and open on the ground so that a bear can nose through them without ripping them to shreds.* And stay away from dead animals and berry bushes—these are *Le menu* for bears.

If you see a bear at a distance, calmly walk (don't run) in the other direction. If it seems interested, some old hands recommend waving your arms or a long stick above your head and talking loudly; the bear's dull vision gives it the impression that you're much taller than a person, and it may (if you're lucky) decide that *you* are threatening to *it*. Always shine a flashlight when walking at night: bears will clear out if given sufficient warning. If you stumble upon a sweet-looking bear cub, leave immediately, lest it's over-protective mother stumble upon you. If attacked by a bear, get in a fetal position to protect yourself, put your arms over the back of your neck, and play dead (maybe it will think you're hibernating). The aggressiveness of bears varies from region to region. Ask local rangers for details before entering any park or wilderness area.

ORGANIZED ADVENTURE

Begin by consulting tourism bureaus, which can suggest parks, trails, and outfitters as well as answer more general questions. *Outside Magazine,* 1165 N. Clark St., Chicago, IL 60610 (312-951-0990), publishes an Expedition Services Directory in each issue. The **Sierra Club,** 730 Polk St., San Francisco, CA 94109 (415-923-5630), plans a variety of outings. So does **Trekamerica,** P.O. Box 470, Blairstown, NJ 07825 (800-221-0596); call or write for more information.

■ Outdoor Sports

WATER SPORTS

The latticework of fast-flowing rivers in the Pacific Northwest is ideal for canoeing, kayaking, and whitewater rafting. Boating opportunities are suggested in the Activities sections throughout the book. Travel agents and tourism bureaus can recommend others.

The **River Travel Center,** P.O. Box 6, Pt. Arena, CA 95468 (800-882-RAFT or 7238), can place you in a whitewater raft, kayak, or sea kayak through one of over 100 outfitters. Trips range in length from three to 18 days. British Columbia rafting trips (half day $42, full day $89) are planned by **Clearwater Expeditions Ltd.,** R.R. 2, Box 2506, Clearwater, BC V0E 1N0 (604-674-3354). **Hells Canyon Adventures, Inc.,** Box 159, Oxbow, OR 97840 (800-422-3568; in OR, 503-785-3352; fax 503-785-3353), is the place to call for Snake River whitewater rafting, whitewater jet boat tours, and fishing charters. Rafting trips cost $90 per person for a one-day trip; jet boat tours start at $25.

Sierra Club Books publishes a kayaking and whitewater rafting guide entitled *Wildwater* ($12). The club offers kayaking trips to the Pacific Northwest and Alaska every year. *Washington Whitewater* ($19) and *Canoe Routes: Northwest Oregon* ($11), published by The Mountaineers Books, might also interest you.

Swimmers in the North country should consult locals before diving into any unsupervised lake or gravelly pit. Some of these may contain the feisty larvae which can lead to **"swimmer's itch."** Symptoms include red and irritated skin beginning almost immediately and usually lasting seven to ten days.

SNOW SPORTS

Tourism bureaus can help you locate the best sports outfitters and ski areas. *Let's Go* suggests options in the Activities sections throughout the book. For Oregon and Washington skiing guides and information (both downhill and cross country), write the **Pacific Northwest Ski Areas Association,** P.O. Box 2325 Seattle, WA 98111-2325 (206-623-3777). The Sierra Club publishes *The Best Ski Touring in America* ($11), which includes Canada as well. The Mountaineers Books publishes good skiing guides for Oregon and Washington.

Pay attention to cold weather safety concerns. Know the symptoms of hypothermia and frostbite (see Health above), and bring along warm clothes and quick energy snacks like candy bars and trail mix. Drinking alcohol in the cold can be par-

ticularly dangerous: even though you *feel* warm, alcohol can make you rather cold-blooded, slowing your body's ability to adjust to the temperature and thus making you more vulnerable to hypothermia.

FISHING AND HUNTING

Should you wish to take advantage of the regions' well-stocked lakes and streams, contact the appropriate department of fisheries for brochures that summarize regulations and make sport fishing predictions. Some fishing seasons are extremely short, so be sure to ask when the expected prime angling dates occur. Licenses are available from many tackle shops, or you can purchase them directly from the state or provincial department of fisheries. You need not reside in a state or province in order to hunt there, but steep license and tag fees will probably discourage you. Consult the appropriate departments of game to purchase licenses and receive regulations pamphlets.

Alaska: Fish and Game Licensing, P.O. Box 25526, Juneau, AK 99802-5525 (907-465-2376; fax 465-2604; open Mon.-Fri. 8:30am-4:30pm). Nonresident fishing license $10 for 1 day, $15 for 3 days, $30 for 14 days, $50 for a year. Nonresident hunting licenses $85 ($20 for small game only), plus tags from $150 (deer) to $1100 (musk ox). $135 combined license for hunting and fishing.

Alberta: Fish and Wildlife Service, 9945 108th St., Edmonton T5K 2G6 (403-427-3590). Nonresident fishing license CDN$15 for Canadians, CDN$30 for non-Canadians. Nonresident hunting license CDN$22 (wildlife certificate and resource development stamp), plus tags from CDN$24 (wolf) to CDN$306 (sheep). CDN$20 limited 5-day fishing license for non-Canadians.

British Columbia: Fish and Wildlife Information, Ministry of Environment, 780 Blanshard St., Victoria, BC V8V 1X4 (604-387-9737). Non-Canadian angling license CDN$22.50 for 6 days, CDN$35 for a year; CDN$45 for steelhead tags. Non-Canadian hunting license CDN$155, for wolf CDN$27, for grizzly bear CDN$535; prices for other animals range somewhere in between.

Oregon: Department of Fish and Wildlife, 2501 S.W. 1st Ave., P.O. Box 59, Portland 97207 (503-229-5400). Nonresident fishing license $35.75, plus $5.50 each for salmon/steelhead, sturgeon, and halibut tags. Nonresident hunting license $125.50 for nonresidents. Combination license $24.75 (residents only).

Washington: Department of Fisheries, P.O. Box 43135, Olympia 98504-3135 (206-902-2200). Nonresident personal use license for food fish $10, plus $4 for salmon and $3 for sturgeon tags. Freshwater fishing licenses available through Department of Wildlife.

Washington: Department of Wildlife, 600 Capitol Way, Olympia 98501-1091 (206-753-5700). Nonresident game fishing license $48. Nonresident hunting license $150. Combination license $29 (residents only).

Yukon Government, Department of Renewable Resources, Fish and Wildlife Branch, 10 Burns Rd., P.O. Box 2703, Whitehorse Y1A 2C6 (403-667-5221). Non-Canadian fishing license CDN$5 for 1 day, CDN$20 for 6 days, CDN$35 for a year. Non-Canadian small-game hunting license CDN$20 for 1 year; large-game hunting license CDN$150 for a year, plus tags from CDN$5 (moose) to CDN$25 (grizzly bear). All Non-Canadians must work with a registered guide when hunting large game.

Many outfitters plan fly-in fishing trips or boating trips designed for anglers. These expeditions are expensive. If interested, consult a travel agent or tourism bureau for possibilities.

■■■ KEEPING IN TOUCH

■ Mail

Individual offices of the **U.S. Postal Service** are usually open Monday to Friday from 9am to 5pm and sometimes on Saturday until about noon; branches in many larger cities open earlier and close later. All are closed on national holidays. **Postcards** mailed within the U.S. cost 19¢; **letters** cost 29¢ for the first ounce and 23¢ for each additional ounce. Domestic mail takes from two to three days to reach its destination. To Canada, it costs 30¢ to mail a postcard, and 40¢ to mail a letter for the first ounce and 23¢ for each additional ounce. It costs 30¢ to mail a postcard to Mexico; a letter is 35¢ for a half-ounce, 45¢ for an ounce, and 10¢ for each additional half-ounce up to two ounces. Each additional ounce after two ounces and up to 12 ounces costs 25¢. Postcards mailed overseas cost 40¢, and letters are 50¢ for a half-ounce, 95¢ for an ounce, and 39¢ for each additional half-ounce up to 64 ounces. **Aerogrammes,** printed sheets that fold into envelopes and travel via air mail, are available at post offices for 45¢. Mail to northern Europe, Canada, and Mexico takes a week to 10 days; to southern Europe, North Africa, and the Middle East, two weeks; and to South America or Asia, a week to 10 days. Of course, all of the above estimated times of arrival are dependent on the particular foreign country's mail service as well. Be sure to write "Air Mail" on the front of the envelope for the speediest delivery. Large cities' post offices offer an **International Express Mail** service, which is the fastest way to send an item overseas (guaranteed delivery to a major city overseas in 48-72 hr.; often takes but a day). A half-ounce letter costs 50¢, a one-ounce letter 95¢; each additional ounce after one ounce costs 50¢.

In **Canada** mailing a letter (or a postcard, which carries the same rate as a letter) to the U.S. costs CDN$0.49 for the first 30 grams and CDN$1.10 if the letter is between 31 and 100 grams. To every other foreign country, a 20-gram letter costs CDN$0.86, a 21- to 50-gram letter CDN$1.29, and a 51- to 100-gram letter CDN$2.15. The domestic rate is CDN$0.43 for a 30-gram letter, and CDN$0.86 for a letter between 31 and 100 grams. Aerogrammes can be mailed only to other locations in Canada (CDN$0.86). Letters take from three to eight working days to reach the U.S. and a week or two to get to an overseas address. **General Delivery** mail can be sent to any post office and will be held for 15 days. Canada Post's most reliable and pricey service is **Priority Courier,** which offers speedy delivery (usually next-day) to major American cities (CDN$23.50 for a document). Delivery to overseas locations usually takes two days and costs CDN$63 for a document. Guaranteed next-day delivery exists between any two Canadian cities and costs CDN$8.10 within a single province and CDN$11.50 between provinces; for the purposes of Priority Courier, Quebec and Ontario represent one region, so that mail traveling between those provinces costs CDN$8.10.

The U.S. is divided into postal zones, each with a five-digit **ZIP code** particular to a region, city, or part of a city. Some addresses have nine-digit ZIP codes, used primarily for business mailings to speed up delivery. Writing this code on letters is essential for delivery. The normal form of address is as follows:

Jessica Raft
Fulfillment Manager (title or name of organization, optional)
4000 Northup Way, Suite 290 (address, apartment number)
Bellevue, WA 98009 (city, state abbreviation, ZIP)
USA (country, if mailing internationally)

In Canada, **postal codes** are the equivalent of U.S. ZIP codes and contain letters as well as numbers (for example, H4P 1B8). The normal form of address is nearly identical to that in the U.S.; the only difference is that the apartment or suite number can *precede* the street address along with a dash. For example, 23-40 Sherbrooke St. refers to Room #23 at 40 Sherbrooke St.

If in the U.S. and ordering books and materials from abroad, always include with your request an **International Reply Coupon**—a method of "pre-paying" in the U.S. for postage on letters to be mailed from foreign countries that belong to the Universal Postal Union (95¢). IRCs should be available from your home post office. Be sure that your coupon has adequate postage to cover the cost of delivery. Canada Post also offers an IRC service (CDN$1.25).

Depending on how neurotic your family is, consider making arrangements for them to get in touch with you. Mail can be sent **General Delivery** to a city's main branch of the post office. Once a letter arrives it will be held for about 30 days; it can be held for longer at the discretion of the Postmaster if such a request is clearly indicated on the front of the envelope. Family and friends can send letters to you labeled like this:

Mr. John <u>DuFresne</u> (underline last name for accurate filing)
c/o General Delivery
Main Post Office
Berkeley, CA 94702

American Express does not automatically offer a Poste Restante service, but offices throughout the U.S. and Canada will act as a mail service for cardholders if you contact them in advance. Under this free **"Client Letter Service,"** they will hold mail for 30 days, forward upon request, and accept telegrams. For a complete list of offices and instructions on how to use the service, call 800-528-4800.

Most major cities features the **Postal Answer Line (PAL),** which provides information on first-class surface mail at ext. 319, International Express Mail at ext. 318, Parcel Post at ext. 317, customs at ext. 308, special services at ext. 142, and IRCs at ext. 307.

■ Telephones

Most of the information you will need about telephone usage—including area codes for the U.S., foreign country codes, and rates—is in the front of the local **white pages** telephone directory. The **yellow pages,** published at the end of the white pages or in a separate book, is used to look up numbers of businesses and other services. Federal, state, and local government listings are provided in the **blue pages** at the back of the directory. To obtain local phone numbers or area codes of other cities, call **directory assistance** at 411. Dialing "0" will get you the **operator,** who can assist you in reaching a phone number and provide you with general information. For long-distance directory assistance, dial 1-(area code)-555-1212. The operator will help you with rates and other information, and will give assistance in an emergency. You can reach directory assistance and the operator free from any pay phone.

Telephone numbers in the U.S. consist of a three-digit area code, a three-digit exchange, and a four-digit number, written as 123-456-7890. Only the last seven digits are used in a **local call. Non-local calls** *within* the area code from which you are dialing require a "1" before the last seven digits, while **long-distance calls** *outside* the area code from which you are dialing require a "1" and the area code. For example, to call Harvard University in Cambridge, MA from Las Vegas, NV, you would dial 1-617-495-5000. Canada and much of Mexico share the same system. Generally, **discount rates** apply after 5pm on weekdays and Sunday and **economy rates** every day between 11pm and 8am; on Saturday and on Sunday until 5pm, economy rates are also in effect.

Many large companies operate **toll-free numbers** to provide information to their customers at no charge. These consist of "1" plus "800" plus a seven-digit number. To obtain specific toll-free numbers, call 800-555-1212. Be careful—the age of technology has recently given birth to the **"900" number.** Its area code is deceptively

T
E
L
E
P
H
O
N
E
S

similar to the toll-free code, but "900" calls are staggeringly expensive. Average charges range from $2-5 for the first minute, with a smaller charge for each additional minute. You can have phone sex, make donations to political candidates, or hear about the Teenage Mutant Ninja Turtles, but it'll cost you.

Pay phones are plentiful, most often stationed on street corners and in public areas. Be wary of private, more expensive pay phones—the rate they charge per call will be printed on the phone. Put your coins (10-25¢ for a local call depending on the region) into the slot and listen for a dial tone before dialing. If there is no answer or if you get a busy signal, you will get your money back after hanging up; connecting with answering machines will prevent this. To make a long-distance direct call, dial the number. An operator will tell you the cost for the first three minutes; deposit that amount in the coin slot. The operator or a recording will cut in when you must deposit more money. A second, rarer variety of pay phone can be found in some large train stations and charges 25¢ for a one-minute call to any place in the continental U.S.

If you are at an ordinary telephone and don't have barrels of change, you may want to make a **collect call** (i.e., charge the call to the recipient). First dial "0" and then the area code and number you wish to reach. An operator will cut in and ask to help you. Tell him or her that you wish to place a collect call from Blackie Onassis, or whatever your name happens to be; anyone who answers may accept or refuse the call. If you tell the operator you are placing a **person-to-person collect call** (more expensive than a regular, station-to-station collect call), you must give both your name and the receiving person's name; the benefit is that a charge appears only if the person with whom you wish to speak is there (and accepts the charges, of course). The cheapest method of reversing the charges is MCI's new 1-800-COL-LECT (205-5328) service: just dial 1-800-COLLECT, tell the operator what number you want to engage (it can be anywhere in the world), and receive a 20% to 44% discount off normal rates (discounts are greatest when the rates are cheapest). Finally, if you'd like to call someone who is as poor as you, simply bill to a third party, also by dialing "0," the area code, and then the number; the operator will call the third party for approval. Note that in some areas, particularly rural ones, you may have to dial "0" alone for any operator-assisted call.

In addition to coin-operated pay phones, AT&T and its competitors operate a **coinless** version. Not only can collect and third-party calls be made on this kind of phone, but you can also use a **telephone credit card;** begin dialing all calls with "0." Generally, these phones are operated by passing the card through a slot before dialing, although you can always just punch in your calling-card number on the keypad—a desirable alternative if you happen to be traveling in an area where carrying around credit cards is unwise. AT&T calling cards (free for customers) are available in the United Kingdom, Ireland, Australia, and New Zealand, but not in South Africa; Canadians can use their Bell calling cards. Many of these phones—especially those located in airports, hotels, and truckstops—accept Visa, Mastercard, and American Express as well. The cheapest way to call long-distance from a pay phone is by using a calling card or credit card.

You can place **international calls** from any telephone. To call direct, dial the universal international access code (011) followed the country code (see Appendix for various codes), the city code, and the local number. Country codes and city codes may sometimes be listed with a zero in front (e.g. 033), but when using 011, drop successive zeros (e.g., 011-33). In some areas you will have to give the operator the number and he or she will place the call. Rates are cheapest on calls to the United Kingdom and Ireland between 6pm and 7am (Eastern Time); to Australia between 3am and 2pm; to New Zealand between 11pm and 10am; and to South Africa between 5pm and 6am.

TELEGRAM

■ Telegram

Sometimes cabling may be the only way to contact someone quickly (usually by the next day). For foreign telegrams, **Western Union** (800-325-6000) charges a base fee of $8, in addition to a per-word rate, which applies to the name, address, and signature as well as the message. For Canada, the rate is 50¢ per word; for Great Britain and Ireland, 56¢ per word; and for Australia, New Zealand, and South Africa, 61¢ per word. Western Union offers a variety of services for domestic telegrams. The most expensive option ensures same-day service ($29.90 for 15 words, $36.90 for 16-25 words, and $44.90 for 26-35 words). For a same-day phone call and a letter on the next mail-day, it costs $16 for the first 15 words, $23 for 16 to 25 words, and $30.95 for 26 to 35 words. Finally, a "Mailgram" costs $18 for 50 words and will arrive on the next mail-day.

■■■ CLIMATE

In **Alaska,** the weather varies from the coast inland. In general, summer and early fall (i.e. June-Sept.) are the warmest and sunniest times of year. However, wet, windy, and cold days even during the summer should be no real surprise. In Anchorage, the average temperature is around 20°F in January and 60°F in July. In Alaska's interior, the temperatures range from the 70s in the summers to the -30s in the wintertime. As you progress farther north, summer days and winter nights become longer. In Alaska and the Yukon, summer days may last from 6am to 2am.

In **Alberta,** the north and south of the province differ in temperature, although the entire area tends to be dry and cool. In January, the average temperature is around 15°F in the south, closer to -20°F in the north; in the summer, both regions warm to around 70°F.

In British Columbia, Washington, and Oregon, the key weather-making factor is the **mountains.** West of the mountains it rains quite a bit; to the east it is relatively dry. On the B.C. coast, the average temperature is about 35°F in January and a cool 65°F in the summer. Inland, winter temperatures hover around 0°F, while summer temperatures rise near 70°F. Temperatures in Washington range from an average of 35°F in January to 70°F in July—the west slightly colder, the east slightly warmer in the summer, and the other way around in the winter. Oregon is, on average, a little warmer than Washington.

■■■ ETIQUETTE

American etiquette (despite the shock you might feel at seeing those two words in conjunction) takes the form of several conventions which more invite your awareness than demand your adherence. In the United States, a brief shaking of hands is the most prevalent form of greeting among acquaintances, and, to a somewhat lesser extent, among friends. In social relationships, people often refer to one another by first name from the moment they are introduced. Prevalent in America's larger cities is the practice of "civil inattention," or the purposeful ignorance of every person one sees.

Waiters and waitresses in America's **restaurants** are usually not addressed as Sir and Miss. In many restaurants, your check will be delivered before you ask for it; you should not consider this a personal affront or, necessarily, a subtle hint that it's time to leave. Because they do not employ people to bus tables, most fast food restaurants expect you to throw away your own waste after you have finished eating.

Smoking in the United States, although still common, has acquired a slew of negative associations in the perception of the American public. It is prohibited in nearly all theaters, auditoriums, and museums. Most restaurants have designated sections in which smoking is allowed. As a general courtesy to fellow lung-bearers, ask people in your immediate vicinity if they mind inhaling your smoke before you light up.

ALASKA

Alaska's beauty is born of extremes. Here lie the highest mountain, the deepest gorge, and the broadest expanse of flatlands in North America. Alaska's oceans and rainforests teem with wildlife, and its icy wastelands receive less rainfall than most deserts; the largest land carnivore lives in Alaska (the Kodiak brown bear), as does its only hunter. In a land so vast, the human presence is still so small as to be negligible—harsh weather and an unforgiving landscape resisted successful human habitation in Alaska's interior until the 19th century. Yet greed for fur, gold, and oil has left an indelible mark.

The native Aleuts, who thrived for millennia on the harsh Aleutian island chain, called the spectacular and enormous expanses to the northeast "Alashka," meaning "The Great Land." To the Europeans and followers of "manifest destiny" who journeyed into the northwestern hinterlands, Alaska was the "Last Frontier." For the tourists and the sunlight-starved, the region is the "Land of the Midnight Sun," where you can start a pick-up game of softball at 2am in the summer months. One name which does not aptly describe Alaska is "frozen waste"—for half the year, all but the northernmost reaches turn green with vegetation.

In terms of physical attributes, Alaska truly is "The Great Land." The state contains one-fifth of all of America's land mass—586,000 sq. mi.—which averages to 1.03 sq. mi. per resident, in comparison to .03 sq. mi. per resident in Manhattan. The 33,000-mi. coastline (11 times the distance from New York to San Francisco) encompasses more than 3 million lakes larger than 20 acres, nearly all of which abound with grayling, arctic char, and steelhead trout. Alaska is home to Wrangell-St. Elias, the largest national park in America, comprising an area of 13 million acres—twice the size of Massachusetts. Nineteen Alaskan peaks reach over 14,000 ft., and several glacial ice fields occupy areas larger than the state of Rhode Island. Four major mountain ranges cross the state: the Wrangell Mountains, the Chugach Mountains, the Brooks Range, and the Denali-topped Alaska Range.

Despite its great natural endowments, Alaska has something of a love-hate relationship with Mother Nature. Located at the edge of the Pacific Plate on the "Ring of Fire" and almost due north of the Hawaiian volcanic chain, the Aleutian Islands are perpetually wracked by earthquakes and active volcanoes. Since 1964, Alaskans have justifiably scoffed at Californian neuroses about earthquakes. The Good Friday quake, centered in Miner's Lake (located between Whittier and Valdez), registered 9.2 on the modern Richter Scale and lasted eight terrible minutes. Its aftershocks continued for several days. Many coastal towns, including Kodiak and Whittier, were demolished by the *tsunami* which followed the earthquake. Valdez was completely destroyed and had to be rebuilt on a new site.

Although the Sound's wounds linger, a trip to Alaska will still thrill nature lovers. Photographers will find the wilderness full of quarry—caribou, bear, moose, Dall sheep, and even scattered mountain goats. Anglers will be sated by millions of spawning salmon, off-shore halibut which can weigh over 500 lbs., and trophy-sized grayling and trout churning in countless untouched interior lakes. And for hikers and campers, Alaska provides unparalleled opportunities for a truly solitary wilderness experience. Only one-quarter of Alaska is accessible by highway, and the rest can be reached only by plane, snow machine, or dogsled. Because of this isolation, the true bushwhacker can easily find opportunities for backcountry exploration in virgin forests. But you do not need to be a hard-core outdoorsperson to see much of the state's beauty—many of Alaska's stunning glaciers are accessible by road.

Alaska

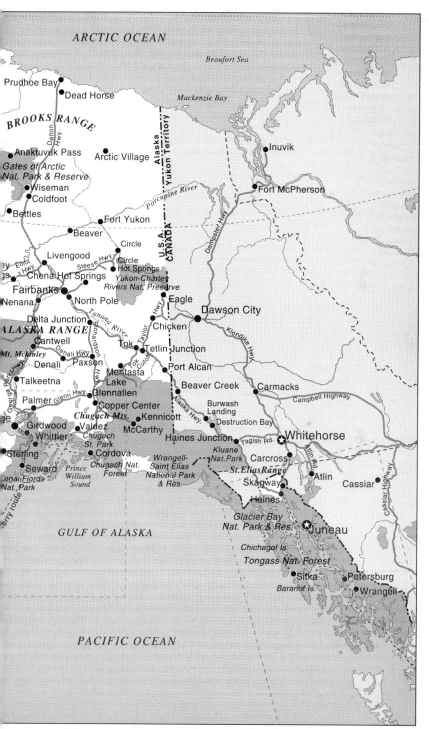

Geography

Alaska is home to several distinct geographic zones. On the archipelago of the **Southeastern Panhandle,** the isolated state capital of Juneau resides among numerous fjord-scarred islands, verdant rainforests, and primordial swamps known as *muskeg*. **Southcentral Alaska**—home of Kodiak Island, the Kenai Peninsula, and Prince William Sound—is filled with an abundance of wildlife, including the Kodiak brown bear. To the north and east from Anchorage, the interminable flatlands of the **Interior** are dominated by the highest mountain in North America: 20,320-ft.-tall Denali (Mt. McKinley). The **Bush** encompasses the vast and empty areas north and west of the Interior—the Brooks Range and the Arctic Circle, the Seward Peninsula, and all of western Alaska along the Bering Sea. The Alaska Peninsula and the storm-swept **Aleutian Islands** poke into the extreme southwestern reaches of the Bush, offering small purchase to a handful of hardy human inhabitants.

History

The first humans arrived in the region some 20,000 years ago, migrating over the Bering Land Bridge from Siberia to Alaska. Today, four distinct native ethnic groups inhabit Alaska. The Southeast is home to the Tlingit and Haida peoples, who are renowned for their exquisitely carved totem poles and nearly impenetrable wooden forts, from which they almost staved off Russian invaders in the 19th century. The Interior and Southcentral regions harbor the once-nomadic Athabasca nation, and the Aleutian Island Chain is populated largely by the Aleuts, a peaceful people who were enslaved by the Russians as fur trappers. Eskimos, also called Inuits, reside almost exclusively within the Arctic Circle and share a common language and heritage with the Native Siberians across the Bering Strait.

In 1733, Russian seafarers, under orders from Peter the Great to find a route from the Arctic to the Pacific, landed on Kayak Island of Prince William Sound. Bering's expedition brought the fur of sea otters back to Russia and inaugurated an intense competition for control of the lucrative trade in "soft gold." The Russian Company soon began a massive colonization of the Alaskan wilderness. The Russians located their bases of operation primarily in the southern coastal region, which even today retains an unmistakably Slavic imprint. By the mid-1800s, the once-bountiful supply of fur-bearing animals was nearly exhausted, the populations of Aleuts had shrunk through forced labor, and the Russians welcomed an American bid for the "dead land." Such frenzied and profit-seeking exploitation of natural resources, ending only with total depletion, would provide the pattern for much of Alaska's future.

On October 18, 1867, in the territorial capital of Sitka, the United States purchased Alaska for $7,200,000, or approximately 2¢ per acre. Critics mocked the transaction, popularly known as "Seward's Folly" after President Johnson's Secretary of State who negotiated the deal. Alaska's native peoples at this time restated their claims to their ancestral lands and received limited recognition from Washington. The issue went unresolved, though, and titles would be held in abeyance for more than a century.

James Seward was vindicated a scant 15 years post-purchase when large deposits of gold were unearthed in the Gastineau Channel and the Eldorado-esque Juneau was born. As deposits on the Gastineau began to give out, other rivers such as the Yukon, the Charley, the Fortymile, and the Klondike all in turn were swarmed by gold-panning prospectors. Hundreds of millions of dollars in gold eventually made their way pipeline-style down to the continental U.S.

In 1959, decades after the last major deposits of gold had been pulled from the ground, Alaska became the 49th state. Under the Statehood Act, the new government was granted the right to select 102 million acres of land which had until then been under federal control. Throughout the 1960s, Alaskan Natives watched with growing consternation as the federal and state governments divvied up vast tracts of land without regard for the Natives' 20,000-year-long occupancy. The discovery in

1968 of huge oil deposits beneath the shore of the Beaufort Sea in the Arctic Ocean brought matters to a head. Natives increased the pressure for settlement of their claims which had for so long been ignored, seeking to claim their share the anticipated economic boom.

In January of 1971 the Department of the Interior issued a study which pushed the profitable prospects of the oil fields closer to reality. It dealt with the necessity of a trans-Alaskan pipeline to transport the oil south from the Arctic to an ice-free port on Prince William Sound. The Department of the Interior claimed that while such a pipeline would unavoidably lead to environmental damage (a concern raised by native peoples and early conservationists), it was nonetheless necessary in the name of national security. Among the most actively supportive of Alaskan commercialization was once-and-future Governor of the state Walter J. "Wally" Hickel.

In December of 1971, the federal government finally made its peace with the native peoples, state and federal courts, and environmental groups by passing the Alaska Native Claims Settlement Act (ANCSA). The natives, who then numbered around 60,000, received $1 billion and 40 million acres of land. Of the $1 billion, half was paid from the U.S. treasury over an 11-year period, and half came from oil and other mineral revenues collected from state and federal lands. The money was distributed to 12 regional native corporations, all of which were (and continue to be) controlled and administered by the local tribes. Each native person received stock in a corporation according to tribal affiliation. The corporations are in purpose akin to trust funds, their main goals being to provide social and educational benefits to their shareholders; corporations invest and attempt to increase their holdings, and shareholders earn dividends whenever their corporations turn a profit. The natives became, collectively, rich; but their victory came at the cost of a revolution in thinking. In a land where natives once could follow caribou over lands without borders and fish for subsistence without permits, "no trespassing" signs have shot up, and the native corporations have become more focused on the profits to be made by selling off natural resources.

Moreover, ANSCA designated some 80 million acres of Alaskan land to be considered for federal protection as national parks, forests, wildlife refuges, and "wild rivers." While environmentalists and state legislators battle over which lands should be preserved for the public, federal controls have significantly reduced private homesteading rights, and the frontiersperson who once could have taken to the woods and built a cabin must now wait for the government to designate and sell off subdivisions.

In 1973, the Alyeska Pipeline Service Company received the official go-ahead to build a pipeline from Prudhoe Bay to Valdez—800 mi. through the heart of the Alaskan wilderness. The pipeline has brought jobs, money, and people to Alaska, and with them, many of the undesirable features of the lower 48 states: pollution, overcrowding, and profligate spending. It is hard to imagine overcrowding in a land so huge; then again, it is hard to believe that a single pipeline, in relative size only as thick as a thread across Staten Island, could have such a drastic effect on the state's political, social, and economic landscape. By 1981, four years after the Trans-Alaska pipeline was installed, $7,200,000 worth of crude oil flowed from the Arctic oil field every 4½ hours, forever ending criticism of "The Folly." State revenues from oil taxation have created a trust fund in the name of the people of Alaska, providing the government with enough money to operate without the need for any additional private taxation.

Twenty-five years to the day after the Good Friday earthquake of '64 which leveled the port city of Valdez, the Exxon oil tanker *Valdez* ran aground on Bligh Reef, spilling over 250,000 barrels (11 million gallons) of syrupy crude into the blue waters of Prince William Sound and onto shores as far away as Kodiak Island, several hundred miles to the south. Thousands of marine mammals and birds, saturated with the sticky black sludge, suffered horrible deaths. Clean-up crews were completely unprepared, grossly underfunded, and grossly understaffed. A full 10% of the

Sound suffered from oil poisoning, and 2% of Alaska's total coastline was polluted. Though by the summer of 1990 no oil was visible to the casual observer, the long-term effects of the spill are uncertain at best; in addition to poisoning thousands of marine mammals and birds, the oil has disrupted feeding cycles in the sound.

Exxon has spent $2.5 billion to clean up the spilled oil, and in October, 1991, the company agreed to pay an additional $900 million over the next 11 years for future clean-up operations, plus $100 million in restitution to the state and federal governments and $25 million in criminal fines. Hundreds of lawsuits filed against Exxon by private individuals, including Native Alaskans, are still pending. But the payments have put little more than a dent in the oil company's earnings, while recent federal and state environmental reports have revealed that marine biologists (and the courts) have underestimated the extent of the damage caused by the spill.

The tremendous uproar surrounding the spill helps to underscore the present shift taking place within the Alaskan economy. As the pipeline's profits have been securely divided among the oil companies, the native corporations, and the state and federal governments, the rush which sprang up around its discovery and exploitation has begun to subside. In its place has come an environmentally-spurred interest in the state's pristine wilderness. Such vast stretches of unspoiled land are not to be found anywhere else in the U.S., and they are at present Alaska's hottest commodity. The astounding extent of Exxon's payment (and the serious threat that it may be required to pay still more) attests to the growing political clout of those controlling and promoting the state's unpopulated lands.

In 1990, political eccentric Walter Hickel, mentioned above as the former governor and strong proponent of the pipeline, swept into the governor's mansion once again on an independent ticket supported by a small but dedicated party of Alaskan secessionists. Hickel's early support of the oil companies has since been followed by a slew of further attempts at commercializing the state: he bears the dubious distinction of being the person who introduced the shopping mall to Alaska, he has proposed construction of a gigantic "garden hose" through which Alaskan fresh water would be pumped to drought-stricken California, and he once suggested building an "ice highway" over the top of the world to Norway in order to spur trade with Europe.

In the fall of 1992, with Hickel still at the state's helm, the Alaska Board of Game voted to allow the tracking and shooting of wolves from the air, hoping that a smaller population of wolves would lead to larger herds of moose and caribou, and, in turn, to larger crowds of tourists to the state's public park lands. A *New York Times* article quoted David Kelleyhouse, director of the Alaska Division of Wildlife Conservation: "We feel we are going to create a wildlife spectacle on par with the major migrations in East Africa. Mom and pop from Syracuse can come up here and see something that they can't see anywhere else on earth." Kelleyhouse's grand vision was clearly in keeping with that of Governor Hickel, who had appointed both Kelleyhouse and the members of the state Board of Game following his election in 1990. Before Hickel's election, the state's policies toward wolf-killing had been moving in much the opposite direction.

The vote by the Board of Game quickly drew vociferous protest, both from within Alaska and from the Lower 48. The Fund for Animals, Inc., took out a prominent ad on the *Times's* Op-Ed page displaying a large picture of a wolf, tongue lolling from its mouth. The ad exhorted readers to "make a call for the wild" by contacting the Governor and voicing their dissent (his address is: P.O. Box A, Juneau, AK 99811). On December 5, the *Times* published a selection of the reader mail it had received on the matter, the gist of which was captured in the section's accompanying illustration: a wolf blindfolded and roped to a stake, the muzzles of five rifles pushing into its chest.

Such negative publicity was certainly not what Hickel had hoped for, and, following several governmental gatherings in early 1993, the state Board of Game rescinded its decision to allow shooting and tracking from the air, opting instead to permit shooting from the ground only, and solely by officers of the state's Department of Fish and Game. The hunting is to take place in a more limited area than was first proposed, and the newly-revised goal of the hunting is more specific and more acceptable—to reverse the decline of a certain herd of caribou near Fairbanks whose numbers had been falling for several years. Mom and pop from Syracuse will have to wait.

Literature

A good way to catch up on Alaska's ABCs is to peruse some of the following writings: John McPhee's *Coming Into the Country*—a must-read—sketches a fascinating overview of Alaskan issues and wilderness life-styles; Thomas Burger's *Village Journey* gives a first-hand perspective on emerging Native corporations; Lael Morgan's *Art and Eskimo Power* depicts Eskimo culture and heritage; and Walter Hickel's *Who Owns America* outlines the Governor's plans for future development of the state. The venerable Native newspaper *Tundra Times,* founded in part by the legendary Eskimo journalist Howard Rock, publishes out of Anchorage and provides the most up-to-date discussions of current Indian issues, without skirting their own internal diversity and factionalism. Finally, *Going to Extremes* by Joe McGinniss and *Alaska: The Sophisticated Wilderness* by Jon Gardey both acquaint the reader with Alaskan settlers seeking refuge from the lower 48. (Eccentrics or mavericks? You decide.)

   Alaska by James Michener; *Never Cry Wolf* by Farley Mowat; *Travels in Alaska* by John Muir; *Alaska: The Sophisticated Wilderness* by Jon Gardey; *The Spell of the Yukon and Other Poems* by Robert Service; and *The Call of the Wild* by Jack London all give less topical, more imaginatively descriptive introductions to the state.

PRACTICAL INFORMATION

Capital: Juneau.
Visitors Information: Alaska Division of Tourism, 33 Willoughby St. (465-2010). Mailing address: P.O. Box 110801, Juneau 99811-0801. Open Mon.-Fri. 8am-5pm.
Alaska Public Lands Information Center, 605 W. 4th Ave. #105, Anchorage, 99501 (271-2737 or 258-PARK for a recording). Help in crossing any and all wilderness areas. Branch office in Fairbanks; others under construction in Ketchikan and Tok. Open daily 9am-7pm.
Alaska State Division of Parks, Old Federal Bldg., Anchorage 99510 (762-2617). Open Mon.-Fri. 8am-4:30pm.
United States Forest Service, 1675 C. St., Anchorage, AK 99501-5198 (271-4126). General information regarding national parks and reserves. Open Mon.-Fri. 8am-5pm.
National Park Service, Parks and Forests Information Center, W. 4th Ave., Anchorage 99503 (271-2737). Open Mon.-Fri. 9am-7pm.
Alaska Department of Fish and Game, P.O. Box 25526, Juneau, AK 99802-5526 (465-4210). Hunting and fishing regulations available here.
Alaska State Employment Service, 10002 Glacier Highway, Suite 200, Juneau 99801 (790-4562).
Alaska Department of Labor, P.O. Box 22509, Juneau 99802 (465-4839). For those hunting jobs, not game. Branch offices in Anchorage, Ketchikan, and Petersburg.
Legislative Information Office, 716 W. 4th Ave. #200, Anchorage 99501-2133 (558-8111). For those who would like to delve into Alaska's juicy political debates. Or call the **Alaska State Government General Information** service at 561-4226.
United States Customs Service: 202-927-6724. This Washington, DC office will connect you with the Canadian Customs and Excise office for information regarding the rules and regulations of traveling through Canada on your way to Alaska.

INTRODUCTION

Payphones: In many towns, phones will not return coins, even if the party you're calling doesn't answer. Dial, wait until party picks up, and *then* deposit coins. They will understand the lag.

Population: 550,000. **Nicknames:** The Last Frontier; Land of the Midnight Sun. **Motto:** North to the Future. **Flower:** Forget-Me-Not. **Bird:** Willow Ptarmigan. **Tree:** Sitka Spruce. **Date of Incorporation:** Jan. 3, 1959 (49th state). **Land Area:** 570,373 sq. mi.

Emergency: 911.

Avalanche and Mountain Weather Report: 243-7675.

State Troopers: 269-5511 in Anchorage, 452-2114 in Fairbanks.

Time Zones: Alaska (most of the state; 4 hr. behind Eastern); Aleutian-Hawaii (Aleutian Islands; 5 hr. behind Eastern).

Postal Abbreviation: AK

Drinking Age: 21.

Area Code: 907.

GETTING AROUND

The cost of travel both to and through Alaska is exorbitant no matter how you go. Bringing a car is not necessarily the wisest plan—if at all feeble, the car may not survive the rocky drive up the largely unpaved **Alaska Highway.** Even if you and your car do arrive safely, there often aren't enough usable roads to justify the time and expense of driving (gas is expensive, breakdowns are common, and traveling with a car on the ferry is costly). Many people do, of course, venture onto Alaska's roads despite the difficulties, and anyone so inclined should consult the By Car: Driving in Alaska section of the Essentials chapter.

The shortcomings of Alaska's sketchy road and rail networks are quick to explain why one in 36 Alaskans has a pilot's license. Given Alaska's size, air travel is often a necessity, albeit an exorbitantly expensive one (the hourly rate exceeds $100). Several intrastate airlines, almost exclusively based at the Anchorage airport, transport passengers and cargo virtually to every village in Alaska: **Alaska Airlines** (to larger Bush towns and Cordova; 800-426-5292); **Mark Air** (to larger Bush towns, Kodiak, and the Aleutians; 800-426-6784); **ERA Aviation** (southcentral; 243-6633); **Southcentral Air** (southcentral; 243-2761); **Reeve Aleutian Airways** (Aleutians; 243-4700); and **Ryan Air Service** (practically anywhere in the Bush; 561-2090). Many other charters and flight-seeing services are available. Write **Ketchum Air Service Inc.,** P.O. Box 190588, Anchorage 99519 (243-5525), on the North Shore of Lake Hood, to ask about their charters. One-day flights and overnight or weekend trips to isolated lakes, mountains, and tundra usually range from $165 up.

Those who intend to hit the ground running—and keep running—would be smart to check out the **Alaska Pass.** The pass offers unlimited access to Alaska's railroad, ferry, and bus systems; a 15-day pass sells for $569, a 30-day pass for $799. The fare may seem expensive, but with a network that extends from Bellingham, WA to Dutch Harbor on the Aleutian Islands, the pass is a good deal for those who want to see a lot of Alaska in a short amount of time. If interested, call 800-248-7598, 7am-7pm (Alaska time).

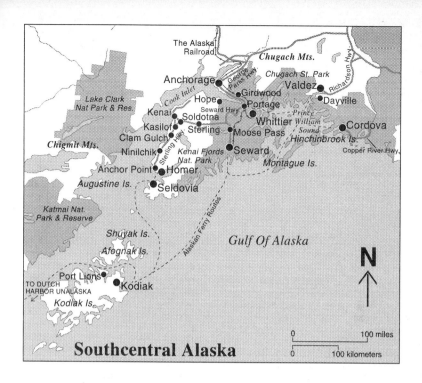

Southcentral Alaska

Southcentral Alaska

Southcentral Alaska may provide a model in miniature of Alaska's future. The regions which make up this part of the state—Anchorage, Prince William Sound, the Kenai Peninsula, and Kodiak Island—are becoming less isolated as an expanding network of well-maintained roads (still a rare convenience in the northland) draws more and more people up from the Lower 48. As the population increases and municipal economies merge, the cost of living is creeping down toward the levels found in the rest of the country.

An amazing and varied spread of wilderness—massive and challenging peaks, rivers churning with fish, and a catalogue of animal life large enough to cast several episodes of *Wild Kingdom*—can be reached in less than a day from Anchorage. But as the state makes itself more presentable to guests and export industries, the kinds of nature which to many people define Alaska—the pristine and untouched expanses devoid of human presence—are receding into a distance open only to the most diligent.

Valdez is the southern terminus of the Alaskan pipeline, attracting score upon score of heavy tankers to pump themselves full at this colossal proto-gas station. It was in this area that the tanker Exxon *Valdez* made its toxic (and intoxicated) blunder, defacing countless miles of coastline. Exxon and its oily brethren have in recent times butted heads with the Southcentral region's other huge export industry, fishing (the fleet which runs out of Kodiak Island is the nation's third-largest). Many of those who work within it feel that the Exxon spill has had a harsh affect on the size of their catches—so much so, in fact, that in August, 1993, a number of boats block-

ANCHORAGE

aded Valdez harbor in protest of the oil conglomerate's insufficient efforts at compensation and cleanup.

■■■ ANCHORAGE

Only 80 years ago cartographers wasted no ink on what is now Alaska's major metropolis. Not surprisingly, the city has an aroma of prefabrication—writer John McPhee called it "condensed, instant Albuquerque." Approximately half the state's population—some 250,000 people—live in "Los Anchorage," the moniker that some rural residents use to mock the city's urban pretensions. A decentralized jumble of fast-food joints and discount liquor stores, Anchorage also supports a full range of popular and high-brow culture: semi-professional baseball and basketball teams, frequent performances by internationally known orchestras and pop stars, dramatic theater, and opera. The Anchorage Daily News won a Pulitzer Prize in 1989 for its reporting on suicide and alcoholism among Native Americans in the region. Even though moose and bear not only frequently wander downtown but can actually be hunted legally within the municipality, this is as close to "big city" as Alaska gets.

Anchorage's history is anomalous for Alaska—no one ever struck gold here, Russian imperialist Baranov and his countrymen didn't stop by, and it is not located at a natural travel hub. But the Alaska Railroad's 1914 decision to move its headquarters to a small rail camp converted Anchorage into the state's Grand Central Station. While Juneau remained the Alaskan capital, Anchorage was the organizational headquarters and staging area of a massive military buildup conducted by the federal government during and after World War II. Today Anchorage's international airport is among the world's busiest, ferrying passengers en route to and from the Far East.

Downtown Anchorage, centered on 4th Avenue, was until recently a red-light district filled with adult bookstores. But the state has hosed down the filth with a quick spray from the petrodollar hydrant, replacing it with new federal and state buildings. While the area between A St. and Fairbanks St. is still strewn with bars, porno theaters, and pull-tab joints, it's difficult to maintain a nocturnal netherworld in a city where night in the summertime may last as little as an hour.

PRACTICAL INFORMATION AND ORIENTATION

Visitors Information: Log Cabin Visitor Information Center, W. 4th Ave. at F St. (274-3531). Open daily 7:30am-7pm; Sept. and May 8:30am-6pm; Oct.-April 9am-4pm. The Log Cabin is usually crammed with visitors and a staff of volunteers. Plenty of maps and brochures. Smaller visitors information **outlets** are located at the **airport,** in the domestic terminal near the baggage claim, and in the overseas terminal in the central atrium, as well as in the **Valley River Mall,** first level.

Visitor Language Assistance: 276-4118. Pre-programmed assistance in languages from Laotian to Finnish. Anchorage is home to **consulates** from most Western European countries and Japan.

Alaska Public Lands Information Center, Old Federal Bldg. (271-2737), 4th Ave. between F and G St. An astounding coagulation of 8 state and federal offices (including the **National Park Service, U.S. Forest Service, Division of State Parks,** and the **U.S. Fish and Wildlife Service**) all under one roof provides the most current information on the entire state. Here you will find popular topographic maps, a computerized sportfishing map, and an interactive trip-planning video unit. Films daily at 12:15 and 3:30pm, or upon request. Open daily 9am-6pm.

Alaska Employment Center, P.O. Box 107224, 3301 Eagle St. (269-4800). Take bus #3 or 60. Open Mon.-Fri. 8am-noon and 1-4:30pm.

Airport: Alaska International Airport, P.O. Box 190649-VG, Anchorage 99519-0649 (266-2525). Serviced by 7 international carriers, including **British Airways** (248-1803) and **Korean Airlines** (243-3329); 5 domestic carriers, including

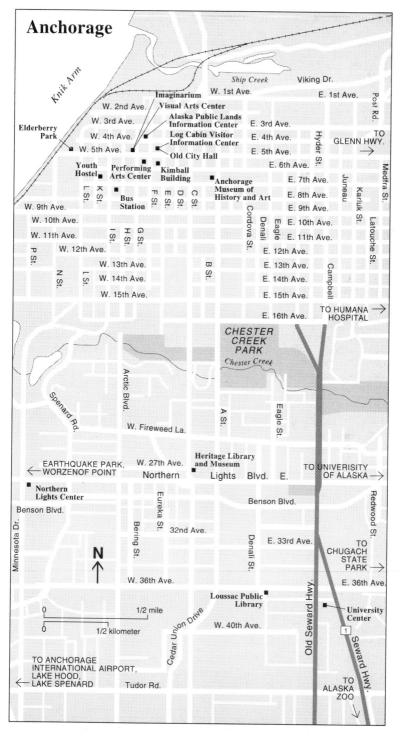

Anchorage

Knik Arm

Ship Creek

Viking Dr.

W. 1st Ave.

E. 1st Ave.

Post Rd.

Imaginarium

W. 2nd Ave.

Visual Arts Center

W. 3rd Ave.

Alaska Public Lands
Information Center

E. 3rd Ave.

TO
GLENN HWY.

Elderberry
Park

W. 4th Ave.

Log Cabin Visitor
Information Center

E. 4th Ave.

Hyder St.

W. 5th Ave.

Old City Hall

E. 5th Ave.

E. 6th Ave.

Youth
Hostel

Performing
Arts Center

Kimball
Building

Anchorage
Museum of
History and Art

E. 7th Ave.

Juneau

Karluk St.

Medfra St.

Latouche St.

K St.

L St.

Bus
Station

F St.

E St.

D St.

C St.

E. 8th Ave.

E. 9th Ave.

Cordova St.

Denali

Eagle

W. 9th Ave.

W. 10th Ave.

I St.

H St.

G St.

E. 10th Ave.

E. 11th Ave.

W. 11th Ave.

P St.

W. 12th Ave.

E. 12th Ave.

N St.

L St.

W. 13th Ave.

B St.

E. 13th Ave.

W. 14th Ave.

E. 14th Ave.

W. 15th Ave.

E. 15th Ave.

E. 16th Ave.

TO HUMANA
HOSPITAL

Campbell

CHESTER
CREEK
PARK

Chester Creek

Arctic Blvd.

Spenard Rd.

W. Fireweed La.

A St.

Eagle St.

EARTHQUAKE PARK,
WORZENOF POINT

W. 27th Ave.

Heritage Library
and Museum

Northern

Lights

Blvd.

E.

TO UNIVERSITY
OF ALASKA

Northern
Lights Center

Benson Blvd.

Benson Blvd.

Minnesota Dr.

Bering St.

Eureka St.

32nd Ave.

Denali St.

E. 33rd Ave.

Redwood St.

TO
CHUGACH
STATE
PARK

N
↑

W. 36th Ave.

E. 36th Ave.

0   1/2 mile

0   1/2 kilometer

Loussac Public
Library

W. 40th Ave.

Cedar Union Drive

Old Seward Hwy.

University
Center

Seward Hwy.

1

TO ANCHORAGE
INTERNATIONAL AIRPORT,
LAKE HOOD,
LAKE SPENARD

Tudor Rd.

TO
ALASKA
ZOO

Delta (249-2110), **Northwest Airlines** (266-5636), and **United** (241-6522); and 3 Alaskan carriers, including **Mark Air** (243-6275 or 800-426-6784; daily flights to Kenai $25, Homer $40, and Kodiak $65—all fares one way with 21-day advance purchase). Nearly every airport in Alaska can be reached from Anchorage, either directly or through a connecting flight in Fairbanks.

Alaska Railroad, 411 W. 1st Ave., Anchorage 99510-7500 (265-2494, 800-544-0552 out of state), at the head of town. To: Denali ($85), Fairbanks ($120), and Seward ($40). In winter, 1 per week to Fairbanks; no service to Seward. A summertime "flag-stop" also runs between Anchorage and Hurricane (a stop between Talkeetna and Denali) on Wed., Sat., and Sun. The train will make unscheduled stops anywhere along this route—just wave it down with a white cloth and wait to be acknowledged with a whistle. For more information write to Passenger Service, P.O. Box 107500, Anchorage. Office open daily 6am-11pm; ticket sales from 6:15am to 5pm. May be closed if no trains are arriving.

Buses: Alaska Denali Transit, P.O. Box 2203, Anchorage (273-3331 24 hr. for recorded message, or 733-2601 9am-5pm for reservations). Several trips per week to: Talkeetna ($25), Denali ($35), Fairbanks ($55), and Haines ($99). Pickup at Anchorage Youth Hostel (see Accommodations) at 8am. Schedules vary widely, so call ahead. **Caribou Express,** 501 L. St. (278-5776). To: Portage (2 per day, $20), Fairbanks (1 per day, $75), Valdez (1 per day, $75). **Moon Bay Express** (274-6454). To Denali (1 per day, $35). Pickup at Anchorage Youth Hostel (see Accommodations) at 8am. **Homer and Seward Bus Lines,** 800-478-8280. To: Seward (1 per day, $30), Homer (1 per day, $35). **Alaskon Express,** 800-544-2206. To: Valdez (4 per day, $89) and Haines (4 per day, $189). **Alaska Direct,** 277-6652. To Whitehorse, YT (Mon., Wed., and Sat. at 6am, $145). **Alaska Backpacker Shuttle,** 344-8775, van service daily at 7am from the hostel to trailheads north and south of Anchorage ($5-10 depending on distance).

People Mover Bus: (343-6543), in the Transit Center, on 6th Ave. between G and H St., just up the street from the Anchorage Youth Hostel. Buses leave from here to all points in the Anchorage Bowl (including a few per day to the airport) 6am-10pm; restricted schedule on weekends. Cash fare $1, tokens 90¢, day pass $2.50. Exact change. The downtown region, border by 5th Ave., Eagle St., 7th Ave. and K St., is a **free fare zone** Mon.-Fri. 9am-3pm and 6-8pm, Sat. 9am-8pm, Sun. 11am-6pm. The Transit Center office is open Mon.-Fri. 8am-5pm and sells a helpful transit map (50¢).

Alaska Marine Highway, 333 W. 4th St. (272-4482), in the Post Office Mall. No terminal, but ferry tickets and reservations. Open Mon.-Fri. 8am-4:30pm.

Taxi: Yellow Cab, 272-2422. **Checker Cab,** 276-1234. **Alaska Cab,** 563-5353.

Car Rentals: Allstar Rent-A-Car, 561-0350. $40 per day, unlimited mileage. **Payless,** 243-3616. $45 per day, unlimited mileage. **Budget,** 243-0150. $45 per day, unlimited mileage. For all three, must be at least 21 with major credit card. All are located at the **airport.** Ask about a free drop-off and pick-up downtown.

Road Conditions: 243-7675.

Bicycle Rental: at the **Anchorage Youth Hostel** (see Accommodations). $7 per day. Also at the **Royal Alaska** (243-2300), on Spenard just east of Minnesota. Close to the Coastal Bike Trail. $5 per hr., $24 per 24 hr.

Camping Equipment: Recreational Equipment, Inc. (REI), 1200 Northern Lights Blvd. (272-4565), near Spenard, at Minnesota. High-quality packs, clothing, tents, stores, and dried foods. Open Mon.-Fri. 10am-9pm, Sat. 9:30am-6pm, Sun. noon-5pm. Take bus #7. The **Army-Navy Store,** on 4th Ave. across from the Post Office Mall, offers even lower prices. Open Mon.-Fri. 9am-8pm, Sat. 9am-6pm, and Sun. 11am-5pm. For buying or selling **used equipment,** try **Play It Again Sports** (278-7529), at 27th and Spenard near REI. A frequently-rotating inventory of quality fishing and camping equipment at discount prices.

Library: ZJ Loussac Library (261-2975), at 36th Ave. and Denali St. The most architecturally-intriguing building in Anchorage. Take bus #2 or 60. Devotes an entire wing to Alaska material. Open Mon.-Thurs. 11am-9pm, Fri.-Sat. 10am-6pm; in winter also Sun. 1-5pm.

Bookstore: Cyrano's Bookstore and Cafe (274-11730), on D St., between 4th and 5th Ave. Anchorage has come a long way since writer John McPhee reported

A
C
C
O
M
M
O
D
A
T
I
O
N
S

2 decades ago that books were selling for 47¢ per lb. Leftist films screened Thurs.-Sat. nights. For a dog-eared copy of *White Fang*, try **C&M Used Books,** 215 E. 4th Ave. (278-9394). Open Mon.-Sat. 10am-7pm. Also try **Title Wave,** 505 E. Northern Lights (278-9283). Open Mon.-Sat. 10:30am-6:30pm.

Secondhand Tickets: An entire section of the classified ads in the *Daily News* lists tickets for travel within the state and to the Lower 48. **The Ticket Exchange,** 505 W. Northern Lights (274-8153), also buys and sells tickets at rates between the newspaper and over-the-counter prices. Open Mon.-Sat. 9am-6pm. **Warning:** if someone travels under someone else's name, the airline is under no obligation to honor the ticket. Before paying for a secondhand ticket, call the airline and ask if they require identification at check-in with the particular ticket you want to buy. Be especially careful about frequent-flyer tickets.

Laundromat: K-Speed Wash, 600 E. 6th St. (279-0731). Wash $1.50, 7½-min. dry 25¢. Open Mon.-Sat. 7am-10pm. **Anchorage Youth Hostel** (see Accommodations) also has laundry facilities. Wash $1, dry 50¢.

Weather: 936-2525. **Motorists and Recreation Forecast:** 936-2626. **Marine Weather Forecast:** 936-2727.

Crisis Line: 562-4048. Mon.-Fri. 8:30am-5pm. **Rape Crisis Line:** 276-7273. 24 hr.

Disabilities Access Line: Challenge Alaska (563-2658). The Log Cabin Visitors Center (see listing above) is equipped with a **TTY** for people with communications disabilities.

Hospital: Humana, 2801 DeBarr Ave. (264-1224).

Emergency: 911. **Police:** 786-8901.

Post Office (277-6568), W. 4th Ave. and C St. on the lower level in the mall. Open Mon.-Fri. 10am-5:30pm, Sat. 10am-4pm. **General Delivery ZIP Code:** 99510. The **state's central post office** (266-3259) is located next to the international airport. It does *not* handle general delivery mail, but is open 24 hr.

Directory Assistance within Alaska: 411. Free.

Area Code: 907.

From its seat 114 mi. north of Seward on the Seward Hwy., 304 mi. west of Valdez on the Glenn and Richardson Hwy., and 358 mi. south of Fairbanks on the George Parks Hwy., Anchorage is the hub of Southcentral Alaska.

Anchorage can be reached by road, rail, or air. **Anchorage International Airport** (see above), a few mi. southwest of downtown off International Airport Rd., is served by all Alaskan airlines, as well as by major American and international airlines. The **People Mover Bus** (see above) runs from the airport to downtown (3 per day); the visitors center near the baggage claim can direct you a short distance from the terminal to more frequently-serviced routes. Numerous **courtesy vans** run from the airport to the larger hotels downtown.

Military bases to the north, the Chugach Mountains to the east, and the Knik and Turnagain Arms of the Pacific to the west and south frame the **Anchorage Bowl,** within which the city sprawls some 50,000 acres. The **downtown area** of Anchorage is laid out in a grid. Numbered avenues run east-west, and addresses are designated East or West from **C Street.** North-south streets are lettered alphabetically west of **A Street,** and named alphabetically east of A Street. The rest of Anchorage spreads out—*way* out—along the major highways. The **University of Alaska, Anchorage** campus lies on 36th Ave., off Northern Lights Blvd.

ACCOMMODATIONS

Although Anchorage is blessed many times over with affordable lodgings, few are good enough to build their inns downtown. The best option is the hostel (see listing below). Several **Bed and Breakfast** referral agencies have set up shop in Anchorage. Try **Alaska Private Lodgings,** 1236 W. 10th Ave., Anchorage 99511 (258-1717), or **Stay With a Friend,** 3605 Arctic Blvd., Suite 173, Anchorage 99503 (278-8800). Both can refer you to singles from $50 and doubles from $60.

Those who truly lack the funds to stay elsewhere can find a bed at the **Rescue Mission,** 2328 E. Tudor Rd. (563-5603)—take bus #75. Accommodations are minimal and the curfew 9pm, but it's free. Budget travelers usually avoid the St. Francis shelter, which is primarily a long-term respite for people stuck in poverty.

Anchorage Youth Hostel (HI/AYH), 700 H St. (276-3635), at 7th, 1 block south of the Transit Center downtown. A great gateway hostel in a convenient location. 3 kitchens, 2 balconies, and scads of info. on traveling throughout the state. Family and "couple rooms" available. Frequently filled to the rafters in summer; write ahead for reservations. The **Alaska Black Book,** in the 2nd floor reference room, is an invaluable compendium of previous travelers' (mis)adventures all over Alaska. Wheelchair accessible. Lockout noon-5pm. Curfew midnight. 4-day max. stay in summer. Members $12, nonmembers $15. Weekly and monthly rates during the off-season's "winter community" program. Overflow and long-term guests are directed to a smaller, less convenient hostel near the airport.

Eagle Crest (276-5913), 9th Ave. and Eagle St. Clean and well-managed by the Salvation Army. For many, the next stop after they've stayed their limit at the hostel. Many long-term residents. Common kitchen and laundry. Free coffee. No curfew. Bed in 4-person room $15. Singles $27.50, and doubles $40, both with private baths. Low weekly and monthly rates.

International Backpackers Inn, 324 Mumford (274-3870 or 272-0297), at Peterkin. Take bus #45 to Bragaw and Peterkin. As you watch the bus depart, turn left and walk 3 blocks. The office is upstairs. Anchorage's "other hostel," this quiet, family-run complex houses 25 dorm-style beds, common kitchens, bathrooms, and TVs. Free local phone and linen. Chore required. Key deposit $10. Beds $12-15 (go for the $15 building). Tentsites $10. Weekly and monthly rates available.

Inlet Inn (277-5541), 6th and H St. near the Anchorage Youth Hostel (see above). Nice rooms with cable TV. Singles $55. Doubles $60. Smaller rooms for 1-2 people, with sink and bathroom down the hall, $40 each.

Caribou Inn, 501 L St. (272-0444). 3 floors of comfortable, carpeted rooms in a good downtown location near the Coastal Bike Trail. You'll see Cook Inlet if you crane your neck. Singles $49. Doubles $59. Bath on hall. Full breakfast included.

Midtown Lodge, 604 W. 26th (258-7778), off Arctic Blvd. Take bus #9. Simple, spotless rooms with shared bath. Free continental breakfast; free soup and sandwiches in the lobby for lunch—these people get an "A" for effort. Singles $43. Doubles $48. Reservations essential up to 2 weeks ahead in summer.

Alaska Budget Motel, 545 E. 4th Ave. (277-0088). On the wrong side of the tracks, but the rooms are nice enough. Cable TV, free local calls. Singles $49. Doubles $59.

CAMPING

Both camping areas within the city welcome tents and RVs. Many of the state's best sites lie in the free **State Division of Parks and Outdoor Recreation campgrounds,** just outside the city limits (water and toilets). Most sites hide along dirt roads off the highway. Bring your own food and supplies. Among the best of the state campgrounds are **Eagle River** (688-0998) and **Eklutna** (EE-cloot-nah; 694-2108), which are, respectively, 12.6 mi. and 26.5 mi. northeast of Anchorage along Glenn Hwy. For more information on these and other campsites, contact the USDA Forest Service (271-2500) or the Alaska Parks and Recreation Dept. (762-2617).

Centennial Park, 8300 Glenn Hwy. (333-9711), north of town off Muldoon Rd.; look for the park sign. Take bus #3 or 75 from downtown. 72 sites for tents and RVs. Showers, dumpsters, fireplaces, pay phones, and water. 7-day max. stay. Check-in before 6pm in the summer peak-season. Sites $13, Alaskans $11.

Lions' Camper Park, 5800 Boniface Pkwy. (333-9711), south of the Glenn Hwy. In Russian Jack Springs Park across from the Municipal Greenhouse, 4 blocks from the Boniface Mall. Take bus #12 or 45 to the mall and walk. Connected to the city's bike trail system. Overflow for Centennial Park. 10 primitive campsites with water station, fire rings, and showers. Self-contained vehicles only. 14-day max. stay. Sites $13. Open May-Sept. daily 10am-10pm.

John's Motel and RV Park, 3543 Mt. View Dr. (277-4332). Only 2 mi. from downtown. Take bus #45. 50 RV sites. Full hookups $18.

FOOD

With a considerably diverse population and the advantage of an economy of scale, Anchorage presents budget travelers with the most affordable and varied culinary fare in Alaska. Although most restaurant menu prices are inflated to the bloated proportions of the rest of the state, Anchorage is pocketed with eateries offering surprisingly inexpensive food. A number of these places lie outside of the downtown tourist zone, but even there one can ferret out some interesting meals.

Cheap Eats

In addition to the places listed below, check out the following: **Nordstrom's Cafe,** in the second floor of the department store on 603 D St., pours a bottomless 25¢ cup of coffee (open Mon.-Fri. 9am-9pm, Sat. 9am-6pm, Sun. 11am-6pm); yesterday's sandwiches are half-price at the **4th Avenue Theater** (see Entertainment below)— today's remaining sandwiches achieve yesterday-status at about 8pm; the affable **hot dog man** who sets up shop at 4th Ave. and G. St. not only serves a large Polish dog with chips for $3, but he's also a friend to half the city; the **Wonder and Hostess Bakery Thrift Shop,** on Spenard and 23rd Ave., purveys discount bread and they-keep-forever Twinkies (open Mon.-Sat. 9am-7pm, Sun. 10am-5pm).

The closest grocery to downtown is also the cheapest in the city. **Save U More,** at 13th and I St., carries many bulk foods and no-name brands (open Mon.-Sat. 10am-7pm, Sun. noon-6pm). For a wider selection of brand name groceries, the 24-hour **Carr's** (277-2609), at 13th and Gamble, is a 1½-mi. walk from the hostel. After dark take bus #11—this neighborhood isn't one of Anchorage's finest.

Downtown

Federal Building Cafeteria (277-6736), in the Federal Building on C. St., between 7th and 8th Ave. Good, hot daily entrees like chicken dijon or Mongolian beef with rice and a roll ($3.35-$5.25) that aren't just for paper-chasers anymore. Daily soups ($1.25 per cup, $2.50 per bowl). After 1:30pm, entrees are $1 less and soups are ½-price. Open Mon.-Fri. 7am-3:30pm.

White Spot Cafe, 109 W. 4th Ave. (279-3954). An unrivaled cheeseburger with homecut fries ($3.50) has made this tiny establishment an Anchorage favorite since 1959. 2 eggs, potato, toast, and coffee ($2.75). Open daily 6:30am-7pm.

Wing and Things, 529 I St. (277-9464), between 5th and 6th St. Unbelievably good chicken wings barbecued amid wing memorabilia and inspirational poetry. The "nuke" sauce is a wonderfully masochistic experience. 10 wings for $6. Open Mon.-Sat. 10:30am-10pm.

Maharaja's, 328 G St. (272-2233), between 3rd and 4th Ave. The finely-gilded decor and spicy lunch buffet provide a feast for all the senses at this authentic Indian restaurant. All-you-can-eat buffet ($7) served Mon.-Fri. 11:30am-2pm. Vegetarian dinner specialties ($6.50-8.50) served 5:30-10pm.

Legal Pizza, 1034 W. 4th Ave. (274-0686). Home to the other Anchorage lunch buffet—all-you-can-eat pizza, salad bar, soup, and beverages ($6) served Mon.-Fri. 11:30am-3pm. Arrive by 12:30 for the best selection of pizzas. Open Mon.-Tues. 11am-11pm, Wed.-Sat. 11am-midnight, Sun. noon-9pm.

Thai Cuisine, 444 H St. (277-8424). Therrific Thai fare on white linen and patio furniture. Huge bowl of soup ($6.25-7). 18 vegetarian dishes ($7-8). Lunch specials include entree, soup, and salad ($6.50). Open Mon.-Sat. 11am-10pm, Sun. 4-10pm.

Kumagoro Restaurant, 533 4th St. (272-9905). The combination of Alaskan fish and Japanese expertise make this an excellent, reasonably priced sushi restaurant. Daily lunch specials (served 11:30am-2pm), such as halibut teriyaki with soup, rice, and vegetables ($6). Chicken teriyaki ($6.50). At night, karaoke crooners ham it up at the mike. Bar open daily 10am-2am; restaurant open daily 11am-10pm, although food is available until 1am.

Burger Jim's (277-4386), in the Transit Center. Jim packs 'em in for indigestible, greasy burgers. Try the lunch special—burger, fries, and a bottomless soda ($4.75). Open Mon.-Fri. 10am-8:30pm, Sat. 11am-8:30pm.

Midtown Restaurants

Twin Dragons, 612 E. 15th Ave. (276-7535). Fill a bowl heaping-full from the fresh meat- and vegetable-buffet and watch the master Mongolian barbecuer fry it with an amazing flourish. Opulent decor and private, pagoda-like booths. Soup and appetizer included with the barbecue. Once through with the lunch buffet ($6), forge ahead into the all-you-can-eat dinner ($9). Open for lunch Mon.-Sat. 11am-3:30pm, Sun. 2-3:30pm; open for dinner Mon.-Thurs. 3:30pm-1am, Fri.-Sat. 3:30-10:30pm, Sun. 3:30-9:30pm.

Alaska Flapjacks, 1230 W. 27th Ave. (274-2241). The best breakfast spot in town advertises itself as a family restaurant—possibly because you could almost feed a family with a single one of their breakfast specials. 3 eggs, 2 pancakes, bacon, gravy, and hash browns ($6). Superstack of 5 pancakes ($4). Open daily 6am-8pm.

Mama O's, on Spenard Between 26th and 27th Ave., near Alaska Flapjacks. A Japanese fried seafood joint "where batter-dipped halibut is King." The King is served with fries, rice, or salad ($7). Japanese *Udon* noodles ($5.50). Calamari with rice ($5.25). Open Mon.-Sat. 11am-8:30pm.

SIGHTS AND ACTIVITIES

Watching over Anchorage from Cook Inlet is **Mt. Susitna,** known to locals as the "Sleeping Lady." For a fabulous view of Susitna, as well as Denali (Mt. McKinley) on a clear day, head to the top of the parking garage over the People Mover Transit Office (see Practical Information above). The same view is available from a more attractive setting about 4 mi. from downtown at **Point Warzenof,** on the western end of Northern Lights Blvd. **Earthquake Park** recalls the 1964 Good Friday earthquake, a day Alaskans refer to as "Black Friday." The quake was the strongest ever recorded in North America, registering 9.2 on the current Richter scale. Either drive, walk, skate, or bike along the **Tony Knowles Coastal Trail,** an 11-mi. paved track that skirts Cook Inlet on one side and the backyards of Anchorage's upper-crust on the other. Built for a million dollars per mile, critics originally complained that the trail would only be an expensive invitation for burglars to prey on wealthy homeowners. Fears have proved unfounded, though, and the heavily-traveled trail has become a major asset. In the winter it is groomed for **cross-country skiing.**

A four-hour **walking tour** of downtown Anchorage begins at the visitors center (see Practical Information). Street-corner signs give a detailed description of the neighborhood's history, and you can absorb the tour in smaller segments while wandering about downtown. The **Captain Cook Monument,** at 5th and K, presents an interesting synopsis of this restless explorer's travels from Antarctica to the Aleutian Islands. The omnipresent **Grayline** (277-5581) offers a 3½-hour Anchorage city tour, leaving daily at 3pm ($21, under 12 $10).

The public **Anchorage Museum of History and Art,** 121 W. 7th Ave. (343-4326), at A St., is without a doubt the best of the public and private museums that fill downtown Anchorage. The museum features permanent exhibits of Alaskan Native artifacts and art, as well as a Native dance series three times per day in summer ($4). The Gallery gives free tours daily at 11am and 1pm. (Open daily 9am-6pm; Sept. 16-May 14 Tues.-Sat. 10am-6pm, Sun. 1-5pm. Admission $4, seniors $3.50, under 18 free.) The **Imaginarium,** 725 5th Ave. (276-3179), a hands-on "science-discovery center," recreates Arctic marine environments, glacier formation, and other scientific oddities of the North (open Mon.-Sat. 7am-6pm, Sun. noon-5pm; admission $4, under 12 $3).

The golden-glass **ARCO Tower** (263-4545), on G St. between 7th and 8th Ave., is the tallest building in Alaska—although not in the least bit menacing. ARCO screens documentary-type films on Alaskan industry in the lobby and also maintains a small collection of pipeline paraphernalia. The **Heritage Library** (276-1132 or 265-2834), in the National Bank of Alaska Office Building at Northern Lights Blvd. and C St., contains a display of rare books and Native artifacts (open Mon.-Fri. 1-5pm; free).

To see real Alaskan wildlife without the danger of being trampled or otherwise mauled, visit the **Alaska Zoo,** Mile 2 on O'Malley Rd. (346-2133). Take bus #91. Here you can say hello to **Binky the Bear** and other orphaned Alaskan animals. For a heavy-duty dose of culture, watch **Arabell the Elephant** paint (Fri.-Sun. at 12:30 and 3:30pm in summer). Her paintings are on sale in the gift shop. (Zoo open daily 9am-6pm. Admission $5, senior citizens $4, ages 13-18 $3, ages 3-12 $2.) **Star the Reindeer** lives in a fenced-in courtyard close to downtown at 10th Ave. and I St. He has paced this tiny plot for a quarter-century, in the process becoming Anchorage's mascot—feed him carrots if you wish. In salmon season, walk down C St. to the water and watch fin-to-fin traffic jams heading upstream. Best viewing is from the plant lookout.

SHOPPING

If you want a smell of authenticity while you shop, head to the close confines of the non-profit gift shop at the **Alaska Native Medical Center,** 3rd and Gampbell (257-1150). Many Native Alaskans pay for medical services with their own arts and handicrafts, and the Alaska State Museum in Juneau has sent buyers here to improve its exhibitions. Walrus bone *ulus* (knives used by Natives, $17-60), fur moccasins, Eskimo parkas, and dolls highlight the selection (open Mon.-Fri. 10am-2pm, and occasionally Sat. 11am-2pm). Downtown holds several more traditional shops.

Craftworks from Alaska's Bush country, similar to those on display at the Museum of History and Art (see Sights), are sold at the **Alaska Native Arts and Crafts Showroom,** 333 W. 4th Ave. Birch baskets (from $10), beadwork and other jewelry ($14-20), and ivory carvings ($30) tempt you here (open Mon.-Fri. 10am-6pm, Sat. 10am-5pm, Sun. noon-5pm). **Bering Sea Originals** (561-1650), in University Mall on the old Seward Hwy., features a wide range of Alaskan handicrafts, including *Ulus* (from $10) and ivory carvings ($25). (Open daily 10am-9pm.) The **Stonington Gallery,** behind the visitors center on F St., carries an excellent variety of photos, pottery, prints, and other contemporary crafts (open Mon.-Fri. 10am-8pm, Sat. 11am-5pm, Sun. noon-5pm). Although it's entirely unpredictable, artists in different states of sobriety often offer patrons at Darwin's Theory (see Nightlife below) single pieces of top-quality work for a fraction of what they would cost in a gallery.

ENTERTAINMENT

Trek to the **Alaska Experience Theater,** 705 W. 6th Ave. (276-3730), to see brown bears and Native dances come alive on the inner surface of a hemispherical dome. The 70mm film (40-min.) is guaranteed to make your head spin (every hr. daily 9am-10pm; admission $6, children $4). An earthquake exhibit at the theater will cost you another $5. The **Capri Cinema,** 3425 E. Tudor Rd. (275-3799), runs a mix of art flicks and intelligent mainstream works (oxymoron though it may seem) that have finished their first run. Take bus #75 (shows $4). On a rainy day, park yourself at the **Denali Theater** (275-3106), on 27th Ave. at Spenard, where double-features of popular movies in limbo between the big screen and video release show for $1.

Yearning for a touch of Arctic Broadway? The **4th Avenue Theatre,** 630 W. 4th Ave., 1 block west of the Log Cabin visitors center (see Practical Information) and 5000 mi. west of Broadway, has been faithfully restored to its original 1940s decor. The neon-clad building now contains a cafeteria, gift shop, and a big-screen movie house that shows free films from the afternoon into the evening (although you have to look out at the screen over the light of the mammoth gift shop).

NIGHTLIFE

Downtown bars get nastier around C St., but several places on the west side of town fill each night with merry tipplers. The **F Street Station,** on 4th at F, attracts half the yuppies in Alaska on a weekend night. They offer free cheddar cheese and crackers and serve yuppie sandwiches from their kitchen. **Darwin's Theory,** on G St. between 4th and 5th Ave., can be packed with a friendly, local crowd. Darwin dishes out free popcorn to get your thirst up. The **Pioneer Club,** 739 W. 4th Ave., claims to be the oldest bar in Anchorage (which means that it's still probably younger than your grandparents).

Around midtown, Anchorageans from all of Uncle Sam's tax brackets party at **Chilkoot Charlie's,** 2435 Spenard Rd. (272-1010), at Fireweed. Take bus #7 or 60. Six bars fill this huge and heavily commercial space, in addition to a rockin' dance floor and a quiet lounge. Ask about the nightly drink specials; otherwise you'll end up paying an outrageous amount. Two different bands at each end of this behemoth "log cabin" play nightly from 9pm.

Less crowded and more interesting is **Mr. Whitekey's Fly-by-Night Club,** 3300 Spenard Rd. (279-SPAM/7726). Take bus #7. Mr. Whitekey's is a "sleazy bar serving everything from the world's finest champagnes to a damn fine plate of Spam." The Monty Python-esque house special gives you anything with Spam at half-price when you order champagne (free with Dom Perignon). Try Spam nachos or Spam and cream cheese on a bagel ($3-7). Nightly music ranges from rock to jazz to blues. The *Whale Fat Follies*—a new anti-tourist tourist attraction or "musical off-color follies"—plays nightly at 8pm (bar open 3pm-2:30am). The **Great Alaskan Bush Co.,** 631 E. International Airport Rd. (561-2609), is a world-famous strip-joint where there is no cover for guests, and definitely not for employees.

SEASONAL EVENTS

For more spontaneous entertainment, watch for annual events celebrated Alaska-style. Call the **event hotline** (276-3200) to see what's coming up. The **Anchorage Music Festival** has been held from mid-June through early July since 1956. For information and tickets for this mostly classical festival, call 263-ARTS/2787. The summer solstice (June 21) brings dancing to the streets and runners from all over the world to the inspirational **Mayor's Marathon.** The **Iditarod,** a grueling 1049-mi. sled dog race traversing two mountain ranges, 150 mi. of the frozen Yukon River, and the ice pack of the Norton Sound, begins in Anchorage on the first weekend in March. Twelve to 18 days later, the winner (and, with luck, some of the other competitors as well) arrives in Nome. The tortuous route commemorates and duplicates a part of the heroic journey of early-day Anchoragean mushers who carried serum to halt a diptheria epidemic in Nome. The **Fur Rendezvous,** held the second week of February, revives the era when fur trappers gathered to whoop it up. Today, affectionately referred to as "Fur Rondy," it includes the world sled-dog championship races, a grand prix, and snowshoe softball games.

The Anchorage Bucs (274-3627) and Pirates (277-2827), the city's two **semi-professional baseball** teams, play a more traditional version of the game in the summer. Games take place at Mulcahy Park on 16th Ave. and A St.; call ahead for times and ticket prices. Reggie Jackson and Dave Winfield once impressed the Anchorage crowds here.

OUTDOORS: HIKING

To counteract urban claustrophobia, head for the summit of **Flattop Mountain** in the "Glenn Alps" of the Chugach Range near Anchorage. The excellent view of the city and—if it's clear—sun-soaked Denali is well worth the hour-long hike. The most frequently climbed trail in Alaska is deceptively difficult due to its steepness and slippery shale, but even novices will find it manageable. Wear long pants, as you may find yourself sliding down bum-first. To reach the trailhead, jump on bus #92 to the intersection of Hillside Rd. and Upper Huffman Rd. From there walk ¾ mi. along upper Huffman Rd. and take a right on Toilsome Hill Dr. Proceed for 2 mi. Trail signs at the park entrance point the way up the 4,500-ft. mountain.

   People Mover bus #92 will also bring you to the foot of 4455-ft. **Wolverine Peak,** which watches over eastern Anchorage. At the intersection of O'Malley Rd. and Hillside Dr., head east ½ mi. along O'Malley to Upper O'Malley Rd. Turn left at the intersection with Prospect Dr. and head 1.1 mi. to the park entrance. The return hike from bus stop to the peak is a long 13.8 mi., but the views of the Alaska Range and Cook Inlet will keep your steps light.

   Rabbit Lake is a beautiful alpine bowl which collects water in the shadow of 5,000-ft. Suicide Peak. People Mover bus #92 is again your montane chariot; hop off at the corner of Hillside Dr. and De Armoun Rd. Follow Upper De Armoun Rd. from here 1 mi. east, and then turn right onto Lower Canyon Rd. for 1.2 mi. The roundtrip from where you debark the bus to the lake is a gentle 15.4 mi. Camping at the lake or along the way makes a pleasant two-day hike.

   Although neither the Forest Service nor the City of Anchorage publishes a guide to nearby trails, the widely available *55 Ways to the Wilderness in Southcentral Alaska* by Helen Nienhueser and Nancy Simmerman (The Mountaineers Books, 306 2nd Ave. West, Seattle, WA 98119; $11) offers an excellent description of many trails around Anchorage and the Kenai Peninsula.

■ Near Anchorage: South

The Seward Hwy. runs south along the **Turnagain Arm** of the Cook Inlet. This body of water, with tidal fluctuations second only to those in New Brunswick's Bay of Fundy, received its name from Captain Cook when he entered looking for the Northwest Passage and left deflated, having had only to turn again. Miles of the arm are temporarily uncovered at low tide, only to be inundated by 10-ft. high "bores"— waves created as the 15mph riptide races in. **Warning:** although you might be tempted to stroll around on the exposed sand at low tide, *don't do it.* The beach is composed of a fine, quicksand-like silt, and you wouldn't be the first person to get stuck and perish in the incoming tide—the water in Cook Inlet is so cold that you wouldn't survive for more than five minutes. In the very unfortunate event that you do walk on the beach and do get stuck, experts recommend that you lie down, distribute your weight evenly, and call for help.

   Fifteen mi. down the arm sits the **Potter Section House Historical Site** (345-5014), the last of the Alaska Railroad's original roadhouses. The site now houses a **ranger station** for Chugach State Park (for info. on Chugach State Park see below; open Mon.-Fri. 8am-4:30pm). To catch a glimpse of an incoming bore tide or a pod of Beluga whales chasing salmon up the inlet, pull over at **Beluga Point,** about 4 mi. south of the section house. The bore tides generally reach Turnagain Arm two hours after the low tide in Anchorage; consult the *Daily News* for a tidal report.

   Dall sheep often appear in the rocky crevices of **Bird Ridge,** another 9 mi. down the highway at Mile 102. Sheep even wander down to the roadside in summer. A convoy of RVs pulled over beside the ridge is usually the first giveaway that something is astir.

   The **Birdhouse Bar** sits off the highway in a sunken cabin a few mi. past the ridge. A large blue and orange bird protrudes from the cabin wall—the only exterior indication of the hilarious antics that go on within. Every square inch of the small bar room is padded with the personal effects of past patrons—from business cards and lingerie to a prosthetic leg—many believe it's all that holds the place together. (Note the two *Let's Go* researcher-writer ID cards supporting the ceiling over the front left corner of the bar.) The decor creates a hushed and intimate acoustic, all the better to hear the bartenders' endless supply of jokes. The bar itself slants at the 20° angle it achieved in the 1964 earthquake; a few key knotholes provide a purchase for your beer. Before leaving, ask to call the ptarmigans, or better yet ask for a friend—a special horn brings them right to the window.

   Off of Seward Hwy. lies the **Alyeska Ski Resort** (783-2222), a site perennially proposed to host the Winter Olympics. The resort is open November to April for skiing (a full-day lift ticket runs about $30). While in Alyeska, stay at the **Girdwood-Aly-**

eska Home Hostel (HI/AYH), run by the same folks who manage the Anchorage Hostel (276-3635; see Accommodations above). To get there, turn left onto Alyeska Blvd. off Seward Hwy., right on Timberline Dr., then right on Alpina. The hostel has six beds and a sauna, but no hot showers ($8, nonmembers $10). Winter or summer, it's worth the detour into Alyeska just to visit the Bake Shop, an outstanding restaurant below the Alyeska Resort. People from across the state sing the praises of their towering sweet rolls ($2), bottomless bowls of soup ($3.75), and sourdough ($1.25). (Open Mon.-Fri. and Sun. 7am-7pm, Sat. 7am-8pm.)

Four mi. up Crow Creek Rd. is Crow Creek Mine, a National Historic Site with eight original buildings and an active gold mine (run by transplanted New Yorker Cynthia Toohey and her children). The $6 admission for miners includes a pan, a sluice box, and instructions. Most people turn up a few flakes, but don't expect to pay back your entrance fee. This strike predates even those in Fairbanks and the Klondike, and the site is the non-restored real McCoy. (Campsites with water and toilets $5; hikers and sightseers $3.) As you leave Crow Creek Rd., stop in at the Double Musky (783-2822), set back from the road in the trees. The "Musky" deserves its reputation as one of the best restaurants in Alaska. If you can't swing a spicy Cajun-style dinner ($16-30), at least treat yourself to a drink or dessert (about $4). The jambalaya and the double musky pie (a blend of chocolate and pecans) deserve special attention (open Tues.-Thurs. 5-10pm, Fri.-Sun. 4-10pm).

Portage Valley

Four roadside glaciers sit staunchly along the Portage Valley, grinding channels through the earth in a tradition that dates back to the Ice Age. As the glaciers gradually recede, massive ice cubes fall into Portage Lake and float to within a snowball's throw of shore. Perched on the lakeside, the Begich-Boggs Visitors Center (783-2326) has the strangest name and most modern displays of virtually any Alaskan information outlet. The center's exhaustive glacial exhibitions and historical movie attract throngs of visitors (open daily 9am-7pm; in winter Sat.-Sun. 11am-4pm). To reach the center, take the 5-mi. detour off Seward Hwy., south of Alyeska, along the well-paved Portage Hwy.

Two state-run campgrounds on Portage Hwy. have excellent sites ($6) with panoramic glacial views. Black Bear and Williwaw provide water and toilets; Williwaw also boasts a short hiking trail and a viewing ledge overlooking salmon-spawning areas (salmon run from early July to late August). Naturalists introduce travelers to the easy hiking trails that begin from the visitors center. For more information on the hikes and trails, call the Anchorage Ranger District Office (271-2500), or write to Chugach National Forest, Anchorage Ranger District, 201 E. 9th Ave., #206, Anchorage 99501. The Alaska Public Lands Information, 605 W. 4th, Anchorage 99501 (271-2737) has information on the Chugach as well.

Portage is 45 minutes from downtown Anchorage by car along the Seward Hwy. Rides are reportedly easy to find, although Let's Go does not recommend hitchhiking (see Kenai Peninsula introduction). In addition, every tour group and its brother runs day trips to Portage. The cheapest may be the one given by Grayline (277-5581), which conducts the six-hour, mother-of-all-tours tour of Portage Glacier, including stops at the Begich-Boggs Visitor Center and at Alyeska Ski Resort (daily tours at 8:30am and noon; $50, under 12 $25).

■ Near Anchorage: North

If Flattop doesn't satisfy your craving for wilderness (see Outdoors: Hiking above), head for Chugach State Park, which covers 495,000 acres north, east, and south of the city. The Eagle River Visitors Center (694-2108) is at Mile 12.7 on Eagle River Rd., off Glenn Hwy. In addition to the wildlife displays, hiking trails, and a new outdoor telescope, they can explain the many hiking opportunities in this area (open Thurs.-Mon. 11am-7pm). If you're long on time and short on dollars, take People Mover bus #74, 76, or 78 on a 48-mi. round-trip excursion to the satellite communities of **Eagle River, Chugiak,** and **Peters Creek,** north of Anchorage. Even without getting off the bus, you're likely to catch a glimpse of a moose between Fort Richardson and Eagle River.

Due north is **Matanuska Valley,** an area settled by Scandinavian-American farmers in 1935 as part of a New Deal program. President Franklin Roosevelt wanted to transplant families from the depressed Midwest to Alaska to experiment with agriculture. The idea never gained enough popularity to ignite the hoped-for exodus, but enough people moved to create growth of which the President never dreamed—namely, 75-lb. cabbages. Long summer daylight has turned garden-variety vegetables into mastodon-sized meals; fist-sized strawberries are popular snacks. In summer, fresh produce is available (in bulk, of course) from roadside stands along Glenn Hwy. between its junction with George Parks Hwy. and the town of Wasilla. The drive through the Matanuska is powerfully beautiful, running parallel to glacier fingers, winding through steep, lush passes, and crossing and re-crossing turbid rivers of glacier silt.

The valley's biggest annual event is the **Alaska State Fair,** on the fairgrounds at Mile 40.2 on Glenn Hwy. The 11-day event, ending on Labor Day, includes parades, rodeos, livestock, and agricultural sideshows starring the aforementioned cabbages. (Open daily 10am-10pm. Admission $6, senior citizens $3, ages 6-12 $2.) For more information, call 745-FAIR/4827.

But wait—there's more to the Matanuska than vegetables on steroids. Relive the halcyon days when dog sleds carried medical supplies across miles of subfrozen tundra (-40°F) at the **Knik Museum and Mushers Hall of Fame** (376-7755), at Mile 14 on Knik Rd. While not quite Cooperstown, the museum features mushing memorabilia and famous dog sleds in its Canine Hall of Fame. (Open June-Aug. 31 Wed.-Sun. noon-6pm. Adults $2, seniors $1.50, under 18 free.) **Independence Mine State Historic Park** (745-5897), 22 mi. from downtown Wasilla in Hatcher Pass, features hiking, fishing, restored mine buildings, and a lodge. Take either Glenn Hwy. to Mile 50 and the Fishhook-Willow Rd. to the park, or Parks Hwy. to Mile 71, the other end of Fishhook-Willow Rd. (Open Fri.-Mon. 11am-6pm. 1-hr. tours at 1:30 and 3:30pm, Sat.-Sun. also at 4:30pm. Admission $3, seniors and children under 12 $2.)

Head to **Big Lake** (Mile 52 on Parks Hwy.) and **Nancy Lake** (Mile 67.5 on Parks Hwy.) for excellent camping, lodging, canoeing, fishing, and more. Or splash in white water on the lower **Matanuska River** for a fair price with **NOVA Riverrunners** (745-5733). NOVA also runs thrilling whitewater trips including the 14-mi. class IV Lionshead (featuring a 16-ft. drop when the water is high), and the boiling class V Sixmile Creek which requires previous whitewater experience. These trips cost $80 and $100 respectively. Call collect for reservations, or write NOVA, P.O. Box 1129, Chickaloon, AK 99674.

Palmer

Palmer has long been Alaska's major educational and commercial center north of Anchorage. Learn more about its history at the **visitors center** (745-2880), a log cabin downtown, across the railroad tracks on South Valley Way at E. Fireweed Ave. (open May-Sept. daily 8:30-7pm). Explore the wonderful world of Alaskan agriculture at the **University of Alaska Experiment Station** (746-5450), on Trunk Rd., ½ mi. north of the junction of Glenn and Parks Hwy. (tours June-Aug. daily).

A few mi. off Parks Hwy., on Hatcher Pass Rd. at Mile 50.1 of the Glenn Hwy., lies the world's only **domesticated musk-ox farm** (745-4151). Neither bovines nor producers of perfume, these beasts are actually hairy cousins of sheep. Natives weave the *qiviut* locks of these creatures into scarves and hats. The musk-ox was once indigenous to Alaska but was hunted to extinction by Natives centuries before the arrival of Europeans. Today's herds have been transplanted from the Eurasian continent across the Arctic Circle (open daily 9am-7pm; admission $6, seniors and students $5, under 6 free).

Fall asleep to the distant bellows of these furry behemoths at the **Matanuska River Park,** at Mile 18 of the Glenn Hwy. Sites with water and pit toilets $6.

Wasilla

Wasilla, which actually means "breath of air," shares Palmer's overgrown agricultural heritage. Despite its location only 42 mi. north of Anchorage on the Parks Hwy., the town lives in the wild outback of rough frontier days, a fact reflected by the nearby **Dog Musher's Hall of Fame.** If you want try dog mushing, call **Mush Alaska,** P.O. Box 871752, Wasilla 99687 (376-4743). Half-hour excursions start at $20 per person.

The **Wasilla Museum** (376-2005) and the town's **visitors center** are on Main St. off the Parks Hwy. Behind the museum is **Frontier Village,** containing Wasilla's first school, sauna, and ferris wheel (open daily 10am-6pm; admission $1.50, children under 13 free). The **Alaska Historical and Transportation Museum,** at Mile 46 of the Parks Hwy. (745-4493), displays implements from the loggers, miners, fisherfolk, and farmers of Alaska past (open Mon.-Sat. 10am-6pm; admission $3, ages 6-12 $1.50, family $7).

Anchorage's **Stay-With-A-Friend B&B** (344-4006) projects its sphere of influence north to Wasilla (singles start at $50, doubles at $55). Campers should continue south toward Anchorage for another 13 mi. to **Eklutna Campground,** a state-run spot with water and toilets. For more information on the area, contact the **Wasilla Chamber of Commerce,** P.O. Box 871826, 1801 Parks Hwy., #A-8, Wasilla 99687 (376-1299).

KENAI PENINSULA

■ Hope

Most people know Hope, the only town on the southern side of Turnagain Arm, as a twinkle of lights seen across the water from the Seward Hwy. Without a major salmon run or ferry terminal, this former gold rush town of 200 remains untrampled, unlike other communities within a daytrip of Anchorage.

Prospectors made an early gold strike at Hope in 1889. This town—now the closest to Anchorage on the Kenai Peninsula—grew to 3000 people before Anchorage was even a clearing in the bushes. The boom was short-lived but many of its relics remain, and much of the federal land around Hope is still open to recreational mining. Hope lies at the end of the scenic 17-mi. Hope Hwy. This paved road joins the Seward Hwy. 71 mi. outside of Anchorage, just where it turns sharply south down the Peninsula toward its namesake.

Practical Information and Sights The Hope **visitors center** (782-3268) doubles as BJW Mining and Gifts and can be reached by heading ¼ mi. out on Palmer Creek Rd., just before the townsite (open daily 10am-7pm; in winter Sat.-Sun. noon-6pm). The center provides information on mining and hiking near Hope; more thorough literature on mining is found at the Ranger Station in Seward. The USDA Forest Service permits amateur mining along Sixmile Creek from Mile 1.5 to 5.5 on the Hope Rd. They will even allow you to bring a dredge in here from May 15 to July 15 with a permit. Closer to town, another 20-acre claim (beginning at the Resurrection trailhead foot bridge of Resurrection Trail Rd.) is also open to weekend sourdoughs.

Paystrike (277-8904), at the end of Resurrection Creek Rd., offers mining on private claims along with gold pans and instructions for $20 per day. They also offer the perfect Mother's Day gift—a one-day instructional course in operating a suction dredge and wearing a dry suit ($100). Resurrection Creek at the edge of town supports a healthy run of **pink salmon** in early August. The tiny **Hope Museum** on the first road into the townsite hopes to m ove across the street into a larger building— maybe then it will be open more than two hours per week (Sat. 2-4pm). The **post office** sits next to the museum (open Mon.-Fri. 8:30am-4:30pm, Sat. 10am-2pm; **General Delivery ZIP Code:** 99605).

Accommodations, Camping, and Food   Hope is happily endowed with a number of affordable accommodations. At about Mile 14 of the Hope Hwy., the **Trusters of Hope Hostel** (782-3158) stands back in the bushes beside Henry's 1-Stop Grocery. This friendly, recently resurrected establishment boasts eight bunks in a small cabin, a wood stove sauna, and a rudimentary kitchen (bunks $8, tentsites $5, showers $2 at Henry's). The manager is a wealth of hiking information waiting to be mined.

In town, the **Seaview Motel** (782-3364) occupies a choice location near the mouth of Resurrection Creek. Their rooms with separate baths go for the reasonable rate of $25 (for both singles and doubles). They also rent private cabins which sleep from two to five people ($25 for 2, on up to $50 for 5). Campers will find sweet respite at the Chugach National Forest **Porcupine Campground,** at the end of the Hope Hwy. (sites $6 with water and pit toilets).

In the late afternoon, the sun slants into the peaceful **Seaview Cafe** (782-3364), and a light breeze blows through the screen door. Don't deprive yourself of their all-you-can-eat ribs, chicken, and pork chop barbecue with baked beans, potato salad, and a sourdough roll ($9). Do, however, decline the unremarkable pie ($3). Heaping plate of fries ($1.75) and onion rings ($2.25).

Outdoors   **Hiking** around Hope is generally excellent. In addition to enjoyable dayhikes, this is the northern terminus of a 70-mi. series of trails which cross the Kenai Peninsula from Seward to Hope.

The **Gull Rock Trail,** an easy 5.1-mi. trek along Turnagain Arm, affords fine views of the water, the shore, and even Denali on an exceptionally clear day. The trek initially follows an old wagon road out of the Porcupine Campground at the end of the Hope Hwy. It passes the site of an old sawmill and a homestead along the way to the rock. The terrain does not favor camping, so plan on making the four- to six-hour round-trip.

Also beginning from the Porcupine Campground, the **Hope Point Trail** is a more challenging hike up to a peak above treeline. This 5-mi. round-trip initially follows Porcupine Creek and then climbs steeply up to treeline and on to Hope Point. The trail becomes somewhat less distinct after passing a microwave tower but is still not difficult to follow.

The **Resurrection Pass Trail,** originally a 19th-century gold miner's byway, leads 39 mi. through the Chugach National Forest from Hope to the Sterling Hwy. This popular hike traverses a beautiful area of abundant wildlife. To reach the trailhead in Hope, turn south onto Resurrection Creek Road at Mile 15 of the Hope Hwy. The trail begins 4 mi. in at a parking area. No less than seven **Forest Service cabins** punctuate this hike. They can be reserved in Anchorage (and usually have been far in advance) and also at the Seward Ranger Station (see Seward). Fine fishing in Juneau and Trout Lakes comes as a reward near the end of the trail. The southern trailhead lies on the Sterling Hwy. near Cooper Landing, 106 mi. south of Anchorage and 53 mi. east of Soldotna. An alternative endgame is to take the **Devil's Creek Trail** just south of Resurrection Pass, 19 mi. along the trail from Hope, and end up on the Seward Hwy. instead. For more information on the Resurrection Pass Trail and the extension to Seward, contact the USDA Forest Service for the Seward Ranger District, P.O. Box 390, 334 4th Ave., Seward 99664 (224-3374).

■■■ SEWARD

Seward (SUE-urd) traces its origins to a nearby Russian shipyard built by the legendary Russian explorer Alexander Baranov in the 1830s. The town expanded to its present form in 1904 as the southern terminus of the Alaska railroad, and it is from here that the Iditarod Dogsled Trail led early gold prospectors into the Interior (even though the famous race now begins in Anchorage). Today, Seward is also accessible by road, via the Seward Hwy.—the only nationally designated "Scenic Byway" in Alaska. (That means it's *really pretty*.)

The city itself offers little to attract outsiders other than fine hiking and halibut fishing, but Seward holds paramount importance as the gateway to the stupendous **Kenai fjords**. It also commands a little respect for surviving the 1964 earthquake ("Black Friday") that rang in at 8.3 on the old Richter scale (9.2 on the new scale) and sent six successive *tsunamis* sweeping across the peninsula.

Like Homer, Seward is divided into two distinct parts—one near the ferry dock and one near the small-boat harbor. The former is where natives live, the latter a pricey tourist enclave. The streets in Seward are named after the U.S. Presidents from Washington to Van Buren, in chronological order, so read up on your history before you visit.

PRACTICAL INFORMATION AND ORIENTATION

Visitors Information: Chamber of Commerce (224-8051), Mile 2 on Seward Hwy. The usual assortment of pamphlets (and free coffee to boot). Open daily 9am-6pm; Labor Day-Memorial Day Mon.-Fri. 9am-5pm. Also operates a **railroad car** (224-3094), 3rd and Jefferson St., where you can pick up a self-guided walking tour and mark your home town on the world map. Open in summer daily 11am-5pm.

National Park Service Visitors Center, 1212 4th Ave. (224-3175), at the small-boat harbor. Information and maps for the spectacular **Kenai Fjords National Park.** Dockside talks on marine life daily at 3pm. Open in summer daily 8am-7pm; in winter Mon.-Fri. 8am-noon and 1-5pm. **Seward Ranger Station, Chugach National Forest (USFS),** 334 4th Ave. (224-3374), at Jefferson. Extensive trail information, maps, and advice on trails close to town, as well as the complete Iditarod route. Chugach cabin reservations ($20 per night, 3-day max. stay; see Hope: Outdoors). Open Mon.-Fri. 8am-5pm.

Employment Office, Seward Employment Center, P.O. Box 1009, Seward (224-5276), 5th and Adams, on the 2nd floor of the City Bldg. Open Mon.-Fri. 8am-4:30pm.

Airport: Located 2 mi. north of town on Seward Hwy. No regularly scheduled flights to Anchorage. **Harbor Air** offers charters and hour-long flightseeing trips over the fjords ($85 per person; 3-person min.).

Alaska Railroad, (224-3133, 278-0800 for reservations), depot at the northern edge of town. To Anchorage (May 23-Sept. 6, 1 per day, 6pm, $40).

Buses: Homer and Seward Bus Lines, 550 Railway Ave. (224-3608). To Anchorage (1 per day, 9am, $30). Call about service to Homer.

Alaska Marine Highway (224-5485), ferry dock, 4th and Railway Ave., on the southern edge of town. Served by the *M/V Tustumena*. About 1 per week in summer (and occasionally only 1 every 2 weeks) to: Kodiak ($52), Valdez ($56), and Homer ($94). Call for schedule.

Trolley: 224-7373, ext. 03210. Just wave it down and it will take you anywhere on its route through town ($1, round-trip $2, all day $3). Or call for pickup. Operates daily 10am-8pm.

Taxi: Independent Cab, 224-5000. **PJ's Taxi,** 224-5555. Both 24 hr.

Car Rental: Seward Tesoro (224-86111). $49 per day with 200 free mi., 20¢ per extra mi. Must be at least 25 with credit card.

Kayak Rental: Sea Kayak (224-3960), next to the National Park Visitors Center. Single-seat $30 per day, two-seat $40 per day. Open daily 9am-6pm.

Bike Rental: Grizzly Bike Rental (224-3960), at the small-boat harbor. Road bikes $7 per hr., $25 per day. Mountain bikes $8 per hr., $32 per day. Open daily 9am-6pm.

Laundromat and showers: Seward Laundry, 4th and C St. Wash, dry, and fold $1.30 per lb. Showers $3 (unlimited time). Open daily 8am-10pm. **Public Showers,** also at the Harbormaster Bldg. 5-min. shower $1.

Public Restrooms, on the waterfront near Adams St., and at the Harbormaster Building.

Pharmacy: Seward Drug, P.O. Box 127, Seward (224-8989), at 224 4th Ave. Open Mon.-Sat. 9am-9pm, Sun. 10am-6pm; in winter Mon.-Sat. 9am-6:30pm.

Fishing Rods and Tackle: Rod rentals from **Seward Drug** (see above) $10 per day with a $50 deposit. No tackle included. Buy tackle from **The Fish House,** across from the Harbormaster. A wide selection of all necessary equipment. Open daily 6am-10pm.

Crisis Line: 224-3027. 24 hr.

Hospital: Seward General (224-5205), 1st Ave. and Jefferson St.

Emergency: 911.

Police: 244-3338.

Post Office: (224-3001), 5th Ave. and Madison St. Open Mon.-Fri. 9:30am-4:30pm, Sat. 10am-2pm. **General Delivery ZIP Code:** 99664.

Population: 3000.

Area Code: 907.

Seward is located on the southeast side of the Kenai Peninsula, alongside beautiful **Resurrection Bay.** Anchorage, 127 mi. due north, is connected to Seward by the **Seward Hwy.** Seward, Nebraska is 4135 mi. due southeast.

ACCOMMODATIONS AND CAMPING

The only hostel on the Kenai Peninsula lies 16 mi. outside Seward and lacks a telephone, but the hotel rates in town may give you the adrenaline you'll need to hike there. A rooming crunch in Seward has sent the price of accommodations up through the hole in the ozone layer. Seward's municipal campground is clean and inexpensive, though there are private alternatives which offer more solitude.

Snow River International Home Hostel (HI/AYH), at Mile 16 of Seward Hwy. No phone; call the central hostelling number in Anchorage (276-3635). Beautiful new house in a scenic (if incredibly inconvenient) location with 14 beds, showers, and laundry facilities. $10, nonmembers $13.

Van Gilder Hotel, 308 Adams St. (224-3079), just off 3rd Ave. A well-preserved 77-yr. old National Historic Site that could be the setting of any frontier Western. Beautiful rooms with TV and sink. Singles and doubles $50, with bath $85. (It's amazing what some people will pay for a private bath.) Reservations necessary, especially on weekends.

The New Seward Hotel, 217 5th Ave. (224-3045). Singles $48 in the bargain-basement with flaming-red carpet, exposed pipes, a small window, and bath down the hall. Doubles $72, with bath $92.

Municipal Waterfront Campground, stretching along Ballaine Rd. from Railway Ave. in the south to D St. in the north (with numerous Presidents in between). Tent lawns and RV lots occupy some of Seward's choicest (and windiest) real estate, with a stunning view of the mountains across Resurrection Bay. Most tenting between Adams and Jefferson St. Toilets are scattered throughout the campground, and restrooms with showers are located at the Harbormaster Bldg. 2-week max. stay. Check-out 4pm. Open May 15-Sept. 30. Sites $5, parking spots $6; collected by strict honor code.

Bear Creek RV Park (224-5725). Turn off Seward Hwy. at Mile 6.6 and take Bear Leg Rd. ½ mi. Laundry and hot showers $2.50. Small area for tents $2.50 per person. Full hookup $16.

Wildflower RV Park (224-8294), 4th Ave. and Van Buren St. Gravel parking lot near the boat harbor. No tents. Full hookup $15.

SEWARD

FOOD

Seward offers the usual spread of greasy diners and *très chic* tourist traps; stock up on groceries at the **Eagle Quality Center** at Mile 2 of Seward Hwy. (open 24 hr.). It's a bit of a walk from downtown, but you can reward yourself with a massive $1 ice cream cone from the in-store soda fountain.

Don's Kitchen, 4th Ave. and Washington St. Big breakfast specials 75¢-$9. Their weighty biscuits-and-gravy plate ($4) is available by the ½- and ¼-order. 2 eggs, 2 hotcakes or hashbrowns, and 2 sausage links ($5). Open 24 hr.

Breeze Inn (224-5298), in the small-boat harbor. Not your average hotel-restaurant. Breeze in for the huge all-you-can-eat lunch buffet ($8). Slighter appetites should try the two-trips-to-the-soup-and-salad-bar ($4.25). Breakfast all day. Open daily 6am-9pm.

Peking, 338 4th Ave. (224-5444), at Jefferson St. Tasty lunch specials with rice and soup ($5.45-6.45) served 11:30am-3pm. Open Mon.-Fri. 11:30am-10:30pm, Sat.-Sun. noon-10:30pm.

Harbor Dinner Club, 240 5th Ave. (244-3012), across from the New Seward Hotel. Where Joe Seward takes his wife on their anniversary. Try the Champion Burger—cheese, onions, mushrooms and peppers heaped onto a ¾-lb. fresh beef pattie ($7.50). Known for their taco salad ($5.50). Open Mon.-Sat. 11am-2:30pm and 5pm-whenever, Sun. 11am-whenever.

Niko's Restaurant, 4th Ave. and Railway Ave. Cavernous pizza joint and bar. Large 15-in. pizza ($12). Wide variety of Italian and Mexican fare, too. Open daily noon-midnight.

Marina Restaurant (224-3202), across from the small-boat harbor on 4th Ave. Tasty Mexican dishes and pizza with open-air seating on an outdoor patio. 3 eggs and hashbrowns for breakfast ($3.75), slice of pizza with soup or salad for lunch ($5), and a 15-in. cheese pizza for dinner ($14).

SIGHTS AND SEASONAL EVENTS

The self-guided **walking tour** of Seward, detailed on the map available at the visitors center, passes many turn-of-the-century homes and businesses. A complete tour takes two to three hours. The **Resurrection Bay Historical Society Museum,** in the Senior Center, 3rd and Jefferson St., exhibits Native artifacts including a fine collection of woven baskets. (Museum open Memorial Day-Labor Day Mon.-Fri. 11am-5pm, Sat.-Sun. noon-6pm. Extended hours when tour ships are in town. Admission $1, children 50¢.) From June 15 to Labor Day you can see *Seward's Burning* (the "Earthquake Movie," as residents call it) at the **Seward Community Library** (224-3646), 5th Ave. and Adams St. No, it doesn't star Charlton Heston, Ava Gardner, or even Charo; this movie shows actual footage of the 1964 Good Friday earthquake (with a supporting cast of fires and tidal waves), which destroyed much of Seward and Southcentral Alaska. (Library open Mon.-Fri. noon-8pm, Sat. noon-6pm. Screenings Mon.-Sat. at 2pm. $1.50 donation requested.) **Liberty Theater,** 304 Adams St. (224-5418), projects the flicks in which you may find Heston and Gardner.

The **Silver Salmon Derby** opens each year on the second Saturday in August and closes eight days later. Prizes are awarded for the largest fish (up to $5000) and the tagged fish (up to $10,000). To date, no one has actually caught the tagged fish during the derby, only after.

The other annual event that gets Seward hopping is the **Mountain Marathon** on the 4th of July. Alaska's oldest footrace, the marathon began when one sourdough challenged a neighbor to make it up and down the 3022-ft. peak in less than an hour. That was in 1915, and the poor guy just couldn't do it. The current record for men (42 min.) and women (50 min.) demonstrate that humankind is on the move. The race has been joined by a parade, the governor, and hundreds of enthusiasts running, sliding, falling, and bleeding down the steep mountainsides to the shores of Resurrection Bay. Thousands of sadistic spectators set up lawn chairs anywhere in town and watch the painful spectacle with binoculars. The **Annual Seward Sil-**

ver **Salmon 10K Run** takes off during the Labor Day weekend, and the **Exit Glacier 5K and 10K Run** kicks off in mid-May. Though these races may sound tough, Seward's truest test of physical endurance comes in the third weekend of January during the **Seward Polar Bear Jump,** which sends participants right into the hypothermia-inducing water. The event is surrounded by three days of activities.

OUTDOORS

Known as the "Gateway to Alaska" because of its position at the southern terminus of the railroad, Seward is also the point of entry into the **Kenai Fjords National Park.** The **Park Service Visitors Center** sits near the small-boat harbor (see Practical Information above). The park protects a coastal mountain system packed with wildlife and glaciers. The best way to see this area is from boats in the bay; pick up the list of charters and prices at the Chamber of Commerce (see Practical Information) or from shops along the boardwalk next to the harbormaster's office. Most trips run $80-100 per day, $50-65 per half-day, but prices are likely to change due to frequent price wars. For more information, contact **Alaska Renown Charters** (224-3806), **Mariah Charters** (243-1238), **Kenai Coastal Tours** (224-7114), and **Kenai Fjord Tours** (224-8030). These tours are worth every dime, gratifying visitors with incredible sights: glaciers larger than some eastern states, herds of orcas berthing and gliding under the boat, sea lions cavorting in the sea, and a Greenpeace pamphlet-full of your favorite marine mammals.

For a less-expensive glimpse of wildlife loiter near the small-boat harbor when the charter fishing trips return in the evening. A sea lion often prowls below the docks waiting for remains of fish tossed into the water as the catch is cleaned.

Seward is a great base for **day hikes.** Nearby **Mt. Marathon,** of race fame (see Sights, above), offers a great view of the city and ocean. From 1st and Jefferson St., take Lowell St. to the very end to reach the trail. The trail begins with a steep ascent up a rocky stream bed. Once above vegetation, a number of criss-crossing trails continue up the rocky ledge to the left. Another route climbs through loose rocks (scree) to the right. The rocky route provides better footing for the ascent, and the scree can be fun to run through on the way down. Unless you're training for the race, plan on a two-hour climb to the top and a 45-minute hop-and-slide to come down. There is no final peak at the end of the trail, but the views out over Resurrection Bay are phenomenal.

Exit Glacier—billed as Alaska's most accessible—is 9 mi. west on the road that starts at Mile 3.7 of Seward Hwy. If you're feeling energetic, take the steep and slippery 4-mi. trail from the ranger station to the magnificent **Harding Ice Field** above the glacier. The rangers will prevent you from getting within 50 ft. of the glacier's face, as chunks of ice weighing several tons are continually breaking off, or "calving." Check the ranger station (see Practical Information) for information on a campground and other trails in the Seward area.

Fishing is heavenly in the Seward area. Salmon and halibut can be caught in the bay, grayling and dolly varden right outside of town. Charters are available for both halibut and salmon throughout the summer; prices run from $90-100, with all gear provided. Call **The Fish House** (800-478-8007; see Practical Information), the largest charter-booking service in Seward. You can also fish for free off of the docks.

■ Near Seward: Moose Pass

Known, barely, for Ed Estes's waterwheel (an allegedly "Internationally Known Landmark"), tiny Moose Pass began as a flag-stop for the Alaska Railroad and now has dropped out of the bigger picture. Moose Pass offers a **Solstice Festival** on the weekend nearest every solstice with lots of beer, a carnival, and other fun for kids and adults. Located at Mile 29 on Seward Hwy., the town has four **campgrounds** with excellent fishing: **Primrose** at Mile 18, **Ptarmigan Creek** at Mile 23, **Trail River** at Mile 24, and **Wye** at Mile 36. All are run by the **Chugach National Forest;** write Alaska Public Lands Information, 605 W. 4th, Anchorage 99501 (271-2737).

The **Moose Pass Inn** (288-3110) lies at Mile 30. Rooms are expensive ($72 and up), but nonetheless reservations are necessary.

■■■ SOLDOTNA

Soldotna (from the Russian word for "soldier"), once merely a fork in the road on the way to Homer, Kenai, or Seward, has become the Kenai Peninsula's center of government and recreation. The peninsula's premier fishing spot, Soldotna (pop. 3900) draws vacationers *en masse* from as far away as Prudhoe Bay. Prize-winning salmon are caught regularly in the Kenai River, a few minutes from downtown. Kenai Riverbend Campground, halfway between Soldotna and Kenai, offers a $10,000 reward to the person who catches a salmon weighing more than 97 lb., the current record (that's $103.09 per lb.)—such a sum goes a long way toward paying for a budget vacation (even in Alaska).

Although both Soldotna and neighboring Kenai resemble a slice of greater Anchorage more than typical Alaskan towns, at least Soldotna provides budget travelers with a comfortable campground. If you have to overnight in one of these service strips, and you're not a singleminded angler, Soldotna is the clear choice. The best option (though perhaps not the safest) might be to close your eyes and drive on through.

PRACTICAL INFORMATION AND ORIENTATION

At the north end of town, the **Sterling Highway** forks in one direction to continue to Anchorage, and in the other as the **Kenai Spur Road** to Kenai. This fork is known as the **Soldotna Y,** and many businesses describe their locations in relation to it. The 22-mi. **Kalifornsky Beach Road** (no, that's not Russian for "California") also intersects Sterling Hwy. at the southern end of town and begins its mile marking from the Kenai end. Hence an address located at Mile 3 is actually 19 mi. from Soldotna.

Visitors Information: Visitors Center, P.O. Box 236 (262-1337), between Miles 95 and 96 on Sterling Hwy., just across the river from downtown. Modern facility with photo displays, friendly staff, and stairs down to the river. The world-record 97-lb. king salmon caught in the Kenai River is here on permanent display, as well as a multitude of mounted local mammals. Open daily mid-May to Labor Day 9am-7pm. **Chamber of Commerce,** P.O. Box 236, Soldotna 99669 (262-9814), next door to the visitors center. Especially good for Bed and Breakfast lists, trail information, and sundry Soldotna souvenirs. Open Mon.-Fri. 9am-5pm.

Division of Parks and Outdoor Recreation, P.O. Box 1247 (262-5581), on Morgans Rd. between Miles 84 and 85 on Sterling Hwy. Information on campgrounds and fishing.

Fishing Licenses: available at any sporting goods store or **Pay and Save.** 1-day $10, 3-day $15, 14-day $30, annual $50. Alaska residents $15 for the year.

Car Rental: Ford Rent-A-Car, 43465 Sterling Hwy. (262-5491). $43 per day, unlimited mi. Must be at least 21 with credit card. **Hertz** (262-5857), based at Kenai Airport but will deliver. $45 per day, unlimited mi. Must be at least 25 with credit card.

Buses: Homer and Seward Bus Lines, 800-478-8280. To: Homer (1 per day, $17), Seward (1 per day, $25), and Anchorage (1 per day, $30).

Taxi: AAA Taxi, 262-1555.

Laundromat: Alpine Laundromat (262-9129), on Sterling Hwy. next to the Dairy Queen. Wash $1.75, 7-min. dry 25¢. Shower $3. Open daily 8am-9pm.

Showers and Hot Tubs: Arctic Oasis (800-770-3114), near the Y. 15-min. shower in a private wood-paneled room $3. Hot tub and shower for 1 hr.: for 1 person $13.50, for 2 $21.50, for 3 $27.50, for 4-8 $33. Open Mon.-Sat. 9am-1am, Sun. 1pm-1am. Showers also at Alpine Laundromat (see above).

Pharmacy: Payless Drug, next to the Safeway on Sterling Hwy. Open Mon.-Fri. 9am-9pm, Sat. 9am-6pm, Sun. 10am-6pm.

Crisis Line: 283-7257. 24 hr.
Ambulance: 262-4792.
Hospital: Central Peninsula General, 250 Hospital Pl. (262-4404).
Emergency: 911.
Post Office: (262-4760), Corral and Binkley St., downtown. Open Mon.-Fri.
8:30am-5pm, Sat. 10am-2pm. **General Delivery ZIP Code:** 99669.
Area Code: 907.

Soldotna is 140 mi. southwest of Anchorage on Sterling Hwy., at its junction with
Kenai Spur Rd. Take the Seward Hwy. south from Anchorage and turn right onto
Sterling at the second fork in the road (the Hope Hwy. is the first).

ACCOMMODATIONS AND CAMPING

Soldotna is mobbed by thousands of crazed anglers willing to pay any price for a
room or campground close to the Kenai River—especially during **"the run,"** a
three-week period in July when the river is choked with millions of love-struck
salmon. Competition for rooms and tentsites has driven prices up; your best rooming option may be a bed and breakfast. The Chamber of Commerce (see Practical
Information above) has a complete list of local establishments starting at $45 a night.
Fortunately for itinerant pedestrian campers, the Soldotna city elders have decreed
a price of only $2 per night at the attractive municipal campgrounds.

The Duck Inn (262-5041), Mile 3 on Kalifornsky Beach Rd., by the Red Diamond
Mall. Tiny, clean rooms with private bath and TV. Singles and doubles with 1
queen-sized bed $59.50.
The Bunkhouse Inn (262-4584), across the river from the visitors center. Recently
remodeled rooms with cable TV and full bath. 10% discount for senior citizens.
Singles $75. Doubles $90.
Swiftwater Park Municipal Campground, south on Sterling Hwy. at Mile 94, and
Centennial Park Municipal Campground, off Kalifornsky Beach Rd. near the
visitors center. Both are in the woods, both have boat launches on the river, and
both offer excellent fishing spots and tables set aside for cleaning fish. 1-week
max. stay. Pit toilets and water. Quiet, well-groomed sites $2, with a vehicle $7.
River Terrace RV Park (262-5591), next to the Bunkhouse Inn (see above).
Caters mostly to RVs but offers limited space for tents. Laundry facilities. Showers
$2. River access. Office open Mon.-Sat. 8:30am-9pm, Sun. noon-9pm. RV sites $20
for full hookup, $25 during the run. Tentsites $10, during the run $15

FOOD

The Kenai-Soldotna area has boomed in the past 20 years, attracting swarms of fast-
food joints. However, there are many good local restaurants for true budget travelers who can't stomach another "Kangaroo Burger." The 24-hr. **Safeway** downtown,
located on Sterling Hwy., is the place for groceries, and in the summer they sell
cheap and delicious **fresh fruit** out of a tent in the parking lot. A weekly **Farmer's
Market** takes place next to the fire department on Sterling Hwy. (Sat. 10am-2pm).

Sal's Klondike Diner, 44619 Sterling Hwy. (262-2220), ½ mi. from the river and
several hundred mi. from the Klondike. Amply adorned with Alaskana; a model
train circles overhead. Menu "loded" with gold rush trivia. Newspaper columns of
breakfast items ($3.50 each or 2 for $6) served all day. The massive $3 cinnamon
roll is a meal in itself. Open 24 hr.
Black Forest Restaurant, 44278 Sterling Hwy. (262-5111). Nostalgic foreign travelers and polyglots should stop in, as the owners—fluent in English, French, German, and Filipino—love swapping stories in any language. They also speak the
international language of the budget diner. Whopping ½-lb. cheeseburger
($5.25), 12-in. submarine sandwiches ($4.75-5.50). Try a fresh banana shake
($2.50). Open Mon.-Fri. 11am-8pm, Sun. noon-7pm.

Bull Feathers (262-3844), in the back of the Peninsula Center Mall, on Sterling Hwy. Substantial ½-lb. burger with 3 "Jo Jos" (deep-fried potato slices) and a packed "burger fixin's bar" ($5). Open Mon.-Sat. 9am-9pm, Sun. 10am-7pm.

Diamond K Cafe, in the small mall at Sterling Hwy. and the Kenai Spur Rd. A family-run restaurant with no-nonsense American food. The Hungry Man's breakfast could satisfy a grizzly—3 eggs, bacon, pancakes, biscuits and gravy, and coffee ($7.50). Wide range of sandwiches ($4.85-6.65). Open 24 hr.

SIGHTS AND SEASONAL EVENTS

The reclusive **Soldotna Museum** sits up in the woods just before the entrance to Centennial Park. It houses relics from the homesteading era of the 1940s and 50s, when Soldotna was settled (open Tues.-Fri. 10am-4pm, Sat.-Sun. noon-4pm).

Soldotna Progress Days, celebrated at the end of July, commemorates the completion of the natural gas pipeline in 1961. Festivities include a parade, rodeo, and airshow. Mid-June brings the ecology-oriented **Kenai River Festival,** held across from the Soldotna Safeway.

If you feel like stomping your heels, check out the **Maverick Saloon** (262-7979) on Sterling Hwy., across from the Bunkhouse Inn, for live country music (Mon. 9:30pm-4:30am; club open daily 8am-5am). A little bowling to pass the time? **Gold Strike Lanes,** behind Sal's Klondike Diner (262-9065), is both highly recommended and cheap—$2 per game, $1 to rent shoes. Frequent specials drop the price of a game to 99¢ (open daily 2-10pm).

OUTDOORS

The **Kenai River** wriggles with wildlife of the scaly sort. Pink, king, red, and silver salmon glide through at various times during the summer, and steelhead and dolly varden do the underwater tango all summer long. Numerous **fishing charters** run the river, usually charging $100-125 for a half-day of either halibut or salmon fishing (or $150 for both kinds of fishing). Contact the visitors center for more information. Such expense isn't necessary, however. The downtown area is loaded with equipment rental shops that will fully outfit you with everything from bait to licenses for under $15 per day, and you can angle from the shore. **Kenai Motorboat Rental** (262-3736), by the bridge on Sterling Hwy., provides 16-ft. power boats ($125 per day plus a $5 launching fee; gas not included). The best places to throw out a line are those where the current runs slowly (e.g. near a bridge), since salmon often rest in such pockets on their journeys upstream.

If you're tired of oversexed seafood and maniacal, rubber-suited anglers, wander over to the **Kenai National Wildlife Refuge Visitors Center** (262-7021), off Funny River Rd. at the top of Ski Hill Rd., directly across from the Soldotna visitors center. A great source of information on this 197-million acre refuge for moose, Dall sheep, and other wild animals, but don't count on seeing any beasts from here—most of them are amid the several million acres. The center also houses dioramas and various victims of taxidermy. You can scratch-and-sniff wooly patches of caribou, moose, and sheep hair, or pick up a phone to talk to a loon or wolf. Several nature trails are nearby (open Mon.-Fri. 8am-5pm, Sat.-Sun. 10am-6pm).

Fast-paced rivers weave into the **Kenai National Wildlife Refuge,** and dozens of one- to four-day **canoe routes** wind their way through the forest. **The Sports Den** (262-7491) has canoes for $35 per day, $25 per day for three days or more (sometimes lower during price wars; open daily 8am-8pm). Boats are also available alongside the highway, where residents put their vessels in their front yards and hang "for rent" signs on them. Boat rentals are far from inexpensive, but it's hard to put a price on the peacefulness to be found gliding through some of the nation's most remote waterways. For free **canoe route maps** drop by the visitors center (above), or write or call the Refuge Manager, Kenai National Wildlife Refuge, P.O. Box 2139, Soldotna (262-7021).

■■■ KENAI

Kenai (pronounced KEEN-eye), the second oldest non-native settlement in Alaska, is the largest and fastest-growing town on the peninsula. Named for the Kenaitze Indians who first settled here, it later attracted Russians seeking sea otters and Captain Cook seeking the fabled Northwest Passage. Because of its strategic location, the Russians built Fort St. Nicholas here in 1791, and the U.S. Army erected Fort Kenay in 1868—the earliest (and coldest) battlements of the Cold War.

But it was not until the 1950s that "black gold" was discovered off the coast, forever changing the pace of life in Kenai and Alaska as a whole. Now the logos on the refineries and platforms that ribbon the shore read like a *Who's Who* of the oil world: Amoco, Shell, Mobil, Texaco, Phillips, UNOCAL, Marathon, et al. Rigs with pet names like "Spark" and "King Salmon" pump out about 70,000 barrels of crude oil per day. In the shadows of the oil rigs, jumbled remnants of each historical era lie scattered among the strip malls and RV parks that constitute Kenai (pop. 6500). And during the summer months, Alaska's largest collection of Beluga whales dodge the hunks of metal as they chase spawning salmon through the mouth of the Kenai River.

If this is you're first look at an Alaskan town outside of Anchorage, don't despair—this is the exception rather than the rule. Not every town can lay claim to the largest Kmart on the planet.

PRACTICAL INFORMATION AND ORIENTATION

Visitor and Cultural Center, 11471 Kenai Spur Hwy. (283-1991), just past the corner of Spur and Main St. A veritable palace of visitation, erected for the town's 1991 bicentennial. Usual array of pamphlets is supplemented by a room full of stuffed native wildlife, an area dedicated to Native artifacts, and a small theater with films on the area's development ($1 suggested donation for exhibits). Open Mon.-Fri. 9am-6pm, Sat. 10am-5pm, Sun. noon-5pm; in winter Mon.-Fri. 9am-5pm.

National Park Service, 502 Overland Dr., P.O. Box 2643, Kenai 99611 (283-5855). Best source of information on **Lake Clark National Park and Preserve,** located across Cook Inlet from Kenai. Hours vary.

Airport, 1 mi. north of downtown. Take Kenai Spur Rd. to Willow St., follow signs for Airport Loop. Serviced by **ERA** (800-426-0333), and **Mark Air** (800-478-0800, from out of state 800-426-6784). To Anchorage ($50, 3-day advance $35, 21-day advance $25).

Taxi: Alaska Cab, 283-6000. **Inlet Cab,** 283-4711. Both open 24 hr.

Car Rental: National (283-9566), $35 per day, unlimited mi. Must be 21 with credit card. **Avis** (283-7900), $36 per day, unlimited mi. Must be 21 with credit card. **Hertz** (283-7979), $45 per day, unlimited mi. Must be 25 with credit card. All three located at the airport.

Buses: Homer and Seward Bus Lines (278-0800). One per day to Anchorage ($30) and Homer ($17).

Library, 163 Main St. Loop (283-4378). Open Mon.-Thurs. 8:30am-8pm, Fri.-Sat. 8:30am-5pm.

Laundromat and Showers: Wash-n-Dry (283-9973), Lake St. and Kenai Spur Rd. Wash $1.50, 7-min. dry 25¢. 20-min. shower $3.50. Open daily 8am-10pm.

Pharmacy: Kenai Drug Inlet Pharmacy (283-3714), in the Sea Plaza, at Spur and McKinley. Open Mon.-Sat. 10am-6pm.

Crisis Line: 283-7257 (24 hr.).

Women's Resource Center, 325 S. Spruce St. (283-9479). 24 hr.

Hospital: Central Peninsula General Hospital, 250 Hospital Pl., Soldotna (262-4404).

Emergency: 911.

Police: 283-7879.

Post Office, 140 Bidarka (283-7771). Open Mon.-Fri, 8:45am-5:15pm, Sat. 9:45am-1pm. **General Delivery ZIP Code:** 99611.

Area Code: 907.

KENAI

Kenai, on the western Kenai Peninsula, is about 148 mi. from Anchorage and 81 mi. north of Homer. It can be reached via **Kalifornsky Beach Rd.,** which joins Sterling Hwy. from Anchorage just south of Soldotna, or via **Kenai Spur Rd.,** which runs north through the Nikishka area and east to Soldotna. Kalifornsky **mile markers** measure distance from Kenai, while the Kenai Spur mile markers measure distance from Soldotna. Both roads lay open the peninsula's lakes and peaks: on a clear day, you can see the 10,000-ft. **Mt. Redoubt Volcano** across Cook Inlet.

ACCOMMODATIONS AND CAMPING

As in Homer, tourists and anglers have conspired to put Kenai's hotel rates into orbit. Check the visitors center (see Practical Information) for listings of local bed and breakfasts, which start at $45. Backpackers used to stay in a free municipal campground which has since banned overnight camping. This leaves not a single affordable accommodation in Kenai, although one lodge 9 mi. out of town offers inexpensive bunks (men only; see North Star Lodge below).

Katmai Hotel, 10800 Kenai Spur Hwy. (283-6101), 1 block from downtown. Small rooms with nice decor and cable TV. Singles $79. Doubles $89.

Kenai Merit Inn Hotel, 260 S. Willow St. (283-6131), just off the Kenai Spur Hwy. Courtesy vans, cable TV. Singles and doubles $85.

North Star Lodge, Mile 21 Kenai Spur Hwy. (776-5259). A hotel and restaurant 9 mi. north of town with space for 12 men in a bunkhouse. Free showers, no kitchen. $10. Rooms from $55.

Overland RV Park, P.O. Box 326 (283-4227), next to the visitors center. Full hookup $16. Right behind it is **Kenai RV Park,** P.O. Box 1913 (283-3196). Showers $1. Full hookup $12.

FOOD

Carr's Quality Center (283-7829), in the Kenai Mall next to the K-Mart on Kenai Spur Rd. is the city's largest grocery store. Bakery, fruit and juice bar, natural foods section, pharmacy, and fast food for reasonable prices (open 24 hr.).

Little Ski-Mo's Burger-n-Brew (283-4463), on Kenai Spur Hwy. across from the visitors center. Stunning array of burgers. Try the Polynesian ($6.50) or the Shaka burger ($5.25). Burger-n-brew or soda ($5) all day, every day. Open Mon.-Sat. 11am-11pm, Sun. 11am-10pm.

Katmai Hotel Restaurant, 10800 Kenai Spur Rd. (238-6101), near Kaliforsky Beach Rd. Full platters of lip-smacking (artery-stopping) fried foods. 2 eggs, ½-order of biscuits and gravy, and coffee ($5). Third-pound deluxe burger with fries ($5). Tall iced tea ($1). Open 24 hr.

Arirang Chinese Restaurant, 145 S. Willow St. (283-4662), off Kenai Spur Rd. Refuel at the all-you-can-eat lunch buffet ($7) served Mon.-Fri. 11:30-2pm. Open daily 11am-10pm.

SIGHTS AND ACTIVITIES

The most breathtaking sight in Kenai is **Cook Inlet,** framing miles of white sand, two mountain ranges, and volcanic Mt. Augustine and Mt. Redoubt. Imbibe the magic of the inlet and its beluga whales, salmon, and gulls from the overlook at the end of Main St. A small **caribou** herd, often spotted trotting along Kenai Spur Hwy. or Kalifornsky Beach Rd., roams the flatlands between Kenai and Soldotna. The town itself is a diffuse jumble of asphalt and malls that has more in common with the sprawl of suburban New Jersey than with Alaska's frontier towns.

The only worthwhile indoor attraction in Old Kenai is the town's oldest building, the **Holy Assumption Russian Orthodox Church,** on Mission St. off Overland. Originally built in 1846 and rebuilt in 1896, this National Historic Landmark contains a 200-year-old Bible (tours in summer daily 11am, 1, and 3pm). Cultural Kenai is closeted inside the cement-block **Kenai Fine Arts Center** (283-7040), at Main and

Cook. The **Kenai Peninsula Artists Exhibit** rests in the Gallery (open Mon.-Sat. 10am-4pm).

Recreational opportunities in the Kenai area abound. Check at the Chamber of Commerce for fishing charter information (prices are comparable to those in Soldotna), or with the Forest Service (see Practical Information) for canoeing and hiking activities. The **Captain Cook State Recreation Area,** 30 mi. north of Kenai at the end of Kenai Spur Rd., offers swimming, fishing, free **camping,** and landing points for canoes on the Swanson River. Contact the State Division of Parks for rules and regulations. **Nikiski,** an unincorporated village a few miles north of Kenai, is home to a **geodesic-domed pool** behind the school. The dome is a stunning contrast to its forest setting, and in winter you can swim next to the snowdrifts that pile high outside the arched windows. (Open Tues.-Fri. 7am-5pm and 6-9pm, Sat. noon-5pm, Sun. 6-9pm. Admission $2.50, ages over 62 free, ages 17 and under $1.) If swimming under a dome has you tuckered out, take the gravel paths at the end of Spruce St. in Kenai to lounge on the local **beaches.**

■ Clam Gulch and Ninilchik

South of Kenai and Soldotna on the Sterling Hwy. sits **Clam Gulch,** populated by 141 people and 141 zillion clams. Clamming requires a sports fishing license, and there is a daily limit of 60 clams per person. Rubber gloves and waterproof footgear are highly recommended, as well as a clam-digging shovel (which you can pick up at any sporting goods store in Kenai for $5-10). Clam Gulch claims only one cot-cluttered corner store, the **Clam Shell Lodge,** Mile 118.3 of Sterling Hwy. (262-4211). The lodge has clean hotel rooms, a bar/restaurant, and showers (singles in July $60; June and Aug. $50; May and Sept. $40, on down to $25 Nov.-Feb.). The cook's specialty? Clam chowder, of course (bowl $3.50, open 11am-6pm). The Lodge will also set you up for clamming with equipment and guide ($25 per person, $30 per couple). Clamming carries on throughout the year in any minus tide. Other good places for madcap clammers are Deep Creek, Ninilchik, and Homer Spit. The **Tustumena 200, Clam Gulch Classic,** and other **dog sled races** attract mushers in January and February as qualifying races for the March Iditarod.

The **Clam Gulch Post Office** (262-5137) sits just next to the Clam Shell Lodge on Mile 118.3 of Sterling Hwy.—it's a great place to pick up a postmark (open Mon.-Fri. 8am-4pm, Sat. 9am-1pm).

Ninilchik, between Clam Gulch and Homer on the Sterling Hwy., is another small town (pop. 845) with spectacular fishing and fantastic scenery. Its strong Russian heritage, however, distinguishes it from other hamlets on the peninsula. The only sightseeing attractions are the old **Russian fishing village** on Village Rd. north of town, and the **Holy Transfiguration of Our Lord Orthodox Church,** built in 1901. Both overlook Cook Inlet, and the church, high up on a bluff, offers an unparalleled view of the Redoubt and Iliamna volcanoes. The church and cemetery are still in use, but the Russian village sits disintegrating and half-abandoned.

The nearby **Deep Creek Recreation Area** is one of the most popular on the peninsula. Locals stake the claim that it has the world's best salt-water king salmon fishing; dolly varden and steelhead trout swim here as well. During the third weekend in August, the **Kenai Peninsula State Fair**—Ninilchik's "Biggest Little Fair in Alaska"—features a horse show, 4-H exhibits, livestock competition, and arts and crafts. For more information, contact the Fair Association, Box 39210, Ninilchik 99639.

If you decide to stay in town for the night, head for the **Beachcomber Motel and RV Park** (567-3417) on Village Rd. Each of the motel's four cabins has a shower, full kitchenette, TV, and unimpeded view of Mt. Redoubt across the Cook Inlet. (Singles $45. Doubles $55. Full hookups for RVs $12.) For campers the choice is obvious: stay at one of the **state campgrounds** near town—each with water and toilets (sites $6). Superb sites in **Ninilchik State Recreation Area** are less than 1 mi. north of the library. RV hookups rattle and hum closer to town at **Hylea's Camper Park,** Mile 135.4 of Sterling Hwy. (567-3393).

Groceries can be bought at the **General Store** (567-3378) on Sterling Hwy. The **Happy Wok** (567-1060), next door, sells pricey Chinese specials ($8) and a bacon double cheeseburger ($6). (Open daily 11am-midnight.) Just before the general store, on the left side of Sterling Hwy. as you head toward Homer, a long low restaurant and bar sits back on a gravel plot. The **Inlet View Cafe,** Mile 135.4 on Sterling Hwy. (567-3337), offers a sterling view of the Cook Inlet and hearty sandwiches named for the mountains you can see across the water: the Redoubt, Iliamna, and others ($5.50-9). Halibut basket, cole slaw, and fries ($7.25). (Open daily 5:30am-midnight.) The **bar** is a laid-back local hangout (open 10am-whenever).

The library's visitor information section is also the local **visitors center** (567-3333; open Mon.-Sat. 11am-4pm). The library is across the street from the Happy Wok.

■■■ HOMER

The happy Shangri-la of Homer is the product of a large artists' enclave combined with (and sometimes overlapping) a traditional fishing village. At first glance Homer may seem little different than other small coastal towns in Alaska—dented pickup trucks barrel over dusty roads, a large fleet of commercial halibut boats strain at their moorings in the harbor, and sitting remote from all this an indifferent backdrop of immense natural beauty.

But Homer has more dimensions than most of the other towns it resembles. This spirited community supports its own theater group, scores of galleries stocked with the work of local artists, and one of the best small newspapers in Alaska. Geologically, too, Homer has no match. The town rises up on bluffs above Kachemak Bay at one end with wide views of the blue mountains and pale glaciers across the water. The other end of town actually extends into the bay along the improbable 3½-mi. tendril of sand and gravel known as the **Spit.**

The ruggedly beautiful island and wilds of **Kachemak State Park** lie across the Kachemak Bay, where the southern end of the **Kenai Mountains** reaches the sea. Also on the south side of the bay are the artist/fishing colony of **Halibut Cove,** the Russian/hippy **Yukon Island,** the **Gull Island** bird rookery, and the Russian-founded town of **Seldovia.**

PRACTICAL INFORMATION AND ORIENTATION

Visitors Information, about 1 mi. from the ferry docks, the second building on your right as you head onto the Spit. This small blue building has all the necessary information and pamphlets for the region. Open Memorial Day-Labor Day daily 9am-9pm. If you can't make it here, go to the **Pratt Museum,** 3779 Bartlett St. (235-8365), for brochures. Open daily 10am-5pm.

Park Information: Alaska Maritime National Wildlife Refuge Visitor Center, 202 Pioneer Ave. (235-6546). Wildlife exhibits, marine photography, and helpful advice on backcountry adventures in Kachemak Bay. Open Mon.-Fri. 8:30am-5pm, Sat.-Sun. 10am-5pm. **Southern District Ranger Station,** Kachemak Bay State Park, P.O. Box 321, Homer 99603 (235-7024), 4 mi. outside town on the Sterling Hwy.

Fishing Licenses: $15 for 3 days, available at local sporting goods stores and charter offices, or contact the **Alaska Dept. of Fish and Game,** 3298 Douglas St., Homer 99603 (235-8191).

Job Service, Ste. 123, Kachemak Center Mall (235-7791), on Pioneer Ave. Open daily 8am-noon and 1-4:30pm.

Airport: Turn left at the beginning of the Spit. **Mark Air,** 800-478-0800 in Alaska, 800-426-6784 outside Alaska. To: Anchorage ($60, 3-day advance $50, 21-day advance $40) and Kodiak ($209, but from Anchorage it's only $85).

Buses: Homer and Seward Bus Lines, 235-8280 from Homer, 278-0800 from Anchorage. Daily to: Soldotna ($17), Kenai ($17), and Anchorage ($35). Call for prices and schedule to Seward.

Alaska Marine Highway, P.O. Box 355, Homer 99603 (235-8449, 800-500-2256 in Alaska, 800-551-7185 outside Alaska). Ferry terminal just across the road beyond the small boat harbor. Ferry office just before Land's End—toward the end of the Spit, on the right. Open Mon.-Fri. 10am-noon and when ferry is in. The *M/V Tustumena* sails from Homer to Cordova ($136), Seward ($94), Seldovia ($16), Kodiak ($46), and once a month to Dutch Harbor ($240).

Taxi: Lynx Taxi, 235-5969. **Nick's Taxi,** 235-6921. To downtown from the airport ($4) or ferry ($8).

Bike Rental: Quiet Sports, 144 W. Pioneer Ave. (235-8620). Mountain bikes 4 hr. $12, 8 hr. $20. They also have the best selection of **camping equipment** in town. Open Mon.-Fri. 10am-6pm, Sat. 10am-5pm. **Homer Rental Center** on the Spit (see below). Mountain bikes 4 hr. $10, 24 hr. $18.

Homer Rental Center (235-5211), just past Pier 1 Theater on the Spit. All manner of tools and toys for hire. Fishing poles $10 per day. Clamming shovels $5 per day. Camp stove $8.75 per day. Firewood $3 per bundle. Open daily 6am-10pm.

Bookstore: The Bookstore, next to the Eagle Quality Center on Sterling Hwy. Open Mon.-Sat. 10am-7pm, Sun. noon-5pm.

Library (235-3180), on Pioneer Ave. near Main St. Open Tues. and Thurs. 10am-8pm, Wed. and Fri.-Sat. 10am-6pm.

Laundromat and Showers: Homer Cleaning Center, Main St. (235-5152), downtown. Wash $2, 7-min. dry 25¢. Last load 1 hr. before closing. 30-min. shower $2.25, towel included. Open Mon.-Sat. 8am-9pm, Sun. 9am-9pm. **Washboard** (the Kenai's new laundry dynasty!), 1204 Ocean Dr. (235-6781), not far off the Spit, 2 doors up from Sourdough Express. Wash $1.50-2, 8-min. dry 25¢. 30-min. shower $3. TV, sunbeds, lockers, and a panoply of dirt-purging projects. Open daily 8am-9pm; in winter daily 8am-8pm. **Homer Rental Center,** on the Spit (see above). Wash $2, dry $1. Shower $3.75, towel and soap included.

Women's Crisis Line: 235-8101. 24 hr.

Hospital: South Peninsula Hospital, 4300 Bartlett (235-8101), off Pioneer.

Emergency: 911. **Police:** 235-3150.

Post Office: 3261 Wadell Rd. (235-6125), off Homer Bypass. Open Mon.-Fri. 8:30am-5pm. **General Delivery ZIP Code:** 99603.

Area Code: 907.

Surrounded by 400 million tons of coal, Homer rests on **Kachemak ("Smoky") Bay,** named after the mysteriously burning coal deposits that greeted the first settlers. Mild 20° weather in January and 60° days in June have since earned Homer the dubious title "Banana Belt of Alaska."

Homer sits cozily on the southwestern Kenai Peninsula, on the north shore of Kachemak Bay. The Sterling Hwy. links it with Anchorage (226 mi. away) and the rest of the Kenai Peninsula.

ACCOMMODATIONS AND CAMPING

The visitors center (see Practical Information) has a list of bed and breakfasts, starting at $50 per night. Contact them at P.O. Box 541, Homer (235-5300), for further information. Homer's closest approximation to a hostel, the Seaside Farm lies in the meadows outside of town, on East End Rd. Of Homer's two **municipal campgrounds,** one is in town and one is on the Spit. Most budget travelers choose the oceanfront locale and become "Spit rats." Town camping and Spit camping are two different animals, each with its own set of rules.

Seaside Farm, 58335 East End Rd. (235-7850), by the shore, 4½ mi. out. Equestrian Bed and Breakfast with bunks for backpackers ($12 with shower). Tentsites $6.

Heritage Hotel, 147 W. Pioneer (235-7787 or 800-478-7789 in AK), in the middle of downtown. A large log cabin building with 3 types of accommodations: rooms with shared baths, rooms with private baths, and a suite. Rooms are spacious and have TVs. Singles $55. Doubles $65. Oct.-March rooms begin at $47.

Driftwood Inn, 135 W. Bunnell (235-8019), a short walk from downtown. Take the Homer Bypass, turn right on Main St., then right again on Bunnell. Rustic and family-run with barbecues on the large porch. Originally Homer's first schoolhouse. Courtesy van. Singles with shared bath $60, private bath $65.

Ocean Shores Motel, 3500 Crittendon (235-7775), off Sterling Hwy. 1 block from downtown. Fair to excellent mountain and ocean views, depending on the room. Singles from $50, in winter from $35.

Homer Cabins, 3601 Main St. (235-6768). 7 tidy owner-built cabins, each with a flower box in the window, kitchenette, shower, and double bed. For 1-2 people $65, for 3 people $80. Weekly rates available.

Municipal Campgrounds on the Spit: Harbormaster's Office, 4350 Spit Rd., Homer 99603 (235-3160). *Do* camp on the beach or on the 30-acre fill north of Harbor. *Don't* camp between road and harbor, within 50 ft. of road, on private property east of road before the Harbor, between freight deck and Land's End (used for barge landings), or on beach near Spit Lagoon. (Got it?) Check with the office for specifics. Portable toilets at the top of each harbor ramp and in camp areas. 2 permanent city restrooms with fresh water. Pitch tents high to avoid the extremely high tides, or you may wake up in the water. Windy, but voluptuously scenic. Campers can usually share a bonfire built by cannery workers in their tent enclaves. Sites $3. RVs $7. Pay next to the visitors center.

Municipal City Campground, office at Parks and Recreation Dept., City Hall, 491 E. Pioneer (235-8136). Take Pioneer to Bartlett St., go uphill, and take a left at the hospital entrance on Fairview St. Water and pit toilets. Tentsites $3. RVs $7.

Homer Spit Campground (235-8206), 200 yd. from the ferry dock. Privately owned. Caters more to the RV crowd and provides full hookups, showers ($1 for guests and $2 for the general public), city water, and sewage dump. Tentsites $10. RV sites with central water and dump $15.

Kachemak Bay State Park, 7 water mi. across from the Spit (it may cost you $40-50 just to get there, by boat). Free. No facilities. For further information, contact: State of Alaska Division of Parks, Kenai area, Box 1247, Soldotna 99603. March-Oct., call 235-7024.

FOOD

Homer's grocery stores range from the earthy **Smoky Bay Cooperative,** 248 W. Pioneer Ave. (235-7252), which carries only health food and houses an excellent lunch counter (open Mon.-Fri. 8am-8pm, Sat. 8:30am-7pm, Sun. 10am-6pm; lunch counter open daily 11am-3pm); to the 24-hr. **Eagle Quality Center,** 436 Sterling Hwy. (235-2408), a spinoff from the Carr's Chain. The **Save-U-More** in the Kachemak Center Mall on Pioneer Ave. will do just that. They sell discount booze as well as food (open Mon.-Sat. 10am-7pm, Sun. 11am-6pm).

On the Spit, you can usually hook or snag a salmon from the **Fishing Hole.** Buy fresh seafood for campfire cookouts directly from fishermen or at one of the large retail outlets: **Icicle Seafood Market,** 842 Fish Dock Rd. (235-3486), near the mouth of the harbor; or **The Exchange** (235-6241), just up the road. Those seeking a restaurant meal in Homer will find themselves buffeted with buffets—no less than five restaurants advertise reasonable all-you-can-eat specials within as many blocks.

Downtown

Cafe Cups, 162 Pioneer Ave. (235-8330). A gathering place for artists and young travelers. Tasty, unusual sandwiches ($6-8 with salad). Espresso milkshake ($4.50). Attractive abstract oil paintings inside. Outdoor seating as well. Open daily 7am-10pm.

Fresh Sourdough Express Bakery and Coffee Shop, 1316 Ocean Dr. (235-7571), on the main drag to the Spit. Dine indoors or out on the deck, or just pick up some fresh baked goods. Try the all-you-can-eat breakfast buffet ($9); it includes almost everything on the breakfast menu—great sourdough rolls, organic coffee, fresh fruit, sausage gravy and biscuits, bread pudding with blueberries, and more. Filling ½-sandwiches ($3.75). Open daily 6am-10pm.

The Thai and Chinese Restaurant, 601 E. Kachemak Center. Food is of varying quality, but the all-you-can-eat Thai and Chinese buffet ($6) is the best of the bunch (served 11am-3pm). Much of the same fare appears again for the dinner buffet ($7, served 5-9pm). Open daily 11am-10pm. Similar lunch buffets are served for the same price at **Young's Oriental Restaurant,** next door, and at the **Blue Dragon Chinese Restaurant,** on Lake St. between the Homer Bypass and Pioneer Ave.

Kachenak Bowl and Beachcomber's Restaurant, Lake St. and Pioneer Ave. A favorite with anglers, especially for breakfast. The all-you-can-eat sourdough hotcakes ($3.50) will keep you anchored all day. Open daily 6am-9pm.

Pioneer Pizzeria, 265 E. Pioneer Ave. (235-7312). Order the all-you-can-eat pizza dinner ($7, served 5:30-9pm), which includes soda and small salad bar. Decent pizza lets you lose count of the pieces. 8-in. personal pizza with 1 topping ($3.50). Open Mon. 4-11pm, Tues.-Sat. 11:30am-11pm.

On the Spit

Betty's, near the end of the Spit. A mobile provender of substantial, inexpensive Mexican meals. Bulging bean burritos ($1), tostadas with beans, cheese, guacomole, and sour cream ($1.50). Picnic table seating. The whole operation may pack up and roll away for the Talkeetna Bluegrass Festival during August.

Addie's Big Paddies (235-8132), on the Spit. Conveniently located near the boat harbor for the early fisherman, and near the Salty Dawg for the late night partier. The food is greasy but guaranteed to fill you up. Big sandwiches and burgers ($5-6.50). Open Sun.-Thurs. 5am-2am, Fri.-Sat. 4am-2am.

Boardwalk Fish 'n Chips (235-7749), at the end of Cannery Row Boardwalk, across from the Harbormaster's Office. A local favorite. Respectable halibut with chips ($7). Open daily 11:30am-10pm.

Lands End Resort, P.O. Box 273 (235-2500). As the name suggests, it's at the end of the Spit. Mouth-watering food is justifiably expensive. Breakfast specials include eggs Benedict and potatoes ($6). Lunch specials $6.75-12, dinner specials $15.50-28. Or just sit on the patio and sip cocktails while watching the sea otters frolic. Open daily 7am-10pm.

SIGHTS AND SEASONAL EVENTS

The **Pratt Museum,** 3779 Bartlett St. (235-8635), is the best museum on the peninsula. Recently remodeled, the Pratt houses a gallery of local art and historical exhibits of Kenai artifacts. "Eclectic" doesn't quite capture it—displays range from homesteader cabins to Eskimo and Denali Indian artifacts, and some of the best displays of dead and living marine mammals. View the skeleton of the Bering Sea beaked whale or take part in the feeding frenzy in the live salt water aquarium (fish frenzied Tues. and Fri. 4-5pm). If you're at the Pratt on a Friday afternoon, be sure to help feed the resident octopus. In addition, the museum houses a permanent exhibit on the March, 1989, Exxon *Valdez* oil spill, which dumped 11 million gallons of oil into Prince William Sound. (Open daily 10am-6pm; Oct.-Dec. and Feb.-April Tues.-Sun. noon-5pm. Admission $3, seniors and students $2.)

Homer has any number of **art galleries,** such as **Homer Artists,** 202 W. Pioneer (235-8944; open Tues.-Fri. 10am-6pm, Sat. 10am-5pm), and **Ptarmigan Arts,** 471 Pioneer Ave., with the work of over 40 Alaskan artists and craftspeople. The town's active theater group performs at **Pier One** (235-7333), near the start of the buildings on the Spit. You can catch plays there on the Main Stage throughout the summer (Fri. and Sat. at 8:15pm; tickets $9, seniors $8, children $6). A series of other performances take place from Sunday to Thursday, many featuring Homer's most famous son, Tom Bodett, of National Public Radio and Motel 6 ("We'll leave the light on for ya") fame. Check the *Homer News* for up-to-date schedules. **Homer Family Theater** (235-6728), at Main St. and Pioneer Ave. features current blockbusters and feel-good movies. Tickets $5.

Homer never sleeps in the warmer months; nightlife ranges from beachcombing at low tide in the midnight summer sun to investigating whether the sourdough-filled **Salty Dawg Saloon** under the log lighthouse at the end of the Spit ever actually closes (open 11am-whenever, as the sign says). **Land's End Resort,** at the very end of the Spit, has an expansive if expensive view of Kachemak Bay; for cheaper spirits head to **Alice's Champagne Palace,** 196 Pioneer Ave. (235-7650), a wooden barn with honky-tonk music (Tues.-Sat. from 10pm into the morning). **Rowley's Road-house,** Mile 4.5 of East End Rd. (235-8644), features local bands every Sunday in June 9pm-2am (bar open Sun.-Thurs. 11am-2am, Fri.-Sat. 11am-5am). The **Water-front Bar,** 120 Bunnell Ave. (235-9949), has all the gritty character of its name, smoke-filled pool room and all (live music Wed.-Sat. 10pm-3am; bar open daily 1pm-5am). Beware of the **moose crossing** outside the bar with their calves in June. (No, you haven't been drinking too much.)

Since Homer is often billed as the halibut capital of the world, it should perhaps come as no surprise that a massive halibut derby is the town's most popular annual event. The **Homer Jackpot Halibut Derby,** from May 1 to Labor Day, offers prizes from $250 to $20,000 for catching the biggest fish and the tagged fish. Every year several would-be winners are left crying at the scales after they land prize-winning fish with no ticket. Tickets are available in local tackle shops on the Spit. But Homer celebrates more than just its halibut—the annual **Winter Carnival,** held during the first week in February, features sled dog races and snow machine competitions.

OUTDOORS

Nearly everyone who comes to Homer spends some time on the **Homer Spit.** Here one can admire the view and wonder how the heck this 3½-mi. strip of sand was created and preserved in the unruly Pacific. The Spit is home to many fishing charter services and typical boardwalk candy and ice-cream stores. Near the start of the boardwalks on the bay side of the Spit, the **Fishing Hole** offers almost anyone who can hold a rod the chance to catch a salmon. A vigorous stocking program plants salmon fry in this tidal lagoon, which then grow and return years later to spawn. It's all a cruel ruse, though—the lagoon is unsuitable for spawning, and anglers manage to hook or snag most of the fish that return. About 3000 king salmon, the same number of pinks, and nearly 6000 silvers were taken from the hole last year.

Fleets of **halibut charters** depart from the Homer Spit daily in summer, many of which are run by **Central Charters** (235-7847), near the middle of the Spit's buildings. Full-day trips run $125-175, depending on boat size and meals provided. A fishing license (3 days $15) earns you a daily two-fish limit. Scads of smaller charters, some just for touring, have offices on the boardwalks up and down the Spit. Choosing a charter, like the fishing itself, is something of a crap shoot. Although most charter companies run reputable business, there are some that strip their customers more cleanly than a filleted halibut. Check with the tourist office for a list of companies in the Homer Charter Association; not every reliable business will necessarily be a member, but those that are should be reputable. Have your 300-lb. halibut vacuum-packed and deep-frozen at **The Coal Point Trading Co.,** across the street from Central Charters (65¢ per lb.).

The easiest way to see the sloping bluffs that rise behind Homer is to cruise **Skyline Drive,** which runs along the rim of the bluffs. Wildflowers (mostly fireweed, accompanied by scattered bunches of geranium, paintbrush, rose, etc.) bloom here from June to September. On a clear day, the view of the Kenai Mountains is unrivaled.

■ Near Homer

Kachemak Bay

For a closer look at the Kachemak Bay and its wildlife, hike or boat into **Kachemak Bay State Park,** State of Alaska Department of Natural Resources, Pouch 7-0001,

Anchorage 99510 (262-5581 in Soldotna). Contact them for park regulations and precautions. The park's trails offer the best (and really the only) hiking near Homer, but visitors' facilities are limited. A **water taxi** run by St. Augustine's Charters in Homer will bring you to the park any morning and arrange for a flexible pick-up date and time. ($40 per person round-trip with a 2-person min. For reservations call Inlet Charter at 235-6126 and ask for Seabird.) Pick up *The Kachemak Bay Park Pamphlet* at the Spit's visitors center (see Homer: Practical Information) for details on eight varied **trails.** Central Charters (235-7847) also offers **kayaking** daytrips to the Park, with equipment, guide, and lunch ($140).

One of the best natural history tours of Kachemak Bay is conducted by the non-profit **Center for Alaskan Coastal Studies.** Their daily expedition passes by the 15,000 nesting seabirds on **Gull Island,** surveys beaches and intertidal areas, and includes discussion of Indian and Eskimo prehistory. For reservations, call Rainbow Tours (235-7272; outing from 9am-6pm $49, seniors $39, children $29). **St. Augustine Charters** (235-6126) runs a two- to three-hour wildlife cruise including Gull Island and the south slope of Kachemak Bay. For an additional $18, they will also do a drop-off and pick-up for people interested in hiking to a glacier. **Kachemak Bay Adventures** offers a quick $10 tour of Gull Island (departs daily at 10am, returns at 11:30am).

Halibut Cove

Danny J. Cruise Tours (235-7847) leaves from the small-boat harbor in Homer for Halibut Cove daily at noon and returns at 5pm ($35 round-trip, seniors $28, children $17.50). The tour passes **Gull Island** for a close view of puffins, ptarmigans, red-legged cormorants, and other birds up from the Aleutian chain to roost for the summer. The charter stops for three hours at the artist/fishing colony of **Halibut Cove,** with its few dozen residents. Walk the raised boardwalk village to the **Experience Art Gallery** and view a collection of works by residents (including Marian Beck, Danny Greene, Alex Lombs, and Diana Tillion). Then head to the **Saltry** (296-2223), the cove's only restaurant, for lunch. Their menu offers a variety of raw and cooked fish. Try the halibut salad ($8), the chocolate cheese cake, or the nori maki ($8). The *Danny J.* also makes a daily dinner trip to the Saltery at 5pm, returning at 9pm ($17.50 round-trip). On Thursday nights the trip is half-price ($8.75); reservations are critical.

Get your hands on the octopus-ink paintings at **Diana Tillion's Cove Gallery.** She extracts ink from stranded octopi with a hypodermic needle, eats the octopi, and then paints with their body fluids. She and her husband were the first artists to raise a family here and begin the integration of fish and art that now characterizes Halibut Cove. **Alex Combs'** private oil gallery lies at the end of the beach in the two small red buildings.

Make your visit to Halibut Cove a daytrip—the only places to stay in town are **Halibut Cove Cabins,** Box 1990, Homer (296-2214), which charges $65 for singles and $75 for doubles (bring your own bedding and food), and the **Quiet Place Lodge Bed and Breakfast** (296-2212), which charges $100 for double rooms in individual cabins. Unfortunately, camping is out of the question because Halibut Cove lies on a privately owned island without public access to the surrounding wilderness.

Anchor Point

Proudly billing itself as the westernmost point on the U.S. Highway system, the otherwise obscure village of **Anchor Point** lies 16 mi. northwest of Homer on Sterling Hwy. The town is quickly becoming a suburb of expanding Homer; like its neighbor, it also has a **Salmon Derby,** in mid-May. If you decide to spend the night, go to the **Anchor River Inn** (235-8531), Mile 157, just off Sterling Hwy. in front of the bridge (singles with shower $40, doubles $45; 24-hr. grocery store).

Nikolaevsk

Visitor-shy but extremely interesting is **Nikolaevsk,** perhaps the only village in the U.S. where Russian is the primary language. Nikolaevsk's Old Believers are Russian Orthodox schismatics whose migrations in the past 200 years have taken them to China, Brazil, Oregon, and Kenai, venturing ever farther from decadent, *pagoni* influences. The economy centers on fishing and a shop plying traditional handmade Russian clothing. To find Nikolaevsk, take North Fork Rd. (in the center of Anchor Point) east to the Nikolaevsk sign post; from here, go down the gravel road until you get to the village. *Don't* hitchhike, because you'll never get out, and try not to act like a tourist—for the Believers, religion is a higher priority than visitors.

■ Seldovia

Directly across Kachemak Bay from Homer, this small town has been virtually untouched by the tourist mania prevailing on the rest of the peninsula. The Russians named Seldovia for its herring; indeed, the fishing industry has kept the town afloat for centuries. Seldovia predates Homer as the first community in Kachemak Bay— mail and groceries arrived here when Homer was a mere homesteading plot. At the same latitude as Oslo, Norway, Seldovia overlooks four active volcanoes—**Mts. Augustine, Iliamna, Redoubt,** and **Spur.**

Stop by the small **museum,** 206 Main St. (234-7625), sponsored by the Seldovia Native Association (open Mon.-Fri. 8am-5pm). On a hill overlooking the water, the beautiful **St. Nicholas Orthodox Church** was built in 1891 (open daily 1-2pm).

As part of the **Alaska Marine Highway System,** the ferry *M/V Tustumena* runs between Homer and Seldovia several times per week ($32 round-trip). You have the choice of spending either two hours (while the *Tustumena* refuels) or two days (until the next ferry arrives) in Seldovia. If you decide to stay, you can sleep on **Outside Beach,** 2 mi. out of town. Public rest rooms, water, and showers are all located at the Harbormaster's Office. To avoid roughing it in the sand, make reservations before you leave Homer at the **Boardwalk Hotel** (234-7816; singles $58, doubles $85).

If you're tired of playing games with the ferry schedule, **Kachemak Bay Adventures** (235-8206) offers two reasonably priced alternatives to experience Seldovia: a six-hour afternoon cruise ($35), which gives you a few hours to explore the town; and an overnight cruise which includes a night at the Boardwalk Hotel and a flightseeing trip back to Homer.

Seldovia triples in size on **Independence Day.** The old-fashioned celebration draws visitors from all over the peninsula and includes parades, log-rolling, a naked baseball game, and (presumably non-naked) greased pole climbing, as well as a potluck picnic.

KODIAK ISLAND

Aptly nicknamed Alaska's "Emerald Isle," Kodiak Island is both astonishingly beautiful and the victim of amazingly hard luck. The island has in this century been rocked by earthquakes, washed over by *tsunamis,* hit by the oil of the Exxon *Valdez,* and blanketed in nearly 2 ft. of volcanic ash—all of which is compounded by the dreary fact that half the days of every year see rain.

Cursed as it may seem, Kodiak Island's superlatives more than dwarf such past misfortunes. The island is the largest in Alaska (and the 2nd-largest in the U.S. behind the Big Island of Hawaii). Much of this vast acreage is preserved in the Kodiak National Wildlife Refuge, home to an estimated 2600 Kodiak brown bears and countless other furry creatures ranging from little brown bats to beavers. The refuge's 800 mi. of coastline ring the island's sharp, gemlike peaks. As for Kodiak's

K
O
D
I
A
K

human population, the rich waters around the island have made its fishing and crabbing fleet the state's most productive, drawing flocks of young people each summer to work its canneries. The largest Coast Guard station in the U.S. is based less than 10 mi. from Kodiak City, patrolling against poachers. Islanders here take their seafood (and especially their crab) seriously.

■ ■ ■ KODIAK

Kodiak was the first capital of Russian Alaska (1792-1804) before Alexander Baranov moved the Russian-American Company headquarters to Sitka. It was here that the Russians committed their worst atrocities, importing Aleut natives and enslaving them to hunt Kodiak Island's sea otters to near extinction.

Modern residents would much rather have had Mt. Katmai extinct instead—the volcano erupted in 1912, covering Kodiak Island with 18 in. of ash and obliterating much of the area's wildlife; traces of ash remain in the forests today. In 1964, the biggest earthquake ever recorded in North America shook the area, creating a tidal wave that destroyed much of downtown Kodiak and causing $24 million in damage. The swamped fishing port was rehabilitated by the Army Corps of Engineers and local resourcefulness; one 200-ft. vessel, *The Star of Kodiak,* was cemented into the ferry dock and converted into a cannery.

PRACTICAL INFORMATION AND ORIENTATION

Visitors Information: Information Center (486-4070), at Center St. and Marine Way, right in front of the ferry dock. Hunting and fishing information, charter arrangements, and a self-guided-walking-tour map. Open Mon.-Fri. 8am-5pm and for most ferry arrivals. **U.S. Fish and Wildlife Headquarters and Visitor Center,** just outside Buskin State Recreation Site, 4 mi. southwest of town. Wildlife displays, 150 films to choose from, and information on the Kodiak National Wildlife Refuge and its cabins. Open Mon.-Fri. 8am-4:30pm, Sat.-Sun. noon-4:30pm.

State Department of Parks: at Fort Abercrombie (486-6339). Has information on local state parks and campgrounds.

Sport Fishing Division: Alaska Department of Fish and Game, Box 686, Kodiak, at 211 Mission Rd. (486-1880). Information on fishing regulations and seasons.

Employment: Alaska State Employment Service, 305 Center St. (486-3105), in Kodiak Plaza. Open Mon.-Fri. 8am-4:30pm.

Airport: Located 4 mi. southwest of town on Rezanof Dr. Served by **Mark Air,** 487-9798 at the airport, 800-478-0800 in Alaska, 800-426-6784 out of state. To Anchorage $85, with 3-day advance purchase $75, with 21-day advance $65. To Homer $209.

Alaska Marine Highway: Terminal next to the visitors center (800-526-6731 or 480-3800). The *M/V Tustumena* docks in Kodiak May-Sept. 1 to 3 times per week; in winter less frequently. To: Homer ($46); Seward ($52); and Valdez or Cordova ($96). 5-day run to Dutch Harbor once every month ($200).

Car Rental: Rent-A-Heap (486-5200), at the Mark Air terminal. $25 per day and 25¢ per mi. **National Car Rental,** 122 Rezanof Dr. (487-4435). $39 per day; unlimited mileage. Must be 25 with a credit card or a $500 cash deposit for both.

Taxis: A&B Taxi, 486-4343. $3 base fee plus $2 per mi. $13.40 to the airport from downtown. 24 hr.

Camping and Fishing Equipment: Mack's Sports Shop, 117 Lower Mill Bay (486-4276), at the end of Center Ave. Open Mon.-Sat. 7am-7pm, Sun. 9am-5pm. Also, **Cy's Sporting Goods,** on Shelikof St. near the harbor. Open Mon.-Sat. 8am-7pm, Sun. 10am-5pm.

Bookstore: Shire Bookstore, in the alley beside Kraft's Grocery (see Post Office below). Open Mon.-Sat. 9:30am-7pm, Sun. 1-5pm.

Library: on Lower Mill Bay Rd. Has a **courtesy phone** for free local calls. Open Mon.-Fri. 10am-9pm, Sat. 10am-5pm, Sun. 1-5pm.

Laundromat and showers: Ernie's, 218 Shelikof (486-4119), across from the harbor. Wash $1.50, 4-min. dry 25¢. 20-min. shower $3.25. Drop-off available. Open daily 8am-8pm.

Weather: Local forecasts, 487-4313. **Marine forecasts,** 487-4949.

Pharmacy: Wodlinger Drug and Photo (486-4035), on Marine Way across from the harbormaster. Pharmacy open Mon.-Fri. 10am-6pm.

Hospital: Kodiak Island Hospital and Care Center, 1915 E. Rezanof Dr. (486-3281).

Emergency: 911.

Post Office: on Lower Mill Bay Rd. Open Mon.-Fri. 9am-5:30pm, Sat. 10am-4pm. **General Delivery ZIP Code:** 99615. Substations in **Kraft's Grocery,** 111 Rezanof, and **Safeway,** on Mill Bay Rd. Open Mon.-Sat. 10am-6pm.

Population: Kodiak Island 15,575. Kodiak township 6365.

Area Code: 907.

The city of Kodiak is on the eastern tip of Kodiak Island, 100 mi. off the Kenai Peninsula and roughly 200 mi. south of Homer. Kodiak Island is, at 3670 sq. mi., approximately the size of the state of Connecticut. One hundred mi. of rutted gravel roads follow the scenic coastlines north and south of the city.

ACCOMMODATIONS AND CAMPING

A dearth of affordable hotel rooms makes Kodiak a good place to check out the local B&Bs; close to a dozen go for rates as low as $45 a night. Call the visitors center (see Practical Information) for a list and remember to reserve well in advance; finding a room becomes almost impossible when the airport shuts down due to bad weather (which is often).

Backpackers can head for **Gibson Cove,** 2 mi. west of Kodiak on Rezanof. Built by the city for transient cannery workers, Gibson Cove looks and feels like a gravel parking lot and stinks of fish—but at $2 a night with free hot showers, who can quibble? If you can't deal, 2 mi. farther off Rezanof is the prettier and less fishy **Buskin River Recreation Area.**

Shelikof Lodge, 211 Thorsheim Ave. (486-4141), a small street to the right of McDonald's. Comfortable rooms with cable TV. Courtesy van to the airport. Singles $60. Doubles $65.

Star Motel, 119 Yukon St. (486-5657), a small street to the left of McDonald's. Dreary exterior masks equally dreary rooms. Gets rowdy when the fleet's in. Singles and doubles $55.

Gibson Cove Campground (Tent City), 2 mi. from ferry terminal. From terminal take Center St. to Rezanof and turn left. 45 tentsites. Quiet transient-worker community may fill up when the fleet's in. Friendly, on-site manager. Raised gravel platforms for tents, hot showers, toilets, drinking water. No max. stay. Sites $2.

Fort Abercrombie State Park Campground, 4 mi. northeast of town on Rezanof-Monashka Rd. Water, shelters, and outhouses. No RV hookups; designed for backpackers. WWII ruins, a trout-fishing lake, and spectacular sunsets. Historic tours June-Aug. Sun., Tues., and Fri. at 2:30pm ($1). 7-night max. stay. Sites $6.

Buskin River State Recreation Site, 4½ mi. southwest of the city. Water and pit toilets. Over 50% of Kodiak's sport fish is caught on the Bushkin River. 14-night max. stay. Sites $6.

Pasagshak State Recreation Site, 40 mi. from the city at the mouth of the Pasagshak River, which reverses direction 4 times daily with the tides. Water and toilets. Noted for king salmon fishing. 14-day max. stay. 7 sites. Free.

FOOD

Restaurants in Kodiak, though tasty, tend to hit hard on the wallet. The enormous **Safeway,** 2 mi. out of town on Mill Bay Rd., claims to be the largest on the West Coast. Besides cheap groceries and a wide selection of produce, the store houses a popular **Chinese deli** (store open daily 6am-midnight). Other markets in town include **Kraft's Grocery,** 111 Rezanof (open daily 7am-midnight) and **Cactus Floats Natural Foods,** 338 Mission St. (open Mon.-Sat. 10am-6pm). Hobgoblins of conformity can always trudge to **McDonald's,** at Rezanof and Lower Mill Bay Rd., **Subway,** at 326 Center Ave., or **Pizza Hut,** on Mill Bay Rd. in front of Safeway.

El Chicano (486-6116), in the nameless gray building across from the Orpheum Theater on Center St. Although this authentic Mexican restaurant presents no sign to passers-by in the street, it could advertise some of the best and biggest Mexican specialties north of the border. Try a bowl of black-bean soup with homemade Mexican bread ($4.75) or a filling burrito ($4.75-7.25). Complimentary corn chips and salsa. Open Mon.-Sat. 11am-10pm, Sun. noon-9pm.

Henry's Sports Cafe (486-2625), in the mall on Marine Way. Surprisingly swank for Kodiak with a circular bar and shaded lamps, but the sandwich prices remain within the realm of reason. Egg-salad sandwich and fries $4.75, burgers with fries or cottage cheese $5.75-7.25. Open Mon.-Thurs. 11am-11pm, Fri.-Sat. 11am-midnight, Sun. 5-10pm.

Fox Inn, 211 Thorsheim (486-4300), a windowless room in the Shelikof Lodge. Although service can be slow, locals rave about the Fox's straightforward American fare. Soup and sandwich specials ($6). Waffle, eggs, and bacon ($5.25). Reindeer-sausage and cheese omelette ($5.75). Open Tues.-Sat. 7am-9:30pm, Sun. 8am-9pm.

Beryl's (486-3323), in the alley off Center St., to the right of the First National Bank of Anchorage. $5.45 sandwiches and a wide variety of ice cream and sweets. Try a pineapple milkshake ($2.50). Open Mon.-Fri. 7:30am-6am, Sat. 10am-6pm, Sun. noon-5pm.

Peking and Sizzler, 116 W. Rezanof (486-3300). Come at lunch on a weekday for the sweet and sour pork, soup, wonton, and rice ($5.25; served 11:30am-2:30pm). Open Mon.-Sat. 11:30am-10pm, Sun. noon-10pm.

SIGHTS AND SEASONAL EVENTS

Built in 1808 as a storehouse for sea-otter pelts, the **Baranov Museum,** 101 Marine Way (486-5920), is the oldest Russian structure standing in Alaska—as well as the oldest wooden structure on the entire West Coast. The museum displays Russian and native artifacts, and a library displays period photos and literature ranging from the Russian colony to the present. (Open Mon.-Fri. 10am-4pm, Sat.-Sun. noon-4pm; Labor Day-Memorial Day Mon.-Wed. and Fri. 11am-3pm, Sat. noon-3pm. Admission $1, under 12 free.) The **Resurrection Russian Orthodox Church** (486-3854), not far from the museum, houses the oldest parish in Alaska. Built in 1794, its elaborate icons date back to the early 19th century, and its church bells are still rung by hand (call for tours by appointment; open Mon.-Fri. 1-3pm).

Several interesting sights in Kodiak make little effort at self-promotion. The **Alutiiq Culture Center,** 214 W. Rezanof Dr. (486-1992), displays numerous archaeological treasures from recent digs around the island as well as a model of a communal Alutiiq dwelling (open Mon.-Fri. 10am-5pm; free). The **St. Herman's Seminary,** up the hill from the double-domed church on Mission St., contains a small collection of icons, clothing, and Aleut prayer books for viewing (open Mon.-Fri. noon-3pm). Across the bridge on Near Island, engineers at the **Fisheries Industry Technology Center** rack their brains trying to invent new mass-marketable fish foods. Stop by to tour their laboratories and sample tomorrow's fish products (open Mon.-Fri. 8am-5pm).

In past years, Alaska's only outdoor theater, the **Frank Brink Amphitheater** on Minashka Bay, staged the historical play *Cry of the Wild Ram* on August weekends. The production, which covered 30 years in the life of Alexander Baranov (who established the first colonies in Kodiak and the Kenai Peninsula), was discontinued in the summer of 1993 due in part to squabbles over whether the Russian explorers should be portrayed as heroes or exploiters. A revised version of the play may be performed in 1994. For more information, write the Kodiak Arts Council, P.O. Box

1792, Kodiak, or call them at 486-5291. Meanwhile, you can count on first-run films at the **Orpheum Theater** (486-5449), on Center St. (tickets $5, balcony seats $6).

Beautiful **Fort Abercrombie State Park,** 3½ mi. north of town, was the site of the first secret radar installation in Alaska (shh!). The fort is also the site of a WWII defense installation; after several islands in the Aleutian chain were attacked by the Japanese in 1942, American military minds assumed that Kodiak would be the next target. Some bunkers and other reminders of the Alaskan campaign remain, including an old naval station 6½ mi. southwest of Kodiak. The station is now home to the largest Coast Guard base in the U.S.

The **Kodiak Crab Festival,** held during Memorial Day and the five days previous, celebrates a bygone industry with parades, fishing derbies, kayak and crab races, and a blessing of the fleet. The event culminates with the **Chad Obden Ultramarathon,** a superhuman race along 42 mi. of hilly roads from Chiniak to Kodiak. **St. Herman's Days** (486-3524), held August 7 to 9, celebrates the first saint of the Russian Orthodox Church in North America (canonized in 1970). On one of these days, depending on the weather, visitors are welcome to join the faithful in an annual pilgrimage to St. Herman's former home on Spruce Island. Throughout the year, the Thursday evening service at the Resurrection Church also relates a narrative of the life of St. Herman. The **State Fair and Rodeo,** beginning in early September, includes crafts and livestock.

OUTDOORS

Kodiak Island is home to one of the largest commercial-fishing fleets in Alaska; the sheer number of fish in the island's rivers and surrounding waters can leave you reeling. The 100-mi. road system permits access to a number of productive **salmon streams.** Right in Kodiak, surfcasting into Mill Bay around high tide often yields a pink or silver salmon. **Red salmon,** which run from early June to the beginning of August, appear in the Buskin and Pasagshak Rivers along the road system. **Pink salmon** run up the Buskin, Russian, American, and Olds Rivers in astounding numbers from July 20 to August 20. Better-tasting but not so numerous **silver salmon** run up the same rivers from about August 20 into September. **Dolly varden,** the most frequently hooked fish on Kodiak, may be taken year-round from the Pasagshak and Buskin Rivers.

On a clear day **hikers** can obtain a commanding view stretching from the Kenai Peninsula to the Aleutian Peninsula atop **Barometer Mountain.** To reach the trailhead, take the first right past the end of the airport runway on the way out of town. After passing through thick alders, the trail climbs steadily and steeply along a grassy ridge marked by several false peaks before arriving at the summit. Most hikers require about two hours to reach the top, and they usually descend in half that time. The trail up **Pyramid Mountain,** beginning from the parking lot at the pass on Anton Larsen Bay Rd., is another popular hike near town.

A large **bison herd** roams a private ranch at the end of Rezanof Hwy. at the southeast tip of Kodiak near Ugak Island. The animals were transplanted to Kodiak and have managed to defend themselves against marauding brown bears; imported cattle herds have not fared so well.

If you have an automobile, the 42-mi. coastal drive to Chiniak offers the chance to see beautiful seascapes with small coastal islands muted in fog (as well as a multitude of mufflers lying along the jarringly rough road). If the potholes haven't rearranged your dental work, stop in for a deluxe high-rise hamburger with fries ($5) at the **Road's End Restaurant and Bar** in Chiniak. They also serve a generous grilled-cheese sandwich with fries ($3.50) and premier pies ($3.50 per slice) of many kinds (open Tues.-Thurs. 11am-9pm, Fri.-Sun. 11am-10pm).

Shuyak Island State Park, an undeveloped area with ample hunting, fishing, and kayaking, lies 54 mi. north of Kodiak. The park rents four **cabins,** each with room for two to six people ($50 per night; in winter $30 per night). Reserve in advance at the Division of Parks and Outdoor Recreation, SR Box 3800, Kodiak (486-6339), or call for more information.

■ Kodiak National Wildlife Refuge

The Wildlife Refuge, on the western half of Kodiak Island, was inaugurated in 1941 and has grown to nearly two million acres. An estimated 2600 Kodiak bears live on the island along with a variety of other mammals and several hundred bald eagles. The bears are most commonly seen in July and August during their fishing frenzy. They hibernate from December to April, bearing cubs in February and March. Though the bears are half-vegetarian and usually avoid contact with humans, be careful: Kodiaks are the largest and most powerful carnivores in North America, and they can—and do—kill humans. Because of the bears' relatively small numbers, hunters are permitted to kill only one Kodiak apiece every four years.

Other mammals native to the area are red foxes, land otters, weasels, tundra moles, and little brown bats. Deer, snowshoe hares, beavers, muskrats, Dall sheep, mountain goats, and red squirrels have been transplanted from other parts of the state to Kodiak. The refuge's 800-mi. coastline is home to thousands of waterfowl and about 20 seabird species. Off the coast, whales, porpoises, seals, sea otters, and sea lions frolic.

Because it was established for the enjoyment of animals rather than humans, the refuge remains undeveloped and expensive to access. For the same reason, those intrepid (or monied) few who visit the refuge will be rewarded by one of the world's most pristine wilderness experiences. About the only affordable way to access the refuge is to join a scheduled **Mark Air** (487-9798) mail run to any of the several small villages scattered throughout the wilderness. Although stopovers (possible for an extra fee) are brief, the aerial view of the island is stunning. The flights to Karluk and Larsen Bay and to Old Harbor are two of the best. Both routes are flown frequently and the passenger fare is $99. Call for schedules and information.

A **float plane** can be chartered from any of the dozen companies in Kodiak for about $400 an hour; the planes usually carry five passengers with gear. To protect visitors from the elements and the bears, the refuge has 10 **cabins** (all accessible by float plane) in various locations for $10 per night (7-night max. stay). Cabins are frequently available if guests are prepared to visit remote sights for short blocks of time. For information about the park as well as cabin reservations, contact the **Kodiak National Wildlife Refuge Managers,** 1390 Buskin River Rd., Kodiak 99615 (487-2600). If you're in Kodiak, drop by the **U.S. Fish and Wildlife Headquarters and Visitor Center** (see Kodiak: Practical Information).

PRINCE WILLIAM SOUND

■■■ WHITTIER

Whittier, a well-placed rest-stop hedged in on all sides by massive glaciers and waterfalls, is a town of beauty as well as of convenience. Whittier is named for one of the nearby glaciers, which, in turn, was named after the poet John Greenleaf Whittier. Native and Russian fur traders bivouacked here before crossing the 13-mi.-long isthmus known as the Portage Pass, and in the late 19th and early 20th centuries, this pass was heavily traveled by throngs of gold seekers and intrepid mail carriers. However, it wasn't until World War II—when the U.S. Army drilled a railroad tunnel connecting the Sound's ice-free seaport with the Alaska Railroad—that Whittier became a permanent community. Today, with the flotilla of boats in the harbor outnumbering the 300 residents in the town, Whittier serves as a staging ground for pleasureseekers from Anchorage and beyond.

According to the town's advertising slogan, Whittier is "unique even to Alaska," and the claim is undeniably accurate. Social life—as well as everything else in this condensed town—rallies around the 14-story **Begich Towers,** the refurbished army officers' quarters where a hive-like 85% of the town's residents now live. Although most people see Whittier only in passing (and without a doctor or a bank the town isn't prepared for much more) this is a highly unusual town well worth exploring on a sunny day.

PRACTICAL INFORMATION AND ORIENTATION

Visitors Center, P.O. Box 604 (472-2379), located in the center of town, slyly camouflaged in a refurbished railroad car next to the railroad tracks. Information on hiking, boating, camping, and fishing. Open daily 11am-6pm.

Harbormaster Office: P.O. Box 608 (472-2320 or 472-2330), in small boat harbor. **Showers** available—$3 for a 17½-min. pressure-wash. Open 24 hr.; in winter daily 8am-midnight.

Alaska Railroad, 265-2494 for an operator, 265-2607 for a recording. 6 runs between Portage and Whittier daily in summer ($13, $16 round-trip).

Buses: Caribou Express (278-5776) leaves Portage for Anchorage twice daily in summer ($20).

Alaska Marine Highway (272-4482), located ½ mi. east of town, next to the small boat harbor. To: Valdez ($56), Cordova ($34 direct, $56 via Columbia Glacier or Valdez).

Fishing License: at the **Harbor Store** near the Visitors Center. Open Mon.-Thurs. and Sun. 9am-7:30pm, Fri.-Sat. 9am-9pm.

Kayak Rental: Prince William Sound Kayak Center (562-2866 or 472-2452), at Billings and Glacier St. Single boats $35 per day, doubles $60 per day. Call ahead and leave a message to arrange a rental.

Library: 2nd floor of the Begich Towers. Open Tues. 10am-noon and 2-5pm, Wed.-Thurs. 2-5pm and 7-9pm, Sat. 11am-4pm.

Laundromat: Anchor Inn (472-2354), on Whittier St. Wash $1.25, 10 min. dry 25¢. Also in the **Begich Towers.** Wash $1.50, dry 25¢. Open daily 10am-midnight.

Medical Services: There are trained EMTs in Whittier, but no doctors and no clinic. Over-the-counter pharmaceuticals available at the **Anchor Inn Grocery** (472-2354).

Emergency: 911.**Police:** 472-2340.

Post Office: On 1st floor of Begich Towers. Open Mon., Wed., Fri. 11:30am-5:30pm. **General Delivery ZIP Code:** 99693.

Area Code: 907.

Whittier, Portage, Billing's, and Maynard Glaciers surround the town of Whittier, which lies 63 mi. southeast of Anchorage and 105 mi. west of Valdez. As with the other towns in the Sound, Whittier is no stranger to rain. More than 15 ft. drips on this soggy hamlet each year.

ACCOMMODATIONS AND CAMPING

There is only one public campground in Whittier, the **Whittier Camp Grounds,** located behind Begich Towers next to the Whittier Glacier Falls. It has limited facilities, including water and toilets. Don't keep any food in your tent, however—the summer bear trail passes right through camp. Take showers at the Harbormaster Office (see Practical Information). Sites are $5 on the honor box system, and there is no maximum stay.

There are two hotels in Whittier. The **Sportsman Inn** (472-2352), on Eastern Ave. near the Army Dock, has clean, comfortable rooms which are likely to be more expensive than the Anchor Inn. The **Anchor Inn** (472-2354) has spiffy, newly remodeled rooms (singles $52 and doubles $57, both with baths).

The lone B&B in Whittier offers you a chance to sleep in the honeycombs of Begich Towers. The **Whittier B&B** (472-2396) has singles for $35 and doubles for $50.

FOOD

Whittier's several restaurants offer standard Alaskan fare at standard Alaskan prices. The **Anchor Inn** (472-2354) is the best place to buy groceries, but beware: a box of cereal can run a nightmarish $6.35! (open daily 8am-10pm, Wed.-Sun. 8am-10pm).

Hobo Bay Trading Company (472-2374), in Harbor Area. Babs, the proprietor and "pro-piemaker," presides over a political salon that doubles as a first-rate short-order restaurant. Come in to eavesdrop on the spirited political banter, and try a hearty taco ($2) or a piece of fresh baked pie ($2.50). The halibut fish and chips perfects this culinary genre ($7.50).

Irma's Outpost (472-2461), in the Triangle. Jumbo sandwiches ($6). Scrumptious muffins and pie slices ($2.50). Also the only liquor store in town, with—by Alaskan standards—surprisingly cheap booze. Open daily 8am-10pm.

Anchor Inn (472-2354), on Whittier St. Seafood-loaded menu includes salmon burger, fries, and coffee ($5.75). Stack of pancakes ($4.50). Open 6am-midnight.

Cafe Orca & Bakery (472-2496), in the Triangle, by the ferry. Serves a respectable bagel for this latitude—with Arctic Lox ($3) cheap! Tasty sandwiches $5.50-6.75. And, of course, espresso ($1.25)—no Alaskan town's complete without it—along with espresso coffee cake ($1.50). Open Wed-Sun. 10:30am-6:30pm.

SIGHTS

The Begich Towers also house the **Whittier Museum,** which contains rare shellfish specimens, 1964 earthquake memorabilia, and even an orca's skull (open daily in summer 1-5pm). At the top of the Towers is a **sun room,** with an outstanding view of the surrounding glaciers and waterfalls, although visitors are not permitted above the second floor without an accompanying resident. The huge, bare concrete Soviet-style building on the Whittier skyline is the **Buckner Building,** an army complex that once housed 1,000 people along with a bowling alley and jail. The building is now decrepit and unsafe to enter. At night, residents head to Whittier's bar: the multi-faceted **Anchor Inn** (see Food) has live rock'n'roll from 9pm-5am.

Hiking opportunities abound; the best day hike climbs the 4½-mi. **Portage Pass Trail** to the stunning Portage Glacier overlook. To reach the trailhead, take W. Camp Rd. out of town along the railroad tracks and cross the tracks towards the airstrip; the trail forks off to the left.

Tour boats operate daily from Whittier. **Phillips' Cruises and Tours** (800-544-0529 or 276-8023) conducts a popular cruise to 26 glaciers ($120 from Whittier, $160 including bus from Anchorage which leaves from the **Captain Cook Inn** daily at 8:30am). **Major Marine Charters** (274-7300) runs a half-day cruise ($89 per person) which includes an all-you-can-eat salmon bake. **Honey Charters** (344-3340) hires out boats for personalized tours ($77 per person for 3-hr. cruise; $165 per person for an 8- to 11-hr. cruise). A nice daytrip is a cruise up the nearby **College Fjord** to see the **Harvard** and **Yale Glaciers.** The Harvard Glacier is the bigger of the two.

■■■ VALDEZ

Evidence of the lingering Spanish influence in Alaska, Valdez was named by explorer Don Salvador Fidalgo after the Marine Minister for Spain, Valdes y Basan. Although not nearly as famous as the Klondike Trail, it was from Valdez in 1897-98 that gold-seekers streamed into the Interior to follow the tortuous "all-American route" to the newly-tapped gold deposits (other overland routes passed mainly through Canada). Ironically, Valdez today has the converse distinction of being a terminus of wealth, rather than the start of the trail for goldpanners. The Trans-Alaska Pipeline deposits its "black gold" into waiting oil tankers in Valdez.

VALDEZ

Whether approached by land or by sea (or by pipeline), the journey into Valdez is unavoidably beautiful. The final 30 mi. of the Richardson Hwy. before it reaches town pass by the face of a glacier, through a canyon, and beside two high waterfalls. Coming into Valdez by boat, the trip across Prince William Sound leads past the **Columbia Glacier,** the second largest glacier to spill into the ocean in North America. Valdez itself (pop. 3500) has earned the nickname of "Little Switzerland," and indeed nearly every spot in this busy port affords a gorgeous alpine view. The only town on Prince William Sound with direct access by road, there is also scarcely a spot in Valdez without a prominent view of an RV park. Opponents of road-building projects in Cordova and Whittier often build their case around the example of camper-ridden Valdez.

The infamous Exxon *Valdez* oil spill of March 1989 despoiled the shores a few mi. away from Valdez, although you won't see much evidence of the disaster in the town itself. In fact, the mayor of Valdez appeared in a series of television commercials in 1991 to promote the (overestimated) success of Exxon's cleanup. To obtain the most thorough, impartial, and up-to-date information on the spill and the ongoing clean-up measures, contact **APLIC** (Alaska Public Lands Information Center) in Anchorage (see Anchorage Practical Information and Orientation).

PRACTICAL INFORMATION AND ORIENTATION

Visitors Information: Valdez Convention and Visitor Bureau, P.O. Box 1603 (800-874-2749 or 835-2984), at Fairbanks and Chenega St. Information on sights, accommodations, hiking, and camping. Shows movies about the devastating 1964 earthquake every hr. on the hr. daily 9am-7pm. Admission $2.50. Open daily 8am-8pm in summer, Mon.-Fri. 8:30am-5pm in winter. Free local phone. **Parks and Recreation Hotline:** 835-2555.

Job Service (835-4910), on Meals Ave., in the State Office Bldg. Info on working at the 3 canneries in Valdez. Open Mon.-Fri. 8am-noon and 1-4:30pm.

Fishing Information: Alaska Dept. of Fish and Game, 310 Egan Dr., (835-2802). Numerous canneries in Valdez attest to the abundance of fish in the Valdez Arm.

ATM Machine: First National Bank of Anchorage, 101 Egan Dr. **National Bank of Alaska,** 329 Egan Dr.

Telegrams: Western Union, at Eagle Quality Center. Open 7am-midnight.

Airport: Valdez Airport, 4 mi. out of town off Richardson Hwy. Serviced by **Mark Air** (800-478-0800) and **Alaska Airlines,** 800-426-0333. One-way to Anchorage $109, with 1-day advance purchase $70, 3-day $60, 21-day $50.

Buses: Caribou Express (278-5776) runs from Valdez to Anchorage on Wed., Fri., and Sun. at 3:20 pm ($75, bus leaves from the visitors center). **Alaskon Express** (800-544-2206) makes the same trip on Tues., Thurs., Fri., and Sun. ($89, leaves from the Westmark Hotel).

Alaska Marine Highway, P.O. Box 647 (835-4436), located in the City Dock at the end of Hazelet Ave. To: Whittier ($56), Cordova ($28), and Seward ($56). Whittier run makes a stop at Columbia Glacier.

Taxis: Valdez Yellow Cab, 835-2500. 4-mi. trip to airport will cost you $7, each additional person $1.

Car Rental: Valdez-U-Drive, P.O. Box 852 (835-4402), at the airport. $35 per day with 100 free mi., plus 25¢ per additional mi. **Avis** (800-835-4774), also at the airport. $52 per day, with unlimited mileage.

Camping Supplies: The Prospector, beside the Post Office on Galena Dr. One of the best places in the state. Immense supply of clothing, shoes, tarps, freeze-dried food, and fishing tackle. Open Mon.-Sat. 8am-10pm, Sun. 9am-6pm.

Kayak Rental: Keystone Raft and Kayak Adventure, P.O. Box 1486 (835-2606), at Pioneer and Hazelet. Valdez is within easy reach of superb whitewater, with rapids ranging from class II to IV. 1-hr. trip $30, daytrip $65. Make reservations at least 1 day in advance. **Anady Adventures** (835-2814), on South Harbor Dr. Guided daytrips begin at $135. Single kayak $45 per day. Damage deposit ($200-300) and a 2-hr. orientation class ($15) required.

Library: 200 Fairbanks Dr. Open Mon. 10am-6pm, Tues.-Thurs. 10am-8pm, Fri. 10am-6pm, Sat. noon-6pm.

Laundromat: Like Home Laundromat, 110 Egan (835-2913). Wash $1.50, 7 min. dry 25¢. Open 8am-10pm daily.

Public Showers: $3 for 10 min. at the Harbormaster, or you can cough up another $1 and go to **Bear Paw RV Park** (see Accommodations and Camping). You'll get a spotlessly clean private bathroom with sink, etc., plus all the time you want.

Weather: 766-2491. Live from the National Weather Service, Valdez.

Crisis Line: 835-2999. 24 hr.

Pharmacy: Valdez Drug and Photo, 321 Fairbanks Dr. (835-4956). Open Mon.-Fri. 9am-9pm, Sat. 9am-6pm, Sun. noon-5pm.

Hospital: Valdez Community Hospital, 911 Meals Ave. (835-2249).

Emergency/Ambulance: 911. **Police:** 835-4560.

Post Office: 835-4449, at Galena St. and Tatitlek St. Open Mon.-Fri. 9am-5pm, Sat. 10am-noon. **General Delivery ZIP Code:** 99686.

Area Code: 907.

Valdez resides 304 mi. east of Anchorage at the head of the Valdez Arm, in the northeast corner of Prince William Sound. From Valdez, the spectacular **Richardson Hwy.** runs north to Glennallen, where it intercepts the Glenn Hwy. to Anchorage.

CAMPING AND ACCOMMODATIONS

The **South Harbor Dr. Campground,** home to many of Valdez's transient cannery workers, is also the cheapest place for transient budget travelers. The Visitors Bureau (see Practical Information) also lists over 70 bed and breakfasts, which generally charge about $65 for singles and $75 for doubles (about $30 less than a hotel room). The **free reservation center** (835-4988) for Valdez will hook you up with bed and breakfasts, glacier tours, rafting trips, helicopter tours, etc.—"One call does it all."

South Harbor Drive Campground (835-2531), on S. Harbor Dr. (surprise), overlooking the small boat harbor. This campground occupies a prime location on a bluff overlooking town but the hard gravel surface and late-night expletives exchanged between the cannery workers who occupy most of the sites may sour your sleep. 50 sites with wooden tent platforms, water, and pit toilets. Sites $5, collected in an honor box.

Valdez Glacier Campground (835-2531), located 5½ mi. east of town on the Richardson Hwy., 1½ mi. past the airport. Look for small sign on left. 110 campsites, first-come, first-served. Amazing view of the Valdez glacier. On the site of Old Valdez, destroyed in the 1964 earthquake, this campground is difficult to reach without a car or bicycle, although rides are reportedly easy to find given the steady stream of traffic to and from the airport. As always, it could be dangerous to accept them. *Let's Go* does not recommend hitchhiking. Be extra careful storing food here; as bounteous signs warn, it's a favorite bear hangout. Water and pit toilets. 14-day max. stay. Sites $7.

Bear Paw Camper Park, P.O. Box 93 (835-2530), in the small boat harbor downtown. RV sites $12, with hookups $18. A separate colony of tentsites covers a small hill, $12 for 1 person, $2.50 per additional person. Free showers for guests.

Sea Otter RV Park, P.O. Box 947 (835-2787), on S. Harbor Dr. 200 sites. Free showers for guests. Full hookups $15, with water and electricity only $12. Tentsites $10.

Gussie's Bed and Breakfast, 354 Lowe St., ½ mi. from downtown. Located in a quiet residential neighborhood. Clean comfortable rooms. Single with shared bath $55. Double with shared bath $60. And of course, Gussie the dog comes at no extra charge.

FOOD

The bustling-est town on Prince William Sound, Valdez supports a variety of restaurants. For those who must stick to tight budgets, there's always the **Eagle Quality**

Center (835-2100) at Meals and Pioneer (open 24 hr.), or the **Red Apple Market** (835-4496) on Egan, which has a deli where a 3-piece chicken dinner with Jo-Jo's is $4 (open daily 6am-midnight). If you're staying at the Valdez Glacier Campground, **Top Dog** (835-2001), at the airport, serves up inexpensive chili and assorted fast-food items.

Oscar's (835-4700), on N.Harbor Dr., next to Bear Paw RV. The best bet for break-fast in town, and the locals know it. Stack of pancakes ($4). Sausage, hashbrowns, 2 eggs, biscuits and gravy ($7). Homemade chowder in a sourdough bread bowl ($3.75). Open daily 6am-midnight.

Mike's Palace (also called the Pizza Palace), 201 N. Harbor Dr. Locals and tourists alike line up along the sidewalk here for the great Italian-Mexican-American fare. Large pizza ($14). You know you're in Alaska when the "low-calorie plate" con-sists of cottage cheese, fruit, and a beef patty for $6. Baklava ($2.75).

Valdez Christian Book & Coffee Shop (835-5881), on Pioneer Dr. An overwarm and pungent eatery. Bottomless bowl of soup and never-ending bread ($4).

Alaska Halibut House (835-2788), at Meals Ave. and Pioneer Dr. A small halibut basket with fries with emphasis on the fries ($5.75). Ketchup pumps, plastic trays, and his-and-hers halibuts on the restroom doors. Open daily 10am-11pm.

A Rogue's Garden & Wildflower Cafe, 328 Egan (835-5580). A small selection of natural foods. Healthy sandwiches on homemade bread with chips ($6.25). Open Mon.-Fri. 10am-5pm, Sat. 11am-4pm. Sandwiches served 11am-2pm.

Fu Kung, 203 Kobuk St. (835-5255), in the Quonset Hut. Tasty Chinese dinners $8.50-12. Lunch specials with rice, soup, and appetizer from $6.25. Open Mon.-Sat. 11am-11pm, Sun. 5-11pm.

No Name Pizza (835-4419), on Egan Dr., next to the Like Home Laundromat. Pizza that would make Goldilocks smile—12 in. Mama ($12) and 16 in. Papa ($17), each with up to 3 toppings. The pizza bomb ($8.50) is "just right." Open daily 3pm-midnight.

SIGHTS AND SEASONAL EVENTS

After an 800-mi. journey from the fields of Prudhoe Bay, the **Trans-Alaska Pipeline** dumps its oil at Valdez. Located across the bay from town, the monolithic terminal spews millions of gallons of rich crude oil every day into the maws of awaiting tank-ers. **Alyeska** (835-2686) offers free two-hour tours that leave eight times per day from their visitors center at the airport. The tours strive to make Alyeska appear "environment-friendly." Nonetheless, even Greens and solar-energy proponents will be impressed by the company's descriptions of how the Play-Doh-like crude is trans-ported and processed. (Reservations required; see Practical Information about taxis from the airport).

If fish are more your style, the **Salmon Gulch Hatchery** (835-4874), on Dayville Rd. 14 mi. out of town, off the Richardson Hwy., offers guided tours (6 per day, $1). Half a mile outside of town on the Richardson Hwy., tour buses pull over at Cripple Creek where a strong run of silver salmon battle their way upstream in July.

In town, head to the **museum** (835-2764) on Egan Dr. Inside, you'll see Valdez's original 1907 Ahrens steam fire engine, and a North Pacific Fur Fish, a creature amazingly well-adapted to thrive in regions with cold waters and gullible tourists. Valdez is also home to **Prince William Sound Community College,** which features an absolutely stunning 30-ft. carved wooden head by renowned Native American sculptor Peter Toth, on the front lawn near the corner of Meals Ave. and Pioneer Dr.

In an attempt to spice up small-town life and milk tourists for all they're worth, Valdez created the **Gold Rush Days** celebration (slated for August 3-7 in 1994). The month-long town fund-raiser includes a fashion show, banquet, dance, and even an ugly vehicle contest. Look out for—hell, run after (if you're 21 plus and have dead-ened tastebuds)—the traveling jail, which picks up aimless tourists and makes them drink gallons of warm beer. If you'd rather pay to have your beer cold, head to the **Pipeline Club and Lounge,** 112 Egan Dr. (835-4332). Dance to live bands Tuesday through Saturday nights from 9:30pm to 1am. (Bar open Mon.-Thurs. and Sun.

10:30am-2am, Fri.-Sat. 10:30am-4am.) The **Glacier Bar,** 113 Fairbanks (835-4794), "rocks" to live rock 'n' roll Tuesday through Saturday 10pm to 3am.

OUTDOORS

For all its mountainous grandeur, Valdez has few developed hiking trails. A good place to begin is the 1.2-mi. **Mineral Creek,** just north of downtown, which follows a magnificent gorge through uninhabited backcountry (but look out for bears). The trail begins 8 mi. down a gravel road at the end of Mineral Creek Dr. and winds up at a turn-of-the-century gold mine. The 1.3-mi. **Solomon Gulch** trail starts 150 yd. northeast of the hatchery on Dayville Rd. near Valdez's hydro-electric plant (which, surprisingly, supplies 80% of the power for this oil-soaked region) and ends at breathtaking **Solomon Lake.** The **Goat Trail** follows an Indian footpath that was the only route from Valdez to the Interior prior to the opening of the Richardson Hwy. It begins near Mile 13½ of the highway, just past Horsetail Falls, and accompanies the Lowe River for 5 mi.

By boat, helicopter, or plane, you can investigate two of the Sound's most prized possessions: **Columbia** and **Shoup Glaciers. ERA Helicopter** (835-2595) will give you a one-hour tour of both ($155 per person). **Stan Stephens Charters** (800-478-1297 or 835-4731) offers a 5½-hour red-eye (7am) economy cruise to Columbia ($61.50 per person), while **Glacier Charters** (835-5141) offers a five-hour cruise ($55). For a *real* economy cruise, simply take the **Alaska Marine Hwy.** (see Practical Information) from Whittier to Valdez (or vice-versa). The *MV Bartlett* makes a brief 10- to 15-minute stop at Columbia and gets about as close as the other tours. The price ($58) is the same and you'll be getting somewhere as you sightsee.

Backcountry Connections (822-5292) now offers van service from Valdez to McCarthy on Monday and Wednesday at noon for $72. They also run from McCarthy to Valdez at 2pm on Friday. (See Wrangell-Saint Elias National Park for information on McCarthy.)

■■■ CORDOVA

A town more isolated today than it was 80 years ago, Cordova marks the convergence of several rich ecological systems—the Chugach National Forest, the Copper River delta, and the Pacific Ocean. It is the ocean that keeps this fishing town of 2500 afloat, where scarcely a single sail can be seen among the blocky seiners and gill-netters that crowd Cordova's harbor. Not fish, however, but copper originally placed Cordova on the map. With only horses and manual labor, the engineer Michael J. Heney (who had already made railroad history in constructing the White Pass and Yukon route) built the 200-mi. Copper River Railroad from Cordova to the Kennicott mines deep in the Wrangell Mountains. Three hundred million dollars worth of copper ore passed through Cordova from 1911 until the mine was exhausted in 1938. The railroad had fallen into disrepair even before the 1964 earthquake snapped its longest bridge, and a controversial plan to reopen the route as the Copper River Hwy. has many modern Cordovans preferring it left that way.

The town is within easy reach of Child's Glacier, one of the least visited and most spectacular sights in all of Alaska. Fortified by rugged mountains of volcanic rock and its salmon-filled seas, Cordova has been known to lure visiting nature-lovers and anglers—and never let them go. It is easily one of the most beautiful and welcoming places on the Prince William Sound.

PRACTICAL INFORMATION AND ORIENTATION

Visitors Information: Cordova Chamber of Commerce, P.O. Box 99, 622 1st St. (424-7260), next to the bank. Information on accommodations, transportation, and attractions. Open Tues.-Sat. 1-5pm. **USDA-Chugach National Forest District,** Cordova Ranger District, Box 280 (424-7661), on the 3rd floor at the building at 2nd between Browning and Adams. Excellent information on hiking trails and fishing. Also a good place to head for pamphlets when the Chamber is closed. Reserve any of the 18 **Forest Service cabins** here. Open Mon.-Fri. 8am-5pm.

Fishing Information: Alaska Dept. of Fish and Game, Box 669 (424-3212).

Airport: 13 mi. east of town on the Copper River Hwy. Serviced by **Alaska Airlines** (800-426-0333 or 424-3278) and **Mark Air** (800-478-0800 or 424-5982). One way to: Juneau ($176), Anchorage ($102, or $77 with 1-day advance purchase, $67 with 3-day advance, $52 with 21-day advance).

Alaska Marine Highway, P.O. Box 1689, Cordova 99574 (800-642-0066 or 424-7333), 1 mi. north of town on Ocean Dock Rd. One way to: Valdez ($28), Whittier ($56 via Valdez, $34 direct), Seward ($56), Kodiak ($96), and Homer ($136).

Taxis: A-Cab, 424-7131. **Harbor Cab Co.,** 424-7575. **Wild Hare Taxi,** 424-3939. All 24 hr. Rates start at $3 and go nowhere but up.

Car Rental: Imperial Car Rental (424-5982), at airport. $55 per day with unlimited mileage. With only 6 cars in stock, you should definitely call ahead. Must be over 25 with major credit card. **Reluctant Fisherman Inn** (424-3272). $50 per day, $55 per day for mini-van. 25¢ per mi.

Camping Equipment: Flinn's Clothing & Sporting Goods Store (424-3282), on 1st St. Open Mon.-Sat. 9am-6pm, Sun. 9am-1pm.

Laundromat: Club Speedwash (424-3201), in the Prince William Motel on Council Ave. Wash $2, 5-min. dry 25¢. Open Mon.-Sat. 8am-8pm, Sun. 9am-8pm.

Showers: at **Club Speedwash** (above), $2.50 plus 25¢ for every 5 min. Also at the **Harbormaster's,** $3 for 5 min. Tokens available Mon.-Fri. 8am-5pm.

Swimming: Cordova Pool (424-7000), by the Small Boat Harbor. Swim and shower, $4 for first ½ hr., $1 per additional ½ hr. Open Sun.-Thurs. 3-5pm and Fri.-Sat. 1-5pm. Also open Mon.-Sat. 7-9pm.

Pharmacy: Cordova Drug Co., P.O. Box 220, (424-3246), on 1st St. Open Mon.-Sat. 9:30am-6pm.

Hospital: Cordova Community Hospital (424-8000), on Chase St. off Copper River Hwy.

Ambulance: 424-6100.

Police: 424-6100.

Emergency: 911.

Post Office: at Council St. and Railroad Ave. (424-3564). Open Mon.-Fri. 10am-5:30pm, Sat. 10am-1pm. **General Delivery ZIP Code:** 99574.

Population: 2500 in city, 3500 in Copper River Delta area.

Area Code: 907.

Cordova is located on the east side of Prince William Sound on **Orca Inlet,** connected to the outside world only by boat or plane. It should be noted that the airline rates listed above for flying into Cordova from Juneau or Anchorage can, with advance purchase, be cheaper than taking a bus from Haines or Skagway to Valdez—and, needless to say, you'll have a much faster and more pleasant trip. West of town, the braided channels of the Copper River weave a wide delta where 20 million migrating shore birds pause to feed on their way to the Arctic.

ACCOMMODATIONS AND CAMPING

Cordovan accommodations reflect in many ways the lack of concern that residents have for the tourist trade; most of the hotels look like hell. If camping is your game, there is always **"Hippy Cove,"** a private (and extremely odd) place where you can crash for free. A municipal campground offers a more peaceful alternative, with showers, for $3. Unsanctioned tents often spring up near the reservoir at the top of a rocky trail off of Whiteshed Rd., and near the ski area behind town.

> **Hippy Cove,** ¾ mi. north of the ferry terminal on Orca Inlet Dr. With its own unique social life, Hippy Cove is guaranteed to keep you entertained. Most of its inhabitants are short-term cannery workers, although there are some lifers left over from the Psychedelic Era. There is also a woodstove **sauna,** where townspeople and Cove dwellers gleefully roast at temperatures up to 200° and then quench themselves in an icy stream-fed bath. The dress code suggests a birthday

suit. Hippy Cove is free (so is love) and has drinking water. Town officials discourage visiting and camping at Hippy Cove.

Odiak Camper Park (424-6200), 2 mi. outside of town on Whiteshed Rd. Tentsites (with water) by the water for $3, with a vehicle $10. Free showers for guests; pick up a token in town at City Hall. Open May-Sept.

Alaskan Hotel and Bar, P.O. Box 484 (424-3288), on 1st St. The only building on the street with a fresh coat of paint. Clean, simple rooms occupy the upper floors. However, rooms above the bar are a bit noisy at night. Singles $37, with bath $47. (And by the way, don't you wonder why their sign is upside down?)

Cordova House Hotel (424-3388), 1st St., adjacent to the Alaskan. Not the tightest ship, this is a true frontier hotel—nothing to warm the hearts of tourists, just basic shelter. Small, musty rooms. Bath and color TV. Singles and doubles $40.

Harborview Bed and Breakfast (424-5356), on Observation Ave. off 1st St. Nice room, private bath and a great view of the inlet. $50 with breakfast, $45 without. Also has referral for 2 other B&Bs.

FOOD

Restaurants in Cordova are fairly expensive, so get ready either to whip out a credit card or fire up a camp stove. Groceries can be bought at **Davis' Super Foods** on 1st (open Mon.-Sat. 8am-8pm, Sun.10am-4pm), or **A.C. Company** (424-7141) on Council St. next to the post office (open daily 5am-midnight).

Club Cafe (424-3405), on 1st St., behind the Club Bar. The angler's breakfast spot of choice. They gather around a single table in an ever-widening circle. "Hot and Hearty Breakfast Specials" include the pancake sandwich, 2 eggs, 2 pancakes, and 2 strips of bacon ($5.25). Burgers ($6.50-8) with potato salad and french fries. Open Mon.-Sat. 6am-9pm, Sun. 7am-5pm. Take-out window open Mon.-Sat. 6am-midnight, Sun. 7am-9pm.

OK Restaurant (424-3433), on 1st St. next to the Cordova Hotel. Wide-ranging Chinese/Korean/American menu with lunch specials starting at $7. Kim Chee with rice and soup ($9). Open daily 11:30am-midnight.

The Reluctant Fisherman's Restaurant, 407 Railroad Ave., near the harbor. A bright and cheery dining area with service to match. A full stack of pancakes "as light as the first blush of dawn" ($4). 2 eggs, 2 biscuits, and excellent gravy ($5.75). Cup of soup and half-sandwich ($5). Open daily 6:30am-9pm. The **Lounge,** next door, has drawn a crowd in previous summers with a $3.50 cheeseburger and fries special (with the purchase of a beverage; served 11:30am-6pm). Drop by to see if the madness continues.

Killer Whale Cafe (424-7733), on 1st St. It seems that every Alaskan town, no matter how tiny it is, has at least one earthy espresso-laden cafe; Cordova is no exception. Located in the back of the oh-so-groovy Orca Bookstore, the cafe serves killer sandwiches ($5.50-8), espresso (50¢), and cappuccino ($2). Open Mon.-Sat. 7:30am-4pm.

Alaskan Bakery and Deli (424-5698), on 1st St., catty-corner to the Alaskan Hotel. Great view of the harbor. Large pinwheel cinnamon roll ($1.50), decent donuts ($1). Half-sandwich and full bowl of soup ($5). Open Mon.-Fri. 8am-5pm.

Baja Taco (424-5599), in a red bus by the Small Boat Harbor. A rolling taco stand whose owner goes south of the border in winter for research and development. Breakfast burrito ($5.75), chicken burrito ($6.25). Open Mon.-Fri. 8am-4pm, Sat. 9am-4pm, Sun. 10am-4pm.

SIGHTS AND SEASONAL EVENTS

If it's raining (and since this area averages 200 in. of rain a year, it probably is), stop by the **museum,** in the same building as the library on 1st St. Inside the museum you'll find real iceworms (*Mesenchytraeus solifugus*) which live inside the glaciers. Bigger and more exciting is Prince Willie, an erratic leatherback turtle who strayed several thousand miles and wound up in a local fisherman's net (museum open Mon. and Thurs.-Sun. 1-5pm, Wed. 1-9pm).

For the past 31 years, Cordova residents have held an **Iceworm Festival** in order to honor the semi-legendary creature and relieve cabin fever. The celebrations break loose the first weekend in February (Feb. 4-6 in 1994) and include the parade of a 100-ft. iceworm propelled by Cordova's youngsters down frozen 1st Street. Like most coastal towns in Alaska, Cordova also hosts an annual **Salmon Derby** in late August. At other times of the year, locals seek solace from the rainy nights at the **Alaskan Hotel and Bar** (424-3288), which still houses the original oak barfront circa 1906 (open Mon.-Fri. 8am-2am, Sat.-Sun. 8am-4am). For music fans, most nights feature live blues and rock bands from 10pm 'til closing.

OUTDOORS

Childs Glacier is a rare gem in Alaska's wealth of treasures—an icefield that is both as breathtaking as Glacier Bay on the Panhandle and as accessible as Mendenhall near Juneau. Under the heat of the summer sun, the glacier calves ten-story chunks of ice which fall·hundreds of feet before crashing into the Copper River's deep silty water. The largest ice falls are capable of sending 20-ft. waves washing over the observation area on the opposite bank of the river, ¼ mi. from the glacier. Broken trees and boulders strewn throughout the woods are evidence of the awesome power of this water. Although falls of this size might happen only once a season (if at all), they are unpredictable events and—as several alarming signs suggest—viewers should literally be prepared to run. Another set of signs warns of prohibitions against harvesting the salmon tossed into the woods by the waves. They have been left high and dry in the parking lot. The Childs Glacier provides an incredible chance to see geological change occurring in human time. If you come to Cordova and don't see this glacier, you are simply missing the point of traveling to Alaska.

Childs is located 50 mi. north of Cordova along a rough gravel road optimistically called the **Copper River Hwy.** If you don't have your own transportation, there are several ways to get to the glacier. Groups should try to rent one of **Imperial Car Rentals'** six cars (see Practical Information), then pack a picnic lunch and make a day of it. Travelers have been known to hitchhike—and get stranded, since Childs is not (yet) a major tourist attraction. If you're traveling alone or can't get a rental car, go with **Footloose Tours** (424-5356), based in Cordova, which offers a free ride to town and complimentary refreshments.The tour lasts seven hours (noon-7pm) and includes a delicious lunch spread during the three-hour stopover at Childs. The standard price is $35, but if you're in a big group you might be able to secure a lower rate.

While you're at the glacier you might also want to explore the **Million Dollar Bridge,** only a few hundred yards from the glacier viewing area. Built in 1910 by Michael J. Heney, the bridge was considered an engineering marvel due to its placement between two active glaciers. (One has retreated; Childs, on the other hand, is now less than ½ mi. away.) The structure was heavily damaged in the 1964 earthquake and a primitive patch job keeps it standing today; you can drive across the entire span, but it is not recommended.

Closer to town along the Copper River Hwy. is the vast expanse of the **Copper River Delta,** a preserve which covers an area of over 700,000 acres. **Fishing** here is superb as all five species of Pacific Salmon—king, silver, red, chum, and pink—spawn seasonally in the Copper River. The Delta swarms with bears, moose, foxes, wolves, coyotes, eagles, and even sea otters.

Hiking in the Delta is often wet, tough work, but the neighboring **Chugach Mountains** provide dry trails and excellent climbing opportunities. An easy hike from town is the 2.4-mi. **Crater Lake Trail,** which can be reached via Power Creek Rd., 1½ mi. north of Cordova. From Crater Lake cradled high in an alpine bowl, there are excellent views out across the sound, delta, and mountains. For a more strenuous and increasingly scenic hike, continue along a 5½-mi. ridge (occasionally occupied by mountain goats) to connect with the **Power Creek Trail.** The ridge-route meets the Power Creek Trail midway on its 4.2-mi. ascent to a **Forest Service**

cabin, the only one of seven in the Cordova area easily accessible by foot. The Power Creek Trail terminates on Power Creek Rd., 5 mi. from town. The Crater Lake Trail with the Power Creek connection is a 13-mi. hike. Other, shorter trails branch off the Copper River Hwy.; check with the USDA Forest Service (see Practical Information) for an excellent pamphlet on hiking around Cordova.

■■■ WRANGELL-SAINT ELIAS NATIONAL PARK

Wrangell-St. Elias National Park and Preserve is Alaska's best-kept secret. The largest national park in the U.S., it could contain more than 14 Yosemites within its boundaries. Four major mountain ranges converse within the park: the Wrangells, St. Elias Mountains, Chugach Mountains, and the Alaska Range. Nine peaks tower at more than 14,000 ft. within the park, including the second highest mountain in the U.S. (18,008-ft. **Mt. St. Elias**). The heights are enveloped with eternal snow and ice; the Basley Icefield is the largest non-polar icefield in North America and the Malaspina Glacier, a piedmont glacier near the coast, is larger than the state of Rhode Island. Mountain sheep populate the jagged slopes within the park and moose and bear are commonly sighted in the lower elevations.

The park is located in the southeast corner of Alaska's mainland and is bounded by the Copper River to the west and the Alaskan boundary to the east. Kluane National Park in the Yukon lies adjacent to the east and the two parks together are designated a World Heritage Site. Park access is through two roads: the **McCarthy Road** which enters the heart of the park and the **Nabesna Road,** which enters from the northern park boundaries and is frequently washed out. Home to Alaska's grandest, most rugged, and wildest wilderness, the majority of tourists remain ignorant of its very existence: fewer than 45,000 people visited the park in 1992 (compared to the 600,000 in Denali). If you have any time at *all* to spend in Alaska, come *here*, although the condition of the McCarthy Rd. is a deciding factor in your ability to get here, so be sure to check ahead.

The **visitors center** (822-5234) can be found 1 mi. off the Richardson Highway on the side road towards **Copper Center.** (Open in summer daily 8am-6pm, in winter Mon.-Fri. 8am-5pm.) Informed rangers will give you the low-down on all the to-dos (and to-sees) in the park. There are also **ranger stations** in **Chitina** (CHIT-na; 823-2205, open Fri.-Sun. 9am-6pm) and in **Slana** on the northern park boundary (822-5238, open daily 8am-5pm).

■ From the Perimeter into McCarthy

Most visitors travel to **McCarthy,** a small town of fewer than 50 permanent residents smack-dab in the middle of the park. The **Edgerton Highway** leaves the Richardson Highway 33 mi. south of Glennallen and heads east for about 34 mi. to the town of **Chitina.** There is a gift shop and grocery store here, and this is the last place to buy groceries (there's no store in McCarthy). On a clear day along the Edgerton Hwy., you can look north to see 12,010-ft. Mt. Drum, 16,237-ft. Mt. Sanford (Alaska's fifth-highest), and 14,113-ft. Mt. Wrangell (Alaska's tallest active volcano). Steam can be seen rising from the flat summit of Mt. Wrangell on exceptionally clear days.

From Chitina, the **McCarthy Road** follows the old roadbed of the **Copper River and Northwestern Railway** for 58 mi. to the Kennicott River. This road is arguably the roughest state road in Alaska (Dalton Hwy. included). Severe washboard, potholes, and the occasional railroad spike in the road make this a two- to three-hour one-way trip (bring a spare tire). Because of trees and brush, the drive is not particularly scenic, although the 525-ft. long **Kuskulana Bridge** (a former railroad trestle) at Mile 17 passes 238 ft. above the underlying Kuskulana River and was justifiably called the greatest thrill of the McCarthy Road before it was upgraded and guard rails were added in 1990. The road terminates on the western edge of the Kennicott

River, a silt-laden river originating within the Kennicott Glacier. There are two parking lots here, and it is recommended that visitors park in the upper lot as sudden glacial releases of water can raise the river several feet in a matter of minutes, submerging the lower lot. Be especially wary in late July and early August. The only way across the river is by a hand-operated **tram** (a metal "cart" with two seats, running on a cable). It is far easier to have somebody pull you across than to do it yourself, so return the favor if somebody helps you out. Just riding the tram over the roaring river is almost worth the drive out here. McCarthy is an easy ½-mi. walk from the opposite side of the river.

In the early 1900s, the richest copper ore ever discovered was found in the nearby mountain ridge on the east side of the Kennicott Glacier. The ore averaged a 12.79% copper content but ranged as high as 70% pure copper (today's mined ore averages only around 2% copper). The find attracted Stephen Birch, a young mining engineer, who gained backing from men such as the Guggenheim brothers and J.P. Morgan. In 1906, the Kennecott Copper Corporation was formed. (Misspelled, the company and mine's name remained Kennecott while the town and glacier are named Kennicott.) To transport the ore, the Copper River and Northwest Railway was constructed between 1908-1911. The CR&NW (jokingly called "Can't Run and Never Will") did run for 196 mi. from the Kennecott mines to the warm-water port of Cordova. A company town with a reputation for being very proper and maintaining strict conduct rules, **Kennicott** was home base for the mining operations until 1938, when falling copper prices forced the mine to shut down. The last train left in November of 1938, after having transported more than $200 million worth of copper ore during its 27-year life-span. Today, Kennicott remains remarkably intact, and has earned the name of "American's largest ghost town."

■ McCarthy

McCarthy, 5 mi. south of Kennicott, developed originally for miners' recreation. Both alcohol and women, prohibited in Kennicott by the male powers-that-were, made the town more attractive to male miners. Today, McCarthy clusters along a few mainly nameless streets.

Practical Information Walking from the river, the first building encountered houses the rather unimpressive **McCarthy-Kennecott Historical Museum** which has artifacts and documents from the mining days (open daily 8am-6pm). This is a good place to get general info about the area and pick up a walking tour of Kennicott and McCarthy ($1 donation).

Getting to McCarthy isn't too difficult. Drive on your own if you want to test your car's suspension. **Backcountry Connections** (822-5292) will take you aboard their roomy, comfortable vans replete with friendly and knowledgeable drivers. One-way from Glennallen is $55, from Chitina $35. Vans go every day of the week except Tuesday, and the company prides itself as "the independent traveler's touring service." They also offer van service from Valdez to McCarthy on Monday and Wednesday at noon for $72. They make the return trip at 2pm on Friday. **Wrangell Mountain Air** (see below in the Outdoors section) flies here daily from Chitina for those who'd rather not tackle the highway ($60 each way). Regular traffic makes hitchhiking a possibility (although *Let's Go* does not recommend it).

No **phones** in McCarthy—everybody is connected via the "bush phone" (a CB system) and most businesses have "phone bases" elsewhere. The McCarthy Lodge has **showers** for $5. There is no **post office.** (Local mail is flown in weekly.)

Accommodations, Camping and Food McCarthy Lodge (333-5402) in downtown McCarthy has rooms from $95 and the **Kennicott Glacier Lodge** (258-2350) in Kennicott has rooms from $109, but **camping** is free on the west side of the Kennicott River (no water, pit toilets). Because almost all of the land around McCarthy and Kennicott is privately owned and local drinking water comes from nearby creeks, camping is prohibited in all areas on the eastern side of the Kennicott River, with the exception of land north of Kennicott. Keep it clean!

A **cafe** adjacent to the Historical Museum (see above) purveys monster muffins for $1.25 (open daily 8am-6pm). The town has no general store, though the **Nugget Gift Shop** has some snacks and fruit (open daily 9am-12:30pm and 3-8pm). The **McCarthy Lodge** (see above) serves an affordable breakfast ($5-8), and enormous "McCarthy burgers" for lunch ($9). Dinner is more expensive ($14-17). Rumor has it that a pizzeria is soon to open in town, which will hopefully make its own dough rather than taking most of yours.

■ Outdoors in the Park

If you go **flightseeing** anywhere in Alaska, this is the place to do it. Because of the close proximity of 16,390-ft. Mt. Blackburn and the spectacular glaciers, a short 35-minute flight offers amazing views of even more incredible scenery. **Wrangell Mountain Air** (800-478-1160 for reservations), based in downtown McCarthy, offers the best deals. A 35-minute flight takes you up and over Kennicott and the amazing icefalls of the Kennicott and Root Glaciers ($40). A 50-minute trip will take you up the narrow Chitistone Canyon to view the thundering Chitistone Falls and over 15 glaciers and five mountain peaks ($55). You'll fly completely around majestic Mt. Blackburn in a 70-minute flight ($70) or fly out to see 18,000-ft. Mt. St. Elias and 19,800-ft. Mt. Cogan in a longer 90-minute flight ($100). There is a three-person minimum on all flights. **McCarthy Air,** also in McCarthy, offers similar flights and rates.

St. Elias Alpine Guides (277-6867) organizes numerous day trips (a ½-day glacier walk costs $55) but their coolest trip is a two-week "First Ascents" expedition whereby you can climb a peak that has *never* been scaled before by human being. (not for the budget traveler, though; costs $2500). You can rent bikes here to explore some of the old, obscure roads that are everywhere around town ($25 per day, ½-day $15). **Copper Oar** (522-1670), located at the end of the McCarthy Rd., offers a two-hour whitewater trip down the Kennicott River for $40. Get wet! For those on a serious shoe-string, just walking around McCarthy and Kennicott is plenty interesting, as many original buildings remain in both towns, and Kennicott is nearly intact. A **shuttle bus** runs out to Kennicott from McCarthy on a fairly regular schedule ($8 round-trip). It's a 5-mi. hike between the two towns.

Most **hikers and trekkers** use the McCarthy Road or McCarthy as a diving board. The park maintains no trails, but miners and other travelers from decades past have established various routes and obscure roads that follow the more exciting pathways. The most common route, a hike out past Kennicott to the Root Glacier, takes from one to three days for the 16-mi. round-trip and follows road-bed and glacial moraine with three moderate stream crossings. A hike to **Dixie Pass** has the advantage of easy accessibility (it starts from Mile 13 of the McCarthy Road) and hikers should allow three to four days for the 24-mi. round-trip. Those with a little more money and a thirst for real adventure should try the **Goat Trail.** The trail is a 25-mi. one-way trek from Lower Skolai Lake to Glacier Creek and traverses the ridge high above **Chitistone Canyon and Falls,** one of the park's more exciting features. Access is only by air taxi. Wrangell Mountain Air (see above) offers the best service. Allow between $150-200 per person for the drop-off and pick-up. Though only 25 mi., the extremely rugged terrain and numerous stream crossings make this a four- to eight-day trek for experienced hikers only. For any overnight trip, the park service requests a written itinerary (though it's not required, it's in your own best interest since you could get stuck out there). This is bear country, so be aware of the precautions necessary to reduce risk. (See Bear Necessities in the Essentials: Camping & the Outdoors section at the beginning of the book.) Make sure to have extra food, warm clothing, and know what you're doing (especially in stream crossings). And travel with someone, so you can make it back and share the memories.

Southeastern Alaska (The Panhandle)

Southeastern Alaska embraces the waters of the Inside Passage, spanning 500 mi. north from the breathtaking Misty Fjords National Monument up past Juneau to the city of Skagway at the foot of the Chilkoot Trail. This network of islands, inlets, and saltwater fjords hemmed in by mountains is distinguished by temperate rain-forest conditions, 60-odd major glaciers, and 15,000 bald eagles.

While the communities of Interior and Southcentral Alaska have experienced urban sprawl (by Alaskan standards), the towns in the southeast cling to the coast. Gold Rush days haunt such towns as Juneau, others like Sitka hearken back to the era of the Russian occupation, and throughout the region the native Tlingit (KLING-kit) and Haida (HI-duh) tribes attempt to preserve and persevere.

The Alaskan Marine Highway system provides the cheapest, most exciting way to explore the Inside Passage. In order to avoid the high price of accommodations in towns without hostels, plan your ferry trip at night so that you can sleep on deck.

SOUTHERN PANHANDLE

■■■ KETCHIKAN

"People don't tan in Ketchikan," according to a local proverb, "they rust." If the 14,600 locals didn't learn to ignore the rain in this fishing and lumber town, they would scarcely step outside. Fourteen feet of rain per year explain the ubiquitous awnings projecting over the streets of Alaska's southernmost and fourth-largest city. Cradled at the base of Deer Mountain, Ketchikan is also the first stopping point in Alaska for northbound cruise ships and ferries, which disgorge loads of tourists and dump hordes of students in search of the big summer bucks offered at the canneries. If you're one of those would-be fish slimers, be forewarned that jobs in Ketchikan are catch-as-catch-can: plan your arrival cautiously to within one week before each major fishing season. (For example, salmon usually start running the first week of July.) If you are serious about getting employment, it's also worth contacting the Alaska Employment Service upon arrival (see Practical Information), even though this is no substitute for trekking from door to cannery door. In fact, those who bypass the employment center and hit the canneries directly have had the best luck in recent years. Leave yourself time to find scarce apartment space, or prepare for the deluge with a hammock and a plastic tarp or a good tent and a few wooden pallets. Most campgrounds set weekly limits, and the youth hostel will only guarantee you four nights out of the rain. Many backpackers risk the wrath of the Ketchikan police by illegally camping in the state forest north of town, where they are largely undisturbed. However, getting rousted from your campsite is not an impossibility.

Many of the boats and float planes continually buzzing through Ketchikan's busy harbor travel to nearby Misty Fjords National Monument. Only 20 mi. from Ketchikan at its nearest point, this region of long, narrow waterways and old-growth forests, home to both killer whales and mountain goats, invites hikers and kayakers to play in a wilderness the size of Connecticut.

Ketchikan sits on Revillagigedo island 235 mi. south of Juneau, 90 mi. north of Prince Rupert, BC, and 600 mi. north of Seattle, WA.

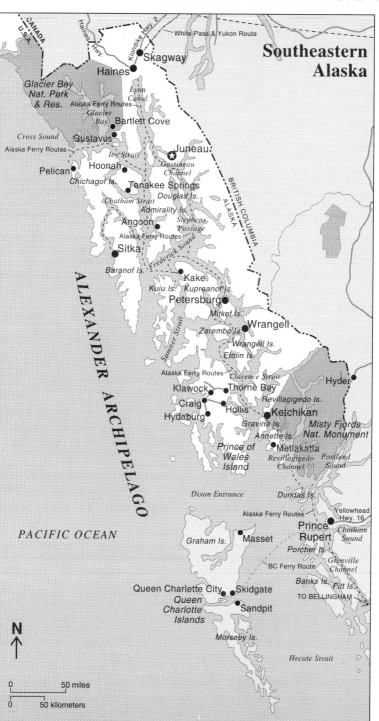

KETCHIKAN

CANADA
USA

Haines Hwy.

Klondike Hwy. 2

White Pass & Yukon Route

Skagway

Haines

Southeastern Alaska

Glacier Bay
Nat. Park
& Res.

Lynn
Canal

Alaska Ferry Routes

Glacier
Bay

Bartlett Cove

Cross Sound

Gustavus

Alaska Ferry Routes

Icy Strait

Pelican

Hoonah

Juneau

Gastineau
Channel

Chichagof Is.

Tenakee Springs

Douglas Is.

Chatham Strait

Admirality Is.

Angoon

Stephens
Passage

Alaska Ferry Routes

Sitka

Baranof Is.

Frederick Sound

BRITISH COLUMBIA

ALASKA

Kake

Kuiu Is.

Kupreanof Is.

Petersburg

Mitkof Is.

Sumner Strait

Zarembo Is.

Wrangell

Wrangell Is.

Etolin Is.

Alaska Ferry Routes

Clarence Strait

Hyder

Klawock

Thorne Bay

Revillagigedo Is.

Craig

Hollis

Hydaburg

Gravina Is.

Ketchikan

Misty Fjords
Nat. Monument

Annette Is.

Metlakatla

ALEXANDER ARCHIPELAGO

Prince of
Wales
Island

Revillagigedo
Channel

Portland
Sound

Dixon Entrance

Dundas Is.

Alaska Ferry Routes

PACIFIC OCEAN

Graham Is.

Masset

Yellowhead
Hwy. 16

Prince
Rupert

Chatham
Sound

Porcher Is.

BC Ferry Route

Grenville
Channel

Banks Is.

Pitt Is.

Queen Charlotte City

Skidgate

TO BELLINGHAM

Queen
Charlotte
Islands

Sandpit

Morseby Is.

Hecate Strait

N

0   50 miles

0   50 kilometers

KETCHIKAN

PRACTICAL INFORMATION AND ORIENTATION

Visitors Information: Ketchikan Visitors Bureau, 131 Front St. (225-6166 or 800-770-3300), on the cruise ship docks downtown. Offers map of a good walking tour, along with friendly advice and a cup of coffee. Open Mon.-Fri. 8am-5pm, and Sat.-Sun. depending on cruise ship arrival times.

United States Forest Service: Ranger District Office, Federal Building at 648 Mission St. (225-2148). Informational packets on hiking and paddling in Misty Fjords and the Ketchikan area (free). They also sell a kayaker's map of Misty Fjords ($3) and reserve cabins around Ketchikan and Prince of Wales. Ask for the little green guide to recreation facilities for complete cabin listings. Open Mon.-Fri. 7:30am-4:30pm, and, in summer only, Sat.-Sun. 8am-4:30pm.

Alaska Employment Service, 2030 Sea Level Dr., Suite 220 (225-3181), at the west end of town. Open Mon.-Fri. 8am-noon, 1-4:30pm. This facility is helpful for researching fishing seasons in advance and offers the guide *How to Find Work in the Alaskan Salmon Fisheries.*

Public Phones: Alascom Teleservices Center, 315 Mill St. (225-9700). Sixteen phones for long-distance calls with metered charges that allow you to pay at a cash register rather than plugging in fistfulls of dollars. Hours vary with cruise ship schedules, posted on door (or call ahead from a public phone!).

Airport: Located across from Ketchikan on Gravina island. A small ferry runs from the airport to just above the state ferry dock ($3). The Alaska Marine Highway terminal is only a short walk from the airport ferry dock. **Alaska Airlines** (225-2141 or 800-426-0333), in the Ingersoll Hotel at the corner of Front and Dock St., provides flight information from Ketchikan. Daily flights to Juneau $124. Open Mon.-Fri. 9:30am-5pm.

Alaska Marine Highway (225-6181), at the far end of town on N. Tongass Hwy. Turn right leaving the terminal to reach the city center. Buses run into town until 6:45pm; after that you have to pay the $8 cab fare or risk hitching.

Buses: The basic fare in the local transit system is $1, under 11 and senior citizens 75¢. Buses run every ½ hr. Mon.-Sat. 6:40am-7pm. The main bus route runs a loop with turnaround points at the post office near the ferry terminal at one end, and Dock and Front St. downtown at the other. Stops about every 3 blocks.

Taxi: Sourdough Cab, 225-5544. **Alaska Cab,** 225-2133. **Yellow Taxi,** 225-5555. These can be chartered for $40-45 per hour.

Air Taxis and Tours: Taquan, 225-9668. **Ketchikan Air Service,** 225-6608. **Misty Fjords Air and Outfitters,** 225-5155. Tours range from $35 to $150.

Car Rental: Alaska Rent-A-Car, airport office (225-2232) or 2828 Tongass Ave. (225-5123 or 800-662-0007). Free local pick-up and delivery. $40 per day, with unlimited free mileage. Open Mon.-Sat. 8am-5pm, Sun. 8am-3pm.

Kayaking: Southeast Exposure, 507 Stedman St. (225-8829). Required 1½-hr. orientation class $20. Single fiberglass kayak rental, $35 per day; 4 or more days, $30 per day. Double kayak, $45 per day; 4 or more days $40 per day. $200 damage deposit. Open daily 8am-5pm.

Bookstore: Ms. Lillian's (Parnassus), 5 Creek St. (225-7690). An upstairs bookshop with an eclectic selection of used and new books. Discernible emphasis on women's studies. Open daily noon-7pm; in winter closed on Mon.

Seamen's Center (225-6003), on Mission St. next to St. John's. A warm, dry lounge where workers and others can clean up, watch television, and sometimes find free food. Meals served on weekends in summer 6-8pm. Showers $1.50, laundry 75¢. Open daily in June 6-10pm, July-Aug. 3-10pm; in winter, open 3 days per week. Volunteers can help cook or clean for 2 hours any evening.

Public Radio Station, KRBD 105.9. Drop by their station at 123 Stedman St. (225-9655) to learn about who's playing and where.

Laundromat: The Mat, 989 Stedman St. (225-0628). Wash $2-5.25, 7-min. dry 25¢. Also has showers ($2.64 for 15 min.), TV, and play area. Open 6am-11pm, in winter 7am-10pm.

Pharmacy: Downtown Drugstore, 300 Front St. (225-3144). Open Mon-Sat. 8am-6:30pm., Sun. 10am-4pm.

Hospital: Ketchikan General Hospital, 3100 Tongass Ave. (275-5171).

Fire Department: Main St., near Dock St. Will sometimes let you leave your pack with them for the day (at your own risk).

Police Station: Main St. and Grant St. (225-6631), across from the hostel.

Post Office: (225-9601) Main office next to the ferry terminal. Open Mon.-Fri. 9am-5pm. **General Delivery ZIP Code:** 99901. Substation in the back of The Trading Post, at Main and Mission St. Open Mon.-Fri. 9am-5pm.

Area Code: 907.

ACCOMMODATIONS

Besides hostels, rooms here are relatively expensive. The **Ketchikan Bed and Breakfast Network,** Box 3213, Ketchikan 99901 (225-8550), provides rooms from $50-75.

Ketchikan Youth Hostel (HI/AYH), P.O. Box 8515 (225-3319), at Main and Grant St. in the basement of the United Methodist Church. Although there are no beds, 4-in.-thick foam mats on the floor are quite comfortable if you have a sleeping bag. Clean kitchen, common area, 2 showers, tea and coffee. Houseparents change, and their management styles vary widely. Lockout 9am-6pm. Lights off at 10:30pm, on at 7:00am. Curfew 11pm. Call ahead if coming in on a late ferry. $7, nonmembers $10. No reservations. 3- or 4-day limit subject to availability. Overflow sleeps in the sanctuary. Open June 1-Sept. 1.

New York Hotel, 207 Stedman St. (225-0246). A painstakingly restored 8-room hotel beside the Creek St. boardwalk. Cable TV, queen-size beds, and luxurious bath tubs. May-Sept. $69; Oct.-April $49.

Shelter, 628 Park Ave. (225-4194). 28 beds in the 3 rooms with separate quarters for men and women. Check-in 7-10pm, check-out 7:30 am. Kitchen facilities and luggage storage for residents. 5-night max. stay. Free, but $3 donation requested of those who can afford it.

CAMPING

If you plan well in advance, camping provides an escape from Ketchikan's high accommodation prices. The sporting goods stores in town tend to cater more to the fatigues-and-fishhooks crowd than to backpackers, but you may want to check out **The Outfitter,** 3232 Tongass (225-6888), or **Plaza Sports,** in the Plaza Mall (225-1587). Campgrounds have time limits of a week or two, but the occasional cannery worker has been spotted carrying supplies to tent illegally up in the public forests for longer periods. There is no public transportation to the campgrounds, so plan on hiking, biking, or paying the exorbitant cab fare out there. **Ketchikan Ranger District** (225-2148) runs the **Signal Creek, Last Chance,** and **Three C's Campgrounds** and will also supply information about cabins with stoves ($20) in remote locations in the **Tongass National Forest.**

Signal Creek Campground, 6 mi. north on Tongass Hwy. from the ferry terminal. 25 units on the shores of Ward Lake. Water, pit toilets. Sites $5. Open in summer.

Last Chance Campground, 2 mi. north of Ward Lake's parking lot entrance. 25 sites, mainly RV. Water, pit toilets. Sites $5. Open in summer. 2-week limit.

Three C's Campground, ½ mi. north of Signal Creek. Four units for backpackers. Water, pit toilets, firewood. Sites $5. 2-week limit.

RV Dumpstation, 3291 Tongass Ave., 2 blocks north of the ferry terminal. Open 24 hrs., year-round. Free. (If only everything in Ketchikan were this simple.)

Clover Pass Resort, P.O. Box 7322-V (247-2234), 14 mi. north of Ketchikan. 35 complete RV hookups with electricity, sewer, water, laundry, and a dump station. Rates vary, so call ahead.

FOOD

The supermarket most convenient to downtown is **Tatsuda's,** 633 Stedman at Deermount St. just beyond the Thomas Basin, (225-4125). Open daily 7am-midnight. You can pick up single items at **Junior's Convenience Store,** at Dock and Main St., including a mean 85¢ microwave burrito for the truly desperate. As always, **McDonald's** plies the cheapest meal at the Plaza Mall, 1 mi. north of the tunnel (and a prayer meeting is held here every Wed. morning at 7:30am—"What you want is what you get."). The freshest seafood swims in Ketchikan Creek; anglers frequently hook King Salmon from the docks by Stedman St. in the summer, and, if you should be so lucky, **Silver Lining Seafoods,** 1705 Tongass Ave. (225-9865), will custom-smoke your catch for $2 per lb. Also look for boats along the waterfront selling shrimp. **KetchiCandies,** on Dock St. next to the Trading Post, is an aromatic experience not to be missed; even if you're worried you won't be able to keep yourself from the Frangelica Truffles ($15 per lb.).

5 Star Cafe, 5 Creek St. (247-7827). Savory salads and scrumptious sandwiches smothered in sprouts—try the smoked turkey on dark rye ($5.50) or the smoked salmon potato salad ($4.25). An art gallery in the back gives you an excuse to linger. Open Mon.-Wed. 8am-7pm, Thurs.-Fri. 8am-8pm, Sun. 8am-5pm.

Harbor Inn, 320 Mission St. (225-2850).Generous portions in a friendly fishermen's hangout. 3 eggs, gravy, hashbrowns, and bacon $7. Seafood specials $7-16. Open 24 hrs.

Diaz Cafe, Stedman St. This long-standing Chinese, Flipina, and American eatery inspires fierce loyalty among many of Ketchikan's more frugal sons and daughters. The deluxe burger with a heap of sweet and sour rice ($4.75) explains why. Open Mon.-Fri. 11:30am-2pm, 4-8:30 pm, Sat. 11:30am-8:30pm, Sun. noon-8pm.

Jimbo's Cafe, 307 Mill St. (225-8499), across from the cruise ship docks. Try a 1-lb. Alaskan burger for $9. Stack of 3 pancakes $3.75. Where the inebriated head after the bars have closed. Open daily 6am-3 or 4am.

Chico's (225-2833), at Dock and Edmond St. Tortellini meets the tortilla. Zesty Mexican/Italian decor and music. Spicy dinners $7.50-9. Large pizza $13. Open daily 10am-11pm.

Latitude 56 Restaurant, in the bowling alley across from the mall. Great breakfast bargains—3-egg omelette, hash browns, and toast ($5.25); stack of pancakes, 2 eggs, and sausage ($4.75). Breakfast served Mon.-Fri. 6-11am, Sat.-Sun. 6am-1pm.

SIGHTS AND ENTERTAINMENT

Fortune-seeking prospectors turned Ketchikan into a mining boom-town, and a little bit of this history is preserved on **Creek Street,** a thriving red light district where it is often said that sailors and salmon went upstream to spawn until 1954. Creek St. itself is a wooden boardwalk on pilings lined with shops along Ketchikan Creek—there is no actual street. Curiosity may lead you into the sordid past of **Dolly's House,** 24 Creek St. (225-6329), a former- brothel-turned-museum. There are countless antiques from the '20s and '30s set amidst bawdy colors and secret caches. Young women tastefully dressed as past employees give you the true history of each room as you visit. Hours vary with cruise ship arrivals; call ahead (admission $2.50).

Also on the walking tour is the **Totem Heritage Center,** 601 Deermount St. (225-5900), which houses 33 well-preserved totem poles from Tlingit, Haida, and Tsimshian villages, the largest collection of authentic totem poles in the U.S. (Open daily 8am-5pm. Admission $2, under 13 free, Sun. afternoon free.) Across the creek, at the **Deer Mountain Fish Hatchery,** a self-guided tour explains artificial salmon sex. (Open daily 8am-5pm. Free.) The **Tongass Historical Museum** (225-5600), on Dock St., explains the town's historical pastiche of Native Americans, rain, salmon, and prostitutes. (Open mid-May to Sept. daily 8am-5pm. Admission $1, under 18 free; free Sun. afternoon.) Under the same roof as the museum, the **Ketchikan Library,** overlooking a waterfall and rapids, is the best place to pass a rainy day (Open Mon. and Wed. 10am-8pm, Tues., Thurs., Fri., and Sat. 10am-6pm, Sun. 1-5pm.) A free **funicular** ascends the street slope behind Creek St. near the library. You get more than you paid for in the view of the harbor from the top lobby at Westmark Hotel.

Some of the finest ancient and contemporary totems inhabit Ketchikan and the surrounding area. Pick up the guided walking totem tour at the visitors bureau.

World-renowned totem carver Nathan Jackson lives here; his work stands in front of the Federal Building. If you can see only one thing in Ketchikan, visit the best and largest totem park in the world—the **Saxman Native Village,** 2½ mi. southwest of Ketchikan on Tongass Hwy ($8 by cab). The native village has a tribal house, native dancers, and an open studio where artisans carve new totems. (Open daily 9am-5pm and on weekends when a cruise ship is in.) Also, 13½ mi. north of Ketchikan on Tongass Hwy. is **Totem Bight,** or **"Totem Cove,"** featuring 13 totems. Entry to both parks is free, and visitors are welcome during daylight hours. For those interested in purchasing authentic native art, **Shotridge Studios,** 407 Stedman St., is both a commission gallery with the best prices in town and the workshop of master carver Israel Shotridge (open Mon.-Sat. 10am-4pm).

Bars jostle for position along Water St. leading towards the ferry. In town, the **Frontier Saloon** at 127 Main St. (225-4407), has live music Tuesday though Sunday in summer (open daily 10am-2am). The **Arctic Bar** (225-4709) on the other side of the tunnel is a fishermen's land-lubbing haunt (open Sun.-Wed. 8am-midnight, Thurs.-Sat. 8am-2am). Throughout the year, **Ketchikan's First City Players** present an intriguing variety of plays to sell-out crowds on Friday nights at 7 and 8pm. In July and August, check out the bawdy *Fish Pirate's Daughter,* a melodrama about Prohibition Ketchikan. Shows are $6, and performed at the **Main Street Theatre,** 338 Main St. (225-4792). Like most towns in the Alaskan Southeast, Ketchikan celebrates the Fourth of July with a vengeance. Ketchikan's festivities coincide with the annual **Timber Carnival,** a spirited display of speed-chopping, axe-throwing, choker-setting virtuosity. August brings crafts, food, and live music to the streets along with a fiercely contested **slug race.**

OUTDOORS: HIKING AND PADDLING

Although Ketchikan stands as the gateway to the boundless hiking and kayaking opportunities within the nearby **Misty Fjords National Monument,** you scarcely have to go beyond the city limits to find a trailhead leading into the hills. A good day-hike from Ketchikan is 3,001-ft. **Deer Mountain.** Walk past the city park on Fair St.up the hill towards the town dump. The marked trail head branches off to the left just behind the dump. A steep but manageable ascent leads 2 mi. up the mountain, and although most hikers return the same way they came up, an extended route leads over the summit and past an A-frame shelter that can be reserved at the ranger station in town. The trail continues above treeline along a sometimes steep-sided ridge where snow and ice may remain into the summer. **Blue Lake,** an alpine pond stocked with trout, lies at the middle of the ridge walk. At the summit of the 3,237-ft. John Mountain, the **John Mountain Trail** descends from the ridge passing the Stivis lakes on its way down to the Beaver Falls Fish Hatchery and the South Tongass Highway, 13 mi. from Ketchikan. This section of the hike is poorly marked and may test hikers' ability to read topographic maps. The entire hike, manageable for well-shod, experienced hikers in one full day, is 10 mi. long. A less strenuous and equally accessible outing is the trek along a boardwalk built over muskeg up to Perseverance Lake. The **Perseverance Trail,** beginning 6 mi. north of the city just before the Three C's campground, climbs 600 ft. over 2.3 mi. to a montane lake with trout fishing opportunities.

The magical **Misty Fjords National Monument** lies 20 mi. east of Ketchikan and is accessible by kayak, power boat, or float plane. This 2.2-million-acre park offers excellent camping, kayaking, hiking, and wildlife viewing. Walls of sheer granite, clearly scoured and scraped by retreating glaciers, rise up to 3,000 ft. from saltwater bays. More than 12 ft. of annual rainfall as well as the runoff from large ice fields near the Canadian border feed the hundreds of streams and waterfalls which empty into two long fjords—Behm Canal (117 mi.) and Portland Canal (72 mi.)—on either side of the monument. Four first-come, first-serve shelters (free) and fourteen forest service cabins dot the preserve, all but two of which require a chartered floatplane to reach. Even the two cabins accessible by boat may be available in mid-week during the summer—it's always worth asking at the ranger station (225-2148).

Although seasoned kayakers prepared to navigate the difficult currents between Ketchikan and Behm Canal can paddle straight into the park, another option is to have **Outdoor Alaska** (225-6044) bring you and your boat along on one of their five sightseeing tours per week. They will drop off paddlers and pick them up again anywhere along their route for $175. Walker Cove, Punchbowl Cove and Rudyard Bay, off Behm Canal, are several of the destinations of choice for paddlers. In planning a trip, keep in mind that these waters are frigid and extended stretches of coast have no good shelter. A reliable cooking stove is also essential since wood in Misty Fjords tends to be soggy.

A slew of charter operations visit the monument; plan on spending at least $140 for a day trip. **Outdoor Alaska** (again, 225-6044) offers a 10-hour **boat tour** with meals. An **air tour** of the park will cost you more than $1 for every minute in the air, with the length of the flight depending on what your wallet can sustain. Call the Ketchikan Visitors Bureau (see Practical Information) for more on tours.

■■■ PRINCE OF WALES ISLAND

Prince of Wales Island, the third largest in the U.S. (after Kodiak and the Big Island of Hawaii) sits quietly west of Ketchikan by less than 30 mi. Most beautiful at its edges where countless bays and protected inlets cradle calm waters, the island lies beneath a dense rain forest broken only by mountain peaks, patches of muskeg, and large clear-cuts. A branch line of the Alaska ferry makes reaching Prince of Wales a cinch, and a 900-mi. road system (albeit gravel, but for 30 paved mi.) allows mountain bikers and drivers thorough access to the island. Even so, few people other than relatives of the 6000 residents make this detour beyond the foaming wakes of the main ferry route. The small communities on the island, only four of which have been incorporated, meet visitors with a combined expression of warmth and bemusement. These fish and timber towns where two trucks never pass without a wave offer few standard services to visitors, but an excellent chance to see Alaskans—even in the summer—plying the tourist trade only as an afterthought.

The extensive logging on Prince of Wales recently uncovered a vast network of limestone caves in the north of the island. Most of these have yet to be mapped, and only two are now easily accessible. But speleologists are all abuzz over the discovery of another Alaskan superlative—the deepest cave in the U.S.—and paleontologists take interest in a prehistoric bear that fell to its death and was preserved at the bottom of another cave. To ensure that visitors don't meet a similar fate, the Forest Service only provides the public with information on two easily accessible caves, both equipped with visitor facilities. If you want to dig deeper, contact **Glacier Grotto,** Alaskan Chapter of the National Speleological Society, P.O. Box 376, Haines 99827.

The Alaska state ferry **Aurora** makes the 2¾-hour crossing from Ketchikan to Hollis on Prince of Wales roughly eight times per week ($18). **The Prince of Wales Transporter** (755-2348) meets almost every ferry and rolls on to Craig ($17). Hitchhikers are rarely seen waiting long for rides. Both **Ketchikan Air** (826-3333) and **Taquan Air** (826-9800) buzz over to Craig and Klawock ($65) and Thorne Bay ($50) about eight times per day in the summer.

■ Craig

Craig, on the west coast of Prince of Wales and the local service center, is the most "visitable" town on the island. A short causeway flanked by two small harbors leads out to a small hump of an island where from the town's center there are views of peaceful waters and islands in nearly every direction. With Craig's commercial enterprises spilling out of town and breaking ground along the road to Klawock, the town seems to be riding a different economic wave than other island communities.

After absorbing the sunset from the docks and inspecting a faded fish-packing plant, visitors can mingle with fishermen and loggers in the triangle marked out by three local bars. Both the **Hill Bar** and the **Craig Inn** resound with live music at least five nights a week, more when the fleet is in town. The Inn (which has no accommodations) displays the most hostile decor (and atmosphere) in town with its chiseled and slashed bar top. **Ruth Ann's,** a quieter, more intimate spot, lines its walls with photos from the fishing days of yore.

Although most of Prince of Wales Island falls within the Tongass National Forest, which allows free unimpaired camping, Craig is surrounded by Native lands where camping is prohibited. There are several campsites within city limits beside the baseball field on Graveyard Island—follow Hamilton Dr. out along the water to reach them—but the city has posted signs discouraging camping there. The **TLC Laundromat and Rooms** (826-2966), on Cold Storage Rd. behind the supermarket, offers the only affordable slumber space in Craig. Their singles ($27-36) and doubles ($44) with hall baths fill fast in summer. The state-of-the-art laundromat ($1.75 wash, 25¢ dry) also has showers costing $1.50 for 5 min. (open daily 7am-9pm).

Several island communities do their food shopping in Craig and the **ShopRite** on Craig Clawack Rd. will not disappoint (open Mon.-Sat. 8am-8pm, Sun. 10am-6pm). **Lacie's Pizza** (826-3925), across the street from the market, serves up satisfying slices at lunch time for $1.75 plus 30¢ per topping (open Tues.-Thurs. 11:30am-8pm, Sat. 11:30am-9pm, Sun. 4-8pm). **Sub Mania,** on Water St., offers substantial sandwiches at reasonable prices, including their vegetarian special, "The Empty Net" ($4). Their soft-serve ice-cream cone is the most calories to be had for a buck in Craig. There's always a place for the hungry traveler at the **Captain's Table** on Front. St. The captain serves a soup and sandwich ($6) and a big breakfast special ($7) of 2 eggs, 3 hotcakes, and bacon (open daily 5am-9pm).

The **Public Library** (826-3281) up the hill on Third St. shelves a strong Alaskan section. (Open Mon. 7-9pm, Tues.-Fri. 10:30am-12:30pm and 2:30-5:30pm, also Tues.-Thurs. 7-9pm, Sat.-Sun. 2:30-5:30pm.) For information on the 19 wilderness cabins on Prince of Wales, caves, and camping, drop by the **Forest Service Office** at Ninth Ave. and Main St. (826-3271; open Mon.-Fri. 8am-5pm). **Wards Cove Packing Co.** sells **fishing licenses** (open Mon.-Sat. 8am-5pm); **JT Brown** handles tackle (open Mon.-Sat. 9am-6pm).

■ Klawock, Thorne Bay, and Hydaburg

Seven mi. north of Craig, the village of **Klawock** sits by a river of the same name. Klawock, home to Alaska's first cannery (built in 1878) still revolves around fishing. The local totem park, the largest on Prince of Wales, contains 21 original and replicated totems from the abandoned village of Tuxekan.

A narrow, dusty logging road cuts northeast across the island from Klawock to **Thorne Bay,** an unpretentious town recently created through the incorporation of a logging camp. For many of the helicopter pilots, tree-fellers, and mechanics working in the logging industry, Thorne Bay is one in a long series of temporary homes that move with the timber harvest. For others living in float houses and cabins along the beautiful bay, the town is primarily a postal address and grocery supply point. Thorne Bay provides attractive waters to kayakers; its tributary rivers wins the praise of anglers. Unlike Craig, Thorne Bay lies fully within national forest lands and campers may pitch tents for up to two weeks on any suitable site. **Sandy Beach Picnic Area,** 6 mi. north of Thorne Bay on Forest Road 30, offers campers a view and a toilet, as does **Gravely Creek Picnic Area** 4 mi. northwest of town on Thorne Bay Rd. (free). The flocking hordes of tourists support one place of lodging in Thorne Bay, **Brenda's Beehive B&B** (828-3945) on Bayview Rd., which in turn has just one bed in the summer—fortunately, it's very comfortable ($55, $70 with dinner). Brenda and her husband can also field questions about the Tongass Forest. You may see them again at the **Forest Service Station**(828-3304) in town. The **Thorne Bay Market,** where a gallon of milk goes for $4, sits back in a cove beyond the docks (open Mon.-Sat. 8am-8pm, Sun. 9am-6pm). **Some Place to Go,** the outdoor hamburger stand beside the high school, serves a tasty cheeseburger for $3.50—not bad for a monopoly. Pack your dirty laundry up the hill beside St. John's church to **Dan's Laundromat** for a $2 wash and $1 dry (open daily 8am-9pm).

Hydaburg, the Alaskan stronghold of the Haida people, lies 20 mi. off the Hollis-Craig highway. The predominantly Native community receives few visitors but welcomes those that come. The only standard attraction in this little village centered on fishing and subsistence activities is the colorful totem park in front of the school. Fran Sanderson (228-3139) offers a room and three meals in her home across from the totem park for $75 (ask about student discounts). Caroline Natkong (283-3301) does the same for $70 in her home by the Hydaburg River.

■ Hyder and Stewart

Once a week the state ferry Aurora heads south from Ketchikan to the natural Portland Canal, and then threads its way back north through this scenic waterway to the twin towns of Hyder, Alaska and Stewart, British Columbia. The towns lie within 2 mi. of each other at the terminus of this turquoise-hued fjord. In the surrounding mountains, framed perfectly in the view down the main street of either town, glaciers slide down out of the clouds, feeding streams and waterfalls that pour into the canal. Most events in this little international community, including the arrival of the ferry, take place in Stewart—chiefly because, with about 900 people, residents of Stewart outnumber those of Hyder by ten to one. Hyderites deal in Canadian currency (except at the post office), use a British Columbia area code, and send their children to school in Stewart. No checkpoint or even a sign marks the border between the towns, but Hyder's assimilation isn't complete. Half of Hyder sets their clocks by British Columbia's time zone, the others remain an hour earlier on Alaska time—an excellent recipe for confusion. **(Times listed here are in BC time unless otherwise noted.)** From July1-4, the two communities celebrate an extended birthday party for both nations.

Practical Information and Sights A left turn from the ferry terminal takes you to Hyder, a right turn to Stewart. Hyder's **information center** displays the *Hyder Weekly Miner* from 1919-1934 on microfiche for free perusal (open Thurs.-Tues. 10am-2pm). The major tourist activity in Hyder is to sidle up to the bar in the historic **Glacier Inn** and ask to be "Hyderized." Thousands of signed bills line the walls of this bar where early miners would tack up cash as insurance against ever returning to town too broke to buy a drink. **The First and Last Chance Saloon** is another popular beer hall. In Stewart, a little **museum** which also houses the **information center** delves into mining and fashion (miners' fashions?) in the area (open Mon.-Fri. 8:30am-4:30pm, Sat.-Sun. 9:30am-4:30pm). Bears can often be seen plucking salmon from **Fish Creek** 4 mi. from Hyder. **Bear Glacier,** 30 mi. east of Stewart in British Columbia, sits in plain view of the road.

Many visitors never stay overnight in Hyder at all because if they travel by **ferry,** spending one night means spending a week. The Aurora's weekly trip from Ketchikan to Stewart/Hyder ($36) includes a three-hour layover that almost gives pedestrians enough time to see both towns. Rent a bike at the ferry from **Portland Mountain Bikes** ($20 per day, $5 per hour) and have time to spare. Route 37A runs 30 mi. from these towns to the Cassiar Hwy. Inquire at the Cornell Travel Agency in Stewart about **bus service** to Terrace, BC. Two **mail flights** each week zip over to Ketchikan ($100); talk with Sue Hickman (636-9150) for details.

The **Hyder post office** (636-2662) in the HCA building accepts only U.S. currency (open Mon.-Fri. 8am-noon and 1-4pm, Sat. 9:30-11:30am *Alaska time*) **Stewart's post office** is at Brightwell St. and 5th Ave. (open Mon.-Fri. 8:30am-5:30pm, Sat. 8:30am-12:30pm). Hyder's **library** (236-2498) also resides in the HCA building (open Tues.-Sat. 1-4pm *Alaska time*); as does the **U.S. Forest Service** (636-2367;

open Fri.-Sun. 9-10am and 1-2pm, Mon. 9am-noon and 1-2pm). The **Mounties** are posted at 8th Ave. and Conway St. The **area code** is 604.

Camping, Accommodations, and Food Both towns boast campgrounds and the difference between them may be a reflection of national character. Stewart's **Lion's Campground** (636-2537) is orderly and quiet—tentsites ($9 for 2 people, $2 per additional person), sites with electricity ($12), showers ($1). It's a little difficult to tell exactly where the nearby horse pasture ends and Hyder's **Camp Runamuck** begins (tentsites with picnic tables $5). The **Sealaska Inn** (636-2445) offers the most reasonable hotel rates in Hyder (singles $38, doubles $42). Larger groups achieve economies of scale at the **Alpine Motel** (636-2445), at 6th Ave. and Conway St. in Stewart. A suite with twin beds, kitchen, bath, and fold-out couch goes for $80.50. The same set-up for two people is $64.40.

    Cut-Rate Foods on 5th Ave. in Stewart fulfills its calling with scores of no-name products for cheap (open daily 9am-9pm). **The King Edward Hotel Coffee Shop,** on 5th Ave., serves a deluxe burger with fries for quite less than a prince's ransom ($4.50), and a sandwich, soup, and fries special ($6; open daily 7am-9pm). In Hyder, the **Border Cafe** advertises an "internationally famous" burger (U.S. + Canada = International) with potato salad and fries ($6.25). They also do breakfast all day. (Open Tues. and Thurs.-Fri. 8:30am-7pm, Wed. 8:30am-6:30pm, Sat. 8:30am-4pm.)

■■■ WRANGELL

The only place in Alaska to have been ruled by four different nations, the tidy town of Wrangell (pronounced Wrangle) harvests the riches of the forest and the sea amidst a wealth of sights and history. Founded as a fort in 1834 by the Russian-American company as Redoubt-St. Dionysius, this spot near the mouth of the torrential Stikine River had long supported a Tlingit Indian village. The Russians, who originally established the fort to block the British from the Stikine River fur trade, later leased their holding to the British-owned Hudson Bay Company in 1840. The townspeople saluted the Union Jack until the American purchase of Alaska in 1867. As the only gateway to Canada's interior between Prince Rupert and Skagway, the Stikine River became a key transportation corridor during three gold rushes over the next four decades. Meanwhile Wrangell exploded into a staging ground for miners travelling to and from the goldfields. The renowned explorer and ecologist John Muir passed through the town in this era and was entirely underwhelmed: "It was a lawless draggle of wooden huts and houses, built in crooked lines, wrangling around the boggy shores of the island."

    Present day Wrangell presents a more appealing front to visitors. An orderly, prosperous town with a postcard of a harbor, Wrangell's attractions are convenient enough to allow a brief visit during a ferry layover and plentiful enough to merit a night's stay. A new youth hostel and a free campground make this an easy option.

PRACTICAL INFORMATION AND ORIENTATION

    Chamber of Commerce Visitors Center (874-3901), in the A-frame on Outer Dr. beside City Hall. Open Tues.-Wed. and Fri. 10am-4pm, Mon. 9am-noon and 3-6pm, Thurs. 10am-2pm and 6-8pm, Sat. 3:30-6:30pm, Sun. when ferries are in.

    USDA Forest Service, 525 Bennett St., ¾ mi. north of town (874-2323). Open Mon.-Fri. 8am-5pm. Reserve cabins here.

    Alaska Marine Highway (874-2021), at Stikine Ave. and 2nd St., 5 min. from the visitors center. Frequent service to Sitka ($36), Juneau ($54), and Ketchikan ($22). 24-hr. recording of arrivals and departures (874-3711). Open 2 hr. before arrivals and Mon.-Fri. 10am-4pm. Luggage lockers 25¢.

    Airport: Alaska Air (874-3308) makes daily stops in Wrangell year-round, once on a northbound flight to Petersburg and Juneau, and again on a southbound flight to Ketchikan and Seattle.

    Taxi: Star Cab, 874-3622. In service from 6am-3am.

WRANGELL

Laundromat: Thunderbird Laundromat, at Front St. and Outer Dr. Wash $2, dry 25¢. Open daily 7am-8pm.

Weather: Wrangell receives an average of 80 in. rain per year. Ketchikan airport weather report (874-3232).

Library (874-3535), on 2nd St. beside the museum. Very respectable Alaskana section. Open Tues.-Thurs. 1-5pm and 7-9pm, Mon. and Fri. 10am-noon and 1-5pm, Sat. 9am-5pm.

Emergency: 911. **Police** (874-3304) and **Fire** (874-3223), both located in the Public Safety Building on Zimoula Hwy.

Hospital: (874-3356), next to the elementary school on Airport Rd.

Post Office, on the corner across from the library. The town rejected proposed delivery boxes in 1983 in favor of maintaining the ritual of coming in to check P.O. boxes. Open Mon.-Fri. 8:30am-5pm, Sat. 11am-1pm. **ZIP Code:** 99929.

Area Code: 907

Wrangell (pop. 2600) lies on the northern tip of Wrangell Island, about 85 mi. northwest of Ketchikan and 150 mi. southeast of Juneau. Five mi. north of town, the Stikine River flows down from British Columbia and, after passing through Alaska for the last 30 mi. of its run, empties into the Pacific. At its mouth the river branches out into a wide, sandy delta where the world's second-largest congregation of bald eagles gathers in the spring.

ACCOMMODATIONS AND CAMPING

First Presbyterian Church Hostel, 202 Church St. (874-3534). An independent hostel run with high and admirable standards. Sleep on foam mats, 5 to a room. Bring your own sleeping bag. Showers, kitchen, and piano. $10. Open mid-June to Labor Day daily 5pm-9am.

City Park, 1 mi. south of town on Zimovia Hwy. (2nd St. changes names several times before becoming Zimovia Hwy. south of town.) The park is immediately beyond the cemetery and the baseball field. Picnic tables and shelters, toilet, bumpy tent spots, and a beautiful view of the water. Perhaps a little too close to the sewage treatment plant. No drinking water. 24-hr. max. stay. Free.

Shoemaker Bay RV Park, 5 mi. south of town on the Zimovia Hwy. 29 RV sites, wooded tent camping area, picnic tables, and water tap. Trail to Rainbow Falls (¾ mi.) across the highway. Sites $8.

Pats Lake, 11 mi. south of town, near where the Zimovia Hwy. becomes a narrow Forest Service road. Same facilities as Shoemaker Bay with drinking water from Pats Creek. Trout swim in the lake and the creek, and salmon also run up the creek in the fall. Sites $8.

Rooney's Roost B&B (874-2026 or 874-3622), on 2nd St. Tired tourists flock in to nest in Rooney's 3 rooms. $45-$55.

FOOD

Not a wellspring of haute cuisine, Wrangell's eateries fry most of their fare. Buy eggs at **Benjamin's Groceries** on Outer Drive and poach them yourself at the hostel. (Open Mon.-Sat. 8am-8pm.)

Duke's Diner (874-2589), on Outer Drive near Front St. The place to eat a late night breakfast before going to bed. Biscuits and gravy $4; 3 eggs, ham, hashbrowns and toast $6.50; chicken burger with fries $5.25.

Diamond Cafe, beside the laundromat on Front St. A homestyle favorite of Wrangellites (and about the only place open before noon on a Sunday). Sausage and cheese omelette with hashbrowns and toast $7; fish and chips $7.50. Open Mon.-Fri. 6am-8pm, Sat.-Sun. 6am-4pm.

SIGHTS AND THE OUTDOORS

If the ferry schedule permits you to spend at least 45 minutes of your life in Wrangell, a walk out to **Shakes Island** might be the best use of your time. Follow

Front St. to Shakes St. and a short bridge leads out to the island in the middle of Wrangell's small, snug harbor. Outdoor totems stand before the **Shakes Tribal House,** a meticulous replication of the communal home of high caste Tlingit Indians. A Civilian Conservation Corps work team built the house during the Depression era without the aid of a sawmill or a single nail. Inside, finely carved totems and a sunken floor stand below large timbers showing the countless adze marks which hewed them into shape. The house is open during the summer whenever a ship or ferry docks for more than one hour and also at these scheduled times: Mon.-Tues. 2-4pm, Wed. 10am-1:30pm, Fri. 1-3pm. (Also by appointment (874-2023) for a donation of $10 or more. Regular donation $1.)

The **Wrangell Museum** (874-3770), on 2nd St., occupies the town's original schoolhouse. Besides the interesting but predictable collections of Native American artifacts and more recent historical material, the library devotes one entire room to local artists. (Open May to mid-Sept. Mon.-Sat. 1-4pm and when ferry ships are in; mid-Sept. to April, Wed. 1-4pm, or by appointment. Admission $1, under 17 free.) The museum is also the place to buy permits to try your hand at mining garnets from the **Wrangell Garnet Ledge.** Previously owned by the first all-female corporation in America, the mine was deeded to the Boy Scouts and children of Wrangell in 1962. The children now chip garnets out of the rock by hand and line up to hawk their wares whenever a ship arrives. The mine, located by the mouth of the Stikine River, can only be reached by boat. Permits are $10 per day and 10% of the garnets must be left with the Scouts.

Garnets aren't the only interesting rocks in Wrangell. Strewn across **Petroglyph Beach,** ¾ mi. north of the ferry terminal on Evergreen Ave., are the stone carvings of Wrangell's first inhabitants. Archaeologists remain uncertain about the age of these petroglyphs—estimates range from centuries to millennia. But, then again, who trusts archaeologists? They'll date anything. Unlike the garnets, you can't take these rocks home with you. Many people make rubbings with nearby ferns on a special rice paper which is sold by several stores in town.

Hikers can follow in John Muir's footsteps and scramble up nearby Mt. Dewey to an observation point with a commanding view of town and the Stikine River flats. Walking down 2nd St. towards the center of town, McKinnon St. is on the left. Follow McKinnon St. 2 blocks away from the water where it intersects with 3rd St. Turn left on 3rd St. and look for a white sign marking the trailhead.

Three mi. beyond City Park on Zimovia Hwy., **Rainbow Falls Trail** runs 1km up to the waterfall and then continues on as the Institute Creek Trail. This trail climbs steeply through Spruce and Hemlock forest and then follows a boardwalk past several muskeg openings to a ridgetop with views and space to pitch a tent. A three-sided Forest Service shelter sits on the ridge, open on a first-come, first-served basis.

Charter boat operations regularly run up the Stikine and over to Garnet Lodge. There are six Forest Service cabins throughout the Stikine delta and two bathing huts at **Chief Shakes Hot Springs,** a few miles up the river. Talk with **TH Charters** (874-3613 or 874-2085) or **Boathouse** (874-3813 or 874-2554) for information.

■■■ PETERSBURG

Named after Peter Buschmann, a Norwegian immigrant who built the first cannery here, Petersburg lays claim to the world's largest halibut fleet and a strong Scandinavian legacy. The greeting signs at the ferry dock proclaim *Velkommen*, not Welcome, and it's more than a tourism gimmick: nearly everyone in town claims to be descended from Buschmann, and Petersburg clings fast to a hard-fishing, hard-playing Norwegian character.

By virtue of its position at the top of the Wrangell Narrows, a section of the Inside Passage that challenges ferry captains to navigate within a shallow, narrow channel subject to ferocious tidal currents, Petersburg (pop. 3500) lies outside the range of the large cruise ships. Such isolation seems to have lent this island community an uncommon cohesiveness: when one of the canneries a few years ago found itself understaffed with a heap of salmon to process, the management went through the phone book calling for extra hands—retirees, housewives, and people just home from work all rallied to help.

Unfortunately, Petersburg's strong communal sense has made it somewhat suspicious of strangers. If you're a student or backpacker planning to stay in the city, be forewarned that there are no youth hostels and no storage facilities for packs. Rumor has it that townspeople consider such visitors "transients."

PRACTICAL INFORMATION AND ORIENTATION

Visitors Information: Chamber of Commerce and Forest Service Visitors Center, P.O. Box 649, Petersburg 99833 (772-3646), located at 1st and Fram St. Home of a replica of the world-record 126½-lb. king salmon. Reserve Forest Service cabins here. Helpful, informed staff. Open Mon.-Fri. 8am-5pm, Sat. 10am-4pm., Sun. noon-4pm; in winter Mon.-Fri. 10am-3pm.

Airport: Alaska Airlines (772-4255), 1 mi. from the Federal Bldg. on 1506 Haugen Drive. To Juneau ($105); Seattle ($346). For sightseeing, contact **Temsco Air** (772-4220).

Alaska Marine Highway (772-3855), terminal at Mile 0.9 on the Mitkof Hwy., 1 mi. from the center of town. To: Ketchikan ($36), Sitka ($24), Wrangell ($16), and Juneau ($42).

Taxi: City Cab, 772-3003. Rates start at $4. Open 24 hr.

Car Rental: All-Star Rent-A-Car (772-4281), at the Scandia House Hotel. $40-45 per day with unlimited mileage. Also rents 18-ft. **boats** ($150 per day, $125 for guests of the hotel).

Bike Rental: Northern Bikes, 114 Harbor Way (772-3777). $4 for the first hr., $2.25 each additional hr.

Bookstore: Sing Lee Alley Books, 11 Sing Lee Alley. Open Mon.-Sat. 10am-5pm, Sun. noon-4pm.

Theater: Viking Theater, 306 Nordic at Excel St. First-run movies $6, students up to 18 $5, seniors $3.

Employment: Petersburg Job Service (772-3791), at Haugen Dr. and 1st St. Provides information on all 4 canneries. Openings posted in the window. Write ahead for the straight-talking pamphlets *Alaska Job Facts* and *Seafood Processing Jobs in Alaska*. Open Mon.-Fri. 8am-noon and 1-4:30pm.

Laundromat: Glacier Laundry, downtown on Nordic and Dolphin (772-4400). Will dry-clean sleeping bags for $14. Wash $1.75, 7-min. dry 25¢. Open daily 8am-10pm. Also at **LeConte RV Park** (772-4680), at 4th and Haugen.

Showers: LeConte RV Park (772-4680), at 4th and Haugen, **Tent City** (see Accommodations and Camping below), and **Glacier Laundry** ($1.75 for 7 min.).

Pharmacy: Rexall Drug, 215 Nordic Dr., downtown. Open Mon.-Fri. 8am-9pm, Sat. 8am-6pm, Sun. 11am-6pm.

Library: at Haugen and Nordic above the Fire Hall. Open Mon.-Thurs. noon-9pm, Fri.-Sat. 1-5pm.

Hospital: Petersburg General Hospital (772-4291), at Fram and N. 1st St.

Emergency: City Police, 772-3838. **State Troopers,** 772-3100.

Post Office: (772-3121) at Haugen and Nordic Dr. Open Mon.-Fri. 9am-5:30pm, Sat. 11am-2pm. **General Delivery ZIP Code:** 99833.

Area Code: 907.

If you're looking for Nordic Drive, Main St., or Mitkof Hwy., you're probably on it. The main drag goes by several names, but it's an illusion of development—there's only one. The ferry drops you off 1 mi. south of downtown; be prepared to walk, as no bus operates here. Cabs to the center run about $4, $6 out to Tent City.

ACCOMMODATIONS

The only two places in town for backpackers are often packed sardine-like with summer cannery workers. A stagnant swamp surrounding Petersburg means the next nearest campground is 17 mi. away. Contact the Visitor's Center (see Practical Information above) for more comprehensive bed and breakfast listings.

Tent City (772-9864), on Haugen Dr. past the airport, 2.1 mi. from the ferry. This ramshackle collection of tarps and wooden platforms rests atop one of Alaska's most fascinating terrains—muskeg swamp—and is home to most of Petersburg's "transient" workers. Now administered by Parks and Recreation, the city has added several amenities (pay phone, griddle, hot-plate, cooking appliances, and a barn-like shelter with no walls) and a dose of order to what used to be largely self-governed. A true Alaskan experience. Water, toilet, 4 showers (50¢) and pit fires with wood. Open May-Sept. $4 per night. Weekly and monthly rents too.

LeConte RV Park, P.O. Box 1548 (772-4680), at 4th and Haugen. 1 mi. from ferry, 3 blocks from downtown. Limited space for tentsites ($5); rates vary for RV hook-ups. Grounds are worn but still close to town. A **coin-op laundry** (wash $1, dry 75¢) and **showers** ($1.25 per 9 min.) are open to the public.

The Narrows, Box 1048 (772-4284). Mile 1 of Mitkof Hwy., across from the ferry. Surprisingly pleasant, clean rooms. 25 units. Singles $55. Doubles $65. Call for summer reservations before June.

Jewels By the Sea, 806 Nordic Dr. (772-3620), ¼ mi. north of the ferry terminal. Small B&B with a great view of the mountains and the Wrangell Narrows. Beautifully furnished rooms, with a shared bath—but only three of them. Airport or ferry pickup and delivery. Singles $50. Doubles $60. Make reservations well in advance. Hotel office open in conjunction with ferry arrivals and departures.

Scandia House, 110 Nordic Dr. (772-4281), between Fram and Gjoa (JOE-uh) St. Exceptionally clean rooms, with TV and free HBO. Courtesy van available. Boat and car rental offices based here. Singles $50, with bath $65, $5 each additional person. Hotel open 24 hr. for registration and check-out.

Ohmer Creek Campground, Mile 22 of Mitkof Hwy. Maintained by Forest Service. 15 sites. 14-day max. stay. Gravel trail will take you to the perfect spot for first-hand fish habitat voyeurism. Water, pit toilets. Free.

FOOD

Although it should be like finding fish in the sea, reasonably priced seafood is a rare commodity in Petersburg. **Hammer and Wikan** (772-4246), on Nordic Dr., has a huge selection of groceries and also sells camping gear and insect repellent (open Mon.-Sat. 8am-6pm). **The Trading Union** (772-3881), on Nordic and Dolphin, has a similar selection (open Mon.-Fri. 8am-7pm, Sat. 8am-5:30pm, Sun. 9am-5pm). Crowds assemble for free soup and sandwiches every Wednesday from 5 to 6:30pm at the St. Andrews church at 3rd and Excel from June 2 to August 11.

Homestead Cafe (772-3900), Nordic Dr. at Excel, across from the general store. Run by fishermen's wives who understand large appetites. Go ahead and try to finish their stack of pancakes ($3.50)—we dare you. Prodigious plate of biscuits and gravy $5.50. Hearty Viking burger and fries $6.75. The good ol' boys of Petersburg convene at the counter. Open Mon.-Sat. 24 hr.

Helse-Health Foods and Deli (772-3444), on Sing Lee Alley off Nordic Dr. With flowers, ferns, little wooden stools, and plenty of reggae, this earthy place is a favorite port of call for the Rastafarian halibut fleet. Soup and bread $5, "Cheese Breeze": avocado, shrimp, mushrooms, and havarti ($6.75). Chocolaty brownie $1.35. Open Mon.-Fri. 9am-5pm, Sat. 10am-3pm.

Pellerito's Pizza (772-3727), across from the ferry. Where the locals get stuffed. Try the chicken primavera on noodles with garlic bread ($6.65) or, if you're really hungry, order a football-sized calzone ($9). Avoid the nachos. Open Mon.-Thurs. 11am-10pm, Fri.-Sat. 11am-11pm.

Harbor Lights Pizza, Sing Lee Alley (772-3424), overlooking the harbor. Decent pizza but the use of the sound-system to call out orders can be grating. 15-in. cheese pie $15.70, spaghetti dinner with garlic bread $7.45. One of the few places to eat on a Sun. night. Open Sun.-Thurs. 11am-10pm, Fri.-Sat. 11am-11pm.

SIGHTS AND ENTERTAINMENT

This is the best place on the Panhandle to see a fishing town at work (as long as the fish are biting). Only one of the town's four canneries is open to the public: Patty Norheim leads groups of four or more on three-hour tours through the shrimp cannery next to the harbormaster's office, as well as through the rest of the city, a hatchery, and finally back to her home for cocktails. Find out about the **"Patty Wagon"** ($25) at 772-4837 or stop in at the Tides Inn.

To understand the development of this pristine Norwegian village, head to the **Clausen Memorial Museum,** at 2nd Ave. and Fram St., which displays native artifacts and a truly inspiring history of fishing techniques. Outside the museum is the bizarrely attractive **Fisk Fountain,** dedicated to the fish on which Petersburg thrives (open daily noon-5pm; admission $2, under 12 free).

Petersburg is surrounded on all sides by scenic hiking trails and fishing sites. Pick up the *Petersburg Map* at the Chamber of Commerce for a complete illustration of the trails and logging roads on Mitkof Island. Of the several Forest Service cabins around Petersburg, only one is easily accessible by foot. The trail to the Raven's Roost cabin begins near the large orange and white tanks behind the airport. After traversing a section of muskeg on a boardwalk, the trail climbs steeply to an alpine region with excellent views of Petersburg and the Wrangell Narrows. The cabin with a second-story sleeping loft sits at the end of the 4-mi. trail.

On the weekend closest to May 17, Petersburg joins its international brethren in joyous celebration of Norwegian independence from Sweden. During the **Little Norway Festival,** mock Vikings hunt their own furs, wear horns, and sail in Viking boats. Memorial Day weekend brings the **Salmon Derby,** with its ubiquitous salmon bakes. The **Fourth of July** in Petersburg is a merry flight, especially during the competitive herring toss.

OUTDOORS NEAR PETERSBURG

The well-planked **Petersburg Creek Trail,** ½-mi. across the narrows, runs 11½ mi. up to Petersburg Lake through a wilderness area to another Forest Service cabin. If the tide is high enough, you can also go up the creek a few mi. by boat to make a 6½-mi. hike in to the lake. Although many charter operators in town ferry people across the narrows and rent skiffs, this can cost more than $100. Try asking at the Harbormaster's office about boats making the crossing with space for a passenger. A small number of people also live across the narrows—look for someone making the afternoon commute home.

Twenty-two mi. south of town on Mitkof Hwy., Three Lake Loops Rd. runs up to **Three Lakes Loop Trail.** This easy 3-mi. loop passes (would you believe?) three small lakes, all known for their trout fishing. Another 1½-mi. trail leads from the middle lake out to **Ideal Cove** on Frederick Sound. Adjacent to Tent City, **Frederick Boardwalk** leads to the sea through the local flora; a 1-mi. walk each way provides a chance to see muskeg quagmire without even wetting a toe. A common, though foolhardy, dusk activity for Tent City campers is to follow Nordic Dr. 1 mi. north to the city dump, a gourmet restaurant for local wildlife such as black bears. This can be extremely dangerous— the hungry bears here no longer fear humans.

To access the **Stikine Wilderness and Icefield,** rent a skiff in town, take it 35 mi. south to the end of Mitkof Hwy., and jump in. Green Rocks Lodge, P.O. Box 110 (772-3245), offers affordable four-day package tours to fish salmon at **Blind Slough.** The package is cheaper than four nights at a local bed and breakfast, and includes hot breakfast, kitchen facilities, 16-ft. skiff with radio, fishing gear, protective wear, and transportation.

■■■ SITKA

The only major Panhandle town with direct access to the Pacific Ocean, Sitka was settled by the Russians in 1799. The native Tlingits grew to resent the Russians' presence, and in 1802 they razed the settlement with only a few occupants escaping alive. Two years later the manager of the Russian-American Company, Alexander Baranov, sailed into Sitka harbor and began bombarding the fort which the Tlingits had constructed in anticipation of attack. After a bloody ten-day battle, the Tlingits retreated late in the night.

Baranov consolidated his spoils by making Sitka the capital of Russian Alaska. For the next 63 years, the city was the "Paris of the Pacific," with a larger population than either San Francisco or Seattle. After the Russian Tsar sold Alaska to America in 1867 (the transaction was officiated in Sitka), Sitka became the territory's capital from 1884 until 1906. Travelers from all nations came here to profit from the trade in sea otter pelts and to enjoy the trappings of glittering society life. The legacy of this cultural preeminence in the Northwest remains; Sitka is currently the fifth-largest city (pop. 8600) in the state and a center for the arts in Southeast Alaska.

The historic remnants of Russian and Tlingit settlement and beautiful natural sights around Baranov Island—none more impressive than the gentle broken cone of Mt. Edgcumbe rising up across the sound—draw pods of cruise line leviathans into Sitka's shores. Although for many years the town's economy has rested on the sturdy tripod of tourism, fishing, and timber, last summer's closure of a $70 million pulp mill that employed 20% of Sitka's workforce is likely to increase ties to tourism. For their part (and pride), residents of Sitka would much prefer three legs to two.

PRACTICAL INFORMATION AND ORIENTATION

Visitors Information: Chamber of Commerce, Centennial Bldg., 330 Harbor Dr. (747-3225). The visitors bureau is extremely organized. Open Mon.-Sat. 8am-5pm, Sun. when cruise ships are in and when the Centennial Bldg. hosts events.

U.S. Forest Service, Sitka Ranger District, Tongass National Forest, 204 Siqinaka Way, Sitka (747-6671), off Katlian St. Open Mon.-Fri. 8am-5pm. Pick up a copy of *Sitka Trails* at the **information booth** at the corner of Lincoln and Lake St. Donation $1. Open May-Sept. daily 8am-5pm.

Public Phone: Make local calls for free at **Coffee Express** and **Market Center** (see Food below).

Airport: Alaska Airlines, 800-426-0333 or 966-2266. Service to Juneau ($87) and Ketchikan ($124). Also to Seattle, Anchorage, Wrangell, and Petersburg.

Alaska Marine Highway, 7 Halibut Rd. (747-8737 or 800-642-0066), 7 mi. from town. To: Ketchikan ($52), Petersburg ($24), and Juneau ($24).

Buses: Sitka Tours (747-8443) runs a shuttle and tour guide service from the ferry terminal, whenever ferries are in port ($2.50). Tours $5-8. The shuttle will also pick you up or drop you off at the AYH Hostel on the way to or from the ferry.

Taxis: Arrowhead Taxi, 747-8888. **Sitka Taxi,** 747-5001.

Car Rental: All-Star Rent-A-Car, 600 C Airport Rd. (800-426-5243 or 966-2552). $36 per day with unlimited mileage. **Avis** (966-2404), in airport, too. $49 per day. Must be at least 21 with a credit card for both.

Commercial Fisheries: Sitka holds two main processing plants: **Seafood Producers Cooperative (SPC),** 507 Katlian Ave., specializes in high-quality salmon, and **Sitka Sound Seafood,** along the docks. Jobs are available through both plants directly, though employment is not easy to come by. However, if you persevere, SPC will usually find you something to do. The city has no central employment office.

Bank/ATM: First National Bank of Anchorage, 318 Lincoln St. **National Bank of Alaska,** 300 Lincoln St.

Laundromats and Shower Facilities: Homestead Laundromat, 713 Katlian Ave. (747-6995). Wash $1.75, 30-min. dry $1.25. Showers $2. Open Mon.-Sat. 7am-8pm, Sun. 8am-5pm. **Duds 'n Suds Laundromat,** 908 Halibut Point Rd. (747-5050), near hostel. Wash $1.75, 8-min. dry 25¢. Shower $2 for 10 min. Open Mon.-Fri. 7am-8pm, Sat. 8am-8pm, Sun. 9am-10pm.

Bookstore: Old Harbor Books, 201 Lincoln (747-8808). Superb Alaskana section and lots of information about local arts events. They also carry marine charts and topographical maps. The owner, a member of Greenpeace, is infamous for chaining himself to the mill to protest their former lack of pollution control. Open Mon.-Fri. 9am-6pm, Sat.-Sun. 9am-5pm.

Luggage Storage: Both fire station and visitors center will hold packs for free.

Kayak Rental: Sheldon College fish hatchery, 747-5209. Both single and double fiberglass kayaks —both for the ultra-reasonable price of $7 per ½ day, $14 per day. **Baidarka Boats** (747-8996), on Lincoln St. above Old Harbor Books. Single $25 per ½ day, $35 per day. Double $35 per ½ day, $45 per day. Rates less with longer rentals. Required 1 hr. instructional class for novices ($25).

Bike Rental: J&B Bike Rental (747-8279), on Lincoln St. near Southeast Diving & Sports. Mountain bikes $4 per hr., $24 per day.

Library: Ketchikan Memorial Library, 320 Harbor Dr. (747-8708). Open Mon.-Thurs. 10am-9pm, Fri. 10am-6pm, Sat.-Sun. 1-5pm.

Pharmacy: Harry Race Pharmacy, 102 Lincoln St. (747-8666), near Castle Hill. Open daily 9am-6pm.

Hospital: Sitka Community Hospital, 209 Moller Dr. (747-3241), near the intersection of Katlian and Halibut.

Post Office: 1207 Sawmill Creek Rd. (747-3381), a long hike from downtown. Open 8:30am-5:30pm. In town (and for all General Delivery mail), go to the **Pioneer Station** at 201 Katlian (747-5525), inside the Sitka Teen Resource Center across from the old post office building. Open Mon.-Sat. 8:30am-5pm. **General Delivery ZIP Code:** 99835.

Area Code: 907.

Sitka inhabits the western side of **Baranov Island,** 95 mi. southwest of Juneau and 185 mi. northwest of Ketchikan. The O'Connell Bridge connects downtown to Japonski Island and the airport. The snow-capped volcano of **Mt. Edgcumbe** dominates the western Sitkan horizon. Although not as wet as other parts of the Panhandle, Sitka still receives a full fathom (6 ft.) of rain each year.

ACCOMMODATIONS AND CAMPING

HI/AYH has established a hostel in Sitka. Camping facilities are decent, but are at least 5 mi. from town. Cannery workers practice renegade camping closer to town along the Indian River and Gavon Hill trails. Sitka also has 20 **Bed and Breakfasts** from $40 a night up. The Chamber of Commerce keeps a list of rates and numbers.

Sitka Youth Hostel (HI/AYH), 303 Kimshan St., Box 2645 (747-8356). In the United Methodist Church on Edgcumbe and Kimsham St. Find the McDonalds 1 mi. out of town on Halibut Point Rd., and walk 25 yd. up Peterson St. to Kimsham. A roomy hostel with 24 army cots, kitchen facilities, free local phone calls, and a TV and VCR (with several movies—rentals are hard to find). Houseparents change yearly, but in the past they've been friendly. Lockout 8:30am-6pm. Curfew 11pm. $7, nonmembers $10. Will store packs during the day.

Sheldon Jackson College Campus Housing (747-2518), at the east end of Lincoln St., next to the Sheldon Jackson Museum. A reasonably priced dormitory alternative (without curfew) to the hostel. 85 units at "S.J." may be full of conventioneers, so call ahead. Provides bedding, towel, and shared bath. Meals available in the cafeteria. Rooms available summer only; register in Sweetland Hall. Singles $30, doubles $50.

Sitka Hotel, 118 Lincoln St. (747-3288). Cheap, clean, and quiet rooms with tacky decor. 60 units. Singles $49, with bath $54. Doubles $54, with bath $60. Key deposit $5.

Sawmill Creek Campground, 14 mi. SE of the ferry terminal, 7 mi. out of town. Take Halibut Point Rd. to Sawmill Creek Rd. junction in Sitka. Follow Sawmill Creek Rd. to pulp mill, then take left spur for 1.4 mi. Unmaintained 9-unit campground with spots for tents and RVs. Boil water from Sawmill Creek. No showers. Picnic tables, fireplaces, 2 outhouses. Great scenery and decent fishing in nearby Blue Lake. 14-day max. stay. Free.

Starrigaven Creek Campground, at the end of Halibut Point Rd., 1 mi. from the ferry terminal, 8 mi. from town. A USFS campground. 30 sites for tents and RVs. Water, pit toilets. 14-day max. stay. Sites $5.

Sealing Cove. From ferry go south on Halibut Point Rd. to Lake St. Follow Lake St. across the bridge to Sealing Cove. 26 RV spots. Water and electricity. 15-day max. stay. Sites $10.

FOOD

Do your grocery shopping with the friendly people at the **Market Center Grocery,** at Biorka and Baranov St., uphill from the Bishop's House (open daily 5am-midnight), or close to the hostel at **Lakeside Grocery,** 705 Halibut Point Rd. (open Mon.-Sat. 9am-9pm, Sun. 11am-7pm). You can also pick up fresh seafood from fisherfolk along the docks or at **Alaskan Harvest,** a new store run by Sitka Sound Seafood (open Mon.-Sat. 8am-6pm). Though Sitka Sound is going upscale, the cooler people work at **Seafood Producers Coop,** at 507 Katlian Ave.

Sheldon Jackson College Cafeteria, at the east end of Lincoln St. The best deal in Sitka if not the state, "S.J." is a refuge in the Alaskan wilderness of overpriced, often under-nourishing eateries. Bow to your god or goddess of budget travel and come ready to feast. All-you-can-eat breakfast ($4.50), lunch ($5.50), dinner ($8). No breakfast on Sun. Open daily 6:45am-8am, noon-1pm, and 5-6pm.

Coffee Express, 104 Lake St. (747-3343), in downtown. Excellent coffee (80¢), and filling soup and sandwich ($7). Cinnamon rolls rolled big and buttery ($1.85), and muffins ($1.25). Open Mon.-Fri. 7am-4pm, Sat. 8am-4pm.

The Bayview Restaurant, 407 Lincoln St. (747-5440), upstairs in the Bayview Trading Company. Everything from *piroshki,* a Russian delicacy (complete with salad and cup o' borscht, $7) to tandem toad in the hole (2 eggs and toast) with potatoes, gravy, and sausage ($5.50). More than 25 variations on the hamburger theme. Open Mon.-Sat. 6:30am-7pm, Sun. 6:30am-4pm.

Lane 7 Snack Bar, 331 Lincoln St. (747-6310), next to the Cathedral. Chomp on hotter 'n hell chili dogs ($3), mini salads ($4), and ice cream cones ($1-$1.75) while you bowl some turkeys (games $2.25, seniors $1.25). Open Mon.-Sat. 7am-11pm, Sun. 7am-10pm.; Sept. 15-May 15 Mon.-Sat. 10am-11pm, Sun 10am-10pm.

Ginny's Kitchen, 236 Lincoln St. (747-8028). Deli sandwiches on freshly baked bread for $5.25, milkshake $1.75. Ginny is also the source of all the baked goods at Coffee Express. Open Mon. 9am-6:30pm, Tues.-Thurs. 7:30am-6:30pm, Fri. 9:30am-6:30pm, Sat.-Sun. 10am-5pm.

The Backdoor, 104 Barracks St. (747-8856), behind Old Harbour Books. An amicable coffee shop and salon (and thus a popular college hangout) with attractive watercolors on display and unpredictable poetry readings (after-hours cookie-baking on Wed. evenings tends to be a fertile time). 16-oz. Buzzsaw (coffee with espresso) for $1.75, salad plate-sized chocolate chip cookies for $1. Open Mon.-Sat. 7am-5pm, Sun. 11am-4pm.

Channel Club, 2906 Halibut Point Rd. (747-9916), 3 mi. from downtown. The restaurant every Sitkan will recommend. Fantastic salad bar with over 35 individual salads ($12). Open Sun.-Thurs. 5-10pm, Fri.-Sat. 5-11pm.

Staton's Steak House, 228 Harbor Dr. (747-3396), down the street from the Centennial Bldg. Delicious, well-sized portions. Dinner tends toward the exorbitant but lunch specials include deep-fried halibut with heaps of french fries ($7.50) and sandwich with soup ($6.25). Open Mon.-Sat. 11:30am-2:30pm and 5-9pm.

SIGHTS AND ENTERTAINMENT

Modern Sitka treasures its rich Russian heritage. Its lasting symbol of Slavic influence is the onion-domed **St. Michael's Cathedral,** built in 1848 by Bishop Innocent. In 1966, fire claimed the original structure, though Sitka's citizens saved the majority of priceless artifacts and paintings. The Cathedral was promptly rebuilt in strict accordance with plans for the first building, and today haunting icons gleam on its walls. Among the Cathedral's most valued works are the *Sitka Madonna* and the *Panto-*

crator, both by Vladimir Borbikovsky, as well as several neo-Baroque paintings from a movement supported by Catherine the Great. Services are open to the public, and are conducted in English, Tlingit, and Slavonic (old Russian). (Hours vary with cruise ship schedules; generally open Mon.-Sat. 11am-3pm. $1 "donation".)

Two blocks farther down Lincoln is the **Russian Bishop's House,** home of Ivan Veniaminov, the builder of St. Michael's Cathedral. The cathedral was such a success that Veniaminov was canonized as St. Innocent in 1977. It took the Park Service 15 years and $5 million to restore his home to its original 1842-3 condition, but the results are spectacular. The house is one of four remaining Russian colonial buildings in the Americas, and it has been refurbished with the exact materials, colors, and patterns which Veniaminov himself used to decorate his home. Upstairs is a magnificent chapel, dedicated to the Annunciation of the Virgin Mary and adorned with beautiful gold and silver icons (which, unlike those in St. Michael's, may be photographed). For history and architecture buffs, this sight is a must (open 8:30am-4:30pm, tours every ½ hr.).

The **Sheldon-Jackson Museum** (747-8981), at the east end of Lincoln St., is perhaps one of Alaska's best museums for native artifacts and history. Housed in a single octagonal room, the first concrete structure built in Alaska, the well-organized collections date back to the 1880s and represent Athabascan, Aleut, Eskimo, and Northwest Coast styles. Don't miss the pull-out drawers holding the Eskimo children's toys and the raven helmet worn by Chief Katlean, the Tlingit hero in the battle of 1804 (open daily 8am-5pm; admission $2, free with student ID).

For naturalists, the **Alaska Raptor Rehabilitation Center** (747-8662), in Island Community College on Sawmill Creek Rd., has a fantastic collection of recovering bald eagles and owls. The center stages free open houses and self-guided tours during the summer (Mon. 5-7pm, Fri. 4-6pm). When ships are in town, which includes most summer days, there are also guided tours every half-hour throughout the day for $6. Call ahead to confirm. The second best place to view eagles in town is from the McDonalds by the water on Halibut Point Rd.

Stroll down the enchanting, manicured trails of the **Sitka National Historic Park** (Totem Park, as locals call it), at the end of Lincoln St. (747-6281), 1 mi. east of St. Michael's. The trails pass by 15 masterfully replicated totems placed in a well-suited setting along the shoreline among old growth trees. At one end of the 1-mi. loop stands the site of the **Tlingit Fort** where the hammer-wielding chieftain Katlean almost held off the Russians in the battle for Sitka in 1804. The park **visitors center** offers an audio-visual presentation on the battle and the opportunity to watch native artists at work in the Native American Cultural Center. There is also a small museum here, dedicated entirely to the local Kiksadi Tlingits (open daily 8am-5pm).

Across town from the college are numerous well-preserved sites of historical interest. **Castle Hill,** site of Baranov's Castle and Tlingit forts, provides an incredible view of Mt. Edgecumbe, the inactive volcano known as the "Mt. Fuji of Alaska." Castle Hill was also the site of negotiations for Alaska's sale to the United States in 1867, facilitated by the Busch benefactor, Mr. Seward (open daily 6am-10pm).

The June **Sitka Summer Music Festival** ranks as one of the state's most popular events and draws world-renowned musicians to play chamber music. The concerts, held in the Centennial Building on Tuesday, Friday, and some Saturday evenings, can be crowded—reservations are a good idea. Rehearsals, however, are free and rarely crowded. (All shows $12; $72 seasonal passes are available. Contact the visitors bureau at 747-8601 for information and advance ticketing.) The **New Archangel Dancers,** a local all-women troupe, perform energetic Russian folk dances in the Centennial Building throughout the summer ($4, check the variable schedule at the visitors bureau). Peruse the local paper for occasional dance performances by the Sitka Tribe of Alaska; Keith Perkins (747-3207) can also provide information.

The **All-Alaska Logging Championships** take place the weekend before Independence Day. Other summer-time events include the **King Salmon Derby** at the end of May. A permit costs $10 for a day, but the person who catches the largest salmon wins $6,000. The summer climaxes with the **Mudball Classic Slowpitch,** on Labor Day. If you're in town in October, check out the **Alaska Day** celebrations marking the sale of Alaska to the U.S. on October 18, 1867 (it's a statewide holiday).

The **Pioneer Bar** (747-3456) on Katlian St. is clearly the nightspot of choice for both permanent and transient Sitkans (open daily 8am-2am). **Ernie's Old Time Saloon,** 130 Lincoln St. (747-3334), a down-home pool-hall, is also popular (open Mon.-Sat. 8am-2am, Sun. noon-2am).

OUTDOORS

The Sitka area offers excellent **hiking** opportunities—don't forget to bring rain gear, and make sure to pick up the thick booklet *Sitka Trails* at the USFS information booth or office. One of the gentlest and most intimately beautiful walks is the **Indian River Trail,** a 5½-mi. riverside trek up to the base of Indian River Falls. The walk begins close to town where Indian River Rd. meets Sawmill Creek Rd. beside the Public Safety Academy. Salmonberries abound along this stretch, as do squatters from the canneries. At the pump house at the end of the road the trail branches off into the old growth forest and meanders through muskeg and tall trees alongside the clear pools of the Indian River. The rocky Sisters Mountains occasionally come into view, and it is sometimes possible to see spawning salmon in early fall. The trail gains no more than 250 ft. in elevation; plan on a four- to five-hour round-trip.

A shorter, steeper hike leads from downtown up to the summit of **Gavan Hill.** With excellent views of Sitka and the Sound, this 2500-ft. ascent breaks out above the tree-line at about 2100 ft. Find the trailhead just past the house at 508 Baranof St. walking towards the Old City Cemetery. If you plan to camp in the alpine areas around Gavan Hill, be sure to bring along a canteen, since no water is available in the higher regions. Plan on a six- to eight-hour round-trip.

The **Mount Verstovia Trail** offers another direct route to the views. Beginning beside the Kiksadi Restaurant 2 mi. from town on Sawmill Creek Hwy., this strenuous hike begins as an easy stroll through alder groves to the site of the Old Russian Charcoal Pits. The trail soon begins to climb with a series of switchbacks and, at approximately 2 mi., breaks out onto a sparsely vegetated ridge. Many hikers choose to turn back after the ridge meets a steep hillside topped by a rocky outcrop. Stalwarts can continue on through beautiful displays of alpine flowers to reach the summit in another hour. The round-trip to the outcrop takes about four hours.

A fine 3-mi. walk from downtown crosses the runway at the Japonski Island airport, heading across the old WWII causeway which leads past abandoned fortifications, finally arriving all the way out at **Makhanati Island.** Access by small boat is best, since waltzing across the runway without special permission is illegal, but the airport manager (966-2960) also arranges infrequent crossings.

■ Tenakee Springs

In a state where most towns are dedicated to the hurried pursuit of some resource—whether fish, oil, timber, or gold—Tenakee Springs stands apart. The only thing people seriously pursue in Tenakee is relaxation, and of this they have an abundance. Tenakee's main (and only) street is a dirt path beside a row of houses and outhouses along the shore of Tenakee Inlet. Flowers and berries spill into this path along which residents push their belongings in hand carts. Tenakee's traffic code favors technological simplicity—ATVs yield to bicycles which yield in turn to pedestrians. An oil delivery truck and an ambulance make rare appearances as the only automobiles in town.

The **state ferry** LeConte makes a one-hour stopover in Tenakee on its Friday-evening and Sunday-morning trips between Juneau and Sitka. The Friday ferry leaves you in Tenakee for about 21 hours before the next returning boat to Juneau, the Sunday ferry for about 30 hours. The one-way fare to Tenakee from either Sitka or Juneau is $20. **Bellair** (747-8636) flies from Sitka to Tenakee ($76); **Wings of Alaska** (789-9863) soars from Juneau to Tenakee (8am and 5:30pm, $61).

The Hot Spring Tenakee's namesake, a natural hot spring that bubbles up into the public bath house, is the town's epicenter and directly up from the ferry dock. Miners and fishermen have been soaking out their aches and worries in these therapeutic 106° waters for more than a century. Tenakee's present population of retirees and urban refugees from Juneau continue to poach themselves daily in this sublimely soothing bath. A trip to Tenakee, though no less expensive than other small Alaskan towns, could actually save you money—a cheaper solace would be hard to find.

Activities in Tenakee begin, and often end, at the public bath. Since the weathered yellow bathhouse sits on the end of the ferry dock, the one-hour layover in Tenakee on trips between Juneau and Sitka provides ample time for a good soaking. Bathing in Tenakee follows a simple but strict protocol: no clothes in the bath, wash beside the pool before entering, and observe the different hours for men (2-6pm and 10pm-9am) and for women (9am-2pm and 6-10pm). The bathhouse includes a changing room, heated in the winter, from which a door opens onto steps leading down to the pool set in a concrete floor. The sun or stars shining through an overhead skylight provide the only illumination. The bath is free but donations are welcome at Snyder Mercantile across the street.

To reach an even higher echelon of relaxation, follow the bath with a visit to **Moon Feather Therapeutic Massage.** Diane Ziel runs this business out of her home just around the corner from the bath beside the Blue Moon Cafe (½ hr. $20, 1 hr. $35, 1½ hr. $50).

Camping, Accommodations, and Food Walking from the ferry dock to town, a right turn on the dirt path leaves you facing east. After about ¾ mi. in this direction, the path leads into a wooded area with several free, primitive **campsites.** Another ¾ mi. along the trail, the **Indian River Campground** provides tentsites, a shelter, and picnic table beside the Indian River (free), a spot favored by bears in the summer. Before a fire ravaged Tenakee in July 1993, the **Tenakee Inn** stood between the harbor and the bath. The Inn served as a plush bunkhouse, and bunk rates ranged from $15-20. This operation belongs to the same friendly family that runs the Alaskan Hotel in Juneau and hopefully plans for reconstruction of the Inn will be formed and fulfilled.

Locals say **don't drink the water** in this area—not even from the spigots along the main path in town. Though many locals drink it themselves, they say visitors often have a lower tolerance for the Tenakee brand of *giardia.*

Other than the berries along the main path, food in Tenakee can be difficult to come by. **Snyder Mercantile** stocks a small supply of groceries but little that doesn't require a can opener as a fourth utensil. At first glance, Tenakee seems wellendowed with restaurants. This is in part because the ghosts of restaurants past haunt Tenakee's street, places that haven't seen a customer in years and yet still leave out a sign. The **Blue Moon Cafe,** unassuming as it may appear, is a Tenakee institution. If Rosie is there, and if she feels like cooking, try the french fries. No meal escapes the microwave at the **Quick Stop Cafe** (open daily 6am-10pm). The ham and cheese sandwich with chips and ice cream ($3.50) will bring back visions of elementary school cafeterias. The **Tenakee Restaurant** grills an average cheeseburger ($5.50) but offers an extraordinary place to eat it on their back deck (open daily 6am-10:30pm).

Outdoors Tenakee's street extends several mi. in either direction from town. To the west it leads along the water past a communal saw mill and small homesteads which become increasingly far apart. Tread carefully around private land here— some residents greet tourists with a reserve bordering on antipathy. A couple of mi. from town the path turns out onto the shore of the inlet where silver salmon leap from the water in midsummer and smooth rocks make good footing for an extended walk along the beach.

To the east, the wide beach may make for better walking than the faint path through the woods that parallels the shore. About 4 mi. from town an abandoned cannery decays by the water. An extensive network of **logging roads** intersect at a nearby timber loading yard. With a map of this road system, available at the Juneau or Hoonah Forest Service offices, it is possible to ride and occasionally carry a **mountain bike** all the way to Hoonah. Bear in mind that only Admirality Island has a denser population of grizzlies than does this area.

An excellent **paddling** adventure begins in Hoonah and follows the long inlet of Port Frederick back to its end. From there a 100-yd. portage leads to the upper region of Tenakee Inlet. Paddlers can explore the unbroken shores and hidden coves of the inlet on their way out to Tenakee Springs. The 40-mi. trip could also be done in the reverse direction but the hot springs are probably best savored at the end. Rent a kayak in Juneau for this trip, since they are not available in Hoonah or Tenakee, and bring it over on the ferry for $6.

For **chartered expeditions** to fish, view wildlife, and learn the intricacies of the inlet from someone who has been on the water around Tenakee all his life, contact Jason Carter (736-2311). His day-long trips, including lunch, cost $90 per person for two, $80 each for three, etc. Jason also does ½-day trips and transports kayaks.

NORTHERN PANHANDLE

■■■ JUNEAU

Confined within a tiny strip of land at the base of imposing Mt. Juneau, Alaska's capital city (pop. 28,000) refuses to accept its small size. Instead, Victorian mansions crowd up against log cabins, and hulking state office buildings compete for space with simple frame houses. The only state capital in the nation inaccessible by road, Juneau's early settlers didn't have civic planning in mind when they founded the city. In October, 1880, Tlingit chief Kowee led Joe Juneau and Richard Harris to the gleaming "mother lode" in the hills up Gold Creek. By the next summer, boatloads of prospectors were at work in the already-claimed mines of Juneau. Twenty-five years later, the city replaced Sitka as capital of the territory of Alaska.

Mining ended in Juneau in 1941, but by then fishing, lumber, and legislation had stepped in to support the city's economy. With the huge injection of funds from the Alaskan pipeline in the early 1970s, the city's dependence on petro-dollars grew to addictive proportions. Towards the end of the decade, when many Alaskans favored moving the capital to a location more proximate to state population centers, elected officials sunk enormous amounts of money into the construction of impressive office-buildings and parking garages, knowing that if the capital were to be moved such buildings would go to waste.

Many residents favored the capital move, seeing it as an opportunity to loosen the government's stranglehold on the city's economy, and they proposed new investment in the area's long-dormant mines and other promising industries. Although the capital move never happened, the conflict left Juneau bitterly divided between those who cannot help but see the word "capital" in both of its inextricably tied senses and those who would rather see the city less sleek and streamlined, more relaxed and comfortable.

PRACTICAL INFORMATION AND ORIENTATION

Visitors Information: Davis Log Cabin, 134 3rd St., Juneau 99801 (586-2284 or 586-2201), at Seward St. Excellent source for pamphlets on walking tours, sights, and the natural wonders in the vicinity. Open Mon.-Fri. 8am-5pm, Sat.-Sun. 9am-

5pm; Oct.-May Mon.-Fri. 8:30am-5pm. **Marine Park Kiosk** (no phone), Marine Way at Ferry Way, right by the cruise-ship unloading dock (*not* the ferry dock). Manned by enthusiastic volunteers armed with pamphlets and information. Open May-Sept. according to cruise-ship schedules.

U.S. Forest and National Park Services, 101 Egan Dr. (586-8751), in Centennial Hall. Helpful staff and extensive pamphlets provide information on hiking and fishing in the Juneau area, as well as particulars pertaining to **USFS cabins in Tongass Forest.** Write here for Tongass reservations. Also pick up a copy of the valuable *Juneau Trails* booklet ($3) listing numerous 5- to 12-mi. hikes. Free and informative 20-min. films on 16 topics, from wildlife to Glacier Bay, are shown upon request. Open in summer daily 8am-5pm, in winter Mon.-Fri. 8am-5pm.

Department of Fish and Game, 465-4180. **Fishing Hotline,** 465-4116.

Airport: Juneau International Airport, 9 mi. north of Juneau on Glacier Hwy. Serviced by Alaska Air, Delta Airlines, and local charters. **Alaska Air** (789-0600 or 800-426-0333), on S. Franklin St. at 2nd St., in the Baranov Hotel. To: Anchorage ($222, with 21-day advance purchase $125); Sitka ($87); Ketchikan ($124); and Gustavus ($40-65). Flights every morning and afternoon. Open Mon.-Fri. 10am-5pm. Closed holidays. Check **Log Cabin Visitors Center** for schedules and routes of all airlines.

Buses: Capital Transit, 789-6901. Runs from downtown to Douglas, the airport, and Mendenhall Glacier from 7am-10:30pm daily. To get to Mendenhall Campground, tell the bus driver to let you off at the nearest point on the loop and walk the 2 mi. from there. The closest stop to the ferry is at Auke Bay, 1½ mi. from the terminal. The fare is $1.25 to all points; drivers cannot make change.

Ferry Express, 789-5460. Call between 6-8pm to reserve a ride from any major hotel to the airport or ferry (whether you're staying at a hotel or not). Rides $5. From the hostel, the Baronov is the closest hotel. Also offers a 2½-hr. guided tour of Mendenhall Glacier ($9). Tour times vary; call ahead.

Alaska Marine Highway, P.O. Box R, Juneau 99811 (800-642-0066 or 465-3941). Ferries dock at the Auke Bay terminal 14 mi. out of the city on the Glacier Hwy. To: Bellingham, WA ($216, vehicle up to 15 ft. $518); Ketchikan ($72, vehicle up to 15 ft. $177); Sitka ($24, vehicle up to 15 ft. $52); and Haines ($18, vehicle up to 15 ft. $39). Prices higher for larger vehicles and for those who want to make a stopover before their final destination.

Taxis: Capital Cab, 586-2772. Juneau's lowest rates: to Mendenhall Glacier $46 (1 hr.), to the ferry $20. **Taku Taxi** (586-2121) does the same for about 20% more.

Car Rental: Rent-A-Wreck, 9099 Glacier Hwy. (789-4111), next to the airport. $30 per day with 100 free mi. plus 15¢ per extra mi. Must be at least 21 with a credit card or piles of cash.

Kayak Rental: Alaska Discovery, 234 Gold St. (463-5500). Single kayak $40 per day, $60 for weekend (Fri. afternoon to Mon. 5pm). Also offers guided kayak tours to Glacier Bay (up to 10 days) and elsewhere. Open daily 9am-5:30pm.

Camping Equipment: Alaska Discovery sells deeply discounted used tents and equipment from their branch in Auke Bay. In town, try the **Foggy Mountain Shop,** 134 Franklin St. (586-6780), at 2nd. High-quality, expensive gear. Open Mon.-Fri. 10am-7pm, Sat. 10am-6pm, Sun. noon-5pm.

Luggage Storage: In a free unlocked closet at the **hostel.** More secure is the **Alaskan Hotel** at $1.50 per bag per day (see Accommodations below).

Bookstore: Big City Books, 100 N. Franklin St. (586-1772). Open Sun.-Fri. 9am-8pm, Sat. 9am-6pm. **The Observatory,** 235 2nd St. (586-9676). A used and rare bookstore with a knowledgeable proprietress and many maps and prints. Open Mon.-Fri. 10am-5:30pm, Sat. noon-5:30pm; in winter Mon.-Sat. noon-5:30pm.

Library: Over parking garage at Admiral Way and S. Franklin. It's worth coming up just for the views and a great stained-glass window. Open Mon.-Fri. 10am-5:30pm, Sat. noon-5:30pm. The **State Library** and the **Alaska Historical Library,** which hold extensive collections of early Alaskan photographs, are both on the 8th floor of the State Office Bldg. (see Sights below). Both open Mon.-Fri. 9am-5pm.

Laundromat: The Dungeon Laundrette (586-2805), at 4th and Franklin St. Wash $1.25, dry $1.25. Open daily 8am-8pm. Also at the **Hostel** (see Accommodations below). Wash $1.25, dry 75¢.

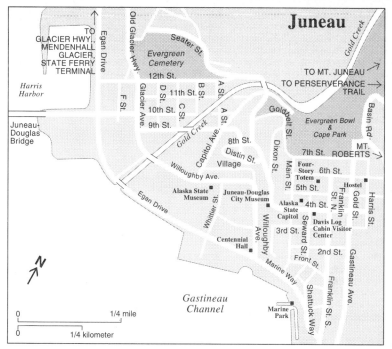

Juneau

JUNEAU

Events Hotline: 586-5866.
Weather: 586-3997.
Pharmacy: Juneau Drug Co., 202 Front St. (586-1233). Open Mon.-Fri. 9am-9pm,
Sat. 9am-6pm, Sun. 10am-7pm.
Hospital: Bartlett Memorial (586-2611), 3½ mi. off Glacier Hwy., north of down-
town.
Emergency and Ambulance: 911. **Police,** 210 Admiral Way (586-2780), near
Marine Park. Visitors can pick up a permit here to allow 48-hr. **parking** in a 1-hr.
zone. Open for permits Mon.-Fri. 8am-4:30pm. RVs exempt.
Post Office: Main Office 709 W. 9th St. (586-7138). Open Mon. 8:30am-5pm,
Tues.-Fri. 9am-5pm. Pick up packages Mon.-Fri. 6am-5pm, Sat. 6am-3pm. **General
Delivery ZIP Code:** 99801. **Substation** (outgoing mail only, no deliveries), 109
S. Seward St. (586-2214). Open Mon.-Fri. 9:30am-5pm, Sat. 9:30am-2pm.
Area Code: 907.

Juneau stands on the Gastineau Channel opposite Douglas Island, 650 mi. southeast
of Anchorage and 900 mi. north of Seattle. **Glacier Hwy.** connects downtown, the
airport, the residential area of the Mendenhall Valley, and the ferry terminal.

ACCOMMODATIONS AND CAMPING

If you can't get into Juneau's hostel, the **Alaska Bed and Breakfast Association,**
P.O. Box 3/6500 #169, Juneau 99802 (586-2959), will provide information on
rooms in local homes year-round. Most Juneau B&Bs are uphill, beyond 6th St., and
offer singles from $45 and doubles from $55. Reservations are recommended. Both
campsites within Juneau's vicinity are carefully groomed by the Forest Service (see
Practical Information).

Juneau Youth Hostel, 614 Harris St. (586-9559), at 6th at the top of a steep hill. A
spotless and highly efficient hostel that operates by a structured set of rules.

JUNEAU

Kitchen facilities and common area. 48 beds. Will store packs during the day. Showers (5 min., 50¢), laundry (wash $1.25, dry 75¢), sheets (75¢). 3-day max. stay if beds are full. Lockout 9am-5pm. The 11pm curfew is not negotiable. Beds $10. Make reservations by May for expected stays in July and Aug.

Alaskan Hotel, 167 Franklin St. (586-1000 or 800-327-9347 from the lower 48 states). A handsome hotel built of dark wood, right in the center of downtown. Has been meticulously restored to its original 1913 decor. Bar on the 1st floor features live jazz. Hot tubs noon-4pm $10 for 1 hr., after 4pm $21. Luggage storage at the desk $1.50. Singles $45, with bath $61. Doubles $55, with bath $72.

Inn at the Waterfront, 455 S. Franklin (586-2050), over the Summit Restaurant. Clean and comfortable carpeted cubicles with attractive wooden dressers, double bed, and hall bath. Singles $42. Doubles $51. 1 room has a futon.

Mendenhall Lake Campground, Montana Creek Rd. Take Glacier Hwy. north 9 mi. to Mendenhall Loop Rd.; continue 3½ mi. and take the right fork. If asked, bus driver will let you off within walking distance (2 mi.) of camp (7am-10:30pm only). A cool view of the glacier, with trails that can take you even closer. 61 sites. Fireplaces, water, pit toilets. 14-day max. stay. Sites $5.

Auke Village Campground, on Glacier Hwy., 15 mi. from Juneau. 11 sites. Fireplaces, water, pit toilets. 14-day max. stay. Sites $5.

FOOD

Juneau tries to accommodate those seeking everything from fresh salmon to filet-o'-fish sandwiches. The local grocery store is the **Foodland Supermarket,** 631 Willoughby Ave., near the Federal Building (open daily 7am-9pm). More expensive health-food items can be bought at **Rainbow Foods** (586-6476), at 2nd and Seward St. Open Mon.-Fri. 10am-7pm, Sat. 10am-6pm, Sun. noon-6pm. Seafood lovers haunt **Merchants Wharf,** next to Marine Park. **Alaska Seafood Co.,** 479 S. Franklin St., sells halibut-leather wallets and silver lox ($11 per lb.). The recently renovated **Federal Office Building cafeteria** on the second floor above the post office is known for its good government cooking (open Mon.-Fri. 6am-4pm).

Armadillo Tex-Mex Cafe, 431 S. Franklin St. (586-1880). Fantastic food and always packed with locals and tourists alike. Hunker down to a heaping plateful of T. Terry's nachos ($8). The *chalupa*—a corn tostada heaped with chicken, beans, guacamole, and cheese—goes for $7.50. 2 enchiladas $6. Open Mon.-Thurs. 11am-9pm, Fri.-Sat. 11am-10pm.

Fiddlehead Restaurant and Bakery, 429 W. Willoughby Ave. (586-3150), ½ block from the State Museum. Fern-ishings for the sprouts-lovin' set. Lures mobs with its beef, salads, seafood, exquisite desserts, and fresh Alaskan sourdough. Great sandwiches and burgers on fiddlehead buns with soup or salad $9-10. Big, buttery ginger-crinkle cookies $1. Dinner $8-14. Open Sun.-Thurs. 8:30am-9pm, Fri.-Sat. 6:30am-10pm. The **Fireweed Room** upstairs serves more expensive fare with weekend jazz throughout the summer. Come just to listen. Open Sun.-Thurs. 11am-1pm and 6-10pm, Fri.-Sat. 6pm-midnight.

Heritage Coffee Co., 1745 Franklin St. (586-1088), across from the Senate Bldg. A popular place to escape for an hour or two from Juneau's often wet and tourist-ridden streets. Jocular staff puts together large sandwiches ($5) and pours excellent 16-oz. cups of coffee ($1.25). Open Mon.-Wed. and Fri. 6:30am-10pm, Thurs. 6:30am-6pm, Sat.-Sun. 8am-10pm. Sandwiches can be had only before 6:30pm.

Channel Bowl Cafe, across from Foodland on Willoughby Ave. A small breakfast spot with blaring blues and an aspiring musician manning the grill. Try the pancakes with berries, pecans, and real maple syrup ($5). Open daily 6:30am-2pm.

Pat's Grub Stake (586-6414), up the steep dirt hill at the end of 3rd, underneath the Bergman Hotel. A local miners' favorite, this subterranean steakhouse serves stout meals for reasonable prices. "The Grubber" fills with an 8-oz. N.Y. sirloin, potatoes, and a carafe of wine ($15). Open Tues.-Sun. 6pm-10pm.

Thane Ore House Salmon Bake, 4400 Thane Rd. (586-3442). A few mi. outside of town, but "Mr. Ore" will pick you up at your hotel. All-you-can-eat salmon, ribs, and fixings ($17.50).

SIGHTS

The **Alaska State Museum,** 395 Whittier St. (465-2910), leads you through the history, ecology, and cultures of "The Great Land" and its four main Native groups (Tlingit, Athabascan, Inuit, and Aleut). It also houses the famous "First White Man" totem pole, on which the artist carved the likeness of Abraham Lincoln. (Open Mon.-Fri. 9am-6pm, Sat.-Sun. 10am-6pm; Sept. 16-May 14 Tues.-Sat. 10am-4pm. Admission $2, senior citizens and students free.) The **Juneau-Douglas City Museum,** 114 W. 4th St. (586-3572), provides unrivaled insight into Juneau's history. There are displays on mining, hand-woven quilts, Native crafts, and a flattering antique scale which knocks a few pounds off your actual weight. (Open Mon.-Fri. 9am-5pm, Sat.-Sun. 11am-5pm; in winter Thurs.-Sat. noon-4:30pm; closed Jan.-Feb. Admission $1, students and children free.)

The remarkably unimpressive and domeless **State Capitol Building** is located at 4th and Main. Tours are offered daily from 9am to 5pm in the summer, but your time is better spent wandering uphill to check out the **St. Nicholas Russian Orthodox Church** on 5th St. between N. Franklin and Gold St. Built in 1894, the church is the oldest of its kind in southeastern Alaska. Services are conducted in English, Slavonic (old Russian), and Tlingit. Open to the public (a $1 donation is requested). The **State Office Building** (affectionately called the S.O.B. by locals) has an eighth-floor **observation platform** overlooking Douglas Island and the channel. A large atrium on the same floor contains a totem pole and a pipe organ fired up for a free concert every Friday afternoon.

Farther downhill along N. Franklin, the **Historic Senate Building** lures tourists with specialty shops, including a surprisingly authentic Russian gift store. In nearby **Marine Park,** rambunctious children play as tourists picnic and watch the slow passage of ships through the **Gastineau Channel.** Free Friday night concerts are held from mid-June to mid-August from 7pm to 8:30pm. Check a newspaper or call 586-2787 to find out who's playing. The **House of Wickersham,** 213 7th St. (586-9001), was home to one of the state of Alaska's founding fathers, Judge James Wickersham. As a U.S. District Court judge, Wickersham sailed around Alaska to oversee a region extending from Fort Yukon to the Aleutian Islands. His contributions to the state include founding the Alaska Railroad, establishing the University of Alaska, and pushing for statehood as early as 1917 (open Sun.-Fri. noon-5pm; free).

Juneau's own microbrewery, the **Alaska Brewing Co.,** 5429 Shaune Dr. (780-5866), offers free tours complete with a free sample of its award-winning brew (which sells for $5.50 per pint at the Alaskan Hotel). To reach the brewery, take the hourly city bus to Lemon Creek—turn onto Anka Rd. from the Glacier Hwy., and Shaune Dr. is the first on the right. (Tours available on the ½ hr. May-Sept. Tues.-Sat. 11am-4:30pm; Oct.-April Thurs.-Sat. 11am-4:30pm.)

ENTERTAINMENT

The doors swing and the cash registers ring at the **Red Dog Saloon,** 278 S. Franklin (463-3777), Juneau's most popular tourist trap. Live music can be enjoyed on weekends (open daily 11:30am-12:30am). The **Alaskan Hotel,** 167 Franklin St., hosts frequent live jazz. Locals hang out farther uptown. The **Triangle Club,** 251 Front St. (586-3140), attracts the more hard-drinking set, while young people and the cruise-ship crowd congregate at the **Penthouse** (463-4141), on the fourth floor of the Senate Building (open 8pm-whenever). The **Lady Lou Revue** (586-3686), a revival of Gold Rush days based on Robert Service's poems, presents weekly toe-tappin' musicals. A major family and tourist attraction, the revue is performed in the **Perseverance Theatre** in Merchants' Wharf, 2 Marine Way. Tickets can be purchased at the door or in local bookstores ($15, children $7.50). Call ahead for show times.

OUTDOORS

Near Juneau

If you're looking for the best view of the Juneau area and you want to burn a few calories, go to the end of 6th St. and head up the trail to the summit **Mt. Roberts** (3576 ft.)—a steep 4-mi. climb—but it's worth it. Though mining in these hills is (for the moment) no longer an active industry, the mines remain in business as tourist sights and frequently host salmon bakes. The **Alaska-Juneau Mine** was the largest in its heyday.

Juneau is one of the best hiking centers in southeast Alaska—after a half-hour hike from downtown, one can easily forget the city ever existed. In addition to the ascent of Mt. Roberts, **Perseverance Trail,** which leads past the ruins of the historic **Silverbowl Basin Mine** behind Mt. Roberts, makes for a pleasant day's trek. To reach this trailhead, follow Gold St. uphill until it turns into Basin Rd. The trail begins on the left side of the road just past a bridge. For more details on this and other area hikes, drop by the state museum bookstore, the Park Service Center, or any local bookstore to pick up *Juneau Trails,* published by the Alaska Natural History Association ($2.50). Rangers provide free copies of- maps from this book at the Park Service Center. (See U.S. Forest and National Park Service under Practical Information.)

During the winter the slopes of the **Eaglecrest Ski Area** on Douglas Island offer decent alpine skiing (155 S. Seward St., Juneau 99801, 586-5284 or 586-5330; $23 per day, children grades 7-12 $16, up to 6th grade $11; rental of skis, poles, and boots $20, children $14). The Eaglecrest Ski bus departs from the Baranof Hotel at 8:30am and returns at 5pm on winter weekends and holidays (round-trip to the slopes $5). In the summer, the Eaglecrest "Alpine Summer" self-guided nature trail is a good way to soak in the mountain scenery of virtually untouched Douglas Island.

Mendenhall Glacier

Three thousand years ago, the "Little Ice Age" froze over much of what is now southeastern Alaska, creating thousands of giant ice cubes whose descendants dot the region today. The most visited of these is the **Mendenhall Glacier,** about 10 mi. north of downtown Juneau. Mendenhall is only one of 38 glaciers in the **Juneau Ice Field,** which covers an area of over 1500 sq. mi. At the **Glacier Visitors Center,** rangers will explain everything you could possibly want to know about the glacier (open daily 9am-6:30pm). The rangers also give an interesting walking tour Sunday through Friday at 9:30am, beginning from the flagpole. The best view of the glacier without a helicopter is from the 3½-mi. **West Glacier Trail.** The cheapest way to reach the glacier is to hitchhike from anywhere along Glacier Hwy. A safer option is to take the local public bus down Glacier Hwy. and up Mendenhall Loop Rd. until it connects with Glacier Spur Rd. ($1.25). From there it's less than a half-hour walk to the visitors center. **Taxi tours** give you only 20 to 30 minutes at the glacier and run $46. **Ferry Express** organizes excellent tours (see Practical Information and Orientation), though a tour is by no means necessary to appreciate this hulking mass of ice.

■ Glacier Bay National Park and Preserve

In 1879, when naturalist John Muir became the first white man to see what nature had uncovered in Glacier Bay, he wrote, "These were the highest and whitest mountains, and the greatest of all the glaciers I had yet seen." He wasn't kidding. Crystal boulders float in the 65-mi.-long fjords of Glacier Bay, while humpback whales glide smoothly through the icy blue depths. **Glacier Bay National Park** encloses 16 tidewater glaciers as well as Mt. Fairweather of the St. Elias Range. Charter flights, tours, and cruise ships all make the spectacular voyage into **Muir Inlet,** offering close-up views of glaciers, rookeries, whales, and seals.

Because of the sensitive habits of wildlife in the area, the number of people allowed into the park is limited. Visitors should contact the **park superintendent** at Glacier Bay National Park and Preserve, Gustavus 99826 (697-2230). Wilderness camping and hiking are permitted throughout the park, and tour-boat skippers drop passengers off at points designated by the park service; you'll have to make arrangements to be picked up later.

Any visit to this park is expensive. The least costly way to get to the island is by **Alaska Airlines** (800-426-0333), which flies twice daily to Gustavus for $40-65 ($80-130 round-trip). Flights depart Juneau at 8:15am and 4:45pm daily and depart from Gustavus at 8:45am and 6pm daily. Gustavus is only 10 mi. from the park, and those who risk it say it's an easy hitch to Bartlett Cove, though a bus is available (round-trip $20). An **information center** is maintained in **Bartlett Cove** by the park service (open June-Sept. daily 9am-5:30pm. In winter, call 789-0097 Mon.-Fri. 8am-4:30pm). Once at Bartlett Cove, backpackers can stay in the free state campground, which has 25 sites and is rarely full.

In order to see the most impressive part of the park, the **West Arm,** it is necessary to take a boat tour. The *Spirit of Adventure* conducts an 8-hour tour of the glaciers for $145. For an extra $25, the boat will drop off campers or kayakers, and pick them up again at pre-arranged times. The *Spirit* is owned by the **Glacier Bay Lodge** (800-622-2042), which is next to Bartlett Cove and offers six different **sightseeing packages** for the glacier. The cheapest one includes bed and breakfast for $99. Singles at Glacier Bay Lodge run $115, doubles $138. **Puffin Travel, Inc.** (789-9787) runs a bed and breakfast and provides free bicycles and transfers to and from the airport (singles $40, doubles $60, each additional person $12). Puffin also operates a travel-booking service for other accommodations, as well as sightseeing, fishing, and photography tours. For more information, write to Puffin Travel, Inc., Box 3-LG, Gustavus, AK 99826. They also sell a package trip including round-trip airfare between Juneau and Gustavus, one night at the Puffin B&B, and a one-day tour of the park on the *Spirit of Adventure* for $300 per person (slightly lower for groups of 3 or 4).

Cruises into the park are also available, though they are quite expensive. **Alaska Sightseeing Tours** (800-426-7702) operates a three-day, two-night trip from Juneau that includes both the east and west arms of the bay ($500-700 per person). The cruise sails from May 28 to September 11 every Monday, Wednesday, and Friday at 4pm. **Alaska Discovery** organizes guided kayaking trips into Glacier Bay from Juneau (see Juneau: Practical Information).

■■■ HAINES

Haines occupies one of the most strikingly beautiful settings of any city on the Southeast Coast, with its clear blue water, granite coastal range, high percentage of sunny days, and abundance of breathtaking trails winding in and out of beaches, forest, and mountains. The area's star attraction arrives between November and January, when warm upwellings in the Chilkat River encourage an out-of-season salmon run that draws over 3000 bald eagles—more than double the town's human population—to the Chilkat Peninsula's "Council Grounds" for a midwinter feast.

Taking its name from a wealthy female patron who never visited the place, the city only became known as Haines in 1881 with the establishment of a Presbyterian mission (it was originally named Dershu, Tlingit for "The End of the Trail"). At the turn of the century, the military moved in to share space with the mission. Fort William H. Seward, a picturesque collection of white frame houses around a central nine-acre green, stands in sharp contrast to the haphazard layout of the rest of town. For nearly 20 years, this now decommissioned fort was the only army post in Alaska.

Haines (pop. 1240) now marks the end (or beginning) of the **Haines Hwy.,** the most heavily traveled overland route from the Interior and the Yukon into Southeastern Alaska. Built in the early 1890s by adventurer Jack Dalton, the highway was originally an improved Native American trail from Pyramid Harbor up to the Yukon. Dalton's investment paid off during the Gold Rush of 1897-99, when stampeding gold-seekers paid outlandish tolls to cross the quickest road to the Klondike.

PRACTICAL INFORMATION AND ORIENTATION

Visitors Information Center: (766-2234, 766-2202, or 800-458-3579, from British Columbia and the Yukon 800-478-2268), 2nd Ave. near Willard St. Information on accommodations, hiking around town, and surrounding parks. Make sure to pick up the free pamphlet *Haines is for Hikers*. Free tea and a place to stash your pack inside. Open Mon.-Sat. 8am-8pm, Sun. 10am-6pm; Oct.-April Mon.-Fri. 8am-5pm.

State Park Information Office, 259 Main St. (766-2292), above Helen's Shop. Legendary Ranger Bill Zack can tell you all you need to know about hiking in the area, the dangers of bears, and the Chilkat Bald Eagle Preserve. Open Tues.-Sat. 8-8:30am and 4-4:30pm.

Bank: First National Bank of Anchorage, Main St. (766-2321). Open Mon. 10am-5pm, Tues.-Fri. 10am-4pm. No ATM in town.

Air Service: L.A.B. Flying Service (766-2222), and **Wings of Alaska** (766-2030) both fly several times per day to Juneau ($50, round-trip $90). Wings has the cheapest flight to Gustavus near Glacier Bay ($85).

Buses: Alaskon Express, Box 574 (766-2030 or 800-544-2206), on 2nd Ave., across from the Visitors Center in the Wings of Alaska office. Buses leave Haines traveling north along the Haines Hwy. on Tues., Wed., Fri., and Sun., with an overnight stop in Beaver Creek, YT, near the Canadian border. To: Anchorage ($189), Fairbanks ($165), and Whitehorse ($76). Open Mon.-Sat. 7am-6pm. **Alaska-Direct** (800-770-6652) also makes runs to Anchorage ($175) and Fairbanks ($150) on Tues., Fri., and Sun.

Alaska Marine Highway: 766-2111. Terminal on 5 Mile Lutak Rd., 4 mi. from downtown. Hitchers can usually get into town—if they decide to risk it. A taxi runs $5. Daily ferry to Juneau ($24), to Skagway ($12).

Water Taxi: 766-3395. To Skagway, on a 40-ft. passenger boat (2 per day, $18, round-trip $29).

Taxi: Haines Taxi, 766-3138. **Other Guy's Taxi,** 766-3257. $5 from ferry to downtown Haines. 24 hr.

Ride Board: on the bulletin board in **Howser's Supermarket** on Main St. Many offers to share expenses to Anchorage or Fairbanks; few posted offers of rides.

Car Rental: Hertz (766-2131), in the Thunderbird Hotel. $35 per day, 40¢ per mi. **Independent Car Rental** (766-2891), at Eagle's Nest Motel. $42 per day, 100 mi. free, 30¢ for each extra mi.

Library: (766-2545), on Third Ave., 1 block below Main St. Open Tues. and Thurs. 10am-4:30pm and 7-9pm, Fri. 10am-4:30pm, Sat. 1-4pm, Sun. 2-4pm.

Laundromat and Showers: Port Chilkoot Camper Park (766-2000), across from Halsingland Hotel. Wash $2, 7 min. dry 25¢. Showers $1.50. Open daily 7:30am-9pm. **Susie Q's,** Main St. near Front St. Wash $2, dry 50¢. Showers $2. Open daily 8am-8pm; in winter daily 8am-6pm.

Health Center: 766-2521.

Ambulance and Emergency: 911. **Police:** 766-2121.

Post Office: On Haines Hwy., between 2nd Ave. and Front St. Open Mon.-Fri. 9am-5:30pm, Sat. 1-3pm. **General Delivery ZIP Code:** 99827.

Area Code: 907.

Haines lies on a thin peninsula between the Chilkat and Chilkoot Inlets. Below this narrow neck of land, the two inlets merge into **Lynn Canal.** Don't confuse your Chilkats and Chilkoots—the former refers to the "big baskets of fish" taken from that river, and the latter to the "big baskets of *even bigger* fish" in the other. Both the U.S. and Canada have **customs offices** (767-5511 and 767-5540) at Mile 42 of the Haines Hwy. (open daily 7am-11pm). Travelers must have at least $150 and a credit card, as well a valid proof of citizenship to cross into Canada, although the border officials generally enforce this requirement at their whim.

ACCOMMODATIONS AND CAMPING

There are a number of choices for backpackers in Haines. In addition to the spots listed below, there are several **state campgrounds** in and around Haines which vie for budget travelers. **Portage Cove,** ¾ mi. from town on Beach Rd., accepts only backpackers and bicyclists. **Chilkat State Park,** 7 mi. south on Mud Bay Rd., offers 32 sites by the sea with good fishing and guided nature walks. **Chilkoot Lake,** 10 mi. north of town on Lutak Rd., provides fresh-water views and fishing. **Mosquito Lake,** 27 mi. north on the Haines Hwy. is a smaller spot with only seven sites to better acquaint you with the bloodsuckers. All state campground sites have water and toilets for $6.50.

Bear Creek Camp and Hostel (HI/AYH), Box 1158 (766-2259), on Small Tract Rd. 2 mi. outside of town. From downtown, follow 3rd Ave. out Mud Bay Rd. to Small Tract Rd. A ring of very basic cabins around a circular drive, 2 of which are hostel dorms. Rarely full. Many guests work in the area and hang around the hostel to kill time. Somewhat unclean kitchen facilities, free showers for guests, and laundry (wash $1.50, dry 25¢). No curfew. Call from ferry terminal for pickup. Members $10, nonmembers $15, family cabins $35. Tentsites for $5 may be the best way to go ($2 per for each additional person).

Hotel Halsingland, Box 1589MD, Haines 99827 (800-542-2525 or 766-2000). The coolest hotel in town, located in the old Ft. Seward officers' quarters. Intriguing decor. Rooms $30, with bath $75. Next door is **The Officers' Inn Bed and Breakfast.** Bathless singles $50. Doubles $55.

Fort Seward Lodge, Box 307-RG, Haines 99827 (766-2009). Fine view of Lynn Canal from another historic Fort Seward building. 10 rooms at reasonable rates. Singles with shared bath $40. Doubles from $45. Oct-April rooms are $10 less.

Mountain View Inn (766-2900), at the entrance to Ft. Seward on Mud Bay Rd. 8 units with HBO and kitchenettes. Singles $61. Doubles $67. Triples $72. Quads $78. Frequently full, so call ahead.

Summer Inn Bed and Breakfast, 247 2nd Ave., P.O. Box 1198 (766-2970). Nice rooms, full breakfast, and great view of the Lynn Canal and surrounding mountains. Singles $55. Doubles $65. Triple $85.

Port Chilkoot Camper Park, Box 473 (766-2755), across from Hotel Halsingland. 60 sites for tents ($6.75) and RVs (full hookup $15). Laundromat (see Practical Information), showers ($1.50), and telephone available.

Haines Hitch-Up RV Park, P.O. Box 383, Haines 99827 (766-2882), ½ mi. west of town on Main St. Laundry (wash $1.50, 7-min. dry 25¢), free showers. 92 full-hookup units $16.

FOOD

Those wishing to forego restaurant fare can hit **Howser's Supermarket** (766-2040) on Main St. The store has a great salad bar with a large pasta selection ($3 per lb.), and a deli counter with surprisingly good chow—try the 5 Jo-Jos (deep-fried potato wedges) and golden 3-piece fried chicken ($4). (Open daily 8am-8pm. Deli open daily 7am-7pm.) You can pick up bulk health foods at **The Mountain Market** (766-2962) at Haines Hwy. and 3rd Ave. (open Mon.-Sat. 9am-6pm). For retail seafood at wholesale prices, try **Alaska Salmon and Seafood** (766-2904), at 4th Ave. and Main.

Porcupine Pete's (766-9199), Main and 2nd Ave. Rustic, cheap food. The carved duo depicted on a totem by local artist David Stead is meant to represent "Pete" and his porcupine mascot from mining days in the Porcupine mines. The hamburger pita, a tasty sourdough-calzone concoction, fills your plate like a small bowling ball. Open daily 11am-10pm.

Commander's Room (766-2000), in Hotel Halsingland. Expensive fare with one notable exception: the soup and all-you-can-eat salad and taco bar lunch special ($7). Open daily 7am-2pm and 5:30-10pm.

Chilkat Restaurant and Bakery (766-2920), on 5th Ave., near Main. Family-style restaurant with healthy portions. Gentlemen prefer Haines' *best* baked goods: bread loaves ($2.10), cinnamon rolls ($1.25). All-you-can-eat soup-and-salad bar ($8). Sandwiches $3.50-5.25. Open Mon.-Sat. 7am-9pm, Sun. 9am-9pm.

Bamboo Room (776-9109), 2nd Ave. near Main St., next to the Pioneer Bar. Great breakfast spot, always crowded with fisherfolk on their way out to the nets down-

ing the buckwheat hotcakes and coffee ($4.25), and omelettes with hashbrowns
and toast (from $6.25). Lunch specials $6, dinner specials $10-13. Breakfast til
3pm. Open daily 6am-10pm.

Cottonwood Cafe (766-3122), Union and Main St. 2 eggs, hashbrowns, and toast
($4.75). Biscuits and gravy ($5). Breakfast til 8pm. Looks like we've got a breakfast war right here in Haines! Open Wed.-Mon. 8am-8pm.

Port Chilkoot Potlatch (766-2000), at the Tribal House of Ft. Seward. All-you-can-
eat salmon bake and BBQ with all the trimmings ($19.75). The Potlatch is a tourist
trap, but the salmon is unbeatable. Reservations recommended, since tickets are
pre-sold to cruise ships. Salmon served nightly 5-8pm except Thurs.

SIGHTS

Fort William Seward, on the west side of town, was originally established in 1901
to assert an American presence during a border dispute with Canada. With little else
to do other than shovel snow and watch for fires, the post quickly became known
as a gentle assignment. Boredom was in fact the soldiers' only enemy: "Even among
men with the most modern arms, time is the hardest thing to kill," lamented one
observer in a 1907 newspaper. After being declared surplus at the end of WWII, five
veterans bought the entire 400-acre compound, sight unseen, with plans of making
a commune out of the old fort. Their utopian venture never succeeded, but most of
these settlers became (free-) enterprising members of the community and today
Fort Seward lies at the center of Haines's tourist activity. In the middle of the
grounds sits a replica of a **Totem Village** (766-2160), complete with a tribal house.
The **Chilkat Dancers** perform traditional Native dances here Thursdays at 8pm ($8,
students $4, children under 5 free). The village is also home to the local salmon bake
(see Food above) and the Sea Wolf studio (below). Crossing to the far side of the
parade grounds takes you to the **Alaska Indian Arts Center** (766-2160). Inside, visitors are welcome to watch Native artisans in their workshops and marvel at the craft
of totem pole carving. (Open Mon.-Fri. 9am-noon and 1-5pm. The Chilkat Dancers
perform here as well on Mon., Wed., and Sat. nights.)

In town, the worthwhile **Sheldon Museum,** 25 Main St., houses Native art and
artifacts upstairs and exhibits on the history of Haines downstairs. Movies about
Haines are shown starting at 1:30pm (open in summer daily 1-5pm; admission
$2.50). The museum's benefactor acquired his first piece in collection at the tender
age of eight. Haines is also something of an artists' colony. Check out the works of
local artists in galleries near the visitors center; the **Northern Arts Gallery** (766-
2318, open daily 10am-5pm), the **Chilkat Valley Arts** (766-2990; open daily 9am-
6pm), and the **Sea Wolf Studio** (766-2540; open Mon.-Fri. 9am-5pm) in Fort Seward
are particularly noteworthy. Galleries here offer unusually high quality craft work in
fur, wood, and photography rather than the usual tourist cache.

Capitalizing on the natural grandeur surrounding Haines, Hollywood producers
chose to shoot the film version of Jack London's novel *White Fang* here in 1990.
The stage set for the movie, essentially a scaled-down front of an Old West town, has
been recycled into the tourist mill of **Dalton City.** Located about 1 mi. out of town
on the Haines Hwy. at the fairgrounds, this small array of souvenir shops and eateries offers little that is any more authentic than the piped-in ragtime music. The proprietors seem to be modifying this newly opened operation as they go—check the
Haines Visitors Guide for a list of activities before schlepping out to the Fairgrounds.
(Dalton City is open in summer Mon.-Sat. 10am-8pm, Sun. noon-8pm. Free.)

OUTDOORS: HIKING

The Haines Hwy. winds 40 mi. from Haines through the **Chilkat Range** and up
through the Yukon Territory in Canada. The views are guaranteed to blow you
though the back of your Winnebago. **Chilkat State Park,** a 19-mi. drive up the highway, protects the largest population of bald eagles in North America—3500 of
them. From November through January, travelers can see great numbers of eagles
perched on birchwoods in the rivers or flying overhead. To get the best view of

these rare birds, go see the most excellent Ranger Zack for trail tips. (You can pick up *Haines is for Hikers* there or at the Visitors Information Center; see Practical Information.)

Three main **trails** head into the hills around Haines. The closest trailhead to the hostel is that of the moderate hike up to the 1760-ft. summit of **Mt. Riley,** where heads spin with the amazing 360° view. The trail begins at a marker about 1½ mi. down Mud Bay Rd. past the hostel. Little water lies along the 2.1-mi. route which clears the treeline only just before reaching the summit.

Two other, longer trails also lead up Mt. Riley from closer to town. To reach the **Port Chilkoot trail,** walk out the FAA road behind Officers' Row in Fort Seward. After 1 mi., the road leads into a city water route, and 2 mi. along this byway a five-minute spur trail branches off to connect with the Mud Bay route. From Fort Seward to the summit is a 3.8-mi. trek.

The third route, called the **Portage Cove route,** follows the road along the cove and then the level Batter Point trail beside the shore. Just before the Batter Point trail reaches the beach, a right fork leads up to Mt. Riley. This approach is a 5½-mi. hike.

The long but not very laborious **Seduction Point trail** offers 6¾ mi. of birds, beaches, ocean bluffs, berry picking, wildflowers, and a view of alpine glacier Davidson. Take Mud Bay Rd. out of Haines 7 mi. and look for the trailhead. Try to time the last part of the hike along David's Cove to coincide with low tide.

Mt. Ripinsky, the 3920-ft. massif looming over town to the north, provides a challenging hike over two summits connected by an alpine ridge. On a clear day, the view from the ridge extends all the way to Juneau. To reach the trailhead, follow 2nd Ave. north to Lutak Rd. Branch off Lutak onto Yung St. at the hill, and then turn right along a buried pipeline for 1 mi. The trail cuts off to the left a few yards after the pipeline right of way begins to descend steeply towards the tank farm. After cresting at the 3610-ft. **North Summit,** the trail dips down along the ridge where it may be difficult to follow in poor weather. At the end of the ridge, it climbs again to the 3920-ft. peak, and then descends steeply to its terminus at Mile 7 of Haines Hwy. This 10-mi. hike makes for a long day's walking or a more relaxed overnight trip.

Alaska Nature Tours, P.O. Box 491 (766-2876), leads you to the eagles for a three-hour tour ($45, fall only). The people with Nature Tours are experts at observation and photography of bears, moose, and sea lions. **Chilkat Guides,** P.O. Box 170 (766-2491), leads four-hour raft trips down the Chilkat River, leaving several times daily in the summer. Rubber boots, ponchos, and transportation to and from the river are provided ($70, children $30). The **Southeast Alaska State Fair** lights up the fairground here August 10-14 in 1994, while concurrently blues and bluegrass artists strut their stuff at the **Alaska Bald Eagle Music Festival**.

Locals ham it up in the Friday- and Sunday-night Vaudeville "The Smell of the Yukon." Catch it at the Chilkat Center for the Arts (8pm; tickets $7, ages 5-18 $4).

The **Master Anglers Tournament** runs in late August, and **Alcan 200 Snowmobile Races** on January 22 in 1994 makes the winter considerably livelier for those in the area.

■ ■ ■ SKAGWAY

In 1896, George Carmack, Skookum Jim, and Tagish Charley made an unlikely discovery in a tributary off the Klondike River—gold lying thick between slabs of rock "like cheese in a sandwich." Within two years, Skagway and nearby Dyea (DY-ee) were besieged by legions of crazed stampeders heading for the Klondike gold. Each town marked the head of a trail over the coastal mountains and down to the headwaters of the Yukon River. From Skagway, the stampeders pushed their pack horses mercilessly along the rocky but relatively gradual White Pass Trail. Nearly 3000 horses expired along this route in the winter of 1897-98, thereby earning it a more fitting name—the Dead Horse Trail. The Chilkoot Trail, starting in Dyea, climbs too steeply for pack animals. The average gold-seeker, in the course of lugging a ton of food and supplies over the mountains, traversed this route 30 to 40 times.

While most opportunists labored along these trails in hopes of hitting gold, others seized upon more illicit means of striking it rich. Almost all of the operators in this business took orders from one Soapy Smith, the legendary crime boss of Skagway. Soapy's ingenious schemes to fleece those rushing heavy-laden off the Klondike included a mock telegraph office, even though countless miles of wilderness separated Skagway from the nearest telegraph cable. And yet Soapy ensured that a return message came through—always collect. An enigmatic figure who established an orphanage for stray dogs as readily as he robbed people blind, Soapy died in a shoot-out with his opponent Frank Reid, a local hero whose headstone reads, "He gave his life for the honor of Skagway."

Today, Dyea is little more than a ghost town. But Skagway, kept alive by the rail-road built along the White Pass Trail, has been restored wholesale by the National Park Service to its original 1898 condition—right down to the wooden sidewalks. Visitors come to revel in Skagway's history as well as to enjoy an amazing array of hiking opportunities second only to those found around Juneau. A scant 29 in. of annual rainfall means that hikers are almost always rewarded with clear views. And, largely because of the sheer bluffs which line the way, the one-hour ferry ride from Haines to Skagway is considered to be one of the Inside Passage's most impressive stretches.

PRACTICAL INFORMATION AND ORIENTATION

Visitors Information: Klondike Gold Rush National Historical Park Visitor Center (983-2921), 2nd and Broadway. Walking tours daily at 10:30 and 11:15am, 3:15 and 5:15pm. An excellent introduction to Skagway's history is the film *Days of Adventure, Dreams of Gold,* narrated by Hal Holbrook and shown on the hr. Open May-Sept. daily 8am-8pm. **Skagway Convention and Visitors Bureau** (983-2855), in the Arctic Brotherhood building on Broadway, between 2nd and 3rd. Pick up the free Skagway Trail Map here. Performs the *Skagway Story* at 10am, 12:15, 2:45, and 4:45pm; $2.50. Open daily 8:30am-5:30pm.

Long Distance Phone: Alascom Phone Service (983-9150), on Broadway, between 5th and 6th. Open when cruise ships are in.

Flights: Skagway Air Service, 983-2218. 7 flights per day to Juneau ($70).

Trains: White Pass and Yukon Route, P.O. Box 435 (800-343-7373 or 983-2217), 1 block off Broadway on 2nd. 3-hr. round-trip excursion to White Pass Summit, on one of the steepest railroad grades in North America. Trains leave daily at 8:45am and 1:15pm ($72, under 13 $36). Combined train and motorcoach service to and from Whitehorse, YT. Train leaves daily at 12:45pm. ($92 one-way, under 13 $46).

Buses: Alaskon Express (800-544-2206 or 983-2241), in the Westmark Inn, 3rd Ave. between Broadway and Spring. Buses Tues.-Wed., Fri., and Sun. at 7:30am. To: Anchorage ($200) and Fairbanks ($189). All trips include an overnight stop in Beaver Creek near the border. Also 1 per day in summer to Whitehorse, YT ($52) at 7:30am. **Alaska Direct** (800-770-6652) runs vans from the hostel and hotels. To: Whitehorse ($35) daily, with connections on Tues., Fri., and Sun. to Fairbanks ($120), and Anchorage ($145).

Alaska Marine Highway: 983-2941. Ferries daily to Haines ($12, vehicle up to 15 ft. $53) and Juneau ($24, vehicle up to 15 ft. $85).

Water Taxi: 776-3395. A 40-passenger boat cruises twice daily to Haines ($18, round-trip $29).

Taxi: Pioneer Taxi, 983-2623. To Dyea and Chilkoot Trail ($15). Combination tour of town, waterfront, and White Pass ($24). **Klondike Tours** (983-2075) also runs from the hostel to the Chilkoot Trail head daily 6:45am, 5, and 9:30pm ($10).

Car Rental: Sourdough Shuttle (983-2525), at 6th Ave. and Broadway, is by far the cheapest at $25 per day. **Avis** (983-2247), 2nd and Spring. $46 per day, 100 free mi., plus 35¢ per additional mi. Must be 25 with a credit card for insurance.

Bike Rental: Corner Cafe, 4th and State St. Bikes rent out quickly at $3 per hr., $5 per 2 hr., $7 per day. **Sockeye Cycle** (983-2851), on 5th Ave. off Broadway. Rates begin at $5 per hr., $15 per day.
Bookstore: Skagway News Depot (983-2354), Broadway between 2nd and 3rd. Small collection of Alaskan travel books. Open daily 8:30am-7:30pm.
Library: 8th Ave. and Broadway. Open Mon.-Fri. 1-9pm, Sat. 1-5pm.
Laundromat: Service Unlimited Laundromat, 2nd Ave. and State St. Wash $2, dry 25¢. Open daily 8am-9pm.
Hospital: Skagway Medical Service, 983-2255 or 983-2418.
Post Office: Broadway and 6th, next to the bank. Open Mon.-Fri. 8:30am-5pm. **General Delivery ZIP Code:** 99840. Lobby open 24 hr. for postage machine.
Area Code: 907.

At the same latitude as Stockholm, Sweden and at the northernmost tip of the Inside Passage, Skagway is the terminus of the Alaska Marine Hwy. From here, travelers on wheels can connect to the Alaska Hwy. by taking Yellowhead Hwy. 2 to Whitehorse via Carcross. Haines is located only 12 mi. away by water, but 359 mi. away by road. Hitchers say they do better by spending $12 on the ferry to Haines and try the more heavily traveled Haines Hwy. to the Interior. (*Let's Go* does not recommend hitchhiking.)

Only about 700 people spend the winter in Skagway, another 1500 arrive for summer jobs in the tourist industry, and on a busy day 3000 visitors may spill off the cruise ships in search of the ultimate bauble.

ACCOMMODATIONS

With a recently refurbished bunkhouse and an unbelievably friendly hostel, Skagway does well by budget travelers. Campers can either shell out $8 for sites at **Hanousek Park,** on 14th at Broadway, or head out for the **Chilkoot Trail** in Dyea, 9 mi. from Skagway, to stay at the free ranger-staffed campground there. It is wise to make reservations at least one month in advance at all Skagway hotels. Also see the **Forest Service cabins** mentioned in the Outdoors: Hiking section below.

Skagway Home Hostel (983-2131), 3rd and Main, 1 mi. from the ferry. Located in a turn-of-the-century house, this is not just another hostel—it's nothing less than an experiment in group living. Unique in that the owners have chosen to share all their facilities and supplies with guests, this hostel operates largely on the same trust and consideration which bind a family. Hostelers are welcome to join in the family dinner for a contribution of $5 or for free if they would like to cook. Pick up at every ferry. No lockout, free showers, kitchen. $3 for wash, dry, and detergent. 19 beds and 2 rooms for couples. Chore required. Will store packs. Check-in 5:30-9pm. $10, nonmembers $12. Reservations by phone recommended.
Skagway's Pullen Creek Bunkhouse, 285 8th St. (983-2737), between Spring and Broadway, beside Rolf's Rabbit Ranch. More formal than the hostel, and no chore required. 16 bunkbeds, kitchen, TV, showers ($1). No max stay. $9 per night.
Hanousek Park (983-2768), on Broadway at 14th, 1½ mi. north of the ferry. Privately run. Drinking water, modern bathrooms with showers (25¢ for 2 min.), fire rings. Sites $8, with RV hookup $16.
Irene's Bed and Breakfast (983-2520), Broadway and 6th Ave. Small, pleasant singles $38. Doubles $54. Shared bath.
Portland House and Inn (983-2493), 5th Ave. and Main. A no-frills cheap-sleep above the Greek place. 1 bed in a 3-bed room, $30. Doubles $45. Shared bath.
Golden North Hotel, P.O. Box 431 (983-2294), at 3rd Ave. and Broadway. A splendid hotel, the oldest operating in the state. Each room is restored to period style in unique fashion, some with canopy beds, claw-footed bathtubs, and the like. Singles $40, with bath $60. Doubles $45, with bath $75.
Skagway Inn, P.O. Box 500 (983-2289), on Broadway at 7th. Built in 1897 as a brothel, the inn is now respectably refurbished—except for the names of the

former businesswomen tacked up on the walls. Courtesy van to the Chilkoot Trail head. Shared bath. Hearty breakfast included. Singles $55. Doubles $66.

Dyea Camping Area, 9 mi. southwest of Skagway on the Dyea Rd. This free campground is near the base of the **Chilkoot Trail,** and contains 22 sites. Pit toilets, fire rings, but no drinking water or showers. 2-week max. stay.

Pullen Creek Park Campground (983-2768) on the waterfront, by the small boat harbor. Showers and 42 RV sites with full hookup. Sites $16.

FOOD

Campers can pick up last-minute groceries for the Chilkoot trail at the small **Fairway Supermarket** at 4th and State (open daily 8am-10pm). The majority of restaurants in Skagway are located in the Historic District, on Broadway between 2nd and 7th St.

Corner Cafe, 4th and State. Where the locals head for grub. Open-air seating lets you avoid the smoke. Stack of sourdough pancakes ($3.25); biscuits and gravy ($3.75). Burgers and sandwiches $4-6. Open daily 6am-9pm.

Prospector's Sourdough Restaurant (983-2865), on Broadway between 3rd and 4th Ave. All-you-can-eat salad bar and soup ($7 11am-4pm, $8 after 4 pm). Open daily 6am-10pm.

Sweet Tooth Cafe (983-2405), on Broadway between 3rd and 4th St. Sandwiches and soup or salad ($4.75-5.60). The cheapest halibut burger in town ($5.60). This cafe scoops a mean ice cream cone ($1.60). Open daily 6am-6pm.

The Popcorn Wagon, Broadway and 5th. Down on your luck, or just plain tired of sit-down meals? Stop here for chili ($2.50) and a large lemonade ($1.50).

SIGHTS AND SEASONAL EVENTS

Most of Broadway (which is most of town) is preserved in pristine 1898 form as the **Klondike Gold Rush National Historic Park.** The Park Service has assembled a small museum beside the visitors center and restored a vintage saloon on Broadway. Many other period pieces have been leased to local businesses. Check out the worthwhile hourly film at the Park's visitors center (see Practical Information). Then wander down Broadway to peep at the **Red Onion Saloon,** Skagway's first bordello, on 2nd Ave. In the ol' days, each lady marked her availability by placing one of the dolls on the rack downstairs in the appropriate position—upright or prostrate. Goodness. Now the Red Onion is a locally favored bar with an enviable collection of bed pans adorning one wall. Come for live afternoon jazz on ship days or for the open jam on Thursday nights, and check out the fading photos of past *femmes fatales* (open daily 11am-whenever; free).

Farther down Broadway is the 1899 **Arctic Brotherhood Hall,** Alaska's first goldmining fraternity. Founded in 1899 as the fraternal order of Klondike Gold Stampeders, it had as its motto "No Boundary Line Here." Twenty-thousand pieces of driftwood cover the façade of the Hall, making for a rather bizarre example of Victorian rustic architecture.

True gold rush buffs can mine for pleasure at the **Trail of '98 Museum,** on the second floor of City Hall, at 7th Ave. and Spring St. (open daily 9am-5pm; admission $2, students $1). Check out the world's only duck-neck robe patterned out of throttled mallard throats and view the Frank Reid-Soapy Smith paraphernalia for some real frontier flavor. Soapy's blood-stained tie hangs here. If you care to delve deeper into this titanic clash between the forces of good and evil, wander out along State St. until it meets 23rd Ave. and look for the sign pointing to Soapy's grave across the railroad tracks in the **Gold Rush Cemetery.** Frank Reid pushes up grass here, too, along with many other stampeders who never made it to the gold fields. Beyond the cemetery and farther out of town **Reid Falls** gently cascade 300 ft. down the mountainside.

If you happen to be in the vicinity of these Elysian fields at 10:30pm on July 8, you can witness the celebration of **Soapy's Wake**—an ironic event that was never meant to be an event at all. Several years ago on the anniversary of Soapy's death, a few locals gathered in the cemetery to down some Champagne, recite amateur poetry, and relieve themselves on Frank Reid's grave. Tour guides publicized the impromptu gathering as an "event" and people began arriving to see the spectacle. A small group now obliges the crowd with a perfunctory wake, but the police have begun to make noises about the defacing of public monuments. For a more genuine display of Skagway's town spirit, try the lively **Solstice Party** every June 21.

Back in town, the museum in the back of the **Corrington Alaskan Ivory Co.** (983-2580), 5th and Broadway, contains an intriguing display of carved bone and ivory pieces, most of which are affordable—if you've managed to strike gold recently yourself (open daily 9am-9pm). **Inside Passage Arts** (983-2585), Broadway and 4th St., sells some of the finest works of local Native artists. Come in to view even if you can't buy (open daily 9am-5pm; later when cruise ships are in).

At night, go to the **Skagway Days of '98** show in the Eagles Dance Hall (983-2234), 6th and Broadway. The show, in its 68th year, features song and dance, play-money gambling by the audience, and audience-actor interaction—definitely worth the money (tickets $14, kids $7). You'll learn all you ever wanted to know about Soapy Smith here (daily in summer; 7:30pm gambling, 8:30pm show). Check the marquee for frequent morning performances that vary with cruise ships ($12, kids $6).

Built as the gold craze calmed in 1900, the **railroad cars** of the White Pass & Yukon Route have been resurrected from the West's locomotive graveyards and now run from Skagway to the summit of Whitepass and back. The scenery of this narrow passage is overwhelmingly beautiful. (Trains run May 24-Sept. 27 daily at 8:45am and 1:15pm. Irregular service before May 24. Fare $72, under 13 $36.)

Dyea, near the head of the Chilkoot Trail, lies 9 mi. out of Skagway on the unpaved Dyea Rd. The town fell into a precipitous decline following the gold rush, and scavengers quickly moved in to dismantle houses, banks, hotels, and other buildings for scrap wood. Today the only evidence of Dyea's former glory are scattered foundations, the remnants of wooden pilings that once supported a large wharf, and **Slide Cemetery** where victims of a terrible avalanche on the Chilkoot Pass are buried. The Park Service runs daily walking tours of Dyea during the summer at 1:30pm. They will explain, among other things, why the wharves are now hundreds of feet from the water (which, so you won't be left in suspense, is due to glacial rebound—the land is rising as glaciers melt). The taxi fare to Dyea is roughly $10, but you can rent a bicycle for the day and peddle there for $7 (see Practical Information above).

OUTDOORS: HIKING

Although the Chilkoot Trail is the marquee name in Skagway hiking, there are a number of excellent shorter hikes in the area with both inspiring views and fewer people around you to block them.

The **Dewey Lake Trail System** provides some of the best hikes near town, ranging from a 20-min. stroll to a strenuous climb up to a 3700-ft. elevation and two alpine lakes. To reach the trail system, walk east toward the mountains along 2nd. Ave. Cross the railroad tracks and follow a dirt road to the left, where you'll shortly find signs pointing out the trail.

Lower Dewey Lake, a long, narrow pond surrounded by woods, lies less than a mile up the trail. Here one trail branches out around the lake (about 2 mi.), and another towards **Icy Lake** and Upper Reid Falls (about 1½ mi.). Both of these walks are very gentle, with little or no change in elevation.

A third trail to **Upper Dewey Lake** branches off the Icy Lake trail near the northern end of Lower Dewey Lake. A steep climb leads 2¼ mi. up to the upper lake, which occupies a stunning amphitheater of serrated peaks. A small **cabin** with space for four and a permanent smell of smoke sits by the lake. It is available on a first-come, first-served basis. The best **camping sites** are along the opposite shore. An extension of the Upper Dewey trail leads south from the lake 1 mi. across a rocky alpine bench to the limpid waters of the **Devil's Punchbowl.** Excellent views of the inlet below make this sidetrip well worthwhile. Chunks of snow float in this transparent pool well into midsummer, and the water is so clear that you'll have no trouble spotting the freckles on the trout. Plan on a three-hour trip one-way from town to the Punchbowl.

A.B. Mountain, so named for the pattern created by the melting snow on its side each spring, dominates the skyline on the west side of town. The **Skyline Trail** leads up this mountain. A 1½-mi. walk from town leads out to the Skyline Trailhead. Cross the Skagway River footbridge at the north-west end of First Ave., and turn left on Dyea Rd. The trailhead lies to the right at the crest of a hill. It is a poorly marked and steep 5-mi. hike to the 3500-ft. summit.

Two other hikes near Skagway combine cabins, glaciers, and the White Pass and Yukon Route railroad. The trail to the **Denver Glacier** begins just short of milepost 6 on the WP and YR railroad. This trail passes below the towering walls of the Sawtooth Range and winds down in the brush of the Denver Glacier moraine. The 4½-mi. hike ends near a Forest Service **cabin** close to the glacier. Enquire at the Park Visitor Center (see Practical Information above) about the availability of the cabin. Don't chance a walk out to the trailhead along the tracks. The WP and YR train will deposit hikers at the trail on its two daily trips to White Pass and make a flag stop to bring them back to town ($10).

The **Laughton Glacier Trail,** beginning at milepost 14 along the train tracks to White Pass, makes an easy 1½-mi. ascent to an immense wall of hanging glaciers. The **cabin,** a cozy spot for up to six people, sits about 1 mi. from the ice at the junction of two rivers. The round-trip train fare to and from the trailhead is $30.

■ The Chilkoot Trail

The winter of 1898 saw nine out of every ten Klondike-bound stampeders slog through Skagway and neighboring Dyea. Formerly a Native American footpath, the Chilkoot Trail extends 33 mi. from the ghost town of **Dyea** to the shores of **Lake Bennett** over the precipitous **Chilkoot Pass.** The four- to five-day hike (3 days for seasoned hikers) is littered with wagon wheels, horse skeletons, and other ballast the prospectors jettisoned, as well as informative plaques placed by the National Park Service.

Although the Chilkoot is considered one of the best trails in Alaska, it is also one of the busiest. Although the traffic is nothing compared to the height of the stampede—when gold-seekers stepped on each other's heels as they trudged ant-like over the pass—the trail remains well-worn with 50 hikers setting out per day in the summer. This adventure offers grand scenery and an exciting chance to retrace history, if not a solitary communion with the mountains. Despite its popularity, the Chilkoot is an extremely demanding trail. Weather conditions change rapidly, especially in the Summit area; avalanches are not uncommon even well into June. Be sure to check with the ranger at the visitors center at 2nd and Broadway in Skagway (see Practical Information) for current trail conditions before you leave. Rangers patrol the U.S. side of the trail and are also usually at the trailhead in Dyea (daily 5-7pm). If planning to continue into the Yukon Territory, be sure to call **Canadian customs** (403-821-4111) before leaving Skagway (Dyea has no phones), and have proof of solvency ($150 and a credit card, plus a valid photo ID and birth certificate) before crossing the border.

To return to Skagway, leave the trail between Lake Bennett and Bare Loon Lake and follow the White Pass railroad tracks (be careful, this is private property) back to the Klondike Hwy. Rides are reportedly easy to find.

The Interior

Alaska's vast Interior sprawls between the Alaska Range to the south and the Arctic Brooks Range to the north, covering 166,000 sq. mi. of the nation's wildest and most startling terrain. Most of the Interior alternates between flat patchworks of forest and marshy, treeless tundra; the drainages of numerous rivers have created the sloughs, inlets, lakes, bogs, and swamps that sustain the world's largest waterfowl population. The unofficial state bird, the mosquito, outnumbers all other animals by over 1000 to 1 in the summer. (Natives love to joke that "there is not a single mosquito in the state of Alaska—they're all married and have kids.") Earth-bound inhabitants include moose, grizzlies, wolves, caribou, Dall (bighorn) sheep, lynx, beavers, hares, and very few mammals of the two-legged variety; outside Fairbanks (the state's second-largest city), the region is sparsely inhabited.

Interior Alaska is the home of the Athabascan Native Americans, many of whom still trap, hunt, and fish within the Interior's network of waterways. These nomadic hunters' traditional domain was an area much larger than that of the Inuits; they followed the migration of caribou and the spawning cycles of salmon. Unlike Native Americans in the Lower 48, Athabascans have not been confined to reservations; instead, they own title to their own land, a result of the Alaska Native Land Claims Settlement Act. Although many have left their remote villages and traditional lifestyle for modern living in Fairbanks and Anchorage, their pride in their unique cultural heritage—as well as in their physical endurance—is preserved in traditional stories and games. Today Athabascans still compete in dogsled races and in the annual World Eskimo-Indian Olympics, where thousands of spectators watch spectacles of pain and stamina, including races that involve tying 10-lb. weights to participants' earlobes.

Awesome Denali (Mt. McKinley) towers above its 14,000-ft. neighbors in the Alaska Range. In summer the mountain can be seen from as far away as downtown Anchorage, 250 mi. to the south. In the winter, long days are supplanted by eternal night, and the splendorous vision of Denali is replaced by the northern lights. Some native traditions hold the lights to be representative of the spirits of the dead.

■■ KLUANE NATIONAL PARK (AND HAINES JUNCTION)

On July 16, 1741—St. Elias Day—Captain Vitus Bering, on board a sealer out of Russia, sighted the mountains of what is now the southwest Yukon. The pristine St. Elias Mountains have remained almost completely undeveloped. A brief gold rush in the early 1900s and the later construction of the Alaska Highway in 1942 have led to what limited development there is around the perimeter of the mountains. Also in 1942, a privy council order established a wildlife reserve in the St. Elias mountains. In 1976, the Canadian government gazetted the entire southwest corner of the Yukon and proclaimed it **Kluane** (Kloo-AH-nee) **National Park.** ("Kluane" is a southern Tutchone word, meaning "the place of many fish.") Kluane is Canadian wilderness at its most rugged, unspoiled, and beautiful.

The "Green Belt" along the eastern park boundary, at the feet of the mountains' Kluane Range, supports the greatest diversity of plant and animal species in northern Canada. Beyond the Kluane loom the glaciers of the Icefield Range—home to Canada's highest peaks, including the tallest of all, 19,850-ft. Mr. Logan. Beset by harsh and moist Pacific winds, these glaciers and mountains cover nearly two-thirds of the park and are accessible only to the most intrepid alpinist and adventurer.

Practical Information Before heading for the hills pick up plenty of free information at the **Haines Junction Visitor Centre,** on Logan St. in Haines Junction (Canadian Park Service 634-2251; Tourism Yukon 634-2345; open mid-May to mid-Sept. daily 9am-9pm), which also sponsors a number of guided hikes and campfire talks from mid-June through August, or at the **Sheep Mountain Visitor Centre,** at Alaska Hwy. km 1707 (841-5161; open June to mid-Sept. daily 8am-5pm). Visitors may also write to Superintendent, Kluane National Park and Preserve, Parks Service, Environment Canada, Haines Junction, YT Y0B 1L0 for information.

Kluane's 22,015 square km are bounded by Kluane Game Sanctuary and the Alaska Hwy. to the north, and Haines Rd. to the east. The town of Haines Junction is located at the eastern park boundary, 158km west of Whitehorse. **Alaska Direct** (800-770-6652, in Whitehorse 668-4833) runs three buses per week from Haines Act. to Anchorage, AK (US$125), Fairbanks, AK (US$100), Haines, AK (US$30), and Whitehorse (US$20).

You can catch Yukon Gold (CKYN), the **visitor radio** station, at FM96.1. **Emergency numbers** in Haines Junction include: **medical,** 634-2213; **fire,** 634-2222; and **police,** 635-5555 (if no answer, call 1-667-5555). There is a **laundromat** in the Gateway Motel (see below; wash $1.50, 5-min. dry 25¢; open daily 7am-midnight). The **post office** (634-2706) is in Madley's General Store (see below; open Mon. and Wed.-Thurs. 9-10am and 1-5pm, Tues. 9am-noon and 1-5pm, Fri. 9am-1pm). The **Postal Code** is Y0B 1L0. The **area code** is 403.

Camping, Accommodations, and Food If you're seeking accommodations in Kluane, you have two choices: stay outdoors and fall victim to bloodthirsty mosquitoes, or head for shelter and fall victim to exorbitant hotel rates. Do yourself a favor and buy some **insect repellent** (it works, really). **Kathleen Lake Campground** (634-2251), 27km south of Haines Jct. off Haines Rd., is close to good hiking and fishing and features water, flush toilets, fire pits, firewood, and occasional "campfire talks" (sites $7.25; open June-Oct.). The Yukon government runs four campgrounds, all with hand-pumped cold water and pit toilets (sites $8; call Tourism Yukon at 634-2345 for more information): **Pine Lake,** 7km east of Haines Jct. on the Alaska Hwy.; **Congdon Creek,** 85km west of Haines Jct. on the Alaska Hwy.; **Dezadeash Lake,** 50km south of Haines Jct. on Haines Rd.; and **Million Dollar Falls,** 90km south of Haines Jct. on Haines Rd., near the BC border. RVers should head to the **Kluane RV Kampground** (634-2709), on the Alaska Hwy. ¼ mi. west of Haines Jct. (sites $10, full hookup $16.50).

Indoor accommodations can be found at **Kathleen Lake Lodge,** 25km south of Haines Jct. (634-2319). Enormous rooms and private bathtub, but no shower (singles $37, doubles $47). **The Gateway Motel,** at Haines Rd. and the Alaska Hwy. in Haines Jct. (634-2371), offers clean, spare rooms with private bath and TV (singles $53, doubles $59, 8 RV sites $12.50).

Haines Junction restaurants offer standard highway-side cuisine; for groceries, head for **Madley's General Store,** at Haines Rd. and Bates (634-2200; open daily 8am-8pm; Oct.-April daily 8am-6:30pm). You could live for days on a monster croissant (95¢) or sourdough loaf ($2.25) from the **Village Bakery and Deli** (634-2867), on Logan St. across from the Visitor Centre. (Open May-June and Sept. daily 9am-6pm; July-Aug. daily 9am-9pm.) The **Cozy Corner Cafe** (634-2511), on the Alaska Hwy. 500 ft. west of Haines Rd., draws highway crowds for big, cheap portions: burgers & fries from $6 (open daily 7am-11pm).

Outdoors in the Park Kluane National Park offers an opportunity to explore wild wilderness. There are few actual trails in the park; the major ones are the 4km **Dezadeash River Loop** (dez-uh-DEE-ush) which begins at the Haines Junction Visitor Centre, the 15km **Auriol Trail** which starts from Haines Rd. km 248 and is an excellent overnight hike, and the 85km **Cottonwood Trail,** a four- to six-day trek beginning either 27 or 55km south of Haines Junction on Haines Rd. Cottonwood is

a loop trail which offers 25km of trail above tree-line and a short detour up an adjacent ridge which provides a view of the Ice Field Ranges and Mount Logan on clear
days.

The park also offers numerous **"routes"** which follow no formal trail and are not
maintained by the park. These are reserved for more experienced hikers, since
route finding, map reading, and compass skills may all be called for. Perhaps the
most popular are the **Slims East** and **Slims West** routes which both begin 3km
south of the Sheep Mountain Information Center (see above); both follow the Slims
River (each on its respective side) for 23-30km (one-way) to ridges overlooking the
mighty **Kaskawalsh Glacier.** Both routes take from three to five days; due to
increased bear activity in this area, the park mandates the use of bear canisters for
the storage of food on all overnight trips. These are available free of charge at the
Sheep Mountain Information Center. *All* hikers camping in the backcountry must
register at one of the visitor centers. These two trailheads lie in a dry, windy valley
which is frequently smothered by dust blowing down from the glacier. Needless to
say, trying to catch a ride while being blanketed can be most unpleasant, especially
since the road is not heavily trafficked; if at all possible, you should arrange a return
ride in advance.

Anglers are invited to put the park's name to the test (that is, if you speak Tutchone). **Kathleen Lake** (see below) is home to lake and rainbow trout, arctic grayling,
and Kokanee salmon. Grayling abound in **Jaruis Creek,** halfway between Haines Jct.
and Sheep Mountain. Visitors can obtain a National Parks fishing permit ($7 weekly,
$13 annually) at either visitor center (see above). Limits on both the size and num-
ber of fish which may be kept have been established to maintain the natural stock;
anglers are required to use barb-less hooks. **Canoe rental** ($25 per day) is available
from **Kruda-Ché** (634-2378), in Haines Junction across from the Kluane RV Kampground (see above).

You can't miss (no matter how hard you try) the **Haines Junction Big Game Monument,** at the intersection of the Alaska Hwy. and Haines Rd. This faux-mountain
landscape, fitted with a number of crude wildlife sculptures, has the distressing
appearance of a giant wild-animal-berry muffin. Right next door, you can inscribe
your name (and a few well-chosen words) in the enormous **Alaska Highway Guest
Book.**

■ Near Kluane: Burwash Landing and Beaver Creek

The small town of **Burwash Landing** lies 124km north of Haines Jct., on the shores
of beautiful Kluane Lake. This tiny town offers only one thing to do: visit the **Kluane
Museum of Natural History** (841-5561; open mid-May to mid-Sept. daily 9am-9pm;
admission $3). The museum is directly on the highway and despite its isolation is
arguably the best museum along the entire length of the Alaska Highway. Life-like
animals lie waiting in their glass display cases, ready to pounce upon prey (that
would be you) meandering through the clean and polished interior. A definite must-
see. For those who find the museum too arresting to drive on, lodging can be found
at the **Burwash Landing Resort** (841-4441), a short drive off the main highway (you
can't miss the signs). The resort has rooms from $50, a restaurant (burger & fries
from $5, mega-expensive breakfasts from $6; open daily 6:30am-11pm), and offers a
spot to pitch your tent for a nominal fee (no facilities).

Kluane's "northern gateway" is **Beaver Creek,** 176km north of Burwash Landing,
Canada's westernmost community and the site where the final link was made in the
construction of the Alaska Highway. In spite of that, the best reason to stop here is
to do some laundry at the **Westmark Inn RV Park** (862-7501), right alongside the
highway, where a load of wash is a solo buck ($1, that is) and you get 10 minutes
drying time for only 25¢ (open 7am-midnight). Oh, and you can also spend the night
here (sites $10, full hookup $18). Visitors also have free access to the Westmark

Inn's Rec Room and mini-golf (oh, boy!). **The Visitor Infocentre** (862-7321), across the street, provides information on current road conditions (open mid-May to mid-Sept. daily 9am-9pm). You really don't want to spend the night indoors here (the cheapest single in town is over $60), or eat here either: a meal anywhere in town will easily cost over $10. The **post office** (862-7211; open Mon. 9am-5pm, Wed. 1:30-4:30pm, Thurs. 1-5pm; **Postal Code:** YOB 1AO) and **bank** (862-7322; open Tues. and Thurs. 9:30-11:30am) are both located in the back of Community Hall (going north on the highway, turn left immediately after the visitor's center). The adjacent swimming pool is open Tuesday through Saturday in the afternoons and evenings (pick up a schedule there or at the post office; a day-pass is $3). The Westmark Inn has a nightly vaudeville theater for $10 and a free (but moth-eaten) wildlife exhibit. The **health center** can be reached at 862-7225. In an **emergency,** call the police at 862-5555.

THE ALASKA HIGHWAY (CONT.)

■ Tok

Tok (TOKE) is the first town of note along the Alaska Highway which is actually *in* Alaska (the border lies 150km southeast), and has thus garnered the nickname "The Gateway to Alaska." Located at the intersection of the Alaska Highway and Tok Cutoff, the town also has the nick-name of "Main Street, Alaska," due to the fact that the entire town lies directly along the two highways.

Practical Information For those debating whether to continue on towards Fairbanks or head south along the cut-off towards Anchorage, do some deep thinking at the recently constructed (and cavernous) **Visitors Center** (883-5775), located at the intersection of the two highways. Directions are unnecessary, though, since it's hard to miss the largest single-story log building in Alaska (open mid-May to mid-Sept. daily 7am-9pm). Adjacent to the visitor center is the **Public Lands Information Center** (883-5667), which has information regarding all public lands (go figure. . .). Public lands include all national and state parks, monuments, and preserves, so stop by to plan your field trips. (Open daily 8am-8pm; in winter Mon.-Fri. 8am-4:30pm). Also offered in the center are a wildlife exhibit and hourly videos on various national parks.

Hitchhiking is notoriously bad in Tok. If you're stuck, **Alaska Direct** (800-770-6652) runs buses which leave three times a week from the front of Northstar RV Park (see below). Buses to Fairbanks Tues., Fri., and Sun., $40; to Anchorage Tues., Fri., and Sun., $65; and to Whitehorse Mon., Wed., and Sat., $80.

The **post office** (883-5880) is near the intersection. (Open Mon.-Fri 8:30am-5pm, Sat. 11:30am-3pm. **ZIP Code:** 99780.) There is also a **laundromat** at the Northstar RV Park (see below; wash $1.25, 7-min. dry 25¢). Emergency numbers include: **health clinic/ambulance,** 883-5855; **police,** 883-5111; and **fire,** 883-2333.

Accommodations, Camping, and Food Tok has numerous and varied accommodations. The **Tok Youth Hostel (HI/AYH)** (883-3745), located an incredibly inconvenient 9 mi. west of town on Pringle Dr., is a huge canvas tent reminiscent of M*A*S*H. (Members $7.50; open May15-Sept. 15; kitchen facilities, no showers or phones.) If you're looking to pitch a tent, the better-situated **Northstar RV Park** (883-4501), ½ mi. east of the visitor center on the Alaska Highway, has tentsites for only $5 (free with a gas fill-up), though a shower will cost you another $3.50 (full hookup with 2 free showers $17). The cheapest hotel in town is the **Snowshoe Motel** (883-4511), across from the visitor center (singles $50, doubles $60).

For sustenance, Tok offers plenty of standard (read: expensive) roadside fare. The town's one exception (meaning it's still pricey, just not standard) is the **Gateway Salmon Bake** (883-5555), on the western edge of town where you can have all the grilled King Salmon you want for $16, or all the beef ribs for $13. A free shuttle is available from numerous spots in town to take you there (open Mon.-Sat. 11am-9pm, Sun. 4-9pm). For red-eyed travelers, a dose of caffeine can be had from the **Alcan Espresso Coffee Shop,** tucked just off the highway halfway into town, (mocha $2.25, espresso $2; open Mon.-Sat. 6am-5pm, Sun. 8am-4pm). Tok's answer to wholesale shopping, **Frontier Foods,** is also across from the visitor center; non-restaurant-eaters will rejoice in reasonably priced bulk items (open daily 7am-11pm).

Sights Besides contemplating which way to go, the only other thing to do in Tok is scrounge around among the gift shops. Check out **Burnt Paw Northland Specialties** (883-4121), ¼ mi. west of the intersection on the Alaska Highway, which offers nightly sled-dog demonstrations at 7:30pm (open daily 7am-9pm).

■ Delta Junction

Like Tok, Delta Junction exists primarily because it lies at the intersection of two main highways, the Alaska and Richardson. The huge post in front of the visitor center declares Delta Junction to be the terminus of the Alaska Highway (though Fairbanks justifiably argues otherwise), and for $1 you can buy a macho certificate stating that you've successfully reached its end.

Practical Information The **visitor center** (895-5069) is found (you guessed it) at the intersection of the two highways (open mid-May to mid-Sept. 8:30am-7:30pm). **National Bank of Alaska** (895-4691) is just north toward Fairbanks (open Mon.-Thurs. 9am-5pm, Fri. 10am-6pm). The **post office** (895-4601) is across the street from the bank. (Open Mon.-Fri. 9:30am-5pm, Sat. 10:30-noon. **General Delivery ZIP Code:** 99737.) Important phone numbers: **police,** 895-4344; in an **emergency,** 895-4800; **health clinic,** 895-4879.

Camping, Accommodations, and Food Tenters should head to **Delta State Recreation Site,** ½ mi. from the visitor center towards Fairbanks (sites $8, drinking water, pit toilets). The **Delta Youth Hostel (HI/AYH)** (895-5074), is as inconveniently located as the one in Tok, 3 mi. off the road from Mile 272, and has simple but adequate accommodations. (Open June 1-Sept.1. Members $7, nonmembers $8; sleeping bag required.) **Kelly's Country Inn Motel** (895-4667) is ¼ mi. from the intersection towards Fairbanks and has cheery rooms with big country quilts (singles $50, doubles $60).

Delta Junction doesn't offer much in the way of food. **Pizza Bella Restaurant** (895-4841), near the visitor center, has pizzas from $9 as well as plenty o'pasta. Gung-ho grocery grabbers should hit the **Delta Shop-Rite** (895-4653), just north towards Fairbanks (open Mon.-Sat. 7am-11pm, Sun. 8am-9pm).

Sights and Entertainment Attractions in the area include a roaming herd of buffalo and the government-subsidized **Delta Agriculture Project,** which raises lots of barley and hay; 1994's harvest will be its 14th. Nearby **Fort Greely** is manned by only 614 soldiers (although many have families there as well), and provides some more economic backbone to the Delta area. If you stumble into town on the first weekend in August, then welcome to the **Deltana Fair!** The most exciting event of the fair is undoubtedly the **Great Alaskan Outhouse Race** which features numerous outhouses on wheels, pulled or pushed by four competitors, while one lucky individual sits on the "throne" for the length of the race. The winners receive the coveted "Golden Throne Award" (2nd place, "The Silver Plunger", 3rd place, "the Copper Snake"). Ten mi. north of town is **Big Delta Historic Park,** home of **Rika's**

Roadhouse (895-4201), a restored roadhouse full of lewd pioneer spirit. If you're thirsty for an engineering marvel, observe the Trans-Alaska Pipeline as it hangs suspended over the Tanana River.

■■■ FAIRBANKS

If E.T. Barnette hadn't gotten stuck with his load of trade goods at the junction of the Tanana and Chena Rivers, and if Felix Pedro, the Italian immigrant-turned-prospector, hadn't unearthed a golden fortune nearby, and if territorial Judge James Wickersham hadn't been trying to woo political favors from an obscure Indiana senator (one Charles Warren Fairbanks by name), then this town might never even have existed—and it certainly wouldn't have been named for somebody who never even set foot in Alaska.

But it did happen, and so Fairbanks exists, although nowadays far more riches flow through the Trans-Alaskan pipeline than were ever extracted from the golden pebbles of Alaskan streams. And as it was at the century's start, the city is now largely a service and supply center for the surrounding Bush, maintaining the rough-and-ready flavor of an old frontier town. Men far outnumber women, and the streets are filled with four-wheel-drive steeds, complete with a wolf dog in the back (part of the package from the dealer). To the south, the needles of black spruce and their underlying sheets of permafrost roll out a green and gold carpet below Denali and the Alaska Range. To the north, the mighty Yukon completes its long arching sweep through the Interior and above the Arctic Circle, bridged only by the lonely Dalton Highway as it escorts the pipeline north through the jagged Brooks Range to its beginning at Prudhoe Bay.

PRACTICAL INFORMATION AND ORIENTATION

Visitors Information: Convention and Visitors Bureau Log Cabin, 550 1st Ave., Fairbanks 99701 (456-5774 or 800-327-5774). Pick up the free *Visitor's Guide,* which maps out a self-guided walking tour of Fairbanks and lists tourist offices, transportation services, maps, annual events, activities, and shops. Open daily 8am-8pm; Oct.-April Mon.-Fri. 8am-5pm, Sat.-Sun. 10am-4pm. The **Fairbanks Chamber of Commerce** is at 709 2nd Ave. (452-1105).

Fairbanks Information Hotline: 456-INFO. 24-hr. recording for coming events.

Alaska Public Lands Information Center (APLIC) (451-7352), at 3rd and Cushman St. Exhibits and recreation information on different parks and protected areas of Alaska. Free daily films. Staff welcomes requests for information about hiking; write to 250 Cushman St., #1A, Fairbanks. Open daily 9am-6pm; in winter Tues.-Sat. 10am-6pm. Fairbanks is also home to the headquarters for the nearby **Gates of the Arctic National Park,** 201 1st Ave. (456-0281; open Mon.-Fri. 8am-4:30pm) and the **Arctic National Wildlife Refuge,** 101 12th St., Room 266 (456-0250; open Mon.-Fri. 8am-4:30pm).

American Express, Vista Travel, 1211 Cushman (456-7088). Open Mon.-Fri. 8:30-6pm, Sat. 10am-4pm.

Airport: Located 5 mi. from downtown on Airport Way, which doubles as the George Parks Hwy. Served by: **Delta** (474-0238), to the lower 48; **Alaska Air** (452-1661), to Anchorage ($184) and Juneau ($283); **Mark Air** (455-5104), to larger Bush towns, including Barrow ($235); **Frontier Flyer Services** (474-0014), to smaller Bush towns: Bettles ($99). These are all immediate departure prices; cheaper fares are possible with advance reservations, but rates vary.

Alaska Railroad, 280 N. Cushman (456-4155), next to the *Daily News-Miner* building. An excellent way to see the wilderness. From May-Sept., 1 train daily to: Nenana ($18), Anchorage ($120), and Denali National Park ($45). Ages 2-11 ½-price. Depot open Mon.-Fri. 7am-9:45pm, Sat.-Sun. 6pm-10pm; get there 1 hr. before the train leaves. During the winter, a train leaves for Anchorage every Sunday ($70).

Buses: Denali Express, 800-327-7651. Daily to Denali ($25). **Alaskan Express,** 800-544-2206. Daily to Anchorage ($105); 4 times per week to Haines ($165;

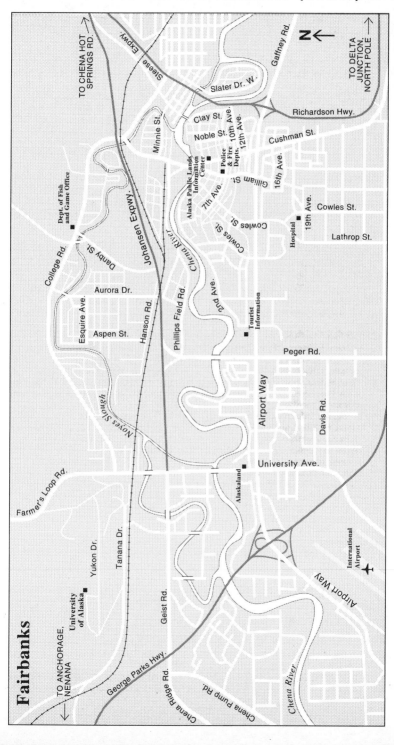

Fairbanks

accommodations during overnight stay in Beaver Creek not included). **Alaska Direct** (1-800-770-6652) has buses to Denali twice weekly ($23). **Fireweed Express** (488-7928 or 452-0521) provides private van service each day to Denali ($25, round-trip $45). They pick-up at the hostel; call for times and reservations.

City Bus: MACS (456-3279), at 6th and Cushman St. Two routes (the red and blue lines) through downtown Fairbanks and the surrounding area. Fare $1.50; senior citizens, high school students, and people with disabilities 75¢; under 5 free. Day pass $3. Transfers good within 1 hr. of stamped time. Pick up a schedule at the Convention and Visitors Bureau (see above).

Taxi: Golden Nugget Cab, 451-8294. **Fairbanks Taxi,** 452-3535. Both 24 hr.

Car Rental: Rent-a-Wreck, 105 Cushman St. (452-1606). $33 per day, 100 free mi. per day, 20¢ each additional mi. **U-Save Auto Rental,** 3245 College Rd. (479-7060). $35 per day, 100 free mi., 26¢ each additional mi. At the airport is **Avis** (474-0900 or 800-331-1212). $39 per day, unlimited free mileage.

Road Conditions: 456-ROAD.

Bike Rental: Beaver Sports (479-2494), across from College Corner Mall on College Rd. Mountain bikes $11 per ½-day, $17 per day, $60 weekly. $250 deposit required (cash or credit). Open Mon.-Fri. 10am-7pm, Sat. 9am-6pm, Sun. 1pm-5pm.

Camping Equipment: Clem's Backpacking Sports, 315 Wendell (456-6314), near the visitors bureau. Open Tues.-Sat. 10am-6pm. **Rocket Surplus,** 1401 Cushman (456-7078). Fine camouflage fashions. Open Mon.-Sat. 9am-6pm. **Apocalypse Design, Inc.,** 101 College Rd. (451-7555), at Illinois. Fast repairs on zippers and straps. Open Mon.-Fri. 9am-6pm, Sat. 10am-4pm. **Beaver Sports** (see above).

Laundromat and Showers: B & C (479-2696), at University and College, in Campus Mall. $1.75 wash, 8-min. dry 25¢. Showers $2.50. Open Mon.-Sat. 7am-10:30pm, Sun. 9am-10:30pm. **B & L** (452-1355), at 3rd and New St. on Eagle Rd. Wash $1.50, dry $1.50. Showers $2.50 for 20 min. Open daily 8am-11pm.

Bookstore: Gulliver's New and Used Books, 3525 College Rd. (474-9574), in College Corner Mall. Open Mon.-Fri. 10am-8pm, Sat. 10am-6pm, Sun. noon-6pm. Also in the Shopper's Forum, 1255 Airport Way (456-3657). Open Mon.-Fri. 10am-9pm, Sat. 10am-6pm, Sun. noon-6pm.

Market: Carr's Foodland, 526 Gaffney (452-1221 or 800-325-6000 for **Western Union** information). Open 5am-midnight.

Weather: 452-3553.

24-hr. Help Lines: Rape Emergency, 452-7273. **Poison Control Center,** 456-7182. **Crisis Line,** 452-4357; also provides contacts with gay and lesbian support groups.

Pharmacy: Payless Drugstore, 38 College Rd. in the Bentley Mall (452-2072). Open Mon.-Sat. 9am-9pm, Sun. 10am-6pm.

Hospital: Fairbanks Memorial, 1650 Cowles St. (452-8181), off Airport Hwy.

Emergency: 911

Alaska State Troopers: 452-2114.

Post Office: 315 Barnette St. (452-3203). Open Mon.-Fri. 9am-6pm, Sat. 10am-2pm. **General Delivery ZIP Code:** 99707.

Population: Fairbanks City, 30,000; Greater Fairbanks Borough, 77,000.

Area Code: 907.

Fairbanks lies 882 mi. northwest of Ketchikan and 508 mi. north of Kodiak Island; Anchorage is 358 mi. away via the **George Parks Hwy.,** and Prudhoe Bay can be reached by 480 mi. of the gravelly **Dalton Hwy.** The city is primarily distributed downtown and along Airport Way, College Rd., and University Ave.

ACCOMMODATIONS

For information on bed and breakfasts, go to the visitors bureau (see Practical Information) or write **Fairbanks B&B,** 902 Kellum St., Anchorage (452-4967). The visitors bureau also distributes a flyer listing all the local hostel services. Don't be afraid to shop around, though. There is a wide range of quality and convenience.

Fairbanks Youth Hostel (HI/AYH), 1641 Willow St. (456-4159). The hostel has moved around a lot in the past few years so call Paul Schultz (at 456-4159) to check on availability of beds ($10), floor space ($8), or tent space ($6). And have fun—the friendly atmosphere in the hostel breeds immediate camaraderie, since the intrepid travelers who make it this far north all share a common adventurous spirit. Paul has a wealth of information about the area and is always willing to direct hostelers toward adventure (including Prudhoe Bay). No curfew, no lockout, free showers, laundry ($2.50 for wash and dry), bike rental ($10 per day) and all too many hungry beavers. Write P.O. Box 721196, Fairbanks for information.

Billie's Backpackers Hostel, 479-2034. Take Westwood Rd. 1 block off College to Mack Rd. Look for the "Billie's B&B" sign. 4 beds in a simple, clean cabin and 4 beds in the renovated upstairs of the main house. Showers and kitchen. Train and airport pickup available. $13.50, plus $5 for a full breakfast.

Noah's Rainbow Inn, 474-3666 or 800-770-2177. Take Gcist Rd. off University to Fairbanks; make a left and it's right there. During the winter, Noah's rents mainly to U. of Fairbanks students. During the summer, it's a cheap, clean, rarely-crowded, dorm-style hotel. TV, kitchen and laundry facilities available. Shared bathrooms. Singles $35. Doubles $40. $5 less if you can live without a TV.

Gaffney Motel, 741 Gaffney Rd. (452-3534). One side of this hotel is a light-tight cinder-block wall; the other side is paneled with wood and has sliding glass doors and balconies. Singles or doubles, $40; 3 or 4 people, $70. Reserve early; often booked by 6pm.

Alaskan Motor Inn, 419 4th Ave. (452-4800), near Lacey. One of the few affordable hotels in the central downtown area. Big rooms with cable TV. Spotlessly clean. Singles $65. Doubles $75.

Aurora Motel and Cabins, 2016 College Rd., (451-1935). Cabins lack TV and phones, but they're a bargain. Singles $40. Doubles $45. 2-room hotel suites with TV and kitchenette $60 single, $7.50 each additional person.

CAMPING

Tanana Valley Campground, 1800 College (456-7956), next to the Aurora Motel and Cabins. Noisy, but the closest campground to the downtown. Caters to RVs, but no hookups available. Free showers, laundromat ($1 wash and dry). Sites $10.

Chena River State Campground (451-2695), on University Ave. First-come, first-served. Usually full despite unjustifiably high rates. Water and toilets. Sites $12.

Alaskaland (459-1091), on Airport Way. RVs can park here for $7 per night. Water and toilets, no electricity. No tentsites.

FOOD

Fairbanks ferments with fast-food frieries; just about every fast-food chain in existence can be found along Airport Way and College Road, and they seem to have squeezed out most of the locally-owned competition. Groceries are available round the clock at **Carr's,** 526 Gaffney (452-1121), and at **Safeway,** 3627 Airport Way at University Center (479-4231). If you're really stocking up, **Pace Membership Warehouse,** 48 College Rd. (451-4800), will let nonmembers buy in bulk for an additional 5% of the total price (open Mon-Fri. 9am-9pm). **Green Gopher Produce,** at College and Antoinette, sells the cheapest fresh fruit in town during the summer (open Mon.-Sat. 8am-8pm, Sun.10am-8pm). Catch the best homemade ice cream in Alaska (and occasional live jazz) at **Hot Licks** (479-7813), located in the Campus Corner Mall at the intersection of College and University (open Mon.-Fri. 7am-11pm, Sat. 11am-11pm and Sun. noon-10pm).

The Whole Earth (479-2052), in College Corner Mall, below Gulliver's Used Books. A health food store, deli, and restaurant all in one. Lots of plants, soft lighting, and funky wall murals. You can sit here all day over a cup of organic coffee and a Natchester Sandwich (beans, cheese, Greek peppers, and spices in a spread, $4). Locals praise the giant No Bull Burger ($4.25). All sandwiches served on fresh homemade whole-wheat rolls. Store and seating open Mon.-Fri. 10am-7pm, Sat. 10am-6pm, Sun. noon-5pm. Hot food served Mon.-Sat. 11am-3pm.

Souvlaki, 112 N. Turner (452-5393), across the bridge from the visitors center. You can almost get your fill on the heavenly aroma. Succulent stuffed grape leaves (3 for $1.15). Salad in a pita ($3). Open Mon.-Fri. 10am-8pm, Sat. 10am-6pm.

Puffin Deli with Mama Heidi's Subs and Sandwiches (451-6725), at 1st and Cushman. Mama Heidi is a sweetheart, and her deli is a house o' deals. Big, fresh sandwiches $4, with salad $4.75. Top it off with a healthy $1 scoop of ice cream. Open Mon.-Fri. 10am-6pm.

Speedy Submarine Sandwich Shop, 1701 Cushman St. (456-7995). Speedy's is straight out of Chicago and makes the best foot-long subs in Fairbanks ($3.75-6.25). Open daily 10am-6pm.

Food Factory, 36 College Rd. (452-3313), and at 18th and Cushman St. (452-6348). Caters to the Alaskan appetite ("Food just like Mom used to send out for!"). Foot-long hoagies $6.50-8, but their forte is beer (106 international varieties). Open Mon.-Thurs. 10:30am-11pm, Fri.-Sat. 10:30am-midnight, Sun. noon-10pm.

Royal Fork Buffet, 414 3rd St. (452-5655), at Steese Hwy. Part of a national all-you-can-eat chain dedicated to stuffing gluttonous patrons with cafeteria food. Different menu every day. Lunch ($6), dinner ($8.65), and Sunday brunch ($6). Open Mon.-Thurs. 11am-8:30pm, Fri.-Sat. 11am-9pm, Sun. 9am-8pm.

(The Inimitable) Denny's Farthest North, Airport Way near Wilbur. OK, it's Denny's, but it's Denny's *Farthest North,* and this time, it's an experience. And it's always open, 24 hr. a day. Veggie cheese melt only $5; Breakfast $5-7.

Godfather's Pizza, 3401 Airport Way (479-7652), near Market St. Their all-you-can-eat lunch buffet (pizza, garlic bread, potato wedges) is a miracle of modern mass consumption ($4.29). Open Sun.-Thurs. 11am-10pm, Fri.-Sat. 11am-11pm.

Alaska Salmon Bake (452-1091), at Airport Way and Peger Rd. inside Alaskaland. Genuinely tacky but still the best salmon bake in town. $17 buys enough salmon, halibut, ribs, and fixin's to satisfy even the most ravenous of travelers. Lunch noon-2pm ($9). Open mid-June to mid-Sept daily 5-9pm.

The Pumphouse Restaurant and Saloon, Mile 1.3 Chena Pump Rd. (479-8452). Rave local spot. This place is so cool that one of the city's bus lines goes out of its way to drop you here. Out-of-this-world lunch buffet ($9.79). Dinner entrees $10-15. Open daily 11:30am-2pm and 5-10pm. Bar open weekends until 2am.

Two Rivers Lodge, Mile 16 Chena Hot Springs Rd. (488-6815). You'll need a car. *Twin Peaks*-esque place to stop on the way back from Chena Hot Springs. Hefty, reasonably priced appetizers $6-10 make a light dinner, especially if you'd like to try the best and only alligator served in Alaska ($10)—check out the mounted, fuzzy one on wall. Entrees $15.95-71.95(!?), but the food is so good locals drive out to eat here. Of the series of grapefruit specialties, the grapefruit pie with complimentary grapefruit schnapps is heavenly. Open Mon.-Sat. 5-10pm, Sun. 3-9pm.

SIGHTS

One of Fairbanks's proudest institutions is the **University of Alaska-Fairbanks,** at the top of a hill overlooking the flat city-scape. Both bus lines stop at the **Wood Campus Center** (474-7033), which has pool tables, lots of video games, and the Student Activities Office, which posts listings of movies ($4-5.50), outdoor activities and occasional music fests. The **University of Alaska Museum** (474-7505), a 10-minute walk from there up Yukon Dr., houses a fascinating array of exhibits ranging from Russian Orthodox vestments to native baskets to a mummified prehistoric bison—all in one huge room! The most popular exhibit is a seven-minute video of the *aurora borealis* (northern lights). (Open daily 9am-7pm; May and Sept. 9am-5pm; Oct.-April noon-5pm. Admission $4, senior citizens and students $3, families $12.50. Oct.-April, free on Fri.) Weekdays at 10am, the university offers free two-hour tours of the campus beginning in front of the museum. At the **Agriculture Experimental Station** cabbages grow to the size of basketballs in the all-day summer sunshine. The **Large Animal Research Station** offers tours on Tues. and Sat. at 1:30pm and 3pm, and on Thurs. at 1:30pm only ($5, students $2, families $10).

Alaskaland, P.O. Box 1267, Fairbanks 99707, on Airport Way, is a would-be Arctic Disneyland. What it lacks in rides, it exacerbates with gift shops, *faux* can-can shows, some authentic pioneer homes, gunfights, a sternwheel riverboat, a pioneer museum, mini-golf, nightly theater, and lots of kids. The quintessential tourist trap. But hey, at least there's no general admission.

The **Dog Mushers Museum** (456-6874), at 3rd and Cushman in the Courthouse Square, is little more than a room full of sleds and other mushing paraphernalia, but some cool videos are screened in the theater (open daily 9am-6pm, admission $2).

Outside town lie all sorts of trivialities. Head out on Farmers Loop Rd. to see the abandoned **"permafrost houses,"** which melted the tundra and now look like giant accordions. **Pedro's Monument** marks the original site of Pedro Felix's 1902 gold discovery at Mile 16 Steese Hwy., 5 mi. north of Fox. It'll cost you $20 to catch a tour of a gold mine and try your luck at goldpanning at the **Little El Dorado Gold Camp,** 1132 Lakeview Terrace (479-7613), 9 mi. out of Fairbanks on Elliot Hwy. Should you decide to shell out the dough, don't blame us if it doesn't pan out. For more golden fun check out **Gold Dredge No. 8,** at Mile 8 of the Old Steese Highway, where a tour of the long-retired dredge and another gamble at gold-panning can be had for $10 (open daily 9am-6pm).

View a technological wonder of the world, the **Trans-Alaska Pipeline,** at Mile 8 of the Hwy. heading out of Fairbanks. The pipeline was elevated on super-cooled posts to protect the tundra's frozen ecological system from the 108°F oil.

Fairbanks features an extensive **bike trail** system. None of the urban trails is particularly scenic, but it's a lot quicker than walking. **Beaver Sports** (see Practical Information) offers the best deal on bike rentals.

ENTERTAINMENT

With nothing but black spruce to keep them company in the surrounding tundra, Fairbanksians turn to the bars at night. Come carouse with stiff drinks and boisterous, rugged types fresh from the North Slope oil fields. UAF students head for the **Howling Dog Saloon** (457-8780), 11½ mi. down Steese Hwy. for live rock-and-roll. Look for a colorful old wooden structure in the middle of nowhere encircled by pickup trucks. The local eye doctor and his wife, conservatively dressed, dance next to bikers, who dance next to field guides from Denali. . . get the picture? Volleyball and horseshoe games go on until 4am or so, as does the band (open Tues.-Fri. 5pm-5am, Sat.-Sun. noon-5am).

Frank's Place, 1705 S. Cushman (452-9890). A biker bar for blues. Get your gear at Harley Davidson's Farthest North (Airport Way and Cushman), then step into a mellow Easy Rider crowd. Don't be fooled by the sign outside that says, "C'mon in, if you're not scared." Open daily 8am-whenever.

Sunset Inn, 345 Old Richardson Hwy. (456-4754). Looks like a warehouse, but since Fairbanksians need only the bare necessities (drinks, dance floor, pool tables), it's usually jam-packed. Live top-40 dance music. Open Wed.-Thurs. and Sun. 10pm-3:30am, Fri.-Sat. 9:30pm-whenever.

Senator's Saloon, Mile 1.3 on Chena Pump Rd. (479-8452), in the Pump House Restaurant. The only (and the farthest north?) oyster bar in Fairbanks. Take drinks out to the deck and watch float planes land and river boats whiz by. Open Sun.-Thurs. 11:30am-1am, Fri.-Sat. 11:30am-2am.

Fox Roadhouse and Motherlode, Mile 11.5 Steese Hwy. (457-7461), across from the Howling Dog. Don't be surprised if you see horses hitched up to the post out front, and try not to stare (or be caught off guard) when they collect shotguns at the front door. Dinner ($13-26) is served daily 5:30-10:30pm. Open Sun.-Thurs. 5pm-midnight, Fri.-Sun. 5pm-2am.

SEASONAL EVENTS

The best time to visit the city is in mid-July—citizens don Gold Rush rags and throw parades, sales, and many other gala events for **Golden Days,** a celebration of Felix Pedro's much-celebrated discovery. Watch out for the traveling jail; if you haven't purchased the silly-looking button commemorating the event, you may be taken prisoner and forced to pay a steep price to spring yourself. (Most stores and businesses in town sell the buttons.) The budget traveler might want to stay on board the paddywagon—it's a free ride and goes all over Fairbanks. For details, contact the Fairbanks Chamber of Commerce (see Practical Information). Make hotel reservations several months in advance if you're coming to town during Golden Days.

The **Tanana Valley Fair** (452-3750), in the second week of August, features variegated shows and competitions as well as a bona fide rodeo. Follow the line of cars down College Rd. to the fairgrounds. (Admission $6, senior citizens $3, ages 6-17 $3; $40 family pass covers all family members throughout the fair.)

For a sports spectacular with native flavor, see the **World Eskimo-Indian Olympics,** P.O. Box 72433, Fairbanks (452-6646). At the end of July, Natives from all over Alaska compete in shows of strength and endurance, and celebrate folklore and traditional dance.

Some of the wildest events occur in the days surrounding the June 21 summer solstice. The **Yukon 800 Marathon Riverboat Race** sends some real intense fellas in low-slung powerboats on an 800-mi. quest up the Tanana and Yukon Rivers to the town of Galena and back again. A few days before the solstice, the 10km **Midnight Sun Run** happens on a well-lit night, beginning at 10pm in the evening. The annual **Midnight Sun Baseball Game** occurs on the solstice itself. Featuring the Fairbanks Goldpanners pitted against another minor-league team, the game begins at 10:30pm, as the sun sets, features a short pause near midnight for the celebration of the midnight sun, and ends its final innings as the sun begins to rise once again. The Goldpanners play more than 30 home games throughout the summer and have won five minor league national championships since 1970, spawning such major league talents as Barry Bonds and Dave Winfield. Games are played at **Growden Memorial Park** near Alaskaland (451-0095; admission $4).

The **Fairbanks Folk Festival** runs roughly from July 12 to July 14. Stompin' bluegrass, but still more sedate than February's **Yukon Quest** Dog Sled Race which runs between Fairbanks and Whitehorse, starting in Fairbanks in even years, and in Whitehorse in odd. The Quest is far more rigorous than the more famous Iditarod: fewer dogs, fewer stops, and less compassion for the human condition. Ask about it at the Visitor's Information Office (see Practical Information).

■ Near Fairbanks

Fairbanks may very well be the only city in the country from which you can pick any direction, drive a scant 20 minutes, and find yourself fully enmeshed in complete and utter wilderness. Wowsers! Go soak your feet (or your head) in the plentiful lakes and nearby hot springs.

Two major roads lead south of Fairbanks. George Parks Hwy. heads southwest by way of Denali National Park, and Richardson Hwy. runs to Valdez in the Prince William Sound. Two minor roads head north (into the Bush). The Steese Hwy. heads north to Circle, an outpost on the mighty Yukon River. The Elliot Hwy. takes you past to the start of the Dalton Highway and then continues onwards to Manley Hot Springs.

Chena River and Lakes

The **Chena River Recreation Area** (451-2695), at Miles 26-51 on Chena Hot Springs Rd., covers 254,080 acres, proffering fishing, hiking, canoeing, and camping around the Upper Chena River. Tentsites convenient to Chena Hot Springs Rd. are available at **Rosehip Campground** (Mile 27) and **Granite Bluff** (Mile 39.5) for $6 (pit toilets and pump water). Hiking trails include: **Granite Tors** (trailhead at Mile 39 campground), a 12- to 16-mi. round-trip hike to granite rocks—great for overnight campouts; **Angel Rocks** (starting at Mile 48.9 campground), an easy 3½-mi. trek through exquisite wilderness; and **Chena Dome Trail** (beginning at Mile 15.5), a more remote 29-mi. adventure overlooking the river valleys. A shooting range is located at Mile 36.5—duck!

Harding Lake (Mile 321.4 on Richardson Hwy.), **Birch Lake** (Mile 305.5 on Richardson Hwy.), and **Quartz Lake** (Mile 277.8 on Richardson Hwy.) are Sunday anglers' dreams. The state stocks the lakes with salmon and trout for that extra-tough fishing challenge. Boat ramps ($3) and campsites ($6) are provided at Harding and Quartz Lake. Birch Lake has primitive camping facilities.

Chena Hot Springs

Fifty-seven mi. northeast of Fairbanks on Chena Hot Springs Rd., the **Chena Hot Springs Resort** (in Fairbanks 452-7867, at the resort 369-4111) allows you the chance to soak out of the rain. Expect fine fishing near this inn once the water temperature has dropped from the spring snow melt. The chalet accommodations are expensive (singles $80, Alaskans $70), although pool admission is included. Non-patrons may use the hot pool for $8, ages 4-11 $4. Handsome hiking trails and tent and RV campsites ($8, with electricity $10) are nearby. **Two Rivers Lodge and Restaurant** (488-6815) sits at Mile 16 Chena Hot Springs Rd., grilling up succulent ribs and Alaskan specialties (see Fairbanks: Food above for listing).

The Arctic Circle Hot Springs (520-5113), discovered in 1893, are three hours north of Fairbanks on Steese Hwy. The hostel on the fourth floor charges $20 for attic accommodations, $60 for a room. Several campgrounds line Steese Hwy. nearby, amid stunning scenery. Or just camp directly on the banks of the Yukon. Gaze up at Eagle Summit while diving into the Olympic-sized hot springs or indulging yourself at the ice cream parlor. At the peak of summer (June 21-22), you can watch the midnight sun glide across the horizon without setting.

Steese National Conservation/White Mountain National Recreation Areas

The one-million-acre White Mountain National Recreation Area and the 1.2-million-acre Steese National Conservation Area lie side-by-side along the Steese and Elliot Hwy., and boast the best hiking and wilderness fishing in the Fairbanks area. The region's most popular trail, the 27-mi. **Pinnel Mountain National Recreation Trail** in Steese, begins at Mile 86 of the Steese Hwy. and ends at Mile 107, and is equipped with two cabins for emergencies en route. Allow at least three days for the trek. With proper timing you can bask in the midnight sun (June 18-24) from many points along the trail. Would-be prospectors should head for **Nome Creek,** where the Bureau of Land Management has established a 4-mi. stretch open to the general public for recreational gold panning. Access is via the Steese Highway to Mile 57, and from there a 6-mi. drive north on U.S. Creek Rd. It is a primitive road that requires at least one crossing of Nome Creek. Most two-wheel drives can easily accomplish the drive, but high ground clearance is recommended due to the large rocks present in the streambed and along the road. White Mountain's **Birch Creek** offers 60 mi. of white water. For more information on the region call the Fairbanks office of the **U.S. Bureau of Land Management** (474-2350). Detailed topographic maps of the area are available at the **U.S. Geologic Survey** (456-0244), in the Federal Building at the end of 12th Ave. in Fairbanks. (Also see section on the Steese Hwy.)

Arctic Circle

It's not a place, it's a latitude—66°30'. The **Northern Alaska Tour Company,** P.O. Box 82991 (474-8600), offers numerous one- and multi-day tours across the imaginary line. In one of their single-day adventures you can bus up and back for $95, and receive your very own certificate proving that yes, indeedy, you were there! (For information on driving there, see Dalton Highway below.)

Cripple Creek Resort

Seven mi. south of Fairbanks (Mile 351.7 on the George Parks Hwy.) lies historic **Cripple Creek Resort.** This authentic, turn-of-the-century gold camp, reconstructed with all the creature comforts of the 1990s, comes as welcome relief from the hackneyed gift shops of Alaskaland.

A **bus** makes the circuit of 10 Fairbanks hotels before heading south to the resort (round-trip $4). To make the necessary reservations, call 479-2500. The resort offers a phenomenal all-you-can-eat buffet ($14, with crab $19; Wed., with crab is only $16) which features such local delicacies as reindeer stew (sorry, Rudolf) and fresh Alaska Dungeness Crab (flown in from Yakutat daily). The crab is sumptuous, and dinner is served in a former miner's mess hall and bunkhouse. After dinner, the resort offers two forms of entertainment. *The Crown of Light,* a film shown twice per night in the Firehouse Theatre, projects the *aurora borealis* onto a giant 30-ft. screen while symphonic music plays over the speakers ($5; shows 7pm, 8pm). Or sidle through the swinging doors onto the sawdust floor of the **Malemute Saloon.** Shows occur daily at 9pm ($4) and are replete with can-can dancers, period costumes, and a recital of Robert Service's famous ballad, "The Shooting of Dan McGrew." An RV and tent **campground** are but a skip from the saloon (sites $9, showers included) or you can stay in the **hotel** above the dining hall. (Singles $50. Doubles $56. Shared bath. Continental breakfast included.) Call or write for room or show reservations: Cripple Creek Resort, P.O. Box 109, Ester 99725, 479-2500.

North Pole

Yes, Charlie Brown, there is a town called **North Pole.** It's 13 mi. south of Fairbanks on Richardson Hwy., and its **post office (ZIP Code:** 99705) receives thousands of letters each Christmas from credulous kids clamoring for contributions to their toy closets. Unfortunate for the peace of mind of Santa and his elves, the town's population has doubled in the last four years. Four shopping malls scar the landscape, and a monstrous overpass guards Badger Road from the perils of the highway.

Only those heading in or out of Fairbanks will find a visit worthwhile. The Chamber of Commerce operates a **visitors center** (488-2242) on the side of the highway (open daily 9am-6pm) which will direct you to the town's only place of interest: **Santa Claus House** (488-2200). Just off Santa Claus Lane, the house is guarded by the world's largest statue of St. Nick (you'd better watch out). The house is packed with expensive trinkets and souvenirs; surprised? (Open May 10am-6pm, June-Aug. 8am-8pm, Sept.-Dec. 10am-6pm.)

Nenana

Nenana (pronounced nee-NAN-nuh) lies 53 mi. south of Fairbanks on George Parks Hwy. Once the terminus of the Alaska Railroad, Nenana is situated at the confluence of the Tanana and Nenana Rivers, and is now famous for the Nenana Ice Pool. Alaskans and Canadian residents of the Yukon Territory—bored out of their skulls during the long winter months—bet on the exact minute when the ice will give out in the spring, thereby dislodging two large tripods ceremoniously stuck there. The pot regularly amounts to over $150,000. Today this tradition is just one of the events at the Nenana Ice Classic, a festival that attracts people from far and wide. For more information write P.O. Box 272, Nenana 99760 (832-5446). The town's nightlife revolves around the two ornery-looking corner bars next to the train station. There are no hotels of note, and the nearest campgrounds are another 20 mi. south on George Parks Hwy. The Alaska Railroad stops here en route to Anchorage.

■■■ DENALI NATIONAL PARK

Established in 1917 to protect wildlife and greatly enlarged in 1980, Denali National Park is also the home of Denali (Athabascan for "The Great One"), the highest mountain in North America. Despite the audacity of the Princeton-educated prospector who in 1896 renamed the peak after Republican presidential nominee William McKinley, locals and visitors alike refer to it as Denali or simply "the mountain." From base to summit, Denali is the greatest vertical relief in the world—unlike other mountains of similar stature, the mountain rises straight from the surrounding meadows with nary a hill intervening. More than 18,000 ft. of rock scrapes upward toward the sky—even mighty Mt. Everest rises only 11,000 ft. from its base on the Tibetan Plateau. Denali is so big that it manufactures its own weather (earning it the nickname "Weathermaker"); when moist air from the Pacific collides with the cold mountaintop, sudden storms encircle the peak. Denali's top is visible only for about 20% of the summer, but even if you can't see the peak, you can still experience the glories of the park's tundra, taiga, wildlife, and lesser mountains.

PRACTICAL INFORMATION AND ORIENTATION

Denali National Park commands respect. If you land in the park unprepared, you'll probably lose a day or more gaining your bearings. Even those fully prepared should allow at least three days for getting a space on a shuttle bus or in a campsite, and obtaining a backcountry permit usually requires an in-park wait as well.

Denali is not a park that can be covered in one day. If you go no farther than the last campground accessible by private vehicle—Savage River, at Mile 12 of the 85-mi. park road—you'll be missing out on 90% of the park's landscape and wildlife. Keep in mind that each quadrant of the park has a different kind of terrain. The first few units of the park consist of spongy tundra and dense taiga forest with a small bear population; walking on natural mattresses quickly loses its novelty. Some of the choicest hiking and wildlife-viewing is smack in the middle of the park, near the Toklat River, Marmot Rock, and Polychrome Pass.

Summer Visitors Information: Visitor Access Center (VAC) (683-1266 or 683-2294; 24-hr. emergency number 683-9100), 0.7 mi. from Rte. 3. The headquarters of the shuttle-bus service; registration or park entrance fee ($3, families $5) includes unlimited bus service for 7 days. Maps, shuttle-bus schedules, and free permits for campground and backcountry camping. Information on campsites, wildlife tours, sled-dog demonstrations, and campfire talks. All travelers are asked to stop here for orientation. Denali Park's indispensable publication *Alpenglow* is also available (free). The center is new and has installed a backcountry simulator which provides useful information for wilderness hikers. Open in summer daily 7am-6pm. 1st shuttle bus departs 5am. Lockers outside 50¢. **Eielson Visitors Center,** 66 mi. into the park, is staffed by helpful rangers who post day-to-day sightings of the mountain and is accessible by shuttle bus. Open in summer daily 9am-8pm. Year-round write to **Denali National Park and Preserve,** P.O. Box 9, Denali Park 99755 (683-1266), for information on the park; or consult one of the **Public Lands Information Centers** (see Practical Information section of either Anchorage or Fairbanks).

Winter Visitors Information: Skiing and sled-dog racing are popular winter-time activities in Denali. Visit the Park Headquarters (683-2294) at Mile 3.5, on the left side of the park road. For information write to Denali National Park and Preserve, P.O. Box 9, Denali Park 99755.

Alaska Railroad, P.O. Box 107500, Anchorage 99510 (683-2233, out of state 800-544-0552). Terminal located 1½ mi. from the park entrance. To: Fairbanks (1 per day, 4pm, $45); Anchorage (1 per day, 12:30pm, $85). Check bags at least ½ hr. prior to departure.

Buses: Denali Express, 800-327-7651. To: Fairbanks (1 per day, 5:30pm, $25); Anchorage (1 per day, 7:30pm, $75). **Moon Bay Express,** 274-6454. To Anchorage (1 per day, 3pm, $35). **Caribou Express,** 278-5776. To: Fairbanks (Mon., Wed., Fri. 3pm, $35); Anchorage (Tues., Thurs., Sat., 10:55am, $54). **Fireweed Express** (488-7928 or 452-0521), in Fairbanks, provides private van service each day to Fairbanks ($25). Call for times and reservations.

Bike Rental: Denali Mountain Bike, P.O. Box 14, Healy 99743 (683-1295), next to the Denali Hostel. Mountain bikes $7 per hr. and $25 per day. Repairs and 1- and 2-day guided tours. Unlike private vehicles, bikes *are* permitted on all 85 mi. of the park road.

Laundromat and Showers: McKinley Campground, P.O. Box 340, Healy 99743 (683-1418), 12 mi. north of park entrance. Showers and the only public laundromat in the area (wash $2, dry $1). **Mercantile Gas and Groceries,** 1½ mi. into the park. Unlimited showers $2. Showers open daily 7:30am-12:45pm and 2-9pm.

Medical Clinic: 683-2211, in Healy. Open Mon.-Fri. 9am-5pm.

Emergency: 911.

Post Office: next to Denali National Park Hotel, 1 mi. from the VAC (see above). Open Mon.-Fri. 8:30am-5pm, Sat. 9:30am-12:30pm; Oct.-May Mon.-Sat. 9:30am-12:30pm. **General Delivery ZIP Code:** 99755.

Area Code: 907.

Denali Park is accessible by asphalt, steel track, and the wide blue sky. The park entrance is 237 mi. north of Anchorage and 121 mi. south of Fairbanks along the scenic **George Parks Hwy.** Thirty mi. south of the park, the 90-mi. gravel **Denali Hwy.** (see Denali Hwy. section) connects Cantwell with **Paxson,** a town located midway between Delta Junction and Glennallen. This bouncy stretch of road, which is closed in the winter, is one of Alaska's most breathtaking, skirting the foothills of the Alaska Range amid countless lakes and streams teeming with grayling, trout, and Arctic char. Denali Park is located in the geographic center of the state and stretches across more than five million acres (a slightly larger area than that of the state of Massachusetts).

GETTING AROUND

Crack Denali's color-coded bus maze and your access to the park will expand exponentially (it's all like a real-life game of "Super Mario Bros"). **Full-Size Yellow School Buses** are **shuttle** and **camper buses,** both free with your $3 park admission. In order to ride the buses, you need to obtain one of three coupons from the VAC—either a same-day coupon, a next-day coupon, or a two-day advance coupon; all three are granted on a space-available basis. Same-day and next-day buses are almost always booked by mid-morning, so it's best to show up at the VAC as close to when it opens as possible (7am). Space on buses leaving in two days begins to get tight starting in late-afternoon.

Shuttle buses leave the VAC between 5am and 3pm to the **Eielson Visitor Center** (about ¾ of the way into the park at Mile 66; buses leave every 20 minutes) and to **Wonder Lake** (at Mile 85). Go for the less frequent Wonder Lake bus if you can, as the best views of Denali are beyond Eielson. The 11-hr. round-trip to Wonder Lake sounds grueling, but if the sun and the wildlife are out, you'll be glad you went. If it's raining, you can always hop off at Eielson and catch another bus back to the VAC (round-trip to Eielson is 8 hr.). You can get on and off these buses at anytime and flag the next one down when you want to move on, a good strategy for day hiking. **Camper Buses** move faster, transporting *only* people with campground and backcountry permits. Camper buses leave the VAC five times daily. The final bus stays overnight at Wonder Lake and returns at 8am the following morning.

Riley Creek Loop Bus runs along the 30-minute loop between the VAC, the Denali Park Hotel, the railroad depot, and the Riley Creek Campground. **Tan School Bus** covers the same route as the free shuttle and camper buses, in the guise of an overpriced ($45) "wildlife tour" of the park offered by the Denali Park Hotel—and even with the fee, the bus only goes about halfway in, to Mile 52 at the Toklat River. **Blue and White School Bus** is a courtesy bus owned by the chalets and makes runs from the Denali Park Hotel to the chalet near Lynx Creek Pizza. Hop on one and head to dinner.

ACCOMMODATIONS AND CAMPING

In the Park

With one exception, accommodations within the park are open in the summer only. Any hotel room in or near the park will be expensive. **ARA Outdoor World,**

Ltd., 825 W. 8th Ave., #240, Anchorage 99501 (276-7234), runs the park's tourist services, including the **Denali National Park Hotel** (683-2215), which more closely resembles Grand Central Station than a wilderness outpost. Nearby are the railroad station, the airstrip, nature trails, the park headquarters, a grocery store, and a gas station. You'll pay through the nose for the railroad-station motif and for easy access to tourist services (open May-Sept.; singles $119, doubles $130).

Hardsiders are going to have a hard time in Denali. There are few hookups or dump stations, and driving is allowed on only 12 mi. of Denali Park Rd. RV drivers can pay $12 per night to park at **Riley Creek, Savage River,** and **Teklanika River Campgrounds** in the middle of it all—the hotel, the visitors center, the train depot—or they can head to the numerous RV parks huddled near the park entrance.

As with the shuttle buses, campgrounds work on the coupon system, allowing access on the same day you visit the VAC, the next day, or two days ahead. All three are given on a space-available basis, so get to the VAC early in the morning two days in advance if you want to assure yourself of a site.

Backpackers waiting for a backcountry permit or a campsite within the park are assured a space for $3 a night in **Morino Campground,** next to the hotel (with water and pit toilets). Permits are distributed on a first-come, first-served basis, so park your tent where you can and arrive at the visitors center as early as possible in the morning. Many people find it helpful to set up camp in Morino the first day while they take the shuttle bus in and preview potential campsites within the park. A wait of several days to get a permit is not uncommon, so be patient and make sure you've brought along plenty of food.

> **Riley Creek,** Mile ¼ Denali Park Rd. The only year-round campground in Denali (no water available in winter). 102 sites. Often has the only sites still open at midmorning. Piped water, flush toilets, and a sewage dump. Sites $12.
>
> **Morino Creek,** Mile 1.9 Denali Park Rd., next to the train tracks. 60 sites for backpackers without vehicles. Water, chemical toilets. 14-day max. stay. Self-registered sites $3. Nearest showers at the Mercantile, ¼ mi. back up the road.
>
> **Savage River,** Mile 12 Denali Park Rd. Flush toilets and water. Accessible only by shuttle bus or by a vehicle with a permit. 33 sites, $12.
>
> **Sanctuary River,** Mile 22 on Denali Park Rd. Chemical toilets but no water. Accessible only by shuttle bus. 7 sites, $12.
>
> **Teklanika River,** Mile 29 Denali Park Rd. Piped water and chemical toilets. Accessible only by shuttle bus or by a vehicle with a permit. 3-day min. stay for RVs. 50 sites, $12.
>
> **Igloo Creek,** Mile 34 Denali Park Rd. "Igloo" means "house"—any kind of house—so you won't see any ice-block domes here. For that matter, you won't see any houses, either. Pit toilets but no water. Accessible only by shuttle. No vehicles allowed. 7 tentsites, $12.
>
> **Wonder Lake,** Mile 85 Denali Park Rd. You are a happy camper indeed if, when you reach the park, Wonder Lake is not full. Spectacular views of Denali. Piped water, flush toilets. No vehicles allowed. 56 quadrillion mosquitoes (give or take a few trillion). Tents only. 28 sites, $12.

Outside the Park

Several accommodations cluster around the entrance to the park, providing a consolation prize to those who did not get a lucky Denali coupon.

> **Denali Hostel,** P.O. Box 801 (683-1295), Denali Park. Drive 9.6 mi. north of park entrance, turn left onto Otto Lake Rd., drive 1.3 mi. 2nd house on the right is the hostel. Friendly owners preside over bunks, showers, and kitchen facilities. Morning shuttles to the park and daily pick-ups from the VAC (see Practical Information) at 5pm and 9pm. Beds $22.
>
> **The Happy Wanderer Hostel** (683-2690 or 683-2360), Parks Hwy., 1 mi. north of the park entrance, across from Lynx Pizza. 8 beds, limited kitchen facilities, pit

toilets, no running water. Nearest shower is at the Mercantile, 1 mi. farther in toward the park. Beds $15.

Denali Grizzly Bear Cabins and Campground (683-2696), P.O. Box 7, Denali Park, 7 mi. south of park entrance. Cabins range from $49 for 2 people without bath to $90 for 4 people with bath. Tent-cabins for 1-2 people $21. Tent and vehicle sites $15, RV sites with full hookup $21. Showers 75¢ for 2 min.

McKinley-Denali Cabins (683-2733), P.O. Box 90, Denali Park, 1 mi. north of park entrance. 12 economy tent-cabins for 1-2 people ($60) or 3-4 people ($65). Separate building houses heat, electricity, and full bath.

Sourdough Cabins (683-2773), P.O. Box 118, Denali Park, 1 mi. north of park entrance, down below Lynx Creek Pizza. Cabin with 2 double beds and private bath $109.

Lynx Creek Campground (683-2548), 1 mi. north of park entrance. The closest private campground. Showers. Tentsites and RV sites $15, with hookup $20. Reservations not accepted.

McKinley Campground (683-1418), P.O. Box 340, Healy 99743, 11 mi. north of park entrance. Showers and the only public laundromat in the area (see Practical Information). Tentsites for 1-2 people $15.75, $4.50 per additional person; full hookup $26.

BACKCOUNTRY CAMPING

Although day hiking is unlimited wherever there are no wildlife restrictions, only two to 12 hikers can camp at one time in each of the park's 44 units. Select a few different areas in the park in case your first choice is booked. The rangers will usually leave two or three zones open to unlimited backcountry camping, but these areas tend to be undesirable, thick with mosquitoes and set back from the road behind other quadrants. Some quadrants are temporarily closed following a fresh kill or a "bear encounter." Sable Pass, a romping place for bears, has been closed since 1955.

Rangers at the backcountry desk will not give recommendations for specific areas because they want to disperse hikers as widely as possible. Generally, though, the areas on the southern side of the park road are the best for trekking. River bars and alpine tundra mean excellent footing and fewer mosquitoes. Areas 9, 10,11, 12, and 13 are especially good (and popular).

No matter where you camp, you must keep within the zone for which you signed up, and you have to pitch your tent completely out of sight of the road (so as not to spoil the view for passers-by). To keep from getting lost, you can obtain **topographic maps** ($2.50) at the VAC (see Practical Information). Before you even leave the VAC, rangers will give you a brief introduction to bear management. *All* zones require that you carry a black, cylindrical **bear-resistant food container,** available free at Riley Creek. Bells (for alerting bears to your presence) are available for 75¢ at the Mercantile. Read **Bear Necessities** in the **Essentials** section of this book before you camp in the backcountry. Though no one has ever been killed by a bear in Denali, you don't want to be the first to claim the honor.

FOOD

Food in Denali is expensive, but government controls mean that prices are probably not as high as you'd expect. Try to bring groceries into the park with you. Provisions in the park are available at **Mercantile Gas and Groceries,** 1½ mi. along Denali Park Rd. (683-2215). A microwaveable burrito can be had for $1 (open daily 7am-10pm). The **Lynx Creek Grocery** (683-2548) has similarly priced items 1 mi. north of the park entrance and is open 24 hr.

Lynx Creek Pizza (683-2547), 1 mi. north of park entrance. Monster portions of Italian and Mexican favorites ($7-8) and good pizza (16 in. from $15.50). Go for the slice-salad-soda-scoop lunch special ($6.50). Open daily 11am-11:30pm.

Whistle Stop Snack Shop (683-2215), in the Denali Park Hotel. Decent fast food with a variety of sandwich platters ($4-6). Open daily 11am-11:45pm.

McKinley/Denali Steak and Salmon Bake Restaurant (683-2733), 1 mi. north of park entrance. Reasonably priced tourist trap doles out pounds of food in a picnic setting. If you're up to it, try the Sourdough Breakfast (scrambled eggs, ham, reindeer sausage, potatoes, juice, coffee, and all-you-can-eat blueberry pancakes) for $8. All-you-can-eat soup, salad, rolls, and pudding available all day for $9. Open daily 5am-11pm.

Cruiser's Cafe (683-2282), in the Harbor Lodge next to the Lynx Creek complex. Snazzier fare for snazzier prices. Sandwiches ($6), burgers and chicken dishes ($6-8). Breakfast buffet daily 5-8am ($5). Open daily 5-8am and 11am-midnight.

OUTDOORS IN THE PARK

Catching a glimpse of both Denali's peak and its many residents takes perfect timing and even better luck. Dall sheep generally dawdle near the Igloo and Cathedral Mountains as well as along Primrose Ridge near Savage River in the summer; look for them near Polychrome Pass in the fall. Caribou congregate in alpine meadows in the summer and move to the hills between the Eielson Visitors Center and Wonder Lake in the fall. Moose meander everywhere but are especially visible during early mornings and late evenings near the Riley Creek Campground, in the Savage River, and between the Teklanika and Igloo campgrounds. Grizzly bears are everywhere; 200 to 300 reside in Denali Park.

The most impressive views of the mountain materialize in the morning and late in the evening. Denali emerges completely only about once every three days, but odds are a little better in the late fall (Sept.-Oct.). During the summer, fog usually shrouds the "Weathermaker." In any season, the best viewpoints are the highway from Anchorage and the Wonder Lake Campground. Otherwise, take a shuttle to the Stony Hill Overlook, the Eielson Visitors Center, or the overlook near the Savage River Campground (at the rise in Sable Pass). If the sky is clear at 2:30am on summer nights, Wonder Lake campers can watch the tip of Denali catching the sun before it is even visible over the horizon. If you yourself are feeling like a Great One and want to try a climb to the summit, it takes 30 days round-trip and costs thousands of dollars (and besides, what do you think you're looking for advice on scaling Denali in a budget travel guide?). **Denali Air** can get you there faster and cheaper (call 683-2261 or talk to someone at the Denali Park Hotel desk). Scheduled 60-minute flights depart from the airstrip (daily every other hr. 8am-8pm, $135 per person). Better, less expensive flightseeing tours fly out of Anchorage, Fairbanks, and especially Talkeetna.

Park rangers organize one-hour **tundra walks** daily at 1:30pm from Eielson (take a bus from the VAC at 9:30am at the latest). Check boards at the VAC entrance for other guided hikes, which are conducted twice daily. Meet at the arranged milepost (at approx. 8am and 1:30pm), and park rangers will lead an "interpretive" hike which often lasts four or five hours. The Denali Wilderness Film shows daily at the VAC (check times), and numerous other talks and naturalist programs are posted there as well. The **sled-dog demonstrations** are another worthwhile free offering. The dogs play a critical role in the winter, when the park is only accessible to sled-dog teams and skiers. Buses leave the VAC at 9:30am, 1:30pm, and 2:30pm.

Most of Denali Park is a trail-less wilderness, but a good way to kill time while waiting for your date with the shuttle bus is to explore the well-maintained **trails** which snake around the VAC and the Denali Hotel. **Horseshoe Lake Trail** is a gentle ½-mi. trail connecting the hotel to an overlook of the lake; there is also a steep 0.7-mi. trail leading down to the lake. The 2-mi. **Rock Creek Trail,** near the Park Headquarters at Mile 3.5 of the park road, terminates at the hotel. The hike to **Mt. Healy Overlook** is a steep 2½ mi. from the hotel. If you feel unchallenged, you can keep going up the ridge to the top of 5700-ft. Mt. Healy. Other popular established trails include the 9-mi. **Triple Lakes Trail,** which runs along the railway tracks, and the 1.5-mi. **Morino Loop Trail,** which begins and ends in Riley Creek campground.

You can day-hike within the heart of the park by riding the shuttle bus to a suitable embarkation point for your hike and asking the driver to let you off. Upon completion, you can flag down a shuttle bus heading towards your camp. Remember, most hiking is done on unmarked terrain, for Denali offers few trails. Before heading out, ask rangers about units which may be closed off for wildlife protection. In addition, check the visitors center for interpretive pamphlets on the flora and fauna you may encounter on your way.

Several rafting companies run the rapids of Denali's **Nenana River.** The best deal in town is at **McKinley Raft Tours** (683-2392), which offers a four-hour combination float trip and whitewater run (daily at noon; $48) and a shorter, more intense two-hour whitewater run (daily 9am, 2:30pm, and 6:30pm; $33). Similar packages at slightly higher prices are offered by **Owl Rafting** (683-2215) and **Denali Rafting Adventures** (683-2234).

■ Near Denali: Talkeetna

Talkeetna, located at the confluence of the Talkeetna, Susitna, and Chulitna Rivers, was a base camp for goldpanners until the waters stopped sparkling in the 1940s. Decades later, the town has been reborn as a base camp of a different sort—Talkeetna is now the most popular flight departure point for climbers of **Denali,** only 60 air mi. to the north. Every year between April and June, hundreds of well-financed climbers from across the globe converge on Talkeetna, creating an international village in an unlikely place. From the town, they are flown to an icy airstrip on the Kahiltna Glacier at 7200 ft., and from there it's all uphill. Deaths are not uncommon. In the spring and summer of 1992, 11 climbers lost their lives on the unforgiving slopes—the costliest season in the history of Denali ascents.

With a small population of 500, consisting mostly of climbers and Bush pilots, Talkeetna is known far and wide for its character. Despite the constant pressures of tourism, the settlement is just far enough off the beaten path to maintain the small-town charm that has made it a welcome oasis for tired climbers and thirsty goldpanners alike.

Practical Information Visitors information (733-1686) for Talkeetna, including pamphlets about local air charters and walking tours, is located in the **"Three German Bachelors Cabin"** at Main St. and Talkeetna Spur (open mid-May-Labor Day 10:30am-5:30pm). If it's closed, **Talkeetna Gifts and Collectibles** (733-2710) next door has most of the same information (open daily 9am-7pm).

Talkeetna is 113 mi. north of Anchorage, 280 mi. south of Fairbanks, and 14 mi. off the Parks Hwy. on Talkeetna Spur Rd. (Mile 98.5). The **Alaska Railroad** runs through the station near the Bachelors Cabin. To: Denali (1 per day, $36); Anchorage (1 per day, $34.50); and Fairbanks (1 per day, $66). Call 800-544-0552 for ticket information. **Caribou Express** (278-5776), **Alaska-Denali Transit** (277-7282), and **Moon Bay Express** (274-6454) run buses to Denali, Anchorage, and Fairbanks.

The **Sunshine Community Health Clinic** (733-2273) is located 14.5 mi. from town on the Talkeetna Spur. **Emergency numbers: ambulance,** 733-2478; **fire,** 733-2443. The **Post Office** (733-2275) is in town on the Spur (open Mon.-Fri. 9am-5pm, Sat. 10am-2pm; **General Delivery ZIP Code:** 99676).

Accommodations, Camping, and Food Budget travelers will cheer for the town's clean, pleasant, and affordable accommodations. The **Fairview Inn** (733-2423), on Main St., has good, cheap rooms (singles $30, doubles $40). The **Talkeetna Roadhouse** (733-1351 or 733-2341), at Main and C St., is surprisingly cheap as well (singles $35, doubles $50). Make reservations well in advance during the climbing season (mid-May to July).

Backpackers should head for the free **River Park Campground,** which is quiet despite its location near the center of town. The park has unimproved sites for tents and RVs (no facilities), but the neighboring **Three Rivers Tesoro Gas Station** (733-2620), on Main St., has a **laundromat** (wash $1.50, 10-min. dry 25¢) and **showers** ($2). (Open Mon.-Sat. 8am-9pm, Sun. 9am-7pm.)

The best budget food in town is at **McKinley Deli** (733-1234), at Main and C St., and the half-sandwich, bowl of soup, and slice of melon special ($4.50) is their tastiest deal (open daily 6am-11pm). The **Roadhouse Cafe** (733-1351), in the (you guessed it) Talkeetna Roadhouse, is home to the nationally distributed Homestead BBQ Sauce. Try their famous Porky Joe ($4.25) or a stack of authentic sourdough pancakes ($4), made from a 1902 recipe (open Mon.-Sat. 7am-3pm and 5:30-8:30pm, Sun. 9am-2pm and 5:30-8:30pm). The best chefs in town serve up excellent fresh seafood at the **Latitude 62° Restaurant** (733-2262), a ½ mi. from town on the Talkeetna Spur. Try the Halibut Sauté ($11.50) and the mountainous McKinley Sundae ($4). (Open daily 6am-11pm.)

Sights and Entertainment If it's raining, check out the **Museum of Northern Adventure,** on the Talkeetna Spur (733-2710), which offers a gruesome recreation of "the cremation of Sam McGee" (open daily 11am-7pm; admission $3.50, under 12 $2.50). The **Talkeetna Historical Society Museum** (733-2487), off C St., has high-quality displays on Alaskan transportation and mountaineering, including an 8-ft. model of Mt. McKinley (open in summer daily 10am-5pm; admission $1).

In mid-May, Talkeetna celebrates its golden history with a parade, etc., on **Miner's Day.** Mid-July brings the **Moose-Dropping Festival** (no, we're not talking about chucking hapless quadrupeds from a helicopter), capped by the infamous "gilded moose dropping toss." The coolest, mellowest concert in Alaska is the **Alaska Music Festival** in early August, a 72-hr. orgy of live bluegrass, rock 'n' roll, and tie-dye in Susitna Bluffs, 30 mi. south of Talkeetna at Mile 86 of the Parks Hwy.

Outdoors Near Talkeetna You may not be able to climb the mountain, but at least you can look at it. The Denali **overlook,** 1 mi. from town down the Talkeetna Spur, boasts the state's best road-accessible view of Denali. If the clouds cooperate, you will be treated to a view of rock—nearly 4 mi. of it, climbing straight up to the sky.

Fishing opportunities and river tours abound in the waterways around town. **McKinley View Tours** (733-2223), **Talkeetna Riverboat Service** (733-2281), **Denali River Guides** (733-2697), and **Mahay's Riverboat Service** (733-2223) all offer access to the wet 'n' wild wilderness. If you'd rather head out on your own, rent a bike ($15 per 8 hr.) or canoe ($25 per day) from **Bikes, Flights, Etc.** on Main St. (733-1351), across from the gas station. The more adventurous can try dog-mushing expeditions (winter only) for $30 per hr. (open daily 10am-6pm).

After the climbing season (mid-May through July), **Talkeetna Airport** (733-2277), across the train tracks in east Talkeetna, is full of charter planes with no place to go—so the four local companies offer Denali flightseeing tours at some of the lowest rates in Alaska. **K2 Aviation** (733-2291) offers a one-hour tour for $75 with a four-person minimum passenger restriction. For $90, you can experience the sheer terror of a glacier landing at the 5600-ft. level with **Talkeetna Air Taxi** (733-2218), which makes a brief stop at the Ruth Amphitheater (4-person min.).

■ The Denali Highway

Running 133 mi. through the foothills of the Alaska Range, the Denali Hwy. gives you a preview of what lies ahead in Denali National Park—you pass by the same mountains, the same kinds of wildlife—but with fewer people, fewer hassles, and no lines for campsites. All that's missing is Denali itself. The road stretches from Cantwell, 17 mi. south of the Denali Park entrance, to Paxson on the Richardson Hwy. From 1957 to 1972 (when the Parks Hwy. was completed), the highway provided the only access to Denali National Park. Overlooked by tour buses and the majority of RVs, the road offers an escape from Alaska's more tourist-traveled routes.

Except for the 21 mi. west of Paxson, the Denali Hwy. is entirely gravel. It is nevertheless well-maintained with few major bumps—a boon to travelers whose suspensions are nearly comatose. At Mile 21 (heading west), the BLM manages the free

Tangle Lakes Campground (water, toilets), and, ¼ mi. further on, the **Tangle River Campground,** also free (water, toilets). Situated in extremely scenic locations, both campgrounds provide easy access to the **Delta River Canoe Route** (a 35-mi. canoe route with one difficult stretch of class III rapids) and the **Upper Tangle Lakes Canoe Route** (an easier paddle beginning at Tangle River and ending at Dickey Lake, 9 mi. to the south). Topographic maps are a necessity for both routes.

On a clear day, spectacular scenery awaits along the rest of the highway, interrupted by an occasional roadhouse or cafe. At Mile 36, **MacLaren Summit** (4086 ft.) is the site of the second-highest highway pass in Alaska (after the Antigun Pass on the Dalton Hwy.). Glacial features are also much in evidence—lakes and a pingo lie at Mile 41, eskers at Mile 59. At Mile 111 rests the free **Brushkana River Campground** (water, toilets).

Backpackers can camp out anywhere along the length of the highway (no permit needed), although topographic maps are necessary since there are no marked trails. Before hitting the road, pick up the BLM's *Denali Highway Points of Interest* pamphlet, available at most local roadhouses, visitors centers, and pit stops.

NORTH FROM THE ALASKA HIGHWAY

■ The Taylor Highway

The Taylor Hwy. extends 160 mi. north from its junction with the Alaska Hwy. to the historic town of Eagle on the Yukon River. Frost heaves, potholes, and sections of washboard abound along the length of the hwy., making this a long and bumpy ride. At **Tetlin Junction,** 12 mi. east of Tok, the highway also connects with the Top-of-the-World Hwy., which heads east toward Dawson City, YT. Unfortunately, no scheduled bus service follows this route, and those without a car are forced to hitchhike, a difficult proposition in light of the fact that traffic is dominated by the "we-don't-pick-up-hitchers-no way-uh-uh-forget it" RV crowd. Most hitchers have a good book handy and start early in the morning. *All* travelers headed to Dawson should keep in mind that the border is open only from 8am to 8pm Alaska time, and entertainment is scarce for those bedding down at the border.

From **Mile 0,** the Taylor Hwy. begins to climb to over 3500 ft. as it winds toward 5541-ft. Mt. Fairplay. An interpretive sign at Mile 35 explains the history of the Taylor Hwy. and offers a good opportunity to stretch your legs and your mind. At Mile 49, the BLM manages the **West Fork Campground,** with 25 sites but no water.

The megalopolis of **Chicken** lies 17 mi. farther north. Like most Interior Alaskan towns, Chicken was developed in pursuit of the golden egg. According to popular myth, miners congregating toward the Yukon discovery in 1896 wished to name the town, now called Chicken, after the many ptarmigan in the area. But none of the miners knew how to spell "ptarmigan," and so Chicken it became. Historic Chicken is off a private road to the west of the highway, while modern "downtown" Chicken is a ¼ mi. east of the highway. Free walking tours of historic Chicken leave daily at 1pm from the parking lot in front of the saloon and are the only way to see some of the original pre-Klondike cabins and the roadhouse where "Tisha" (subject of a nonfictional book about a woman teaching in the Alaskan Bush) taught. Downtown, the **Chicken Cafe** has burgers ($6, or a reindeer burger for $8), but not much more (open daily 8am-7pm). Tent campers can put down on the lawn next to the cafe in Chicken for free (water and pit toilets available). The folks in Chicken aren't scared of expansion: they're set on creating a bigger and brighter future, so expect some moves, price changes, and a few new facilities for 1994. You might even find a phone in Chicken, although none existed in the summer of 1993. The **post office** is a ¼ mi. down the highway from the downtown Chicken turn-off. The **ZIP Code** in Chicken is 99732.

The **Jack Wade Dredge** lies rusting away right next to the highway at Mile 86. The dredge has deteriorated considerably and isn't all that safe, but that doesn't stop most people from wandering around its hollow insides. At **Jack Wade Junction** the road forks: north for 64 mi. to Eagle and east for 79 mi. via the Top-of-the-World Hwy. to Dawson. Don't forget that the border closes at 8pm and that customs agents often seem to have vendettas against hitchhikers. Make sure you have proof of funds or you might fall victim to an arbitrary decision and get stuck in Alaska 120 mi. from the nearest settlement. The last 64 mi. from the junction to Eagle remain bumpy and dusty—they also hide several prickly hairpin turns.

■ Eagle

Like most towns along the Yukon, Eagle came into being primarily as a result of the Klondike Gold Rush. Established in 1898 as a permanent mining community, Eagle's central location in the Interior led the secretary of war to establish an adjacent military base in the same year, and hasty construction of Fort Egbert began in 1899. In 1900 Congress approved criminal and civil codes for Alaska that, among other things, provided for three judicial districts. Eagle was chosen as headquarters for the third judicial district, which stretched from the Arctic Ocean out to the Aleutians and covered nearly half the state. Eagle's first judge had a courthouse and jail built in 1901. That same year, the federal approval of Eagle's charter made it the first incorporated city in Interior Alaska. Ensuing gold strikes in Nome and Fairbanks, however, soon stripped Eagle of its one-time glory. The court was moved to Fairbanks and Fort Egbert was almost completely abandoned in 1911. North of town, several original buildings from Fort Egbert sit restored.

Today, Eagle still retains its turn-of-the-century mystique. Extensive restoration work by the BLM and Eagle Historical Society has returned many of the town's buildings to their original conditions. With a stable population of 160, Eagle sits on the banks of the Yukon River and the brink of vast stretches of wilderness.

Sights and Practical Information Eagle has arguably more square feet of museum space for its size than any other town, city, or village in Alaska. The only way to access all of the town's historic buildings and displays is through the town's daily three-hour walking tour ($3), which leaves at 10am from the **Courthouse Museum** on Berry St. The courthouse is also open to the general public throughout much of the day. Walking around unguided is interesting but not nearly as informative. **Amundsen Park,** on 1st St. at Amundsen, honors the Norwegian explorer who hiked into Eagle in the winter of 1905 from Canada's Arctic Coast. He used Eagle's telegraph to inform the world that he had successfully navigated the Northwest Passage. Several weeks later, Amundsen mushed back to his ship, frozen in the ice floes of the Arctic Ocean. Nine months later he completed the first successful journey from the Atlantic to the Pacific via the Arctic Ocean.

Bikes can be rented from the Village Store for $10 per day (open Mon.-Sat. 9am-6pm, Sun. 9am-5pm). In case of a **medical emergency** call 547-2300. The **post office** (547-2211) is on 2nd St. at Jefferson (open Mon.-Fri. 8:30am-4:30pm). **ZIP Code:** 99738.

Camping, Accommodations, and Food Campers will find Eagle a heavenly haven. **Eagle Campground** is a 1-mi. hike from town past Fort Egbert (no fee, no water, pit toilets). Eagle's "mall" is on Front St. The **Eagle Trading Co.** (547-2220) in the mall has it all: groceries (at Bush prices), showers ($4), laundromat ($4 per load), RV hookups ($15), and rooms for rent (singles $50, doubles $60). (Open daily 9am-8pm.) The adjacent **Riverside Cafe** (547-2250) has delicious burgers ($5) and Idaho-sized baskets of fries ($2). (Open daily 7am-8pm.) Groceries and hardware can also be had from the **Village Store** (547-2270), ¼ mi. east of town.

The Float from Eagle to Circle The National Park Service makes Eagle its headquarters for the **Yukon-Charley Rivers National Preserve.** The **visitors center** (547-2233) is on the western end of 1st St. and can provide detailed information on the geography and wildlife of the area (open daily 8am-5pm). The 158-mi. float through the preserve from Eagle to Circle is a popular one. The full trip usually takes four to six days and passes through some of Alaska's wildest country. Bear, moose, and beaver abound, as do mosquitoes, though campers can generally avoid them by camping on the numerous gravel bars in the river. Canoes and inflatable rafts are the most common forms of transportation—investigate outfitters in Eagle or check with the Park Service by writing Superintendent, P.O. Box 64, Eagle, AK 99738.

■ The Steese Highway

The Steese Hwy. heads northeast of Fairbanks for 162 mi. to the town of Circle on the Yukon River. En route it passes Central and the short side roads that leads to the **Arctic Circle Hot Springs,** as well as several potential hikes and floats. The pavement ends at Mile 44, with the exception of a few miles in and near Central. The road is generally good gravel, although the last 20 mi. coming into Circle can get rather b-b-bumpy.

The Steese Hwy. heads out of Fairbanks as the **Steese Expressway** but becomes the more modest two-lane highway 8 mi. out. Three mi. later comes the junction of the Elliot Hwy. Keep going straight if you're driving to the Dalton Hwy. or just headed for a soak in the Manley Hot Springs, but take a right if you want to follow the Steese. On the highway's north side, at Mile 16, sits a plaque honoring Felix Pedros's 1902 gold discovery which spawned the city of Fairbanks.

Campgrounds at Mile 39 and 60 provide access to the **Chatenika River Canoe Trail,** which parallels the Steese for nearly 30 mi. The stream is clear and Class II, and its biggest dangers to paddlers are low water and overhanging trees.

At **Central** (Mile 127), a small town of about 400 summer residents, the Circle Hot Springs Rd. takes the waiting head-soaker 8 mi. to the **Circle Hot Springs Resort** (520-5113), which has hostel accommodations for $20 ($10 for each additional person; sleeping bags required). Pool use is free for those staying overnight at the resort. Otherwise, a dip in the warm, mineral-rich water will cost $7.

Circle is the pothole at the end of the road (the Steese Hwy., that is), 35 mi. beyond Central. Few diversions present themselves other than a peek at the Yukon River and the opportunity to have your picture taken in front of the "Welcome to Circle City" sign. For those left starving by the trip, the **Yukon Trading Post** (773-1217) has groceries at Bush prices and a café that isn't much cheaper (open daily 9am-8pm). You can find free camping near the river (water, pit toilets). The only historic site is the **Pioneer Cemetery,** a ½ mi. east of town. Follow the road east until you come to a lawn fenced off by sawhorses. Cross the lawn lightly and the cemetery will soon be in view.

Useful phone numbers: **medical emergency,** 773-SICK/7425; **village protection safety officer** (the police of Circle): 773-VPSD/8773. There is a **post office** (773-1220) in the trading post (open Mon., Wed., Fri. 10am-3pm; Tues.-Thurs. 10am-2:30pm). **ZIP Code:** 99733.

The Bush

Nome, Prudhoe Bay, Kotzebue, and Barrow are places of which all Alaskans know but few have ever seen. The Bush is the Alaska where polar bears still ride the ice floes, and where hundreds of thousands of caribou still freely roam the tundra. It's the place where Native settlements are few and far between, accessible only by plane, boat, or dogsled. It's the place where cannery workers and oil drillers swarm to make the big money, knowing it's theirs to save because they'll have nowhere to spend it. This is where the large-scale, big-budget documentaries about the "Last Frontier" are made.

Known variously as the Country, the Wilderness Rim, and the Bush, this vast expanse of frozen tundra and jagged coastline is sparsely dotted with small settlements, narrow landing strips, and other insignificant traces of human presence. This harsh country occupies millions of acres in the northeast, northwest, and southwest sections of the state.

Each area of the Bush has distinctive features. The **Southwest** includes the flat, buggy terrain of the Yukon-Kushkowin delta and the mountainous **Alaska Peninsula,** a volcanic arc that is home to some of the worst weather on earth. **Western Alaska** includes mostly the Seward Peninsula, a treeless, hilly land of tundra. **Nome,** on the coast of the Bering Sea, is frequently swept by harsh storms. The **Brooks Range,** Alaska's Arctic crown, stretches from the northwest to the Canadian border, while the flat, endless expanses of tundra on the **North Slope** spread northwards from the Brooks to the Arctic Ocean. The Bush is made to order for the traveler seeking a wilderness experience that *National Geographic* would gladly have grace its pages. Adventure and self-reliance are key concepts when traveling in the Bush—most towns won't spend time entertaining guests. Soak in the isolation, be prepared to rough it, and remember—bears always have the right of way.

Transportation in the Bush is not cheap. Tour outfitters abound, ready and willing—for a steep price—to lead you out into the wilds to fish, hunt, hike, kayak, canoe, or photograph, and if they don't take you home with them they'll at least take your money. Larger commercial operators like **Alaska Airlines** (800-426-0333) and **Mark Air** (800-478-0800) service the more sizable Bush communities such as Nome, Kotzebue, and Barrow, while smaller companies like **Larry's Flying Service** (474-9169 in Fairbanks) and **Frontier Flying Services** (474-0014 in Fairbanks) fly to the more remote spots like Anaktuvuk Pass and Fort Yukon. Chartering a plane, while costing upwards of $250 an hour, is a necessary evil—it's the only way to get into the middle of the wilderness, away from even the most remote communities.

THE DALTON HIGHWAY

No road anywhere in the world can compare with the Dalton Hwy. It's nearly six times as long as Denali Park Road, far more breathtaking, and runs along the pipeline from Fairbanks to Prudhoe Bay. Myths abound as to the actual accessibility of the highway for the general public, but the truth goes something like this: *Technically,* the highway is open for the general public up to Disaster Creek (Mile 211) and to travel further demands that you appropriate a permit—requiring a "legitimate commercial purpose" for continuing—from the **Dept. of Transportation,** 2301 Peger Rd., Fairbanks 99707 (451-2209). Realistically, however, anybody can drive the length of the highway without difficulty. In previous years, the oil companies stationed a guard at Disaster Creek who warned tourists that a permit was required for further travel. But the guard had no legal authority or power to turn back permit-less travelers. Now all the warning that remains at Disaster Creek is a weather-beaten sign.

The visitor center in Fairbanks spins a different yarn to inquisitive tourists, and with good reason: to discourage ignorant yokels from blithely attempting 500 mi. of extremely rough, dangerous road, where the very limited services are more than *200 mi.* apart. Besides, the highway's primary function is that of a haul road. Truckers populate the highway, their 36-wheel rigs spitting rocks and billowing dust up to crack your windshield and coat your car. So a tip: when a truck is approaching, *slow down* to reduce potential danger, and make sure those windows are rolled up (or you'll soon have enough dirt inside your vehicle to start your own small forest).

The *entire* highway is dirt, and is often interspersed with tennis-ball sized rocks, frost heaves, and *large* potholes. So bring *at least* one spare tire, spare fuel, and spare supplies. Or else, you could spend the rest of your life paying the towing bill.

Hitchhiking the highway is also possible. Hitchers should be prepared for long waits by the roadside and shouldn't expect any truckers to stop. A recent accident involving a truck rolling over a dead hitchhiker (along with over $20 million in lawsuits) has reduced the possibility of catching a ride with that group to nil. Some private traffic does exist on the highway, and although hitchers may spend hours waiting before a single private vehicle passes by, the chances of them stopping are extremely good. Who's gonna leave somebody stranded alone in the middle of nowhere?

■ From Fairbanks to the Arctic Circle

The journey begins with an 80-mi. jaunt from Fairbanks along the **Elliot Hwy.** to Mile 0 of the Dalton Highway. Enjoy the 40 mi. of pavement as you head out from Fairbanks. It's the last you'll see for almost 900 mi. Once it becomes gravel, the Elliot Highway remains a good road and not too difficult to drive. So also is the first stretch of the Dalton Highway, although you can bet your left leg that there'll be more than a few rough spots. The first landmark heading north is the **Yukon River** crossing. This wood-planked bridge is the only one crossing the mighty Yukon and unlike most other bridges, it has a very noticeable pitch to it. Heading north on the bridge, you could virtually put your car in neutral and coast the downhill grade. On the north side of the river exists one of the two **service stations** that can be found on the highway. You can get unleaded gas at **Yukon Ventures** (655-9001) for $1.65 a gallon or rent a room for $50 a person. The gas station and adjacent restaurant are open daily 7am-midnight.

The road next winds through its first tundra region as it gains in elevation and passes by **Finger Rock** (to the east) and **Caribou Mountain** (a distance away to the west). You'll pass over several steep hills with names like "Happy Man" and "Beaver Slide." The **pipeline** runs along the highway (as it does for the whole length). The "fins" sticking out of the pipeline's support posts are "thermal siphons" designed to divert the heat of the 108°F oil flowing within from the pipeline supports, which would otherwise conduct the heat and melt the underlying permafrost.

Next comes the **Arctic Circle.** A recently constructed "pull-out" (or a place to pull off the road) here has several picnic tables and presents the visitor with four placards discussing the Arctic seasons. The enormous "Arctic Circle" sign is great for pictures, and the spot in general is good for (free) camping, albeit with no facilities.

■ From the Arctic Circle to Prudhoe Bay

Continuing onward, over 1500-foot **Gobblers Knob** (is that a cool name or what?), past Prospect Camp and Pump Station No. 5, over the Jim River and the South Fork of the Koyukuk River, you'll rattle along to the town of **Coldfoot,** the last **services** available before Prudhoe Bay (240 mi. away). Coldfoot, "the northernmost truck stop in North America," was originally a mining town which, at its peak, boasted "one gambling hall, two road houses, seven saloons, and 10 prostitutes." Its name originated in 1898, when a group of timid prospectors got "cold feet" about wintering above the Arctic Circle and headed south again. It was probably a smart move on their part. (In the winter of 1989, an all-time Alaskan low temperature of -82°F was recorded here.) "Downtown" consists of a huge and muddy parking lot. Around the perimeter of the field is the **Coldfoot Cafe** (678-5201), which is open 24 hours and has good, hot, and (surprise!) expensive food; burgers and fries start at around $7. The **general store** is open daily noon-9pm and has limited supplies. Gas will cost you about $1.50 a gallon for unleaded ($1.32 for diesel). The **Arctic Acres Inn** (678-5224) has renovated an old construction-worker bunkhouse into a hotel. (Singles with shared bath $90. Doubles $105.) Several RV sites (full hookups $20) and tentsites ($7.50) are adjacent, but if you just hike a mi. out of town in any direction so that you're out of sight, nobody will really care where you pitch your tent. (Clean up after yourself, though!) You can take a **shower** at the hotel for $3.50 or wash and dry a load of **laundry** for $4. Just north and around the corner is the **Coldfoot Visitor Center** (678-5209), which is managed jointly by the National Park Service, Bureau of Land Management, and Alaskan Fish and Game. This is an excellent source of information if you're planning on doing some intense trekking or paddling in the Brooks Range. (Open daily 1-10pm, nightly slide presentations 8:30pm.) For a bit of history, walk across the highway and down the road. You'll pass by the **Coldfoot Cemetery** on your way to historic **Coldfoot,** on the banks of the Koyukuk River, which consists of two weather-worn, broken down cabins dating from the turn of the century. The **post office** is located next to the general store. (Open Mon., Wed., and Fri. 1:30-6pm. **ZIP Code:** 99701.)

Twelve mi. north of Coldfoot is the junction for the historic village of **Wiseman.** Three mi. off the beaten path, this town was immortalized by Robert Marshall in his 1933 book, *Arctic Village,* which details the winter he spent in and amongst its citizens. Perhaps the wildest frontier town accessible by road in Alaska, Wiseman is home to many of the dogs appearing in the Walt Disney movie, *White Fang* (including White Fang himself), as well as about 25 year-round residents. The **Wiseman Trading Post** (est. 1910) will substantiate what you've imagined about the frontier general store and is located at the end of the road leading into Wiseman, across a narrow footbridge. You can pitch a tent behind the store for $2.50. Wiseman is a true part of the Last Frontier, so make the short side trip. It's worth it.

From Wiseman, the highway pierces through the heart of the Brooks Range. Wildlife abounds; keep your eyes open for moose, Dall sheep, bear, hawks, ground squirrels, etc. At Mile 235, **the last tree** found along the highway, a surprisingly tall and majestic spruce, is marked by a sign. Then begins the steep and awe-inspiring ascent towards **Atigun Pass** (4752 ft.), the highest highway pass in Alaska. The highway cuts steeply into the mountainside as it approaches the pass and offers spectacular views of the Dietrich River Valley. Check out the glacial cirque (an amphitheater-shaped depression) on the mountainside east of the highway. Once the mountains are breached, the long descent toward the Arctic Ocean commences.

In the final stretch of the highway, the mountains gradually transform into low bluffs and hills (with names like "Oil Spill Hill"), and ultimately into a broad, flat expanse of nothing but tundra. The road along the final 100 mi. is the worst of the highway. Lots of sharp gravel and small boulders litter the highway. Driving at speeds of more than 25mph could very well rattle the teeth out of your skull and cause your car's suspension and tires to spontaneously disintegrate. The land is generally unattractive. The tundra is perpetually brown except for a short month-long summer in July to August. Walking on the tundra, although it looks flat and easy, is a nightmare. It is filled with bumps and lumps of moss, and is underlain by tremendous amounts of water unable to escape through the frozen ground. Try a tundra walk and you're guaranteed a wet, soggy, difficult hike. Yet despite the rough terrain, caribou roam freely and without difficulty throughout the North Slope. You'll see your share. Even with the presence of the perpetual sun, the temperature is noticeably cooler on the North Slope, typically in the low 40s much of the summer.

Approximately 10 mi. from Deadhorse, the land becomes enshrouded in a layer of coastal fog, blocking the sun and causing the temperature to plummet. Deadhorse and Prudhoe Bay suddenly appear on the horizon in the last few miles of highway. And then you're there. End of the line. The northernmost point accessible by road in North America. Fun, wasn't it? Now you just have to get back.

■ Prudhoe Bay

Named by Sir John Franklin in 1826 after the fourth duke of Northumberland, Baron Prudhoe, Prudhoe Bay may not seem an entirely ample reward for those who've endured the grueling 500-mi. trek up the Dalton Highway. Oil was discovered here in 1968. It took less than 10 years for full-fledged oil extraction to begin, and for the 800-mi. Trans-Alaska Pipeline to be strung from Prudhoe Bay south to the warm-water port of Valdez. Oil extraction continues today, and more than 2 million barrels of oil is contained within the length of the pipeline at any given time, slowly moving south at a rate of 6-7mph.

The weather is wretched. Covered by fog and swept by Arctic winds, the temperature can drop below freezing any day of the year—and with windchill, the temperature usually *is* below freezing. In winter, the official record low-chill factor was clocked at -135°F. Prudhoe receives 64 days of perpetual daylight and 55 days of eternal night each year. In winter, the land is blanketed with snow and ice, and the Beaufort Sea freezes solid. It is not uncommon for polar bears to wander into town off the Arctic ice floes in search of seals—or perhaps a hapless ARCO employee.

This is not a regular community. Everything exists for and because of oil. Every building and structure contributes in some manner towards oil production. No permanent residents, no tourist facilities, no "town proper" to be found in Prudhoe Bay. The camp of **Deadhorse** is situated around the southern perimeter of **Lake Colleen,** at the terminus of the Dalton highway. The town owes its home to the gravel company who brought the first road-building materials north, and whose motto was: "We'll haul anything, even a dead horse."

Sights and Practical Information Prudhoe Bay lacks a visitors center, but any of the hotel desks or travel agencies can supply you with information. If you're interested in getting a look at the oil fields, you'll need to head for Deadhorse. It's the only publicly accessible section of the oil fields, although more than 255 mi. of roads run through them. They are privately owned by the oil companies and access is controlled by two guarded checkpoints. The only way to check them out is aboard a tour. **Arctic Caribou Inn,** Pouch 3401111, Deadhorse 99734 (659-2368), offers excellent tours for $60. You'll stand next to Mile 0 of the pipeline, check out the interior of the worker's bunkhouses (surprisingly nice), and dip your fingers into the icy waters of the Arctic Ocean, among other things. You're here, so you might as well take the tour. What *else* are you going to do? You can either drive the Dalton Hwy. to Deadhorse, take a tour bus to Deadhorse, or fly to Deadhorse. Driving is the most exciting and adventurous route (see Dalton Highway above). Fill up your car for $2 a gallon at the **Goodyear** at the end of the Dalton Highway.

Tours up the highway are expensive. **Princess Tours** (479-9660) offers a three-day, two-night tour of the Dalton Highway and Prudhoe Bay for $505; you bus one way, fly the other. You could also fly directly to Prudhoe Bay from Fairbanks. The **Deadhorse airport** is serviced by **Mark Air** (from Fairbanks $248) and **Alaska Airlines,** which offers a flying tour to Prudhoe Bay for $435.

You can take a **shower** at the North Star Inn for $5 or do a load of **laundry** for $10 (!!). There is an **American Express** outlet (569-2569) next to the Arctic Caribou Inn (open daily 7:30am-7:30pm). In case of an **emergency**, call the ARCO operator at 659-5900, as there are no "public" rescue services. Don't expect ARCO to be too happy about it, though. Prudhoe Bay is a dry "community." No alcohol or firearms allowed. The **post office** (659-2669) is located in the general store. (Open daily 1-3:30pm and 6:30-9pm. **ZIP Code: 99734**.) The **area code** is 907.

Accommodations and Food All of the hotels in Prudhoe Bay are run by the Northwest Alaska Native Corporation (NANA). The **Arctic Caribou Inn** (659-2368) will send "casuals" (individuals not associated with tour groups) over to **"NANA camp"** next door for $65 singles or doubles with shared bath. **North Star Inn** (659-3160) has singles for $90 and shared doubles for $75, both with shared bath. The **Prudhoe Bay Hotel** (659-2520) has singles for $90 and shared doubles for $65 (shared bath, meals included). All of the hotels are basically the same. Converted bunkhouses, all contain spacious rec rooms with large TV, darts, pool, and ping-pong. Each hotel has its own cafeteria (the only places to eat in town) where meals cost $15 each if they're not included with your room. The North Star Inn even has its own salon, where you can get a haircut for $15. If you're thinking of camping to avoid the high hotel prices, forget it. There is nowhere to pitch a tent. The best bets for cheap stays are your car or the hotel rec rooms, where travelers can sometimes stretch out on their big couches without getting booted.

As far as food and other necessaries are concerned, the **Prudhoe Bay General Store** (659-2425), next to the Arctic Caribou Inn, is like a miniature mall and the prices aren't all that steep, considering where you are (open daily 8am-9pm).

THE BROOKS RANGE

Defining Alaska's north coast, the magnificent **Brooks Range** describes a tremendous semicircle from the Chuchki Sea in the west, through the Noatak National Preserve and **Gates of the Arctic National Park,** to the **Arctic National Wildlife Refuge (ANWR)** and the Beaufort Sea in the east. Too far from Fairbanks to draw tourists, too isolated (with the exception of Anaktuvuk Pass) to support human habitation, too huge to be patrolled by park rangers, the Brooks Range is the last stretch of virgin wilderness in U.S. possession. A few remote settlements and the thin trail of the Dalton Highway are the only signs of man's encroachment.

Accessing the Brooks Range and the parks that encompass it is neither difficult nor expensive. Beautiful stretches of the Gates of the Arctic National Park lie just off the Dalton Hwy., near Wiseman (just past Coldfoot) and Atigun Pass. Talk to park officials before planning a trip into the Brooks (the headquarters for both Gates and ANWR are located in Fairbanks; see Fairbanks: Practical Information).

■ Anaktuvuk Pass

In the heart of the Central Brooks Range, the Nunamiat (Noon-ah-mute) are making their last stand. North America's last true nomads, this inland Eskimo people began to forge permanent settlements only in the last 45 years. Surrounded by **Gates of the Arctic National Park** (see below) and nestled in a tundra mountain pass high on the Arctic Divide, the Nunamiat struggle to maintain their subsistence lifestyle amidst the pressures and developments of the 20th century. The mountain backdrop encircling the pass is one of the world's most beautiful—this is the side-trip to make if you head out anywhere into the Alaskan Bush.

Larry's Flying Service (474-9169) offers daily flights to Anaktuvuk Pass (round-trip from Fairbanks $242). If you can stop your stomach from staging a coup, the flight over the tops of the awe–inspiring Brooks Range is itself worth the money. Wilderness so pristine and beautiful is found few places else on earth. Once in Anaktuvuk, visitors should head to the **Simon Panaek Museum** (661-3413), which has extensive displays on traditional Nunaimut culture. The **Hans van der Laan Brooks Range Library** is also inside and has a huge collection of material on the people and land of Alaska's Far North (open Mon.-Fri. 8:30am-5pm; both free). Gorgeous day-hiking opportunities abound around the village. Any of the river valleys radiating away from the town will more than fit the bill. Be prepared for some tough tundra hiking, however, and be sure not to head out in shorts and a T-shirt. Even with bug dope, the mosquitoes will eat you alive.

The town has no rooms for rent, but visitors can camp anywhere just outside of town. The hills on the other side of the John River (which runs through town) are often good camping spots. The **Nunamiut Corporation Store** (661-3327) has groceries at steep Brooks Range prices (open Mon.-Fri. 10am-6pm, Sat. noon-6pm). A small hole-in-the-wall restaurant, the **Nunamiut Corp. Camp Kitchen** (661-3123) on the south end of town has burgers ($5.50) and lobster ($16). (Open Mon.-Sat. 7am-7pm, Sun. 10am-7pm.) The **washeteria** (661-9713), next to the enormous blue-roofed school, has **showers** (free!) and **laundry** facilities (wash $1, 10-min. dry 25¢). **Emergency numbers: medical/fire,** 611; **public safety officer,** 661-3911. The **post office** (661-3615) is next to the airstrip (open Mon.-Fri. 8:30am-11:30am, 12:30pm-5:30pm). **ZIP Code:** 99721.

■ Gates of the Arctic National Park

With 7.2 million acres of protected wilderness, Gates of the Arctic National Park is designed to preserve forever the majestic central Brooks Range. Six national wild rivers run through the park and provide excellent floating opportunities. The heavy glaciation has carved huge V-shaped valleys throughout the park that are excellent for hiking and route-finding.

The park is most accessible to those either decidedly wealthy or simply determined. Budget backpackers can hitch up the Dalton Hwy. and hike in from several access points along the road. Those with a bit more money can fly commercially into Anaktuvuk Pass and head out from there. Those with still more cash to spare can charter a plane and immerse themselves in true isolation. The town of **Bettles** sits south of the mountains on the Middle Fork of the Koyukuk River and is the jumping-off point for those chartering a plane. Several companies offer charter service. Ask around for the best deal, and expect to pay several hundred dollars an hour for a plane. **Larry's Flying Service** (474-9169 in Fairbanks) will get you there for starters (round-trip $180).

Facility with a compass, bear awareness, and other backcountry skills are necessity for any backpacker heading into the park. Extremely variable temperatures can quickly lead to hypothermia or exposure. For more information, contact **Park Headquarters,** 201 1st Ave. (456-0281) in Fairbanks, or write Superintendent, Gates of the Arctic National Park Preserve, P.O. Box 74680, Fairbanks, AK 99707-4680. The Park Service operates a **Gates of the Arctic Field Station** (692-5494) in Bettles for those seeking information (open daily 8am-5pm). In Bettles, **Sourdough Outfitters** (692-5252) offers guided and unguided adventures in the Brooks Range. Canoes and other kinds of equipment are available for rent, and guides are extremely knowledgeable about the park. Stop by for tips before adventuring out.

Ask around about good places to pitch a tent, or stay in the **Bettles Lodge** (692-5111). The lodge has a bunkhouse ($15, sleeping bag required), which is a better deal than regular rooms ($60 and up). The lodge's **restaurant** has good cheeseburgers ($6.50). (Open daily 8am-10pm.) The **Bettles Trading Post** (692-5252) sells some expensive groceries (open Mon.-Sat. 9am-5:30pm, Sun. noon-5pm).

At the lodge, you can also take a **shower** ($3.50) or do some laundry ($7.50 per load). The **post office** (692-5236) is at the northern end of town (open Mon.-Fri. 8am-noon, 1-5pm, Sat. 1-3pm). **ZIP Code:** 99726.

■ Arctic National Wildlife Refuge

Covering a huge northeast swath of Alaska, the Arctic National Wildlife Refuge (ANWR) encompasses more than 20 million incredibly remote acres. The porcupine caribou herd has its calving grounds here. The Brooks Range's highest mountains are here. The oil companies want to move in for exploration. Three national wild rivers flow in the refuge. The only and very expensive way in is by charter plane. There are wolves. There are bears. There are 53 quintillion mosquitoes. Hike it, float it, soak it up. And know what you're doing. This is wilderness.

■ Fort Yukon

Fort Yukon sits at the convergence of the Porcupine and Yukon Rivers, 8 mi. north of the Arctic Circle. An outpost of the Hudson Bay Trading Company from 1847 to 1969, it is the largest modern-day Native community in Alaska. The town, flat and tucked between vistas of the miles-wide arms of the Yukon, is rich in relics of Native and American history. The town's walking-tour pamphlet (available at **Frontier Flying Services** and the local **Sourdough Hotel**) guides you through a collection of sights—a ghost town, St. Stephen's Church (with its WWI beaded-moose-skin altar cloths), the Fort Yukon replica (which now houses the health center), a museum, and a small town-center. Check out the Fort Yukon branch of the **University of Alaska,** which educates mostly Natives from the surrounding towns of Arctic Village, Beaver, Birch Creek, Central Chalkyitsik, Circle, Circle Hot Springs, Rampart, Stevens Village, and Venetie. Visitors are welcome, and classes offering degree programs are in session throughout the year. The log building that houses the university contains unusual Native crafts as well, including a huge wood-block print of the five local Gwich'in chiefs. **Frontier Flying Services** (in Fairbanks at 474-0014) flies twice daily to Fort Yukon (round-trip $166). Home-cooked meals are available for $5 to $7 at the time-warped **Sourdough Hotel** (662-2402). It's a bit musty but spacious and clean with friendly service. (Singles or doubles $65 with shared bathroom).

SEWARD PENINSULA

■■■ NOME

Alaska's gaudy and lawless equivalent to the Yukon's glittering Klondike, Nome owes its existence to the "three Lucky Swedes" who discovered gold on nearby Anvil Creek in 1898. By 1899, news of the strike had reached Dawson City and thousands of prospectors flocked once again towards potential riches. Another discovery was made at Nome in 1899. The beaches themselves were found to be rich in placer gold! Unprecedented in the annals of Northern mining, the situation presented a myriad of problems involving claim size and claiming rights. And unlike the Klondike, the situation was complicated by an utter lack of law and order. Still a territory, Alaska had no law enforcement and extremely limited government—Nome law was reduced to an anarchic "might makes right." Even when a territorial judge was appointed to settle mining disputes in the Nome area, the appointed judge (corrupted by a Washington lobbyist) was completely incompetent; one of his more infamous rulings debunked the three Lucky Swedes from their original (and exceedingly rich) discovery claims on Anvil Creek on the grounds that they were not American citizens. The judge and his lobbyist took millions out of the repossessed claims before justice was finally served and the land was returned to its rightful owners.

It is believed that Nome received its name from a spelling mistake. In the 1850s a British ship officer exploring the Seward Peninsula noted on a manuscript map that a nearby prominent point was not identified and consequently wrote "? Name" on the map. When the map was recopied, another draftsman thought that the "?" was a C and the A in "name" was an O, and thus a mapmaker in the British Admiralty christened it Cape Nome. A contesting theory says that the name was derived from the Eskimo phrase *Ku-no-me,* meaning "I don't know," the presumable reply when an Eskimo was asked the name of the area.

Stricken by two major fires and assailed by numerous violent storms (the most recent in 1974), little of historic Nome remains, and the little that does is generally unexciting. The Nome of today is a transportation hub for much of western Alaska, where mining remains the economic lifeblood. Built almost entirely upon permafrost, buildings are elevated on pilings to prevent melting, and almost all have extremely ramshackle exteriors. One of the few "wet" towns in the Bush, Nome has an infamous penchant for partying.

PRACTICAL INFORMATION

Visitors Center: P.O. Box 240, Nome 99762 (443-5535), located on Front St. (like everything else) next to the Nugget Inn. Amazing number of flyers. Free nightly slide shows at 7:30pm. Open in summer daily 9am-9pm.

American Express: 443-2211, in the old Federal building on Front St. Open Mon.-Fri. 8am-7pm, Sat. 11am-4pm.

Airport: Located about 1 mi. west of town. Taxi to downtown $5. The airport is served by **Mark Air,** 443-5578; round-trip from Anchorage with 14-day advance purchase $406; **Alaska Airlines** (800-468-2248) offers circuit tours from Anchorage to Nome to Kotzebue (for the touristy route).

Taxis: Checker Cab, 443-5211. **Gold Rush Taxi,** 443-5922. **Nome Cab,** 443-3030. All 24 hr. Standard fare is $3 for places in town.

Car Rental: Bonanza (443-2221), 2-wheel-drive pickup $65 per day, 4-wheel-drive pickup $80 per day, unlimited mileage. **Budget Rent-a-Car** (443-5778), compact $65 per day, van $75 per day, unlimited mileage. For all car rentals you've got to be 21 with a major credit card. **Gas** sells for around $2.10 per gallon.

Bookstore: The **Arctic Trading Post** (443-2686), across from the Nugget Inn, has the most extensive selection of local literature. Open daily 7am-11pm.

Library: Kegoayah Kozga Library (443-5133), above the museum on Front St. Open Tues.-Fri. noon-8pm, Sat. noon-6pm.

Laundromat/Public Showers: Blizzard Laundromat (443-5335), at Seppala St. and C St. The only laundromat in town. Wash $3, dry $3, showers $3. Open Mon.-Fri. 10am-6pm, Sat. 10am-7pm. Also shower at the **rec center** (443-5431) on the northern edge of town on East Sixth Ave. Free with the $3 admission price.

Weather: The box outside the visitors center will give you the day's forecast.

Hospital/Pharmacy: Norton Sound Hospital (443-3331), at the end of Bering St.

Emergency: 911. **Alaska State Troopers:** 443-2835.

Post Office: 240 Front St. (443-2401). Open Mon.-Fri. 9am-5pm. **ZIP Code:** 99762.

Population: 4500.

Area Code: 907.

ACCOMMODATIONS

Beds in Nome aren't too costly but camping is **free.** Camping is permitted on Nome's flat, good beaches and along the 280-mi. road system through the countryside. No facilities, though. The beach is about a 1-mi. walk east along Front St. past the sea wall. Gold miners dot the slightly golden beaches, so enjoy the company!

Betty's Igloo (443-2419), a luxurious bed and breakfast on the eastern edge of town on East Third Ave. Clean and comfortable with kitchen facilities, a spacious common room, and friendly hosts. Singles $50, doubles $60. Shared bath. Reservations strongly recommended.

Ocean View Manor B&B (443-2133), halfway between the visitor center and the beach on Front St. Offers a deck-side view out across Norton Sound and the Bering Sea. TV, phones, shared bath. Singles $45. Doubles $50.

Ponderosa Inn (443-5737), at Spokane and Third Ave. near the visitor center. Generic, clean. TV, phone in some rooms, private bath. Singles $65. Doubles $75.

Nugget Inn (443-2323), next to the visitor center. Tourist groups remain. Lots of "historic" decorations inside. TV, phone, private bath. Singles $85. Doubles $95.

Polaris Hotel (443-2000). It's quite visible from the Nugget Inn. Don't be tempted by its central location. The rooms are grungy, the sinks are stained, the carpet is pitted. Get the picture? Rock-bottom prices: Singles $40. Doubles $80.

FOOD

Don't be scared by the oftentimes dilapidated exteriors of Nome's restaurants. Almost all of the buildings are like that. Stock up on groceries and supplies at the **Alaska Commercial Company** (443-2243) on Front St. (open daily 9am-midnight), or **Hanson's Trading Company** (443-5454) on Bering St. (open Mon.-Sat. 8am-9pm, Sun. 10am-6pm). The rowdy bars in town are grouped together on Front St.

Fat Freddie's (443-5899), next to the visitors center. *The* popular place in Nome. Soak in the blue expanses of the Bering Sea while you chow down on a "Poco Loco" (fried chicken patty) for $5.75. Breakfast omelettes for around $6.50. Don't be frightened by the foreboding entrance. Open daily 6am-10pm.

Billikin Bakery/Deli (443-3636), on Front St. The cheapest place in town. Mega-variety of burgers $3.50, sandwiches $4-5. Open Mon.-Sat. 11am-9pm.

Milano's Pizzeria (443-2924), in the old Federal building on Front St. Pizzas start at $9.75. Italian dinners $10-11. Open daily 11am-11pm.

Nacho's (443-5503), also in the old Federal building. Expensive but tasty Mexican food. Meals $8-10. Open Mon.-Fri. 7am-9pm, Sat. 9am-9pm, Sun. 9am-4pm.

SIGHTS AND ACTIVITIES

Pick up a free *Historical Walking Tour* pamphlet at the visitors center to see what little history has survived through Nome's numerous natural disasters. One of the more interesting buildings is the office of the **Nome Nugget,** the oldest existing newspaper in Alaska (est. 1901). Walk along Nome's famous beaches a mi. east of the visitors center. The beaches are public and anybody can try a hand at **gold-panning** for that elusive nugget. It's free with your own gold pan, available at the Alaska Commercial Company (see above) for $3.39. The Nugget Inn offers interesting **tours** for $25 which take you out to chat with a local dog musher and long-time resident (after the dog sled demo) and then out towards Anvil Mountain (near the original discovery claims on Anvil Creek) where you get to pan. Tours run twice a day. Stop by the Nugget Inn for specifics.

At present, the **Carrie McClain Museum** (443-2566), on Front St. still exists and charges no admission, but its future is in doubt due to lack of funds. It's unfortunate that an area as rich with history as Nome supports only this one museum (open Tues.-Sat. 1-6pm). For general hangin' out, the **rec center** (443-5431), on E. 6th Ave., offers hoop courts, a sauna, and jacuzzi for $3 admission, and also has bowling for $2.50 per game (open Sun.-Fri. noon-9:30pm). Gift shoppers should head for **Maruskiya's of Nome** (443-2955) on Front St., for their extensive collection of carved ivory and other Native art (open daily 9am-10pm).

SEASONAL EVENTS

Being isolated from the rest of the world seems to cause Nomeites to do some strange things, as is evidenced by their often wacky seasonal festivities. The hilarious **Bering Sea Ice Golf Classic** is held in March on the frozen Bering Sea. Standard golf rules apply (with some interesting exceptions) in this six-hole course. Contestants' bright orange balls skirt the course's unique hazards: crevices, ice chunks, bottomless snow holes, and frost-leafed greens. Extremity-warmers (whisky and Bacardi rum) are provided with contestants' entry fee. Course rules dictate: "If you hit a polar bear with your golf ball (Endangered Species List), you will have three strokes added to your score. If you recover said ball, we will subtract five strokes." The biggest event of the winter, however, is naturally the **Iditarod dogsled race.** The race finishes in mid-March beneath the log "banner" visible year-round next to City Hall. Thousands of spectators journey in, and it isn't uncommon for all local accommodations to be booked nearly a year in advance.

Summer festivities include the **Midnight Sun Festival** on the weekend closest to the solstice (June 21st). After a parade and chicken BBQ, the **Nome River Raft Race,** the city's largest summer event, commences. Home-made contraptions paddle their way down the 1- to 2-mi. course hoping to clinch the prestigious fur-lined Honey-Bucket. On Labor Day, the **Bathtub Race** sends tubs mounted on wheels down Front St. The bathtub must be full of water at the start and have at least 10 gallons remaining by the finish. Teammates outside the tub wear large brim hats and suspenders while the one in the tub totes a bar of soap, towel, and bath mat.

OUTDOORS

Three highways radiate outwards from Nome and allow exploration of the Seward Peninsula. The **Council Hwy.** travels 76 mi. from Nome to Council, a former gold-rush town turned ghost-town, although some Nomeites make it their summer home (it's appealingly below the treeline). En route, the highway goes around Cape Nome, passes the ghost-town of Solomon and the fascinating **"Last Train to Nowhere,"** a failed railroad project whose only remnants are the engine and cars that sit slowly rusting on the tundra.

The **Taylor Hwy.** (also known as the Kougarok Road) heads north from Nome for 86 mi., though it pretty much peters out without ever reaching a final destination of note. Along the way is **Salmon Lake,** near Mile 40. Popular with locals, the lake offers excellent fishing and has primitive campsites. North of Salmon Lake and off an 8-mi. gravel road from the highway, **Pilgrim Hot Springs** is an historic landmark. During the gold rush, it was a recreation center for miners with its spa baths, saloon, dance hall, and roadhouse. (The saloon and roadhouse burned down in 1908.) From 1917 until 1941, a mission and orphanage existed here, housing up to 120 children. And the weary can still soak in the springs. The **Kigluaik Mountains** are accessible via this highway and offer some good hiking opportunities. Evidence of the **Wild Goose Pipeline,** a failed project intended to bring fresh water to Nome, can still be found on the south side of the Grand Central Valley, in the mountains.

The **Nome-Teller Hwy.** winds westwards from Nome for 76 mi. to the small Native village of Teller. Nothing too exciting exists on this route. A side road heads to **Wooley Lagoon,** where Native families set up summer fish camps (and don't see too many tourists; remember to smile!).

All three highways are entirely gravel and can make for rough going. The only solution is to rent a car from any of the companies in Nome (see Practical Information). There are some excellent fishing rivers along the highways including the Nome River and Pilgrim River (both accessible via the Taylor Highway).

There are numerous **gold dredges** around Nome. Three of them still operate 24 hours a day in the summer. These monstrous machines are littered throughout the Nome vicinity. Ask at the visitors center for locations.

Bering Land Bridge National Preserve encompasses much of the northern Seward Peninsula. The preserve commemorates the prehistoric peopling of North America as the Pleistocene Ice Age exposed Beringia, a land bridge between Siberia and Alaska, that enabled the first humans to enter the continent. The preserve has few recreational opportunities and even fewer facilities. **Serpentine Hot Springs** is accessible by small plane and has a bunk house and baths, but that's about it. **Park headquarters** (443-2522) is stationed in Nome, below the post office, and is open Mon.-Fri. 8am-5pm. For more information write the Superintendent, Bering Land Bridge National Preserve, P.O. Box 220, Nome, AK 99762.

Small plane charter from Nome will get you to some of the most remote places in Alaska, like Savoonga on St. Lawrence Island or Little Diomede Island (U.S. territory), which is a scant 1½ mi. from Big Domede Island (Russian territory). Plane charters cost several hundred dollars but offer a *serious* adventure and a chance to experience culture and settlements to whom the notion of "progress" is alien.

■ Kotzebue

Home of the tundra-covered **Kotzebue National Forest** (comprised of only one tree), Kotzebue is situated on the tip of the Baldwin Peninsula, 160 mi. northeast of Nome and 25 mi. north of the Arctic Circle. Kotzebue is primarily a native settlement (approximately 80%) and functions principally as a hub for native settlements and other small communities in Alaska's Arctic Northwest. The **Northwest Alaska Native Corporation (NANA)** has its headquarters here. All of the roads are gravel and everybody seems to drive around on their personal four-wheeled ATVs. A settlement revolving about subsistence living, for the independent traveler the town offers little more than the opportunity to subsist.

Practical Information The town is situated on a sand spit; the original native name for the town meant "land that is almost an island." But the present name comes from Baron von Kotzebue who explored the region in 1826. The **visitors center** (442-3760) is a half-block from the airport on Second Ave. Managed jointly by the National Park Service, the BLM, and Fish and Wildlife, the center is geared towards providing information about the national parks, preserves, and wildlife refuges found in the vicinity of Kotzebue. They also offer a free map of Kotzebue (open daily 8am-6pm).

The **airport** is situated on the western edge of town, a 10-minute walk from "downtown." **Mark Air** (442-2737) flies to Anchorage (2 per day, $406 round-trip with 14-day advance purchase) and Nome (1 per day, $132 one-way). **Alaska Airlines** (442-3474) has near-identical rates and planes leave 4 times daily for Anchorage. Believe it or not, you'll find three **taxi** companies here. If somebody has lopped off your feet and you can't walk the 6 blocks across town, call either Polar Cab (442-2233), Solis Taxi (442-2777), or Midnight Sun Cab (442-3394) to get you there.

There is a **National Bank of Alaska** (442-3257) on 2nd Ave. (open Mon.-Thurs. 9am-5pm, Fri. 10am-6pm). **Laundry** facilities can be found at the Nullagvik Hotel ($2 wash, $1.25 dry), as well as probably the world's most expensive **public shower** ($15!). There is a **library** in Chukchi College on 3rd Ave. (open Tues.-Fri. noon-8pm, Sat. noon-4pm). **Emergency** numbers include: **hospital,** 442-3321; **police,** 442-3222; **fire,** 442-3404; and of course 911. The **post office** (442-3291) is on Front St. (Open Mon.-Fri. 9am-5pm. **ZIP Code:** 99752.)

Accommodations, Camping, and Food It is extremely difficult to find a place to stay in Kotzebue. There are no campgrounds or designated camping areas. Much of the land surrounding Kotzebue is either privately owned, difficult to camp on, or both. Residents of surrounding villages set up summer fish camps along the beaches to the east and west of town. Campers can walk around these areas in search of an open or uninhabited spot, although they should be aware of the land rights of those already setting up summer fish camps. The thick brush, flocks of mosquitoes, and slanted beaches also make camping out rather difficult. It can be done, though. Otherwise, there are two hotels in town. The **Bay Side Restaurant/ Hotel** (442-3600) on Shore Ave.—all the locals refer to Shore Ave. as Front St. so don't get confused (it's the road paralleling the beach)—has a single for $75 and doubles for $95. The hotel is almost brand-new and the rooms are squeaky clean. **Nullagvik Hotel** (*nullagvik* means "place to stay", 442-3331) is next door and caters more towards tourist groups. A single will cost travelers $140 (OUCH!).

Kotzebue holds four restaurants. The **Bay Side Restaurant** (442-3600), on Shore Ave., offers a view across Kotzebue Sound and the Chukchi Sea and has burgers for around $7 (open Mon.-Sat. 7am-10pm, Sun. 8am-10pm). The **Nullagvik Hotel** (442-3331) also has a restaurant. Grab a bowl of reindeer soup for $2.75. A full meal will cost $10-13 (open daily 6:30am-2pm and 6-8:30pm). The **Arctic Dragon** (442-3770) is on the other side of the Bay Side and serves up Chinese lunch specials for $6-8 (open Mon.-Sat. 11am-10pm, Sun. noon-10pm). **Pizza House** (442-3432) is a block off Front St. on 2nd Ave. and has pizzas from $11, sandwiches for $4-7. Or you can always do your own shopping: **Hanson Trading Co.** (442-3101) on Front St. has the best supply of groceries. (Open Mon.-Fri. 8am-9pm, Sat. 9am-9pm, Sun. 11am-7pm.) You'll pay through the nose, though.

Sights Perhaps the most interesting activity in Kotzebue is just to take a stroll along the beach where nets and drying fish give evidence to the subsistence lifestyle led by many of the locals. Front St. also provides the best location to watch the midnight sun dip down and come back up without setting between June 10 and July 2. The town's commercial offering is to hop on a tour bus with **Tour Arctic** (442-3301). Based in the **NANA Museum of the Arctic** (442-3747) on Second Ave. next to the airport, the regularly scheduled tours cost $50 and last three to four hours. You'll see a traditional native camp, dig down to look at the permafrost, take a tundra walk, and watch a presentation of traditional Eskimo dancing. The tours are extremely informative and the guides are friendly and knowledgable. If you just want to check out the NANA Museum and the presentation, the museum is open daily 9am-8pm and admission to watch the program is $20 (given daily at 3:30pm and 5:30pm). Also in town is the **Ootukahkuktuvik Museum** ("place having old things") which has old whaling artifacts, old Russian remnants, and other old stuff. The museum runs irregular summer hours. Ask around about getting in.

NORTHWEST ALASKA

There are more than nine million acres of protected wilderness in Northwest Alaska. **Kobuk Valley National Park, Noatak National Preserve,** and **Cape Krusenstern National Monument** comprise approximately 11% of all the land administered by the National Park Service in the United States. Subsistence hunting by local residents is permitted and goes on in all three park units.

The Northwest Alaska Areas are wilderness at its wildest, and their remoteness all but guarantees that they will remain that way, accessible for only the most dedicated (and rich) outdoorsperson. The **visitors center** for all of the Northwest Alaska Areas is in Kotzebue. For information call 442-3760, or write Superintendent, Northwest Alaska Areas, National Park Service, P.O. Box 1029, Kotzebue 99752.

Cape Krusenstern National Monument was established primarily for archaeological reasons. Within its gravels, in chronological order, lie artifacts from every known Inuit occupation of North America. The monument borders the coastlines of the Chackchi Sea on the west and Kotzebue Sound to the south. Lots of marshy tundra. Some hiking is possible in the rolling Igichuk or Mulgrave Hills, and kayaking along the coast and in the monument's numerous lagoons is another potential activity. Generally, though, the area is best left to the archaeologists. The only way in is by charter plane from Kotzebue (about $275 an hour for a plane).

1.7 million-acre **Kobuk Valley National Park** occupies a broad valley along the central Kobuk River, some 25 mi. north of the Arctic Circle. One of the more surprising features in the park are the 25 sq. mi. **Great Kobuk Sand Dunes,** a small piece of the Sahara in Alaska's Arctic, although visitors should watch more for grizzlies here than for camels. The most popular activity is floating the Kobuk. Popular put-in spots are the village of Ambler on the park's eastern edge and at the river's headwaters in Walker Lake, deep in the Brooks Range. The sand dunes are accessible via a short overland hike from the Kobuk River (once you've floated to within hiking range). The region is accessible via regularly scheduled flights from Kotzebue. **Ryan Air** (442-3342) flies to Ambler from Kotzebue for $215.

The 6.5 million-acre **Noatak National Preserve** contains a broad, gently sloping valley through which most of the Noatak River flows. This westward-flowing river has the largest undisturbed watershed in North America and is designated a National Wild and Scenic River. The preserve has been named an International Biosphere

Reserve by the United Nations and most visitors see the area by floating. Noatak floaters drift from the arboreal forest's northern edge into a treeless expanse of tundra as they proceed down the river. Wildlife abounds, especially members of the region's 400,000-strong caribou herd. The float is not a difficult one, although its remoteness presents some difficulties. Fewer than 100 visitors floated the Noatak in the 1992 season. The only way in is by (you guessed it) charter airplane, although there are scheduled flights from Noatak, a popular take-out spot on the preserve's western boundary, to Kotzebue for $60.

■ Barrow

The world's largest Inuit village, Barrow truly sits at the top of the world. It is the northernmost point in all of North America. In April and May, villagers carry on the tradition of the whale hunt, both to sustain their culture and (more immediately) to sustain themselves. The entire community participates, some hunting, some hauling, others carving up the whale (a bowhead whale can feed entire villages even today). This event culminates in the *pièce de résistance:* the **walrus-hide blanket toss,** which bounces Eskimos high into the air. **Mark Air** (800-478-0800) flies from Fairbanks daily (21-day advance purchase round-trip $298).

THE ALEUTIAN ISLANDS

Marking the fiery boundary between two tectonic plates, the string of snow-capped volcanoes and volcanic remnants that makes up the Alaska Peninsula and the Aleutian Islands stretches like an icy tendril more than a thousand miles into the stormy North Pacific. The Aleutians comprise one of the most remote locations on earth, with the westernmost islands coming within a few hundred miles of Siberia. The lava-scarred cones on these verdant but treeless isles are whipped by some of the world's worst weather. Here, vicious storms packing winds well in excess of 100 miles per hour can rise up at any moment, playing havoc with those rugged few who live in this cloudy corner of America.

Throughout thousands of years of human habitation, only twice has this jagged archipelago captured the world's attention. In the latter half of the 18th century, an abundance of Aleutian sea otters convinced the Russian Czar's disciples that Alaska was a land worthy of exploitation. The Aleutians (and the Aleut people) served as the steppingstones for Russian domination of the region, which lasted until the sale of Alaska to the U.S. in 1867. Seventy-five years later, during World War II, the world once again turned its eyes toward this hidden world when the Japanese Navy bombed the Aleutian town of Dutch Harbor and then occupied the outer islands of Attu and Kiska in June of 1942. A year later, the U.S. military stormed Attu, touching off a surprisingly bloody and little-known battle which left 3000 American and Japanese soldiers dead or dying on the wind-swept tundra.

Things have quieted down significantly since the 1940s. Today the Peninsula and the islands are home to an assortment of Native Aleut villages, small military installations, and larger towns dedicated to big-time deep sea fishing. Throughout most of the year, the region remains remote due to its harsh climate and limited transportation network. In the summer, hundreds of dedicated tourists flock here both to explore the inherent natural beauty of this volcanic wilderness and to view the millions of migratory seabirds that stop here on their way north. Several species of *aves* nest here and nowhere else in the world.

GETTING THERE

A quick glance at a map will tell you that there are only two ways to see the Aleutians: **plane** or **boat.** Both methods are fairly expensive—traveling to any place this remote is not dirt cheap. A round-trip flight from Kodiak to **Dutch Harbor,** the largest town on the Aleutians, costs around $1000 and lasts about four hours. The same trip on the **Alaska Marine Hwy.** costs $400 and takes about five days. The latter option is far and away the better choice; after all, the whole point of traveling to the Peninsula and the Aleutians is not merely to get somewhere (there is, in the end, really no place to go) but instead to spend time absorbing the unique panoramas and wildlife. The bi-monthly summer ferry trips to Dutch Harbor provide a reasonably affordable opportunity to do just that. Don't think of this as an expensive ferry trip—think of it as a very cheap five-day cruise. This is a once-in-a-lifetime side trip that is well worth the investment. If you are seriously considering a ferry voyage to the Aleutians, consider purchasing the **Alaska Pass,** which might make the trip more affordable (see the Introduction to Alaska above).

THE ALASKA MARINE HIGHWAY

If you choose to take the ferry, remember that the Alaska Marine Highway makes this trip only seven times a year between May and September. It is best to go in July, when the weather is at its mildest. Make reservations at least two weeks in advance; the boat may fill up during the peak tourist season.

While on the trip you will be confined to the *M/V Tustumena*. Fortunately, extensive renovations have restored this elder statesman of the ferry system to a condition very near that of the Panhandle boats; the boat features a dining room with decent food (although a bit pricey—you'd be wise to buy supplies in Kodiak before you leave), showers (25¢ for 10 minutes), and a TV room where the on-board naturalist from the Fish and Wildlife Service regularly gives slide shows and films on the various flora and fauna that glide past the ship. Abovedecks are a solarium and observation lounge where cabinless passengers can sleep and hang out. (Avoid the solarium; not only does it lack lounge chairs, but it is literally right next to the exhaust tower of the 3200 horsepower diesel engine.)

Your companions for the trip will probably be a motley crew consisting mostly of senior citizens who are taking advantage of the $390 they save on discount tickets, along with a scattering of families, students, fisherfolk, and maniacal birdwatcher types who run around with binoculars the size of small children screaming, "Oh my God, it's a Whiskered Auklet!"

The ferry stops briefly at several small towns, ranging from quaint fishing villages to prefabricated cannery quarters. However, it might be best to stay on board until the end of the trip; though intriguing, most of these towns lack tourist facilities. Besides, the grandest part of the voyage is the final day-long approach to Dutch Harbor, the most interesting town in the archipelago.

One last note: stock up on Dramamine or another seasickness remedy before you leave. You'll be weathering 5- to 15-ft. seas; they don't call the *Tustumena* the "Vomit Comet" for nothing.

■■■ DUTCH HARBOR/UNALASKA

Dutch Harbor/Unalaska is nestled at the foot of stunning Unalaska Bay, on the eastern coast of Unalaska Island. For many years there was no actual town of Dutch Harbor—Dutch Harbor was just that, the harbor, and the town was called Unalaska (from the Aleut word for "this great [or] beautiful land"). In recent years a town of Dutch Harbor, complete with its own zip code, has arisen about a half mile from "the old town" of Unalaska.

In terms of budget travel, Dutch Harbor/Unalaska is something of a nightmare. Remoteness and unusually high incomes (over $130 million in seafood goes through this port every year) have conspired to produce extremely high prices. Don't despair, however; there are bargains to be had, and the view—treeless snow-capped mountains soaring thousands of feet from Unalaska Bay's chilly blue waters—is free.

PRACTICAL INFORMATION AND ORIENTATION

Visitors Bureau: Although there is no formal visitors bureau, you can get local information from anyone at the **Department of Parks, Culture, and Recreation** in the Community Center Building at 5th and Broadway in downtown Unalaska (581-1297; open Mon.-Fri. 8am-5pm) or from the desk attendant at the Unisea Hotel in downtown Dutch Harbor (open 24 hr.).

Department of Fish and Game: Upstairs in the Intersea Mall, downtown Dutch Harbor (581-1239 or 581-1219). Will fill you in on local fishing and birdwatching opportunities. Open Mon.-Fri. 8am-noon and 1-4:30pm.

Alaska Marine Hwy.: Docks at City Dock about 1½ mi. from Dutch Harbor and 2½ mi. from Unalaska. Arrives about once every 3-4 weeks in the summer. There is no terminal; call 800-642-0066 or Port of Dutch Harbor (581-1254) for schedule information. One-way to Kodiak: $200.

Airport: Located about ¼ mi. from City Dock on the main road into town. Served by **Reeves Aleutian** (800-544-2248), **Mark Air** (800-426-6784), and **Pen Air** (581-1383). One way to Kokiak about $650. One way to Anchorage about $500 with advance purchase.

Taxis: If you're tired of walking, don't worry—one of the town's 13 different cab companies is sure to hunt you down. Try hard to resist; every company charges the same outrageous prices. Tours of the towns are $1 a minute.

Bike Rental (581-1297). In the Community Center at 5th and Broadway, in Unalaska. Mountain bikes $5 per day—a great way to avoid taxi fares.

Pharmacy: Alaska Commercial Company ("The A.C."), in the Intersea Mall in downtown Dutch Harbor (581-1245). Open Mon.-Sat. 9am-9pm, Sun. 10am-6pm.

Emergency: Police and Fire, 911.

Hospital: Iliuliuk Family and Health Services (581-1202, 581-1233 for after-hours emergencies), near 5th and Broadway.

Post Office: In **Unalaska** (581-1232), between 2nd and 3rd on Broadway. Open Mon.-Fri. 9am-5pm, Sat. 1pm-5pm. **General Delivery ZIP Code:** 99685. In **Dutch Harbor,** in the Intersea Mall (581-1657). Open Mon.-Fri. 9am-5pm, Sat. 1pm-5pm. **General Delivery ZIP Code:** 99692.

Population (Unalaska): 3450.

Area Code: 907.

Unalaska Island is located just east of the border between the Hawaii/Aleutian and Alaska time zones, about 300 mi. from the tip of the Alaska Peninsula. Unlike many larger Alaskan towns, Dutch Harbor/Unalaska has a refreshing lack of concern for the tourist trade; the big money here is in seafood, not tourism (you will find very few tacky t-shirt shops here). Deviating from the usual Alaskan calendar, the liveliest months in Dutch Harbor/Unalaska are in the fall and winter when the local fish and crab seasons begin. In the summer the two towns are pleasantly sleepy.

ACCOMMODATIONS AND CAMPING

Perhaps the biggest drawback to being a tourist in Unalaska/Dutch Harbor is the profound lack of accommodations. Most of the potentially cheap hotels have been bought out by canneries or converted into monthly apartments, which leaves the stray tourist a choice among one hotel, one B&B, and one primitive campground.

Unisea Inn, across from the Intersea Mall, in downtown Dutch Harbor (581-1325). Snazzy first-class hotel mostly for visiting seafood corporate types. Expensive; it has almost no competition. Great rooms, HBO. Singles $105. Doubles $135.

Katies B&B, at 2nd and Broadway next to the Elbow Room Bar. 3 units with full bath and "hearty continental breakfast." Singles $100. Doubles $130.

Summer Bay. From the City Dock or the airport, hike 2½ mi. through Dutch Harbor and Unalaska. Pick up Summer Bay Rd., headed out of town, for another 2 mi. to Summer Bay. A bridge, some sand dunes, and a few picnic tables and barbecues mark the spot; there are no other facilities. Take care to set your tent in a sheltered location, or the 100-mph wind gusts will introduce your possessions to Unalaska Bay.

FOOD

The cheapest grocery in town is the **Alaska Commercial Company or "AC"** (581-1245), in the Intersea Mall in downtown Dutch Harbor. (Open Mon.-Sat. 9am-9pm and Sun. 10am-6pm.) Remember, however, that "cheap" is a relative term.

Stormy's Pizzeria, 2nd and Broadway (581-1565), Unalaska. Slightly off the beaten track and thus slightly less expensive. Great 15-in. pizzas $13-20. Sandwiches and burgers $5-7. Large variety of Mexican, Italian, and Oriental dinners in the $10-20 range. Open daily 11am-11pm.

Ziggy's, about ½ mi. from the airport on the main road to town. A favorite local hang-out. Full stack of sourdough pancakes $4.50. Sandwiches and burgers $6-8. Mexican dinners $9-16. Open daily 7am-10pm.

Unisea Inn Restaurant, in the Unisea Inn (581-1325; see Accommodations). Steak and seafood dinners in the $15-25 range; go for the filling lunch sandwiches, $5.50-7.50. Open daily 7am-10pm.

SIGHTS

If you are traveling by ferry, you have three options: stay three to four hours while the boat refuels, wait three to four weeks until the *Tustumena* returns, or fly back to the mainland, which will cost a minimum of $500. Although Dutch Harbor/Unalaska is an intriguing town, the former option is probably the wisest.

Get a cab (see Practical Information) to drive you the 3 mi. to the **Unalaska Cemetery and Memorial Park** on the eastern edge of Unalaska. These two sights focus on Dutch Harbor's past military significance, including a description of the Japanese air attacks of June 1942. You can still see the bow of the *SS Northwestern,* sunk during the attack, slowly rusting in the bay.

Heading back toward Unalaska on Beach Front Rd., you will eventually reach the **Holy Ascension Orthodox Church** (built 1824-27, expanded in 1894) and the **Bishop's House** (built in 1882). Looking every one of its 168 years, the "nation's most endangered church" is about to undergo restoration. This area was once the center of orthodox missionary activity in Alaska; Ivan Veniamov called Unalaska home for a number of years before moving on to bigger things in the Panhandle (see Sitka).

Right after you cross the "bridge-to-the-other-side" on the way back to the ferry, you will come up alongside **Bunker Hill** (no, not the one near Boston). A quick 420-ft. climb straight up is a large concrete bunker and a spectacular view of the surrounding bays and mountains. Sticking to the main road about ½ mi. after Bunker Hill and ¼ mi. before the airport, you will pass a **grove of trees,** planted by Russians in 1805. The average spruce grove is about as exciting as a field of wheat, but on the treeless Aleutians, this copse merits its title as the only national landmark of its kind.

Those planning to stay longer than three to four hours should ask the locals about the numerous trails and military doo-dads strewn across the local countryside—a number of interesting day hikes are possible.

If you happen to be in Unalaska on any night except Sunday, check out the **Elbow Room Bar** (581-1470) between 2nd and 3rd on Broadway. The Elbow Room was recently voted the second-rowdiest bar in the world.

THE PACIFIC NORTHWEST

Is there such a thing as the "Pacific Northwest region"? Certainly enough travel guides have thus designated the area encompassed by Oregon, Washington, British Columbia, Alberta, and the Yukon. The three Canadian provinces probably have more in common with America's libertarian West (many of their settlers hail from the American West, after all) than with the rest of Canada. While the descendants of French monarchists and English tories in the East are comfortable with Canada's active federal government, Western opposition parties led by anti-government politicos such as Preston Manning are growing in popularity. Regionalism in the Northwest has undergone a revival in recent years, but it is unlike that found in other parts of North America. While Californians draw attention to their paradise on the West Coast, New Englanders take haughty pride in their historic sensibilities, and Southerners lay claim to a better paced way of life, inhabitants of the Pacific Northwest seem content to keep their blessings to themselves. Emmett Watson's "Lesser Seattle" movement has even gone so far as to publish negative (and often misleading) statistics concerning the city in an attempt to dissuade people from moving there. And with good reason—invaders from California, eastern Canada, and the Lower 48 threaten to bring their plastic cities and pollution to North America's last frontier, and to some degree they have succeeded.

Those traveling to the Northwest from other parts of the U.S. or Canada will probably find it by turns charming, awe-inspiring, relaxing, and somewhat familiar. Visitors may, however, want to keep a handful of miscellaneous points in mind. Drivers do not like to honk very much, and pedestrians do not jaywalk in the major cities. In general, lines form themselves and tend to proceed just a little more strictly, and slowly, than in some other regions. Northwesterners call long Italian sandwiches "subs" (not hoagies, heroes, or grinders), and the legumes that look and taste like chick-peas are "garbanzo beans." You'd be wrong to think that folks are friendly in or-a-GON, but residents of the Beaver State will be quick to welcome you to OR-uh-gun.

Canadians celebrate both **national** and **provincial holidays.** All government offices and most businesses close on national holidays, except on Easter Monday and Remembrance Day. Check in local newspapers for a list of what is and isn't open. Those in the U.S. celebrate, as a general rule, only national holidays. For a complete list of both countries' major holidays in 1994, see the Appendix toward the end of this book.

If you will be traveling between the U.S. and Canada, remember that a Canadian dollar and a U.S. dollar are identical in name only. Also remember to take into account the 7% **Goods and Services Tax (GST),** as well as the **Provincial Sales Taxes (PSTs)** in Canada, which can reach 10% and higher. Tourists who save their original receipts can get a GST refund on goods and accommodations excluding luxury items, transportation, camping fees, and gasoline. For information on Canadian currency and the GST, see Money in the Essentials section at the front of this book. **Unless otherwise specified, prices listed in Canadian provinces of this book (British Columbia, Alberta, and the Yukon Territory) are given in Canadian dollars and do not include GST.**

History

Scholars still debate who first set foot on North America—the foot may have been Egyptian, Greek, Etruscan, Chinese, or according to age-old Native American legends, Japanese. The current consensus is that the first American immigrants were Siberians who, some 20,000 years ago, followed the great mammal herds across the frozen grassy plain that was eventually submerged by the Bering Strait.

The luckiest of the newcomers settled in the expanse of land from the Alaskan tundra down to the Northern California coast, where natural wealth and good seafood were plentiful. The natives took advantage of the environment's natural resources, converting the abundant timber into harpoons for whaling and river weirs for snaring the salmon that spawned in the inland waters. The abundance of food allowed Coastal dwellers to abandon their nomadic lifestyle and establish the first permanent settlements in North America.

Life on the coast was so good that altruism became a status symbol in the ceremony of the potlatch ("gift"), in which the chief distributed names, privileges, and material goods such as blankets, copper sheets, and (as times have changed) washing machines and dryers. This was proof of a wealth so great that the owner could afford to lose it. Coastal natives were rich in culture and artwork as well; they crafted elaborately symbolic totem poles, inscribed with family crests and animal signs denoting the hereditary lineages through which clans organized social interaction.

Inland on the Plateau region that stretched between the Cascades to the west and the Rockies to the east, life was more difficult and natural snack foods harder to come by. Plateau natives were on the move nine months of every year, hunting the migratory herds. Their semi-nomadic life-style kept tribal ties in flux, necessitating an egalitarian social system with consensual government. Even wider nomadism was encouraged by the arrival of wild horses around 1730—the advance guard of the European cavalries.

The first claims that Europeans made in the Pacific Northwest region were merely titular, and, more often than not, they were misguided. In 1592 the Greek sailor Apostolos Valerianos claimed to have sailed the apocryphal Northwest Passage from the Pacific to the Atlantic Coast. Later explorers discovered that the "passage" was, in fact, an inlet to the Puget Sound. In 1741, Russian seafarers captained by the Dane Vitus Bering landed on Kayak Island of Prince William Sound. Bering's expedition brought the fur of sea otters back to Russia, inaugurating and then monopolizing the lucrative trade in animal pelts. In 1776 English explorer James Cook traded some rusty nails for a few ragged pelts in Nootka Sound, in the unclaimed land between Russian and Spanish holdings. The furs fetched a fortune in China during Cook's return trip, and the fur frenzy was on.

The fur trade represented the outpost of the European empire, with the English Hudson's Bay Company engaged in cutthroat competition with the French, whose Montreal-based North West Company, the "Nor'westers," used Mafia-like tactics. The only thing that tied these warring fortune-hunters together was the trading language of the Chinook, who served as the mercenary go-betweens of the Northwest. This *lingua franca* incorporated about 300 Indian, French, English, and sign words, from "hiack" for "hurry up" to "Boston" for "American."

Pelts eventually led to pioneers and to political battles between London and Washington. The Spanish had skulked off to Northern California, having made only nominal conquests in towns like Cordova and Valdez, and the Russians were content to stay in Alaska to extract tributes in furs from local tribes. President Jefferson, ostensibly eager to attain "geographical knowledge of our own continent" but far more eager to divert some of the Northwestern pelts south and east, commissioned Meriweather Lewis and William Clark to explore the region in 1803. Guided by the indomitable squaw Sacajawea, the expedition traveled 4000 mi. to and from the mouth of the Columbia and strengthened American claims to the region. London, for its part, sent Captains James Cook and George Vancouver to map the extensive waterways of the Pacific Northwest. In 1818 the two nations at last hammered out an agreement that divided their claims as far west as the Rockies at the 49th parallel of latitude.

The Northwest was slowly emptied of the native population, partly as a result of whites' deliberate machinations and partly due to a malevolent trick of nature. Along with pans and plows, settlers brought with them unfamiliar diseases, such as measles, small pox, and influenza, which wiped out as much as 90 percent of the natives by the late 1800s. Missionary fever was an additional ill. A wave of whites responded in horror to the Chinook custom of flattening babies' foreheads, and crusaders such as Marcus and Narcissa Whitman rushed west to Walla Walla to "save" souls and profiles. The Whitmans would have done better to save themselves; Cayuse warriors killed them, convinced that the missionaries were poisoning their tribe to clear the area for white settlers. The indignation aroused by the incident was a crucial motivating factor in making Oregon an American territory. Those natives who survived the white invasion were herded, nation by nation, onto reserves containing some of the worst land in the region.

Stronger opposition was offered by the British, prompting James K. Polk to win the White House with a "manifest destiny" platform and the shibboleth "54° 40' or fight." But President Polk pursued neither pledge, and in 1846 extended the 49th parallel as the dividing line between British and American territories, leaving the Russian stake above the 54th parallel intact. Thus secured, the Oregon Territory split in half. Oregon claimed statehood in 1859, and the territory to the north joined it 30 years later, reluctantly giving up the name "Columbia" (reserved for the congressional district back east) for "Washington." Farther north, in 1856, miners struck gold near Vancouver, and prospectors swarmed up the coast from Sacramento. Where revenue went, government followed—the governor of Vancouver Island enlarged his jurisdiction to establish a real provincial administration over the mainland in Canada. In 1866, the arrangement was official, and the coastal colony above Washington became British Columbia.

Burdened by debts from the Crimean War, Russia was less resistant to the idea of extending the American presence in the region. U.S. President Andrew Johnson, showing unusual foresight, allowed Secretary of State Seward to purchase Alaska from the Russians at about 2¢ an acre in 1867. Originally mocked as "Seward's Folly" and "Seward's Ice Box," the purchase came to seem wiser in hindsight with the Klondike gold strikes of the late 1880s and 90s. Similarly, the Yukon, which shared Alaska's mineral wealth, and Alberta, whose fertile agricultural plains would later yield valuable oil, became a Canadian territory in 1898 and a Canadian province in 1905, respectively.

Capitalizing on the natural wealth of the land called for settlers, and they were culled from all four corners—malcontents from the Midwest and New England, eager to establish farms and to log huge evergreen trees; as well as Irish, Scandinavians, and Eastern Europeans lured by promotional literature of the New Eden. This boosterism did not extend to the Chinese who had come to region as railroad workers; Sinophobes drove them from Washington in the 1880s. However, the Chinese stuck it out, establishing North America's second largest Asian community in Vancouver. The region's population boomed when the railroad finally roared to the coast (the race to build cross-continental tracks in the U.S. and Canada finished in a virtual "tie" in 1883).

By the beginning of the twentieth century, Northwest history loses its distinct outlines and becomes national history. But the region has retained a character of its own, and the attachment to populist politics in both Western Canada and the Northwest, from the Wobblies labor movement of the early 1900s to B.C.'s Social Credit Party of the 1940s, remains fierce. The Pacific Northwest has spawned history-making liberals such as Washington's Supreme Court Justice William O. Douglas, Senator Henry "Scoop" Jackson, and current Speaker of the House Tom Foley. On the economic scene, however, the region has been forced to relinquish some of its distinctiveness, and the floundering lumber industry has largely been replaced by high technology. Rather than trying to emulate New York or Los Angeles, Northwestern cities in recent years have looked westward to the Pacific Rim to develop trade links with Japan and other Pacific nations.

Throughout the first two years of this decade, environmental concerns were at the forefront of the Pacific political scene. The high-tech, smokestack-less industries of the region's big cities seemed to spread a huge urban umbrella against the recession beating down on the rest of the continent. Few cities in America upped employment as quickly as did Seattle, which further developed its base in the computer software, biotechnology, and airplane industries. Such widespread prosperity allowed environmentalists to raise the banner of the endangered spotted owl against the evil spectre of the Bush administration. Active support for such issues seemed to dissolve rapidly, though, when in February 1993 Seattle-based Boeing told the city that it would likely cut close to 20,000 jobs in the Puget Sound area within the coming 18 months.

As the recession began more to press more severely on the region in 1993, attention became more sharply focused on economic and trade-related issues. A front-page article in the *New York Times* captured national attention in mid-August with the title "Trade Rift Over Apples Sours U.S. Ties to Japan." The dispute centered around Japan's refusal to open its markets to American fruit-growers—an issue which has been much contested as Japan's trade surpluses have continued to balloon. The article explained that the apples' significance was more symbolic than dollar oriented: "Apples are to Japanese and American trade policy what intercontinental missiles were to the cold war. Both sides have them. They have long been a bargaining chip. And now one sides says it is time to put up or shut up." With the recession lingering, such issues of trade and restricted markets continue to catch the national eye.

Arts

In the centuries before European settlement, the Kwakiutl tribe on the B.C. coast enacted world-renewal ceremonies which included theatrical effects like tunnels, trapdoors, ventriloquism, and bloody sleight-of-hand beheadings, all while costumed in fantastical, supernatural cedar masks. The performing arts have been dazzling audiences in the Northwest ever since.

Native American artists were publicly dormant during most of the 20th century, awakening only with the renaissance of tribal identity in the 1960s. In its many forms, Native art is a striking and powerful merger of the human, the animal, and the spiritual. Today, some of the best collections of Native art and artifacts are showcased in the Provincial Museum in Victoria, B.C. and the Thomas Burke Museum at the University of Washington in Seattle; the Portland Art Museum also houses an impressive collection.

The contemporary art scene in the Northwest adopts a generally convivial tone; on the first Thursday evening of each month, Portland and Seattle art galleries fling open their doors (and often their wine cellars) for public browsing. And the cities' 1% tax on capital improvements is funneled into the creation and acquisition of public art.

Contemporary Northwest artists have found an aesthetic silver lining in the clouds that often blanket the region. B.C. painter Emily Carr blended Native elements with her work to create original Northwest images; in the 1950s, the Northwest School, comprised of the mystic troika Morris Graves, Mark Tobey, and Kenneth Callahan, made magical scenes out of the rainy climes.

The Northwest has imported artistic treasures as well, such as the Oregon Shakespeare Festival in Ashland, where an estimated annual audience of 450,000 spends a day or a week every summer enjoying the excellent in- and outdoor performances. A number of actors of note have performed here, including William Hurt in *Long Day's Journey into Night* and Kyle MacLachlan (of *Twin Peaks* fame) as Romeo in *Romeo and Juliet*. Seattle, which has a repertory theater community second only to New York in size, offers a twinkling assortment of new dramas in its many fine theaters.

There is entertainment for the discriminating listener as well. Seattle Opera puts on a show with classical and modern productions and has earned an international reputation for its Wagner. Orchestral music aficionados can trek down to the Bach

Festival in Eugene, OR, where Helmut Rilling waves his exquisite Baroque baton. If you're in the mood, you can make your way south in for the Mt. Hood Jazz Festival in Gresham, OR—the event has played host to such greats as Wynton Marsalis and Ella Fitzgerald. Or wander north to check out what's playing in Alberta's two Jubilee Auditoriums, or at Bumbershoot, Seattle's blow-out festival of folk, street, classical, and rock music.

This is just a survey—*Let's Go* guides you to the arts, theater, and music in the Sights and Entertainment sections throughout the book.

Literature and Film

The Northwest has produced no major literary school of its own, but many writers who have lived or wandered there testify to the liberating effect of the frontier and the mountains. Travelers such as John Muir and John McPhee have celebrated the natural wonders of the region and written detailed descriptions of travelers' struggles to stay alive. Stories and novels by Raymond Carver and Alice Munro provide insight into the people and society of the region. Other authors—such as Ursula K. Le Guin and Jean M. Auel—have simply drawn from the surroundings as they write about other matters completely. Poet Theodore Roethke taught at the University of Washington in Seattle, bequeathing his lyric sensibility to a generation of Northwestern poets. Bernard Malamud taught for many years at Oregon State University as he wrote several of his best-known works.

Recent film makers and writers, many of them displaying an oddly outrageous comic sense, have lifted the Northwest's veil of fog and introduced the region into the pop culture pantheon. NBC's popular *Northern Exposure,* set in Alaska but filmed in Washington's Cascade range, peels back the surface from an isolated, anachronistic timber town, revealing the inhabitants' bizarre eccentricities. Gary Larson, the Seattle-bred creator of the outlandish cartoon strip "The Far Side," has deified the cow. Matt Groening, creator of the "Life is Hell" strip and FOX's *The Simpsons,* hails from Portland. So does John Callahan, whose unconventional comics have taken the "politically correct" world by storm. Northwestern pop culture tends not to pay homage to traditional hero figures.

What follows is a brief and idiosyncratic list of books by regional authors and about the region, from travel diaries to children's works. Check your local bookstore or library for other suggestions: *Where I'm Calling From* and *Fires* by Raymond Carver; the *Ramona* series by Beverly Cleary; *I Heard the Owl Call My Name* by Margaret Craven; *Go East, Young Man* by William O. Douglas; *Instructions to the Double* by Tess Gallager; *Julie of the Wolves* by Jean Craighead George; *Notes from the Century Before: A Journal of British Columbia* by Edward Hoagland; *The Country Ahead of Us, The Country Behind* by David Guterson; *Sometimes a Great Notion* by Ken Kesey; *The Lathe of Heaven* by Ursula K. Le Guin; *Journals of Lewis and Clark* by Merriwether Lewis and William Clark; *The Assistant* by Bernard Malamud; *Stories of Flo and Rose* by Alice Munro; *Zen and the Art of Motorcycle Maintenance* by Robert Pirsig; *Another Roadside Attraction* by Tom Robbins; *The Lost Sun* by Theodore Roethke; *Sacajawea: American Pathfinder* by Flora Warren Seymour; *Traveling Through the Dark* by William Stafford; *Paul Bunyan* by James Stevens; and *Poet in the Desert* by Charles Erskine Scott Woods.

In addition, the Northwest is a popular setting for movies and films—most notably, Cameron Crowe's *Singles, Say Anything,* and *Fast Times at Ridgemont High,* and David Lynch's *Twin Peaks: Fire Walk With Me.* To get a visual sampling of the area before you go, take a look at some of the following; most are widely available at the corner video rental store: *Drugstore Cowboy; An Officer and a Gentleman; Immediate Family; Ice Station Zebra; Orca; Never Cry Wolf; Shoot to Kill;* and *Vision Quest.* And, of course, flip on the TV for *Northern Exposure* (see Cascade Range: Roslyn, in Washington) and reruns of *Twin Peaks* (see Near Seattle: Snoqualmie, in Washington).

British Columbia

British Columbia attracts so many visitors that tourism has become the province's second largest industry after logging. Although Canada's westernmost province does offer excellent skiing year-round, most tourists arrive in the summer and flock to the beautiful twin cities of Vancouver and Victoria and to the pristine lakes and beaches of the Okanagan Valley.

As you head north, clouds begin to replace the crowds. Thick forests, low mountains, and occasional patches of high desert are interrupted only by such supply and transit centers as Prince George and Prince Rupert. Still farther north, even these outposts of civilization defer to thick spruce forests, intermittently tainted by the touch of the voracious logger or blackened by lightning fires.

The Canadian and British Columbian governments have prudently taken steps to preserve much of their undeveloped natural areas—almost 6000 sq. km of land fall under either provincial or federal protection. This extensive and accessible park system allows for an affordable escape from urbandom. While the government may view such escapes in terms of pecuniary possibility, to most of those who get away to the wilderness these escapes climb high onto the list of necessities.

PRACTICAL INFORMATION

Capital: Victoria.
Visitors Information: Call 800-663-6000 or write the **Ministry of Tourism and Provincial Secretary,** Parliament Bldgs., Victoria V8V 1X4 (604-387-1642). Ask especially for the *Accommodations* guide, which lists prices.
Park Information: Canadian Parks Service, 220 4th Ave. SE, P.O. Box 2989, Station M, Calgary, AB T2P 3H8. **BC Parks,** 800 Johnson St., 2nd Floor, Victoria, BC V8V 1X4 (604-387-5002).
Motto: *Splendor sine Occasu* (Splendor without Diminishment). **Year of Royal Naming:** 1858, by Queen Victoria. **Year to Join Confederation:** 1871. **Provincial Flower:** Pacific Dogwood. **Provincial Tree:** Douglas Fir. **Provincial Bird:** Heron. **Provincial Stone:** Jade.
Emergency: 911.
Time Zone: Mostly Pacific (1 hr. behind Mountain, 2 behind Central, 3 behind Eastern). Small eastern part is Mountain (1 hr. behind Central, 2 behind Eastern).
Postal Abbreviation: BC.
Drinking Age: 19.
Traffic Laws: Mandatory seatbelt law.
Area Code: 604.

TRAVEL

British Columbia is Canada's westernmost province, covering over 890,000 sq. km, bordering four U.S. states (Washington, Idaho, Montana, and Alaska) and three Canadian jurisdictions (Alberta, the Yukon Territory, and the Northwest Territories). Vancouver, on the mainland, can be reached via interstate highway from Seattle; Victoria, on Vancouver Island to the southwest of Vancouver, requires a ferry trip from Anacortes, Port Angeles, Seattle, or the Tsawwassen Terminal near Vancouver. However you travel, get used to thinking of distances in terms of kilometers in three or four digits.

Road travel throughout the province varies with the diverse terrain. If you decide to take your own vehicle, avoid potential hassles by obtaining a **Canadian non-resident interprovincial motor vehicle liability card** from your insurance company before leaving. Border police may turn you away if you are not properly insured. In the south, roads are plentiful and well-paved, but farther north both asphalt and towns yield to the Arctic winds. Above Prince George, travel along the two major roads—the **Alaska Hwy.** and the **Cassiar Hwy.**—is complicated by stretches of

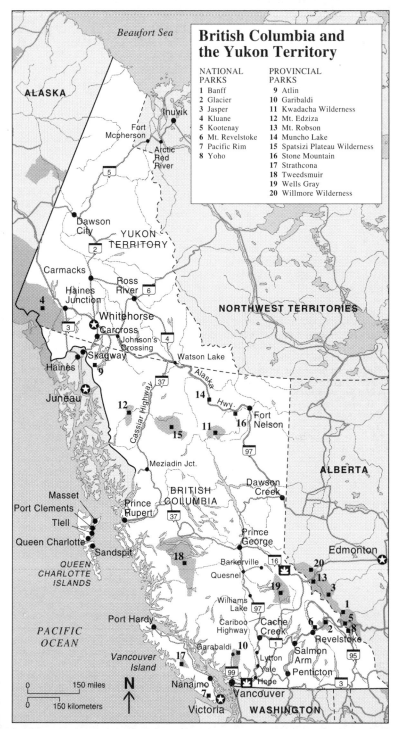

British Columbia and the Yukon Territory

NATIONAL PARKS
1 Banff
2 Glacier
3 Jasper
4 Kluane
5 Kootenay
6 Mt. Revelstoke
7 Pacific Rim
8 Yoho

PROVINCIAL PARKS
9 Atlin
10 Garibaldi
11 Kwadacha Wilderness
12 Mt. Edziza
13 Mt. Robson
14 Muncho Lake
15 Spatsizi Plateau Wilderness
16 Stone Mountain
17 Strathcona
18 Tweedsmuir
19 Wells Gray
20 Willmore Wilderness

Beaufort Sea

ALASKA

Inuvik

Fort Mcpherson

Arctic Red River

5

Dawson City

YUKON TERRITORY

Carmacks

Ross River

6

Haines Junction

4

Whitehorse

3

Carcross

Johnson's Crossing

4

NORTHWEST TERRITORIES

Haines

Skagway

9

Juneau

Watson Lake

Alaska

12

Cassia Highway

Hwy.

14

16

Fort Nelson

37

15

11

97

Meziadin Jct.

BRITISH COLUMBIA

Dawson Creek

ALBERTA

Masset

Port Clements

Tiell

Queen Charlotte

Sandspit

Prince Rupert

37

Prince George

Edmonton

QUEEN CHARLOTTE ISLANDS

18

Barkerville

16

20

13

3

Quesnel

19

1

PACIFIC OCEAN

Williams Lake

97

Port Hardy

Cariboo Highway

Cache Creek

6

2

8

Revelstoke

5

Garabaldi

10

1

Salmon Arm

95

Vancouver Island

17

Lytton

Yale

Penticton

0   150 miles

N

Nanaimo

99

Hope

3

0   150 kilometers

7

Victoria

Vancouver

WASHINGTON

"chip-seal," a cheaper and substantially rougher version of asphalt. Much of B.C. is served by **Greyhound** (662-3222 in Vancouver; 800-231-2222 from the U.S.).

The **Coquihalla Hwy.** (Hwy. 5, more popularly known as "The Coca-Cola") was completed in 1986 to carry tourists comfortably from Hope to Kamloops, a city roughly halfway between Vancouver and Alberta's Banff and Jasper National Parks. The Coquihalla Hwy. costs $10 to ride, but is a much more direct route and constitutes a substantial time savings. Unfortunately, the terrain is very hilly and has assassinated more than one transmission. If you don't think your car is up to snuff, you can always enjoy the Fraser River Canyon's scenery via the Trans-Canada Hwy. instead. The **Yellowhead Hwy.** (Hwy. 5) brings you from Kamloops on to Jasper.

For information about **crossing the U.S.-Canada border** and for customs regulations, see the Essentials: Documents and Formalities section.

■■■ VANCOUVER

Canada's third largest city (after Toronto and Montreal), Vancouver will thrill even the most jaded metropolis-hopping traveler. With its seamless public transit system, spotless sidewalks, and shining safety record, Vancouver could be Sweden or Switzerland with a North American twist. Although there are a few dingy back alleys scattered through the city, the streets are broad, clearly laid out, and well-marked. Moreover, Vancouver's citizens display a kind gentility rare in a city this size.

Vancouver is fast joining the post-industrial age; the unemployment rate has fallen by half in recent years, and electronics and international finance are supplanting timber and mining as the city's economic base. Additionally, a growing wave of Chinese immigrants is orienting Vancouver's culture and economy toward the Far East. Immigration is increasing from Hong Kong in particular; cynics say their city is becoming "Hongcouver" and predict racial tensions will rise. Others regard Vancouver as the archetype of a modern multi-ethnic metropolis. The debate over defining Vancouver's identity remains unsettled, but Mayor Gordon Campbell promises that his city will "not become like a city in the United States."

The range of things to do in Vancouver and its environs is astounding. You can go for nature walks among 1000-year-old virgin timber stands, windsurf, take in a modern art exposition, or get wrapped up in a flick at the most technologically advanced movie theatre in the world—and never leave downtown. Filled with beaches and parks, the cultural vortex that is Vancouver has swallowed hordes of unsuspecting vacationers. If you insist on purchasing a return trip ticket in advance, be sure to allot yourself ample time to appreciate this marvelous city.

PRACTICAL INFORMATION

Visitors Information: Travel Infocentre, 1055 Dunsmuir St. (683-2000), near Burrard St., in the West End. Help with reservations, and tours. If the racks of brochures don't answer all your questions, the staff will. Open daily 8am-6pm.

BC Transit Information Centre, 261-5100. Fare $1.50, exact change. Day passes ($4.50) available at all 7-11 stores, the Post Office, the Waterfront stop, or the Vancouver International Hostel.

Parks and Recreation Board, 2099 Beach Ave. (681-1141). Open Mon.-Fri. 8:30am-4:30pm.

The Gray Line, 200-399 W. 6th. (879-3363), in Hotel Vancouver. Expensive but worthwhile city tours with a number of package options. Basic tours leave daily and last 3½ hr. $30, senior citizens $26.75, children $17. Reservations required.

Taxis: Yellow Cab, 681-3311. **Vancouver Taxi,** 255-5111. Both 24 hr.

Car Rental: Rent-A-Wreck, 180 W. Georgia St. (688-0001), in the West End. (Also 340 W. 4th at Manitoba.) From $45 per day; 150km free plus 15¢ per additional km. Must be 19 with credit card. Open Mon.-Fri. 7am-7pm, Sat. 9am-5pm, Sun. 10am-3pm. Also **ABC Rental,** 255 W. Broadway. Starts at $200 per week.

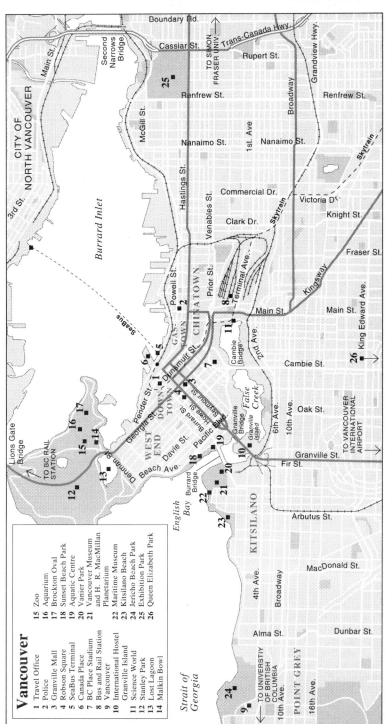

Vancouver

1 Travel Office
2 Police
3 Granville Mall
4 Robson Square
5 SeaBus Terminal
6 Canada Place
7 BC Place Stadium
8 Bus and Rail Station
9 Vancouver
10 International Hostel
11 Science World
12 Stanley Park
13 Lost Lagoon
14 Malkin Bowl
15 Zoo
16 Aquarium
17 Brockton Oval
18 Sunset Beach Park
19 Aquatic Centre
20 Vanier Park
21 Vancouver Museum and H. R. MacMillan Planetarium
22 Maritime Museum
23 Kitsilano Beach
24 Jericho Beach Park
25 Exhibition Park
26 Queen Elizabeth Park

Bike Rental: Bayshore, 745 Denman St. (688-2453). Convenient to Stanley Park. Practically new bikes $5.60 per hr., $20 per 12 hr., $25 per day. Open May-Sept. daily 9am-9pm. Winter hours vary with the amount of sunlight.

Bicycling Association of BC, 1367 W. Broadway, #332, Vancouver V6H 4H9 (731-7433 events line, 737-3034 office). One-page cycling map of city ($2.30); more detailed maps available through the mail. Open Mon.-Fri. 9am-5pm.

Road Conditions: 525-4997. 24 hr.

Camping Equipment Rentals: Recreation Rentals, 2560 Arbutus St. (733-7368), at Broadway. Take bus #10 or 14 from Granville Mall. Backpacks ($8 per day, $20 per week), 2-person tents ($12 per day, $36 per week), and every other kind of camping or sports equipment under the sun. Open Mon.-Wed. 8am-6pm, Thurs. 8am-7pm, Fri. and Sun. 8am-8pm, Sat. 8am-6pm.

Scuba Rentals: The Diving Locker, 2745 W. 4th Ave. (736-2681). Complete outfit $50 first day, $25 per additional day. Open Mon.-Thurs. 9:30am-7pm, Fri. 9:30am-8pm, Sat. 9:30am-7pm, Sun. 10am-4pm.

Public Library: 750 Burrard St. (665-2280, 665-2276 for a recording), at Robson St., downtown. Open Mon.-Thurs. 10am-6pm, Fri.-Sat. 10am-9pm; Oct.-March also Sun. 1-5pm.

Bookstores: Spartacus, 311 W. Hastings (688-6138). Extensive and unique collection spans topics in politics, race relations, and art. Open Mon.-Fri. 10am-8:30pm, Sat. 10am-6pm, Sun. 1-4pm. **Little Sisters Book and Art Emporium Inc.,** 1221 Thurlow (669-1753). Grand selection of literature concerning gays and lesbians. Open daily 10am-11pm.

Arts Hotline: 684-2787. 24 hr.

Weather: 664-9032.

Distress Line: Vancouver Crisis Center, 733-4111. 24 hr.

Women's Services: Rape Crisis Center, 255-6344. 24 hr. **Rape Relief Center,** 872-8212. 24 hr. **Emergency,** 872-7774. 24 hr.

Women's Resource Center, 1144 Robson St. (681-2910), in the West End between Thurlow and Bute St. Open July-Aug. Mon.-Fri. 10am-2pm; in winter Mon.-Fri. 10am-4pm, Sat. 1-4pm.

Senior Citizen's Information and Support Network, 531-2320 or 531-2425. Open Mon.-Fri. 10am-4pm.

BC Coalition of People with Disabilities, 204-456 W. Broadway (875-0188). Open Mon.-Fri. 8am-4pm.

Gay and Lesbian Switchboard, 2-1170 Bute St., 684-6869. Counseling and information. Open daily 7-10pm.

AIDS Vancouver: 687-2437. Open Mon.-Thurs. 10am-9pm, Fri. 10am-6pm, Sat. 10am-3pm.

Poison Control: 682-5050.

Pharmacy: Shoppers Drug Mart, 2979 W. Broadway at Carnarvon (733-9128). Open Mon.-Sat. 9am-9pm, Sun. 11am-6pm.

UBC Hospital: 822-7121.

Emergency: 911. **RCMP Emergency Line:** 666-5343. **Police:** at Main and Powell (665-3321).

Post Office: Main branch, 349 W. Georgia St. (662-5725). Open Mon.-Fri. 8am-5:30pm. **Postal Code:** V6B 3P7.

Area Code: 604.

GETTING THERE

Vancouver is located in the southwestern corner of the Canadian British Columbia mainland, across the Georgia Strait from Vancouver Island and the city of Victoria. **Vancouver International Airport,** on Sea Island 11km south of the city center, makes connections to major cities on the West Coast and around the world. To reach downtown from the airport, take BC bus #100 to the intersection of Granville and 70th Ave. Transfer there to bus #20, which arrives downtown heading north on the Granville Mall. The private **Airport Express** (273-9023) bus leaves from airport level #2 and heads for downtown hotels and the Greyhound station (every 15 min. 6:15am-12:30am, $8.25 per person.

Greyhound makes several runs daily between Seattle and Vancouver. The downtown bus depot provides easy access to the city's transit system. **VIA Rail** runs one train per day on the famed **Trans-Canada Railway,** bound for eastern Canada. The **BC Rail** station in North Vancouver launches trains toward northern British Columbia. **BC Ferries** regularly connects the city of Vancouver to Vancouver Island and the Gulf Islands. Ferries leave from the **Tsawwassen Terminal,** 25km south of the city center. To reach downtown from the ferry terminal, take bus #640 to the Ladner Exchange and transfer to bus #601, which arrives downtown on Seymour St.

Greyhound, 1150 Station St. (662-3222), in the VIA Rail, see below. Service to the south and across Canada. To: Calgary (7 per day, $90), Banff (6 per day, $85), Jasper (4 per day, $83), and Seattle (4 per day, $25). Open daily 5:30am-midnight.

Pacific Coach Lines, 150 Dunsmuir St. (662-5074). Serves southern BC—including Vancouver Island—in conjunction with Greyhound. To Victoria $20, including ferry and service into downtown Victoria.

VIA Rail, 1150 Station St. (800-561-8630 or 669-3050), at Main St. Sky Train stop. To: Jasper (3 per week, $115.60), Edmonton (3 per week, $160.50). Open Thurs.-Tues. 7:30am-9:30pm, Wed. 7:30am-2:30pm.

BC Rail, 1311 W. 1st St. (984-5246), just over the Lions Gate Bridge in North Vancouver. Take the BC Rail Special Bus on Georgia or take the SeaBus downtown to North Vancouver, then bus #239 west. Daily to: Garibaldi ($11.50), Whistler ($14), Williams Lake ($54), Prince George ($74.50), and points north. Open daily 6:30am-8:30pm.

BC Ferries (669-1211 general information, 685-1021 recorded information, Tsawwassen ferry terminal 943-9331). Ferry goes to Victoria, the Gulf Islands, Sunshine Coast, Mainland to Vancouver Island ($6, car and driver $26.50, motorcycle and driver $15.50, bicycle and rider $8; ages 5-11 ½ price). The terminal serving Victoria is actually located in Swartz Bay, north of Victoria. (See Getting There in Victoria for more information.)

Bicyclists will find many excellent routes both in the city itself and outside of it, including routes in the Fraser River Canyon, along the shore of Georgia Bay, on the Gulf Islands, and on Vancouver Island. The Bicycling Association of BC (see Practical Information) can recommend specific trips, and Tourism BC publishes a thorough pamphlet on bicycling. Note that the George Massey Tunnel on Hwy. 99, under the Fraser River (which you must use to get to and from the Tsawwassen terminal), is closed to bicycles. A shuttle service transports cyclists through the tunnel. Call the **Bicycling Association of British Columbia** (731-7433) for information on times and fares. (Shuttle service operates daily in summer, less frequently in winter.)

ORIENTATION AND GETTING AROUND

Vancouver's neighborhoods are more cohesive today than in the past, when marsh waters connecting False Creek with Burrard Inlet would detach the downtown peninsula from the rest of the city at high tide. The miracle of landfill has brought residents closer together, but the profusion of waterways can still confuse even the most diligent map reader. Most of the city's attractions are concentrated on the city center peninsula and the larger rhino-snout-shaped land to the south. The residential area of the city center peninsula, bounded by downtown to the east and Stanley Park to the west, is known as the **West End.** The western portion of the southern peninsula (west from around Alma Ave. to the University of British Columbia campus) is known as **Point Grey,** while the central area on the same peninsula (east from Alma Ave. to the Granville Bridge) is referred to as **Kitsilano,** or "Kits".

Don't try to make any distinction between streets and avenues in Vancouver—there is no apparent standard, and most maps usually omit the surname. The one exception to this madness are the numbered arterials, which are always *avenues* in Vancouver proper (running east-west), and always *streets* in North Vancouver (running every which way but loose), across Burrard Inlet. In the downtown, private vehicles are not allowed on Granville between Nelson and West Pender St., which is called the **Granville Mall.** Both **Chinatown,** stretching from east to west between Hastings and East Pender from Carrall Ave. to Gore Ave., and **Gastown,** on Alexander as it runs into Water St., are easily reached on foot from the Granville Mall.

Vancouver's **BC Transit** covers most of the city and suburbs, with direct transport or easy connecting transit to the city's points of departure: Tsawwassen, Horseshoe Bay, and the airport (see Getting There for specific bus lines). Often one bus will run along a route in one direction while a bus of a different number will run in the other direction; ask a local or bus driver for assistance. Be forewarned: despite the good transit system, it takes longer to get around in Vancouver than you expect.

BC Transit subdivides the city into three concentric zones for **fare** purposes. You can ride in BC Transit's central zone one way for $1.50 (senior citizens and ages 5-11 80¢) at all times. During peak hours (6:30-9:30am and 3-6:30pm), it costs $2 (seniors and ages 5-11 $1) to travel between two zones and $2.75 to travel through three zones. During off-peak hours, passengers pay only the one-zone price. **Day-passes** are $4.50, and transfers are free. Single fares, passes, and transfers are also good for the **SeaBus** and **SkyTrain** (running southeast from downtown to New Westminster). Timetables are available at 7-11 stores, public libraries, city halls, community centers, and the Vancouver Travel Infocentre (see Practical Information). To retrieve **lost property,** call 682-7887 (Mon.-Fri. 9:30am-5pm); otherwise stop by the lost property office in the Sky Train Stadium station.

BC Transit's **SeaBus** operates from the Granville Waterfront Station, at the foot of Granville St. in downtown Vancouver, to the Lonsdale Quay at the foot of Lonsdale Ave. in North Vancouver. The fares are the same as one-zone bus fares, and all transfers and passes are accepted. While waiting, study *The Buzzer,* BC Transit's weekly pamphlet on transit updates and community events, available on buses and wherever transit timetables are distributed.

Driving in Vancouver is a serious hassle. Rush hour begins at dawn and doesn't end until dusk. Beware of the 7-9:30am and 3-6pm restrictions on left turns and street parking; fines are steep. If you can't find parking at street level, look for underground lots (try the lot below Pacific Centre at Howe and W. Georgia St., sometimes called "Garageland.") One-way streets are a curse throughout the city, but many maps have arrows indicating directions. The free Tourism BC maps don't cover the area outside the city center in detail; purchase the larger-scale street map, available from the Infocentre (see Practical Information) for $2.

If you have a car, consider using **Park'n Ride** from New Westminster to circumvent the city's perpetual rush hour. Exit Hwy. 1 at New Westminster and follow signs for the Pattullo Bridge. Just over the bridge, you'll see signs for the Park 'n' Ride lot to your right, between Scott Rd. and 110th Ave. A bus will be waiting, where you can purchase tickets for the bus, SkyTrain, and SeaBus, or one-day passes for $4. Parking is free, and taking the SkyTrain downtown is faster than driving.

ACCOMMODATIONS

Greater Vancouver is a rabbit warren of bed and breakfast accommodations. Cheaper than their American equivalents (but still not as affordable as English B&Bs), these private homes are usually comfortable and have personable proprietors. Rates average about $45-60 for singles and $55-75 for doubles. The visitors bureau (see Practical Information) has a four-page list of B&Bs. Several private agencies also match travelers with B&Bs, usually for a fee; get in touch with **Town and Country Bed and Breakfast** (731-5942) or **Best Canadian** (738-7207). Always call for reservations at least two days in advance.

South of Downtown

Vancouver International Hostel (HI-C), 1515 Discovery St. (224-3208), in Jericho Beach Park. Turn north off 4th Ave., following the signs for Marine Dr., or take bus #4 from Granville St. downtown. Granville is 1 block north of Seymour.

Comely semi-suburban location in park, with a superlative view of the city from Jericho Beach. 285 beds in dorm rooms and 8 family rooms. Good cooking facilities, TV room, laundry facilities, and a convenient—if expensive—cafeteria. Ask about occasional opportunities to spend a few hours cleaning in exchange for a room. 5-day limit enforced in summer, but flexible during other parts of the year. Registration open 7:30am-midnight. Bedding $1.50. $13.50, nonmembers $18.50. Reserve at least 2 weeks in advance during summer. Rents top-quality mountain bikes for $20 per day.

Vincent's Backpackers Hostel, 927 Main St. (682-2441), next to the VIA Rail station, above a big green store called "The Source." Take bus #3 (Main St.) or #8 (Fraser). Not as clean or as structured as the HI-C hostel and Globetrotter's. Narrow, dark hallways, with exposed pipes. Kitchen, fridge, TV, stereo, and the music of the nearby Greyhounds gleefully revving their engines until late at night. 1 washer, 1 dryer. Rents mountain bikes for $5 per day. Office open 8am-midnight. Check in before noon for your best shot at a bed. Shared rooms $10. Singles with shared bath $20. Doubles with shared bath $25. Weekly rates: shared rooms $60, singles $100, doubles $130. Pay before 10am after first night for 20% discount on all rates.

Paul's Guest House, 345 W. 14th Ave. (872-4753), at Alberta. Take bus #15. Nestled in a beautiful residential area. Shared baths. Complimentary full breakfast. Paul's is part of a network of B&Bs mainly in the Kitsilano and City Hall areas; if Paul's is booked, they can arrange your stay at one of these other B&Bs. Check in before 11pm. Call ahead for reservations. Tidy and cozy singles $36. Doubles $46. Rates $5 lower in winter.

Simon Fraser University, (291-4503) in Burnaby 20km east of the city center. Take buses #10 or 14 north on Granville Mall and transfer to bus #135. 190 singles and 9 doubles available May-Aug. Shared bath. Call Mon.-Fri. 8:30am-midnight. Check-in 2-4:30pm. Check-out 11am. Singles $20. Doubles $40. With linen and towels: singles $26, twins $46. No reservations necessary.

University of British Columbia Conference Centre, 5959 Student Union Mall, Walter Gage Residence (822-1010), at the end of Vancouver's largest peninsula. Take bus #4 or 10 from the Granville Mall. Dorm-style rooms available May-Aug. Draws swarms of conventioneers in summer. Check-in after 2pm. 3 types of rates: dorm-style singles with shared bath $19, doubles $38; B&B-style singles with shared bath $22, doubles $44; private singles $29, doubles $68.

Downtown

YWCA, 580 Burrard St. (800-633-1424 or 662-8188), at Dunsmuir, 7 blocks from the bus depot. For women, male-female couples, families, and men (when the YMCA is full). Recently remodeled and clean, but expensive. High-quality sports facilities for female guests over age 15 (free). Kitchens on every other floor and cafeteria in basement. Staff on duty 24 hr., but building locked at midnight—buzz for entry. No male visitors allowed upstairs. Some singles smaller than others, so ask to see a few before choosing. 4-week max. stay. Singles $44. Doubles $64. 10% discount for YWCA members, senior citizens, students, and groups. Weekly and monthly rates available when there are sufficient vacancies.

YMCA, 955 Burrard St. (681-0221), between Smithe and Nelson, 4 blocks south of the YWCA. Newly renovated. Concerned staff on duty 24 hr. Pool, gymnasiums, ball courts, and weight rooms (free). All rooms have shared washrooms and showers. Cafeteria open Mon.-Fri. 7am-4pm, Sat. 8am-2pm. Singles $31. Doubles $47.Rooms with TV $3 extra. Weekly and monthly rates available when there are sufficient vacancies.

Dufferin Hotel, 900 Seymour St. (683-4251), at Smithe. Clean rooms, color TV. Safer than many other hotels in the area. No visitors after 11:30pm. Check-out noon. Singles $60. Doubles $65.

Nelson Place, 1006 Granville (681-6341), at Nelson St., 1 block from the Dufferin. Borders on Vancouver's small and tame red-light district. Great access to downtown. Small rooms with TV and bath. Singles $40. Doubles $45. $5 less in winter.

North of Downtown

Globetrotter's Inn, 170 W. Esplanade (988-5141), in North Vancouver. As close to downtown as the hostel. Take the SeaBus to Lonsdale Quay, then walk 1 block east to W. Esplanade and Chesterfield. Kitchen facilities and shared baths. $13 per night. Private singles $27. Doubles $33, with bath $38.

Sylvia Hotel, 1154 Gilford St. (681-9321), at Beach St., 2 blocks from Stanley Park in a quiet residential neighborhood. Take bus #19 on Pender. Beautiful, ivy-shrouded building overlooking English Bay, with magnificent rooms to match. Singles and doubles from $55. Additional cots $10. Reservations recommended.

Horseshoe Bay Motel, 6588 Royal Ave. (921-7454), in W. Vancouver/Horseshoe Bay. Perfect location for passengers on the BC Ferry. Singles $60. Doubles $65. Rates $20 lower in winter. Kitchen units $10 extra.

CAMPING

Greater Vancouver has few public campgrounds; campers must resort to expensive, private ones. The visitors bureau (see Practical Information) has a complete list of campgrounds outside Vancouver, but many are for RVs only. **Recreation Rentals** offers tents (see Practical Information), but the high cost makes it more sensible to spend the money on a bed at a hostel. The town of **White Rock,** 30 minutes south-east of Vancouver, has campgrounds with room for tents. Take bus #351 from Howe St. downtown.

Richmond RV Park, 6200 River Rd. (270-7878), near Holly Bridge in Richmond. Take Hwy. 99 to Westminster Hwy., then follow the signs. Unquestionably the best deal within 15km of downtown. Sites offer little privacy, but the showers and a soothing staff are sure to wash those cares right out of your hair. Sites $15, with hookups $18.50-20. Open April-Oct.

Hazelmere RV Park and Campground, 18843 8th Ave. (538-1167), in Surrey. Off Hwy. 99A, head east on 8th Ave. Quiet sites on the Campbell River with beach access. Showers 25¢. Sites for 1-2 people $14, with hookups $18; add $2 for each additional person.

ParkCanada, 4799 Hwy. 17 (943-5811), in Delta, about 30km south of downtown. Take Hwy. 99 south to Tsawwassen Ferry Terminal Rd., then go east for 2.5km. The campground, located next to a waterslide park, has flush toilets and free showers, though the lines tend to be long. Sites $12, with hookups $20.

Dogwood Campground, 15151 112th Ave. (583-5585), 31km east on Hwy. 1 in Surrey. Flush toilets and free showers. Sites $16.50, with hookups $23.50.

FOOD

Steer clear of restaurants hawking "Canadian cuisine"—the phrase could be officially certified by the International Oxymoron Commission. The city's best eateries are the diverse ethnic and natural-foods culinaria. Vancouver's **Chinatown** is second in size only to San Francisco's in all of North America, and the East Indian neighborhoods along Main, Fraser, and 49th St. serve up the spicy dishes of the subcontinent. Groceries, shops, and restaurants also cluster around E. Pender and Gore St.

Restaurants in the **West End** and **Gastown** compete for the highest prices in the city; the former caters to executives with expense accounts, while the latter bleeds money from tourists fresh off the cruise ships. Many of the greasy spoons along Davie and Denman St. stay open late or around the clock. **Buy-Low Foods** at 4th and Alma (597-9122), near the HI-C hostel in Jericho Village, will help keep costs down. (Open Mon.-Sat. 9am-9pm, Sun. 9am-6pm.)

The **Granville Island Market,** under the Granville Bridge, off W. 4th Ave. across False Creek from downtown, intersperses trendy shops, art galleries, and restaurants with countless produce stands selling local and imported fruits and vegetables. Take bus #50 from Granville St. downtown. The range of delicacies offered by the stalls at the north end of the island will stun your palate. Slurp cherry-papaya yogurt soup (from an edible sugar waffle bowl), down cheese blintzes and potato knishes,

LET'S GO® Travel

1994 CATALOG

We give you the world
at a discount!

•Discount Flights •Eurails •Travel Gear

LET'S PACK IT UP

Let's Go Supreme

Innovative hideaway suspension with parallel stay internal frame turns backpack into carry-on suitcase. Includes lumbar support pad, torso and waist adjustment, leather trim, and detachable daypack. Waterproof Cordura nylon, lifetime guarantee, 4400 cu. in. Navy, Green or Black.

A • • • • • • • • • • • • $175

Let's Go Backpack/Suitcase

Hideaway suspension with internal frame turns backpack into carry-on suitcase. Detachable daypack makes it 3 bags in 1. Waterproof Cordura nylon, lifetime guarantee, 3750 cu. in. Navy, Green or Black.

B • • • • • • • • • • • • • • • $130

Let's Go Backcountry

Full size, slim profile expedition pack designed for the serious trekker. New Airflex suspension. X-frame pack with advanced composite tube suspension. Velcro height adjustment, side compression straps. Detachable hood converts into a fanny pack. Waterproof Cordura nylon, lifetime guarantee. Main compartment 6530 cu. in. extends to 7130 cu. in.

C • • • • • • • • $210

Undercover NeckPouch

Ripstop nylon with soft Cambrelle back. 3 pockets. 6 x 7". Lifetime guarantee. Black or Tan.

D • • • • • • • • • • • • • • $9.95

Undercover WaistPouch

Ripstop nylon with soft Cambrelle back. 2 pockets. 12 x 5" with adjustable waistband. Lifetime guarantee. Black or Tan.

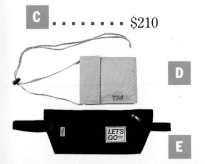

E • • • • • • • • • • • • • • $9.95

LET'S GO BY TRAIN

Eurail Passes

Convenient way to travel Europe. Save up to 70% over cost of individual tickets.

EURAILPASS	
FIRST CLASS	
15 days	$498
21 days	$648
1 month	$798
2 months	$1098
3 months	$1398

EURAIL FLEXIPASS	
FIRST CLASS	
Any 5 days in 2 months	$348
Any 10 days in 2 months	$560
Any 15 days in 2 months	$740

EURAIL SAVERPASS**	
FIRST CLASS	
15 days	$430
21 days	$550
1 month	$678

**Price per person for 2 or more people travelling together. 3 people required between April 1 - September 3.

EURAIL YOUTHPASS*	
SECOND CLASS	
15 days	$398
1 month	$578
2 months	$768

*Valid only if passenger is under 26 on first date of travel.

EURAIL YOUTH FLEXIPASS*	
SECOND CLASS	
Any 5 days in 2 months	$255
Any 10 days in 2 months	$398
Any 15 days in 2 months	$540

*Valid only if passenger is under 26 on first date of travel.

LET'S GO BY PLANE

Discounted Flights

Over 150 destinations including:

LONDON

MADRID

PARIS

ATHENS

ROME

Domestic fares too!
For prices & reservations
call 1-800-5-LETS-GO

EURAIL COUNTRY PASSES

**POLAND HUNGARY
AUSTRIA FRANCE
SCANDINAVIA
FINLAND
LUXEMBOURG
GREECE SPAIN
CZECHOSLOVAKIA
GERMANY PORTUGAL
NETHERLANDS
BRITAIN SPAIN**

Call for prices, rail n' drive
or rail n' fly options.
Flexotel passes too!

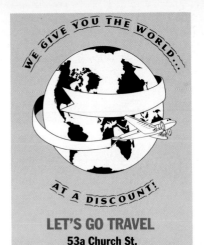

WE GIVE YOU THE WORLD...

AT A DISCOUNT!

LET'S GO TRAVEL
**53a Church St.
Cambridge, MA 02138
(617) 495-9649 or 1-800-5-LETS-GO
FAX (617) 496-8015**

LET'S GO HOSTELING
1994-95 Youth Hostel Card
Required by most international hostels. Must be a U.S. resident.

F1 Adult (ages 18-55) $25

F2 Youth (under 18) $10

Sleepsack
Required at all hostels. Washable durable poly/cotton. 18" pillow pocket. Folds into pouch size.

G $13.95

1993-94 Youth Hostel Guide (IYHG)
Essential information about 4000 hostels in Europe and the Mediterranean.

H $10.95

LET'S GET STARTED
Please print or type. Incomplete applications will be returned

Last Name	First Name	Date of Birth

Street	*We do not ship to P.O. Boxes. U.S. addresses only.*	

City	State	Zip Code

Phone		Date Trip Begins

Item Code	Description, Size & Color	Quantity	Unit Price	Total Price

Shipping & Handling

If order totals: . . . . . Add
Up to $30.00 . . . . . . $4.00
30.01-100.00 . . . . . . $6.00
Over 100.00 . . . . . . $7.00

Total Merchandise Price	
Shipping & Handling (See box at left)	
For Rush Handling Add $10 for continental U.S., $12 for AK & HI	
MA Residents (Add 5% sales tax on gear & books)	
Total	

Mastercard/Visa Order

Cardholder name_____

Card number_____

Expiration date_____

Allow 2-3 weeks for delivery. Rus orders delivered within one week our receipt.

Enclose check or money order payable to:
Harvard Student Agencies, Inc.
53a Church St. Cambridge, MA 0

Prices subject to change without notice

or pick up some duck or shrimp stock to take back to the hostel's stew pot. The bakeries also sell day-old bread and bagels at half-price. Picnics tend to break out spontaneously in the parks, patios, and walkways that surround the market. (Market complex open daily 9am-6pm; Labor Day to Victoria Day Tues.-Sun. 9am-6pm.)

Downtown

Frannie's Deli, 325 Cambie (685-2928), at W. Cordova St. near Gastown. Doesn't look like much from outside (or inside), but let your stomach be the judge. A variety of sandwiches, including a ($3.25) vegetarian. A common ground for casually dressed Canadian capitalists. Open Mon.-Sat. 6:30am-6:30pm.

Chinatown

The Green Door, 111 E. Pender St. (685-4194). Follow the alley off Columbia St. to find the hidden entrance. This legendary, wildly green establishment takes a prominent place in the annals of Vancouver hippie lore. Huge portions of slightly greasy Chinese seafood ($6-7). BYOB (no liquor license). Open Thurs.-Tues. noon-10pm; Oct.-May Wed.-Mon. noon-10pm.

The Japanese Deli House Restaurant, 381 Powell (681-6484). Take-out deli with restaurant across the street. All-you-can-eat sushi ($10; take-out only). Open Mon. 11:30am-3pm, Tues.-Sat. 11:30am-8pm, Sun. 11:30am-6pm.

The Only Seafood Cafe, 20 E. Hastings St. (681-6546), at Carrall St., within walking distance of downtown. Large portions of great seafood at decent prices and a reputation that has spread throughout the Northwest. They've been around since 1912, but they *still* haven't gotten around to building a rest room. Fried halibut steak ($9.75). Open Mon.-Sat. 11:30am-9:30pm, Sun. noon-7pm.

Phnom Penh, 244 E. Georgia (682-1090), near Main St. Take bus #3 or #8 from downtown. Unquestionably the best Vietnamese food in Vancouver. The truly adventurous can sample the *phnom*enal jellyfish salad ($9). The diverse menu can accommodate less daring tastebuds as well. Entrees $5-10. Open Wed.-Mon. 10am-9:30pm.

West End

Hamburger Mary's, 1202 Davie St. (687-1293), at Bute. Heralded for the best burgers in town, which come in many varieties ($4-7). Open daily 6am-4am.

Stephos, 1124 Davie St. (683-2555), at Thurlow. Much more elegant than The Souvlaki Place, and the prices are only slightly higher. Full *souvlaki* meal ($6-10), humus and pita ($3.75), baklava ($2.75). Open Mon.-Sat. 11:30am-11:15pm, Sun. 4-11:15pm.

Cafe La Brocca, 1098 Robson St. (687-0088), at Thurlow. Energetic staff probably carbo-loads on the amazing pasta ($8). Breakfast served. Open daily 8am-10:30pm.

Near Stanley Park

The Souvlaki Place, 1181 Denman (689-3064). This Greek place pulsates with wailing Mediterranean music. *Spanikopita* ($3.25); *souvlaki* ($5). Open daily 11:30am-11pm.

Slice of Gourmet, 1152 Denman (689-1112). The pick for tantalizing pizza with original toppings. Try a filling slice of the peppery potato or Devil's Delight pizza ($3). Open Sun.-Thurs. 11:30am-midnight, Fri.-Sat. 11:30am-1am.

Commercial Drive

Nuff-Nice-Ness, 1861 Commercial Dr. (255-4211), at 3rd. Still P. Hudson's home for Jamaican cuisine and located on a hip strip. Vegetable and meat patties ($1.87 each). Jerk chicken with salad and rice $7.50. Daily specials offered in the late afternoon for $5.50. Open Tues. 12:30-8pm, Wed.-Sat. 11am-8pm, Sun. 1-6pm.

Nick's Spaghetti House, 631 Commercial Dr. (254-5633), between Georgia and Frances, in the Italian District. Take bus #20. An old restaurant under new management. Standard Italian food in a traditional atmosphere. The spaghetti is *mag-*

nifico ($9.10). Open Mon.-Thurs. 11:30am-11pm, Fri. 11:30am-midnight, Sat. 4pm-midnight, Sun. 4-10pm.

Cafe Du Soleil, 1393 Commercial Dr. (254-1145), near Kitchener. Romper Room meets Boulangerie—a veggie cafe serving breakfast all day, with lots of toys for the kids. 2 eggs, toast, and hashbrowns ($3.25). Mix-and-match sandwiches with soup ($4.75). Open Mon.-Fri. 10am-9pm, Sat.-Sun. 10am-6pm.

Granville Island

Isadora's Cooperative Restaurant, 1540 Old Bridge Rd. (681-8816), 1 block on your right near the "Kids Only" complex. This socially conscious natural food restaurant sends its profits to community service organizations. For entertainment, watch the younguns douse each other with garden hoses in the wading pool next door. Sandwiches $7, dinner entrees $10-13. *Khatsah lano* burger made with filet of salmon ($8). Open Mon.-Thurs. 7:30am-9pm, Fri.-Sun. 9am-9pm. Closed Mon. evenings in winter.

Kitsilano

The Naam, 2724 W. 4th Ave. (738-7151), at Stephens. Bus #4 or 7 from Granville. Vancouver's oldest natural-food restaurant. With a fireplace and patio, the Naam is truly a delight. Tofu-nut-beet burgers ($5), spinach enchiladas ($8.25), and salad bar ($1.25 per 100g). Live music nightly from 7-10pm. Open 24 hr.

Nyala, 2930 W. 4th Ave. (731-7899), down the street from The Naam. Tasteful, festive environs can't upstage the authentic Ethiopian fare. Marinated chicken with ginger root and cardamon ($9.75). Vegetarian options ($7-8). Open Mon.-Thurs. 11:30am-2:30pm and 5-11pm, Fri.-Sat. 11:30 am-2:30 pm and 5pm-2am, Sun. 5-10pm.

Near Broadway and Cambie St.

Nirvana, 2313 Main St. (876-2911), at 7th. Take bus #8, 3, or 9. Smells like...authentic, savory, and possibly spiritual Indian cuisine. Find or lose yourself in the chicken curry ($6.50) or vegetable *biryani* ($8). Open Mon.-Fri. 11:30am-11pm, Sat.-Sun. noon-11pm.

Tomato Fresh Food Cafe, 3305 Cambie (874-6020), at 17th. Just about every dish here includes some of that red round thing that hovers between the fruit and vegetable categories. Try Tomato's tomato sandwich ($5.25) or the more exotic Santa Fe corn pie ($6.75). Great selection of fruit and vegetable drinks ($2.50-3.75). The tomatoe juice is Dan Quayle's favorite. Open Tues.-Sat. 9am-10pm, Sun. 9am-3pm.

The Sitar, 564 W. Broadway (879-4333), between Cambie and Ash. Take bus #10 or 14 from Granville. Standard Indian food in a standard Indian setting. You'll have a one-night love affair with the *tandoori* chicken ($9), *mulligatawny* ($3), or full dinners ($12). Lunch specials ($5). The curry cuts like a knife. Open Mon.-Sat. 11am-10:30pm, Sun. 4-10:30pm.

Singapore Restaurant, 546 W. Broadway (874-6161), near Cambie. Take bus #10 or #14 from Granville. The mix of Malaysian, Chinese, and Indian cuisine corresponds to the tangled demography of Singapore. Fried noodles ($6), prawns and ginger ($9.50), beef or chicken *satay* ($1.20 each). Lunch specials ($4.50). Open Mon.-Fri. 11am-2:30pm and 5-10pm, Sat. 11am-10pm, Sun. noon-10pm.

SIGHTS AND ACTIVITIES

Vancouver's attractions range from urbane architectural spectacles to serene parks and beaches.

World's Fair Grounds and Downtown

Expo '86 was the first world's fair to be held in two different locations. The **main grounds,** between Granville and Main St., are now gradually devolving into office space, housing for senior citizens, and a cultural center. The Canada Pavilion, now called **Canada Place,** is about 0.5km away and can be reached by SkyTrain from the main Expo site. The cavernous pavilion is a conventioneer's dream and an agoraphobe's nightmare; its roof, constructed to resemble gigantic sails, dominates the harbor. The shops and restaurants inside are outrageously expensive, but the promenades around the complex are terrific vantage points for snapshots of North Vancouver or for gawking at one of the more than 200 luxury liners that dock here annually. There's a tour **information booth** in front of Canada Place (688-8687; open Mon.-Fri. 8am-5pm).

Also under the sails is the five-story **CN IMAX Theatre** (682-4629). The flat screen doesn't draw you in as much as the domed Omnimax screen, but has unsurpassed image clarity with no peripheral distortion. So there. (Tickets $6.25-9.25, senior citizens and children $5.25-8.25. Open daily noon-9pm.)

The real big-screen star of Expo '86 is the **Omnimax Theatre,** part of the **Science World** complex at 1455 Quebec St. (687-7832) on the Main St. stop of the Sky Train. Gazing on everything from asteroids to zephyrs, you will find yourself delightfully sucked into this celluloid wonderland. The 27m sphere is the largest, most technologically advanced theatre in the world. **Science World** also features more tangible hands-on exhibits for children. (Admission to both attractions $11, seniors and children $7. Admission to only Science World $7 and $4.50. Tickets for the Omnimax alone can be purchased after 4pm for $9. Shows Sun.-Fri. 10am-5pm, Sat. 10am-9pm. Call 875-6664 for details.)

One block south of Chinatown on Main St. at 777 S. Pacific Blvd. is the domed **BC Place Stadium.** Vancouver's so-called "mushroom in bondage" is home to the Canadian Football League's BC Lions. Don't miss the **Terry Fox Memorial** at the entrance to the stadium, erected in honor of the Canadian hero who, after losing a leg to cancer, ran 3318 mi. across Canada to raise money for medical research. Because of his efforts, a nation of only 26 million people raised over $30 million (that's more than $1.15 per Canuck). A few blocks to the north, at 8 W. Penter St., is squeezed the **world's skinniest building**. In 1912, the city expropriated all but six feet of Chang Toy's land in order to expand the street. In a fit of stubbornness, he decided to build on the land anyhow. Currently, the 100 ft. by 6 ft. building is home to Jack Chow's Insurance Company, which might well operate on a very slim profit margin.

Newly renovated, the **Lookout!** at 555 W. Hastings St. (649-0421), offers fantastic 360° views of the city. Tickets are expensive!, but they're good for the whole day ($5.35!, seniors and students $3.75!); after passing a pleasant and panoramic afternoon there, you can leave and come back for the romantic night skyline (open daily 8:30am-10:30pm; 50% discount with HI membership or receipt from the Vancouver International Hostel).

The **Vancouver Art Gallery,** 750 Hornby St. (682-5621), in Robson Sq., has a small but well-presented collection of classical and contemporary art and photography. An entire floor devoted to the works of Canadian artists features British Columbian **Emily Carr's** surreal paintings of trees and totem poles. The Gallery compensates for its limited holdings with innovative exhibitions. Free tours are frequently given for large groups; just tag along. (Open Mon.-Wed. and Fri.-Sat. 10am-5pm, Thurs. 10am-9pm, Sun. noon-5pm. Admission $4.75, seniors and students $2.50. Thurs. 5-9pm free, but donations requested.)

Gastown and Chinatown

Gastown is a revitalized turn-of-the-century district viewed with disdain by most locals as an expensive tourist trap. The area is named for "Gassy Jack" Deighton, the glib con man who opened Vancouver's first saloon here in 1867. His statue now stands at the confluence of Water, Powell, and Alexander St. In 1886, a fire leveled 1000 buildings, including the infamous saloon, in 45 minutes. In the 1960s, community groups led the fight for restoration. Today the area overflows with tourist-oriented craft shops, nightclubs, restaurants, and boutiques. Take the time to stroll along **Water Street,** and stop to listen to the steam-powered clock on the corner of

Cambie St. It's the first one in the world, the only one on the continent, and it eerily whistles the notes of the Westminster Chimes on the quarter hour.

Gastown is a fairly long walk from downtown or a short ride on bus #22 along Burrard St. to Carrall St. It is bordered by Richards St. to the west, Columbia St. to the east, Hastings St. to the south, and the waterfront to the north.

Chinatown, just east of Gastown, is within walking distance of downtown. You can also take bus #22 on Burrard St. northbound to Pender and Carrall St., and return by bus #22 westbound on Pender St. The area is rundown and unsafe by some standards. At night, women walking alone should exercise particular caution. A safer—albeit expensive—way to see this area is through Gray Line Tours (see Practical Information).

Parks

Stanley Park

Founded in 1889, the 1000-acre **Stanley Park,** at the westernmost end of the center peninsula, is testament to the foresight of Vancouver's urban planners. Surrounded by a seawall promenade, the thickly wooded park is crisscrossed with cycling and hiking trails and remains one of the city's most alluring sites. Within the boundaries of the park are occasional restaurants, tennis courts, the **Malkin Bowl** (an outdoor theater), and fully equipped swimming beaches. The **Brockton Oval,** located on the park's small eastern peninsula of Brockton Point, is a cinder running track, with hot showers and changing rooms. Nature walks are given May-Sept. Tues. at 10am and July-Aug. at 7pm. They start from the Lost Lagoon bus loop (in the morning in May, June, and Sept.) or from Lumberman's Arch Water Park (all other times). **Lost Lagoon,** an artificial lake next to the Georgia St. entrance, bristles with a number of fish and bird varieties, including the rare trumpeter swan. Other exotic aquatic species pace within their glass habitats at the **Vancouver Aquarium** (682-1118), on the eastern side of the park not far from the entrance. The British Columbian, Tropical, and Amazonian Halls are named for the geographical climes they skillfully replicate. The marine mammal complex features orca and Beluga whales in a sideshow revue. Weather permitting, the aquarium stages several performances per day; on rainy days, you'll have to settle for fish flicks. (Open daily 9:30am-8pm. Admission $9.50, senior citizens and students $8.25, under 12 $6.25.) Stanley Park's small and crowded, but free, **zoo** next door is worth visiting just to see the maniacal monkeys taunt the poor polar bears next door. In the future, the zoo plans to phase out exotic species and replace them with fauna indigenous to the region (open daily 9:30am-dusk). Without a doubt, the best way to see the park is on bike (see Bike Rental under Practical Information). If you don't feel like biking or hoofing your way around, horse-drawn carriages will take you on a 50-minute tour (every ½ hr., daily 11am-4pm, $10). Call 681-5115 for more information.

Vanier Park

During the summer, a tiny **ferry** (684-7781) carries passengers from the Aquatic Centre across False Creek to Vanier (pronounced Van-YAY) Park and the museum complex located there. (Ferries daily, every 15 min. 10am-8pm. Fare $1.25, youth 50¢.) Another ferry runs from the Maritime Museum in Vanier Park to Granville Island ($2.50). Vanier Park can also be reached by bus #22, heading south on Burrard St. from downtown. Once you reach the park, visit the circular **Vancouver Museum,** 1100 Chestnut St. (736-4431), fronted by an abstract crab fountain. The museum displays artifacts from Native American cultures in the Pacific Northwest and several rotating exhibits. (Open June-Aug. 10am-9pm daily, Sept.-May Tues.-Sun. 10am-5pm. Admission $5, students, seniors, and kids under 18 $2.50, families $10.) The museum also sponsors dance performances and workshops during the summer.

Housed in the same building, the **H. R. MacMillan Planetarium** (736-4431) runs up to four different star shows per day. Laser shows set to rock music illuminate the roof Tues.-Sun. (Star shows $5, laser shows $7, senior citizens free on Tues.; call for showtimes and programs.) The adjacent **Gordon Southam Observatory** is also open to the public, weather permitting. (Open Fri. 7-11pm, Sat.-Sun. noon-5pm and 7-11pm. Call ahead at 738-2855 to check times. Free.)

The **Maritime Museum** (737-2211) is also part of the complex in Vanier Park. The museum exhibits photographs and models that trace the growth of Vancouver's harbor and port. An exception to the otherwise pacific atmosphere is the well-restored *St. Roch*. This 1928 Royal Canadian Mounted Police Arctic patrol service vessel gained its fame during WWII, when it became the first ship to negotiate the Northwest Passage through the Arctic. The boat is displayed in its hulking entirety, and guided tours of its Leviathan hull are given daily. (Open daily 10am-5pm. Admission $5, senior citizens, students, and under 13 $2.50, families $10. Tues. free for seniors. Combination tickets to the Maritime Museum, Vancouver Museum, and Planetarium available.) The Maritime Museum displays more wooden boats in the **Heritage Harbour.** You can wander free of charge here at any hour, day or night. The museum holds a "shanty sing" on the dock every Wednesday evening in the summer.

More Parks

Another adored city park in Vancouver is the **Van Dusen Botanical Garden,** 37th Ave. and Oak St. (266-7194). Take bus #17 from Granville Mall. Floral collections in the 55-acre park range from a Sino-Himalayan garden to a growth of heather to an indoor exhibit of Japanese bonsai trees. The garden is also the site of summer concerts and craft shows, as well as special days for senior citizens and people with disabilities. (Open daily 10am-9pm; in winter 10am-4pm. Admission $4.50, seniors and children $2.25, families $9.)

Only a few blocks away, **Queen Elizabeth Park,** at 33rd Ave. and Cambie St. (872-5513), has metamorphosed from a quarry into an ornamental sunken garden. Take bus #15 from Burrard St. Atop the hill, the **Bloedel Conservatory** gathers a spray of tropical plants and birds together into a geodesic dome overlooking the city center. (Open daily 10am-8pm; in winter daily 10am-5pm. Admission $2.85, senior citizens and ages 6-18 $1.40.)

The **Dr. Sun Yat-Sen Classical Chinese Garden,** 578 Carrall St. (689-7133), is yet another escape from urban bustle. Designed and built by artisans brought to Vancouver from China, the garden brandishes many imported plantings and carvings. (Open daily 10:30am-4pm. Admission $3.50, senior citizens, students, and children $2.50, families $7.)

Beaches

Most of Vancouver's beaches are patrolled by lifeguards from Victoria Day (late May) to Labor Day daily from 11:30am to 9pm. Even if you don't dip a foot in the cold northern Pacific, you can frolic in true West Coast spirit by participating in Sport BC's weekly **Volleyball Tournament,** featuring all levels of competition. Scare up a team at the hostel, then call 737-3096 to find out where to go to make your opponents eat leather.

For a large city, Vancouver has a remarkably large collection of bacteria- and medical waste-free beaches. Follow the western side of the Stanley Park seawall south to **Sunset Beach Park** (738-8535), a strip of grass and beach that extends all the way to the Burrard Bridge. At the southern end of Sunset Beach is the **Aquatic Centre,** 1050 Beach Ave. (665-3424), a public facility with a 50m indoor saltwater pool, sauna, gymnasium, and diving tank. (Open Mon.-Thurs. 7am-10pm, Sat. 8am-9pm, Sun. 11am-9pm; pool opens Mon.-Thurs. at 7am. Gym use $3.20, pool use $2.85.)

Kitsilano Beach (731-0011), known to Vancouverites as "Kits," on the other side of Arbutus St. from Vanier, is a local favorite. Its heated outdoor saltwater pool has lockers and a snack bar. (Pool open June.-Sept. Mon.-Fri. 9am-8:30pm, Sat.-Sun. 10am-8:30pm. Admission $3, senior citizens $1.50, children $2.)

Jericho Beach, to the west, tends to be less heavily used than Kits Beach, though it harbors the massive youth hostel (see Accommodations) and has free showers. North Marine Dr. runs along the beach, and a great cycling path at the edge of the road leads up to the westernmost edge of the UBC campus. Bike and hiking trails cut through the campus and crop its edges. From the UBC entrance, several marked trails lead down to the unsupervised **Wreck Beach**.

Universities

The high point of a visit to the **University of British Columbia (UBC)** is the university's **Museum of Anthropology,** 6393 NW Marine Dr. (822-3825 for a recording, 822-5087 for an operator). To reach the campus, take bus #4 or 10 from Granville. A high-ceilinged glass and concrete building provides a dramatic setting for the museum's totems and other massive sculptures crafted by the Native Americans of the Pacific Northwest coast. The *Guide to the UBC Museum of Anthropology* ($1), available at the entrance desk, sorts out the cultural threads of the various nations that produced these works; much of this information does not appear on exhibit labels. Hour-long guided walks will help you find your way through the maze of times and places. (Open Tues. 11am-9pm, Wed.-Sun. 11am-5pm. Admission $5, seniors and students $2.50, under 6 free. Tues. after 5pm free.)

Behind the museum, in a weedy courtyard designed to simulate the Pacific coastal islands, the **Outdoor Exhibit** displays memorial totems and a mortuary house built by the Haida nation. Each carved figure represents one aspect of the ancestral heritage of the honored dead. Even if you don't make it inside the museum itself, don't miss this silent soliloquy of the Haida culture.

Caretakers of the **Nitobe Memorial Garden** (822-4208), to the south of the museum across Marine Dr., have fashioned a small immaculate garden in traditional Japanese style. (Open daily 10am-8pm; Sept.-June 10am-3pm. Admission $2, senior citizens and students $1.25. Wed. free.) The **Asian Centre,** 1871 West Mall (822-2746), near the gardens, often showcases free exhibits of Asian-Canadian art. The **Asian Centre Library** contains the largest collection of Asian materials in Canada. (Open Mon.-Fri. 9am-5pm. Call for a schedule of events.)

All of UBC's gardens fall under the official rubric of the **Botanical Garden** (822-4208). The **Main Garden,** which is in the southwest corner of the campus at 16th Ave. and SW Marine Dr., may not be worth the bother, especially to the non-horticulturist. Although pebbles outnumber pistils, the **Physick Gardens** are fascinating; signs alert you to the poisonous nature of some of the plants. In the 30-acre **Asian Garden,** through the tunnel and across the street, quiet paths lead past blue Himalayan poppies and rhododendrons. For more specific information, as well as general and tour information on all the gardens, you can call the Botanical Garden office weekdays 8:30am-4:30pm. (Open daily 10am-6pm. Admission $3.75, students and seniors $1.50. Wed. free.)

Large maps at entrances to UBC's campus indicate other points of interest and bus stops. In addition to its gardens, UBC also has a public swimming pool in the **Aquatic Centre** (822-4521), a free **Fine Arts Gallery** (822-2759), free daytime and evening concerts (822-3113), and a museum of geology (822-5586). (Museums and pool open Mon.-Fri. 8:30am-4:30pm.) To arrange a walking **tour** of the campus between May and August, call 822-3131.

Vancouver's other major academy is the relatively new and somewhat isolated **Simon Fraser University (SFU).** Built in 1965, the campus blends architecture and landscaping with soothing results; the **Main Mall** and **Academic Quadrangle** alone are worth the 35-minute bus ride to the top of "the hill." Take bus #10 or 14 to Kootenay Loop, then the #135-SFU. The **Athletic Services Department** (291-3611) can fill you in on the details of using the university's gyms and pools, and the **Outdoor Recreation Office** (291-4434; open Mon.-Fri. 10am-4pm) will give you maps for the numerous hiking trails around the campus. Free **walking tours** leave the

Administration Bldg. every hour on the half-hour daily 10:30am-3:30pm. Call 291-3439 or 291-3210 for more information.

The Pub in the Main Mall at SFU has the cheapest beer on the lower mainland, as well as a great atmosphere. (Open Mon.-Fri. 9pm-midnight, Sat.-Sun. 9pm-4am.) To find out what else is happening around campus, grab the free weekly *The Peak,* which includes an extensive arts section on city happenings, in drop-boxes scattered around campus.

Shopping

Granville Mall, on Granville Ave. between Smithe and Hastings St., is one of the few open-air pedestrian malls in Vancouver. Vehicles other than buses are prohibited. From Hastings St. to the Orpheum Theatre, most shops and restaurants on the mall cater to young professionals and business executives on their power-lunch hours. Beyond W. Georgia St., the mall takes a much-needed adolescent twist as expensive department stores defer to theaters, leather shops, and raucous record stores.

A few blocks to the west, the **Harbour Centre,** 555 W. Hastings St., flaunts a mall with distinctly non-budget restaurants, and a fantastic **skylift** which provides uplifting views of the cityscape. (See Sights and Activities: Downtown.) If you are dying to fill your matching luggage set with chic purchases, head to the ritziest mall west of Long Island: the **Park Royal Shopping Centre** on Marine Dr. in West Vancouver. Take bus #250, 251, or 252 on Georgia St. downtown. Graced with pseudo-European delicatessens and shops, the **Robsonstrasse** shopping district, on Robson St. between Howe and Broughton St., inveigles patrons to throw around their money under kaleidoscopic awnings. The recently renovated **Pacific Centre,** 700 W. Georgia St., is located at the Granville SkyTrain station. For more reasonable prices and "idiosyncratic" offerings, stroll down Commercial Dr. for funky stuff, or browse through the numerous boutiques and second-hand clothing stores lining 4th Ave. and Broadway between Burrard and Alma.

ENTERTAINMENT

To keep abreast of the entertainment scene, pick up a copy of the weekly *Georgia Straight* (an allusion to the body of water between mainland BC and Vancouver Island) or the new monthly *AF Magazine,* both free at newsstands and record stores. The 25¢ *West Ender* lists entertainment in that lively neighborhood and also reports on community issues, while the free *Angles* serves the city's growing gay readership. Believers in the New Age should peruse the free *Common Ground,* a quarterly with listings and advertisements for restaurants, services, events, bookstores, and workshops. Music of all genres can be heard in Vancouver's pubs and clubs; both *Georgia Straight* and the less-thorough *West Ender* have the rundown. Unfortunately, most clubs and bars shut down at 2am.

The Fringe Cafe, 3124 W. Broadway (738-6977). Hip, working-class crowd mixes with UBC students to create one of the hottest bars in town. Open Sun.-Thurs. noon-midnight, Fri.-Sat. noon-2am.

The Arts Club Lounge, Granville Island (687-1354). Sophisté divas frequent this bar between rehearsals and performances at the theatre. Have a mixed drink ($4.25) on the terrace overlooking False Creek. Live music (with a $4 cover) Wed., Fri., and Sat. nights. Open daily noon-2am.

Graceland, 1250 Richards St. (688-2648). Warehouse space pulses to house music on Fri. and Sat. nights, reggae on Wed. Open Mon.-Fri. 9pm-2am, Sat. 8:30pm-2am, Sun. 8pm-2am.

Celebrities, 1022 Davie St. (689-3180). Very big, very hot, and very popular with Vancouver's gay community. Sun. features techno music, Mon. spins classic disco. Open Mon.-Sat. 9pm-2am, Sun. 9pm-midnight.

Luv-A-fair, 1275 Seymour St. (685-3288). Trendy dance space pipes alternative music into the ears of black-clad clubsters. Experiment with the live underground bands Wed. night.

Basin St. Cabaret, 23 West Cordova St. (688-5351). Bluesy jazz nightly. Local talent who play "cause they love the music" jam til the small hours. With cheap beer (pint $3, glass $1.50), a dance floor, and a terrace over the back alley—this new club is one of the hippest in Vancouver. No cover. Open daily 9pm-2am.

Spats, 1222 Hamilton St. (684-7321), in the warehouse district. Enter on the side facing Pacific Blvd. Most innovative of the dozen gay and lesbian clubs in the city. Open Mon.-Sat. 9pm-2am.

The **Vancouver Symphony Orchestra (VSO)** plays in the refurbished **Orpheum Theater,** 884 Granville St. (280-4444). The VSO ticketline is 280-3311. The 52-year-old **Vancouver Bach Choir** (921-8012) sometimes performs with the VSO in the Orpheum. Smaller groups, such as the Warblin' Rosen Trio, appeal to a variety of musical tastes—check the *West Ender* for listings.

Robson Square Conference Centre, 800 Robson St. (660-2487), sponsors events almost daily during the summer and weekly the rest of the year, either on the plaza at the square or in the Centre itself. Their concerts, theater productions, exhibits, lectures, symposia, and films are all free or nearly free. The Centre's monthly brochure *What's Happening at Robson Square* is available from the visitors bureau (see Practical Information) or establishments in the square.

Vancouver has an active theater community. The **Arts Club Theatre** (687-1644) hosts big-name theater and musicals, and the **Theatre in the Park** program (687-0174 for ticket information), in Stanley Park's Malkin Bowl, puts on a summer season of musical comedy. The annual **Vancouver Shakespeare Festival** (734-0194; June-Aug. in Vanier Park) often needs volunteer ticket-takers and program-sellers, who work in return for free admission to the critically acclaimed shows. **UBC Summer Stock** (822-2678) puts on four plays during the summer at the Frederick Wood Theatre.

The **Ridge Theatre,** 16th Ave. and Arbutus (738-6311), often shows European films and works that more commercial theaters may bypass ($6). The **Hollywood Theatre,** 3123 W. Broadway (738-3211), also runs some art films. (Tickets Mon. $2.25, Tues.-Sun. $3.25. Doors open at 7pm.) **Cinema Simon Fraser,** Images Theatre, SFU (291-4869), charges $2.50 for a variety of films (open Sept.-May). The **Paradise,** 919 Granville (681-1732), shows double features of first-run movies (triple features on weekends) for $2.50.

Cultural activities at Vancouver's universities never cease. The **SFU Centre for the Arts** (291-3514) offers both student and guest-professional theater, primarily from September to May. For **UBC's** activities, call Public Events Information at 822-3131 or pick up a free copy of *Ubyssey.* UBC's film series (228-3698) screens high-quality flicks on Thursday and Friday nights for $2.50.

SEASONAL EVENTS

Attend one of Vancouver's annual fairs, festivals, or celebrations to confirm rumors of the city's cosmopolitan nature. The famed **Vancouver Folk Music Festival** is held in mid-July in Jericho Park. For three days the best acoustic performers in North America give concerts and workshops. Tickets can be purchased for each day or for the whole weekend. (Tickets $26 per evening, $37 for the whole day.) Buy a whole-weekend ticket before Christmas and pay last year's price; early-birds who purchase their tickets before mid-June receive a substantial discount. For more details, contact the festival at 3271 Main St., Vancouver V6V 3M6 (879-2931).

The annual **Du Maurier International Jazz Festival Vancouver** (682-0706) in the third week of June features over five hundred performers and bands like Randy Wanless's Fab Forty and Charles Eliot's Largely Cookie. The 10-day festival is hot. Call 682-0706 or write to 435 W. Hastings, Vancouver V6V 1L4 for details. Ask about the free concerts at the Plaza, in Gastown, and on Granville Island.

Vancouver's Chinese community fetes its heritage on **Chinese New Year** (usually early to mid-Feb.). Fireworks, music, parades, and dragons highlight the celebration. The **Folkfest** (736-1512) in early June features two weeks of multicultural merriness in Gastown and Robson Sq. All the festivities are free. Italians and Greeks whoop it up in July and the last week of June, respectively. Food stands, musical performers, carnivals, and more food stands cluster around each community's center.

Vancouver celebrates its relationship with the sea several times per year. The Vancouver Maritime Museum in Vanier Park (see Sights and Activities) hosts the annual **Captain Vancouver Day** (737-2211) in mid-June to commemorate the 1792 exploration of Canada's west coast by Captain George Vancouver. Thrills include free tours of the Heritage Harbor, tall ships, boat model building, sled dog rides, and appearances by the **Shanty Singers.** In mid-July, the **Vancouver Sea Festival** (684-3378) schedules four days of parades, concerts, sporting events, fireworks, and salmon barbecues. All events take place in English Bay at the BC Enterprise complex and are free, but you have to pay for the salmon. The headline attraction is the notorious **Nanaimo to Vancouver Bathtub Race,** a journey across the rough waters of the Strait of Georgia for Gilgameshes with rubber duckies (see Central and North Vancouver Island: Nanaimo, above).

■ Near Vancouver

North of the City

For an easy hike that still offers fantastic views of the city, head for **Lynn Canyon Park** in the district of North Vancouver. The suspension bridge here is free and uncrowded, unlike its more publicized twin in Capilano Canyon. Often called a rip-off by Vancouverites, a walk across the "world's longest suspension footbridge" in Capilano will cost the gullible tourist $4.50. Try Lynn instead. Take bus #228 from the North Vancouver SeaBus terminal and walk the 0.5km to the bridge. While there, take in the concise exhibits of the **Lynn Canyon Ecology Centre** (987-5922; open daily 10am-5pm, closed weekends Dec.-Jan.; free).

Grouse Mountain is the ski resort closest to downtown Vancouver and has the crowds to prove it. Take bus #246 from the North Vancouver SeaBus terminal; at Edgemont and Ridgewood transfer to bus #232, which will drop you off at the **Supersky Ride,** an aerial tramway. (Tram runs from 9am to 10pm. Adults $14.50, students $12.50.) The slopes are lit until 10:30pm from November to May, and the tram ride is popular with sightseers in summer. On sunny days, helicopter tours leave from the top of the mountain, starting at $30 per person. For more information contact Grouse Mountain Resorts, 6400 Nancy Greene Way, North Vancouver V7R 4K9 (984-0661, ski report 986-6262). Ski rental is $21 per day, no deposit required. Adult lift tickets are $28.

For a secluded and esoteric park, head out across the Lions Gate Bridge from Stanley Park along North Marine Dr. to **Lighthouse Park.** Getting there makes for a fantastic and challenging bicycle daytrip; it's a 50km round-trip from downtown, and the inclines can be daunting. This is not for puny pedalers. Bus #250 from downtown will take you right to the park's entrance. From there, numerous trails with peaceful water views will take you all over the 185-acre preserve. The point is preponderated by one of the few remaining human-operated lighthouses, and free guided tours (the only way you can get to the top) ascend on the hour (Wed.-Sun. 11am-5pm).

Puff along on the **Royal Hudson Steam Locomotive** (688-7246), operated by BC Rail. After a two-hour journey along the coast from Vancouver to Squamish (the gateway to Garibaldi Provincial Park), passengers are loosed for 90 minutes to browse in town before they head back. (Excursions June-Sept. 20 Wed.-Sun. Fare $26.65, senior citizens and ages 12-18 $22.45, ages 5-11 $16.55.) The train departs from the BC Rail terminal, 1311 W. 1st St., across the Lions Gate Bridge in North Vancouver. Reservations are required.

52km north of Vancouver (on the way to Whistler) is the **BC Museum of Mining** in Britannia Beach (688-8735 or 896-2233). An electric mine train pumps passengers through an old copper artery into the mountain that poured out the most metal in the British empire: 1.3 billion pounds. (Open mid-May to June Wed.-Sun. 10am-5pm; July-Labor Day daily 10am-5pm; Sept. to mid-Oct. Weds.-Sun. 10am-4pm. Admission seniors $8, students $6, students $5, children under 5 free, families $22; pre-booked $1 off.)

Whistler lies about 110km north of Vancouver on Hwy. 99. Expensive development projects have shaken the peaceful foundation of this ski resort town. It seems that only the beautiful hostel allows Whistler to remain on the budget-skiers' itinerary. **Whistler Hostel (HI-C),** 5678 Alta Lake Rd. (932-5492), is a timber cabin with a kitchen, wood stove, sauna, ski tuning room, and ski lockers. They offer free use of their canoes in Alta Lake (i.e. the backyard). (Check-in 8-10am and 5-10pm; $13.50. Reservations advised Nov.-March.) Outfitters in town have mountain bikes, canoes, kayaks, and ski equipment for rent. For those seeking some solitude, hiking in nearby **Garibaldi Provincial Park** is an option to explore. **B.C. Rail** stops at Whistler on its route from Vancouver and will stop at the hostel if requested.

East of the City

To the east, the town of **Deep Cove** maintains the salty atmosphere of a fishing village. Sea otters and seals cavort on the pleasant Indian Arm beaches. Take bus #210 from Pender St. to the Phibbs Exchange on the north side of Second Narrows Bridge. From there, take bus #211 or 212. **Cates Park,** at the end of Dollarton Hwy. on the way to Deep Cove, has popular swimming and scuba waters and is a good destination for a day bike trip out of Vancouver. Bus #211 also leads to **Mount Seymour Provincial Park.** Trails leave from Mt. Seymour Rd., and a paved road winds the 8km to the top. One hundred campsites ($8 per site) are available, and the skiing is superb.

South of the City

The **Reifel Bird Sanctuary** on Westham Island, 16km south of Vancouver, is just northwest of the Tsawwassen ferry terminal. Bus #601 from Vancouver will take you to the town of **Ladner,** 1½km east of the sanctuary. Two-hundred forty species of birds live in the 850 acres of marshlands, and spotting towers are set up for long-term birdwatching. (Open daily 9am-4pm; nominal fee $3.25, seniors and children $1.) For information contact the **BC Waterfowl Society** at 946-6980.

VANCOUVER ISLAND

Named after Captain George Vancouver, the first white man to circumnavigate the island (he did it accidentally in 1787 while looking for passage to China), Vancouver Island stretches almost 500km along continental Canada's southwest coast, and is one of only two points in Canada which extends south of the 49th parallel (London, Ont. is the other). The cultural and administrative capital of the island is Victoria, located on its extreme southern tip. Victorians are forthright about their British roots, and the city basks in English charm.

Vancouver Island is like New York State: there's the big city—Victoria—and then there's the rest. But while "the rest" may be culturally dwarfish from an urban perspective, it is in actuality much bigger than the "big city," and much less expensive. The Trans-Canada Hwy., approaching the end of its 8000km trek, leads north from Victoria to Nanaimo, the social hub of the central region. Nanaimo's heritage combines aspects of Native American culture and Welsh coal-miner society, with a dash of Anglo-Canadian pastry chefs' cooking thrown in. Beyond Nanaimo, the towns shrink in size. Port Alberni, at the tip of the Alberni Inlet, and Campbell River, along Hwy. 19, are homebases for sublime hiking and fishing—some of the world's largest salmon have met their smoker here. Campbell River guards the entrance to triangle-shaped Strathcona Provincial Park. Hornby Island, off the island's eastern side, is a

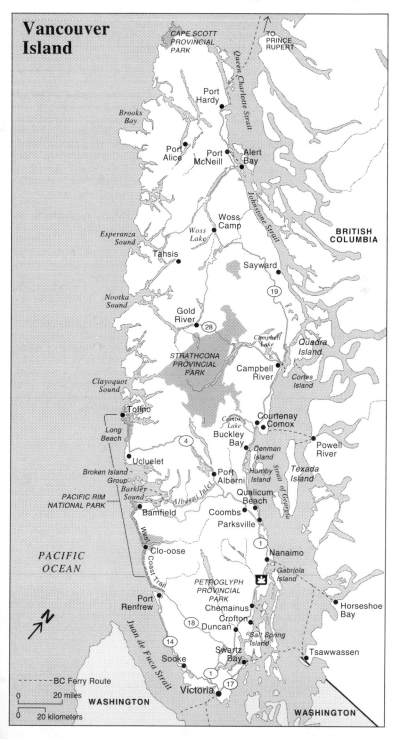

Vancouver Island

CAPE SCOTT
PROVINCIAL
PARK

TO
PRINCE
RUPERT

Queen Charlotte Strait

Brooks
Bay

Port
Hardy

Port
Alice

Port
McNeill

Alert
Bay

Johnstone Strait

BRITISH
COLUMBIA

Woss
Camp

Esperanza
Sound

Woss
Lake

Tahsis

Sayward

(19)

Nootka
Sound

Gold
River

(28)

Campbell
Lake

Quadra
Island

STRATHCONA
PROVINCIAL
PARK

Campbell
River

Cortes
Island

Clayoquot
Sound

Tofino

Comox
Lake

Courtenay
Comox

Long
Beach

(4)

Buckley
Bay

Powell
River

Ucluelet

Denman
Island

Broken Island
Group

Barkley
Sound

Port
Alberni

Homby
Island

Texada
Island

PACIFIC RIM
NATIONAL PARK

Qualicum
Beach

Strait of Georgia

Alberni Inlet

Bamfield

Coombs

Parksville

(1)

PACIFIC
OCEAN

West Coast Trail

Clo-oose

Nanaimo

Gabriola
Island

PETROGLYPH
PROVINCIAL
PARK

Chemainus

Horseshoe
Bay

Port
Renfrew

Crofton

Duncan

(18)

Salt Spring
Island

(14)

Swartz
Bay

Tsawwassen

Sooke

Juan de Fuca Strait

(1)

(17)

------- BC Ferry Route

0   20 miles

Victoria

0   20 kilometers

WASHINGTON

WASHINGTON

VICTORIA

remarkable post-hippie settlement. Continuing along Rte. 19 into the northern third of Vancouver Island—known to the residents as "North Island"—residents shift from Peugeots to pickups, Bacardi to Black Label, crumpets to clamburgers.

■■■ VICTORIA

The sun may have set on the British empire years ago, but like an aging, eccentric Redcoat, Victoria still dresses up and marches to the beat of a bygone era. Set among the rough-hewn logging and fishing towns of Vancouver Island, this jeweled capital city of British Columbia evinces enough reserve and propriety to chill even the Windsors. A walk along the Inner Harbour barrages the traveler with all the charms of London. Tourist-filled double-decker buses, festively decorated with the Union Jack, meander through the streets (albeit on the right side of the road). Decked in kilt and sporran, a bagpiper plies his street trade at the corner of the Parliament Buildings, stately stone edifices which measure up to the standard of Westminster. The ivy-shawled Empress Hotel, also named for the dour queen, gazes regally at its own image in the water. On warm summer days, Anglophilic residents sip their noon teas on the lawns of Tudor-style homes in the suburbs, while downtown, horse-drawn carriages clatter through the streets.

Despite Victoria's refined modern-day image, today's citizens are not at all ashamed of the ornery prospectors who swilled beer in front of the town's rowdy brothels on their way to the Cariboo mines during the 1858 gold rush. The Hudson's Bay Company moved its western headquarters to the southern tip of Vancouver Island because the site of its former headquarters in Astoria, Oregon was declared U.S. property. When the Canadian Pacific Railway reached the Pacific Coast, Victoria managed to tease out an additional stretch across the Strait of Juan de Fuca from Vancouver, and the city stole Vancouver's distinction as Canada's western railroad terminus. In 1869, Victoria was named the capital of British Columbia, partially on the assumption that the promised railroad would cause the city to explode into a booming metropolis. The railroad pipe-dream was never fully realized, however, and Victoria did not undergo industrialization as expected—much to its own benefit. Instead of pollution and ugly factory chimneys, Victoria has 250,000 well-heeled citizens who delight in the blessedly un-British annual rainfall of only 27 in. per year.

PRACTICAL INFORMATION AND ORIENTATION

Visitors Information: Tourism Victoria, 812 Wharf St., Victoria V8W 1T3 (382-2127), in the Inner Harbour. An unbelievable number of pamphlets on the area. Open daily 9am-9pm; winter daily 9am-5pm.

VIA Rail, 450 Pandora St. (383-4324 for departure/arrival information; 800-561-8630 for general information and tickets). Near the Inner Harbour.

Bus Service: Pacific Coast Lines (PCL) and its affiliate **Island Coach Lines,** 700 Douglas St. at Belleville (385-4411). Connects all major points and most minor ones, though fares can be steep. To: Nanaimo (7 per day, $14.70), Vancouver (8 per day,$20.75), Seattle (daily 10am, $28.60). Lockers $2 per 24 hr.

Greyhound Information, 700 Douglas St., at Belleville St. (388-5248), in the bus depot. This is an information and ticketing booth only, as Greyhound offers no service on the island or to Vancouver. Buses run exclusively out of the Vancouver terminal (see Vancouver).

BC Ferry, 656-0757 for a recording, 386-3431 for an operator. Between Swartz Bay (Victoria) and Tsawwassen (Vancouver), 20 per day 5:30am-10pm ($6.50, bike $2.50, car $20). Between Tsawwassen and Nanaimo (north Vancouver Island), 10 per day 7am-9pm, same rates. Take bus #70 ($2) to reach the ferry terminal.

Washington State Ferries, 381-1551. From Sidney, BC to Anacortes, WA, via the San Juan Islands: 2 per day in summer, 1 per day in winter. Buy your ticket straight through to Anacortes and stop over in the San Juans for as long as you like; you can rejoin the ferry at any point for no charge as long as you continue

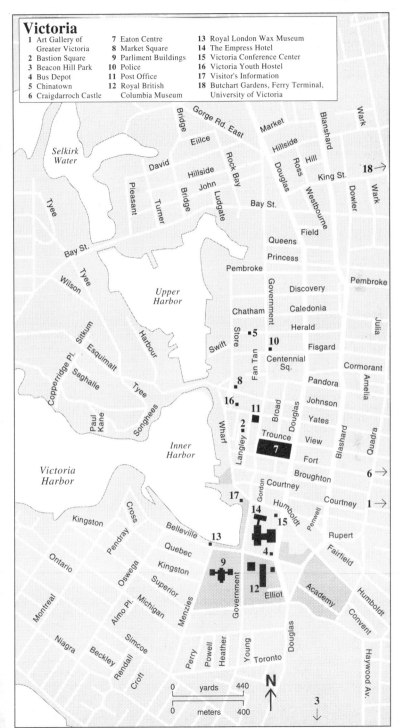

Victoria

1 Art Gallery of
   Greater Victoria
2 Bastion Square
3 Beacon Hill Park
4 Bus Depot
5 Chinatown
6 Craigdarroch Castle

7 Eaton Centre
8 Market Square
9 Parliment Buildings
10 Police
11 Post Office
12 Royal British
    Columbia Museum

13 Royal London Wax Museum
14 The Empress Hotel
15 Victoria Conference Center
16 Victoria Youth Hostel
17 Visitor's Information
18 Butchart Gardens, Ferry Terminal,
    University of Victoria

VICTORIA

traveling eastward (see the San Juan Islands section for more detail). Fare $6, over 64 and 5-11 $4, under 5 free; car and driver $31.25 ($26 off-season). Vehicle reservations for travel from Sidney to Anacortes are recommended June 14-Sept. 19 (call 206-464-6400 a day in advance). Fares vary by season (call for exact rates and schedules). Take bus #70 ($1.75) to reach the ferry terminal.

Victoria Clipper, 1000-A Wharf St. (382-8100). The only direct ferry service from Victoria to Seattle. April 15-June 5, 2 per day; June 6-Sept. 27, 4 per day; Sept. 28-Dec., 1 per day. Fares vary by season: one way $46-52, round-trip $74-85.

Black Ball Transport, 430 Belleville St. (386-2202). Connects Victoria with Port Angeles, WA. Mid-May to late-Sept., 4 per day; early-Oct. to late-Nov. and mid-March to mid-May, 2 per day; Dec. to mid-March, 1 per day. Fare $6.80, car and driver $27.80, ages 5-11 $3.40. Off-season fare $6, car and driver $24.

Victoria Regional Transit: 382-6161.

Car Rental: Sigmar Rent-A-Car, 752 Caledonia Ave. (388-6686). $19-24 per day plus 10¢ per km. Must be 21 with a major credit card. Open Mon.-Sat. 8am-5pm. **Budget Discount Car Rentals,** 727 Courtney St. (388-7874). (Not to be confused with the far more expensive Budget Rent-A-Car on the same block.) Must be 19 with a major credit card. Used cars in excellent condition from $22 per day plus 10¢ per km. Open daily 7:30am-5:30pm.

Canadian Automobile Association, 1075 Pandora (389-6700). Offers full range of services for AAA members. Open Mon.-Sat. 9am-5pm.

Taxi: Victoria Taxi, 383-7111. **Westwind,** 474-4747.

Bike Rental: Biker Bill's, 1007 Langley St. (361-0091). 18-speed mountain bikes $5 per hr., $20 for 24 hr. Lock and helmet included. Deposit required. Open daily 8am-8pm. **Harbour Scooter,** 843 Douglas St. (384-2133). Mountain bikes $5 per hr., $15 per day. Lock and helmet included. Open daily 9am-6pm.

Scooter Rentals: Harbour Scooters (see above). $5 per hr., $25 per day.

Camping Supplies and Rentals: Jeune Brothers, 570 Johnson St. (386-8778). 2-person tent $25 for 3 days, $41 per week. Open Mon.-Thurs. 9:30am-6pm, Fri. 9:30am-9pm, Sat. 9:30am-5:30pm, Sun. 11am-5pm.

Library: 735 Broughton (382-7241), at Courtney. Open Mon., Wed., Fri., Sat., 9am-6pm; Tues., Thurs. 9am-9pm.

Laundromat and Showers: 812 Wharf St., 1 floor below Tourism Victoria.

Crisis Line: 386-6323. 24 hr.

Rape Crisis: 383-3232. 24 hr.

Gay and Lesbian Information: 361-4900. Volunteer staff; hours vary.

Disabilities Services: 727-7811. 8am-11:30pm.

Tourist Alert Board: 380-6136. If you need to reach someone in an emergency, this number will put a message at every tourist office in the city and at major tourist attractions.

Poison Control: 595-9211. 24 hr.

Pharmacy: London Drugs, 900 Yates St. (381-1113), at Vancouver, in the Wilson Centre. Open Mon.-Sat. 9am-10pm, Sun. 10am-8pm.

Emergency: Police/Fire 911. **Police:** 625 Fisgard at Government St. (384-4111 for non-emergency). Staff sergeant on duty 24 hr.

Post Office: Victoria CRO, 714 Yates (363-3887). Open Mon.-Fri. 8:30am-5pm. **Postal Code:** V8W 1L0.

Area Code: 604.

Ferries and buses connect Victoria to many cities in British Columbia and Washington (see Practical Information above). The city of Victoria enfolds the Inner Harbour; **Government Street** and **Douglas Street** are the main north-south thoroughfares. Traditional tourist attractions crowd this area, and locals are few and far between. Residential neighborhoods form a semicircle around the Inner Harbour, the more popular and wealthy weighting the beaches in the east. **Victoria Regional Transit** (382-6161) serves the whole city seven days per week, with major bus connections at the corner of Douglas and Yates St. downtown. Travel in the single-zone area costs $1.50, multi-zone (north to Sidney and the Butchart Gardens) $2. Daily passes for unlimited single-zone travel are available at the visitors center (see above) and 7-11 stores for $4 (ages over 65 and under 12 $3). Transit maps and a riders' guide cost 25¢ and are available wherever day passes are sold; pick up the free pamphlet Explore Victoria by Bus at the visitors center.

ACCOMMODATIONS

Victoria Youth Hostel (HI-C), 516 Yates St., Victoria V8W 1K8 (385-4511), at Wharf St. downtown. 104 beds in the newly remodeled Victoria Heritage Building. Big, modern, and spotless. Extensive kitchen and laundry facilities. Family rooms available. Open daily 7:30am-midnight. $13.50, nonmembers $18.50.

University of Victoria (721-8395), 20 min. northeast of the Inner Harbour by bus; take bus #7 or 14. Private rooms with shared baths. Coin-operated laundry machines. Register in the Housing Office, near the Coffee Gardens entrance that faces University Dr. Registration after 3pm. Singles $32.75. Doubles $47.81. Breakfast included. Reservations advisable. Open May-Aug.

Salvation Army Men's Hostel, 525 Johnson St. (384-3396), at Wharf St. Men only. Modern, immaculate, and well run on a first-come, first-sleep basis. Dorms open daily at 4pm. You need a late pass if you plan on returning after 11pm. Dorm beds $15, private rooms $19. Meals cost as follows: breakfast $1.75, lunch $2.50, dinner $3.50. Weekly room and board $133.

YWCA, 880 Courtney St. (386-7511), at Quadra, within easy walking distance of downtown. *Women only.* Heated pool and private rooms with shared baths. Check-in 8:30am-6pm. Check-out 6-11am. Singles $36.27. Doubles $53.82.

Victoria Backpackers Hostel, 1418 Fernwood Rd. (386-4471). Take buses #1, 10, 11, 14, 27, or 28 to Fernwood and Douglas. No curfew. Shared rooms $10, private $25-30.

Battery Street Guest House, 670 Battery St. (385-4632), 1 block in from the ocean between Douglas and Government St. Dutch is spoken in this spacious bed and breakfast. Non-smokers only. Singles $35-55. Doubles $55-75.

Cherry Bank Hotel, 825 Burdett Ave. (385-5380), at Blanchard. 90-year-old bed and breakfast; very traditional. Spotless rooms along winding corridors. *Trivial Pursuit* played incessantly in the lounge—they even advertise it outside. Singles from $39.50. Doubles from $46.

CAMPING

The few grounds on the city perimeter cater largely to wealthy RV drivers. Be forewarned that many campgrounds fill up in July and August; reservations are a good idea.

McDonald Park (655-9020), less than 3km south of the Swartz Bay Ferry Terminal, 30km north of downtown on Hwy. 17. Primitive sites. No showers, and no beach access. Government-run. 30 tent and RV sites.

Thetis Lake Campground, 1938 Trans-Canada Hwy. (478-3845), 10km north of the city center. Serves traffic entering Victoria from northern Vancouver Island. Sites are peaceful and removed (maybe too removed—it can be long walk to the bathroom). Metered showers and a laundromat. Sites $10 for 2 people, 50¢ per additional person. Full hookups $15.

Fort Victoria Camping, 127 Burnett (479-8112), 7km NW of downtown, off the Trans-Canada Hwy. Free hot showers. Laundromat. Sites $15 for 2 people. Full RV hookups $18.

Goldstream Park, 2930 Trans-Canada Hwy. (387-4363). Government-run, set in a deeply forested area along a river, 20km northwest of Victoria. Great short hiking trails, swimming, and fishing. In Nov., the river is crowded by salmon with a death-wish. Flush toilets and firewood available. 150 gorgeous gravelly sites ($15.50). The nearby **Freeman King Visitor Centre** relates the history of the area from the Ice Age to the welfare state. Naturalists will take you for a walk, or roam down the self-guided nature trail. Open in summer daily 8:30am-4:30pm; in winter by appointment only.

Weir's Beach Resort, 5191 William Head Rd. (478-3323), 24km west on Hwy. 14. You'll pay through your teeth for the great beach location. Metered showers and a swimming pool. Sites $13 for 2 people, plus $1 per additional person. Full hook-ups $18.

French Beach, farther west on Hwy. 14, nearly 50km out. Right on the water, park has 70 sites with pit toilets, swimming, and hiking trails. No showers. Sites $8.

FOOD

Victoria's predilection for anachronisms surfaces in its culinary customs. Victorians actually do take tea—some only on occasion, others every day. No visit to the city would be complete without participating in the ceremony at least once.

As in every big city, the ethnic diversity of Victoria is a recipe for flavorful restaurants. **Chinatown,** west of Fisgard and Government St., fills the air with exotic aromas; more Occidental offerings take over by the time you get to Wharf St. If you feel like cooking, head down to **Fisherman's Wharf,** four blocks west at the corner of Harbour and Government St., between Superior and St. Lawrence St. On summer mornings, you can buy the day's catch as it flops off the boats. For bulk food, try **Thrifty Foods** at Simcoe and Menzies, six blocks south of the Parliament buildings. (Open daily 8am-10pm.)

Eugene's, 1280 Broad St. (381-5456). Vegetarian souvlaki $3, dinners $5-7.50. *Rizogalo* or *bougatsa* is a nice change for breakfast ($2). Eugene tells take-out customers, "call when you leave and it will be ready on your arrival." Ring from a pay phone next door and freak him out. Open Mon.-Fri. 8am-8pm, Sat. 10am-8pm.

Goodies, 1005 Broad St., 2nd floor (382-2124), between Broughton and Fort. Build your own omelette for $4.45 plus 65¢ per ingredient, or choose from a list of sandwiches like the "Natural High" (mushroom, cheese and avocado $5). Tex-Mex dinners $6-8. Breakfast served until 3:30pm, $1 discount on omelettes Mon.-Fri. 7-9:30am. Open daily 7am-9pm.

Fan Tan Cafe, 549 Fisgard St. (383-1611), in Chinatown. Fan-tastic food at reasonable prices. Combo plate (chicken chow mein, chicken chop suey, and sweet and sour pork) $6. Fan-cy dinners $7-9. Open daily 10am-9pm.

Bennie's Bagelry, 132-560 Johnson St. (384-3441), between Wharf and Pandora. Whole-grain, environmentally safe, kid-tested, parent-approved bagels 65¢, with cream cheese $2.10. Sandwiches $4.25. Open Mon.-Sat. 7am-7pm, Sun. 10am-7pm.

Rising Star Bakery, 1320 Broad St. (386-2534). Giant cheese croissant, fresh out of the oven and still rising ($1). Curried lentil humble pies $2. Day-old bread $1 per loaf. Open Mon.-Sat. 7:30am-5:30pm, Sun. 8:30am-2:30pm.

Old Victoria Fish and Chips, 1316 Broad St. (380-9994). Classic Brit-style fish-and-chips joint. One-piece platter of—what else?—fish and chips $3.75. Open Mon.-Sat. 11am-7pm, Sun. noon-7pm.

Ferris' Oyster and Burger Bar, 536 Yates St. (360-1824), next to the hostel. BC smoked oysters $1.75 each. Almond tofu burger ($4.25) is a rare find; have it with sweet potato fries ($2). Open Mon. 11:30am-8pm, Tues.-Fri. 11:30am-10pm, Sat. 11:30am-11pm. HI members discount.

Cross' Deli, 1310 Douglas St. (384-2631). The deli has been around awhile; the meat is fresh. Locals pick up soup and sandwich for $3. Open Mon.-Fri. 8am-5:30pm, Sat. 8am-5pm.

Scott's Restaurant, 650 Yates St. (382-1289), at Douglas St. Real diner feel; you just *know* they serve a mean chicken à la king. "Breakfast 222" (2 hotcakes, 2 eggs, 2 sausages) will cost you $4.25. Daily dinner specials a good bet ($5.25-7). Open 24 hr.

The Blethering Place, 2250 Oak Bay Ave. (598-1413), at Monterey St. in upright Oak Bay. "Blether" is Scottish for "talk volubly and senselessly"—a fact of little relevance concerning this superb tearoom frequented by mousey elementary school teachers. Afternoon tea served with scones, Devonshire cream tarts, English trifle, muffins, and sandwiches all baked on the premises ($9). Ploughman's Lunch ($7) is a cheesier alternative. Dinners $10. Open daily 8am-9pm.

James Bay Tearoom, 332 Menzies St. at Superior (382-8282). Portraits of Queen Victoria, King George V, Chuck and Di, Winston Churchill and a royal family tree from 900 AD set the scene for regal afternoon tea ($6), daily 1-4:30pm. The place is crowded until 2:30pm. Open Mon.-Sat. 7am-9pm, Sun. 8am-9pm.

SIGHTS AND ACTIVITIES

Victoria is a small city; you can wander the **Inner Harbour,** watch the boats come in, and take in many of the city's main attractions, all on foot. The elegant residential neighborhoods and the city's parks and beaches farther out are accessible by car and public transportation.

The first stop for every visitor should be the **Royal British Columbian Museum,** 675 Belleville St. (387-3014 for a tape, 387-3701 for an operator). Arguably the best museum in Canada, it chronicles the geological, biological, and cultural history of the province and showcases detailed exhibits on logging, mining, and fishing. The extensive exhibits of Native American art, culture, and history include full-scale replicas of various forms of shelter used centuries ago. The gallery of **Totem Art** is particularly moving. **Open Ocean** is a tongue-in-cheek re-creation of the first descent in a bathysphere. (Open daily 9:30am-7pm; Oct.-April 10am-5:30pm. Admission $5; senior citizens, people with disabilities, and students with ID or HI card $3; ages 6-18 $2. Free after 5:45pm and on Mon. Oct.-Apr. Hang on to your ticket— it's good for 2 days.) Behind the museum, **Thunderbird Park** is a striking thicket of totems and longhouses, backed by the oxidized copper towers of the **Empress Hotel.**

Also on the grounds of the museum is **Helmcken House,** a Heritage Conservation building, part of which dates from 1852. Originally the home of Dr. John Helmcken, the frontier medic of Fort Victoria, the house still contains many of the family's furnishings and displays some of the doctor's medical instruments. Needlework and paintings in the house—crafted by members of the family's first Canadian-born generation—will bore all but the most hard-core domestic-history buffs (open daily 11am-5pm; admission $3.25, students $2.25).

Across the street from the front of the museum are the imposing **Parliament Buildings,** 501 Belleville St. (387-3046), home of the provincial government since 1898. The 10-story dome and Brunelleschi-esque vestibule are gilded with almost 50 oz. of gold. At night, over 300 lights line the façade, imparting the feel of a Disney-land electrical parade. Free tours leave from the main steps daily 9am to 5pm, departing every 20 minutes in summer, every hour in winter.

Just north of Fort St. on Wharf is **Bastion Square,** which earned Victorians the Vincent Massey Award for Excellence in Urban Environment in 1971. The **Maritime Museum,** 28 Bastion Sq. (385-4222), exhibits ship models, nautical instruments, and a modified 13-meter Native American canoe that shoved off from Victoria in 1901 on a daring (but ultimately doomed) trip around the world. (Open June-Aug. daily 9am-6:30pm. Admission $5, ages 12-17 $3, 6-11 $2, under 6 free.)

Around the corner on Wharf St. is the **Emily Carr Gallery,** 1107 Wharf St. (387-3080). Carr was a turn-of-the-century BC painter whose originality lay in her synthesis of British landscape conventions and Native American style. The gallery's collection includes many of her paintings of Native totems and life-styles, forged in a conscious attempt to preserve what she saw as "art treasures of a passing race." Also on display are photographs and manuscripts of other period artists, politicians, and prominent citizens. Free films on Carr's life and work show at 2:30pm. (Open Tues.-Sun. 10am-5:30pm. Admission $2, senior citizens $1.)

North on Fisgard St., the Government St. entrance to the now-tiny **Chinatown** is marked by the large "Gate of Harmonious Interest." Once a sprawling maze of streets, the area is now just as tailored as the rest of the city. Still, the great restaurants and inexpensive trinket shops make Chinatown a rewarding place for a meal and a jaunt.

South of the Inner Harbour, **Beacon Hill Park** surveys the Strait of Juan de Fuca (take bus #5). Here you can picnic amidst flower gardens, 350-year-old garry oaks, and network of paths. East of the Inner Harbour, **Craigdarroch Castle,** 1050 Joan Crescent (592-5323), embodies Victoria's wealth. (Take bus #10, 11, or 14.) The castle was built in 1890 by Robert Dunsmuir, a BC coal and railroad tycoon, in order to lure his wife from their native Scotland to the West Coast. The interior detail is impressive; the tower has a mosaic floor and the dining room a built-in oak sideboard. (Open daily 9am-7pm; in winter 10am-5pm. Admission $5, students $4.)

One block back towards the Inner Harbor, on Fort St. at 1040 Moss, is the **Art Gallery of Greater Victoria** (384-4101), never the same museum twice. The museum has no permanent collection save a wooden Shinto shrine and instead hosts a succession of temporary exhibits culled from local and international sources. (Open Mon.-Sat. 10am-5pm, Thurs. 'til 9pm and free after 5pm, Sun. 1-5pm. Admission $4, seniors $2.)

Point Ellice House (387-4697), a Heritage Conservation House dating from 1861, is decorated exactly as if the residents had just stepped out for a few short polo matches. The dining table is set, the chess set stands ready in the drawing room, and cast-iron pots and period kitchen utensils are strewn about the kitchen. (Guided tours given. (Open daily 10am-5pm. Adults $3.45, students $2.25.) To get to Point Ellice, head in the opposite direction from Inner Harbor and hop on bus #14, or take Bay St. west off Government and stop just before crossing the Port Ellice Bridge.

Across the bridge, you'll find **Craigflower Farmhouse** (387-4697), at the corner of Craigflower and Admirals Rd. (take bus #14), a complex of historical buildings on a farm built by Hudson's Bay Company in the 1850s. Craigflower is more rustic than Point Ellice, though the kitchen is equipped with the Cuisinart-esque equivalents of its day. (Open Wed.-Sun. 10am-3:45pm. Adults $3.25. Students $2.25.) At **Fort Rodd Hill National Historic Park,** on Ocean Blvd. off Hwy. 1A (388-1601) old defense batteries and **Fisgard Lighthouse,** the first of Canada's West-Coast beacons, compete for attention with excellent views of the strait. Take bus #50 or 61 to Western Exchange, transfer to #60, get off at the end of Belmont St., and walk along the path to the park. (No bus service in the evening, on Sun., or holidays. Park open daily 8am-sunset.)

Almost worth the exorbitant entrance fee are the stunning **Butchart Gardens,** 800 Benvennto, 22km north of Victoria (652-5256 for a recording, 652-4422 for an operator Mon.-Fri. 9am-5pm). Established by Jennie Butchart in 1904 in an attempt to reclaim the wasteland that was her husband's quarry and cement plant, the gardens are a maze of pools and fountains. Rose, Japanese, and Italian gardens cover 50 acres in a blaze of color. From mid-May through September, the whole area is lit at dusk, and the gardens, still administered by the Butchart family, host variety shows and cartoons. On Saturday nights in July and August, the skies shimmer with fireworks displays, while seventy thousand Christmas lights compensate for the lack of vegetation in December. Take bus #75 from Douglas and View northbound right into the Gardens, or #70 and walk 1km. The last #75 from the Gardens to the Inner Harbour is at 9:59pm. Motorists should consider approaching Butchart Gardens via the **Scenic Marine Drive,** following the coastline along Dallas and other roads. The 45-minute route passes through sedate suburban neighborhoods and offers a memorable view of the Olympic Mountains across the Strait of Juan de Fuca. (Gardens open year-round daily 9am; call for closing times. Admission in summer $10.50, ages 13-17 $7.50, ages 5-12 $3; in winter $7, $5, and $2. Hang on to your ticket: readmission within 24 hr. only $1.)

ENTERTAINMENT AND SEASONAL EVENTS

Nightlife in Victoria doesn't really get off the ground until Thursday night, but once the weekend's under way, the entire city grooves to the rhythms of jazz, blues, country, rock, folk, and more jazz. You can get an exhaustive listing of what's where in the free weekly *Monday Magazine* (inexplicably released every Wednesday), available at the hostel, most hotel lobbies and tourist attractions. On Tuesdays first-run movies at Cineplex Odeon theatres are half-price ($4). For more off-beat and foreign films, head to the University of Victoria's **Cinecenta** (721-8365 for show information) in the student union (bus #7 and 14). Nonmembers pay $5.75, but if you can convince them you're a student, the price is only $3.50.

The **Victoria Symphony Society,** 846 Broughton St. (385-6515), performs regularly under conductor Peter McCoppin, and the **University of Victoria Auditorium,** Finnerty Rd. (721-8480), is home stage to a variety of student productions. The **Pacific Opera** performs at the McPherson Playhouse, 3 Centennial Sq. (386-6121), at the corner of Pandora and Government St.

Harpo's Cabaret, 15 Bastion Sq. (385-5333), at Wharf St. An eclectic mix of jazz, blues, folk, and whatever else is in town. Open Mon.-Sat. 9pm-2am, Sun. 8pm-midnight; cover around $5.

The Forge, 919 Douglas St. (383-7137), at Courtney, in the Strathcona Hotel. Specializes in mid-70s rock with a wattage that could bend steel. Open Mon. and Fri.-Sat. 7:30pm-2am, Tues.-Thurs. 8pm-2am. Cover $3, $5.50 weekends.

Spinnakers, 308 Catherine (386-2739). Across the Johnson St. bridge. Locals escape from the tourists here and sample from the 38 beers brewed on the premises. Live music nightly ranging from jazz to rockabilly. No cover. Open daily 11am-11pm.

Rumors, 1325 Government St. (385-0566). Gay and lesbian clientele; drinking and dancing. Open Mon.-Sat. 9pm-3am.

The **Folkfest** in late June and early July celebrates Canada's birthday (July 1) and the country's "unity in diversity" with performances by "P.C." and "C.D." (Culturally Diverse) musicians. Occurring at the same time, the **JazzFest** is sponsored by the Victoria Jazz Society (388-4423 or 386-2441). The **Classic Boat Festival** is held Labour Day weekend and displays pre-1955 wooden boats in the Inner Harbour. Free entertainment accompanies the show. Contact the visitor and convention bureau for more information on all Inner Harbour events, or pick up a free copy of *Victoria Today* from the Infocentre (see Practical Information above).

■ Near Victoria

Sooke

West of Victoria on Hwy. 14 lies the town of Sooke, named for the native T'sou-ke tribe and host to the logging events and festivities of **All Sooke Day** on the third Saturday in July. **The Sooke Region Museum** (642-6351), just off Hwy. 14 at 2070 Phillips Rd., delivers an excellent history of the area (open daily 9am-6pm; free). The museum also houses a **travel infocentre.** Next to the park where all Sooke Day takes place, on Phillips Rd. past the museum, is the **Sooke River Flats Campsite** (642-6076) which has a phone, showers, toilets, and running water (gates locked 11pm-7am; sites $10). To get to Phillips Rd. from the city, take the #50 bus to the Western Exchange and transfer to #61. Sooke is mostly a haven for the wealthier Victorians, making cheap indoor accommodations hard to come by. If you can't get back to the city, try the **Blackfish B&B** (642-6864), 7 mi. west of Sooke's sole stoplight (singles $35, doubles $40). Large groups should ask about the great **bungalow** down on the pebble beach with free laundry and a full kitchen (sleeps 9; $100 per night).

North of Sooke are some of the comeliest beaches for beachcombing on the southern island. Hwy. 14 continues along the coast, stringing together three provincial parks: **China Beach** and **Loss Creek** (both day use), and **French Beach** which offers tentsites (May-Oct.; $9.50).

Gulf Island Archipelago

Just off the southeastern coast of Vancouver Island lies British Columbia's Gulf Island Archipelago. Five are serviced by **BC Ferries** (call 656-0757 for details). The three principal members of the chain are **Salt Spring, Pender,** and **Mayne.** Pick up a free copy of *The Gulf Islander* on the ferry to Victoria for a complete listing of area activities. For information on the five main islands, call the **tourist information centres** in Salt Spring (537-5252), Pender (382-3551), Mayne (539-5311), Galiano (539-2233) or Saturna (382-3551). Find an **HI-C hostel** at 640 Cusheon Lake Rd. (537-4149), on Salt Spring Island ($13, nonmembers $16).

Chemainus

About 70km north of Victoria on Hwy. 1 lies the town of Chemainus. When the closure of the town's sawmill threatened economic disaster in 1980, an ambitious revitalization program—centered on a series of more than 30 enormous murals of the town's history—helped turn things around. In mid-July **Chemainus Daze** offers arts and crafts and a chance to meet with the mural artists. The **Horseshoe Bay Inn**, 9576 Chemainus Rd. (246-3425) at Henry, has singles for $30, doubles for $38. The **Senior Drop-In Centre,** on the corner of Willow and Alder (246-2111), is open daily 10am-4pm with coffee, tea and muffins for anyone who drops in. Call the **Chamber of Commerce** in Chemainus at (246-3944) for more information.

■■■ NANAIMO

In the 19th century, Robert Dunsmuir's path to riches led through Nanaimo's coal mines. The supply is still here, but demand for the coal industry floundered after WWII, and BC's first settlement shifted its focus from coal to logging and fishing. When the logging economy turned to pulp throughout the province, Nanaimo, like the rest of BC, turned to tourism to supplement its revenue. The combination of affable, outgoing people, easy accessibility by car or ferry, and a slow-paced, relaxing atmosphere has drawn vacationers—especially anglers—from all parts of the continent. The local populace includes immigrants and their descendants from, among other countries, the United Kingdom, China, Finland, and Poland.

PRACTICAL INFORMATION AND ORIENTATION

Visitors Information: Travel Infocentre, 266 Bryden St. (754-8474), on the Trans-Canada Hwy., just northwest of downtown. Mine of information on all of Vancouver Island. Call before you visit the area for accommodation referrals. Open daily 8am-7pm.

BC Ferry, 680 Trans-Canada Hwy., Nanaimo V9S 5R1 (753-6626 for recorded information, 753-1261 for an operator). To Vancouver (8 per day leaving between 5:30am and 11pm; passenger $5.50, car and driver $25.50). Ferries leave from a terminal at the northern end of Stewart Ave. (Take the ferry shuttle from Gordon St. Exchange downtown.) Check in 15 min. before departure.

Via Rail, 321 Selby St. (800-561-8630). To Victoria (1 per day, $16).

Island Coach Lines, 753-4371. At Comox and Terminal, behind Tally Ho Island Inns. To: Victoria (6 per day, $14.70); Port Hardy (1 per day, $57.75); Port Alberni (3 per day, $10.50, with connecting service to Tofino and Ucluelet).

Car Rental: Rent-A-Wreck, 41 Nicol St. (753-6461). Very-used cars start at $25 per day plus 14¢ per km. Must be at least 21 with a major credit card. Open Mon.-Sat. 8am-6pm, Sun. 10am-4pm. **Budget,** 753-1195. $200 per week with unlimited mileage. Must be at least 19.

Bus Information: 390-4531. Terminal at Front and Wharf. 10 bus routes serve the area. Fares $1, senior citizens 75¢. Day passes $2.50, senior citizens $2.

Laundromat: at Nicol and Robins at the **Payless Gas Station.** Open 24 hr.

Crisis: 754-4447. 24 hr.

Pharmacy: London Drugs (753-5566), in Harbour Park Mall at Island Hwy. and Terminal Ave. Open Mon.-Sat. 9am-10pm, Sun. 10am-6pm.

Hospital: 1200 Dufferin Crescent (754-2141). Open 24 hr.

Police: 303 Pridaux St. at Fitzwilliam (754-2345; **emergency** 753-2212). **Fire:** 753-1234. At Fitzwilliam and Milton.

Post Office: 60 Front St., at Church St. Open Mon.-Fri. 8:30am-5pm. **Postal Code:** V9R 5J9.
Area Code: 604.

Nanaimo lies on the eastern coast of Vancouver Island, 111km north of Victoria on the Trans-Canada Hwy., 391km south of Port Hardy via Hwy. 19. The two highways merge downtown at the waterfront and become the major road in town. The ferry terminal is 2km north of the junction on Stewart Ave.

ACCOMMODATIONS AND CAMPING

Nicol St. Mini-Hostel (HI-C), 65 Nicol St. (753-1188), 7 blocks southeast of the Island Bus Lines Depot. If you're coming into Nanaimo from the south, ask the driver to let you off by the Nicol St. Hostel, and save yourself a walk. Great management. Members $13, nonmembers $15. Tentsites $8. Laundry (wash and dry) $2.50.

Thomson Hostel (HI-C), 1660 Cedar Hwy. (722-2251), 10km south of Nanaimo. Take bus #11, or the free shuttle from the bus depot 6-9pm. Accommodates 12 in 6 bedrooms, in addition to camping space. Kitchen facilities. Ping-pong table, billiards, and piano. Registration 9am-11pm. Laundry facilities $2.50. Free use of bicycles, canoes and kayaks. No Canadian guests. $12. Open year-round.

Malaspina College (754-6338), on 4th St. approximately 2km west of downtown. Private rooms with shared baths. Coin-operated laundry, TV rooms, refrigerators, pay phones. Singles $24. Open May-Aug.

Colonial Motel, 950 N. Terminal Ave. (754-4415), on the Trans-Canada Hwy. Immaculate rooms. Kitchenettes available. Singles $41. Doubles $46.

Big 7 Motel, 736 Nicol St. (754-2328). Loud, blue-and-pink motel decor, but the rooms are O.K. Waterbed units available for those who don't want to give up that seasick feeling after a long day of open-ocean fishing. Singles $34. Doubles $38.

Westwood Lake (753-3922), west of town off Jingle Pot Road. Full facilities. 66 sites. $12, $16 with hookups (GST incl.). Take bus #5.

Jingle Pot (758-1614), west on Island Hwy. off Jingle Pot Road. 22 sites $12, with hookup $15 (GST incl.). Full facilities.

Brannen Lake Campsite, 4228 Biggs Rd. (756-0404), 6km north of ferry terminal. Follow the signs from Hwy. 19. On a ranch and definitely worth the trip. Clean bathrooms with hot showers (25¢). Free hayrides every night, and you can help with the animals. Hike to a nearby waterfall. Sites $10, with hookup $12.

FOOD

Look out Twinkies and Suzy Q's—here comes the **Nanaimo Bar,** a local concoction comprised of three layers of satanically delicious graham crackers, butter, and chocolate. Residents take great pride in their hometown confection; a 1986 contest uncovered nearly 100 separate recipes. Most of the neighborhood restaurants and bakeries offer their own renditions, and the conscientious traveler will sample several (just to get a real feel for the place, of course). Leaving the city without trying a Nanaimo Bar is like hitting a home run and forgetting to touch third.

The Scotch Bakery, 87 Commercial St. (753-3521). The acknowledged home plate of Nanaimo Bar aficionados (75¢). Don't ignore the macaroons ($1) or sausage rolls either. Open Mon.-Fri. 8:30am-5:30pm, Sat. 8:30am-5pm.

New York Style Pizza, 426 Fitzwilliam (754-0111), at Richards. Classy framed posters of Gotham and Louis Armstrong ease the disappointment of pizza that doesn't taste anything like Ray's of Greenwich Village. Live music 6 nights a week. 6-in. pizza $3, pasta specials $7.25. Open Mon.-Thurs. 11:30am-2:30pm and 5-9pm, Fri. 11am-2:30pm and 5-11pm, Sat. noon-11pm.

Doobee's (753-5044), at Front and Church St. Delicious sandwiches $3-4.50. Sidewalk tables, sunshine, espresso for $1, and cappuccino for $1.75 will keep you singing. Open Mon.-Fri. 7am-5pm, Sat. 8:30am-5pm.

Nanaimo Harbour Lights Restaurant (NHL), 1518 Stewart Ave. (753-6614). The owner, ex-NHL referee Lloyd Gilmour, is more than willing to "talk puck."

Surf-and-turf entrees also let you face off with the salad bar ($9-12). Lunches $6. Open Mon.-Thurs. 11:30am-3pm and 5-9pm, Fri.-Sat. 11:30am-3pm and 5-10pm.

SIGHTS

The **Nanaimo Centennial Museum,** 100 Cameron St. (753-1821), next to the bus terminal, crystallizes all aspects and eras of Nanaimo history with fossilized remains of plants and animals, coastal Salish artifacts, and a full-scale walk-through model of a coal mine. The small museum makes a particular effort to pay tribute to the imported "Coolie" laborers who supported Nanaimo's vitality long before the Chinese-Canadians' struggle for equality had begun. Only 300m from the museum on the water's edge is the **Bastion,** constructed by the Hudson's Bay Company as a storehouse and safehouse against Native attacks. A six-pound cannon booms daily at noon. (Open Mon.-Fri. 9am-6pm, Sat.-Sun. 10am-6pm; in winter Tues.-Sat. 9am-5pm. Admission $2, senior citizens and students $1, children 50¢.)

About 2.5km west of town is the **Nanaimo Art Gallery** (755-8790). The gallery features various rotating exhibitions of local and international art and culture. Bus #6 will save you the 30-minute walk uphill. About 1km farther west up Nanaimo Lakes Ave. by the city reservoir is the **Morrell Nature Sanctuary.** The tranquil trails are a perfect place to digest those Nanaimo bars.

Three km south of town on Hwy. 1 (also Hwy. 19) is the **Petroglyph Provincial Park.** Hundreds of generations of Salish shamans have carved figures of various animals and mythical creatures into the soft sandstone. Rubbings can be made from concrete replicas at the base of the trail leading to the petroglyphs.

Eight km further south stretches the ever-expanding **Bungy Zone** (753-5867), a dimension of sight, sound, and giant rubber bands. Thrill seekers from all over the continent make a pilgrimage here to drop 140 feet into a narrow gorge, secured against certain death only by a thick elastic bungy cord. The short but exhilarating trip down costs $95 (2 for 1 if you rent a car from Budget). You can also get a video immortalizing you on your plungy from 'da bungy. To get there, take Hwy. 1 south to Nanaimo River Rd. and then follow the signs (open daily).

Departure Bay washes onto a pleasant beach in the north end of town off Stewart Ave. **North Island Water Sports,** 2755 Departure Bay Rd. (758-2488), rents bikes ($8 per hr., $25 per day), kayaks ($35 per day), and scuppers (they're like kayaks, but you sit on top of them; $8 per hr., $30 per day). **Newcastle Island Provincial Park** has campsites for $9.50 (no hookups), pit toilets, and a fantastic swimming beach. There's no auto access to the park, however, so you'll have to shell out the $3.50 (round-trip) for the foot ferry (runs every hour on the hour daily 10am-9pm).

The annual **Nanaimo Theatre Group Festival** presents plays about the city's history in late June and early July. All plays take place at Malaspina College (tickets $6-12). For reservations, contact the festival at P.O. Box 626, Nanaimo V9R 5L9 (754-7587), or stop by the office above the Travel Infocentre.

The week-long **Marine Festival** is held during the second week of July. Highlights include the **Silly Boat Race** and the renowned **Bathtub Race.** Bathers from all over the continent race porcelain tubs with monster outboards from Nanaimo to Vancouver across the 55km Georgia Strait. The organizer of this bizarre but beloved event is the **Royal Nanaimo Bathtub Society,** P.O. Box 656, Nanaimo V9R 5L5 (753-7233). They hand out prizes to everyone who makes it across, and ceremoniously present the "Silver Plunger" trophy to the first tub that sinks.

■ Hornby Island

In the 1960s, large numbers of young Americans fled the draft to settle peacefully on quiet Hornby Island, one of the two small chunks of land off Vancouver's eastern coast, halfway between Nanaimo and Campbell River. Today, Hornby Island and her sister, **Denman,** comprise an interesting mélange of inhabitants: the descendants of pioneering families circa 1850, and hippie-holdovers who offer spiritual awareness readings and home-grown. Living in a curious symbiosis, the two groups share a thinly veiled disdain of tourists.

With its light traffic and paved roads, Hornby Island is best explored on two wheels. You can rent bikes ($5 per hr., $20 per day) from **Zucchini Ocean Kayak Centre,** at the Co-op (335-2033; open daily 10am-6pm). Zucchini also rents kayaks and sailboards ($20 per 4 hr., $30 per day), and wetsuits ($10 per 4 hr., $20 per day). Low tide at **Tribune Bay** and **Whaling Station Bay** uncovers over 300m of the cleanest, finest sand on Vancouver Island. Tribune, lapping at the base of Central Rd., is the more accessible of the two beaches. Whaling Station Bay is about 5km farther north.

On the way to Whaling Station Bay from Tribune Bay is Helliwell Rd., the cut-off for stunning **Helliwell Provincial Park.** A well-groomed trail takes you on a one-hour hike through old-growth forest to bluffs overlooking the ocean. Cormorants are everywhere, diving kamikaze-style into the ocean to surface moments later with trophy-quality fish. Bald eagles cruise on the sea breezes.

The **Hornby Festival** draws musicians, comedians, and artists from all over Canada for ten days in early August. Call the Hornby Festival Society (335-2734) for details. For more information, contact **Denman/Hornby Tourist Services,** Denman Island V0R 1T0 (335-2293), or the post office on Hornby (see below).

If you plan on spending more than a day here, bring a tent and food. The **Hornby Island Resort** (335-0136), right at the ferry docks, is a versatile establishment—pub/restaurant/laundromat/hotel/campground. The pub fare is standard but reasonably priced; the restaurant has breakfast plates from $4 (restaurant open daily 9am-9pm; sites $13-15 per night, hookup $3). **Bradsdadsland Country Camp,** 1980 Shingle Spit Rd. (335-0757), offers standard plots to pitch your tent (sites for 1-2 people $14-16 per night, $1.50 per additional person; full hookup $3). **Tribune Bay,** at the Co-op at the eastern end of Central Rd. (335-2359), has 120 sites on wonderful (you guessed it) Tribune Bay. (Sites $14.50-17; 8 sites with electricity $17-19.50. Coin-op showers. Bike rentals. Open Easter-Labor Day.) The **Joy of Cooking** (335-1487), by the Co-op, serves up BC-style sushi in the form of *nori* rolls, smoked salmon and rice wrapped in seaweed ($3; open daily 8:30am-8pm). **The Co-op,** at the end of Central Rd. by Tribune Bay (335-1121), is a well-stocked grocery store with a deli and post office (open daily 9am-7pm).

Island Coach Lines has a flag stop at **Buckley Bay,** on Vancouver Island Hwy. 19, where the ferry docks. **BC Ferries** sails nine times per day (round-trip $4.50, car and driver $12.50). It's a 10-minute ride from Buckley Bay to Denman; disembark and make the 11km trek across the island to the Gravely Bay docks for another 10-minute ride to Hornby. Once on Hornby, there are only two roads to worry about: **Shingle Spit Road** (try saying that 10 times fast) and **Central Road,** separated by the docks. Central Rd. extends to the eastern shore, where all the "action" is—however, it's 15km away, and there's no public transit.

A lot of this area is difficult without a car, so some foot-travelers ask friendly faces for lifts at Denman or on the ferry. Those who decide to risk hitching should appear neat—islanders can be somewhat reticent. If you need a **taxi,** call 335-0521. **Emergency Numbers: ambulance,** 338-9112; **fire,** 338-6522; **police,** 338-6551. The **post office** is at the Co-op at the terminus of Central Rd. (335-1121), on the eastern shore of the island. **Postal Code:** V0R 1Z0. The **area code** is 604.

■ The Comox Valley

Billing itself as the "recreation capital of Canada," the Comox Valley area is comprised of Courtenay, Comox, and Cumberland. The area has become an intellectual oasis of sorts in Vancouver Island's rural north. It boasts the highest concentration of artists in Canada, the many museums and galleries sprinkled through the valley showing and selling their wares. And, along more scientific lines, the discovery of the 80 million year old "Courtenay Elasmosaur" in 1989 has transformed the valley into a minor mecca of paleontology as well.

If talk of arts and sciences brings nasty visions of college and coursework, then find relief in nearby Strathcona Provincial Park. The park's southern regions of are just a llama's trot away from the "Three C's."

Practical Information The **Tourist Office** in Courtenay is located at 2040 Cliffe Ave. (334-3234), and in Cumberland on Dunsmuir (336-8313). **Island Coach** (334-2475), in Courtenay at Fitzgerald and Cumberland, connects the area to points north and south along Hwy. 19. **BC Ferries** (339-3310) connects Comox with Powell River on the mainland.

Some useful numbers: **Weather,** 339-5044; **Police,** 338-6551, non-emergency 338-1321; **Fire,** 338-6522; **Ambulance,** 338-7471; **Hospital,** 339-2242. Find the **Women's Resource Center** on Cliffe 2km before the Info. Center. The **Post Office** sits on Fourth St. at Cliffe, across from the museum in Courtenay. **Area Code:** 604.

Accommodations, Camping, and Food Many pricey motels line the highway south of Courtenay. B&Bs abound and are a better bet—get a listing at the Infocentre or try the **Mountain View Bed and Breakfast,** 605 Ellcee Place, Courtenay, BC V9N 7G3 (338-0157), which offers charming rooms, spotless bathrooms, TV lounge area, and a good view from the balcony (singles from $25, doubles from $40; reservations recommended). Campers should try **Kin Beach** (339-4079), Astra Road, Comox. Their 7 tentsites and 8 RV sites are $6.50. **Miracle Beach** (337-5720), Miracle Beach Drive, Black Creek has trails, picnic tables, BBQ pits and a playground. Nicer than Kin Beach, but not too accessible (showers, flush toilets; $14.50).

Area restaurants are more reasonable than are hotels, and the many **Farmers Markets** in the area provide a still less expensive (and fresher) option. A convenient one is **Farquharson Farms,** 1300 Comox in Courtenay (338-8194). **The Bar None Cafe,** 244 4th St. (334-3112), off Cliffe in Courtenay, purveys exceptional all-vegetarian fare. Choose your own rice and pasta dishes, salads, and fresh salsas, and pay $1.40 per 100 grams. Also an espresso bar, homemade juices (apple, lime, and mint, $2). (Open Mon.-Sat. 8am-8pm, Fri. night coffee-house until 11pm.) The price is right at **Babe's Cafe,** 2702 Dunsmuir (336-2763), in Cumberland (sandwiches under $3, dinners under $6). **Safeway** and **Shopper's Drug Mart** are both located on 8th St. in Courtenay.

Sights and Activities The **Arts Alliance,** 367 4th St. (338-6211), in Courtenay, is a focal point for the local arts community, housing a craft gallery and a shop which essentially functions as another gallery.

The Courtenay and District Museum, 360 Cliffe Ave. (334-3611; open daily in summer 10am-4:30pm), houses permanent exhibits on pioneer life, native culture and art, industry, and geology. A special paleontology annex, next door to the museum, holds in storage the bevy of dinosaur bones uncovered in the area (tours can be arranged through the museum). **The Comox Air Force Museum** (339-8635) at the Canadian Forces Base, Ryan and Little River Rd. in Comox, will tell you everything you ever wanted to know (but were afraid to ask) about the Royal Canadian Air Force. Future exhibits will chronicle Native artists who have served.

Horne Lake Caves Provincial Park, south of Courtenay on Horne Lakes Rd., opens its caves to the public; equipment is available.

■ Strathcona Provincial Park

Near the heart of Vancouver Island, Strathcona Provincial Park doesn't present too striking a contrast to the modestly developed regions around it—an extensive network of hiking trails, a total lack of pricey hotels and stores—especially since the park itself has been modestly developed for recreation. Elk, deer, marmots, and wolves all inhabit the more than 200,000 hectares of Strathcona, one of the best preserved and most beautiful wilderness areas on Vancouver Island. **Buttle Lake,** which is found on Hwy. 28 between Gold River and Campbell River, and **Mt. Washington/Forbidden Plateau** are the park's two visitors centres. The two official campgrounds, sharing 161 campsites between them, are Buttle Lake and Ralph River, both on the shores of Buttle Lake and accessible via Hwy. 28 and secondary roads (follow the highway signs). **Buttle Lake,** closer to Campbell River, has comfortable sites, a playground, and the sandy beaches of the lake itself ($12). **Ralph River,** slightly less crowded, provides convenient access to the park's best hiking trails. Visitors wishing to forego the campgrounds and hide themselves away in Strathcona's **back-country areas** must camp 800m from main roads. To minimize environmental impact, camp at least 100 ft. away from water sources as well. Back-country campers, while missing out on more modern facilities, are rewarded by lakes, water-falls, ancient cedar and fir-forests, and wild-flower meadows. Campfires are discouraged in the park. Those entering the undeveloped areas of the park should notify the park service of their intended departure and return times, and should be well-equipped (maps are essential, and perhaps a parasol might be useful due to frequent rain). The Forbidden Plateau and Mt. Washington, which lie outside the park boundaries, hit their high-seasons in the winter with a heavy influx of skiers. For information on the park, contact BC Park, District Manager, Rathtrevor Beach Provincial Park, Box 1479, Parksville, BC V9P 2H4 (604-248-3931 or 755-2483).

■ Campbell River

Although 67km south of the acknowledged boundary of "North Island," Campbell River is close enough in spirit to be included among its northern neighbors. Its tourist economy is geared toward fishing, diving, and hiking.

News of the enormous salmon regularly wrestled from the river by Cape Mudge natives sparked a tremendous influx of sport fishermen in the early 1800s. They could never have expected that today every pamphlet, billboard, and menu would shout "Salmon Capital of the World" in obtrusively large print.

Practical Information The **Travel Infocentre,** 923 Island Hwy. (286-0764), has a helpful staff (open daily 8am-8pm; in winter open Mon.-Fri. 9am-5pm, Sat. 10am-5pm).

Island Coach Lines (287-7151) is at 13th and Cedar. **BC Ferries** runs from Campbell River to Quadra Island (15 daily; $2.50, cars $7.50; bikes free). Find **Rent-a-Wreck** (287-8353) at 1353 Island Hwy. in Lakeland.

A local laundromat is **Sunrise Laundry Ltd.** (923-2614) in Sunrise Square. Some useful numbers: **Crisis Hotline,** 287-7743; **Hospital,** 287-7111 for information; **Poison Control,** 287-7111; **Ambulance,** 286-1155; **Police,** 286-6221.

Accommodations, Camping, and Food Finding inexpensive lodging here is like swimming upstream. The best bet is camping in Strathcona Provincial Park (see below). The **Ocean Front Motel,** 834 South Island Hwy. (923-6409), close to city centre at least gets points for location (singles from $28, doubles $29). The **Parkside Campground** (287-3113), 5km west of Campbell River on Hwy. 28, has appealing wooded sites and hot showers in private, quiet surroundings (sites $14, with hookup $18).

As far as food goes, good budget fare is hard to find. The **Overwaitea Market,** at 13th and Elm St., offers decent sandwiches and other casual cuisine, and it's the best you'll do if you're not cooking your dinner yourself (open daily 9am-9pm).

Sights and Activities Sockeye, Coho, Pink, Chum, and Chinook salmon are lured each year from the waters of the Campbell River. The foolish can shell out a small fortune paying for guides and charters, but the savvy can reap deep-sea prizes from **Discovery Pier** in Campbell Harbour (fishing charge $1; rod rentals $2.50 per hr., $6 per ½ day). The pier has 200m of boardwalk plants and an artificial underwater reef built to attract astigmatic fish.

National Geographic once praised Campbell River's **scuba diving** as "second only to the Red Sea." Unfortunately, unless you spy some real treasure in Discovery Pier's artificial reef, it'll be hard to come up with the requisite cash to rent equipment. **Beaver Aquatics,** 760 Island Hwy. (287-7652), advertises a $25 snorkel package that includes suit, mask, snorkel, and fins.

No visit to the self-proclaimed "Salmon Capital of the World" would be complete without a tour of the **Quinsam River Salmon Hatchery** (287-9564). They monitor more smolts before 9am than most people do all day (open daily 8am-4pm). An audio-visual extravaganza introduces you to shiny, happy little fish who are blissfully unaware of the rods and reels lying ahead.

If you don't like to fish, your only (albeit temporary) respite from the salmon-centered masses may be the **Campell River District Museum** (287-3103) in the same building as the Travel Infocentre.

About an hour north of Campbell River up Hwy. 19 is the **Valley of 1000 Faces** in Sayward. Painted faces of a variety of public figures (including JFK, C3PO, and John Travolta) gaze out quizzically from their positions on the tree trunks. Conceived and executed by local artist Hetty Fredrickson, the valley is poignant testimony to the ecstatic indefatigability of the postmodern mind (open May-Aug. daily 10am-5pm).

■ Port Hardy

In a sense, Port Hardy is the modern Canadian equivalent of Liverpool. Port Hardy was completely content to be a quiet logging and fishing community until the BC Ferry made it the drop-off point for southbound visitors from upper BC and Alaska. Virtually overnight, the formerly unassuming town etched a name for itself as a major transportation port, complete with a chainsaw-carved welcome sign. Unlike Liverpool, however, Port Hardy remains a mild coastal town, an excellent place for ferry passengers to spend the night, and the loser in the race to export popular 60s rock stars with Cockney accents.

Practical Information Pick up a restaurant menu guide and tour maps at the **Travel Infocentre,** 7250 Market St. (949-7622). Take Hardy Bay Rd. off Hwy. 19 to Market St. (open Mon.-Fri. 8am-8pm, Sat.-Sun. 9am-8pm). **Buses** leave from **Island Coach Lines** (949-7532), on Market St. across from the Travel Infocentre (to Victoria 1 per day, $72.45). **BC Ferry** (949-6722) is located 3km south at Bear Creek. (Service between Prince Rupert and Port Hardy every other day, one way $90). **North Island Taxi** can be reached at 949-8800. **North Star Cycle and Sports,** at Market and Granville, rents bikes for $8 per hour. Other outdoor equipment needs may be taken care of at **MacLean's True Value** on Market. Clean those stinkin' clothes at **Payless Gas Co.** (949-2366), on Granville St. Open 24 hr.

Some helpful phone numbers: **crisis line,** 949-6033; **police,** 7355 Columbia Ave. (949-6335); **Coast Guard** (974-5413) at Alert Bay; **hospital,** 949-6161; and **ambulance,** 949-7224. Port Hardy's **postal code** is V09 2P0. The **area code** is 604.

On the northern tip of Vancouver Island, Port Hardy serves as the southern terminus for ferries carrying passengers down from Prince Rupert and Alaska. Hwy. 19 runs south from the center of downtown.

Accommodations, Camping, and Food Despite the fact that many of the ferry arrivals bring along RVs, the demand for hotel rooms is just as high as you would expect in any port town. Take Byng Rd. off Hwy. 19 toward the airport to arrive at the **Airport Inn** (949-9434), which has singles from $55 and doubles from $65. Extra persons add $6. Kitchen units about $6 extra. Stream to the **Pioneer Inn** (949-7271), off Hwy. 19 on Old Island Hwy., 2km south of town, for rooms next to a salmon hatchery. The Pioneer has laundry facilities and a dining room (singles $54, doubles $60). For current **B&B** listings call 949-7622 (singles from $45). For a more sylvan setting, tent it at the **Quatse River Campground,** 5050 Hardy Bay Rd. (949-2395), across from the Pioneer Inn. Quiet, wooded setting with private sites. Toilets come in a choice of flush and pit. Showers and laundromat. (Sites $12, full hookups $15.) **Wildwoods Campsite** (949-6753), on the road from the ferry within walking distance of the terminal, has comfortable sites strewn with pine needles. Plenty of spaces are crammed into a relatively small forest area, but they are well-designed to afford maximum privacy. Hot showers, but expect a line in the morning. (Sites $10, with hookup $15.)

Port Hardy maintains its excellent cuisine in the face of growing ferry traffic. A brigade of superb budget restaurants serve dinners for under $10. **Brigg Seafood House** (949-6532), at Market and Granville St., serves seafood in a large old house. Their "you catch it, we'll cook it" service can get you dinner with all the trimmings for $5; bistro dinners from $7. Children's menu available (open Sun.-Wed. 11:30am-3pm and 5-10pm, Thurs.-Sat. 11:30am-3pm and 5:30-11pm). **Sportsman's Steak & Seafood House** (949-7811), on Market St. across from the Infocentre, offers lunch sandwiches stuffed with meat from $4. Salad bar is well-stocked, and a few surf-and-turf entrees under $9 (open daily 11:30am-2pm and 5pm-"whenever"). The **Road-house,** a family restaurant at the Pioneer Inn on Old Island Hwy., has sandwiches ($3.80) and pasta entrees ($6-8). Several **markets** line (aptly enough) Market St.

Sights For a peek at vignettes of city history, head to the **Port Hardy Museum,** 7110 Market St. (949-8143), near the Infocentre (see above). The small library/museum holds early Native artifacts and some yellowed photographs; not very heady stuff, but it's free. The only other real attraction in town is a leisurely stroll along the **seawall,** which brings you near to the town's coastal beauty.

■ Port McNeill and Alert Bay

Port McNeill, 65km south of Port Hardy on Hwy. 19, began as the operations base of the Pioneer Timber Company, Ltd. in 1937. Rumor has it that in these first years locals fought swarming bugs on the government dock by lighting sticks of dynamite (with their pipes, no less), and dropping the sticks into holes in the dock's pilings. More recent approaches to local annoyances aren't quite so extreme, but the exceptionally friendly locals are still willing to lend a hand (or a pipe) to those in need.

Practical Information Find **travel information** in **Port McNeil** by the ferry dock. Find it in **Alert Bay,** on Cormorant Island, at 116 Fir St. (974-5213). **BC Ferries** (956-4533) operates a tri-island ferry which runs between Port McNeill, Sointula, and Alert Bay (ferries run daily 8:40am-9:50pm). **Island Coach Lines** runs from Port McNeill to Victoria (1 per day, $65, departs from the Dalewood Inn). Those whose car breaks down should call **Port McNeill Auto Body** (956-3434, 24-hr. towing). You can grab a shower at the pool on Campbell Way past the skating arena (956-3638; $2, $1 for children).

Some useful numbers: **Ambulance,** 949-722; **hospital,** 956-4461 in Port McNeill; **RCMP,** (956-4441. The **Area Code** is 604.

Accommodations A fabulous **hostel** (604-974-2026) plays host in Alert Bay, complete with piano and a bay view ($13, nonmembers $15). Reservations are recommended as group programs can sometimes fill the beds; if the hostel is full, though, lodging can often be arranged elsewhere.

Sights Alert Bay is one of the richest sources of native culture on Vancouver Island. Half the community is a Nimpkish reserve. The tallest totem pole in the world, at 173 ft., is located behind the U'Mista cultural centre (974-5403; open Mon.-Fri. 9am-5pm, Sat.-Sun. noon-5pm; winter Mon.-Fri. only). The totem tells the story of the Kwkiutl Indian Nation, and the cultural centre houses breathtaking bronzes and masks used in the Potlatch (gift-giving ceremony). These works of art had formerly been held captive by the Canadian government.

The island straits near Alert Bay and Port McNeill boast the continent's highest concentration of **orcas.** Sighting charters are everywhere (and expensive); instead, you can catch a glimpse of the pods synchronously surfacing to the water by the ferry or just outside the harbor at Alert Bay.

■ Cape Scott Provincial Park

If you feel a need to sum up Cape Scott (and sound like a brochure while you're doing it), "Wet and Wild" is the phrase of choice. The elements have spelled doom for two attempts at human settlement. The park is now accessed by 60km of rough logging roads which are still very active (so use caution—nothing ruins a trip like 20 tons of angry "big rig" bearing down on you). Parking lots lie near the trailheads, providing easy access to the trails which are, in turn, the only access to the park. Most trailheads begin from the parking lot on **San Josef Rd.** near the entrance to the park.

Wilderness camping in the park is not restricted to wilderness sites, although **San Josef Bay** and **Nels Bight** are popular because fresh water is available. Make sure that you're not so near the shore that your camp will be swamped at high tide, and, as always, practice "minimum impact" camping. Good topographic maps will be helpful to enterprising trekkers (available from **Maps BC,** Ministry of Environment, Parliament Bldgs., Victoria BC V8V 1XS). For more detailed information on the park, pick up the Cape Scott Provincial Park pamphlet at one of the travel infocentres elsewhere in the region, since none exist anywhere near the park. And finally, while the wildlife you see may vary, one thing is certain—IT WILL RAIN, so be prepared.

■■■ PACIFIC RIM NATIONAL PARK

So different in landscape and seascape are the three regions of Pacific Rim National Park—West Coast Trail, Broken Group Islands, and Long Beach—that only the homogenizing hand of government could have combined them under the same jurisdiction.

Constructed in 1907 to give shipwrecked sailors a path to civilization, the 77km **West Coast Trail** between Port Renfrew and Bamfield is the most demanding and potentially dangerous section of the park. It can be traversed only on foot, and takes anywhere from six to ten days. About halfway along the trail near **Clo-oose** (pronounced KLO-ooze) is the **Carmanah Valley** where the tallest Sitka spruce in the world tower 90m above the forest floor. This route is for serious hikers only.

Barkley Sound intrudes between Bamfield and Ucluelet (pronounced you-CLUE-let), and here you'll find the **Broken Group Islands** unit of the park. Accessible only by boat, these islands are untouched.

Gentle trails and broad vistas of Douglas fir and Western cedar characterize the 23-km **Long Beach,** between Ucluelet in the south and Tofino in the north. Long Beach has two camping facilities (see Accommodations and Camping below).

Each spring, you can witness the commute of some of the 22,000 gray whales streaming past the park. The area also crawls with orcas, sea lions, black-tailed deer, and black bears. Dress for wet weather here; even the mosquitoes wear raincoats.

■ West Coast Trail: Port Renfrew and Bamfield

Port Renfrew, still making the switch from a logging economy to one based on tourism, is the point of departure for those embarking on the West Coast Trail. It offers only a minimum of resources for hikers and tourists, so prepare in advance.

The West Coast Trail, linking Port Renfrew and Bamfield, is 77km of unadulterated coastal hiking weaving through forests and waterfalls and scaling steep wooden ladders and slopes. The treacherous shoreline has been the sinker of many ships. Only experienced hikers should attempt this slick trail, and never alone—gray whales, sea otters, and black bears along the route may provide company, but they can't help you in an accident. A maximum of 52 people per day are permitted to tackle this legendary trail; write the Park Superintendent, Box 280, Ucluelet, BC V0R 3A0, or call ahead for reservations (726-7721). You can order maps, tide tables, information on ferry crossings within the trail, and brochures on trail safety from the Park Superintendent as well.

The **Botanical Beach Provincial Park** is nearly as much a source of local pride as is the Pacific Rim. Nature enthusiasts have access to varieties of intertidal life, as well as sandstone, shale, quartz, and basalt formations. The park is only accessible to four-wheel-drive vehicles; those without must park and make the 45-minute trek to the beach.

Anyone heading into Bamfield will have to pass over a few socket-jarring kilometers of gravel logging roads which provide the only route into town. Luckily, the breathtaking **Lake Cowichan** offers ample reward for the ride. The few patches of clear-cut dotting the lakeshores prove that these roads have been more than decorative (and still active, so be careful). The tactful Forest Service explains that "landscape principles were not fully applied at the time of harvest"; they note, however, that everything will "green-up" as logging continues to decline. **Pacheenaht Bus Service** (647-5521) operates in the area. Take it—your car will thank you (see Practical Information below). The town of Bamfield itself is located on two sides of an inlet, and lacks a bridge to connect the halves. A water taxi from Kingfisher Marina is the only way to reach the rest of the town (see Practical Information).

Practical Information Seek out maps and information on the area and registration information for the West Coast Trail at the **Trail Information Center** in Port Renfrew (647-5434; open May-Sept. daily 9am-5pm). The info. center in Bamfield is deserted and lacks even a phone.

The **Pacheenaht Bus Service,** 155 Tataxawo, Port Renfrew (647-5521) offers one-way service to Bamfield ($35), Lake Cowichan ($24), and Duncan ($25). In Bamfield, try **Western Bus Lines,** 723-3341. For a **taxi** by road, try **Hawkeye's Marina** (728-3491) in Bamfield. For one by water, try **Bamfield Kingfisher Marina,** 728-3228.

Do your **laundry** and take a **shower** at the Port Renfrew Hotel. The local hospital is the **Bamfield Red Cross Hospital.** The **post office** is in Bamfield, across the inlet near the Bamfield Inn.

Accommodations, Camping, and Food Choices in town are limited, and camping in the park is the best of the lot. The **Seabeam Fishing Resort and Hostel (HI-C)** (728-3286)—turn right in Bamfield past the Kamshee Store and it's up the hill on the right—is the only non-camping budget option and includes a kitchen, laundry, showers, and separate rooms. And Bob Hope stayed here once, to boot ($15). Campers should head to **Camp Ross** at the West Coast Trailhead in an amazing shore-side spot (outhouses, pay phone; 3-day max.; free).

The **General Store** (647-5587) in Port Renfrew (647-5587) and the **Kamshee Store** (728-3411) in Bamfield are both good markets. Finding a good, cheap restaurant in the area will be hard, if it's possible at all.

■ Long Beach: Ucluelet and Tofino

Ucluelet and Tofino, at the southern and northern ends of Long Beach, respectively, are both small-town communities complementing the park's outdoor recreational opportunities. From the spring through the fall, Ucluelet transforms into a town-sized pair of binoculars for sightseeing migrators to watch the whales busy with their own migration. Tofino, an intriguing congregation of artists and environmentalists, is also willing to fulfill tourist demands, although perhaps without trading privacy for dollars.

Practical Information Find **visitor information** in Long Beach, 3km into the Long Beach unit of Hwy. 4, close to the **Port Alberni** junction (726-4212; open mid-April to mid-Oct.); in **Tofino** at 351 Campbell St. (725-3414; open July-Aug. daily 9am-8pm, March-June and Sept.-Oct. Sat.-Sun. 9am-5pm); and in **Ucluelet** at 1620 Peninsula Rd. (726-7289; open July-Aug. daily 9am-8pm). The **Park Superintendent** can be contacted for advance information at Box 280, Ucluelet, BC V0R 3A0 (726-7721).

Island Coach Lines, 700 Douglas St., Victoria (385-4411; in Port Alberni at 724-1266; in Nanaimo at 753-4371). Service along the eastern half of Vancouver Island connects Victoria to: Nanaimo (6 buses per day, $14.70); Port Alberni (3 per day, $25.20); Campbell River (4 daily, $33.60); Port Hardy (2 daily, $77.70). **Orient Stage Lines** (in Port Alberni at 723-6924) connects with Island Coach Lines at Port Alberni. During the week they send two buses and on the weekend only one to Ucluelet ($12), and Tofino ($14). **Alberni Marine Transportation, Inc.,** P.O. Box 188, Port Alberni, V9Y 7M7 (723-8313), operates the ferry *M.V. Lady Rose* year-round to Bamfield (4 per week, $15, round-trip $30), Ucluelet (3 per week, $18, round-trip $35), and Gibraltar Island in the **Broken Group Islands** (3 per week, $16, round-trip $32); canoe and kayak rental available. **Great Escapes** (725-2384), on Meares Landing in Tofino, rents mountain bikes for $20 per day.

The **laundromat** is Koin Laundrette in Davison's Shopping Plaza on Peninsula in Ucluelet. The area **bank,** CIBC on Main St., Ucluelet (also at First and Campbell in Tofino) has a 24-hour **ATM** serving Visa and PLUS cards. **Hospital:** 261 Neill St., Tofino (725-3212). **Emergency: Coast Guard,** 725-3231; **RCMP,** 725-3242, in Tofino. **Post Office:** at 1st and Campbell in Tofino (open Mon.-Fri. 8:30am-5:30pm, Sat. 9am-1pm). **Area Code:** 604.

Accommodations, Camping, and Food This is campground country. There are no hostels around, and cheap beds are rare. **Ucluelet Hotel** (726-4324), on Main St. offers shared bath, but no phone and no TV, and is located above a rockin' bar (singles and doubles $28.75-34.50). **Dolphin Motel** (725-3377), 5km south of Tofino near the beach has singles from $37, and doubles from $40.

The 1km-long trail necessary to reach **Schooner Campground,** at the northern end of Long Beach, drastically reduces demand for this backpacker's villa, supplied with cold water and outhouses. Unfortunately, high tides threaten the grounds every other week during the winter (sites $6). **Green Point Campground** (726-4245), 10km north of the park information centre, has 94 sites equipped with hot water, flush toilets, and fireplaces, and swarms with campers and mosquitoes in July and Aug. (Interpreter-led programs. No reservations; June-Sept. work by waiting list each day; April-June first come, first served. Sites mid-June to Aug. $13; Sept.-March $5; April to mid-June $8.50). **Ucluelet Campground,** at Ucluelet Harbor (726-4355) offers showers and toilets for $14 per site, with electricity $2, water $1, and sewer $1 (open March-Oct.).

The small, funky, and colorful **Alleyway Cafe** (725-3105), in Tofino at 305 Campbell at 1st lets you try the clamburger ($5.80) or the unique taco-in-a-bowl ($4.80; open daily 8am-9pm; closed in winter). At the **Common Loaf Bake Shop,** in Tofino at 131 1st St. (725-3915), everything is dense, delicious and satisfying. The chocolate chunk cookie (75¢) and peasant bread ($1.85) are uncommonly good; so is the conversation (open daily 8am-9pm; in winter 8am-6pm). **Porky's Too Pizza and Burgers,** in Ucluelet at 1950 Peninsula (726-7577), has locals squealing over their burgers ($3.20). Quick service, too (open Mon.-Thurs. and Sat. 11am-9pm, Fri. 11am-11pm).

Sights and Activities **Whale watching** is the premier outdoor activity on Long Beach from March to November. Local boatsmen will gladly take you on a three-hour ride to observe the grays closely ($30-45). Smooth rides in large boats are available, but the daring venture out in **Zodiacs,** hard-bottomed inflatable rafts with massive outboard motors that ride the swells at 30 knots. **Remote Passages** (725-3330) offers Zodiac adventures supplemented by an interpretive discussion of the coastal environment (tickets start at $35, under 12 $20). **Subtidal Adventures** (728-7336) offers cruises to the Broken Group Islands ($37, ages 6-12 $21, under 6 $10).

Radar Hill, a few km north of Green Point and connected to the highway by a short paved road, allows you to see far and wide. Learn about the indigenous wildlife and culture at the **Wickaninnish Centre** (726-4212), 3km off Hwy. 4 just past the park entrance (open daily mid-May to Labor Day; free).

Most visitors take advantage of the park's magnificent **hiking trails.** Pick up a *Hiker's Guide* for the Long Beach stretch at the visitors center for a list of nine hikes ranging from 100m to 5km in length. Away from the established trails the park offers infinite opportunities for wandering. When the rain finally overwhelms you, seek refuge in the Native American art galleries in Ucluelet and Tofino. Ucluelet's **Du Quah Gallery,** 1971 Peninsula Rd. (726-7223), is more modest than Tofino's **Eagle Aerie Gallery,** 350 Campbell St. (725-3235), which protects unusual and striking paintings behind the $17,000 carved wooden doors.

■ Port Alberni

Located on Rte. 4, about halfway between Nanaimo and Pacific Rim National Park, this historically lumber-based city is, like many others in the area, shifting toward the tourism industry. And, again like its neighbors, Port Alberni bills itself as the "Salmon Capital of the World," and hosts an annual **Salmon Festival** each Labor Day weekend. The town itself is geared more toward those passing through than to those stopping over. A few attractions do exist, though. Brochures and advice on the general area can be found at the Port Alberni **Infocentre,** on Hwy. 4 (724-6535; open daily 8am-8pm, Sept.-May daily 9am-5pm). **Nosegaard's,** a bountiful farmer's market off Hwy. 4 just west of town, lets you pick your own strawberries for 90¢ per lb. (open mid-June to mid-July 8am-9pm). **Sproat Lake Provincial Park** (248-3931),13km west of Port Alberni off Hwy. 4, offers space to explore mysterious petroglyphs, boat, swim, fish, and camp (sites $12). Moored on Sproat Lake in the summer are the **Martin Mars Bombers,** the last two working flying boats of this type in the world. Originally WWII troop carriers, they are now used to fight fires.

SOUTHEASTERN BRITISH COLUMBIA

■■■ PENTICTON

Native Americans named the region between Okanagan and Skaha Lakes *Pen-tak-tin,* "a place to stay forever." Today, the original inhabitants would spin in their graves if they knew the extent to which their eternal paradise has been insulted by heated pools, waterslides, and luxury hotels. Hot weather, sandy beaches, and proximity to Vancouver, Seattle, and Spokane have ushered in the Tourist Age, and it may strain your budget to spend a weekend here, let alone eternity. The human scale of the area still remains small in relation to the surrounding scenery, though, and the warm water and sprawling beaches of the Okanagan and Skaha Lakes make for ideal swimming, sailing and fishing—so camp out or stay at the hostel and head away from the city. The less neon you see the more fun you'll have (and the less money you're likely to spend).

PRACTICAL INFORMATION AND ORIENTATION

Visitors Information: Penticton Visitors Information Centre, 185 Lakeshore Dr. (493-4055). Take Riverside Dr. north off Hwy. 97, then right on Lakeshore. A fount of travel brochures and an attentive staff. Open daily 8am-8pm; Sept. to mid-June Mon.-Fri. 9am-5pm, Sat.-Sun. 10am-4pm. In summer, the city also sets up an **Information Centre** on Hwy. 97 S, 7km from downtown. While not as expansive as the main office, it carries an ample supply of literature. Open mid-June to Sept. daily 8am-6pm.

Greyhound, 307 Ellis (493-4101). To: Vancouver (5 per day, $39), Vernon (7 per day, $12), Kelowna (7 per day, $7). Open daily 5:45am-7pm and 9pm-12:45am.

Buses: Penticton Transit System, 301 E. Warren Ave. (492-5602). Bus service $1, senior citizens and students 75¢, under 5 free. All drivers carry complete schedules. Service to Naramata $1.50 (4 buses per day Mon.-Fri., 3 on Sat.). Catch the bus at Wade and Martin St. Transit office open Mon.-Fri. 8am-5pm.

Taxi: Klassic Kabs, 492-6666. **Penticton Taxi,** 492-5555.

Car Rental: Budget Rent-A-Car (493-0212), in the main terminal at the Penticton Airport. $40 per day with 100 free km, 15¢ per additional km. Weekend rate of $30 per day with unlimited km. Must be at least 21 with major credit card.

Bike Rental: Skaha Bike Rental, on Yorktown Ave. (490-8575), at the waterslide. Mountain bikes $8 per hr., $25 per day. Open mid-June-Sept. daily 10am-9pm.

Laundry: Plaza Laundromat, 417-1301 Main St. (493-8710).

Weather: 492-6991.

Crisis Line, 493-6622. **Women's Shelter,** 493-7233.

Hospital: 550 Carmi Ave. (492-4000).

Emergency: 911. **Police:** 1103 Main St. (492-4300).

Post Office: 187 W. Westminster Ave. (492-8394). Open Mon.-Fri. 8:30am-5pm. **Postal Code:** V2A 5M0.

Area Code: 604.

Penticton lies 400km east of Vancouver on Hwy. 3. It is the southernmost stomping ground of the Lake Okanagan tourist region, the warmest and driest of the trio of towns that includes **Vernon** on the north and **Kelowna** in the middle. Lake Okanagan borders the north end of town, while the smaller Skaha Lake lies to the south. Main Street bisects the city from north to south.

ACCOMMODATIONS AND CAMPING

Because Penticton is a year-round resort city, hotels here charge more than those in the surrounding towns, making the new hostel nothing short of a godsend. Since you'll be paying through the nose for camping anyway, you might as well try to find a campground on the shores of Okanagan Lake. Make reservations well in advance; vacant sites are rare in July and August.

Penticton Hostel (HI-C), 464 Ellis St. (492-3992). Conveniently located ½ block from a bus stop and 10 min. from the beach. Comfortable lounge and patio, kitchen, laundry facilities, gas grill. Sign on for a few days if the fruit-pickings are slim. Accommodates 45. $13.50, nonmembers $18.50. Under 17 $6.25, under 6 free (with parent). Linen $2.

Riordan House, 689 Winnipeg (493-5997). Infinitely more elegant than the neon-lighted concrete-box motels on Lakeshore Dr.—and not a penny more expensive. The gorgeous Victorian-style mansion was built in 1921 with stressed oak and fir imported from Nova Scotia. 3 enormous rooms are impeccably decorated and include such modern amenities as plush carpeting, TVs, and VCRs. The house even has a library. Breakfast is included in the room fee and features whatever local fruit is in season—rhubarb, strawberries, or cherries. 6 blocks from the beach and 2 from the center of town. Rooms are $50-70.

Kozy Guest House, 1000 Lakeshore Dr. (493-8400). Great location on Okanagan Lake Beach. Each room features a revolutionary revolving television invented by the owner; you can even watch it from the bathroom. Showers in every room. Singles and doubles $50.

Wright's Beach Camp, Site 40, Comp. 4, R.R. 2 (492-7120). Directly off Hwy. 97 on the shores of Skaha Lake at the south end of town. Nearby traffic is often noisy. Adequate washrooms and showers. Sites $18, with hookups $22-24. Make reservations at least 2 weeks in advance.

South Beach Gardens, 3815 Skaha Lake Rd. (492-0628), across the street from the beach, east of the Channel Parkway. Serviced sites $18-21. Unserviced sites $15.

Park Royal RV Park, 240 Riverside Dr. (492-7051), off Hwy. 97. Extensive facilities grace 60 shaded sites. 2-person tentsites $17, RV sites $19, full hookups $23. Additional persons $2.50, additional children $1.50.

FOOD

Intransigent budget travelers may have to swallow their pride and heed the economical call of the Golden Arches or Burger King. However, a few local sandwich shops do provide workable alternatives. Stock up on corned-beef hash at **Foodland,** 698 Westminster Ave. (492-3869; open daily 8am-10pm).

Judy's Deli, 129 W. Nanaimo (492-7029). Take-out only; you'll find a large, splinter-free bench in front of the radio station next door. Healthy beach-goers stop here for hearty homemade soups ($1.65-2) and butter-laden sandwiches ($2.30-3). Open Mon.-Sat. 9am-5:30pm.

Elite Restaurant, 340 Main St. (492-3051). The Elite has been serving quality meals since 1927. The decor is more up-to-date, however, recalling the days of sideburns, the reign of the Chevy Impala, and Jack Lord. Burgers $4-5.50, sandwiches $3.75-6.75. Soup-and-sandwich lunch special $4. Dinner special includes salad or soup, pudding or jello, tea or coffee, and a roll ($8). Open daily 6am-8pm.

Spotted Dog Coffee Bar, 320 Milton. Soda-fountain atmosphere meets a full-espresso bar menu. Go figure. Light food choices. Open Mon.-Fri. 7am-10pm, Sat. 8am-10pm, Sun. 10am-4pm.

SIGHTS AND SEASONAL EVENTS

Known throughout Canada for its bountiful fruit harvests, the **Okanagan Valley** lures visitors with summer blossoms, sleepy towns, and tranquil lakes. Tourists with cars should explore the subtle pleasures of lake-lined Hwy. 97; camp in an orchard bursting with newly-ripened cherries, eat the fruit at a family stand, sample the wines at a local vineyard, or fish in one of the pristine lakes.

The Penticton tourist trade revolves around **Okanagan Lake.** A long, hot summer, in addition to sport facilities on the lake, make Okanagan a popular hangout for a chic young crowd. **Sail Inland** (492-2628 or 493-8221) arranges cruises, charters, and lessons. **The Marina,** 293 Front St. (492-2628), offers rentals of ski boats and fishing equipment. **California Connection** (493-0244), on the beach next to the Delta Lakeside Hotel, offers windsurfing rentals (from $35 per ½ hr.) and lessons.

At the west end of Okanagan Beach, you can step aboard the restored paddle-wheel steamer **S.S. Sicamous** (492-0403), which transported livestock, produce, logging equipment, and passengers up and down Okanagan Lake from 1914 to 1935. You never saw the good side of Penticton until you took a ride on a riverboat queen. (Well, no rides, but open Mon.-Fri. 7am-8:30pm. Admission $2).

For a sample of local culture, take a trip to the **Art Gallery of the South Okanagan,** 11 Ellis St. (493-2928), at Front St. This lovely beachfront gallery exhibits on local and international levels. And the best part is, it's absolutely free. (Open Tues.-Fri. 10am-5pm, Sat.-Sun. 1-5pm.) The **Penticton Museum** (a.k.a. the **R.N. Atkinson Museum),** at 785 Main St. (492-6025), presents one artist's potpourri of Western Canadiana, tracing the history of the region with Native artifacts and wildlife displays. (Open Mon., Wed., and Fri.-Sat. 10am-5pm, Tues. and Thurs. 10am-8:30pm; in winter Mon.-Sat. 10am-5pm.) In the Park on Main St. across the road from the lake, the town sponsors free **summer evening concerts** at the Gyro Bandshell.

Masquerading as an East African wildlife preserve, the **Okanagan Game Farm,** (497-5405) on Hwy. 97 just south of Penticton, covers 560 acres and protects 130 animal species from crazy summer life on the lake. All creatures roam free of fences and bars. Cars can drive throughout the park, and animal checklists should keep the kiddies entertained (open 8am-dusk; admission $8, ages 5-15 $6).

The colorful **Blossom Festival** in April welcomes the fresh flowers blooming in hundreds of apple, peach, and cherry orchards. The city shifts into full gear with the **Peach Festival** and the hellacious **Ironman Canada Triathalon** in mid-August. The Peach Festival offers recreational and aquatic activities for all ages, while the non-stop triathlon commits true athletes to 4km of swimming, 180km of bicycling, and 45km of running.

The mists and mellow fruitfulness of fall mark the ripening of the wine season. There are a number of wineries within easy driving distance of Penticton; the closest one, **Cartier Wines,** 2210 Main St. (492-0621), offers regular tours and free tasting. (Tours given Tues.-Fri. at 11am, 1 and 3pm; in winter Tues.-Fri. at 2pm.) The **Okanagan Wine Festival** (490-8866) to be held September 30 to October 9, 1994, is fun for those fond of feeling thick pulp squish between their toes. Nearby, **Apex Alpine,** P.O. Box 1060 (492-2880), provides winter diversion with six ski lifts, 44 runs, and a 670m vertical drop. (Open Nov. to late April. Lift tickets $30, students $25, senior citizens and children $20. Cross-country skiing $5.)

■■■ REVELSTOKE

Named after the British banker who supplied the money to build a much-needed railroad into the wilderness, the 19th-century Revelstoke was straight out of a Sam Peckinpah Western, with dust-encrusted megalomaniacs maiming each other amidst the gold-laden Selkirk Mountains. Today, Revelstoke attracts an older, Winnebago-driving crowd, but is trying to entice the younger set of skiers and hikers with a new large-scale ski resort at Mt. MacKenzie, 5km south of town. The projected influx of money and tourism threatens to turn this sleepy relic, wedged between the impressive snow-capped peaks of the Selkirk and the Monashee Mountains, into a Banff-like tourist draw—an unwelcome prospect to many Revelstokians. Until the threatened deluge takes place, however, Revelstoke remains quiet, beautiful, and blessedly unexploited.

PRACTICAL INFORMATION AND ORIENTATION

Visitors Information: Travel Information Centre, junction of Hwy. 1 and Hwy. 23 N. (837-3522). Open early May-Sept. daily 9am-6pm. **Chamber of Commerce,** 300 W. 1st St. (837-5345), downtown. Useful and convenient. For more information write to the Chamber of Commerce, P.O. Box 490, Revelstoke, BC V0E 2S0. **Canadian Parks Service,** at Boyle Ave. and 3rd St. (837-7500). Open Mon.-Fri. 8am-noon and 1-4pm.

Greyhound, 1899 Fraser Dr. (837-5874), just off Hwy. 1. To: Calgary ($45.50); Vancouver ($54.50); Salmon Arm ($10.65). Open daily 5:30am-6pm and 10pm-midnight.

Taxi: Johnnie's, 314 Townley St. (837-3000).

Car Rental: Tilden Car Rental, 301 W. 1st St. (837-2158). New cars at decent rates. $40 per day with 100 free km plus 15¢ per additional km. Must be 21 with a credit card.

Bicycle Rental: Revelstoke Cycle Shop, 118 Grizzly Plaza (837-2648). Rents mostly mountain bikes ($5 per hr., $21 per day) and the occasional 10-speed. Open Mon.-Sat. 9am-5:30pm.

Ambulance, 374-5937. **Police,** 320 Wilson St. (837-5255).

Post Office: 307 W. 3rd St. (837-3228). Open Mon.-Fri. 8:30am-5pm. **Postal Code:** V0E 2S0.

Area Code: 604.

Revelstoke is situated on the Trans-Canada Hwy., 410km west of Calgary and 575km east of Vancouver. The town is relatively small and can be easily covered on foot or by bicycle. **Mount Revelstoke National Park** itself is much larger; including the town, it covers 263 sq. km. Mild temperatures, a relatively long growing season, and large amounts of rain endow this portion of the Columbia Mountains with lush vegetation and bountiful wildlife. Revelstoke and its easterly neighbor, Glacier National Park, contain sections of the Columbia Rainforest. The 1000-year-old cedars let you appreciate why residents are so concerned over the logging industry's clear-cutting.

ACCOMMODATIONS AND CAMPING

Numerous hotels line Revelstoke's rim along the Trans-Canada Hwy. In town you'll find a bed for the same moderate price, further removed from the sounds and smells of interprovince traffic. Local campgrounds tend to favor RV drivers over tenters.

King Edward Hotel, 112 Second St. E. (837-2000), at Orton.Hall bathrooms, the nearby train depot, and the lounge beneath often make for less-than-tranquil snoozing. But the bathtubs are decadent, the management friendly, and the prices the lowest in town. Singles $26.45, tax included.

Hidden Motel, 1855 Big Eddy Rd. (837-4240). Take Hwy. 23 south from Trans-Canada Hwy., turn left on Big Eddy Rd. to reach this cozy, comfortable family-operated hotel. Each room has its own stove, refrigerator, kitchen sink, and cable TV. Dutch spoken. Singles and doubles $42, double with twin beds $48. Each additional person $6.

Ol' Frontier Motel (837-5119), at Trans-Canada Hwy. and Hwy. 23 N, next to the infocentre. 28 small but adequate rooms. Color TV, sink, and shower for contortionists. Popular restaurant next door is run by the same management. Store open 24 hr. Singles $33. Doubles $37. Prices drop $3 in winter.

Smokey Bear Campground (837-9575), on Hwy. 1, 5km west of Revelstoke. Convenient, but close to the noisy highway. Clean bathrooms, metered showers, laundromat, and amply stocked store. Both RVs and tents are welcome. 30 sites, $10-15. Each additional person 75¢. Electricity $2, sewer $1. Open May-Oct.

Canyon Hot Springs (837-2420), Hwy. 1, 35km east of Revelstoke on the border of Mt. Revelstoke National Park. The staff is pleasant, and the scenic location—near both Mt. Revelstoke and Glacier National Parks—is convenient for exploring the mountains. Caters more to RVs than to backpackers. Unserviced sites $14, serviced $18. Includes showers and firewood. Group rates available on request. Open late May-late Sept.

FOOD

The downtown dining scene is dominated by Chinese and Western restaurants. You'll have to head many kilometers to the west along Hwy. 1 for a Whopper or that much-coveted box of McDonaldland Cookies. Pick up a five-pound can of beans at **Cooper's Supermarket,** in the Alpine Village Centre on Victoria St. (837-4372; open daily 9am-6pm, Fri. until 9pm. Local hangout.)

Manning's Restaurant, 302 MacKenzie Ave. (837-3258). The best Chinese food in town, plus a wide array of reasonably priced Continental dishes. Beef and broccoli ($6.70), sweet and sour spareribs ($7), 8-oz. steaks ($10). Open Mon.-Sat. noon-10pm, Sun. 4-9pm.

Ol' Frontier Restaurant (837-5119), at the junction of Hwy. 1 and Hwy. 23 N. Wagon wheels and checkered tablecloths recollect the restaurants of the Ol' West. The "Ranchhand" is a ½-lb. cheeseburger with the works ($7.40). Tenderfoots may prefer the sparer "bareback" ($4.70), a plain hamburger with nothing on it. Open daily 6am-9pm.

A.B.C. Family Restaurant (837-5491), in the Alpine Village Centre on Victoria St. Link in a chain of "family" restaurants, but nonetheless maintains an original atmosphere. Huge dinner menu ranges from $7.40-10.60. Soup and sandwich $6.50; don't pass up a slice of fresh pie ($3-4). Open daily 6am-10pm.

Alphaus, 604 W. 2nd St., at Garden Ave. (837-6380). The quaint white stucco and brown shingles seem jarring in Revelstoke. Sandwiches on homemade rye run

SALMON ARM

$3.25-5.50, and authentic German dinner specialities run $7.50-12.50. If young Werther were still with us, perhaps he'd drown his sorrows in a $2.75 bottle of Okanagan Stout. Open daily 8:30am-8pm.

SIGHTS

All tourism in town revolves around the **Revelstoke Dam,** 5km north of Hwy. 1 on Hwy. 23 (837-6515 or 837-6211). The **visitor centre** underscores the dam's mechanical marvels by means of a free tour via "talking wand." Hum along with the four monster generators to keep yourself awake, and then take the elevator to the top of the dam for an impressive view. (Open daily mid-March to mid-June 9am-5pm; mid-June to mid-Sept. 8am-8pm; mid-Sept. to late Oct. 9am-5pm. Wheelchair accessible.) The **Revelstoke Museum and Archives** (837-3067), 315 1st St. W., like most small town museums, resides in an old government building (the post office) and exhibits a modest ensemble of local turn-of-the-century artifacts. (Open June-Aug. Mon.-Fri. 1-8pm; May, Sept., and Oct. Mon.-Fri. 1-4:30pm; Nov.-April Mon., Wed., and Fri. 1-4:30pm.)

Mt. Revelstoke National Park has many of the scenic attractions one comes to expect from Canadian national parks. This tiny park (260 square km) teems with all sorts of animals that eat, drink, move around, and copulate right before your very eyes. A number of excellent **fishing** lakes can be reached by 35km of established trails; apply at the park information center (see Practical Information) for a permit (weekly $6, annual $13). At the summit of Mt. Revelstoke are some of the few vehicle-accessible alpine meadows in Western Canada; **Summit Road** branches off from the Trans-Canada Hwy. 1.5km east of Revelstoke and takes about an hour to drive. The **Canadian Parks Service** (see Practical Information) has park information.

Two special **boardwalks** just off Hwy. 1 on the eastern border of the park allow exploration of the local brush in depth. One trail leads through "acres of stinking perfection"—brambles of skunk cabbage plants that grow to heights of over 1.5m. The other wanders into a forest full of giant cedar trees, some over 1000 years old.

Revelstoke has tried some curious variations on **downhill skiing** to spice up its winter season. **Mount Mackenzie,** P.O. Box 1000, 5km outside of town (call collect at 837-5268), gives you a chance to climb deep bowls of powdered snow in motorized snow cats. Experts (rich experts, that is) may want to try **helicopter skiing** in the Selkirks. (Write to Selkirk Tangiers Heli-Ski Ltd., P.O. Box 1409, Golden, BC or call 837-5378 or 344-5016 for arrangements.) **Cross-country** skiers will find more than enough snow and trails in the nearby national parks to keep them busy all winter long. Contact **Revelstoke Cycle Shop** (837-2648) for information and rentals ($24 per day). Summer vacationers will want to contact **Monashee Outfitting,** P.O. Box 2958 (837-3538), which sponsors just about every outdoor activity imaginable, including horse rides, fishing trips, hunting trips, and gold panning.

■ Salmon Arm

Salmon Arm is a small, honky-tonk town just like thousands of others that aren't immortalized in the pages of *Let's Go,* but its setting is extraordinary. Lake Shuswap is sublime, and the mountains which cradle the town are breathtaking, especially when the leaves change in autumn.

Practical Information The **Travel Infocentre,** Box 999 (832-6247), is just off the Trans-Canada Hwy. in the center of town (open Mon.-Fri. 8:30am-5pm, Sat.-Sun. 9am-5pm; in winter weekdays only).

You can wash out your grubbies at the **B-Line Laundromat,** 456 Trans-Canada Hwy. (832-5500), in the Smitty's shopping center (wash $1.25, 12-min. dry 25¢; open daily 6am-11pm). Emergencies in Salmon Arm are answered by the **ambulance** (374-5937); the **hospital** is at 601 10th St. NE (832-2182); and the **police** are at 501 2nd Ave. NE (832-6044). Address general delivery letters to **Postal Code** V1E 4M6. The **area code** is 604.

Accommodations, Camping, and Food When in Salmon Arm, your best option is to overnight at the **Cindosa Bed and Breakfast,** 3951 40th St. NE (832-3342), where the Cindosas will pamper you with nice beds and fantastic, home-cooked breakfasts with ingredients from the farm out back. They'll even pick you up at the bus station (singles $35, doubles $45). **Glen Echo Resort,** 6592 Trans-Canada Hwy. NW (832-6268), 7 mi. west on Hwy. 1, is smack on Lake Shuswap, with a sandy beach, excellent swimming all summer long, and a gregarious owner (open Victoria Day-Sept.; 65 sites, $8).

Despite its name, Salmon Arm's culinary establishments showcase neither fish nor limbs. Restaurants offer standard surf 'n' turf fare with a pronounced emphasis on the turf. Try **Mr. Mike's** (832-8428) on Hwy. 1 across from the waterslide. The $6.40 all-you-can-eat salad bar includes soup and dessert. Beat the system—construct primitive, outlaw sandwiches from shredded ham and oddly shaped pieces of French bread. (Open Mon.-Tues. 11am-8:30pm, Wed.-Sat. 11am-9pm, Sun. 11am-8pm.) The **Eatery,** 361 Alexander St. (832-7490), serves "Big Magilla" sandwiches (turkey, roast beef, and lamb $4.50) along with other gargantuan concoctions (open Mon.-Thurs. and Sat. 6am-5pm, Fri. 6am-6pm).

Sights Visit **Heritage Park,** just south of the junction of Hwy. 1 and 97B (832-5243), to experience turn-of-the-century life. Period buildings include a church, a schoolhouse, and the meticulously restored **Haney Heritage House.** The **Salmon Arm Museum,** located next to the church, displays an extensive collection of photographs from the early part of the century (open June-Oct. daily 10am-6pm; admission $2, children $1, preschoolers free).

Learn what curds and whey actually are at **Gort's Gouda Cheese Factory,** 1470 50th St. S.W. (832-4274). The free tours only last a few minutes, getting you to the tasty cheese samples that are exhausted much more quickly (tours Mon. and Fri. at 2pm; call to arrange tours at other times).

The Salmon Arm area teems with wildlife. Relax at **McGuire Park,** on Hwy. 1 next to the hospital, to view Canada geese, muskrats, turtles, and ducks. Fish or swim in **Lake Shuswap,** go white water rafting on nearby **Adams River,** or hike out to **Margaret Falls,** just west of town. Follow the signs for **Heral Park** off Hwy. 1. A 10km detour and a short hike on the manicured slopes will bring you to the striking falls.

Salmon Arm is also home to world-famous talking horse **Shag-ra** and his faithful companion **Shamus the Wonderdog.** Shag-ra has appeared on network television and performs regularly at local fairs and festivals. In the face of skepticism and plagued with an unappetizing tooth discoloration, Shag-ra perseveres, undaunted: "Undaunted, I Persevere" reads the sign. For more information about Shag-ra, contact the Chamber of Commerce or the Travel Infocentre.

■ Glacier National Park

For a $5000 salary bonus and immortality on the map, Major A.B. Rogers discovered a route through the Columbia Mountains which finally allowed East to meet West in Canada's first transcontinental railway. Completed in 1885, the railway was a dangerous enterprise; more than 200 lives were lost to avalanches during its first 30 years of operation. Today, **Rogers Pass** lies in the center of Glacier National Park, and 1350 sq. km commemorate the efforts of Rogers and other hardy explorers who united British Columbia with the rest of Canada.

Practical Information The Trans-Canada Hwy.'s numerous **scenic turn-offs** offer picnic facilities, bathrooms, and historical plaques. For a detailed description of the park's 19 hiking trails, contact the **Park Administration Office** (837-7500), at 3rd and Boyle west of the park in Revelstoke (open Mon.-Fri. 8am-4:30pm), or pick up a copy of *Footloose in the Columbias* at the **Rogers Pass Information Centre,** located along the highway in Glacier. The Centre has enough computerized information, scale models, and exhibits to warrant a visit—don't miss the free 25-minute movie *Snow War,* which is shown on the hour and includes a chilling scene from an actual avalanche rescue (open daily 8am-8pm; in winter daily 9am-6pm). **Park passes** are available at the Centre and cost $5 per day, $10 for four days, $30 per year. For more information about Glacier, write the Superintendent, P.O. Box 350, Revelstoke V0E 2S0.

Glacier lies right in the path of the Trans-Canada Hwy., 262km west of Calgary and 723km east of Vancouver. **Greyhound** (837-5874) makes four trips daily from Revelstoke to Glacier ($6.15). In an emergency, call the **Park Warden Office** (837-6274; open daily 7am-11pm; in winter daily 24 hr.). The **area code** is 604.

Accommodations, Camping, and Food The only beds in the park are under the roof of the **Best Western Glacier Park Lodge** (837-2126), Trans-Canada Hwy., The Summit, Rogers Pass. If you absolutely must have a comfortable mattress and a clean bathroom, be prepared to turn your head and cough up $90 for a single or $95 for a double (10% discount for senior citizens, children under 12 free).

There are two campgrounds in Glacier: **Illecillewaet** (ILL-uh-SILL-uh-watt) and **Loop Brook.** Both offer flush toilets, kitchen shelters with cook stoves, drinking water, and firewood (open mid-June-Sept.; sites for both $10.50). Illecillewaet stays open in winter without plumbing; winter guests must register at the Park Administration Office at Rogers Pass. **Backcountry campers** must pitch their tents at least 3km from the highway and register with the Administration Office beforehand.

The only **restaurant** in the area is at the **Best Western** (see above), where prices are prohibitive, and proper attire is required. The **Petro-Canada station** at Rogers Pass sells soggy ham-and-cheese subs for $4; you'd do well to drop by a supermarket in Golden or Revelstoke before you enter the park.

Outdoors A century after Rogers' discovery, Glacier National Park remains one of the few unspoiled wilderness areas in the interior of British Columbia. The jagged peaks and steep, narrow valleys of the Columbia Range prevent development within Glacier—one would literally have to move mountains to establish a "townsite" here. The Trans-Canada Highway cuts a thin ribbon through the center of the park, affording spectacular views of over 400 glaciers. More than 140km of challenging trails lead away from the highway, inviting rugged mountain men and women to penetrate the near-impenetrable. Try to visit the park in late July or early August, when brilliant explosions of mountain wildflowers offset the deep green of the Columbia rainforests. Glacier receives measurable precipitation one out of every two days during the summer, but don't despair—the clouds of mist that encircle the peaks and blanket the valleys only add to the park's astonishing beauty. Hikers not directly descended from Sir Edmund Hilary should avoid the park in winter, as near-daily snowfalls and the constant threat of avalanches often restrict travel to the Trans-Canada Hwy.

Eight popular **hiking trails** begin at the Illecillewaet campground, 3.4km west of Rogers Pass. The relaxing, 1km **Meeting of the Waters** trail leads to the confluence of the Illecillewaet and Asulkan Rivers. The 4.2km **Avalanche Crest** trail offers spectacular views of Rogers Pass, the Hermit Range, and the Illecillewaet River Valley; the treeless slopes below the crest testify to the destructive power of winter snowslides. From early June to late August, the Information Centre runs daily **interpretive hikes** through the park beginning at 9am. Come prepared for one of these four- to six-hour tours with a picnic lunch, a rain jacket, and a sturdy pair of walking shoes. Due to the steepness of the terrain, there is no biking on the trails in Glacier. The park's glacial meltwaters, a startling milky-aqua color due to the fine bits of sediment suspended in the current, don't support many fish; determined anglers can try their luck with the cutthroat in the Illecillewaet River.

Northern British Columbia and the Yukon

Although the Yukon and Northern British Columbia were the first regions of North America to be settled some 20,000 years ago, today they remain largely untouched and inaccessible. With an average of only one person per 15 sq. km, the loneliness of the land is overwhelming—as is its sheer physical beauty, a reward for those willing to put up with poor road conditions and millions of biting insects.

FRASER RIVER CANYON

Simon Fraser, Canada's single rough equivalent of Lewis and Clark, braved 1300km of turbulent water to reach Vancouver from Mt. Robson in 1808. Today, a slightly easier path (the **Trans-Canada Hwy.**) snakes down the Fraser River between the towns of Hope and Cache Creek. Fraser's 200km of coiling rapids are not quite exciting as the Infocentre's pamphlets would have you believe, but the sheer size of the towering, pine-covered canyon walls makes it a very striking scene.

■ Hope

Plastered with pics and posters, the **Travel Infocentre** in Hope, 919 Water Ave. (869-2021), is quick to welcome newcomers to the very same area used to stage the original "Rambo" blockbuster, *First Blood*. Perhaps inspired by that movie's sizable gross, *Shoot to Kill*, with Sidney Poitier and Kirstie Alley, and the box-office bomb *Fire with Fire* were also filmed in this small town of 3500. Besides providing a tour of the town on the "Rambo Walking Tour," the Infocentre also disseminates exhaustively hopeful information on the town and region surrounding the Fraser River Canyon. (Open daily 8am-8pm; Oct.-May daily 9am-5pm).

Even in the absence of hordes of gaffers and DPs, Hope—located 150km east of Vancouver and 190km south of Cache Creek—remains the largest town in the Fraser Canyon. The **Greyhound station,** 833 3rd Ave. (869-5522), is centrally located and provides an easy reference point for visitors. Buses arrive almost hourly from Vancouver and continue onwards toward Dawson Creek or Calgary. Those without the patience (or the cash) to wait for the next departing bus north can hitch a ride along Hwy. 1 without too much difficulty. Those averse to hitching can rent a car at **Gardner Chev-Olds,** 945 Water St. (869-9511), next to the Infocentre ($30 per day with 100km free, plus 13¢ per additional km; optional damage/collision waiver $9 per day; rent for a week for the price of 6 days. Open Mon.-Sat. 8:30am-6pm.) The **RCMP** in Hope (869-5644) is at 670 Hope-Princeton Hwy., just off Hwy. 3 (but no, they don't rent horses).

If you decide to stay overnight, trek an entire block north from the bus station to Wallace St. and hang a left. The **Hope Motor Hotel,** 272 Wallace St. (869-5641), rents rooms for $40.25 (single or double); be sure to request one of the recently renovated rooms. Excepting July or August, breakfast is included in the price of the room. Campers can try **Coquihalla River Park,** 800 Kawkawa Rd. (869-7119), off

Hwy. 3 via 7th Ave. (just before the Coquihalla River Bridge), which provides free showers (116 sites, $14, with electricity and water $18).

Hope has its share of fast-food joints (there's a Dairy Queen right on the highway), but if you prefer to order your meal from a resting position, try either the **Cariboo Restaurant** (867-5413), which gives a good generic meal (hamburger and fries for $5), or **The Suzie Q Family Restaurant** (869-5515) which serves both cheap Western *and* Japanese cuisine (hmm…). Both are located a block north of the bus station at the intersection of Wallace and 6th.

■ Yale

Yale, 30km north of Hope on the Trans-Canada Hwy., not only is the site of the oldest church in British Columbia and birthplace of the colony's first white child, but also boasted a gold boom population of 20,000 in 1858, when it was the largest North American city west of Chicago and north of San Francisco. But the city's unfortunate name has forever condemned it to second-rate status—Yale has floundered, and the population has dwindled to below 250. Find out everything there is to know about the town at the **Yale Historical Society Museum** (863-2324), next to the church at the convergence of Hwy. 1, Douglass St., and Albert St., near the town's only stoplight (open June-Oct. daily 9am-5pm; "requested contribution" $2, students $1). If you're not frightened by psychedelic woolly red and orange carpet, the **Gold Nugget Motel** (863-2446), on the highway, offers singles for $28 (cable TV, no phones). Across the street is **Barry's Trading Post** (863-2214), a small general store which serves up cheap fried food—and lots of it. The **Emery Creek Provincial Park,** 5km south on the highway, maintains 34 sites April through October ($10, no reservations; firewood and running water available).

Farther north along Hwy. 1, hard-core campers will enjoy roughing it at **Gold Pan River Campground,** 16km west of **Spences Bridge.** The 12 sites ($6) offer no privacy but are a mere hop from the rushing **Thompson River.** Less intrepid campers can opt for **Skihist Provincial Park Campground,** 12km east of **Lytton.** The 50 sites ($9.50) are protected by gates which are locked from 11pm to 6am; water and flush toilets are provided.

■ Outdoors In The Canyon

To get a closer look at the Fraser River, you've got plenty of options. It is worthwhile to set out on one of the moderately difficult **hikes** that start from trailheads near Hope. The 20-minute, lush **Rotary Trail** starts off at Wardle St. and runs into the confluence of the Fraser and Coquihalla Rivers. If you seek something a bit more challenging, try the two-hour climb to the summit of **Thacker Mountain.** To reach the foot of this trail, cross Coquihalla River Bridge, take a left on Union Bar Rd., and then go left again on Thacker Mtn. Rd. The car park at the road's end marks the beginning of a 5-km gravel path to the peak, which features clear vistas of Hope and the Fraser River. While hiking to the trailhead, pause for a pleasant diversion at Kawkawa Creek off Union Bar Rd., which was recently "enhanced" to aid the mid- and late-summer salmon spawnings. The boardwalk along the creek leads to a swimming hole and popular picnicking spot.

For those with a car, the **Coquihalla Canyon Recreation Area** is a 5 to10- minute drive out of Hope along Kawkawa Lake Rd. The **Othello Quintet Tunnels** located here provide mute evidence of the impressive engineering that led to the opening of the Kettle Valley Railway in 1916. Blasted through solid granite, these rough tunnels overlook the Coquihalla River, which has itself done an impressive job on the granite by carving out the 300 ft.-deep channel through which it now flows. Take a right on Othello Rd. off Kawkawa Lake Rd., and then take another right on Tunnel Rd. Allow half an hour to walk through the tunnels.

If you're based in Yale and want to get out and enjoy the river, head north and take the first right after the stoplight (remember, there's only one), and then follow the gravel road about 1km; you'll find a close-up view of the majestic **Lady Franklin Rock,** which splits the Fraser into two sets of heavy rapids. If you're interested in actually getting *on* the river, **Fraser River Raft Expeditions** (863-2336), located just south of town, is undoubtedly the way to go. Although the $90 fee for a full-day trip might seem as steep as the canyon walls, those who can pull together the funds shouldn't miss the opportunity to get their hearts pounding and their bodies drenched. One- and multi-day trips down the Fraser, Thompson, Nahatlatch, and Coquihalla Rivers are available, and the friendly guides serve up great meals.

When Simon Fraser made his pioneering trek down the river that now bears his name, he likened one particularly tumultuous stretch of rapids to the "Gates of Hell." The white foaming waters of **Hell's Gate,** 25km north of Yale on Hwy. 1, make the success of Fraser's journey seem miraculous indeed. When melting snow floods the river in spring, the 60m-deep water rushes through the narrow gorge with such force that the air around it vibrates and sizzles. A cluster of overpriced gift shops and eateries are now embedded in the precipitous cliffs where Fraser once advised "no human beings should venture." The gondolas of **Hell's Gate Airtram** will "fly" you 502 ft. across the canyon ($17.50 for four—count 'em, *four*—minutes aloft); those wishing to stay grounded should opt for the free hike down to the river.

THE CARIBOO HIGHWAY

The portion of Hwy. 97 known as the **Cariboo Hwy.** runs south to north for approximately 450km between Cache Creek and Prince George. The road stretches through relatively flat terrain characterized by its mostly unimpressive scenery. Dry winds and sagebrush bound along much of the highway as it winds through a series of small towns—many punctuated with such lackluster names as "100 Mile House" and "108 Mile Ranch" (whose claim to fame is possession of the world's largest pair of cross-country skis). Generally unexciting, the highway's best pit stops are the towns of Williams Lake, at Mile 155, and Quesnel (pronounced kwuh-NEL), half-way between Williams Lake and Prince George. The **Travel Infocentre** in **Williams Lake** is on the highway and can give you the scoop on activities and events in the area (392-5025; open daily 8am-6pm, Labour Day-Victoria Day Mon.-Fri. 9am-5pm). The **Greyhound** station in William's Lake is located halfway through town, directly off the highway. Buses going north leave three times daily.

You can secure a roof over your head at the **Valley View Motel** (392-4655), off the highway (A/C; singles $36, doubles $38). Just next door is the **Lakeside Motel** (392-4181), with singles for $41. Williams Lake is home to the province's most active cattle marketing and shipping industry; the town celebrates its "cowboy" heritage each July with the four-day **Williams Lake Stampede,** held Canada Day Weekend. The festivities include a rodeo, parade, and "pony chuckwagon races."

In **Quesnel,** the **Infocentre,** at 703 Carson Ave. in Le Bourdais Park (992-8716), offers information and, for $1.50 admission, a museum of local history. (Open May-June daily 8am-6pm, July-Aug. daily 8am-6pm, Labour Day-Victoria Day Mon.-Fri. 8:30am-4:30pm.) The **Cariboo Hotel,** 254 Front St. (992-2333), has rooms starting from $45 (includes continental breakfast), with cable TV, phones, and jacuzziesque baths. **Roberts Roost Campground,** 3121 Gook Rd. (747-2015), is in **Dragon Lake,** 8km south of Quesnel. Open April to October, the campground has showers, flush toilets, laundry facilities, and a swimming beach (sites $14, full hookup $18).

Barkerville, 80km east of Quesnel, lures tourists with its "living museum"—an 1870s gold rush town replete with wild-west costumes, period buildings, and gold-panning. Between mid-June and Labor Day you'll have to pay admission to enter the town ($7.50, students $6), although you can walk in and stroll around for free after 5pm. There are three provincial campgrounds within 2km of Barkerville. **Lowhee** and **Forest Rose Campgrounds** both offer showers and sites for $12. **Government**

Hill Campground has sites for $9.50 (pit toilets only). Check with the Quesnel Travel Infocentre (see above) or the **Visitors Services Office** in Barkerville (994-3332; open June 19-Sept. 6 8am-8pm) for a full schedule of the town's shenanigans. For coverage of the entire Cariboo region, pick up a free copy of *Cariboo Chilcotin Coast*, available at hotels, tourist attractions, and infocentres along the highway.

Hard-core outdoorspeople should chase to **Bowron Lake Provincial Park,** 28km east of Barkerville, accessible only by dirt road. The park's 116km canoe circuit roughly traces its perimeter; allow seven to 10 days for the trip. For those who've gone beyond hard-core and off the deep end, the **Alexander Mackenzie Heritage Trail** might be the ultimate challenge. The 250km trail begins from Hwy. 97 just north of Quesnel and stretches across western British Columbia as it retraces the final leg of Mackenzie's exploratory journey of 1793, finally terminating in **Bella Coola** on the remote central coast. Allow 14 to 21 days to cover the entire trail.

■ Prince George

Named for the British heir whom Shelley unaffectionately described as "mud from a muddy spring," Prince George is a simple town sustained by the timber industry. Pulp and lumber mills labor beyond the city limits, while the city itself harbors more than 100 spotted-owl-friendly parks. Though nothing spectacular awaits the incoming traveler, residents are friendly, the museums pleasant, and the city's 60 baseball fields offer an opportunity to enjoy the diamond outdoors.

Practical Information Prince George is roughly equidistant from four major Canadian cities: 780km northeast of Vancouver, 720km southeast of Prince Rupert, 735km west of Edmonton, and 790km northwest of Calgary. You can pick up a free, detailed map of Prince George at either of the two **Travel Infocentres,** the first at 1198 Victoria St., at 15th Ave. (562-3700), and the second at the junction of Hwy. 16 and 97 (563-5493). Both are open May-Sept. Mon.-Fri. 8:30am-8pm, Sat.-Sun. 9am-8pm; the first remains open in the off-season Mon.-Fri. 9am-5pm.

If you're up to an attempt at deciphering the schedules at **BC Rail** (561-4033), at the end of Terminal Blvd., 2km south on Hwy. 97, or **VIA Rail,** 1300 1st Ave. (564-5233 or 800-561-8630; open Tues.-Thurs. 5pm-1am), at the foot of Quebec St., then try your luck with the infrequent services south to Vancouver and Edmonton (but a little bad luck could have you hanging out in Prince George for several days before your train arrives). Rather not wait? Try **Greyhound,** 1566 12th Ave. (564-5454; open Mon.-Sat. 5:30am-midnight, Sun. 5:30-9:30am, 5-6:30pm, and 8:30pm-midnight), across from the Infocentre, which has buses to Whitehorse, YT (3 per week, $200), Edmonton, AB (2 per day, $83), Vancouver (3 per day, $80), Prince Rupert (2 per day, $77), and Dawson Creek (2 per day, $45). Lockers are available for $1.

The **public library** is located at 887 Dominion (563-5528 for a recording, 563-9251 for an operator. Open Mon.-Thurs. 10am-9pm, Fri.-Sat. 10am-5:30pm). Those in need of a **pharmacy** or **laundromat** shouldn't have any trouble finding one—they exist in plenty. **Prince George Regional Hospital** is located at 2000 15th Ave. (565-2000; emergency 565-2444). The **RCMP** are at 1325 5th Ave. (561-3155). The **post office** is at 1323 5th Ave. (561-5184; open Mon.-Fri. 8:30am-5pm; **Postal Code:** V2L 4R8). The **area code** is 604.

Accommodations, Camping, and Food If you're only stopping in Prince George to get a good night's sleep and stock up on provisions, the closest thing to budget accommodations—and it's not very close—can be found at the **Queensway Court Motel,** 1616 Queensway St. (562-5068; singles $40, doubles $46), or at the **Camelot Motel,** 1600 Central St. (563-0661; singles $45, doubles $50; indoor swimming pool). The **Red Cedar Inn,** on Bear Rd. (964-4427), 8km west off Hwy. 16, has campsites ($11, full hookups $14) and rooms (singles $30, doubles $34) and is close to the highway. Farther from the highway—but plagued by RVs—the **South Park Trailer Park** (963-7577), 5km south of Prince George on Hwy. 97, has grassy sites

($11, hookups $16) with clean bathrooms and one metered shower per gender. The closest campground to downtown, however, must be the **City Campground** (563-2313), an approximately 20-minute walk along 15th Ave. from the Infocentre (after a lengthy walk, take a left on Ospikn Blvd., and then a right on 18th Ave.) which has showers and a secure fence (gates closed 11am-6pm; sites $11, with full hookup $13).

Those seeking to cheaply sate their hunger should seek out **Safeway,** 1600 15th Ave., across the intersection from the downtown Infocentre. Restaurant fare can be had at **Nick's Place,** 363 George St. (562-2523), where a large plate of good spaghetti costs $7 (open Mon.-Sat. 11am-3:30am, Sun. 4-10pm), or at the **Camelot Court,** right next to the Camelot motel, which serves up major portions of burgers, sandwiches, and fries for minor prices.

Sights **Cottonwood Island Nature Park,** a 3km walk from downtown along Patricia Blvd., has plenty of comfortable walking trails. For a bird's eye view of the rich landscape, climb atop **Connaught Hill Park,** off Queensway on Connaught Dr. **Fort George Park,** on the bands of the Fraser River off 20th Ave., offers huge expanses of green grassy lawns, picnic tables, and barbecue pits. If all the excitement drives you indoors, seek refuge in the **Fort George Regional Museum** (562-1612), which houses an array of frontier artifacts including several primitive chain saws. (Open daily 10am-5pm; mid-Sept. to mid-May Tues.-Sun. noon-5pm. "Requested donation" $3, students $2.) For a thorough introduction to Canadian rail history, choo-choo-ch'boogie on over to the **Prince George Regional Railway and Forest Industry Museum** (563-7351) on River Rd. Visitors can climb aboard and explore the growing collection of rolling stock; the highlight is an original 1914 Grand Trunk Station, one of only three that remain (open Victoria Day to Labour Day daily 10am-5pm; $2.50, students $2).

Prince George's royal events and festivities "range from the sublime to the ridiculous and beyond." **Mardi Gras,** which lasts for 10 days in late February, features events such as sno-golf, softball in the snow, and jousting with padded poles. For information call 564-3737 or write P.O. Box 383, Station A, Prince George. Summertime events include the **Canadian Northern Children's Festival,** a four-day event held in mid-May which includes live theatre, vaudeville, and plenty of music; and **Sandblast,** the daring third Sunday in August which sends a group of skiers down the steep and sandy Nechako Cutbanks. Prince George's **Oktoberfest** is held on an early October weekend. Enjoy traditional Bavarian oom-pah-pah music while taking in plenty of the three B's: beer, bands, and bratwurst.

■ Prince Rupert

When wealthy entrepreneur Charles Melville Hays dreamt of completing a second trans-Canada railroad, he planned to make its terminus the then-uninhabited Kaien Island, home to the third-largest ice-free harbor in the world. In order to secure shareholders, Hays traveled to England, only to return on the ill-fated *S.S. Titanic.* While the Grand Trunk Pacific Railway eventually established a company city on the island and named it Prince Rupert after the second cousin of King Charles II, Hays' good intentions are remembered by a statue downtown.

Prince Rupert never lived up to Hays's vision of a port city to rival Vancouver in economic muscle, but the docks steadily welcome the produce of the North Canadian plains. Prince Rupert is yet another of Western Canada's "gateways"—towns that offer few bona fide tourist attractions, but nonetheless draw hordes of travelers headed for more interesting destinations. As a point of embarkation for those who want to explore the Alaskan Panhandle to the north, the Queen Charlotte Islands to the west, and Vancouver Island to the south, Prince Rupert is perhaps best viewed from the stern of an outbound ferry.

Practical Information Most visitors come to Prince Rupert either for its fishing or its ferries. An afternoon in a guided fishing boat costs upwards of $100; thus, pass the hours before your ship comes in browsing the 15 downtown blocks. The **Travel Infocentre**, 1st Ave. and McBride St. (624-5637; open May 15 to Labor Day daily 9am-9pm; in winter Mon.-Sat. 10am-5pm), has maps for a self-guided tour which includes the Infocentre's free museum, a cornucopia of totem poles, the manicured Sunken Gardens, and a Native American carving shed.

The only major road into town is **Hwy. 16,** which becomes McBride at the city limits and then curves left to become 2nd Ave. downtown. **Prince Rupert Bus Service** (624-3343) provides local, limited service around downtown Mon.-Sat. (fare $1, senior citizens 60¢, students 75¢; day pass $2.50, senior citizens and students $2). The #52 bus runs from 2nd Ave. and 3rd St. to within a five-minute walk of the ferry terminal. Or try **Skeena Taxi**, 624-2185 (open 24 hr.).

From Prince Rupert, **Air BC**, 112 6th St. (624-4554), flies to Vancouver ($322). **Canadian Airlines** (624-9181), on the bottom floor of the mall on 2nd Ave. W, offers the same service at the same price. Ask about standby flights which can be cheaper than the bus or train. **VIA Rail** (627-7589), on the water at the end of 11th St. (by car) or down the ramp from the corner of 1st Ave. and 2nd St. (by foot), runs trains to Vancouver (3 per week, $199) and Prince George, 720km to the east ($45 with 7-day advance purchase). (Open Mon., Thurs., and Sat. 1-4:30pm; Tues., Fri., and Sun. 9am-12:30pm.) **Greyhound,** 822 3rd Ave. near 8th St. (624-5090), runs buses twice daily to Prince George ($77), Vancouver ($157), and Seattle ($182). (Open Mon.-Fri. 8:30am-8:30pm, Sat.-Sun. and holidays 9-11:15am and 6-8:30pm.) The **Alaska Marine Highway** (627-1744) runs ferries north from Prince Rupert to Ketchikan (US$32, car US$87), Wrangell (US$50, car US$139), Petersburg (US$62, car US$172), Juneau (US$98, car US$277), and Haines (US$112, car US$316). **BC Ferries** (624-9627), at the end of Hwy. 16, serves the Queen Charlotte Islands (6 per week, $18, car $69) and Port Hardy (4 per week, $90, car $185). Reservations are required at least three weeks in advance for vehicles. Ferrygoers are not permitted to leave their cars parked on the streets of Prince Rupert. A number of establishments charge a daily rate for storage; pick up a list at the Infocentre (see above).

King Koin Laundromat (624-2667) spins at 7th St. and 2nd Ave. (Wash $1.50, 5 min. dry 25¢. Open Mon.-Sat. 7am-10pm, Sun. 8am-9pm.) The **library** is on McBride at 6th St. (627-1345; open Mon. and Wed. 1-9pm, Tues. and Thurs. 10am-9pm, and Fri. and Sat. 1-5pm; in winter also open Sun. 2-5pm). **Star of the West Books,** 518 3rd. Ave., stocks a fine collection of regional titles. (Open May-Dec. Mon.-Fri.9am-9pm, Sat. 9am-6pm; Jan.-April Mon.-Sat. 9am-6pm.)

Prince Rupert's **hospital** is located at 1305 Summit Ave. (624-2171); in an **emergency,** call 911. The **Mounties** are at 100 6th Ave. (624-2136). You can receive general delivery mail at the main **post office** at 2nd Ave. and 3rd St. (627-3085; open Mon.-Fri. 9am-5pm), but only the two substations sell stamps and postal supplies. One is in the Shoppers Drug Mart at 3rd Ave. and 4th St. (open Mon.-Fri. 9:30am-9pm, Sat. 9:30am-7pm, Sun. 11am-6pm); the other lurks upstairs in the 2nd Ave. Mall (open Mon.-Sat. 9am-6pm). The **Postal Code** is V8J 3P3. The **area code** is 604.

Accommodations, Camping, and Food Nearly all of Prince Rupert's hotels are located within the six-block-square area circumscribed by 1st Ave., 3rd Ave., 6th St., and 9th St. Everything fills up when the ferries dock, so call a day or two ahead. **Pioneer Rooms,** 167 3rd Ave. E (624-2334), has floors clean enough to eat from, a microwave and TV downstairs and great management. Pick your own berries in the backyard. (Singles with shared bath $15-20. Doubles $25-30. Showers $3.) Primarily a social-service agency for the unemployed, the **Friendship House,** at 7th St. and Fraser St. (627-1717), offers barracks-style accommodations and three meals for $10. The House doesn't discourage budget travelers but clearly has a different mission than a hostel, and is free to those who need it. The **Ocean View Hotel,** 950 1st Ave. W (624-6259), just a short stagger upstairs from the first-floor tavern, has singles for $30 and doubles for $34. The only campground in Prince Rupert is the **Park Ave. Campground,** 1750 Park Ave. (624-5861 or 800-667-1994), less than 2km east of the ferry terminal via Hwy. 16 (tentsites $9, RVs $16).

The best budget-food options in Prince Rupert begin in the bulk food department at the colossal **Safeway** at 1st. St. and 1st. Ave. (open daily 9am-9pm). **New Moon,** 630 3rd Ave. (627-7001), serves an all-you-can-eat smorgasbord and salad bar for lunch ($7) and dinner ($8.25, children $7); served daily noon-1:30pm, 4:30-8pm. When local fisher-families out for seafood, they head to **Smiles Seafood Cafe** on the waterfront at 113 George Hills Way (624-3072). Entrees hover around $13, but the heaping fish and chip platter for $7.50 is a fine feed (open daily 10am-10pm).

Sights Few visitors realize that Prince Rupert Harbor has the highest concentration of archeological sites in North America. Large piles of discarded clam shells on nearly every island in the harbor attest to the 10,000-year inhabitance of native peoples (and their mollusk-intensive diets). Three-hour **archeological boat tours** leave from the Infocentre daily. A local expert will take you across the waves to **Digby Island,** the site of an ancient Native settlement, then over to the modern Native community of **Metlakatla** and back to Prince Rupert. Unfortunately, some of the most interesting petroglyphs are inaccessible to the tour boat, so that although the narrative is interesting, the hefty fee leaves you staring at your feet (too) much of the time. (Tours depart June 14-30 daily 12:30pm, July to mid-Sept. daily 1pm. $20, children $12, under 5 free.)

The grassy hills of **Service Park,** off Fulton St., offer a panoramic view of downtown Prince Rupert and the harbor beyond. **Diana Lake park,** 16km east of town along Hwy. 16, provides a picnic area set against an enticing lake.

QUEEN CHARLOTTE ISLANDS

The Queen Charlotte Islands are perched in the Pacific Ocean 130km west of Prince Rupert. Sometimes referred to as the "Canadian Galapagos," these remarkable islands contain one of the only two regions in Canada not covered by glaciers during the last Ice Age (the other is the southern tip of Vancouver Island). The Charlottes describe a tapering archipelago made up of two principal islands, Graham and Moresby, and 148 surrounding islets. Graham, the northern island, is home to all but one of the Charlottean communities as well as the world's only known Golden Spruce tree and a particularly potent (and illegal) strain of hallucinogenic mushroom. Hot springs whisper amidst the mists of Moresby Island and its smaller neighbors to the south, and the massive wooden monuments of the islands' first denizens decay by the shore in Canada's newest national park.

The Queen Charlottes were the first place in British Columbia to be given a European appellation. In 1778, Captain George Dixon inscribed the islands on the map, lending them the name of his ship. Despite the European presence, the islands' natives, the Haidas (pronounced HIGH-duhs), have outlasted most other first nations in maintaining the integrity of their culture; they make up a large percentage of the population, and an even larger proportion of the islands' many artists. Students in the public schools have a choice between learning Haida or French as a second language, and a recent initiative sought to restore the use of the original Haida name for the islands.

Logging has played a central role in the recent history of the islands. Many locals staunchly defend the industry that provides one of the islands' economic mainstays, while others would put an end to local logging operations altogether. In the 1980s the debate attracted national attention when environmentalists and Haidas demonstrated in an effort to stop logging on portions of Moresby Island. In 1988, the Canadian government established Gwaii Haanas South Moresby National Park, encompassing the southern third of the Queen Charlottes. Perhaps not coincidentally, the area's steep terrain makes it unsuitable for heavy logging.

The frequently riotous waters of the Hecate Strait insulate the Queen Charlotte Islands from British Columbia's usual summer tourist moil. The southern Charlottean beaches are rocky and the water cold, but kayakers and anglers heap lavish praise on the archipelago. Without a boat of your own, though, or the requisite mint to join a charter group, the region remains largely inaccessible. When traveling about these islands, keep in mind that cities on Graham and Moresby Islands are not within walking distance of eachother, and that there is no public transportation. Some travelers try to find others to share the steep car rental fees; many others hitch the 110km between Queen Charlotte City on the south shore of Graham Island and Masset on the north. (*Let's Go* does not recommend hitchhiking.)

■■■ QUEEN CHARLOTTE CITY

Queen Charlotte City grew up around a sawmill and still relies on logging as its major industry, as the bald hills surrounding the town soberly attest. More than any other settlement on the islands, Queen Charlotte City has unrolled a welcome mat to tourists, and visitors enjoy spending time along the attractive waterfront. Still teetering on the brink of modernity, this small town of about 1000 people has yet to undergo large-scale development.

Queen Charlotte City sprawls inland from the water at the southern end of **Graham Island.** The city stretches for 2km along 3rd Ave., which turns into Hwy. 16 to the east, leading to Skidegate, Tlell, Port Clements, and Masset. The city lies 4.5km west of Skidegate's ferry terminal. Red and golden salmonberries, found in summertime along almost every roadside in the Charlottes, make the walk more palatable.

PRACTICAL INFORMATION AND ORIENTATION

Visitors Information: Travel Infocentre, 3922 Hwy. 33 Box 337, Queen Charlotte, BC V0T 1S0 (559-4742). Follow 3rd Ave. east out of town for 2km; located in a jewelry store. Offers the *Guide to the Queen Charlotte Islands* ($4.23). The zealously helpful staff will amplify the already comprehensive book. Several years ago, a container ship dropped 40,000 Nike running shoes into the ocean and they have been washing up along the BC coast ever since. The tourist office has two of them, a matching pair, serving as flower pots in front of the building.Open Mon.-Tues. 9am-5pm, Wed.-Sun. 9am-7pm; Oct.-May Mon.-Sat. 9am-5pm.

Canadian Parks: Gwaii Haanas Park Information (559-8818), on 3rd Ave. downtown. Knowledgeable staff will acquaint you with Canada's newest (and least accessible) national park. Register here before setting out into the Park (or at the office in Sandspit). Open Mon.-Fri. 8am-noon, 1-4:30pm.

Ministry of Forests (559-8447), on 3rd Ave. in a new blue bldg. at the far west end of town. Information on free, primitive campsites maintained by the Forest Service on Graham and Moresby Islands.

BC Ferry: terminal in Skidegate Landing (559-4485), 4.5km east of Queen Charlotte City. To Prince Rupert (6 per week July-Aug., 5per week Sept., 4 per week Oct.-June, $18, car $69). Reserve for cars at least 3 weeks in advance.

Interisland Ferry, 559-4485. Runs between Skidegate Landing on Graham Island and Alliford Bay on Moresby Island (12 trips per day, $2.50 round-trip, car $7).

Taxi: Twin Services, 559-4461.

Car Rental: Rustic Rentals, west of downtown at the Chevron Station (559-4641). Anachronistic autos at contemporary prices. $39 per day plus 15¢ per additional km. Must be 21 with a credit card. Open Mon.-Fri. 8:30am-6pm, Sat. 9am-5:30pm. Will pick up at the ferry terminal in Skidegate.

Bike and Kayak Rental: Wavetrack Adventures (559-8838), on 3rd Ave. Mountain bikes $24 per day. Kayaks $45 per day—includes free transportation to Moresby Camp on Moresby Island. Open May-Sept. daily 8am-6pm.

Laundromat: 121 3rd Ave. (559-4444). Wash $1.50, dry 25¢. Open daily 7am-9pm.

Pharmacy: (559-8315), downstairs in the hospital building. Open Mon.-Fri.
10:30am-12:30pm and 1:30-5:15pm (Wed. open 1:30-5:15pm only).
Hospital: (559-8466), on 3rd Ave. at the east end of town.
Emergency: Police (RMCP), 3211 Wharf St. (559-4421). **Ambulance,** 559-4506.
Fire, 559-4488.
Post Office: in the City Centre Bldg. on 3rd Ave. (559-8349). Open Mon.-Fri.
8:30am-5:30pm, Sat. noon-4:30pm. **Postal Code:** V0T 1S0.
Area Code: 604.

ACCOMMODATIONS AND CAMPING

The small hotels of Queen Charlotte City are clean, cozy, friendly, and expensive.
During the summer, make reservations or arrive early in the day to secure a room.

Spruce Point Lodging, (559-8234), on the little peninsula across from the Chevron station at the west end of town. 6 new hostel beds in a co-ed dorm for $17.50.
Reservations accepted for groups. Laundry and cooking facilities. Bed and breakfast upstairs. Singles $50, doubles $55.

Jo's Bed and Breakfast, 4813 Ferry Loop Rd. (559-8865). Follow the road from
the ferry terminal up the hill to the white house with blue trim. Wonderfully
clean and convenient. The wood stove will warm your bones after a long day of
hiking. Continental breakfast. Singles $22, doubles $32. Reservations a good idea.

The Premier Hotel, 3101 3rd Ave. (559-8401). This friendly hotel dates to 1910
and has been beautifully renovated with veranda and balcony. Singles with shared
bath from $25, with balcony from $56. Doubles with own bath $45.

Hecate Inn (559-4543 or 800-665-3350), at 3rd Ave. and 4th St. Clean, comfortable
rooms with private bath and TV. Shared kitchen and refrigerator make Hecate an
inn for anglers and work crews. Singles $50. Doubles $55, twin $60.

Haydn Turner Park Campsite, at the west end of 4th Ave.; a 25-min. walk from
the town center. Forested sites and free firewood. A few spots at the end overlook the water. Toilets and water (boil before drinking). Tents $3, RVs $5.

Joy's Island Jewellers, 3rd Ave. at the east end of town (559-4742). A few sites
available in the yard next door, with some of the islands' best drinking water from
a private spring (free). No toilet facilities. Tents $5, RVs $8, full hookups $10.

FOOD

Culinary offerings in Queen Charlotte City are limited in selection and high in price.
Buy your own grub at **City Center Stores Ltd.,** (559-4444) in the City Center Building (open Tues.-Fri. 9:30am-9pm, Mon. and Sat. 9:30am-6pm).

Margaret's Cafe, 3223 Wharf St. (559-4204), at the east end of town. Smoke and
locals linger over filling breakfast and lunch specials. BLT $4.50. Sandwich, soup,
gravy, and fries $6. Open Mon.-Fri. 6:30am-1:30pm.

Claudette's Place, 233 3rd Ave. (559-8861), just west of city centre. Pleasant
patio/garden out front. Best breakfasts in town—Denver omelette ($6.50), or 2
eggs, hashbrowns, and toast ($4). Open daily 8am-10pm.

John's Cafe, on 3rd Ave. just west of the City Centre Building. Tasty Chinese dishes
around $8.50, burgers from $3.50. Open Tues.-Sat. 11:30am-3pm and 4:30-9pm,
Sun. noon-3pm and 4:30-9pm.

SIGHTS

Displays of contemporary Haida artwork sparkle at **Rainbows Art Gallery and Gift
Shop,** on 3rd Ave. at Alder (559-8420), a gallery brimming with silver, gold, and
argillite (black shale) carvings (open Mon.-Sat. 9am-5pm, Sun. 1-5pm).

In Queen Charlotte City, just south of town, is the **city dump.** Not known merely
for its garbage, the dump is a scavenging site for the 40-plus bald eagles and half-
dozen black bears that meet there nightly. Go in a car, as garbage bears are capable
of trashing any tourist, and the broken glass underfoot tends to put them on edge.

■ Near Queen Charlotte City: Skidegate

Skidegate Mission, known as "the Village," is a cluster of small, worn houses on Rooney Bay, 2km east of the ferry landing. Skidegate has been a Haida village for centuries; today's community of 500 is a nexus of Haida art and culture. Visit the **Skidegate Band Council Office** (559-4496), in a Haida longhouse built in 1979 according to ancient design specifications. The frontal totem pole is a favorite perch of bald eagles. Ask the receptionist for permission to view the artwork and old photographs inside (office open Mon.-Fri. 9am-noon and 1-4:30pm). Halfway between Skidegate Landing and Skidegate Mission is the **Queen Charlotte Islands Museum** (559-4643), housing totem poles from remote village sites, an extensive collection of stuffed birds, and beautiful contemporary Haida prints and carvings. The shed next door protects the 50-ft. cedar canoe carved by renowned Haida artist Bill Reid for Vancouver's Expo '86. (Open June-Aug. Mon.-Fri. 10am-5pm, Sat.-Sun. 1-5pm. Admission $2.50, children free.) On the beach 1km north of Skidegate rests **Balance Rock,** a memento left by a glacial movement thousands of years ago. Search for fossils in the surrounding bedrock, but don't rock the Rock.

■ Tlell

Tlell isn't really even a town; it consists of a few houses and farms spread thinly along a 7km stretch of Hwy. 16. Its central location and friendly residents make it a perfect stopover for those on their way between Queen Charlotte City and Masset. Here the rocky beaches of the south give way to sand, and the Tlell River offers excellent trout fishing and water warm enough for swimming.

In December 1928, the wooden log barge **Pezuta** ran aground just north of Tlell. A two-hour hike to the wreck from the Naikoon Park Picnic lot traces the Tlell River and crosses sand dunes and agate-strewn beaches. Spot land otters on the way.

Citizens of Tlell occasionally complain that the exceptionally pure air in their town puts them to sleep. Well, then Tlell is a good place for a traveler to relax. **Body Currents Cappuccino Bar,** 1km south of Richardson Ranch on Wiggins Rd. (557-4793), serves great chocolate chip cookies and cappuccino. The adjacent **gallery** exhibits and sells handmade jewelry and crafts (open Mon.-Sat. 10am-5pm, Sun. noon-5pm). **Riverworks Farm & Store** (557-4363), 2km south of Wiggins Rd. next to the post office, boasts island-grown produce and eggs (open daily 10am-5:30pm).

Pitch a tent at **Misty Meadows Campground,** just south of the Tlell River Bridge. Pit toilets, picnic tables, and water grace 30 sites (call Naikoon Provincial Park Headquarters at 557-4390). Or sink into the lap of luxury at **Hltunwa Kaitza Bed and Breakfast** (557-4664), just north of Richardson Ranch on the sea-side of the road; singles start at $25. The friendly folk of Hltunwa Kaitza rent mountain bikes and kayaks. Out front in the **Glass Shack** Gayle displays her gorgeous stained glass windows; bring her the bottles you find washed up on the beach and she'll sandblast you a custom design. Ask nicely to sniff the whale skull. Just north of the Tlell River Bridge, the **Bellis Lodge** (557-4434) offers hostel accommodations for 10 ($12).

Tlell lies on Hwy. 16 on the east coast of Graham Island, 30km north of Skidegate and 24km southeast of Port Clements. The **post office** is on Hwy. 16 2km south of Wiggins Rd. (557-4391; open Mon.-Fri. 2-5pm, Sat. 9-10am; **Postal Code:** V0T 1Y0).

■ Port Clements

While Queen Charlotte City is the islands' administrative center and Masset is dominated by the Canadian Forces station, Port Clements is primarily a blue-collar town. A tangled network of logging roads stretches inland from the port; these bumpy byways are open to public use and provide access to the heavily forested (for now) interior (stop at the Village Office for maps, see below). Port Clements faces west onto Masset Inlet; the town claims the best sunsets in the Charlottes.

The world's only known **Golden Spruce** grows beside the Yakoun River south of Port Clements. A rare mutation causes the tree's needles to be bleached by sunlight. To reach the albino tree, drive 5.5km south of town to a roadside pullover; from there it's a 10-minute walk. 8km south of the pullover, a trail leads to an unfinished **Haida canoe.** The wood-be boat was uncovered by loggers and remains in its original site. Nearby stumps are riddled with test holes where the early builders sampled other trees for their canoe potential. On your way to the spruce, stop by **Golden Spruce Farms,** 1km south of town on Bayview Dr. (557-4583), the "westernmost farm in Canada." Dave sells rabbit meat ($2.50 per lb.) and an astonishing variety of fresh vegetables (considering it's nearly impossible to grow potatoes here).

The handful of "reasonably priced" accommodations in Port Clements include the **Golden Spruce Motel,** 2 Grouse St. (557-4325; singles $36, doubles $40) and **Swan's Keep Bed and Breakfast,** 197 Bayview Dr. (557-2408; singles $40, doubles $60). The only restaurant in town is the **Yakoun River Inn** on Bayview Dr. (557-4440). Good burgers start around $6; at night, toss back a few pints and indulge in some "boneheadedness" with the loggers (open Mon.-Sat. noon-2am, Sun. noon-midnight). For the raw stuff, head to **Bayview Market,** on Bayview Dr. (557-4331; open Tues.-Sat. 10am-6pm).

Port Clements is located 24km northwest of Tlell on Hwy. 166. Bayview Dr. is the main artery; it follows the shore of Masset Inlet, then breaks south toward the Golden Spruce. The **Port Clements Village Office** (557-4295), on Cedar Ave. between Tingley and Pard St., offers information and free maps of the logging roads (open Mon.-Fri. 1-5pm). You can browse for more information at the **Port Clements Islands Regional Library,** at Tingles St. and Cedar Ave. (557-4402; open Wed. 3-5pm and 7-9pm, Fri. 2-6pm). The **Queen Charlotte Islands Health Care Society** operates a medical clinic on Park St. (557-4478) next to the elementary school. (open Mon.-Fri. 9am-4:30pm). In an **emergency,** call 557-4777. The nearest **police** station is in Masset (626-3991). The **post office** is on Tingley St. between Hemlock and Spruce Ave. (open Mon.-Fri. 8:30am-12:30pm and 1:30-5:30pm, Sat. 1:30-5:30pm; **Postal Code:** V0T 1R0). The **area code** is 604.

■■■ MASSET

At 1600 inhabitants, Masset and the neighboring Haida village of Old Masset make up the largest community on the Queen Charlottes. The dispersal of residents among these two settlements and a self-contained Canadian Forces Station belie this fact, however, and visitors may search in vain for a focal point to this scattered community. The beautiful beaches of Naikoon Provincial Park stretch to the east, inviting beachcombers to search for greatly-prized Japanese fishing floats (glass balls that Japanese fishermen use to float their nets) and elusive razor clams. Masset is at the north end of Graham Island on Hwy. 16, and Collison Ave. is the main drag. Old Massett Village lies 2km farther up the road.

PRACTICAL INFORMATION AND ORIENTATION

Visitors Information: Travel Infocentre, Old Beach Rd. (626-3982), at Hwy. 16. Plenty of local history and trail maps for choice birdwatching. Open July-Aug. daily 9am-8pm. The **Masset Village Office** on Main St. (626-3995) will give you further information. Open Mon.-Fri. 9:30am-4pm.

Car Rental: Tilden Rentals, 1504 Old Beach Rd. (626-3318), at the Singing Surf Inn. New cars from $40 per day, plus 22¢ per km. Must be 21 with a credit card.

Taxi: Jerry's Taxi, 626-5017.

Library, at Collison Ave. and McLeod St. (626-3663). Open Tues. and Sat. 2-6pm, Thurs. 2-5pm and 6-8pm.

Emergency: Ambulance, 626-3636; **Fire,** 626-5511; **Police** (626-3991), on Collison Ave. at Orr St.

Post Office, on Main St. north of Collison (626-5155). Open Mon.-Fri. 8:30am-5:30pm, Sat. 8:30am-12:30pm. **Postal Code:** V0T 1M0.

Area Code: 604.

ACCOMMODATIONS AND CAMPING

It's an understatement to say the options in Masset are limited. Rooms in a bed and breakfast cost at least $35 per night, and they fill quickly during the summer. There is free camping on the beach1km past Tow Hill (about 30km east of Masset).

Naikoon Park Motel (626-5187), on Tow Hill Rd. about 8km east of town. Close to the beach. 13 rooms at $35, with kitchen $50.

Harbourview Lodging (626-5109), on Delkatla Rd. just north of Collison. B&B right on the harbor. The "blue," "brown," and "pink" rooms downstairs have color TV, shared bath, and sauna. Singles $40. Call for reservations in summer.

Copper Beech House (626-3225), on Delkatla Rd. at Collison. B&B that looks more like an eclectic private museum. Singles $50. Doubles $75.

Masset-Haid Lions RV Site and Campground, on Tow Hill Rd. next to the wild-life sanctuary. 22 gravelly sites, toilets, pay showers. Sites $8, with electricity $10.

Agate Beach Campground, 26km east of town in Naikoon Provincial Park. 32 beachfront sites with an area reserved for tenters. Picnic shelter, firewood, water, flush toilets. Free clamming. Sites $10 May-Sept., free in winter. For more information call Park Headquarters (557-4390).

FOOD

Free razor clams on Agate and North Beach! Best roasted on a stick or chowderized, these clams are rarely affected by the ultra-toxic red-tide (but check the hotline anyway). Other types of shellfish, however, should be approached with caution. Ask locally or call the BC red-tide hotline (604-666-3169). You can pick up some lemons at **Masset Grocery** on Old Beach Rd. (626-3666), directly across from the bridge (open daily 11am-11pm).

Pizza Plus (626-3222), on Main St. next to the post office. Comes closest to offering a local specialty—"pizza with pizzazz." Sandwiches $3-4, subs $6-10. Small pizza from $8.50, large from $15. Open Mon.-Sat. 9am-11pm.

Sam's Chicken House (626-5666), at Collison Ave. and Main St. Take-out fish and chips ($6.15) and chicken (1 piece with fries $3.64).

Daddy Cool's (626-3210), at Collison Ave. and Main St. The only bar in town. Imposing arsenal of disco lights, live music every night. Occasional 99¢ cheeseburger specials. Open Mon.-Sat. noon-2am, Sun. noon-midnight.

SIGHTS AND ACTIVITIES

Search for agates, seashells, and razor clams along the shores of **Agate Beach,** 26km east of Masset in **Naikoon Provincial Park**. **Tow Hill,** just to the east, rises 100m above Dixon Entrance. The hill is a half-hour walk from the parking area at the Hiellen River; on a clear day you can see Alaska from the top. Another short trail leads to the **Blow Hole,** or "gun"—a small cave that erupts with foaming water when the tide comes in. Across the Hiellen River, **North Beach** is the site of the Haida creation myth, where Raven discovered a giant clam full of tiny men.

Red-breasted sapsuckers, orange-crowned warblers, glaucous-winged gulls, great blue herons, and binocular-toting tourists converge on the **Delkatla Wildlife Sanctuary,** off Tow Hill Rd. in Masset. The best paths from which to observe the 113 airborne species originate from the junction of Trumpeter Dr. and Cemetery Rd.

With 600 residents, **Old Massett Village,** 2km west of town at the terminus of Hwy. 16, is the largest Haida village on the Charlottes. Many of the houses/stores that line the streets sell Haida prints and carvings. The **Ed Jones Haida Museum** (626-9337), located in the old schoolhouse at the north end of town, houses a jumbled collection of old photographs and artifacts from abandoned village sites. The Eagle and Raven totems out front are reproductions of poles from the old village of Yan, across Masset Sound (museum open in summer daily 8am-noon and 1-4pm;

free). You can apply for permits to visit abandoned Haida villages on Graham Island at the Masset Band Council Office, in the large cedar-and-glass building at the east end of town (626-3337; open Mon.-Fri. 8:30am-noon and 1-4:30pm).

■ Sandspit

Located on a thin strip of land that projects into Hecate Strait, Sandspit is the only permanent community on **Moresby Island.** The town grew up in the 1940s around a Royal Canadian Air Force airfield; today, the logging operations of Fletcher Challenge are the mainstay of the Sandspit economy. The sandy beaches of the spit are a pleasant change from the tidal flats around Queen Charlotte City; birds and shells proliferate on these shores. The best time to visit may be late May or early June when the sawdust flies as axe-wielding men and women climb, chop, and saw in the annual **Loggers Day** competitions.

Practical Information **Gwaii Haanas Park Information** (637-5362) is located off Beach Rd. at the north end of town (open mid-June to mid-Sept. daily 9am-5pm). Register here or at their office in Queen Charlotte before venturing into the park.

Sandspit is 13km east of the Alliford Bay ferry landing on Moresby Island. There's not much traffic on the connecting road; those hitching from Sandspit to catch a late ferry are known to have a hard time finding a ride. **Interisland Ferry** (559-4485) runs between Skidegate Landing on Graham Island and Alliford Bay on Moresby Island (12 trips per day; $2.45 round-trip, car $6.50). **Budget Rent-A-Car** (637-5688), at Beach and Blaine Shaw Rd., rents cars from $56 per day, plus 25¢ per km (must be 21 with a credit card). Another office is at the airport.

The **library** (637-2247) sits off Beach Rd. at the north end of town (open Tues. 3-6:30pm, Thurs. 3-5pm and 7-8:30pm). The **health clinic** (637-5403) is on Copper Bay Rd. in the school building. (Open Mon.-Fri. 10am-noon; after hours, call the **Queen Charlotte City Hospital** at 559-8466). **Emergency** numbers: **ambulance,** 559-4506; **fire,** 637-2222; **police,** 559-4421 in Queen Charlotte City. The **Post Office** is at Beach and Blaine Shaw Rd. (637-2244; open Mon.-Fri. 8:30am-5:30pm, Sat. 9am-noon; **Postal Code:** V0T 1T0). The **area code** is 604.

Accommodations, Camping, and Food The sandy beaches of the spit are the cheapest overnight option (including 20 primitive campsites on the shores of Gray Bay; see Outdoors below)—but if you're unwilling to sleep with the fish be prepared to shell out a few clams. The **Moresby Island Guest House** (637-5305), on Beach Rd. next to the post office, provides eight cozy rooms with shared washrooms, kitchen, and billiard table. In the morning, they provide the ingredients and you make the breakfast. (Singles $25. Doubles from $50 can accommodate up to four. Overflow cots for $15—feign desperation.) Just up the road towards Spit Point, the **Seaport Bed and Breakfast** (637-5678) offers island hospitality with plush couches, cable TV, and breakfast with fresh eggs from the henhouse out back. Reservations nearly essential in summer. (Singles $25, doubles $35.)

Ramble to **Dick's Wok Inn,** 388 Copper Bay Rd. (637-2275), where a heaping plate of fried rice costs $8 and up (open daily 5-10pm). Or rest your cheeks at the **Bun Wagon,** at 396 Copper Bay Rd. (637-5446). $2 dogs and $4.74-6.50 burgers will satisfy even the most discriminating pioneer (open Wed.-Thurs. 11am-2pm, Fri. 11am-2pm and 4-7pm, Sat.-Sun. 11am-7pm). The **BC Agency Supermarket** resides in the mini-mall near the spit (open Mon.-Tues. and Thurs.-Sat. 9:30am-6pm, Wed. 9:30am-7:30pm).

Outdoors Stroll to the end of the spit for spectacular sunrises and sunsets. Anglers can cast for silver salmon in the surf. Bumpy logging roads lead 20km south of Sandspit to **Gray Bay;** check with the **Fletcher Challenge Information Centre** on Beach Rd. (637-5436; open Mon.-Fri. 8am-5pm) to find out when the roads are open to the public (logging trucks are VERY big). Twenty primitive **campsites** line the unspoiled beach (free). A 4.5km trail follows the shore south to **Cumshewa Head; Moresby Camp,** at the end of Cumshewa Inlet (also accessible by logging road) is a perfect launching point for kayakers who wish to explore South Moresby National Park. **Wavetrack Adventures** (see Queen Charlotte City: Practical Information) includes free transportation with its kayak rental.

In the summer, **Fletcher Challenge** will take you out to see the trees (and the stumps) on their free 4.5-hour **logging tour.** The tour provides a view of an active logging site and the chance for a frank discussion of logging practices. Some may wince at the sight of glorious spruce trees being reduced to 2x4s, but this is one of the best ways to get away from the highway into the backcountry. Tours leave from the office on Beach Rd. at noon on Wed. and Fri.; call their Information Centre for further information (see above).

Unfortunately, since there's no public relations incentive for any company to take you to South Moresby, the road to Haida Gwaii inevitably begins in your wallet. **Moresby Explorers,** based in Sandspit, offers wilderness trips on a demand basis to points of interest along South Moresby. These include Hot Springs Island and the abandoned Haida villages of Skedans and Minstints. Day trips are $110 per person; overnight trips, on which guests sleep on a 40 by 70 ft. spruce raft, are $140 per person. Contact Doug Gould (637-2215) for information.

THE CASSIAR HIGHWAY

Most travelers journey between British Columbia and Alaska via the Alaska Hwy. (see below) or aboard Alaska Marine Hwy. ferries. But a third (and largely ignored) route runs along 750km of **Hwy. 37,** commonly known as the **Cassiar Hwy.** This lonely road slices through spectacular extremes of charred forest, logged wasteland, and virgin wilderness from Hwy. 16 (between Prince George and Prince Rupert) to Mile 655 of the Alaska Hwy. (near the Yukon border). The Cassiar's long stretches of unpaved road and flying rocks chip windshields, crack headlights, and generally gum up the car's works. Nevertheless, for those with older autos that won't mind a scratch or two, and who know their way around an engine, this route is a good way to cut hundreds of kilometers off the Alaska Hwy. Gas stations are few and far between, so bring along a spare tire and an emergency gas supply. *A Complete Guide for Highway 37,* available at the most BC infocentres, offers a partial list of facilities and campgrounds on the route. Hitchhikers on the Cassiar find locals and truckers friendly but RV drivers unfriendly.

The road is divided into three sections. From Hwy. 16, the intrepid motorist follows 172km of paved road to **Meziadin Junction.** The **Meziadin Infocentre** will load you down with brochures and point you in the right direction (north). The primitive pit toilets outside are a sobering indication of what lies ahead; take a deep breath, step away, and get ready for...

Dirt. The 100km to the **Bell II Service Plaza** make mountain access roads look like interstates. Gaping craters alternate with gravel patches layered so thickly that you'll have trouble steering (drive slowly, and remember to turn *into* a skid). At Bell II, fuel up and grab a burger. Even more difficult driving along 240km of hard-packed dirt will bring you to **Dease Lake.** Here the **Boulder Cafe** defies traditional budget traveler logic, serving prohibitively expensive breakfasts but reasonably priced dinners (open Mon.-Sat. 6am-10pm, Sun. 7am-10pm). **The Tanzilla Cold Beer and Wine Store** (771-4513) rents 10 rooms upstairs, each with private bath and TV (singles $46, doubles $52).

The final leg of the trip is the most scenic, as each turn of the paved road to the Alaska Hwy. reveals a new lake or mountain. These last 237km reward the adventurer with one of the best (and best-named) restaurants on the Cassiar: **Yukon Ma's**

Cafe, at the junction with the Alaska Hwy. Here yu kon try their Salisbury steaks, then cleanse the palate with a few burgers.

THE ALASKA HIGHWAY

Built during World War II, the Alaska Highway maps out an astonishing 2647km route between Dawson Creek, BC, and Fairbanks, AK. After the Pearl Harbor attack in 1941, worried War Department officials were convinced that an overland route—far enough inland to be out of the range of carrier-based fighters—was necessary to supply the U.S. Army bases in Alaska. The U.S. Army Corps of Engineers completed the daunting task in just eight months and twelve days; the one-lane dirt trail curved around swamps and hills (landfill would come only later). Do not use the arbitrarily placed mileposts as official calibration standards, but rather as a general guide. The new kilometer posts are less frequent, though more accurate.

Travelers on the highway should be prepared for heavy-duty driving. Don't bring your shiny new sportscar or your junkheap with worn-out springs. For much of the route, pavement gives way to chip-seal, a layer of packed gravel held in place by hardened oil. In the dry summer weather, dust and rocks fly freely, virtually guaranteeing shattered headlights and a chipped windshield. Drivers should fit their headlights with plastic or wire-mesh covers. Most locals protect their radiators from bug splatter with large screens mounted in front of the grill. Travel with at least one spare tire and some spare gas; if you're crazy enough to drive the highway in winter, bring along a full set of arctic clothing and prepare your four-wheel-drive (you *will* have a four-wheel drive) for subzero conditions.

For you and your car's sake, don't underestimate the distance involved. The Alaska Highway is over 1500 mi. long. Ever driven halfway across the States? Even if you have, it wasn't on roads like these. Finally, try to take the time to learn some of the history of the highway and the area it runs through. You can make the scenery interesting where it might otherwise get monotonous.

Before setting out on your epic Alaskan journey, pick up the exhaustive listing of *Emergency Medical Services* and Canada Highway's *Driving the Alaska Highway* at a visitors bureau, or write the Department of Health and Social Services, P.O. Box H-06C, Juneau, AK 99811 (907-465-3027). The free pamphlet *Help Along the Way* lists emergency numbers along the road from Whitehorse to Fairbanks.

■ Dawson Creek

Dawson Creek, BC (not to be confused with Dawson City, YT) is the Highway's official starting point **(Mile 0)** and has calmed down considerably from the heyday of construction, which included the accidental explosion of 60 cases of dynamite close to downtown on February 13, 1943. Needless to say, the business district was completely leveled.

Practical Information Before you head out on the highway (lookin' for adventure), a quick tour of the town might excite your wanderlust. The **Tourist Information Centre,** 900 Alaska Ave. (782-9595), in the old train station just off Hwy. 97, provides the little information available on the town, and the addended museum can fill you up with local history ("requested donation" $1, families $2).

If you're stuck in Dawson Creek, **Greyhound,** 1201 Alaska Ave. (782-3131), can bus you to Whitehorse, YT (3 per week, $155), Prince George (2 per day, $45), and Edmonton, AB (2 per day, $67).

The **King Koin Laundromat,** 1220 103rd Ave. (open daily 8am-9pm), has showers for $2.75 and (oh, yeah) you can do a load of wash for $2; 4.5- min. dry 25¢. In an emergency, call for an **ambulance** (782-2211) or contact the **police** (782-5211) at

Alaska Ave. and 102nd Ave. The **post office** (782-2322) sits at 104th Ave. and 10th St. **Postal Code:** V1G 4J8.

Accommodations, Camping, and Food Indoor accommodations can be had at the **Cedar Lodge Motel**, 801 110th Ave. (782-8531; singles $30, doubles $39) or the **Sizzler Inn**, 10600 8th St. (782-8136; singles $40, doubles $45). RVers should head for **Tubby's RV Park**, at 20th St. and Hwy. 97 (782-2584; open May-Oct.; sites $10, full-hookups $16, with laundry and showers), while tenters should head for greener pastures at **Mile 0 City Campground,** 1km west of Mile Zero on the Alaska Hwy. (782-2590; sites $10 with laundry and showers). If foraging on your bug-splatted windshield has failed to sate you, a great place for nourishment in Dawson Creek is the **Alaska Cafe & Pub** (782-7040), "55 paces south of the Mile 0 Post" on 10th St., which has excellent burgers and fries for $6. The Golden Arches of **McDonald's** beckon enticingly at 11628 8th St., just down Hwy. 2 (and who knows how long it's been there—have you ever heard of a McDonald's closing down?).

Sights The town's most inspiring sights have less to do with the town than with the highway running through it: the **Mile 0 Cairn,** on the edge of the rotary next to the Infocentre, marks the beginning of the highway, and the **Mile 0 Post,** located a block toward downtown at 10th and 102nd, commemorates the construction of the highway and is much more a photo-op. Chronically stressed travelers might take a dip in Dawson Creek's **Centennial Swimming Pool,** at 10th and 105th (782-7040; $2.50 per session, students $2.25); the pool also houses a spiraling slide which plunks you down in the pool's center.

■ Northwest Along The Highway

Tired after only 76 km? Then make a quick pit-stop in **Fort St. John.** The **Travel Infocentre,** 9323 100th St. (785-6037; open daily 8am-8pm), will quickly make it clear to you that there's really nothing to do or see. The adjacent **museum** might well be the only sight in town. The city provides live entertainment on the (also) adjacent oil derrick at **Doin's at the Derrick** every evening from mid-June to mid-August. For those without any recourse but to spend the night, the **Four Seasons Motor Inn,** 9810 100th St., has singles for $34 and doubles for $38. **Centennial RV Park** is located right behind the Infocentre (785-9980; sites $10, full hookup $15; showers and laundry). The only cheap food to be had in town is produced by the flock of fast-food joints lining 100th.

Fort Nelson, 480 (of the highway's most unexciting) km north of Dawson Creek, is the highway's next pit-stop town on the way to Whitehorse. The **Infocentre** (774-6400) hides itself in the Rec Center on the western edge of town (open daily in summer 8am-8pm) and provides a small brochure dealing with Fort Nelson, though the fact that the supermarkets are highlighted indicates how much excitement you can expect. The **Fort Nelson Heritage Museum** (774-3536), however, is an exception. Across the highway from the Infocentre, the museum features several beautiful vintage cars and highlights (no, not supermarkets) local history (museum open daily in the summer 8:30am-7:30pm; admission $2.50). Rest up at the **Mini-Price Inn** (774-2156), which is hidden a block off the highway at 5036 51st Ave. (singles $30; doubles $35; kitchenettes $5 extra). Campers should continue another km west to **Westend Campground** (774-2340), a veritable oasis with hot showers (25¢ per 3 min.), a laundromat, a free car wash, and free firewood (sites $12, full hookups $17). Fort Nelson cuisine consists of standard hotel fare and fast food.

Small hotels, plain but expensive, pockmark the remainder of the highway every 80 to 160km on the way to Carcross, Whitehorse, and the Alaska border. Campers' needs are satisfied by the provincial parks that spring up along the road. **Stone Mountain Campground,** about 160km past Fort Nelson, is a park campsite set beside Summit Lake. Tenters should continue on for 19km to the grassy areas (towards the beaver dam) at **One Fifteen Creek.** Each park has sites with toilets and fresh water for $12. 40km farther down the road lies **Toad River,** a booming town of 60. The **Toad River Cafe** (232-5401) makes an interesting stop to peek up at the 3400 hats hanging from the ceiling—how often do you see *that?* Food is also available at surprisingly reasonable prices (burgers from $4).

After winding its way along the achingly beautiful Muncho Lake, the highway reaches the **Liard River Hot Springs** near the 800km mark. Soothe your weary bones and ease your frazzled, dazed mind in these naturally warm (to very hot) pools (free). The park service manages **campsites** here ($12) as well as a free day-use area. Get here early, though, if you want to spend the night. The campground is often full by early afternoon.

Near the BC-Yukon border, the road winds through vast areas of land scorched by forest fires; gray arboreal skeletons stretch in all directions as far as the eye can see. At night, this area offers prime winter viewing of the *aurora borealis,* as there are no city lights to pollute the view.

The Alaska Highway's winding route crosses the BC-Yukon border several times before it passes through Whitehorse. Just after it crosses into the Yukon for the second time (as you travel west), the highway passes through the small town of **Watson Lake** and the famed **"Sign Post Forest,"** at Mile 635. The "forest," was born in 1942 when a homesick Army Engineer erected a sign indicating the mileage to his hometown of Danville, Illinois. More than 17,000 travelers have since followed suit; if you look hard enough, you'll probably find a sign from a town near you. The **Info-centre** is hidden amidst the forest (open daily 8am-8pm). Throughout the Yukon summer, visitors can tune in to 96.1 FM for information on weather and road conditions and for a little bit of light rock.

■ Carcross

"Caribou Crossing," as Carcross was once known, at the narrows between Bennett and Nares Lakes, has been the site of a seasonal hunting camp of the Tagish Native Americans since time immemorial. During the Klondike Gold Rush of the 1890s, the town grew into a key distribution and transfer center for the White Pass & Yukon Railway. As boom faded to bust, many rail towns were abandoned. But "Carcross" survived—albeit three syllables shorter—nourished by the tourism and mining industries of the Yukon's southern lakes district. Carcross was connected to civilization when the Alaska Hwy. construction crew rolled into town during World War II, but the past 75 years have brought few other changes to this frontier town of 350.

Practical Information The wooden facades of the **Caribou Hotel, Matthew Watson's General Store,** and the old **White Pass & Yukon Railway Depot** have stood up to the Yukon's fierce and gritty winds for 80 years. Old photographs and displays trace the railroad's history in the **Carcross Visitor Reception Centre,** inside the depot (821-4431; open mid-May to mid-Sept. daily 8am-8pm).

Carcross is located at the narrows (Natasaheenie River) between Bennett and Nares Lakes. The **South Klondike Hwy. (Hwy. 2)** connects Carcross with Whitehorse, 74km to the northwest, and with Skagway, AK, 106km to the southwest. The **Atlin Express** (604-651-7617) connects Carcross with Atlin, BC ($17.50, senior citizens $13, children $8.75, under 5 free) and with Whitehorse ($13, senior citizens $9.50, children $6.50, under 5 free). The Express, which serves double-duty as the mail van, stops at the Carcross post office Monday, Wednesday, and Friday year-round. The **Sourdough Shuttle** (907-983-2523 or 800-478-2529) connects Carcross with Skagway, AK ($20).

The two-story red building in Carcross houses the **health station,** 821-4444. Emergency numbers: **ambulance,** 821-3333; **fire,** 821-222; **police,** 821-5555—if no answer call 1-667-5555. Do your laundry at **Montana Services** (see below; wash $2.25, 4 min. dry 25¢). The **post office** is the white building with red trim on Bennett Ave. (Open Mon., Wed., and Fri. 8:30am-noon and1-2pm, Tues. and Thurs. 10-

WHITEHORSE

11:45am; **Postal Code:** Y0B 1B0.) Tune in to **visitor's information** on 96.1 FM. The **area code** is 403.

Accommodations, Camping, and Food Travelers seeking accommodations in the Crossing may choose to check out the **Caribou Hotel** (821-4501), the oldest operating hotel in the Yukon. The original structure was destroyed in a 1909 fire; the present building was erected shortly thereafter. "She may be old, but she's clean and friendly." (Shared bath. Singles $30. Doubles $35. Yukon residents receive a $10 discount.) The only other "budget" beds in town are housed in rustic cabins (no electricity or water; $40) at **Spirit Lake Lodge** (821-4337), 7km north of town on Hwy. 2. The lodge also maintains forested tentsites overlooking the lake ($4, with shower $6). The Yukon government maintains 14 rocky sites ($9) with drinking water, firewood, and pit toilets at **Carcross Campground,** 1km north of town on Hwy. 2 (turn at E.J.'s Diner). RVers can park at **Montana Manor** (821-3708) at the Chevron Station on Hwy. 2, for $9.50 (showers $3).

Perogies—Russian dumplings—are a local specialty. You can buy beef perogies by the half-dozen ($6) at **Waldemar's Cafe** (821-3100), below the Caribou Hotel. Burgers, too ($6 and up). (Open daily 8am-10pm.) Herbivores can get cheese and potato *perogies* at the **Spirit Lake Restaurant** (821-4337), in the Spirit Lake Lodge. Burgers $5 and breakfast $4.70. (Open daily 7am-11pm.) If you've brought your mom's *perogy* recipe from home, you can shop for ingredients at the **Matthew Watson General Store** (821-3803; open May-Sept. daily 9am-6pm) or **Montana Services** (821-3708), at the Chevron Station on Hwy. 2 (open May-Sept. daily 7am-11pm, Oct.-April daily 8am-9pm).

Sights The tiny steam locomotive *Duchess,* built in 1878 to haul coal and passengers for Dunsmuir and Diggie Co., is on display next to the depot which houses the Reception Centre (see above). George and Kate Carmack, Skookum Jim, and Dawson Charlie—whose 1896 discovery sparked the Klondike Gold Rush—were natives of Carcross. Kate, Skookum, and Dawson returned to their hometown when the boom died out; you can visit their graves at the **Carcross Cemetery,** take the first left on Hwy. 2. Itinerant anglers can cast for lake trout and grayling from the footbridge that spans the river.

The **Carcross Desert,** the world's smallest, is located 2km north of town on Hwy. 2. This desert—once the sandy bottom of a large glacial lake—was exposed by glacial retreat, and harsh winds from Lake Bennett have discouraged the growth of vegetation. Alternating shallows and deep pools create a mottled blue-and-green appearance at **Emerald Lake,** 8km farther north. You can rent canoes ($5 per hr., $25 per day) from the **Spirit Lake Lodge** (821-4337), 7km north of town on Hwy. 2.

The **Museum of Yukon Natural History** (667-1055), 1km north of the desert, presents mounted animals in life-like settings, including the largest polar bear ever mounted (open mid-May to mid-Sept. daily 8am-5:30pm; $3, children $2). The **Frontierland Heritage Park,** next to the museum, fills six acres with reconstructed Native dwellings and trappers' cabins, as well as a pen housing a pair of (understandably) irritable lynx (open mid-May to mid-Sept. daily 8am-5:30pm; $6, children $4).

■■■ WHITEHORSE

Named for the once-perilous Whitehorse Rapids (now tamed by a dam) whose crashing whitecaps were said to resemble an entourage of galloping pale mares, Whitehorse marks the first navigable point on the Yukon River. The bone-weary Sourdoughs of the '98 Gold Rush often stopped here to wring themselves out after successfully navigating the rapids, and then continued on with the floating armada of expectant gold-seekers headed for the Klondike.

Capital of the Yukon since 1953, Whitehorse now boasts a population of more than 20,000 and is as cosmopolitan as one might expect a city of its size to be—yet it still maintains much of its century-old gold rush architecture and serves as a gateway to the surrounding country.

PRACTICAL INFORMATION AND ORIENTATION

Visitors Information: Whitehorse Visitor Reception Centre (667-2915), on the Alaska Hwy. next to the airport. The Centre's state-of-the-art bathroom is one of the great unsung pleasures of the Canadian North. An entire forest's worth of free brochures and maps, an excellent video overview of the city, and a really spectacular slide-show highlight the Yukon's history and wilderness. Open mid-May to mid-Sept. daily 8am-8pm. You can also get information by writing to **Tourism Yukon,** P.O. Box 2703, Whitehorse, YT Y1A C26. The **City of White-horse Information Centre,** at 3rd Ave. and Wood St. (667-7545), offers the same brochures and maps, without the film or the polished fixtures. Open mid-May to Sept. daily 8am-8pm; Oct.-April Mon.-Fri. 9am-5pm.

Canadian Airlines, 668-4466, for reservations 668-3535. To: Calgary (in summer, 3 per day Mon.-Fri., 2 per day Sat.-Sun.; in winter, 2 per day; $519), Edmonton (3 per day, $448), and Vancouver (3 per day, $448).

Buses: Greyhound, 2191 2nd Ave. (667-2223). All buses run Tues., Thurs., and Sat. at noon. To: Vancouver ($281), Edmonton ($222), and Dawson Creek ($155). There is *no* Greyhound service to Alaska. Open Mon.-Fri. 8:30am-5:30pm, Sat. 8am-noon, Sun. 5-9am. **Alaskan Express,** in the Greyhound depot (667-2223). Buses run late May to mid-Sept. To: Anchorage (4 per week, US$179), Haines (4 per week, US$76), Fairbanks (4 per week, US$149) and Skagway (daily, US$52). **Norline,** in the Greyhound depot (668-3355). Service to Dawson City (3 per week in summer, 2 per week in winter; $73).

Local Transportation: Whitehorse Transit, 668-2831. Limited service downtown. Buses leave/arrive downtown next to Canadian Tires on the northern edge of town. Mon.-Fri. 6am-7pm, Sat. 8am-7pm. Fare $1.25, senior citizens 50¢, children and students 85¢.

Taxi: Yellow Cab, 668-4811. 24 hr.

Car Rental: Norcan Leasing, Ltd., 8 Alaska Hwy. at Mile 917 (668-2137 or 800-661-0445). Cars from $38 per day with 100 free km, plus 15¢ per additional km. Must be 21 with credit card.

Bike Rental: The Bike Shop, 2157 2nd Ave. (667-6501). Mountain bikes $10 per day. Credit card imprint needed as deposit. Open Mon.-Sat. 10am-6pm.

Bookstore: Mac's Fireweed Books, 213 Main St. (668-2434). An extensive collection of Northern literature. Open Mon.-Sat. 9am-9pm, Sun. 10am-7pm.

Library: 2071 2nd Ave. (667-5239). Open Mon.-Fri. 10am-9pm, Sat. 1-6pm, Sun. 1-9pm.

Market: Food Fair, 2180 2nd Ave. (667-4278). Open Mon.-Wed. 8:30am-7pm, Thurs.-Fri. 8:30am-9pm, Sat. 8:30am-6pm, Sun. 10am-6pm.

Laundromat: Norgetown (667-6113). Wash $1.90; Dryer 50¢ per 7.5 min. Open daily 8am-9pm.

Public Showers: 4th Ave. Residence, 4051 4th Ave. (667-4471). $3.20, with towel $3.75.

Crisis Line: 668-9111.

Pharmacy: Shoppers Drug Mart, 311 Main St. (667-7304). Open Mon.-Fri. 8am-9pm, Sat. 9am-6pm, Sun. 11am-6pm.

Hospital: (667-8700), on the east side of the Yukon River on Hospital Rd., just off Wickstrom Rd.

Police: 4th and Elliot (667-5555). **Ambulance:** 668-9333.

Post Office: No main office. For general services: 211 Main St. (668-5847). Open Mon.-Fri. 8am-6pm, Sat. 9am-5pm. For general delivery: 3rd and Wood, in the Yukon News Bldg. (668-3824). Open Mon.-Sat. 7am-7pm. General Delivery **Postal Code** for last names beginning with the letters A-L is Y1A 3S7; for M-Z it's Y1A 3S8.

Area Code: 403.

WHITEHORSE

To reach Whitehorse by car, take the downtown exit off the Alaska Hwy. Once there, park the car since the downtown is relatively compact. The airport is a short ride to the west, and the bus station is a short walk from downtown on the north-eastern edge of town.

ACCOMMODATIONS AND CAMPING

Call the **Northern Network of Bed and Breakfasts** (993-5649 in Dawson City) to reserve a room in a Klondike household. Singles average $50 and doubles $60, plus $15 per extra person. Camping in Whitehorse is a problem—there is only one RV campground and one tenting park near the downtown area. Tenters praying for a hot shower should wend their way to the group of campgrounds clustered 10 to 20km south of town on the Alaska Hwy.

Fourth Avenue Residence (HI-C), 4051 4th Ave. (667-4471). Offering long- and short-term housing, this well-run residence boasts cooking and laundry facilities, good security, and free use of the city pool next door. Hostel beds (in a shared triple) $16, nonmembers $18. Private singles $38. Doubles $50. Call ahead to reserve a bed.

Fort Yukon Hotel, 2163 2nd Ave. (667-2594), near shopping malls and Greyhound. Rooms are old but untarnished. Singles from $40. Doubles from $45.

Hi Country RV Park, at S. Access Rd. and Alaska Hwy. (667-7445). Pay phones, showers, laundromat, firewood, and a pelt-ridden general store. 150 shady sites: tenters $10, back-in $15, pull-though $18.

Robert Service Campground, 1km out on South Access Rd. A convenient (but expensive) stop for tenting folk. Firewood, fire pits, playground, picnic area, drinking water, toilets, metered showers. Island Nature Walk nearby. Open late May to early Sept. Gate closed midnight-6am. 40 sites, $13.

FOOD

Don't be discouraged by the dilapidated exteriors of many Whitehorse gastro-centers; the insides are usually well-worn but cozy. The prices are reasonable by Yukon standards (which still means expensive to outsiders).

No Pop Sandwich Shop, 312 Steele (668-3227). This artsy alcove is very popular with Whitehorse's small suit-and-tie crowd. You can order a Beltch (BLT and cheese, $4.50), but don't commit the egregious *faux pas* of ordering a coke here—it's strictly fruit juice and milk. Open Mon.-Thurs. 8am-9pm, Fri. 8am-10pm, Sat. 10am-8pm, Sun. 10am-3pm.

Talisman Cafe, 2112 2nd Ave. (667-2736). Good food in a nondescript environment. Try to get your 4 food groups in a few Russian *peroshki* ($9). Burgers from $5 and breakfasts around $5.50. Open daily 6am-10pm.

Mom's Kitchen, 2157 2nd Ave. (668-6620), at Alexander. Breakfast is a specialty. Mom whips up some great omelettes ($6-9). Lunch on the three-course Chinese special for $7.50. Open Mon.-Fri. 6:30am-8pm, Sat. 6:30am-5pm, Sun. 7am-3pm.

Mr. Mike's, 4114 4th Ave. (667-2242). Whopping burgers on sourdough rolls, and excellent fries. (Mmm, mmm good.)

SIGHTS AND ACTIVITIES

Considering the size of its city, the Whitehorse welcoming committee has assembled an astonishing array of scheduled tours and visitor activities. In July and August, the **Yukon Historical and Museum Association,** 3126 3rd Ave. (667-4704), sponsors free daily tours of downtown called **Heritage Walks.** The tours leave from Donnenworth House, in Lepage Park next to the Infocentre (Mon.-Fri. 6 tours daily, Sat.-Sun. 4 tours daily). The **Yukon Conservation Society,** 302 Hawkins St. (668-5678), arranges free hikes Monday through Friday during July and August to explore the Yukon's natural beauty.

The restored *S.S. Klondike,* on S. Access Rd. (667-4511), is a dry-docked stern-wheeler that recalls the days when the Yukon River was the city's sole artery of survival. Pick up a ticket for a free and fascinating guided tour at the information booth at the parking lot entrance (open May-Sept. daily 9am-6pm). The **Whitehorse Rapids Fishway** (633-5965), at the end of Nisutlin Drive 2km southeast of town, allows salmon to bypass the dam and continue upstream in the world's longest salmon migration (open mid-June to mid-Sept. daily 8am-10pm; free). Two km south of town on Miles Canyon Rd. off of South Access Rd. whispers **Miles Canyon.** Once the location of the feared Whitehorse rapids, this dammed stretch of the Yukon now swirls silently under the first bridge to span the river's banks.

Visitors desiring a taste of local culture can feed their heads at the **MacBride Museum,** 1st Ave. and Wood St. (667-2709). The exhibits feature memorabilia from the early days of the Yukon, including photographs of Whitehorse as a tent city. The log cabin in the museum courtyard, built by Sam McGee in 1899, has thus far managed to avoid the flames that consumed its occupant. (Open daily in May and Sept. noon-4pm; June and Aug. 10am-6pm; July 9am-6pm. Admission $3.25, senior citizens and students $2.25, families $7.50.) The **Old Log Church Museum,** 303 Elliot St. (668-2555), at 3rd, has converted its aisles into a museum that fully explicates the history of missionary work in the territories. Built by its pastor, the church required only three months of labor; sub-zero weather has a way of motivating people. (Open June-Aug. Mon.-Sat. 9am-6pm, Sun. 12:15-4pm. Museum admission $2.50, children $1.) The incredible three-story **Log Skyscrapers** at 3rd Ave. and Lambert St. were built single-handedly in the 1970s by a local septuagenarian. Vacationing scholars are welcome to browse and research at the **Yukon Archives,** 80 Range Rd. (667-5321), in the Yukon College site (open Tues.-Fri. 9am-9pm, Sat. 10am-6pm).

The **Sarsparilla Sisters Show** at the Pioneer RV Park 5 mi. south of town (668-5944) is a tongue-in-cheek rendition of the Yukon's colorful history. (Shows Tues.-Sun. at 7:30pm. Admission $8, children $4.)

Two-hour river tours are available on two different lines. From June to September, the **Youcon Kat** (668-2927) will take you on a jaunt downstream from the hydro-electric dam. Boats leave daily at 1, 4, and 7pm from the ramshackle pier at 1st and Steele. ($14, children $7.) The **Yukon Gardens** (668-7972), 3km southwest of town at the junction of the Alaska Hwy. and South Access Rd., blossom with 22 acres of wildflowers and plants from around the world. (Open early June to mid-Sept. daily 9am-9pm. Admission $5, senior citizens $4.50, students $3.75, children $1.50.)

Before moving on, needed supplies and fun-time browsing can be had downtown at the **Hougan Center,** on Main St. between 3rd and 4th, which has numerous specialty shops (open Mon.-Fri. 8am-9pm, Sat. 9am-9pm, Sun. 10am-7pm).

THE DEMPSTER HIGHWAY

Named after Sergeant W.J.B. Dempster—one of the most courageous officers to wear the red of the Royal Canadian Mounted Police—the 741km (460-mi.) Dempster Hwy. is the only public highway in North America to cross the Arctic Circle. The highway remains the sole access road to Canada's isolated Mackenzie Delta communities of **Fort McPherson, Arctic Red River,** and **Inuvik** (pronounced in-NEW-vik; see below) in the Northwest Territories.

■■■ DAWSON CITY

Gold. Gold! GOLD! Of all the insanity ever inspired by the lust for the dust, the creation of Dawson City must surely be ranked among the most amazing. For 12 glorious, crazy months—from July 1898 to July 1899—Dawson City, on the doorstep of the Arctic Circle and 1000 mi. from any established settlement, was the largest Canadian city west of Toronto and every bit as cosmopolitan as San Francisco or Seattle. Its 30,000-plus residents, with names like Swiftwater Bill, Skookum Jim, Arizona Charlie Meadows, and The Evaporated Kid, had each somehow floated more than 1000 lb. of provisions down the Yukon River and made portages over some of the region's most rugged terrain—all driven by the desire to be filthy, stinkin' rich.

When the torrent of gold slowed to a trickle in 1900, the city proved less hardy than its inhabitants and quickly devolved into a ghost town. It wasn't until the early 1960s that the Canadian federal government, recognizing the historical importance of Dawson, brushed away the tumbleweeds and began to restore the Arctic version of El Dorado to its former glory. There is no tacky Hollywood à la Yukon show-biz here but rather a faithful re-creation of one of the greatest gold rushes that ever was. More than three-quarters of a century after its moment in the midnight sun, Dawson City is once again the jewel of the Yukon.

PRACTICAL INFORMATION AND ORIENTATION

Visitors Information: Visitor Reception Centre (993-5566), Front and King St. Historic movies as well as extensive information on local history. Open mid-May to mid-Sept. daily 9am-9pm, mid-Sept. 9am-8pm. For info. from afar, write Box 40, Dawson City, YT Y0B 1G0. The **Northwest Territories Visitors Center** (993-6167) is across the street and has plenty of info. on driving the Dempster Hwy. (open daily 9am-9pm). **Tourist radio** (96.1 FM) broadcasts weather, road conditions, and seasonal events.

Buses: Norline Coaches Ltd. (993-5331), at Arctic Drugs on Front St. Service to Whitehorse 3 times per week (2 times in winter) for $72.75. **Gold City Tours** (993-5175) runs buses up the Dempster Hwy. Fri. and Mon. at 8am (round-trip to Inuvik $350).

Ferry: The **MV Yukon Queen** makes daily trips up and down the Yukon to and from Eagle, AK. The boat leaves Dawson daily at 8:30am. Make reservations at **Yukon Queen River Cruises** (993-5599), on Front St. next to the dock (one-way $90 or US$72; round-trip $159 or US$129).

Taxi: Dawson City Cab, 993-6699.

Library (993-5571), at 5th and Princess. Open Tues.-Wed. and Fri. 9am-7pm, Thurs. 1-8pm, Sat. noon-5pm.

Laundromat and Showers: River West (993-5384), at Front and York. Wash $2.50, dry $2.50. 5-min. shower $1. Open Mon.-Sat. 7am-9pm, Sun. 11am-5pm.

Pharmacy: Arctic Drugs (993-5331), on Front St. next to the visitors center. Open Mon.-Fri. 9am-8pm, Sat.-Sun. 9am-6pm.

Medical Emergency: 993-2222.

Police: RCMP (993-5555; if no answer 1-667-5555), on Front St. north of Craig St., in the southern end of town.

Post Office (993-5342), 5th Ave. and Princess St. Open Mon.-Fri. 8:30am-5:30pm, Sat. 8:30am-12:30pm. **Postal Code:** Y0B 1G0.

Area Code: 403.

To reach Dawson City, take the Klondike Hwy. 533km north from Whitehorse, or follow the Top of the World Hwy. about 100km east from the Alaskan border.

ACCOMMODATIONS AND CAMPING

The hostel and the campground on the west side of town are the cheapest options; the ferry across the river is free and runs 24 hours.

Dawson City River Hostel (no phone). Across the river from downtown; take the 1st left when you come off the ferry. This is the hostel to end all hostels—brand-new bunks in brand-new log cabins with wood-heated "prospector's bath," refreshingly icy showers, cozy lounge with wood stove, and a beautiful hilltop view of the Yukon River and the city beyond. Friendly staff. Rates $12.50-15, tentsites $6 per person.

The Bunkhouse (993-6164), Front St. and Princess. Brand-new and in a great location. Wood-planked rooms and tiny shared bathrooms (singles $45, doubles $50).

Dawson City Bed and Breakfast, 451 Craig St. (993-5649). Fantastic rooms and wonderfully accommodating management. Singles $59. Doubles $69. Shared bath. Make reservations at least a week in advance, 2 weeks for a weekend stay.

Yukon River Campground. Ride the ferry to the west side of Dawson City and take the 1st right. A haven for budget travelers who want to return to nature. Remember to boil drinking-water for 3 min. Pit toilets. RVs welcome, but no hookups available. Sites $8.

Gold Rush Campground (993-5247), 5th and York St. Gold Rush has a monopoly on RV sites anywhere close to downtown, so it's wise to phone ahead. Campsites are fairly crowded and too rocky for tenters. Laundromat, convenience store, showers, and dump station. Solicitous management. Sites $10, electric hookups $15, full hookups $18.

FOOD

There's not a lot around, but prices are reasonable by Yukon standards—especially compared to Thanksgiving Day in 1899, when a single turkey fetched over $100. Snag a bag o' groceries at the **Dawson City General Store** (993-5474) at Front and Queen St. (open Mon.-Sat. 9am-8pm, Sun. 10am-6pm).

The Jack London Grill (993-5346) in the Downtown Hotel at 2nd and Queen St. Don't be scared off by the well-furnished dining room. Terrific dinners go for a measly $7-8. Open daily 6:30-11am and 11:30am-10pm.

Klondike Kate's (993-6527) at 3rd and King St. The veggie sandwich ($5) should keep scurvy at bay, and the K.K. Special ($4) is the best breakfast deal in town. Open mid-May to mid-Sept. daily 7am-11pm.

'98 Drive In (993-5226), Front St. Styled after a 1950s American drive-in, but named for the 1898 Klondike Gold Rush and comes complete with that era's boom-town prices. Deluxe burgers ($5.75), ice cream ($1.60). Open May daily noon-8pm; June-Sept. daily 11am-9pm.

SIGHTS AND ENTERTAINMENT

Perhaps to compensate for the cost of everything else, Dawson City sponsors a wide variety of free tours and attractions. Free 90-minute **walking tours** leave from the visitors center four times per day and from St. Paul's Church once per day. The guides are well-informed, and these tours are one of the best ways to appreciate the city.

The **Robert Service Readings** are in front of the very cabin on 8th Ave. at Hanson where the Bard of the Yukon penned such immortal ballads as "The Cremation of Sam McGee" and "The Shooting of Dan McGrew" (2 shows daily, 10am and 3pm).

Down the street, on 8th Ave. at Grant, is the re-located **Jack London Cabin.** The great Yukon author's life and times are recounted during interpretive readings daily at 1pm. Tours of Arizona Charlie's marvelously restored **Palace Grand Theatre** at 2nd and King are given daily at 10am and noon. The **Gaslight Follies** (993-5575) are on display at the Palace Grand—an original melodrama and a vaudeville revue are shown on alternate nights (Wed.-Mon. at 8pm). Together these shows form the best period performances available in the Yukon ($11.50 and $13.50, children $5.75).

The **Dawson City Museum** (993-5007), on 5th St. south of Church, elaborates on the history of the region with exhibits ranging from the mastodons of millennia gone by, to modern mining machinery. The museum holds shows by local artists and has hourly events, including the half-hour documentary **City of Gold** (which sparked the federal government's interest in renovating Dawson City), showing daily at 3pm (open daily 10am-6pm; admission $3.25, students and seniors $2.25).

Cutting-edge nightlife in Dawson is dominated by **Diamond Tooth Gertie's,** at 4th and Queen, one of Canada's few legal gambling halls. For a $4.75 cover you can try your hand at roulette, blackjack, and Texas hold' em; or just take in one of the two nightly floor shows at 8:30 and 10pm—a good bet (open nightly 7pm-2am).

The goldfields of **Bonanza** and **Eldorado Creeks** held some of the richest lodes discovered. Nearly 10 mi. of maintained gravel road follows Bonanza Creek to the former site of **Grand Forks** (which was chewed up to non-existence when the dredges came through). En route are **Gold Dredge #4** and **Discovery Claim**—the site of George Carmak's discovery of August 16, 1896, that inspired the whole mad rush in the first place.

If you're interested in learning about the modern gold-mining operations (last year's take was 100,000 oz.) or panning on your own, check in with **Gold City Tours** (993-5175) on Front St. The three-hour tour (daily 1pm, $29) provides enough history and information to cause a mental meltdown (open daily 9am-6pm). The Park Service also maintains a national historical sight at **Bear Creek,** 13km south of town on the Klondike Hwy. The mining operations here were halted all at once in 1966, leaving behind tools, machinery, and the haunting feeling that all the people should be *somewhere* nearby.

For those hunting their own fortunes in gold, numerous businesses will let you pan gold for around $5, but anyone can pan for free at the confluence of the Bonanza and Eldorado Creeks (you need your own pan though). Panning anywhere else along the creeks will most likely lead to a *very* unpleasant encounter with the owner/miner of the claim you're jumping.

■ North Along The Highway

This is not a drive to be taken lightly. Despite the service centers and campgrounds along the way, you'll be left all to yourself for long stretches. Hitching the route is strongly discouraged. For four and a half days each autumn, the 150,000-member **Porcupine Caribou herd** migrates across the highway and usurps the right of way. Two **ferries** service the route, at the **Peel River** and at **Arctic Red River** (both free). Operation depends on the weather; call 800-661-0752 for current status. The pamphlet *The Dempster* is available at the tourist-information centers in Whitehorse and Dawson City (see Practical Information for these cities) and is a must for anyone venturing out along the highway.

For current road conditions, up-to-date maps, and information, contact the **Western Arctic Visitors Centre** (993-6456), Front St. at King in Dawson City, YT (open June-Sept. daily 9am-9pm). **Gold City Tours** (993-5175), Front St. in Dawson City, provides bus service along the Dempster from Dawson City to Inuvik (2 per week, $198, round-trip $350) via Arctic Red River ($153) and Fort McPherson ($138). (Open daily 9am-6pm.)

■ Inuvik

Inuvik—"place of man" in Inuvialuktun—was built in 1958 to house the oft-flooded Canadian Arctic administrative center in nearby Aklavik. A planned community, the town is also a flourishing cultural center, where three Arctic peoples live together in remarkable harmony: the Inuvialuit of the Beaufort sea coast, the Gwich'in of the Mackenzie River Delta, and transplants from southern Canada. Inuvik's 3200 inhabitants have adapted to the Arctic's peculiar seasonal rhythms, hibernating during the nine-month-long winter and emerging in the summer to celebrate their enduring place in the frozen North.

Practical Information Stop by the **Inuvik Visitor Information Centre** (979-4518), on Mackenzie Rd. at Distributor St., to pick up information on tours of the Mackenzie Delta and the Beaufort Sea's coast (open June-Sept. daily 8am-midnight).

Inuvik is located on the Mackenzie River Delta, 741km northeast of Dawson City and 100km south of the Beaufort Sea, in the Northwest Territories (you're not in the Yukon anymore). The **Arctic Tour Co.,** 175 Mackenzie Rd. (979-4100 or 800-661-0721), runs buses (June to early Sept.) to Arctic Red River (3 per week, $45), Fort McPherson (3 per week, $60), and Dawson City, YT (3 per week, $198). Local transportation is provided by **Inuvik Taxi** (979-2525; 24 hr.). For **ferry and road information,** call 800-661-0752.

Yup, they're everywhere: **Inuvik Rexall Drugs** (979-2266) is at Mackenzie Rd. (open Mon.-Sat. 9am-6pm). The **hospital** (979-2955) is also on Mackenzie Rd. at the south end of town. In an **emergency,** call 979-4357 or the **police** (979-2935), located on Distributor St. at Mackenzie Rd. **Inuvik Laundry and Dry Cleaners** (979-2392), on Mackenzie Rd., will solve your embarrassing ring-around-the-collar problem (open Mon.-Tues. and Thurs.-Fri. 9am-5:30pm). The **post office** (979-2252) is on Distributor St. at Mackenzie Rd. (open Mon.-Sat. 9am-5:30pm; **Postal Code:** X0E 0T0). The **area code** is 403 (same as the Yukon Territory).

Camping, Accommodations, and Food Inuvik offers two categories of accommodations: $100-a-night hotel rooms for the bored well-to-do and campgrounds for the rugged adventurer (that's you). The **Happy Valley Campground** (979-2607), on Happy Valley Rd. in the northwestern part of town, has a playground, firepits, flush toilets, showers, and a laundromat (wash $1.75, dry $1.50). The 20 gravelly sites feature a nice view of the Mackenzie River ($12, full hookup $17). The **Chuk Territorial Campground,** 4km south of town on the Dempster Hwy., has firepits, flush toilets, showers, and a 20m observation tower with a spectacular view of the Mackenzie Delta (38 sites, $10). The cheapest bed in town is at the **Gardiner Guest House** 22 Kingmingya Rd. (979-4408), at the northern end of town (singles $75, doubles $80).

A number of Inuvik's restaurants offer northern delicacies such as caribou and Arctic char. None of these tastes anything like chicken. **The Back Room,** 108 Mackenzie Rd. (979-2002), is a dimly lit back room featuring burgers (from $6.50) and a huge stuffed polar bear (open daily 11am-1am). **To Go's,** 69 Mackenzie Rd. in the town center (979-3030), has beef burgers (from $3.75), caribou and musk-ox burgers ($5; we warned you), and "the best pizza this side of the 60th parallel" (small $9.25). (Open Mon.-Thurs. 7am-1am, Fri-Sat. 7am-2:30am, Sun. 10am-11pm.)

Sights, Outdoors, and Entertainment The visitors center will help you to make arrangements to visit **Our Lady of Victory Church,** on Mackenzie Rd. The "igloo church," built in the late 1950s without blueprints and on a shoestring budget—but winterproof nonetheless—reflects the blend of European and Arctic cultures that is unique to Inuvik. **Inhamo Hall,** on Mackenzie Rd. at the northern end of town, is the meeting place and cultural center of the Gwich'in; a number of celebrations and special events are open to the public. The three-story building was constructed from more than 1000 logs cut in southern Canada and floated up the Mackenzie River, the longest Arctic river in the world.

As the days grow longer and longer (and longer), winter ski trails become summer **hiking** trails. Several trails 3 to 5km in length depart from Loucheaux Rd. behind Grollier Hall. Prime birdwatching rewards those who make the short walk to the **Lagoon,** off Navy Rd. at the west end of town. You can rent a **bicycle** ($3 per hr., $20 per day) from **Northern Recreation,** 60 Franklin Rd. (open Mon.-Thurs. and Sat. 10am-6pm, Fri. 10am-8pm). If you want to get a little farther out of town, the **Arctic Tour Company** (979-4100) sponsors wildlife scenic tours and a number of boating and fly-in excursions to the delta communities of Aklavik and Tuktoyaktuk.

Inuvik makes the most of its short, sunny summer with a host of festivals and special events. The summer solstice is ushered in with street dancing and nocturnal chicanery during **Midnight Madness.** The **Northern Games** in late July include three days of non-stop activity, including a blanket toss and seal skinning (with free tasting for hungry onlookers). The 10-day **Great Northern Arts Festival** (979-3536), also in July, attracts the Arctic's finest artists and artisans for workshops; media range from soapstone to antler. The two-day **MusicFest** coincides with the Arts Festival and offers free performances by a number of way-northern bands.

Alberta

Alberta's glitter is concentrated in the west of the province; the icy peaks and turquoise lakes of Banff and Jasper National Parks reign as Alberta's most prominent landscapes. To the east, less sublime vistas of farmland, prairie, and oil fields fill the yawning expanses. As a whole, Alberta boasts thousands of prime fishing holes, world-renowned fossil fields, and centers of Native American culture; many of the province's most fascinating attractions, such as Waterton Lakes National Park, Head-Smashed-In Buffalo Jump, and the Crowsnest Pass, are located within easy traveling distance of the U.S. border.

Petrodollars have fostered the growth of gleaming, modern cities on the once-barren prairie. Calgary caught the world's eye when it hosted the XV Winter Olympics in 1988, and is annual host to the wild and wooly Stampede. Edmonton, slightly larger than its intense rival to the south, is home to the world's largest shopping mall and damned with faint praise.

More than half of the province lies to the north of Edmonton, but this is the uninhabited land of midnight twilight. The north is devoid of large cities, although the ethereal charm of rural towns might lure you up toward the Arctic Circle.

PRACTICAL INFORMATION

Capital: Edmonton.

Visitors Information: Alberta Tourism, 3rd floor, 10155 102 St., Edmonton T5J 4L6 (800-661-8888, 427-4321 in Alberta). Information on Alberta's provincial parks can be obtained from **Provincial Parks Information,** Standard Life Centre #1660, 10405 Jasper Ave., Edmonton T5J 3N4 (427-9429). For information on the province's national parks (Waterton Lakes, Jasper, Banff, and Wood Buffalo), contact the **Canadian Parks Service,** Box 2989, Station M, Calgary T2P 3H8 (292-4401). The **Alberta Wilderness Association,** P.O. Box 6398, Station D, Calgary T2P 2E1, distributes information for off-highway adventurers.

Motto: *Fortis et Liber* (Strong and Free). **Provincial Bird:** Great Horned Owl, chosen by Albertan schoolchildren in a 1977 province-wide vote. **Provincial Flower:** Wild Rose. **Provincial Tree:** Lodgepole Pine.

Emergency: 911.

Time Zone: Mountain (2 hr. behind Eastern).

Postal Abbreviation: AB.

Drinking Age: 18.

Traffic Laws: Mandatory seatbelt law.

Area Code: 403.

GETTING AROUND

Hwy. 16 connects Jasper with Edmonton, while the **Trans-Canada Hwy.** (Hwy. 1) connects Banff with Calgary, 120km to the east. **Hwy. 3** runs from Medicine Hat to Vancouver, BC, passing a plethora of historical signposts along the way. The extensive highway system facilitates bus connections between the major points of interest—use Calgary as a base. **Greyhound** runs from Calgary to Edmonton to Jasper, as well as from Calgary to Banff. **Brewster,** a subsidiary of Greyhound, runs an express bus between Banff and Jasper. Alberta's major **airports** are located in Calgary and Edmonton.

You must leave the Trans-Canada Hwy. to explore rural Alberta—a feat easier said than done. **Writing-On-Stone Provincial Park** and **Elk Island National Park,** two of the province's most intriguing destinations, lie off of the usual tourist trail. To reach out-of-the-way (but worthwhile) sights, consider renting a car.

More adventurous travelers should have no problem discovering alternative methods of transportation in Alberta. From the glaciers of Jasper National Park to the huge northern lakes, the Ice Age sculpted the landscape with the hiker, ice climber,

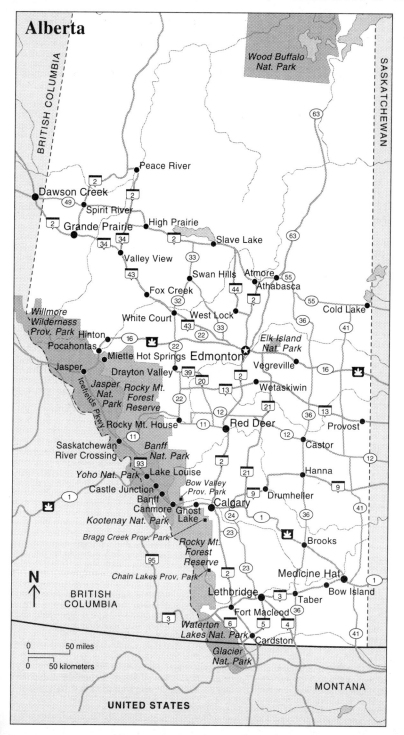

canoer, and bicyclist firmly in mind. **Hikers, mountaineers,** and **ice climbers** will find the most—and the best—rambling terrain in the Canadian Rockies of Banff and Jasper National Parks and Kananaskis Country. **Canoeing centers** encircle the lakes of northern Alberta and the Milk River in the south. The wide shoulders of Alberta's highways make **bicycle** travel relatively easy; some highway segments, such as the stretch of the Trans-Canada that runs between Banff and Calgary, have special bike lanes marked on the right-hand shoulder of the road. Consider renting a mountain bike instead of a 10-speed; you and your bike will have an easier time on the rough rural roads, and you'll be able to enjoy the Rocky Mountain backcountry. The national parks have made an effort to improve Alberta's budget travel situation by erecting a string of **hostels** between Banff and Jasper and by establishing campsites that accommodate only hikers and bicycliSt.

■■■ EDMONTON

What is most striking about Edmonton is its sheer size—190 streets and 180 avenues and the largest shopping mall in the world. Beyond its immensity, however, the vacuous gaze of the mall-goer betrays Edmonton's fundamental drabness. When Edmonton devoured its younger neighbor Strathcona in 1912, it gained both a long-hoped-for railway and a drop of interesting diversity, but it is a drop that has been for the most part swallowed by the gaping maw of countless convenient stores and fast-food restaurants. Edmonton continues to sprawl across its oil-rig-dotted landscape, firmly convinced that it can make up in acreage what it so sorely lacks in everything else.

PRACTICAL INFORMATION AND ORIENTATION

Visitors Information: Edmonton Tourism, 9797 Jasper Ave. (422-5505). Information, maps, brochures, and directions. Helpful staff. Open daily 8:30am-4:30pm; in winter Mon.-Fri. 8:30am-4:30pm. Also at **Gateway Park** (988-5455), on Hwy. 2 south of the city. Open daily 8am-9pm; in winter Mon.-Fri. 8:30am-4:30pm, Sat.-Sun. 9am-5pm. The tourism people also operate 2 smaller offices on Hwy. 16 during the summer. One is in the **western section** of the city near 190 St., and the other is in **East Edmonton** near -23 (minus 23) St. NE. Both are open daily 9am-5pm. For information about the rest of the province, head to **Alberta Tourism,** 10155 102 St. (427-4321), on the main floor. Open Mon.-Fri. 8:15am-4:30pm.

American Express, 10305 Jasper Ave. (421-0608). Holds mail free of charge for cardholders. **Postal code:** T5J 1Y5. Open Mon.-Fri. 8:30am-5:30pm.

Greyhound, 10324 103 St. (421-4211). To: Calgary (nearly every hr. 8am-8pm, $29), Jasper (5 per day, $41), Vancouver (6 per day, $103), Yellowknife ($103). Open daily 5:30am-1am. Locker storage $1.50 per 24 hr.

VIA Rail, 10004 104 Ave. (422-6032 for recorded information, 800-501-8630 for reservations), in the CN Tower, easily identified by the huge red letters on the front of the building. More expensive than the bus. To: Jasper ($72, students $65) and Vancouver ($170, students $153). Open Mon., Thurs., and Sat. 7am-3:30pm; Tues. and Fri. 8:30am-9:30pm; Wed. 8:30am-4pm; Sun. 10:30am-9:30pm.

Edmonton Transit, 423-4636 for schedule information. Buses and light rail transit (LRT) run frequently and all over this sprawling metropolis. You can ride free on the LRT Mon.-Fri. 9am-3pm and Sat. 9am-6pm if you stay in the downtown area (between Grandin Station at 110 St. and 98 Ave. and Churchill Station at 99 St. and 102 Ave.). Otherwise the fare for bus and LRT is $1.35 ($1.60 Mon.-Fri. 5-9am and 3-6pm), those over 65 and under 15 80¢. No bikes are allowed on the transit system. For more information, stop by the **Downtown Information Centre,** 100 A St. and Jasper Ave. Open Mon.-Fri. 9am-5pm; or call 421-4636, Mon.-Fri. 6:30am-10:30pm, Sat. 8am-5pm, Sun. 9am-5pm.

Taxis: Yellow Cab, 462-3456). **Alberta Co-op Taxi,** 425-8310.

Car Rental: Rent-A-Wreck, 10140 109 St. (423-1755). $27 per day with 200 free km, 10¢ per additional km. Must be 21. Under 25 subject to $12 per day insurance

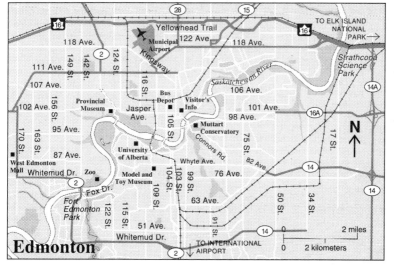

Edmonton

surcharge and $500 deductible; over 25 $10 surcharge and $250 deductible. Open Mon.-Fri. 7:30am-7pm, Sat.-Sun. 9am-5pm. **Tilden,** 10135 100A St. (422-6097). $35 per day with 100 free km, 12¢ per additional km. Weekend special $20 per day. Must be 21. Open Mon.-Fri. 7am-6pm, Sat.-Sun. 8am-4pm.

Bike Rental: Edmonton Hostel (see Accommodations below) rents mountain bikes for $12 per day.

Weather Information: 468-4940.

Pharmacy: Mid-Niter Drugs, 11408 Jasper Ave. (482-1011). Open daily 8am-midnight.

Hospital: Edmonton General, 11111 Jasper Ave. (482-8111).

Emergency: 911.

Police: 423-4567.

Post Office: 9808 103A Ave. (495-4105), adjacent to the CN Tower. Open Mon.-Fri. 8am-5:45pm. **Postal Code:** T5J 2G8.

Area Code: 403.

Although Edmonton has the distinction of being the northernmost major city in North America, it's actually in the southern half of Alberta, making it an easy 3½-hour drive from Calgary on Hwy. 2 and four hours from Jasper on Hwy. 16. **Greyhound** and **VIA Rail** let you off downtown, but the **airport** sits far south of town, a prohibitively expensive cab fare away. The **Grey Goose Airporter Service** runs a shuttle to the downtown area for $11. Those not willing to pay $11 are known to hop on an airport shuttle bus taking travelers to downtown hotels.

Like Calgary, Edmonton uses a system of streets and avenues; **streets** run north-south, and **avenues** run east-west. Street numbers increase to the west, and avenue numbers increase to the north. "0 St." and "0 Ave." were, presumably, placed by a group of intoxicated city planners over a century ago; thus, "City Centre" sits around 105 St. and 101 (Jasper) Ave., and East Edmonton is saddled with the shame of "negative" street addresses. If you're crazy enough to drive around here, transit maps are available all over town.

ACCOMMODATIONS

The liveliest place to stay in Edmonton is the hostel, though you'll have more privacy at St. Joseph's College or the University of Alberta.

Edmonton International Youth Hostel (HI-C), 10422 91 St. (429-0140), off Jasper Ave. Take bus #1 or 2. A long walk from the bus station. Much of the eccentric clientele consists of older men in from the oil rigs on their nights off. The area surrounding the hostel is not the finest; you'll feel safer walking via Jasper Ave., which is busy and well-lighted. The hostel rarely turns anyone away, no matter what the hour nor how full the beds. $10, nonmembers $15.

St. Joseph's College (492-7681), 89 Ave. at 114 St., in the University of Alberta neighborhood. Take bus #43. The rooms here are smaller, less institutional, and cheaper than those at the university nearby. Shaded lawn out front. In summer, make reservations—rooms fill up fast. Singles $20, weekly $119. Doubles $30 (limited number). Cold breakfast $2.25, hot breakfast $3.25.

University of Alberta (492-4281), 87 Ave. between 116 and 117 St. on the ground floor of Lister Hall. Classic institutional rooming units. Work up a good head of steam freeing your immovable mattress (wedged under the shelves that are perma-fastened to the walls), or just use the weight room and steam room (free). Singles $24. Doubles $34. Tanning $1.25.

YWCA, 10305 100 Ave. (429-8707). Men not allowed on the residential floors. Women slumber in quiet rooms, many with balconies. Free use of pool and unlimited local calls for $1 per day. Dorm-style beds $11. Singles $23.50, with bath $29.

YMCA, 10030 102A Ave. (421-9622). Conveniently close to the bus and VIA Rail stations. A lively, clean building with rooms available for both men and women. More secure rooms especially appropriate for women are available on the 4th and 7th floors. Singles $25, 4th- or 7th-floor rooms $27.50. Doubles $35. Dorm bunk beds $18 per night (3 beds in 1 room, with lockers; 2-night max. stay).

FOOD

One might hypothesize that citizens of Edmonton—the self-labeled "City of Champions"—kick off their day with a bowl of Wheaties. Little evidence can be found to support this theory. The city's restaurants seem to have trouble with substantial repasts, but both **downtown** and **Old Strathcona,** a region along 82 (Whyte) Ave. between 102 and 105 St., sizzle and crack with a number of eateries.

Lunch with politicians in the main cafeteria of the **Alberta Legislature Building** when the legislature is in session (cafeteria open 7am-3:30pm and 5-7pm). Or try the private sector cafeterias of the **YWCA** (men allowed; open Mon.-Fri. 7am-5pm, Sat. 9am-2pm, Sun. 10am-2pm) and the **YMCA** (open Mon.-Fri. 7am-6:30pm).

Real Pizza & Steaks, 9449 Jasper Ave. (428-1989), near hostel. Pizza and steaks are nothing to write home about, but the blueberry pancakes are superb (no wimpy soft berries—just good, firm ones). Good breakfast special (2 eggs, toast, bacon, and hash browns) for $4.50. Open 10am-2am.

Patisserie Kim's Cafe, 10217 97 St. (422-6754). No frills here, just fast, cheap food. For $2.25 dine on 2 eggs, hash browns, toast, and coffee, or for $2.85, a hamburger and fries. Not the safest location, but the law courts are just across the street. Open Mon.-Fri. 6:30am-8pm, Sat.-Sun. 6:30am-7pm.

Polo's Cafe, 8405 112 St. (432-1371). Contemporary Asian cuisine in a predominantly pink setting. Large stir fry and noodle dishes $6-8, salads $3-6. The "Malaysian Wave"—a heaping helping of beef/chicken, vegetables, and spicy egg noodles—is a favorite of U. of A. students. Open Mon.-Fri. 11am-midnight.

Veggies, 10331 82nd Ave. in Old Strathcona. Creative vegetarian cuisine. Hummus plate ($5.50). Open Mon.-Fri. 11am-10pm, Sat. 9am-10pm, Sun. 9am-9pm.

New York Bagel Cafe, 8209 104 St. in Old Strathcona. Part of a continent-wide trend towards subjecting the bagel to all kinds of unnecessary and humiliating bastardizations—for instance, chicken liver pâté. 007 fanatics can contemplate (but probably can't afford) what would be a James Bond favorite—bagel with Malasol Beluga caviar ($45). Wash it all down with a pineapple or raspberry milk cocktail ($3.35), or choose from 9 types of coffee. Open daily 11am-midnight.

SIGHTS

The "oh-my-god-that's-*obscenely*-huge" **West Edmonton Mall** (444-5200 or 800-661-8890) sprawls across the general area of 170 St. and 87 Ave. With the Milky Way's largest conglomeration of retail stores under one roof, The Mall is simply the talk of the town. Though It keeps Edmontonians warm during the sub-zero winters, It leaves most tourists with a cold impression of the town. When It first landed, Its massive sprawl of boutiques and eateries seized 30% of Edmonton's retail business, effectively suffocating the downtown shopping district and sucking the downtown life out of the city.

Encompassing a water park, an amusement park, and dozens of pathetically caged exotic animals, The World's Biggest Mall appears even Bigger than It is thanks to the mirrors plastered on nearly every wall. Among Its many attractions, The Mall boasts twice as many submarines as the Canadian Navy, a full-scale replica of Columbus' *Santa Maria,* and **Lazermaze,** the world's first walk-through video game. You can get to The Mall via bus #10. (Open Mon.-Fri. 10am-9pm, Sat. 10am-6pm, Sun. noon-5pm.)

After sampling the "achievements" of the late 20th-century malls, the late 19th century will seem a welcome relief as you head for **Fort Edmonton Park** (428-2992), off Whitemud Dr. near the Quesnell Bridge. At the end of the park (farthest from the entrance) sits the fort, a 19th-century "office building" for Alberta's first entrepreneurs—ruthless whiskey traders. Between the fort and the park entrance are three long streets (1885 St., 1905 St., and 1920 St.), each bedecked with period buildings—apothecaries, blacksmith shops, and barns—keyed to the streets' respective years. Appropriately clothed park volunteers greet visitors with the inquisitiveness of a 19th-century schoolmarm or the geniality of a general-store owner. (Park open Victoria Day-late June Mon.-Fri. 10am-4pm, Sat.-Sun. 10am-6pm; late June-Labour Day daily 10am-6pm; Labor Day-Thanksgiving Sun., Mon., and holidays 10am-6pm. Admission $6, senior citizens and ages 13-17 $4.50.) The park can be reached on bus #123 or 32.

After visiting the fort, stop in at the **John Janzen Nature Centre** next door to pet the salamanders. (Open late June-Labour Day Mon.-Fri. 9am-6pm, Sat.-Sun. 11am-6pm.) Then, sprint across Hwy. 2 to the **Valley Zoo** (496-6911), at 134 St. and Buena Vista Rd.—and yes, it *does* have more species than The Mall. (Open early May-Sept. daily 10am-6pm. Admission $4.75, senior citizens $3.50, youths $2.50. Open fall and winter Sat.-Sun. noon-4pm. Admission $3.25, senior citizens $2.40, children $1.65. Closed in April.)

From the imprisoned fauna of the Valley Zoo, turn to the imprisoned flora of the **Muttart Conservatory,** 9626 96A St. (428-5226 for a recording). Here plant species from around the world serve their life sentences in the climate-controlled comfort of four ultramodern glass-and-steel pyramids. Palm trees and banana plants tower over orchids and hibiscus in the humid Tropical Pavilion; cacti and desert shrubs flourish in the dry heat of the Arid Pavilion. Take your wedding photos in the Show Pavilion, which presents brilliant floral displays that change from season to season. If you happen to be traveling with an ailing plant, Muttart will diagnose the problem for a "minimal" fee. (Open year-round Sun.-Wed. 11am-6pm. Admission $4, senior citizens and youths $3, children $2.) Bus #51 whisks you to Muttart.

The **Alberta Legislature Building,** 97 Ave. and 109 St. (427-7362), is as stately and ornate as any capitol building in Alberta. The free tour guides you to the magical "Magic Spot," where water sounds as if it's pouring down torrentially from above (an echo from the fountain three floors below). (Tours given every ½-hr. Victoria Day-Labour Day Mon.-Fri. 9am-8:30pm, Sat.-Sun. 9am-4:30pm; call in winter.)

On sunny summer days, crowds throng to the magnificent fountains and greens that stretch before the steps of the capitol building. If you're not in the mood to frolic with the children in the **Wading Pool,** escape to the darkness of the **Government Centre Pedway,** a network of subterranean walkways connecting the Legislature Building with other government offices. If you'd prefer to observe Edmonton from on high, check out the **AGT Vista 33** on the 33rd floor of the Alberta Telephone Tower, 10020 100 St. (493-3333). This lookout spot also includes a small **telephone museum.** A number of hands-on displays just might make the elevator trip well worth the nominal admission fee. (Open Mon.-Sat. 10am-8pm, Sun. noon-8pm. Admission $1, children 50¢, senior citizens and pre-schoolers free.)

You can retrace the steps of Alberta's pioneers along **Heritage Trail.** The self-guided tour begins at 100 St. and 99 Ave. and winds past the Legislature Building, Edmonton's first schoolhouse, and other historic landmarks. Just follow the red brick road. Another self-guided tour, the **Walking Tour of Old Strathcona,** starts at 8331 104 St. (433-5866) in the Old Strathcona Foundation Building (open Mon.-Fri. 8:30am-4:30pm). The **Old Strathcona Model and Toy Museum,** McKenzie Historic House, 8603 104th St. (433-4512), is a pleasant way to spend a few minutes. Examine over 200 paper reconstructions of such historic buildings as St. Basil's Cathedral and the Taj Mahal, and of such ships as the *Mayflower* and the *Titanic.* The paper caricatures of Canadian Prime Ministers are particularly well-done. (Open Wed.-Fri. noon-8pm, Sat. 10am-6pm, Sun. 1-5pm. Free.) Take bus #43.

More substantial artifacts may be found at the **Provincial Museum of Alberta,** 12845 102 Ave. (453-9100), which caches all kinds of Albertan relics. Despite the impressive collection, the museum fails to create a cohesive picture of either pioneer or Native life. Marvel at a clump of cow dung "representing the buffalo dung used in a secret ceremony of the Blackfoot Horn Society," or at a turn-of-the-century veterinary textbook (complete with pop-up pictures). The museum does, however, contain one of the only photographs of downtown Edmonton taken before the oil boom spiked the area with skyscrapers. (Open Victoria Day-Labour Day daily 9am-8pm; in winter Tues.-Sun. 9am-5pm. Admission $3, children $1. Tues. free.) Take bus #1 or 2.

ENTERTAINMENT AND ACTIVITIES

Led by Wayne Gretzky, the NHL's **Edmonton Oilers** skated off with four of five consecutive Stanley Cups in the 80s. The Great One departed for the Los Angeles Kings, but the Oilers still play from October through April in the **Northlands Coliseum,** 7424 118 Ave. (471-2191).

If the violence of NHL brawl's doesn't intoxicate you enough, head to one of the bars in the downtown area. Homesick Brits hold support groups at **Sherlock Holmes,** 10012 101A Ave. (426-7784), an English-style pub known for its sing-alongs and a passel of staple British ales on tap. Country fans should mosey on over to **Cook County Saloon,** 8010 103 St. (432-2665), while Charlie Parker aficionados will dig **Yardbird Suite** at 10203 86 Ave. (432-0428). The **Sidetrack Cafe** at 10333 112 St. (421-1326) and **Blues on Whyte** at the Commercial Hotel, 10329 82 Ave. (439-3981), are the best blues clubs in the city.

For a more cerebral evening, buy tickets to the **Princess Theatre,** 10337 82 (Whyte) Ave. (433-0979, 433-5785 for a recording). Watch for the Princess's **Grazing on Film** festival in June. (Tickets $7, senior citizens and children $2.25.) Check the *Edmonton Bullet* (free) for theater, film, and music listings. The "Live-Line" (424-5483) updates the performance scene.

SEASONAL EVENTS

Edmonton, presumably jealous of Calgary's success with the Stampede, conjured its own summertime carnival a few years back. Held for 10 days at the end of July, **Klondike Days,** like the Stampede, occasions the painting of cartoon figures on storefront windows and causes an epidemic of free (or nearly free) breakfaSt. Klondike Days recalls the turn-of-the-century Yukon Gold Rush when Edmontonians lured treasure-seekers to their city, advertising an apocryphal "Klondike Trail" from Edmonton to Dawson City. (Write to Edmonton's Klondike Days Exposition, P.O. Box 1480, Edmonton T5J 2N5, or call 471-4653 for information.) In mid-July is the **International Street Performers Festival** (425-5162).

Each summer, alternative entertainment dominates the Old Strathcona district along 82nd (Whyte) Ave. The **Fringe Theatre Event** (448-9000; mid-Aug.) features 150 alternative theatre productions in area parks, theaters, and streets. The **Edmonton Folk Music Festival** (429-1899; early Aug.) brings country and bluegrass banjo-pickin' to the city. The **International Jazz City Festival** (432-7166; late June-early July) jams together 10 days of club dates and free performances by some of Canada's (and the world's) most noted jazz musicians. This musical extravaganza coincides with a visual arts celebration called **The Works** (426-2122).

■ Near Edmonton

Wilderness beckons a mere 35km to the east at **Elk Island National Park.** In 1906, civic concern prompted the establishment of the park in order to protect endangered herds of elk. Since then, all sorts of exotic mammals (plains bison, wood bison, moose, hikers) have moved in, along with 240 species of birds. Pick up your copy of *You Are in Bison Country* at the **Park Information Centre,** just off Hwy. 16, and learn that bison are dangerous; in fact, they're faster than horses and fifty times bigger than Marge Simpson's hair. The shore of **Astotin Lake** is the center of civilized activity in the park. The **Astotin Interpretive Centre** (992-6392) answers questions, screens films, and schedules activities (open Sat.-Sun. 3-6pm). Questions can also be fielded by the information office at the south gate (922-5833; open daily 10am-6pm) or the administration office of the park (992-6380). Admission to the park is $5 per vehicle. Backcountry **camping** is allowed in certain areas with a **free permit,** obtainable at the Information Centre. The park also features 12 well-marked **hiking trails,** most 3-17km in length, which double as cross-country and snowshoeing trails in the winter.

WESTERN ALBERTA

■■■ JASPER NATIONAL PARK

Before the Icefields Parkway was built, few travelers dared to venture north from Banff into the untamed wilderness of Jasper. But those bushwhackers who made it returned with rave reviews, and the completion of the Parkway in 1940 paved the way for everyone to appreciate Jasper's astounding beauty. Today, the yearly influx of vehicles (and tourists) is estimated to be in excess of one million.

In contrast to its glitzy southern peer, Jasper townsite manages to maintain the look and feel of a real small town. The houses of Jasper's permanent residents rise away from Connaught Drive and blend peacefully with the surrounding landscape. The only conspicuous traces of Jasper's tourist trade are the blue-and-white signs advertising "approved accommodations" and the imitation totem pole at the VIA Rail station, which keeps its back turned to the town in a gesture toward good taste.

PRACTICAL INFORMATION AND ORIENTATION

Visitors Information: Park Information Centre, 500 Connaught Dr. (852-6176). Trail maps and information on all aspects of the park. Open daily 8am-8pm; early Sept. to late Oct. and late Dec. to mid-May daily 9am-5pm; mid-May to mid-June daily 8am-5pm. **Alberta Tourism,** 632 Connaught Dr. (800-222-6501 in AB, 800-661-8888 elsewhere). Open Victoria Day-Labour Day daily 8am-8pm. **Jasper Chamber of Commerce,** 632 Connaught Dr. (852-3858). Open Mon.-Fri. 9am-5pm. For further information, write to **Park Headquarters,** Superintendent, Jasper National Park, 632 Patricia St., Box 10, Jasper T0E 1E0 (852-6161).

VIA Rail, 314 Connaught Dr. (800-852-3168). To: Vancouver (Mon., Thurs., Sat., $126), Edmonton (Tues., Fri., Sun., $73), and Winnipeg (Tues., Fri., Sun., $200).

10% discount for senior citizens and students. Children ½ fare. Coin-operated lockers $1 for 24 hr.

Greyhound, 314 Connaught Dr. (852-3926), in the VIA station. To: Edmonton (4 per day, $42), Kamloops ($45), and Vancouver ($82.50).

Brewster Transportation and Tours, 314 Connaught Dr. (852-3332), in the VIA station. To Banff (full-day tour $59.50, daily 4¼-hr. express $38.50) and Calgary (daily, 8 hr., $47).

Taxi: Heritage Taxi, 611 Patricia (852-5558), offers a flat rate of $8 between town and Whistler's hostel, and a 30% discount from regular fares to HI members.

Car Rental: Tilden Car Rental, in the bus depot (852-4972). $44 per day with 100 free km. Must be 21 with credit card. $2500 insurance deductible for drivers under 25.

Bike Rental: Freewheel Cycle, 611 Patricia Ave. (852-5380). Mountain bikes $5 per hr., $13 per 5 hr., $20 per day. Open in summer daily 9am-8pm; in spring and fall Tues.-Sun. 10am-6pm. **Home Hardware,** 623 Patricia Ave. (852-5555). Mountain bikes $4-5 per hr., $15-18 per day. Open Mon.-Fri. 8am-9pm, Sat. 9am-9pm, Sun. 11am-5pm. **Whistlers Mountain Hostel** rents mountain bikes for $13 (nonmembers $17) per day (see Accommodations for address).

Laundry and Showers: Jasper Laundromat and Showers, on Patricia St. near the Post Office. Wash $1, 42-min. dry $1. 10-min. showers $1. Open daily 9am-10pm.

Pharmacy: Whistler Drugs, 100 Miette Ave. (852-4411). Open daily 9am-10:30pm; early Sept. to mid-June 9am-9pm.

Hospital: 518 Robson St. (852-3344).

RCMP Emergency: 852-4848. **Ambulance and Fire:** 852-3100.

Police: 600 Pyramid Lake Rd. (852-4848).

Post Office: 502 Patricia St. (852-3041), across from the townsite green. Open Mon.-Fri. 9am-5pm. **Postal Code:** T0E 1E0.

Area Code: 403.

All of the above addresses are found in **Jasper townsite,** which is located near the center of the park, 362km southwest of Edmonton and 287km north of Banff. **Hwy. 16** transports travelers through the northern reaches of the park, while the **Icefields Parkway** (Hwy. 93) connects to Banff National Park in the south. Buses run to the townsite daily from Edmonton, Calgary, Vancouver, and Banff. Trains arrive from Edmonton and Vancouver. Renting a bike is the most practical option for short jaunts within the park; bikes can also be rented for one-way trips between Jasper and Banff. Hitching is popular along the Icefields Parkway; some locals swear by it, but *Let's Go* does not recommend it.

ACCOMMODATIONS

Hotels in Jasper townsite are too expensive to be viable budget options. You may, however, be able to stay cheaply at a **bed and breakfast** (singles $20-35, doubles $25-45). Most are located right in town near the bus and train stations. Ask for the *Private Homes Accommodations List* at the Park Information Centre or the bus depot (see Practical Information). Since few visitors know of the list, space in B&Bs may be available on short notice. If you have some sort of transportation (preferably with wheels) and would like to get away from the townsite, head for one of Jasper's hostels (listed below from north to south). Reservations, as well as information on closing days and on the winter "key system," are channeled through the Edmonton-based **Northern Alberta Hostel Association** (439-3139; fax 403-433-7781).

Maligne Canyon Hostel (HI-C), 11km east of townsite on Maligne Canyon Rd. (852-3584). Small, recently renovated cabins on the bank of the Maligne River. An ideal place for viewing wildlife; the knowledgeable manager is happy to lead guided hikes through nearby Maligne Canyon. Accommodates 24. $8, nonmembers $12. Closed Wed. in winter.

Whistlers Mountain Hostel (HI-C), on Sky Tram Rd. (852-3215), 7km south of the townsite. Closest to the townsite, this is the park's most modern (and crowded) hostel. Usually full in summer. Bring your own food, leave your shoes at the front door, and struggle to hold your own against the staff in an all-out game of volleyball. Accommodates 69. Curfew midnight. $12, nonmembers $16.

Mt. Edith Cavell Hostel (HI-C), on Edith Cavell Rd., off Hwy. 93A. The road is closed in winter, but the hostel welcomes anyone willing to ski 11km from Hwy. 93A; see reservations number above. Really. Accommodates 32. $8, nonmembers $12. Open mid-June to early Oct., key system in winter.

Athabasca Falls Hostel (HI-C), on Hwy. 93 (852-5959), 30km south of Jasper townsite, 500m from Athabasca Falls. Huge dining/recreation room with wood-burning stove. Accommodates 40. $9, nonmembers $14. Closed Tues. in winter.

Beauty Creek Hostel (HI-C), on Hwy. 93, 78km south of Jasper townsite. Next to the stunning Sunwapta River. Accommodates 24. Accessible through a "key system" in winter (groups only). $8, nonmembers $12. Open May to mid-Sept., closed Wed.

CAMPING

The campsites below are listed from north to south. For campground updates, tune in 1450AM on your radio when nearing the townsite. For detailed information, call the Park Information Centre (852-6176).

Pocahontas, on Hwy. 16, at the northern edge of the park, 50km east of the townsite. Closest campground to the Miette Hot Springs. Flush toilets, hot and cold running water. 140 sites, $9.25. Open mid-May to early Sept.

Snaring River, 16km east of the townsite on Hwy. 16. Kitchen shelters, dry toilets. 56 sites, $7.25. Open mid-May to early Sept.

Whistlers, on Whistlers Rd., 3km south of the townsite. If you're intimidated by wilderness, the occupants of the 781 neighboring sites will keep you company. Hot and cold running water, showers. Tent sites $13, full hookups $17.50. Open mid-May to mid-Oct.

Wapiti, on Hwy. 93, 2km south of Whistlers. RV central. 366 Winnebago-laden sites. Showers. Sites $14, with electricity $15. Open mid-June to early Sept.

Wabasso, on Hwy. 93A, about 20km south of Jasper townsite. Flush toilets, hot and cold running water, trailer sewage disposal. 238 sites, $9.25. Open late June to early Sept.

Mount Kerkeslin, on Hwy. 93, about 35km south of Jasper townsite. Kitchen shelters, dry toilets. 42 sites, $8. Open mid-May to early Sept.

Honeymoon Lake, on Hwy. 93, about 50km south of the townsite. Kitchen shelters, dry toilets, swimming. 35 sites, $8. Open mid-June to Oct.

Jonas Creek, on Hwy. 93, about 70km south of the townsite. Kitchen shelters, dry toilets. 25 sites, $8. Open mid-May to Oct.

Columbia Icefield, on Hwy. 93, 103km south of the townsite, at the southern border of the park. Close enough to the Athabasca Glacier to receive an icy breeze on the warmest summer night, but crowded nonetheless. Kitchen shelters, dry toilets. 33 sites, $8. Open mid-May to Oct.

Wilcox Creek, on Hwy. 93, at the southern park boundary. Kitchen shelters, dry toilets, trailer sewage disposal. 46 sites, $8. Open mid-June to mid-Sept.

FOOD

It's a good idea to stock up on food at a local market or bulk foods store before heading for the backcountry. For grocery supplies at any time of night or day, stop at **Wink's Food Store,** 617 Patricia St. (852-4223), or **Super A Foods,** 601 Patricia St. **Nutter's,** 622 Patricia St. (852-5844), offers bulk grains, nuts, and dried fruits. They also sell deli meats, canned goods, and freshly ground coffee. (Open Mon.-Sat. 9am-10pm, Sun. 10am-8pm.)

Roony's, 618 Connaught Dr. (852-5830). Although the pizza and subs are only fair, the Egyptian food will make your mouth light up like a pinball machine. Try the *kofta,* spicy ground beef with parsley and onions on toasted bread ($7). Burgers are cheap ($3.25-3.75). Open daily noon-2am; in winter 2pm-2am.

Mountain Foods and Cafe, 606 Connaught Dr. (852-4050). Stake out a table at this popular streetside cafe. The menu has both hot and cold running sandwiches ($3.50), soups, and desserts—all of them nutritious. Pita melt with avocado, turkey, and tomato $7. Hearty bowl of lentil soup ($2.40). Frozen yogurt ($1.60). Prepare for the New Age by stocking up on bulk grains and holistic books. Open daily 8am-10pm.

Scoops and Loops, 504 Patricia St. (852-4333). Average food at great prices. Croissant sandwiches ($3) and bran muffins (60¢) are fine for lunch, but definitely save room for dessert. Monstrous selection of hard and soft ice cream, pies, and pastries. Open daily 10am-10pm.

Mondi's, 632 Connaught Dr. Pasta dishes and entrees $8.25-12, but between 5 and 6pm, all entrees are 2-for-1.

OUTDOORS

An extensive network of trails connects most parts of Jasper; many paths start at the townsite itself. Information Centres (see Practical Information for locations) distribute free copies of *Day Hikes in Jasper National Park* and a summary of longer hikes. The trails listed cover the park's three different ecological zones. The **montane zone** blankets the valley bottoms with lodgepole pine, Douglas fir, white spruce, and aspen. Subalpine fir and Engelmann spruce inhabit the middle part of the canopy, called the **subalpine zone,** comprising 40% of the park. Fragile plants and wildflowers struggle for existence in the uppermost, **alpine zone,** covering another 40% of Jasper. Hikers should not stray from trails in the alpine area, so as to avoid trampling endangered plant species. Kick off any foray into the wilderness with a visit to the Information Centre in the townsite. Experts will direct you to appropriate hiking and mountain-biking trails. The Icefield Centre, on Hwy. 93 at the southern entrance to the park (see Icefields Parkway), provides similar services.

Mt. Edith Cavell, named after a German nurse who was executed during WWI for providing aid to the Allies, will shake you to the bone with the thunderous roar of avalanches off the Angel Glacier. Take the 1.6km loop trail Path of the Glacier to the top or the 8km hike through **Cavell Meadows.** Edith rears her enormous head 30km south of the townsite on Mt. Edith Cavell Rd.

Not to be outdone by Banff, Jasper has a gondola of its own. The **Jasper Tramway** (852-3093), the longest and highest tramway in Canada, offers a panoramic view of the park as it rises 2.5km up the side of **Whistlers Mountain.** The gondola draws crowds and packs the parking lot. (Fare $9.65, ages 5-14 $4.85, under 5 free. Open mid-April to early Sept. 8am-9:30pm; Sept. to mid-Oct. 9am-4:30pm. Closed mid-Oct. to mid-April.) A steep 10km trail starting from the Whistlers Mountain Hostel also leads up the slope; take the tram ride down ($5) to spare your quadriceps. No matter which way you go, be sure to bring along a warm jacket and sunglasses to protect against rapidly changing weather conditions at the summit.

Maligne Lake, the largest glacier-fed lake in the Canadian Rockies, is located 50km southeast of the townsite at the end of Maligne Lake Rd. In Maligne's vivid turquoise waters you can enjoy every conceivable water sport. Reservations for boat cruises and whitewater rafting trips can be made through the **Maligne Tours** office, 626 Connaught Dr. (852-3370). Farther north in the valley and 30km east of the townsite, the Maligne River flows into **Medicine Lake**—but no river flows out. The trick? The water escapes underground through tunnels in the easily dissolved limestone, re-emerging 16km downstream in the **Maligne Canyon,** 11km east of the townsite on Maligne Canyon Rd. (This is the longest known underground river in North America. Pretty sneaky, eh?)

Whitewater Rafting (Jasper) Ltd. (852-7238) offers several rafting trips from $35; a two-hour trip down the Maligne River costs $45. Register by phone or stop at the Esso station in the townsite. **Rocky Mountain River Guides** (852-3777), in On-Line Sport and Tackle, offers a three-hour trip ($50). **Sekani Mountain Tours** (852-

ICEFIELDS PARKWAY

5337) offers various trips with discounts to HI members. **Boat rental** is available at **Pyramid Lake** (852-3536; canoes $10 for 1 hr., $8 each additional hr.; motorboats $15 for 1 hr., $12 each additional hr.; $20 or a valid ID required for deposit) and **Maligne Lake** (852-3370; canoes $10 for 1 hr., $6 each additional hr., $30 per day; ID required for deposit). For a less strenuous tour of Maligne Lake, **Maligne Lake Scenic Cruises** offers narrated cruises in cozy, heated tour boats. Reservations are recommended ($27, seniors $24, children $13.50).

Trout abound in Jasper's spectacular lakes during the month of May—but so do anglers. The key to finding a secluded **fishing** spot at Jasper is to go someplace inaccessible by car. One such remote area is **Beaver Lake,** located about 1km from the main road at the tip of Medicine Lake. The lake is beautiful, never crowded, and here even novice fisherfolk can hook themselves a dinner. Rent equipment at **Currie's,** in the Sports Shop at 416 Connaught Dr. (852-5650; rod, reel, and line $10; one-day boat rental $25).

Let your steed do the sweating on a **guided horseback trail ride.** Three-hour rides at Maligne Lake cost $45; 1½-hour rides cost $25 at the Jasper Park Lodge (852-5794). Guided rides at Pyramid Lake are $17 per hour (852-3562).

The saddle-sore can revive their numbed buns at **Miette Hot Springs** (866-3939), north of the Townsite off Hwy. 16 along the clearly marked, 15km Miette Hotsprings Rd. The 1986-vintage Hot Springs building contains lockers and two pools (one of which is wheelchair accessible and neither of which is especially transfixing). Free from nutrient-filled additives and the rotten-egg reek of sulfur, the pools are heated via external pipes through which the spring water is pumped from the smelly source. Unfortunately, the 40°C (102°F) water is off-limits in winter. (Open May25-June 24 Mon.-Fri. 12:20-8pm, Sat.-Sun. 10:30am-9pm; June 25-Sept. 5 daily 8:30am-10:30pm. Admission $2.50, children $1.50. Suit rental $1.25, towels $1, lockers 25¢.) Rotten-egg-lovers can wallow in the sulfur-soused spring itself; a short trail leads south from a picnic area near the modern pool complex to one of the steamy outlets. Don't drink the water—it's 55°C (131°F) and full of untamed microscopic beasties.

Intrepid hikers should attempt the three-faced **Mystery Lake Trail,** leading east and uphill from the pools. The trail metamorphoses from a paved path into a dirt road into a serious trek in the course of the 11km journey to Mystery Lake. Be warned that you will need to ford a major river that becomes unpassable after periods of heavy rainfall; contact the trail office at the Information Centre for a report on trail conditions.

Winter may keep you away from the hot springs, but you can always warm up on the ski slopes of **Marmot Basin,** near Jasper townsite (852-3816). A full-day lift ticket costs $33, half-day $27. Ski rental is available at **Totem's Ski Shop,** 408 Connaught Dr. (852-3078). A full rental package (skis, boots, and poles) runs $9.50 per day. (Open daily 9:30am-10pm; Labor Day to Victoria Day Sun.-Fri. 8am-6pm, Sat. 8am-9pm.) Maligne Lake offers cross-country ski trails from November through May.

The extra-adventurous who do not consider hiking, fishing, boating, skiing, and sightseeing stimulating enough will find Jasper a challenging site for feats of daredeviltry. **Jasper Climbing School,** 806 Connaught Dr. (852-3964), offers an introductory three-hour rappelling class ($25) for those who want a closer look at the imposing cliffs which surround Jasper. **Caving** is a little-talked-about and extremely dangerous pursuit, and is not permitted in the national parks without a permit; one should try it only with an experienced guide. Ben Gadd (852-4012), author of *Handbook of the Canadian Rockies,* leads tours to the **Cadomin Caves** and charges a flat rate of $250 for up to 15 people. Because these caves are outside the National Park, a permit is not required.

■ Icefields Parkway

The Icefields Parkway (Hwy. 93), dubbed the "window on the wilderness," is a glacier-lined, 230km road connecting Jasper townsite with Lake Louise in the south.

The Parkway snakes past dozens of ominous peaks and glacial lakes; pull over at the head of one of 17 trails into the wilderness, or stop at one of 22 scenic points to take in a spectacular view. The 10-minute trail to **Bow Summit** affords a magnificent view of **Peyto Lake,** with its unreal fluorescent blue-green coloring—especially vivid at the end of June. Marvel at the **Weeping Wall,** where water seems to seep from the rock, or at **Bridal Veil Falls'** beautiful series of small cascades. Whether driving or biking, set aside at least three days for the Parkway; its challenging hikes and endless vistas are never monotonous. Thanks to the extensive campground and hostel networks which line the Parkway, extended trips down the entire length of Jasper and Banff National Parks are convenient and affordable. (See Accommodations and Camping under each park.) All points on the Parkway are within 30km of a location where you can roll out your sleeping bag.

Before setting your wheels on the road, pick up a free map of the *Icefields Parkway,* available at park Information Centres in Jasper and Banff. The pamphlet is also available at the **Icefield Centre,** at the boundary between Banff and Jasper. The Centre is within view of the **Athabasca Glacier,** the most prominent of the eight major glaciers which flow from the 325-sq.-km **Columbia Icefield,** one of the largest accumulations of ice and snow south of the Arctic Circle. Its meltwater runs into streams and rivers that terminate in three different oceans—north to the Arctic, east to the Atlantic, and west to the Pacific Ocean. Summer crowds have snowball fights on the vast icefields to the side of the road. **Brewster Transportation and Tours** (762-2241) carries visitors right onto the Athabasca Glacier in monster buses called "Snocoaches." This 75-minute trip will set you back $18.50 (ages 6-15 $9). Or explore the icy expanse on your own from the parking lot. (Tours given early May to mid-Oct. daily 9am-5pm; late Oct. daily 10am-4pm.)

If you a bone-chilling curiosity to know about the geological history of the glaciers, sign up for a guided interpretive hike on the Athabasca (offered mid-June to Labor Day). A three-hour hike called "Ice Cubed" costs $17 (ages 8-17 $7), and the five-hour "Icewalk Deluxe" is $22 (children $10). Write **Athabasca Glacier Icewalks,** Attn.: Peter Lemieux, Box 2067, Banff T0L 0C0, or call 762-3891.

A warmer alternative to journeying out onto the glacier is the 13-minute explanatory film inside the cozy **Icefield Centre.** (Open mid-June to Aug. daily 9am-7pm; mid-May to mid-June and Sept. 9am-5pm.) Although closed in winter, the Parkway is closed only after heavy snowfalls, and then only until the plows clear the way.

If you only have time for a quickie, try the **Parker Ridge Trail.** The 2.4km hike (one-way) guides you away from the Parkway, past the treeline, and over Parker Ridge. At the end of the trail awaits an amazing view of the **Saskatchewan Glacier.** The trailhead is located 1km south of the **Hilda Creek Hostel,** which is itself located 8.5km south of the Icefields (see Banff: Accommodations below).

■■■ BANFF NATIONAL PARK

Banff is Canada's best-loved and best-known natural preserve. It offers 2543 sq. mi. (6600 sq. km) of peaks and canyons, white foaming rapids and brilliant turquoise lakes, dense forests and open meadows. Yet it was not simple love of natural beauty that motivated Prime Minister Sir John MacDonald to establish Canada's first national park in 1885. Rather, officers of the Canadian Pacific Railroad convinced him of Banff's potential for "large pecuniary advantage," and were quick to add, "since we can't export the scenery, we shall have to import the tourists."

The millions who come to Banff every year can afford to dismiss such callous assessments, though. The Park's priceless greenery clearly does grow on trees, offering an abundance of unspoiled backcountry opportunities to novices and experts alike. And while every year the government gets its share of the millions of dollars poured into the overpriced, colorless shops of Banff townsite, it is still up to those who visit Banff to decide how much they want to buy and pay, how much comfort they require, and how much wilderness they wish to experience.

PRACTICAL INFORMATION AND ORIENTATION

Visitors Information: Banff Information Centre, 224 Banff Ave. (762-1550). Includes **Chamber of Commerce** (762-8421) and **Canadian Parks Service** (762-4256). Open daily 8am-8pm; Oct.-May 9am-5pm. **Lake Louise Information Centre** (522-3833). Open mid-May to mid-June daily 10am-6pm; mid-June to Aug. daily 8am-10pm; Sept.-Oct. daily 10am-6pm. Both Centres dispense detailed maps and brochures, and provide information about ski areas, restaurants, activities, accommodations, and cultural attractions.

Park Administration, Superintendent, Banff National Park, Box 900, Banff T0L 0C0 (762-1500).

Bank: Bank of America Canada, 124 Banff Ave. (762-3666). Open Mon.-Thurs. 10am-7pm, Fri. 10am-8pm, Sat.-Sun. noon-8pm. **Bank of Montreal,** 762-2275. **CIBC,** 762-3317.

American Express, 130 Banff Ave., Box 1140 (762-3207). Holds mail free of charge for cardmembers. **Postal code:** T0L 0C0.

Greyhound, 100 Gopher St. (762-6767). Operates out of the Brewster terminal. To: Lake Louise (5 per day, $6.40), Calgary (5 per day, $14.65), Vancouver ($89).

Brewster Transportation, 100 Gopher St. (762-6767), near the train depot. Monopoly on tours of the area; runs 1 express daily to Jasper ($35.50). Does not honor Greyhound Ameripasses. Depot open daily 7:30am-midnight.

Taxis: Legion Taxi, 762-3353. **Lake Louise Taxi,** 522-2020.

Car Rental: Banff Used Car Rentals, junction of Wolf and Lynx (762-3352). $34 per day with 100 free km, 10¢ per additional km. Must be 18 with major credit card. **Avis,** 209 Bear St. (762-3222). $44 per day with 100 free km, 19¢ per additional km. HI-C members get 50 free km. Must be 21 with credit card.

Bike Rental: Bactrax Rentals, 337 Banff Ave. (762-8177). Mountain bikes $5 per hr., $20 per day. HI-C member discount: $2.50 per hr., $12 per day. Open daily 8am-8pm.

Laundry: Laundry Co., 203 Caribou St. (762-2090). $1.75 wash, 7-min. dry 25¢. Open Mon.-Fri. 8am-9pm, Sat. 9am-9pm, Sun. 10am-6pm. **Lake Louise Laundromat,** Samson Mall (522-2143). $2 wash, 8 min. dry 25¢. Open daily 8am-9pm.

Pharmacy: Harmony Drug, 111 Banff Ave. (762-5711). Open daily 9am-9pm.

Hospital: Lynx and Wolf St. (762-2222).

Emergency: Banff Warden Office (762-4506). **Lake Louise Warden Office** (522-3866). Both open 24 hr. **Police:** 762-2226, between Lynx St. and train depot.

Post Office: 204 Buffalo St. (762-2586). Open Mon.-Fri. 9am-5:30pm. **Postal Code:** T0L 0C0.

Area Code: 403.

Banff National Park hugs the Alberta-British Columbia border, 120km west of Calgary. The **Trans-Canada Hwy.** (Hwy. 1) runs east-west through the park; **Icefields Parkway** (Hwy. 93) connects Banff to Jasper National Park in the north. Greyhound links the park to major points in Alberta and British Columbia. Civilization in the park centers around the townsites of Banff and **Lake Louise,** 55km northwest of Banff on Hwy. 1. Buses between the townsites are expensive. If you're hitching, expect plenty of competition. (Let's Go does not recommend hitchhiking.)

ACCOMMODATIONS

Although the budget traveler may have difficulty finding an affordable restaurant in town, inexpensive lodging is abundant. Fifteen residents of the townsite offer rooms in their own homes—many year-round, and the majority in the $20-40 range. Ask for the *Banff Private Home Accommodation* list at the Banff Townsite Information Centre (see Practical Information). A string of Hosteling International-Canada (HI-C) hostels runs from Banff to Lake Louise on to Jasper. The **Pika Shuttle** (800-363-0096) will take you to the next hostel on the route. Buy tickets at the hostels, and confirm through the Banff Hostel. Call for reservations; prices vary depending on destination.

Banff International Hostel (HI-C), Box 1358, Banff T0L 0C0 (762-4122), 3km from Banff townsite on Tunnel Mountain Rd., among a nest of condominiums and lodges. BIH has the look and setting of a ski lodge. In winter, a large fireplace warms the lounge area for cross-country and downhill skiers. Clean quads with 2 bunk beds. A hike from the center of the townsite, but the modern amenities and friendly staff make the trek worthwhile. Ski and cycle workshop. Cafeteria, laundry facilities, TVs, hot showers. Wheelchair-accessible. Registration 6-10am and 4pm-midnight. $16, nonmembers $21. Linen $1.

Banff YWCA, 102 Spray Ave. (762-3560). Welcomes both men and women. Antiseptic white everywhere confirms that this was once a hospital. Cafeteria. Singles $45. Doubles $51. Bunks $16, weekly $80. Prices drop about $10 during winter (Oct. 1-May 15).

Hilda Creek Hostel (HI-C), 8.5km south of the Icefield Centre on the Icefields Parkway. The most noteworthy feature is a primitive **sauna** that holds about 4 people—uncomfortably. In the morning, guests must replenish the water supply with a shoulder-bucket contraption. Full-service kitchen. Accommodates 21. Excellent hiking and skiing nearby at Parker's Ridge. $8, nonmembers $13. Call BIH (above) for reservations.

Rampart Creek Hostel (HI-C), 34km south of the Icefield Centre. Rampart's proximity to several world-famous ice climbs (including **Weeping Wall,** 17km north on Icefields Parkway) makes it a favorite of winter mountaineers. Accommodates 30 in rustic cabins. Sauna, full-service kitchen, wood-heated bathtub. $8, nonmembers $13. Call BIH for reservations.

Mosquito Creek Hostel (HI-C), 103km south of the Icefield Centre and 26km north of Lake Louise. Close to Wapta Icefield. Accommodates 38. Fireplace, sauna, full-service kitchen. $8, nonmembers $13. Call BIH for reservations.

Lake Louise International Hostel (HI-C), Village Rd. (522-2200), 0.5km from Samson Mall in Lake Louise townsite. Brand-new super-hostel à la Banff International. Accommodates 100. Cafeteria, full-service kitchen, hot showers. Wheelchair-accessible. The adjacent Canadian Alpine Centre sponsors various programs and events for hikers and skiers. $15, nonmembers $22. Call BIH for reservations and information.

Castle Mountain Hostel (HI-C), on Hwy. 1A (762-2367), 1.5km east of the junction of Hwy. 1 and Hwy. 93. Recently renovated. Accommodates 36. $9, nonmembers $14. A common area with store and windows which offer frequent bear sightings.

CAMPING

There are hundreds of campers looking to be happy in Banff, and none of the campgrounds takes reservations, so arrive early in the day to stake your claim. Each site holds a maximum of two tents and six people. **Mosquito Creek, Lake Louise, Johnston Canyon,** and **Tunnel Mountain Village** have the best facilities and are located closest to a townsite; contact the Banff or Lake Louise Information Centres (see Practical Information) for detailed information. The campgrounds below are listed from north to south.

Cirrus Mountain, 24km south of the Icefield Centre, 105km north of Hwy. 1 on Hwy. 93. 16 sites, $8. Open late June to early Sept.

Waterfowl, 57km north of Hwy. 1 on Hwy. 93. 116 sites, $10.50. Flush toilets. Hiking and canoeing nearby. Open mid-June to early Sept.

Mosquito Creek, 103km south of the Icefield Centre and 26km north of Lake Louise. Near the Mosquito Creek Hostel. 32 sites (20 during winter), $7.25 (free in winter). Open mid-June to early Sept.

Lake Louise. Not on the lake, but the toilets flush. 220 tentsites, $10.50. Hiking and fishing nearby. Open mid-May to late Sept.

Protection Mountain, 11km west of Castle Junction on Hwy. 1A. 89 sites, $10.50. Flush toilets. Cycling nearby. Open late June to early Sept.

Castle Mountain, midway between Banff and Lake Louise along Hwy. 1A. 43 sites, $10.50. Flush toilets. Cycling nearby. Open late June to early Sept.

Johnston Canyon, 26km northwest of Banff on Hwy. 1A. 132 sites, $13. Flush toilets, showers. Excellent trail access; cycling nearby. Open mid-May to mid-Sept.

Two Jack Main, 13km northeast of Banff. 381 tentsites, $9.50. Flush toilets. Canoeing and cycling nearby. Open late June to early Sept.

Tunnel Mountain Village, 1km past the International Hostel, closest to Banff townsite. 620 tentsites, $13. Flush toilets, showers. Self-guiding trail to Hoodoos. Open mid-May to late Sept.

FOOD

The restaurants in Banff generally charge high prices for mediocre food; the fast-food joints in Banff generally charge moderate prices for poor food. Luckily, the Banff **(Cafe Aspenglow)** and Lake Louise **(Bill Deyto's Cafe)** International Hostels serve affordable, wholesome meals for $3-6. Your best option, however, is to pick up a propane grill and a 10-lb. bag of potatoes and head for the mountains (baked potatoes, potato skins, hash browns, french fries, potato salad...). Do your shopping at **Safeway** (762-5378), at Marten and Elk St. (open daily 8am-10pm).

Aardvark's, 304A Caribou St. (262-5500). This small pizza place does big business late at night, when the bars close. Excellent pizza anytime. Small $6-8, large $12-19. Subs $3-7, wings $5. 10% discount with an HI card. Open daily 11am-4am.

TJ's, 130 Banff Ave. Pasta $5.75-8. Small pizza $6.50-8.50, large $11.50-14. Often has $6 dinner specials. Open daily 11:30am-9:30pm.

Laggan's Deli (522-3574), in Samson Mall at Lake Louise townsite. Savor a thick sandwich on whole-wheat bread ($3.65) with a Greek salad ($1.65), or take home a freshly baked loaf ($1.50-1.75) for later. Always crowded; nowhere better in Lake Louise Village. Open daily 6am-8pm.

Btfsplk's Diner, on Banff Ave. For those who hate vowels but like Ceasar salads ($6) and BBQ burgers ($7).

ENTERTAINMENT

Banff's bartenders contend that the real wildlife in Banff is at the bars. Most of the bars are concentrated along Banff Ave. where you can drink 'til you barff.

Rose and Crown, 202 Banff Ave. (762-2121). Waits of up to an hour are not uncommon to get into this popular English-style pub. Live music almost every night. During happy hour (5:30-7:30pm), drafts are $2.75, highballs $2.50. Open daily 11am-2am.

Barbary Coast, upstairs at 119 Banff Ave. (762-4616). Sports paraphernalia dominates the decor at this fashionable laid-back bar. Live music every night ranges from blues to light rock. 35¢ chicken wings on Tues. and 60-oz. pitchers of beer $9 on Wed. Open 11am-2am.

Silver City, 110 Banff Ave. (762-3337). Formerly the scene of countless drunken brawls, this "Hall of Fame Sports Bar" has mellowed with age. Billiards $1.25. Happy hour 4-7pm. Open 4pm-2am.

SIGHTS AND SEASONAL EVENTS

The palatial **Banff Springs Hotel,** Spray Ave. (762-6895), is perched high over the townsite. In 1988, this enormous 825-room castle celebrated its 100th birthday with a series of posh parties and its own special brand of beer (which has since been watered down at the request of hotel guests). You probably won't have enough money to spend the evening here, or even order dinner, but you can take in a Centennial Ale, a basket of bread, and a fantastic view for $3.50 at the **Grapes Wine Bar** on the second level. During the summer, the hotel offers free guided tours of the grounds daily at 4:30pm. The tour, a good pastime for a rainy day, reveals fascinating secrets about the hotel and offers a grand opportunity to view lavish architecture and museum-quality artifacts. The hotel also offers horseback riding (daily 9am-5pm; $18 for 1 hr., $28 for 2 hr., $34 for 3 hr.; reservations recommended).

Other rainy-day attractions include Banff's small but illuminating museums. The **Whyte Museum of the Canadian Rockies,** 111 Bear St. (762-2291), provides an interesting look at the history of Canadian Alpinism. Exhibits in the museum's Heritage Gallery explain how the townsite developed—very rapidly, unchecked, and catering to the whims of wealthy guests at the Banff Springs Hotel. The galleries downstairs display local artists' paintings of the mountains and their inhabitants. (Open daily 10am-6pm; mid-Oct. to mid-May Mon.-Wed. and Fri.-Sun. 1-5pm, Thurs. 1-9pm. Admission $3, senior citizens and students $2, children free.) The **Banff Park Museum** (762-1558), on Banff Ave. near the bridge, is a taxidermist's dream (or a preservationist's nightmare); here all species indigenous to the park (and many that aren't) are stuffed and displayed under glass. The museum also contains a well-stocked reading room where you can discover the differences between buffalo and bison or peruse clippings that detail recent violent encounters between elk and automobiles (open daily 10am-6pm; free). Less than a block away, on the second floor of the Clock Tower Village Mall, the **Natural History Museum,** 112 Banff Ave. (762-4747), rounds out Banff's archival troika. The complete tour includes a thrilling 20-minute video documentary focusing on the eruption of Mt. St. Helens. (Unfortunately, the early-80s soundtrack is not available for purchase.) On your way out be sure to make faces at the eight-foot-tall "authentic" model of Sasquatch. (Open daily May-June 10am-8pm, July-Aug. 10am-10pm, Sept. 10am-8pm, in winter 10am-6pm. Admission $2, senior citizens and teens $1, under 10 free.)

The culture industry moves into Banff every year for the summer-long **Banff Festival of the Arts,** producing drama, ballet, jazz, opera, and other aesthetic commodities. Pick up a brochure at the Information Centre or call 762-6300 for details.

OUTDOORS

Hike to the **backcountry** for privacy, beauty, over 1600km of trails, and trout that will bite anything. The pamphlet *Drives and Walks,* available at the Information Centres (see Practical Information), describes day and overnight hikes in the Lake Louise and Banff areas. You need a permit to stay overnight in the backcountry; get one free of charge from information centers and park warden offices. All litter must leave the backcountry with you, and no wood may be chopped in the parks. Both the Banff International Hostel (see Accommodations) and the Park Information Centre have the *Canadian Rockies Trail Guide,* with excellent information and maps.

Two easy but rewarding trails lie within walking distance of the Banff townsite. **Fenland** winds 2km through an area creeping with beaver, muskrat, and waterfowl. Follow Mt. Norquay Rd. out of Banff and look for signs either at the bridge just before the picnic area or across the railroad tracks on the left side of the road. The summit of **Tunnel Mountain** provides a spectacular view of Bow Valley and Mt. Rundle. Follow Wolf St. east from Banff Ave. and turn right on St. Julien Rd. to reach the head of the 2.3km trail.

About 25km out of Banff toward Lake Louise along the Bow Valley Parkway, **Johnston Canyon** offers a moderately taxing but popular half-day hike. The 1.1km hike to the canyon's lower falls and the 2.7km trip to the canyon's upper falls consist mostly of a catwalk along the edge of the canyon. Don't stop at the falls, though; proceed along the more rugged trail for another 3.1km to seven blue-green cold-water springs known as the **Inkpots.**

After a strenuous day of hiking, consider driving one of the many scenic routes in the Banff area. **Tunnel Mountain Drive** begins at the intersection of Banff Ave. and Buffalo St. and proceeds 9km past Bow Falls and up the side of Tunnel Mountain. Several markers along the way point to splendid views of the Banff Springs Hotel, Sulphur Mountain, and Mt. Rundle. Turn right onto Tunnel Mountain Rd. to see the **hoodoos,** long, finger-like projections of limestone once part of the cliff wall and thought by Native Americans to encase sentinel spirits.

Drive west along Vermillion Lakes Drive, which branches off Mt. Norquay Rd. just before the overpass. When the sun sets gloriously over the snowy mountains and shimmering lakes, remember to keep both eyes on the road.

Bicycling is permitted on public roads and highways and on certain trails in the park. Spectacular scenery and the proximity to a number of hostels and camp-grounds make the Bow Valley Parkway (Hwy. 1A) and the Icefields Parkway (Hwy. 92) perfect for extended cycling trips. The brochure *Trail Bicycling in National Parks in Alberta and British Columbia,* available at the Information Centres in Banff and Lake Louise, lists trails on which bikes are permitted. Trail cyclists should remember to dismount and stand to the downhill side if a horse approaches. Also be forewarned that the quick and quiet nature of trail bicycling is more prone to sur-prise a bear than is the tromping of hikers.

When Canada's first national park (and the world's third) was established in 1885, it was called the Hot Springs Reserve and its featured attraction was the **Cave and Basin Hot Springs.** The **Cave and Basin Centennial Centre** (762-4900), a refur-bished resort circa 1914, now screens documentaries and stages exhibits. Explore the original cave or relax in the hot springs pool where lifeguards wear sexy pre-World War I bathing costumes. Walk along the Discovery Trail to see the original spring discovered over 100 years ago by three Canadian Pacific Railway workers. The Centre is southwest of the city on Cave Ave. (Open daily 10am-7pm; in winter 10am-5pm. Pool open early June to late Aug. only. Pool admission $3, senior citizens and children $2.)

A particularly scenic walk lies just beyond the Cave and Basin in **Sundance Can-yon.** Allow about an hour and a half for the uphill trail. If you find Cave and Basin's 32°C (90°F) water too chilly, follow the rotten-egg smell to the **Upper Hot Springs pool** (762-2056), a 40°C (104°F) sulphurous cauldron up the hill on Mountain Ave. (Open year-round Mon.-Thurs. 12:30-9pm, Fri.-Sun. 8:30am-11pm. Admission $3, senior citizens and children $2. Bathing suit rental at either spring $1.50, towel rental $1, locker rental 25¢.)

Taking a **gondola** to the top of a peak is an expensive way to see the park, but it saves your legs for hiking at the summit. The **Sulphur Mountain Gondola** (762-5438), next to the Upper Hot Springs pool, lifts you 700m to a view of the Rockies normally reserved for birds and mountain goats. (Open daily 8:30am-8pm. Fare $8.50, ages 5-11 $3.75, under 5 free.) The **Summit Restaurant** (Canada's highest), perched atop Sulphur Mountain, serves an "Early Morning Lift" breakfast special for $4.25. Grab a table by the window.

Brewster Tours (762-6767) offers an extensive array of guided bus tours within the park. If you don't have a car, these tours may be the only way to see some of the main attractions, such as the Great Divide, the Athabasca Glacier, and the spiral rail-road tunnel (trains are often so long that you can see them entering and exiting the mountain at the same time). The tour-guide/drivers are professional, knowledge-able, and entertaining. If you were planning on taking the regular Brewster bus from Banff to Jasper ($35.50), you might want to spend $24 more to see the sights in between. (One way $59.50, 9½-hr. round-trip $83. A walk on the Columbia Icefields is $17.50 extra. Tickets can be purchased at the bus depot.)

If you'd prefer to look up at the mountains rather than down from them, the nearby lakes provide a serene vantage point. **Fishing** is legal virtually anywhere you can find water, but you must hold a National Parks fishing permit, available at the Information Centre ($5 for a 7-day permit, $10 for an annual permit). Superb trout fishing rewards those willing to hike the 7km to **Bourgeau Lake.** Closer to the road, try **Herbert Lake,** off the Icefields Parkway between Lake Louise and the Columbia Icefield, or **Lake Minnewanka,** on Lake Minnewanka Rd. northeast of Banff town-site, rumored to be the home of a half-human, half-fish Indian spirit. You can find out about this myth during a 1½-hour guided tour sponsored by **Minnewanka Tours Ltd.** (762-3473; $20, children $6). Lake Minnewanka Rd. also passes **Johnson Lake,** where the sun warms the shallow water to a swimmable temperature, and **Two Jack Lake,** just beyond Lake Minnewanka, easily explored by boat or canoe.

Those who prefer more vigorous water sports can **river raft** the white waters of the **Kootenay River. Kootenay River Runners** (604-347-9210) offer half- and full-day trips for $49 and $69 respectively, as well as a more boisterous full-day trip on the **Kicking Horse River** for $69. Tickets are available at **Tickets** (762-5385), located on the corner of Caribou St. and Banff Ave. A particularly good deal is offered by the **Banff International Hostel** (see Accommodations)—rafting on the Kicking Horse River (transportation included) for $44. A stop in a pub is promised afterwards.

LAKE LOUISE

The spectacularly clear waters of Lake Louise often serve North American filmmakers' need for Swiss Alpine scenery; on a clear day, the view from the lakeside chateau evokes the feel of St. Moritz. Unfortunately, most visitors spend only enough time at the lake to snap a couple photos. Few stay as long as explorer Tom Wilson did in the 1880s, when he wrote of its majesty, "I never in all my explorations...saw such a matchless scene."

To gain a deeper appreciation of the soothing blue lake and its surrounding glacier, consult the **Lake Louise Information Centre** at Samson Mall (522-3833; open May 19-June 23 8am-6pm, June 24-Sept. 4 8am-8pm, Sept. 5-Oct. 9 10am-6pm, winter 9am-5pm). The brand-new $4.4 million complex is a museum in itself, with exhibits and a short film on the formation of the Rockies. Don't forget that the **bank** in Lake Louise is closed on weekends; bring plenty of money to avoid getting stuck. Renting a canoe from the **Chateau Lake Louise Boat House** (522-3511) will give you the closest look at the lake ($20 per hr.; open 9am-8pm). Several hiking trails begin at the water; as an incentive, aim for one of the two **teahouses,** tucked away at the ends of the 3.4km **Lake Agnes Trail** and the 5.3km **Plain of Six Glaciers Trail.** Be prepared to pay dearly for this mountainous meal both in physical effort and in cash—all the food must be flown in by helicopter (open in summer daily 9am-6pm).

Many find **Lake Moraine** to be even more stunning than its sister Lake Louise, which lies nearby. The lake, also explorable by canoe or boat, lies in the awesome **Valley of the Ten Peaks.** Among the ten peaks is the glacier-encrusted **Mountain Temple,** the third-highest mountain in the park. If you don't get a chance to visit Lake Moraine, just get your hands on a Canadian $20 bill; the Valley of Ten Peaks is pictured on the back.

Timberline Tours (522-3743), located off Lake Louise Dr. near Deer Lodge, offers guided horseback rides through the area. The 1½-hour tour costs $23, and the day-trip $65 (lunch included). The **Friendly Giant sightseeing Lift** (522-3555), which runs up Mt. Whitehorn, across the Trans-Canada Hwy. from Lake Louise, provides another chance to gape at the landscape. (Open mid-June to late Sept. daily 9am-6pm. Fare $9, students $8, ages 5-12 $4. "One-way hiker's special" $5.50.) Like its counterpart at Sulphur Mountain, Lake Louise's lift offers a $3.50 breakfast deal; just make sure to purchase your lift ticket by 10am. Coupons worth $2 off sometimes appear in the *Where?* booklet available at the Park information centres.

■ Kananaskis Country

Tucked away between Calgary and Banff, Alberta's most conspicuous tourist magnets, is a 4000-sq.-km conglomeration of provincial parks—**Bow Valley, Peter Lougheed,** and **Bragg Creek**—and so-called "multi-use recreational areas" (**Spray Lakes** and **Highwood/Cataract Creek** are two of the largest). Even in high season, the wilderness of Kananaskis remains tranquil and unspoiled.

For outdoorsy types, Kananaskis Country offers skiing, snowmobiles, windsurfing, golfing, biking, and hiking. Eager staff members at the five Park Information Centres can help design itineraries for visitors. Expect to be showered with maps and elaborate brochures describing your activity of choice. **Visitor Centres** lie within (or nearby) each of the three provincial parks. The **Bow Valley** centre (673-

3663) is located north of Hwy. 1 between Seebe and Exshaw (open daily 8am-7pm); the **Elbow Valley** centre is located on Hwy. 66 near **Bragg Creek** (949-3754); the cozy, chalet-style centre in **Peter Lougheed Park** (591-7222), complete with a fireplace, a wooden deck, and informative displays and videos, is located on the Kananaskis Lakes Trail (hours vary from season to season). The Alberta Parks System has a central office on **Barrier Lake,** near the junction of Hwy. 40 and 68 (673-3985; open daily 9am-7pm, 9am-5pm in winter). **Travel Alberta** maintains a helpful office in **Canmore,** just off Hwy. 1A near the northwest border of K-Country (678-5508; open Sun.-Thurs. 9am-6pm, Fri.-Sat. 8am-8pm). In an emergency, call the **Canmore RCMP** (591-7707).

Kananaskis' **hiking trails** accommodate all kinds of nature lovers. Those with limited time or endurance will enjoy the hour-long interpretive hikes. The 1.9km **Canadian Mt. Everest Expedition Trail**, for example, provides a majestic view of both Upper and Lower Kananaskis Lakes. More serious hikers will find Gillean Dafferns' *Kananaskis Country Trail Guide* (published by Rocky Mountain Books) the definitive source on area trails, detailing 337 hikes through the area. For additional hints and trail updates, ask a staff member at an Information Centre (see above for locations). Bikers will also find the park staff helpful in planning treks along the untraveled highways and trails.

Buses do not service K-Country directly. However, if you are absolutely determined to reach the area, you can take one of the frequent buses to Banff, which will drop you off about 20km from the region's northwestern boundary at Canmore (see Calgary Practical Information). Once in Kananaskis, hitchhiking is possible but difficult; for safety reasons, *Let's Go* does *not* recommend hitchhiking.

No less than 3000 campsites are accessible via K-Country roads, and camping is unlimited in the backcountry as long as you set up camp at least 1km from a trail. Most established campsites in Kananaskis cost at least $10.75 per night. The **Ribbon Creek Hostel** (591-7333), near the Nakiska Ski Area, 24km south of the Trans-Canada Hwy. on Hwy. 40, accommodates 48 people. The hostel's private family rooms hold four beds each, and its living room has a fireplace. Be warned: the overly-friendly hostel cats will molest you if you venture outdoors (members $9, nonmembers $14). **William Watson Lodge** (591-7227), a few km north of the Information Centre in Peter Lougheed Park, accommodates disabled visitors. Although only senior citizens and residents of Alberta who have disabilities may make reservations to stay in the cabins, the main lodge is open year-round, and anyone may drop by to enjoy the accessible local trails. (Lodge open 8am-10pm; in winter 8am-9pm.)

■■■ CALGARY

The Northwest Mounted Police were sent to south-central Alberta in the 1870s to put an end to illegal whiskey trade and to discourage American expansion into the Canadian wilderness. In 1875, Inspector Denny described the Mounties' arrival at the confluence of the Bon and Elbon Rivers: "Before us lay a lovely valley, bordered to the west by towering mountains with their snowy peaks.... The knowledge that a fort was to be built here gave us the greatest satisfaction." Ranchers and farmers were soon attracted by the low prices of the prairie land, and with the arrival of the Canadian Pacific Railroad in the 1880s the population boomed.

Although "Calgary" is Gaelic for "clear running water," the city now thrives on a less transparent liquid. The discovery of huge oil reserves in the 1960s and the onset of a global energy crisis in the 1970s made the transformation from cowtown to major metropolis possible. Nowadays, office buildings rise higher than oil derricks, businesstypes scurry about in suits toting leather briefcases, and a newly built public transport system soundlessly threads through immaculate downtown streets.

Calgarians take pride in their well-oiled city. They treasure memories of hosting the XVth Winter Olympic Games in 1988. They are also inexplicably proud that bits of *Superman III* were filmed downtown (the filmmakers liked the effect of the mir-

CALGARY

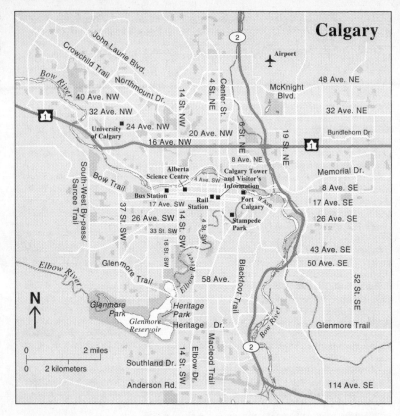

Calgary

John Laurie Blvd.
Crowchild Trail
Bow River
Northmount Dr.
40 Ave. NW
32 Ave. NW
University of Calgary
24 Ave. NW
16 Ave. NW
14 St. NW
4 St. NE
Center St.
20 Ave. NW
6 St. NE
8 Ave. NE
Airport
McKnight Blvd.
48 Ave. NE
32 Ave. NE
Bundlehorn Dr.
19 St. NE

Alberta Science Centre
4 Ave. SW
Calgary Tower and Visitor's Information
Memorial Dr.
8 Ave. SE
Bow Trail
South-West By-pass/ Sarcee Trail
Bus Station
17 Ave. SW
37 St. SW
26 Ave. SW
14 St. SW
33 St. SW
16 St. SW
Rail Station
4 St. SW
Fort Calgary
9 Ave.
Stampede Park
17 Ave. SE
26 Ave. SE
43 Ave. SE
50 Ave. SE
52 St. SE
Blackfoot Trail
Elbow River
Glenmore Trail
58 Ave.
N
Glenmore Park
Glenmore Reservoir
Heritage Park
Heritage Dr.
Macleod Trail
Elbow Dr.
14 St. SW
Southland Dr.
Anderson Rd.
Glenmore Trail
114 Ave. SE
Bow River
2

0   2 miles
0   2 kilometers

rored buildings in the flying sequences). And of course, everyone puts on their cowboy hats and Wranglers when the **Stampede** yahoos into town in July.

PRACTICAL INFORMATION AND ORIENTATION

Visitors Information: Calgary Convention and Visitors Bureau, 237 8th Ave. SE (263-8510). Call or write for help finding accommodations, especially around Stampede time. Open daily 8am-5pm. There are 2 **Information Centres** in the city: **Tower Centre,** ground floor of Calgary Tower at 101 9th Ave. SW (263-8510, ext. 507), open daily 8:30-5pm; **Calgary International Airport** on the arrivals level of the main terminal (292-8477), open daily 7am-10pm; **Visitor Information Phone Line,** (262-2766; Mon.-Fri. 8am-5pm, Sat.-Sun. 10am-5pm). For the cost of a local call, the **"Talking Yellow Pages"** provides a wide range of information, from local events and attractions to the latest in vomit-stain removal techniques (no joke). Dial 521-5222 and the appropriate 4-digit code, listed in the front of the Yellow Pages.

Bank: Bank of Canada, 404 6th Ave. SW (261-3400); many banks downtown.

American Express, 200 8th Ave. SW (269-3757). **Postal code:** T2P 2S8

Trans-Canada Highway Office, 6220 16th Ave. NE. Open daily 8am-9pm; Sept.-June 10am-5pm. **Travel Alberta,** 455 6th St. SW (297-5038, 800-222-6501 in AB), on the main floor, distributes information about the entire province. Open June-Sept. Mon.-Fri. 8:15am-4:30pm.

Greyhound, 877 Greyhound Way SW (from outside Calgary 800-661-TRIP/8747; from within Calgary 260-0846). Frequent service to Edmonton ($26) and to Banff ($14.66). Morning and evening Mon.-Fri. bus to Drumheller $15.25. 10% senior citizen discount. Free shuttle bus from C-Train at 7th Ave. and 10th St. to bus depot (every hr. on the ½-hr., 6:30am-7:30pm, with additional buses at 9am, 6, and 9pm).

Other Buses: Brewster Tours, 221-8242. Operates buses from the airport, to: Banff (3 per day, 12:30, 3, and 6pm, $26); Lake Louise (2 per day, 12:30 and 3pm, $28), and Jasper (1 per day, 12:30pm, $49.50). **Pacific Western Tours,** 221-1992. Operates a 3:30pm bus from the Airport to Banff ($25) and to Lake Louise ($28).

Calgary Transit: Information and Downtown Sales Centre, 206 7th Ave. SW. Bus schedules, passes, and maps. Open Mon.-Fri. 8:30am-5pm. Fare $1.50, ages 6-14 90¢, under 6 free. Exact change required. Day pass $4.50, children $2.50. Book of 10 tickets $12.50, children $8.50. **Information line** (262-1000) open Mon.-Fri. 6am-11pm, Sat.-Sun. 8:30am-9:30pm.

Taxi: Checker Cab, 299-9999. **Yellow Cab,** 250-8311.

Car Rental: Dollar, 221-1888 at airport, 269-3777 downtown. Cars start at $37 per day with unlimited mileage. Weekend special for $33 per day. Must be 23 with a major credit card. If under 25, a mandatory $9 per day surcharge for collision insurance. Open daily 7am-midnight. **Rent-A-Wreck,** 287-9703. Cars start at $30 per day, 200 free km. Discount of $5 per day to HI members. If under 25, there is a mandatory $14 per day surcharge for collision insurance. Open Mon.-Fri. 8am-7pm, Sat.-Sun. 9am-5pm. Because most companies increase their rates during the summer, especially during Stampede time, you should call for the exact rates.

Bike Rental: Global Sports Rental, 7218 Macleod Trail SW (252-2055). $17 per day. **Abominable Sports,** 1217 11th Ave. SW (245-2812). Mountain bikes $25 per day; during the summer, there are often specials for $12.50 per day.

Laundromat: Beacon Speed Wash & Dry, 1518 Centre St. N. (230-9828). Open daily 8am-11pm.

Time and Weather: 263-3333.

Gay Lines Calgary: 223 12th Ave. SW (234-8973), on the 3rd floor. Recorded phone message provides gay community information; peer counseling available at the office. Phone and office open Mon.-Sat. 7am-10pm.

Women's Resource Centre, 320 5th Ave. SE (263-1550), at the YWCA. For women of all ages seeking any kind of assistance. Open Mon.-Fri. 8:30am-4:30pm.

Sexual Assault Centre: 237-5888. Open daily 9:30am-5pm.

Crisis Line: 266-1605.

Hospital: Calgary General, 841 Centre Ave. E. (268-9111).

Emergency: 911.

Police: 316 7th Ave. SE (266-1234).

Post Office: 220 4th Ave. SE (292-5512). Open Mon.-Fri. 8am-5:45pm. **Postal Code:** T2P 180.

Area Code: 403.

Calgary is accessible by several highways, including the **Trans-Canada Hwy.** (Hwy. 1). Planes fly into **Calgary International Airport** (292-8400 for the Airport Authority; 292-8477 for general information, Mon.-Fri. 8am-4:30pm), approximately 5km northwest of the city center. **Cab** fare from the airport to the city is about $25. Bus #57 provides sporadic service from the airport to downtown (call for schedule). Unless you take a cab or have impeccable timing, you will probably end up taking the **Airporter Bus** (291-3848), which offers frequent and friendly service to major hotels in downtown Calgary for $7.50; if you ask nicely they just may drop you off at an unscheduled stop.

Calgary is divided into quadrants: **Centre Street** is the east-west divide, and the **Bow River** divides the north and south sections. The rest is fairly simple: avenues run east-west, streets run north-south. Pay careful attention to the quadrant distinctions (NE, NW, SE, SW) at the end of each address. You can derive the street from an avenue address by disregarding the last two digits of the first number: thus 206 7th Ave. is at 2nd St., and 2339 Macleod Trail is at 23rd St. You should definitely pick up a **city map** at convenience stores or at any of the Information Centres.

Public transportation within the city is inexpensive and efficient. **Calgary Transit** operates both buses and streetcars ("C-Trains"). Buses run all over the city and cost $1.50. You need only call 276-7801 to find out how to get from here to there. Though they cover less territory, C-Trains are free in the downtown zone (along 7th Ave. S.; between 10th St. SW and City Hall); you pay the $1.50 fare only when you leave downtown. Most of what you'll need—lodging, food, and sights—is within the C-Train's free zone anyway.

ACCOMMODATIONS

Cheap lodging in Calgary is rare only when packs of tourists Stampede into the city's hotels—reserve ahead for the month of July. Contact the **B&B Association** of Calgary (403-284-0010) for information and availability on this type of lodging. Prices for singles range from $20-50, doubles $30-70.

Calgary International Hostel (HI-C), 520 7th Ave. SE (269-8239). Conveniently located several blocks south of downtown with access to the 3rd St. SE C-Train station and public buses. Snack bar, meeting rooms, cooking and barbeque facilities, laundry, and a cycle workshop. Wheelchair accessible. Discount tickets for the Calgary Tower can be purchased by showing your hostel card at the Tower. Curfew 2am. Front desk closes at midnight. Members $13, nonmembers $18.

University of Calgary, 3330 24th Ave. (220-3203), in the NW quadrant of the city. A little out of the way, but easily accessible via bus #9 or the C-Train. If you can't make the Olympic squad, at least you can sleep in their beds—U of C was the Olympic Village home to 1988 competitors and offers clean rooms at competitive prices. A virtually unlimited supply of rooms is available May-Aug.; rooms are *not* available at other times. With student ID, singles $21, doubles $31.50. Without student ID, singles $29, doubles $36. More lavish suites with private bathrooms are available in Olympus Hall or Norquay Hall for approximately $30. Booking for all rooms is coordinated through **Kananaskis Hall,** 3330 24th Ave., a 12-min. walk from the University C-Train stop (open 24 hr.).

St. Regis Hotel, 124 7th Ave. SE (262-4641). Friendly management and clean, comfortable rooms. Tavern and snack bar downstairs. Singles $37, with TV $40, with TV and bath $48. If you're feeling particularly ascetic, try "the sleeping room"—a closet-like single with no TV, bath, or windows for $37.

FOOD

Finding food is relatively easy in Calgary. Ethnic and cafe-style dining spots line the **Stephen Avenue Mall,** 8th Ave. S between 1st St. SE and 3rd St. SW. Good, reasonably-priced food (there's no such thing as "cheap" food in Calgary) is also readily available in the **"Plus 15" Skyway System.** Designed to provide indoor passageways during bitter winter days, this futuristic mall-in-the-sky connects the second floors of dozens of buildings throughout downtown Calgary—just look for the blue and white "Plus 15" signs on street level. **Safeway** supermarkets dot the city.

For more expensive, trendy restaurants, go to the **Kensington District,** along Kensington Rd., between 10th and 11th St. NW. Take the C-train to Sunnyside or use the Louise Bridge to reach the area. Other good and lively cafe-restaurants are on 4th St. SW (accessible via the #3 and 53 buses) and 17th Ave. SW (#7 bus).

City Hall Cafeteria, (268-2463) in the City Hall Municipal Building at the intersection of 7th Ave. SE and Macleod Trail, or take the back entrance to City Hall. Backpackers and briefcases guzzle cheap coffee (50¢) and gobble muffins (85¢). Stop by for a cheap breakfast special ($2.80) on your way downtown. Open Mon.-Fri. 7am-4pm.

Hang Fung Foods Ltd., 119 3rd Ave. SE (269-5853), located in the rear of a Chinese market with the same name (one of a number of Asian restaurants on this stretch of 3rd Ave.). Enormous bowl of plain *congee* (rice broth) $1.50. Combination dinners which include won ton soup, a spring roll, pork fried rice, and a large entree for $8.50. Bring your own silverware if you haven't mastered chopsticks. Open daily 9am-9pm.

4th Street Rose, 2116 4th St. SW (228-5377). California cool pervades this fashionable restaurant on the outskirts of town: high ceilings, tile floors, and the positively groovy "Aztec Room" upstairs. Sit among cacti in the skylit interior or join the "in crowd" on the patio. The house specialty is the Caesar Salad ($4), served in a large Mason jar. Gourmet pizzas and homemade pastas $4-9. Open Mon.-Thurs. 11am-1am, Fri. 11am-2am, Sat. 10am-2am, Sun. 10am-midnight.

Kaos Cafe, 718 17th Ave. SW (228-9997). Headbangers and little old ladies sit side by side in colonial chairs, sipping cappuccino ($1.75) beneath dangling strings of tiny illuminated cows. Popcorn and chunks of smoked salmon punctuate the Caesar Salad. Kaos indeed. Dinners (from stir fry to Tex-Mex) $6-10. Live jazz and blues music Fri. and Sat. nights (sometimes a cover). Open daily 9am-midnight.

Picadilly Grill, 216 7th Ave. SW (261-6699). A pleasant restaurant/cafe in the heart of downtown with turquoise tables, a checkered floor and mirrored walls. They didn't film *Grease* here, but they could have. Try the breakfast specials (light and fluffy hot cakes and bacon, for example) for $2.75. Burgers and sandwich entrees $6-8. Dinners under $10. Great daily specials like 2-for-1 steaks. Take out or sit down. Open Mon.-Fri. 6:30am-10pm, Sat. 8am-10pm, Sun. 10am-8pm.

Island Experience, 314A 10th St. NW (270-4550). Specializes in Caribbean treats (borrowed from India), including Rotis (flat bread, filled with curry), Banana Date Chutney ($1), and Peanut Punch ($2). Entrees 6.25-7.50. Open daily 11am-9pm.

The Roasterie, 312 10th St. NW (270-3304), near Kensington Rd.; also 2212 4th St. SW (541-0960). No meals here, just cookies, muffins, and about 20 kinds of coffee, ranging from Rioberry ($2.25) to HiTest ($1.75) to Vietnamese Iced Coffee ($3.25)—all served in giant bowls. Decide for yourself whether there's any truth to their claim that "caffeine saves the brain." Hot chocolate ($1.25) and tea ($1). Open Mon.-Sat. 8am-midnight; Sun. 9am-midnight.

Golden Age Club Cafeteria, 610 8th Ave. SE (262-6342), upstairs from the club. Very convenient to the hostel, this center for the retired welcomes the hungry of all ages. Patio furniture and bright lights create a cheerful, relaxing atmosphere. Daily hot lunch specials ($4.45) include potato, vegetable, and roll plus coffee or tea. Daily breakfast specials ($2) include two pancakes/waffles/French toast, one egg, and ham/bacon/sausage. Open Mon.-Fri. 8am-3pm.

SIGHTS

Don't just gaze at the **Calgary Tower** (266-7171), 101 9th Ave. SW; ride an elevator to the top for a spectacular view of the Rockies on clear days (admission $2.75, children $2, after 10:30am $4.25, seniors, students, and HI members $3, 7:30-10:30am $2.75). The 190m tower also affords a 360° view of the city. The revolving **Panorama Dining Room** atop the tower can be expensive, but the "Breakfast in the Sky" special, a full morning meal for $9.50 (children $5.25, under 6 $2.25), includes a free elevator ride in the price (elevator pass is valid throughout the day). (Rides Mon.-Sun. 8am-11pm.)

The **Glenbow Museum,** 130 9th Ave. SE (268-4100), just across the street from the Tower, is a nexus of cultural pride in this boomtown. There's something for everyone in the Glenbow's odd mix: a plaster statue of Queen Victoria stares past a reconstructed log cabin at a collection of mineral samples, and the proximate placement of such unrelated artifacts as Indian bronzes, pre-Columbian pottery, and 19th century firearms endows the museum with the feel of the world's-most-expensive-garage sale. (Open Tues.-Sun. 10am-6pm. Admission $4.50, senior citizens, students and children $3, under 7 free; free on Sat.) Less than a block northeast of the museum, the **Olympic Plaza** still attracts crowds on sunny days five years after the flame left town. The site of the medal presentations during the Winter Games, this open-air park now hosts a variety of special events, including free concerts during the **Calgary Jazz Festival** in June. For an update on Olympic Plaza programming, call 268-5207 during business hours. One of the park's most interesting features, the **walkway,** was constructed out of more than 20,000 bricks, each purchased for $20-

30 and engraved with the name or personal message of the patron. Try to decipher such cryptic messages as "NGF 1959 BN B IN YYC" and "Pam and Nick Forever."

Five blocks down 8th Ave. to the west and about 50 ft. straight up are the **Devonian Gardens.** Located on the fourth floor of Toronto Dominion Sq. (8th Ave. between 2nd and 3rd St. SW), this 2.5-acre indoor garden contains sculptures, fountains, waterfalls, bridges, and over 20,000 plants, representing 138 local and tropical species. Sit on a rock and feed the goldfish as you watch your reflection in the mirrored windows of the skyscrapers across the street. (Open daily 9am-9pm. Free.)

Farther west, roughly 4.3 light-years from Alpha Centauri, is the **Alberta Science Centre and Centennial Planetarium** (221-3700, 11 St. and 7th Ave. SW near the Greyhound Bus Terminal). **Discovery Hall** contains hands-on exhibits directed primarily at children. Several different planetarium shows are presented in the **Star Theatre,** each geared to a specific age group. Most of the shows for children are in the afternoon and those for adults after 6pm. For baby-boomers, laser shows feature music from Pink Floyd and the Rolling Stones.

Just a stroll away from the Science Centre is **Prince's Island Park,** which can be reached by footbridges from either side of the Bow River. Many evenings during the summer at 7:30pm, a local college puts on free Shakespeare plays in the park. When an airplane flies overhead, drowning out all the actors, a bizarre whistle is blown and everyone on stage freezes until the plane is gone. Call 240-6359 for information. The park is laced with biking and fitness trails. Though usually quiet, the park sometimes hosts such events as the **Caribbean Cultural Festival,** held in June.

Calgary's other island park, **St. George's Island,** is accessible by the river walkway to the east and is home to the marvelous **Calgary Zoo** (232-9300). The Canadian Wilds exhibit, opened in July of 1992, re-creates in the heart of the city the sights, the sounds, and, yes, the smells of Canada's wilderness. A pamphlet available at he zoo's entrance gate lists animal feeding times; visitors are invited to watch big animals eat little animals. The squeamish must content themselves with a stroll through the **botanical gardens** or the **prehistoric park,** or a visit to the **children's zoo.** (Open 9am-6pm in summer; 9am-4pm in winter. Admission $7.50, senior citizens $4.75, children $3.75. "Tuesdays are Special:" adults $5, senior citizens free.)

Although the Olympic flame has been extinguished in Calgary, the world-class athletic facilities retain their touristy pull, drawing the recreational athlete and the architecture buff alike. The two most impressive arenas are the **Olympic Oval** (220-7954) an indoor speed-skating track on the University of Calgary campus (open Mon.-Fri. 9am-4:30pm; call for more information), and **Canada Olympic Park,** (286-2632), 10 minutes from downtown Calgary on Hwy. 1 west, the site of the bobsled, luge, and ski jumping competitions. A guided tour of Olympic Park costs $8 (senior citizens and children $4)—the one-hour trip around the facilities includes a chance to stand in the bobsled track and to glance down the slope from atop the 90m ski jump tower. (Tours daily 10am-3pm; mid-May to mid-Sept. tours on weekends only.) The **Olympic Hall of Fame** (268-2632), also located at Olympic Park, honors Olympic achievements past and present with displays, films, and videos. (Open daily 8am-5pm. Admission $3.75; senior citizens, students, and children $2.70.) The Grand Olympic Tour includes a visit to the Park and the Olympic Hall of Fame for $8.50 (children and senior citizens $4.50).

For non-vicarious downhill excitement, turn to the slopes of **Nakiska at Mount Allan** (591-7777), 99 km west of Calgary on Hwy. 40 in Kananaskis Country, the site of Olympic alpine events and freestyle moguls. Nordic skiers can tread where Olympians once trod for free at the **Canmore Nordic Centre** (678-2400), in Kananaskis Country just outside the town of Canmore. Of the 56km of trails, one is designed for beginners; the rest are all Olympic level. If you have brought along your biathalon association membership card and a rifle, you are cordially invited to use the **shooting range** and, in summer, the **roller-ski course.**

THE STAMPEDE

Even those who think that rodeo is grotesque and silly have trouble saying "Calgary" without letting a quick "Stampede" slip out. Indeed, Calgarians take great pride in their "Greatest Outdoor Show on Earth"; it seems that the more cosmopolitan the city becomes, the more firmly it clings to its frontier origins. Every year around Stampede time, locals in 10-gallon hats command tour groups to yell "yahoo" in the least likely of circumstances. Simply put, the entire city of Calgary flips out.

And why not? Any event that draws millions from across the province, the country, and the world deserves some gratuitous hype—and your attention. Make the short trip out to **Stampede Park,** just southeast of downtown, for a glimpse of steer wrestling, bull riding, wild cow milking, and the famous chuckwagon races. You can visit the past at an authentic Native American encampment and a re-created Wild West town, or perch yourself atop the wild, thrashing back of a roller coaster at the **Stampede Midway,** or try the gaming tables at the **Frontier Casino.**

Parking is ample, but the crowd is always more than ample in July—instead of driving, take the C-Train from downtown to the Stampede stop. For official information and ticket order forms, write **Calgary Exhibition and Stampede,** Box 1860, Station M, Calgary T2P 2L8, or call 800-661-1260 (261-0101 in Calgary). Ticket prices range from $15 to $38 depending on the event and seats. Inquire about rush tickets, available for $7.50 (youth $6.75, seniors and children $3.50).

Even if you can't be there in July, Stampede Park has sights to amuse and educate year-round. Jog over to **Lindsay Park Sports Centre,** 2225 Macleod Trail S. (233-8393), across from Stampede Park. This bubble, often mistaken for the Saddledome, offers four swimming pools, an indoor track, numerous basketball courts, a weight room, and aerobics. Built in 1983 for the Western Canada Summer Games, Lindsay Park is primarily a "competition and training" facility for Canadian athletes of all levels. Call ahead to be sure it is open to the public on a particular day. (Admission $5.50, children $1.70. Open Mon.-Fri. 5am-11pm, Sat.-Sun. 6am-10pm.)

ENTERTAINMENT

After a long, hard day pounding barrels of local crude, many young Calgarians like to pound bottles of local brew along **"Electric Avenue,"** the stretch of 11th Ave. SW between 5th and 6th St. Swimming in neon, the avenue brings a touch of Sodom and Gomorrah to the heart of the Stampede City. Beware of Electric Avenue during hockey playoff time: the streets are closed off and the lines for bars and clubs wind around the block. Last call in Calgary is at 2am, and is observed rigidly.

Bottlescrew Bill's Pub, at 10th Ave. SW and 1st St. (263-7900). If Electric Avenue has left you on the verge of sensory overload, take refuge in the relaxed atmosphere of this "Old English Pub." Bill's offers the widest selection of beers in Alberta ($3-15). If you feel bold, try a pint of Bill's own Buzzard Breath Ale ($3.50). Open Mon.-Wed. 11am-1am, Thurs.-Sat. 11am-2am.

Ranchman's Steak House, 9615 Macleod Trail S. (253-1100). One of Canada's greatest honky-tonks. Experience Calgary's Wild West tradition firsthand in the live C&W or in the not-so-subtle flavor of Calgary Stampede beer. Open Mon.-Wed. 9pm-2am, Thurs.-Sat. 8pm-2am. Opens earlier during the Stampede.

Mad Jack's Saloon, 438 9th Ave. SE (262-1680). Below the King Edward Hotel. The big daddy of Calgary blues bars, with blues Mon.-Fri. 9:30pm-2am and jam sessions Sat. 2:30pm-7pm and Sun. 7pm-1am. Cover $3-6. Drinks from $2.75. A bit expensive, but worth it.

The Stadium Keg, 1923 Uxbridge Dr. NW (282-0020). Where the "Dinos" from the nearby University of Calgary eat, drink, and be merry. Good rock 'n roll blasted at a level which still allows you to hear yourself think. 2 large TVs. Drink specials nightly 6-9pm. Thurs.-Fri. 12-oz. drafts $1.50. Chicken wings 25¢ per basket on Thurs. Mon. is Margarita night ($1.75). Open daily 4:30pm-2am-ish.

■ Near Calgary

You won't lose the crowds by going to the **Tyrrell Museum of Paleontology** (403-823-7707), near Drumheller, but you will lose your sense of self-importance. The world's largest display of dinosaur specimens forcibly reminds one that humanity is a mere crouton in the Caesar salad of Earth's history. From the Big Bang to the Quarternary Period (that's where we are), Tyrrell (rhymes with "squirrel") covers it all with a dizzying array of displays and videos. And if you're not side-tackled by a hyperactive kindergartner who's run away from his class trip, you may just get to build your own "Sillysaurus" on one of the museum's educational computers. The food at the museum cafeteria is surprisingly inexpensive and tasty. Grab a seat beneath an umbrella on the patio and beat the heat with a breakfast or lunch special (about $5). (Open daily 9am-9pm in summer; Labor Day-Victoria Day Tues.-Sun. 10am-5pm. Admission $5, senior citizens and children $3. Tues. free.) The Calgary Hostel offers a full-day **"dinosaur tour"** ($27) which takes you here, the badlands, and the hoodoos. The museum is on **Secondary Hwy. 838**, a.k.a **North Dinosaur Trail**, 6km from Drumheller. From Calgary, it's a 90-minute drive via Hwy. 2 north to Hwy. 72 and 9 east. Tyrrell isn't directly served by public transportation, but you can take Greyhound from Calgary to Drumheller (2 per day, one-way $14.70) and hoof it.

Tyrrell lies in the heart of the Alberta **badlands,** where prehistoric wind, water, and ice carved 70 million years of geological history out of the sedimentary rock. Tyrrell offers free 90-min. interpretive walks through the surrounding badlands (weekends and holidays only, 11am and 3pm), but **Horseshoe Canyon,** about 20km west of Drumheller on Highway 9, offers the most impressive landscapes. With its inhospitable terrain and grotesquely twisted rock formations, the canyon will give you a good idea of what hell must look like. Carry at least one quart of water if you want to explore the canyon during hot weather.

The **Old Midland Mine Office** (823-1754 or 823-1755) is located 2km east of the museum in **Midland Provincial Park** (823-1751). This renovated coal miners' credit union office now dispenses maps of the park and information about the coal mines that fueled the economy of Drumheller Valley before the discovery of Alberta's vast oil and natural gas reserves.

While the staff at Tyrrell will tell you the dinosaurs vanished from the earth 65 million years ago, a stroll through nearby **Drumheller** will reassure you that the "terrible lizards" continue to reign supreme at the heart of Drumheller's tourist economy. Tacky dinosaur statues on the outskirts of town threaten to come to life and ravage its few attractions, including a number of shops that sell dinosaur t-shirts, dinosaur mugs, little plastic dinosaurs, and other forms of local bad taste.

There are two campgrounds in Drumheller, located across from each other on North Dinosaur Trail at the intersection with Highway 9: **Shady Grove Campground** (823-2576) and **Dinosaur Trailer Park** (823-3291). Tentsites are about $13 per night. Don't be surprised to find these campgrounds overrun by RVs, the dinosaurs of the automotive age. If you must, try the **Dinosaur Motel** on Riverside Drive in Drumheller (823-3381).

The **Field Station** (378-4587) for the Tyrrell Museum is located 48km east of **Brooks** in **Dinosaur Provincial Park.** The station contains a small museum that complements Tyrrell, but the main attraction is the **Badlands Bus Tour,** which runs four to 10 times per day between Victoria Day and Thanksgiving. For $4.50 (youth $2.25, children free), be chauffeured into this restricted archaeological hot spot of dinosaur discoveries and fossil finds. Many fossils still lie within the eroding rock; if you make a discovery, however, all you can take home with you are memories, Polaroids, and a coveted "Fossil Finder Certificate"—but not the actual goods. The **campground** (378-4587) in the park is shaded from the summer heat, and grassy plots cushion most campsites. Although it stays open year-round, the campground is fully serviced only in summer. (Sites $10.75. Park open Victoria Day-Labor Day Sun.-Thurs. 1-9pm, Fri.-Sat. 8am-11pm. After Labor Day, you must make an appointment for a tour.) For more information, contact the Field Station, Dinosaur Provincial Park, Box 60, Patricia T0J 2K0. From Drumheller, follow Hwy. 56 S. for 65km, then take Hwy. 1 about 70km to Brooks. Once in Brooks, go east along the well-marked Hwy. 873 and 544. Bikers should be especially cautious since much of the route from Brooks is paved only with loose gravel.

SOUTHERN ALBERTA

While central Alberta—propelled by the increasingly intense rivalry between the oil-rich metropoli of Calgary and Edmonton—limps toward post-modernity, oil-free southern Alberta remains a revolution or two behind the times. Farms and ranches fill the vast prairie expanses to the east; burnt-out coal towns slumber at the foothills of the Canadian Rockies to the west. This part of the province turns instead to devolution and funnels its money into promoting the past—some of North America's best-preserved Native archaeological sites are located in the parks of this region, including Head-Smashed-In Buffalo Jump and its $10 million interpretive center. Aficionados of large-scale cataclysms should make a point of visiting Crowsnest Pass, where they can view the sites of several massive mining disasters.

■ ■ ■ LETHBRIDGE

Lethbridge doesn't quite fit into southern Alberta. Set admist minuscule farming towns that dot the prairie, this city of 60,000 is home to two universities, one of Canada's most interesting historical parks, and a lush Japanese garden. Lethbridge's urbanization—along with its frequent gusty winds—make the city seem like a minor-league version of Chicago. Nonetheless, Alberta's third-largest city manages to retain a somewhat tempered rustic pride characteristic of the region as a whole.

PRACTICAL INFORMATION AND ORIENTATION

Visitors Information: Chinook Country Tourist Association, 2805 Scenic Dr. (320-1222), at Scenic and Mayor Magrath Dr. The staff will gladly help you plan a tour of southern Alberta. Maps, brochures and guides to the city and the region. Open May-Labour Day daily 8am-9pm; Labour Day to mid-Oct. daily 9am-5pm; in winter Mon.-Sat. 9am-5pm. A newer **Information Centre,** located on Brewery Hill, at 1st Ave. S. off Hwy. 3 (320-1223), provides the same maps and pamphlets and features an intoxicating vista of Brewery Gardens, formerly a disposal site for coal ashes. Open May-Labour Day daily 8am-9pm; Labour Day to mid-Oct. Mon.-Fri. 9am-5pm; in winter Tues.-Sun. 9am-5pm.

Greyhound, 411 5th St. S. (327-1551). To: Calgary (5 per day, $23.70) and Edmonton (4 per day, $52.60). Open Mon.-Sat. 7:30am-7pm, Sun. 8-11:30am and 1-7pm.

Buses: Lethbridge City Transit operates 9 routes which blanket the city. You can catch the buses at the intersection of 4th Ave. S. and 6th St. S. Fare $1.10, students (up to grade 12) 85¢, senior citizens and children 55¢. For more information call 320-3885.

Taxi: Lethbridge Cabs, 327-4005. Senior discount 10%. 24 hr.

Car Rental: Rent-A-Wreck, 2211 2nd Ave. N. (328-9484). Must be 21 with credit card. $32 per day with 100 free km, 12 per additional km. Open Mon.-Sat. 8:30am-5pm.

Women's Shelter: Harbour House, 604 8th St. S., run by the YWCA (320-1881; phone staffed 24 hr.).

Sexual Assault Crisis Line: 327-4545 or 800-552-8023.

Hospital: Lethbridge Regional Hospital, 960 19th St. S. (382-6111).

Emergency: 911.

Police: 444 5th Ave. S (328-4444).

Post Office: 704 4th Ave. S. (320-7133). Open Mon.-Fri. 8:30am-5pm. **Postal Code:** T1J 0N0.
Area Code: 403.

Lethbridge lies on Hwy. 3, also known as the **Crowsnest Hwy.** Highways 4 and 5 run into the city from the south. From Calgary or Edmonton, drive south on Hwy. 2 until it intersects Hwy. 3, then travel 50km east. In the city, avenues run east-west and streets north-south.

ACCOMMODATIONS

The reputable motels along Mayor Magrath Dr. run about $45 a night and invariably flash vacancy signs in summer. Unless your coffers are empty, stay away from the sleazy, ultra-cheap hotels in the city center.

University of Lethbridge (329-2584), across the Oldman River from the city but easily reached by bus #7 and 8. In summer, the residence office, Room C-442 in University Hall, rents rooms to students and others. If you're hungry and unwilling to make the 15-min. trek to the West Village Mall, the University's vending machines serve up a mean pizza sub for $2. Singles $27. Suites with kitchen and private bath $34 per person.

YWCA, 604 8th St. S. (329-0088). Women traveling alone will feel safe here. Comfortable, homey place complete with shared kitchenette, TV room, and laundry on each floor. *Women only.* Male visitors permitted in the lobby only. Singles $22, weekly $80. Shared rooms $20.

Parkside Inn, 1009 Mayor Magrath Dr. (328-2366), next to the Japanese Gardens, Heritage Lake, and the golf course. Take bus #1 from downtown. Large rooms with A/C, cable TV, and unlimited local phone calls. Singles $40, doubles $42.

Henderson Lake Campgrounds (328-5452), on Parkside Dr., at Henderson Lake in the southeast corner of the city. Shaded sites for tenters; virtual driveways for RVs. When it rains, the lower tenting area floods on a Biblical scale. Closed to cars daily midnight-7am. Max. stay 14 days. Open April 1-Oct. 31. Tentsites $11, with electricity and water $15.50.

FOOD

It is difficult to find interesting budget food in Lethbridge. Fast-food joints line Mayor Magrath Dr. and cluster near the city cente. Your best option is **Top Pizza and Spaghetti House.** You can pick up groceries at **Allwest Foods,** 110 Columbia Blvd. (381-1600), in the West Village Mall (open daily 9am-9pm).

Top Pizza and Spaghetti House, 11th St. and 4th Ave. S. (327-1952). Top-notch pizza at rock-bottom prices: small $5.50, medium with pepperoni and mushroom $9.10. Struggle with gobs of cheese in the incredible $4.95 baked lasagna lunch special. Open Mon.-Thurs. 11am-1am, Fri.-Sat. 11am-3am, Sun. noon-midnight.

Kassandra's, at 3rd Ave. and Scenic, serves up plain but good comestibles. Breakfast specials from $1.79, lunch from $4, dinner from $6. Open Mon.-Sat. 7am-8pm, Sun. 8am-8pm.

The Duke of Wellington, 132 Columbia Blvd. W. (381-1455), in the West Village Mall. Students and encumbered nobility dine here infrequently; it's close to the university but somewhat expensive. Daily sandwich specials (under $5.50) include soup and fries. Open Mon.-Sat. 11am-10pm.

SIGHTS

Fort Whoop-Up (329-0444), located in **Indian Battle Park** on the east bank of the Oldman River, is a replica of the notorious whiskey trading outpost which originally stood some 10km from present-day Lethbridge. Dressed in period costumes, guides at the **Interpretive Centre** explain the history of the whiskey and fur trades. Europeans introduced the Native Americans to make-shift whiskey, a potpourri of pure grain firewater flavored with tobacco, lye, dirt, and whatever else was handy at the time, and in the process bilked local tribesmen. A generally unbiased slide show is projected on request. (Interpretive Centre open May-Labour Day Mon.-Sat. 10am-6pm, Sun. noon-8pm. Admission $2, students and seniors $1, children free.) An additional 50¢ buys you a 20-minute tour of the park and the Oldman River Valley aboard the **Whoop-Up Wagon Train,** a motorized modern-day stagecoach. No public transportation serves this area. Drive or trek 20 minutes down a regional trail which begins at 3rd and Scenic.

Young children and naturalists alike will appreciate the **Helen Schuler Coulee Centre and Nature Reserve** (320-3064), a section of Indian Battle Park created to protect local vegetation, prairie animals, and the occasional porcupine. (Open Sun.-Thurs. 10am-8pm, Fri.-Sat. 10am-6pm; spring and fall Tues.-Sat. 1-4pm, Sun. 1-6pm; winter Tues.-Sun. 1-4pm.) A short trail leads outside the Reserve to the **Coal Kiosk,** which outlines the progress of Lethbridge's coal industry from the first excavation in 1881 through the city's incorporation in 1906. The kiosk lies beneath the spectacular **High-Level Bridge,** the longest and highest of its kind in the world. The black steel skeleton opened to trains in 1909 and is still in use today, supporting traffic many times heavier than its designers envisioned.

The **Nikka Yuko Japanese Garden** (328-3511) in the southeast corner of town is the city's most trumpeted attraction. Constructed and reconstructed (just to be safe) in Japan, then dismantled and shipped to Lethbridge for another reconstruction, the main pavilion blends surprisingly well with Albertan placidity. An informative hostess appears at each point of interest to guide you through the garden. (Open mid-May to mid-June daily 9am-5pm; mid-June to late August daily 9am-8pm; late Aug. to late Sept. daily 9am-5pm. Admission $3, seniors and youth $2, children free.) The **rose garden** immediately outside the Japanese garden is an ideal resting or picnicking spot. Take bus #1 to the garden. For more information call 320-3020.

The **Southern Alberta Art Gallery,** 601 3rd Ave. S. (327-8770), offers about 20 different exhibits each year, focusing mainly on contemporary Canadian art.

■ Near Lethbridge

Fort Macleod

In 1873, alarmed by the lawlessness, violence, and exploitation of Native Americans engendered by the whiskey trade, the Northwest Mounted Police (NWMP) dispatched 300 men to Fort Whoop-Up. In a performance worthy of the Keystone Cops, the Mounties got lost *en route,* giving the whiskey traders time to escape south of the border down the Montana way. When the force finally arrived, it was greeted by a hail of gunshots from the sole remaining liquor vendor. Unable to purchase Fort Whoop-Up from the conniving moonshiner, the Mounties instead founded nearby **Fort Macleod** in order to keep the whiskey traders in check.

The **Fort Macleod Museum** (553-4703) at 219 25th St., a 1957 replica of the 1874 fort, exhibits typical NWMP uniforms, guns, tools, and furniture. Although the Interpretative Center at Fort Whoop-Up (see Lethbridge Sights above) presents a better synopsis of the area's history, Fort MacLeod offers a fascinating exhibit on Native American life. (Fort and museum open May 1 to late June daily 9am-5pm; late June to early Sept. 9am-8:30pm; early Sept.-Oct. 15 9am-5pm; Oct. 16-late April Mon.-Fri. 9:30am-4pm. Admission $3.50, ages 13-18 $1.25, under 13 75¢.) Four times daily during July and August, the Fort Museum's **Mounted Patrol Musical Ride** takes its song-and-dance to the streets. If you can't catch the real thing, check out the picture of the Mounties in similar formation on the back of the Canadian $50 bill.

Providing endless nighttime fun in Fort Macleod, the **Great West Summer Theatre** puts on a summer production at the **Empress Theatre** (553-4404), on Main St. If you appreciate bad jokes, zany madcap antics, and off-key singing, you'll just love it. Even if you don't, it's the only nightlife in the area. (Tickets $9, senior citizens and students $8, children $5.) If you are compelled to spend the night in Fort Macleod, the friendly **DJ Motel,** (553-4011) at 416 24 St., has 15 comfortable rooms with bath and cable TV. (Singles from $33.60. Doubles from $34.)

Greyhound (553-3383) runs to Fort Macleod from Lethbridge (3 per day, $5.50). Step into the bus station for a bite to eat at the **Java Shop** (553-3063). Sleepy townsfolk congregate here for the quick and filling breakfast special—sausage and two eggs ($4.60). Coffee and muffin special $1 (open daily 5am-7:30pm). For supper, head on over to **Luigi's Pizza and Steak House,** 537 Main St. (555-4555), 1km east of the Greyhound depot. Small specialty pizza $6, medium $9.50, baked pasta $7. (Open Mon.-Thurs. 11am-midnight, Fri.-Sat. 11am-2am, Sun. 11:30am-11pm.)

Head-Smashed-In Buffalo Jump

Coveted as a source of fresh meat, sustenance, tools, and shelter, the buffalo was the victim of one of history's most innovative forms of mass slaughter: the buffalo jump. Agile Blackfoot tribesmen of southern Alberta—clad in coyote skins—would slither behind a herd, skillfully maneuver it into a "gathering basin," and then spook some 500 nearly-blind bison into a fatal stampede over a 10m-high cliff. For over 5500 years, Native Americans in Southern Alberta created instant all-you-can-eat buffets with this technique. No buffalo jump is as well-preserved as the **Head-Smashed-In Buffalo Jump,** named about 150 years ago in memory of a young thrill-seeking warrior who was drowned by a waterfall of buffalo as he watched the event from the base of the cliff.

Although UNESCO will fine you $50,000 if you forage for souvenirs in the 10m-deep beds of bone, you can learn about buffalo jumps and local Native American culture at the **Interpretive Centre** (553-2731), a $10-million, 7-story facility built into the cliff itself. The center screens reenactments of the fatal plunge which were filmed with frozen rather than live buffalo. Two km of walking trails lead to the top of the cliff and to the kill site below. (Open daily 9am-8pm; Labour Day-Victoria Day 9am-5pm. Admission $5, youth $2, under 6 free, Tues. free.)

There is not yet any public transportation to this unique North American spectacle. Rent a car or arrange a ride from Lethbridge or from Fort Macleod, 18km southeast of Head-Smashed-In along Secondary Rte. 785.

■■■ CROWSNEST PASS

Crowsnest Pass is an easy daytrip from Lethbridge and an irresistible stopover for disasterophiles *en route* to southern Alberta via British Columbia. With an unmistakable tremor of pride in their voices, locals speak of frequent shootouts and train robberies during the wild rum-running days of the 1920s. They speak more soberly of disasters at the Bellevue Mine, the Hillcrest Mine, and the legendary town of Frank, buried in 1903 under 82 million tons of limestone from the summit of Turtle Mountain. In its glory days nearly a century ago, the Pass was heralded as the "Pittsburgh of Canada," and immigrants flocked to the mountains with dreams of digging a quick fortune—or at least enough to retire to a farm or ranch on the prairies.

In order to reach the coal seams, miners tunneled deep into the mountains, leaving pillars of natural rock to support the tunnel roof. When a seam was exhausted, miners often could not resist the temptation to extract what little coal was left in the pillars—usually worth enough cash for a big night in a tavern, no more—leaving the mine roof to collapse behind (or, in the worst cases, on top of) them. As mines were mangled and the demand for coal diminished, the putative Pittsburgh perished, preserving Crowsnest Pass in a state of arrested development. Several Hollywood directors have taken advantage of the sleepy streets and brick storefronts to recreate scenes from the Depression Era.

The grim history of Crowsnest Pass prompts many visitors to overlook its natural beauty; southern Alberta's "Gateway to the Rockies" remains surprisingly tourist-free. Moose, Dall sheep, and bears stroll among the area's stately pines and brilliant mountain wildflowers, and the town of Crowsnest Pass is minutes away from numerous opportunities for fishing, hiking, and mountain climbing.

ACCOMMODATIONS, CAMPING, AND FOOD

Grand Union International Hostel, 7719 17th Ave. (563-3433), in downtown Coleman. Has the feel of an over-a-tavern motel, but rooms are clean and the staff is friendly. The band on the first floor can be a bit loud; the hostel manager will furnish you with a free pair of earplugs at check-in. "Beer" brand beer only $1.75 in the hostel lobby; tastes as good as its name implies. Kitchen and laundry facilities. Accommodates 62. Members $10, nonmembers $13. Check-in 8am-11pm.

Chinook Lake Campground (Alberta Forest Service, 403-427-3582). Follow Hwy. 3 west from Coleman for 9km, then follow the signs up Allison Creek Rd. Virtually inaccessible to the traveler on foot. Bring a sleeping pad to cushion the 70-odd stony sites. $7.50, senior citizens $5.50.

Crowsnest Campground (562-2932), just off Hwy. 3A in Blairmore. More commercial than most in the Pass, this campground offers hot showers, a heated pool, and 64 sites for RVs or tenters. Sites $12, full hookups $18.

Chris and Irvin's Cafe, 7802 17 Ave. (563-3093), in downtown Coleman. This classic diner serves up chicken burgers ($2.60) and the Miner's Deluxe ($4.65). Fantastic fries. Open Mon.-Fri. 6am-10pm, Sat. 7am-10pm, Sun. 8am-7pm.

Robinson's Department Store (562-8811), in Crowsnest Mall, Blairmore, off Hwy. 3A. A small cafeteria sits on a platform at the back of the store. The corner tables afford breath-taking views of the menswear department. $3 breakfast special includes 2 eggs, bacon, and hashbrowns. $4-5 sandwich platter includes fries and 20% off a pair of wool socks. (Just kidding.) Open Mon.-Wed., Fri., Sat. 9:30am-5pm; Thurs. 9:30am-9pm.

SIGHTS AND ACTIVITIES

For a good introduction to the history of the Pass, start at the **Leitch Collieries** (562-7388), on Hwy. 3 at the east end of the Pass. Nineteenth-century miners dug their picks into the hills about 2km from the road, but the coal was processed in a complex of buildings, now weed-covered ruins alongside Hwy. 3. Casually-clad interpreters who will decipher the coal miner's sign lingo for you. (Open May 15-Sept. 15 daily 9am-5pm; off-season tours can be arranged. Free.)

Located just west of Leitch Collieries on Hwy. 3 is the **Bellevue Mine,** (564-4700) opened in 1903. On December 9, 1910, a rock fall generated sparks which ignited the methane gas in the mine, destroying the mine's only ventilation fan. The resulting buildup of carbon dioxide and carbon monoxide killed 30 of the 42 men working at the time. Despite this disaster, the mine reopened only a few weeks later and remained operational until 1962. Don a miner's helmet and following guides for 366m along the same path taken by coal miners. (Open late June-early Sept. daily 10am-5:30pm. Tours given every half hour for $4, senior citizens and children $2.)

Heavy mining turned Crowsnest Pass into a modern Pompeii in 1903, when one tunnel too many sent Turtle Mountain tumbling like a giant sandcastle. Ninety million cubic feet of stone spilled into the town of Frank, burying 70 people and their houses in less than two minutes. Today, a decapitated mountain and a mile-long river of boulders are all that remain. The **Frank Slide Interpretive Centre,** also on Hwy. 3 (562-7388), gives you a notion of what Frank was like before the straw broke the Turtle's back; its award-winning multimedia presentation details the lives, origins, and attitudes of the miners (lesson: "you're only as safe as the stupidest guy in the mine." For a close look at a mining ghost town, take a half-day hike to **Lille,** 8km from the Centre and inaccessible by auto. (Centre open daily 9am-8pm; Labour Day-Victoria Day 10am-4pm. Admission $3, children $1. Tues. free.)

If you've had enough of death and destruction, the Pass offers a host of more cheerful diversions. The **trout fishing** in the **Crowsnest River, Castle River,** and **Old Man River** is reputed to be among the best in all of the Rockies. Crowsnest Pass is also home to the **Gargantua Cave,** the second longest and deepest cave in all of

Canada. Known simply as "The Cave," Gargantua is located near the Alberta-British Columbia border at the site of Old Man River's spill into Crowsnest Lake. Drop by the Frank Slide Interpretive Centre (above) for a look at topographic maps and for information on how to safely explore the cave.

According to Albertan legend, in the late nineteenth century two prospectors—**Lemon** and **Blackjack**—discovered a huge vein of gold somewhere in the Crowsnest Pass area. Driven to madness by greed, Lemon split his partner's head with an axe and fled the scene, only to return years later unable to relocate the mother lode. In 1989, Edmonton scientists and technicians concluded from mineral samples that there is, indeed, "gold in them thar hills." But despite the unflagging efforts of R.F. McDermott, the Lost Lemon Mine remains lost. Perhaps you'll have better luck.

If you are heading north into **Kananaskis** and **Banff,** consider taking the scenic but dusty **Forestry Trunk Rd.,** which meets Hwy. 3 near Coleman. The drive offers spectacular vistas of mountains colored in vibrant hues of green, red, brown, and purple. The road is lined with Forest Service campgrounds such as **Dutch Creek, Old Man River,** and **Cataract Creek** (sites $7.50, senior citizens $5.50). Call 562-7307 for information. An **Alberta Tourism Information Centre** (563-3888) is located 8km west of Coleman on Hwy. 3 and can provide further information on sights in the area. (Open May 15-Labour Day daily 9am-7pm.)

■■■ WATERTON-GLACIER INTERNATIONAL PEACE PARK

Waterton-Glacier transcends international boundaries to unite two of the most pristine but relatively accessible wilderness areas on the continent. Symbolizing the peace between the United States and Canada, the park provides sanctuary for many endangered bears (the parks' prize possessions), bighorn sheep, moose, mountain goats, and now the grey wolf—and for tourists weary of the more crowded parks farther south and north.

Technically one park, Waterton-Glacier is, for all practical purposes, two distinct areas: the small Waterton Lakes National Park in Alberta, and the enormous Glacier National Park in Montana. Each park charges its own admission fee (in Glacier, $5 per week; in Waterton Lakes, CDN$5 per day, CDN$10 per 4 days), and you must go through customs to pass from one to the other. Several **border crossings** pepper the park: **Chief Mountain** (open May 15-May 31 daily 9am-6pm, June 1-Sept. 15 daily 7am-10pm, closed in winter); **Piegan/Carway** (in U.S., open all year daily 7am-11pm; in Canada open March 1-Nov. 1 7am-11pm, off-season 9am-6pm); **Trail Creek** (open June-Oct. daily 9am-5pm); and **Roosville** (open year round 24 hr.).

Since snow melt is an unpredictable process, the parks are usually in full operation only from late May to early September. To find the areas of the park, hotels and campsites that will be open when you visit, contact the headquarters of either Waterton or Glacier (888-5441). Also, there is the newspaper *Waterton Glacier Guide* published at the beginning of the summer. This has dates and times of trail, campground, and border crossing openings.

■ Waterton Lakes National Park, Alberta

The Canadian section of Waterton is only a fraction of the size of its south-of-the-border neighbor, but it nonetheless offers much of the same scenery and many similar activities and is generally less crowded than Glacier during the peak months of July and August. (See Glacier National Park, Montana for information on this park.)

Practical Information You don't have a choice—the only road from Waterton's park entrance leads 5 mi. south to **Waterton townsite.** On the way, grab a copy of the *Waterton-Glacier Guide* to local services and activities, at the **Water-**

ton Information Office, 215 Mountain View Rd. (859-2224), 5 mi. south of the park entrance (open Mon.-Fri. 8am-4pm).

If you're on four wheels, drive either the **Akamina Parkway** or the less traveled **Red Rock Canyon Road.** Both leave the main road near the townsite and end at the heads of popular backcountry trails. You can rent wheels two at a time from **Pat's Texaco and Cycle Rental,** Mount View Rd., Waterton townsite (859-2266; mountain bikes $5.50 per hr. plus $20 damage deposit).

In an **emergency,** call the ambulance (859-2636). Waterton's **post office** is on Fountain Ave. at Windflower, in Waterton townsite (open Mon.-Fri. 8:30am-4:30pm). The **Postal Code** is T0K 2M0. The **area code** is 403.

Accommodations, Camping, and Food As you enter the park, marvel at the enormous **Prince of Wales Hotel** (859-2231), where you can have tea while maintaining a proper distance from the common townsite. Pitch a tent at one of the park's three campgrounds. RV drivers flock to the hot showers of the **Townsite** campground, at the south end of town (sites $13; full hookups $17.50). **Crandell** (sites $10.50), on Red Rock Canyon Rd., and **Belly River** (sites $7.25), on Chief Mountain Hwy., are cheaper and farther removed from the hustle and bustle characteristic of townsite life. **Backcountry camping** is free but requires a permit from the Information Office (see above) or from **Park Headquarters and Information,** Waterton Lakes National Park, Waterton AB T0K 2M0 (859-2224; open Mon.-Fri. 8am-4pm). If you must stay indoors, drop by **Dill's General Store,** on Waterton Ave. (859-2345), and ask to sleep in one of the nine rooms of the **Stanley Hotel** (singles or doubles $45; no shower or private bath).

Waterton is sorely lacking in budget restaurants; the most attractive option in the Townsite is the **Zum Burger Haus,** 116 B Waterton Ave. (859-2388), which serves decent cheeseburgers for $4 on a pleasant patio. (Open daily 7:30am-9pm). Stock up on dried meat and granola at the **Rocky Mountain Foodmart** (859-2526) on Windflower Ave. (open daily 8am-10pm; hours vary in winter).

Outdoors If you've brought only hiking boots to Waterton, set out on the **Crypt Lake Hike,** which stretches 4 mi. from Waterton townsite; you'll feel entombed as you pass through a natural tunnel bored through the mountainside. The **International Hike** delivers you to Montana some 5 mi. after leaving the Townsite.

Fugitives and non-fugitive anglers alike will appreciate Waterton's **fishing.** Fishing in the park requires a **license** ($5 per 7 days), available from the Park offices, campgrounds, wardens, and service stations in the area. Lake trout and pike cruise the murky depths of **Cameron** and **Waterton Lakes;** for flycasting, try the small (nameless) creek that spills from Cameron Lake about 200m to the east of the parking lot. A two-hour boat tour of Upper Waterton Lake leaves from the **Emerald Bay Marina** (859-2362) in the townsite (5 per day mid-May to mid-Sept.; $14, ages 4-12 $7). You can rent a **rowboat** at Cameron Lake for $10 per hour. **Alpine Stables,** 2½ mi. north of the Townsite (859-2462, in winter 653-2449), conducts trail rides of varying lengths. (1-hr. ride $11, all-day $48.)

In the evening, take in an **interpretive program** at the **Falls** or **Crandell Theatre.** "The Fall of the Roamin' Empire" examines the annihilation of the great buffalo herds; "Salamander Suicides and Other My-newt Tragedies" exposes the soft white underbellies of the park's tiniest residents. (Programs in summer daily at 8:30pm; contact the Information Office for schedule information. Free.)

■ Glacier National Park, Montana

Practical Information Glacier's layout is simple: one road enters through West Glacier on the west side, and three roads enter from the east—at Many Glacier, St. Mary and Two Medicine. West Glacier and St. Mary provide the two main points of entry into the park, connected by **Going-to-the-Sun Road** ("The Sun"), the only road that traverses the park. Fast-paced **U.S. 2** runs between West and East Glacier along 82 mi. of the southern park border.

Stop in at the **visitors centers** at **St. Mary**, at the east entrance to the park (732-4424; open daily in early June 8am-5pm, late June-early Sept. 8am-9pm), or at **Apgar**, at the west park entrance (open daily early June 8am-5pm, late June-early Sept. 8am-8pm). A third visitors center graces **Logan Pass** on Going-to-the-Sun Rd. (Open daily mid-June 9am-5pm, late June-early Sept. 9am-6pm.) An **info center** (888-5743) for Alberta is in West Glacier; ask any questions there before hiking. (Open daily 8am-7pm.)

Amtrak (226-4452 locally, or 800-872-7245) traces a dramatic route along the southern edge of the park. Daily trains huff and puff to West Glacier from Whitefish ($7), Seattle ($123), and Spokane ($61); Amtrak also runs from East Glacier to Chicago ($208) and Minneapolis ($179). **Intermountain Bus Lines** (862-6700) is the only line that comes near the park (Kalispell, MT). One bus a day runs from Kalispell to Missoula, MT ($24.75). A car is the most convenient mode of transport, particularly within the park. **Rent-a-Wreck** rents used cars from Kalispell, 1194 U.S. 2 E. (755-4555; $35 per day), and from East Glacier, at the Sears Motel (226-9293; $50 per day with 125 mi. free per day plus 25¢ each additional mi.). You must be over 21 and have a major credit card.

The Glacier **post office** is at Lake McDonald Lodge, in the park. (Open Mon.-Fri. 9am-3:45pm.) **General Delivery ZIP code** is 59921. The **area code** is 406.

Accommodations and Camping Glacier Park, Inc. handles all lodging within the park and offers only the **Swiftcurrent Motor Inn** for budget travelers. Cabins without bathrooms at the Swiftcurrent are $20, $29 for two bedrooms (each additional person $2; open late June-early Sept.). The Swiftcurrent has a motel, but rooms cost twice as much. Reservations can be made through Glacier Park, Inc. From mid-September to mid-May, contact them at 925 Dial Tower Mail Station, Phoenix, AZ 85077 (602-207-2600); from early May to late September at East Glacier Park, 59434 (406-226-5551). Other than the Swiftcurrent, seven pricier lodges open and close on a staggered schedule, beginning in mid-May.

Excellent, affordable lodging can be found just across the park border in **East Glacier**, which sits on U.S. 2, 30 mi. south of the St. Mary entrance, and about 5 mi. south of the Two Medicine entrance. East Glacier boasts the **Backpackers Inn,** 29 Dawson Ave. (226-9392), a home-away-from-home behind **Soranno's restaurant.** The owners of the Inn offer excellent advice about trails and activities. The Inn offers clean beds and hot showers for only $8 per night (bring a sleeping bag or rent one for $1). The Mexican food at Soranno's is reasonably priced ($4-11) and tasty.

There is also a hostel at **Brownies Grocery (HI/AYH),** 1020 Rte. 49 (226-4426), in East Glacier. It offers comfortable accommodations in its dorm which is rumored to have once been a brothel. Offers a great view from the porch. ($10 members, $13 nonmembers), private rooms (singles $15, $18 nonmembers; doubles $20, $23 nonmembers), and a family room ($30, 4-6 people). The **Kalispell/Whitefish Home Hostel,** 2155 Whitefish Stage Rd., Kalispell 59901 (756-1908), beckons 25 mi. from Glacier's west entrance, between U.S. 93 and U.S. 2. The home has comfortable beds (bring a sleeping bag), kitchen utensils, and rents mountain bikes ($10).

Camping offers a cheaper and more scenic alternative to indoor accommodations. All developed campsites are available on a first-come, first-camped basis ($8-10); the most popular sites fill by noon. However, "Campground Full" signs sometimes stay up for days on end; look carefully for empty sites. All 11 campgrounds accessible by car are easy to find. Just follow the map distributed as you enter the park. **Sprague Creek** on Lake McDonald has many peaceful sites near the lake, but arrive early to avoid those near the road; there are only 25 sites total. Some sites at Sprague, Apgar, and Avalanche remain reserved for **bicyclists;** towed units are prohibited. Campgrounds without running water in the surrounding national forests offer sites for $5. Check at the Apgar or St. Mary visitors centers for up-to-date information on conditions and vacancies at established campgrounds.

Outdoors **Backcountry trips** are the best way to appreciate the pristine mountain scenery and the wildlife which make Glacier famous. The **Highline Trail** from Logan Pass is a good day hike through prime bighorn sheep and mountain goat territory, although locals consider it too crowded. The visitors center's free *Nature with a Naturalist* pamphlet has a hiking map marked with distances and backcountry campsites. All travelers who camp overnight must obtain a free **wilderness permit** from a visitors center or ranger station 24 hr. in advance, in person; backcountry camping is allowed only at designated campgrounds. The **Two Medicine** area in the southeast corner of the park is well traveled, while the trek to **Kintla Lake** rewards you with fantastic views of nearby peaks. It's easy to find your own backcountry trails. Rangers at any visitors center or ranger station will instruct you on the finer points of keeping bears at bay (also see Camping and the Outdoors: Bear Necessities in the Essentials chapter).

    Going-to-the-Sun Rd., the only road traversing the park, may be the most beautiful 52-mi. stretch of road in the world. Even on cloudy days when there's no sun, the constantly changing views of Alpine peaks will have you struggling to keep your eyes on the road. Snow keeps the road closed until late June, so check with rangers for exact dates. Vehicles must be less than 24 ft.by 8ft. (including mirrors).

    Although The Sun Rd. is a popular **bike route,** only experienced cyclists with appropriate gear and legs of titanium should attempt this grueling stint. The sometimes nonexistent shoulder of the road creates a hazardous situation for cyclists: in the summer (June 15-Sept. 2), bike traffic is prohibited from the Apgar turn-off at the west end of Lake McDonald to Sprague Creek, and from Logan Creek to Logan Pass, 11am-4pm. Bikes are not permitted on any hiking trails. **Equestrian** explorers should check to make sure trails are open; fines for riding on closed trails are steep.

    While in Glacier, don't overlook the interpretive programs offered by the rangers. Ask about "jammers," the red buses that snake around the park. Inquire at any visitors center for the day's menu of guided hikes, lectures, bird-watching walks, and children's programs. At the Backpacker's Inn, ask about **Sun Tours,** guides through the park which try to include a Native American perspective. The tour guide is extremely knowledgable about wildlife and vegetation.

    Boat tours explore all of Glacier's large lakes. At Lake McDonald and Two Medicine Lake, one-hour tours leave throughout the day. (Tours at Lake McDonald $6.50, ages 4-12 $3.25; at Two Medicine $6 and $3.) The tours from St. Mary (90 min.) and Many Glacier (75 min.) provide access to Glacier's backcountry. (From St. Mary $8, ages 4-12 $4; from Many Glacier $7.50 and $3.75.) The $7 sunset cruise proves a great way to see this quotidian phenomenon which doesn't commence until about 10pm in the middle of the summer. **Glacier Raft Co.,** in West Glacier (800-332-9995 or 888-5454) hawks full- and half-day trips down the middle fork of the Flathead River. A full-day trip (lunch included) costs $57, under 13 $28; half-day trips ($29, under 13 $18) leave in both the morning and the afternoon. Call for reservations.

    Rent **rowboats** ($5 per hr., $25 per 10 hr.) at Lake McDonald, Many Glacier and Two Medicine; **canoes** ($5 per hr.) at Two Medicine and Many Glacier; and **outboards** ($10 per hr., $50 per 10 hr.) at Lake McDonald. All require a $50 deposit. **Fishing** is excellent in the park—cutthroat trout, lake trout, and even the rare Arctic grayling challenge the angler's skill and patience. No permit is required; right outside the park, however, on Blackfoot Indian land, you need a special permit. Anywhere else in Montana you need a Montana permit.

Washington

Geographically, politically, and culturally, Washington is divided by the spine of the Cascade Mountains. The personality difference between the state's eastern and western halves is pervasive, long-standing, and polarizing. The division stretches back to the 1840s, when Stephen A. Douglas, chairman of the Senate committee on boundaries, purportedly dragged his cane down the spine of the Cascade Range on a map of the Oregon Territory and urged the committee to make this the Territory's eastern border. Douglas' cane traced a boundary that to this day is plagued by a bloodless yet passionate war. To "wet-siders" who live near Washington's coast, the term "dry-siders" conjures images of rednecks tearing through the eastern deserts in their Chevy trucks, slurring the endangered spotted-owl and avidly hooting for its destruction. In the minds of dry-siders, the residents of Seattle and the rest of western Washington are yuppified, liberal freaks too wealthy to recognize or care that in saving owls they sacrifice people.

What does unify Washingtonians—whether from the wet or dry side—is an independent frame of mind. State voters do not register their political affiliation, which is fitting since the spectrum of elected officials varies so markedly. In 1988, twenty years after a Republican governor founded the first "alternative" state university (Evergreen), ultra-conservative evangelist Pat Robertson won the backing of the state's delegates at the Republican National Convention.

The western part of the state finds strength in its numbers. Most of Washington's population is clustered around Puget Sound, a prosperous international port sustained by commerce and aerospace engineering. Life in the West, especially in Seattle, is intimately tied to the arts; the *New York Times* has been known to lament that there is more good theater in Seattle than on Broadway (backhanded compliments are compliments nonetheless). The East is less congested; residents and tourists enjoy its rolling countryside without having to buck for space. Native American reservations dot the area; rodeos and wineries share the land with equanimity.

The collective palate of western Washington is sated by abundant seafood. Salmon and shellfish are available at the Pike Place Market in Seattle or closer to the source at spots like Dungeness—as in the crab—on the Olympic Peninsula. But pity not the residents of eastern Washington. The orchards of Wenatchee and Yakima produce apples, apricots, and other fruits by the bushel.

Like its ideological spectrum, Washington's terrain is all-encompassing: deserts, volcanoes, Pacific beaches, and the world's only non-tropical rain forest all lie within state boundaries. You can raft on the Skagit, Suiattle, Sauk, Yakima, and Wenatchee Rivers; sea kayak around the San Juan Islands; and build sand castles on the Strait of Juan de Fuca. Mount Rainier has fantastic hiking, while the Cascades boast perfect conditions for nearly every winter recreational activity. Seattle and Spokane drape themselves over handsome green landscapes, proving that natural beauty can be its own selling point. Best of all, Washington is a compact state by Western standards, and most destinations are within a day's trip.

PRACTICAL INFORMATION

Capital: Olympia.

Visitor Information: State Tourist Office, Tourism Development Division, 101 General Administration Bldg., Olympia 98504-0613 (206-586-2088 or 206-586-2102, 800-544-1800 for vacation planning guide). Open Mon.-Fri. 9am-5pm. **Washington State Parks and Recreation Commission,** 7150 Cleanwater Lane, KY-11, Olympia 98504 (206-753-5755, May-Aug. in WA 800-562-0990). **Forest Service/National Park Service Outdoor Recreation Information Center,** 915 2nd Ave. #442, Seattle 98174 (206-553-0170). Open Mon.-Fri. 8am-5pm.

WASHINGTON

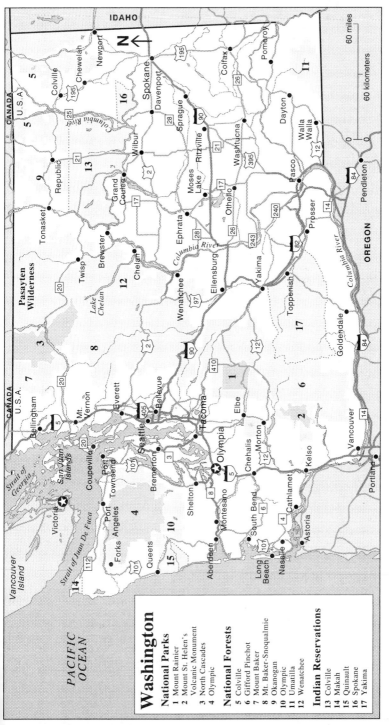

Washington

National Parks
1 Mount Rainier
2 Mount St. Helen's Volcanic Monument
3 North Cascades
4 Olympic

National Forests
5 Colville
6 Gifford Pinchot
7 Mount Baker
8 Mt. Baker-Snoqualmie
9 Okanogan
10 Olympic
11 Umatilla
12 Wenatchee

Indian Reservations
13 Colville
14 Makah
15 Quinault
16 Spokane
17 Yakima

State Motto: *"Alki,"* an Indian word meaning "by and by," which looks to the future greatness of the state. **Nickname:** Evergreen State. **State Song:** "Washington, My Home." **State Flower:** Coastal Rhododendron. **State Dance:** Square Dance. **State Rock:** Petrified Wood. **State Mollusk:** Geoduck. **State Bird:** Goldfinch. **State Tree:** Western Hemlock.
Area: 68,192 sq. mi.
Emergency: 911.
Time Zone: Pacific (3 hr. behind Eastern).
Postal Abbreviation: WA.
Drinking Age: 21.
Traffic Laws: Mandatory seatbelt law.
Area Codes: 206 in western Washington, 509 in eastern Washington.

GETTING AROUND

Bus remains the cheapest way to travel long distances in Washington. Greyhound (800-231-2222) serves the two main transportation centers, Spokane and Seattle, along with other major cities in between. Local buses cover most of the remaining cities, although a few areas (such as the northwestern Olympic Peninsula) have no bus service. There is an **Amtrak train** line from Los Angeles to Vancouver with many stops in western Washington; another line extends from Seattle to Spokane and on to Chicago. Amtrak serves most large cities along these two lines.

Hitchhiking in the San Juans and on the southern half of Whidbey Island is locally accepted if not legal. Hitching on the Olympic Peninsula is less speedy; hitching in other parts of western Washington is neither speedy nor safe. "No hitchhiking permitted" signs are posted on all highways. Opportunities for thumbing decrease as one goes east. *Let's Go* does not recommend hitchhiking, especially for women traveling alone.

ACCOMMODATIONS AND CAMPING

With the exception of those in Seattle, Washington's **hostels** are generally uncrowded, even during July and August. Cheap hotels exist in downtown areas of most large cities, but safety is not assured.

State park **campgrounds** have less expensive, more secluded sites than private campgrounds; additionally, they provide better access to trails, rivers, and lakes. Drivers will find state park campgrounds (standard sites $11) more accessible than Department of Natural Resources (DNR) and National Forest campgrounds. Most campgrounds have sites for hikers and bikers for $5.50 with vehicle access, $4 without. The state park system charges $14 for hookups and $4-5 for extra vehicles. Six-minute showers cost 25¢. Some parks allow self-registration; others have rangers register campers at their sites in the evening. Expect long, slow lines if the campground requires registration at the office. Campers who arrive after dusk needn't register until a ranger checks the sites in the morning. The gates open at dawn (about 6:30am in summer and 8am October 16-March 31) and close at dusk (about 10pm in summer). Pets must be leashed and accompanied by owners at all times.

Be aware that several state parks—including Belfair, Birch Bay, Fort Flagler, Steamboat Rock, Fort Canby, Twin Harbors/Grayland Beach, Lake Chelan, Pearrygin Lake, and Moran—accept reservations for Memorial Day through Labor Day and may be filled up weeks in advance, especially during July and August. Reservations can be made in January, and must be made two weeks in advance.

Drivers can enjoy the solitude of the many National Forest and DNR sites. National Forest campsites cost from nothing up to $8 (most cost about $6). Call MISTIX at 800-365-2267 to reserve campsites in the national forests or national parks. National Park campgrounds accessible by road cost $8 on average and are generally in the best settings. Olympic National Park has some free campgrounds accessible by car. Campgrounds that can be reached by trail only are usually free.

■■■ SEATTLE

Seattle's mid-19th century pioneers originally named their city New York Alki, meaning "New York By and By," but nowadays, the mere mention of the big Big Apple is enough to make a native skittish. Prompted by Seattle's alarming expansion, a local organization called Lesser Seattle works to further their city's reputation as the rain capital of the U.S. in an effort to keep Seattle to themselves. Nonetheless, the Space Needle is no Tower of Babel; Seattle has integrated its population into a cohesive and successful modern city where no single culture dominates. Even Seattle's former Chinatown is now known as the "International District."

Given its diversity, Seattle has been a prolific and creative cradle. The city has spawned such venerable musicians as Jimi Hendrix and Heart, and even the Big Apple has been caught smelling the teen spirit of this corner of the country. The roar of the grungy "Seattle Sound"—best exemplified by groups like Nirvana, Pearl Jam, Soundgärden, and the Screaming Trees—has outshined all other recent developments in rock and roll. The theater community supports Broadway shows and alternative vaudeville, while the opera consistently sells out. In relative size, the repertory theater community ranks second only to New York among U.S. cities. Seattle supports a dynamic palette of large-scale museums and parks, small galleries, and personable bistros throughout the downtown and even in the dreaded suburbs. (Say "suburbs" too loud, and most Seattlites will flinch.) In other words, there's a lot more to Seattle than is visible from the top of the Space Needle.

Surrounded by water on three sides, with mountain ranges to the east and west, every hilltop in the city offers an impressive view. Unfortunately, Seattle spends nearly three quarters of the year blanketed by clouds. Undaunted, residents spend as much time as possible in the great outdoors, biking around the many parks or skiing in the nearby Cascades. Even the police ride mountain bikes. Don't be dismayed by the drizzle, because although the clouds may seem almost as permanent as the mountains they mask, Seattle actually soaks up less precipitation per year than many other cities. The temperature hovers between 40°F and 70°F year-round; it is rarely cold enough for snow. A light drizzle is standard in winter. Occasionally the skies clear and "the mountain is out," and Seattlites run for their cars and into the country.

PRACTICAL INFORMATION

Visitors Information: Seattle-King County Visitors Bureau, 666 Stewart St. (461-5840), on the Galleria level of the Convention Center. Enter at Union and 7th. Well-stocked with maps, brochures, newspapers, and transit schedules. Information on the rest of Washington. Helpful staff. Open Mon.-Fri. 8:30am-5pm, Sat.-Sun. 10am-4pm. Weekend hours summer only. From 5-7:30pm, call the airport branch at 433-5218. **Tourism BC,** 720 Olive Way, Seattle 98101 (800-663-6000). Information on travel to British Columbia. Open Mon.-Fri. 9am-5pm.
Seattle Parks and Recreation Department, 5201 Green Lake Way N., Seattle 98103 (684-4075). Open Mon.-Fri. 8am-6pm. **National Park Service, Pacific Northwest Region,** 915 2nd Ave. #442 (220-7450). Open Mon.-Fri. 8am-4:30pm.
Currency Exchange: Thomas Cook Foreign Exchange, 906 3rd Ave. (623-6203). Open Mon.-Fri. 9am-5pm. **Mutual of Omaha** (243-1231) behind the Continental Airlines ticket counter at **Sea-Tac Airport.** Open daily 6am-9:30pm.
Airport: Seattle-Tacoma International (Sea-Tac) (433-5217 for General Information) on Federal Way, south of Seattle proper. **Sea-Tac Visitors Information Center** (433-5218), in the central baggage claim area across from carousel 10, helps with basic transportation concerns for arriving visitors. Open daily 9:30am-7:30pm. Foreign visitors should contact **Operation Welcome** (433-5367), in the customs and immigration areas, where staff members answer questions on customs, immigration, and foreign language services in just about every language.
Amtrak (800-872-7245), King Street Station, 3rd and Jackson St. Trains daily to: Portland (3 per day, $23); Tacoma (3 per day, $8); Spokane (1 per day, $65); San Francisco (1 per day, $153). Station open daily 6am-10pm; ticket office open 6:30am-4:30pm.

Greyhound (800-231-2222 or 628-5526), 8th Ave. and Stewart St. Buses daily to: Sea-Tac Airport (2 per day, $3.50); Spokane (4 per day, $35); Vancouver, BC (4 per day, $21.75); Portland (8 per day, $19). Ticket office open daily 5am-9pm and midnight-1:30am.

Green Tortoise (324-7433 or 800-227-4766); buses leave from 9th Ave. and Stewart. Departs on Tues., Thurs., and Sun. at 8am to Portland, OR ($15), Eugene, OR ($25), Berkeley, CA ($69), San Francisco, CA ($69), and Los Angeles ($89, Thurs. trip only). Reservations are required and should be made 5 days in advance. See Getting There and Getting Around: By Bus in the Essentials section at the beginning of this book for more information.

Metro Transit: Customer Assistance Office, 821 2nd Ave. (24-hr. information 553-3000. TTD service 684-1739), in the Exchange Building downtown. Open Mon.-Fri. 8am-5pm. Fares are based on a two-zone system. Zone 1 includes everything within the city limits ($1.10 during peak hours, 85¢ off-peak); Zone 2 comprises anything outside the city limits ($1.60 peak, $1.10 off-peak). Ages 5-18 pay 75¢. With reduced fare permits costing $1, ages over 64 and people with disabilities pay 25¢ to go anywhere at any time. Peak hours in both zones are generally weekdays 6-9am and 3-6pm. Exact fare required. Weekend all-day passes are $1.70. Between 4am-9pm, ride free within the "Magic Carpet" area bordered by Jackson St. on the south, 6th Ave. and I-5 on the east, Battery St. on the north, and the waterfront on the west. Transfers valid for 2 hr. and for Waterfront Streetcars as well. See Getting Around below for more information.

Ferries: Washington State Ferries, Colman Dock, Pier 52 (464-2000 for recording, ext. 4 for schedule and fare info.; in WA 800-542-0810 or 800-542-7052). Service to Bremerton (on Kitsap Peninsula), Winslow (on Bainbridge Island), and Vashon Island (passenger ferry only). Ferries leave daily (and frequently) 6am-2am. Fares from $3.30; car and driver $6.65 ($5.65 in winter).

Car Rental: A-19.95-Rent-A-Car, 804 N. 145th St. (365-1995). $19.95 per day ($25 if under 21), plus 15¢ per mi. more than 100. Free delivery. Drivers under 21 welcome, but must have verifiable auto insurance. Credit card required. The cheapest and least convenient is also worth a try: **Auto Driveaway** (235-0880) hires people to drive their cars to various locations across the U.S.

Automobile Club of Washington (AAA), 330 6th Ave. N. (448-5353), 2 blocks east of the Space Needle. Provides maps and tourbooks to AAA members. Open Mon.Tues. and Thurs.-Fri. 8:30am-5pm, Wed. 8:30am-6:30pm.

Ride Board: 1st floor of the Husky Union Building (the HUB), behind Suzallo Library on the University of Washington main campus. Matches cars and riders for destinations across the country. Check the bulletin board at the hostel as well.

Bike Rentals: The Bicycle Center, 4529 Sand Point Way (523-8300). $3 per hr. (2-hr. min.), $15 per day. Credit card or license required as deposit. Open Mon.-Thurs. 10am-8pm, Fri.-Sat. 10am-6pm, Sun. noon-5pm. **Alki Bikes,** 2622 Alki Ave. SW (938-3322). Mountain bikes $9 per hr., $20 per 24 hr. Credit card or license required as deposit. Open Mon.-Thurs. 10am-7pm, Fri. 10am-8pm, Sat. 10am-6pm, Sun. noon-5pm; in winter Mon.-Fri. 3-7pm.

Seattle Public Library: 1000 4th Ave. (386-4636). Quiet and relaxed modern facility. Pick up a copy of the SPL *Events* newsletter for listings of free lectures, films, and programs. Tours leave the information desk Wed. noon and Sat. 2pm. **Quick Information** (386-4697) answers questions about everything from a Plato quote to the phone number of a Vietnamese deli. Open Mon.-Thurs. 9am-9pm, Fri.-Sat. 9am-6pm, Sun. 1-5pm; June-Aug. open Mon.-Sat. only.

Ticket Agencies: Ticket Master, located in record stores across the city; hours depend on the store. **Ticket/Ticket,** 401 Broadway E (324-2744), on the 2nd floor of the Broadway Market. Half-price day-of-show tickets to local theater, music, concerts, comedy, and dance performances. Cash only. Open Tues.-Sun. 10am-7pm. Also in the Pike Place Market, open Tues.-Sun. noon-6pm.

Laundromat: Downtown-St. Regis, 116 Stewart St., attached to the St. Regis Hotel (see Accommodations). A somewhat scary area, so bring a friend and watch your laundry. Wash $1.25, dry 75¢. Open 24 hr. **Queen Anne Maytag Center,** Queen Anne N. and W. Boston (282-6645). On the top of Queen Anne hill, north

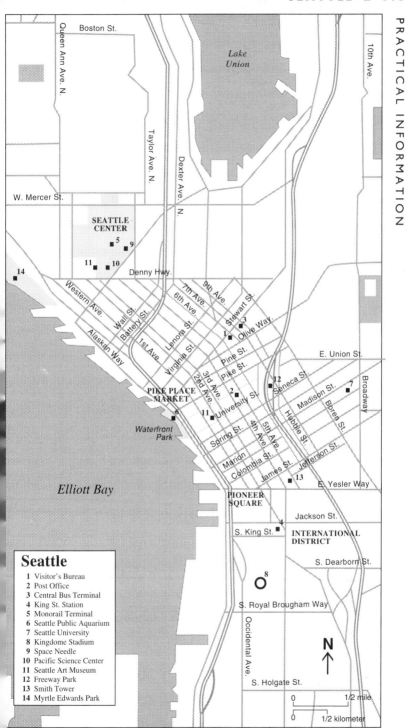

Queen Ann Ave. N.

Boston St.

Lake Union

10th Ave.

Taylor Ave. N.

Dexter Ave. N.

W. Mercer St.

SEATTLE CENTER

■ 5 ■ 9

■ 11 ■ 10

■ 14

Denny Hwy.

Western Ave.

Wall St.

Battery St.

1st Ave.

Lenora St.

Virginia St.

6th Ave.

7th Ave.

9th Ave.

Stewart St.

Olive Way

■ 1 ■ 3

Alaskan Way

Pine St.

Pike St.

E. Union St.

3rd Ave.

2nd Ave.

University St.

Seneca St.

■ 12

Madison St.

Boren St.

Broadway

■ 7

PIKE PLACE MARKET

■ 2

■ 11

Waterfront Park

■ 6

Spring St.

4th Ave.

5th Ave.

Hubble St.

Marion

Colombia St.

James St.

Jefferson St.

■ 13

E. Yesler Way

Elliott Bay

PIONEER SQUARE

Jackson St.

S. King St. ■ 4

INTERNATIONAL DISTRICT

S. Dearborn St.

○ 8

Occidental Ave.

S. Royal Brougham Way

N
↑

S. Holgate St.

0 _____ 1/2 mile

0 _____ 1/2 kilometer

Seattle

1 Visitor's Bureau
2 Post Office
3 Central Bus Terminal
4 King St. Station
5 Monorail Terminal
6 Seattle Public Aquarium
7 Seattle University
8 Kingdome Stadium
9 Space Needle
10 Pacific Science Center
11 Seattle Art Museum
12 Freeway Park
13 Smith Tower
14 Myrtle Edwards Park

of downtown. Attended facility. Take bus #3, 4, or 13. Wash 75¢ Tues.-Thurs., $1 Fri.-Mon.; 17 min. dry 25¢. Open daily 7:30am-10:30pm.

Crisis Clinic: 461-3222. 24 hr. **Seattle Rape Relief:** 1905 S. Jackson St., #102 (632-RAPE or 7273). Crisis counseling, advocacy, and prevention training. 24 hr.

University of Washington Women's Information Center: (685-1090), Cunningham Hall, in the main campus. Monthly calendar, networking, and referral for women's groups throughout the Seattle area. Open Mon.-Fri. 9am-5pm.

Senior Citizen Information and Assistance: 1601 2nd, #800 (448-3110). Open Mon.-Fri. 9am-5pm.

Travelers' Aid: 909 4th Ave., #630 (461-3888), at Marion, in the YMCA. Free services for stranded travelers who have lost wallets, grandmothers, or their marbles. Open Mon.-Fri. 8:30am-9pm, Sat. 9am-1pm.

Operation Nightwatch: 2419½ 1st Ave. (448-8804). Emergency aid in the downtown area. Street ministry operates nightly 9pm-1am. Answering machine 24 hr.

International District Emergency Center: 623-3321. Medics with multilingual assistance available. 24 hr.

Poison Information: 526-2121. 24hr.

AIDS Hotline: (796-4999). Open Mon.-Fri. 8am-5pm.

Gay Counseling Service: 200 W. Mercer, suite #300 (282-9307). Open Mon.-Fri. noon-9pm.

Lesbian Resource Center: 1208 E. Pine (322-3953). Support groups, drop-in center, lending library, workshops, and job referrals. Open Mon.-Fri. 2-7pm.

Health Care: Aradia Women's Health Center, 112 Boylston Ave. E. (323-9388). Appointments are necessary and should be made 1 week in advance; urgent cases are given priority. Staff will refer elsewhere when booked. Open Mon.-Fri. 10:30am-5:30pm. **Country Doctor Community Clinic,** 500 19th Ave. E. (461-4503). Family care. Open Mon. 9am-9pm; Tues. 9am-5pm; Wed. 1-9pm; Thurs.-Fri. 9am-5pm (closed noon-1pm daily for lunch). Appointments necessary.

Emergency: 911. **Police Department,** 610 3rd Ave. (625-5011).

Post Office: (442-6340), Union St. and 3rd Ave. downtown. Open Mon.-Fri. 8am-5:30pm. **General Delivery ZIP Code:** 98101.

Area Code: 206.

GETTING THERE AND GETTING AROUND

Seattle is a long, skinny city stretched out north to south between long, skinny **Puget Sound** on the west and long, skinny **Lake Washington** on the east. The head of the city is cut from its torso by Lake Union and a string of locks, canals, and bays. These link the saltwater of Puget Sound with the freshwater of Lake Washington. In the downtown area, avenues run northwest to southeast and streets southwest to northeast. After Western Ave., the avenues run numerically up the hill to 6th Ave. Downtown streets run south to north in pairs: Jefferson, James, Cherry, Columbia, Marion, Madison, Spring, Seneca, University, Union, Pike, Pine. To remember the order of the pairs keep repeating the helpful mnemonic "Jesus Christ Made Seattle Utterly Perfect" (or "Under Protest," depending on whether or not it's raining).

Outside the downtown area everything is simplified—avenues run north to south and streets east to west, with only a few exceptions. The city is split into **quadrants:** 1000 1st Ave. NW is a long hike from 1000 1st Ave. S. City maps and phone books include grids that impart spatial significance to this alpha-numeric cipher.

The city is easily accessible by **car** via I-5, which runs north-south on the eastern side of the downtown area, and by I-90 from the east, which ends its transcontinental path from Boston just south of the city center. From I-5, get to downtown by taking any of the exits from James to Stewart St. (including **Pioneer Square, Pike Place Market,** and the **waterfront).** Take the Mercer St./Fairview Ave. exit to the **Seattle Center.** The Denny Way exit leads to **Capitol Hill,** and farther north, the 45th St. exit will take you to the **University District.** Getting on the freeway from the downtown area is a challenge. The freeway is always visible; just drive around until you spot a blue I-5 sign. I-99 skirts the western side of downtown, offering some of the best views from the Alaskan Way Viaduct. I-99 is less crowded than I-5 and is often the better choice when driving to the northwestern part of the city.

Transportation options from the mammoth **Seattle-Tacoma International Airport (Sea-Tac)** are numerous. **Gray Line coaches** (626-5208) and **limousines** both will whisk you to and from downtown ($7 each way, $12 round-trip). **Greyhound** makes the trip (2 per day, $3.50 one-way). **Metro buses** #174 and 194 are cheaper and run daily every half-hour from 6am to 1am. A taxi ride from the airport to downtown Seattle costs about $22.

Seattle's **Metro Transit** system provides extensive, reliable, and inexpensive service by bus and electric trolley throughout the city and major suburbs (see Practical Information above for fares). A **monorail** operates from Westlake Center to the Seattle Center. The hassles of downtown traffic jams and expensive parking can be avoided by taking the bus. However, making connections all across the city often entails long waits, especially in the evening. Buses operate daily from 6am to 1 or 2am, and a few buses offer "night owl service" from 1:30 to 4:30am. Express buses do not run on weekends. All passes, as well as timetables and a free, comprehensive map, are available from the **Metro Customer Assistance Office** (see Practical Information). Timetables and maps are also available at public libraries, the hostel, the University Book Store, the visitors bureau, and on the buses themselves.

Routes and buses equipped with lifts are marked by blue **wheelchair accessibility** signs. **Bike racks** with capacity for two bicycles are also placed on the front of the buses that run from downtown Seattle to Bellevue and Kirkland. Not all buses are equipped with racks, and bikes can be loaded only at designated stops; check out Metro's *Bike & Ride* pamphlet, available at the visitors center and hostel (see Practical Information and Accommodations respectively).

Metro extends into Seattle's outskirts, covering the whole of King County east to North Bend and Carnation, south to Enumclaw, and north to Snohomish County, where Metro bus #6 hooks up with **Community Transit**. This line runs to Everett, Stanwood, and well into the Cascades. Metro bus #174 connects in Federal Way to Tacoma's Pierce County System. (See Near Seattle for more information.)

PUBLICATIONS

The city's major newspaper is the *Seattle Times* (464-2121). The paper's "Tempo" section, published on Fridays, lists upcoming events. The *Seattle Weekly* is the popular alternative to the dominant daily; it pumps out fresh opinions every Wednesday. *Arts Focus,* a free magazine available at most bookstores, carries information on the performing arts, and *Seattle Arts* published by the Seattle Arts Commission is especially good for events in the visual arts. Both are published monthly. The *Rocket,* the *Wire,* and *Hype* are sources of information on the music scene. *Seattle Gay News* is an established weekly catering to the gay community. The University of Washington puts out two papers that also list upcoming events and give a sense of Washingtonian attitude: *University Herald* and *The Daily U of WA General.* Various suburban publications include the *Belltown/Brainfever Dispatch,* the *Capitol Hill Times,* and the *Ballard News Tribune;* though somewhat harder to find, most of these can be found in cafes and in bookstores (see Practical Information).

ACCOMMODATIONS

The **Seattle International Hostel** is the best option for the budget traveler staying downtown. For those tired of the urban scene, the **Vashon Island Hostel** (sometimes called "Seattle B") is ideal (see Vashon Island). **Pacific Bed and Breakfast,** 701 NW 60th St., Seattle 98107 (784-0539), can set you up with a single room in a B&B in the $40-70 range (open Mon.-Fri. 9am-5pm).

Downtown

Seattle International Hostel (HI/AYH), 84 Union St. (622-5443), at Western Ave. Take Metro #174, 184, or 194 from the airport. 139 beds, common kitchen which never closes, immaculate facilities, plenty of modern amenities, and a friendly, knowledgeable staff. Check-in may be tedious but security is tight. The location is convenient and the crowd alluring. Loads of information about Seattle in the library and on the brochure racks. The view of the bay will mollify your temper when the traffic gets too loud. Hostel is always full in summer so make reservations (participates in international reservations system). During the summer, there is a supplemental hostel for overflow. Offers discount tickets for Aquarium and Omnidome. Sleep sacks required (linen rental $2). 5-day max. stay in summer. Front desk open 7am-midnight. Check-out 10:30am. $14, nonmembers $17. Members priority in the summer.

YMCA, 909 4th Ave. (382-5000), near the Madison St. intersection. Men and women welcome; must be over 18. Small but well-kept rooms. Good location; tight security, with a staffed security desk. TV lounge on each floor (color TVs in some rooms), laundry facilities, and use of swimming pool and fitness facilities. Bring your own bedding for the bunk-room and your own lock for lockers. Check-out by noon. No curfew. HI/AYH members: bunk-room $18, singles $33, doubles $36. Nonmembers: singles $39, with TV and bath $53; doubles $43.50, with TV and bath $57. Weekly rates for all visitors: singles $167; doubles $190.

YWCA, 1118 5th Ave. (461-4888), near the YMCA. Take any 4th Ave. bus to Seneca St. *Women only, ages under 18 require advance arrangement.* Great security, with the front desk open and staffed 24 hr. Good, central location. Shared kitchen facilities. 2-week max. stay. No curfew. Singles $31, with bath $36. Doubles $42, with bath $48. Weekly: singles $186, with bath $216. Health center use $5. Key deposit $2.

Moore Motel, 1926 2nd Ave. (448-4851), at 2nd and Virginia. Next to the historic Moore Theater. Big rooms include 2 beds, bath, and TV. Singles $34. Doubles $39. Those turned away from the full hostel, with a HI\AYH membership card, get singles for $20 and doubles for $25.

Commodore Hotel, 2013 2nd Ave. (448-8868), at Virginia. Clean and relatively safe. The rates are worth sacrificing a private bath. Singles $33, with bath $42, with 2 beds and bath $49. One shared double with shared bath $37.

St. Regis Hotel, 116 Stewart St. (448-6366), 2 blocks from the Pike Place Market. Pleasant management, good security, but the neighborhood is a little squalid and the rooms a little bare. No visitors after 10pm. Laundromat on the first floor. Singles $32, with bath $36. Doubles $38, with bath $44. $1 key deposit.

Other Neighborhoods

Vincent's Guest House, 527 Malden Ave. E (323-7849). This hostel-like guest house in Capitol Hill is a bit removed from downtown proper, but a friendly and funky alternative if the Seattle Hostel is full. Kitchen facilities and fresh herbs from the garden (but no, not *that* herb). No curfew. Checkout 11am. Private rooms available. Shared rooms $12.

Park Plaza Motel, 4401 Aurora Ave. N. (632-2101). Just north of the Aurora bridge; take Metro #6 to 46th Ave. or #5 to 43rd and Fremont. Friendly and surprisingly quiet. Unfortunately, the external orange decor is replicated on the inside as well. Bare rooms and halls. Singles $30. Doubles from $35.

Nites Inn, 11746 Aurora Ave. N. (365-3216). Take bus #6. One of the many motels that line Aurora north of 85th St., but better and larger than most. Cable TV and free local calls. Singles $38. Doubles $42.

Motel 6, 18900 47th Ave. S. (241-1648), exit 152 off I-5. Take bus #194. Near Sea-Tac Airport, but very inconvenient to Downtown. Crowded; make reservations. Singles $30. Doubles $36.

The College Inn, 4000 University Way NE (633-4441). European-style B&B in the University District. Antiques and individual wash basins in every room. The rooms facing 40th are the quietest. All rooms have shared shower and bath, but a cozy diner-style breakfast is included, served in a finely refurbished attic. Singles from $39. Doubles from $55.

FOOD

As the principal marketplace for Washington's famous fishing industries and orchards, Seattle is practically aswarm with salmon and apples. You will be hard-pressed to avoid the catch of the day. However, in spite of the fresh food flopping constantly into their laps, Seattle restaurateurs seem equally inclined to stick their heads (and breads) in ovens: bakeries proliferate alongside endless espresso stands, and few Seattlites seem to be able to move in the morning without an *espresso americano* and sticky-bun fuel-up. The best fish, produce, and baked goods can be purchased from various vendors in **Pike Place Market** (see below for more information). If you have the facilities and faculties to cook for yourself, you can buy fish right off the boats at **Fisherman's Wharf,** at NW 54th St. and 30th Ave. NW in Ballard, along the route of bus #43. The wharf is usually open from 8am to 3 or 4pm. Or visit one of Seattle's active **food coops,** such as those located at 6518 Fremont N. (in Greenlake) and at 6504 20th NE (in the Ravenna District north of the university). Also in Ravenna is a fine produce stand, **Rising Sun Farms and Produce,** 6505 15th Ave. NE (524-9741). (Open Mon.-Sat. 8am-8pm, Sun. 8am-7pm.)

Seattlites are serious about coffee. When civic leaders visited Philadelphia a few years ago, they brought their own beans with them. **Uptown Espresso,** 525 Queen Anne N. (281-8669) at the base of Queen Anne, has a well-established reputation. Most Seattlites have strict loyalties to several obscure street corner carts for their espresso; brand-wise, the best bet is the locally roasted **Starbuck's** or **SBC** (Stuart Bros. or "Seattle's Best"). Both have many shops downtown.

One final word for those culinary kamikazes with thin wallets and a thick tolerance for greasy pizza: **Godfather's Pizza** has an all-you-can-eat lunch special for $3.75. They have locations throughout the city, including one at 1414 Alaskan Way (621-7835), downtown.

Pike Place Market

Farmers have been selling their own produce here since 1907, when angry Seattle citizens demanded the elimination of the middle-merchant. A nasty fire in 1941, the World War II draft, and the internment of Japanese-Americans almost did away with the market, but in the last 15 years a rehabilitation drive has restored it. Lunatic fish- and produce-mongers bellow at customers and at each other while street performers offer their own entertainment to the crowds. The market's conglomeration of self- and full-service restaurants allows you to escape the crowded aisles for space at a crowded table. Chic shops and restaurants proliferate, but the farmers and fishmongers are the mainstays of the market.

The most hospitable time to visit the market is between 7 and 9am, when the fish are yawning and the fruit still glistens in the sun. In summer between 10am and 5pm, tourists flood the market in such numbers that it becomes nearly impossible to navigate. You might want to show up late and hunt around for end-of-the-day specials on produce, or linger at **Pike Place Fish** (86 Pike Place), where they will sing your order in chorus and then fling it over the counter. The monthly *Pike Place Market News,* available free in the market, has a map and the low-down on the market's latest events, new merchants, and old-timers. An information table in front of the bakery in the main market can answer your questions. (Table open Mon.-Sat. 10am-6pm, Sun. noon-6pm. Market open Mon.-Sat. 6:30am-6pm, Sun. 6:30am-5pm.)

Soundview Cafe (623-5700), on the mezzanine level in the Main Arcade just to the left of the largest fish stall. This wholesome self-serve sandwich-and-salad bar offers fresh food, a spectacular view of the Sound (naturally), and occasional poetry readings. Get a View Special (eggs and potatoes) for $2.70, try the West African nut stew ($2.15), or bring a brown-bag lunch—the cafe offers public seating. Open Mon.-Sat. 7am-5:30pm, Sun. 9am-3:30pm.

Three Girls Bakery (622-1045), at Post and Pike Pl. Order to go or sit in the cafe. The rows of bread and pastry in the display alone will make you drool, not to mention the aroma. Mammoth apple fritters (95¢). Open Mon.-Sat. 7am-6pm.

Athenian Inn, 1517 Pike Pl. (622-4881). Great Greek food. Try the Athenian steak ($6), the spinach salad ($7), or any other item off the huge menu. Open Mon.-Sat. 6:30am-7pm.

Copacabana, 1520½ Pike Pl. (622-6359). Music and passion are always in fashion. The outdoor tables are probably the best place in the market to watch the harried crowds go by. Try the Bolivian *salteña* ($3), a meat and raisin pastry and the house specialty. Open Mon.-Sat. 11:30am-9pm, Sun. 11:30am-5pm.

Emmett Watson's Oyster Bar, 1916 Pike Pl. (448-7721). Watson is a local newspaper columnist and California-basher who founded the Lesser Seattle movement in order to dissuade tourists and new residents with the candid motto, "Keep the Bastards Out." The restaurant isn't as interesting as the wise old huckster himself, but the patio is pretty and the oysters plentiful. You haven't really experienced a vitamin E high until you've tried the Oyster Bar Special ($5.65). Open Mon.-Wed. 11:30am-8pm, Thurs.-Sat. 11:30am-9pm, Sun. 11:30am-5pm.

Delcambre's Ragin' Cajun, 1523 1st Ave. (624-2598). Good food, tremendous portions. Breakfasts are overwhelming—the $6 *huevos rancheros* keep you going until the next morning. Open Tues.-Wed. 9am-3pm, Thurs.-Sat. 9am-8pm.

Lowell's Restaurant, 1519 Pike Pl. (622-2036). Great view of the Sound—at least for those tall enough to see over the top of one of their immense seafood specials ($7). Head to the upper dining room to avoid the bustle of the market and the harried servers. Open Mon.-Fri. 7am-5pm, Sat. 7am-5:30pm, Sun. 8am-3pm.

International District

Along King and Jackson St., between 5th and 8th Ave., Seattle's International District crowds together immigrants—some of them excellent chefs—from China, Japan, the Philippines, and Southeast Asia. Fierce competition keeps prices low and quality high. Any choice here will probably be a good one as three out of any four restaurants have been named (at one time or another) the best in town by a *Seattle Times* reviewer. Don't shy away from a shabby exterior—the quality of the façade is often inversely proportional to the quality of the food. **Uwajimaya,** the largest Asian retail store in the Pacific Northwest, is at 519 6th Ave. S. (624-6248). A huge selection of Japanese staples, fresh seafood (often still swimming), a wide variety of dried and/or instant foods (great for camping), a sushi bar, and a bakery make this Seattle institution a must-visit (open daily 9am-8pm; take bus #7 or 14).

Tai Tung, 655 S. King St. (622-7372). The busiest hours at Tai Tung are 1-3am, when the munchies take hold of university students. Waiters here rise to the occasion—they're likely to learn your name by the second night you're in. 10-page menu taped up around the dining room, with entrees $7-8. Open Mon.-Sat. 10am-3:30am, Sun. 10am-1:30am.

Ho Ho Seafood Restaurant, 653 S. Weller St. (382-9671). Casually elegant. Generous portions. Great seafood. Check the blackboard list for daily specials. Entrees $4.50-11.50. Open Sun.-Thurs. 11am-1am, Fri.-Sat. 11am-3am.

House of Hong Restaurant, 409 8th Ave. S. (622-7997), at Jackson. The most popular *dim sum* in town at $1.80-3 per dish; served daily 11am-3pm. Open Mon.-Thurs. 11am-10pm, Fri. 11am-midnight, Sat. 10:30am-midnight, Sun. 10:30am-10pm. Reservations recommended.

Phnom Penh Noodle Soup House, 414 Maynard Ave. S. (682-5690). Phnomenal Cambodian cuisine. Head to the tiny upstairs dining room for a good view of the park and a large bowl of noodles. Try the Phnom Penh Noodle Special ($3.70); some people come here weekly and never order anything else. Open Mon.-Tues. and Thurs.-Sun. 8:30am-6pm.

Viet My Restaurant, 129 Prefontaine Pl. S. (382-9923), off of 4th and Washington. Hard to find, but the consistently delicious Vietnamese food at great prices is worth the search. Try *bo la lot* (beef in rice pancakes, $3.50) or shrimp curry ($4.25). Avoid the lunch rush. Open Mon.-Sat. 11am-9pm.

Chau's Chinese Restaurant, 310 4th St. (621-0006), at 4th and Jackson. The best in late night seafood, though not in decor. Try the geoduck with ginger sauce

($6.50). Open Mon.-Thurs. 11am-midnight, Fri. 11am-1am, Sat. 4pm-1am, Sun. 4-11pm.

Mon Hei Bakery, 669 Main St. Some of the best finds in the international district can be had in tiny bakeries like this. Pastries (from 35¢) and gloriously sweet rice cakes (50¢). Open 11am-8pm daily.

A Little Bit of Saigon, 12th and S. Jackson (325-3663). Large Vietnamese restaurant at the back corner of Asian Plaza. A favorite with Vietnamese-Americans as well as a trendy restaurant-hopping crowd fed up with Thai food. Entrees $3.50-7. Open daily 9am-10pm.

Pioneer Square and the Waterfront

Historic Pioneer Square is an area of *haute couture* and *haute* prices. The Waterfront lures tourists with wharf-side fare that's more suited to be thrown to the seagulls. The best option is a picnic in Occidental Park or Waterfall Park.

Panchitos, 704 1st Ave. (343-9567). This Mexican cafeteria may lack table service and big prices, but nothing is lacking in the food. Enchiladas ($2.50), burritos with all the fixings ($4). Open daily 11:30am-9pm daily.

Seattle Bagel Bakery, 1302 Western Ave. (624-2187). Two blocks in from the waterfront, 1 block west of Pier 56. The best buy in Seattle—yummy, fat, affordable bagels (40¢) that could take over Manhattan. Also bagel sandwiches (from $3.25). Open Mon.-Fri. 7:30am-6:30pm, Sat.-Sun. 8:30am-5:30pm.

Ivar's Fish Bar, Pier 54 (624-6852), on the waterfront. One of a string of seafood restaurants founded by and named for the late Seattle celebrity and shipping magnate Ivar Haglund. For years Ivar donated the fireworks to Seattle's 4th of July celebration. Indulge those patriotic stirrings (or not—the food is still good) with fish and chips ($3.89), or definitive Seattle clam chowder ($1.39). Dine with the gulls and pigeons in covered booths outside. Open daily 11am-2am.

Trattoria Mitchelli, 84 Yesler Way (623-3883), at Yesler and Western. A cozy pizza place which evolves into an elegant late-night cafe as the sun sets. Also relaxing brunch spot (Sun. until 3pm). Open Tues.-Fri. 7am-4pm, Sat. 8am-4am, Sun. 8am-11pm, Mon. 7am-11pm.

Grand Central Bakery, 214 1st Ave. S. (622-3644). Walk-up cafe and deli in the Grand Central Arcade. Buy a loaf of bread ($2.90) or Irish soda bread (85¢). Come early—these famous pastries sell out fast. Eat at outdoor tables in the attractive antique arcade or just outside in Occidental Park. Open Mon.-Fri. 7am-6pm, Sat.-Sun. 9am-5pm.

Capitol Hill

With dance steps paved into the sidewalks, Capitol Hill offers a chance to two-step away from tourist traps to the imaginative shops, elegant clubs, and espresso houses of **Broadway Avenue.** The eclectic array of restaurants that lines the avenue serves largely as an excuse for patrons to watch the parade of people walking by, and although the food is not especially cheap, it is some of the best the city has to offer. **15th Street,** also on the hill, is more sedate—a swanky and pleasant lane with a twist. Bus #7 goes along Broadway, and #10 goes along 15th St. If dining in, ignore the metered parking on Broadway and head east from that street for the free angle park spots behind the reservoir park.

The Gravity Bar, 415 Broadway E (325-7186), also in the Broadway Market. Newton's Own fruit and vegetable juices. Blast off from a table or kneel at the bar. Among the infamous fruit and vegetable drinks are Daily Planets, Moonjuice (a lemon/lime concoction; $3.50), and Mr. Rogers on Amino Acid (16oz., $3.75). Also has a small closet outlet in Pike Place Market off Pine St. (443-9674). Open Mon.-Thurs. 8am-10pm, Fri.-Sat. 8am-11pm, Sun. 9am-10pm.

Dick's, 115 Broadway Ave. E (323-1300). A Broadway institution, recently made famous in Sir Mix-A-Lot's rap "Broadway." The first place homesick Seattlites go when they return after a long trip, this local drive-in burger chain also has locations in Wallingford, Queen Anne, and Lake City. Dick's Deluxe Burger ($1.60), and a good shake ($1.10). Open daily 10:30am-2am.

Hamburger Mary's, 401 Broadway E (325-6565), in the ritzy Broadway Market. Rockin' and racin' with the Broadway Ave. step, this branch outlet of Portland's famous H.M. is a hot-spot for the gay community. Nightly specials offer less meaty options than the obvious fare. Hamburgers around $5. Entrees under $12. Open Mon.-Fri. 10am-2am, Sat.-Sun. 9am-2am.

Cafe Paradiso, 1005 E. Pike (322-6960). A bit off the geographical beaten-path, this proud-to-be-alternative cafe gives you your RDA of both caffeine and counter-culture. Open Mon.-Thurs. 6am-1am, Fri. 6am-4am, Sat. 8am-4am, Sun. 8am-1am.

The Cause Célèbre, 524 15th Ave. E (323-1888), at Mercer St. The special province of Seattle's well-fed left. Stay away if you don't like alternative music or discussions on Serbian atrocities. *Al fresco* dining on the spacious porch. Extensive vegetarian selection; try the eggplant parmigiana ($5). Great Sun. brunch ($4-6). Lunch sandwiches ($4-5). Open Mon.-Sat. 9am-9pm, Sun. 9am-5pm.

Rocket Pizza, 612 Broadway Ave. E (329-4405). A slice here will set you back $1.35, but the prime location for people-watching makes this a popular hang-out from within and without. Open Mon.-Sat. 11am-11pm, Sun. noon-10pm.

Deluxe Bar and Grill, 625 Broadway E (324-9697). An indoor/outdoor joint where you can enjoy great breakfasts for under $6. Watch out for the ravenous "potato crowd." The humongous spuds have been a favorite here since the 1930's. Grill open Sun.-Thurs. 11am-midnight, Fri. 11am-1am, Sat. 10am-1am. Bar open Mon.-Wed. 10am-1am, Thurs.-Fri. 10am-2am, Sat.-Sun. 9am-2am.

Siam, 616 Broadway E. (324-0892). The interior may lack the old world atmosphere of Thai Garden but the food is equally good and less expensive. Did you know that *pad thai* ($5.25) translates from the Thai as "Delicious Thai food which every Thai restaurant everywhere shall sell..."? Open Mon.-Thurs. 11:30am-10pm, Fri. 11:30am-11pm, Sat. 5-11pm, Sun. 5-10pm.

Hana Japanese Restaurant, 219 Broadway Ave. E (328-1187). This small and elegant spot gets packed early with sushi fanatics out for the $1-per-plate deal. Open Mon.-Sat. 11am-11pm, Sun. 4-10pm.

Matzoh Mamma's, 509 15th E (324-MAMA or -6262), at 15th and Republican. Kosher-style (not *glatt* kosher) deli and restaurant. Try the chicken soup ($2.75) or the *Nudnik* sandwich ($7 for a triple-decker). Eat, eat, eat—you're looking *so* thin. Open Mon.-Fri. 8am-9pm, Sat.-Sun. 4-10pm.

Giorgina's Pizza, 131 15th Ave. E (329-8118). Great New York-style pizza, across the street from Group Health. Varied veggie toppings as well as the usual stuff. 13 in. cheese ($7.50), 16 in. ($10). Slices ($1.40) also available upon request. Open Mon.-Fri. 11am-10pm, Sat.-Sun 4-10pm.

Espresso Roma, 202 Broadway Ave. E (324-1866). The pleasant service and propitious placement of this light and airy cafe make it a cut above the plethora of Seattle espresso bars and cafes. Open Mon.-Fri. 7am-midnight, Sat-Sun. 8am-midnight.

Kokeb Restaurant, 926 12th Ave. (322-0485). Behind Seattle University at the far south end of Capitol Hill, near the First Hill neighborhood. One of Seattle's best ethnic restaurants, this Ethiopian eatery serves hot and spicy meat or vegetable stews on spongy *injera* bread. Watch Ethiopian videos while you eat. Entrees $7-11. Open Mon.-Fri. 10:30am-2pm and 5-10pm, Sat.-Sun. 5pm-2am.

University District

The titanic **University of Washington,** set north of downtown between Union and Portage Bays, supports a colorful array of funky shops, ethnic restaurants, and a slew of coffeehouses. Most of the good restaurants, jazz clubs, cinemas, and cafes are within a few blocks of **University Way.** Ask for University Way, however, and be prepared for puzzled looks—it's known around here as **"The Ave"** (one contracted syllable). To reach the University, take any one of buses #70-74 from downtown, or bus #7 or 43 from Capitol Hill.

Last Exit on Brooklyn, 3930 Brooklyn Ave. NE (545-9873), 1 block west of University Way at NE 40th St. The Exit was established in 1967 and never quite left the 60s; aging hippies watch aspiring chessmasters battle it out in a large smoky room. Dirt-cheap espresso (65¢). Try the espresso float ($2) or the cream cheese cupcakes (85¢). Open mike for music Mon. at 9pm. Open Mon.-Tues. 7am-midnight, Wed.-Thurs. 24 hr., Fri. 7am-2am, Sat. 11am-2am, Sun. 11am-midnight.

Morningtown Cafe, 4110 Roos. Way NE (632-6317). Away from the fray behind a dry cleaners. A sunny, non-smoking alternative to the Last Exit that seems to exist in a world of its own—one without additives or preservatives. Blue corn pancakes with organically grown blueberries ($2.75). Healthful serving of black beans and rice with blue corn chips ($3). Open Mon.-Fri. 11:30am-8:45pm, Sat.-Sun. 10am-8:45pm.

Silence-Heart Nest, 5247 University Way NE (524-4008). Vegetarian and Indian food served up by followers of Sri Chinmoy. Try *calananda* (described as an East Indian calzone) or the Bliss-Burger ($4.75 for either). Open Mon.-Tues., Thurs. 11am-9pm; Wed. 11am-3pm; Fri.-Sat. 11am-9pm.

Asia Deli, 4235 University Way NE (632-2364). No corned beef here—this atypical deli offers quick service and generous portions of delicious Vietnamese and Thai food (mostly of the noodle persuasion). Try the sauteed chicken and onions ($3.75). Almost all the dishes are under $4 and all are prepared without MSG. Open Mon.-Sat. 11am-10pm, Sun. noon-9pm.

Grand Illusion Cinema and Espresso, 1405 50th St. NE (525-9573), at University Way. Relaxing coffeehouse with an overstuffed green couch in front of the working fireplace. Small, beachy wooden terrace and in-house theater (see Entertainment). Hot and cold coffees (75¢-$2.15) to make both Jean and his *père* Auguste proud. Try the whole-wheat cream scone (70¢). Open Mon.-Thurs. 8:30am-11pm, Fri.-Sat. 8:30am-11:30pm, Sun. 8:30am-10:30pm.

Tandoor Restaurant, 5024 University Way (523-7477). Their all-you-can-eat lunch buffet ($4) is a *superfind!* Open Mon.-Fri. 11am-2:30pm and 4:30-10pm, Sat.-Sun. 11am-10:30pm.

Pizzeria Pagliacci, 4529 University Way NE (632-0421). Voted Seattle's best pizza, at $1.15 a slice it's also one of the city's best values. Open Mon.-Thurs. and Sun. 11am-11pm, Fri.-Sat. 11am-1am.

Dankens, 4507 University Way NE (545-8596). Known nationally for their "Chocolate Decadence" ice cream (made in the store) and for their infamous "Seattle Sludge." Get a 2-for-1 special by showing the scoopers a picture of your parents, or try your luck at Trivial Pursuit. During happy hour every afternoon (5-7pm), one scoop is $1. (Normally $1.45 per scoop.) Open Mon.-Thurs. 11am-11pm, Fri.-Sat. 11am-midnight, Sun. noon-10pm.

Espresso Roma Cafe, 4201 University Way NE (632-6000). Its selling point is its location in the heart of "The Ave." Muffins ($1.30). Open Mon.-Fri. 7am-11pm, Sat. 8am-11pm, Sun. 9am-11pm.

Ezell's, 4216 University Way NE (548-1455). Possibly the best fried chicken outside the deep South. Order the spicy version of the snack pack (one piece, fries, and a roll) for $3.32. Ezell's poundcake ($1.03 a slice) and other scrumptious desserts are impossible to pass up. (Oprah Winfrey broke her famous diet—yeah, that one—here, when she couldn't resist them.) The original Ezell's (501 23rd, across from Garfield High School) is in the Central District. Open Mon.-Sat. 10am-10pm, Sun. 11am-10pm.

The Unicorn Restaurant, 4550 University Way (634-1115). In contrast to the macrobiotic atmosphere of the rest of the University District, this place is renowned for its large collection of obscure English ales ($2.50-3). The most popular is the highly intoxicating Welsh Ale or Mad Man's Mash. The Unicorn also cooks up a mean steak-and-kidney pie ($7). Their afternoon special, a snack and a draft ($5), is sold all day long. Open daily 11:30am-10pm.

Other Neighborhoods

The Dog House, 2230 7th Ave. (624-2741), 3 blocks north of Greyhound between Bell and Blanchard St. This 24-hr. Seattle favorite is perfect for the night you arrive in the city via Greyhound with no place to go. The waitresses will call you "honey," and Dick Dickerson will serenade you on the electric organ (Fri.-Sat.

9pm-1:30am). Although the diner caters almost exclusively to locals, prices run on the high side. Try the Mutt Burger ($3.75). Full bar open Mon.-Thurs. 8am-midnight, Fri.-Sat. 8am-2am, Sun. 10am-10pm. Restaurant open 24 hr., 365 days a yr.

Burk's Cafe-Creole and Cajun, 5411 Ballard Ave. (782-0091). A relaxed Creole cafe. Lunch sandwiches reasonably priced at $5, dinners $7-11. Try the crawfish with *remoulade* sauce ($5). A bowl of pickled okra sits on every table. Open Tues.-Sat. 11am-10pm.

Spud, 6860 E. Greenlake Way N. (524-0565), across the lake from Greenlake Jake's. Serving the Seattle staple of fish and chips ($2.60) for 51 years—but don't worry, they're made fresh daily. Clams and chips ($2.90). Open daily 11am-10pm. Also located in West Seattle right on the beach at Alki. 266 Alki SW (938-0606).

Zesto's Burger and Fish House, 6416 15th NW (783-3350). This Ballard High hangout has been serving students and frying fish since 1952, and even local fishermen rave about Zesto's "oriental-style" batter. Filling fish and chips dinners run $6.25, and the distinctive "snowshoe" fries make the deal a good one. Good burgers ($2.20-3.10), too. Open Mon.-Thurs. 9:30am-10pm, Fri. 9:30am-11pm, Sat.-Sun. 11am-11pm.

Greenlake Jake's, 7918 E. Greenlake Dr. N. (523-4747), on the north shore of Green Lake. Great breakfasts: 2 blueberry muffins ($1.70). Large lunches with salads $6-7. Open daily 7am-9pm.

Honey Bear, 2106 North 55th (545-7296). *The* best cinnamon rolls in town ($1.60). Green Lake exercisers come here to refuel. Dinners are simple soup-and-pizza style (around $3). Open 6am-11pm daily.

Julia's 14 Carrot Cafe, 2305 Eastlake E. (324-1442), between Lake Union and I-5 at Lynn St. Only Julia's could make edible nut burgers which don't crumble, dry up, or stick in the back of your throat ($3.50). Great baked goods, too. Open Mon.-Fri. 7am-3pm, Sat.-Sun. 7am-4pm.

SIGHTS AND ACTIVITIES

If you are a latter-day Phineas Fogg with only a day to spare in Seattle, despair not— just *don't* pack up and head for the Space Needle. The best way to take in the city skyline (including the Space Needle) is from any one of the **ferries** that leave from the waterfront at frequent intervals. The finest view of Seattle, however, is a bit of a secret, not to mention an exclusively female privilege. The athletic club on the top floor of the **Columbia Tower** (the big black building at 201 5th Ave.) has floor-to-ceiling windows in the ladies room, which look out over the entire city and its surroundings.

It takes only two frenetic days to get a closer look at most of the city sights, as most are within walking distance of one another or are within Metro's Free Zone (see Getting Around above). Just be sure not to ignore the more relaxing natural sights. Take a rowboat out on Lake Union, bicycle along Lake Washington or hike through the wilds of Discovery Park.

Downtown

The new **Seattle Art Museum,** 100 University Way (654-3100), near 1st and University Way, boasts a stunning design by Philadelphia architect Robert Venturi. Don't forget there's art *inside* the building, too. Call for current information on films and lectures. (Free tours Tues.-Sat. 2pm, Sun. 1pm, Thurs. 7pm; special exhibitions 30 min. later. Museum open Tues.-Sat. 10am-5pm, Thurs. 10am-9pm, Sun. noon-5pm. Admission $5, senior citizens and students $3. Free on the first Tues. of every month.) One block north of the museum on 1st Ave., inside the Alcade Plaza Building, is the **Seattle Art Museum Gallery** which features current art, sculpture, jewelry, and prints by hot local artists. Come browse for free.

Westlake Park, with its Art Deco brick patterns and Wall of Water, is a good place to kick back and listen to steel drums. This small triangular park, on Pike St. between 5th and 4th Ave., is bordered by the original **Nordstrom's** and the gleaming new **Westlake Center.** Nordstrom's is an upscale department store which emphasizes superlative customer service. (Travelers toting *Let's Go* may find **Nord-strom's Rack,** at 2nd and Pine, more appealing.)

Many of the business-district high-rises warrant a closer look. **The Pacific First Centre** at 5th and Pike displays a breathtaking collection of glass art commissioned from the prestigious Pilchuk School. Other notable buildings include the **Washing-ton Mutual Tower** on 3rd Ave. and the complex of buildings around 6th and Union.

Bristling with excitement and only a short walk down Pike St. is the **Pike Place Market,** a public market frequented by tourists and natives in equal proportions. (See Pike Place Market in the Food section.)

The Waterfront District

The **Pike Place Hillclimb** descends from the south end of the Pike Place market down a set of staircases, leading past more chic shops and ethnic restaurants to Alas-kan Way and the **waterfront.** (An elevator is also available.) The **Seattle Aquarium** (386-4320) sits at the base of the Hillclimb at Pier 59, near Union St. Outdoor tanks re-create the ecosystems of salt marshes and tidal pools, employing marine birds and mammals as well as members of the finny tribe. The aquarium's star attraction—the underwater dome featuring the fish of the Puget Sound—is alone worth the admis-sion price. Don't miss the daily 11:30am feeding. (Open daily 10am-5pm. Admission $6.50, senior citizens $5, ages 6-18 $4, ages 3-5 $1.50.)

Next to the Aquarium is **Omnidome** (622-1868). The only good thing about this large wrap-around movie screen is that you get to watch two movies for the price of one. The theater and the screen are of marginal quality, and neither film shown uses the Omnidome format particularly well. *The Eruption of Mt. St. Helens* offers strik-ing photography but little else. (Films shown daily 10am-8pm. Tickets to 2 movies $6, senior citizens and students $5, ages 3-12 $4; with admission to aquarium $10.75, senior citizens and ages 13-18 $6.75, ages 6-12 $5.75.) You might want to save money and see the IMAX at the Pacific Science Center instead (see below).

Pier 59 and the aquarium sit smack in the middle of the waterfront district. Explore north or south by foot or by **streetcar.** The circa-1927 cars were imported from Melbourne, Australia in 1982 because Seattle had sold its original streetcars to San Francisco, where they now enjoy international fame as cable cars. (Streetcars run every 20 min. Mon.-Sat. 7am-11pm, Sun. 10:15am-9:45pm; in winter every ½ hr. until 6pm. 60¢ for 1½ hr. of unlimited travel. Metro passes are good on the streetcar. On Sun., children under 16 ride free if accompanied by 1 paying passenger.)

North of Pier 70's pricey shopping arcade, **Myrtle Edwards Park** stretches along the water to the granaries on Piers 90 and 91. Despite lovely grassy areas and equally good views, Myrtle Edwards affords more seclusion than other downtown parks.

South of the aquarium, two companies offer tours of the **Elliott Bay Harbor.** Again, a **ferry** ride is the best and cheapest option for exploring Puget Sound. The Youth Hostel offers discount tickets for some of the tours, but even the discount doesn't knock the wind out of the heavy-weight prices. An exception is **Tillicum Tours,** off Pier 56 (443-1244), which actually docks on Blake Island so that you can explore Tillicum Village, in the Native American reservation. They have a package that includes a salmon dinner and a "rare presentation" of Native dance. The best part of all is that the hostel offers an $11 discount. Two four-hour trips sail per day ($40 without the discount, senior citizens $38, teens $26, children $16).

Among the many tourist shops along the waterfront, **Ye Olde Curiosity Shop** on Pier 54 deserves note. Founded in 1899, this locally famous museum-*cum*-store dis-plays such items as the dehydrated body of "Sylvester" and Siamese twin calves.

Colman Dock, Pier 52, is now the departure point for the **Washington State Ferry** to Bremerton and Bainbridge Island (see Getting There above). Even if you're on the road to nowhere and simply come straight back, taking a ferry to Bremerton or Winslow (on Bainbridge Island) is a glorious way to see Seattle. Round-trip fare is $3.30 for a pedestrian, $6.65 for a car and driver ($5.55 in winter). The dock has gone through a number of incarnations and was at one time the home base of the

Mosquito Fleet. Today, Colman Dock forms a pale and uninspiring comparison to its past. Those addicted to dock-history should pick up a free copy of the *Historic Old Colman Dock* pamphlet inside the terminal.

The Seattle Center

Take the **monorail** (75¢) from the third floor of the Westlake Center to **Seattle Center.** The 74-acre, pedestrians-only park was originally constructed for the 1962 World's Fair and still attracts plenty of perusers daily. Located between Denny Way and W. Mercer St., and 1st and 5th Ave., the Center has eight gates, each equipped with a model of the Center and a map of its facilities. The **Pacific Science Center** (443-2001), within the park, houses some of Seattle's most enthralling entertainment: a **laserium** (443-2850) and an **IMAX theater** (443-4629). Evening IMAX shows run Wednesday through Sunday. (Science Center open daily 10am-6pm; Labor Day-June Mon.-Fri. 10am-5pm, Sat.-Sun. 10am-6pm. Admission $5.50, senior citizens and ages 6-13 $4.50, ages 2-5 $3.50. Laser and IMAX shows are each an additional $1. A ticket to the IMAX show without museum admission costs $4.50, senior citizens and ages 6-13 $3.50, ages 2-5 $2.50.) The evening laser shows quake to music by groups like U2, Genesis, and Led Zeppelin (shown Tues.-Sun.; $5.50). Don't miss the Tuesday evening laser-show special for only $2.50.

The **Space Needle** (443-2100), sometimes known as "the world's tackiest monument," has an observation tower and restaurant. On clear days, the view from atop is without peer; on cloudy days, forget it. (Observation Deck open daily 8am-midnight. Admission $6, senior citizens $5, ages 5-12 $4.)

Although Seattlites generally disdain the Center (leaving it to tourists and suburbanites), it is the home of the renowned **Pacific Northwest Ballet Company,** the **Opera,** and the **Seattle Symphony** (see the Entertainment: Music and Dance section below). Locals lower their noses and turn out in numbers for its frequent performances, special exhibits, and festivals. For information regarding special events and permanent attractions at the Center, call 684-8582 or 684-7200. The Center has an **information desk** (625-4234) on the court level in the Center House (open daily 1-4pm). The visitors bureau also runs another **information booth** (447-4244) next to the monorail terminal (open Memorial Day-Labor Day daily 10am-6pm). See Seasonal Events, below, for information on the ever-popular **Seafair, Folklife Festival,** and the **Bite of Seattle,** all held annually at the Center. Over Labor Day weekend, Seattlites prove their partygoing endurance at the four-day **Bumbershoot,** a festival of folk, street, classical, and rock music. Free concerts are also held during the summer at the **Seattle Center Mural Amphitheater** and feature a variety of local rock bands. Check the "Tempo" section of the *Seattle Times* for listings.

Pioneer Square and Environs

From the waterfront, it's just two blocks to historic Pioneer Square, where 19th-century warehouses and office buildings were restored in a fit of prosperity during the 70s. The *Complete Browser's Guide to Pioneer Square,* available in area bookstores, includes a short history and walking tour of the area, in addition to listings of all the shops, galleries, restaurants, and museums in the square. After an aborted attempt by pioneers to claim the land on Alki Beach (now West Seattle) in 1851, the earliest Seattlites set up camp instead on the site which is today Pioneer Square; this area became Seattle's first city center. "Doc" Maynard, a notorious early resident, gave a plot of land here to one Henry Yesler on the condition that he build a steam-powered lumber mill. No sooner said than done, the mill was fed with logs dragged down the steep grade of Yesler Way, earning that street the epithet **"Skid Row."** Years later, the center of activity moved north, precipitating the decline of Pioneer Square and giving the term "skid row" its present meaning as a neighborhood of poverty and despair.

When Seattle nearly burned to the ground in 1889, an ordinance was passed to raise the city 35 ft. At first, shops below the new elevated streets remained open for business and were connected to the upper city by an elaborate network of ladders. In 1907 the city moved upstairs permanently, and the underground city was sealed off. Tours of the vast underworld are now given by **Bill Speidel's Underground Tours** (682-4646). Speidel spearheaded the movement to save Pioneer Square from urban renewal, and his company's tours are informative, irreverent glimpses at Seattle's origins; just ignore the rats that infest the tunnels. Tours (which last 1½ hr.) leave from Doc Maynard's Pub at 610 1st Ave. (6-8 per day, 10am-6pm). Reservations should be made at least one day in advance. (Office open daily 9:30am-4pm. Admission $5.50, senior citizens $4.50, students 13-17 or with college ID $4, ages 6-12 $2.25.)

Once back above ground, learn about the next major event in the city's historical chronology at the **Klondike Gold Rush National Historic Park,** 117 S. Main St. (553-7220). Not really a park, this "interpretive center" depicts the lives and fortunes of miners. A slide show weaves together seven photographers' recordings of the miners' mostly unsuccessful ventures. To add some levity to this history of shattered dreams, the park screens Charlie Chaplin's 1925 classic, *The Gold Rush,* on the first Sunday of every month at 3pm (open daily 9am-5pm; free).

While in Pioneer Square, browse through the numerous local art galleries, which distribute for many of the Northwest's prominent artists. The first Thursday evening of each month, the art community sponsors **First Thursday,** a well-dressed and well-attended gallery walk. A few of the Square's notable galleries are **Flury and Co. Gallery,** 322 1st Ave. S. (587-0260), which features vintage photographic portraits of Native American life (open Mon.-Sat. 10am-6pm, Sun. noon-5pm); **Linda Farris Gallery,** 322 2nd Ave. S. (623-1110), which promotes innovative Seattle artists (open Tues.-Sat. 11:30am-5pm, Sun. 1-5pm); **Native Design Gallery,** 108 Jackson St. (624-9985), housing imported art from Africa, South America, and India (open Tues.-Sat. 11am-5pm); and **Sacred Circle Gallery,** 607 1st Ave. (285-4425), guardian of an acclaimed collection of contemporary Native American art (open Wed.-Sat. 10am-5pm, Sun. noon-5pm). Stop in also at the **Seattle Indian Arts and Crafts Shop,** 113 Cherry St. (621-0655), run by the American Indian Women's Service League. A non-profit business, the shop features Native American art of the Pacific Northwest. Proceeds benefit the local Native American community (open Mon.-Fri. 10am-5pm, Sat. 11am-4pm). For a different twist on American art, visit **Animation USA, Inc.,** 104 1st St. (625-0347), Mickey's favorite gallery. Tours of **In Public: 1991**—a project for which the Seattle Arts Commission hired 37 artists and spent $567,000 in public arts funds—leave from the Convention Center (Visitors Info.) at noon ($5). Another important landmark of the Pioneer Square area is the **Smith Tower,** for many years the tallest building west of the Mississippi. The 21-story tower was commissioned in 1911 by L. C. Smith at a cost of $1,500,000, and was later owned by local celebrity and fish-and-ships mogul Ivar Haglund.

Many Seattlites consider the **Kingdome,** 201 S. King St. (340-2100 or 340-2128), down 1st Ave., the only serious challenger to the Boeing factory for the distinction of being the city's ugliest building. Nonetheless, with the excitement of the **Seattle Mariners** running the bases and the **Seattle Seahawks** tearing up the gridiron, fans manage to ignore the architecture under the world's largest self-supporting concrete roof. For a schedule, call 800-950-FANS. Tickets for Mariners games start at $4.50 (206-628-0888). Sunday is senior citizens discount day. If you prefer to skip the game and just take in the wonder of an indoor stadium, tours of the stadium include a stop at the **Royal Brougham Sports Museum.** (Tours leave daily from Gate D on the north side of the dome at 11am, 1, and 3pm; April-Sept. at 1pm only. Otherwise, stadium only open during sporting events. Museum admission $3, senior citizens and children $1.50.)

The International District

Three blocks east of Pioneer Square, up Jackson on King St., is Seattle's International District. Though sometimes still called Chinatown by Seattlites, this area is now home to immigrants from all over Asia, and their descendants. The **Nippon Kan Theater,** 628 Washington St. (624-2151), built in 1909 to house weddings and cultural events, is a good place to start your tour of the district.

Other landmarks of the International District include the **Tsutakawa sculpture** at the corner of S. Jackson and Maynard St. and the gigantic dragon mural in **Hing Hay Park** at S. King and Maynard St. The community gardens at Main and Maynard St. provide a peaceful and well-tended retreat from the downtown sidewalks. Duck into the **Wing Luke Memorial Museum,** 414 8th St. (623-5124). This tiny museum houses a permanent exhibit on the different Asian groups which have settled in Seattle as well as temporary exhibits by local Asian artists, such as sculptor George Tsutakawa. There are occasional free demonstrations of traditional crafts. Thursdays are always free. (Open Tues.-Fri. 11am-4:30pm, Sat.-Sun. noon-4pm. Admission $2.50, senior citizens and students $1.50, ages 5-12 75¢.)

Capitol Hill

Capitol Hill inspires extreme reactions from both its residents and its neighbors. In any case, the former wouldn't live anywhere else. The district's leftist and gay communities set the tone for its nightspots (see Entertainment below), while the retail outlets include a large number of collectives and radical bookstores. The numerous coffee shops and restaurants (see Food: Capitol Hill above) offer the best sites for people-watching. You can also saunter down Broadway or its cross streets to window-shop, or walk a few blocks east and north for a stroll down the hill's pretty residential streets, lined with well-maintained Victorian homes. Bus #10 runs along 15th St. and #7 cruises along Broadway.

Volunteer Park, between 11th and 17th Ave. at E. Ward St., north of the main Broadway activity, welcomes tourists away from the city center. Named for the "brave volunteers who gave their lives to liberate the oppressed people of Cuba and the Philippines" during the Spanish-American War, the park boasts lovely lawns and an outdoor running track. Be aware, however, that the park has an unsavory reputation after dark. Climb the water tower at the 14th Ave. entrance for a stunning 360° panorama of the city and the Olympic Range. The views rival those from the Space Needle, and what's more, they're free. On rainy days, hide out amid the orchids inside the glass conservatory (free).

The **University of Washington Arboretum** (543-8800), 10 blocks east of Volunteer Park, has superb cycling and running trails, including Lake Washington Blvd., a smooth bicycling road which runs the length of the arboretum from north to south and then continues along the western shore of Lake Washington as far south as Seward Park. The Arboretum boasts 4000 species of trees and shrubs and 43 species of flowers, making for an Edenesque stroll. A tranquil **Japanese Garden** (684-4725) is located in the southern end of the arboretum at E. Helen St. Take bus #11 from downtown. The nine acres of sculpted gardens encompass fruit trees, a reflecting pool, and a traditional tea house. (Park open March-Nov. daily 10am-8pm. Arboretum open daily dawn to dusk. Greenhouse open Mon.-Fri. 10am-4pm. Admission $2; senior citizens, people with disabilities, and under 19 $1.)

University District

With 33,000 students, the **University of Washington** is the state's cultural and educational center of gravity. The "U District" swarms with students year-round, and Seattlites of other occupations take advantage of the area's many bookstores, shops, taverns, and restaurants. Stop by the friendly and helpful **visitors center,** 4014 University Way NE (543-9198), to pick up a map of the campus and to obtain information about the University (open Mon.-Fri. 8am-5pm).

On the campus, visit the **Thomas Burke Memorial Washington State Museum** (543-5590), at NE 45th St. and 17th Ave. NE, in the northwest corner of the campus. The museum houses artifacts of the Pacific Northwest's Native American tribes. The scrimshaw displays especially will be inscribed in your memory. (Open daily 10am-

5pm, Thurs. until 8pm. A donation of $2.50 for adults and $1.50 for senior citizens and students is requested.) The astronomy department's **observatory** (543-0126) is open to the public for viewings on clear nights. The grounds and gardens of the University are a popular and beautiful place to stroll, and the campus' enormous **Red Square** serves as a great meeting place and relaxation area.

The **Henry Art Gallery,** 15th Ave. NE and NE 41st St. (543-2280), has excellent exhibits. Stop in before you stroll the campus lawns. (Open Tues.-Wed. and Fri.-Sun. 10am-5pm, Thurs. 10am-9pm. Admission $3, senior citizens and students $1.50; free Thurs.) The **UW Arts Ticket Office,** 4001 University Way NE (543-4880), has information and tickets for all events (open Mon.-Fri. 10:30am-4:30pm). To reach the U-District, take buses #71-74 from downtown, or #7, 43, or 48 from Capitol Hill.

Students often descend to the waterfront area for drinks by the bridges to Queen Anne (see Entertainment below), and the area of **Freemont** seems to have gone haywire under the influence of this jovial atmosphere. A statue entitled "Waiting for the Inner-city Urban" depicts several people waiting in bus-purgatory and is frequently dressed up in moments of inspiration and sympathy by passers-by. Another interesting comment on civilization is the statue of a large, mean **troll** who sits beneath the Freemont Bridge (on 35th St.) grasping a Volkswagen Bug (recently covered in cement to prevent vandalism). Freemont is also the home of **Archie McPhee's,** 3510 Stone Way (545-8344), a shrine to popular culture and plastic absurdity. People of the punk and funk persuasion make pilgrimages from as far as the record stores of Greenwich Village in Manhattan just to handle the notorious **slug selection.** You can get to Archie's on the Aurora Hwy. (Rte. 99), or take bus #26. The store is east of the Hwy. between 35th and 36th, 2 blocks north of Lake Union (open Mon.-Fri. 10am-6pm, Sat. 10am-5pm).

Waterways and Parks

A string of attractions festoon the waterways linking Lake Washington and Puget Sound. Houseboats and sailboats fill **Lake Union.** Here, the **Center for Wooden Boats,** 1010 Valley St. (382-2628), maintains a moored flotilla of new and restored small craft for rental (rowboats $8-12 per hr., sailboats $10-15 per hr.; open daily 11am-6pm). **Kelly's Landing,** 1401 NE Boat St. (547-9909), below the UW campus, rents canoes for outings on Lake Union. (Sailboats $10-20 per hr., also day rates. 2-hr. min. Hours determined by weather, but normally Mon.-Fri. 10am-dusk, Sat.-Sun. 9am-dusk.) **Gasworks Park,** a much-celebrated kite-flying spot at the north end of Lake Union, was reopened a few years ago by the EPA after being shut for a time due to an excess of toxins. Don't be daunted by the climb up a large hill. At the top is a gorgeous view and an "interactive sundial," in which your body acts as the pointer. **Gasworks Kite Shop,** 1915 N. 34th St. (633-4780), is 1 block north of the park. (Kite shop open Mon.-Fri. 10am-6pm, Sat. 10am-5pm, Sun. noon-5pm. Park open dawn-dusk.) To reach the park, take bus #26 from downtown to N. 35th St. and Wallingford Ave. N. The popular **Burke-Gilman Trail** runs from Latona St. at NE Northlake, just next to the Washington Ship Canal Bridge and I-5, through the university, past Sand Point and Magnuson Park, north to NE 145th.

Farther west, the **Hiram M. Chittenden Locks** (783-7001) draw good-sized crowds to watch Seattle's boat lovers jockeying for position in the locks. A circus atmosphere develops at peak hours, as all the boats traveling between Puget Sound and Lake Washington try to cross over (viewing hrs. daily 7am-9pm). If listening to the cries of frustrated skippers ("Gilligan, you nitwit!") doesn't amuse you, climb over to the **fish ladder** on the south side of the locks to watch trout and salmon hurl themselves over 21 concrete steps on their journey from the sea. Take bus #43 from the U District or #17 from downtown. The busiest salmon runs occur from June to November; steelhead trout run in the winter, cutthroat trout run in the fall. Afterwards, you can listen to summertime lectures held in the **visitors center** (783-7059) on Tuesdays at 7:30pm. The U.S. Army Corps of Engineers gives talks with captivating titles like "The Corps Cares About Fish" and "A Beaver in Your Backyard?" (Visitors center open daily 11am-8pm; Sept. 16-June 14 Thurs.-Mon. 11am-5pm.)

Farther north, on the northwestern shore of the city, lies the **Golden Gardens Park,** in the Loyal Heights neighborhood, between NW 80th and NW 95th. A small boat ramp lies at the southern end, which is an ideal spot for a picnic, especially as the sun sets over Shilshole Bay. Several expensive restaurants line the piers to the south, and unobstructed views of the Olympic Mountains almost justify the prices of their uniformly excellent seafood.

Directly north of Lake Union, exercisers run, roller skate, and skateboard around **Green Lake.** Take bus #16 from downtown Seattle to Green Lake. The lake is also given high marks by windsurfers, but woe to those who lose their balance. Whoever named Green Lake wasn't kidding; even a quick dunk results in gobs of green algae clinging to your body and hair. A more pleasant way to experience the lake is by renting a boat from **Green Lake Rentals** (527-0171) on the eastern side of the lake (sailboards $12 per hr., pedalboats, canoes, and kayaks $7 per hr., rowboats $6 per hr.). But watch out: on sunny afternoons the boat renters, the windsurfers, and energetic scullers can make the lake feel more like rush hour on I-5. Next to the lake is Woodland Park and the **Woodland Park Zoo,** 5500 Phinney Ave. N. (684-4034), best reached from Rte. 99 or N. 50th St. Take bus #5 from downtown. The park itself is a bit shaggy, but this makes the animals' habitats seem all the more realistic. The African Savannah and Gorilla Houses reproduce the wilds, while the Nocturnal House reveals what really goes on when the lights go out. The newly opened **elephant habitat** has enhanced the zoo's international reputation for creating natural settings. It's one of only three zoos in the U.S. to receive the Humane Society's highest standard of approval. (Open daily 9:30am-6pm; in winter, closing time depends on day length. Admission $6, ages 6-17, senior citizens, and people with disabilities $3.50, ages 3-5 $1.50.)

A number of other worthwhile parks and attractions are spattered across the city. **Discovery Park,** on a lonely point west of the Magnolia District and south of Golden Gardens Park, at 36th Ave. W. and Government Way W., is comprised of acres of minimally tended grassy fields and steep bluffs atop Puget Sound. Take bus #24. At the park's northern end is the **Indian Cultural Center** (285-4425), operated by the United Indians of All Tribes Foundation. (Open Wed.-Fri. 8:30am-5pm, Sat.-Sun. 10am-5pm. Free.)

Seward Park (723-5780) is the southern endpoint of a string of beaches and forest preserves along the western shore of Lake Washington. Take bus #39. The park has a number of beaches, wooded areas, and walking and biking trails, as well as a fishing pier, picnic shelters, tennis courts, and an arts center. After exercising in the park, refresh yourself with a tour of the **Rainier Brewery Co.,** 3100 Airport Way S. (622-2600), off I-5 at the West Seattle Bridge. Take bus #123. Attentiveness is rewarded with complimentary beer (root beer for those under 21) and cheese and crackers (tours Mon.-Fri. 1-6pm; free).

Directly to the west is **Alki Beach Park,** a thin strip of beach wrapped around residential West Seattle. Take bus #36. The water is chilling, but the view of downtown Seattle in one direction and of the Olympics in the other will warm your bones. The Coast Guard's **Alki Point Lighthouse,** 3201 Alki Ave. SW (932-5800), is open for tours (Sat.-Sun. noon-4pm, Mon.-Thurs. by appointment only; call one day in advance). The first white settlers of Seattle set up camp here in 1851, naming their new home New York Alki. By the time the settlement moved to Pioneer Square, parvenu Doc Maynard suggested that perhaps "New York By and By" was too deferential a name and that the city should be named for his Native American friend Chief Sealth. Because Sealth's tribe did not believe in pronouncing the names of the deceased, the city's name was later changed to "Seattle." A monument to the city's birthplace is located along Alki Beach at 63rd Ave. SW, south of Alki. Just south of **Lincoln Park,** along Fauntleroy Way in the Fauntleroy section of the city, is the departure point for **ferries** to Vashon Island (see Vashon Island, below). Take bus

#18 to Lincoln Park. The park has a number of playing fields, tennis courts, picnic tables, swimming beaches, bicycling trails, and the Colman Pool, open only during the summer.

SPORTS AND RECREATION

Seattle parks are a never-ending outdoor carnival of running and cycling trails, tennis courts, and playing fields. There are more than 200 road races each summer in the Northwest. Pick up a copy of the pamphlet *Your Seattle Parks and Recreation Guide,* available at the visitors bureau or the Parks Department (see Practical Information), or the monthly *Sports Northwest,* available at most area sports outfitters (free). The paper includes calendars of competitive events in the Northwest, as well as book reviews, and recreation suggestions.

Road bicyclists should gear up for the 192-mi., 1600-competitor **Seattle to Portland Race.** Call the **bike hotline** (522-2453) for more information. The Seattle Parks Department also holds a monthly **Bicycle Sunday** from May to September, when Lake Washington Blvd. is open only to cyclists from 10am to 5pm. Contact the Parks Department's Citywide Sports Office (684-7092) for more information. Dear to the heart of many Seattle speed-cyclists is **Marymoor Velodrome** (282-8356), in Redmond off Rte. 520 at the Rte. 901 exit. The velodrome is open to the public when not in use for competition and offers classes on the ways of the track. Pack a picnic supper and sit on the lawn to watch the sweaty races, sponsored by the Washington State Bicycling Association from May through August on Friday nights at 7:30pm. All the buses that cross Lake Washington have bike racks—call Metro (447-4800) for more information.

Whitewater river rafting has become extremely popular in Washington in the last fifteen years. While the rapids all lie at least two hours from Seattle by car, many outfitters are based in the Seattle area. River running is currently unregulated, and over 50 companies compete for a growing market. The best way to secure an inexpensive trip is to call a number of outfitters and quote competitors' prices at them; they are often willing to undercut one another. Scour the "Guides" section in the Yellow Pages. In recent years rafting companies have attempted to subject themselves to a regulatory bureaucracy of their own making, **River Outfitters of Washington (ROW)** (485-1427), which sets safety guidelines for its members. Even if your outfitter does not belong to ROW, be sure it lives up to ROW's basic safety standards, succinctly summed up as follows: under no circumstances should a single raft navigate a river unaccompanied; guides should possess basic water and safety skills and should have been trained at least twice on each river that they run commercially; all guides should have Standard First Aid and CPR certification; and all rafts should be rigged with bail buckets, throw lines, and extra paddles. Some of the larger companies have on-shore support staff at all times. Don't hesitate to spend the extra dollars to ensure the highest level of safety. Private boaters should remember that whitewater is unpredictable and potentially dangerous; *always* scout out new rivers before running them. ROW has a list of tips for private boaters, and outfitters can give you the scoop on navigable Washington rivers.

The **Northwest Outdoor Center,** 2100 Westlake Ave. (281-9694), on Lake Union, holds a number of instructional programs in whitewater and sea kayaking during the spring, summer, and fall. (2-evening introduction to sea kayaking $40 if you have your own boat. Equipment rentals available.) The center also leads a number of excursions—sea kayaking through the San Juan Islands or backpacking and paddling through the North Cascades (open Mon.-Fri. 10am-8pm, Sat.-Sun. 10am-6pm).

With the glorious Mt. Rainier ever present on the horizon and all that powder just a few hours from downtown Seattle, it's no surprise that natives and visitors alike go ski-crazy in the winter. **Alpental**, **Ski-Acres,** and **Snoqualmie** have lumped themselves together for an information number (232-8182) which can give out conditions and lift ticket rates for all three. **Crystal Mountain** (663-2265), the region's newest resort, can be reached by Rte. 410 south out of Seattle and offers ski rentals, lessons, and lift ticket packages.

Ever since the days of the Klondike rush, Seattle has been one of the foremost cities in the world for outfitting expeditions into the wilds. Besides a host of ordinary army-navy surplus stores and campers' supply shops (try **Federal Army and Navy Surplus,** 2112 1st Ave.; 443-1818), the city is home to many world-class outfitters. **Recreational Equipment Inc. Coop (REI Coop),** 1525 11th Ave. (323-8333), is the favored place to buy high-quality mountaineering and water recreation gear. Take bus #10. For a few dollars you can join the coop and receive a year-end rebate on your purchases. REI has a bulletin board where lone hikers advertise for hiking companions. The company also offers its own backpacking and climbing trips and clinics, in addition to presenting free slide shows and lectures on topics such as trekking through Nepal, bicycling in Ireland, or improving your fly-fishing techniques. Call or stop by the store for a full schedule. (Open Mon.-Tues. 10am-6pm, Sat. 9:30am-6pm, Wed.-Fri. 10am-9pm, Sun. noon-5pm.) **North Face,** 4560 University Way NE (574-6276), also has its headquarters in Seattle, though prices are so steep you'll have to scale them (open Mon.-Fri. 9am-8pm, Sat. 10am-7pm, Sun. noon-5pm).

Some Seattlites do take time out from their own outdoor activities to spectate. Besides the action in the **Kingdome** (see Pioneer Square), there's also pro basketball in town. The Seattle **Supersonics** (281-5800) (known more casually as the "Sonics") is the only Seattle team ever to win a national title, and their basketball games in the Coliseum in Seattle Center attract a religious following. The **University of Washington Huskies** lap up local popularity as well. The football team has been dominant in recent years and always plays to full crowds in Husky Stadium (where some—mostly Seattlites—say the ubiquitous "wave" was invented). They crushed Iowa to win the Rose Bowl in 1991, but in August, 1993, they were suspended from postseason play by the NCAA for recruiting violations. Call the **Athletic Ticket Office** (543-2200) for schedules and price information.

Opening Day (the first Sat. in May) in the University District's Mont Lake Cut, the channel between Lake Washington and Portage Bay, is a big spring rowing event. Crowds flood the banks to watch streams of sailboats (usually dressed up to follow a theme) and, most importantly, to watch the University of Washington crews challenge international competitors in 2000m sprint races. Take the Bellevue exit off I-5.

ENTERTAINMENT

During lunch hours in the summertime, the free, city-sponsored **"Out to Lunch"** series (623-0340) brings everything from reggae to folk dancing to the parks and squares of Seattle. The **Seattle Public Library** (386-4636) shows free films as part of the program and has a daily schedule of other free events, such as poetry readings and children's book-reading competitions. *Events,* published every two months, is a calendar of the library's offerings (available at libraries throughout the city).

Music and Dance

The **Seattle Opera** (443-4700) performs in the Opera House in the Seattle Center throughout the winter. The popularity of the program requires that you order tickets well in advance, although rush tickets are sometimes available 15 minutes before curtain time ($8 and up). Write to the Seattle Opera, P.O. Box 9248, Seattle 98109. The **Seattle Symphony Orchestra** (443-4747), also in Seattle Center's Opera House, performs a regular subscription series from September through June (rush tickets $4 and up) under the talented baton of Gerard Schwarz, as well as special pops and children's series. In recent years, the symphony has played summer series in the gorgeous, renovated **Fifth Avenue Theater.** The **Pacific Northwest Ballet** (547-5900) starts its season at the Opera House in December with the spectacular Maurice Sendak-designed version of the *Nutcracker.* The season continues through May with four or five slated productions (tickets $10 and up). The **University of**

Washington offers its own program of student recitals and concerts by visiting artists. Call the Meany Hall box office (543-4880).

For a truly off-beat but rewarding experience, try a concert at the **Paramount Theatre,** 907 Pine St. (682-1414), where they host everyone who's anyone from Bonnie Raitt to the Butthole Surfers. Ticket prices vary as widely as the performers. Also check out the **Moore Theater,** 1932 2nd Ave. (443-1744), which runs the gamut from punk through pop to hypnotism. Ticket prices vary.

Theater

Devotees of the stage would argue that the best thing about Seattle is its theater, and with good reason. Boasting the second-largest number of professional companies in the U.S., Seattle hosts an exciting array of first-run plays (many eventually move on to New York) and alternative works, particularly in the many talented semi-professional groups. Although touring companies do pass through, they are nowhere near as interesting as the local scene.

You can often get **rush tickets** at nearly half price on the day of the show (with cash only) from **Ticket/Ticket** (324-2744).

Seattle Repertory Theater, 155 Mercer (443-2222), in the wonderful **Bagley Wright Theater** in Seattle Center. Artistic director Daniel Sullivan and the repertory company won the 1990 Tony for Regional Excellence. Their winter season combines contemporary, original, and classic productions (usually including Shakespeare). Recent plays that eventually reached Broadway but got their start at the Rep include *The Heidi Chronicles* and *Fences.* 1994 will include Shakespeare's *Pericles.* Tickets for weekends and opening nights range $16-31.50. Other nights and Sun. Matinee $13.50-29.50. 10 min. before each show a senior and student rate of $7 is available with ID.

A Contemporary Theater (ACT), 100 W. Roy (285-5110), at the base of Queen Anne Hill. A summer season of modern plays, often off-beat premieres. Tickets $12-23.

Annex Theatre, 1916 4th Ave. (728-0933). Refreshing emphasis on company-generated material. New "1-week wonders" are a good bet—they're experimental shows staged between the regular 4-week-long productions. Every Fri. during the summer sees an "Improv. Night" at 11pm for $2, or free with a ticket for the evening show. Regular tickets $7-12.

The Empty Space Theatre, 3509 Fremont Ave. N. (547-7500), 1½ blocks north of the Fremont bridge. It almost folded a few years ago, but this space is not empty yet; the zany comedies rollick onward. Tickets $13-18, preview tickets (first 4 performances) $10.

Intiman Theater at the Playhouse in Seattle Center (626-0782). Their season (May-Dec. 1) usually snags the most talented local actors for a classical repertoire. Tickets $13.50-21.

Bathhouse Theater, 7312 W. Greenlake Dr. N (524-9108). This small company is known for its popular restaging of radio skits and transplanting Shakespeare to unexpected locales (e.g., a Wild West *Macbeth,* Kabuki *King Lear,* and *Midsummer Night's Dream* set in the 50s). Tickets $10-18.

Seattle Group Theatre, 3940 Brooklyn NE (441-1299), next to the Last Exit Restaurant, in the U District. Home to **The Group,** one of Seattle's most innovative small theater ensembles, performing original and avant-garde works. Tickets $11-18, senior citizens half price, students $5.

Alice B. Theater, Broadway Performance Hall (32-ALICE or 25423), at Broadway and Pine. This gay/lesbian theater company keeps getting better. Their witty musicals are sparkling. Tickets $10-14.

New City Theater, 1634 11th Ave. (323-6800), on Capitol Hill. The farthest gone of the alternative theaters, the size and type of their offerings swings wildly. Ticket prices change accordingly.

University of Washington School of Drama Theaters (543-4880 or 543-5986). The 3 UW theaters—the Penthouse, Meany Hall, and Glenn Hughes Playhouse—offer a wide variety of works, from children's shows to classical and contemporary theater. Of particular interest is the free open-air Shakespeare in the summer. Call for information on the wide variety of UW cultural activities. Tickets $22-35.

Taverns and Clubs

One of the joys of living in Seattle is the abundance of community taverns which bypass the traditional focus of imbibing alcohol and scoping, and look instead to providing a relaxed environment for dancing and spending time with friends. In Washington, taverns may serve only beer and wine; a fully-licensed bar or cocktail lounge must adjoin a restaurant. You must be 21 to enter bars and taverns. The Northwest produces a variety of local beers, some sold in area stores but most only on tap in bars. Popular brews include **Grant's, Imperial Russian Stout, India Pale Ale, Red Hook, Ballard Bitter, Black Hook,** and **Yakima Cider.**

The best spot to go for guaranteed good beer, live music, and big crowds is **Pioneer Square.** Most of the bars around the Square participate in a **joint cover** ($10) that will let you wander from bar to bar and sample the bands you like. **Fenix Cafe and Fenix Underground** (343-7740), **Central Tavern** (622-0209), and the **Swan Cafe** (343-5288) all rock and roll consistently, while **Larry's** (624-5288) and **New Orleans** (622-2563) feature great jazz and blues nightly. The **J and M Cafe** (624-1670) is also in the center of Pioneer Square but has no music—only the classic bar hum and click. All the Pioneer Square clubs shut down at 2am Friday and Saturday nights, and at around midnight during the week. Another option is to catch an evening of live **stand-up comedy** in one of Seattle's many comedy clubs, such as Pioneer Square's **Swannie's Comedy Underground,** 222 S. Main St. (628-0303). Tickets are $5 or so; acts are daily at 9 and 11pm.

Red Door Alehouse, 3401 Tremont N (547-7521), at Tremont and 34th Ave. N, across from the Inner-Urban Statue. Throbbing with University students who attest to the good local ale selection. Open daily 11:30am-2am.

The Trolleyman Pub, 3400 Phinney N (548-8000). In the back of the Red Hook Ale Brewery, which rolls the most popular kegs on campus to U of W students. Early hours make it a mellow spot to listen to good acoustic music and contemplate the newly-made bubbles in a fresh pint, especially if it is a pint of Nut Brown Ale. Open Mon.-Fri. 8am-11pm, Sat. 11am-11pm, Sun. noon-6pm.

The Blue Moon, 712 45th NE (545-8190), in the U District. Mellow, inviting atmosphere where ex-hippies converge—even the pool table sports tie-dye. Sun. is Grateful Dead Night, a striking contrast to Mon., when the Moon goes opera. Open daily noon-2am.

Kells, 1916 Post Alley (728-1916), at Pike Place. A raging Irish pub with nightly Irish tunes and a crowd that guarantees good "crack," as the Irish would say. Live music Wed.-Sat. with cover charge Fri.-Sat. only. (Open Wed.-Sat. 8am-2am. $3 cover Fri. and Sat.)

Off Ramp, 109 Eastlake Ave. E (628-0232). One of the most popular venues of the local music scene. Always loud and wild at times. Open 5pm-2am daily. Varied cover.

Under the Rail (448-1900), 5th and Batluy. This newest and largest downtown club offers local music (cover $4-5) and the occasional national tour. DJ and dancing on nights without concerts. Open 9pm-2am daily.

OK Hotel, 212 Alaskan Way (621-7903), just below Pioneer Square towards the waterfront. Lots of wood, lots of coffee. No liquor but great live bands with hot alternative sound. Grab breakfast here and rub elbows with the many local artists who live in the Pioneer Sq. area. Open Sun.-Thurs. 6am-3am, Fri. and Sat. 8am-4am. Occasional cover charge up to $6.

Comet Tavern, 922 E. Pike (323-9853), in the Capitol Hill area. Mixed crowd, no cover—and you can add your tip to the growing sculpture of dollar bills stuck to the ceiling. Open daily noon-2am.

RKCNDY, 1812 Yale Ave. (623-0470). Shares the spotlight with the Off Ramp as the venue of choice for bands peddling the now-classic "Seattle sound." Open 9pm-2am Wed.-Sun.

Weathered Wall, 1921 5th Ave. (448-5688). An audience as diverse and artistic as its offerings (poetry readings to punk). The Weathered Wall is always interesting. Open Tues.-Sun. 9pm-2am. Cover $3-7.

The University Bistro, 4315 University Way NE (547-8010). Live music (everything from blues to reggae) nightly. Happy hours (4-7pm) feature pints of Bud for $1.25, pitchers $4. Cover Tues. $2, Wed.-Sat. $3-5, no cover Sun.-Mon. Open Mon.-Fri. 11am-2am, Sat. 6pm-2am.

Murphy's Pub (634-2110), at Meridian and N. 45th St., in Wallingford, west of the U District. Take bus #43. A classic Irish pub with a mile-long beer list. Popular with a young crowd, Murphy's has live Irish and folk music Fri. and Sat (cover $2). Open mike on Wed. Open daily 11am-2am.

Re-Bar, 1144 Howell (233-9873). A gay bar for those who like dancing on the wild side, depending on the night. Open daily 8pm-2am.

The Vogue, 2018 1st Ave. (443-0673). A rockin' dance place for the black-clad and/or angst-ridden. Features alternative music (i.e., local bands). Open nightly 7pm-3am

Cinema

Seattle is a *Cinema Paradiso*. Most of the theaters that screen non-Hollywood films are on Capitol Hill and in the University District. Most matinee shows (before 6pm) cost $4—after 6pm, expect to pay $6.50. Seven Gables has recently bought up the Egyptian, the Metro, the Neptune, and others. $20 buys admission to any five films at any of their theaters.

The Egyptian, 801 E. Pine St. (323-4978), at Harvard, on Capitol Hill. This handsome Art Deco theater shows artsy films and is best known for hosting the **Seattle Film Festival** (although some films are screened at other theaters) held the last week of May and the first week of June. The festival includes a retrospective of one director's work with a personal appearance by the featured director. Festival series tickets are available at a discount. Regular tickets $6.50, senior citizens and children $4, first matinee $4.

The Harvard Exit, 807 E. Roy (323-8986), on Capitol Hill. Quality classic and foreign films. Half the fun of seeing a movie here is the theater itself, a converted residence—the lobby was once someone's living room. Arrive early for complimentary cheese and crackers over a game of chess, checkers, or backgammon. Admission $6.50, senior citizens and children $4, first matinee $4.

Neptune, 1303 NE 45th St. (633-5545), just off University Way. A repertory theater, with double features that change daily. *The Rocky Horror Picture Show* has been playing at midnight for as many Saturdays as anyone can remember. Admission $6.50, senior citizens and children $4.

Seven Gables Theater, 911 NE 50th St. (632-8820), in the U District, just off Roosevelt, a short walk west from University Way. Another cinema in an old house. Shows independent and classic films. Admission $6.50, senior citizens and children $4, first matinee $4.

Guild 45th, 2115 N 45th (633-3353). Shows slightly off the beaten track features—but the real attraction is the building, neon pink stucco, a prominent fixture in the landscape and local art.

Grand Illusion Cinema, 1403 NE 50th St. (523-3935), in the U District at University Way. A tiny theater attached to an espresso bar, showing films made on 1930s-type budgets. Admission $6, senior citizens and children $3, matinees $4.

Metro Cinemas, 45th St. and Roosevelt Way NE (633-0055), in the U District. A large, generic 10-theater complex. Half the screens show mainstream movies; the other half are reserved for contemporary art films. Admission $6.50, senior citizens and children $4, 1st matinee $4.

Bookstores

University Book Store, 4326 University Way NE (634-3400). The second-largest college bookstore in the country. Textbooks are in the basement. Good collection of children's books on the 2nd floor. Open Mon.-Wed. and Fri.-Sat. 9am-6pm, Thurs. 9am-9pm, Sun. noon-5pm.

Left Bank Books, 92 Pike St. (622-0195), in the Pike Place Market. A large leftist bookstore quietly awaiting the Revolution. Good prices on new and used books. Open Mon.-Sat. 10am-9pm, Sun. noon-6pm.

Shorey's Book Store, 1411 First Ave. (624-0221), downtown. One of the oldest and largest bookstores in the Northwest, Shorey's sells new, used, and rare books. Open Mon.-Sat. 10am-5pm, Sun. noon-6pm.

Elliott Bay Books, 101 S. Main St. (624-6600), in Pioneer Sq. Vast collection. The store sponsors reading and lecture series. Open Mon.-Sat. 10am-11pm, Sun. noon-6pm.

Red and Black Books, 432 15th E. (322-7323). Features multicultural, gay, and feminist literature and frequent readings. Open Mon.-Thurs. 10am-8pm, Fri.-Sat. 10am-9pm, Sun. noon-8pm.

Beyond the Closet, 1510 Belmont Ave. E. (322-4609). Nearly exclusively gay/lesbian material. Open Sun.-Thurs. 10am-10pm, Fri.-Sat. 10am-11pm.

SEASONAL EVENTS

Seattlites don't let raindrops dampen their spirits. Pick up a copy of the Seattle-King County visitors center's *Calendar of Events,* published every season, for event coupons and an exact listing of innumerable area happenings. One of the most notable events is the **Northwest Folklife Festival,** held on Memorial Day weekend at the Seattle Center. Artists, musicians, and dancers congregate to celebrate the heritage of the area. The Japanese community celebrates the third week of July with the traditional **Bon Odori** festival in the International District, when temples are opened to the public and dances fill the streets. **Street fairs** throughout the city are popular conglomerations of crafts and food stands, street music, and theater. Especially of note are those in the University District during mid- to late-May, the Pike Place Market over Memorial Day weekend, and the Fremont District (633-4409) in mid-June. The **Bite of Seattle** (232-2980) is a celebration of food, held in mid-July in the Seattle Center (free). The summer is capped off with the massive **Bumbershoot** (622-5123), held in the Seattle Center over Labor Day weekend. This fantastic 4-day arts festival attracts big-name rock bands, street musicians, and an exuberant crowd (Fri. free, Sat.-Sun. $4 at the door, $3 in advance).

Seattle does not forget its Sea. Tack on up to Puget Sound to take in the yachting season, which falls in May. **Maritime Week** (467-6340 or 329-5700), during the third week of May, should buoy your spirits, and the **Seattle Boats Afloat Show** (634-0911) in mid-August gives area boaters a chance to show off their craft. At the beginning of July, the Center for Wooden Boats sponsors the free **Wooden Boat Show** (382-2628) on Lake Union. Don't go without your blue blazer, deck shoes, and skipper's cap. Size up the entrants (over 100 traditional wooden boats) and then watch a demonstration of boat-building skills. The year-end blow-out is the **Quick and Daring Boatbuilding Contest,** in which hopefuls go overboard trying to build and sail wooden boats of their own design, using a limited kit of tools and materials. Plenty of music, food, and alcohol make the sailing smooth.

The biggest, baddest festival of them all is the **Seattle Seafair** (728-0123), spread out over three weeks from mid-July to early August. All of the city's neighborhoods contribute with street fairs, parades large and small, balloon races, musical entertainment, and a seafood fest. The festival ends with the totally insane **Emerald City Unlimited Hydroplane Races,** in which everybody grabs anything that will float and heads to Lake Washington for front row seats. As the sun shines more often than not during these weeks, half the city seems to turn out in inner tubes.

The year ends with the annual **Christmas Cruise** in early December. Sparkling boats promenade along Lake Washington and Elliott Bay, with local choirs belting out seasonal music nightly.

■ Near Seattle

Fatigued? Exhausted? Hectic big-city life got you down? Float on over to **Lake Washington.** Simply cross the lake on the two floating bridges to arrive in a biker and picnicker's dream vision. In general, the towns in this region are of no interest to the sightseer, but the spacious parklands and miles of country roads delight those who have an affinity for the outdoors. Seattle's outskirts are astonishingly rural; only **Bellevue** across Lake Washington has developed anything akin to urban flair. Although bowling and movie-going draw big evening crowds in this affluent suburb, Bellevue is beginning to show signs of a developing nightlife in its downtown restaurants and clubs. The July **Bellevue Jazz Festival** (455-6885), in particular, attracts both the local jazz cats and national acts.

If nothing else, a jaunt to suburbia grants a fine view of Seattle against a mountainous backdrop. The hills due east of the city, known affectionately as the **"Issaquah Alps,"** are ridden with good hiking trails.

Head farther out for lovely country excursions. Take I-90 to **Lake Sammamish State Park,** off exit 15, for excellent swimming and water-skiing facilities, volleyball courts, and playing fields. You might want to continue onward to the towns of **Snoqualmie** and **North Bend,** 29 mi. east of Seattle. In Snoqualmie, the **Puget Sound Railroad Museum,** 109 King St. (746-4025), on Rte. 202, houses a collection of functional early steam and electric trains in the old Snoqualmie Depot. Train rides on these antique beasts run to North Bend, offering views of Snoqualmie Falls (see below). Trips run on the hour and the full round-trip takes an hour. (Open April-Sept. Sat.-Sun. 11am-5pm. Round-trip rides $6, senior citizens $5, children $4.) In North Bend, the **Snoqualmie Valley Museum,** 320 North Bend Blvd. S. (888-3200 or 888-0062), resurrects a *fin-de-siècle* parlor and kitchen and displays locally unearthed Native American artifacts. (Open Sat.-Sun. 1-5pm and occasionally during the week; call for information.) North Bend operates a **visitors information booth** (888-1678) in summer at North Bend Blvd. and Park Ave.

Back in North Bend, take bus #210 or Rte. 202 north to view the astounding **Snoqualmie Falls.** Washington State residents are quick to mention that the falls are 100 ft. higher than Niagara. Formerly a sacred place for coastal Native Americans, the falls now answer to the secular needs of Puget Power; the hydroelectric plant has had the capacity to turn the falls on and off since 1898. Puget Power maintains public picnic facilities at the falls. The falls were featured in David Lynch's cult TV series *Twin Peaks,* and the small town of Snoqualmie has been host to hordes of "Peaks freaks" (strangely, mostly Japanese) since the release two summers ago of the show's big-screen flick, *Fire Walk With Me.*

A number of **u-pick berry farms** line Rte. 202 north along the Snoqualmie River and open up in the spring and summer. In **Woodinville** is the **Ste. Michelle Vintners,** 14111 145th St. NE (488-4633), a leader in the recent move to popularize Washington wines. 45-minute tours of the facility, which resembles a French château, finish with wine tasting for those 21 and over (tours given daily 10am-6pm; free). To reach Woodinville from downtown Seattle, take bus #310 during peak hours only.

The Seattle area is surrounded by the facilities of the **Boeing Aircraft Industry,** Seattle's most prominent employer. When last seen in the 1950s, evasive author Thomas Pynchon (*Gravity's Rainbow*) was working for this glittering jewel of the military-industrial complex, writing technical manuals. Free tours of one Boeing plant are given 25 mi. north of Seattle in **Everett,** where 747s and 767s are assembled in one of the world's largest buildings. Take I-5 to exit 189, then Rte. 526 west. Tickets for the twice-daily tour are available on a first-come, first-served basis at 8:30am at the plant. Get there early—they go fast. Call the **Everett Tour Center** (342-4801) for more information. At Boeing Field to the south of Seattle is the **Museum of Flight,** 9404 E. Marginal Way S. (767-7373). Take I-5 south to exit 158 and turn north onto E. Marginal Way S., or take bus #123. The museum is in the restored Red Barn where William E. Boeing founded the company in 1916. Inside, photographs and artifacts trace the history of flight from its beginnings through the 30s, including an operating replica of the Wright Brothers' wind tunnel. Rare aircraft sometimes participate in special events on the grounds nearby. The July 13-14 **Airshow** is always a soaring success (open Fri.-Wed. 10am-5pm, Thurs. 10am-9pm; admission $5, ages 6-15 $3).

Just south of **Des Moines** on Rte. 509 off Rte. 99 is **Saltwater State Park.** Take bus #130. The park has extensive foot trails through the Kent Smith Canyon, a beach for swimming and clamming, and 53 campsites with pay showers and flush toilets (sites $9).

From Colman Dock (Pier 52) on Seattle's waterfront, ferries run to the town of **Bremerton,** on the Kitsap Peninsula, home of the **Puget Sound Naval Shipyard** (round-trip $3.30; see Kitsap Peninsula for more information).

Ferries also depart from Colman Dock for the town of **Winslow** on **Bainbridge Island,** a charmingly rural idyll homesteaded by late-19th-century Swedish and late-20th-century Californian immigrants. In Winslow, follow the photographic record of these settlements at the **Bainbridge Island Historical Museum** on High School Rd. (open Sat. 10am-4pm; free), or satisfy a hunger of the non-historical kind at the firecracker- and flower-festooned **Streamliner Diner,** 397 Winslow Way (842-8595), where the amazing, eccentric natural food and rich pies (slice $2.50) tempt the Northwest traveler. (Open Mon.-Fri. 8am-3pm, Sat.-Sun. 8am-2:30pm.) Wash it down with a bottle of Ferry Boat White from the **Bainbridge Island Vineyards & Winery** (842-9463). Here you can sample the local grape, or tour the fields where it is grown; just turn right at the first white trellis on Rte. 305 as you come from the ferry (open Wed.-Sun. noon-5pm, tours Sun. 2pm; free).

For less decadent fun, head for one of Bainbridge Island's state parks. **Fort Ward,** southwest of Winslow, offers boat launches, picnic facilities, and an underwater scuba diving area (day-use only). **Fay-Bainbridge,** on the northern tip of the island just 1½ mi. from **Cliffhaven,** has good fishing and 36 **campsites** with pay showers and flush toilets (sites $8). Ferries to the island run each day 5am-2am at 45-minute to two -hour intervals.

■ Vashon Island

Only a 25-minute ferry ride from Seattle, Vashon Island has remained seemingly (and inexplicably) invisible to most Seattlites. The small-town lifestyle of the islanders is virtually unblemished by the proximity to city speedways, and so is Vashon's wealth of natural beauty. About 75% of the island is undeveloped—green forests of Douglas firs, rolling cherry orchards, strawberry fields, and wildflowers cover the island during the summer. The remainder of the island includes a tiny town and several unimposing factories. Taking a trip to Vashon from Seattle is like taking a breath of fresh air on the back porch—surprisingly necessary at times, no matter how nice the house.

Practical Information Vashon Island stretches between Seattle and Tacoma on its eastern side and between Southworth and Gig Harbor on its western side. From Seattle, driving south on I-5, take exit 164 down to Western Ave. and the waterfront or exit 163A (West Seattle/Spokane St.) down Fauntleroy Way to Fauntleroy Cove. From Tacoma, off I-5, take exit 132 (Bremerton/Gig Harbor) to Point Defiance Park.

Washington State Ferries (800-84-FERRY or 843-3779 in WA, or 464-6400) can get you to Vashon Island. Ferries leave from Fauntleroy (in Seattle) and Southworth for the northern end of Vashon and from Point Defiance (in Tacoma) for the southern end. The passenger-only Seattle ferry departs from Coleman Dock at Pier 50 and takes 25 minutes. There are nine departures Monday through Friday between 6am and midnight, six departures Saturday between 9:30am and 11:30pm. The Fauntleroy ferry takes 15 minutes and departs about 25 times per day (6am-2am). The Point Defiance ferry takes 15 minutes and departs about 18 times per day (6am-10pm).

Round-trip fare is $3.30 in Seattle and $2.15 in Fauntleroy and Point Defiance ($7.50 for car-and-driver round trip). There is a $1.50 surcharge on car fares between June 25 and Sept. 30. Hostels give discounts on ferry tickets.

Buses #117, 118, and 119 run from downtown Seattle onto the island; vans also service the island, beginning their runs from the ferry landing. Unlike the buses, the vans can be flagged down anywhere. Fares are the same as in the rest of the system: $1 for travel in one zone, $1.50 for two-zone travel. The island is all within one zone. Buses #54 and 55 from the Fauntleroy ferry to downtown Seattle are the only ones that run on Sunday.

The **Vashon Manny Senior Center** (463-5173) is downtown on Bank Rd. So is **Joy's Village Cleaner,** 17500 Vashon Hwy. (463-9933; wash and dry 75¢ each; open Mon.-Sat. 7am-10pm, Sun. 7am-9pm). Emergency numbers: **medical,** 911; **police,** 463-3618; **Coast Guard,** 463-2951. Vashon's **post office** is on Bank Rd. (463-9390; open Mon.-Fri. 9am-5pm; **General Delivery ZIP code:** 98070). The **area code** is 206 (from Seattle—dial 1 and then the 7-digit number).

Accommodations and Food

The **Vashon Island Ranch/Hostel (HI/AYH)** (sometimes called **"Seattle B"**) is really the island's only accommodation, and it is in itself one of the main reasons to come here. The hostel is located at 12119 SW Cove Rd. (463-2592); to get there, jump on any bus at the ferry terminal, ride it until it gets to Thriftway Market, and call at the pay phone inside the market, marked with an HI/AYH sticker. Judy will come pick you up if the hour is reasonable, and she has never turned a hosteler away. "Seattle B" is a wonderful retreat from "Seattle A," with all the comforts of home—free pancakes for breakfast, free use of old bikes (at your own risk), free campfire wood, free volleyball games in the afternoon, and a caring manager. The hostel accommodates 14 in bunk rooms, but those are for the weak of heart—the romantic will go for the huge teepees under the stars. When all beds are full, you can pitch a tent (open year-round; tents and beds $8, nonmembers $11). If for some unfathomable reason you can't make it to the hostel, call for information on **B&Bs** (463-3556).

Most hostelers get creative in the kitchen with supplies from **Thriftaway and Becks,** which are both downtown (open Mon.-Sat. 8am-9pm, Sun. 8am-7pm). However, there are other options for those who are allergic to dishwashing. **Cafe Tosca,** 9924 Bank Rd. (463-2125), has the best food in town and a charming low-key atmosphere. Entrees will run you around $10. (Open Mon.-Fri. 11am-9pm, Sat. 4:30-9:30pm, Sun. 4:30-10pm.) You'll find better-than-average Chinese and American cuisine at **Happy Gardens,** Vashon Village (463-9109). Sweet and sour chicken ($6.75) and vegetable chow mein ($4.50) are both popular. (Open daily 7:30am-11pm, popular lounge open till 2am.)

Sights and Seasonal Events

The island is wonderful for **biking.** Don't be deceived by the short distances—Vashon's hills will turn even a short jaunt into an arduous affair. A sweaty exploration will be rewarded, however, with rapturous scenery. **Point Robinson Park** is a gorgeous spot for a picnic (from Vashon Hwy. take Ellisburg to Dockton to Pt. Robinson Rd.). **Wax Orchards** is also a fulfilling destination (take 204 to 111 Ave. SW to SW 220, then to Wax Orchard Rd.). More than 500 acres of hiking trails weave their way through the woods in the middle of the island, and several lovely walks start from the hostel.

With one in every 10 residents of the island a professional artist, you can count on some culture no matter when you visit. **Blue Heron Arts Center** (463-5131) coordinates most activities. Call for information on upcoming classes and events (gallery and craft shop open Tues.-Sat. noon-5pm).

At **Tramp Harbor** on a calm day you can rent a sea kayak or rowboat at the **Quartermaster Arena** (463-3624). The **Strawberry Festival,** held over the second weekend in July, seems to awaken even the mainland to Vashon's existence, and people flood the island to cheer soap derby races down those infamous Vashon hills. Local and national bands inspire street dancing well into the night, and small children are known to metamorphose into giant strawberries among the miles of food and craft stands.

■ Tacoma

Although spending time in Tacoma rather than in nearby Seattle is somewhat like hanging out in Newark instead of New York, Tacoma does boast a few worthwhile outdoor attractions suitable for a day-trip.

Practical Information Visitors Information in Tacoma can be obtained at the Pierce County Visitor Information Center, 906 Pacific Ave. (627-2836), downtown on the fourth floor of the Seafirst Center. (Open Mon.-Fri. 8:30am-5pm.) Useful phone numbers: **Emergency,** 911;. **Crisis Line,** 759-6700; **Rape Relief,** 474-7273; **Safeplace,** 279-8333. The Tacoma **post office** is on 11th at A St. (Open Mon.-Fri. 8am-5:30pm. **General Delivery ZIP Code:** 98402.)

Accommodations and Food If you're (inexplicably) planning on staying the night in Tacoma, don't go out alone. One of the best hotels is the **Valley Motel,** 1220 Puyallup Ave. (272-7720), which is clean and feels safe (singles $25, doubles $29). Large rooms are $1 more than regular ones and include kitchenettes ($2 key deposit). There's also that old standby, **Motel 6,** at 1811 S. 76th St. (473-7100), south of downtown, which offers the usual comfortable sterility. The pool and hot tub make up for spending a few extra dollars (singles $32, doubles $38).

Stop in at **Antique Sandwich Company,** 5102 N. Pearl St. (752-4069), near Point Defiance, for some great natural food, an open mike on Tuesday nights, and live music on Friday night. "Poor boy" sandwich are $5.75; espresso shakes are $3.25. (Open Mon. and Wed-Fri. 7am-8pm, Tues. 7am-11pm, Sat. 7am-7pm, Sun. 8:30am-7pm.) On your way home, you might want to visit the monkeys (named Java and Jive) at **Bob's Java Jive,** 2102 S. Tacoma Way (475-9843), south of downtown, directly beneath the I-5 Skyway. The Java Jive is a locals-only hangout and at 9pm the cabaret starts up. Hamburgers and sandwiches around $3 (open Mon.-Thurs. noon-11pm, Fri. noon-2am, Sat. 3pm-2am).

Sights Tacoma's waterfront is home to **Point Defiance Park** (591-3681), one of the most attractive parks in the Puget Sound area. To reach the park, take a short detour off I-5 onto **Ruston Way** north of downtown; the route replaces the stifling clouds of Tacoma's famous smokestacks with views of Mt. Rainier. Continue toward Point Defiance Park; a 5-mi. loop passes by all the park's attractions and offers postcard-perfect views of the Puget Sound and miles of woodland trails as well. If you happen by in the spring, stop to smell the flowers; the enormous tulip and daffodil garden can be overwhelming. **Owen Beach** looks across at Vashon Island and is a good starting place for rambles down the beach. The loop then brushes by the spot where Captain Wilkes of the U.S. Navy proclaimed in 1841 that if he had guns on this and the opposite shore (Gig Harbor) he could defy the world (hence the name Point Defiance).

The park's prize possession is the **Point Defiance Zoo and Aquarium** (591-5335). Penguins, polar bears, and scary sharks populate the aquarium, and the zoo features a reproduction of Southeast Asia (scaled down, of course). (Open daily 10am-7pm; Labor Day-Memorial Day 10am-4pm. Admission $6.25, seniors $5.75, ages 5-17 $4.50, ages 3-4 $2.25, under 3 free.) The meticulously restored **Fort Nisqually** (591-5339), in the park, also merits a visit. The British (now Canadian) Hudson's Bay Company built the fort in 1832 to offset growing commercial competition from Americans. The indoor **museum** delves into the sound's history. (Fort open daily 11am-6pm; in winter Wed.-Fri. 9am-4:30pm, Sat.-Sun. 12:30-4:30pm. Museum open daily noon-6pm; in winter Tues.-Sun. 1-4pm. Free.) **Camp Six Logging Museum** (752-0047), also in the park, retrieves an entire 19th-century logging camp from the dustbin of history. The camp includes buildings and equipment and offers a 1-mi. ride ($2, senior citizens and children $1) on an original steam-powered logging engine. (Open Memorial Day-Labor Day Wed.-Fri. 10am-6pm, Sat.-Sun. 10am-7pm. Admission $2, senior citizens and children $1.) The **Tacoma Art Museum** (272-4258), on the northeast corner of 12th and Pacific, has a rotating exhibit downstairs and a stupendous collection of photographs by the eccentric Weegee upstairs (admission $3, senior citizens and students $2, ages 6-12 $1; open Tues.-Sat. 10am-5pm, Thurs. 10am-7pm, Sun. noon-5pm).

PUGET SOUND

According to Native American legend, Puget Sound was created when Ocean, wishing to keep his children Cloud and Rain close to home, gouged out a trough in western Washington and molded the dirt into a wall of mountains. Ever since then, Cloud and Rain have kept near the sea, rarely venturing across the Cascade Range to the interior tablelands. The majority of Washington's residents also stick close to the water, making their homes in the sound's labyrinth of inlets, bays, and harbors.

From Bellingham in the north through Seattle to industrial Tacoma, cities and towns along the sound form an almost continuous East Coast-style megalopolis along I-5. The bay's southern shore curves past Lacey to Olympia, the state capital, and beyond that to the Kitsap Peninsula. A few dozen islands speckle the sound, providing tranquil retreats for harried city dwellers. The San Juan Islands off Anacortes receive the brunt of the tourist traffic, while Vashon Island, between Seattle and Tacoma, remains quieter.

Puget Sound attracts as many water breathers as city dwellers. Although pods of orcas can be sighted anywhere in the Sound, the southwest coast of San Juan Island is the favorite haunt of the highly intelligent, black-and-white cetaceans.

An extensive web of roads and ferries ensnares the cities and islands of Puget Sound. Information on ferries to specific destinations is given in the Practical Information and Orientation sections of each city or area. If you're driving, you should arrive at the ferry terminal early and get in the line that matches your destination (cars are boarded according to their exit points). Cyclists and pedestrians travel cheaply by ferry and never have to wait in line. Try to avoid ferries across the Sound during commuter rush hours and the San Juan ferry on Friday afternoons. Larger cars and RVs may have to wait for a place; RVs pay an extra fee.

■■■ OLYMPIA

Olympia was once a peaceful, easy-going fishing and oystering port at the southernmost end of Puget Sound. While still peaceful and easy-going, the city has made the transition from small seaport to small state capital quite smoothly. The sprawling Capitol Campus, with its whitewashed buildings and perfectly manicured lawns, dominates the downtown area. The rest of downtown is home to a host of turn-of-the-century buildings and tiny specialty shops. And, as capital of the Evergreen State, it is only fitting that Olympia draws on its natural setting. The shimmering waters of Puget Sound assure that it remains a seaport in appearance if not in function.

PRACTICAL INFORMATION AND ORIENTATION

Visitors Information: Greater Olympia Visitors Convention Bureau (586-3460), exit 105a off of I-5 at 14th and Capitol Way. Brochures, information, and Sound advice. Open Mon.-Fri. 8am-5pm, Sat.-Sun. 10am-4pm. **Department of Trade and Economic Development, Tourism Division,** General Administration Bldg., #G-3 (800-544-1800). **City of Olympia Parks and Recreation Department,** 222 N. Columbia Ave. (753-8380). Open Mon.-Fri. 8am-10pm.

Washington State Parks and Recreation Commission: 7150 Cleanwater Lane (753-5755; write to P.O. Box 42650, Olympia WA, 98506-2650 for information/ reservation packet). All the latest on the state parks. Immensely helpful staff. Open Mon.-Fri. 8am-5pm.

Department of Natural Resources (DNR), 111 Washington St. (902-1000). The *Guide to Camp and Picnic Sites* points out free DNR sites throughout the state. Ask for their guide to waterfront areas in the Puget Sound area. Open Mon.-Fri. 8am-4:30pm.

Department of Fisheries, 111 Washington St. (902-2200). Information on saltwater fishing and shellfish, including season and limit designations. Open Mon.-Fri. 8am-5pm.

Department of Wildlife, 600 N. Capitol Way (753-5700). Information and licensing for freshwater fishing and game hunting. Open Mon.-Fri. 8am-5pm.

Greyhound, 107 E. 7th Ave. (357-5541). To: Seattle (7 per day, $10); Portland (7 per day, $18); Spokane (3 per day, $36.50). Open Mon.-Fri. 7:30am-8:30pm, Sat.-Sun. 8am-4pm.

Buses: Intercity Transit (I.T.), 526 S. Pattison (943-7777). Office open Mon.-Fri. 8am-5pm; phone-staffed Mon.-Fri. 7am-7pm, Sat. 8am-5pm. Buses run Mon.-Fri. 6am-11:30pm, Sat. 8am-5pm. Limited service Sun. afternoon and early evening hours. Buses service the area bounded by Columbia St. station in the north, Tumwater Square in the south, Capitol Mall and Evergreen State College in the west, and Hawks Prairie Mall in the east. Fare $1, seniors and people with disabilities 50¢. Day passes 50¢ with reduced-fare cards. All buses begin and end their routes at 4th and Columbia. The **Capitol Shuttle** is free to the public. Buses run between the campus and downtown every 10 min. Call I.T. for information. **Custom buses** run where normal fixed routes stop—these run Mon.-Fri. (standard fares). Supplementary transport is provided for seniors and travelers with disabilities by **Special Mobility Services** at 320 Dayton SE (754-1200 or 754-9430).

Taxi: Red Top Taxi, 357-3700. **Budget Taxi,** 786-8294. Both 24 hr.

Car Rental: U-Save Auto Rental, 3015 Pacific Ave. (786-8445). $26 per day plus 20¢ for each additional mi. over 100. Must be at least 21 with credit card.

Bike Rental: Olympic Outfitters, 407 E. 4th Ave. (943-1997). Mountain bikes $30 per day. $100 deposit, unless you leave a credit card number. This enormous sports shop also rents tents, skis, and mountain climbing gear. Bikes rented here can be taken to Olympic National Park. Open Mon.-Fri. 10am-8pm, Sat. 10am-6pm, Sun. noon-5pm.

Public Library: (352-0595), E. 8th and S. Franklin St. Open Mon.-Thurs. 10am-9pm, Fri.-Sat. 10am-5pm. In winter also open Sun. 1-5pm.

Lesbian/Gay Resource Center: (866-6000, ext. 6544), at Evergreen State College, erratic summer hours.

Women's Shelter: Safeplace, 754-6300. Counseling, housing referrals. 24 hr.

Emergency: 911.

Post Office: 900 S. Jefferson SE (357-2286). Open Mon.-Fri. 7:30am-6pm. **General Delivery ZIP Code:** 98501.

Area Code: 206.

Greyhound stops in downtown Olympia on its I-5 journey. The Amtrak depot is about 8 mi. southeast of the city, and is not connected by bus service to downtown, with the exception of the Custom Bus system for which you must call ahead (see listing above). Intercity Transit provides limited service between the three area cities: Olympia, Tumwater, and Lacey (see listing above).

ACCOMMODATIONS AND CAMPING

The hotels and motels in Olympia generally cater to lobbyists and lawyers rather than to budget tourists. The two local universities reserve all their rooms for their own students, so your choices here are limited. Camping is the most financially prudent option.

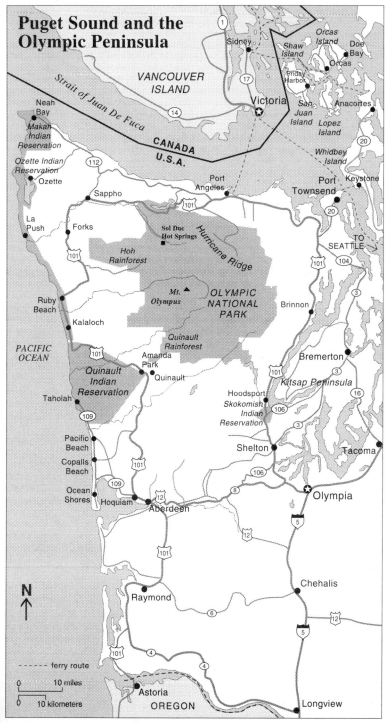

Puget Sound and the Olympic Peninsula

ferry route

0   10 miles

0   10 kilometers

N

The Golden Gavel Motor Hotel, 909 Capitol Way (352-8533). The most inexpensive downtown option. Clean and comfortable with cable TV and phones. Singles and doubles $41-44.

The New Holly Motel, 2816 Martin Way (943-3000), on a main east-west drag, east of town. Take exit 107 off I-5, or bus #61 or 62. The beds are a little narrow, but the rooms are blessedly roach-free. Singles from $28. Doubles from $40.

Bailey Motor Inn, 3333 Martin Way (491-7515), just off exit 107 of I-5. Clean, comfy rooms and an indoor heated pool. Singles from $32. Doubles from $36.

Motel 6, 400 W. Lee St. (754-7320), in Tumwater. Take Exit 102 off I-5 and head east on Trosper Rd., then south 1 block on Capitol Blvd., and west on W. Lee St. Or take bus #13 from downtown. Comfortable rooms near the freeway. Color TV and swimming pool. Singles $30. Doubles $36. Each additional person $6.

Millersylvania State Park, 12245 Tilly Rd. S. (753-1519), 10 mi. south of Olympia. Take Exit 99 off I-5, then head south on Rte. 121. 216 crowded and open sites for camping, with pay showers and flush toilets. Facilities for the disabled. Primitive hiker/biker sites available. Standard sites $10, RV hookups $14.

Capital Forest Multiple Use Area, 15 mi. west of Olympia. Administered by the DNR. 50 campsites scattered among 6 campgrounds. Camping is free and requires no notification or permit. Pick up a forest map at the visitors bureau or at the state Department of Natural Resources office (see Practical Information).

FOOD

There is potential for good eating along the bohemian 4th Ave., east of Columbia, especially when the pace picks up during the school year. The **farmer's market** (866-6835), at Capital Way and Thurston Ave., lets you take pride in cutting out the middleman (open April-Oct. Thurs.-Sat. 10am-3pm).

Smithfield Cafe, 212 W. 4th Ave. (786-1725). This cozy cafe with mellow jazz and modern art serves coffee ($1), cappuccino ($1.34), and espresso ($1.15). The relaxed, eclectic crowd digs the food, especially the deluxe burrito ($4.50) and the vegetarian and vegan options. The lucky shouldn't miss the free condoms in the bathroom. Open Mon.-Fri. 7am-8pm, Sat.-Sun. 8am-8pm.

Jo Mama's Restaurant, 120 N. Pear St. (943-9849), in an old house at State St. Homemade pizza served in an all-wood, "old-tavern" atmosphere. The food is somewhat pricey (the 10-inch vegetarian pizza—$14.75—feeds 2 hungry people), but the ambience compensates. Open Mon.-Thurs. 11am-10pm, Fri. 11am-11pm, Sat. 4-11pm, Sun. 4-10pm.

Olympia Soup and Sub, 915 Capitol Way S. (786-6742). A tiny sandwich shop that barely has enough room for a cash register. Try the foot-long subs with rocket-powered flavor ($5-7), or the suspenseful "special of the month" ($3.50). Open Mon.-Fri. 10am-7pm, Sat.-Sun. 11am-7pm.

The Falls Terrace Restaurant, 106 S. Deschutes Way (943-7830). Take exit 103 off I-5. Elegant (but not fancy-schmancy) with dinner prices to match. Lunches ($6-8) are a better deal, and you can still enjoy the great view of Tumwater Falls. Open Mon.-Fri. 11am-9pm, Sat. 11:30am-9pm, Sun. 11:30am-8pm. Reserve.

SIGHTS

Begin your exploration of the capitol area at the **State Capitol Information Center** (586-3460), on Capitol Way between 12th and 14th Ave. (Open Mon.-Fri. 8am-5pm, Sat.-Sun. 10am-4pm; Labor Day-Memorial Day Mon.-Fri. 8am-5pm.) The staff here can provide you with information on the Capitol Group and save you a trip to the Chamber of Commerce (open Mon.-Fri. 8am-5pm). Take a free tour of the **Legislative Building** (586-8687) to sneak a peek at the public sphere. The building's spectacular dome (at 287 ft. high, the fifth-tallest dome in the world) is accessed by a spiralling staircase of some 200 steps. The panoramic view of Olympia from the top justifies the sweaty trip up. An enormous wool, velvet, and velour carpet covers over 1200 sq. ft. of the State Reception Room's teakwood floor; when the handpainted rug was completed, the original pattern was destroyed so it could not be replicated elsewhere. To frustrate state employees' tendency to roll back the carpet and dance the Charleston jitterbug after work, many pieces of heavy furniture were purchased in 1929 and placed on the carpet's perimeter. Even those who aren't carpet connoisseurs will enjoy the informative tours given by a knowledgeable corps of guides (45 min., daily 10am-3pm).

Capitol Lake Park is a favorite retreat for runners, sailors, and swimmers. Spawning salmon head for Tumwater Falls from late August through October; you can spot the lox leaping through the air as they cross the lake. The **State Capitol Museum,** 211 W. 21st Ave. (753-2580), exhibits local artwork and historical fragments (open Tues.-Fri. 10am-4pm, Sat.-Sun. noon-4pm; free).

Budget deals in Olympia come out after dark. The **State Theater,** 204 E. 4th Ave. (357-4010), shows first-run movies for $1.50. During the summer, the city schedules free jazz, ensemble, and symphony concerts at **Sylvester Park** (Wed. at 7:30pm and Fri. at noon; call 753-8183 for confirmation of schedule). Since 1985 the band Beat Happening and their label, K Records, have made Olympia one of the centers of the international pop-music underground; the Kill Rock Stars label, and sometimes their flagship feminist band Bikini Kill, live here too. Ask in record shops about cool shows or look for posters.

■ Near Olympia

The **Mima Mounds** (753-2400), unusual geologic formations, are preserved in a Department of Natural Resources prairie park 10 mi. south of Olympia. The self-guided interpretive trails are wheelchair-accessible (open daily 8am-dusk). Take I-5 south to exit 95; 1 mi. west of Littlerock, follow Wadell Creek Rd. west.

The **Nisqually National Wildlife Refuge** (753-9467), located off I-5 between Olympia and Tacoma (at exit 114), has recently pitted neighbor against neighbor in the quiet Nisqually delta. Environmentalists seek to preserve the delta's diverse marsh and marine life, but developers hope to cast some of their bread upon the water and its environs. For the time being, you can still view the protected wildlife from blinds or walk the trails that wind through the preserve. Trails open daily during daylight hours (office open Mon.-Fri. 7:30am-4pm; admission $2).

Olympia Beer (754-5177), actually brewed south of the capital city in **Tumwater,** has been taken over by the Pabst Company, which now produces a number of different beers on the premises. You can tour the facility and have a brewski on the house (open daily 8am-4:30pm; free). The brewery, visible from I-5, can be reached by taking exit 103 in Tumwater. Nearby, **Tumwater Falls Park** practically begs for picnickers.

Ten mi. south of the city is **Wolfhaven** (264-4695). Established in 1982 as refuge for 20 wolves, the haven now preserves 40 wolves of six different species. Tour the grounds ($3, children $2) or take part in the Howl-In (every Fri. and Sat. 7-10pm; $4, children $2.50). Groups tell stories 'round a campfire to the accompaniment of the howling residents (open daily 10am-5pm; Oct.-April Wed.-Sun. 10am-4pm).

■ Kitsap Peninsula

Resembling a half-completed landfill project jutting into Puget Sound, the Kitsap Peninsula occupies much of the area between the Olympic Peninsula and Seattle. The peninsula, rife with natural deep-water inlets, is an excellent natural naval base and provides safe haven to some of the U.S. Marine Corps' most sophisticated military machinery. This aesthetic drawback aside, travelers without Top Secret clearance can still enjoy the area's varied terrain. The peninsula's numerous backroads and campgrounds lay out the blueprints for a cyclist's paradise.

Bremerton is the economic hub of the Kitsap Peninsula. This naval-base town of 35,000 boasts one of the largest U.S. Navy repair yards in the world. You'll swear you've stepped into a Tom Clancy novel; every third person has a Navy security pass swinging from his or her neck.

In 1990, *Money* magazine designated Bremerton and surrounding communities as "America's Most Liveable City." However, the relatively undeveloped downtown area and the restricted nature of the Naval Yard—its major attraction—are apt to leave travelers saying, "It's a nice place to live, but I wouldn't want to visit there." The town contains enough sights to hold the attention of the casual visitor for a few minutes and provides an excellent home berth for those wishing to explore the peninsula and nearby Hood Canal.

Practical Information The **Bremerton Kitsap County Visitor and Convention Bureau,** 120 Washington St. (479-3588), is just up the hill from the ferry terminal and will help you navigate the area. The office puts out a flotilla of pamphlets on Bremerton and nearby towns, and the lively staff tries hard to cover up the city's fundamental drabness. (Open Mon.-Fri. 9am-5pm, Sat. 10am-4pm; Labor Day-Memorial Day Mon.-Fri. 9am-5pm.) The **post office** (373-1456) is stationed at 602 Pacific Ave. (open Mon.-Fri. 9am-5pm; **General Delivery ZIP Code:** 98310).

Getting to the Kitsap Peninsula from Seattle is easy: **ferry service** to either Bremerton (the main town on the Peninsula-proper) or Winslow (on nearby Bainbridge Island—see the Near Seattle section), starts daily at 6am. To reach the area from south of Seattle, take the ferry from Fauntleroy (toward the southern end of the Seattle Metropolitan area) to Southworth (which lies on the Peninsula-proper south of Bremerton). North of Seattle, Edmonds is connected to Kingston (north of Bremerton at the top end of the peninsula), and ferry service is frequent. The fare—$3.30 for passengers and $5.55 for car and driver ($6.65 in summer)—is the same for all three ferries. The full, round-trip fare for passengers without vehicle is collected on the westbound segment; half the fare for passengers with vehicle is collected in each direction. (Call 464-6400 Mon.-Fri. 9am-5pm for schedule info.)

Once there, getting around is fairly simple. **Kitsap Transit** (373-2877) maintains several buses connecting population centers. (Fares 50¢, senior citizens and passengers with disabilities 25¢.) Call ahead for times or pick up schedules at the Winslow, Bremerton, or Kingston ferry terminals. Keep in mind, however, that the buses are designed to serve commuters, and that many lines stop running after 6pm and do not service the Winslow terminal on Saturday or Sunday. The area is compact and a bike will be sufficient to get you most places.

Accommodations, Camping, and Food Kitsap Way (the road which bus #11 from Bremerton to Winslow follows) is peppered with $30-and-up **hotel** chains; for cheaper lodgings, consider spending the night in Seattle. If you're intent on spending the night here, your best bet is to camp. Those traveling by foot will find **Illahee State Park** (478-6460) wonderfully convenient. To get there, hop on bus #29 at the ferry terminal in Bremerton and take it to the corner of Perry and Sylvan. From there, walk ¼ mi. up the hill on Sylvan until you reach the entrance. The park has 51 campsites replete with water, bathrooms, and that necessary luxury—hot showers (sites $10, walk-in sites $5). Another possibility is **Scenic Beach State Park** (830-5079), near the village of Seabeck on the west coast of the peninsula. The park has 52 campsites with water and bathrooms (sites $10, walk-in sites $5). From Silverdale, take Anderson Hill Rd. or Newberry Hill Rd. west to Seabeck Hwy., and then follow the highway 7 mi. south to the Scenic Beach turnoff. Cyclists should be prepared for the staggering hills along this route.

In general, culinary choices in Bremerton are about as appealing as those in the gallies next door. Locals head for the slightly upscale **Boat Shed,** 101 Shore Dr. (377-2600), on the water immediately below the northeast side of the Manette Bridge. Terrific seafood, sandwiches, and super nachos—all in the $5 range (open Mon.-Sat. 11am-11pm, Sun. 3-10pm).

Sights and Seasonal Events Next door to the Visitor's Center (see above), you'll find the **Bremerton-Naval Museum** (479-7447). Thrill to the sight of large action photos from WWII and transparent models of destroyers and aircraft carriers measuring up to 10 ft (open Tues.-Sat. 10am-5pm, Sun. 1-5 pm; free, though donations are requested). The Navy also plans to open the destroyer *Turner Joyce* (of Tonkin Bay infamy) to the public in the near future (call 792-2457 for updated information). The **Naval Undersea Museum** (396-4148) in Keyport (a.k.a. "Torpedo Town, U.S.A.") exhibits undersea artifacts including a K-10 torpedo and a Japanese Kamikaze aircraft used in WWII (open Wed.-Sun. 10am-4pm; free).

For those *really* interested in getting an up-close look at the Naval Yard, join the Navy. Otherwise, take the **foot ferry** across the Sinclair Inlet to **Port Orchard.** (Ferry leaves every hr., on the ¼-hr. Fares run 70¢ from the Bremerton ferry terminal.) The ride across affords an excellent view of the shipyards. While waiting for the ride back, have a gander at Port Orchard's many antique shops and art galleries.

If you ask nicely, the driver of bus #90 will let you off at the Longhouse Convenience Store. Follow the road 1 mi. to the fascinating **Suquamish Museum** (sue-QUAH-mish; 598-3311). If you're driving, you'll find the museum 7 mi. north of Winslow, on the north side of the Agate Pass Bridge on Rte. 305. Run by the tribe on the Port Madison Indian Reservation, this small museum is devoted entirely to the history and culture of the Puget Sound Salish Native Americans. Striking photographs, artifacts, and quotations from tribal elders piece together the lives of those who inhabited the peninsula before the great invasion (open daily 10am-5pm; admission $2.50, senior citizens $2, under 12 $1). **Chief Sealth,** for whom Seattle was named, belonged to the Salish nation, and his grave is located up the hill, about a 15- minute walk away. The chief's memorial of cedar war canoes over a Christian headstone is an excellent example of the melding of Catholic and Native North American religions attempted briefly in the 19th century. Next to the gravesite is a Suquamish city park that was once the site of **Old Man House,** a cedar loghouse burned by federal agents in 1870 in an attempt to destroy Native Americans' communal lifestyle, which was regarded as immoral and conducive to the transmission of smallpox.

■■■ WHIDBEY ISLAND

Whidbey Island, the longest island in the continental U.S., sits in the rain shadow of the Olympic Mountains. The clouds, wrung dry by the time they finally pass over Whidbey, release a scant 20 in. of rain on Whidbey each year, endowing the sigma-shaped island with one of America's highest amounts of average sunshine. Rocky beaches lead back to bluffs crawling with wild roses and blackberry brambles.

The island was named in 1792 for Captain Joseph Whidbey, who sailed through Deception Pass, north of the island, on *H.M.S. Discovery.* Pioneer homesteaders followed in the mid-19th century. The town of Coupeville has been designated a national historic reserve, maintaining nearly 100 original homes and buildings.

PRACTICAL INFORMATION

Chambers of Commerce: Oak Harbor, 5506 Hwy. 20 (675-3535), about 1½ mi. north of the town center. Open Mon.-Fri. 9am-5pm, Sat. 9am-6pm, Sun. 10am-4pm; Sept.-May open Mon.-Fri. 9am-5pm. **Coupeville,** 504 N. Main St. (678-5434). Open Mon.-Fri. 9am-noon, 2-5pm. **Langley,** 124½ 2nd St. (321-6765), behind the Star Bistro Cafe (see Food), fronting the alley between 1st and 2nd St. Open Mon.-Fri. 10am-3pm.

Ranger Station: Deception Pass, 5175 N. Rte. 20, Oak Harbor (293-3861). **Fort Ebey State Park,** Coupeville (678-4636).

Bike Rental: See Getting There and Getting Around below.

Library: Oak Harbor Public Library, 7030 70th St. E. (675-5115), in City Hall, lower level. Open Mon.-Thurs. noon-9pm, Fri.-Sat. 9am-5pm.

Crisis Center: 678-5555 or 321-4868. 24 hr.

Pharmacy: Langley Drug, 105 1st St. (221-4359), across from the Post Office. Open Mon.-Sat. 9am-7pm, Sun. 10am-4pm.

Hospital: Whidbey General, 101 N. Main St. (678-5151), in Coupeville.

Emergency/Police/Fire: 911.

Post Offices: Oak Harbor, 7035 70th St. NW (675-6621). Open Mon.-Fri. 8:30am-5pm. **General Delivery ZIP Code:** 98277. **Coupeville,** 201 N.W. Coveland (678-5353). Open Mon.-Fri. 9:30am-4:30pm, Sat. 11am-1pm. **General Delivery ZIP Code:** 98239. **Langley,** 115 2nd St. (321-4113). Open Mon.-Fri. 8:30am-5pm. **General Delivery ZIP Code:** 98260.

Area Code: 206.

GETTING THERE AND GETTING AROUND

The southern tip of Whidbey Island lies 40 mi. north of Seattle, as the puffin flies. The 20-minute **ferry** to Clinton, at the southern end of the island, leaves from **Mukilteo** (pronounced mu-kul-TEE-o), a small community just south of Everett. Take I-5 north from Seattle and follow the large signs to the ferry (exit 189). Avoid commuter traffic eastbound in the morning and westbound at night.

Ferries leave Mukilteo every half-hour from 6am to 11pm, and leave Clinton every 25 minutes from 4:40am to 1:30am. The exact schedule changes with the seasons; call Washington State Ferries at 800-542-7052 for detailed information. (Car and driver $4.50, each additional passenger $1; bicycle and rider $2.65. Walk-on $2.15; ages over 65, ages 5-12 and travelers with disabilities 50¢; under 5 free.)

Public transportation from Seattle is slightly more difficult. Take Metro Bus #6 from downtown Seattle to the Aurora Village Transit Center ($1, during rush-hour $1.50). From there, catch the Community Transit Bus #170 to the Mukilteo ferry terminal (fare 40¢). Be warned that the last bus from the ferry terminal back to Aurora Village runs away at 6:30pm.

You can also reach Whidbey Island from **Port Townsend** on the Olympic Peninsula. **Ferries** leave the terminal in downtown Port Townsend for Keystone, on the west side of the island (8 per day 7am-10pm). Ferries return from Keystone to Port Townsend (8 per day 7:45am-10:40pm). Hours are reduced in winter, so call ahead; additional daily ferries shuttle large crowds in August. (35 min. Car and driver $5.55, summer $6.65; bicycle riders $3.50. Walk-on $1.65; ages over 64, ages 5-12 and travelers with disabilities 80¢; under 5 free.) For more information, call Washington State Ferries (800-84-FERRY or 800-843-3779).

To reach Whidbey from the north, take exit 189 off I-5 and head west toward **Anacortes.** Be sure to stay on Rte. 20 when it heads south through stunning Deception Pass State Park (signs will direct you); otherwise you'll end up in Anacortes. **Evergreen Trailways** runs a bus to Whidbey from Seattle. The bus leaves Seattle at 4:30pm and arrives in Anacortes at 8pm (Mon., Wed., and Fri.). It returns to Seattle from the Anacortes ferry dock at 8:25am, stopping in downtown Anacortes at 8:35am and arriving in Seattle at 11:55am (Mon., Wed., Fri.).

Unfortunately, **Island Transit** (678-7771 or 321-6688) runs only one intra-island bus line—King Automobile still reigns. There is, however, only one main road: Rte. 525 on the southern half of the island, which transmutes itself into Rte. 20 around Coupeville. **The Pedaler,** 5603½ S. Bayview Rd., Freeland (321-5040), 7 mi. from Clinton, rents bicycles for $4 an hour, $18 a day, and $48.50 per week. Bicycle helmets come at no extra cost. Transporting bikes on the ferry is also easy and inexpensive (see above). Bicyclists will have safer and more scenic rides away from Rte. 525/20 (where motorists are often demented and shoulders are narrow). A less heavily traveled and more scenic detour off Rte. 20 is **Smugglers Cove Rd.** running along the west coast of the island.

Stop at one of the real estate offices in Clinton, or in one of the state parks, to pick up a free map of the island. Roads are not well-marked, and it's easy to become lost.

ACCOMMODATIONS AND CAMPING

Inexpensive motels are few and far between on Whidbey, and those that do exist are often run-down. Making reservations is always sensible, especially in rain-free July and August. A number of B&Bs offer pleasant, homey rooms for a few dollars more. Contact **Whidbey Island Bed and Breakfast Association,** P.O. Box 259, Langley 98260 (321-6272) for a full listing; reservations are necessary. Four **state parks** on a 50-mi.-long island can hardly be missed. They are listed here south to north.

Tyee Motel and Cafe, 405 S. Main St., Coupeville (678-6616), across Rte. 20 from the town proper, toward the Keystone ferry. Clean, standard motel rooms, with showers, but no tubs. The setting is bleak—you might forget you're on an island—but it's within walking distance of Coupeville and the water. Cafe open Mon.-Sat. 6:30am-8:30pm. Singles and doubles from $43. You can also check in at the lounge (open 11:30am-2am) if the cafe is closed.

Crossroads Motel, 5622 Rte. 20 (675-3145), on northern edge of Oak Harbor. Cinderblock construction suggests cheap military housing, but the rooms are immaculately kept and the ship-shape management adds a feeling of security. Senior and military discounts. Singles $32. Doubles $40. Rooms with kitchens $45.

Fort Ebey State Park, 395 N. Fort Ebey Rd. (678-4636). North of Fort Casey and just west of Coupeville. Take the Libbey Rd. turn-off from Rte. 20. Miles of hiking trails and easy access to a pebbly beach make this newest of Whidbey's campground, also its best. 50 sites for cars and RVs $8 (Oct.-April $6). 3 hiker/biker sites $4. Pay showers.

South Whidbey State Park, 4128 S. Smuggler's Cove Rd. (321-4559), 7 mi. northwest of Freeland via Bush Point Rd. and Smuggler's Cove Rd. On a cliff in a virgin stand of Douglas fir. Steep ¼-mi. trail leads down to a broad but rocky beach. 54 sites; deer browse by RVs. Sites $8. Open year-round.

Fort Casey State Park, 1280 S. Fort Casey Rd. (678-4519), right next to the Keystone ferry terminal, 3 mi. south of Coupeville on Fort Casey Rd. Sites snuggle with 35 others in an open field. This campground isn't full because of its aesthetic appeal—the ferry is two steps away. Sites $11. Open year-round.

Deception Pass State Park, 5175 N. Hwy. 525 (675-2417), 8 mi. north of Oak Harbor. The highway passes right through the park on Deception Pass Bridge. The park has 8½ mi. of hiking trails and freshwater fishing and swimming. Jets flying overhead from Oak Harbor Naval Air Station will lull you right to sleep. 250 standard sites $11. 4 rustic hiker/biker sites $4. Open year-round.

FOOD

Smoked salmon is the dish of choice on Whidbey. In Oak Harbor, your best bet is the **Safeway** grocery store on Rte. 20.

Doghouse Tavern, 230 1st St. (321-9996), in Langley, on the main drag of a 1-block town. A local hangout that serves 10¢ 6-oz. beers with lunch (limit 2). Eat $5 sandwiches, burgers, burritos, and BBQ, either in the tavern or around the back in the "family restaurant." Open Mon.-Fri. 11am-9:30pm. Sat.-Sun. 11am-10pm. Bar open till 1-2am.

Star Bistro Cafe, 201½ 1st St. (221-2627), in Langley. Dinners are expensive ($8.50-13), but the ever-present view is enticing and the live music good. Open Mon. 11:30am-3pm, Tues.-Thurs. 11:30am-9pm, Fri.-Sat. 11:30am-10pm, Sun. 10am-8pm.

Toby's Tavern, 8 Front St. (678-4222), Coupeville, in the 1890 Whidbey Mercantile Company Bldg. Like everything else in Coupeville, the building is a historical landmark. Inside, the tavern (a favorite with locals) serves burgers ($4.25), sandwiches ($4.50), and beer ($1). Open daily 11:30am-11pm, sometimes later.

SIGHTS AND ACTIVITIES

You could spend days exploring Whidbey Island, or only a few hours as you wait for transport connections. Whichever interval you choose, spend no more time in **Clinton** than is required to get off the ferry, scratch your mosquito bites, and get up the hill. Keep an eye out for loganberries and Penn Cove mussels, Whidbey's biggest exports. In general, the island's interior regions are uninspiring; Whidbey's real beauty lies in its circle of beaches.

Follow Rte. 525 about 3 mi. from the center of Clinton and turn right (north) onto Langley Rd. to reach the little town of **Langley,** located just to the west of a small shopping plaza. Langley has gone for the Old West motif—wooden sidewalks connect false fronts of antique shops and taverns—but it's not nearly as tasteless as it could be. Poke around the various arts and crafts shops on 1st St. During the second weekend in July, the townspeople close down 1st St. for the **Choockokam Arts Festival,** which showcases jewelry, pottery, and other local artworks. Call the Childer's Proctor Gallery (221-2978) for more information. The stairs at 2 Front St. lead down to **Seawall Park,** which has several picnic tables scattered along a grassy stretch by the water.

On the west side of **Useless Bay,** still towards the south end of the island on the side opposite Clinton, 1½ mi. of uninterrupted beach along **Double Bluff Park** wait to be combed. The bay can be reached by Double Bluff Rd., about 5 mi. west of Langley Rd. and 1 mi. east of Freeland on Rte. 525. Perhaps the single most impressive vista on the island is the view of Seattle and Mt. Rainier from the parking lot at the southern end of Double Bluff Rd. A more ideal spot for the Blythe spirit is **South Whidbey State Park,** 4128 S. Smuggler's Cove Rd. (321-4559), about 7 mi. north of Freeland off Rte. 525. The park's 87 acres of virgin forest and beach wrap around the west coast of the island, from Lagoon Point in the north to a lighthouse on Bush Point in the south. (See Camping for the park's overnight facilities.)

Around the bend to the north lies **Fort Casey State Park,** 1280 S. Fort Casey Rd. (678-4519), right next to the Keystone ferry terminal, 3 mi. south of Coupeville. The park is situated on the site of a late 1890s fort designed to defend against a long-anticipated attack from the Pacific. Tours of the fort's remnants are given on weekends at 2pm and start at the main gun sites. Fort Casey also operates camping facilities and shower rooms for scuba divers.

Fort Ebey State Park, 395 N. Fort Ebey Rd. (678-4636), is accessible by turning west onto Libbey Rd. from Rte. 20 north of Coupeville, by Valley Drive's park entrance. The way from the highway to the park is well-marked, but the way back to the highway is not—leave a trail of breadcrumbs or remember your route. The park is also the driest spot on the island; prickly pear cacti grow on the parched bluffs. Public beach lands, perfect for all-day expeditions, stretch from the southern tip of Fort Casey to Partridge Point, north of Fort Ebey.

Both parks and the town of **Coupeville** are contained within **Ebey's Landing National Historical Reserve,** established by the federal government for the "preservation and protection of a rural community." Many of Coupeville's homes and commercial establishments date from the 19th century. Two fortified buildings at the west end of town, the **John Alexander Blockhouse** and the **Davis Blockhouse,** stand as reminders of the early settlement's standoff with the native Skagit tribes. **Rhododendron Park,** 2 mi. southeast of Coupeville on Rte. 20, has picnic areas and six free campsites which almost always fill early during summer months. During the second weekend in August, Coupeville's **Arts and Crafts Festival** draws artists from all over the Northwest. For information on other Coupevilliana, contact the **Central Whidbey Chamber of Commerce,** P.O. Box 152, Coupeville 98239 (678-5434).

Oak Harbor, on Rte. 20 facing Oak Harbor Bay at the northern end of the island, was named for the Garry oaks that once dominated the landscape. Fast-food restaurants generally have greater dominance in the town now. **City Beach Park,** downtown, maintains a free swimming pool, kitchens, and tennis courts. (Buildings and facilities open April-Nov.; park open year-round.) In mid-July the city sponsors **Whidbey Island Race Week,** a colorful yacht regatta. A few miles north on Rte. 20, the sword and plough share the field at **U-Pick Strawberry Farms,** where the roar from low-flying Navy jets virtually rattles the fruit from the plants.

When the Skagit tribe lived and fished around Deception Pass, the area was often raided by the Haida tribe from the north. A bear totem of the Haidas now occupies the north end of West Beach in **Deception Pass State Park,** 5175 N. Rte. 20 (675-2417), at the northern tip of the island. The pass itself was named by Captain George Vancouver, who found the tangled geography of Puget Sound as confusing as most visitors do today. This is the most heavily used of Whidbey's four state parks, and its vistas are magnificent. A brand-new **interpretive center** in the Bowman area, just north of the WPA bridge on Rte. 20 E., describes the environmental army that built so many of the park facilities in the Pacific Northwest during the Great Depression. There are camping facilities, a saltwater boat launch, and a freshwater lake for swimming, fishing, and boating. (A fishing license, available at most hardware stores, is required for fishing in the lake; the season runs from mid-April to Oct. Park open year-round.)

SAN JUAN ISLANDS

The San Juan Islands are an accessible treasure. Bald eagles spiral above haggard hillsides, pods of killer whales spout offshore, and despite the lush vegetation it never seems to rain. To travelers arriving from teeming summer resorts, the islands seem blissfully serene. It's possible to drive the back roads in seclusion even in mid-summer, rarely passing another car. For this reason, islanders don't begrudge admission to their towns and campsites. Although tension is starting to build between locals and transplants from Seattle and California who are buying up huge chunks of the islands at exorbitant prices, well-behaved tourists and their dollars are still very welcome on the San Juans.

An excellent guide to the area is *The San Juan Islands Afoot and Afloat* by Marge Mueller ($10), available at bookstores and outfitting stores on the islands and in Seattle. *The San Juans Beckon* is published annually by the *Islands Sounder,* the local paper, and provides maps and up-to-date information on island recreation. You can pick it up free on the ferries and in island stores. The *San Juanderer* also has useful information, including tide charts and ferry schedules (free on ferries or at the tourist centers).

GETTING THERE

Washington State Ferries serve the islands daily from **Anacortes** on the mainland. To reach Anacortes, take I-5 north from Seattle to Mt. Vernon. From there, Rte. 20 heads west to the city, and the way to the ferry is well-marked. **Gray Line** (624-5077) buses to Anacortes depart Seattle from the Greyhound depot at 8th Ave. and Stewart St. at 5:55am daily ($13.25). Call for more information.

Of the 172 islands in the San Juan archipelago, only four are accessible by ferry. **Ferries** depart Anacortes about nine times per day on a route that stops at **Lopez, Shaw, Orcas,** and **San Juan Islands.** In summer, two additional ferries per day travel directly to San Juan Island, and one ferry per day continues to the town of **Sidney, BC,** just north of Victoria on Vancouver Island. Not every ferry services all the islands, so check the schedule (800-843-3779 or 464-6400). The ferry system revises its schedule seasonally.

You can purchase **ferry tickets** in Anacortes. You pay only on westbound trips to or between the islands; no charge is levied on eastbound traffic. A money-saving tip: travel directly to the westernmost island on your itinerary and then make your way back to the mainland island by island. Foot passengers travel in either direction between the islands free of charge. Fares from Anacortes to San Juan Island are $4.65 (seniors and ages 5-11 $2.35), $6.25 for bikes, $8.30 for motorcycles, and $19 for cars ($16 in winter). Fares to the other islands en route are generally a few dollars cheaper. Inter-island fares average $2.25 for bikes and motorcycles, $7.75 for cars. The one-way fare to Sidney is $6.05, $7.55 for bikes, $9.60 for motorcycles, and $31.25 for cars in summer ($26.05 in winter). Some car spaces are available from the islands to Sidney. Reservations for Sidney are strongly recommended; call before noon the day before your trip to ensure a space. For specific departure times and rates, call Washington State Ferries (206-464-6400; in WA 800-542-0810). On peak travel days, arrive with your vehicle at least one hour prior to scheduled departure. The ferry authorities accept only cash or in-state checks as payment.

■■■ SAN JUAN ISLAND

The history of San Juan Island is an oddball chronicle. The 1846 Treaty of Oregon had not assigned the San Juans to either Canada or the U.S., and when the Canadian Hudson's Bay Company established a salmon-curing station and a sheep farm on the island, the Company assumed its ownership would go undisputed. However, in 1853 the Territorial Congress of Oregon declared the islands its property, ignoring British claims. By 1859, 25 Americans and many more animals lived on San Juan Island. The cold-blooded shooting of a British pig found rooting one morning in an American farmer's potato patch left both countries with no choice but to send in troops, thus initiating perhaps the least-known international dispute in U.S. history—"The Pig War." For 12 years, two thoroughly bored garrisons yawned across the island at each other, occasionally rousing to join in horse races and Christmas dances. According to local historians, 16 Americans died in the conflict, mostly of disease. The soldiers' descendants now direct their energies to more peaceful pursuits, primarily the bustling tourist industry on this island.

Lime Kiln State Park provides the best ocean vista of all the islands for whale-watching. San Juan may be the last stop on the ferry route, but it is still the most frequently visited island and provides the traveler with all the beauty of San Juan and all the comforts of **Friday Harbor,** the largest (although still modest) town in the archipelago. Since the ferry docks right in town, this island is also the easiest to explore.

PRACTICAL INFORMATION AND ORIENTATION

Visitors Information: Chamber of Commerce (378-5240) on Front St. at the Ferry Terminal. **National Park Service Information Center** (378-2240), northeast corner of 1st and Spring. Both answer questions about San Juan and Friday Harbor. Park Service open Mon.-Fri. 8am-4:30pm, Sat.-Sun. 9am-4:30pm; closed on weekends in winter.

U.S. Customs: 271 Front St. (378-2080 or 800-562-5943 for 24-hr. service).

Tours: The Inn at Friday Harbor, 410 Spring St. (378-4351), takes 10-12 people on a bus around the island via English Camp and Lime Kiln Park (for whale-watching) daily 2pm ($10).

Ferry Terminal: 378-4777. Information line open 24 hr. Waiting room opens ½ hr. before scheduled departures.

Taxi: Primo Taxi, 378-3550. Open daily 5am-3am.

Car Rental: Friday Harbor Rentals, 410 Spring St. (378-4351), in the Inn at Friday Harbor. $45 per day, unlimited mileage. Major credit card required. Only rents to people 21 and over with their own insurance.

Bike Rental: Island Bicycles, 380 Argyle St., Friday Harbor (378-4941). 1-speeds (kids only) $10 per day, 5-speeds $15 per day, 10-speeds $20 per day, mountain bikes $25 per day. Locks and helmets included. Also rents child carriers and trailers. Provides maps of the island and suggests bike routes. Credit card required. Open daily 10am-5:30pm; Labor Day-Memorial Day Thurs.-Sat. 10am-5:30pm.

Moped Rental: Susie's Mopeds (378-5244), in Churchill Sq. above the ferry lanes on Nichols St. between A and B St. Mopeds $12 per hr., $45 per day. Credit card required. Open March-Oct. daily 9:30am-6pm.

Laundromat: Wash Tub Laundromat (378-2070), in the San Juan Inn on Spring St., ½ block from the ferry dock. $1.50 wash, 10-min. dry 50¢. Open daily 7:30am-9pm.

Senior Citizens' Center: at the Gray Top Inn (378-2677). Open Mon.-Fri. 9am-4pm.

Red Tide Hotline: 800-562-5632.

Pharmacy: Friday Harbor Drug, 210 Spring St. (378-4421). Open Mon.-Sat. 9am-7pm, Sun. 10am-4pm.

Medical Services: Inter-Island Medical Center, 550 Spring St. (378-2141). Open Mon.-Fri. 9am-5pm. 24-hr. emergency service.
Emergency: 911. **Sheriff:** 135 Rhone St., at Reed St. (non-emergency 378-4151).
Post Office: (378-4511), Blair and Reed St. Open Mon.-Fri. 8:30am-4:30pm. **General Delivery ZIP Code:** 98250.
Area Code: 206.

With bicycle, car, and boat rentals all within a few blocks of the ferry terminal, Friday Harbor proves a convenient berth for exploring the islands. Miles of road make all corners of the island accessible, but the roads are poorly marked. It's smart to plot your course carefully on one of the free maps available at the information center in town (see above). If the information center is closed, stop at one of the island's real estate offices, most of which distribute free maps outside their doors.

CAMPING

San Juan's campgrounds have become wildly popular of late; show up early in the afternoon to make sure you get a spot.

San Juan County Park, 380 Westside Rd. (378-2992), 10 mi. west of Friday Harbor on Smallpox and Andrews Bays. Cold water and flush toilets. No RV hookups. Sites for those with vehicles $14. Biker/hiker sites $4.50.

Lakedale Campgrounds, 2627 Roche Harbor Rd. (378-2350), 4 mi. from Friday Harbor. Pay showers ($1), fishing in nearby fertile waters ($4, no permit required), canoe rentals ($4.50 per hr., $18 per day), and swimming in freshwater lakes (non-campers $1.50, under 12 $1). Sites with vehicle access for 1-2 people $15 (July-Aug. $18), plus $3.50 each additional person. Biker/hiker sites $5 (Sept.-July-Aug. $6.50). Open April 1-Oct. 15.

FOOD

Stock up at **King's Market,** 160 Spring St. (378-4505; open daily 8am-10pm).

Vic's Driftwood Drive-In (378-8427), at 2nd and Court. Amiable management with great burgers ($1.60) and shakes so thick you'll get dimples trying to drink them ($1.50). Open Mon.-Fri. 6am-7pm, Sat. 6am-2pm.

Katrina's, 65 Nichols St. (378-7290), behind the Funk 'n Junk "antique" store. Hard to find, but worth it. The tiny kitchen cooks up a different menu every day, but they always have local organic salads, freshly baked bread, and gigantic cookies (50¢) to fill a picnic basket. Open Mon.-Sat. 12-5pm.

The Hungry Clam, 130 1st St. (378-3474), near Spring St. The unmistakable spout of the fast-food leviathan. Clam basket $5.50, burger $2.75. Open Tues.-Sat. 11am-7pm, Sun. 11am-3pm.

SIGHTS AND ACTIVITIES

Friday Harbor is less than charming when the tourists are out in full force, but quite appealing at other times, especially in winter. Take the time to poke around the galleries, craft shops, and bookstores. The **Whale Museum,** 62 1st St. (378-4710), stars skeletons, sculptures, and information on new research. The museum even has a toll-free **whale hotline** (800-562-8832) to report sightings and strandings. (Open daily 10am-5pm; in winter daily 11am-4pm. Admission $3, seniors and students $2.50, under 12 $1.50.) The **San Juan Historical Museum,** 405 Price St. (378-3149), in the old King House across from the St. Francis Catholic Church, explodes with exhibits, furnishings, and photographs from the late 1800s. Pick up the pamphlet mapping out a free walking tour of Friday Harbor. (Open Wed.-Sat. 1-4:30pm; Labor Day-May Thurs.-Fri. 1-4pm. Free.)

A drive around the perimeter of the island takes about 90 minutes, and the route is flat enough for cyclists. The **West Side Road** traverses gorgeous scenery and provides the best chance for sighting **orcas** (killer whales) offshore. For those without private transportation, **The Inn at Friday Harbor** (378-4351) runs a two-hour sightseeing tour of the island every afternoon, stopping at Roche Harbor, English and American Camps, and Lime Kiln Lighthouse (see Practical Information).

To begin a loop of the island, head south out of Friday Harbor on Mullis Rd., which merges into Cattle Point Rd. on the way to **American Camp** (378-2907), 5 mi. south of Friday Harbor. The camp dates to the Pig War of 1859, when the U.S. and Britain were at loggerheads over possession of the islands. Two of the camp's buildings still stand. An interpretive shelter near the entrance to the park explains the history of the conflict, and a self-guided trail leads from the shelter through the buildings and past the site of the British sheep farm. Every weekend (June-Sept. noon-3pm), volunteers in period costume re-enact daily life at the camp (free). If the weather's clear, make the ½-mi. jaunt farther down the road to **Cattle Point,** which offers views of the distant Olympic Mountains.

Returning north on Cattle Point Rd., consider taking the gravel **False Bay Rd.** to the west. The road will guide you down the straight and narrow to **False Bay,** a true bay that is home to a large number of nesting **bald eagles** and a great spot for watching them. During the spring and summer, walk along the northwestern shore (to your right as you face the water) at low tide to see the national emblems nesting.

Farther north on False Bay Rd., you'll run into **Bailer Hill Rd.,** which turns into West Side Rd. when it reaches Haro Straight. (You can also reach Bailer Hill Rd. by taking Cattle Point Rd. to Little Rd.) Slopes overflowing with wildflowers rise to one side, while rocky shores descend to the ocean on the other.

Whale-watching at **Lime Kiln Point State Park,** a few miles north, is best during salmon runs in the summer. Check the whale museum for day-to-day information on your chances of sighting the orcas and minkes looming offshore.

The Pig War casts its comic pallor over **British Camp,** the second half of **San Juan National Historical Park.** The camp lies on West Valley Rd. on the sheltered **Garrison Bay** (take Mitchell Bay Rd. east from West Side Rd.). Here, four original buildings have been preserved, including the barracks, now used as an **interpretive center.** The center chronicles the "War" and sells guides to the island. It also shows a relatively interesting 13-minute slide show on the epic struggle. (Park open year-round; buildings open Memorial Day-Labor Day daily 8am-4:30pm. Free.)

Roche Harbor Resort, Roche Harbor Rd. (378-2155), on the northern side of the island, began as a lime mine and kiln built by the British during their uneventful occupation. After its establishment by megalomaniacal industrialist John S. McMillan in 1886, Roche Harbor became a full-fledged company town. In 1956, the entire town was delivered from the company to be converted into a resort. The **Hotel de Haro,** built by McMillan in 1887, is the center of this vacationland. Stop by the information kiosk in front for a copy of the $1 brochure, *A Walking Tour of Historic Roche Harbor,* which tosses a little history of the "town" in with architectural and social commentary. Most of the grounds are open to the public. Don't miss the bizarre mausoleum that McMillan had built for himself and his family. The Masonic symbolism that garnishes the structure is explained in the *Walking Tour.*

If you're eager to **fish** or **clam,** pick up a copy of the Department of Fisheries pamphlet, *Salmon, Shellfish, Marine Fish Sport Fishing Guide,* for details on regulations and limits. The guide is available free at **Friday Harbor Hardware and Marine,** 270 Spring St. (378-4622). Hunting and fishing licenses are required on the islands, and can be obtained from the hardware store (open Mon.-Sat. 8am-6pm, Sun. 10am-4pm). Check with the **red tide hotline** (800-562-5632) if you'll be gathering shellfish; the nasty bacteria can wreak deadly havoc on your intestines.

Several small-scale entrepreneurs run charters or rent out boats to visitors for expeditions on the water or to neighboring small islands. **San Juan Kayak Expeditions,** P.O. Box 2041, Friday Harbor 98250 (378-4436), leads two- to four-day trips in two-person sea kayaks. These excursions (given June-Sept.) offer a peaceful and personal way to see the hidden niches of the archipelago. They supply equipment and camping gear. ($160 for a 2-day trip, $220 for a 3-day trip, and $275 for a 4-day trip, including 2 hot meals per day.)

The annual **San Juan Island Traditional Jazz Festival** brings several swing bands to Friday Harbor on the last weekend in July. A $40 badge ($45 if purchased after July 1) will gain you admission to all performances, but you'll have just as much fun for free by joining the crowds of revelers in the streets outside the clubs. Single performance tickets range from $10-25. For more information, contact San Juan Island Goodtime Classic Jazz Association, P.O. Box 1666, Friday Harbor 98250 (378-5509).

■■■ ORCAS ISLAND

Mount Constitution overlooks much of Puget Sound from its 2409-ft. summit atop Orcas Island, the largest island of the San Juan chain. In the mountain's shadow dwells a small population of retirees, artists, and farmers tending to understated homes surrounded by the red bark of madrona trees and greenery. With an enchanting state park and funky youth hostel, Orcas has perhaps the best tourist facilities of all the islands. The one problem is that much of the beach access is occupied by private resorts and is closed to the public. The DNR trail to **Obstruction Pass Beach** is the best of the few ways to clamber down to the rocky shores.

PRACTICAL INFORMATION AND ORIENTATION

Visitors Information: North Beach Rd., ½ block north of Horseshoe Hwy. next to the museum (see Sights). An unstaffed shack with racks of pamphlets. Call the **Chamber of Commerce** (376-2273) for other information or stop at a real-estate office along North Beach Rd. for free maps.

Ferries: Washington State Ferry, 376-4389 or 376-2134. 24 hr. The only way onto the island from Anacortes. **Island Shuttle Express,** 671-1137. Service to Bellingham and Friday Harbor (1 per day, $18). Walk-on or bicycle passengers only. Departs from the Obstruction Pass dock.

Taxi: Adventure Taxi, 476-4994.

Bike Rental: Wildlife Cycle (376-4708), A St. and North Beach Rd., in Eastsound. 21-speeds $5 per hr., $20 per day. Open Mon.-Sat. 10:30am-5pm.

Moped Rental: Key Moped Rentals (376-2474), just north of the fire station on Prune Alley in Eastsound; also at ferry landing. $12 per hr., $45 per 8-hr. day. Driver's license and $10 deposit required. Helmets, gas, and maps included. Open May-Sept. daily 10am-6pm.

Library: (376-4985), at Rose and Pine in Eastsound. Open Tues.-Wed. 10am-7pm, Thurs. 10am-9pm, Fri.-Sat. 10am-4pm.

Senior Services Center: (376-2677), across from the museum on North Beach Rd. in Eastsound. Open Mon.-Fri. 9am-4pm.

Pharmacy: Ray's (376-2230, after-hours emergencies 476-4756), next to Templin's in Eastsound. Open Mon.-Sat. 9am-6pm, Sun. 10am-6pm.

Emergency: 911.

Post Office: (376-4121), A St. in Eastsound Market Place, ½ block north of the Chamber of Commerce. Open Mon.-Fri. 9am-4:30pm. **General Delivery ZIP Code:** 98245.

Area Code: 206.

Because Orcas is shaped like a horseshoe, getting around is a bit of a chore. The ferry lands on the southwest tip. Travel 9 mi. northeast to the top of the horseshoe to reach **Eastsound,** the island's main town. Olga and Doe Bay are an additional 8 and 11 mi. from Eastsound, respectively, down the eastern side of the horseshoe. Stop in one of the shops at the landing to get a free map (most are open daily 8:30am-6:30pm).

Gas prices on Orcas often run 40¢ per gallon higher than on the mainland, so tank up in Anacortes. The only **gas stations** on the island are located in Deer Harbor and Eastsound and at the ferry landing.

ORCAS ISLAND

ACCOMMODATIONS AND CAMPING

Avoid the bed and breakfasts (upwards of $60 per day) of the "Healing Island" and stay at the hostel. If the hostel is full, try a campground.

Doe Bay Village Resort, Star Rte. 86, Olga 98279 (376-2291 or 376-4755), off Horseshoe Hwy. on Pt. Lawrence Rd., 8 mi. out of Moran State Park. On a secluded bay. No single-sex dorms. The resort comes with kitchen facilities, a health food store, an organic cafe, and plenty of grounds on which to wander. The crowning attraction is the steam sauna and mineral bath ($3 per day, nonlodgers $6; bathing suits optional). Beds $12.50, nonmembers $14.50. Camping $8.50. Cottages from $32.50. Imaginative and flexible work-trade program.Guided kayak trips $30 per 4 hr. (see Sights). Reservations recommended (only 8 bunks). Open year-round.

Outlook Inn (376-2200), P.O. Box 210, Eastsound 98245. On the north side of Horseshoe Hwy. in the center of Eastsound. If the island's many beach-cabin resorts don't appeal to you (or your wallet), this elegant inn by the shore is a good alternative. Singles from $64. Doubles $69. Reservations required. Rates $10 less in winter.

Moran State Park, Star Rte. 22, Eastsound 98245 (376-2326). Follow Horseshoe Hwy. straight into the park. All the best of San Juan fun—swimming, fishing, and hiking. Arresting grounds, amiable staff. 4 different campgrounds with a total of 151 sites. About 12 sites remain open year-round, as do the restrooms. Backcountry camping prohibited. Rowboats and paddleboats $8-9 for the 1st hr., $6 per hr. thereafter. Standard sites with hot showers $11. Hiker or biker sites $5. **Information booth** at park entrance open Memorial Day-Labor Day daily 2-11pm. Park open daily 6:30am-dusk; Sept.-March 8am-dusk. Reservations strongly recommended May-Labor Day. Send $16 ($11 per site plus a $5 reservation fee).

Obstruction Pass: the state DNR maintains 9 primitive sites, accessible only by boat or foot. Just past Olga, turn off Horseshoe Hwy. and hang a right to head south on Obstruction Pass Rd. Soon you'll come to a dirt road marked "Obstruction Pass Trailhead." Follow the road for about 1 mi. The sites are a ½-mi. hike from the end of the road. No drinking water, so bring plenty. Pit toilets. A rocky but well-maintained trail to a beach overhang. Sites free.

FOOD

All the essentials can be found at **Island Market,** on Langdell St. (376-6000; open Mon.-Sat. 8am-9pm, Sun. 10am-8pm). For loads of fresh local produce, try the **Farmer's Market** in front of the museum (every Sat. 10am).

Bilbos Festivo (376-4728), Prune Alley and A St. Good Mexican cooking and *great* salsa. You can try the peppy Christmas burrito year-round ($7). Homemade chocolate desserts $3-4. Artistic decor, patio dining. Open Mon.-Fri. noon-2:30pm and 5-9:30pm, Sat.-Sun. 5-9:30pm.

The Lower Tavern (376-4848), on Langdell St. behind the Island Market, Eastsound. Boasts the town's best burgers (with fries, $4.75). Avoid the lunchtime rush. Open Mon.-Sat. 11am-midnight, Sun. noon-7pm.

Rose's Bakery Cafe (376-4220), in Eastsound Sq. Upbeat, offbeat staff serves up croissants ($1) and sandwiches ($6). Buy bags of day-old pastries at half price. Open Mon.-Sat. 8am-5pm, Sun. 10am-3pm.

Cafe Olga (376-5098), in the Orcas Island Artworks Bldg. at the Olga crossing a few mi. beyond Moran State Park. A cooperative gallery converted into an artsy-pricey coffeehouse. Soup and Sandwich special $5.50, blackberry pie $3.25. Open March-Dec. daily 10am-6pm.

Portofino Pizzeria (376-2085), Prune Alley. 10-in. pizza $7.50, and only 93¢ for a slice. Open Tues.-Thurs. 11:30am-8:30pm, Fri.-Sat. 11:30am-9pm.

SIGHTS AND ACTIVITIES

Trippers on Orcas Island don't need to travel with a destination in mind. At least half the fun lies in simply tramping about—pick a side road, select a particularly moving vista, and meditate on llife, llove, and llamas.

Eastsound offers great views from the highway and from the adjacent beach. Stop in at the picturesque and peaceful **Emmanuel Church** (376-2352), on Main St. just across from the library. Built in 1885, the islanders transcend their sectarian differences and worship, both in this one building. A path behind the church leads to a rock-ledge seat that hangs over the surfline.

Moran State Park is unquestionably Orcas's greatest attraction. Over 21 mi. of hiking trails cover the park, ranging in difficulty from a one-hour jaunt around Mountain Lake to a day-long constitutional up the south face of **Mt. Constitution,** the highest peak on the islands. Pick up a copy of the trail guide from the **rangers station** (376-2837). From the summit of Constitution, you can see other islands in the group, as well as the Olympic and Cascade Ranges, Vancouver Island, and Mt. Rainier. The stone tower at the top was built in 1936 by the Civilian Conservation Corps as an observation tower fro tourists and a fire lookout. It's a torturous climb to the top of the mountain; if you don't have a car, you may not want to try it. And be warned: rental mopeds are not powerful enough to reach the summit. For an easier jaunt, drive up Mt. Constitution and hike part-way down to **Cascade Falls—** which is spectacular in the spring and early summer. Down below, you can swim in two freshwater lakes easily accessible from the highway or rent rowboats ($8 per hr.) and paddleboats ($9 per hr.) from the park. Head out from the lake to the lagoon for an oceanside picnic.

Olga is a minuscule collection of buildings that stretches the definition of "town." At the Olga crossing stands an old strawberry-packing plant, now converted by an artists' cooperative into **Orcas Island Artworks** (376-4408), a shop carrying high-quality, high-priced local crafts and clothing (open March-Dec. daily 10am-6pm). Off Horseshoe Hwy., on West Beach Rd., is **The Right Place,** which gives you an eye-witness view of glass-blowers in action. Continue along Horseshoe Hwy. to **Doe Bay Village Resorts** (376-2291), where you can soak in the natural mineral waters, sweat in the sauna, and see prophetic visions as you jump into the cold bath (bathing suits are the exception; see Accommodations and Camping). The **Sea Kayak Tour** of the surrounding islands is a fascinating, albeit expensive, "water-hike" of the north end of Puget Sound. ($25 per 4-hr. tour. Tours leave June-Sept. Mon.-Fri. at 1pm, Sat.-Sun. at 10am and 2pm, and include a ½ hr. of dry-land training.) The resort grounds are secluded and make for good wandering. Check first with the manager to learn the perimeters and parameters of the resort.

■ Lopez Island

Smaller than either Orcas or San Juan, Lopez (or "Slow-pez," as it's called) is an island of 1200 fisherfolk and farmers. Lopez lacks some of the tourist facilities of the other islands and some of the tourists as well. Keep a hand free while you're passing through—you'll need it to return the genial waves of the locals.

Lopez Island is ideal for those seeking solitary beach-walking or tranquil bicycling. It is, for the most part, free of both imposing inclines and heavy traffic. Since **Lopez Village** (which, with all of 14 buildings, is the largest town on the island) is 3½ mi. from the ferry, it's best to BYOB (bring your own bicycle). If you need to rent a bike, head to **Lopez Bicycle Works** (468-2847), south of the village next to the island's Marine Center. The cheerful staff will give you a detailed map of island roads, complete with distances, even if you don't rent. Ten-speeds cost $4.50 per hour and $18 per day; mountain bikes cost $5 per hour and $23 per day. (Open June-Aug. daily 10am-6pm; call in winter months.)

Shark Reef and **Agate Beach Park**—small parks on the south end of the island that are meant for daytime use—offer a change from mainland campgrounds. Shark

Reef features tranquil and well-maintained hiking trails, and Agate's beaches are calm and desolate. The only other "sight" is the **Lopez Island Historical Society Museum** in Lopez Village (468-2049), 1½ blocks from the New Bay, across from the San Juan County Bank. Besides exhibits on island history, this facility boasts an open shed filled with old canoes and obsolete farm equipment. (Open Wed.-Sun. noon-4pm; May-June and Sept. Fri-Sun. noon-4pm; closed Oct.-April. Free.)

Indoor accommodations can be found in the shape of spartan cabins at **Islander Lopez Marine Resort** (468-2233), on Fisherman Bay Rd. about a ½ mi. south of Lopez Village. You can get a room with all the amenities ($50 per night), or, for a cheaper alternative, try their four-person teepees ($30 per night). **Odlin Park** (468-2496), just off the road and a little over 1 mi. from the ferry terminal, offers 30 sites, a kitchen with a wood stove and cold running water, a boat launch, a volleyball net, and a softball diamond ($10 per vehicle up to 4 people, each additional person $3; hiker/biker sites $2.50). **Spencer Spit State Park** (468-2251), on the northeast corner of the island, about 3½ mi. from the ferry terminal, has 51 sites along 1 mi. of beachfront that provides good clamming year-round ($10; 2 8-bunk covered shelters $14 per person).

Nothin' says lovin' like **Holly B's** oven, in the Lopez Plaza (468-2133). Pastries and bread (from 85¢) as well as day-olds at a discount (open Wed.-Mon. 8am-5pm). If you don't feel like paying for Lopez eateries, stop by **Greg's Smokehouse,** Shoal Bay Lane, which smokes up fresh salmon. **Madiona Farms** (468-3441), at Davis Bay and Richardson Rd., is a good place to pick up a snack of seasonal fruits and berries (open Mon.-Fri. 8am-5pm). **Grayland Gallery** displays local arts and crafts next to **Hermnel Lake,** which is stocked annually and open to the public for fishing.

The **Senior Citizens' Helpline** is 468-2421 (open Mon.-Fri. 9am-4pm). The **emergency number** is 911.You can reach the **post office** at 468-2282. **General Delivery ZIP Code:** 98261.

■ Other Islands

With one store and 100 residents, **Shaw Island** was not designed with tourists in mind. One eclectic building serves island visitors—a combination ferry terminal/ general store/post office/dock/gas station that's run by Franciscan nuns, no less. However, the island's 11 mi. of public roads are endearing to hikers and bikers. The library and museum, near the center of the island, at the intersection of Blind Bay and Hoffman Cove Rd., are open only on Mondays and Saturdays. **Shaw Island County Park,** on the south side of the island, has eight campsites ($6), which fill quickly. There are no other accommodations on the island.

Washington State Parks operates over 15 **marine parks** on some of the smaller islands in the archipelago. These islands, accessible by private transportation only, have anywhere from one to 51 mainly primitive campsites. The park system publishes a pamphlet on its marine facilities that is available at parks or hardware and supply stores on the larger islands. One of the most popular destinations is **Sucia Island,** site of gorgeous scenery and rugged terrain. Canoes and kayaks can easily navigate the archipelago when the water is calm, but when the wind whips up the surf, only larger boats (at least 16 ft.) go out to sea. Navigational maps are essential to avoid the reefs and nasty hidden rocks that surround the islands.

The Department of Natural Resources operates three parks; each has three to six free campsites with pit toilets but no drinking water. Cypress Head on **Cypress Island** has wheelchair-accessible facilities.

■■■ BELLINGHAM

Founded by Whatcom loggers and coal miners in the 1850s, the town flightily decided on Sehome for its name, next alighted ephemerally on Whatcom City, and finally landed on Bellingham. Local poet Ella Higginson once bragged that she had lived in three different cities without ever having moved a block.

Together with its southern neighbor of Fairhaven, Bellingham set its sights on becoming the terminus of the transcontinental railroad. So hell-bent were residents on capturing the ultimate spike that when the famed feminist-anarchist Emma Goldman blew into town, they trooped en masse to jeer her, fearful that her presence would smear Bellingham's all-American image. The townspeople's spleen went for naught, however—the railroad line ended 90 mi. to the south.

PRACTICAL INFORMATION AND ORIENTATION

Visitors Information, 904 Potter St. (671-3990). Take exit 253 (Lakeway) from I-5. Prepare yourself for a flood of Whatcom County trivia and non-trivial information. Extremely helpful staff. Open daily 9am-6pm; in winter 8:30am-5:30pm. **Bellingham Parks and Recreation Department,** 3424 Meridian St. (676-6985).

Greyhound, 1329 N. State St. (733-5251). To: Seattle (4 per day, $11); Vancouver (4 per day, $12); Mt. Vernon (4 per day, $4). Open Mon.-Fri. 7:30am-5pm, Sat.-Sun. 8:30-10am and 1-4pm.

Whatcom County Transit: 676-7433. All buses originate at the terminal in the Railroad Ave. mall on Magnolia St., where maps and schedules are available. Fare 25¢, senior citizens 10¢; no free transfers. Buses run every 15-30 min. Mon.-Fri. 7am-7pm, reduced service Sat. 9am-6pm.

Lummi Island Ferry (676-6730), at Gooseberry Pt. off Hackston Way. 26 trips back and forth each day. The first leaves the island at 6:20am; the last departs the mainland at 12:10am. Fare $1, driver and car $2.

Taxi: Superior Cabs, 734-3478. **Bellingham Taxi,** 676-0445. Both 24 hr.

Car Rental: U-Save Auto Rental, 1100 Iowa (671-3687). Cars from $18 per day with 100 free mi., 15¢ per additional mi. Must be 21, with credit card or $250 deposit. Open Mon.-Fri. 9am-5:30pm, Sat. 9am-4pm.

Laundromat: Bellingham Cleaning Center, 1010 Lakeway Dr. (734-3755). Wash $1, 10-min. dry 25¢. Open daily 7am-10pm.

Public Library: 210 Central (676-6860), in the central business district. Open Mon.-Thurs. 10am-9pm, Fri.-Sat. 10am-6pm.

Ride Board: Viking Union at Western Washington University. Rides most often to Seattle and eastern Washington, but also to other regions of the continent.

Senior Services: Information and assistance 733-4033 (city) or 398-1995 (county); take bus 10B to the corner of Ohio and Cornwall St. Open 8:30am-4:30pm daily.

Crisis Centers: Bellingham (734-7271). Whatcom County (384-1485). Both 24 hr.

Pharmacy: Fountain Super Drug Store, 2416 Meridian (733-6200). Open Mon.-Sat. 9am-10pm, Sun. 10am-7pm.

Hospital: St. Joseph's General, 2901 Squalicum Pkwy. (734-5400). Open 24 hr.

Post Office: 315 Prospect (676-8303). Open Mon.-Fri. 8am-5pm. **General Delivery ZIP Code:** 98225.

Area Code: 206.

Bellingham lies along I-5, 90 mi. north of Seattle and 57 mi. south of Vancouver. Bellingham's downtown is a small shopping and business area centered on Holly St. and Cornwall Ave., "perfumed" by the Georgia Pacific paper plant. Western Washington University climbs a hill to the south along Indian St. Old Fairhaven Village (the "South Side" to locals) fronts the south end of the bay along South State St. suburbs. 130 acres of city parks encircle the entire city of Bellingham. **Whatcom County Transit** provides service throughout the area.

Reach **Fairhaven** either by heading south along State St. from downtown or by taking the Fairhaven exit (#250) off I-5. From the south, take the bayside **Chuckanut Drive** (Rte. 11) instead of I-5. Chuckanut leaves I-5 at exit 231 in Skagit County and follows the water and mountains into Fairhaven Village. Larrabee State Park is along this drive. Startling views of the San Juan Islands and sparkling Puget Sound appear through the trees. This route is not recommended for cyclists; the road is extremely narrow and is a favorite drag stretch for hot-rodders. Cyclists should stick to Rte. 9, a more manageable stretch that pops up on the east side of I-5. Fairhaven is also on Bellingham bus lines 1A, 1B, 2B, 5A, and 7B.

Bellingham may have lost the railroad, but competitive bidding has lured the **Alaska Marine Highway** from Seattle, establishing the northern city as the most important link for trade and transportation to the "Great Land." The ferry cruises up the Alaskan Panhandle offering a spectacular voyage past glaciers, wooded islands, and snowy peaks. Whales, seals, and eagles often escort the ship. The **Tongass National Forest** even trots out an interpretive program when ferries sail by its holdings. For information on schedules, rates, discounts, and vehicle transport see Getting Thereand Getting Around: By Ferry in the Essentials chapter.

ACCOMMODATIONS AND CAMPING

Most of Bellingham's motels serve traveling salespeople and north-bound itinerants, and the rooms lack both tranquility and a bay view. Your best bet is the hostel. The local bed and breakfast association, **Babs,** P.O. Box 5025, Bellingham (733-8642), can assist with reserving you a place to stay; B&B doubles average $50.

Fairhaven Rose Garden Hostel (HI/AYH), 107 Chuckanut Dr. (671-1750), next to Fairhaven Park, about ¾ mi. from the ferry terminal. Take exit #250 on I-5, west on the Old Fairhaven Parkway to 12th St.; bear left onto Chuckamut Dr. Or take bus lines 1A and 1B. If stranded after buses stop running, hostel will pick up from depot or ferry terminal. The accommodations are a bit cramped, but the friendly guests and rosy surroundings compensate. Open Jan. 2-Dec. 23. Check-in 5-9pm. Check-out 10am. Members $8.50, nonmembers $11.50. Call 2 days ahead for reservations if you're planning on staying on Wed. or Thurs., as Alaska-bound travelers fill the beds quickly. Reservations mandatory from Nov.-Feb.

Mac's Motel, 1215 E. Maple St. (734-7570), at Samish Way. Large clean rooms. Pleasant management, and cats—lots of cats—all over the place. Mac loves cats. Cats. Cats. Singles $25. Doubles $32.50. Open 7am-11pm.

Bell Motel, 208 N. Samish Way (733-2520), on the strip. Hard beds and plain decor. Free local calls. Refrigerator in most rooms. Singles $33. Doubles from $35. Some rooms have kitchens available, for $5 extra.

YWCA, 1026 N. Forest St. (734-4820), up the hill, 1 block east of State St., about 4 blocks from Greyhound. Only women over 18 allowed; priority given to long-term residents. A pleasant, older building. Bathroom on the hall. Check-in Mon.-Fri. 8am-9pm, Sat. 9am-5pm. Private singles $20, adjoining singles $15.

Larrabee State Park, Chuckanut Dr. (676-2093), 7 mi. south of Bellingham. 86 sites on Samish Bay. Check out the nearby tidal pools or hike to alpine lakes. For your listening pleasure, trains thunder by nightly. The 3 walk-in tentsites are the most appealing option. Sites $8. Hookups $12.

FOOD

Community Food Co-op, 1059 N. State St. (734-8158), at Maple, has the essentials. Nonmembers pay 6½% more (open Mon.-Sat. 9am-8pm, Sun. 11am-6pm).

Bullie's Restaurant, 1200 Harris (734-2855), in the Fairhaven Marketplace. Decor is enhanced by an old gas pump converted into a cylindrical fish bowl. Burgers ($4.75-6.50); massive beer selection, including micro-brews. Open Mon.-Thurs. 11am-11pm, Fri.-Sat. 11am-midnight, Sun. 11am-10pm.

Tony's Coffees and Tea Shop, 1101 Harris Ave. (733-6319), in Fairhaven Village just down the hill from S. State St. This Fairhaven institution is at once cafe and coffee market. Some tables are inlaid with hand-painted tiles. Coffee, bagels, and pastries in a free floating atmosphere of sitar music and paisley. "Toxic milkshake" $2. Free live music at random. Open daily 7:30am-11pm, garden open 7am-11pm. Same cinnamon rolls for ½-price at the **Great Harvest Bakery** in the Bellingham Mall (671-0873), on Samish Way. Bakery open Tues.-Sat. 9:30am-6pm.

Cafe Akroteri, 1215 Cornwall Ave. (676-5554). Plaster of Paris and accents of Athens. Gyros $4.50, *souvlaki, baklava,* and more let's go to Greece dishes. Open Mon.-Thurs. 11am-9pm, Fri.-Sat. 11am-9:30pm.

SIGHTS AND ACTIVITIES

When the trans-continental railroad bypassed Bellingham and nearby Fairhaven, construction of many buildings stopped short. In Fairhaven especially, the structures were left to rot until 20 years ago, when a developer caught sight of the area (now called the South Side or, more euphemistically, the "historic Fairhaven district") and initiated a revitalization process.

Though odd for any town, it seems especially strange that one spurned by the railroads has so many old railway cars housing restaurants and shops—particularly in the fully restored **Marketplace,** at Harris Ave. and 12th St. *Fairhaven District,* a free brochure at the visitors center, maps out a short walking tour.

The **Whatcom Museum of History and Art,** 121 Prospect St. (676-6981), between Holly, Prospect, and Central St. downtown, dates from the same boom era as the South Side buildings. The towering red Victorian is visible from most of downtown. Once the city hall, it now displays first-rate exhibitions of modern art and local history (open Tues.-Sun. noon-5pm; free).

Western Washington University (676-3424) is the nexus of much of the activity in and around the Bellingham area. The campus ornaments its sylvan setting with 16 pieces of outdoor sculpture, commissioned from local and nationally known artists. A free brochure, available at the Visitor Information Center, guides the visiting critic around campus from piece to piece. Friday nights during the academic year, a program of concerts called **Mama Sundays** heats up the Viking Union on campus. Top-notch folk and bluegrass are the norm ($3-5). In the summer, there are free weekday lunchtime concerts. The **Western Visitors Center** is at the entrance to the college on South College Dr., and information is also available at the Whatcom County Visitors Center in Blaine. Here you can pick up a schedule for the Faculty of Dramatic Arts **Summer Stock Theater** which runs from July to August (676-3873). Take bus #3B, 7B, or 8A to reach the campus. Smart, bouncy and basic; Bellingham natives Crayon are one of the world's best rock and roll bands. See them if possible. Garage-rock label Estrus and their rockin' Mono Men also live and perform here.

OUTDOORS

Like every other city in Northwest Washington, Bellingham isn't far from tranquility. Hike up **Chuckanut Mountain** through a quiet forest to overlook the islands that fill the bay. You can occasionally spot Mt. Rainier to the south. A 2½-mi. hike uphill leaves from Old Samish Hwy. about 1 mi. south of the city limits. The beach at **Lake Padden Park,** 4882 Samish Way (676-6989), delights those who find Puget Sound a little chilly. Take bus #5B or 10A 1 mi. south of downtown. A lifeguard keeps watch from Memorial Day through Labor Day. The park also has miles of hiking trails, a boat launch (no motors allowed), tennis courts, and playing fields. The park is wheelchair-accessible (open daily 6am-10pm).

Whatcom Falls Park, 1401 Electric Ave., due east of town, also has fantastic hiking trails, picnic facilities, and tennis courts. Upper Whatcom Falls Trail (1.6 mi.) leads to the falls themselves, converted into an unofficial waterslide by the locals. Take bus #4A or 11A (open daily 6am-10pm). The fishing is good in both these lakes and also in **Lake Samish** and **Silver Lake,** north of the town of Maple Falls off the Mt. Baker Hwy. (See Near Bellingham for information on Silver Lake County Park.) The lake trout season opens on the third Sunday in April. **Fishing licenses** ($3) are available from the Department of Fisheries (586-1425), at any sporting goods store, and at some hardware stores.

Popular with South Side residents, **Interurban Trail** runs 6.6 mi. from Fairhaven Park to Larrabee State Park along the route of the old Interurban Electric Railway. The trail is less developed than those at Padden and Whatcom Lakes and follows a creek through the forest. Occasional breaks in the trees permit a glimpse of the San Juan Islands. You may stumble onto **Teddy Bear Cove,** along the Interurban Trail, accessible from Chuckanut Drive, 2 mi. south of Fairhaven. This clothing-optional beach offers revealing views of the local wildlife.

SEASONAL EVENTS

Whatcom County hosts a number of annual fairs and festivals that celebrate its modestly colorful past. Held on Gooseberry Point in the Lummi Island Reservation, the **Lummi Stommish Indian Water Carnival** (734-8180) is entering its 46th year. The three-day carnival at the end of June stages traditional dances, war-canoe races, arts and crafts sales, and a salmon barbecue.

Loggers succeeded Natives in Whatcom County, and fete themselves earlier in June at the 28-year old **Deming Logging Show** (676-1089). Tree-fellers converge here from throughout the region to compete in axe-throwing, log-rolling, and speed climbing. To reach the Showgrounds, take Mt. Baker Hwy. 12 mi. east to Cedarville Rd. and head north. Signs lead you to the grounds.

The **Northwest Washington Fairgrounds** (354-4111), in Lynden, hosts a number of blow-out wing-dings throughout the summer, including the **Northwest Washington Fair,** in mid-August.

■ Near Bellingham

Mt. Baker

The *pièce de résistance* of Whatcom County is certainly Mt. Baker (10,778 ft.), which has been belching since 1975; in winter, jets of steam often snort from its dome. Exit 255 off I-5, just north of Bellingham, leads to Rte. 542, the **Mt. Baker Hwy.** Fifty-six mi. of roadway traverse the foothills, affording spectacular views of Baker and the other peaks in the range. Crowning the Mt. Baker-Snoqualmie National Forest, Mt. Baker contains excellent downhill and cross-country skiing facilities, usually open from late October through mid-May. The longest downhill run plummets 6500 ft. The snow tarries long enough here to extend the ski season to July, when the zany **Slush Cup,** a race that started in snow and finished 2000 ft. below in a giant slushie, was held years ago. The environmental consciousness of the 90s has liquefied enthusiasm for the Slush Cup; it is no longer held due to its devastating effects on the meadow where the race ended. Instead, the **Bigfoot at Baker Festival** is now held in early June. For those ca-macho enough events like the Bigfoot look-alike contest and the **Authentic Bigfoot Museum** are sure to be hair-raising. Call 599-2594 for more information; call 734-6771 in Bellingham for more information on the operation and ski resort. On your way to the mountain, stop at the **Mount Bakery,** 3706 Mt. Baker Hwy. (592-5703), for gigantic apple fritters, donuts, and pastries for around 50¢ (open Mon.-Sat. 5am-5pm).

Silver Lake Park, 9006 Silver Lake Rd. (599-2776), 28 mi. east of Bellingham on the Mt. Baker Hwy. and 3 mi. north of Maple Falls on Silver Lake Road, is operated by the Whatcom County Parks and Recreation Department. The park tends 113 **campsites** near the lake along with facilities for swimming, hiking, and fishing. Tentsites are $6, hookups $7.50.

Lummi Island

Lummi Island, off the coast of Bellingham, was for centuries the fishing and hunting ground of the Lummi nation of Native Americans. Now the Lummis are confined to a reservation, and the island has been overrun by hermits. Lummi is distinctly rural, with paved roads only on the northern half. The old logging roads which criss-cross the rest of the island are ideal for hiking up to Lummi Mountain or down to the island's various tidal pools. Bicyclists will find the island roads peaceful.

Lummi Island can be reached by ferry from **Gooseberry Point** on the Lummi Indian Reservation, 15 mi. from Bellingham. Take I-5 north to exit 260; left on Rte.

540 will lead you west about 3½ mi. to Haxton Way. Turn south and follow signs to the ferry terminal. For 10 days in June each year, the ferry is sent to Seattle for maintenance. During this interlude a walk-on ferry is substituted, so call before taking your car (fare: $3 per vehicle or $1 per walk-on; ferry information 676-6730).

Blaine

Twenty mi. north of Bellingham is the border town of **Blaine,** the busiest port of entry between Canada and the U.S. (And judging by the number of BC and Alberta license plates at Blaine's gas stations, a good percentage of that traffic is Canucks filling up on cheap U.S. gas.) A word of warning: those who get turned away from the Canadian border for lack of sufficient identification or funds (you need CDN$500 per car and $50 per extra passenger if you're headed for Alaska) often head for Blaine, and the border patrol prides itself on catching these undesirables with blanket stop-checks.

The main attraction in Blaine is the **Peace Arch Park Heritage Site** (332-8221; open for day use only). Built in 1921 with nickels and dimes volunteered by school children in Washington and British Columbia, the arch commemorates the 1814 signing of the Treaty of Ghent, which terminated the War of 1812 and ushered in an era of peace between Canada and the U.S. The two legs of the arch straddle the international border. With two gates, one hinged on the U.S. side, the other on the Canadian, the gate can be closed only by mutual consent. Summer-time happenings include "hands across the border" events, replete with kids, balloons, and **Rotarians** (open daily 6:30am-dusk; Oct. 16-March 8am-5pm; toilets, kitchen facilities).

The spit of land encompassing **Semiahmoo Park** (371-5513), 5 mi. southwest of Blaine, was first inhabited by the coastal Salish people, who harvested shellfish when the tide was low. Clam digging is still a popular activity. Buckets and shovels may be rented from the park; no license is required. Three buildings from the former Alaska Packers Association cannery, which operated on the spit for 74 years, are now used by the park as an **interpretive center,** preserving the history of both the local canning industries and the natural environment. Take Drayton Harbor Rd. around to the southwestern side of Drayton Harbor (open mid-Feb. to Dec. Wed.-Sun. 1-5pm; free). For information on all Whatcom County Parks, contact the **Parks and Recreation Board Headquarters and Information Center,** 5105 Helwig Rd. (371-2800). The **Blaine Visitors Center,** 900 Peace Portal Dr. (332-4544), is a storehouse of information on these parks as well as American and Canadian points of interest in the area. (Open Mon.-Sat. 9am-5pm, Sun. 10am-4pm.)

The **Birch Bay Hostel (HI/AYH),** building #650 on the former Blaine Air Force Base (371-2180), is one of the Pacific Northwest's biggest (HI/AYH members only). Among its amenities are a spacious common area with cable TV and extensive cooking facilities. The rooms are spotless, and the manager helpful. Take either the Birch Bay-Lynden Rd. exit or the Grandview Rd. exit off I-5 and head west. Blaine Rd. will take you to the Alderson Rd. entrance to the Air Force base (open June-Sept.; $8.50). The **Westview Motel,** 1300 Peace Portal Dr. (332-5501), also offers excellent lodgings (singles $31, doubles $35.50). The best seafood in town, fresh daily, is at the **Harbor Cafe,** on Marine Dr. (332-5176), halfway down the pier. The $7 fish and chips—salad bar and roll included—is hard to resist.

For campers, **Birch Bay State Park,** 5105 Helwig Rd. (371-2800), 10 mi. south of Blaine, operates 167 sites near the water. The Semiahmoo Native Americans used this area and the marshland at the southern end of the park to harvest shellfish and hunt waterfowl; today, 300 species of birds live in the parks's **Terrell Creek Estuary.** The park is also a good area for crabbing, scuba diving, water-skiing, and swimming. To reach the park, take the Birch Bay-Lynden exit off I-5 and turn south onto Blaine Rd. When you run out of road, turn east onto Bay Rd. Turn south on Jackson Rd. and take it to Helwig Rd. The way is well-marked from the freeway (open year-round; sites $8, with hookup $12).

The Blaine **Greyhound Station** uses a drop-off point at the Burger King on the truck route junction. For more information, call the station in Bellingham (733-5251). One bus to Seattle per day ($13.50).

OLYMPIC PENINSULA

In the fishing villages and logging towns of the Olympic Peninsula, locals joke about having webbed feet and using Rustoleum instead of suntan oil. The Olympic Mountains wring the area's moisture (up to 200 in. of rain per year fall on Mt. Olympus) out of the heavy Pacific air. While this torrent supports bona fide rain forests in the peninsula's western river valleys, towns such as Sequim in the range's eastern rain shadow are the driest in all of Washington, with as little as 17 in. of rain per year.

Extremes of climate are matched by extremes of geography. The beaches along the Pacific strip are a hiker's paradise—isolated, windy, and wildly sublime. The seaports of the peninsula's northern edge crowd against the Strait of Juan de Fuca, hemmed in by the glaciated peaks of the Olympic range. To the east, fjord-like fingers cross the Hood Canal. For the most part, however, visitors come to this corner of the country for one reason: the spectacular rugged scenery of Olympic National Park, which sits solidly at the Peninsula's center. Though the park's network of trails now covers an area the size of Rhode Island, these rough and wooded mountains resisted exploration until well into the 20th century.

Because it compresses such variety into a relatively small area, the Olympic Peninsula is one of Washington's most accessible destinations for those seeking wilderness and outdoor recreation. U.S. 101 skirts the edges of the peninsula, stringing together scattered towns and attractions on the nape of the mountains. The numerous secondary roads connecting U.S. 101 with the park's interior were designed with exploration in mind, though many are bare gravel, making biking difficult. Rte. 112 follows the Strait of Juan de Fuca out to Neah Bay, in the Makah Indian Reservation near Cape Flattery. Greyhound runs only as far as Port Angeles to the north and Aberdeen/Hoquiam to the south. Although local transit systems extend public transportation a little farther, the western portion of the peninsula and the southern portion of Hood Canal are not on any regular routes.

Hitchhiking is illegal on U.S. 101 southwest of Olympia. Elsewhere, thumbing can often be slow, and one may well be stranded in the rain for hours. Hitchhiking is always dangerous, and *Let's Go* does not recommend it. Cyclists, too, should beware—bicycling is dangerous in some spots, particularly along Crescent Lake just west of Port Angeles. The shoulders are narrow or nonexistent, the curves are sharp, and the roads are aswarm with speeding logging trucks. Motoring suits the peninsula best, although some of the beaches and mountain wilds can be reached only by foot. The splendid terrain of the area is ideal for the day-tripper and the die-hard hiker alike.

The best time to visit the area is in the summer months when precipitation declines precipitously. Plan to bring rain gear at all times, though. Downpours make for lush vegetation, but they can dampen the spirits of even the cheeriest camper.

CAMPING ON THE PENINSULA

Although many towns on the peninsula harbor numerous motels and resorts, camping will put you closer to the natural splendor you came to see—and it'll be cheaper to boot. Olympic National Park, the state of Washington, and Olympic National Forest all maintain a number of free campgrounds. The free **National Park campgrounds** include Deer Park, Dosewallips, Graves Creek, July Creek, Ozette (all with drinking water), and Queets (with no water but great hiking trails through old-growth rain forest). In addition, the National Park has many standard campgrounds (sites $8). Numerous **State Parks** are scattered along Hood Canal and the eastern rim of the peninsula (sites $8-14; occasional site for only $4-5). The National Forest and Park Services both welcome **backcountry camping** (free everywhere), but a permit is required within the park, available at any ranger station or trailhead. Camping on the **beaches** is especially easy, although you should be sure to bring a supply of water. The beaches in the westernmost corner of Neah Bay, and from the town of Queets to Moclips farther south, fall within Native American reserve land. Visitors should be aware that reservation land is private property—travelers are welcome, but local regulations prohibit the drinking of alcohol, fishing without a tribal permit, and beachcombing. The Quinault Indian Reservation took the spotlight 20 years ago by forcibly ousting vandals.

Washington's **Department of Natural Resources (DNR)** manages the huge tracts of land on the Kitsap Peninsula and near the western shore along the Hoh and Clearwater Rivers, as well as smaller, individual campsites sprinkled around the peninsula. Except in the high summer, DNR camping is generally free and uncrowded, and no reservations are required. Some of these sites allow RVs, some do not have drinking water, and most have good fishing. Unfortunately, many sites cannot be found without a map. The DNR publishes a guide to all its Washington sites and displays additional maps of its Multiple Use Areas (MUAs). The DNR also publishes a guide to **public use shellfish sites** on Hood Canal and the Peninsula. Maps of Hoh-Clearwater MUA and Tahuya MUA (on the Kitsap Peninsula) are available from DNR, Olympic Area, Rte. 1, P.O. Box 1375, Forks 98331 (206-902-6100 or 800-527-3305), and at most DNR campgrounds.

Keep an eye out for other camping possibilities, such as county and city parks and ITT Rayonier's **Tumbling Rapids Park** off U.S. 101 in Sappho, 55 mi. west of Port Angeles. This campground with rest rooms, picnic area, and community kitchen is maintained by the giant company for public use.

Be warned: in the summer, competition for campground space can be fierce. From late June on, most sites are taken by 2 or 3pm, so start hunting early; in the more popular areas of the National Park (such as the Hoh River), find a site before noon or plan on sleeping elsewhere.

■■■ OLYMPIC NATIONAL PARK

Lodged amidst the august Olympic Mountains, Olympic National Park unites 900,000 acres of velvet-green rainforest, sparkling snow-covered peaks, and dense evergreen woodlands. This enormous region at the center of the peninsula allows limited access to four-wheeled traffic. No scenic loop roads cross the park, and only a handful of secondary roads attempt to penetrate the interior. The roads that do exist serve as trailheads for over 600 mi. of hiking. The only people who seem not to enjoy this diverse and wet wilderness are those who come unprepared; a parka, good boots, and a waterproof tent are essential in this area.

PRACTICAL INFORMATION AND ORIENTATION

Visitors Information: Olympic Visitors Center, 3002 Mt. Angeles Rd., Port Angeles (452-0330), off Race St. Main information center. Fields questions about the whole park—camping, backcountry hiking, and fishing—and displays a map of the locations of other park ranger stations. Also houses the **Pioneer Memorial Museum** (see Port Angeles: Sights). Open daily 9am-5pm; in winter daily 9am-4pm.

Park Superintendent, 600 E. Park Ave., Port Angeles (452-4501, ext. 311). Open Mon.-Fri. 8am-4:30pm.

Entrance Fee: $3 per car is charged at the more built-up entrances, such as the Hoh, Heart o' the Hills, and Elwha—all of which have paved roads and toilet facilities. The fee buys an entrance permit good for 7 days. A similar pass for hikers and bikers costs $1.

Park Weather: 452-0329. 24 hr.

Park Radio: 530 AM for road closures and general weather conditions.

OLYMPIC NATIONAL PARK

Park Emergency: 452-4501. Operates daily 8am-5pm, other times phone 911.

The perimeters of the park are well-defined. The Park Service runs **interpretive programs** such as guided forest walks, tidal pool walks, and campfire programs out of its various ranger stations (all free). For a full schedule of events obtain a copy of the park newspaper from ranger stations or the visitors center. The **map** distributed at the park's gates is wonderfully detailed and extremely helpful.

July, August, and September are the best months for visiting Olympic National Park, since much of the backcountry often remains snowed-in until late June, and only the summer provides rainless days with any regularity. Backpackers should come prepared for a potpourri of weather conditions at any time. Always wear a wool hat in winter; hypothermia is a leading cause of death in the backcountry (see Health in the Essentials section at the front of this book). Make sure hiking boots are waterproof with good traction, since during rainy spells trails transform themselves into rivers of slippery mud. **Backcountry camping** requires a free **wilderness permit,** available at ranger stations and some trailheads. The Park Service's backcountry shelters are for emergencies only.

Never, ever drink even one mouthful of untreated **water** in the park. *Giardia,* a very nasty microscopic parasite, lives in all these waters and causes severe diarrhea, gas, and abdominal cramps. Symptoms often don't appear for weeks after ingestion. Carry your own water supply or boil local water for five minutes before drinking it. You can also buy water purification tablets at the visitors center (see above) or at most camping supply stores. **Dogs** are not allowed in the backcountry and must be leashed at all times within the park.

Mountain climbing is tricky business in the Olympic Range. Although the peaks are not high in absolute terms (Mt. Olympus is only 7915 ft. above sea level), they are steep, and their proximity to the sea makes them prone to nasty weather. The quality of rock is poor, and most ascents require sophisticated equipment. Climbers are required to check in at a ranger station before any summit attempt. The rangers urge novices to buddy up with experienced climbers who are "wise in the ways of Northwest mountaineering."

Berry picking ranks high on the list of summer activities, and is easy as pie on the peninsula. Newly cleared regions and roadside areas are best; raspberries, strawberries, blueberries, and huckleberries are all common. **Fishing** within park boundaries requires no permit, but you must obtain a state game department punch card for salmon and steelhead trout at outfitting and hardware stores locally, or at the game department in Olympia. The Elwha River, which bisects the northern half of the park, is best for **trout,** and the Hoh is excellent for **salmon.**

■ Eastern Rim

The eastern section of the Park is accessible through the Olympic National Forest from U.S. 101 along Hood Canal. (See Hood Canal for information on camping in the National Forest.) The auto campgrounds are popular with hikers, who use them as trailheads to the interior of the park. **Staircase Campground** (877-5569), 16 mi. northwest of Hoodsport at the head of Lake Cushman, has a ranger station that offers interpretive programs on weekends (open year-round; 59 sites, $8). **Dosewallips** (doh-see-WALL-ups), on a road that leaves U.S. 101 3 mi. north of Brinnon (27 mi. north of Hoodsport), has 32 free but less well developed sites for cars. The **ranger station,** open from June through September only, has no electricity or telephones. A spectacular trail leads from Dosewallips across the Park to Hurricane Ridge (see Northern Rim below).

■ Northern Rim

Heart o' the Hills Campground (452-2713; 105 sites), 5½ mi. from Port Angeles inside Olympic National Park, has idyllic campsites with drinking water and toilets.

Go up Race Rd. past the Park's visitors center and toward Hurricane Ridge. Both Heart o' the Hills and **Elwha Valley** (452-9191; 41 sites) have interpretive programs and ranger stations, as does **Fairholm Campground** (928-3380; 87 sites), 30 mi. west of Port Angeles at the western tip of Lake Crescent. (All 3 open year-round; sites $8.) The **Crescent Lake** station (928-3380) has an extensive interpretive program but no camping. There is also an information booth here (open July-Aug. daily 11am-4pm). **Soleduck Hotsprings Campground** (327-3534), to the southeast of Lake Crescent, 13 mi. off U.S. 101, is adjacent to the commercial hot springs resort. A roving naturalist is on duty in the afternoon, and there are scheduled programs in the evening (sites $8). The grounds are shut down when it snows.

The **Sol Duc Hot Springs** (327-3583), near the Soleduck ranger station, is where hot-tubbers can soak all day ($5.10, senior citizens $4.10). The cement decks, chlorine smell, and shower-before-you-enter signs detract from this pristine source of naturally hot water (open May 21-Oct.1 9am-9pm; closes at 8pm in Sept.). A better and less well-known way to harness the region's geothermal energy is to hike up to the **Olympic Hot Springs.** Turn off at the Elwha River Road and follow it 12 mi. to the trail head. The natural springs are about a 2½-mi. hike but well worth it. As you go higher up on the mountain, the springs get warmer. They give off an unsavory sulfurous aroma.

For some inspiring **hiking,** head south on Soleduck Road 14 mi. to a trailhead. From there, **Soleduck Falls** and **Lover's Lane** are wonderfully scenic, yet heavily trafficked trails along the Soleduck River. Lover's Lane is the easier hike of the two with little or no incline as it follows the river for 3 mi. to the waterfall. For more secluded hiking, try **Aurora Ridge,** which goes through forested areas instead. For further information and free overnight camping permits, get in touch with the **Soleduck ranger station** (327-3583) on Soleduck Rd. (open June-Aug. daily 8am-5pm).

The main attraction of the northern area, especially for those not planning back-country trips, is **Hurricane Ridge,** with its splendid views of Mt. Olympus, the Bailey Range, and Canada on clear days. The often-crowded ridge is the easiest point from which to grab a hiker's view of the range. Crowds tend to thin out, though, as they head off along the many trails that originate here (including some for senior citizens and people with disabilities). Thick populations of bear and deer roam the woods and meadows. Be alert while in the tourist-ridden parking area—the deer have grown brazen and often graze in the parking lot. Although the snow is often too heavy and wet to be much good for winter sports, the Park Service nonetheless runs cross-country and downhill skiing on Hurricane Ridge during the winter (lift ticket $12). Sledding is discouraged because of past "mishaps."

■ Rain Forest

Washington is home to the only temperate rain forest in the world. Particularly lush growths of gigantic trees, ferns, and mosses canopy the rain forest along the Hoh and Queets Rivers. Although the forest floor is thickly carpeted with unusual foliage and fallen trees, the Park Service keeps the many walking trails clear and well-marked. The first campgrounds along the Hoh River Rd., which leaves U.S. 101, 13 mi. south of the town of Forks, are administered by the Department of Natural Resources (DNR) and accept no reservations (free). Drinking water is available at the **Cottonwood** and **Minnie Peterson** sites only. DNR sites are usually much less crowded than the Hoh, and they are about twice as roomy. You can obtain a separate map of the Hoh-Clearwater MUA from the DNR main office in Forks or at Minnie Peterson (see Olympic Peninsula: Camping on the Peninsula above).

The **Hoh Rain Forest Campground and Visitors Center** (374-6925) is located 19 mi. down the Hoh River Rd. from the junction with U.S. 101 (open in summer daily 9am-4:30pm). Touring the area, even if you have only the afternoon, is rewarding. However, think twice about cycling down if you don't have a car—there are no shoulders, the road has a lot of blind corners, and the damn-the-torpedoes logging truck drivers are scary.

To find shelter from the area's incessant rains, seek out the **Rain Forest Home Hostel** (374-2270) between mileposts 169 and 170 on U.S. 101. Jim and Kay will gladly acquaint you with sites in the region, and their fireplace is a particularly cozy place to chat on a cold, wet night. (Check-in 5-10pm daily. Members and nonmembers $8. Linen $1. Full kitchen facilities and showers.) **Forks,** 57 mi. southwest of Port Angeles on U.S. 101, is the last stop south on U.S. 101 to pick up groceries if you are planning on using the hostel kitchen or cooking over the campfire.

You'll find several worthwhile hikes into the rainforest. The **Hoh River Trail** is for pros, but the **Hall of Mosses** and **Spruce** trails require only an hour; and the mini trail is more wheelchair-accessible than most others. Camping is available year-round and costs $8. Try to camp near the riverbed in loop A (sites open year-round). Deer stroll casually through your campsite here, and herds of elk often walk the riverbed early in the morning. Areas of clearcuts border the road back to U.S. 101.

Farther south, after U.S. 101 rejoins the coast (see Ocean Beaches below), the park's boundaries extend southwest to edge the banks of the **Queets River.** The road here is unpaved and the campground at the top is free (26 sites; open June-Sept.). The Park and Forest Services share the land surrounding **Quinault Lake and River**. The Park Service land is accessible only by foot, but the Forest Service operates a day-use beach and an information center in the **Quinault Ranger Station,** South Shore Rd. (288-2444; open daily 9am-5pm; in winter Mon.-Fri. 9am-5pm).

■ Ocean Beaches

More than 57 miles of pristine coastline await visitors on the park's western section, which edges the Pacific coast from the Quinalt Reservation in the south to the Makah Reservation at its northern border, separate from the park's main body. Piles of driftwood, imposing sea stacks, sculptured arches, and abundant wildlife frame a perfect sunset.

The rugged and deserted beaches along the peninsula's western edge are especially magnificent during winter storms. Beware, though, of incoming tides that can trap you against steep cliffs—clip and carry a tide chart from a local newspaper. Bald eagles are often out on windy days, and whales and seals tear through the sea. Most of the beaches are easily accessible via paved roads followed by trails ranging from ¼ mi. to 3½ mi. in length. The 15 mi. stretch of beaches begins in the north with the dramatic **Ruby Beach** near milepost 165 on U.S. 101. South of Ruby Beach at milepost 160 is Beach #6, a favorite whale-watching spot.

Mora (374-5460), near the Quillayute Indian fishing village of **La Push,** and **Kalaloch** (962-2283) have campgrounds (sites $8) and ranger stations. The **Kalaloch** (pronounce KLAY-lok) **Center,** with 177 sites near the ocean, including a lodge, a general store, and gas station, is the more scenic of the two. A **beach trail** from the mouth of the Hoh River leads to 17 mi. of beach camping and eventually La Push. The total 57 mi. of the peninsula is a protected coastal wilderness for hiking and backcountry camping. **Backcountry camping** is permitted all along the beaches. Pick up use **permits** at trailheads.

■■■ EASTERN PENINSULA

■ Hood Canal

Glaciation carved the notch in the land now known as Hood Canal, but no one is quite sure how the ribbon of water that separates the Kitsap and Olympic Peninsulas came to be called this instead of its original "Lord Hood's Channel." Local historians blame carelessness on the part of cartographers.

U.S. 101 parallels the west bank of the canal, from **Potlatch State Park** in the south to **Quilcene** (Quil-SEEN) in the north. This scenic road, highlighted by a steep pass just outside Quilcene can be cycled—if you don't mind a heavy workout and dangerously nonexistent shoulders. Without a bike or car, abandon any hopes of seeing this area—there are no buses, and hitching is both illegal and foolhardy.

West of the canal, the **Olympic National Forest** rims the eastern edge of the national park. Much of the forest is more developed and more accessible than the park and gives those with little time or small appetite for the outdoors a "taste" of the peninsula's wildlife. Stop by one of the forest's **ranger stations** along the canal to pick up information on camping and trails in the forest. The two stations are in **Hoodsport,** P.O. Box 68, 98548 (877-5552; open daily 8am-4:30pm; Labor Day-Memorial Day daily Mon.-Fri. 8am-4:30pm) and **Quilcene,** U.S. 101 S. (765-3368; open same hours as Hoodsport). Both are marked clearly with signs on the highway. Most forest service campgrounds are cheap, less developed and less crowded options than the State Parks. **Elkhorn Campground,** on Forest Service Rd. 2610, 11 mi. northwest of Brinnon, is only $4.

The following cost $5 per site: **Hamma Hamma,** on Forest Service Rd. 25, 7 mi. northwest of Eldon; **Lena Creek,** 2 mi. beyond Hamma Hamma; and **Collins,** on Forest Service Rd. 2515, 8 mi. west of Brinnon. Also $5 is **Falls View,** on U.S. 101, 3½ mi. south of Quilcene. This easily accesible campground offers views of the falls and a canyon trail down to the river. All are indicated by signs on U.S. 101 and have drinking water, as well as access to good fishing, hiking, and gorgeous scenery. Unfortunately, many of these campgrounds are reached only by gravel roads, which are difficult (if not impossible) to navigate by bicycle. Adjacent to the ranger station in Hoodsport is a **post office** (877-5552; open Mon.-Fri. 8am-12:30pm and 1:30-5pm, Sat. 8:30am-11:30pm; **General Delivery ZIP Code:** 98548).

Lake Cushman State Park (877-5491), 7 mi. west of Hoodsport on Lake Cushman Rd. (paved), is a popular base camp for extended backpacking trips into the National Forest and Park. Situated on a comely lake with good swimming beaches. The park offers showers (6 min. for 25¢) and flush toilets (70 sites $10, and 30 with full hookup $14). **Seal Rock Campground,** 10 mi. north of Brinnon on U.S. 101, offers 41 sites ($6-8). This campsite is one of the only places along the Hood Canal with free public access to oyster beds. Clamming also available. No permit required but a limit of 40 clams and 18 oysters per person. (Oyster season runs from Feb.-July; call the Quilcene Ranger Station for more details.)

Clinging to a quiet cove is **Mike's Beach Resort and Hostel,** N. 38470 U.S. 101 (877-5324), 2 mi. north of Eldon. The hostel, which is not HI/AYH affiliated, lacks a kitchen but contains a small grocery store and is located right on the water. The resort is not primarily a hostel, and you may be elbowed out by RV's and large families. The hostel, with only 2 tiny barracks-like rooms crammed with bunkbeds, is prohibitively small. Call ahead to reserve. (Check-in 7am-10pm, open April 15-Nov. 1. $7.50, nonmembers $10.) The **Hungry Bear Cafe,** N. 36850 U.S. 101 (877-5527), in Eldon, serves burgers ($2.75), and fries ($2.50). (Open daily 7am-9:30pm.)

A breathtaking view of Hood Canal, extending out to Puget Sound, Mt. Rainier, the Space Needle, and Seattle, awaits adventurous travelers atop the **Mt. Walker View Point.** Take U.S. 101, 3 mi. south of Quilcene. A single lane gravel road takes you 4 mi. to the lookout, which, at 2,700 ft., is the highest viewpoint accessible by car. The road is steep, has precipitous drop-offs, and should not be attempted in foul weather (the clouds will obscure the view anyway.)

■■■ NORTHERN PENINSULA

■ Port Townsend

From Port Townsend on Puget Sound to Cape Flattery on the Pacific Ocean, the northern rim of the Olympic Peninsula defines the U.S. side of the **Strait of Juan de Fuca.** This sapphire passage was named for the legendary explorer, allegedly the first European to enter the ocean inlet. The shores are dotted with small towns, many of them old salmon fishing ports past their prime.

The Victorian splendor of Port Townsend's buildings, however, has survived the progression of time and weather, though the bustling salmon industry has not. The entire business district of this "peninsula off a peninsula" has been declared a national landmark.

Although the Port itself has been artificially restored to its former grandeur, sailors and amateur boat-builders alike still congregate in town bars and cafés. Home to a thriving art and music community, Port Townsend stands as a cultural oasis on an otherwise untamed peninsula. Walk down Water Street, and you'll be lured by countless art galleries, book shops, and cafés. It is one of the few places west of Seattle where espresso stands outnumber live bait shops.

Practical Information and Orientation The town's **Chamber of Commerce,** 2437 Sims Way, Port Townsend 98368 (385-2722), lies about 10 blocks from the center of town on Rte. 20. Ask the helpful staff for a free map and visitors guide (open Mon.-Fri. 9am-5pm, Sat. 10am-4pm, Sun. 11am-4pm). Find the **Public Library** at 1220 Lawrence (385-3181), uptown (open Mon. 11am-5pm, Tues.-Thurs. 11am-9pm, Fri.-Sat. 11am-5pm).

By land, Port Townsend can be reached either from **U.S. 101** or from the **Kitsap Peninsula** across the Hood Canal Bridge. **Greyhound's** daily Seattle-to-Port Angeles run connects with Jefferson County Transit in the town of Port Ludlow for the last leg to Port Townsend. By water, Port Townsend can be reached via the **Washington State Ferry** (800-84-FERRY or 33779), which runs in summer (reduced in winter) daily to and from Keystone on Whidbey Island. Ferries land and depart from the dock at Water St., west of downtown. (Operates from 7am to 10pm every 45 min. Mid-Oct. to mid-May service reduced. $1.65 one-way, cars $6.65; off-season $5.55.)

Jefferson County Transit (JCT), 1615 W. Sims Way (385-4777), operates Port Townsend's public transportation as well as connecting the city with nearby destinations. To reach Port Angeles from Port Townsend hop on JCT bus #8 (at Water and Quincy St.) which goes to Sequim (30 min.), and from there you can catch Clallam Transit System bus #30 to Port Angeles (30 min.). JCT also sends the following other buses from Port Townsend: #1 bus to Brinnon and Quilcene (Mon.-Fri.); #7 bus to Poulsbo, Winslow, and Bremerton via Kitsap Transit (Mon.-Sat.). (Fares 50¢ and 25¢ per zone, senior citizens and passengers with disabilities 25¢ and 25¢ per zone, ages 6-18 10¢. Day passes $1.50). A Port Townsend **shuttle bus** loops around the town itself, and other service extends west along the strait to Sequim (50¢, seniors and students 25¢, under 6 free; daily passes $1.50). For a **taxi,** call Key City Transport (385-5972; open 24 hr.).

P.T. Cyclery, 215 Taylor St. (385-6470), rents mountain bikes ($6 per hr., $22.50 per day). Helmet and lock are included (open Mon.-Sat. 10am-5:30pm, Sun 11am-3pm; in winter no Sun. hours). **Field Dock,** Port Ludlow Marina (437-0513), in Port Ludlow, south of Port Townsend, rents 14-ft. sailboats ($6 per hr., $18 per 3 hr., $36 per day). **Sport Townsend,** 1044 Water St. (379-9711), rents camping equipment by the day. A two-person tent is $13 for the first day, $5 per additional day (open Mon-Sat 9am-6pm).

A local pharmacy is **Don's,** 1151 Water St. (385-2622; open Mon.-Fri. 9am-7pm, Sat. 9am-5pm). The Hospital is **Jefferson General,** 385-2200. **Emergency Medical Care** (385-4622) is located on the corner of Sheridan and 9th St. in the west end of town. **Emergency:** 911. **Police:** 607 Water St. (385-2322), non-emergency. **Jefferson County Crisis Line:** 385-0321. 24-hour mental health counseling. **Senior Assistance:** 385-2552. Open Mon.-Fri. 8:30am-4:30pm. Port Townsend's **post office** is at 1322 Washington St. (385-1600. Open Mon.-Fri. 9am-5pm. **General Delivery ZIP Code:** 98368.) The **area code** is 206.

Accommodations and Camping Port Townsend's hostels and campgrounds lie near the town. So many cheap beds in such a small town doesn't make sense, but who's complaining? **Fort Worden Youth Hostel (HI/AYH),** Fort

Worden State Park (385 0655), 2 mi. from downtown, has bulletin boards and trek-kers' log which are good, if somewhat dated, sources of information on budget travel around the Olympics. Also kitchen facilities. (Open Feb.-Dec. 21. Call ahead for Nov.-Feb. Check in 5-10pm; check-out 9:30am; curfew 11pm. $8.50, nonmem-bers $11.50. Cyclists $6. Family rates available.) **Fort Flagler Youth Hostel (HI/AYH),** Fort Flagler State Park (385-1288), lies on handsome Marrowstone Island, 20 mi. from Port Townsend. From Port Townsend head south on Rte. 19, which con-nects to Rte. 116 east and leads directly into the park. Fantastic for cyclists—miles of pastoral bike routes weave through Marrowstone, and the hostel is virtually unoccu-pied, even in summer—great for solitude-seekers. (Open year-round by reservation only. Check in 5-9pm, lockout 10am-5pm. $8.50, nonmembers $11.50. Cyclists $6.) **Point Hudson Resort,** Point Hudson Harbor (385-2828 or 800-826-3854), at the end of Jefferson St., is a collection of faded wooden structures which bespeak a time when Point Hudson was the major resort in the area. Today, amateur boat-builders hammer away outside your window, and a bratty buoy clangs incessantly. Very well-kept rooms. (Singles and doubles start at $45, $53 with bath.)

   Campers should try **Fort Worden State Park** (385-4730) for $15 per night, or **Old Fort Townsend State Park** (385-4730) for $10 per night, $14 with hookup ($5-7 for primitive hiker/biker sites). The latter is 5 mi. south of Port Townsend just off Rte. 20 and is open mid-May to mid-Sept. Fort Worden is open year-round. You can also camp on the beach at **Fort Flagler State Park** (753-2027).

Food and Entertainment   Strap on your Birkenstocks and grab your organic essentials at **Abundant Life Seed,** 1029 Lawrence (385-5660), at Polk. A **Safeway,** 442 Sims Way (385-2806), south of town along Rte. 20 serves the less macrobioti-cally inclined. **Burrito Depot,** 609 Washington St. at Madison (385-5856)—the cacti in their garden may be small, but their servings are *muy grandes.* Try the mouth-watering veggie fajita ($3.70). Big big burritos from just $2.65 (open Mon.-Sat. 10am-9pm, Sun.11am-4pm). **Bread and Roses Bakery and Deli,** 230 Quincy St. (385-1044). Gargantuan raspberry croissants ($1.25), currant scones ($1), and a dozen varieties of muffins for your morning (open daily 6am-5pm).

   Port Townsend's first and finest pizza fills the tiny **Waterfront Pizza,** 951 Water St. (385-6629). 16" pies start at $10 (open 11am-11pm daily). **Landfall,** 412 Water St. (385-5814), on Point Hudson, cooks up seafood, salads, and Mexican food. Din-ners are expensive; go for breakfast or lunch ($4-6). A huge bowl of homemade fish and chips rings in at a salty $5.75, and tasty sourdough French toast at $3. The boat-making crowd hangs out here, seasoning their food with shoptalk about hulls and wind resistance (open Mon.-Thurs. 7am-3pm, Fri.-Sun. 7am-9pm). **Elevated Ice Cream Co.,** 627 Water St. (385-1156), is owned by friendly people receptive to the scruffy traveler. Perhaps the largest ice cream shop in the continental U.S., the Ele-vated serves delicious homemade ice cream and decent espresso (90¢). One scoop of ice cream or 2 mini-scoops of Italian ice $1.15 (open daily 9:30am-10pm; in win-ter 11am-10pm).

Sights and Seasonal Events   Port Townsend's early pioneer settlers built sturdy maritime-style houses, but their wealthier successors preferred huge Queen Anne and Victorian mansions. Of the over 200 restored homes in the area, some have been converted into cozy, but costly, bed and breakfasts; others are open for tours. The 1868 **Rothschild House** (355-2722), at Franklin and Taylor St., has period furnishings and herbal and flower gardens. (Open daily 10am-5pm; Sept. 16-May 14 Sat.-Sun. 11am-4pm. Requested donation $2.) Or peek into the **Heritage House** at Pierce and Washington (open daily 12:30-3pm; admission $1.50).

   Take the steps on Taylor St. down to **Water Street,** the town's quaint main artery. This is reputedly the place where Jack London spent a night in jail on the way to the Yukon. Brick buildings of the 1890s are interspersed with newer shops and cafes with the old-style motif. The **Jefferson County Museum** (385-1003), at

Madison and Water St., showcases vestiges of the town's wild past. Highlights include a dazzling kayak parka made of seal intestines (open Mon.-Sat. 11am-4pm, Sun. 1-4pm; donations $2.)

The red **bell tower** on Jefferson St. called firefighters to their work in Port Townsend for 80 years. The base of the grand tower overlooks the town. An old Romanesque clock tower hovers over the **County Courthouse,** at Jefferson and Walker St. Farther southwest is the **Manresa Castle** (385-5750), on 7th and Sheridan St., built in 1892 and used as a Jesuit school for 42 years. It's now a hotel and open for wandering.

Point Hudson, the hub of the small shipbuilding area, forms the corner of Port Townsend, where Admiralty Inlet and Port Townsend Bay meet. North of Point Hudson are several miles of beach, **Chetzemolka Park,** and the larger **Fort Worden State Park.** Don't let the tide sneak up on you as you walk along the pretty coastline; you could easily find yourself on your own private island with no escape. **Fort Worden** (385-4730), a strategic military post dating from the turn of the century, guards the mouth of Puget Sound and commands fine views of the sound and the Cascades. The fort was pressed back into service in 1981 as a set for the movie *An Officer and a Gentleman.*

Eighteen mi. south of town on Marrowstone Island, **Fort Flagler State Park,** another discharged military post, has slightly more run-down barracks than Fort Worden but only a fraction of the tourists. Explore the gun emplacements, watch the sailboats on Puget Sound from the outpost high above the water, or stroll along the almost deserted beach down below.

From mid-June to early September, the **Centrum Foundation** sponsors a series of festivals in Fort Worden Park. The foundation supports bluegrass, jazz, folk, and classical music along with poetry readings, dance performances, and painting displays. Two of the most popular events are the **Fiddle Tunes Festival** in early July and **Jazz Port Townsend** later in the same month. Tickets are $8-15 for most single events; combination tickets can be purchased to cover the whole of each festival. For a schedule, write the Centrum Foundation, P.O. Box 1158, Port Townsend 98368 (385-3102). Other annual attractions include the **Wooden Boat Festival,** held the first weekend after Labor Day, and the **House Tour,** held the following weekend, when all the mansions are open to visitors free of charge. October's **Kinetic Sculpture Race,** with its bizarre costumes in motion, serves as Port Townsend's gateway to Halloween. For more information contact the chamber of commerce.

■ Port Angeles

Never confuse Port Townsend with Port Angeles, a cheerless industrial complex dominated by paper and plywood mills. Though Port Angelenos are working to eradicate this unflattering image, the town's greatest asset will always be an unparalleled view of the gorgeous blue bay (try to ignore the smoke stacks). Stop in town for information and transportation connections or before driving up to the stupendous Hurricane Ridge, but don't stay around long—the rest of the peninsula awaits.

Practical Information Visitors information for Port Angeles is located at the **Chamber of Commerce,** 121 E. Railroad (452-2363), next to the ferry terminal. In addition to lists of lodgings, the center provides a free telephone for calling motels. (Open daily 8am-9pm; in winter Mon.-Sat. 10am-3pm.) The **Clallam County Parks and Recreation Department** is located in the Courthouse Building (452-7831, ext. 291), at Lincoln and 4th St. (open Mon.-Fri. 8:30am-4:30pm).

Port Angeles is served by **Greyhound,** 1315 N. Laurel (452-8311; to Seattle Mon.-Fri. $13.75) and by water by **Black Ball Transport,** foot of Laurel St. (457-4491; to Victoria $6.25 on foot, $9.25 with bicycle, $25 with car.) **Clallam Transit System ("The Bus"),** 639 Monroe Rd. (800-858-3747 or 452-4511), serves the Port Angeles area and connects with Jefferson Transit in Sequim. (Buses run Mon.-Fri. 6am-7:30pm, Sat. 9am-5pm. Fare 50¢ within downtown.) **Car Rental** is available at **All-**

Star, 602 E. Front St. (452-8001), in Aggie's Motel complex, and at **Budget,** 111 E. Front St. (452-4774; cars from $48; must be 21).

Tents are available at **Browns,** 112 W. Front St. (457-4150), between Laurel and Oak. (Open Mon.-Sat. 9:30am-6pm.) The local **laundromat** is the **Peabody Street Coin Laundry,** 212 Peabody St. (open 24 hr.; wash 75¢, dry $1). The **post office** sits at 424 E. 1st St. (452-9275), at Vine. (Open Mon.-Fri. 8:30am-5pm, Sat. 9am-noon. **General Delivery ZIP Code:** 98362.)

Accommodations, Camping, and Food If you must spend the night indoors in Port Angeles, stay at the **Royal Victorian,** 521 East 1st (452-2316). It's not luxurious, but is fairly safe, comfortable, and convenient, with phones and cable TV (singles $32, doubles $40; rates lower in winter). The closest free campground is **Boulder Creek Campground,** at the end of Elwha River Rd., 8 mi. past Altaire. Park at the end of the road, and hike 2 mi. along an abandoned road. You'll need a free **backcountry permit** (available at the trailhead) to pitch at one of the 50 sites. Be sure to bring your own water as well.

In a town that makes its living off the sea, the scarceness of reasonably priced seafood is inexplicable. About the only reasonable place to sample the local catch is a Mexican restaurant. **La Casita,** 203 E. Front St. (452-2289), stuffs its seafood burrito ($7) with generous amounts of crab, shrimp, and fish, along with giving you all-you-can-eat free tortilla chips and salsa (open Mon.-Sat. 11am-10pm, Sun. noon-10pm). Follow up with strawberry Belgian waffles ($4) at **First Street Haven,** 107 E. 1st St. (457-0352; open Mon.-Sat. 7am-4pm, Sun. 8am-2pm), or try a good espresso at the **Coffeehouse Battery,** 118 East 1st (452-1459). The coffeehouse offers vegetarian dishes ($5), local artwork, and live folk music most weekends (free, with an occasional cover of up to $6; coffeehouse open Mon.-Sat. 7am-8pm, Sun. 8am-5pm).

Sights The only compelling aspect of Port Angeles is the surrounding countryside. Unfortunately, without a vehicle, your only chance of seeing it is by forking over $12.75-16 to **Olympic Van Tours** for three-hour or all-day excursions to Hurricane Ridge. (Check out the kiosk on the sidewalk by the ferry docks, or call 452-3858.) More accessible by foot is the **Arthur D. Feiro Marine Laboratory** at Peninsula College (452-9277), which offers three classrooms of touch tanks with local marine life. (Open June 15-Sept. daily 10am-8pm; in winter Sat.-Sun. noon-4pm. Admission $1, under 12 50¢.) Also on the pier is an observation tower with great views of the port and the Olympic Mountains that overlook the town (open daily 6am-10pm). Beginning at the pier and following the shore for ½ mi. is the **Waterfront Trail,** which affords a nice escape from the dreary downtown area.

The **Olympic National Park Visitors Center,** 3002 Mt. Angeles Rd. (452-0330), at Race St., dispenses free maps and will acquaint you with the majestic environs. (Open Memorial Day-Labor Day daily 8:30am-6pm; in winter daily 9am-4pm.)

■ Neah Bay

The Western Peninsula contains the northwesternmost point in the contiguous U.S. In 1778, the area caught the attention of explorer James Cook, who named the tip Cape Flattery because it "flattered us with the hopes of finding a harbor." It still flatters the visitor with pristine beaches.

At the westernmost point on the strait within Washington State is **Neah Bay,** the only town in the **Makah Indian Reservation.** The Clallam Transit System reaches Neah Bay via Sappho. Take bus #14 from Oak St. in Port Angeles to Sappho (60 min.). Then take bus #16 to Neah Bay (60 min.). Check schedules at the Port Angeles Greyhound Station to avoid excessive layovers. In case of **emergency** in Neah Bay, call 645-2701 (645-2236 in a **marine emergency). General Delivery ZIP Code:** 98357. **Area code:** 206.

Cape Flattery sits in the corner of Neah Bay's backyard, but the dirt road out is hard to follow. Watch for signs reading "cape trails" at the west end of town. Follow the signs (and the dirt road) about 8 mi. to a dead end, where a well-marked trailhead sends you toward Cape Flattery. The half-hour hike rewards those willing to risk twisted ankles with fantastic views of Tatoosh Island just off the coast and Vancouver Island across the strait. A few miles south of Cape Flattery is **Hobuck Beach,** where camping and picnicking are within car's reach. To the south lie the more secluded beaches, which can be reached only by foot. The whole area is private property; visitors are welcome but should stop at the cultural center in Neah Bay and acquaint themselves with reservation regulations.

Back in Neah Bay, the **Makah Cultural and Research Center** (645-2711) houses artifacts from the archaeological site at Cape Alava, where a huge mudslide 500 years ago buried and preserved an entire settlement. A 70-foot-long house, with a sloped roof that was ideally suited to the rainy environment, has been replicated at the museum. (Open daily 10am-5pm; Sept.-May Wed.-Sun. 10am-5pm. Admission $4, senior citizens and students $3.) The Makah nation—whose recorded history goes back 2000 years—still lives, fishes, and produces magnificent art work on its original land. During the last weekend of August, Native Americans from as far away as Canada and La Push come to participate in canoe races, traditional dances and bone games (a form of gambling) during the **Makah Days.** The delicious Salmon Bake is a definite highlight. Contact the cultural center for more information.

SOUTHWEST WASHINGTON

At the climax of its odyssey through Washington, the Columbia River makes a breathless descent into the Columbia River Gorge and forms the border between Oregon and Washington for several hundred miles before ending in the Pacific. Small resort towns cluster at the mouth of the river and around the bays and fishing ports to the north. The landscapes along the coast rarely dovetail smoothly—wild marshlands and grasslands run up against one another. Several stunning state parks and wildlife refuges harbor a variety of coastal fauna. For information on the area, contact the **Tourist Regional Information Program,** SW Washington, P.O. Box 128, Longview 98632. In **emergencies** call the state **police** at 911 or 206-577-2050.

■ Columbia River Mouth

In 1788, British fur trader (and poor loser) Captain John Meares, frustrated by repeated failures to cross the treacherous Columbia River Bar, named the water now known as Baker Bay **Deception Bay** and the large promontory guarding the river's mouth **Cape Disappointment.** Since then, more than 230 vessels have been wrecked, stranded, or sunk where the Columbia meets the ocean—a region aptly named "the graveyard of the Pacific."

Fort Columbia State Park (777-8221) lies on U.S. 101 northwest of the Astoria Megler Bridge, 1 mi. east of Chinook. The fort was built in 1895 and armed with huge guns to protect the mouth of the river from potential enemies who never showed up. The park's **interpretive center** entertainingly re-creates life at the fort and includes an exhibit on the Chinook Native Americans who once occupied this land. A 1-mi.-long woodland trail takes you past several historical sites, including an abandoned observation station. (Park open daily 6:30am-dusk; Oct. 16-March Wed.-Sun. 8am-dusk. Center open Wed.-Sun. 9am-5pm.) What was once the area's hospital is now the **Fort Columbia Youth Hostel,** P.O. Box 224, Chinook (777-8755). Isolated from the center of town and without even a nearby phone, the hostel imbues visitors with a communal spirit. The hostel managers will give you a cookie at check-in and lots of advice on how to explore the hostel's gorgeous grounds and beaches. (Open June to mid-Sept. Registration 5-10pm. $8.50, nonmembers $11.50.) Bus #14 takes you from Astoria to Fort Columbia.

In nearby **Ilwaco** (named after the Native American chief El-wa-cho), **Fort Canby State Park** offers camping and more Lewis-and-Clarkiana. To reach the park, take U.S. 101 to the Ilwaco exit and head 2 mi. southwest. Ignore the many signs pointing right to the park—*that* road is a mile longer. **Pacific Transit** buses (642-9418) connect Ilwaco with the north Washington coast, the Long Beach Peninsula, and Astoria, Oregon (daypass $1.50). From Ilwaco you can walk 2 mi. to reach the park. The park's 190 **tentsites** fill up on summer weekends (sites $11, with hookup $15, hiker/biker $5). To reserve a site, write Fort Canby State Park, P.O. Box 488, Ilwaco 98624, or call the **park office** (642-3078).

The U.S. Coast Guard maintains a **lifeboat station and surf school** in the park. Arduous training in rough winter surf pays off in summer; the students often have to abandon their maneuvers to attend to a real rescue of swimmers or vessels. This is one of the busiest search-and-rescue stations in the United States. The **North Head Lighthouse,** built in 1898, is located in the northwest corner of the park and is accessible by an extremely short, paved trail. The **Cape Disappointment Lighthouse,** built in 1856 and the oldest in the Northwest, is located in the southeast corner of the park and can be reached by a ¼-mi. walk uphill from the Coast Guard station parking lot. A tour of the interior of North Head Lighthouse is given during the summer on Saturdays at 7pm, and a tour of Cape Disappointment Lighthouse is given Fridays at 7pm. For a magnificent beach-level view of both lighthouses, drive past **Waikiki Beach** onto the **North Jetty** and gaze at the sharp cliff on which the beacons are perched. Though not quite like Honolulu, Waikiki Beach is ideal for swimming in summer, beachcombing after storms in winter, and year-round ship-watching. Near Cape Disappointment is the **Lewis and Clark Interpretative Center** (642-3029 or 642-3078), where the legendary expedition is described with journal entries, photos, memorabilia, and equipment—it won't disappoint (open daily 9am-6pm; Oct.-May Wed.-Sun. 9am-5pm; free).

The restored railway depot at 115 SE Lake St. behind the museum runs a miniature train through a scale model of the peninsula as it looked in the 1920s. For a better view of Ilwaco's modern-day economic lifeline, try charter fishing. Stop by **Pacific Salmon Charters,** P.O. Box 519, Ilwaco 98624 (642-3466), in the Port of Ilwaco, where eight-hour salmon fishing tours (providing coffee, lunch, and tackle) start at $59 (trips run Sun.-Thurs. at 6am). For good, inexpensive food with a view of the Ilwaco port, eat at **Smalley's Galley** (642-8700), which serves up tasty clam chowder ($1.75), fish and chips ($5.25), and hamburgers ($2.75). (Open Sun.-Mon. 4am-4pm, Tues.-Fri. 5am-4pm, Sat. 5am-8pm.)

■ Long Beach Peninsula

Long Beach Peninsula, with 28 mi. of unbroken beach, is a mundane combination of kites, seafood, beaches, and more kites. Fishing, swimming, boating, and kite-flying fill the warmer months which allow residents to recuperate from the pounding winter storms. You can beachcomb for peculiar pieces of driftwood and glass balls from Japanese fishing nets. (Permits are required for gathering driftwood in state parks.) Driving on the beach is legal (and common) on the hard, wet sand above the lower **clam beds.** From October to mid-March, look for people chasing the limit of 15 tasty razor clams. To find the fast-digging bivalves, look for dimples or bubbles in the sand. If you're willing to shell out $10.50 for an annual non-resident license (Washington residents $3.50) and spend a few days learning the ropes, you can harvest a seafood feast. The *Chinook Observer's Long Beach Peninsula Guide* and the **state fisheries** (753-6600) in Ocean Park both offer advice on technique. Consult fisheries' regulations before digging in. Free tide tables are available at information centers and many places of business. These are useful both for finding clams and escaping island status when the tide comes in.

You can fill up by **berry picking** in late summer; look for wild varieties in the weeds along the peninsula's roadsides. The peninsula contains nearly 500 acres of cranberry bogs. Be careful about picking on private property.

Pacific Transit buses (in Raymond 642-9418, in Naselle 484-7136, farther north 875-9418) provide local transportation. For 85¢ and a transfer, you can take a bus as far north as Aberdeen. Schedules are available in post offices and visitors centers (service Mon.-Fri. 2-3 times per day).

If you don't like getting sand between your toes, head for the boardwalk in Long Beach, a little more than 10 mi. north. The seemingly infinite walkway stretches along the sand and provides a convenient perch for watching the sunset, the surf, and the kites. Two blocks west of Pacific Ave. you'll find the beach. On 10th St. just behind Marsh's museums, you can rent a horse at Double D Ranch (642-2576) for $10 per hour (a wrangler goes with you). The city of Long Beach has a passion for flying contraptions and invites kite flyers from Thailand, China, Japan, and Australia to the International Kite Festival (642-2400) during the third week of August. Late July brings the Sand Castle Festival to the town. In 1989, a world record trembled when participants built a 3-mi.-long fortress of sand.

The cheapest place in town to sleep is the Sand-Lo-Motel, 1906 Pacific Hwy. (642-2600; singles and doubles $36). For delicious oatmeal cookies (30¢) or a sandwich ($3), go to the Cottage Bakery and Deli (642-4441), just south of the intersection of Rte. 103 and Bolstad St., in Long Beach (open daily 4am-8pm, in winter daily 4am-6pm). Farther up the peninsula, the quiet residential community of Ocean Park is home to Jack's Country Store (665-4988), at Bay and Veron, the place for groceries and hardware. Prices are reasonable (open daily 8am-8pm).

Nearby Nahcotta relies on the oyster for both entertainment and financial solvency. Nahcotta's claim to fame is The Ark (665-4133), easily the finest, most fantastic restaurant in the area (and thus deserving of a paragraph all to itself). Dinner might cost upwards of $15, but you'll be overwhelmed with fresh seafood, homemade baked goods and pastries, and Northwestern specialties—all elegantly prepared and presented (open Tues.-Sat. 5-10pm for dinner and Sun. 11am-8pm for brunch). Make reservations a couple days in advance.

Leadbetter Point State Park, on the Long Beach peninsula's northernmost tip, is a favorite of photographers, nature lovers, and bird watchers. Bring bug repellent to make sure that you don't lose kids and small pets to the carnivorous mosquitoes. Farther down the peninsula, Pacific Pines and Loomis Lake State Parks are also perfect spots for hiking, picnicking, and surf-fishing.

■ Willapa Bay

Willapa Bay, just north of Long Beach, is known for its wildlife. The drive up U.S. 101, culminating with a turn west on Rte. 105 at Raymond, is a feast for the eyes and compensates for the protected bay's prohibitions on swimming and sunning. The smooth, tortuous road along the perimeter of the sharp drop-off down to Willapa Bay assures a rare and wonderful experience (although the several state-troopers patrolling the route can put a damper on it). The small towns along the peninsula are thirsty for tourist dollars and bristle with the usual array of souvenir shops and overpriced seafood restaurants. All of the state parks spread through the region are for day use only. (All parks open daily 6:30am-dusk; Nov.-March 8am-dusk. Call 753-2027 for more information.)

The highlight of the area, north off Long Beach on U.S. 101, is the headquarters of the Willapa National Wildlife Refuge (484-3482), a sanctuary for seabirds and waterfowl. The refuge is comprised of several "units" scattered through the Willapa Bay region, including a unit at Leadbetter Point on the tip of the Long Beach Peninsula and one on Long Island in Willapa Bay. The refuge offers the rare opportunity to observe Canada geese, loons, grebes, comorants, trumpeter swans, and a wide variety of winged creatures. The greatest diversity of birds descends upon the area during the fall and winter months.

Long Island, the largest estuarine island on the Pacific Coast, is Willapa Bay's most superlative attraction. Not only is the island teeming with deer, bear, elk, beaver, otter, and grouse—it's also home to a 274-acre cedar grove, one of the West Coast's last climax forests still producing new trees after 4000 years of growth. The cedars are as much as 11 ft. in diameter and average 160 ft. in height.

Long Island is home to several **campgrounds** which are inaccessible by RV. Reaching the island is *the* problem. No commercial shuttle service exists, and you'll have to find your own boat. If you don't have a boat, you may be able to bum a ride. Don't try to swim the channel; the water is too muddy. Boats should be launched from the Wildlife Refuge Headquarters; the channel at this point is only about 100 yd. wide. After reaching the island and tying up your boat, hike 2½ mi. along the island's main road to reach the **Trail of Ancient Cedars.** The **office** at the Refuge furnishes advice on getting to the island and maps marked with campgrounds.

Thirty mi. farther north and accessible by Pacific Transit, **South Bend's** world is the oyster—harvested from Willapa Bay's 25,000 acres of oyster beds. If you flash your pearly whites—and greenbacks—you too can purchase fresh oysters from the **Hilton's Coast Oyster Company** (875-5557), located at U.S. 101 and Pacific St. ($16 per 4 lbs.). If you'd rather have your food prepared by others, try **Bob's Riverview Dining** (875-6155), an average family-type place located just north of the Oyster Company, where you can get a half-dozen Willapa Bay oysters on the half-shell ($8) or an Oyster burger ($4.50), a local delicacy (open daily 11am-9pm). Also on U.S. 101, the **Pacific County Museum and Visitors Center** (875-5224) has, among other things, reference materials on everybody who's ever lived and died in South Bend (open Mon.-Sat. 11:30am-3:30pm). For a panoramic and fairly atypical view of the Willapa River and its surrounding meadows and hills, stop by the **Pacific County Courthouse,** up Memorial St. off U.S. 101.

■ Grays Harbor

North of Willapa Bay and Raymond, at the far southwest corner of the Olympic Peninsula, the restless waters of Grays Harbor make a sizable triangular dent in Washington's coastline. Long sandbars protect the undistinguished harbor. The spits also extend north and south of the bay, forming wide, fine-grained beaches that stretch for miles. Take advantage of the many beach accesses on Rte. 105 between Willapa Bay and Gray's Harbor. The long, isolated stretches of sand are perfect for beachcombing; be sure to scan the horizon for pieces of driftwood or highly coveted **Japanese glass floats.** These colored glass balls have been carried by a Pacific current known as *Kuroshio* across thousands of miles of ocean from Japan, where they were used to support fishing nets. The glass balls may have traveled for many years before arriving on American shores; those found by beachcombers average more than ten years in age. Digging for **razor clams** is popular on the beaches from October to mid-March. Licenses are available at local establishments; contact the Washington State Dept. of Fisheries (268-0623) for the opening date of the clam season.

On your way up Rte. 105, take a right at Cranberry Rd. and observe the huge **cranberry bogs** for which the area has been dubbed the "Cranberry Coast." Harvesting runs from late September through Thanksgiving. Local pride for the cranberries is warranted; the tart fruit is one of only three native North American fruits (Concord grapes and blueberries are the others).

Westport, on Grays Harbor's southern spit, is known for salmon. At least every other storefront on Westhaven Dr. is devoted to **charter fishing** (including bottom fishing and whale watching), and the ones in between are bait and tackle shops. The least expensive fishing trips start at around $65 for a full day; price lists are available from the Chamber of Commerce. Fishing liscences can also be purchased at most charter offices. The floats in the Westport Marina are some of the best places on the coast to go **crabbing.** No license is required (season runs Dec.- Sept. 15), and the sport itself is simple—just rent a crab ring (a hula-hoop-like contraption with nets attached) for $3-5, load it with fish carcasses, put it in the water, and check every 15 min. Generic clam and chowder joints are almost as ubiquitous as charters.

A nice outdoor attraction is the paved walk from Westport's South Jetty out to the **lighthouse.** For a more interactive experience with the waterfront, **scuba** gear and lessons are available at **Harbor Dive,** 100 N. Montesano St. (268-0080).

Dozens of cheap motels line Rte. 105 in Westport; the motels along the waterfront are slightly pricier. The best deal is at **Breakers Motel,** 971 N. Montesano St. (268-0848). The "sleeping rooms" are large, include a TV, and have a bathroom down the hall (singles $20, doubles $25). The **Chamber of Commerce,** 2985 S. Montesano St. (268-9422), is eager to provide information on accommodations and attractions. (Open Mon.-Fri. 9am-5pm, Sat.-Sun. 11am-4pm; winter hours vary.) **Buses** for Taholah, Westport, and Olympia originate from the east end of Grays Bay at **Aberdeen Station,** Wishkah St. and G St. (800-562-9730 or 532-2770). The fare is 25¢ ($1 to Olympia).

Lying at the mouth of the Chehalis River where it flows into Grays Harbor are the heavily industrialized cities of **Aberdeen** and sister-city **Hoquiam,** both of which suffer from a bad reputation. Residents in the rest of Washington have dubbed these port towns "the mud puddles of the Northwest." In the dry summertime, however, their strategic location and low prices make them fine places to rest and refuel, if not necessarily to linger, between the beaches on the Olympic Peninsula and the inland mountains and cities.

The **Grays Harbor Historical Seaport** (532-8611), 813 East Heron St. in Aberdeen, is a working shipyard which constructs and maintains vintage vessels including replicas of Robert Gray's *Columbia Redivva* (the first American ship to circumnavigate the world) and *Lady Washington* (the first American ship to visit Japan). (Open Mon.-Sat. 10am-5pm, Sun. noon-5pm. Admission $3, seniors and students $2, children $1.) Frequent cruises to Westport and around the harbor are $20-25. If you haven't been camping long enough to yearn for the comforts of a cheap motel, make a stop in **Montesano,** a small town about 20 min. east of Aberdeen on U.S. 12. From Montesano, you can waltz into the hills for an overnight stay and a swim at **Lake Sylvia** (249-3621; sites $10).

Grays Harbor National Wildlife Refuge, 1 mi. south of Rte. 109 in Hoquiam, is a Hitchcockian nightmare—over one million birds gather here on their way south to beat the heat. Put on your rubber boots and hike the muddy 1-mi. trail to Bowerman Basin, the best place to watch species such as sandpipers and dunlin. During peak migration times (mid-April), a **shuttle bus** provides round-trip service from Hoquiam High School (25¢). For information call the refuge's **office** in Olympia (753-9467).

A string of inexpensive motels assures a supply of cheap rooms for those stopping overnight. In Aberdeen, the best option is undoubtedly the **Towne Motel,** 712 E. Wishkah (533-2340), a few blocks east of the bus station. Ignore the slightly dilapidated exterior—the small, tidy rooms have large cable TV with remote, A/C, microwave, in-room coffee, and mini fridges (singles $32, doubles $35). The **Grays Harbor Chamber of Commerce,** 506 Duffy, Aberdeen 98520 (532-1924) can provide information on the area (open Mon.-Fri. 1-5pm, Sat.-Sun. 9am-noon).

A resort area creeps north to Moclips near the **Quinault Indian Reservation.** Mobs of vacationers had invaded the turf of the Quinault nation until August of 1969, when the Quinault people booted the littering and vandalizing visitors off their tribal beaches. This bold move brought a flood of supportive letters to the Quinault's mailboxes. A small museum up the coast in **Taholah,** in the office of the **Quinault Historical Foundation** (276-8211 for the museum), exhibits these political memoranda alongside more ethnological displays (open Mon.-Fri. 8am-4:30pm). You'll see more if the staff is on hand, so call ahead to arrange a guided tour (and to get directions—the museum is a bit tough to find). Take Grays Harbor Transit's bus #50, which stops in Taholah.

CASCADE RANGE

In 1859, Henry Custer—the first explorer to record his observations of the Cascade Range—gushed, "Nowhere do the mountain masses and peaks present such strange, fantastic, dauntless, and startling outlines as here." The Northwestern Native Americans summed up their admiration more succinctly, dubbing the Cascades "The Home of the Gods."

Intercepting the moist Pacific air, the Cascades have divided the eastern and western sides of Oregon and Washington into the lush green of the west and the low, dry plains of the east. The tallest, white-domed peaks of Baker, Vernon, Glacier, Rainier, Hood, Adams, and Mt. St. Helens understandably attract the most attention and have, for the most part, been made accessible by four major roads offering good trailheads and impressive scenery. **U.S. 12** through White Pass approaches Mt. Rainier National Park most closely; **I-90** sends four lanes past the major ski resorts of Snoqualmie Pass; scenic **U.S. 2** leaves Everett for Stevens Pass and descends along the Wenatchee River, a favorite of whitewater rafters **Route 20,** the **North Cascades Hwy.,** provides access to North Cascades National Park from spring to fall. These last two roads are often traveled in sequence as the **Cascade Loop.**

Greyhound covers the routes over Stevens and Snoqualmie Passes to and from Seattle (3-hr. round-trip), while **Amtrak** cuts between Ellensburg and Puget Sound. Rainstorms and evening traffic can slow hitchhiking; locals warn against thumbing across Hwy. 20, as a few hitchers apparently have vanished over the last few years. *Let's Go* **does not** recommend hitching. This corner of the world can only be explored properly with a car. The mountains are most accessible in the clear months of July, August, and September; many high mountain passes are snowed-in the rest of the year. The best source of general information on the Cascades is the joint **National Park/National Forest Information Service,** 915 2nd Ave., Seattle 98174 (206-220-7450).

■■■ NORTH CASCADES (RTE. 20)

A favorite stomping ground for deer, mountain goats, black bears, and even a few pesky, dovian grizzlies, the North Cascades remain one of the last great expanses of untouched land in the continental U.S. The range is an aggregate of dramatic peaks north of Stevens Pass on U.S. 2 and is administered by a number of different government agencies. **Pasayten** and **Glacier Peak** are designated wilderness areas, each attracting hefty numbers of backpackers and mountain climbers. **Ross Lake Recreation Area** surrounds the Rte. 20 corridor, and **North Cascades National Park** extends north and south of Rte. 20. The **Mt. Baker/Snoqualmie National Forest** borders the park on the west, the **Okanogan National Forest** to the east, and **Wenatchee National Forest** to the south. **Rte. 20** (open April-Nov., weather permitting) is the primary means of access to the area and awards jaw-dropping views around each curve; a road designed for unadulterated driving pleasure.

A wide selection of books can assist in planning an expedition in the North Cascades. Ira Springs's *100 Hikes in the North Cascades* (The Mountaineers Press) ranks among the most readable for recreational hikers, while Fred Beckley's *Cascade Alpine Guide* (The Mountaineers Press) targets the more serious high-country traveler and mountain climber.

PRACTICAL INFORMATION AND ORIENTATION

North Cascades National Park, 2105 Hwy. 20, Sedro Woolley 98284 (206-856-5700). Open June-Sept. Sat.-Thurs. 8am-4:30pm, Fri. 8am-6pm; Oct.-April Mon.-Fri. 8am-4:30pm.

National Park/National Forest: Outdoor Recreation Information Office, Jackson Federal Building, 915 2nd Avenue, Room 442, Seattle 98174 (206-220-7450). Open Mon.-Fri. 8:30am-5:30pm.

Wenatchee National Forest, 301 Yakima St., P.O. Box 811, Wenatchee 98801 (509-662-4335).

Snow Avalanche Information: 206-526-6677.

Area Code: 206 west of the Cascades, 509 to the east.

Rte. 20 (exit 230 on I-5) follows the Skagit River to the Skagit Dams and lakes, whose hydroelectric energy powers Seattle; then it crosses the Cascade Crest at Rainy Pass (4860 ft.) and Washington Pass (5477 ft.), finally descending to the Methow River and the dry Okanogan rangeland of eastern Washington.

Greyhound stops in Burlington once per day on the Seattle-Bellingham route, and **Empire Lines** (affiliated with Greyhound) serves Okanogan, Pateros, and Chelan on the eastern slope. Fare runs about $15 from Seattle to the East Cascades. No public transportation lines run within the park boundaries or along Rte. 20.

■ Sedro Woolley to Marblemount

Sedro Woolley, though situated in the rich farmland of the lower Skagit Valley, is primarily a logging town. The city's odd appellation could have been worse—the town was originally called "Bug." Locals forced the local bigwig to change the name to something a mite more dignified, and decided on "Sedro"—a misspelling of the Spanish "Cedro" meaning cedar. The city's surname was added when the nearby town of Woolley merged with Sedro in 1898. The last week of June and first week of July, locals turn out in droves for the **Sedro Woolley Loggerodeo**. Axe-throwing, pole-climbing, and sawing competitions vie for center stage with free-flowing beer and wild-and-woolly rodeo events such as bronco-busting and calf-roping. For information write the **Sedro Woolley Chamber of Commerce,** P.O. Box 562, Sedro Woolley 98284 (855-1841), at 308 Ferry St. (open Mon.-Sat. 9am-5pm). Sedro Woolley also houses the **North Cascades National Park Headquarters** (see Practical Information). Route 9 leads north of town through forested countryside, providing indirect access to **Mt. Baker** via the forks at the Nooksack River and Rte. 542.

As it continues east, Rte. 20 forks at **Baker Lake Road,** which dead-ends 25 mi. later at **Baker Lake.** There are several campgrounds along the way, but only **Horseshoe Cove** and **Panorama Point** offer toilets and potable water (sites $9). All other grounds are free. For more information on the Mt. Baker area, see Near Bellingham in the Puget Sound section above.

You would only have to sneeze four times in succession to miss the town of **Concrete** and its three neighbors—and perhaps you would be wise to do so. Those choosing to investigate will certainly be welcomed; the ratio of "Welcome to Concrete" signs to denizens is comically high. The town was named in 1921 after a fire gutted most of the wooden structures in the area and residents decided to rebuild with non-incendiary materials. If you are driving on an empty stomach, stop at the **Mount Baker Cafe,** 119 E. Main (853-8200); it may be hard to pass up the burger and fries for $3 (open Mon.-Thurs. 5am-9pm, Fri.-Sat. 5am-10pm, Sun. 8am-4pm).

The road from Concrete to Mt. Baker runs past the lakes created by the Upper and Lower Baker Dams. Concrete information and help are available from the **Chamber of Commerce,** 153 Rail Road (853-8400), tucked away in the old depot between Main St. and Rte. 20. (Follow the railroad tracks east upon entering town. Open Mon.-Fri. 8am-4pm, Sat.-Sun. 9am-4pm.)

To the east, neighboring **Rockport** borders **Rockport State Park** (853-8461), which is blessed by magnificent Douglas firs, a trail that accommodates wheelchairs, and 62 fully developed campsites in a densely wooded area ($8, with full hookup $12). The surrounding **Mt. Baker National Forest** permits free camping closer to the high peaks. From Rockport, Rte. 530 stems south to **Darrington**, which, for some unknown reason, is home to a large population of displaced North

Carolinians and therefore to a well-attended **Bluegrass Festival** on the third weekend of June. Darrington's **ranger station** (436-1155) is on Rte. 530 at the north end of town. (Open Mon.-Fri. 7am-5pm, Sat.-Sun. 8am-5pm; Oct.-April Mon.-Fri. 7am-4:30pm. Call for information about Rockport State Park.) If Rockport is full, continue 1 mi. east to Skagit County's **Howard Miller Steelhead Park** on the Skagit River, ideal for fishing and rafting, with 10 tentsites (tents $7, hookups $10).

Stop in **Marblemount** to dine at the **Mountain Song Restaurant,** 5860 Rte. 20 (873-2461), as you continue east from Rockport. The Mountain Song serves hearty meals—if the mountain air and the multitude of signs saying "Last Chance for 89 miles" make you feel romantic, sample the summit sandwich ($8.50) built for two (open Mon.-Thurs. 8am-8pm, Fri.-Sat. 8am-9pm). You can pitch your tent at the free sites in the **Cascade Islands Campground,** on the south side of the Cascade River (get directions in town). Bring heavy-duty mosquito repellent.

From Marblemount, it's 22 mi. up Cascade River Rd. to the trailhead for a 9-mi. hike to **Cascade Pass.** From the pass, the **Park Service shuttle** runs the 26 mi. between **Cottonwood** and the extremely isolated town of **Stehekin** (pronounced steh-HEE-kun) to the southeast, which can only be reached by boat, sea-plane, or foot. (Shuttle runs June-Sept. twice per day at 8am and 2pm, 2 hr., one-way $10. For more information see Lake Chelan.) Shuttle reservations are required; call or check in at the **Marblemount Ranger Station,** P.O. Box 10, Marblemount 98267 (873-4590), 1 mi. north of Marblemount on a well-marked road from the west end of town (open daily 7am-8pm; in winter Mon.-Fri. 8am-4:30pm). Marblemount is the last place to buy supplies (e.g. gas, food, beef jerky) before Winthrop.

■ Ross Lake and North Cascades National Park

Newhalem is the first town on Rte. 20 as you cross into the **Ross Lake National Recreation Area,** a buffer zone between the highway and North Cascades National Park on either side. The town is owned and operated by Seattle City Light Power Company and feels like it was designed by a used-car salesman; everywhere you go, City Light lets you know what a wonderful job they've done in flooding thousands of acres of virgin forest. A small grocery store and hiking trails to the dams and lakes nearby are the highlights of Newhalem. Information is available at the **visitors center** (386-4495), on Rte. 20 (open late June-early Sept. Thurs.-Mon. 8am-4pm).

The artificial expanse of **Ross Lake** (plugged up by Ross Dam on the west) extends back into the mountains as far as the Canadian border and is ringed by 15 campgrounds—some accessible only by boat, others by trail. The trail along **Big Beaver Creek,** at milepost 134 on Rte. 20, leads from Ross Lake over Ross Dam into the Picket Range and eventually to Mt. Baker and the northern unit of North Cascades National Park. The **Sourdough Mountain** and **Desolation Peak** lookout towers near Ross Lake offer eagle's-eye views of the range.

The National Park's **Goodell Creek Campground,** just south of Newhalem, has 22 sites with drinking water and pit toilets which are suitable for tents and trailers, and also a launch site for white-water rafting on the Skagit River (open year-round; sites $5). **Colonial Creek Campground,** 10 mi. to the east, is a fully developed, vehicle-accessible campground with flush toilets, a dump station, and campfire programs every evening. Colonial Creek also serves as the trailhead for several hikes into the southern unit of the North Cascades (open mid-May to Nov.; 164 sites, $7). **Newhalem Creek Campground** is another National Park facility (129 sites; $7).

Diablo Lake lies southwest of Ross Lake; the foot of Ross Dam acts as its eastern shore. The town of Diablo Lake, on the lake's northeast shore, is the main trailhead for hikes into the southern unit of North Cascades National Park (see under North Cascades above). The **Thunder Creek Trail** traverses Park Creek Pass to Stehekin River Rd., in Lake Chelan National Recreation Area south of the park. Diablo Lake supports a boathouse and a lodge that sells groceries and gas, an interpretive center, and several boat-in or hike-in campsites. Check with park rangers about the availability of sites since all North Cascades Parks close at various months in the winter and for some areas a free back country permit is necessary.

■ Winthrop to Twisp

Thirty mi. farther on Rte. 20, the **Pacific Crest Trail** crosses **Rainy Pass** on one of the most scenic and perilous legs of its 2500-mi. Canada-to-Mexico route. The trail leads up through **Pasayten Wilderness** in the north and down past **Glacier Peak** (10,541 ft.), which commands the central portion of the range to the south. (Glacier Peak can also be approached from the secondary roads extending northward from the Lake Wenatchee area near Coles Corner on U.S. 2, or from Rte. 530 to Darrington.) Near Rainy Pass, groomed **scenic trails** of 1 to 3 mi. can be hiked in sneakers, provided the snow has melted (which doesn't occur until mid-July). An overlook at **Washington Pass** rewards a very short hike with one of the state's most dramatic panoramas—a flabbergasting view of the red rocks of upper **Early Winters Creek's Copper Basin.** It's only a five minute walk on a paved trail, which is wheelchair-accessible.

Farther east is the town of **Winthrop,** child of an unholy marriage between Bonanza and Long Island Yuppies who think a rusty horseshoe counts as an antique. Find the **Winthrop Information Station** (996-2125), on the corner of Rte. 20 and Riverside (open Memorial Day-Labor Day daily 9am-5pm). The great billows of hickory-scented smoke draw customers to the **Riverside Rib Co. Bar B-Q,** 207 Riverside (996-2001), which serves fantastic ribs in a "converted prairie schooner" (a covered wagon); they also offer filling vegetarian dinners for $9 (open Labor Day to mid-April Mon.-Fri. 11am-9pm). If it's breakfast you're after, try **The Palace,** at 149 Riverside (996-2245; open Mon.-Fri. 7am-9pm, Sat.-Sun. 7am-10pm).

The summer season is sandwiched by rodeos on Memorial and Labor Day weekends. If you're not there for either, you can always mark time at the **Shafer Museum,** 285 Castle Ave. (996-2712), 1 block west of Riverside Ave. and up the hill that overlooks Winthrop. The museum displays all sorts of pioneer paraphernalia in a log cabin built in 1897 (open daily 10am-5pm; free). You can rent horses at the **Rocking Horse Ranch** (996-2768), 9 mi. north of Winthrop on the North Cascade Hwy. ($20 per 1½ hr.). Mountain bikes are available at the **Virginian Hotel,** just east of town on Hwy. 20 ($5 1st hr., $3.50 per additional hr., $25 full day). The **Winthrop Ranger Station,** P.O. Box 579 (996-2266), at 24 W. Chewuch Rd. in the west end of town, dispenses information on camping in the National Forest (open Mon.-Fri. 7:45am-5pm, Sat. 8:30am-5pm). North of Winthrop, the **Early Winters Visitor Center** (996-2534), outside Mazama, is aflutter with information about the Pasayten Wilderness, an area whose relatively gentle terrain and mild climate endear it to hikers and equestrians (open daily 9am-5pm; in winter weekends only).

Fourteen mi. west of Winthrop on Hwy. 20, **Early Winters** maintains 15 campsites ($6). **Klipchuk,** 1 mi. farther west, tends 46 developed sites ($6). Cool off at **Pearrygin Lake State Park** (996-2370) beach, four mi. down Pearrygin Lake Rd. from Riverside west of town. Sites ($11) by the lake have flush toilets and pay showers. Arrive early, since the campground fills up by late afternoon.

Flee Winthrop's prohibitively expensive hotels and sleep in **Twisp,** the town that should have been a breakfast cereal. Nine mi. south of Winthrop on Rte. 20, this peaceful hamlet offers low prices and far fewer tourists than its neighbor. Stay at **The Sportsman Motel,** 1010 E. Rte. 20 (997-2911), where a barracks-like facade masks tastefully decorated rooms and kitchens (singles $29, doubles $34; Nov. 1-May 1 singles $24, doubles $29). The **Twisp Ranger Station,** 502 Glover St. (997-2131), employs an extremely helpful staff ready to strafe you with trail and campground guides (open Mon.-Sat. 7:45am-4:30pm; closed on Sat. in winter). The **Methow Valley Tourist Information Office,** in the community center-*cum*-karate school at Rte. 20 and 3rd, has area brochures (open Mon.-Fri. 8am-noon and 1-5pm).

Join local workers and their families at **Rosey's Branding Iron,** 123 Glover St. (997-3576), in the center of town. The Iron usually has really cheap specials on the menu (under $3) and offers special menus for dieters, senior citizens, and children. All-you-can-eat soup and salad $6 (open Mon.-Sat. 5am-8pm, Sun. 6am-3pm).

■ Lake Chelan

The serpentine body of Lake Chelan (pronounced shuh-LAN) slithers northwest from the Columbia River and U.S. 97 into the eastern Cascades. Although the lake-shores around the faded resort town of **Chelan** are an unimpressive dry brown, the shores farther north are handsome indeed. The lake, which at points is 1500 ft. deep (the third deepest in the U.S.), extends far into Wenatchee National Forest and pokes its northwesternmost tip into the Lake Chelan Recreation Area, a section of North Cascades National Park.

Sights and Practical Information The **Chelan Ranger Station,** 428 W. Woodin Ave. (682-2576, or 682-2549 for the National Park Service), just south of Chelan on the lakeshore, will explain the byzantine regulations governing the parks, forests, and recreation areas (open daily 7:45am-4:30pm; Oct.-May Mon.-Fri. 7:45am-4:30pm). If you'll be in Chelan for a while, stop by the **Lake Chelan Chamber of Commerce,** 102 E. Johnson (682-3503 or 800-424-3526); it offers plenty of informa-tion on Chelan and nearby Manson, but not much on the surrounding wilds (open Mon.-Fri. 9am-6pm, Sat. 10am-4pm; winter Mon.-Fri. 9am-5pm).

Empire Bus Lines stops at 115 S. Emerson St. (682-4147), by the pony mailbox, and sends three buses daily to Seattle ($33) and Spokane ($29). Chelan's pharmacy is **Green's Drugs,** 212 E. Woodin Ave. (682-2566; open Mon.-Sat. 9am-6pm, Sun. 9am-1pm). The **Lake Chelan Community Hospital** (682-2531) is open 24 hr. Important phone numbers: **emergency,** 911; **24-hr. Crisis Line,** 662-7105; **Police,** 207 N. Emerson St. (682-2588). Wash that grey right out of your clothes ($1 a load; 10-min. dry 25¢) at **Chelan Cleaners,** 127 E. Johnson (open daily 7am-10pm, in winter 7am-8pm). The **post office** (682-2625) is at 144 E. Johnson at Emerson (open Mon.-Fri. 8:30am-5pm; **General Delivery ZIP Code:** 98816). The **area code** is 509.

Accommodations, Camping, and Food Exploiting sun-starved visitors from western Washington, Chelan has jacked up the prices on just about every-thing. Most motels and resorts in town are unaffordable during the summer; two exceptions are **Mom's Montlake Motel,** 823 Wapato (682-5715), at Clifford (sin-gles $40, doubles $45), and the **Travelers Motel,** 204 E. Wapato Ave. (682-4215), around the corner from the bus depot (no single rooms; doubles $35, with kitchen $69; prices $10 higher on weekends). Some visitors choose to sleep for free on the banks of the Columbia River in Pateros, 12 mi. north of Chelan on U.S. 97, although a questionable crowd of vagrants haunts the city park. Less questionable is **Lake Chelan State Park** (687-3710), 9 mi. from Chelan up the south shore of the lake. (Open April-Sept. 144 sites $11, with hookup $15. Reservations necessary: write Lake Chelan State Park, Rte. 1, P.O. Box 90, Chelan 98816.) **Twenty-Five Mile Creek State Park** (687-3610), 18 mi. up the lakeshore beyond Lake Chelan State Park (open Memorial Day to late Oct.; tents $11, with hookup $15) is good as well. Reservations recommended (accepted in Jan. for the coming summer).

The cheapest eats in Chelan can be had at local fruit stands, the farmers' market, or the **Golden Florin's Bear Foods,** 125 E. Woodin Ave. (682-5535), which sells natural foods in industrial quantities (open Mon.-Sat. 9am-7pm, Sun. noon-5pm). **Judy Jane Bakery,** 216 Manson Rd. (682-2151), sells delicious baked goods and deli foods. Sandwich of the day and salad special sell for $2.69 (open Sun.-Thurs. 7am-7pm, Fri.-Sat. 7am-8pm).

Outdoors One mi. east of Chelan in Lakeside is **Lake Chelan Butte Lookout.** Take a hike to the top for a great view of the lake and the hang gliders taking the easy way down. For other hiking try **Twenty-Five Mile Creek,** or better yet, find your way to **Stehekin,** a town inaccessible by road. The **Lake Chelan Boat Company,** 1418 W. Woodin, Chelan 98816 (682-2224), runs one round-trip to Stehekin daily April 15 to October 15, leaving at 8:30am and arriving at 12:30 pm, with a 1½-hour stop. Don't miss the return trip unless you're prepared to camp out (or shell out a small fortune for a cabin) in Stehekin. The dock is 1 mi. south of Chelan on U.S. 97. (Boats also run Oct. 16-April 14 Mon., Wed., Fri., and Sun. $14 one-way, $21 round-trip. Ages 6-11 ½ price; under 6 free.)

A lodge, ranger station, and campground cluster around Stehekin. An unpaved road and numerous trails probe north into the **North Cascades National Park.** A **shuttle bus** ($3) operates along the Stehekin Valley Rd., linking Stehekin and the lakeshore to the national park (buses leave Stehekin Landing at 8am and 2pm). All walk-in campgrounds in North Cascades are open May through October (free). **Backcountry use permits** are mandatory in the park throughout the year and are available on a first-come, first-served basis. Pick one up at the Chelan or Stehekin ranger stations. (For more information, see North Cascades National Park.) An excellent resource for the entire Stehekin area is *The Stehekin Guidebook* (free).

■■■ LEAVENWORTH

"Willkommen zu Leavenworth" proclaims the decorous wooden sign at the entrance to this curious resort/theme-park. After the logging industry exhausted Leavenworth's natural resources and the railroad switching station was transplanted to nearby Wenatchee, the town was forced to invent a tourist gimmick in order to survive. By the mid-1960s, "Project Alpine," as this kitschy endeavor was called, had laid a Bavarian veneer over Leavenworth. One can only wonder at the planners' *Weltanschauung.*

Leavenworth's merchants pay tribute to Oberammergau (their sibling city in the old country) by selling beer steins and dinners served by a phalanx of *lederhosen*-clad waiters. The town's establishments frequently sport names that are freakish fusions of German and English. Have your hair cut at **Das Klip und Kurl,** or shop at a crenellated Safeway market. The German gimmick lures skiers during the peak season from November to March; in the slow summer months, this *kleines Dorf* survives on profits from functionless wooden knick-knacks and taste-tests between the local Mt. Rainier beer and German brew. Today, an estimated one million people visit this living Swiss Miss commercial each year, with massive influxes during the city's three annual festivals. The sidewalks are lined with quaint (read: expensive) stores, and loudspeakers pump the theme from the wedding scene of the *Deer Hunter* into the streets. Never mind that no one knows any German; this town is an experience in bizarre, pseudo-cultural American vacation fun and tackiness.

PRACTICAL INFORMATION AND ORIENTATION

Visitors Information: Chamber of Commerce, 894 U.S. 2 (548-5807), in the Innsbrucker Bldg. Very helpful staff, many of whom see absolutely nothing amusing in their town's *töricht* gimmick. Open Mon.-Sat. 9am-noon and 1-5pm.

Ranger Station, 600 Sherbourne (782-1413 or 548-4067), just off U.S. 2. Pick up a well-organized guide to trails in Wenatchee National Forest and a list of the 8 developed campgrounds within 20 mi. of Leavenworth. Families should consult the page-long list of "relatively easy, short hikes." The **Enchantment Lakes** trail is the most popular, but for experienced hikers only. A permit (free for a day hike; $1 for overnight). Open daily 7:45am-4:30pm; winter Mon.-Fri. 7:45am-4:30pm.

Greyhound, 662-2183. Stops west of town on U.S. 2 at the Department of Transportation. One bus per day to Spokane ($27.50) and two to Seattle ($18.80).

Bike Rental: DerSportsmann, 837 Front St. (548-5623). Mountain bikes for $6 per hour or $20 per day. Cross-country skis $10 der day. Hiking and biking maps too. Open Sun.-Thurs. 10am-6pm, Fri.-Sat. 10am-7pm.

Weather: 663-2619. **Cascade Snow Report:** 353-7440.

Senior Citizens Center, 423 Evans (548-6666), across from Chamber.
Pharmacy: Village Pharmacy, 821 Front St. (548-7731). Open Mon.-Fri. 8:30am-6:30pm, Sat. 9am-5:30pm, Sun. 11am-5pm.
Hospital: Cascade Medical Center, 817 Commercial Ave. (548-5815).
Emergency: 911.
Post Office: 960 U.S. 2 (548-7212). Open Mon.-Fri. 9am-5pm, Sat. 9-11am. **General Delivery ZIP Code:** 98826.
Area Code: 509.

Leavenworth is located in Chelan County, on the eastern slope of the Cascades, near Washington's geographical center. U.S. 2 bisects Leavenworth within 200 ft. of the main business district. The main north-south route through the area is U.S. 97, which intersects U.S. 2 about 6 mi. southeast of town. Leavenworth is approximately 121 mi. east of Seattle, 190 mi. west of Spokane.

ACCOMMODATIONS AND CAMPING

If you can't get a room at the Hotel Edelweiss consider leaving town; most hotels start at $40 for a single. Call ahead for reservations on weekends. **Camping** is plentiful in **Wenatchee National Forest.** Ten mi. from town along **Icicle Creek Road,** a series of Forest Service campgrounds squeeze between the creek and the road. (To get there, take the last left in town on U.S. 2 heading west. All have drinking water; the closest to town is $6, all others $5. The last campground in the group is for horse campers only. You'll find more isolated spots by pulling off the road and hauling your gear down the banks of the Icicle. If you seek solitude, avoid weekend stays after Memorial Day. In any case, come early, or you may not find a spot.

Hotel Edelweiss, 843 Front St. (548-7015), downtown. Plain but clean rooms; bar and cocktail lounge downstairs. "Room" 14 (solitary confinement) has no TV, bath, or windows, but it's only $15. Room 10 is graced with a TV and a window, but no bath or sink ($16). Other singles with bath and TV from $24.
Chalet Park, Duncan Rd. (548-4578), east of town off U.S. 2. This small campground is close to the highway but otherwise quiet. Sites for 1 or 2 people $14, with electricity and water $16, full hookups $18. Baths and showers included.
KOA Kampground, 11401 Riverbend Dr. (548-7709), ¼ mi. east of town on U.S. 2. A corporate campground, with laundry, basketball, volleyball, playground, pool, spa, pool table, video games, and a well-stocked convenience store. Quiet hours 11pm-8am. Tentsite for 1 or 2 people $18, with electricity and water $22 (extra adults $4 per person). RV site $18, full hookup $24. One-room "kamping kabin" (a wooden shack) $30. Showers inkluded. Except for the "kabin," rates are $4 less from March 20-April 30 and Oct. 3-Nov. 1 (closed in winter).

FOOD

Predictably, Leavenworth's food mimics German cuisine; surprisingly, it often succeeds. Those who wish to avoid burgers and hot dogs and scarf down some *schnitzel,* however, should be prepared to pay $8-12 for a full dinner.

Oberland Bakery and Cafe, 703 Front St. (548-7216). The "Europeans" painted on the walls keep you company as you nibble on your Bavarian almond pretzel. $4 gives you rights to a generously large sub. Open daily 9am-5:30pm.
Casa Mia Restaurant, 703 U.S. 2 (548-5621). The food is excellent, and meals are preceded by chips and salsa. The lunch menu offers enchiladas and burritos from $4. The dinners are more expensive but authentic. *Arroz con pollo* is $8.50. Lunch served noon-4pm. Open Sun.-Thurs. noon-9pm., Fri.-Sat noon-10pm.
Bavarian Beer Garden, Bar-B-Que and Sausage Haus, 226 8th St. (548-5998). The place to go for *wurst.* Open 11am til 10pm or when it starts to rain.
Mini-Market, 285 U.S. 2 (548-5027). This run-of-the-mill convenience store merits mention for 10¢ coffee and 50¢ hot cider or egg nog. Open daily 6am-midnight.

SIGHTS AND ENTERTAINMENT

If you are in a riding mood, try the **Eagle Creek Ranch** (548-7798), north on Rte. 209, then right on Eagle Creek Rd. for 5½ mi. Horseback rides ($15 per hour), hay rides ($12), and winter horse-drawn sleigh rides.

On your way up Icicle Rd., stop at the **Leavenworth National Fish Hatchery** (548-7641) to immerse yourself in exhibits about local river life. In the summer, adult salmon (sometimes reaching 30 lbs.) fill the holding ponds—watching them is about as interesting as fishing without a hook. (Open daily 7:30am-3:30pm.)

On your way south to the U.S. 97 junction, stop in **Cashmere** at their **Aplets and Cotlets Factory,** 117 Mission St. (782-2191), for free tours of the plant and ample samples of their gooey candies. (Open Mon.-Fri. 8am-5:30pm, Sat.-Sun. 10am-4pm; Jan.-April Mon.-Fri. 8:30am-4:30pm.)

In Leavenworth, the **Historic Movie and Photo Gallery** at 801 Front St. continuously screens a 30-minute history of the Bavarian village (free). The film has the amateurish quality of a VHS camcorder, but the content is fascinating. The **Washington State Leaf Festival,** a celebration of autumn, runs for nine days during the last week in September and the first week in October. It includes a Grand Parade, as well as art shows, flea markets, and street dances. "Smooshing," a four-person race run on wooden two-by-fours, is the highlight of the **Great Bavarian Ice Fest,** held on the weekend of Martin Luther King, Jr. Day.

■ Roslyn

Don't tell them we told you so, but the people of **Roslyn** play begrudging hosts to the wildly popular television show *Northern Exposure*. The small town's isolated location on Rte. 903 at the edge of Wenatchee National Forest makes it a convincing set for the fictitious town of Cecily, Alaska (the moose was imported). But it doesn't take a Joel Fleischman to diagnose Roslyn's ills—the film crew's presence has driven rents up, forcing some long-time residents out of their homes. Roslyn has managed to hide some sacred antiques, including **The Brick Tavern,** 1 Pennsylvania Ave. (649-2643), the oldest operating tavern in the U.S. While you are in town, terrific food can be found at the **Roslyn Cafe** (649-2763), at 2nd and Pennsylvania.

Gray Line Bus Tours (624-5077), which seems to always pop up at the right time and place, runs a Northern Exposure tour to Roslyn with a stopover at Snoqualmie Falls on the way back ($30). Buses depart from 8th Ave. and Stewart.

■■■ MOUNT RAINIER NATIONAL PARK

Rising 2 mi. above the surrounding foothills, 14,411-ft. Mt. Rainier presides regally over the Cascade Range. Once called "Tahoma," meaning "mountain of God," by Native Americans, Rainier is simply "the mountain" to most modern-day Washington residents. Due to its extreme height, Rainier creates its own weather, jutting up into the warm ocean air and pulling down vast amounts of snow and rain. Clouds mask the mountain up to 200 days per year, frustrating visitors who come to view the famed summit. Some 76 glaciers (only 26 are named) patch the slopes and combine with sharp ridges and steep gullies to make Rainier an inhospitable place for the 3000 determined climbers who clamber to its summit each year.

Those who don't feel up to scaling The Mountain can find many places to ponder and play in the old-growth forests and alpine meadows of Mt. Rainier National Park. With over 305 mi. of trails, solitude is just a step away, whether you choose to hike through a rainforest, past hot springs, across rivers, or alongside wildflowers.

PRACTICAL INFORMATION AND ORIENTATION

Visitors Information: The **Longmire Hiker Information Center** distributes **backcountry permits.** Open Sun.-Thurs. 8am-6pm, Fri.-Sat. 7am-7pm; fall-spring

Sun.-Thurs. 8am-6pm. The **Paradise Visitors Center** offers lodging, food, and souvenirs. Open daily 9am-7pm; late-Sept. to mid-Oct. 9:30am-6pm; mid-Oct. through winter daily 10am-5pm. The **Sunrise Visitors Center** contains exhibits, snacks, and a gift shop. Open summer through mid-Sept. daily 9am-6pm. The **Ohanapecosh Visitors Center** offers information and wildlife displays. Open summer through mid-Oct. daily 9am-6pm. All centers can be contacted by writing c/o Superintendent, Mt. Rainier National Park, Ashford 98304, or by telephoning the park's central operator (569-2211). Additional backpacking and camping information can be obtained by writing or calling to the **Backcountry Desk,** Mt. Rainier National Park, Tahoma Woods, Star Route, Ashford 98304 (569-2211, ext. 3317).

Park Administrative Headquarters, Tahoma Woods, Star Route, Ashford 98304 (569-2211). Open Mon.-Fri. 8am-4:30pm.

Entrance Fee: $5 per car, $3 per hiker. Gates are open 24 hr., with free admission in the evenings.

Gray Line Bus Service, 720 S Forest St., Seattle 98134 (624-5077). Excursions from Seattle to Rainier daily May-Oct. 13 (single-day round-trip $34, under 13 $17). Buses leave from the Sheraton Hotel in Seattle at 8:15am and return around 6pm, giving you about 1½ hr. at Paradise and about 3½ hr. total at the mountain—ample time to tramp through the trails.

Hiking Supplies: RMI (569-2227), in Paradise. Rents ice axes ($7), crampons ($7.25), boots ($15), packs ($15), and helmets ($5) by the day. Expert RMI guides also lead summit climbs, seminars, and special schools and programs. Open May-Oct. daily 9am-5pm. Winter office: 535 Dock St. #209, Tacoma 98402 (206-627-6242).

Ski Supplies: White Pass Sports Hut, U.S. 12, Packwood (494-7321). Alpine package $11.50 per day, Nordic package $9. Also rents snowshoes and snowboards and sells camping equipment. Open daily 9am-6pm; in winter Mon.-Thurs. 8am-6pm, Fri.-Sun. 7am-6pm.

Park Emergency: 569-2211. 24 hr.

Post Office: In the **National Park Inn,** Longmire. Open Mon.-Fri. 8:30am-noon and 1-5pm. Also in the **Paradise Inn,** Paradise. Same hours as Longmire. **General Delivery ZIP Code:** 98398.

Area Code: 206.

To reach Mt. Rainier from the west, drive south from Seattle on I-5 to Tacoma, then go east on Rte. 512, south on Rte. 7, and east on Rte. 706. This scenic road meanders through the town of **Ashford** and into the park by the Nisqually entrance. **Rte. 706** is the only access road open throughout the year; snow usually closes all other park roads from November through May. The total distance from Tacoma is 65 mi.; the total distance from Seattle is approximately 60 mi.

Drivers should bear in mind that the park covers a large area (nearly 236,000 acres), and the only **gas station** is located in Longmire, where supplies are often limited. Make sure to fuel up before entering the park for the day.

Many visitors say that **hitchhiking** opportunities along the mountain roads tend to be exceptionally good. Contrary to what rangers say, Park Service employees will often give lifts to stranded hikers. One should be careful, though, to avoid getting marooned in the middle of nowhere. Those who need help should ask a person in uniform for assistance; personnel here are helpful and friendly, especially on rare sunny days when the peak is visible and spirits are high.

Summer temperatures stay warm during the day but drop precipitously at night. You should pack clothes and equipment and be prepared for rapid changes of weather. The park puts out two brochures on mountain-climbing and hiking that contain helpful hints and a list of recommended equipment for the Mt. Rainier explorer. Party size is limited in many areas, and campers must carry all trash and waste out of the backcountry. Piped water (safe for drinking) is available at most backcountry campsites, but canteens are recommended for daytime use. All stream and lake water should be treated for microorganisms before ingestion. The park is staffed with emergency medical technicians and owns a number of emergency vans. Rangers can provide first aid. The nearest **medical facilities** are in Morton (40 mi. from Longmire) and Enumclaw (50 mi. from Sunrise).

The **Gifford Pinchot National Forest** is headquartered at 6926 E. Fourth Plain Blvd., P.O. Box 8944, Vancouver, WA 98668 (206-750-5000). The section of the **Mt. Baker-Snoqualmie National Forest** that adjoins Mt. Rainier is administered by the **Wenatchee National Forest,** 301 Yakima St., Wenatchee 98807 (509-662-4314). Closer **ranger stations** are located at 10061 U.S. 12, Naches 98937 (509-965-8005), and Packwood Ranger Station, P.O. Box 559 Packwood 98361 (206-494-5515).

ACCOMMODATIONS AND FOOD

Longmire, Paradise, and **Sunrise** offer accommodations and food that are generally out of reach to the budget traveler. The general stores sprinkled throughout the area sell only last-minute trifles like bug repellant and marshmallows, and items are charged an extra state park tax. Stock up and stay in **Ashford** or **Packwood** if you must have a roof over your head. Otherwise, camp—isn't that what you're here for?

Paradise Inn (569-2413, reservations 569-2275), Paradise. This rustic inn, built in 1917 from Alaskan cedar, offers paradisiacal views of the mountain. Wake up early to hike the heavenly **Skyline Trail,** which starts in the heavenly parking lot. Small singles and doubles with shared bath $58 plus 9% tax, each additional person $10. Open late May-early Oct. Reservations required in summer; call at least a month ahead.

National Park Inn (569-2411, reservations 569-2275), Longmire. A less dramatic view than in Paradise but convenient for cross-country skiing. Singles and doubles with shared bath $54, each additional person $10. Reservations required for weekends and recommended for weekdays.

Hotel Packwood, 104 Main St. (494-5431), Packwood. Adorable old motel with very reasonable prices. Singles $20, with bath $38. Doubles $30.

Gateway Inn Motel, 38820 Rte. 706 E, Ashford 98304 (569-2506). Clean, comfortable rooms with bathrooms down the hall. Singles $30. Doubles $35. Individual cabins with TV, fireplace, shower, and 2 double beds from $50.

Sweet Peaks, 38104 Rte. 706 (569-2720). On the way to the Nisqually Entrance. Stop off for a killer cinnamon roll ($1.25) or a loaf of fresh bread ($1.25-2). The bakery also sells an assortment of camping gear. Open daily 5:30am-8pm.

Ma & Pa Rucker's (494-2651), Packwood. This local favorite serves piping hot pizza (small $5, large $9) and typical burgers and chicken sandwiches. A single scoop of their divine peppermint candy ice cream will cost you just $1. Stick around long enough and Ma & Pa will tell you about their son, Fudd. Open Mon.-Thurs. 9am-9pm, Fri.-Sun. 9am-10pm.

CAMPING

Camping at the auto-accessible campsites between mid-June and late September requires a permit ($5-8), which is available at campsites. **Alpine** and **cross-country camping** require free permits year-round and are subject to certain restrictions. Be sure to pick up a copy of the *Wilderness Trip Planner* pamphlet at a ranger station or hikers' center before you set off. Alpine and cross-country access is strictly controlled to prevent forest damage, but auto camping permits are relatively easy to get.

Each auto campground has its own personality. Go to **Ohanapecosh** for the gorgeous and serene high ceiling of old-growth trees; to **Cougar Rock,** near Longmire, for the strictly maintained quiet hours; and to both **White River** in the northeastern corner and **Sunshine Point** near the Nisqually entrance for the panoramas. Open on a first-come, first-camped basis, the grounds fill only on the busiest summer weekends. Sunshine Point is the only auto campground open year-round.

With a **backcountry permit,** cross-country hikers can use any of the free, well-established **trailside camps** scattered throughout the park's backcountry. Most camps have toilet facilities and a nearby water source, and some have shelters as well. Most of these sites are in the low forests, although some are found high up the mountain on the glaciers and snow fields. Adventurous cross-country hikers can test their survival skills in the vast cross-country zones at any of the low forests and in the sub-alpine zone. *Fires are prohibited in both areas,* and there are limits to the number of members in a party. Talk to a ranger for details. **Glacier climbers** and **mountain climbers** intending to go above 10,000 ft. must always register in person at ranger stations in order to be granted permits.

The **national forests** outside Rainier Park provide both developed sites (free-$5) and thousands of acres of freely campable countryside. When free-camping, be sure to avoid eroded lakesides and riverbanks—flash floods and debris flows can catch unwary campers in their paths. Minimum-impact **camping-fire permits,** which allow hikers to burn small fires that don't sterilize the soil, are available at national forest-ranger stations (see Practical Information). Don't count on receiving one, however, since the small number of backcountry sites limits the supply of permits. All permits are issued on a first-come, first-served basis.

OUTDOORS

It should be fairly obvious that Mother Nature is what beckons most to Mt. Rainier. Much of the activity in this area occurs at the park's **visitors centers** (see Practical Information above). Each has displays, a wealth of literature on everything from hiking to natural history, postings on trail and road conditions, and rangers to help point visitors in the right direction—whether they're on foot, in a wheelchair, or behind the wheel of a car. Guided trips and talks, campfire programs, and slide presentations are given at the visitors centers and vehicle campgrounds throughout the park. Check at a visitors center or get a copy of the free program guide, *Tahoma*.

A car tour is a good introduction to the park. All major roads offer scenic views of the mountain and have numerous roadside sites for camera-clicking and general gawking. The roads to Paradise and Sunrise are especially picturesque. **Stevens Canyon Road** connects the southeast corner of the national park with Paradise, Longmire, and the Nisqually entrance, unfolding spectacular vistas of Rainier and the rugged Tatoosh Range. The accessible roadside attractions of **Box Canyon, Bench Lake,** and **Grove of the Patriarchs** line the route.

Mt. Adams and Mt. St. Helens, not visible from the road, can be seen clearly from such **mountain trails** as **Paradise** (1½ mi.), **Pinnacle Peak** (2½mi.), **Eagle Peak** (7 mi.), and **Van Trump Peak** (5½ mi.). For more information on these trails, pick up *Viewing Mount St. Helens* at one of the visitors centers.

Several less developed roads provide access to more-isolated regions, often meeting trailheads that cross the park or lead to the summit. Hiking and camping outside designated campsites is permissible in most regions of the park, but a permit is required for overnight backpacking trips. The **Hiker Centers** at Carbon River and Longmire have information on day and backcountry hikes through the park and dispense necessary camping permits (see Practical Information for hours).

A segment of the **Pacific Crest Trail (PCT),** running between the Columbia River and the Canadian border, crosses through the southeast corner of the park. Geared to both hikers and horse riders, the PCT is maintained by the U.S. Forest Service. Primitive **campsites** and **shelters** line the trail; a permit is not required for camping, although you should contact the nearest ranger station for information on site and trail conditions. Food may be stored at designated food-cache areas in the park. Call 569-2211 for details. The trail, offering glimpses of the snow-covered peaks of the Cascades, snakes through delightful wildlife areas.

A trip to the **summit** of Mt. Rainier requires special preparation and substantial expense. The ascent is a vertical rise of more than 9000 ft. over a distance of 8 or more mi.—usually taking two days, with an overnight stay at **Camp Muir** on the south side (10,000 ft.) or **Camp Schurman** on the north side (9500 ft.). Camp Muir provides a public shelter, but climbers should be prepared to camp if it is full. Each camp has a ranger station, rescue cache, and some form of toilet. Climbers must melt snow for drinking water.

Experienced climbers may form their own expeditions upon satisfactory completion of a detailed application; consult a climbing ranger at the Paradise, Carbon River, or White River stations. Solo climbing requires the consent of the superintendent. Novices can sign up for a **summit climb** with **Rainier Mountaineering, Inc. (RMI),** which offers a one-day basic-climbing course followed by a two-day guided climb; the package costs $320 and requires strength and physical fitness. You must bring your own sleeping bag, headlamp, rain jacket, corset, and pants and carry four meals in addition to hiking gear. For more information, contact **Park Headquarters** or **RMI** (see Practical Information above).

Less ambitious, ranger-led **interpretive hikes** interpret everything from area history to local wildflowers. Each visitors center (see Practical Information) conducts its own hikes on its own schedule. These free hikes complement evening campfire programs, also conducted by each visitors center.

If you are llooking to spend an unusual day in a llovely llocation, **Llama Wilderness Pack Trips,** Tatoosh Motel, Packwood (491-LAMA/7213) offers a llunch with the llamas in the park for $25 per person (4-5-hr. trip). They also llease their llamas for pack trips and have guided trips of their own.

Longmire

Longmire's **museum,** in the visitors center, dwells on Rainier's past. The rooms are filled with exhibits on local natural history and the history of human encounters with the mountain. One interesting display reveals the disappointing secret of the mountain's name: "Rainier" has nothing to do with either a weather report or Monaco's monarch, but rather with a forgotten Tory politician who never even laid eyes on the peak (open in summer daily 9am-5:30pm, in off-season daily 9am-4:30pm).

Programs run by the visitors center in the Longmire area typically include **night meadow walks** and **hikes** into the surrounding dense forest. The **Hikers Center** is an excellent source of information and guidance for all backcountry trips except summit attempts. Free information sheets about specific day and overnight hikes are available throughout the park. The **Rampart Ridge Trail** (a 2½-hr., 4.6-mi. loop) has excellent views of the Nisqually Valley, Mount Rainier, and Tumtum Peak. The path of the **Kaetz Creek Mudflow** of 1947 and **Van Trump Park & Comet Falls Trail** (a steep 4-hr., 5-mi. hike) passes Comet Falls and, in early July, often a mountain goat or two. Check out the Center's relief model of the mountain before plunging into the woods. Remember that a permit is required for backcountry camping. The **Eagle Peak Saddle** trail (a 7-mi. round-trip) ends with a view of Mt. Rainier and the Gifford Pinchot National Forest.

Longmire remains open during the winter as a center for snowshoeing, cross-country skiing, and other alpine activities. **Guest Services, Inc.** (569-2275), runs a **cross-country ski center** (rental $11 per day, lessons $22 per hr., day tour $16, moonlight tour $6). The trails are difficult, but you can snowshoe eight months out of the year. Some diehards even enjoy winter hiking and climbing out of Longmire.

Paradise

One of the most visited places in the park, Paradise is perhaps the only place in Rainier where the sand of bubbling brooks and waterfalls might be drowned out by screaming children. Summer weekends bring city dwellers and families trying to escape to the wilderness; nearby inner-tubing runs attract many to visit just for the day. Nevertheless, if you can manage to avoid the hustle and bustle and arrive on a clear, sunny weekday, the name Paradise won't seem meant to mock you.

The area was first settled by the Longmire family, who saw Paradise's vast meadows of wildflowers as the Valhalla of the Northwest. Sitting well above the timberline, the sparkling snowfields can blind visitors staring down at the forest canyons thousands of feet below, even in mid-June. The road from the Nisqually entrance to

Paradise is open year-round, but the road east through Stevens Canyon is open only from mid-June through October, weather permitting. The **Paradise Visitors Center** offers audiovisual programs and an observation deck for viewing the heavens. From January to mid-April, park naturalists lead **snowshoe hikes** to explore winter ecology around Paradise (Sat.-Sun. at 10:30am, 12:30, and 2:30pm; snowshoe rental $1). You'll need the snowshoes: the world record for snowfall in one season (93.5 ft.) was set here in the winter of 1971-1972.

Paradise is the starting point for a number of **trails** heading through the meadows to the nearby Nisqually Glacier or up the mountain to the summit. Many trails allow close-up views of Mt. Rainier's glaciers, especially the two closest to Paradise, the **Paradise** and the **Stevens** glaciers. The 5-mi. **Skyline Trail** is the longest of the loop trails out of Paradise (4-hr. walk). The marked trail starts at the Paradise Inn, climbing above the treeline. Skyline is probably the closest a casual hiker can come to climbing the mountain. The first leg of the trail is often hiked by climbing parties headed for **Camp Muir** (the base camp for most ascents to the summit). The trail turns off before reaching Camp Muir, rising to its highest elevation at **Panorama Point.** Although only halfway up the mountain, the point is within view of the glaciers, and the summit appears deceptively close. Turn around to witness rows of blue-gray mountaintops, with Mt. St. Helens and Mt. Adams presiding over the horizon. Heading back down the trail, you will cross a few snowfields and do some boulder-hopping. Since route conditions vary, contact a ranger station in Paradise, White River, Sunrise, or Longmire for information on crevasse and rockfall conditions.

The mildly strenuous, 2½-mi. half-day hike up to **Pinnacle Peak,** which begins across the road from Reflection Lakes (just east of Paradise), features a clear view of Mount Rainier, Mt. Adams, Mt. St. Helens, and Mt. Hood. One of the most striking features of hikes out of Paradise is the expanse of wildflowering alpine meadows surrounding them; these are some of the largest and most spectacular in the park.

Hikers should be especially careful to stay on the trails because the meadows are extremely fragile. Erosion and hiker damage can take years to repair; some of the plants in the area bloom only once in several years.

Ohanapecosh and Carbon River

Though located in the far opposite corners of the park, the Ohanapecosh and Carbon Rivers are in the same ranger district. The **Ohanapecosh Visitors Center** and campground are located in a lush forest along a river valley in the park's southeast corner. Here grows the **Grove of the Patriarchs,** one of the oldest stands of original trees in Washington. An easy 2-mi., one-and-a-half-hour walk will take you to these 500- to 1000-year-old Douglas firs, cedars, and hemlocks. The visitors center has displays on the forest and naturalist programs, which include walks to the Grove, Silver Falls, and Ohanapecosh Hot Springs—which is a trickle of warm water in an area returning to the wild after commercialization as a therapeutic resort in the 1920s. For serious hiking, the **Summerland** and **Indian Bar trails** receive rave reviews.

Carbon River Valley, in the northwest corner of the park, is one of the only **rain forests** in the continental U.S., and its trails are on every ranger-in-the-know's top 10 list for hiking. **Spray Park** and **Mystic Camp** are superlative free backcountry campsites. Carbon River also has access to the **Wonderland Trail** (see below). Most visitors to the park miss the chance to go to Carbon River, however, because they don't find out about it until they reach one of the more popular visitors centers and then can't stomach the three-hour drive. However, if you arrive at the park through Carbon River (via Rte. 165), the region is more easily accessible. Your time here will no doubt leave you hoping that Carbon River remains one of the best-kept secrets.

Sunrise

The winding road to Sunrise, the highest of the four visitors centers, swims with visions of the Pacific Ocean, Mt. Baker, and the heavily glaciated eastern side of Mt. Rainier. The mountain views from Sunrise are among the best in the park.

Sunrise provides an abundance of **trails** varying greatly in difficulty; the visitors center has details on hikes ranging from ½ to 13 mi. Two favorites are **Burrough's Mt. Trail,** a 5-mi., three-hour walk affording excellent views of the glaciers, and **Mt. Fremont Trail,** a 5.6-mi., four-hour hike with views of the Cascades, Grand Park, and quite possibly mountain goats.

The often attempted but seldom completed **Wonderland Trail** passes through Sunrise on its way around the mountain. A popular 95-mi. trek circumscribing Rainier, the trail traverses ridges and valleys. The lakes and streams near the path are trout-ridden. The entire circuit takes 10-14 days and includes several brutal ascents and descents. Beware of early snowstorms in September, snow-blocked passes in June, and muddy trails in July—all of which can force hikers to turn back. Rangers can provide information on weather and trail conditions; they also can store food caches for you at ranger stations along the trail. In case of an emergency, you would be at most one hiking day away from a park road or ranger station.

The hike from **Fryingpan Creek Bridge** (3 mi. from the White River entrance) to Summerland is popular for its views of Mt. Rainier; behold elk and mountain goats grazing on the surrounding slopes. The circuit runs 4.2 mi. from the road along Fryingpan Creek to the Sunrise campground, ranger station, and meadows.

■ Cowlitz Valley

The **Cowlitz River** originates from the tip of a Rainier glacier and cuts a long, deep divot west between Mt. Rainier and Mt. St. Helens, pinning the Columbia River along I-5. Although your view of St. Helens and Rainier will be obscured when you sink into the Cowlitz Valley, your loss will be compensated with softer scenery—miles of lush foothills and farmland.

The river forms part of the waterbed for both the **Mt. Adams** and **Goat Rocks Wilderness Areas,** to the west and northwest of Mt. St. Helens, respectively. Both areas are excellent hiking country—accessible only on foot or horseback—and include sections of the **Pacific Crest Trail** among their extensive trail networks. The rugged Goat Rocks area is famed for its herd of mountain goats, while Mt. Adams seduces hundreds of climbers each year with its sensuous snow-capped summit (12,307 ft.). Two **ranger stations** in the valley are located at 13068 U.S. 12, Packwood (206-494-5515) and at 10024 U.S. 12, Randle (206-497-7565). Contact the U.S. Forest Service at one of these locations for trail guides and other information on these wilderness areas.

The Cowlitz passes closest to Mt. St. Helens near the town of **Morton.** This logging town is accessed by U.S. 12 from the east and west (I-15 exit 68), Rte. 508 from the west (I-5 exit 71), and Rte. 7 from the north. Morton and other towns near Mt. St. Helens have capitalized on the public interest in the now *passé* 1980 eruption. Stores sell containers of ash and other St. Helens *dreck* (ash-glass paperweights, pens, thermometers, and Christmas-tree ornaments). The **Morton Chamber of Commerce** (496-6086), in the log cabin just off U.S. 12 as you enter town, can fill you in on local events. The **Cody Cafe** (496-5787), on Main St. serves a Helenic stack of three pancakes ($2.25). Lunches run $3-5 (open Mon.-Fri. 4am-11pm, Sat. 5am-11pm, Sun. 6am-11pm). If you are staying overnight in the area, head for the lime-green **Evergreen Motel,** 111 Main St. (496-5407). The rooms may be plain, but they're still cheap and clean (singles from $22, doubles from $30). Morton's **post office** (496-5316) is located at 2nd and Bingham (open Mon.-Fri. 8am-5pm; **General Delivery ZIP code:** 98356).

The Cowlitz River, once wild and treacherous, has been tamed considerably by a Tacoma City Light hydroelectric project. The **Mayfield** and **Mossyrock Dams** back up water into the river gorge to create two lakes, **Mayfield** and **Riffe,** both much-used recreation areas. **Ike Kinswa State Park** and **Mayfield Lake County Park,** on Mayfield Lake off U.S. 12, offer camping and excellent rainbow- and silver-trout fishing year-round. Ike Kinswa (983-3402) has over 100 sites with showers (sites $10, full hookups $14). Mayfield Lake (985-2364) offers 54 tentsites ($10). Public boat launches provide access to Mayfield, the lower of the two lakes.

Riffe Lake, much larger than Mayfield, was named to memorialize **Riffe,** a town flooded by the building of the enormous Mossyrock Dam. Campers at **Mossyrock Park** (983-3900) on the south shore can drop by the display at Hydro Vista next to the dam (sites $10, with electricity and water $14). Tacoma City Light offers free **guided tours** of the Cowlitz River Dams.

One of the more intriguing aspects of the complex is the **Cowlitz Salmon Hatchery,** south of the town of Salkum just off U.S. 12. The free self-guided tours of the facility include views of fish ladders, the spawning center, and the tanks where the salmon are kept. This facility releases 17½ million young chinook salmon each year. Hatcheries like this one have been constructed all over the Northwest both to encourage salmon fishing and to compensate for changes in the environment wrought by hydroelectric projects.

Below the dams, the Cowlitz River courses through farmland, flowers, and blueberries. Hosts of local farms dot the hillside along the road, many offering **U-pick berry bargains** during the summer harvest season (late June-Aug.).

Two free publications, *The Lewis County Visitors Guide* and *The Morton Journal View*, are available throughout the Cowlitz Valley and provide up-to-date information on local parks, camping, hiking, food, and lodging.

■■■ MOUNT ST. HELENS

On May 18, 1980, the greater part of the top of Washington's Mt. St. Helens was atomized, creating a hole 2 mi. long and 1 mi. wide in what had once been a perfect cone. The blast leveled entire forests, leaving a stubble of trunks on nearby slopes. Because the blast was lateral, not vertical, it proved more destructive, as no energy was dissipated fighting gravity. Ash from the crater blackened the sky for hundreds of miles and blanketed the streets of towns as far as Yakima, 80 mi. away. Debris spewed from the volcano-flooded Spirit Lake, choked rivers with mud, and descended to the towns via river and glacier.

Once the jewel of the Cascades, the **Mt. St. Helens National Monument** (administered by the National Forest Service) is now steadily—albeit slowly—recovering from the explosion that transformed 150 sq. mi. of prime forest land into an ashen desert. The spectacle of disaster is now freckled by signs of returning life—saplings push their way up past their fallen brethren, two insects have flourished near newly formed waterfalls, and a beaver has been spotted in Spirit Lake.

The area surrounding the monument is now the **Gifford Pinchot National Forest.** Much of the monument area is off-limits to the public because of ongoing delicate geological experiments and the unpredictability of the volcanic crater. The "lady of fire," is still considered active and could erupt again.

PRACTICAL INFORMATION AND ORIENTATION

Visitors Information: Mount St. Helens National Volcanic Monument Visitor Center, (206-274-6644, or 206-274-4038 for 24-hr. recorded information), on Rte. 504 5 mi. east of Castle Rock. Take exit 49 off I-5, and follow the signs. The best place to start a trip to the mountain, with information on camping and access to the mountain, as well as displays on the mountain's eruption and regeneration. Interpretive naturalist activities mid-June to Aug. The free 22-min. film *The Eruption of Mt. St. Helens* has graphic footage of the eruption's aftermath. Open April-Sept. 9am-7pm; Oct.-March 9am-5pm.

Information Inside the Monument: Several stations are staffed to answer visitor questions. At **Woods Creek Information Station,** 6 mi. south of Randle on F.R. 25, you not only will find displays, maps, and brochures, but you can also have an attendant answer your questions without even leaving your car. Open May-Oct. 9am-5pm. The **Pine Creek Information Station,** 17 mi. east of Cougar on F.R.

90, shows a short movie to prepare visitors for their adventure to the mountain. Open May-Sept. 9am-5pm. **Apes' Headquarters,** at Ape Cave on F.R. 8303, is the place to go with questions on the lava tube. Open May-Sept. 9am-6pm. The **Monument Headquarters** (247-5473, or 247-5478 for recorded message), 3 mi. north of Amboy on Rte. 503, doles out information on traveling, permits, and conditions. Open Mon.-Fri. 8am-5pm.

Information Outside the Monument: Inhabitants of many nearby small towns have become quite adept at answering questions about Mount St. Helens. The **Woodland Chamber of Commerce,** 1225 Lewis River Rd. (225-9552; open daily 9am-5pm), the **Castle Rock Chamber of Commerce,** 113 Huntington (274-6603; open daily 10am-6pm; Nov.-April Wed.-Sat. noon-4pm), and the **Kelso Volcano Information Center,** 105 Minor Rd. (577-8058; open daily 9am-5pm; Nov.-April Wed.-Sun. 9am-5pm), are well-equipped to discuss the social, economic, and botanical effects of the eruption. Pick up free copies of the *Volcano Review* and the *Tourist Guide to Volcano Country,* two excellent sources of local information, at any one of these visitors centers.

Gifford Pinchot National Forest Headquarters, 6926 E. 4th Plain Blvd., PO Box 8944, Vancouver, WA 98668 (206-750-5000). Camping and hiking information within the forest. Additional **ranger stations** located at: **Randle** (206-497-7565), north of the mountain on U.S. 12 and east of the visitors center; **Packwood** (206-494-5515), farther east on U.S. 12; **Wind River** (509-427-5645), south of the mountain on Forest Service Rd. 30 and north of the town of Carson in the Columbia River Gorge; and **Mt. Adams** (509-395-2501), at Trout Lake, southeast of the mountain on Rte. 141 and above White Salmon in the Columbia River Gorge.

Climbing Permits: Available at Jack's Restaurant and Store (231-4276), Rte. 503, 5 mi. west of Cougar.

Climbing Hotline: 247-5800. Information on snow, temperature, visibility, wind, and other factors that might affect climbing the volcano.

Emergency: 911.

Area Code: 206.

If you can spend only a short time in the area, visit the **Mount St. Helens National Volcanic Monument Visitor Center,** on Rte. 504 (see above). But if you want a closer view of the volcano, plan to spend the whole day in the monument and visit either the **Pine Creek Information Center** in the south or the **Woods Creek Information Center** in the north. While not as large as the center near Toutle, these two centers are each within a mi. of excellent viewpoints (see above). Those wishing to climb the mountain (see Sights below) must apply for permits from the Monument Visitor Center or register at Jack's Restaurant and Store (see Climbing Permits above). All drivers should fill up their **gas** tanks before an excursion into Mt. St. Helens, as fuel is not sold in the monument.

CAMPING

Although the monument area itself contains no campgrounds, many are scattered throughout the surrounding national forest. Free dispersed camping *is* allowed within the monument, meaning that if you stumble upon a site on an old forest service road you can camp out there, but finding a site is a matter of luck; contact a ranger for information. The closest campsite to the scene of the explosion is the **Iron Creek Campground,** just south of the Woods Creek Information Center on Forest Service Rd. 25, near the junction with Rd. 76 (98 sites, $8). For reservations call MISTIX at 800-365-2267.

Farther south is **Swift Campground,** located on Forest Service Rd. 90, just west of the Pine Creek Information Station. Swift is run by Pacific Power & Light (503-464-5035) on a first-come, first-pitched basis (93 sites, $6). West of Swift Campground on Yale Reservoir lie two other PP&L campgrounds, both of which accept reservations and have flush toilets and showers. **Beaver Bay,** with 63 RV and tentsites ($6), lies 2 mi. east of **Cougar,** which offers 45 tentsites ($6).

Seaquest State Park (274-8633), on Rte. 504, 5 mi. east of the town of Castle Rock at exit 49 off I-5, has 92 sites ($10), four of which are primitive and reserved for the hiker/biker set.

OUTDOORS

The first stop for visitors traveling south on Rd. 25 from Randle and U.S. 12 should be the **Woods Creek Information Station**. Drivers continuing south on Rd. 25 can turn east on Rd. 26, or follow Rd. 25; both eventually run into Rd. 99. If you choose Rd. 26, bear in mind that it is a one-laner (with turn-outs) that follows the side of a ridge. Visitors traveling with trailers or in motor homes are advised to stay on Rd. 25. Rd. 26 winds through a valley devastated even though it didn't receive the brunt of the blow (the explosion vented its principal energy west and south of here). Viewpoints along the road are listed on various handouts at the visitors center and include the **Quartz Creek Big Trees** and **Ryan Lake.**

If you decide instead to stay on Rd. 25, continue south 9 mi. farther until you reach Rd. 99 going west. The newly paved, two-lane Rd. 99 passes through 17 mi. of curves, clouds of ash, and precipices. Those with trailers are best off leaving them in the **Wakepish Sno-park,** the designated trailer drop. If possible, allow a few hours to complete this stretch of road. Without stops it takes nearly an hour to travel out and back on Rd. 99, but the numerous talks, walks, and views along the way merit getting out of the car.

On the way west from Rd. 25, **Bear Meadow** provides the first interpretive stop and an excellent view of St. Helens, as well as the last restrooms before Rd. 99 ends at **Windy Ridge.** The monument begins just west of here, where Rd. 26 and 99 meet, at **Meta Lake.** Forest interpreters lead 45 minute walks to this emerald lake during the summer (daily at 12:30pm and 3pm); meet at the old **Miners' Car.**

Farther west along Rd. 99, frequent roadside turnouts offer interpretive information on the surroundings, unbeatable photo opportunities, and numerous trailheads for hikers. **Independence Pass Trail #227** (3.5 mi., 4-hr. round-trip) is a difficult hike with overlooks to **Spirit Lake** and superb views of the crater and dome that improve as you go farther along the trail. Farther west, **Harmony Trail #224** (2 mi., 1½-hr. round-trip) provides the only public access to Spirit Lake. Forest interpreters lead a hike from the Harmony Viewpoint to Spirit Lake along this trail during the summer daily at 1:30pm.

Windy Ridge, at the end of Rd. 99, is worth enduring the winding trip. From here, you can climb atop an ash hill for a magnificent view of the crater from 3½ mi. away. During the summer, forest interpreters describe the eruption during talks held in the Windy Ridge amphitheater (every hr. on the ½ hr., Mon.-Fri. 11:30am-4:30pm, Sat.-Sun. 11:30am-5:30pm.)

The **Pine Creek Information Station** lies 25 mi. south, at the junction of Rd. 25 and 90. From here continue 12 mi. west and then 2 mi. north on Rd. 83 to reach **Ape Cave,** a broken 2½-mi.-long lava tube formed in an ancient eruption. Wear a jacket and sturdy shoes. Lanterns may be rented for $3, or bring your own flashlights (minimum of 2). Forest interpreters lead 30-minute guided lantern walks during the summer through the Western Hemisphere's longest known lava tube (every hr. on the ½ hr., Mon.-Fri. 12:30-2:30pm, Sat.-Sun. 11:30am-4:30pm).

Rd. 83 continues 9 mi. farther north, ending at **Lahar Viewpoint,** site of terrible mudflows which followed the eruption. Interpreters lead a 30-minute walk through this landscape during the summer daily at 1:30 and 4pm, showing travelers how flora and fauna are slowly returning to an area that was wiped clean of life.

Those with a sense of adventure, the proper equipment, and the foresight to have made reservations (required May 15-Oct. 31) can scale the new, stunted version of the mountain to glimpse the lava dome from the crater's rim. Although not a technically difficult climb, the route up the mountain is steep and often unstable (especially at the rim). Climbers are encouraged to bring the whole package: ice axe, hard hat, sunglasses, sunscreen, crampons, rope, climbing boots, and foul-weather clothing. Between May 14 and November 1, the Forest Service allows only 100 people to hike to the crater each day. Reservations can be made in person at the **Mt. St. Helens National Volcanic Monument Headquarters** (see Practical Information), or by writing to headquarters at 42218 NE Yale Bridge Rd., Amboy, WA 98601.

Climbers should visit **Jack's Restaurant and Store** (231-4276), on Rte. 503, 5 mi. west of Cougar, which holds unreserved permits for 40 climbers per day available on a first-come, first-served basis. Each day at 11am, a list is made of those desiring permits for the next day; at 6pm, permits are issued to the first 40 on the list.

Many companies offer to fly helicopters and planes over the crater, though these flights are prohibitively expensive. The Monument Visitors Center (see Practical Information) has a list of most of them.

EASTERN WASHINGTON

Located in the rain-shadow of the Cascades, the hills and vales of the Columbia River Basin once fostered little more than sagebrush and tumbleweed. With irrigation and the construction of several strategically placed dams, the basin now yields bumper crops of nearly every imaginable kind of fruit. The same sun that ripens the region's orchards also bronzes flocks of visitors from the wet-side. East of the river, ranching, wheat farming, and mining dominate the economy. **Spokane** is the largest city east of the Cascades but poses no real threat to the cultural preeminence of Seattle.

U.S. 97, running north-south on the eastern edge of the Cascades, strings together the main fruit centers and mountain resorts of the Columbia River Basin. **Interstate 90** emerges from the Cascades to cut a route through Ellensburg, Moses Lake, and Spokane, while **Interstate 82** dips south through Yakima and Toppenish.

Greyhound (509-624-4116) runs along I-90 and passes Yakima. **Empire Lines** (at the same number) runs from Spokane to Grand Coulee and Brewster, and along U.S. 97 from Oroville on the Canadian border to Ellensburg, passing by Lake Chelan. **Amtrak** (509-624-5144) runs its "Empire Builder" through Spokane, the Tri-Cities, the Columbia River, and then north to Yakima, Ellensburg, and Tacoma.

■■■ SPOKANE

Originally named "Spokan Falls" after the area's pre-Columbian inhabitants, the Spokan-ee Indians, Spokane was the first pioneer settlement in the Pacific Northwest. After the Great Fire of 1889, Spokane's economy quickly re-routed in the lumber, mining, and agriculture industries. The economy is still based on local natural resources, and Spokane remains one of the Northwest's major trade centers. Spokane achieves urban sophistication without typical big-city hassles. The downtown thrives, but the pace is slow. The legacy of Expo '74 includes a museum and theater in **Riverfront Park,** as well as a number of elegant restaurants and hotels.

PRACTICAL INFORMATION AND ORIENTATION

Visitors Information: Spokane Area Convention and Visitors Bureau, W. 926 Sprague Ave. (747-3230), exit 280 off I-90. Overflowing with literature extolling every aspect of Spokane. Open Mon.-Fri. 8:30am-5pm, and most summer weekends Sat. 9am-5pm and Sun. 10am-3pm (depending on volunteer availability).

Amtrak, W. 221 1st St. (624-5144, after business hours 800-872-7245), at Bernard St., downtown. To: Chicago (1 per day, $211); Seattle (1 per day, $65); Portland (1 per day, $65). Depot open Mon.-Fri. 11am-3:30am, Sat.-Sun. 7:15pm-3:30am.

Greyhound, W. 1125 Sprague (624-5251), at 1st Ave. and Jefferson St., downtown. **Empire Lines** (624-4116) and **Northwest Stage Lines** (800-826-4058 or 838-4029) share the terminal with Greyhound, serving other parts of Eastern Washington, northern Idaho, and British Columbia. Northwest Stage Lines to Seattle (6 per day, $20), Lewiston, ID (2 per day, $20). Station open 24 hr.

Spokane Transit System, W. 1229 Boone Ave. (328-7433). Serves all of Spokane, including Eastern Washington University in Cheney. Fare 75¢, ages over 64 and travelers with disabilities 35¢.Operates until 12:15am downtown, 9:15pm in the valley along E. Sprague Ave.
Taxi: Checker Cab, 624-4171. **Yellow Cab,** 624-4321. Both open 24 hr.
Car Rental: U-Save Auto Rental, W. 918 3rd St. (455-8018), at Monroe. Cars from $23 per day with 100 free mi., 20¢ per additional mi. $250 deposit or major credit card required. Must be over 21. Open Mon.-Fri. 7am-8pm, Sat. 8am-6pm, Sun. 9am-6pm.
AAA Office, W. 1717 4th (455-3400). Open Mon.-Fri. 8am-5pm.
Camping Equipment: White Elephant, N. 1730 Division St. (328-3100) and E. 12614 Sprague (924-3006). The Crazy Eddie of camping stores, with every imaginable piece of equipment at bargain prices. Open Mon.-Thurs. and Sat. 9am-6pm, Fri. 9am-9pm. **Outdoor Sportsman,** N. 1602 Division St. (328-1556). Prices are even more insane. Open Mon.-Thurs. 9am-6:30pm, Fri. 9am-7pm, Sat. 10am-6pm, Sun. 9am-5pm.
Public Library: W. 906 Main St. (838-3361). Open Mon.-Thurs. 10am-9pm, Fri. (and Sat. in winter) 10am-6pm.
Laundromat: Ye Olde Wash House Laundry and Dry Cleaners, E. 4224 Sprague (534-9859). Wash (electric, not ye olde tub) 75¢, 12 min. dry 25¢.
Events Line: 747-2787. 24-hr. Recorded information.
Travelers Aid Service, W. 1017 1st (456-7164), near the bus depot. Kind staff, adept at helping stranded travelers find lodgings. Open Mon.-Fri. 1-4:30pm.
Crisis Hotline: 838-4428. 24 hr.
Public Health Clinic: W. 1101 College Ave. (324-1600).
Poison Information: 747-1077. 24 hr.
Senior Center: W. 1124 Sinto (327-2861). Mon.-Sat. 8:30am-5pm, Sun. 2-5pm.
Pharmacy: Hart and Dilatush, W. 501 Sprague (624-2111). Mon.-Fri. 8am-midnight, Sat.-Sun. noon-10pm.
Hospital: Deaconess Medical Center, W. 800 5th (458-7100).
Police: 456-2233. **Ambulance:** 328-6161. Both 24 hr.
Post Office: W. 904 Riverside (459-0230), at Lincoln. Open Mon.-Fri. 8:30am-5pm. **General Delivery ZIP Code:** 99210.
Area Code: 509.

Spokane lies 280 mi. east of Seattle on I-90. The **Spokane International Airport** (624-3218) is off I-90 8 mi. southwest of town. Avenues run east-west parallel to the river, streets north-south, and both alternate one-way. The city is bifurcated north and south by **Sprague Ave.,** east and west by **Division St.** Downtown is the quadrant north of Sprague and west of Division, wedged between I-90 and the Spokane River. I-90 exits 279 to 282 access Spokane. Street addresses begin with the compass point first, list the number second, and the street name third (e.g., W. 1200 Division). Dare to be different. All Spokane Transit System buses start and finish their routes 2 blocks south, at Riverside and Howard St.

ACCOMMODATIONS AND CAMPING

Don't try to sleep in Riverfront Park; the Spokane police *don't* like it. A handful of hotels south of downtown are cheap but sleazy. Most camping areas are at least 20 mi. away. The hostel is your best option.

Brown Squirrel Hostel (HI/AYH), S. 930 Lincoln (838-5968). A steep climb up Lincoln brings you to a large, warm house with a grandfather clock, spacious porch, and delightfully creaky wooden floorboards; a cozy kitchen, laundry, and bath complete the nostalgic atmosphere. The hostel fills up in July and August so make a reservation. Even if you don't have a reservation, show up. They might just squeeze an extra cot in a corner. $10.
Town Centre Motor Inn, W. 901 1st St. (747-1041), at Lincoln St. in the heart of downtown, 4 blocks from the bus depot. Well-kept rooms include a refrigerator and a microwave. Save nearly 20% by exchanging your US$ for CDN$ at one of

the downtown banks beforehand; the Motor Inn accepts north-of-the-border currency at par. Singles $40. Doubles $46.

Motel 6, S. 1580 Rustle St. (459-6120), off of I-90 at exit 277, far from downtown. TV and pool. Singles $30. Doubles $36. Make reservations 2-3 weeks ahead.

Riverside State Park (456-3964), 6 mi. northwest of downtown on Rifle Club Rd. off Rte. 291 or Nine Mile Rd. Take Division north and turn left on Francis. The route is not clearly marked; ask a local. 101 standard sites in an urban setting. Kitchen, shower, bath, and a small park. Wheelchair access. Sites $10.

Mt. Spokane State Park (456-4169), 35 mi. northeast of the city. Take U.S. 395 5 mi. north to U.S. 2, then go 7 mi. north to Hwy. 206, which leads into the park. Popular with winter athletes for its cross-country skiing and snowmobiling trails. Views of 2 states and Canada from the Vista House. 12 sites. Flush toilets; no showers, cold water only. Sites $10.

Smokey Trail (747-9415), 5 mi. west of the city. Take I-90 to exit 272. Follow Hallett Rd. east to Mallon Rd., then 1 mi. south. Warm up with hot showers, free firewood, and laundry facilities. Sites $15, RV hookups $19. Open May 15-Sept. 20.

FOOD

Besides supporting a number of small diners and cafes, Spokane, a trading center for Eastern Washington's agriculture, boasts a cornucopia of fresh produce. On Wednesday, Saturday, and Sunday from May to October, the **Spokane County Market** (482-2627) vends fresh fruit, vegetables, baked goods, and arts and crafts in Riverfront Park. The **Green Bluff Growers Cooperative,** E. 9423 Green Bluff Rd., Colbert 99005, is an organization of 20-odd fruit and vegetable farms, all marked with the big red apple sign 16 mi. northwest of town off Day-Mountain Spokane Rd. Many of the farms have "u-pick" arrangements, and are near free picnic areas.

For a variety of interesting eateries downtown, head to **The Atrium,** on Wall St. near 1st. Ave. **Europa Pizzeria,** one of the restaurants in this small brick building, bakes the best pizza in town. The famished should eat in bulk; many of the chain restaurants clustered along 3rd. Ave. advertise all-you-can-eat specials and buffets.

Dick's, E. 10 3rd Ave. (747-2481), at Division. Look for the pink panda sign near I-90. This takeout burger phenomenon, located in an inexplicably inflation-free pocket of Washington, has been permanently enshrined in the *Let's Go: Did You Know?* Hall of Fame. Burgers 55¢, fries 43¢, sundaes 65¢, soft drinks 43-75¢. Take the panda's advice and buy by the bagful. Dick's is always crowded, but battalions of workers move the lines along quickly. Open daily 9am-1:30am.

Coyote Cafe, W. 702 3rd Ave. (747-8800). This jazzy Mexican joint has *cerveza* signs on the walls, cacti in the windows, and $2.75 margaritas all day. You don't have to be a super genius to enjoy the Wile E. Coyote *chimichanga* ($5.75). "Margarita Madness" on Thursdays offers 75¢ 'ritas. Open Mon.-Thurs. 11:30am-10pm, Fri. 11:30am-11pm, Sat. noon-11pm, Sun. noon-10pm.

Cyrus O'Leary's, W. 516 Main St. (624-9000), in the Bennetts Block complex at Howard St. A Spokane legend. Devour delicious food from a creative 25-page menu offering enormous meals ($7-15). Sandwiches $5.75 and up. Happy hour 4:30-6:30pm. Open Mon.-Thurs. 11:30am-11pm, Fri.-Sat. 11:30am-midnight, Sun. 11:30am-10pm.

Thai Cafe, W. 410 Sprague (838-4783). This tiny restaurant adds plenty of spice (or only a little—your choice) to Spokane's American fare. The traditional *pad thai* and *gai pad* are $5. Open Mon.-Fri. 11:30am-1:30pm and 5-8:30pm, Sat 5-8:30pm.

Benjamin's Burger Inn (455-6771), in the Parkade Plaza. This popular and more gourmet alternative to Dick's sells larger, juicer—and more expensive—burgers ($2). Get a little crazy with the curly fries (90¢), or one of their other home-cookin' menu items. Open Mon.-Fri. 7am-6pm, Sat. 8am-5pm.

Milford's Fish House and Oyster Bar, N. 719 Monroe (326-7251). Don't be fooled by the dingy neighborhood—Milford's is one of the finest restaurants in the entire Pacific Northwest. And though it may well sink your budget, the freshest seafood in town will certainly buoy your spirits. Choose from a placard of fresh specials ($12-18) which are rotated daily; each includes a bowl of clam chowder or a dinner salad along with bread and vegetables. Open Mon. 5-9pm, Tues.-Sat. 5-10pm, Sun. 4-9pm.

SIGHTS

Spokane doesn't aspire to flashy art or high-flown architecture (and probably shouldn't). The city's best attractions concentrate on local history and culture. The **Cheney Cowles Memorial Museum,** W. 2316 1st Ave. (456-3931), near the hostel, houses well-explicated displays on the animals and pioneers of Eastern Washington. The museum's exhibits on Native North and South American art and artifacts have been augmented by the collection from the now-defunct Museum of Native American Cultures. One gallery is also given over to contemporary Northwest art.

Riverfront Park, N. 507 Howard St. (625-6600), just north of downtown, is Spokane's civic center. If the park hadn't been built for the 1974 World's Fair, the populace would have nowhere to stroll on leisurely weekend afternoons. The **IMAX Theatre** (625-6604) boasts a 5½-story movie screen and a projector the size of a Volkswagen. (Admission Tues.-Sun. $4.50, senior citizens $3.50, under 18, $3. Open daily 11am-9pm; shows on the hour.) Another section of the park offers a full range of kiddie rides—including the exquisitely hand-carved **Looff Carousel** (open daily 11am-9pm; $1 a whirl). A one-day pass ($11, children and senior citizens $10) covers admission to the whole works. The park offers ice-skating in the winter ($4, skate-rental $1.25) and often hosts special programs and events.

Hard-core Bingsters will be drawn to the **Crosby Library,** E. 502 Boone St. (328-4220 ext.3132), at Gonzaga University. Here, the faithful exhibit the Bingmeister's relics and gold records. (Open daily, but call for hours since they vary. Free.)

Spokane's collection of two dozen parks includes **Manito Park** (456-4331), on S. Grand Ave. between 17th and 25th Ave. south of downtown, which encompasses a flower garden, tennis courts, a romantic duck pond. The **Dr. David Graiser Conservatory,** also cultivates many tropical and local plant species (open daily 8am-dusk; in winter 8am-3:30pm; free). Adjacent to Manito Park is the **Nishinomiya Garden,** a lush Japanese garden consecrating the friendship of Spokane and her Japanese sister city, Nishinomiya (same hours as Manito Park; free).

ENTERTAINMENT AND SEASONAL EVENTS

The *Spokane Spokesman-Review's* Friday "Weekend" section and the *Spokane Chronicle's* Friday "Empire" section give the lowdown on area happenings. During the summer, the city parks present a free **Out-to-Lunch** concert series at noon on weekdays at various locations around town. Call 624-1393, Mon.-Fri. 8:30am-4:30pm for schedule information.

Spokane supports two minor league sports teams. The **Indians** play ball at N. 602 Havana (535-2922) from June through August (tickets $3.50-5.50), while the **Chiefs** skate at the Coliseum (328-0450) from October through March. All city-sponsored events are ticketed by Select-A-Seat. Call 325-SHOW (7469) for information or 325-SEAT (7328) for reservations.

The Opera House, W. 334 Spokane Falls Blvd. (353-6500). Home to the Spokane Ballet and the Spokane Symphony Orchestra; also stages special performances ranging from rock concerts to chamber music. Open Mon.-Fri. 8:30am-5pm.

Civic Theater, N. 1020 Howard St. (325-1413; 325-1413 for reservations), opposite the Coliseum. Locally produced shows; has a downstairs theater for more "risqué" productions. Tickets Fri.-Sat. $15, Wed.-Thurs. $12, seniors and students $9.

Spokane Interplayers Ensemble, S. 174 Howard (455-7529). A resident professional theater which performs a broad range of plays. 7 productions a season, 20 public performances each. Matinees $9, evening $10 and $12.

Magic Lantern Theatre, S. 123 Wall St. (838-4919). Fantastic films, from American classics to foreign features. Admission $5.50, senior citizens and students $4.50, and for the *Rocky Horror Picture Show* $3.

Outback Jack's, W. 321 Sprague Ave. (747-7539). The place to be among Spokane's younger crowd. Drink specials in a relaxed atmosphere. Nothing to do
with Australia, however. $1 beers on Thurs.-Sun. Cover Thurs.-Sat. $2. Hosts local
bands on Fri. and Sat.

Henry's Pub, W. 230 Riverside Ave. (624-9828). *The* place for live rock Fri.-Sat.
nights. Cover charge varies from $2-6 depending on the band. Local and out-of-
town bands—local favorites include Nice World, Soul Patch, and Motherlode—
slam and thrash here. Draft beer $1.50-1.75. Open Wed.-Sat. 7am-2am.

On the first Sunday in May, Riverfront Park hosts its premature, annual **Bloomsday
Road Race,** the second biggest footrace on the West Coast. The race is the highlight
of the **Lilac Festival,** a week-long hoopla of car shows, art fairs, house tours, and
Special Olympics. For information on these and other events, contact the Chamber
of Commerce (see Practical Information, above).

OUTDOORS NEAR SPOKANE

The state runs two parks in the Spokane area. **Riverside State Park** (456-3964)
embroiders the Spokane River with 7655 acres of volcanic outcroppings, hiking
trails (especially good in **Deep Creek Canyon,** the fossil beds of a forest that grew
there seven million years ago), and equestrian trails in nearby Trail Town (horse
rides $11 per hr., by appointment only; 456-8249). **Mount Spokane State Park**
(456-4169) stands 35 mi. to the northeast of the city. A well-paved road extends to
the summit, which affords views of the Spokane Valley and (on clear days) the distant peaks of the Rockies and Cascades. Mt. Spokane is a skiing center with free
cross-country trails and downhill ski packages (from $20). The area is also good for
hiking, horseback riding (no rentals here), and camping (see Accommodations).
The **U.S. Forest Service** (206-753-2027) has more information on the parks.

Lucky visitors may catch a glimpse of trumpeter swans at the **Turnbull National
Wildlife Refuge** (235-4723), 21 mi. south of Spokane. Numerous blinds have been
set up for photographing at this happy breeding ground for bird species of the
Pacific flyway. To get there, take the Four Lakes exit off I-90 in Cheney, and go left
on Badger Rd. (open daily until dusk. $2 per vehicle).

Don't leave Spokane without tasting a fine Eastern Washington wine. The **Arbor
Cliff House,** N. 4705 Fruithill Rd. (927-9463), offers a tour of the vineyards, a view
of the city, and free wine (daily from noon-5pm). It's worth the trip: take I-90 to the
Argonne north exit, travel north on Argonne over the Spokane River, turn right on
Upriver Dr., proceed 1 mi., and then bear left onto Fruithill Rd. Take a sharp right at
the top of the hill and you're there.

■ Pullman

One local legend suggests that Pullman founder Bolin Farr named this town after his
close friend, George Pullman (who gave his name to the famous boxcar). Another
claims that in 1887 the townspeople held a contest wherein the person who depos-
ited the most dough in the public coffers would have the town named after himself.
According to this particular legend, George Pullman sent a check for $25, along
with a note asking that he not be bothered again.

Practical Information The **Pullman Chamber of Commerce,** N. 415
Grand Ave. (334-3565), enough brochures on "The Other Washington—The State!"
to cause a filibuster in the Washington, DC Congress (open Mon.-Fri. 9am-5pm).

Pullman lies at the junction of Rte. 27 and 270. U.S. 195, running from Spokane
south to Lewiston, bypasses the city to the west. Spokane lies 70 mi. north. Pullman
lies 9 mi. *vostok* of Moscow, Idaho. **Northwestern Trailways,** NW 1002 Nye (334-
1412), runs buses to Boise (1 per day, $38.75), Seattle (2 per day, $50), and Spokane
(2 per day, $13). (Open Mon.-Sat. 8:30am-5pm.) Within the town itself, the three
lines of **Pullman Transit,** 775 Guy St. (332-6535), mostly run between the WSU

campus and the downtown area. (Operates Mon.-Fri. 6:50am-5:50pm. Fare 35¢, senior citizens and under 18 20¢.) **Evergreen Taxi Inc.** (332-7433) runs 24 hr. **Budget Rent-A-Car,** Pullman Airport (332-3511), rents for $25 per day, 30¢ each mi. over 100. (Must be at least 25 with major credit card. Open Mon.-Fri. 8:30am-5:30pm, Sat. hours vary.)

Cleanse your clothes at **Betty's Brite and White,** N. 1235 Grand Ave. (332-3477). A load of wash is 50¢, and a dryer costs 25¢ (open daily 7am-11pm).

The **Pullman Senior Citizen Center,** City Hall (332-1933) is available to seniors (open Mon.-Sat. 11am-4pm). . **Pullman Memorial Hospital** (332-2541) is located at NE 1125 Washington Ave. NE. **Professional Mall Pharmacy,** SE 1205 Professional Mall Blvd. (332-4608; open daily 9am-8pm). Useful phone numbers: **Rape Resource,** 332-4357, 24 hr.; **Emergency,** 334-2131; **Ambulance and Police,** 332-2521. The **Post Office** (334-3212) is on Grand Ave. (open Mon.-Fri. 8:30am-5pm, Sat. 8:30-11:30am; **General Delivery ZIP Code:** 99163). **Area Code: 509.**

Accommodations and Camping   The consistent stream of student travelers through Pullman fosters a decent selection of moderately priced, no-frills motels. Rooms are easy to find, except on home football weekends and during commencement (the first week of May). **Manor Lodge Motel** (334-2511), SE 455 Paradise at Main, 3 blocks from the Greyhound station, is spruce, comfortable, and occupies a great location. Try to get a room with a refrigerator, couch, and bathtub (open 7am-11pm, after hours ring night bell; singles $20, doubles $26). **The Hilltop Motor Inn** (334-2555), off U.S. 270 (Colfax Hwy.) on the northwest edge of town (not very accessible to the Greyhound station), offers comfortable rooms with TV and bath (singles $28, doubles $34). **Kamiak Butte Park,** 10 mi. north of Pullman on U.S. 27, offers 10 campsites with water and toilets but no showers for $5.

Food   **Ferdinand's** (335-4014), on WSU campus next to the tennis courts in the Food Quality Bldg., makes everything with milk from WSU's dairy. Their Cougar Gold cheese ($10 for a 30-oz. tin) may be Pullman's biggest attraction. An ice cream cone ($1) and a large glass of milk (55¢) will do your body good. Sneak around back to their "observation room" and see the cheese being made (open Mon.-Fri. 9:30am-4:30pm). Motor through the drive-through or slide into a booth inside at **Cougar County Drive-In,** N. 760 Grand Ave. (332-7829), a 10-minute walk from downtown. This popular student hang-out offers burgers (from $1.29) and shakes (lots o' flavors, $1.29). Try the Cyclone D ($2)—soft ice cream mixed with candy (open daily 10am-11pm). Enjoy the best Chinese food in the area, prepared with a minimum of MSG, at the **Mandarin Wok Restaurant,** N. 115 Grand Ave. (332-5863). Dinners are expensive, but try the $6 lunch specials (main dish, soup, fried rice, and tea). Good vegetarian specials, too. (Open lunch Mon.-Fri. 11:30am-1pm. Dinner Mon.-Thurs. 5-9pm, Fri.-Sat. 5-9:30pm, Sun. 5-8:30pm.) **The Combine** (332-1774), 215 E. Main St. in the Combine Mall, is the town's best coffee house with sandwiches ($2.75) and a great space upstairs for relaxing. Live bands and poetry readings during the school year (open Mon.-Sat. 7am-midnight, Sun. 9am-10pm).

Sights and Entertainment   Most of Pullman's enterprises lie along Main St. and Grand Ave. Grand runs north to south; Main travels west to east, terminating at the **Washington State University** campus. The campus has consumed the eastern half of town and is Pullman's primary pull. Call or stop by the **University Relations Office** in the French Administration Building, Room 442 (335-4527). The office offers guided tours of the 100-year-old campus every weekday at 1pm. Pick up a copy of *Museums and Collections at Washington State University.* All campus museums are free. The **Museum of Art,** in the Fine Arts Building (335-1910), has a small permanent collection and rotating exhibits of local and international art (open Tues.-Fri. 10am-4pm, Sat.-Sun. 1-5pm; Tues. evening 7-10pm). For an outdoor attraction, head out from WSU to the end of Grimes Way to see **black bears** up close and personal. Good viewing hours are 9am-8pm, or call 335-1119 for more information.

Pullman's surrounding gentle terrain and the broad vistas of Washington's **Palouse region** make the area ideal for exploration by bicycle or automobile. **Kamiak** and **Steptoe Buttes,** north of town off Rte. 27, both make for enjoyable day trips. Pack a picnic lunch and head for the hills.

For those 21 or older, there are nearly as many **bars** as Cougar signs in the Palouse. **Shakers,** NE 600 Colorado St. (334-6467), is big and friendly with pool tables, food, Rainer pitchers at $2, and crowds. Shakers splits top-bar honors with another popular student hangout: **Cougar Cottage,** NE 900 Colorado (332-1265), called The Coug. Drafts are $1.50-1.75 and burgers from $2-4 (open daily 11am-2am).

■ Wine Country

Washington is now the second-largest producer of wine in the nation, and local vineyards have been garnering international acclaim.

Wineries abound in the small towns between Yakima and the Tri-Cities. Almost all offer tours and tastings and many boast spectacular scenery.Many are close to I-82; call ahead for hours. Among the most popular of the over 40 wineries in the locale are **Chateau Ste. Michelle** (882-3928), **Columbia Crest** (875-2061), **Covey Run** (829-6235), **The Hogue Cellars** (786-4557), and **Stewart Vineyards** (854-1882), but smaller new wineries pop up all the time. There are some useful guides available *gratis* in visitor centers across the region. Of particular value are the *Winery Tour: Tri-Cities Area* and the *Yakima Valley Wine Tour,* which overflow with maps.

■ Grand Coulee Area

A long time ago (18,000 years, to be more precise) the weather warmed, and a little glacier blocking a lake in Montana slowly melted and gave way. The resulting flood swept across eastern Washington, gouging out layers of loess and basalt to expose the granite below. The washout, believed to have occurred over an entire month, carved massive canyons called "coulees" out of a sizeable region now known as the **Channeled Scab Lands.** Geologists, who generally assume that changes in the earth's surface take place gradually, were at first baffled by the coulees, but the area is now acknowledged as a striking example of the possibility of violent and rapid geological change. The largest of the coulees is named, appropriately enough, Grand Coulee. The construction of the **Grand Coulee Dam** created the massive **Franklin D. Roosevelt Lake** and **Banks Lake.**

Sights and Practical Information The Dam and its surrounding cities— Grand Coulee, Coulee Dam, and Electric City—constitute the hub of the **Coulee Dam National Recreation Area,** which stretches along the Columbia River from Banks Lake north to the Canadian border. The Dam, celebrated by folk singer Woody Guthrie and others, was a local cure for the economic woes of the Great Depression. From 1934 through 1942, 7000 workers were employed in constructing this engineering marvel. Today the dam irrigates the previously parched Columbia River Basin and generates much of the electrical power used in the Northwest— more power, in fact, than any other hydroelectric plant in the United States. The electricity generated by the dam permitted the Northwest to produce 40% of the aluminum used by the U.S. during World War II.

At the rotund **Visitors Arrival Center** (633-9265), on Rte. 155 just north of Grand Coulee, you can see a 15-minute film (it plays every 15 minutes) called "The Columbia—A Fountain of Life" featuring vintage 1930's footage of the dam's construction, accompanied by Woody Guthrie's music. The visitors center also provides information on fishing and motorboating on the two enormous lakes, hiking and biking trail maps, camping guides, and offers self-guided tours through the power plants. (Open daily late-May through July 8:30am-11pm, Aug. 8:30am-

10:30pm, Sept. 8:30am-9:30pm, Oct.-late May 9am-5pm.) Free guided tours of the dam leave from atop the monolith at the third power plant (station #5) on the half-hour every day in summer between 10am and 5pm. The dam may not be impressive seen behind a mucky car window, but standing on top of it will pique your senses. Return to the dam when night falls during the summer to see a spectacular, multi-colored **laser show** on the concrete walls, along with a narration of the area's natural and human history (late May-late July 10pm, Aug. 9:30pm, Sept. 8:30pm; free).

Across the street from the Visitor's Arrival Center is the Midway Mini Mart which serves as Grand Coulee's bus terminal. **Empire Bus Lines** runs to Spokane (1 per day, $16). Midway Mini Mart has schedule information and tickets inside. **Coulee Cab** (633-2350) charges $5 for a trip from downtown to the Dam.

T&T bowling and Laundry, 412 Midway (633-2695) has $1 washers and 75¢ dryers (open daily 8am-8pm). Friday through Sunday you can bowl while waiting for laundry (open Fri.-Sun. 1-8pm; $1.50 per game). To reach the **Police,** call 633-1411. **Coulee Community Hospital** is found at 404 Fortune Rd. (633-1911). The **post office** is on Midway Ave. across from the Safeway (see below; open Mon.-Fri. 8:30am-4:45pm, Sat. 8:30-11:30am). **General Delivery ZIP Code:** 99133.

Accommodations, Camping, and Food Spokane Way in Grand Coulee is the place for budget motels. **Center Lodge Motel,** 508 Spokane Way (633-0770), has big rooms furnished for munchkins—low beds and tiny sinks. If you're lucky you might meet the owner, Wizard Max. Singles will put you back $25, doubles $35 (rates slightly higher July-Aug.). The **Umbrella Motel,** 404 Spokane Way (633-1691), in Grand Coulee, is also a good deal—smaller rooms, bigger beds, and cheaper than the Center Lodge Motel (singles $25, doubles $30). **Trail West Motel,** 108 Spokane Way (633-3155), offers singles from $27, and doubles for $38 (prices higher in the summer season). Kitchenettes, bath, and pool.

Campers should head to **Spring Canyon** (633-9118), 2 mi. east of Grand Coulee off Rte. 174, in a gorgeous setting on the banks of Franklin D. Roosevelt Lake with 89 sites and a beach area (sites $8, seniors with Golden Age Passport $4). Eight mi. south of the dam on Rte. 155 by the banks of Banks Lake, busy **Steamboat Rock State Park** (633-1304; write P.O. Box 370, Electric City, WA 99123 for summer reservations) has 168 sites set beneath dramatic rock walls (tentsites $8, RV hookup $13). Both campgrounds are wheelchair-accessible and have flush toilets. Steamboat Park has pay showers. Campsites east of Spring Canyon are accessible by boat.

Numerous **free camping areas** line Rte. 155 south of Electric City; information is available at Steamboat Rock State Park. Pull onto any of several unmarked dirt roads that lead to Banks Lake, but keep an eye (and an ear) out for rattle snakes. The **Coulee Playland Resort** (633-2671), in Electric City 4 mi. from the Dam, offers more amenities than the free campsites nearby, but you'll have to pay $12 for a tentsite or $16 for an RV hookup. Call the State Parks summer hotline for more information (800-562-0990; open May 1 to Labor Day, Mon.-Fri. 8am-5pm).

Flo packs 'em in for country cooking and great breakfasts at **New Flo's Place,** 316 Spokane Way (633-3216), in Grand Coulee, and nothing on the menu costs more than $6 (open Mon.-Fri. 5am-2pm, Sat. 6am-1pm, Sun. 6am-noon). **That Italian Place** (633-1818), less than a mile east of Grand Coulee on Rte. 174, serves inexpensive pizza and good calzones ($4) in a more elegant dining atmosphere (open daily 11am-10pm). Find a **Safeway** (633-2411) in Grand Coulee at 101 Midway Ave. (open daily 7am-midnight; winter 7am-10pm).

Oregon

After decades of zealously protecting its rocky shores and inland forests from inter-loping tourists and developers, Oregon has adopted a kinder, gentler attitude toward visitors in the 90s. Excellent youth hostels operate in Ashland, Bandon, and Eugene. Chambers of Commerce throughout the state promote a prize-winning superabundance of superlatives, including the most bomb-proof public settlement in the Western Hemisphere (Sisters), North America's deepest gorge (Hell's Canyon), the world's smallest park (in Portland), and the world's shortest river (in Lincoln City).

Oregon's shady forests have been the wellspring of intrastate conflict in recent years. Rising exports of unmilled logs have deprived the state's lumber mills of business. To protest their predicament, angry timber workers drove enormous trucks through the downtown streets of Portland. Though an uneasy truce was called, the logging crisis resumed in full fury after the federal government's June 1990 decision to protect the endangered spotted owl—thus prohibiting logging on a full one-third of the state's timberland. The result has been a heavy loss of jobs in the timber industry, and much rancor between loggers and the environmentalists who lobbied for the change.

Things were a little more peaceful in Oregon nearly two centuries ago, when the intrepid duo of Meriweather Lewis and William Clark slipped quietly down the Columbia River on the last leg of their transcontinental trek. Later in the 19th century, waves of westward-moving settlers thronged the Oregon Trail. Most modern-day visitors head straight for the Pacific to gape at waves and cliffs which rival California's Big Sur in scenic beauty.

The coastal route is handsome, but you should also venture inland to see some of Oregon's greatest attractions—the prehistoric fossils at John Day National Monument, the volcanic cinder-cones near Crater Lake, and the world-renowned Shakespeare festival in Ashland.

PRACTICAL INFORMATION

Capital: Salem.
Visitors Information: State Tourist Office, 775 Summer St. NE, Salem 97310 (800-547-7842). **Oregon State Parks,** 525 Trade St. SE, Salem 97310 (378-6305). **Department of Fish and Wildlife,** P.O. Box 59, Portland 97207 (229-5403). **Oregon State Marine Board,** 3000 Market St. NE, Salem 97310 (378-8587). **Statewide Road Conditions,** 889-3999.
State Motto: The Union. **Nickname:** Beaver State. **State Song:** "Oregon, My Oregon." **State Flower:** Oregon Grape. **State Animal:** Beaver. **State Fish:** Chinook Salmon.
Emergency: 911.
Time Zone: Mostly Pacific (1 hr. behind Mountain, 2 behind Central, 3 behind Eastern). A small southeastern section is Mountain (1 hr. ahead of Pacific, 1 hr. behind Central, 2 behind Eastern).
Postal Abbreviation: OR.
Drinking Age: 21.
Traffic Laws: Seatbelts required.
Area Code: 503.

■■■ PORTLAND

Casual and idiosycratic, Portland is the quietest big city on a crowded West Coast. Its name was decided by the toss of a coin—one more turn and Oregon's largest metropolis would have been called "Boston, Oregon." The 1970s saw the flowering

PORTLAND

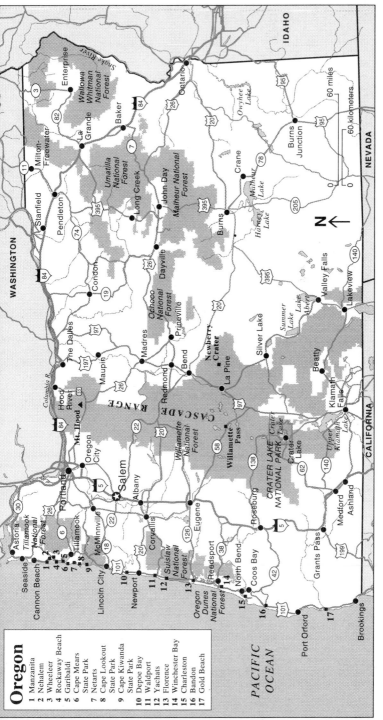

Oregon

1 Manzanita
2 Nehalem
3 Wheeler
4 Rockaway Beach
5 Garibaldi
6 Cape Mears
   State Park
7 Netarts
8 Cape Lookout
   State Park
9 Cape Kiwanda
   State Park
10 Depoe Bay
11 Waldport
12 Yachats
13 Florence
14 Winchester Bay
15 Charleston
16 Bandon
17 Gold Beach

of a permissive spirit in Portland: a popular poster depicted local tavern-owner "Bud" Clark in a trenchcoat flashing a public sculpture. Shortly thereafter, he was elected mayor.

Real-estate barons have discovered this last "underdeveloped" city on the West Coast in the past ten years, summoning forth new superstructures and refurbishing once-crumbling shells into snappy Art Deco office spaces. Funded by a one-percent tax on this new construction, Portland has fostered a growing body of outdoor sculpture and outdoor jazz concerts. Any number of improvisational theaters are in constant production, and the Center for the Performing Arts now lures actors from the renowned Shakespeare Festival in Ashland. This varied artistic scene is anchored by Portland's venerable Symphony Orchestra—the oldest in the U.S. And, knowing that good beverages are essential to the full enjoyment of any highbrow affair, the city's first-rate flock of small breweries pump out barrels of some of the nation's finest ale.

Portlanders take full advantage of their area's natural endowments: drawn by a common need to escape all that's urban, they are consummate hikers, bikers, and runners. Portland harbors both the largest and smallest parks enclosed within any U.S. city, as well as one of only two parks in the world located on a dormant volcano. The Willamette River provides downtown denizens with a range of recreational possibilities, and dense forests at the city's edge cloak miles and miles of well-maintained hiking trails. Attractions within an easy drive of the city prove still more satisfying—on any July day you can schuss down the snow-covered slopes of Mt. Hood in the morning, watch the sun drop into the Pacific Ocean from the warm sand of an empty beach, and still return to town in time to catch an outdoor jazz concert down at the municipal zoo.

PRACTICAL INFORMATION

Visitors Information: Portland/Oregon Visitors Association, 26 SW Salmon St. (222-2223 or 275-9750), at Front St. Distributes extensive information on the city and surrounding area. The free *Portland Book* contains maps, general information, and historical trivia. The free *Easy Reference Guide* offers community and recreation information, maps, and transportation details. Open Mon.-Fri. 9am-5pm, Sat. 9am-3pm. Detailed city road maps are free at **Hertz,** 1009 SW 6th (249-5727), at Salmon. Open Mon.-Fri. 7am-6:30pm, Sat. 8am-4pm.

Park Bureau/Public Recreation, 1120 SW 5th St. (823-2223 or 823-5100). Open 8am-5pm.

Local Events Hotline: 233-3333. Recording.

Amtrak, 800 NW 6th Ave. (800-872-7245, Portland Station 273-4865), at Hoyt St. To: Seattle (3 per day, $23); Eugene (1 per day, $24). Not in the best neighborhood. Open daily 7:30am-6pm.

Greyhound, 550 NW 6th Ave. (800-231-2222). Buses every 1½ hr. to Seattle ($18). To Eugene (8 per day, $16). Ticket window open 5:30am-12:30am. Station open 24 hr.

Green Tortoise, 225-0310 for reservations. Pick-up point 616 SW College Ave. at 6th Ave. To: Seattle (Tues., Thurs., and Sat. 4pm; Sept.-June Tues. and Sat. 4pm; $15) and San Francisco (Sun., Tues., Thurs., and Fri. noon; Sept.-June Thurs. and Sun. noon; $59).

City Buses: Tri-Met, Customer Service Center, #1 Pioneer Courthouse Sq., 701 SW 6th Ave. (238-7433; open Mon.-Fri. 7:30am-5:30pm). Several 24-hr. recorded information numbers are available: how to use the Call-A-Bus information system (231-3199); fare information (231-3198); updates, changes, and weather-related problems (231-3197); special needs transportation (238-3511, Mon.-Fri. 7:30am-5:30pm); TDD information (238-5811); lost and found (238-4855, Mon.-Fri. 9am-5pm); bicycle commuter service (233-0564). Service generally 5am-midnight, reduced Sat.-Sun. Fare 95¢-$1.25, ages 7-18 70¢ (see Getting Around below).

Taxi: Broadway Cab, 227-1234. **New Rose City Cab Co.,** 282-7707. From airport to downtown $21-24. From airport to hostel $17. Both open 24 hr.

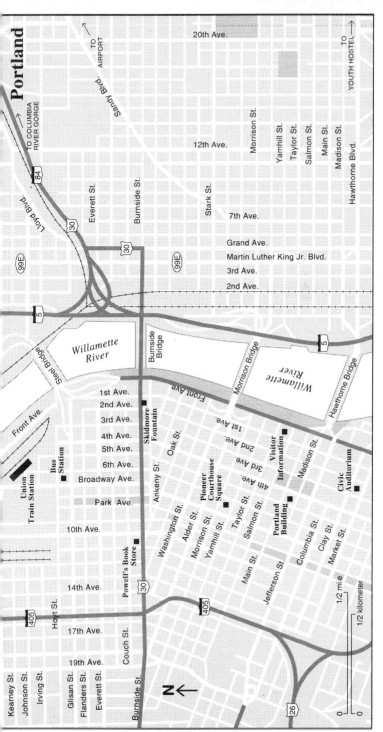

Portland

TO COLUMBIA
RIVER GORGE

TO
AIRPORT

TO
YOUTH HOSTEL

20th Ave.

12th Ave.

Morrison St.
Yamhill St.
Taylor St.
Salmon St.
Main St.
Madison St.
Hawthorne Blvd.

Sandy Blvd.

Everett St.

Burnside St.

Lloyd Blvd.

Stark St.

7th Ave.

Grand Ave.

Martin Luther King Jr. Blvd.

3rd Ave.

2nd Ave.

Willamette
River

Steel Bridge

Burnside
Bridge

Morrison Bridge

Willamette
River

Hawthorne Bridge

Front Ave.

Union
Train Station

Bus
Station

Front Ave.

1st Ave.
2nd Ave.
3rd Ave.
4th Ave.
5th Ave.
6th Ave.
Broadway Ave.

Park Ave.

10th Ave.

14th Ave.

17th Ave.

19th Ave.

Skidmore
Fountain

Oak St.

Ankeny St.

Washington St.

Alder St.

Morrison St.

Yamhill St.

Pioneer
Courthouse
Square

1st Ave.
2nd Ave.
3rd Ave.
4th Ave.

Taylor St.

Salmon St.

Main St.

Jefferson St.

Visitor
Information

Madison St.

Portland
Building

Columbia St.

Clay St.

Market St.

Civic
Auditorium

Powell's Book
Store

Kearney St.
Johnson St.
Irving St.
Glisan St.
Flanders St.
Everett St.
Couch St.

Hoyt St.

Burnside St.

N

1/2 mile

1/2 kilometer

AAA Automobile Club of Oregon, 600 SW Market St., 97201 (222-6734). Second location at 8555 SW Apple Way, 97225 (243-6444). Both open Mon.-Fri. 8am-5pm.

Car Rental: Avis Rent-A-Car, at airport (800-331-1212 or 249-4950). **Practical Rent-A-Car,** 1315 NE Sandy Blvd. (224-8110). $24 per day, 100 free mi., 15¢ per additional mi. Must be at least 21 with credit card or $300 deposit.

Laundromat: Springtime Cleaners and Laundry, 2942 SE Hawthorne Blvd. (235-5080), across from the hostel. Wash 75¢, 10-min. dry 25¢. Open daily 8:30am-10pm.

Ski Conditions: Timberline, 222-2211. **Ski Bowl,** 222-2695. **Mt. Hood Meadows,** 227-7669.

Time/Weather: 778-6000.

Crisis Line, 223-6161. **Women's Crisis Line: General/Rape Hotline,** 235-5333. Both 24 hr.

Women's Services: Women's Counseling of Portland, 19 SW Gibbs St. (242-0230). General counseling Mon.-Fri. 9am-5pm. **West Women's Hotel Shelter,** 2010 NW Kearney St. (224-7718). 24 hr.

Gay and Lesbian Information: Phoenix Rising, 620 SW 5th #710 (223-8299). Counseling and referral for gay men and lesbians. Open Mon.-Fri. 9am-5pm.

Senior Citizens' Services: County Committee on Aging, 248-3646. Open 8am-5pm. **Senior Citizens' Crisis Line,** 223-6161. **Oregon Retired Persons' Pharmacy,** 9800 SW Nimbus Ave., Beaverton (646-0591 for orders, 646-3500 for information). Open Mon.-Fri. 8:30am-5pm, Sat. 9am-1pm.

Emergency: 911. **Police:** 1111 SW 2nd (230-2121). **Fire:** 232-2111.

Post Office: 715 NW Hoyt St. (294-2300). **General Delivery ZIP Code:** 97208. Closer to the mall is the branch across the street from Pioneer Courthouse Square, 520 SW Morrison St. (221-0282). Both open Mon.-Sat. 8:30am-5pm.

Area Code: 503.

ORIENTATION AND GETTING AROUND

Portland is tucked into the Northwest corner of Oregon, just south of the Columbia River and about 75 mi. inland from the coast. The city is 637 mi. north of San Francisco. Portland lies 172 mi. south of Seattle on I-5. East of the city, I-84 (U.S. 30) follows the route of the Oregon Trail through the Columbia River Gorge. West of Portland, U.S. 30 follows the Columbia downstream to Astoria. I-405 curves around the west side of the business district to link I-5 with U.S. 30.

Portland is on the major north-south routes of both **Amtrak** and **Greyhound.** Both stations are located inside Tri-Met's Fareless Square (see Practical Information).

The cheapest way to reach downtown from **Portland International Airport** is to take Tri-Met bus #12 (a nearly 45-min. ride), which will arrive going south on SW 5th Ave. (fare 95¢). **Raz Tranz** (246-3301 for taped information) provides an airport shuttle (4:35am-midnight every ½-hr., 30 min. to downtown, $7).

Portland is divided into five districts. **Burnside Street** divides the city into north and south, while east and west are separated by the Willamette River. **Williams Avenue** cuts off a corner of the northeast sector, which is called simply "North." All street signs are labeled by their districts—N, NE, NW, SE, and SW. **Southwest district** is the city's hub, encompassing the downtown area, the southern end of historic Old Town, and a slice of the wealthier West Hills. The heart of the hub is the downtown mall area between SW 5th and 6th Ave. Car traffic is prohibited here; this is the transit system's turf. Streets in the **Northwest district** also offer metropolitan trendiness; NW 21st and NW 23rd are hot-spots for shopping. The streets in the district are named alphabetically beginning with Burnside and continuing with Couch (pronounced KOOCH) through Yeon. The order is disrupted only where "X" and "Z" should be—you'll find Roosevelt and Reed St. instead. The **Southeast district** is a less-well-to-do residential neighborhood, but it is the hippest part of the city. The city's best ethnic restaurants line **Hawthorne Boulevard,** along with small cafes and theaters catering to the hippie-artist crowd, mostly supported by nearby Reed College's student population. The **North** and **Northeast** districts are chiefl residential, punctuated by a few quiet, small parks. In the past few years, drug traffickers have based their operations in the Northeast.

The **Tri-Met bus system,** one of the nation's better systems of mass transit, weaves together Portland's districts. In the downtown mall, 31 covered passenger shelters serve as both stops and information centers. Southbound buses pick up passengers along SW 5th Ave.; northbound passengers board on SW 6th Ave. Bus routes fall into seven regional service areas, each with its own individual "Lucky Charm": orange deer, yellow rose, green leaf, brown beaver, blue snow, red salmon, and purple rain (strange but true). Shelters and buses are color-coded for their region. A few buses with black numbers on white backgrounds cross town north-south or east-west, transgressing color-coded boundaries.

Most of downtown, from NW Irving St. in the north to I-405 in the west and south and the Willamette River in the east, constitutes **"Fareless Square."** As the name suggests, the buses are free in this zone. The rest of the fare zones comprises three zones defined by concentric squares around downtown. The fare is 95¢ for one or two zones, $1.25 for three zones. Senior citizens and riders with disabilities pay 40¢; children under 7 are free when traveling with fare-paying adults. An all-day ticket is $3. Pick up monthly passes, bus maps, and schedules at the visitors center (see Practical Information), at Willamette Savings branches, or at the Tri-Met Customer Assistance Office. Buses generally run 7am to 12:30am, though Saturday and Sunday service is greatly reduced. Tri-Met also has special services for the disabled. Each of the 90 or so bus routes has its own 24-hr. recorded information line, which will tell you where each bus goes and how frequently (see Practical Information.)

ACCOMMODATIONS AND CAMPING

As Portland moves toward gentrification, cheap lodgings dwindle. **Northwest Bed and Breakfast,** 610 SW Broadway (243-7616), has an extensive listing of member homes in the Portland area and throughout the Northwest. They promise singles from $35 to $60 and doubles from $50 to $80. The **hostel** (see below) is undoubtedly the best option. If it is full, the hostel manager can refer you to a private boarding house. The motel strip on Barbur is also comely and accessible; N. Interstate Ave. and **Motel 6** are generally better for people with wheels. If you are a woman traveling alone, the **YWCA** or Motel 6 is the safest bet other than the hostel. The State Parks don't provide good access to the city for those without cars.

Portland International HI/AYH Hostel, 3031 SE Hawthorne Blvd. (236-3380), at 31st Ave. Take bus #5 (brown beaver). Cheerful, clean, and crowded. Sleep inside or on the back porch when it's warm. Kitchen facilities; laundromat across the street. Fills up early in the summer (particularly the women's rooms), so make reservations ahead (credit card required) or plan to arrive at 5pm to get one of the 12-15 beds saved for walk-ins. 4 times per week the hostel runs daytrips to either Mt. St. Helens or the Columbia River Gorge and Mt. Hood ($24), providing an excellent opportunity for the hosteler without wheels to visit some of Portland's more distant attractions. Don't miss the all-you-can-eat pancakes every morning (a paltry 50¢). Open daily 7:30-10am and 5-11pm. Curfew at midnight. Members $12, nonmembers $15.

Aladdin Motor Inn, 8905 SW 30th St. (246-8241 or 800-292-4466), at Barbur Blvd., a 10-min. ride from downtown. Take bus #12 (yellow rose) from 5th Ave., or take exit 294 from northbound I-5 (exit 296a if coming south). Big rooms, big beds, and cable. A/C and kitchens available. Mention *Let's Go* and get discounts. Singles $32 (with kitchen $37). Doubles $37.

YWCA, 1111 SW 10th St. (223-6281). *Women only.* Situated on the park blocks, close to major sights. Clean and safe. Small rooms. Singles $21, with semi-private bath $25. Shared doubles $16. Hostel with bunk beds $7.

Motel 6, 3104 SE Powell Blvd. (238-0600). Take bus #9 (brown beaver) from 5th Ave. Another cardboard box motel. Small, clean rooms, pool. Singles $32 and doubles $38. Always full; call 3-4 days in advance. Wheelchair access.

Midtown Motel, 1415 NE Sandy Blvd. (234-0316). Take bus #12, 19, or 20 from 6th Ave. Standard rooms with TV and A/C. Singles from $22. Doubles from $26.

Saharan Motel, 1889 SW 4th Ave. (226-7646). Just blocks from the center of town. Clean rooms with A/C and TV. Singles from $32. Doubles from $36.

Bel D'air Motel, 8355 N. Interstate Ave. (289-4800); take the Lumbard West exit off I-5. Take bus #5 (red salmon) from 6th Ave. Its name is a bit pretentious; its decor is decidedly not. But hey, it has TV. Singles $28. Doubles $33.

Milo McIver State Park, 25 mi. southeast of Portland, off Rte. 211, 5 mi. west of the town of Estacada. Fish, boat, and bicycle along the nearby Clackamas River. Hot showers, flush toilets. Sites with electricity $12.

Ainsworth State Park, 37 mi. east of Portland on I-84, along the Columbia River Gorge. Hot showers, flush toilets, and hiking trails. Sites with full hookups $13.

Champoeg State Park, 25 mi. south of Portland off U.S. 99 W (678-1251). Hike, bike, or visit the historic home and log cabin museum. Sites with electricity $12.

FOOD

Portland has more restaurants per capita than any other American city. Just as New York City offers a street or neighborhood to suit any mood, so does Portland offer a restaurant, cafe, tavern, or random roadside attraction for the thirsty, famished traveler. Only in Portland do gas stations proudly serve espresso.

Southwest

Panini, 620 SW 9th Ave. (224-6001). Straight out of the film *La Dolce Vita*—only Vespas parked out front are missing from this indoor/outdoor Italian espresso and panini bar. Delicious fresh calzones ($5.50). Extensive selection of Italian wines and beverages. Excellent service. Open Mon.-Fri. 7am-7pm, Sat. 8am-5pm.

Brasserie Montmartre, 626 SW Park Ave. (224-5552). Paper tablecloths & crayons and live jazz nightly offer diverse diversions for dull dates and similarly-awkward social situations. This beautiful restaurant offers inexpensive food and "fabu atmo." See and be seen as you sit in the bistro section—order the *Mange-à-trois* a trio of *pâtés* ($5.75). Open Mon.-Thurs. 11:30am-2am, Fri. 11:30am-3am, Sat 10am-3am, Sun. 10am-2am.

Kent's Bento, 1022 SW Morrison St. (221-4508). Of the dozen bento places that have opened in the last year alone, Kent takes the big prize. Chicken and vegetable bento ($5). Pretend you're an on-the-go Japanese businessman in need of refueling and guzzle the vitamin beverage Liporitan-D ($1.75). Open Mon.-Sat 11:30am-5pm.

Mummy's, 622 SW Columbia St. (224-7465), across from the *Oregonian* newspaper building. This inconspicuous Egyptian restaurant is underground, and was built to resemble the interior of a pharoah's tomb. Lunch is particularly inexpensive (nothing over $7). The Kutta Kebab (lamb & beef) is especially yummy ($5) On tap bar. Open for lunch Mon.-Sat. 11am-2:30pm; open for dinner Mon.-Fri. 5 10pm.

Western Culinary Institute Chef's Center, 1235 SW Jefferson (242-2433). The testing ground for the cooking school's creative adventures; you'll know you're there when you see the people in tall white hats hanging out in front. All the lunches are under $6. Breakfast is also delicious and cheap—try the gourmet hashbrowns. Good assorted breads ($1 a loaf). Open Mon. 8am-2:30pm, Tues.-Fri 8am-6pm.

Northwest

Fong Chong, 301 NW 4th Ave. (220-0235), in the heart of Chinatown. Portland' best dim sum, but be prepared to move quickly as the harried waiters whiz by with their carts. Expect to spend about $7 for a dim sum meal. The ginger chicken is fabulous. Dim Sum (*the* real reason to go here) served daily 11am-3pm Open daily 10:30am-10pm.

Caffe Mingo, 807 NW 21st Ave. (226-4646). Take bus #17 (red salmon). Easily the best pizza in town. Mayor Vera Katz is a frequent customer, and usually has a slice of "the regular" (cheese, $1.50). Pizza boy-wonder William Nantes is known to occasionally do floor shows as he tosses dough into the air. Open Mon.-Sat. 11am-11pm, Sun. 3-11pm.

Anne Hughes Coffee Room, 1005 W. Burnside St. (228-4651), inside Powell's City of Books. One Sunday afternoon 8 years ago, Anne Hughes read an entire book while sitting on an uncomfortable crate. She craved the inevitable Pacific Northwest espresso, too. Michael Powell gave her the go-ahead to use the bargain-book room as a coffee/reading room. . .and the rest is history. Great place to

Shaker's Cafe, 1212 NW Glisan (221-0011). One of the best diners in Portland. Features blue corncakes ($4.75) and a wonderful staff. Open Mon.-Fri. 6:30am-4pm, Sat. 7:30am-4pm.

Kornblatt's, 628 NW 23rd Ave. (242-0055). Take bus #15 (red salmon). A delicatessen haven for homesick New Yorkers. Never-ending menu includes matzoh ball soup ($3), knishes ($2.25), latkes ($3.50). Crowded, but the wait is worth it. Open Mon.-Tues. 7am-10pm, Wed.-Fri. 7am-11pm, Sat. 7:30am-11pm, Sun. 7:30am-10pm.

Blah-Blah, 300 NW 10th Ave. (223-9160). When the infamous Quality Pie closed, Portland's dining queens and anarchic youth were suddenly homeless—until this year. A late-night nook where almost anything goes, Blah-Blah boasts Portland's most eclectic jukebox and standard diner fare. Try the home-fries ($1.75) or the Soylent Green (spinach) omelette ($4.50). Open 24 hr.

Southeast and Northeast

Nicholas' Restaurant, 318 SE Grand Ave. (235-5123). Take bus #15 (brown beaver) across the bridge to Grand, then walk 5 blocks north. Don't let the unassuming facade fool you—Nicholas serves tantalizing Lebanese and Mediterranean food at incredibly inexpensive prices. Try Meezza ($6), the sample-a-li'l-bit-o'-everything platter, or the Phoenician pizza ($2). Open Mon.-Sat. 11am-6pm.

My Father's Place, 523 SE Grand Ave. (235-5494). Take bus #15 (brown beaver) across the bridge to Grand, then walk 3 blocks north. Old American relics decorate the walls and wait the tables. On any given Sat. or Sun., you can order steak and eggs for the ridiculously low price of $2.85, and complement it with a Bloody Mary for $2 more. Open daily 6am-2:30am.

Pied Cow Coffeehouse, 3244 SE Belmont St. (230-4866). Take bus #15 (brown beaver), right to the front door. Fabulous indoor/outdoor cafe in an old Victorian house. Open Tues.-Thurs. 6pm-midnight, Fri. 6pm-1am, Sat. 10am-1am, Sun. 10am-11pm.

Montage, 2411 SE Belmont St. (234-1324). Take bus #15 (brown beaver). Supercool underground Cajun bistro for hungry disco-fiends and their night-owl brethren. Jambalayas galore (from $6.50). Macaroni & cheese ($1.50). Open Tues.-Sat. 6pm-5am.

Cafe Lena, 2239 SE Hawthorne St. (238-7087). Take bus #5 (brown beaver). The Portland intelligentsia reverently frequent this cafe, known for its open-mike poetry every Tues. 7:30pm. Nightly readings and music accentuate an appetizing menu—try the Birkenstock Submarine ($5). Breakfast served daily until 4pm. Open Tues.-Fri. 7am-midnight, Sat. 8am-midnight, Sun. 8am-2pm.

Cup & Saucer, 3566 SE Hawthorne St. (236-6001). Take bus #5 (brown beaver). Friendly, frantic neighborhood restaurant famous for its pancakes ($3.25) and gardenburgers ($4.25). Smack dab in the middle of the ultimate Pacific Northwest neighborhood—environmentally conscious, lesbian- and gay-friendly, and Clinton-supporting. Open Sun.-Wed. 7am-8pm, Thurs.-Sat. 7am-10pm.

Rimsky-Korsakoffee House, 707 SE 12th Ave. (232-2640). Take bus #15 (brown beaver) to 12th, then walk 2 blocks north. Big red Victorian house converted into a cozy salon which offers a bacchanalian frenzy of desserts and the inevitable array of espresso drinks. Live classical music nightly. Open Sun.-Thurs. 7pm-midnight, Fri.-Sat. 7pm-1am.

Saigon Kitchen, 835 NE Broadway St. (281-3669). Take bus #9 (purple raindrops). Quite possibly the best Vietnamese and Thai restaurant in town. The *chazio* rolls ($3.50) are a perennial favorite. Most entrees $6-8. Open Mon.-Sat. 11am-10pm, Sun. noon-9pm.

Merchant of Venice, 1432 NE Broadway St. (284-4558). Take bus #9 (purple rain-drops). Really cheap gourmet Italian food. Psyched staff are happy to serve every-thing from a slice of pizza *del giorno* ($2) to fresh-made pastas. Don't expect to spend more than $7. Open Mon.-Thurs. 11am-9pm, Fri.-Sat. 11am-10pm.

SIGHTS AND ACTIVITIES

Shaded parks, magnificent gardens, innumerable museums and galleries, and bus-tling open-air markets beckon the city's tourists and residents alike. Catch the best of Portland's dizzying dramatic and visual arts scene on the **"First Thursday"** (of each month), when the numerous small galleries in the Southwest and Northwest all stay open until 9pm. For information contact **The Metropolitan Center for Pub-lic Art,** 1120 SW 5th Ave. (823-5111), or go to the museum to latch onto a **Public Art Walking Tour** (226-2811; museum open Tues.-Sat. 11am-5pm, Sun. 1-5pm).

Downtown

Portland's downtown area is centered on the **mall,** running north-south between 5th and 6th Ave., bounded on the north by W. Burnside St. and on the south by SW Madison St., and closed to all traffic except city buses. At 5th Ave. and Morrison St. sits the **Pioneer Courthouse,** the primogenitor of downtown landmarks. The mon-ument now houses the U.S. Ninth Circuit Court of Appeals and is the centerpiece for **Pioneer Courthouse Square,** 701 SW 6th Ave. (223-1613), which opened in 1983. Forty-eight thousand Portland citizens purchased personalized bricks to sup-port the construction of an amphitheater in the square for live jazz, folk, and ethnic music. During the summer (Tues. and Thurs. noon-1pm) the **Peanut Butter and Jam Sessions** seem to draw the entire 48,000-person cast back to enjoy the music.

Certainly the most controversial building in the downtown area is Michael Graves' postmodern **Portland Building** (823-4000), located on the mall. The build-ing's 1984 opening was attended by King Kong (full-sized and inflatable), perched on the roof. Since then, this amazing confection of pastel tile and concrete has been both praised to the stars and condemned as an overgrown jukebox. Make sure to visit the interior, which looks like something out of the film *Blade Runner*. On a niche outside the building's second floor, *Portlandia* reaches down to crowds below. This immense bronze statue—second in size only to the Statue of Liberty—portrays the trident-bearing woman on the state seal (which to many looks like a man with breasts brandishing a large salad fork). The **Standard Insurance Center,** nearby at 900 SW 5th Ave., has also engendered controversy for the white marble sculpture out front, *The Quest*. The sculpture is more commonly known to locals as *Three Groins in the Fountain*. Also notable is the glass **Equitable Building,** SW 6th and Alder, designed by Pietro Belluschi.

There is room for romping just west of the mall on the **South Park Blocks,** a series of cool, shaded parks down the middle of Park Ave., surrounded by **Portland State University.** Facing the parks is the **Oregon Art Institute,** 1219 SW Park Ave. (226-2811), at Jefferson St., which houses the **Portland Art Museum, The Pacific Northwest College of Art,** and the **Northwest Film and Video Center** (221-1156), which shows classics and offbeat flicks. Tickets are available at the box office, 921 SW Morrison. The Art Museum has an especially fine exhibit of Pacific Northwest Native American art, including masks, textiles, and sacred objects. International exhibits and local artists' works are interspersed. (Open Tues.-Wed. and Fri.-Sat. 11am-5pm, Thurs. 11am-9pm, Sun. 1-5pm. Admission $4.50, senior citizens and stu-dents $2.50, under 12 $1.50. Thurs. senior citizens get in free.)

Across the street, the **Oregon Historical Society Museum and Library,** 1230 SW Park Ave. (222-1741), stores photographs, artifacts, and records of Oregon's past 200 years. The maritime exhibit is especially good. (Open Mon.-Sat. 10am-5pm., Sun. noon-5pm. Admission $3, students $1; seniors free on Thurs.; all are free 1st Thurs. of every month.)

Four separate theaters make up the **Portland Center for the Performing Arts,** 1111 SW Broadway (248-4496), on the eastern side of the Park Blocks. The **Arlene Schnitzer Concert Hall,** a recently refurbished marble-and-granite wonder, shares the corner of Broadway and Main with the brick and glass **Dolores Winningstad Theatre** and the **Intermediate Theater.** The **Civic Auditorium,** 222 SW Clay St., is the Center's fourth component. The modern, glass-fronted, 3000-seat auditorium plays host to opera, ballet, and the occasional jazz or folk concert. Call the center for tickets and schedules.

The view from the Civic Auditorium includes Lawrence Halprin's **Forecourt Fountain** (better known as Ira's Fountain), Portland's most popular foot-soaking oasis. This terraced waterfall, at SW 3rd Ave. and Clay St., circulates 13,000 gallons of water every minute. Retreat to a secluded niche behind the waterfall and discover for yourself what the backside of water looks like.

Old Town, to the north of the mall, resounded a century ago with the clamor of sailors whose ships filled the ports. The district has been revived by the large-scale restoration of store fronts, new "old brick," polished iron and brass, and a bevy of recently opened shops and restaurants. A popular people-watching vantage point, the **Skidmore Fountain,** at SW 1st Ave. and SW Ankeny St., marks the entrance to the quarter. Had the city accepted resident brewmeister Henry Weinhard's offer to run draft beer through the fountain, it would have been a truly cordial watering hole indeed (and much much more popular). Old Town also marks the start of **Waterfront Park.** This 20-block-long swath of grass and flowers along the Willamette River provides locals with an excellent place to picnic, fish, stroll, and enjoy major community events. For a kick, stop at **Where's the Art!!!,** 219 SW Ankeny (226-3671), where for just 25¢ you can pray at the church of Elvis, view the world's first 24-hr. coin-operated art gallery, or get marriage counseling.

The festive **Saturday Market** (222-6072), 108 W. Burnside St., under the Burnside Bridge between 1st and Front St., is overrun with street musicians, artists, craftspeople, chefs, and greengrocers clogging the largest open-air crafts market in the country. Many of these artists sell their work in the city's studios and galleries during the week. (Market runs March-Christmas Sat. 10am-5pm, Sun. 11am-4:30pm.)

The Portland Children's Museum, 3037 SW 2nd Ave. (823-2227), at Wood St. (take bus #1, 12, 40, 41, 43, or 55, all yellow rose), schedules organized games, races, arts activities, and hands-on exhibits (open daily 9am-5pm; admission $3.50, children $3). Tour the facilities and sample some local lager at the **Blitz Weinhard Brewing Co.,** 1133 W. Burnside St. (222-4351), or take a stroll through all 2 ft. of **Printing Press Park,** at SW Front and Taylor St. The tiniest park in the world is the product of a journalist's desire to put some token greenery outside his window. It is now protected from iconoclasts by a chain hanging between two iron columns.

West Hills

Less than 2 mi. west of downtown, the posh neighborhoods of West Hills serve as a manicured buffer zone between the soul-soothing parks and the turmoil of the city below. Take the animated "zoo bus" (#63) or drive up SW Broadway to Clay St. and turn right onto Sunset Hwy. 26 (get off at zoo exit).

Washington Park and its nearby attractions are perhaps the most soulful sites in Portland. The park's gates are open daily 7am to 9pm in an attempt to close out lawless types. Drug traffickers still haunt the park after hours but mostly make themselves unseen. The **Bristlecone Pine Trail** is wheelchair accessible. Obtain maps at the information stand near the parking lot of the arboretum, or refer to those posted on the windows. **Hoyt Arboretum,** 4000 SW Fairview Blvd. (228-8733 or 823-3655), at the crest of the hill above the other gardens, features many a conifer and "200 acres of trees and trails." Free nature walks (given April-Nov. Sat.-Sun. at 2pm) last 60-90 minutes and cover 1-2 mi. The 3-mi. **"Wildwood" Trail** connects the arboretum to the zoo in the south (trails open daily 6am-10pm; visitors center hours daily 9am-3pm).

Below the Hoyt Arboretum lie many of Portland's most popular attractions. Although they can be crowded on hot summer days, each is worth seeing. The **Washington Park Zoo** (226-1561 for an operator, 226-7627 for a recording) is renowned for its successful elephant-breeding and its scrupulous re-creation of natural habitats. Whimsical murals decorate the #63 "zoo" bus from the park to Morrison St. in the downtown mall. A miniature **railway** also connects the Washington Park gardens with the zoo (fare $2.50, senior citizens and students $1.75). The zoo features a number of interesting "animal talks" at various times on weekends and has a pet-the-animals **children's zoo.** If you have time, pull up a seat in the grassy amphitheater and watch as huge birds of prey swoop down over you in a demonstration. (Open daily in summer 9:30am-7pm, gates close at 6pm; in winter daily 9:30am-6pm. Admission $5, senior citizens $3.50, children $3. Free 2nd Tues. of each month.) If you're around in late June, July, and August, grab your picnic basket and check out the zoo-sponsored **Your Zoo and All That Jazz,** a nine-week series of open-air jazz concerts (Wed. 7-9pm), free with zoo admission. **Zoograss Concerts** features a series of bluegrass concerts (Thurs. 7-9pm), also free with admission.

The **World Forestry Center,** 4033 SW Canyon Rd. (228-1367), specializes in exhibits on Northwestern forestry and logging. The eavesdropping trees in *The Wizard of Oz* would have gone bonkers if they had to listen to the Forestry Center's "talking tree" all day long; the 70-ft. plant never shuts up. (Open daily 9am-5pm, Labor Day-Memorial Day daily 10am-5pm. Admission $3, students $2.)

Northwest, North, and Northeast

From Washington Park, you have easy access to sprawling **Forest Park,** the largest park completely within the confines of an American city. The park is laced with hiking trails and garnished with scenic picnic areas. The **Pittock Mansion,** 3229 NW Pittock Dr. (823-3624), within Forest Park, was built by Henry L. Pittock, the founder of Oregon's only daily newspaper, the *Oregonian.* From the lawn of the 80-year-old French renaissance mansion, you can take in a striking panorama of the city. To reach the mansion from downtown, take crosstown bus #20 (orange deer) to NW Barnes and W. Burnside St., and walk ½ mi. up Pittock Ave. (open daily noon-4pm; admission $3.50, senior citizens $3, under 18 $1.50).

Downtown on the edge of the Northwest district is **Powell's City of Books,** 1005 W. Burnside St. (228-4651), a cavernous establishment with more volumes than any other bookstore in the U.S. (almost 500,000). If you tend to dawdle in bookstores, beware—or bring a sleeping bag and several meals. Powell's also features frequent poetry and fiction readings in the afternoons and an extensive travel section on Portland and the Northwest (open Mon.-Sat. 9am-11pm, Sun. 9am-9pm).

Farther out, geographically and spiritually, is the **Grotto,** at the Sanctuary of Our Sorrowful Mother, NE 85th Ave. and NE Sandy Blvd. (254-7371). Take bus #12 (purple rain). The splendid grounds are decorated with depictions of the Stations of the Cross and Mary's Seven Sorrows. You can behold the Columbia River gorge from the cliff. (Open daily 8am-sunset. Donation requested.)

Some find shopping a religious experience in the **Nob Hill** district. Fashionable boutiques run from Burnside to Thurman St., between NW 21st and NW 24th Ave. Shopping Dorothy Hamill wanna-bes make the pilgrimage to **Lloyd Center** (288-6073), a shopping mall with an open-air ice-skating rink ($5.25, children $4.25, skate rental included). Also noteworthy here is the award-winning **Lloyd Cinema** (248-6938), an ultramodern multiplex equipped with comfortable contour chairs.

Southeast

Southeast Portland is largely a residential district with the exception of two colorful and eclectic strips of mercantilism. **Reed College,** a small liberal arts school founded in 1909, sponsors numerous cultural events. The ivy-draped grounds, which encompass a lake and a state wildlife refuge, make up what is certainly one of the most attractive college campuses in the country. In 1968 this transplendent enclave of progressive politics became the first undergraduate college to open its own nuclear reactor. One-hour tours (geared mainly to prospective students) leave Eliot Hall #220, 3203 Woodstock Blvd. at SE 28th, twice per day during the school year (Mon.-Fri. 10am and 2pm; individual tours are available by appointment in summer—call 777-7511). The **Chamber Music Northwest Festival** (294-6400 or 223-3202) holds concerts at the college every summer from late June to late July (Mon. and Thurs.-Sat. at 8pm). Concerts sell out quickly; call ahead for tickets ($12-17). Across the street, in the lovely **Crystal Springs Rhododendron Test Gardens,** SE 28th Ave. (796-5193), at Woodstock (take bus #19), 2500 rhododendrons surround a lake. The rhododendrons and azaleas are in full bloom April and May. (Open daily "in season" during daylight hours. Admission $2 charged Thurs.-Mon. 10am-6pm, but gardens open daily 6am-9pm.)

The **Oregon Museum of Science and Industry (OMSI),** 1945 SE Water Ave. (228-2828), at SE Clay, will keep children and adults mystified with do-it-yourself science, computer, and medical exhibits (including a walk-though heart). The museum also house an impressive OmniMax theater. (Open Sat.-Wed. 9:30am-7pm, Thurs.-Fri. 9:30am-9pm. Admission $6.50, seniors $5.50, ages 3-17 $4.)

Old Sellwood Antique Row, at the east end of Sellwood Bridge, on SE 13th Ave. between Bybee and Clatsop St., has over 30 curiosity shops showcasing stained glass, rare books, and assorted "used" memorabilia at prices that may inspire you to hawk your old Lite-Brites and sea monkey spawnariums. (Hours vary, but all stores open Tues.-Sat.) **Hawthorne Boulevard** (take bus #5 from downtown) has a high concentration of quiet cafes, antique shops, used book stores, and theaters useful for dodging the sporadic Portland rainfall. It ends at the bottom of **Mt. Tabor Park,** one of two city parks in the world on the site of an extinct volcano. Take bus #15 (brown beaver) from downtown, or drive down Hawthorne to SE 60th Ave.

ENTERTAINMENT

Once an uncouth and rowdy port town, Portland manages to maintain an irreverent attitude. Many waterfront pubs have evolved into upscale bistros and French bakeries, but plenty of local taverns still hide away throughout the city. Nightclubs cater to everyone from the casual college student to the hard-core rocker. The best entertainment listings are in the Friday edition of the *Oregonian* and in a number of free handouts: *Willamette Week* (put out each evening and catering to students), the *Main Event, Clinton St. Quarterly, Just Out* (which caters to gay and lesbian interests), the *Portland Guide,* and the *Downtowner* (friend of the upwardly mobile). All are available in restaurants downtown and in boxes on street corners.

Music

Portland has its share of good, formally presented concerts, but why bother with admission fees? You'll find the most exciting talent playing for free in various public facilities around the city. Call the Park Bureau (796-5193) for info, and check the *Oregonian* (see above) for **Brown Bag Concerts,** free public concerts given around the city in a six-week summer series (at noon during the week and Tues. evenings).

Oregon Symphony Orchestra plays in Arlene Schnitzer Concert Hall, 719 SW Alder (228-1353), Sept.-April. Tickets $15. "Symphony Sunday" afternoon concerts $12.

Portland Civic Auditorium, 222 SW Clay St. (248-4496). Attracts the usual hard rockin' arena acts, as well as a few jazz and opera stars. Ticket prices vary ($8-30).

Sack Lunch Concerts, 1422 SW 11th Ave. and Clay St. (222-2031), at the Old Church. Free concert every Wed. at noon (except in the event of rain) during the summer.

Chamber Music Northwest performs summer concerts at Reed College Commons, 3203 SE Woodstock Ave. (223-3202). Classical music Mon., Thurs., Sat. at 8pm. Admission $16, ages 7-14 $9.

Couch Tuesdays and Wallace Thursdays, held Tues. in Couch Park at NW 20th and Glisan, and Thurs. in Wallace Park on NW Raleigh at 25th. These events offer folk, rock, bluegrass, and children's specials, 7-8:30pm during summer.

Noon Lawn Concerts, at the Odell Manor Lawn, Lewis and Clark College (244-6161), 8 mi. south of Portland. Free classical concerts throughout June and July. Wed. noon-1pm.

Starbucks by Starlight, at Pioneer Courthouse Square, hosts quartets, big band, and jazz during the summer. Mon. 5:30-7pm.

Peanut Butter and Jam Sessions at Pioneer Courthouse Square from noon to 1pm every Tues. and Thurs. during the summer months. A potpourri of rock, jazz, folk, and world music.

Theater

While inferior to Seattle (both in variety and quality), Portland's theater scene does benefit from a trickle-down-effect. College shows, held predominantly during the school year, are inexpensive and often worthwhile.

Oregon Shakespeare Festival/Portland (274-6588), at the Intermediate Theater of **PCPA,** at SW Broadway and SW Main. 5-play series, featuring classics as well as modern adaptations, Nov.-April Tickets Fri.-Sat. $11-30, Sun. and Tues.-Wed. $9-26.

Portland Civic Theater, 1530 SW Yamhill (226-4026). The mainstage often presents musical comedy, while the smaller theater-in-the-round features less traditional shows. Tickets $12-20.

Artists Repertory Theater (242-9403), SW 10th, on the 3rd floor of the YMCA. This small theater puts on excellent low-budget productions, many of them experimental. Tickets $15.

Portland State University Summer Festival Theater (229-4440), at the Lincoln Hall Auditorium. Schedules at the box office or the Portland Public Library. Performances mid-June to mid-July. Tickets $8-15.

Portland Civic Auditorium, 222 SW Clay St. (248-4496). Occasional big splashy opera and touring shows, now part of the Portland Center for the Performing Arts (PCPA). Tickets $25-55.

Cinema

Most of Portland's countless movie theaters have half-price days or matinee shows. With the help of the *Oregonian* (see above) it's sometimes possible to dodge the $6 ticket price for the average "major motion picture."

Baghdad Theater and Pub, 3702 SE Hawthorne (230-0895). This magnificently renovated theater shows current movies and boasts an excellent beer menu (pint $2.65). Evening shows are very popular. Doors open 5pm, Sun. matinee. Admission $1.

Aladdin Theatre, 3017 SE Milwaukee Ave. (233-1994). Classic films shown on weekends. An organ concert, serial chapter, and classic cartoons precede the 7pm viewing on Fri. and Sat. nights. Tickets $3.50, senior citizens and students $2.

Cinema 21, 616 NW 21st (223-4515). Clean, attractive cinema showing mostly documentary, independent, and foreign films. Tickets $5; students, children, senior citizens, and matinee $4.

Clinton Street Theater, 2522 SE Clinton St. (238-8899). Classic and foreign films $3.50; free popcorn Wed. nights. Time-warp to the 70s with the *Rocky Horror Picture Show* every Fri.-Sat. at midnight $4.

Laurelhurst Theater, 2735 E. Burnside (232-5511). Inexpensive second-run films. $1.50 all seats.

Northwest Film and Video Center, 1219 SW Park Ave. (221-1156), in the Berg Swann Auditorium at the Portland Art Museum. Mostly documentary films on little-known places and peoples. Tickets $4.50, under 12 $3.50. Open Wed.-Sun.

Sports

Contact the **Portland Park Bureau,** 1120 SW 5th Ave., #502 (796-5150 for indoor athletics or 796-5132 for outdoor recreation), for a complete guide to Portland's many parks, which contain myriad hiking and cycling trails and lakes for swimming and sailing. Forty of the parks have outdoor **tennis courts,** many of which are lighted for night play and free to the public. The following parks have **swimming pools:** Columbia, Creston, Dishman, Grant, Mt. Scott, Montavilla, Peninsula, Pier, Wilson, and Sellwood (pool admission $1.50, children 50¢). Special facilities and programs are provided for senior citizens and people with disabilities (call 248-4328).

The **Coliseum,** 1401 N. Wheeler (248-4496) is home to the **Trail Blazers** (234-9291), Oregon's beloved NBA team. The hard-working Blazers have become a regular fixture in post-season play, although somewhat disappointing in 1993. The **Beavers** play Class AAA baseball (and aspire to become the Minnesota Twins) at Civic Stadium, 1844 SW Morrison St. (248-4345; tickets $4.50, seniors and students $2.50). The **Winter Hawks** (238-6366) of the Western Hockey League, also play the Coliseum. Take bus #9 (brown beaver) or take MAX.

Clubs and Bars

The best clubs in Portland are the hardest ones to find. Neighborhood taverns and pubs may be tucked away on back roads, but they have the most character and best music. The most accessible clubs from downtown are in the Northwest part of the city. Flyers advertising upcoming shows are always plastered on telephone poles around town. Several pubs now selling the locally brewed McMinnamin's beer are favorites of the locals.

Lotus Card Room and Cafe, 932 SW 3rd Ave. (227-6185), at SW Salmon. Twenty-something crowd laps up 80s wave music each Thurs. Techno, house, and hip-hop attract a collegiate crowd on Fri. and Sat. Disco on Sun. is quite possibly the best (and certainly the grooviest) dance experience in the entire city. Well drinks $2.50, beer on tap $2.25-3. Open Mon.-Fri. 9am-2:30am, Sat.-Sun. 8am-2:30am.

Red Sea, 318 SW 3rd Ave. (241-5450). Harry Belafonte's happy hunting ground. Calypso galore. Live reggae on Thurs. Cover $2-3. Well drinks $2.50, Henry Weinhard's $2.25. Vicious carding. Open Thurs. 9pm-1:30am, Fri.-Sat. 9pm-2:30am.

Gypsy, 625 NW 21st Ave. (796-1859). Take bus #17 (red salmon). Fabulous David Lynch-ian decor wasted on unmistakably American crowd. Bring your cool friends for moral support. Groovy hour Mon.-Fri. 4-7pm features beer for $1.50 and appetizers at ½ price. Pool tables and darts abound. Open Mon.-Fri. 9am-11pm, Sat.-Sun. 8am-11pm.

The Space Room, 4800 SE Hawthorne Blvd. (235-8303). Take bus #5 (brown beaver). Judy Jetson smoked way too many cigarettes inside this space-age joint. The cutting-edge, savvy, sassy crowd contemplate the vintage-clothing possibilities as they eye the keno-playing vestiges of the Eisenhower years. One bloody mary ($3) will put you over the edge. Open daily 7am-2:30am.

La Luna, 215 SE 9th Ave. (241-LUNA/5862). Take bus #20 (purple raindrops), get off at 9th, walk 2 blocks south. Too much going on here—live concerts, 2 bars, 1 non-smoking coffee room, and an anything-goes Generation X crowd. All ages admitted (except to the bars). Call ahead for concert listings. The Living Room bar open Thurs.-Sat. 8pm-2:30am, concerts and special events on other nights.

East Side, 3701 SE Division St. (236-5550). Take bus #4 (brown beaver). Despite Portland's high lesbian population, the city's only real bar-offering to the lesbian community is this country-western hideaway *à la* "Desert Hearts." Dancing Tues.-Sat., with lessons on Tues. and Thurs. On Thurs., draft beers 50¢. Open Sun.-Mon. 4pm-2am, Tues.-Sat. 11:30am-2am.

Caribou Bar & Buck's Cafe, 503 W. Burnside St. (227-0245). Two caribou from 1927 oversee this bar which features 125 drinks for $1 each!!! Eclectic clientele (businesspeople to drag queens) and eclectic music (Rolling Stones to Porno for

Pyros) make for one loud and crowded fiesta. Open Mon.-Fri. 11:30am-2:30am, Sat. 4:30pm-2:30am.

Dot's Cafe, 2521 SE Clinton St. (235-0203). Take bus #4 (brown beaver) to 26th, and walk 3 blocks south. Across the street from the Clinton Street Theater. Wig night was a big hit a few months back at this neighborhood hangout. Decor includes an impressive collection of 3-D Jesus iconography and work by local artists. Popular with Reed College students and their bohemian brethren. Open Sun.-Wed. 11am-1am, Thurs.-Sat. 11am-2am.

Brigg and Boxx's Video Bar, 1035 SW Stark (226-4171). Primarily gay bar with dancing beginning at 9pm. Thurs. and Fri. are "buck night." $2 cover on weekends. Open daily 4:30pm-2:30am.

Produce Row Cafe, 204 SE Oak St. (232-8355). Bus #6 (red salmon) to SE Oak and SE Grand, then walk west along Oak towards the river. 21 beers on tap ($1.50-2.50), 72 bottled domestic and imported beers (ranging in origin from China to Belgium), and a lovely outdoor beer garden. Ask one of the friendly bartenders to mix you the house special, a Black and Tan (Guinness Stout and champagne, $3). Open Mon.-Fri. 11am-1am, Sat. noon-1am, Sun. 2pm-midnight.

Mission Theater and Pub, 1624 NW Glisan (223-4031). Serves excellent homebrewed ales as well as delicious and unusual sandwiches ($4.50). Also offers free showings of double features (everything from Bogart to Allen) twice nightly. Relax in the balcony of this old moviehouse with a pitcher of Ruby, a fragrant raspberry ale named after one of Mick Jagger's creations ($1.50 glass, $7 pitcher). Open daily 5pm-1am.

East Avenue Tavern, 727 E. Burnside St. (236-6900). Bus #12, 19, or 20 (all brown beaver). Folk music. Open-mike nights make for unexpected variety: Irish, French, flamenco, bluegrass. Cover $1-5, depending on the name and fame of the performer. Open Mon.-Sat. noon-midnight, Sun. 8pm-midnight.

Key Largo, 31 NW 1st Ave. (223-9919). Airy, tropical atmosphere. You can dance out on the patio when it's not raining. A variety of local and national bands. Rock, rhythm & blues, zydeco, and jazz. Cover $2-8, depending on the band. Open Mon.-Fri. 11am-2:30am, Sat.-Sun. noon-2:30am.

Bridgeport Brew Pub, 1313 NW Marshall (241-7179). Much-acclaimed homebrew and great pizza in a waterhouse that actually fills on weekend nights.

Embers, 310 NW Burnside (222-3082). Hot dancing until 2:30am. High percentage of gay clientele. Beer 75¢, well drinks $2.25.

Hobbit Restaurant, 4420 SE 39th St. (771-0742). The best jazz in the city is tucked away in this not-so-great restaurant and bar. Cover charge before 11pm around $3, depending on the band.

The Laurelhurst Public House, 2958 NE Glisan (232-1504). Local acoustic bands each night. Pool tables. McMinnamin's and microbrews $3 a pint. Open Mon.-Sat. 11am-2:30am, Sun. 4pm-2:30am.

SEASONAL EVENTS

Cinco de Mayo Festival (823-4000 or 292-5752). May 5th. Mexican Independence Day celebration complete with firy food, entertainment, and crafts at SW Front and Salmon.

Rose Festival (call 248-7923 for recording, 277-2681 for offices). First 3 weeks of June. U.S. Navy sailors flood the street while the city decks itself in all its finery for Portland's premier summer event. Waterfront concerts, art festivals, celebrity entertainment, auto racing, parades, an air show, Navy ships, and the largest children's parade in the world (the Rose Junior Parade).

Waterfront Blues Festival (282-0555). Early July. International celebrities and some of the finest regional blues artists participate in this 3-day event. Call 282-0555.

Oregon Brewers Festival (281-2437 or 241-7179). Mid-July. The continent's largest gathering of independent brewers makes for one incredible party at Waterfront Park.

Mt. Hood Festival of Jazz, first weekend in Aug. at Mt. Hood Community College in Gresham (666-3810). It is overpriced, but this is the premier jazz festival of the

Pacific Northwest, with 20 hr. of music over the course of a weekend—Wynton Marsalis and the late Stan Getz have been regulars in the past. Admission around $20 per day, reserve well in advance. Write Mt. Hood Festival of Jazz, P.O. Box 696, Gresham 97030. To reach the festival, take I-84 to Wood Village-Gresham exit and follow the signs, or follow the crowd on MAX to the end of the line.

Artquake (227-2787). Labor Day weekend. Music, mime, food, and neo-situationist hooplah in and around Pioneer Courthouse Square.

Portland Marathon (226-1111). Late-Sept. Feeling in shape? Join the thousands who run this 26.2-mi. race. Many shorter walks and runs are also held.

■ Near Portland

One of Portland's finest attributes is its proximity to natural attractions. The burned-out shell of Mt. St. Helens is a short drive north into Washington State; the Columbia River Gorge—full of colorful windsurfers—is only a 30-minute drive up I-84; and Mt. Hood, a skier's haven, is one and a half hours away. You can retrace the footsteps of early pioneers east along the Oregon Trail. A two-hour jaunt west will take you to the rugged cliffs lining the Pacific, and a slightly longer drive north or south will land you in such coastal towns as Cannon Beach, Seaside, Astoria, or Tillamook.

Oregon City

Take bus #32, 33, or 35 (all green leaf) to Oregon City from 5th Ave. in downtown Portland, or drive approximately 20 minutes down Rte. 43, Rte. 99E, or I-205. On Clackamette Dr. is **Clackamette Park,** the closest **free swimming** (in the Clacka-mas River) to Portland, and the main reason that Portlanders ever head out to sleepy Oregon City.

Sauvie Island

Twenty minutes from downtown Portland, Sauvie Island is a peaceful rural hide-away at the confluence of the Columbia and Willamette Rivers. The island offers great views of the city from its vast sandy stretches. On winter mornings, eagles and geese congregate along the roads, and in spring and summer, berries are every-where. For many Portlanders, a summer trip to the island's **u-pick farms** (family operations announced by hand-lettered signs along the roads) is an annual tradition. The island's beaches are another star attraction, and understandably so, since at night many visitors feel free to swim without the customary distraction of a suit. **Oak Island,** at the North East end, is the best beach area. In light of all these possibil-ities, it might be an easy thing to forget yourself—as long as you don't forget an ample supply of either gas or drinking water. Neither is available on the island.

Columbia River Gorge

Fifteen million years ago, massive flows of lava poured out of rifts in the earth, cov-ering northern Oregon with 25,000 cubic mi. of basalt. The Columbia River began carving its determined path through the rock, forming a narrow channel 3000 ft. deep and 55 mi. long. As a result, walls of volcanic stone rise from either side of the grand river as it surges on its last lap to the sea. To follow the spectacular Columbia River Gorge, take I-84 east to the Troutdale exit onto the **Columbia River Scenic Highway.** This road—first constructed in 1915—follows the crest of the gorge walls and affords legendary views of waterfalls, dams, mountains, and the gorge itself. Numerous free publications, including *Gorge Vistas, The Visitor's Guide to Gorge Fun,* and for those interested in windsurfing, *Northwest Sailboard,* offer excellent information on local sights, camping, accommodations, history, and events. These are available at local visitor centers and chambers of commerce along the Gorge.

Recently, windsurfing enthusiasts have discovered the magnificent power of the Columbia's water and 30mph winds. Vibrantly colored sailboards decorate the Gorge, engaging in obsessive, zany competitions like the "Killer Loop Classic." Sub-lime hiking experiences and vistas are accessible all the way down the Columbia

River Scenic Hwy. For information on trails and a friendly earful of local lore, call **Columbia Gorge National Scenic Area Headquarters** (386-2333).

The famous **Vista House** (695-2240), built in 1918 in Crown Point State Park as a memorial to Oregon's pioneers, now serves as a visitors center. The house hangs on the edge of an outcropping, high above the river. A trail leaves the road a few yards down from the house, ending in a secluded view of both the house and the gorge. Reach Crown Point from the Scenic Hwy. or from the Corbett exit off I-84.

About 2 mi. farther east is one of the 20 waterfalls that line this route—**Latourell Falls**—where you can clamber over jagged black rock to stand behind a plume of falling spray. Six mi. farther, take the steep trail to the top of the skinny but beautiful (and very crowded) **Multnomah Falls** (Exit 31 off I-84). The falls crash 620 ft. into a tiny pool at the bottom. Wading is allowed in the pool, but be aware of the some-times sharp rocks that pepper the bottom.

Hikers who yearn to escape main-trail traffic can follow other paths into **Mt. Hood National Forest;** get an inexpensive trail map from the Multnomah Falls gift shop. A **Nature Center** sits at the base of the falls (open July-Labor Day daily 9:30am-6pm). **Camping** facilities are available in **Ainsworth State Park** (sites $14). Check with a Multnomah Falls park ranger for more information. The Washington side of the river offers decent (and more copious) prospects as well.

Exactly 44 mi. east of Portland is the oldest of the Columbia River hydroelectric projects, the **Bonneville Dam** (Exit 40 off I-84). Pete Seeger was working for the Bonneville Power Co. when he wrote "Roll On Columbia," a salute to the river (and, indirectly, the BPC): "Your power is turning our darkness to dawn, so roll on Colum-bia, roll on." Across the river on the Washington side, a **visitors center** (374-8820) shows tourists a fish ladder and the dam's powerhouse and generator room. Also on this side of the river, don't miss dramatic **Beacon Rock,** the 848-ft.-high neck of an old volcano, which is the largest monolith in the U.S.

At the **Cascade Locks** (Exit 44 off I-84), 4 mi. past Bonneville, take a **paddleboat ride** aboard the *Columbia Gorge* (374-8427, in Portland 223-3928), a replica of the sternwheelers that used to ply the Columbia and Willamette Rivers (2-hr. rides, 3 per day; fare $11, children $6). The **Visitor Information Center** (374-8427) in Cas-cade Locks is full of brochures on camping, hiking, and local sights (open Memorial Day-Oct. daily 8am-5pm).

You can also cross the **Bridge of the Gods** (75¢ toll) at this side of the river. The bridge was constructed at the site of the natural bridge which, according to Native American legend, collapsed when the two warrior gods, Mt. Adams and Mt. Hood, erupted in the fight for the honor of the goddess Mt. St. Helens. The bridge seems fragile even now—if you drive slowly, you can see right through the bridge grating to the river below. Just across the bridge is the town of Carson, where visitors can go to the **Hot Mineral Springs Resort** (427-8292) and relax in a hot mineral bath.

The largest town along the gorge is **Hood River,** located at the junction of I-84 and Rte. 365, which leads to Mt. Hood. Known as the "windsurfing capital of the Northwest," Hood River is also situated on excellent soil, and orchards full of blos-soms and fruits line the roads. Local attractions include the **Mt. Hood Railroad** (386-3556), which connects the mountain and gorge, and the **Columbia Gorge Hotel** (386-5566), a national historic landmark. The **Hood River County Chamber of Commerce** (386-2000 or 800-366-3530), in Port Marine Park, houses information on the gorge and Mt. Hood areas, and also offers complete, well-organized bro-chures on anything you might want to know about Hood River.

Farther east, **The Dalles** was the last stop on the agonizing Oregon Trail. Lewis and Clark camped here in 1805, and French explorers named the area "Le Dalle" (the trough) after the rapids around that section of the river. **Fort Dalles** (296-4547), at 15th and Garrison, a historical museum housed in the original 1856 surgeon's quarters, displays memorabilia of these historical events. For a free map including a walking tour, go to the **Convention and Visitor's Bureau,** 901 E. 2nd St. (296-6616 or 800-255-3385). The visitors center at the **Dalles Lock and Dam** (296-1181) offers free public viewing of its fish ladders, as well as a train tour around the facilities (open June-Labor Day daily 9am-5pm).

A little farther east, crossing the Columbia on U.S. 97, lies the **Mary Hill Museum of Art** (509-773-3733). European and American paintings—including works by Native Americans—and Romanian memorabilia make the museum a major cultural resource for the gorge area.

Mount Hood

Glacier-topped Mt. Hood is located at the junction of U.S. 26 and Rte. 35, 90 minutes east of Portland and less than an hour from Hood River. The 11,235-ft. volcano has been behaving itself for some time now. Skiers can take advantage of the winter trails at three ski areas: **Timberline, Ski Bowl Multorpor,** and **Mt. Hood Meadows.** All three offer night skiing. Timberline (272-3311) offers summer skiing for the truly dedicated (you'll have to yield to the U.S. national team, however). Rental of skis, poles, and boots runs $17 per day ($10 for children) and lift tickets generally cost around $26 per day ($23 in the summer). All three areas offer ski lessons averaging $35 per hour or $15 per person for group lessons. Special packages including rental, lesson, and lift tickets are often available at a much-reduced price; call for current deals. Timberline's **Magic Mile** lift carries nonskiers up above the clouds for spectacular views of the mountain and surrounding environs ($5, children $3). The lodge also has stunning views of the Cascades. For adventurers who wish to really tackle the mountain on foot, **Timberline Mountain Guides,** P.O. Box 464, Terrebonne 97760 (548-0749), offers mountain, snow, and ice climbing courses led by experts. Climbs last one to three days.

Even if you decide to avoid Timberline and ski at Ski Bowl or Mt. Hood Meadows, turn up the 6-mi. road just off **Government Camp** to the WPA-style **Timberline Lodge** (800-547-1406, 231-5400 from Portland), site of the outdoor filming of Stanley Kubrick's *The Shining.* The road to the lodge also offers arresting views of the valley below. Next door is the **Day Lodge,** where skiers can store equipment without staying overnight, and the **Wy'east Kitchen,** a cafeteria alternative to Timberline's expensive dining. Even nonskiers can find non-stop fun on the mountain. Ski Bowl runs an alpine slide, go-kart course, and groomed mountain-bicycle trails. In addition, **hiking** trails circle the mountain. The most popular is **Mirror Lake,** a 4-mi. loop open June through October. Start from the parking lot off U.S. 26, 1 mi. west of Government Camp. For more information drop in at either the **Mt. Hood Visitors Information Center,** 65000 E. U.S. 26., Welches 97067 (622-4822); the **Zigzag Ranger District Office,** 70220 E. U.S. 26, Zigzag 97049 (622-3191); or the **Hood River Ranger Station,** 67805 Rte. 35, Parkdok 97041 (352-6002). Nearby primitive tentsites ($5) with drinking water are available at **Sherwood** and **Robinwood Campgrounds.**

From the Columbia River Gorge, you can also take **Rte. 35** south from Hood River, which wends through apple, pear, and cherry orchards. The drive is particularly memorable in April when the trees are in bloom. The Mt. Hood loop offers adults the diversion of wine-tasting during the summer and fall at the area's vineyards. **Hood River Vineyard** is open to the public daily (1-5pm), except Friday. **Gray Line Tours,** 400 SW Broadway (285-9845), offers an eight-and-a-half-hour ride around Mt. Hood and through the Columbia River Gorge ($30, under 12 $15). Tours leave from the Imperial Hotel (mid-May to early-Oct. Tues., Thurs., and Sat. at 9am).

OREGON COAST

The renowned coastal highway **U.S. 101** hangs close to the shore, from time to time rising in elevation and opening up to a number of lofty viewpoints. From Astoria in the north to Brookings in the south, the highway laces together the resorts and fishing villages that cluster around the mouths of rivers feeding into the Pacific. Its most breathtaking stretch lies between the coastal towns, where hundreds of miles of state and national parks allow direct access to the beach. Wherever the highway leaves the coast, look for a beach loop road—these quiet byways afford some of the finest scenery on the western seaboard. Stop and wander along the huge stretches of unspoiled beach and observe the ocean's more comfortable inhabitants—the seals, sea lions, and waterfowl just offshore.

GETTING AROUND

For the most extensive and rewarding encounter with the coast, travel by car or bike. Cyclists should write to the Oregon Dept. of Transportation, Salem 97310, or to virtually any visitors center or Chamber of Commerce on the coast for the free *Oregon Coast Bike Route Map;* it provides invaluable information on campsites, hostels, bike repair facilities, temperatures, and wind conditions. Remember that Portlanders head down-road to vacation, so most traffic flows south.

For those without a car or bike, transportation becomes a bit tricky. **Greyhound** offers only two coastal runs from Portland per day; one of those takes place under cover of night, when the coast's beautiful scenery is hidden. Along the southern coast, the 10-hour Portland-Brookings route stops at Lincoln City, Newport, Florence, Reedsport, Coos Bay, Bandon, Port Orford, Gold Beach, and every suburb between Portland and the coast. The northern route connects Portland with Tillamook, Cannon Beach, Seaside, and Astoria. Local public transportation links Astoria to Cannon Beach, but vanishes south of Cannon Beach.

Gasoline and grocery **prices** on the coast are about 20% higher than in the inland cities. Motorists should try to stock up and fill up before reaching the coastal highways. When searching for a site to pull in for the night, look to the small villages, as they tend to be the most interesting (and often the cheapest) places to stay. From north to south, Nehalem, Wheeler, Depoe Bay, Winchester Bay, Charleston, Bandon, and Port Orford offer escape from the larger and more commercialized towns of Seaside, Tillamook, Lincoln City, Newport, and Coos Bay. State parks along the coast offer 17 major campgrounds with electricity and showers.

■■■ ASTORIA

The 200-year saga of Astoria, the first American settlement on the West Coast, has been one of gentle rise and persistent fall. Lewis and Clark first arrived here in 1805 at the end of their transcontinental voyage, and John Jacob Astor established a fur-trading post which became the first permanent American settlement on the Pacific in 1811.

Over the next century Astoria built a thriving economy around fisheries, canneries, dairies, and lumber. The tables turned on December 9, 1922, when the town's entire business district was destroyed by fire. Since then Astoria has enjoyed some mini-booms—spawned by the U.S. Army's WWII defense buildup and the post-war salmon industry—but the overall pattern is one of decline. The local waters were over-fished and emptied in the 1950s, causing a mass migration of canneries north to Alaska. The dairies soon followed and most manufacturing as well. Most recently, the timber industry has been cut short by Congressional regulations designed to protect the endangered spotted owl.

With no other natural resources to put into manufacturing, Astoria, like other towns along the Oregon Coast, has found tourism to be the most lucrative (and often least destructive) way to keep themselves afloat. A natural vacation spot for inlanders and city-dwellers seeking to escape the heat, Astoria now promotes museums, parks, and a panoramic view of the Columbia River and Washington coastline.

PRACTICAL INFORMATION AND ORIENTATION

Visitors Information: Greater Astoria Chamber of Commerce, 111 W. Marine Dr. (325-6311), just east of the U.S. 101 toll bridge to Washington. P.O. Box 176, Astoria 97103. Thoroughly stocked with information on Astoria, the Coast, and southwest Washington. Open Mon.-Sat. 8am-6pm, Sun. 9am-5pm; Sept.-May Mon.-Fri. 8am-5pm, Sat.-Sun. 11am-4pm. Also operates a small summer **information hut** at the base of Astoria Column. Open June-Labor Day daily 11am-6pm.

Greyhound (RAZ Transportation), 364 9th St. (325-5641), at Duane St. Leaves Astoria for Portland (2 per day, 9:15am and 7:15pm, $15); leaves Portland for Astoria (2 per day, 6:30am and 4:30pm, $15). Open Mon.-Sat. 9am-noon and 4:30-7:30pm.

North Coast Transit, at the Greyhound station in Seaside (738-7083). Runs from Astoria to Seaside and back, serving towns in between. Leaves Astoria every 2 hr. 9am-5pm. To Seaside ($2.50, round-trip $4). Operates Mon.-Fri.

Pacific Transit System, at the Greyhound terminal (206-642-9418 or 206-875-9418). To Ilwaco and Chinook, WA (fare 50¢). Buses leave Astoria daily at 7:30, 11:40am, 3, and 5:40pm.

TBR Transit, 364 9th St. (325-0563 or 325-5189). Local bus service. Makes a full city loop every 20 min. on the hr. (fare 50¢, students and under 12, 35¢). Service Mon.-Sat. 6:30am-7:15pm.

Taxi: Yellow Cab, 325-3131. 24 hr.

AAA: 5 U.S. 101, Warrenton (861-3118). Open Mon.-Fri. 8am-5pm.

Laundromat: 127 Bond St. (325-7815), behind the visitors center. Wash 75¢, 10-min. dry 25¢. Open daily 6am-10pm.

Clatsop County Women's Crisis Services: 1250 Duane St. (325-5735). 24 hr.

Senior Citizen's Information Service: 818 Commercial St. (325-0123). Legal services and a community rec center. Open Mon.-Fri. 8:30am-noon and 1-3pm.

Pharmacy: Astoria Pharmacy, 840 Exchange St. (325-1123). Open Mon.-Fri. 9:30am-5:30pm, Sat. 9:30am-12:30pm.

Hospital: Columbia Memorial, 2111 Exchange St. (325-4321).

Emergency: 911. **Police:** 555 30th St. (325-4411). **Clatsop County Sheriff:** 355 7th St. (325-8635). **Coast Guard:** Port of Astoria Airport (861-0105), Warrenton. 24-hr. marine and air emergency service.

Post Office: in the Federal Bldg. (325-2141), at 8th and Commercial. Open Mon.-Fri. 8:30am-5pm. **General Delivery ZIP Code:** 97103.

Area Code: 503.

Astoria is the only direct connection between the Oregon coast and Washington. Two bridges run from the city: the **Astoria Bridge,** which spans the Columbia River into Washington, and the **Youngs Bay Bridge,** to the southwest, on which Marina Drive metamorphoses into U.S. 101. Warrenton lies a few mi. west of the latter bridge. U.S. 30 links Portland (100 mi. east) with Astoria. Astoria can also be reached from Portland via U.S. 26 and U.S. 101 at Seaside.

ACCOMMODATIONS AND CAMPING

For some reason most tourists aren't deterred by the high prices of motels in Astoria. If you're going to lay out the dough, be sure to make reservations. The 10-mi. trek to **Fort Stevens Park** will let you pitch a tent near clean facilities in the woods.

Fort Columbia State Park Hostel (HI/AYH), Fort Columbia, Chinook, WA (206-777-8755), within the park boundaries. Across the 4-mi. bridge into Washington, 2 mi. north on U.S. 101. Pacific Transit System will get you there for 50¢ (see Practical Information); otherwise you'll have to pay the $1.50 toll to cross the bridge. A nearly deserted hostel located in what was the army hospital of a turn-of-the-century fort. Glorious grounds and a friendly staff to help you find and explore its hidden trails and coves. A fire on chilly evenings and snacks in the kitchen. Laundry and barbecue facilities. Lockout 9:30am-5:30pm, but hours not strictly enforced. Members $8.50, nonmembers $11.50.

Lamplighter Motel, 131 W. Marine (325-4051). Bright, attractive rooms compensate for the traffic noise. Singles $38. Doubles $48.

Rivershore Motel, 59 W. Marine Dr. (325-2921), 1 mi. east of the bridge, on U.S. 30 along the Columbia. Popular motel with cable TV and phones. Singles $35. Doubles $50.

Astoria City Center Motel, 495 Marine Dr. (325-4211). Nothing fancy, but clean and comfortable—much like Astoria itself. Singles $39. Doubles $55. Rates lower in winter.

The Dunes Motel, 288 W. Marine Dr. (325-7111). Home of Astoria's only hotel swimming pool and jacuzzi. A glance to the heavens will bring the elevated Astoria Bridge entrance ramp into view. Singles $44. Doubles $52.

Martin and Lilly Foard House, 690 17th St. (325-1892). This peach, lemon and lime Victorian home is one of Astoria's treasures—partly because it looks like a storybook gingerbread house come to life, but the more so because it opens its doors as a two-room B&B on weekends and holidays. Rooms $45.

Fort Stevens State Park (861-1671), over Youngs Bay Bridge on U.S. 101 S., 10 mi. west of Astoria. For reservations, write Fort Stevens, Hammond 97121. A huge park with rugged, desolate beaches. 605 sites with hot showers; facilities for people with disabilities. Sites $14-16. Hiker/biker sites $2.

FOOD

Meals in Astoria are generally wholesome, though not especially gourmet. The **Safeway** (325-4662), 11th St. and Duane is open 24 hr. The **Community Store** (325-0027), 14th and Duane, sells natural and bulk foods (open Mon.-Sat. 10am-6pm).

Andrew and Steve's Cafe, 1196 Marine Dr. (325-5762). A local favorite with home-style cookin'. Old Fashioned Steak ($6.25) and "Famous" homemade veal cutlets with cream sauce ($6). Open Mon.-Sat. 6am-9pm, Sun. 7am-8:30pm.

Peri's, 915 Commercial St. (325-5560). A friendly indoor/outdoor deli that serves only a few items, but does them well. Chocolate chip cookies (3 for $1). "Lite" sandwiches ($2.75), "super" ($3.75). Open Mon.-Sat. 11am-4pm.

Pacific Rim, 229 W. Marine Dr. (325-4481), near Washington Bridge. Great food, no frills. Ignore the ugly, diner-like decor, and try the Sicilian-style ravioli with basil and blue cheese. Italian dinners run $5-7 or opt for the lower-priced lunch portion served all day. Open Sun.-Thurs. 11am-11pm, Fri.-Sat. 11am-midnight. Lounge open 11am-2pm.

Columbian Cafe, 1114 Marine Dr. (325-2233). A gem for the vegetarian gourmet. Crêpes, egg dishes $4-6. Fresh pasta made daily, dishes around $8-9. The menu of special seafood dinners depends on the catch of the day. Open lunch Mon.-Fri. 8am-2pm, Sat. 10am-2pm. Dinner Wed.-Sat. 5-9pm.

SIGHTS AND SEASONAL EVENTS

Astoria's prime location is best appreciated from the top of the **Astor Column,** on Coxcomb Hill Rd., which affords a view of Saddle Mt. and lush forests to the south and the mouth of the Columbia River to the north. Erected in 1922, the column is wrapped by 166 steps on the exterior, passing faded, storm-worn friezes which depict the history of the area. Tableaux of historic Astoria include the discovery of the Columbia River by intrepid English sea captain Robert Grey, the arrival of Lewis and Clark, and the settling of Astoria. Open from dawn to 10pm, the column is accessible by the TBR bus (see Practical Information).

Stop by the Chamber of Commerce (see Practical Information) or one of the local historical museums for a copy of the self-guided *Walking Tour of Astoria* ($2.50), which leads you (mostly uphill) past 71 historical sites. Those with less time and energy can walk or drive up 17th St. and traverse **Grand** and **Franklin St.** for a highlight of Astoria's magnificent Victorian houses.

The Historical Society maintains three **museums** in Astoria: the Heritage Museum, the Flavel House, and the Firefighters' Museum (admission to any 2 $4, children $2; admission to all 3 $5, children $2.50). The knowledgeable guides at the

Clatsop County Heritage Museum, 16th and Exchange St. (325-8395), will narrate the story of one of Astoria's most famous sons, Ronald MacDonald (no, not the ubiquitous cholesterol-hawking harlequin). Nearly six years before Commodore Perry arrived in Japan, MacDonald managed to infiltrate the closed island by intentionally capsizing his boat on the Japanese shore. The museum houses photographic exhibitions, the usual assortment of old things, and a fascinating exhibit on Oregon's first Chinese settlers. You'll also learn that Paul Bunyan was an actual logger who became the legend of grade-school cartoons after participating in a French-Canadian rebellion against the British crown. (Open daily 10am-5pm; Nov.-April daily 11am-4pm.)

One of the best turn-of-the-century recreations (of many in the area) is the **Flavel House,** 441 8th St. (325-2563), a beautifully restored Victorian mansion once owned by Astoria's first millionaire. Although the house's original furnishings are gone, the replacements are from the same historical period. Don't miss the basement, which houses such jetsam of history as a turn-of-the-century telephone switchboard and a horse carriage (open daily 10am-5pm; Nov.-April daily 11am-4pm). The **Uppertown Firefighters' Museum** (325-6920), 30th and Marine Dr., displays vintage firefighting equipment (open Fri.-Sun. 10am-5pm; Nov.-April Fri.-Sun. 11am-4pm).

Nearby, the **Columbia River Maritime Museum,** 1793 Marine Dr. (325-2323), at the foot of 17th St., includes, among its wide array of nautical paraphernalia, sailing-ship models, early sea charts, and whaling exhibits. Anchored out front is the *Columbia,* the last lightship to see active duty at the mouth of the Columbia River (museum open daily 9:30am-5pm; admission $5, senior citizens $4, ages 6-17 $2).

One block up from the Maritime Museum, the intriguing owner of the **Shallon Winery,** 1598 Duane St. (325-5978), will give you a tour of his small winemaking facilities, provide his interpretation of the area's history, and proudly display his extraordinary repetoire of wines. A self-proclaimed connoisseur of fine food, he insists you call him "anytime of day or night" before you consider eating at any restaurant within a 50-mi. radius. He'll treat you to a taste of wines made from local berries and the only commercially produced **whey wines** (from Tillamook cheese) in the world. Approach the cranberry and whey wine with caution; its fruity taste belies its alcohol content. Sampling **lemon meringue pie wine** is likely to be the highlight of any trip to the Oregon Coast—the taste is so uncanny that you'd swear you were drinking a puree of grandma's special. The owner even serves the wine with a small cracker to ensure that you receive the correct proportion of crust to pie (open daily noon-6pm).

The **Astoria Regatta** (325-5139), held the second weekend in August, is one of the longest running community events in the Northwest, dating back to 1894. The regatta tradition remains strong and features food and craft booths, a watershow, scenic boat rides, fireworks, dances, and even a sailboat race or two.

■ Near Astoria

Six mi. west of Astoria, the **Fort Clatsop National Memorial** (861-2471) reconstructs the winter headquarters of the ragtag Lewis and Clark expedition, based on descriptions in their detailed journal. The crude fort housed Lewis, Clark, their Native American guide Sacajawea, 24 enlisted men, three officers, a few interpreters and guides, Clark's slave York, Lewis's dog Scannon, and plenty o' fleas. The **visitors center** shows a slide presentation and a few exhibits. (Open daily 8am-6pm; Labor Day to mid-June 8am-5pm. Admission $1, over 62 or under 17 free, families $3.)

Fort Stevens State Park (campground 861-1671; historical area 861-2000), off U.S. 101 on a narrow peninsula 10 mi. west of Astoria, has excellent swimming, fishing, boating facilities, beaches, and hiking trails. Within the park lie the skeletal remains of the 287-ft. British schooner *Peter Iredale,* lost in 1906. The beach near the wreck is the perfect place for beachcombing and relaxation. The water remains a mere 6 in. deep for 50 yards past the wreck; the soft, black mud here is extremely soothing for hot, tired feet. When you've wearied of examining the skeleton of the schooner, lounge on one of the many drift logs that have washed ashore and marvel at the varicolored kites swirling through the air.

Cycling is an excellent way to explore the park. Bicycles are available for rent at **Fort Stevens Bicycle Rentals** (861-0937), next to the Historical Area (open June-Sept. 10am-6pm; $3 per hour, $15 per 24 hr.).

Fort Stevens was constructed in 1864 to prevent Confederate gun boats from entering the Columbia, and its presence was seemingly enough to keep them at bay. From 1897 to 1904, the fort underwent a massive development program, including the construction of 8 concrete-gun batteries. Although the guns have all been removed, nearly all the batteries remain and are the primary focus of a self-guided historical walking tour (about 2 hr.), which begins up the road from the day-use and campground areas. Between Memorial Day and Labor Day, a restored 1954 Army cargo truck takes visitors on narrated tours at 11am, 12:30, 2:30, and 4pm (admission $3, children $1.25). Guided tours of **Battery Mishler** are also available at the same times (admission $2, children $1). The tours leave from the **Fort Stevens Military Museum and Interpretive Center** (861-2000), which contains displays and artifacts spanning the history of the fort (open daily 10am-6pm; winter Wed.-Sat. 10am-4pm; free). **Battery Russell** (861-2471), in the park ½ mi. south of the historical area, bears the dubious distinction of being the only mainland American fort to see active defensive duty since the War of 1812. At 11:30pm on June 21, 1942, a Japanese submarine offshore shelled the fort with 17 rounds. The fort was undamaged and did not return fire. Today it is a military monument.

■■■ SEASIDE

Seaside marked the end of the trail for explorers Lewis and Clark; it was their final and westernmost camp. In the 1870s, eccentric Portland railroad- and ship-builder Ben Holladay developed Seaside into a resort. A zoo and a racetrack were among the town's first structures, and Holladay's ships were ordered to fire cannon shots each time vessels sailed past the town. The years and the tourists, however, have eroded much of Seaside's charm; today, the town is crowded with motels, fast food, and video arcades that clash with the brooding scenery of Oregon's coastline.

PRACTICAL INFORMATION AND ORIENTATION

Visitors Information: Chamber of Commerce, 7 N. Roosevelt St. (738-6391, in OR 800-444-6740), on U.S. 101 and Broadway. Well-versed staff armed and ready for any question about the town. The Chamber of Commerce doubles as a booking agency for most local motels. Open Mon.-Sat. 8am-6pm, Sun. 9am-5pm. Oct.-May Mon.-Fri. 9am-5pm, Sat.-Sun. 10am-4pm.

Greyhound (RAZ Transportation), 201 S. Holladay (738-5121). Leaves Portland at 6:30am for Seaside (2¼ hr.) and Astoria (2¾ hr.). The reverse trip leaves from Seaside at 8:45am and 8pm ($13). **North Coast Transit** (738-7083) provides service Mon.-Fri. only between Astoria and Cannon Beach, with stops *en route* in Warrenton, Gearhart, and Seaside. North and southbound buses leave Seaside in front of Kerwin Rx Drugs at Holladay and Broadway. To: Cannon Beach (2 per day, 9:45am and 4:20pm, 15 min., $2); Astoria (4 per day, 8:10, 10:30am, 2:10, and 5:05pm, 40 min., $2.50).

Taxi: Yellow Cab, 738-3131. 24 hr.

Bike Rental: Prom Bike Shop (738-8251), at 12th and Holladay; also at 80 Ave. A, downtown. Bikes, roller skates, and beach tricycles $4 per hr. and $20 per 24 hr.; tandem bicycles $6 per hr. ID required. Open daily 10am-6pm.

Laundromat: Holladay Coin Laundry, 57 N. Holladay St. (738-3458), at 1st Ave. Wash $1.25, 12 min. dry 25¢. Open daily 6am-10pm.

Senior Citizen's Information Service: 1225 Ave. A (738-7393). Open Mon.-Fri. 9am-4pm.

Women's Crisis Service: 325-5735. 24 hr.

Hospital: Providence Seaside Hospital, 725 S. Wahanna Rd. (738-8463).

Emergency: 911. **Police:** 1000 S. Roosevelt Dr. (738-6311).
Post Office: 300 Ave. A (738-5462). Open Mon.-Fri. 8:30am-5pm, Sat. (for pickup only) 8-10am. **General Delivery ZIP Code:** 97138.
Area Code: 503.

Seaside lies 17 mi. south of Astoria and 8 mi. north of Cannon Beach along U.S. 101. The most direct route between Seaside and Portland is **U.S. 26** ("The Sunset Highway"), which runs into U.S. 101 just south of Seaside along Saddle Mountain State Park. The **Necanicum River** runs north-south through Seaside, approximately two blocks from the coastline, paralleled by U.S. 101 and Holladay Dr. to the east. All three are bisected by **Broadway,** running through the middle of town.

ACCOMMODATIONS AND CAMPING

The prices of motels are directly proportional to their proximity to the beach. Though there are seemingly thousands of motels, the cheapest (i.e. the ones farthest from the beach) hover near $40 per night (and they're cheaper during the off-season). Rooms are invariably full by 5pm; get ahead of the game by the Chamber of Commerce for availability listings. They won't reserve a room for you, but they'll offer advice. Reservations should be made at least a couple of days in advance.

Royale Motel, 521 Ave. A (738-9541), 1 block from the arcades of Broadway. Friendly staff and clean rooms with large, full-length windows which would be amazing if the view were of the ocean and not the parking lot. Cable TV and phones. Singles $45 (in winter $35). Doubles $50 (in winter $40).

Riverside Inn, 430 S. Holladay Dr. (738-8254), next to the Holladay. Cozy bedrooms, with bookshelves, fresh flowers, and raftered ceilings. All rooms have private bath and TV. If you ask nicely, the owners will serve you the included full breakfast on the riverfront deck. Rooms $45-80.

Mariner Motels 430 S. Holladay Dr. (738-8254), parallels U.S. 101 beside the Necanicum River toward the ocean. No phones, no pets, and no one under 21. Small, standard rooms. Free coffee (8:30-10am) in the office. Singles $41. Doubles $52.

Private campgrounds around town are for RVs only, and the closest state parks are **Fort Stevens,** 21 mi. north (see Astoria: Accommodations and also Near Astoria), and **Saddle Mountain** (861-1671), 14 mi. southeast of Seaside off U.S. 26 at Necanicum Junction. Saddle Mountain has ten primitive campsites ($10) with flush toilets, near the base of the Saddle Mountain hiking trail. Closer to Seaside is **Kloochle Creek,** about 300 yd. off U.S. 26, 6 mi. southeast of town. Pitch a tent at the base of the world's largest Sitka Spruce tree (9 sites, $6). Sleeping on the beach in Seaside is illegal, and police enforce this rule.

FOOD

Buck-fifty corn dogs, beachfront burgers, and fried starch are everywhere. Those who are repulsed by such cuisine will have to search hard and spend a few more pennies to satisfy their delicate palates.

Dooger's Seafood and Grill, 505 Broadway St. (738-3773). The best clam chowder in town ($1.50), unadulterated by flour or cornstarch thickeners. Lunch special of sea scallops, salad, and garlic toast ($7.50). Open daily 11am-10pm; Oct.-May daily 11am-9pm.

Miguel's Mexican and Seafood, 412 Broadway (738-0171). A tiny restaurant which fills up fast for $9-10 dinners. Lunch specials are a better budget bet—try the soft tacos ($4). Open Wed.-Thurs. 11:30am-9pm, Fri.-Sat. 11:30am-10pm, Sun. 12:30-8:30pm.

Bee Bop Burgers, 111 Broadway (738-3271). Classic 50s tunes rock around the clock while you enjoy your choice of Bopper ($2.50), Big Bopper ($3.75), or

Teeny Bopper ($1.25). Wash it down with a cherry, chocolate, vanilla, or lemon coke (75¢). Open daily 11am-10pm.

Harrison's Too, 35 Broadway (738-8919), at the Turnaround. A good place to fill up on coffee and doughnuts (25-85¢). The bread is excellent, but can double as birdfood if it sits around too long ($1.50 per loaf). Open Wed.-Mon. 7:30am-9pm.

SIGHTS AND SEASONAL EVENTS

The historical society, in conjunction with the city, publish the free *Walking Tour of Historic Seaside Promenade,* which describes the late-19th- and early-20th-century buildings along the 1-mi. public walkway.

Seaside revolves around **Broadway,** a garish strip of arcades, shops, and salt water taffy joints running the ½ mi. or so from Roosevelt (U.S. 101) to the beach. Indoor miniature golf, bumper cars, and video games are some of the "highlights." The **Turnaround** at the end of Broadway signals the "official" (read: arbitrary) end of the Lewis and Clark Trail. In 1986, the Turnaround underwent a facelift to add to the $1.3 million spent on street improvements in 1982-3, and a statue of Lewis and Clark was erected at the end of the Trail. Eight blocks south of the Turnaround lies the **Saltworks,** a replica of the cairn used by the Lewis and Clark expedition to produce salt for preserving food.

A recent addition to the downtown beachfront culture is located along the Necanicum River. **Quatat** (from the Clatsop word meaning "village by the sea") **Marine Park** spans four blocks between First Ave. and Broadway and boasts peaceful dock walkways and benches removed from the teeming sidewalks of Broadway. Quatat Park also offers water sports of sorts: **Monkey Business** operates off a dock in the park, offering bumper boats (just inner tubes with motors) at $3 for five minutes, and paddle boats at $7 per half- hour for two people.

Drop in and explore the wonders of the sea at the **Seaside Aquarium,** 200 N. Promenade (738-6211). Marvel at the 20-ray starfish and the Leopard Shark, or feed dead fish to the spirited Harbor Seals. (Open Mar.-Oct. Sun.-Thurs. 9am-6pm, Fri.-Sat. 9am-8pm; Nov.-Feb. Wed.-Sun. 9am-5pm. Admission $4.50, children $2.25.)

Seaside's beach front is expansive but crowded nonetheless. Lifeguards are on duty from Memorial Day to Labor Day (daily 10am-6pm), even though the water is always too cold for swimming. Don't even think about swimming on "red flag" days: the surf is too rough. For a quieter beach, head to **Gearhart,** approximately. 2 mi. north of downtown off U.S. 101. The beach has no lifeguard, and in the aftermath of a 1983 drowning accident, town officials have advised against swimming. You can, however, explore the long stretch of sand and dunes on foot or by car.

Saddle Mountain State Park, 14 mi. southeast of Seaside on U.S. 26, is named for the highest peak in the coastal range. A strenuous 6-mi., four-hour hike up to Saddle Mountain's 3283-ft. summit rewards the fit with an astounding view of the Nehalem Bay and the Pacific to the west and the Cascades to the north. (The summit trail is open March-Dec.) Farther east on U.S. 26 lies the **Jewell Meadows Wildlife Area,** a wintering habitat for Roosevelt elk. Parking spaces throughout the refuge allow you to get out and wander about with the elk, present mostly in fall and winter. Black-tailed deer often appear in the spring and summer, and a coyote may turn up any time of year. Take U.S. 26 to Jewell Junction, then head north on the unmarked state road for 9 mi. to Jewell. Turn west and travel 1½ mi. on Rte. 202 to the refuge area.

The **Seaside Beach Run, Promenade Walk,** and **Sand Games** are held in the third week of July. The 8-mi. beach race leaves from Seaside's Turnaround. The real heartbreaker comes at the end of August, when the **Hood to Coast Race** finishes in Seaside to the cheers of 25,000 spectators. Some 750 12-person teams run this 2-day relay race from Mt. Hood in 5-mi. shifts. The Chamber has more information.

■■■ CANNON BEACH

A rusty cannon from the shipwrecked schooner *Shark* washed ashore at Arch Cape, giving this town its name. Distinguished from Seaside by its romance and subtlety and from Astoria by its lack of historical significance, this popular weekend destination for wealthy Portlanders is singularly tasteful and expensive. Cannon Beach tries to blend inconspicuously into the grandeur of the northern Oregon coast, camouflaging its houses in thickets of trees and maintaining an unobtrusive beach front. Aesthetic sensibility rules here; art galleries, pricey craft stores, and theater groups outnumber fast-food joints and neon signs.

PRACTICAL INFORMATION AND ORIENTATION

Visitors Information: Cannon Beach Chamber of Commerce, 201 E. 2nd (436-2623), at Spruce St. P.O. Box 64, Cannon Beach 97110. Extremely helpful; maps. Open daily 11am-4pm; Labor Day-July Mon.-Sat. 11am-4pm.

Buses: North Coast Transit (738-7083). Buses leave downtown Cannon Beach (2 per day, 10am and 4:15pm) to: Seaside, Gearhart, Warrenton, and Astoria, with connections to Portland. North Coast Transit operates the pickup in Cannon Beach upon request only; call ahead to schedule ($2). During the summer, a free **shuttle** service (436-1581) operates within Cannon Beach Fri.-Tues. 10am-6pm. Call the Chamber of Commerce (above) for the schedule.

Bike Rental: Mike's Bike Shop, 248 N. Spruce St. (436-1266), around the corner from the Chamber of Commerce. Offers maps of routes that follow the old, untraveled logging roads. Mountain bikes ($6 per hr. and $20 per day), beach tricycles ($6 per 90 min). Credit card deposit required. Open daily 10am-6pm.

Lifeguard Service: 436-2345. 10am-8pm daily.

Weather: 861-2722.

Hospital: Seaside, 725 S. Wahanna St. (738-8463). **Cannon Beach** (436-1142), walk-in clinic at 171 Larch St. in Sandpiper Sq. Mon.-Fri. 9am-midnight.

Emergency: 911. **Police:** 163 Gower St. (436-2811). **Fire Dept.:** 436-2280.

Post Office: 155 N. Hemlock St. (436-2822). Open Mon.-Fri. 9am-5pm. **General Delivery ZIP Code:** 97110.

Area Code: 503.

Cannon Beach lies 7 mi. south of Seaside and 42 mi. north of Tillamook on U.S. 101, which does not run through the center of town. Watch for signs; Hemlock, Cannon Beach's main drag, connects with U.S. 101 in only four places. Cannon Beach is 79 mi. from Portland via U.S. 26.

ACCOMMODATIONS AND FOOD

Cannon Beach has a variety of pleasant motels, few of which are affordable; camping is the best option for the budget traveler. Many people ignore the "no camping" signs at the incredibly gorgeous **Ecola State Park** (436-2844). Like all Oregon state parks, Ecola has sites for hiker/bikers. To reach them, follow the long, paved road into the park and, heeding the signs, turn right into Indian Beach. A 2-mi. long, northerly trail leads to the camp. Less rugged camping is available at **Oswald West** (see Cannon Beach to Tillamook below), just south of town.

In keeping with the town's character, Cannon Beach cuisine is served in trendy and pricy cafes. Be especially wary of the several overpriced bakeries. **Mariner Market,** 139 N. Hemlock St. (436-2442), is the least expensive grocery store in town—which isn't saying much. You can have peanut butter ground while you wait ($2 per lb.). (Open Mon.-Thurs. 9am-10pm, Fri.-Sat. 9am-11pm, Sun. 9am-9pm.)

McBee Court (436-2569), S. Hemlock and Van Buren Rd., at old U.S. 101, ½ block from the ocean near Haystack Rock. A little south of the commercial center of town, but still on a noisy main street. Pleasant rooms 1 block from the beach. Rooms $37-75, some with kitchens. Separate 2-story townhouse with kitchen, fireplace, 1 double bed, 3 twins, and hide-a-bed $90.

Blue Gull Inn, 632 S. Hemlock St. (436-2714). Big, clean rooms decorated with expensive oil paintings of crashing surf. Set back from the street. TV with cable and laundry facilities. Singles and doubles from $45 in the peak summer season; in spring from $40, in winter from $32. Ask about the 2-for-1 special. Stay 2 or more nights in winter and get 50% off.

Lazy Susan Cafe, 126 N. Hemlock St. (436-2816). A gorgeous restaurant serving health food. Sandwiches $5-6; variety of omelettes $5-7.25. Make sure to order the waffle and fruit special ($5.26) when it's available. Open Mon. and Wed.-Sat. 7:30-11:30am and noon-2:30pm, Sun. 8am-2pm.

Osburn's Deli and Grocery, 240 N. Hemlock St. (436-2234). Hearty sandwiches to go ($4.25, available 11am-5pm). Open daily 8:30am-8:30pm; Labor Day-June 9am-7:30pm. **Osburn's Ice Creamery** (436-2578), next door, scoops cones for $1.25. The fresh strawberry shake ($3.45), available in season, is nectar of the gods. Open Sun.-Thurs. 11am-5pm, Fri.-Sat. 11am-7pm.

Dory's Launch Grill (436-1759), at S. Hemlock and Gower St., on the south end of town. Ignore the fast-food appearance of this place and dig into their hearty burgers ($2.50-3.25) and excellent clam chowder ($2.25). Open daily 11:30am-9pm.

Ecola Seafood Market and Restaurant, 123 S. Hemlock St. (436-9130). Fresh seafood at great prices: Calamari ($7), salmon ($8). Open Mon.-Thurs. 6am-7pm, Fri.-Sat. 6am-8pm.

SIGHTS AND ACTIVITIES

Rather than browse in the overpriced art galleries, you should spend a morning walking on the 7-mi. long stretch of beach. Marking yet another supposed end of the infamous Lewis and Clark Trail, **Ecola State Park** (436-2844) offers a spectacular vantage point of the hulking **Haystack Rock,** which is spotted with (and splattered by) gulls, puffins, barnacles, anemones, and the occasional sea lion. The Rock's tide pools teem with colorful sea life. Digging for mussels and clams is now prohibited and enforced by the **Rock Police.** In an effort to educate the public about the Rock's remarkable self-contained ecosystem, interpreters are present on weekends during especially low tides.

Beyond the Bay's 235-ft. centerpiece, the tenacious old **Tillamook Lighthouse** clings like a barnacle to a wave-swept rock. Construction of the lighthouse—begun in 1879—continued for years in Sisyphean fashion, as storms kept washing the foundations away. Decommissioned in 1957 because of damage caused by storm-tossed rocks, the now privately-owned lighthouse can be reached only by helicopter and only for the purpose of depositing ashes of the dead. From Ecola State Park, take the 12-mi. round-trip hike to **Tillamook Head,** from which you can sometimes glimpse migrating whales. In the fall, ask a knowledgeable local to point out chanterelle mushrooms along the path. The trail is open year-round.

The **Coaster Theater** (436-1242), at 124 Hemlock in Cannon Beach, stages theater productions, music concerts, ballet and modern dance concerts, comedy, and musical revues throughout the year. Write to Coaster Theater, P.O. Box 643, Cannon Beach 97110 for information (tickets $12-15).

Try to schedule your itinerary around Cannon Beach's **Sand Castle Competition.** In late spring, contestants pour in from hundreds of miles away and begin construction early in the morning, creating ornate sculptures from wet sand. By evening the high tide washes everything away, leaving photographs as the sole testimony to the staggering amount of creative energy expended during the day. Such photos are prominently displayed in the Chamber of Commerce.

During the first weekend in November, the community gathers for the **Cannon Beach Arts Festival.** Highlights include gallery shows, a theater production, the "Sunday lunch and brunch," and a choral concert. In December, locals celebrate the holiday season with a three-week festival, opening with an official lamplighting ceremony on the first Friday of the month. Contact the Chamber for more information.

■ **Cannon Beach to Tillamook**

Tillamook County has climbed through various stages of convalescence since the summer of 1933, when a Dante-esque conflagration reduced 500 sq. mi. of the world's finest timber to charcoal. Sixty years later, Tillamook State Forest has been nursed back to health. The sedate beaches and trees of Tillamook County accommodate spillover from the more popular resorts to the north and south. Small towns strung out along the coastline—Manzanita, Nehalem, Rockaway, and Garibaldi—are generally uncrowded and peaceful. Tourist information for the area is available at the visitors information bureau in Tillamook (see Tillamook: Practical Information) or the **Rockaway Beach Chamber of Commerce,** 405 S. U.S. 101 (355-8108; open Mon.-Fri. 9am-5pm, Sat. 10am-3pm).

Oswald West State Park, 10 mi. south of Cannon Beach, is a headland rain forest with huge spruce and cedar trees. The park is accessible only by foot on a ¼-mi. trail off U.S. 101. This doesn't quite qualify as "roughing it," as the State Parks Division provides wheelbarrows for transporting gear from the U.S. 101 parking area to the 36 primitive campsites near the beach (open mid-May to Oct.; sites $9). From the park, take the 4-mi. **Cape Falcon** hiking trail farther out toward the water, or just follow the path from the campground down to one of Oregon's few surfing beaches.

Five mi. south of Oswald West State Park, self-consciously quaint **Manzanita** reclines across a long expanse of uncrowded beach. The **San Dune Motel,** 428 Dorcas Lane (368-5163), just off Laneda St., the main drag through town, has inexpensive, pleasant rooms a mere 5 blocks from the shore (singles and doubles $40, in winter $30). The few restaurants in town are expensive.

Nehalem

Nehalem, a few mi. south of Manzanita, consists of little more than a handful of "made in Oregon" shops marshalled along U.S. 101. On the northern boundary of Nehalem, the **Bunk House** (368-6183), at 36315 U.S. 101, offers one of the Oregon Coast's best deals. The single rooms are pleasant and clean, and some have complete kitchens ($15-35). Stop in at the **Bayway Eatery,** 25870 7th St. (368-6495), for an excellent fish and chips meal ($4.50) or an enormous order of fries ($1.25). This well-worn diner is a favorite Nehalem hangout (open daily 6am-9pm). Three mi. away, south on U.S. 101 to Rte. 53, the **Nehalem Bay Winery,** 34965 Rte. 53 (368-5300), distributes samples of local specialties, including cranberry and blackberry wines, for a $2 tasting fee collected on the honor system (open daily 10am-5pm).

Twenty mi. south of Cannon Beach, just north of Nehalem, **Nehalem Bay State Park** (368-5154 or 368-5943) offers 291 sites with electricity ($15), including some hiker/biker sites ($2) and 17 horse campsites with individual corrals for your steed ($9). Facilities include hot showers, a boat launch, and an airport.

Wheeler

If you prefer indoor accommodations, stop at the newly-renovated **Wheeler Fishing Lodge,** 580 Marine Dr. (368-5858). This motel sports a variety of rooms ranging from $45-105; the premium one looks out on the water and has a jacuzzi. All the rooms have a refreshing, colonial atmosphere, and the owner is a gracious host open to haggling. Free boat mooring is available for guests at the new boat dock, which is also a terrific spot for watching the sunset. The motel lies in the quiet town of Wheeler, whose quirky small-town levity has given way to a more down-to-business attitude, as several of the downtown shops have recently changed hands and been refurbished. **Antiques and Special Occasions,** 489 Nehalem Blvd. (368-3474), across the street from the lodge, houses an unusual collection gathered from the coast and around the world. The **Bayfront Bakery and Deli,** 468 Nehalem Blvd. (368-6599), serves lunch sandwiches ($3.25) and baked goods right out of the oven (open Tues.-Sat. 7:30am-4:30pm). Since seafood along the Coast can be pricey, why not catch your own dinner? **Wheeler Marina,** 278 Marine Dr. (368-5788) rents three hours in a boat ($25;$5 per additional hr.), crab rings ($2), and bait ($1)—all you need to net a crab feast. Crabs caught in Oregon must measure at least 5¾ in. across the shell. Though tempting, a smaller crab carries an $85 price tag.

Garibaldi

If imitation is indeed the sincerest form of flattery, then Hollywood should feel honored by the garishly illuminated "G" on the hillside of Garibaldi, roughly 6 mi. south of Rockaway. An unlikely California wannabe, the town is named after Guiseppi Garibaldi who, it seems, was a fisherman before he united Italy in the 1870s. A highly developed marina juts into the bay here, luring boaters but minimizing ocean and beach access for landlubbers. There are a few good places to eat in town. The **Bayfront Bakery and Deli,** 302 Garibaldi (322-3787), on U.S. 101, has a more extensive menu than its Wheeler branch, including barbecued ribs, pizza, and salads. The pies and baked goods can't be beat (open Tues.-Sun. 4:30am-5:30pm). The **Old Mill Restaurant** (322-0222), 3rd and Americana St. overlooks the boats and water from the Old Mill Marina. Turn west off U.S. 101 over the railroad tracks and follow the signs to the left. Try the daily lunch special ($5), a bowl of clam chowder ($3.50), or a razor clam dinner ($13). (Open daily 8am-10pm.)

■■■ TILLAMOOK

Oregon's finest cheeses are cultured on the eastern shore of Tillamook Bay, where cow pastures (and the accompanying aroma) predominate. Some visitors enjoy a brief jaunt through the surrounding bucolic countryside, but most just hanker for a hunk of cheese.

PRACTICAL INFORMATION AND ORIENTATION

Visitors Information: Tillamook County Chamber of Commerce, 3705 U.S. 101 N. (842-7525), next to the Tillamook Cheese Factory. Open Mon.-Fri. 9am-5pm, Sat. 10am-4:30pm, Sun. 10am-2pm. **Parks and Recreation:** 322-3477. Mon.-Fri. 9am-5pm.

Taxi: Tillamook Taxi, 842-4567. 24 hr.

Senior Citizens' Information: 842-7988. Open daily 8am-5pm.

Tillamook Women's Crisis Center: 842-9486. 24 hr.

Hospital: Tillamook County General Hospital, 1000 3rd St. (842-4444).

Emergency: 911. **Police:** 842-2522, in City Hall. **Fire:** 2310 4th St. (842-7587). **County Sheriff:** 201 Laurel St. (842-2561).

Post Office: 2200 1st St. (842-4711). Open Mon.-Fri. 8:30am-5pm. **General Delivery ZIP Code:** 97191.

Area Code: 503.

Tillamook lies 49 mi. south of Seaside and 44 mi. north of Lincoln City on U.S. 101. The most direct route from Portland is U.S. 26 to Rte. 6 (74 mi.).

ACCOMMODATIONS and CAMPING

Expect inflated lodging prices in high (summer) season.

Tillamook Inn, 1810 U.S. 101 N. (842-4413), between the center of town and the Tillamook Cheese Factory. Generic motel rooms; the highway noise will lull you to sleep. Free coffee. Rates may be lower in the off-season. Senior citizen 10% discount. Singles $36. Doubles $45.

MarClair Inn, 11 Main Ave. (842-7571). Convenient, downtown location. Big, tastefully decorated rooms, pool, and jacuzzi are worth the price. 10% senior citizen discount. Singles $52, off-season $40. Doubles $58, off-season $46.

Kilchis County Park (842-6694), 8 mi. northeast of Tillamook, along Kilchis River Rd. 40 primitive sites near the river and the county ball field. Tentsites $10. Hiker/biker $2.

Cape Lookout State Park, 13000 Whiskey Creek Rd. (842-4981). Hot showers, flush toilets. 53 full hookups, 193 tentsites. Tent $14; hookup $16. Hiker/biker sites $2. Reservations required. (See Tillamook to Lincoln City for more information about the park.)

FOOD

La Casa Medello, 1160 U.S. 101 (842-5768), down the street from El Rancho Motel. Tries hard to stay true to its motif, but what do you expect in Cheesetown, USA? Mild Mexican food prepared to order. Lunch specials $4-5. Massive 12-in. tacos ($6), burritos ($5). Dinners, $6-9, come with rice, beans, and chips. Extremely busy. Open Tues.-Thurs. 11am-9pm, Fri.-Sun. 11am-10pm.

Hadley House, 2203 3rd St. (842-2101), across from the courthouse. More-than-generous helpings of sea (and cheese) products, as well as American standbys. Specials include the baked fish almondine ($10), and the teriyaki burger ($4.50). Sandwiches $4-6. Full dinner $8-15. "Lite eaters" menu $4-6. Open Sun.-Thurs. 11am-9pm, Fri. 11am-10pm., Sat. 4-10pm. Winter closings 1 hr. earlier.

Tillamook Cheese Factory, 4175 U.S. 101 N. (842-4481). Self-guided tours will let you watch from overhead as cheese is cut, weighed, and packaged. Cheap breakfasts served 8-11am. Deli sandwiches $2-5. Homemade ice cream includes exotic flavors such as brown cow, Irish cream fudge, and French silk ($1.25). Plenty o' cheese for sale. Open daily 8am-8pm; Sept. to mid-June 8am-6pm.

SIGHTS AND ACTIVITIES

In Native American parlance, Tillamook means "land of many waters." Whether Tilllamook's original inhabitants were referring to the frequent downpours or not remains a mystery. In any case, the place can be very wet, which may explain why so many of Tillamook's tourist attractions are located indoors. The most visited of these is undoubtedly the **Tillamook Cheese Factory** (see Food), probably for the ice-cream rather than the tour. The place is usually packed in summer. Somewhat less crowded is the **Blue Heron French Cheese Factory,** 2001 Blue Heron Dr. (842-8281), 1 mi. south of the Tillamook factory on the east side of U.S. 101. The "factory" has stopped making cheese, but the sales room is much more generous with samples than at Tillamook (open 8am-8pm, in winter 9am-6pm).

West of the highway—in downtown Tillamook—the **Tillamook County Pioneer Museum,** 2106 2nd St. (842-4553), features all manner of household and industrial goods from the pioneer era. The museum's prized treasure, however, is an impressive collection (considered the best in the state) of animals preserved by taxidermist Alex Walker. (Open Mon.-Sat. 8am-5pm, Sun. noon-5pm; Oct.-March Tues.-Sat. 8am-5pm, Sun. noon-5pm. Admission $1, ages 12-17 50¢, families $5, under 12 free.)

Stop and stare at the gargantuan **Blimp Hangars,** located 2 mi. south of Tillamook at the Port of Tillamook Bay Industrial Park. These behemoths were used during World War II to house a fleet of U.S. Naval blimps. Considered the largest standing wooden structures in the world, the buildings each cover more than 7 acres (enough to hold 6 football fields). If the doors are open, you may see one of the zeppelins flying. (Open daily 10am-6pm, Nov.-mid-May 10am-4pm. Admission $2, ages 6-12 $1.) Five mi. south of the Hangars off U.S. 101, one can admire the sublime **Munson Creek Falls** which, dropping 266 ft. over spectacularly rugged cliffs, ranks as the highest waterfall in the Coast Range. A 1½-mi. road leads to a parking lot from which two trails are accessible. The lower trail is ¼ mi. long and ends at the base of the falls. The upper trail is a bit longer (½ mi.) and a bit more difficult. Passing over rotting wooden catwalks and obstructed by the twisted trunks of uprooted trees, its end rewards with a close view of the wispy, white foam slipping into the canyon.

■ Tillamook to Lincoln City

Between Tillamook and Lincoln City, U.S. 101 wanders eastward into wooded land, losing sight of the coast. Instead of staying on the highway, consider taking the **Three Capes Loop,** a 35-mi. circle to the west that connects a trio of spectacular promontories—Cape Meares, Cape Lookout, and Cape Kiwanda State Parks. The beaches are secluded, and the scenery makes the uncrowded drive worthwhile. Cyclists should beware of the narrow twists and poor condition of the roads.

Cape Meares, at the tip of the promontory jutting out from Tillamook, is home to the **Octopus Tree,** a gnarled Sitka spruce with several trunks. The **Cape Meares Lighthouse,** built in 1890, also stands in the park and now operates as an illuminating on-site interpretive center. Climb to the top for sweeping views and a peek at the original lens of the big light (open May-Sept. daily 11am-5pm; free).

From Cape Meares one can make out the three lonely **Arch Rocks** in the distance. Jutting out of the water like the humps of a ghastly sea monster, the Arch Rocks are a federal refuge for sea lions and birds. You can gain a better view of the sea lions a bit farther south, towards **Netarts Bay.**

From here, continue 12 mi. southwest to **Cape Lookout,** which has trails and facilities for people with disabilities (842-4981; see Tillamook: Accommodations). South of Cape Lookout, the loop undulates through sand dunes, where the sound of the rushing wind competes with the intermittent roar of all-terrain vehicles.

Cape Kiwanda, the third promontory on the loop, is for day-use only (open 8am-dusk). On sunny, windy days, hang gliders gather to test their skill at negotiating the wave-carved sandstone cliffs. The sheltered cape also draws skin divers, and beachcombers come to sink their toes into the dunes. A state park trail overlooks the top of the cape before reaching the ocean. On the cape, just barely north of Pacific City, massive rock outcroppings in a small bay mark the launching pad of the flat-bottomed **Dory Fleet,** one of the few fishing fleets in the world that launches beachside, directly onto the surf. If you bring your own fishing gear down to the cape most mornings around 5am, you can probably convince someone to take you on board; the fee will nearly always be lower than that of a commercial outfitter.

Pacific City, a delightful town missed by most travelers on U.S. 101, is home to the other **Haystack Rock,** just as impressive as its sibling to the north. The mammoth rock has a handle jutting out from its northern edge, suggesting that some prehistoric giant left it here when he got tired carrying it. The **Chamber of Commerce** (965-6161) does not operate a regular office but does have a complete information sign and map posted at 34960 Brooten Rd., in the middle of nowhere.

The **Anchorage Motel,** 6585 Pacific Ave. (965-6773) offers large, pleasant singles for $35 and doubles for $50. Rooms with kitchens start at $51. The undisputed king of nearby Gustation Hill is the **Riverhouse Restaurant,** 34450 Brooten Rd. (965-6722), overlooking the Nestucca River. Chowder and piled-high sandwiches cost $5-7. (Open Mon.-Thurs. 11am-9pm, Fri. 11am-10pm, Sat. 11am-11pm).

Back on U.S. 101 about 8 mi. south, **Neskowin** appears to be little more than a motel by the side of the road. Squeezed into this parking lot complex, however, is the **Deli at Neskowin,** 4505 Salem Ave. (392-3838), a refuge for homesick New Yorkers. Pastrami sandwiches go for $3.50 (open Sun.-Thurs. 8am-9pm, Fri.-Sat. 8am-10pm). Driving south of Neskowin on U.S. 101, be on the lookout for **Siuslaw National Forest.** An 11-mi. road leaves U.S. 101 and passes by huge old trees dripping with moss (this is a northern rain forest). The **Neskowin Creek Campground** (392-3131) lies 5½ mi. beyond Neskowin, keeping 12 primitive tentsites (outhouse only) available for free camping.

U.S. 101 crosses Rte. 18 at **Otis** (about 2 mi. east on Rte. 18). The **Otis Cafe** (994-2813) serves excellent home-style strawberry-rhubarb pie for $1.75 a slice. The cafe is often crowded; your patience will be rewarded with sandwiches on freshly baked bread ($3.10-5) and breakfast specials ($2.50-6). (Open Mon.-Wed. 7am-3pm, Thurs.-Sat. 7am-9pm, Sun. 8am-9pm.)

A dozen wineries line Rte. 18 on the way to Portland. A 9-mi. detour via Rte. 99 W. and Rte. 47 will take you to **Carlton,** home of the **Chateau Benoit Winery,** Mineral Springs Rd. (864-2991 or 864-3666). From Rte. 47 in Carlton, take Road 204 1.3 mi. east, then go 2½ mi. south on Mineral Springs. The winery specializes in Pinot Noir, Sparkling Brut, and Riesling (tasting hours daily 10am-5pm; free).

■■■ LINCOLN CITY

Lincoln City is actually five towns incorporated into one, all conspiring to make you crawl along at 30 mi. per hour past a 7-mi. strip of motels, gas stations, and tourist traps. Bicyclists will find Lincoln City hellish, and hikers should cut 3 blocks west to the seashore. Although it is perhaps the most commercialized town on the Oregon coast (boasting more than 1000 ocean-front motel rooms), Lincoln City is a convenient base from which to explore nearby capes, beaches, and waterways.

PRACTICAL INFORMATION

Visitors Information: Lincoln City Visitor and Convention Bureau, 801 SW U.S. 101 #1 (800-452-2151 or 994-8378). Offers brochures covering everything to do in Lincoln City. Open daily 8am-5pm. **Parks and Recreation Dept.,** P.O. Box 50 (994-2131).

Greyhound, 316 SE U.S. 101 (994-9833), behind the bowling alley. To: Portland (2 per day, $11) and Newport (2 per day, $4.75). A stop only; no depot.

Taxi: 996-2003. 24 hr.

Car Rental: Robben-Rent-A-Car, 3232 NE U.S. 101 (994-5530). $22 per day plus 15¢ per mi. Must be 21 with major credit card.

Laundry: Coin Laundry, 2164 NE U.S. 101. Wash 1$, 10-min. dry 25¢. Open daily 9am-10pm.

Swimming and Showers: Community Pool, 994-5208. Pool $1.75, showers 75¢.

Senior Citizen Center: 2150 NE Oar Place (994-2722 or 994-2131).

Hospital: N. Lincoln Hospital, 3043 NE Park Dr. (994-3661).

Emergency: 911. **Police:** 1503 E. Devils Lake Rd. (994-3636). **Fire:** 1939 NW 25th St. (994-3100). **Coast Guard:** In Depoe Bay (765-2123).

Post Office: (994-2148), on E. Devil's Lake Rd. 2 blocks east of U.S. 101. Open Mon.-Fri. 8:30am-5pm. **General Delivery ZIP Code:** 97367.

Area Code: 503.

ACCOMMODATIONS AND CAMPING

Lincoln City's inexpensive motels cozy up to noisy U.S. 101. Camping is available within walking distance of Lincoln City, but arrive as early as possible—sites tend to fill by mid-afternoon during the summer.

Sea Echo Motel, 3510 NE U.S. 101 (994-2575). Standard rooms with cable TV, phones, and partial ocean view. Singles and doubles $30.

Bel-Aire Motel, 2945 NW U.S. 101 (994-2984), at the north end of town. The decrepit exterior masks large, pleasant rooms. Singles $25. Doubles $30.

City Center Motel, 1014 NE U.S. 101 (994-2612). Rooms are clean with thin walls and some have kitchens. Cable TV and phones. Singles $29. Doubles $30. Prices drop slightly late Oct.-Memorial Day.

Budget Inn, 1713 NW 21st St. (994-5281). Right on the highway, but first-floor rooms are protected from the noise by a scenic earthen embankment; third-floor rooms have balconies. Free coffee. Singles $26, on weekends $32. Doubles $36, on weekends $43. Rates lower in winter.

Devil's Lake State Park, 1452 NE 6th St., Lincoln City 97367 (994-2002). A clearly-marked turn east off U.S. 101 leads to 100 closely spaced sites which fill up quickly in summer. Call before 4pm. Some people swim in the lake, but most choose to avoid its muddy bottom by floating on the surface. Try to avoid campsites too close to the lake or risk being eaten by mosquitoes. Boat moorings available for $5. Sites $14, RVs $16, hiker/biker camp $2. Reservations recommended.

FOOD

Head down to Depoe Bay or Newport for good seafood. The **Safeway** and **Thriftway** markets, both on U.S. 101, are open 24 hr.

Foon Hing Yuen, Inc., 3138 SE U.S. 101 (996-3831). Generous portions of good Chinese food. Lunches can be had for $3.50; the specials will run you $6-9.

Despite the name, the *pork chow yuk* ($6.50) is delicious. This is one of few restaurants in town that doesn't close before 10pm. Take-out available. Bar and restaurant open Sun.-Thurs. noon-midnight, Fri.-Sat. noon-2am.

Lighthouse Brew Pub, 4157 N Highway (994-7238), in Lighthouse Sq. at the north end of town. 240 varieties of beer line the walls ($2.40-2.90), 11 of which are brewed on the premises. Sandwiches and burgers $4-5. You must be 21 to eat (or drink) here. Ask about tours of the brewery (Capt. Neon's Fermentation Chamber). Open daily 11am-1:30am, winter daily 11am-11pm.

Kyllo's, 1110 NW First Ct. (994-3179), at U.S. 101. Dinners are expensive but the seafood is good—try the steamer clams in garlic and beer ($9)—and the view overlooking the beach and ocean is even better. Open daily 11am-9pm.

Williams' Colonial Bakery, 1734 NE U.S. 101 (994-5919). Coffee (35¢), apple fritters (35¢), glazed doughnuts (50¢). Open daily 5am-6pm.

SIGHTS AND ACTIVITIES

Lincoln City's rather dubious claim to fame is the **D.** All public routes to the beach cross the D, and streets in Lincoln City are numbered by it. Trumpeted as "the world's shortest river," the D is a 100- to 300-yd. overflow from Devil's Lake. Thousands of tourists each year pull over, snap a picture, and zoom off faster than you can say, "Who gives a flying. . ."

Drive or cycle along **East Devil's Lake Road,** which leads around the lake to quiet, clearly marked fishing and picnic sites. **Road's End Park,** a couple of mi. past the Lighthouse Square turn-off at the north end of town, features yet another of Oregon's beautiful beaches.

Film buffs should know that *Sometimes a Great Notion*—based on the Ken Kesey novel—was filmed in Lincoln City. The mock old house that was used as the set can be seen by turning east off U.S. 101 onto the Siletz River Hwy. You can enjoy some of Oregon's fine wines, coffee, and food at **Chateau Benoit,** Suite D130 in the Factory Stores (996-3981) in Lincoln City.

One of only three sanctioned road races in Oregon and Washington, the **Soap Box Derby** zooms through Lincoln City every Father's Day weekend. Lincoln City also boasts the self-bestowed moniker "Kite Capital of the World." The D River beach is overrun with kite flyers during the **International Fall Festival** in the last week of September. Call the Chamber for information (see Practical Information).

■ Lincoln City to Newport

Between Lincoln City and Newport, the state park system really gets down to business. There are rest stops and beach access parking lots every few miles, one with overnight camping. The free **North Creek Campground,** a small area within the Siuslaw National Forest with no drinking water, is off County Rte. 229 on Forest Service Rte. 19.

A few mi. south on U.S. 101, diminutive **Depoe Bay** undercuts Portland's "smallest park" and Lincoln City's "smallest river" with its claim to the smallest navigable harbor in the world. While most motels charge at least $40 for a room, the **Ocean West Motel** (765-2789), just north of the harbor's main strip, offers clean singles for $27 and doubles for $30. Stop for lunch at the **Chowder Bowl** (765-2300), on U.S. 101, an off-shoot of the famous Newport restaurant. The excellent chowder ($2.50) is a meal in itself (open daily 11am-9pm).

Watching the sea-life, rather than just eating it, is also popular in Depoe Bay. The best **gray whale viewing points** in the "whale watching capital of the Oregon coast" are along the seawall in town, at the **Depoe Bay State Park Wayside,** and at the **Observatory Lookout,** 4½ mi. south of town. Go out early in the morning on a cloudy, calm day between December and May for the best chance of spotting the huge grays. Several outfitters charter fishing trips from Depoe Bay. **Deep Sea Trollers** (765-2248) offers five-hour trips for $38 per person (trips leave at 6 and 11am). **Depoe Bay Sportfishing and Charters,** on U.S. 101 at the south end of the Depoe

Bay Bridge (765-2222), also heads out on five-hour trips for $40 per person. Reservations are always necessary for charter trips.

Just south of Depoe Bay, take a detour from U.S. 101 to the famous **Otter Crest Loop,** a twisting 4-mi. drive high above the shore which affords spectacular vistas at every bend. A lookout over **Cape Foulweather** has telescopes (25¢) for spotting sea lions on the rocks below. Captain James Cook first struck the North American mainland here in 1778; greeted with gale-force winds, he felt entirely justified in his choice of appellation. Wind speeds at this 500-ft. elevation still often reach 100mph. The incredible **Devil's Punchbowl** is also on the loop. This collapsed seaside cave is best viewed at high tide, when the heavy waves form a frothing cauldron beneath your feet.

Just south of the Punchbowl, the road returns to U.S. 101 and brings eager campers to the much-trafficked **Beverly Beach State Park,** a year-round reservation campground in gorgeous, rugged terrain. Swimming in the crashing surf is permitted, but the cold water and frequent riptides should discourage even the most intrepid swimmers. The views from the hiking trails will satisfy most visitors anyway. Hot showers and facilities for people with disabilities are available, as well as a few hiker/biker spots (sites $11, hookups $13). For reservations during the summer, call 265-9278 or write 198 NE 123rd St., Newport 97365.

New Age nimrods shouldn't miss **Agate Beach Wayside,** off U.S. 101 just north of Newport, an excellent place—as is the entire Newport area—to hunt for semi-precious stones. The Newport Chamber of Commerce (see Newport: Practical Information) puts out a free pamphlet enticingly entitled *Agates: Their Formation and How to Hunt for Them.* The brochure recommends October through May as the prime hunting months, although the stones are, of course, here year-round.

Just north of Agate Beach is the **Yaquina Head Lighthouse,** a photogenic coastal landmark. Although climbing to the top of the lighthouse is not permitted, large decks provide good views of the offshore rocks that are home to one of the few sea bird colonies close to the U.S. mainland. Western gulls, tufted puffins, and cormorants, among others, can be seen in fine detail. The low, flat rock to the south of the headland is home to harbor seals, sea lions, and many small pebbles. Grey whales are sometimes spotted in the waters beyond.

■ ■ ■ NEWPORT

Part tourist mill, part fishing village, and part logging town, Newport is little different from most of the towns that line U.S. 101. The recently renovated waterfront area provides a rare escape from the malls and gas stations, offering the sights and smells of a classic seaport with kitschy shops and bizarre tourist attractions to boot. Originally a turn-of-the-century sea town where wealthy Portlanders could go to escape the mosquitoes, Newport has subtly matured into a late 20th-century sea town where wealthy Portlanders can go to escape the mosquitoes.

PRACTICAL INFORMATION

Visitors Information: Chamber of Commerce, 555 SW Coast Hwy. (265-8801 or 800-262-7844). Friendly office with an abundance of free maps and guides to Newport and surrounding areas. Open Mon.-Fri. 8:30am-5pm, Sat.-Sun. 10am-4pm; Nov.-Jan. Mon.-Fri. 8:30am-5pm.

Newport Parks and Recreation Office, 169 SW Coast Hwy. (265-7783). Open Mon.-Fri. 8am-noon and 1-5pm.

Greyhound, 956 SW 10th St. (265-2253). To Portland (3 per day, $17.25) and San Francisco (4 per day, $79). Open Mon.-Fri. 8am-5pm, Sat. 8am-noon.

Taxi: Yaquina Cab Company, 265-9552. 24 hr.

Car Rental: Surfside Motors, 27 S. Coast Hwy. (265-6686). From $27 per day with 50 free mi., 20¢ per extra mi. Open Mon.-Fri. 8:30am-6pm, Sat. 9am-5pm.

Newport Public Library, 35 NW Nye St. (265-2153). Open Mon.-Thurs. 10am-8pm, Fri. 10am-6pm, Sat. 1-6pm, Sun. 1-4pm.

Laundry: Eileen's Coin Laundry, 1078 N. Coast Hwy. (265-5474). Open Mon.-Sat. 8am-9pm.
Weather: 265-5511.
Hospital: Pacific Communities Hospital, 930 SW Abbey (265-2244).
Emergency: 911. **Police:** 265-5331. **Fire:** 265-9461.
Post Office: 310 SW 2nd St. (265-5542). Open Mon.-Fri. 8:30am-5pm. **General Delivery ZIP Code:** 97365.
Area Code: 503.

ACCOMMODATIONS AND CAMPING

The strip along U.S. 101 provides plenty of affordable motels, with predictably noisy consequences. **Bed and breakfasts** are a tempting alternative, but the prices (most above $50) are often prohibitive. The visitors center provides complete listings.

Brown Squirrel Newport Hostel, 44 SW Brook St. (265-3729). Just a block from the beach, this homey hostel with kitchen and laundry facilities is by far Newport's most accommodating accommodation. Check out 11am. $10.

Newport Bay Motel, 1823 N. Coast Highway (265-4533). Clean, inexpensive rooms with cable TV. Chat with the manager; he has a Ph.D. in Classics and in his spare time translates *Calvin and Hobbes* comic strips into Latin. As a result of his years in the Ivory Tower, he takes pity on students and may give them a bit of a discount. Singles from $35, doubles from $43. Senior citizen discount $2.

Sands Motor Lodge, 206 N. Coast Hwy. (265-5321). Bright, airy rooms with cable TV and telephone. Laundry and sauna access. Singles $48, in winter $36. Doubles $58, in winter $42. Lower prices during the week. 10% senior citizen discount.

Summerwind Budget Motel, 728 N. Coast Hwy. (265-8076). Small rooms with TV, some with kitchenettes. Singles $24. Doubles $28. In winter $16 and $20.

Finding a place to pitch your tent in or around Newport can prove tricky. The few private campgrounds are overrun by RVs, and campground owners have established facilities geared exclusively to these monstrosities. Campers should escape to the many state campgrounds along U.S. 101, where sites average $14 and hookups go for $16. **South Beach State Park,** 5580 S. Coast Hwy., South Beach 97366 (867-4715), 2 mi. south of town, has 254 full hookup sites ($12) and showers. Just north of town lies the best option, **Beverly Beach State Park,** 198 N. 123rd St., Newport (265-9278), which has 152 sites specifically for tents ($14).

FOOD

Don Petrie's Italian Food Company, 613 NW 3rd (265-3663). Incredible lasagna and vegetarian manicotti (each $8.50 a la carte) fit for a pre-SlimFast Tommy LaSorda include all the cheesy garlic bread you care to eat. The spinach fettuccine ($9.25) is equally good. Open for dinner Sun.-Thurs. 4:30-9pm, Fri.-Sat. 4:30-9:30pm. Lunch served Mon.-Fri. 11:30am-2pm.

The Whale's Tale, 452 SW Bay Blvd. (265-8660), on the bayfront at Fall St. This famous place is great fun—carved out of driftwood and decorated with local art and mismatched old wooden chairs and tables. For breakfast, try the internationally celebrated Eggs Newport: Oregon shrimp and 2 poached eggs on an English muffin, topped with Bearnaise sauce, plus home fries ($7). The oft-praised poppy seed pancakes ($3.75) are often praised as well. Dinners can be expensive (*cioppino* $13), but good sandwiches start at $4.25 and come with soup. Live local music on Sat.-Sun. nights. Open Mon.-Fri. 8am-9pm, Sat.-Sun. 9am-10pm.

The Chowder Bowl, 728 NW Beach Dr. (265-7477), at Nye Beach. Renowned bowls of chowder ($2.75). Huge shrimp, clam, or fish basket with fries and garlic bread ($9.75). Open daily 11am-9pm; Labor Day-July 4 Mon.-Thurs. 11am-9pm, Fri.-Sat. 11am-9pm.

Cosmos Cafe and Gallery, 704 NW Beach Dr. (265-7511). Dine on a black bean burrito ($4.80) while surrounded by a galaxy of moon-, sun-, and star-decorated chairs and tables. Fill up on the astronomically large desert selection. Open Mon.-Sat. 11am-10pm.

SIGHTS AND SEASONAL EVENTS

Of the legions of West Coast pioneer museums, Newport's **Lincoln County Historical Society's Burrows House and Log Cabin,** 545 SW 9th (265-7509), stands apart. The exhibits *are* actually unusual, especially the room devoted to Newport Bay's shipwrecks (open Tues.-Sun. 10am-5pm; Sept.-May Tues.-Sun. 11am-4pm; free).

Beside the bay, two tourist traps lie within 100 yd. of one another at 250 SW Bay Blvd. The **Wax Works Museum** crams as many lifelike figures as it can into an already-cramped space. The **Undersea Gardens** across the street are home to 5000 marine specimens, including Armstrong the Giant Octopus. (Each museum $5.25, senior citizens $4.75, children $3.25. Each open daily 10am-7pm; in winter, 10am-5pm. Call 265-2206 for more information.)

Popular festivals in Newport include the **Newport Seafood and Wine Festival** on the last full weekend in February, showcasing Oregon wines, food, music, and crafts (with a focus on the wine and food); and **Newport Loyalty Days and Sea Fair Festival,** the first weekend in May, with rides, parades, fried chicken, and sailboat races. In mid-October, the **Microbrew Festival** features the tiniest beers in the Northwest. Be sure to try a Widmer Hekewiezen. Contact the Newport Chamber of Commerce (see Practical Information) for more information on all seasonal events.

OUTDOORS AND THE COAST

Yaquina Bay State Park, at the southwest end of town, on the north side of the bay, is home to the **Yaquina Bay Lighthouse.** The short-lit lighthouse (in operation from 1871-1874) presides over the fleets of fishing boats that cruise in and out of the bay daily. It's also haunted (gasp!). The legend is verified in a 20-minute video screened within the lighthouse; the video also features footage of the Coast Guard's dramatic rescue of the crew of the *Blue Magpie* in 1983. The crew was salvaged, but not the ship, a portion of which can be seen from the lighthouse on clear days (open daily noon-5pm; free).

The **Mark O. Hatfield Marine Science Center** (867-0100), on the same side of the bridge on Marine Science Dr., is the hub of Oregon State University's coastal research. The Center's museum explains its research and displays Pacific Northwest marine animals in their natural environments. Beginning in the third week of June, the center (named after Oregon's eminent senior U.S. senator) offers a free educational program called Seataugua, in which marine biologists give talks, show films, and lead nature walks. Call the center (867-0100 ext. 226) for a complete schedule (open daily 10am-6pm; Nov.-June 14 10am-4pm; free).

Down the street from the Science Center, the brand-new **Oregon Coast Aquarium,** 2820 SE Ferry Slip Rd. (867-3474), features 2½ acres of wild, wet indoor and outdoor exhibits. The museum serves as a living classroom, teaching visitors about the wondrous wildlife of the Oregon Coast. Stroll through the galleries, where kelp sways, waves crash, and anemones "stick" to your hands. Wander through the aviary, home of the tufted puffin, or peer into the sea otter tank through the underwater windows. The whale theater shows a 10-minute video on those hip, breezy denizens of the deep, the gray whales. ($7, senior citizens and ages 13-18 $5, 12 and under $3. Open daily 9am-6pm, in winter daily 10am-4:30pm.)

If you have the time and money, try **salmon-fishing** or **bottom-fishing** with one of Newport's charter companies. **Newport Tradewinds,** 653 SW Bay Blvd. (265-2101, 24 hr.), offers an assortment of year-round trips (2½-hr. crabbing run, $20; 9- to 12-hr. fishing trips, $9 per hr.). Whale-watching trips ($27) last only three hours and leave daily at 6, 11:30am, and 2:30pm. The local bird watchers club, **Yaquina Birders and Naturalists** (265-2965), welcomes guests to its free field trips (usually on the 3rd weekend of each month).

Some of the sheltered coves in the area, especially those to the north around Depoe Bay, are excellent for **scuba diving.** Rent equipment and get tips from **Newport Water Sports,** S. Jetty Rd., South Beach (867-3742), at the south end of the bridge. (Open daily Mon.-Thurs. 9am-6pm, Fri. 8am-6pm, Sat.-Sun. 8am-8pm. Top-of-the-line gear rental about $25 during the week, $30 on weekends.)

■ Newport to Reedsport

Between Newport and Reedsport, U.S. 101 is dotted with beautiful campgrounds, day-use beaches, and beachside attractions. The largest sea caves on the coast, **Sea Lion Caves,** 91560 U.S. 101 (547-3111), are home to a sizeable colony of sea lions year-round. Viewpoints from within the caves and above ground allow visitors to observe the lions feeding and being beastly during the breeding fights of June and July (wheelchair access; open daily 9am-dusk; $5.50, children $3.50). One mi. north of the caves lies **Devil's Elbow.** The day-use beach requires a $3 parking permit; get your money's worth by walking from the lot up to an amazing and uncrowded viewpoint on the cliffs of the **Heceta Head Lighthouse.** Also along this stretch are the best alternatives to the more expensive and RV-filled campgrounds. **Rock Creek State Park** and **Cape Perpetua** both offer $8 tentsites (flush toilets, drinking water). The **Silver Sands Motel,** 1449 U.S. 101 North (997-3459), offers comfortable rooms at reasonable (for this area) prices with cable TV, phones, and a pool (rooms for 1 or 2 people $42).

The **New Morning Coffeehouse** (547-3848), at 4th and U.S. 101 in Yachats, is a great place for coffee. Try one of the sweet pastries (scones $1.25) and an espresso ($1) in a relaxed atmosphere with the Back Porch Gallery right next door (open daily 9am-4pm). For more information on this area, contact Florence's **visitors information center,** 270 U.S. 101 (997-3128), at the south end of town (open daily 9am-5pm).

■■■ REEDSPORT AND THE DUNES

For 50 mi. between Florence and Coos Bay, the beach widens to form the **Oregon Dunes National Recreation Area.** Shifting hills of sand rise to 500 ft. and extend up to 3 mi. inland (often to the shoulder of U.S. 101), clogging mountain streams and forming numerous small lakes. Hiking trails wind around the lakes, through the coastal forests, and up to the dunes themselves. In many places, no grasses or shrubs grow, and the vista holds only bare sand and sky (although other places feel more like the Gator Bowl parking lot than the Gobi Desert). Campgrounds fill up early with dune buggy and motorcycle junkies, especially on summer weekends. The blaring radios, thrumming engines, and staggering swarms of tipsy tourists might drive you Jim Morrison-like into the sands to seek eternal truth—or at least a quiet place to crash. The **National Recreation Area Headquarters** in Reedsport can tell visitors just how many decibels a dune-buggy engine can produce. They will also provide the trail maps necessary for serene escape.

PRACTICAL INFORMATION AND ORIENTATION

Visitors Information: Oregon Dunes National Recreation Area Information Center, 855 U.S. 101, Reedsport (271-3611), just south of the Umpqua River Bridge. The U.S. Forest Service runs this center and will happily answer your questions or provide you with free guides. Open Mon.-Fri. 9:30am-6pm, Sat. 9am-5pm, Sun. noon-4pm; Labor Day-Memorial Day Mon.-Fri. 8am-4:30pm; Memorial Day-June 15 Mon.-Fri. 8am-4:30pm, Sat. 9am-5pm, Sun. noon-4pm. **Reedsport Chamber of Commerce** (271-3495 or 800-247-2155 in OR), U.S. 101 and Rte. 38, a cute little shack across the street from the Recreation Area office. Open daily 9am-6pm.

Greyhound, 2207 Winchester Ave., Reedsport (271-5223), at the 22nd St. Market. To: Portland (2 per day, $22.50); San Francisco (2 per day, $117). Open Mon.-Fri. 5am-10pm, Sat.-Sun. 7am-10pm.

Taxi: Reedsport Tavern Taxi, 271-2690. About $7 to the dunes, $1 for each extra passenger. 24 hr.

Laundromat: Sud-z-Seagull, U.S. 101 in Winchester Bay. Wash $1, 10-min. dry 25¢. Open Mon.-Fri. 6:30am-9pm, Sat.-Sun. 8:30am-6pm.
Police: 136 N. 4th, Reedsport (271-2109). **Fire:** 124 N. 4th, Reedsport (271-2423).
Coast Guard: near the end of the harbor, at the foot of the mountain in Winchester Bay (271-2137).
Emergency: 911.
Post Office: 301 Fir St. (271-2521). Open Mon.-Fri. 8:30am-5pm. **General Delivery ZIP Code:** 97467.
Area Code: 503.

The dunes' shifting grip of the coastline is broken only once along the expanse, when the Umpqua and Smith Rivers empty into Winchester Bay about 20 mi. south of Florence. **Reedsport** (pop. 5000) is a typical highway town of motels, banks, and fast food places, neatly subdivided by U.S. 101 and Rte. 38, which connects with I-5 60 mi. to the east. The sport to Reedsport, however, is off the main strip on Rte. 38 where traces of the old coastal town remain. You can also avoid the huge stretches of pavement by passing straight through town and heading for **Winchester Bay,** the small fishing village 4 mi. south at the mouth of the bay of the same name.

ACCOMMODATIONS

The more secluded motels in Winchester Bay are no more expensive than those in Reedsport and all are within a few blocks of the water. Reservations are necessary to ensure one of the cheaper rooms, and on weekends during fishing season you may have to pay slightly more to stay in Winchester Bay. All motels (even those in Reedsport) fill up; arrive in the afternoon.

Harbor View Motel (271-3352), Beach Blvd. spitting distance from the boats. Huge glossy pictures of Marilyn Monroe and John Wayne in the lobby. Clean, comfortable rooms are popular with anglers. Singles $25. Doubles $29. Rates $4 lower in off-season.
Salmon Harbor Motel (271-2732), on U.S. 101 at the northernmost point of Winchester Bay. The farthest of the 3 Winchester Bay motels from the harbor (but only by 1½ blocks). Pleasant, despite being on the highway. Singles from $30. Doubles from $33.50, with kitchens $37.50.
Winchester Bay Motel (271-4871), at the end of Broadway, on 4th St. past dock A in Winchester Bay. This clean, quiet 50-room motel is the place to remember the comforts of civilization. Wheelchair access. TV, free continental breakfast. Singles $48. Doubles $58. Kitchens $10 extra. Labor Day-Memorial Day rooms $10 less.
Fir Grove Motel, 2178 Winchester Ave., Reedsport (271-4848). Winchester Ave. runs to the east diagonal to U.S. 101; the motel is at the intersection. The rooms are small but thick walls mute the sound of passing traffic. Color TV, free coffee, outdoor pool. 1- or 2-person rooms $34, in winter $25.

CAMPING

The national recreation area is subsumed by the Siuslaw National Forest; the Forest Service's pamphlet *Campgrounds in the Siuslaw National Forest* covers campgrounds in the dunes as well. The sites closest to Reedsport are in Winchester Bay. The campgrounds that allow dune buggy access—**Spinreel, Lagoon, Waxmyrtle, Driftwood II, Horsfall,** and **Bluebill**—are generally loud and rowdy in the summer. Call 800-283-2267 for more information.

During the summer, RVs dominate all the campsites around Reedsport and Winchester Bay. Summer campers with tents don't have much hope of finding a legal campground free of family screams. Peace in the name of Noel Ranch lies inland along Rte. 38.

Umpqua Lighthouse State Park (271-3546), 5 mi. south of Reedsport on U.S. 101. Hot showers, boat launch, hiker/biker sites ($2). Nearby **Lake Marie** is cold but swimmable with a beach to boot. Sites $12, with hookup $14.

William H. Tugman State Park, 8 mi. south of Reedsport on U.S. 101. All sites have water and electricity. Showers and facilities for campers with disabilities. Hiker/biker sites $2, tentsites $13.

Noel Ranch, 8 mi. down Rte. 38 at Noel Creek off U.S. 101, just north of Reedsport. A National Forest Service campground with no luxuries and no trace of commercialism. Enjoy the long and winding ride or just pick a spot on the way. Free.

Surfwood Campground, ½ mi. north of Winchester Bay off U.S. 101 on the beach side (271-4020). RV central but with all the luxuries: laundromat, heated pool, grocery store, sauna, tennis court, and hot showers. Call a week in advance during the summer. Sites $12, full hookups $14.

Windy Cove Campground (271-5634), adjacent to Salmon Harbor in Winchester Bay. A county park with a foghorn that will keep you company all night long. 75 sites with drinking water, hot showers, flush toilets, and beach access. Sites $8.40, with hookup $10.50.

FOOD

Winchester Bay again wins the contest with Reedsport for culinary charm and originality. Restauranteurs pride themselves on their seafood, especially salmon.

Seven Seas Cafe (271-4381), Dock A, Winchester Bay at the end of Broadway at 4th St. A small diner crowded with marine memorabilia and navigational charts. The local fishing crowd gathers at this self-proclaimed "haunt of the liars" to trade big fish stories. The seafood comes in huge helpings at low prices—try the fish and chips ($4.50). Join in the fishy fun of the all-you-can-eat fish fry every Fri. and Sat. Open daily 7am-9pm.

Seafood Grotto and Restaurant (271-4250), 8th St. and Broadway, Winchester Bay. An unexpected find: excellent seafood restaurant showcasing a large Victorian doll house. Lunches $4-7; for dinner try the large salmon steak ($14). Open daily 11am-9pm.

Sugar Shack Bakery, at 2 locations: in the **Umpqua Shopping Center** (271-3514) and at 145 N. 3rd in **Reedsport.** Excellent, fresh baked goods, all soaked in sugar. Also quick meals—try the chili with a biscuit and a slice of pudding cake ($1.75) or one of the sandwiches ($3-5.50). Open daily 5am-9pm.

OUTDOORS

Romp in the dunes—why else are you here?

Those with little time or low sand-tolerance should at least stop at the **Oregon Dunes Overlook,** off U.S. 101 about halfway between Reedsport and Florence. Steep wooden ramps lead to the gold and blue swells of the dunes and the Pacific. Trails wander off from the overlook, as they do at several other points on U.S. 101. The *Sand Tracks* brochure (available at the Information Center; see Practical Information) has a detailed map of the dunes and the trails inside.

For dune encounters of a closer kind, venture out on wheels. **Oregon Dunes Tours** (759-4777) on Wildwood Dr., 10 mi. south of Reedsport off U.S. 101, gives 30-minute ($18) and hour-long ($30) dune-buggy rides (open daily 9am-6pm). The buggy rides are more fun than the tacky base camp would suggest, and the drivers have lots of good stories. If you really want to tear up the dunes, shell out $30 for an hour on your own dune buggy. Rent from **Dunes Odyssey,** on U.S. 101 in Winchester Bay (271-4011; open Mon.-Sat. 8am-5:30pm, Sun. 9am-5:30pm), or **Spinreel Park,** Wildwood Dr., 8 mi. south on U.S. 101 (759-3313; open daily 9am-6pm).

Inside **Umpqua Lighthouse State Park,** 6 mi. south of Reedsport, the Douglas County Park Department operates the **Coastal Visitor Center** (271-4631), in the old Coast Guard administration building. The center has small exhibits on the shipping and timber industries at the turn-of-the-century (open May-Sept. Wed.-Sat. 10am-5pm, Sun. 1-5pm; free).

When you tire of dune doodling and museum dawdling, you could try deep-sea fishing with one of the many charter companies that operate out of **Salmon Har-**

bor, Winchester Bay. **Gee Gee Charters, Inc.** offers four-hour fishing trips ($40, those over 59 and under 16 $35). The required one-day license for salmon fishing ($5.25) may be purchased at any of the charter offices. Trips leave daily at 6, 10am, and 2pm. They also offer five-hour bottom-fishing trips ($45) daily at 6am and 1pm. Call the 24-hr. phone service the day before you wish to go to secure a reservation (271-3152 office, 271-4134 home).

The penniless should take in the wildlife at the **Dean Creek Elk Viewing Area,** 2 mi. east of Reedsport on Rte. 38. Here, you can observe the Roosevelt Elk, Oregon's largest land mammal, which was named after antler-toting Rough Rider Teddy Roosevelt. Large herds gather in an isolated spot off the road behind and to the right of the viewing area, into which few tourists venture.

Bird watching (lists are available at the National Recreation Area headquarters, across from the tourist office) and **whale watching** (across from the lighthouse in April, November, and December) are also popular diversions. If you would rather catch animals than watch them, you can rent huge nets to nab crabs in Salmon Harbor. Around Labor Day every summer, Winchester Bay merchants sponsor a crabbing contest; the first competitor to find the tagged "Kleo the Crab" wins $1000.

■■■ COOS BAY/NORTH BEND

The largest city on the Oregon Coast, Coos Bay is making an economic turnaround in the face of environmental regulations which have decimated the local lumber industry. The staggering unemployment rate (around 20%) has dropped significantly as the tourist trade has expanded, and businesses are returning to the once-deserted downtown shopping mall. Huge iron-sided tankers have begun to replace quaint fishing boats. Nevertheless, Coos Bay looks like the real McCoy—its seafront has retained its character, replete with rattling traps, rolling logs, and smelly fish.

▶PRACTICAL INFORMATION AND ORIENTATION

Visitors Information: Chamber of Commerce, 50 E. Central (800-824-8486), 5 blocks west from U.S. 101, off Commercial Ave. in Coos Bay. Not as well-stocked as the Chamber of Commerce in Bandon. Good county map $1.50. Open Mon.-Fri. 8:30am-6:30pm, Sat. 10am-4pm, Sun. noon-4pm. **North Bend Information Center,** 1380 Sherman Ave. (756-4613), on U.S. 101, just south of the harbor bridge in North Bend. Open Mon.-Fri. 8am-5pm, Sat. 10am-4pm, Sun. noon-4pm.

Oregon State Parks Information, 365 N. 4th St., Coos Bay (269-9410). Open Mon.-Fri. 8am-5pm. **Coos County Parks Department:** 267-7009. Open Mon.-Fri. 8am-noon and 1-5pm.

Greyhound, 215 Sherman St. (756-4900). To Portland (4 per day, $24) and San Francisco (2 per day, $79). Open Mon.-Fri. 7:30am-5:30pm, Sat. 8am-5pm, Sun. noon-4pm.

Taxi: Yellow Cab, 267-3111. 24 hr. Senior citizen and student discount.

Coos Bay Public Library: 525 W. Anderson (269-1101). Open Mon.-Wed. 10am-8pm, Thurs.-Sat. 10am-5pm.

Crisis Line: 888-5911. 24 hr.

Medical Emergency: Bay Area Hospital, 1775 Thompson St. (269-8085), in Coos Bay.

Emergency: 911. **Police:** 500 Central Ave. (269-8911). **Fire:** 150 S. 4th St. (269-1191). **Coast Guard:** 4645 Eel Ave. (888-3266) in Charleston.

Post Office: (267-4514), 4th and Golden. Open Mon.-Fri. 8:30am-5pm. **General Delivery ZIP Code:** 97420.

Area Code: 503.

After faithfully hugging the coastline for many miles, U.S. 101 slants east to Coos Bay/North Bend. Route 42 heads 85 mi. from Coos Bay (the town) to I-5 and U.S. 101 continues north into dune territory. Coos Bay and North Bend make up the northeast tip of the southern peninsula in Coos Bay (the bay). U.S. 101 skirts the east side of both cities, and the Cape Arago Hwy. continues west to Charleston, at the mouth of the bay.

ACCOMMODATIONS AND CAMPING

The hostel is, as usual, the best bet. The state-run and private campgrounds take full advantage of the breathtaking coast. Always make reservations during the summer.

Seastar Hostel (HI/AYH), 375 2nd St. (347-9632), in Old-Town Bandon, just south of Coos Bay. Comfortable bunkrooms, kitchen, laundry, and cedar-trimmed dining area with wood stove. The helpful owner provides a wealth of information. "No curfew, no pets, no smoking." The Bistro downstairs offers gourmet cuisine and espresso. $12, nonmembers $15, ages 5-12 ½-price. Private rooms also available ($22, nonmembers $27).

Parkside Motel, 1490 Sherman Ave. (756-4124), on U.S. 101 on the north edge of town. Plastic seagulls perched on every door. Rooms with cable TV and phones. Kitchenettes and laundry facilities available. Singles $38. Doubles $42.

Itty Bitty Inn Motel Bed and Breakfast, 1504 Sherman Ave., North Bend (756-6398), on U.S. 101. Tiny (but comfortable) rooms with color TV and refrigerators have been refurbished in cozy Adobe style. For $2 more receive a gift-certificate for $15 at the Virginia St. Cafe. Singles $35. Doubles $38. In winter, about $3 less. Reservations recommended.

Timber Lodge Motel, 1001 Bayshore Dr., Coos Bay (267-7066), on U.S. 101. Close to downtown. Big rooms, restaurant, and lounge. Singles $38. Doubles $42. Prices higher in July and August.

City Center Motel, 750 Connecticut St. (756-5118), at U.S. 101 in North Bend. Fairly pleasant rooms at fairly pleasant rates. Singles $32. Doubles $38.

Captain John's Motel, 8061 Kingfisher Dr., Charleston (888-4041). Next to the small boat basin in Charleston, 9 mi. from the crowds at Coos Bay, closer to state parks and beaches. Within walking distance of the docks. 1-2 person room $32.

Bluebill Forest Service Campground, off U.S. 101, 4 mi. northwest of North Bend. Follow the signs to the Horsfall Beach area. 19 sites with flush toilets. Trails lead to the ocean and dunes. Sites $8.

Bastendorff Beach Park (888-5353). A county park 10 mi. southwest of Coos Bay. Highly developed sites include hot showers (25¢), flush toilets, and hiking trails. No reservations accepted, but the park fills early; arrive before 5pm. Open year round. Sites $11, with hookup $13.

Sunset Bay State Park 13030 Cape Arago Hwy., Coos Bay 97420 (888-4902), 12 mi. south of Coos Bay and 3½ mi. west of Charleston on the Coos Bay/Bandon loop. Akin to camping in a parking lot, but the cove makes the scene feel like Club Med. 298 sites with hot showers and wheelchair-accessible facilities. Reservations accepted by mail. Open mid-April to Oct. Hiker/biker sites $2, tentsites $14. RVs $16.

FOOD

Virginia Street Diner, 1430 Virginia St., North Bend (756-3475). The 50s motif runs rampant here, from the 45s on the wall to your poodle-skirted waitress. Entrees $6-7. Prime rib special every Fri.-Sat. ($8). Open daily 6am-10pm.

Sea Basket (888-5711), in Charleston Boat Basin, 9 mi. west of Coos Bay. Head south on Cape Arago Hwy. Fresh seafood dinners ($8-12)—not to mention steak and an amazing salad bar—attract a sizeable marina crowd. Open daily 5am-9pm.

The Blue Heron, 100 Commercial St., Coos Bay (267-3933), at U.S. 101, Charleston turn-off. Friendly atmosphere and a well-stocked magazine rack. Gigantic muffins ($1.50); lunches $5-7. Dinners a bit more, but sublime—try the seafood on bed of spinach fettuccine ($12.45). Open daily 9am-10pm.

Carolyn's Breakfast Barn (888-4512), in Charlestown Boat Basin just across the bridge. Where the local fishermen like to hang out. Inexpensive egg dishes ($3-4) in a diner setting. Open Mon.-Sat. 5:30am-1:30pm, Sun. 6-11:30am.

SIGHTS AND ACTIVITIES

For those who need to fill a rainy day or are simply tired of water, Coos Bay and North Bend offer a slew of mediocre museums. North Bend is home to the **Coos County Historical Museum** (756-6320), in Simpson Park just off U.S. 101 south of McCullough Bridge. The museum focuses on local Native American and pioneer history, with a special emphasis on the logging and fishing industries and on pioneer children. A 1922 logging train engine stands at the entrance, and inside is a collection of spinning wheels that would have made Rumplestiltskin green with envy (open Mon.-Sat. 10am-4pm, Sun. noon-4pm; admission $1, ages 5-11 25¢).

South of Coos Bay is the **Marshfield Sun Printing Museum,** 1049 N. Front St. (269-1363), at Front St. and U.S. 101, across from the Timber Inn. The first floor remains in its early 20th-century state—some of the equipment dates to the paper's birth in 1891. Upstairs are exhibits on the history of printing, American newspapers, and early Coos Bay *née* Marshfield (open June-Aug. Tues.-Sat. 1-4pm; free).

In North Bend, the **Little Theatre on the Bay** (756-4336), at Sherman and Washington St., presents musical cabaret with a regional flavor on Saturday nights.

OUTDOORS

Near Coos Bay

One of the most dramatic spots in the central coast is also probably one of the most under-appreciated. The **South Slough National Estuarine Research Reserve** (888-5558) protects 4400 acres of estuaries, where salt and fresh water mix. The Slough area teems with wildlife, from sand shrimp to deer to *Homo photographandis*. Numerous hiking trails weave through the sanctuary; take a lunch and commune with the blue heron. **Hidden Creek** (3 mi. round-trip), **Winchester,** and **Wasson Creek Trails** give access to the upper reaches of the freshwater marsh. The trails are usually quiet, but beware—during the academic year, schools of children on field trips swarm into the reserve.

South Slough is virtually inaccessible without a car, but many Bandon hostelers make the Slough a daytrip expedition; you can often round up a shared ride. Take the exit off U.S. 101 or turn south off Cape Arago Hwy. onto Seven Devils Rd. Travel 4 mi. to the new visitors center and headquarters which explains the ecology of the estuarine environment. Guided walks are given during the summer (Wed. 9am-noon, Fri. 1-4pm). Canoe tours ($5) are also available, depending on the tides and provided you have your own canoe. For a summer calendar, write P.O. Box 5417, Charleston 97420 (open daily 8:30am-4:30pm; Labor Day-Memorial Day Mon.-Fri. 8:30am-4:30pm; free). The trails are open dawn to dusk daily.

Freshwater fanatics should drive northeast from Eastside on the Coos River Rd. past the town of Allegany to **Golden and Silver Falls State Park.** There, ¾ mi. up a beautiful trail crossed with downed logs, twin falls (about 1 mi. apart) crash 200 ft. into a grove of red alder and Douglas fir.

Charleston

Coos Bay is one of the few places in western Oregon where life slows down as you near the ocean shore. Escape the industrial chaos by following Cape Arago Hwy. from Coos Bay to Charleston. (The highway signs alternately say Charleston and Ocean Beaches.) A town where crusty old sea salts seem at home, Charleston is a more pleasant place to stay for an extended period than its two bigger brethren.

Make arrangements to tour the **Coast Guard Lifeboat Station** (888-3266) in the Charleston Marina (tours available anytime by prior reservation) or hop on board one of the many charters nearby. **Charleston Charters,** P.O. Box 5032 (888-4846), is one of the largest outfits. Five-hour fishing trips leave at 6 and 11:30am ($45); less energetic bay cruises last two hours and range from $10-20 per person depending on the number of people in the boat.

Charleston is a convenient stop on the way to **Shore Acres State Park** (888-3732). Once the estate of local lumber landlord Louis J. Simpson, the park contains botanical gardens that survived when the mansion was razed. The flowers are a refreshing change of scenery from endless seashell-strewn beaches. The egret sculptures are a more recent addition, courtesy of some artistically-inclined inmates from the state penitentiary. (Open 8am-8pm. $3 per car on weekends and during summer and holidays. Wheelchair access.)

Farther down the same highway is **Cape Arago,** notable mainly for its wonderful tide pools. Large sand bars rise and fade for some distance from the actual shore, giving a misleading impression of water depth. But what keeps ctenophores and other invertebrates happy also caused endless trouble for early sailors.

SEASONAL EVENTS

The most popular event on the coast is the **Oregon Coast Music Festival,** P.O. Box 663, Coos Bay 97420 (269-0938), in mid-July, which includes a series of classical, jazz, and folk performances around town and in Bandon and Reedsport (tickets $9-11, seniors and ages 6-18 $7-9).

In the second week of August, Charleston hosts a refined but nevertheless decadent **Seafood and Wine Festival** in the Boat Basin. In late August, Coos Bay touts a native fruit with the **Blackberry Arts Festival.** Downtown rocks with square dancing, wine tasting, concerts, and crafts. In early September, Oregon memorializes its favorite son in the **Steve Prefontaine 10K Road Race,** named after the great Olympic athlete who died in an automobile accident in the bell lap of his career. The race attracts dozens of world-class runners to the area. For information on these events, contact the Chamber of Commerce in Coos Bay (see Practical Information).

■ Port Orford

The people of Port Orford, the westernmost city in the Lower 48, boast that their town was the earliest pioneer settlement on Oregon's southern coast. In 1851, nine early settlers lost a skirmish against 400 Native Americans at the extravagantly named Battle Rock. Despite the pioneers' ultimate victory and settlement of the area, the lost battle purportedly cast a 100-year "Indian jinx" on the town. The end of the jinx was celebrated in high fashion in 1951. Today, Port Orford, too tiny to deserve even the appellation "small town," is at best worth a daytrip.

Practical Information The **Information Center** (332-8055) at Battle Rock, on the west side of U.S. 101, dispenses more brochures than one would expect a town this size could produce (open daily 10am-4pm).

U.S. 101 nips through Port Orford so quickly that unless you know where Battle Rock is, you'll miss the town entirely. Port Orford is 45 mi. south of Bandon and 30 mi. north of Gold Beach. **Greyhound** (247-7710) stops at the Circle K store, across from the Port Orford Motel, with service to Portland ($29) and San Francisco ($95.50). The **post office** (332-4251) is located at Jackson and 7th St. (open Mon.-Fri. 8:30am-1pm and 2-5pm). **General Delivery ZIP Code:** 97465. **Area code:** 503.

Accommodations, Camping, and Food While in Port Orford, admire the sunburnt-pink buildings and beautiful landscaping of the **Port Orford Motel,** 1034 Oregon St. (332-1685)—or, for $29 a night, admire them from the inside. The Port Orford Motel is closer to the bus line than the waterfront motels, and only 10 min. from the beach. If you must stay on the beach, stay at one of the three campgrounds. **Humbug Mountain State Park** (332-6774), 7 mi. south of Port Orford, has 108 tentsites with stunning scenery ($14, hookups $16). You'll also find magnificent views at **Cape Blanco State Park** (332-6774), 9 mi. north of Port Orford, off U.S. 101 (hiker/biker sites $2, tentsites $15). A bit more off the beaten path lies the **Elk River Campground** (332-2255), on Elk River Rd. off U.S. 101. You'll be rewarded for your trip with clean sites and great fossil-hunting nearby at Butler Bar (sites $9, with full hookups $13).

Though some fry their food better than others, Port Orford's restaurants serve the same seafood and burgers you can get anywhere else along the coast. Locals flock to **The Wheelhouse Restaurant,** 521 Jefferson St. (332-1605), for the clamm fritter sandwich ($5), burgers, homemade soups, and pies (open Mon.-Sat. 6am-8pm, Sun. 7am-7pm).

Sights and the Outdoors The town itself is pleasant and historic. Several houses date from the end of the 19th century. The most impressive building in the area, 9 mi. north of town, is the restored **Hughes House** built by P. Lindberg in 1898, a locally famed Swedish carpenter. (Open May-Sept. Mon. and Thurs.-Sat. 10am-5:30pm, Sun. noon-5pm. "Donation" required.)

The view of the ocean from **Battle Rock** ranks among the most melodramatic on the entire Oregon coast. Take the short, well-worn path from the beach to the top of the mammoth rock outcropping for a view of the crashing waves. During the months of April through May and August through October, this is a prime whale-watching site. In the summer, **Agate Beach,** accessible by Paradise Point Rd., is supposedly studded with agates.

Nine mi. north of town, near Hughes House, is the gorgeous **Cape Blanco State Park.** The Cape reaches out from the coast far enough to see forever, and if you walk out to the end you can be the westernmost human being in the continental U.S. for the duration of your stand. The park's flower-carpeted hills are topped by a postcard-perfect lighthouse.

For other magnificent views, take a walk through **Humbug Mountain State Park,** 7 mi. south of town. Survivors of the 3-mi. hike up the mountain win a tremendous panorama of the entire area. **Fishing** in the two nearby rivers (the Sixes and the Elk) is fantastic. Ask at the information center for details. **Scuba divers** come to the area for Port Orford's protected coves, where the water temperature rises to a mild 65°F and water clarity ranges from 10 to 50 ft. in summer. Water clarity is even better during the winter, when lower water temperatures (45-60°F) drive the plankton away.

Halfway down the road to Gold Beach, 13 mi. south on U.S. 101, the **Prehistoric Gardens,** 36848 U.S. 101 (332-4463), presents visitors with an arrestingly full-sized Tyrannosaurus Rex, among other extinct beasts. The Rex is one of 29 life-sized (although not especially life-like) prehistoric animals carved by sculptor E.V. Nelson. Your six-year-old will never forgive you if you don't spend the $5 to visit (senior citizens and ages 12-18 $4, ages 5-11 $3).

■ Brookings

Brookings, the southernmost stop before California, is one of the few Oregon coastal towns that has remained relatively tourist-free. Here trinket shops do not elbow out hardware stores and warehouses. Although gorgeous beaches and parks surround Brookings, it is accessible only by U.S. 101 and tends to be more of a stop-over than a destination. So while good restaurants and lodgings are not abundant, the beaches are among the most unspoiled on the Oregon coast. Brookings sits in a region often called the "Banana Belt" due to its mild climate—summery weather is not uncommon in January, and Brookings' beautiful blossoms bloom early.

Practical Information The **Brookings State Welcome Center,** 1650 U.S. 101 (800-547-7842), maintains an exceptionally well-stocked office just north of Brookings and answers questions regarding the Oregon coast (open May-Oct. Mon.-Sat. 8am-6pm, Sun. 9am-5pm). The town's **Chamber of Commerce,** 16330 Lower Harbor Rd. (469-3181), is across the bridge to the south, just off the highway (open Mon.-Fri. 9am-5pm, Sat. 9am-1pm). The **Chetco Ranger Station,** 555 5th St. (469-2196), distributes information on this area of the Siskiyou National Forest (open daily 7:30am-4:30pm).

The **Greyhound** station (469-3326), at Tanburk and Railroad, sends two buses north and two buses south each day (open Mon.-Fri. 9am-noon and 4-6pm, Sat. 9am-noon). The **Laundromat** (469-3975), open 24 hr., is known to locals by its sobriquet "The Old Wash House"; you'll find it near the Chamber of Commerce booth, at the Brookings Harbor Shopping Center (open daily 7am-11pm; wash $1, 10-min. dry 25¢). The **post office** (469-2318), is at 711 Spruce St. (Open Mon.-Fri. 9am-4:30pm. **General Delivery ZIP Code:** 97415.)

Accommodations, Camping, and Food Bed down at the **Chetco Inn Hotel,** 417 Fern Ave. (469-5347), a hotel on a hill (behind the Chevron gas station overlooking the town). A clean and gracious interior is matched by the newly-resurrected façade (singles $34, doubles $44). The **Spindrift Motel,** 1215 Chetco Ave. (469-5345), offers airy rooms all with an ocean view (singles $39, off-season $28; doubles $46, off-season $35).

Harris Beach State Park (469-2021), at the north edge of Brookings, has 69 tentsites in the midst of a grand natural setting. The park lies on the beach across from the 21-acre **Goat Island** and is equipped with showers, hiker/biker sites ($2), and facilities for people with disabilities (open year-round; sites $14, with hookup $16). Make reservations if you plan to stay between Memorial Day and Labor Day. **Loeb State Park,** 8 mi. east of Brookings, has good swimming and fishing. A 1 mi. trail leads to a soothing redwood grove. Tentsites ($12) include electricity and water (open year-round; no reservations accepted). For more campsites off the beaten path, continue east another 7 mi. past Loeb to the charming **Little Redwood** campground. Redwood picnic grove, alongside a burbling and salamander-filled creek, has about 35 sites ($4), with pit toilets. For more information contact the **Forest Service Office,** 702 Chetco Ave. (469-6401; open daily 7am-9pm).

Mama's Authentic Italian Food, 703 Chetco Ave. (469-7611), in the Central Mall, is worth the half-hour trip from either Gold Beach or Crescent City. "Mama" Antonia Vallejo delights in stuffing her clientele with fresh bread and pasta. Try the delicious ravioli ($10.25). Senior citizens get a 10% discount; all orders are available without meat. (Open Mon.-Thurs. 11am-10pm, Fri.-Sun. 11am-11pm. In winter, open Mon.-Thurs. 11am-8:30pm, Fri.-Sun. 11am-9pm.) **Plum Pudding,** 1011 Chetco Ave. (469-6961), serves a delicious breakfast of the standard eggs and bacon genre at slightly higher-than-standard prices (around $5). Try the homemade fruit and nut bread ($1.50) if your wallet won't make the stretch to their breakfast menu (open Mon.-Sat. 8am-3pm).

Sights and Seasonal Events In **Azalea State Park** (469-3181), downtown, lawns are encircled by large native azaleas, some of which are more than 300 years old. Two rare weeping spruce trees also grace the park's grounds. Picnic areas and facilities for the disabled are provided. The **Chetco Valley Historical Society Museum,** 15461 Museum Rd. (469-6651), 2½ mi. south of the Chetco River, occupies the oldest building in Brookings. Exhibits include the patchwork quilts of white settlers and Native American basketwork. The museum is hard to miss—the nation's largest cypress tree stands in front (open Wed.-Sat. noon-5pm, Sun. noon-5pm; admission $1, children 25¢).

If you're heading north from Brookings by bicycle, take scenic **Carpenterville Rd.,** which was the only highway out of town before U.S. 101 was built. The twisty, 13½-mi. road features beautiful ocean views. Watch out for cattle and sheep—the road runs through an open grazing range.

From **Gold Beach,** north of Brookings on U.S. 101, you can take part in a 90-year-old tradition as you ride the mail boat up the **Rogue River. Mail Boat Hydro-Jets** (800-458-3511) offers 64-, 80-, and 104-mi. daytrips abounding in scenic views, history, and whitewater (from $27.50, children from $10).

The pride of Brookings is its annual **Azalea Festival,** held in the Azalea Park during Memorial Day weekend. March brings the **Beachcomber's Festival,** which showcases art created from driftwood and other material found on the beach.

INLAND VALLEYS

While the jagged cliffs and coastal surf draw tourists and nature lovers to the Oregon coast, the bulk of the permanent population resides in the lush Willamette, Rogue, and Umpqua river valleys. Vast tracts of fertile land and huge forests support a large agricultural industry and—until federal legislation was passed a few years ago to protect the spotted owl—immense lumber mills.

Interstate 5 (I-5), which runs north-south through the three West Coast states, traverses rolling agricultural land punctuated by comparatively few urban centers. Farthest south, the **Rogue River Valley,** from Ashland to Grants Pass, is generally hot and dry in the summer. Whitewater rafting, fishing, and spelunking offer refuge from the heat. **Eugene,** Oregon's second-largest city and bawdiest college town, rests at the southern extreme of the temperate **Willamette Valley.** This carpet of agricultural land extends 20 mi. on either side of the highway and runs 80 mi. north until it bumps into the suburban hills that house Portland's bedroom communities.

It is possible to travel the 250-mi. stretch of I-5 from tip to toe in less than six hours, but lead-footed out-of-staters should be wary—most Oregonians obey speed limits, and the highways are of poor quality. To make matters worse, the snowy winters make road construction possible only in summer; you may well find yourself baking behind the wheel in traffic jams in 100° weather. But don't despair; the Oregon Parks and Recreation Department maintains rest areas every 30 to 40 mi. along the interstate. Public rest rooms, phones, picnic tables, and "animal exercise areas" are available. Rest areas are shaded, grassy, and generally well-kept, but travelers should bring their own toilet paper. Tents may not be pitched in public rest areas, but those motorists who can stick it out on a back seat may park for up to 18 hours.

■■■ ASHLAND

Before their expropriation by the guardians of high-brow culture, Shakespeare's plays were popular entertainment for 19th-century Americans. Ashland's informal, rural setting on the California border returns the plays to their lost candor each summer with its world-famous **Shakespeare festival.** In its 55-plus year history, the festival has fostered delightful shops, lodgings, and restaurants within the city. Although pricier than its neighbors, Ashland's prices are reasonable when compared with other U.S. towns of equal charm and elegance. Throughout its nine-month season, the festival offers an astonishing number of plays and an accomplished roster of performers. Though the repertory isn't limited to the Renaissance, Shakespeare's works dominate the three stages. The plays are neatly incorporated into the town itself—Ashland's balmy climate allows for nightly summertime performances in the outdoor Elizabethan theater and a refunds in case of rain.

October's rains see the last of the Shakespeare buffs and usher in the college students of **Southern Oregon State.** By Thanksgiving, the nearby Siskiyou Mountains are blanketed with snow and sprinkled with cross-country skiers. Alpine skiers swarm to Mt. Ashland. Spring thaw ushers in the hikers, bikers, and rafters. And yea, the cycle beginneth anew in February, when Shakespeare wakes to walk again.

PRACTICAL INFORMATION AND ORIENTATION

Visitors Information: Chamber of Commerce, 110 E. Main St. (482-3486). A harried, busy staff frantically dishes out play schedules and brochures, several of which contain small but adequate maps. The Chamber of Commerce does *not* sell tickets to Shakespeare performances. Open Mon.-Fri. 9am-5pm.

Oregon Shakespearean Festival Box Office, P.O. Box 158, Ashland 97520 (482-4331), next to the Elizabethan Theater. Rush tickets (½-price) occasionally available ½ hr. before performances that aren't sold out. A better bet might be standing room tickets ($7.50); a limited number are available for sold-out shows at the Elizabethan Theater.

Rogue Valley Transportation (779-2877), in Medford. Schedules available at the Chamber of Commerce. Fare 75¢, plus 25¢ for each zone change. Over 65 and ages 6-11 ½-price. The #10 bus serving Ashland runs every ½ hr., 5am-7:30pm. Service Mon.-Sat. to Medford, and from there to Jacksonville (on bus #30). Also runs a loop through downtown Ashland every 15 min. (25¢).

Taxi: Ashland Taxi, 482-3065. 24 hr.

Laundromat: B.J.'s Homestyle Laundromat, 1712 W. Main (773-4803). Wash 75¢, 45-min. dry 75¢. Open Mon.-Thurs. 8am-4:45pm, Fri.-Sun. 8am-6:45pm.

Equipment Rental: Ashland Mountain Supply, 31 N. Main St. (488-2749). Internal frame backpacks $5 per day for the first 2 days, $3.50 for each additional day ($50 deposit). External frame backpacks $7.50 per day for the first 2 days, $5 per additional day ($100 deposit). Mountain bikes $10 for 2 hr., $25 per day. **The Adventure Center,** 40 N. Main St. (488-2819). Mountain bikes $20 per day. Bike tours (guided) from $34.

Road Conditions: 1-976-7277.

Crisis Intervention Services: 779-4357.

Emergency: 911. **Police:** 1155 E. Main St. (488-2211). **Fire:** 455 Siskiyou Dr. (482-2770).

Post Office: 120 N. 1st St. at Lithia Way (482-3986). Open Mon.-Fri. 9am-5pm. **General Delivery ZIP Code:** 97520.

Area Code: 503.

Ashland is 15 mi. north of the California border, the last Oregon town on I-5 heading south. Rte. 66 traverses 64 mi. of stunning scenery from Klamath Falls to Ashland, but goes no further west. Downtown Ashland centers around E. Main St., packing in restaurants just past the bridge on N. Main St.

ACCOMMODATIONS AND CAMPING

In winter, Ashland is full to bursting with inexpensive hotels; but in summer, rates double in virtually every hotel, and the hostel is impenetrable. Only a rogue or peasant slave would arrive without an advance reservation. Mid-summer nights see vacancy signs only in nearby Medford. And if we make one more atrocious Shakespeare pun, then you have our permission to throw this book out the window.

Ashland Hostel (HI/AYH), 150 N. Main St. (482-9217). In May and June this well-kept hostel swarms with school groups in town for a little culture. The wonderful owner-managers will help you in any way they can, from tracking down theater tickets to suggesting activities on days when tickets aren't available. Laundry facilities. $11, nonmembers $13. Open for check-in 5pm-midnight. Lock-out 10am-5pm. Reservations advised; the earlier you can make them, the better.

Columbia Hotel, 262½ E. Main St. (482-3726). A cozy European-style inn 1½ blocks from the theaters. Splendid decor is from the 1940s, with a magnificent sitting room lifted from the pages of a Jane Austen novel. Bathroom down the hall for some rooms. Singles, available in summer only, $42. Doubles from $46; Nov.-Feb. $26; March-June $32. Children under 12 free. All rooms non-smoking.

Timbers Motel, 1450 Ashland St. (482-4242), near downtown. Pool, phones, color TV. Singles $48. Doubles $52. Rates $10-12 lower in the off-season.

Vista 6 Motel, 535 Clover Lane (482-4423), on I-5 at exit 14. Small rooms. Not center-stage for the main attractions. Friendly staff. TV, A/C, small pool. Singles $26. Doubles $29.50. Winter and spring discounts.

Emigrant Lake (776-7001), 6 mi. southeast on Rte. 66, exit 14 off I-5. Hot showers and laundromat. Sites $10. Open April 15-Oct. 15.

Glenyan KOA, 5310 Hwy. 66 (482-4138), 5 mi. out of town southeast on Rte. 66, exit 14 from I-5. High quality and price of a KOA. Showers, laundromat, pool, and petite grocery store. Sites $15, with hookups $19.50. Reservations required.

Jackson Hot Springs, 2253 Hwy. 99 N (482-3776), off exit 19 from I-5, down Valley View Rd. to Rte. 99 N for about ½ mi. Nearest campground to downtown. Separate tent area in a grassy, open field encircled by RV sites, which might make you feel like you're camping in front of an apartment building. Laundry facilities, hot showers, and mineral baths ($4 per hr.). Sites $10, with hookups $14.

FOOD

Ashland cooks up an impressive spread for its festival guests. The steep prices are aimed at the monied theater patrons, but so are their hours—many restaurants stay open past their posted closing time on show nights. The hostel has kitchen facilities (see Accommodations); **Sentry Market,** 310 Oak St. (482-3521), is open daily 8am-10pm. **Ashland Community Food Store COOP,** 37 3rd St. (482-2237), sells good picnic and hiking supplies (open daily 9am-8pm).

North Light Vegetarian Restaurant, 120 E. Main St. (482-9463). Baked tofu, broiled tofu, steamed tofu, minced and marinated tofu upside-down cake. However it's cooked, North Light serves up great vegetarian fare in a relaxed environment. Bean burrito ($3.75) and curried tofu with noodles ($5.50) are good bets. Outdoor patio. Open Mon.-Thurs. 11am-8pm, Fri. 11am-9pm, Sat. 9am-9pm, Sun. 9am-8pm.

Teresa's Cantina, 76 N. Pioneer St. (482-1107), at Main St. Wholesome Mexican food in a busy, congenial atmosphere. Cover the salsa-smothered, 1-lb. plus *cantina burrito* ($7.50) with some of the best fresh guacamole north of the border. Interesting fajitas ($10-14). Good place for the kids. 10% discount for seniors. Live music every Wed.-Sat. 1-9pm. Restaurant and bar open for lunch daily 11:30am-2:30pm, and for dinner daily 4:30pm-closing.

Geppetto's, 345 E. Main St. (482-1138). A local favorite, Geppetto's is the place to get late-night nosh. An eclectic and large straw-basket collection on the walls complements the eclectic and large dinner crowd. Fantastic eggplant veggie-burger on a sourdough bun ($3.50). Dinners average $10; breakfasts less—try the pesto omelette ($6.50). Lunches $4-6. Open daily 8am-midnight.

Thai Pepper, 84 N. Main (482-8058). Spicy curries and seafood prepared exquisitely—if not entirely traditionally—in an elegant environment. Dinners $9-12. Creekside dining. Open Mon. 5:30-9pm, Tues.-Sat. 11:30am-2pm and 5:30-9pm, Sun. 5-8:30pm.

Brothers Restaurant and Delicatessen, 95 N. Main St. (482-9671). A traditional New York-style deli and cafe, with some off-beat selections (zucchini burger $4). Open Sun.-Mon. 7am-3pm, Tues.-Sat. 7am-8pm.

Backporch BBQ, 92½ N. Main St. (482-4131), north of The Plaza, above the creek. Texas-style barbecue ($9-12) and margaritas ($3.25) consumed outside to the tune of a bubbling creek. Restaurant open June-Aug. daily 11:30am-9pm. Bar open until 2am on weekends. Closed in winter, but the adjacent **Senor Gator** remains open and carries the BBQ torch through the cold season.

The Bakery Cafe, 38 E. Main St. (482-2117). *The* breakfast place. A menu as unique as Ashland itself. Blueberry buckwheat pancakes ($4.25). Always crowded, always delicious. Open Mon. 7am-4pm, Tues.-Sat. 7am-8:30pm.

SIGHTS AND ACTIVITIES

For information on the Shakespeare festival, see the separate heading below.

Before it imported Shakespeare, Ashland was naturally blessed with lithia water, which was reputed to have miraculous healing powers. The mineral springs have given their name to the well-tended **Lithia Park,** west of the plaza off Main St. To quaff the vaunted water itself, head for the circle of fountains in the center of the plaza, under the statue of horse and rider; the water is about as tasty as sulfur. Guided historical tours are given by the **Northwest Museum of Natural History**

(488-1084; June 17-Sept. Sun. and Wed. at 11am) and by **Old Ashland Story Tours** (488-3281 or 488-1993; June-Oct. daily at 10am). Daily events are tabulated in brochures at the Chamber of Commerce (see Practical Information). The park itself has hiking trails, picnic grounds, a Japanese garden, duck and swan ponds, and a creek that trips over itself in ecstatic little waterfalls.

If the park and its infamous waters fail to refresh you, find your way to the **Chateulin Selections,** 52 E. Main St. (488-WINE or 9463), for free wine tasting. Since a sip is never enough, the wines, along with gourmet foods, are also available for sale (open daily 11am-6pm; in winter Tues.-Sun. 11am-6pm).

If your muscles are demanding a little abuse after all this R&R, you can join the **Pacific Crest Trail** as it passes through Ashland. Or take advantage of the variety of rafting companies that offer daytrips on local rivers. **The Adventure Center** (488-2819) has a kiosk on the plaza downtown at 40 N. Main St. They organize rafting, fishing, rock climbing, and horseback riding trips, among other "things." Daily raft trips on the Rogue River start at $40. The Center also rents bikes, jet skis, and hot air balloons (open Mon.-Sat. 8am-8pm, Sun. 8am-6pm; in winter daily 10am-5pm). For a tamer experience, try the double-flumed, 280-ft. **waterslide** at **Emigrant Lake Park** (12 slides for $4), or just practice your freestyle in the lake. The park also offers jet ski rentals (weekdays $20 for ½ hr., $30 per hr.; weekends $25 for ½ hr., $35 per hr.). **Jackson Hot Springs,** 2 mi. north of Ashland on Rte. 99 (482-3776), offers swimming in a pool filled by the hot springs ($2 for a ½-day, $3 all day) and private hot mineral baths ($4, or $6 per couple).

Mount Ashland has 22 **ski trails** varying in difficulty from moguls to "bunny" hills, with four chair lifts. The mountain also boasts 100 mi. of cross-country trails (Open Thanksgiving Day-April daily 9am-4pm, night-skiing Thurs.-Sat. 4-10pm. Day ticket weekdays $14, weekends $22. Full rental $14.) Contact **Ski Ashland,** P.O. Box 220, Ashland 97520 (482-2897; snow conditions 482-2754).

Halloween is an occasion for very high spirits; the Chamber of Commerce may have no comment, but other town officials are rumored to sponsor a free shuttle that transfers ghosts and goblins from one bar to another. In summer, the **Ashland City Band** sets up every Thursday at 7:30pm in Lithia Park (information 488-5340).

THE SHAKESPEARE FESTIVAL

The **Shakespeare Festival,** the brainchild of local teacher Angus Bowmer, began with two plays performed by schoolchildren during a boxing match intermission. Today, professional actors perform four Shakespeare plays and a host of other classic and modern dramas February through October on the three Ashland stages, and any boxing is over the scarce tickets. The **Agnus Bowmer** is a large (600-seat) traditional indoor theater that stages both Shakespeare and more recent plays. The **Elizabethan Stage** is the exclusive province of outdoor Shakespeare. Modeled after a 17th-century London theater, the Elizabeth is open only June to September. The newest of the three theaters is the intimate **Black Swan,** home to small-scale, often alternative productions. Plays that open in the fall of one season often continue in the spring of the next year. The house is dark on Mondays.

Due to the tremendous popularity of the productions, ticket purchases are recommended one to two months in advance. (Admission $7.50-21. For complete ticket information, write Oregon Shakespeare Festival, P.O. Box 158, Ashland 97520, or call 482-4331.) From March to May, half-price rush tickets are often available an hour before every performance that is not sold out. Additionally, some half-price student-senior matinees are offered. In the summer, almost everything is sold out, and obtaining tickets can be very difficult; arrive at the box office by 9:30am on the day of any show. Locals occasionally leave their shoes to hold their place in line, and you should respect this tradition. At 9:30am, the box office releases any unsold tickets for the day's performances. If no tickets are available, you will be given a priority number, entitling you to a place in line when the precious few tickets that festival members have returned are released (1pm for matinees, 6pm for evening performances). The box office sells a very limited number of standing-room tickets for sold-out shows on the Elizabethan Stage ($7.50).

The **backstage tours** ($7, children under 12 $3.50) provide a wonderful glimpse of the festival from behind the curtain. Tour guides (usually actors or technicians) divulge all kinds of anecdotes—from bird songs during an outdoor *Hamlet* to the ghastly events which take place every time they do "that Scottish play." Tours last two hours and leave from the Black Swan at 10am. Admission fee includes a trip to the **Exhibit Center** (482-2111) for a close-up look at sets and costumes (otherwise $2, children under 12 $1). Bring a camera to record your own role in the dress-up room (open Tues.-Sun. 10am-4pm; fall and spring, 10:30am-1:30pm).

One of the highlights of the Shakespeare Festival comes with the **Feast of Will** in mid-June, a celebration honoring the opening of the Elizabethan Theatre. Dinner and merrie madness are held in Lithia Park from 6-6:45pm (tickets $14; call 482-4331 for exact date).

"Give me excess of it, that, surfeiting, the appetite may sicken and so die." Still haven't had enough theater? The **Cabaret Theater** (488-2902), at 1st and Hagarcline, stages light musicals in a "sophisticated" setting with drinks and hors d'oeuvres (tickets $9-15.50; box office open Mon.-Sat. 1-8pm, Sun. 3-8pm). Small groups, such as **Actor's Theater of Ashland, Studio X,** and the theater department at **Southern Oregon State College,** also raise the curtains sporadically throughout the summer. The **Schneider Museum of Art,** at Siskiyou Blvd. and Indiana St. on the Southern Oregon State campus (552-6245), displays college-sponsored contemporary art exhibits that change every six weeks (open Tues.-Fri. 11am-5pm, Sat. 1-5pm; free).

BARS AND NIGHTLIFE

Mark Antony Hotel, 212 E. Main St. (482-1721). "The Mark" has cozy wooden booths, a large circular bar, and consistently excellent music (live music Wed.-Sat. night). No cover. Open daily 11am-2am.

Cook's Playbill Club, 66 E. Main St. (482-4626). Open since 1897, Cook's boasts of being the second oldest gay and straight club west of the Mississippi. Interesting 30s art on the walls. Pool table, dance floor Thurs.-Sat. Mon. night is openmike. Open daily 2pm-2am.

Log Cabin Tavern, 41 N. Main St. (482-9701). The cheapest brew around: $2.50 per pitcher, 65¢ per glass. An older crowd sits beneath older photographs. Open Sun.-Thurs. 10am-midnight, Fri.-Sat. 10am-2am.

O'Ryan's Irish Pub, 137 E. Main St. (482-2951). Come on down, have a pint, and shoot some pool, if you think the luck o' the Irish is with you. Pitchers $5-8.50. Open 11am-2am daily.

■■■ MEDFORD

Jacksonville was once the hub of the Rogue River Valley, while nearby Medford was just a bend in the river. When the railroads came, bringing promises of jobs, trade, and growth, Jacksonville and Medford both wanted in on the deal. But Jacksonville refused to pay the railroad barons the $25,000 kickback they demanded. The lines were laid in Medford instead, and within 20 years Medford's community of log cabins and trappers had seized power (and the county seat) from Jacksonville.

PRACTICAL INFORMATION

Visitors Information: Medford Visitors and Convention Bureau, 304 S. Central Ave. (772-4847), at 10th St. Stacks of maps and directories. Open Mon.-Fri. 9am-5pm. The **Branch Office** is located in the log cabin at 88 Stewart Ave., just off I-5 Exit 27. A small packet of information, including a city map, is sealed with teddy bear stickers and left by the door after they close. Aww. Open June-Sept. daily 8:30am-6:30pm, Mar.-May and Sept.-Oct. daily 9am-5pm.

Greyhound, 212 Bartlett St. (779-2103), at 5th St. To: Portland (8 per day, $34.25); San Francisco (2 per day, $59). Open daily 6am-6:30pm.

Rogue Valley Transportation, 3200 Crater Lake Ave. (799-2877). Connects Medford with: Jacksonville, Phoenix, White City, Talent, and Ashland. Buses leave 6th and Bartlett Mon.-Fri. 8am-5pm. Limited service Sat. 9am-5pm. Fare 75¢ plus 25¢ per zone crossed, seniors and students under 18 pay ½ price.

Taxi: Metro Cab Co., 773-6665. 24 hr.

Car Rental: Budget (773-7023), at the airport. Cars from $25 with 100 free mi. Each additional mi. 30¢. Must be at least 21 with credit card.

Equipment Rental: McKenzie Outfitters, 130 E. 8th St., off Central Ave. (773-5145 or 683-2038 for central office in Eugene). Backpacks from $15 per day; tents $15 per day for 1-3 days; $25 per day for 4-7 days; ice axes $5 per day; crampons $5 per day. Demonstration kayaks, fishing, and boating equipment.

Public Library: 413 W. Main St. (776-7281), at Oakdale Ave. Open Mon.-Thurs. 9:30am-8pm, Fri.-Sat. 9:30am-5pm.

Crisis Intervention Services: 779-4357.

Hospital: Providence, at Crater Lake Ave. and Woodrow St. (773-6611). Emergency care 24 hr.

Emergency: 911. **Police and Fire:** City Hall, at 8th and Oakdale (770-4783).

Post Office: 333 W. 8th (776-1326), at Holly St. Open Mon.-Fri. 8:30am-5:30pm. **General Delivery ZIP Code**: 97501.

Area Code: 503.

Medford lies on I-5 in southern Oregon, at the intersection of Rte. 238. Grant's Pass is 30 mi. to the northwest, Ashland 12 mi. to the southeast. Central Ave. (Rte. 99) has a number of cheap motels and restaurants. Main St. (Rte. 238) intersects Central in the heart of the city and then proceeds west to Jacksonville.

ACCOMMODATIONS

The small, clean motels that line Central Ave. are depressingly similar, though many are cheaper than Motel 6. There are no campgrounds within 15 mi. of town, just several "day-use parks"— grassy areas with wooden picnic tables.

Valli Hai Motel, 1034 Court St. (772-6183). A bit out of the way, but pleasant, with well-scrubbed rooms and dark wood ceilings. TV, A/C. Singles $25. Doubles $32.

City Center Motel, 324 S. Central Ave. (773-6248). Next door to the information center. The worn exterior hides large, comfortable rooms with A/C, cable, and phones. Singles $24. Doubles $28.

Village Inn, 722 N. Riverside (773-5373). Clean and tidy rooms. Singles $25. Doubles $35.

Sierra Inn Motel, 345 S. Central Ave. (773-7727). Better-than-average rooms. TV, A/C. Laundry and kitchen facilities available. Singles $32. Doubles $38.

Motel 6, 950 Alba Dr. (773-4290), on the south of town, at exit 27 off I-5. Located on the other side of the freeway, the "6" is inconvenient for travelers without cars. Swimming pool. Singles $30. Doubles $36. Additional persons $6 each. Reservations essential.

Capri Motel, 250 Barnett Rd. (773-7796). Blue building with large clean rooms and blue bathtubs next to a blue-bottomed pool. Quiet. A/C, phones, and cable. Singles $32. Doubles $37.

FOOD

If you've been contemplating a fast, Medford is the place to start it. You're better off dining in Ashland (a mere 12 mi. away).

C.K. Tiffins, 226 E. Main St. (779-0480). "Naturally good" health food and pastries served cafeteria-style in an airy renovated warehouse. Weekly lunch specials range from veggie whole-grain pizza ($4.75 with salad) to chicken tostada ($5.25). Open Mon.-Fri. 7:30am-3pm.

Las Margaritas, 12 N. Riverside (779-7628). This cavernous Mexican restaurant serves up large and delicious portions—enchiladas and burritos in full ($3.75) and reduced ($2.50) sizes. Receive an additional 10% off 3-5pm. Open Sun.-Tues. 11am-10pm, Fri.-Sat. 11am-11pm.

Yellow Submarine Sandwich Shop, 137 S. Central Ave. (779-7589), at 9th St. Tables inside and out; take out is eminently picnic-able. Subs range from 4 in. ($2.25) to 2 ft. ($10). Open daily 10am-5pm. Closed Sun.

SIGHTS AND ACTIVITIES

Medford's location on I-5 between Grants Pass and Ashland makes it the hub of southern Oregon. But don't leave town yet—Medford does offer some interesting alternatives for the history buff. The **Medford Railroad Park** (770-4586 or 779-7979), at the junction of Table Rock Rd. and Berrydale Ave., offers free rides to the public (May-Sept. 2nd and 4th Sun. of month, 10am-3pm). The **South Oregon History Center,** 6th and Central Ave. (773-6536), houses a research library, history store, and various exhibits (open Mon.-Fri. 9am-5pm; free).

In April, the **Pear Blossom Festival** (734-7327) lures runners to its 10K race. Other activities include a street fair, a band festival, a golf tournament and, of course, a parade. A more recent addition to the Medford social calendar is the **Medford Jazz Jubilee** (779-4847), held in October. Ten bands come from across the nation to blow their horns in Medford.

Harry and David's Original Country Store, 1 mi. south of Medford on Rte. 99 (776-2277), is the L.L. Bean of the fruit world. The factory complex also includes the 43,000-sq.-ft. show garden of **Jackson & Perkins,** the world's most prolific rose growers (open daily 9am-5pm).

■ Jacksonville

The biggest of Oregon's gold boomtowns, Jacksonville played the role of rich and lawless frontier outpost with appropriate licentious zeal. But the gold dwindled, the railroad and stagecoach lines took Jacksonville off their routes, and, in the final *coup de (dis)grâce,* the city lost the county seat to Medford. On the brink of oblivion, Jacksonville was revitalized by one of humanity's strongest emotions: nostalgia. During the 50s, the town was rehabilitated; today, it is a national historic landmark, one of only eight towns in Oregon on the National Register of Historic Places (all of which are on the Oregon Coast, oddly enough). A stroll down Main St. unveils views of balustraded, century-old buildings: the United States Hotel, the Methodist-Episcopal Church and the old courthouse, among others.

Practical Information To reach Jacksonville (or "J-ville" as residents affectionately call it), take Rte. 238 southwest from Medford or catch the #30 bus at 6th and Bartlett St. in Medford (buses run Mon.-Sat.; see Medford: Practical Information). Jacksonville can be reached by bus from Ashland only via Medford.

Drop by the **visitors center** in the old railway station at 185 N. Oregon St. (899-8118), where the eager staff will supply you with directions and pamphlets (open daily 10am-4pm). The **post office** (899-1563) is right next door at 175 Oregon St. (Open Mon.-Fri. 8:30am-5pm. **General Delivery ZIP Code:** 97530.)

Accommodations and Food Try to avoid spending the night in town. There are no campgrounds, and the **Jacksonville Inn,** 175 E. California St. (899-1900 or 800-231-9544), for all its charm, free Belgian waffle breakfasts, and free mountain bikes, has rooms starting at $80. You can savor a thick burger or other chow at the **Mustard Seed** (899-1958), 5th and C St. (Open Mon.-Fri. 7am-4pm, Sat. 8am-4pm, Sun. 10am-4pm). For a more varied menu at subterranean prices, grab a cup of chili ($2) at **The Claim Jumper's,** an outdoor cafe at 115 W. California St. (open Mon.-Sat. 10:30am-5:30pm, Sun. 11am-5pm).

Sights and Seasonal Events The town's greatest attractions are the tours given by costumed guides, including tours at the **Beekman House** (daily 1-5pm), and the informative lecture on 19th-century banking at the **Beekman Bank** on California St., 4 blocks south (tours and lecture given Memorial Day-Labor Day; bank admission $2, children $1). Visit the **Jacksonville Museum** (773-6536) in the County Courthouse on 5th St. (open daily 10am-5pm; Labor Day-May Tues.-Sun. 10am-5pm; admission $2)—and leave the kids locked up next door in the jail (now the **Children's Museum;** same hours as the Jacksonville Museum). Since reliving the past is parching work, sampling free wine is the perfect remedy. The **Wests' Tasting Room,** 690 N. 5th St. (899-1829), offers vintages from the nearby Valley View Vineyard (open daily 10am-7pm; in winter daily 10am-6pm).

For an excellent overview of the town's attractions, catch the 30-minute **trolley tour** (535-5617) at the Beekman Bank. (Runs Memorial Day-Labor Day daily 10am-4pm on the hr. Fare $3.50, under 12 $1.50.) Llazy hikers should trek over to **Siskiyou Llama Expeditions,** P.O. Box 1330 (899-1696), which rents and sells the beasts of burden for wilderness tours. Those who want to get out of the sun can tour the **Oregon Belle Mine.** More than $200,000 worth of gold was taken out of this "Lucky Strike" find, located 8 mi. outside of downtown Jacksonville, before it was closed in 1987. Admission is $8.50, and tickets are available at **Farrago Chocolates Espresso Bar and Cafe,** 157 W. California St. (899-9127. Open daily 7am-8pm. Reservations required. 2½-hr. tours June-Sept. Mon.-Sat. 10am, noon, 2, and 4pm.)

Jacksonville goes schizo every summer under the influence of the **Peter Britt Music Festivals,** P.O. Box 1124, Medford 97501 (773-6077 in OR, or 800-882-7488), named after the pioneer photographer whose hillside estate is the site of the fest. Acts as diverse as Gladys Knight, the Marsalis Brothers, and Sha-Na-Na make up the "jazz" festival, Mozart and Beethoven take a bow for the classical team, and everyone else is lumped together as folk/country. (Tickets for single events run from $10-25, 12 and under $5-9; package deals for groups of all sizes also available. Tickets also available at Farrago Chocolates.)

■■■ GRANTS PASS

Workers building a road through the Oregon mountains in 1863 were so excited by the news of General Ulysses Grant's victory at Vicksburg that they up and named the town after the burly President-to-be. Today Grants Pass serves as a base camp from which both tourists and locals can discover the Rogue River Valley and the Illinois Valley regions, which boast numerous parks offering camping, swimming, and fishing. The seat of Josephine County, Grants Pass is also the gateway to the coast and the Redwood forests.

PRACTICAL INFORMATION AND ORIENTATION

Visitors Information: Visitor and Convention Bureau (476-7717 in OR, or 800-547-5927), at 6th and Midland. Loads of brochures covering all of Josephine County. Eager and pleasant volunteer staff. Open Mon.-Fri. 8am-5pm, and Sat.-Sun. 9am-5pm in summer.

Greyhound, 460 Agness Ave. (476-4513), at the east end of town. To: Portland ($30) and San Francisco ($54). A few storage lockers (75¢ per 24 hr.) lurk next to the station. Open Mon.-Fri. 6:45am-6:30pm, Sat. 6:45am-12:30pm and 4:30-6:30pm.

Taxi: Grants Pass Taxi, 476-6444. 24 hr.

Laundromat: MayBelle's Washtub, 306 S.E. 8th St. (471-1317). Open daily 7am-10pm. Washer 50¢, 10-min. dry 25¢.

Crisis Hotline: 479-4357.

Senior Citizens' Information: Senior Center, 3rd and B St. (474-5440). **Senior Citizen Helpline,** 479-4357. 24 hr.

Information for Travelers with Disabilities: Handicapped Awareness and Support League, 290 N. East C St. (479-4275).

Hospital: Josephine Memorial Hospital, 715 NW Dimmick (476-6831), off A St.
Emergency: 911. **Police:** Justice Building (474-6370).
Post Office: 132 NW 6th St. (479-7526). Open Mon.-Fri. 9am-5pm. **General Delivery ZIP Code:** 97526.
Area Code: 503.

I-5 curves around Grants Pass to the northeast, heading north to Portland; south of the city, U.S. 199 runs along the Rogue River before making the 30-mi. trip down to Cave Junction. The two main north-south arterials are 6th St. (one-way south) and 7th St. (one-way north). 6th St. is the divider between streets labeled East and West, and the railroad tracks (between G and F St.) divide North and South addresses.

ACCOMMODATIONS AND CAMPING

Grants Pass supports a number of ugly jello-molded motels that for some reason vary greatly in price and quality (but they don't jiggle when you shake them). Since Grants Pass is a favorite highway stop, rooms fill up quickly, especially on weekends. Most of the motels are strung along 6th St.

Like the rest of the Inland Valley towns, Grants Pass suffers from a shortage of nearby campgrounds. **Valley of the Rogue State Park,** 3792 N. River Rd. (528-1118), 16 mi. east on I-5, has sites for $11, with hookup $12. **River RV Park,** 2956 U.S. 99 (479-0046), offers grassy, quiet sites for $16. Another option is **Schroeder Campgrounds** (474-5285), 4 mi. south of town; take U.S. 199 to Willow Lane, then follow the signs 1 mi. to the campground. Excellent sites with showers $11, with hookup $13, are often full by mid-afternoon. Call for info. about this and other Josephine County parks.

Fordson Home Hostel (HI/AYH), 250 Robinson Rd., Cave Junction 97523 (592-3203), 37 mi. southwest on U.S. 199. Accessible only by car. Free bicycle loans, a saw mill, and a resident Big Foot make the drive worthwhile. Friendly owner will dispense a mess of information about the Oregon Valley area and the California Redwoods. He will even give you a tour of his property complete with vortex and tractor museum. Discounted admission to Oregon caves. 5 beds and camping available. Members $8, nonmembers $11. Tentsites $3. Reservations required.

The Flamingo Motel, 728 NW 6th St. (476-6601). Delightfully tacky landscaping. Clean but tiny rooms. Small pool. HBO, phones, A/C. Pets allowed. Singles $29. Doubles $32. Rooms with kitchenette $42 for 2 people.

Motel Townhouse 839 NE 6th St. (479-0892). King-sized beds in large rooms. TV, A/C, and refrigerators—kitchen units in some rooms. Singles from $35. Doubles from $40. Rates ½-price in winter.

Hawks Inn Motel 1464 NW 6th St. (479-4057). Clean, large rooms with slightly worn furniture. Friendly staff. Pool with gazebo. A/C, HBO. Weekly rates in winter. Smaller rooms $26 for 1-2 people, larger rooms $32 for 1-2. 3-day advance reservations advised in summer.

Motel 6, 1800 NE 7th St. (474-1331). Low prices for antiseptic rooms. Cable TV, swimming pool, and A/C. Singles $31. Doubles $37. 1- or 2-day advance reservations are usually necessary.

FOOD

Pongsri's, 1571 N.E. 6th St. (479-1345). Combines a down-home atmosphere with spicy Thai food. Thai cuisine aficionados will love it; meat-and-potatoes lovers will broaden their gastronomic horizons. Large portions. Entrees $6. Lunch special $3 (served Tues.-Fri.). Open Tues.-Sun. 11am-9pm.

Matsukaze, 1675 N.E. 7th St. (479-2961). Traditional Japanese food in a simple and tasteful setting. Daily lunch specials are $3.50-4.50. Try the *makunouchi bentu,* a combination-lunch to go served in an ornate box ($7). Open Mon.-Thurs. 11am-2pm and 5-8:30pm, Fri. 11am-2pm and 5-9pm, Sat. 5-9:30pm.

The Brewery, 509 SW G St. (479-9850). Built as a brewery in 1886, this building has housed an apple-packing plant, a grocery store, and an art gallery; now it's a favorite local restaurant known for its prime rib ($15). The lighter-fare dinner menu (served until 7pm) is a deal at $7-10. Open Tues.-Fri. 11:30am-2:30pm and 4:30-9pm, Sat. 5-9pm, Sun. 4:30-9pm.

OUTDOORS: NEAR GRANTS PASS

A few mi. east of Grants Pass in the town of **Rogue River** lies **Valley of the Rogue State Park** (see Accommodations and Camping). You can enjoy the nearby Rogue (one of the few federally protected rivers designated as a "Wild and Scenic River") by raft, jetboat, mail boat, or simply by fishing or walking along its banks. Hop on a two-hour scenic tour given by **Hellgate Excursions, Inc.** (479-7204; $18, ages 4-11 $10). Those in search of longer trips should try the half-day ($30) and full-day ($45) whitewater rafting and kayaking trips run by **Orange Torpedo Trips** (479-5061 or 800-635-2925; daily May 15-Sept. 15; both trips include lunch).

When you've splashed through so much whitewater that a Class IV rapid draws no more than a yawn (if that's possible), you can **hike** in the Rogue State Park or head south if you have a car. While **Gold Hill** (20 mi. east on I-5) is famous for the large cave of bat guano kept under 24-hour watch by local police, it also houses the **Oregon Vortex/House of Mystery** (855-1543). Here, balls roll uphill, pendulums hang at an angle, and people seem to vary in height depending on where they stand. The bizarre phenomena are supposedly due to a local perturbation of the earth's magnetic field. (The owners apologize for any crude imitations of this house that tourists may have seen across the country, and assure visitors that this is the *real* thing. Decide for yourself. Open daily 8am-6pm, last tour at 4:30; Sept.-May daily 9am-5pm. Admission $6.)

The **Oregon Caves National Monument** (592-3400) can be reached by heading 30 mi. south along U.S. 199 to Cave Junction, and then following Rte. 46 east for 20 mi. Here in the belly of the ancient Siskiyous, acidic waters carved out limestone that had been compressed to marble. Dissolved and redeposited, the limestone filled cavernous chambers with exotic formations, whose slow growth is nurtured by the constant 39-43°F climate. This place is *cold*. (75-min. tours are conducted as groups of 16 form. Tours given daily 8am-7pm; May to mid-June and Sept. daily 9am-5pm; Oct.-April daily at 10:30am, 12:30, 2, and 3:30pm. Admission $6.75, under 12 $3.75, under 6 not admitted, but on-site child care is available.)

The town of **Cave Junction**, 30 mi. south of Rogue River along U.S. 199, offers some R&R for the intrepid explorer. You can catch some z's at the **Kerbyville Inn Bed and Breakfast.** Rooms start at $50 and include a complimentary bottle of wine from the nearby **Bridgeview Winery,** 4210 Holland Loop Rd. (592-4698), which operates the inn. The winery is open for free tasting (daily 11am-5pm). Children should float on over to **Noah's Ark,** 27893 Redwood Hwy. (592-3802), a tame petting zoo. (Open daily 9am-6pm; in winter 10am-5pm. Admission $4.50, ages over 60 and 7-12 $3.25, ages 3-6 $2.25. Pony rides are $1.50.) **The Growers' Market,** on C St. between 4th and 5th (476-5375) is the largest open-air market in the state, vending everything a produce-lover could imagine. (Open March 15-Thanksgiving Tues. and Sat. 9am-1pm; July-Halloween only on Sat.)

■■■ EUGENE

Situated between the **Siuslaw** (pronounced see-YOU-slaw) and the **Willamette** (rhymes with dammit) **National Forests,** Oregon's second-largest city sits astride the Willamette River, touching tiny Springfield to the east. Not small or quaint enough to be a town, not big or (despite its efforts) sophisticated enough to be a metropolis, Eugene is a city open to interpretation. City slickers can shop and dine in downtown's pedestrian mall and 5th Street Market. Outdoorsy types can raft the river, bike and run on its banks, or hike in one of the large parks near the city. And as home to the **University of Oregon,** Eugene crawls with art museums, ice cream parlors, and all the other trappings of a college town in the age of mass academia.

The fleet-footed and free-spirited have dubbed Eugene "the running capital of the universe." Only in this city could the annual **Bach Festival** (in late June) be accompanied by the "Bach Run," a 1 to 5km dash through the city's downtown area. The Nike running shoe company, founded in Eugene, sponsors the event which culminates in a performance of the so-called "Sports Cantata" (BWV 12 "Weinen, Klagen, Laufen," or "Weeping, Lamenting, Running").

PRACTICAL INFORMATION AND ORIENTATION

Visitors Information: Eugene-Springfield Convention and Visitors Bureau, 305 W. 7th (800-452-3670 or 484-5307; outside OR 800-547-5445), between Lincoln and Lawrence St. downtown. Maps, brochures, listings, and guides to everything you might want to do in the 2 cities. (Open in summer Mon.-Fri. 8am-5pm, Sat. 10am-4pm.)

Park Information: Willamette National Forest Service, 211 E. 7th Ave. (465-6522). **Eugene Parks and Recreation Dept.,** 22 W. 7th Ave. (687-5333 for general information, 687-5311 for specialized recreation for people with disabilities). Open Mon.-Fri. 8am-5pm.

University of Oregon Switchboard, 1585 E. 13th Ave. (346-3111). Referral for just about everything—rides, housing, emergency services. Open Mon.-Fri. 7am-6pm.

Amtrak, 4th and Willamette St. (800-872-7245). To: Seattle (1 per day, $50), San Francisco (1 per day, $104), and Portland (1 per day, $24).

Greyhound, 9th and Pearl St. (344-6265 or 800-231-2222). Ten buses north, 6 south per day. To: Seattle ($40), San Francisco ($83.50), Portland ($16). Open daily 6am-10pm. Storage lockers $1 per day.

Green Tortoise, 937-3603. To San Francisco (3 per day, $49); Seattle (3 per day, $25) on the same route. Almost half the price of Greyhound. Reservations required; call for details. Open daily 8am-8pm.

Lane Transit District (LTD): (687-5555), at 10th and Willamette St. Provides public transportation throughout Eugene. Pick up a map and timetables at the Convention and Visitors Bureau, the LTD Service Center, or 7-Eleven stores. Many routes are wheelchair-accessible—look for the international accessibility symbol. Fares Mon.-Fri. 75¢, Sat.-Sun. and after 7pm through the week 50¢; seniors and children ½ price.

Ride Board: Erb Memorial Union (EMU) Basement, University of Oregon. Open during the school year daily 7am-11:30pm; mid-June to mid-Sept. 7am-7pm.

Taxi: Yellow Cab, 746-1234. 24 hr.

AAA Office, 983 Willagillespie Rd. (484-0661). Open Mon.-Fri. 8am-5pm.

Bike Rental: Pedal Power, 535 High St. (687-1775), downtown. 6-speeds $3 per hr., $15 per day. Open Mon.-Fri. 9am-7pm, Sat. 9am-6pm, Sun. 10am-5pm. **Paul's Bicycle Way of Life,** 152 W. 5th Ave. (344-4105). Friendly staff offers city/mountain bikes for $15 per day, $3 per hour. Major credit card or $100 deposit. Open Mon.-Fri. 9am-7pm, Sat.-Sun. 10am-5pm.

Laundromat: Club Wash, 595 E. 13th St. (342-1727), at Patterson. Open daily 7am-2am. Wash 75¢, 8-min. dry 25¢.

Crisis Line: White Bird Clinic, 341 E. 12th Ave. (800-422-7558, in Eugene 342-8255). Free crisis counseling and low-cost medical care. Open Mon.-Fri. 8am-5pm with 24-hr. backup.

Rape Crisis: Sexual Assault Support Services, 630 Lincoln (485-6700). Open Mon.-Fri. 9am-5pm. Answering service 24 hr.

Emergency: 911. **Police/Fire:** 777 Pearl St. (687-5111), at City Hall.

Post Office: In Eugene, (341-3611) at 5th and Willamette St., or in the EMU Bldg. at the university. Open Mon.-Fri. 8:30am-5:30pm, Sat. 10am-2pm. **General Delivery ZIP Code:** 97401.

Area Code: 503.

Eugene is located 100 mi. south of Portland on the I-5 corridor. The University of Oregon campus lies in the southeastern corner of town, bordered on the north by Franklin Blvd., which runs from the city center to I-5. 1st Ave. runs alongside the winding Willamette River; Willamette Ave. intersects the river, dividing the city into east and west. Willamette Ave. is the "main drag" and is interrupted by the mall on 7th, 8th, and 9th St., which allows only pedestrian traffic. The city is a motorist's nightmare of one-way streets; bicyclists and joggers prevail.

ACCOMMODATIONS

Eugene has the usual assortment of motels; the cheapest are on E. Broadway and W. 7th St. The **hostel,** though far from downtown, is the least expensive and most interesting place to stay. The closest legal camping is 7 mi. away, although it is said that people camp by the river (especially in the wild and woolly northeastern side near Springfield). Most park hours are officially 6am to 11pm. Lone women should avoid the university campus vicinity at night.

Lost Valley Center, 81868 Lost Valley Lane, Dexter (937-3351). Take Hwy. 58 south 8 mi., turn right on Rattlesnake Creek Rd.; after 4 mi., turn right on Lost Valley Lane, and 1 mi. later you're there. "An intentional community," this oasis of idealism is the perfect spot to contemplate anything and everything. Sleep in large cabins and wake yourself up with a dip in the swimming hole. Come in at night for the organic dinner. Call ahead for reservations or to sign up for a variety of ecology retreats and conferences. Members $7, nonmembers $10. Campsites $5 per person. Dinner (Mon.-Fri.) $6.

66 Motel, 755 E. Broadway (342-5041). Very professional, very cheap and, not surprisingly, very crowded. Cable TV, A/C, and phones. Singles $25. Doubles $31.

Downtown Motel, 361 W. 7th Ave. (345-8739). Where traveling music groups stay. Flowers in every room. Coffee shop next door. Cable TV, A/C. Singles $26. Doubles $40.

Executive House Inn, 1040 W. 6th Ave. (683-4000). No A/C but huge rooms with TV, phones, and sink. Singles $22, doubles $27.

Timbers Motel, 1015 Pearl St. (343-3345 or 800-643-4167), ½ block from Greyhound, so these clean and small rooms are perfect for late-night bus arrivals. Cable TV, A/C. Singles $23. Doubles $25.

CAMPING

Campers with cars should drive the 20 mi. down Rte. 58 into the **Willamette National Forest.** Other than this, you'll find no good camping nearby, and much of what you will find is dominated by RVs. The swamp in the National Forest gives the tree bark and ferns an eerie phosphorescence in some seasons, especially around the **Black Canyon** campground.

Dorena Lake and **Cottage Grove Lake** (942-5631), 20 mi. south of Eugene on I-5. Equipped for camping. Sites $10. **Schwarz Park,** at the west end of Dorena Lake (942-1418) has sites for $8.

Fern Ridge Shores (935-2335), 12 mi. west of Eugene on Rte. 126. Campgrounds on the southwest spit of land that projects into the lake at Fern Ridge Shores. Sites for RVs only, $16-20.

Fall Creek Lake, Lookout Point Lake, and **Hills Creek Lake** (937-2129), 20 mi. southeast of Eugene on Rte. 58, in Willamette National Forest. Camping allowed on all 3 lakes. Sites $5-16.

Eugene KOA Kamping World, 200 S. Stuart Way, Coburg (343-4832 or 800-621-6628). The closest to Eugene, just off the Coburg exit from I-5, about 7 mi. from downtown. 30 tentsites—the other 115 hook up to the RV altar. Sites $14-19.

FOOD AND ENTERTAINMENT

A plethora of bakeries make soup and bread a good option. The best values are found a bit out of town, but worth the hike.

Downtown

The monotony of pizza joints in this university town is broken by a smattering of ethnic restaurants. Some of the best food downtown is in the enormous open-air **City Center Mall,** centered on E. 11th and Willamette St. The granola crowd does its shopping at **Sundance Natural Foods,** 748 E. 24th Ave. (at 24th and Hilyard). This vegetarian wonderland specializes in fruits and vegetables, baked goods, and local dairy products; you can create a salad for $3.89 per lb (open daily 8am-11pm).

Keystone Cafe, 395 W. 5th St. (342-2075). An eclectic local granola co-op which serves up incredible vegetarian and vegan food made from home-grown ingredients. Burgers ($4.70-6.50), huge slices of fresh pie ($2.50), and other breakfast foods served all day. Open daily 7am-3pm.

The Glenwood Restaurant (687-0355), at 13th and Alder. Great vegetarian selection. Live music. Dinners $5-6. Open 24 hr., with limited service after 9pm.

Cafe Navarro, 454 Willamette St. (344-0943). Caribbean and Latin cuisine and decor. Vegetarian dishes compliment a selection of creative entrees, $9-12. Open Tues.-Sat. 11am-3pm and 5-9:30pm. Also breakfast Sat.-Sun. 9am-3pm.

Allann Bros. Bakery and Coffeehouse, 152 W. 5th Ave. (342-3378), in the Farmer's Union Marketplace. Munch delicious baked goods and salads while listening to the occasional local bands in an airy atmosphere. Fill a thermos with coffee for $1.20. Lunch specials $4. Open Mon.-Thurs. 8am-10pm, Fri.-Sun. 6am-midnight.

Ambrosia, 174 E. Broadway (342-4141). Yuppies come here for the red-fringed lamps and amazing Italian food. *Calzone modo nostra* ($8). Sit outside or beneath huge tapestries indoors. Open Mon.-Thurs. 11:30am-10:30pm, Fri.-Sat. 11am-11:30pm, Sun. 4:30-10pm.

Prince Pücker's Ice Cream Parlor, 861 Willamette St. (343-2621). Homemade ice cream from all-natural ingredients. Best ice cream in Eugene—try the raspberry truffle. Experience the "euphoria ultra chocolate" sundae ($2.10), made with locally-produced chocolate sauce and truffles. Open Mon.-Sat. 7am-9pm, Sun. noon-5pm; in winter, Mon.-Fri. 7am-6pm, Sat. 10am-6pm, Sun. noon-5pm.

University Area

The University area hangout is at 13th and Kincaid. Students take to the sidewalk when the multitude of late-night cafes chairs are filled.

Taylor's Collegeside Inn, 894 E. 13th St. (344-6174), right across from the university. Low-key, low-priced; friendly waiters, plenty of beer. Burgers and sandwiches ($3-4.50) and delicious taco soup ($1.75). This mild-mannered restaurant rocks with live music that echoes throughout the campus (Wed.-Sat. at 7pm; cover $2-5). Restaurant open daily 7am-8pm. Nightclub open daily 7pm-2am.

Guido's, 801 E. 13th St. (343-0681). Good Italian dinners that average $7. Try a calzone with choice of filling ($6). Pool tables and a big dance floor. DJ Mon.-Fri. 10pm-2:30am. Open daily 10am-2:30am.

Chez Ray's Cafe, 1437 E. 19th Ave. (342-8596). Indoor/outdoor cafe draws crowds for the *quesadilla buenos días* ($5.75) and Baja chicken sandwich ($6). Open Tues.-Sun. 8am-10pm.

Elsewhere

New Day Bakery, 345 Van Buren (345-1695). The best bread in town is served with a hearty bowl of soup ($2.50) in this quiet cafe. Open Mon.-Sat. 7am-7pm, Sun. 7am-2pm.

Pizza Stop Cafe, 1478 Willamette (345-4811). Locally renowned pizza (also delivered) with great toppings ($9-12 a pie). Also sells delicious unleavened "hikers' bread" ($2.25). The hot rolls will make your day. Open Mon.-Thurs. 10am-9pm, Fri. 10am-10pm, Sat. 11am-10pm, and Sun. 11am-9pm.

Clubs And Bars

New Max's, 550 13th Ave. (342-6365). Oldest pub in town (despite the name). Great blues and other local and national bands (cover $2-5). Open Sun.-Thurs. noon-2:30am, Fri.-Sat. 11am-2:30am.

High St. Cafe, 1243 High (345-4905). Proudly sells McMinnamin's and seasonal fruit ale. Homey, comfortable atmosphere in which to sip their great brew. Mon.-Sat. 11am-1am, Sun. noon-1am.

Club Arena, 959 Pearl St. (683-2360). Underneath Perrie's Restaurant. The only gay dance club in town. Open daily 7pm-2:30am.

SIGHTS AND ACTIVITIES

Despite the roasting temperatures of a Willamette Valley summer, noon is when recreational centers and museums open. Even the Saturday market drags its feet until the sun reaches the magical meridian. Instead, spend your morning at **Alton Baker Park.** Head east along the bank of the Willamette River to the point where N. Adams St. intersects the bike path. Here the **River House** contains the offices for the city's outdoor program and is a meeting place for outdoor activities. The nearby **Owen Memorial Rose Garden,** just under the I-5 overpass, is perfect for a picnic, replete with rumbling traffic.

The **Lane County Historical Museum,** 740 W. 13th Ave. (687-4239), arranges a formal and exalting look at the city's history. (Open Wed.-Fri. 10am-5pm, Sat. noon-4pm. Admission $2, senior citizens $1, children 75¢.)

Reception centers for the **University of Oregon** (U of O) handle tours and distribute campus maps at **Oregon Hall** (346-3014), E. 13th Ave. and Agate St., and at the visitors parking and information booth, just left of the main entrance on Franklin Blvd. Take time to admire the ivy-covered halls that set the scene for National Lampoon's *Animal House*. The **University Museum of Art** (346-3027), on 13th St. between Kincaid and University St., houses contemporary Northwest and American art, as well as an extensive collection from the Pacific Basin. (Open Sept.-June Wed.-Sun. noon-5pm. Free. Call the museum office for tours.) A few blocks away, the **Museum of Natural History,** 1680 E. 15th Ave. (346-3024), at Agate, shows a collection of relics from the peoples of the Pacific Rim that includes a 7000-year-old pair of running shoes—a primitive "swoosh" is still visible (open Wed.-Sun. noon-5pm; free).

The $26 million **Hult Performing Arts Center,** the city's crown jewel, resides at One Eugene Center (687-5000), 6th and Willamette St., and features a spectrum of music from the blues to Bartók. (Free tours Thurs. and Sat. at 1pm. Call 687-5087 for information and reservations.) The Community Center for the Performing Arts, better known as **WOW Hall,** 291 W. 8th St. (687-2746), is an old Wobblie (International Workers of the World) meeting hall that for years has sponsored concerts by lesser-known artists. Brochures announcing these off-beat acts are plastered everywhere (open Tues.-Fri. 3-6pm).

Only a beat away from the heart of tourist country lurks the highly acclaimed **Fifth Street Market** (484-0383), at 5th and High St. This collection of overpriced boutiques and eateries attracts those who are under the mystifying impression that British cuisine is "gourmet." Instead of falling victim to this labyrinth of pseudo-sophistication, head to the **Saturday Market** (686-8885), at 8th and Oak, held weekly between March 30 and Thanksgiving. The food here (ranging from blintzes to berries to burritos) is tastier, healthier and cheaper than that at Fifth.

If you're looking to get closer to nature, **River Runner Supply,** 2222 Centennial Blvd. (343-6883 or 800-223-4326), organizes outdoor experiences from fishing to whitewater rafting on the Willamette River. The visitors information center can supply a list of several other companies. Reservations are recommended on weekends. Check local river conditions and maps, since there are some dangerous areas on the Willamette near Eugene.

If you just have an afternoon hour to spare, canoe or kayak the **Millrace Canal,** which parallels the Willamette for 3 or 4 mi. This shallow waterway passes under many small foot bridges and through several pipes. While not clean enough for swimming, the river is perfect for lazing in the sun. Rent canoes or kayaks from **EMU Waterworks Company,** 1395 Franklin Blvd. (346-4386), run by University of Oregon students (open in summer daily noon-dusk; $4 per hour, $15 for 24 hr.).

SEASONAL EVENTS

The two-week **Bach Festival** beginning the last week of June (346-5666) brings Helmuth Rilling, world-renowned authority on Baroque music, to lead some of the country's finest musicians in performances of Bach's cantatas and concerti. (Write to the Hult Center Ticket Office, One Eugene Center 97401; or call 687-5000 for reservations or further information. Tickets $5-25.) **Art and the Vineyard,** at Alton Baker Park (345-1571), is a happy food fest held in July. The large park is taken over by West Coast artisans and local vineyards, complete with a food festival and live music. The enormous **Oregon Country Fair** takes place in the middle of July and lasts three days ($6 per day; $5 for the 1st day only). To alleviate the yearly traffic jams, LTD provides bus service (25¢) to and from the fairgrounds in Veneta. Buses leave every half-hour in the morning from the LTD Customer Service Center, and take off again before the fairgrounds close at 7pm. The fair is a huge crafts-and-music happening, characterized by a unique mellow spirit and hailed by many as a Woodstock-like reprise. The **Oregon Festival of American Music** (687-6526) takes place the first week in September and often features big-name singers and musicians. For information, exact dates, and other festivals, especially in the summer and fall, call the Eugene Visitors Center.

■ Near Eugene

Eugene lies at the southern end of the Willamette Valley, whose fertile floor and richly forested hills attracted Oregon's waves of pioneer settlers. Wilderness adventures and relics of pioneer days await those who venture off I-5. One of the favored drives in the area runs from Rte. 126 to U.S. 20 and then back to Rte. 126. The 50-mi. loop surveys the McKenzie Valley and the **McKenzie Pass,** where lava outcroppings served in the 1960s as a training site for NASA astronauts preparing for lunar landings.

Fifty mi. north of Eugene is the **Willamette National Forest** and the start of the 13-mi. **McKenzie River Trail.** The trailhead is 55 mi. northeast of Eugene on Rte. 126, 1.2 mi. past McKenzie Bridge. Five **campgrounds** serve the area. Contact the Parks Department or the Willamette National Forest Service (see Eugene: Practical Information).

The small-town scenes in National Lampoon's *Animal House* and the Rob Reiner film *Stand By Me* were filmed in **Cottage Grove,** 20 mi. south of Eugene off I-5, and the town couldn't have needed more than a spit-polish for its big-screen debut. Maps for self-guided car tours of the "Covered Bridge Capital of Oregon" are available at the **Chamber of Commerce,** 710 Row River Rd. (942-2411). Nearby Dorena and Cottage Grove Lakes are popular spots for water sports, hiking, and picnicking.

■■■ SALEM

Salem is a small town trying to dress up for its job as the state capital. While the downtown area is brand new, much of Salem retains the look and flavor of the missionary settlement it was in 1851, when it beat Oregon City in the competition to be capital.

PRACTICAL INFORMATION AND ORIENTATION

Visitors Information: Visitors Center, 1313 Mill St. SE (581-4325), part of the Mission Mill Village complex (see Sights). Brochures on Salem and other parts of the state. Open Mon.-Fri. 8:30am-noon and 1-5pm, Sat.-Sun. 10am-4pm. In fall and winter, Mon.-Fri. 8:30am-5pm. **Chamber of Commerce,** 220 Cottage St. NE (581-1466). Open Mon.-Fri. 8:30am-5pm.

Amtrak (588-1551 or 800-872-7245), at 13th St. and Oak St. SE across from Willamette University. To Portland (1 per day, $12), Seattle (1 per day, $35), and San Francisco (1 per day, $129).

Greyhound, 450 Church St. NE (362-2428), at Center St. To Portland ($7.50). Open daily 6:30am-8:30pm.

Local Transportation: Cherriots (Salem Area Transit), 588-2877. 19 buses originate from High St.; terminals are in front of the courthouse. Fare 50¢. Service Mon.-Fri. 6:15am-6:15pm (most buses every ½ hr. during rush hours), Sat. 7:45am-5:45pm (every hr.).

Taxi: Salem Yellow Cab Co., 362-2411. 24 hr.

Car Rental: National, 695 Liberty St. NE (800-227-7368 or 585-4226). Cars from $33 with 100 free mi, 30¢ per additional mi. Open Mon.-Fri. 8am-5:30pm.

AAA, 2902 Ryan Dr. SE (581-1608). Open Mon.-Fri. 8am-5pm.

Laundromat: Suds City Depot, 1785 Lancaster Dr. NE (362-9845). Open daily 7:30am-9pm. Wash 75¢, 25 min. dry 50¢.

Women's Crisis Center: 399-7722.

Emergency: 911. **Police:** 555 Liberty St. SE (588-6123), in City Hall.

Post Office: 1050 25th St. (370-4700). Open Mon.-Fri. 8:30am-5:30pm. **General Delivery ZIP Code:** 97301.

Area Code: 503.

Halfway between the equator and the North Pole, bordered on the west by the Willamette River and on the east by I-5, Salem is 47 mi. south of Portland.

ACCOMMODATIONS AND CAMPING

You'll have to hunt a good distance from Salem's city center to find inexpensive lodgings, unless you're a woman or a camper. The former should try the **YWCA,** and the latter should stake a claim at the **KOA Kampground.**

YWCA, 768 State St. (581-9922), next to Willamette U. and Capital Park. *Women only.* A scenic and relatively safe location. Rooms $16 for members, $19 for non-members. Key deposit $4.

Holiday Lodge, 1400 Hawthorne Ave. NE (585-2323 or 800-543-5071). Large, comfortable rooms in a convenient location. Pool, phones, A/C, and cable TV. Singles $30. Doubles $40.

City Center Motel, 510 Liberty St. SE (364-0121), about ½ mi. from the city center (despite the name). The budget lodgings closest to downtown. Phones, cable TV, A/C. Singles $36-40. Doubles $45-55.

Motel 6, 2250 Mission St. SE (588-7191), exit 256 off I-5, 1 mi. east of town. Pool, TV, A/C. Singles $30. Doubles $36.

Salem KOA Kampground, 3700 Hagers Grove Rd. SE (581-6736), off Lancaster Dr. This immaculate campground is wonderfully convenient to the city center, but the noise from nearby I-5 may keep you up all night. Showers. Sites $11.

Silver Falls State Park, 20024 Silver Falls SE (Rte. 214), (873-8681), 26 mi. from Salem. Oregon's largest state park offers swimming, hiking trails, and views of multitudinous waterfalls, including a trail leading behind and beneath one of the smaller falls. The tallest (spectacular Double Falls) crashes 178 ft. Campsites $14, with electricity and water use $15.

FOOD

Restaurants in Salem are generally overpriced and not particularly good, though there are a few exceptions. The best options are near **Willamette University.**

Off-Center Cafe, 1741 Center NE (363-9245), in the lime-green shopping center. Appreciably pioneering, with a left-of-center approach and generally delicious food that has become a local favorite. Try the "bibble and squib" ($3.75) or the scrambled tofu and rice ($5.25). Open Tues.-Fri. 6am-2:30pm, Sat.-Sun. 8am-2pm and 6-9pm.

Deja Breeze, 1210 State St. (364-6246). Just a block from the capital, this small deli serves up monumental sandwiches and gardenburgers. Chicken Fajitas ($4) and espresso (75¢). Open Mon.-Fri. 7am-9pm, Sat. 11am-4pm.

SIGHTS AND ACTIVITIES

The **State Capitol** (378-4423), on Court St. between W. Summer and E. Summer St., is capped by a 24-ft. gold-leaf statue of the quintessential "Oregon Pioneer" which gives the building an imposing, temple-like appearance. Fortunately, the Capitol's interior is much more personable. Despite persistent conflicts between loggers and environmentalists, the legislative chambers are designed for laid-back lawmaking. The carpet on the Senate floor is checkered with salmon and sheaves of wheat, while the House's carpet depicts a forest of Christmas trees. Although the tower is closed indefinitely due to the perils of asbestos, the gold-plated pioneer atop the tower remains steadfast. (The Capitol is open for roaming Mon.-Fri. 8am-5pm, Sat. 9am-4pm, Sun. noon-4pm. Free 30-min. tours Mon.-Fri. 9am-4pm.)

Across the street is **Willamette University,** 900 State St. (370-6300). Founded by Methodist missionaries in 1842, it is billed as "the oldest university of the West." **Tours** leave from the admissions office in George Putnam University Center (370-6303) daily at 10am and 2pm; call ahead.

Mission Mill Village, 1313 Mill St. SE (585-7012), is a group of historic houses where employees in pioneer garb demonstrate forest-cooking, carving, and hunting. The village includes a reasonably interesting woolen mill/museum, several stores more closely tied to the contemporary consumer economy, and missionary Jason Lee's horse. Tours of the houses and mill leave hourly (Open Tues.-Sat. 10am-4:30pm, Sun. 1-4:30pm; in winter, open Tues.-Sat. 10am-4:30pm. Admission $2.50 for either the house or the mill, $4 for both. Seniors and students $2 and $3.) The **Marion Museum of History** (364-2128) is part of the village but charges a separate admission fee. Inside, rare relics of the Kalpuyans survive (open Tues.-Sat. 9:30am-4:30pm; admission $1, seniors and children 50¢).

Oregon grapes produce world-class wines, and opportunities for sampling abound. **Honeywood Winery,** 501 14th St. SE (362-4111), Salem's only urban winery, is Oregon's oldest (open for tours and tasting Mon.-Fri. 9am-5pm, Sat. 10am-5pm, Sun. 1pm-5pm). For a sampling of a less fluid form, check out the **Salem Art Tour and Festival,** held during the third week of July in Bush's Pasture Park, 2330 17th St. NE. The Festival showcases the works of Northwestern artists. In August, check out the 123rd annual **Oregon State Fair** (378-3247).

EASTERN OREGON

Hundreds of millions of years ago, the triangle of land between Portland, Bend, and John Day was one of the great centers of volcanic activity on the North American continent. Massive eruptions spewed forth lava and ash, giving rise to the Cascades, which would later be molded into their present shape by glaciers. These rough and jagged mountains are a natural rain barrier, trapping the moisture from Pacific winds and creating a hot, arid inland climate. For generations, this relatively-deserted desert region has challenged its human inhabitants—from the pioneer settlers who crossed it on foot and wagon to the modern farmers who fight to keep their fields green. In this expansive and largely undeveloped region, a car is a boon since distances are great, and the few buses take roundabout routes.

■■■ CRATER LAKE AND KLAMATH FALLS

Mirror-blue Crater Lake, the namesake of Oregon's only national park, was regarded as sacred by Indian shamans, who forbade their people to look upon it. Iceless in winter and flawlessly circular, the lake plunges from its 6000-ft. elevation to a depth of nearly 2000 ft., making it the nation's deepest lake (and the second deepest in the hemisphere). Klamath Falls offers a few diversions for those making a pit stop, but time and money are better spent at Crater Lake.

PRACTICAL INFORMATION AND ORIENTATION

Visitors Information: William G. Steel Center, located next to park headquarters south of Rim Village on Rim Dr. The center provides visitors information and exhibits. You can pick up backcountry camping **permits** here or at Rim Village (free). Also screens a 17-min. movie on Crater Lake every ½ hr. 8am-4:30pm. Open July-Labor Day daily 8am-7pm; June and Labor Day-Sept. 30 daily 10am-6pm. **Crater Lake National Park Visitors Center** (524-2211), on the lake shore at **Rim Village.** Pamphlets and advice regarding trails and campsites. Open daily 10am-6pm. Closed off-season. The **Klamath County Chamber of Commerce,** at 507 Main St. (884-5193), isn't equipped to answer more than simple questions; instead, try their booth at **Veterans Park** on Lake Ewauna. Open Memorial Day-Labor Day Mon.-Sat. 8:30-5pm, Sun. 11am-5pm.

Park Admission: Admission is charged only in summer. Cars $5, hikers and bikers $3, 62 and over free

Amtrak, S. Spring St. depot (884-2822). 1 train per day north and 1 train per day south. To Portland: $64. Open daily 6-10am and 9-11pm.

Greyhound, 1200 Klamath Ave. (882-4616). To: Bend (1 per day); Redding, CA (2 per day). Lockers $1 per 24 hr. Open Mon.-Fri. 6am-5pm, Sat. 6am-4pm.

Taxi: AB Taxi, 885-5607.

Car Rental: Budget, at Airport (885-5421), take South 6th, turn right onto Altamonta. $25 per day Thurs.-Sun. 150 free mi. per day, 25¢ per additional mi. Open Mon.-Fri. 7am-7:30pm, Sat.-Sun. 8am-5pm.

Equipment Rental: All Seasons Sports, 714 Main St., Klamath Falls (884-3863). Rents water skis, wake boards, and knee boards $15 per day, cross-country skis $10 per day, downhill skis $12 per day, and in-line skates $10 per day or $4 for 5 hr. Open Mon.-Sat. 9am-6pm, Sun. noon-5pm.

Laundromat: Main Street Laundromat, 1711 Main St. (883-1784). Wash $1, 12-min. dry 25¢. Open daily 8am-7pm.

Weather and Road Conditions: (recording) 976-7277. Weather and road information are broadcast continuously on radio station 1610 AM.

Crisis: Red Cross, 884-4125. **Poison Control,** 800-452-7165. **Rape Crisis,** 884-0390.

Hospital: 883-6176.

Emergency: 911. **Police: Klamath Falls,** (884-4876); **County,** (883-5130). **Fire:** 885-2056, non-emergency.

Post Office: 317 S. 7th St. (884-9226). Open Mon.-Fri. 9am-5:30pm.

Rte. 62 through Crater Lake National Park is open year-round, but the park's services and accommodations are available only during July and August. After skirting the southwestern side of the lake, Rte. 62 heads southwest to Medford and southeast to Klamath (pronounced kuh-LAM-ath) Falls. To reach the park from Portland, take I-5 to Eugene, then Rte. 58 east to U.S. 97 south. Many roads leading to the park are closed or dangerous during the winter. Crater Lake averages 530 in. of snow per year (that's right), so some roads could be closed as late as July; call the Steele Center for road conditions (see Practical Information). Rte. 138 heads west from U.S. 97 and approaches the lake from the north, but this route can only be used during the summer.

Klamath Falls lies 24 mi. south of the intersection of Rte. 62 and U.S. 97, at the southern tip of Upper Klamath Lake. Many roads lead to this small town: historic Rte. 66 heads east from Ashland; Rte. 39 goes south to Redding; Rte. 140 runs east to Nevada; and U.S. 97 continues south to Reed. Main St. is just that, with most of the restaurants and motels on it or only a few blocks distant. Very little happens around here in the winter. The lake is effectively, if not officially, closed then, and Klamath Falls motels have lots of room.

ACCOMMODATIONS AND CAMPING

Klamath Falls has several affordable hotels; you may be wise to sack out in the town and make your forays to Crater Lake from there. The national park contains two campsites: **Mazama Campground** and the smaller **Lost Creek Campground,** which is often closed when roads are impassable (see below). Backcountry camping is allowed within the park; pick up permits (free) from Rim Village Visitors Center or at the Steel Center (see Practical Information). Food must be stored properly to prevent hungry bears from investigating; talk to the rangers for more details. Make sure you boil any stream water thoroughly before ingesting, as nasty microscopic critters often lurk.

Value 20 Motel, 124 N. 2nd St. (882-7741). Very clean, spacious rooms equipped with kitchenettes, HBO, A/C. Singles $31. Doubles $33. Allows pets.

Maverick Motel, 1220 Main St. (882-6688), down the street from Greyhound in Klamath Falls. A bit north of the action but only a short walk. Small but elegant rooms. TV, A/C, and a Kleenex-sized pool. Singles $28. Doubles $33.

Fort Klamath Lodge Motel (381-2234), on Rte. 62, 6 mi. from the southern entrance to Crater Lake National Park. The closest motel to the lake, the lodge is located in historic Fort Klamath, which consists of little more than a grocery store, gas station, coffee shop, and tons of wildflowers in the spring. Cute, cozy, country-style rooms with knotted-pine walls. TV; no phones in the rooms. Laundry available. Singles $30. Doubles $35.

Mazama Campground (594-2511), in Crater Lake National Park. The 200 sites in this monster facility are usually tyrannized in summer by mammoth RVs, generating all the ambience of a parking lot. Also rents cabins. Firewood for sale. No hookups, but flush toilets, telephones. Pay laundry facilities and shower. Wheelchair accessible. Sites $11. No reservations.

Lost Creek Campground (594-2211), in Crater Lake National Park. Hidden at the southwest corner of the park, this campground has only 16 sites. Try to secure a spot in the morning. Drinking water and pit toilets. No reservations. Usually open by mid-July. Tents only, sites $5.

FOOD

Eating inexpensively in Crater Lake is difficult. Crater Lake Lodge has a small dining room, and Rim Village establishments charge high prices for a skimpy array of foodstuffs. If you're coming from the south, **Fort Klamath** is the final food frontier before you trek into the park. Stock up here at the **Old Fort Store** (381-2345; open summer daily 8am-9pm). There are several affordable restaurants in Klamath Falls and a 24-hour **Safeway** (882-2660) at Pine and 8th St., 1 block from Main St. Healthy and/or vegetarian food is hard to find in Klamath—try **Gigglers,** 4230 6th St. (884-9151), a small health food store (open daily noon-6pm).

Llao Rock Cafe, in the Rim Village has deli sandwiches for $4.50 (open daily 8am-6pm). Upstairs, **The Watchman Eatery and Lounge** has burgers ($4.75 with potato salad) you can munch while looking out on the stillness of Crater Lake. Open June 10-Sept. 2 daily noon-10pm.

Hobo Junction, 636 Main St. (882-8013), at 7th St. The place to stock up for a picnic or to simply relax among the potted plants. Good deli fare, with hearty bowls of chili ($1.65) and 22 varieties of hot dogs. Try #8, the Hobo Dog (cheddar and Swiss cheese, bacon, and salsa, $2.65). Open Mon.-Fri. 11am-5pm.

The Blue Ox, 535 Main St. (884-5308). Slow service but portions of Bunyanic proportions. $4.25 buys a mammoth Oxburger, and just $1.65 gets you 2 eggs, hashbrowns, and toast. The 50¢ coffee is the cheapest in town. Breakfast served all day. Open daily 7am-8pm.

SIGHTS

As you approach **Crater Lake,** you won't see anything remarkable. It's just a lake; it could be any lake. The sky and mountains are initially what capture your attention. As you ascend, however, the lake's reflected blue becomes almost unreal in its placidity. The fantastic depth of the lake (1932 ft.), combined with the fact that it is a closed system, creates its amazingly serene and intensely blue effect. 7700 years ago, Mt. Mazama created this pacificity by means of one of the Earth's most destructive cataclysms. A massive eruption buried thousands of square miles in the western U.S. under a thick layer of ash and left a deep crater to be filled with still waters.

Rim Drive, a route open only in summer, is 33 mi. high above the lake. Points along the drive offer views and trailheads for hiking. Among the most spectacular are **Discovery Point Trail,** from which the first pioneer saw the lake in 1853 (1.3 mi. one-way), **Garfield Peak Trail** (1.7 mi. one-way), and **Watchman Lookout** (.8 mi. one-way).

The hike up **Mt. Scott,** the park's highest peak (just a tad under 9000 ft.), begins from the drive near the lake's eastern edge. Although steep, the 2½-mi. trail to the top gives the persevering hiker a unique view of the lake that justifies the sweaty ascent. Steep **Cleetwood Trail,** a 1-mi. switchback, is the only route to the lake's edge. From here, the **Lodge Company** (594-2511) offers boat tours on the lake (July-Sept. 9 tours daily 10am-4:30pm; fare $10, under 12 $5.50). Both **Wizard Island,** a cinder cone 760 ft. above lake level, and **Phantom Ship Rock** are fragile, tiny specks when viewed from above, yet they are surprisingly large when viewed from the surface of the water. Picnics and fishing are allowed, as is swimming—but surface temperature reaches a maximum of only 50°. Six species of fish have been introduced artificially into the lake, but the water is too pure to support life; only two species have survived. Park rangers lead free walking tours daily in the summer and periodically during the winter (on snowshoes). Call the visitors center at Rim Village for schedules (see Practical Information).

If pressed for time, walk the easy 100 yd. from the visitors center down to the **Sinnott Memorial Overlook**—the view is the area's most panoramic and accessible. For a short lecture on the area's geology and history, attend one of the nightly ranger talks (held Aug.-Labor Day daily at 9pm in the Mazama Campground Amphitheater) or catch the 15-minute film at Rim Village Visitors Center.

The **Favell Museum,** 125 W. Main St. (882-9996), in Klamath just past U.S. 97, displays Native American artifacts, including a collection of 60,000 arrowheads, as well as paintings by premier Western artists (open Mon.-Sat. 9:30am-5:30pm; admission $4, seniors $3, ages 6-16 $1). The **Ross Rogland Theater,** 218 N. 7th (884-5483), puts on a variety of quality productions. Shows mostly start around 7:30pm; tickets span from $2-25 (box office open Mon.-Sat. 9am-3pm, later on show dates).

Each July 4th, Klamath Falls features **Horse and Buggy Days** downtown, and August brings **Tribal Treaty Days. Fort Klamath** (381-2230), 6 mi. south of Crater Lake Park, boasts a museum and park commemorating this frontier post established in 1863. You can visit the gravesites of Captain Jack and three of his Modoc warrior comrades who put up an heroic, if ultimately unsuccessful, resistance to Western settlers in the Modoc Indian War of 1872-73 (open June-Labor Day daily 10am-6pm).

■■■ BEND

Pioneers forded the Deschutes River at "Farewell Bend" in 1824, and in commemoration the city was named "Bend" when it was incorporated in 1905. Although Bend still has its share of river rafters whose vocabulary is limited to terms descriptive of a river's anatomy, the city has grown to become the state's largest urban population east of the Cascades (47,000) and offers more cultural, culinary, and athletic options than many of its neighbors. Bend is now a hub of central Oregon's highway system, where U.S. 97 and U.S. 20 intersect, and here you will find what the rest of eastern Oregon is missing: people, fast-food, traffic jams. The tourist industry, ignited by the commercialization of Mt. Bachelor, burns most brightly during the summer.

Bend experiences the best of both weather worlds: up to 100°F in summer and 60 in. of snow in the winter. Bordered by Mt. Bachelor, the Deschutes River, and a national forest, the city makes an ideal way station for hikers and bicyclists. The lofty peaks of the Cascades, snow-capped even in August, await you (and your skis) out of town to the west. But the city proper does offer at least one good reason for sticking around: the presence of many restaurants both good *and* cheap—an elusive combination in eastern central Oregon, or anywhere else.

PRACTICAL INFORMATION AND ORIENTATION

Visitors Information: Central Oregon Welcome Center, 63085 N. U.S. 97 (382-3221). Located in a spacious new building. Pick up the State Park Guide, Events Calendar, and free maps. Open Mon.-Sat. 9am-5pm, Sun. 11am-3pm.

Parks and Recreation Dept., 200 Pacific Park Ln. (389-7275). Information on everything about parks. Open Mon.-Fri. 8am-5pm.

Greyhound, 2045 E. U.S. 20 (382-2151), a few mi. east of town. 1 bus per day to: Portland ($20), Salem ($24), and Klamath Falls ($18). Open daily 7:30am-5:30pm and 9-10pm.

Transcentral Public Transportation, Inc., 2055 NE Division St. (382-0800 or 382-9371).

Taxi: Owl Taxi, 1917 NE 2nd St. (382-3311). 24 hr.

AAA, 20350 Empire Ave. (382-1303). Open Mon.-Fri. 8am-5pm. For AAA members.

Bicycle Rental: Hutch's Bicycles, 725 NW Columbia Ave. (382-9253). Mountain bikes $14 per day. **Sunnyside Sports,** 930 NW Newport (382-8018), on the way to the College. Mountain bikes $20 per day. Open Mon.-Fri. 9am-7pm, Sat. 8am-6pm, Sun. 8am-5pm.

Laundromat: Nelson's, 407 SE 3rd St. (388-2140). Wash $1, 12 min. dry 25¢. Open daily 6am-11pm.

Central Oregon Battering and Rape Alliance (COBRA): 800-356-2369.

Poison Control: 800-452-7165.

Hospital: St. Charles Medical Center, 2500 N.E. Neff Rd. (382-4321).

Police: 711 NW Bond (388-5550). **Fire:** 388-5533.

Post Office: 2300 NE 4th St. (388-1971), at Webster. Open Mon.-Fri. 8:30am-5pm. **General Delivery ZIP Code:** 97701.

Area Code: 503.

U.S. 97 (also called "3rd St." in Bend) bisects Bend. The downtown area lies to the west along the Deschutes River; Wall and Bond St. are the two main arteries.

ACCOMMODATIONS AND CAMPING

The cheapest motels are just outside town on 3rd St., but don't let the distance deter you; for a tourist town, the rates are surprisingly low. You can stay free at the campgrounds in the **Deschutes National Forest** (pronounced duh-SHOOTS), but tote your own water. Contact the **Deschutes National Forest Office,** 1230 NE 3rd St. (388-2715 or 388-5664), for details.

Bend Alpine Hostel (HI/AYH), 19 SW Century Dr., Bend 97702 (389-3813). From 3rd St., take Franklin (turns into Galveston) to Century Dr./14th St. and turn left; about 1 mi. from downtown. Within 2 blocks of ski, snow-board, and bike rentals, and also the free ski-shuttle to Mt. Bachelor. $12, nonmembers $15.

Holiday Motel, 880 SE 3rd St. (382-4620 or 800-252-0121). Small rooms with thin walls, but the folks are really friendly and the beds really comfortable. Really. Cable and A/C. Singles $30. Doubles $34.

Chalet Motel, 510 SE 3rd (382-6124). Clean, standard rooms, some with kitchens. Shaded grassy area outside is perfect for a picnic. Singles $28. Doubles $37.

Tumalo State Park (388-6055), 5 mi. northwest of town on U.S. 20. 88 sites along the Deschutes River, 20 with full hookup. Solar showers and flush toilets. Open May through the end of Sept. No reservations. Sites $14, with hookup $16.

Elk Lake Recreation Area, on Forest Service Road 46, 36 mi. from Bend in the national forest. 3 campgrounds offer 36 sites with pit toilets and drinking water. No phone. Open June-Sept. Sites $4-10.

Bend KOA Kampground, 63615 N. U.S. 97 (382-7728), 2 mi. north of Bend. Typical KOA, meaning game room, laundry, etc. Reserve 4 weeks ahead July-Aug. Sites $16, with hookup $20.

FOOD

Restaurants in Bend generally maintain high standards. While the downtown offers a host of pleasant cafes, 3rd St. also has a number of decent eateries. Not less than four mega-markets line the east side of 3rd St.—for example the 24-hour **Safeway,** 642 NE 3rd (382-7341). **Nature's General Store** (382-6732) in the Wagner Mall on 3rd St. has bulk food, organic produce, and healthy sandwiches ($3; open Mon.-Fri. 9:30am-9pm, Sat. 9:30am-6pm, Sun. 11am-6pm).

Rolaine's Cantina, 785 SE 3rd St. (382-4944), across from Albertson's. Mexican specials of almost frighteningly large portions. Try the vegetarian *burrito rolaine* ($6.25), and garnish it with gobs of "killer" salsa (available upon request). The non-vegetarian lunch buffet includes a free margarita ($4.75). Wheelchair access. Open Mon.-Fri. 11:30am-10pm, Sat. noon-10pm, Sun. noon-9pm.

Sargent's Cafe, 719 SE 3rd St. (382-3916). A crowded, friendly diner with abundant portions. One pancake ($1.50) is a full meal. All-you-can-eat spaghetti plate $5.50. Wheelchair access. Open daily 5:30am-9:30pm.

Deschutes Brewery and Public House, 1044 NW Bond St. (382-4242). Tasty food and home-brewed beer. Daily specials $6-7. Pint of ale, bitters, or stout brewed on the premises $2. Homemade root beer $1.50. Spirited dancing with a live band out back on random weekend nights. The bar does not permit smoking. Wheelchair access. Open Mon.-Thurs. 11am-11:30pm, Fri.-Sat. 11am-12:30am, Sun. noon-10pm. Minors not allowed after 8:30pm.

Goody's, 975 NW Wall St. (389-5185). Yummy ice cream cones ($1); try coffee bean in a homemade dish ($1.40). Open Mon.-Sat. 10am-10pm, Sun. noon-10pm.

SIGHTS AND ACTIVITIES

Six mi. south of Bend on U.S. 97, the **High Desert Museum** (382-4754) shines as one of central Oregon's cultural gems, offering exhibits on the fragile ecosystem of the Oregon plateau, realistic and audio-visual exhibitions of the West in days past and refreshing temporary exhibitions, such as one on the history of Japanese-American women from 1885 to the present. A new wing opened in 1991 with a "Desertarium," where seldom-seen animals like burrowing ants and colored lizards are presented in a simulated desert habitat. Lack of funding has kept the price of admission high, but definitely worth it (open daily 9am-5pm; admission $5.50, senior citizens $5, ages 6-12 $2.75).

Five mi. farther south on U.S. 97 is **Lava Butte,** which resembles Pilot Butte in height, geology, and its view of the Cascades. The **Lava Lands Visitor Center** (593-2421), at the base of the butte, offers a shuttle ($1.50) to the top. If you hike up, remember there will be no "rock throwing or any of that monkey business" (open March to mid-Oct. daily 10am-4pm). The **Lava River Caves,** 1 mi. farther south on U.S. 97, were formed by ancient lava flow from the nearby volcanoes. Guarded by interminable brambles of juniper bushes, the caves are a welcome change of scenery (and temperature—bring a sweater along). A self-guided 1.2-mi. tour (each way) affords you your own look. (Open mid-April to late Sept. daily 9am-6pm. Admission $1.50, ages 13-17 $1, under 13 free. Lantern rental $1.50.)

West of Bend, **Century Drive** (Cascade Lakes Hwy.—take 3rd to Division North, and follow the signs) makes a dramatic 89-mi. loop over Mt. Bachelor, through the forest, and past the Crane Prairie Reservoir before rejoining U.S. 97. Thirty campgrounds, fishing areas, and hiking trails pockmark the countryside. Allow a full day for the spectacular drive, and pack a picnic lunch. (Drive open Memorial Day to snow-in, usually in Oct.)

If you can ski the 9075-ft. **Mt. Bachelor,** with its 3100-ft. vertical drop, you're in good company; Mt. Bachelor is the home mountain of the U.S. Ski Team. (Daily lift passes $31, ages 7-12 $14.50. Many nearby lodges offer 5-night ski packages. Call 800-800-8334 or 382-8334. For general information call 800-829-2442; for ski report and summer events call 382-7888.) The ski season often extends into the first week of July. Ticket prices rise and fall in proportion to the number of trails open. From Christmas through Easter, free morning and afternoon shuttlebus service is offered for the 22 mi. between the Mt. Bachelor corporate office (in Bend) and the West Village Guest Services Building at the mountain. Chairlifts are open for sightseers during the summer (open 10am-4pm; $8.50, kids $4, senior citizens $6).

Deschutes National Forest has information on the Deschutes mountain bike trail system (388-5664). **Newberry Crater,** 22 mi. south of Bend on U.S. 97, was formed by Oregon's largest ice-age volcano (encompassing 500 sq. mi.). It contains Paulina Lake and East Lake, which offer limitless forms of fishing and water recreation. **The Three Sisters Wilderness Area** can also be explored on a mountain bike or on horseback. Try **Thousand Trails Stables at Bend,** 15 mi. south of Bend at 17480 S. Century Drive (593-6636; 1-hr. ride $17; call 923-2072 for reservations). **Nora Stables** is another option, at Inn of the Seventh Mountain (389-9458; 1-hr. ride $15).

White water rafting, although costly, is the number one local recreational activity. Most resorts offer half- to three-day whitewater rafting expeditions, and most companies will pick you up in town. Trips usually run around $65 per person per day. **Hunter Expeditions** (389-8370), **Bend White Water Supply** (389-7191), and **Sun Country Tours** (593-2161) also offer half-day rides for around $25.

■ Prineville

Located at the junction of U.S. 26 and U.S. 126, about 40 mi. northeast of Bend, the quiet, slow-paced town of Prineville claims about 5315 residents (up from 5000 last year—boom!), which makes it a virtual metropolis compared to the majority of towns in eastern Oregon. And if ever there was such a thing as a backwoods-alternative-life-style-red-meat-eatin'-liberal-flannel-shirt-mecca, this is it. **The Prineville-Crook County Chamber of Commerce,** 390 N. Fairview (447-6304), leaves brochures on the porch after hours (open Mon.-Fri. 9am-noon and 1-5pm).

The vast wilderness surrounding Prineville supplies ample opportunities for skiing, hiking, fishing, and, of course, **digging.** Rockhounds come from all over in search of agates, jasper, petrified wood, and other unusual stones. Free and commercial digs abound; ask the Chamber of Commerce where to plant your shovel.

Only during the **Rockhound Pow-Wow** (447-5564), a digging festival in mid-June, and the **Crooked River Roundup** (447-4479), a rough-and-tumble rodeo in mid-July, does Prineville regain the pep and spunk of yesteryear. During the Roundup, the usual rodeo business follows a town parade, and nearly everyone gets involved in a game of cops-and-robbers in a staged bank robbery.

Ochoco Lake State Park, 7 mi. east of Prineville on U.S. 26, offers gorgeous picnic sites and a refreshing lake for swimming and boating. Primitive campsites with flush toilets and water are also available ($9). Ten mi. farther along U.S. 26, **Prineville Reservoir State Park** provides similar outdoor opportunities, plus improved campsites ($11, full hookups $13) and showers.

Near the spot where Rte. 126 merges with U.S. 20 and splits off to Prineville sits **Sisters,** a charming, restored western village that is an important supply station for backpackers on the Pacific Crest Trail. If you're staying overnight, try the **Sisters**

Motor Lodge, 600 W. Cascade (549-2551), which has rooms from $36-43. The **Sisters Bakery,** 120 E. Cascade (549-0361), serves up delectable treats including maple-covered "pinecones" ($1). One of the largest festivals in the area is the **Sisters Rodeo** (549-0121), held during the second weekend in June (tickets $10). Stop at the **Sisters Ranger Station** (549-2111), on the highway at the west end of town, for directions to the campgrounds around town. **Lava Camp Lake** is a magnificently isolated free campsite located in the lava fields about 20 mi. out of Sisters on the Forest Service byway. For additional information on the area, contact the **Chamber of Commerce,** 151 N. Spruce St. (549-0251; open Mon.-Sat. 10am-4pm, Sun. 11am-4pm).

South of Sisters, U.S. 20 continues along the edge of the **Deschutes National Forest,** which extends south almost to Crater Lake. The forest features five wilderness areas, a string of fishing lakes, a handful of canoeing rivers, and a top-notch ski resort on Mt. Bachelor. Visitors may camp for free at a number of primitive sites in the forest. The **Deschutes National Forest Office,** 1230 NE 3rd St. (388-2715), in Bend, administers the area (open Mon.-Fri. 7:45am-4:30pm).

■ John Day Fossil Beds National Monument

Eastern Oregon wasn't always a barren desert wasteland. As the John Day Fossil Beds National Monument records the history of life well before the Cascades Range was formed, it describes a land of lush, tropical vegetation and ambling dinosaurs. The Park exists in three parts, each representing a different epoch. **Clarno,** the oldest, is located on Rte. 218 (accessible by Rte. 97 to the west and Rte. 19 to the east), 20 mi. west of Fossil. Leave the developed area and be humbled as you confront the embarrassing insignificance of our species in the grand geological scheme—mere tadpoles in the Great Lake of time. And watch out for snakes. **Painted Hills,** 3 mi. east of Mitchel off U.S. 26, focuses on an epoch circa 30 million BC when the land was in transition. The ½-mi. trail to the overlook give a hawk's perspective sure to induce a "wow," especially at dawn or after a rain, when the whole gorge glistens. **Sheep Rock,** 25 mi. west of Mitchel and 5 mi. east of Dayville at the U.S. 26-Rte. 19 junction, houses the monument's **visitors center** and will satiate all angry demands for concrete fossils—i.e., ones you can see and touch. The **Sheep Rock Overlook,** up the hill, offers a view of the fossil rich valley. (All 3 units keep the same hours: open daily 8:30am-6pm, Sept.-Nov. daily 8:30am-5pm, Dec.-Feb. daily Mon.-Fri. 8:30am-5pm.) The **Parks Department,** 420 W. Main St., John Day (575-0271), will also field fossil questions (open Mon.-Fri. 8am-4:30pm).

The **Grant County Visitors Information Center** (575-0547), on Main St. just west of John Day, overflows with information on Oregon in general (open Mon.-Fri. 9am-5pm). For more area-specific facts, try the **Malheur National Forest ranger station** (575-1731) on the eastern edge of town at 139 NE Dayton (open Mon.-Fri. 7:15am-5pm), or the Parks Department.

The **Gold Country Motel,** 250 E. Main (575-2100) has large, attractive rooms with HBO on the tube (singles from $38, doubles from $45). Seven mi. west of John Day on U.S. 26, **Clyde Holliday State Park** (575-2773) offers 30 campsites with electricity and showers ($13). For hearty, basic fare, tap into the **Mother Lode Restaurant,** 241 W. Main (575-2714). Sandwiches $4.50-6. A special menu offers selections for seniors (open daily 5am-9pm; in winter daily 5am-8pm).

In John Day itself, the **Kam Wah Chung and Co. Museum,** on Canton St. near City Park, showcases the personal possessions that Chinese immigrants brought with them to Grant County during the 1862 Gold Rush. The highlight is a large collection of herbal medicines. The building itself, once the community center of Chinese miners in eastern Oregon, dates back to the 1860s. (Open May 1-Oct. 31 Mon.-Thurs. 9am-noon and 1-5pm, Sat.-Sun. 1-5pm. Admission $2, senior citizens $1.50, ages 13-17 $1, under 12 50¢.)

During hunting season (Sept.-Nov.), the whole of John Day heads for the hills of the **Malheur National Forest** (pronounced mal-HERE). The ranger station in town knows next to nothing about licenses to kill black bears, bighorn sheep, mule deer, salmon, steelhead, and trout; if you want to hunt, you can obtain licenses at several local stores. Camp wherever you please in the forest—except, of course, near "no trespassing" signs. Some areas in the forest have cantilever toilets and drinkable water. **Magone Lake** is one of the forest's most popular campgrounds, and the only one with a user fee ($3). The more adventurous might check out the two government-regulated wilderness areas, **Strawberry Mountain** and **Monument Rock.** Get maps and guidance from the ranger station (above) before venturing out.

Or, raft down the rippling waters and rapids of the John Day River. Inflatable kayaks for one to two people are available for $20 per day at **John Day River Outfitters** (575-2386) which also organizes two- to five-day trips.

■ Hells Canyon National Recreation Area

"The government bet you 160 acres that you couldn't live there three years without starving to death," said one early white settler of the region. Hells Canyon's endearing name comes from its legendary inaccessibility and hostility toward human inhabitants. It is North America's deepest gorge: in some places the walls drop 6000 ft. to **Snake River** below. The fault and fold lines in the canyon walls make the cliffs seem to melt with their great wrinkles of grass and rock.

Accessing the area without four wheels or a horse is difficult—hitchhiking can get one in from the gateway towns of Joseph or Halfway, and talking it up with people at campsites can get one out. The **Area Headquarters** (208-628-3916 or 426-4978) is at 88401 Rte. 82, on the West side of Enterprise. This is a good place to start, for the rangers can provide extensive practical information on the area and tips on the best things to see. Detailed maps are well worth the $3 price (open Mon.-Sat. 7:30am-5pm; Sun. 10am-5pm).

Camping in the region can be a spiritual experience for those who have made adequate preparations. You should stock up on food, drinking water, and gas before leaving civilization—and keep in mind that there are no showers or flush toilets anywhere, and little drinking water. If you plan to hike down into the canyon, insect repellent is a must. Because of adverse road conditions, most campsites are only open from July to September. **Copperfield Park,** with 132 sites (a few of them developed) at the southern end of the Snake River by the Oxbow Dam, is the only campsite open all year and also accessed by a paved road. From Halfway, take Rte. 86 to Snake River.

A number of campsites line the lower Imnaha River along Forest Roads 3980 (dirt) and 3965 (dirt)—both are accessible from Rte. 39 (also dirt) and, for those in need of immediate sightseeing gratification, both allow easy access to the **Hell's Canyon Overlook** on F.R. 3965. Those wishing to descend into the canyon could make base camp at **Hat Point Overlook,** about a two-hour drive (24 mi.) from Imnaha (from Joseph, take 350 to Imnaha, then F.R. 4240 to 315—very rough but still negotiable dirt roads). Campsites have self-registration kiosks, although you should let someone know you're going in for emergency purposes. **Campfires** are illegal from July to September, and in all other months can only be made in a metal pan up to within ¼ mi. of Snake River. No permit is required for either camp or fire.

The Forest Service offers more than 1000 mi. of **hiking trails,** most of which are unmarked. Be sure to bring compass and map (which can be purchased at the area center, see above), and definitely use only established trails to descend into the canyon (several trailheads are at Hat Point Overlook, see above). Those on horseback should receive special instruction at the Area Headquarters.

The town of **Halfway** is home to a few comfy motels including **Halfway Motel,** 170 S. Main St. (742-5722), which has singles for $30 and doubles for $40. Halfway is also home to a number of recreational outfits. **Wallowa Llamas,** Rte. 1, Box 84, Halfway 97834 (742-4930), offers several different trips through the Wallowa mountains and into Hells Canyon. Tents, meals, and llamas are supplied—you provide sleeping bags, stamina, and $225-600. A panoply of both jet boat and raft trips for fishing and exploring historical sights are available for those willing to shell out $65-120 per person per day. Although costly, this may be the most exciting hassle-free way to explore the canyon. Make reservations ahead of time. **Hells Canyon Adventures** offers the most varied options and a toll-free number (800-422-3568).

■■■ PENDLETON

Typical of Eastern Oregon's small towns, Pendleton offers little more than a quiet night's sleep for the weary traveler. During the day porch swings are actually used here, and lawn care seems to be the primary recreation. At night, teens and wanna-bes slowly cruise the streets in goosed-up muscle cars, careful not to make too much noise, 'cause everybody knows everybody.

PRACTICAL INFORMATION AND ORIENTATION

Visitors Information: Pendleton Chamber of Commerce, 25 SE Dorion Ave. (276-7411 or 800-547-8911, in OR 800-452-9403). Open Mon.-Fri. 9am-5pm, Sat. in summer 9am-2pm.

Greyhound, 320 SW Court Ave. (276-1551), a few blocks west of the city center. To: Portland (2 per day, $27); Boise, ID (2 per day, $35.50). Open Mon-Sat. 8am-noon and 1-5pm.

Car Rental: Ugly Duckling Rent-A-Car, 309 SW Emigrant Ave. (276-1498). The only way to enjoy the Blue or Wallowa Mts. without your own car. $20 per day plus 20¢ per mi. Credit card required. Must be over 21. Open Mon.-Fri. 8am-5pm, Sat. 8am-noon.

Hospital: St. Anthony's, 1601 SE Court Ave. (276-5121).

Emergency: 911. **Police:** 109 SW Court Ave. (276-4411). **Fire:** 276-1442.

Post Office: Federal Building, 104 SW Dorion Ave. (278-0203), at SW 1st. Open Mon.-Fri. 9am-5pm, Sat. 10am-1pm. **General Delivery ZIP Code:** 97801.

Area Code: 503.

Pendleton is at the junction of I-84 and OR Rte. 11, just south of the Washington border, roughly equidistant (200-230 mi.) from Portland, Spokane, and Boise. **Raley Park,** right next to the Round-Up Grounds, is the spiritual center of town, while Main Street is the geographic hub.

Pendleton's street design is very peculiar. The city has many streets (running east to west) which are named with startling originality—1st St., 2nd St., and so on. Unfortunately, the planners of the town were so pickled with their creativity they decided to use the names again. Consequently, there are *two* 1st Streets, one SE and one SW, *two* 2nd Streets, etc., which are parallel to each other. Go figure.

ACCOMMODATIONS AND CAMPING

During most of the year, lodging in Pendleton is inexpensive. To stay here during the Round-Up, however, you must reserve rooms six months in advance. Rates double, and prices on everything from hamburgers to commemorative cowboy hats are jacked up. Pendleton has no camping areas nearby. For more information on camping in the region, contact **Parks Information,** 800-452-5687.

Longhorn Motel, 411 SW Dorion Ave. (276-7531), around the corner from the bus station. Don't let the scruffy exterior deter you—these are the nicest cheap rooms in downtown Pendleton. Back rooms have HBO, and wheelchair access. Singles $24. Doubles $30 ($32 for twin beds).

Pioneer Motel, 1807 SE Court Pl. (276-4521), just off Rte. 11. Large pleasant rooms. Singles $22. Doubles $25.

Motel 6, 325 SE Nye Ave. (276-3160), on the south side of town. Not in the middle of things, but easy access to I-84. Cable TV, A/C, and heated pool. Singles $26. Doubles $32.

Emigrant Springs State Park, 26 mi. southeast of Pendleton on I-84. The best campground within 50 mi. Numerous sites (and hot showers) in a shady grove of ponderosa pines (see Sights and Activities). Sites $12, with hookup $14.

FOOD

Vegetarians will have more luck grazing in the outlying wheat fields than selecting from the restaurant menus. This is steak country.

Bread Board, 141 S. Main St. (276-4520). Great $2-4 sandwiches and $1 cinnamon rolls in a friendly atmosphere, with national newspapers strewn about. Try the ham, egg, and cheese croissant for breakfast ($2.75). Open Mon.-Fri. 8am-3pm.

The Circle S, 210 SE 5th St. (276-9637). Don't let the 3-ft. axe door handle scare you away from this great Western barbecue restaurant. Drink beverages from Mason jars while you enjoy a teriyaki burger and fries ($4.75) and a *creme de menthe* sundae ($1.75). If you can eat the 72-oz. sirloin ($45) in an hour, like John Candy in *The Great Outdoors,* it's free (weekdays, before 8pm). Smaller portions also available. Open Tues.-Sat. 7am-10pm, Sun. 7am-3pm.

Rainbow Cafe, 209 S. Main St. (276-4120). Where the cowboys chow down. Classic American bar-*cum*-diner with rodeo decor. Good, hearty food. Burger and beer $3-4. Open daily 6am-2:30am.

SIGHTS AND ACTIVITIES

The **Pendleton Round-Up** (276-2553 or 800-524-2984), a premier event on the nation's rodeo circuit, draws ranchers from all over the U.S. for "four glorious days and nights" in the second full week of September. Steer-roping, saddle-bronco riding, bulldogging, and bareback riding are featured, not to mention non-equine attractions such as buffalo-chip tosses, quick draws, and greased pig chases. For information or tickets ($6-12), write to the Pendleton Round-Up Association, P.O. Box 609, Pendleton 97801. The **Round-Up Hall of Fame** (276-2553), under the South Grandstand area at SW Court Ave. and SW 13th St., gives tours by appointment during the week. The hall has captured some of the rodeo's action for all eternity, including Pendleton's best preserved Round-Up hero, a stuffed horse named "War Paint." Lifetime memberships only $100.

Unless you have some special interest in wool you may want to bag the hyper-hyped tour of the **Pendleton Woolen Mills,** 1307 SE Court Ave. (276-6911; tours given Mon.-Fri. at 9am, 11am, 1:30pm, and 3pm; open Mon.-Fri. 8am-4:45pm, Sat. 8am-2pm; Oct.-April Mon.-Fri. 8am-4:45pm, Sat. 9am-1pm; free).

A newer tourist attraction is the **Pendleton Underground Tours,** 37 SW Emigrant St. (276-0730). A hammed-up and fun look at the wild days of yesteryear, the tour examines the tunnels used by Chinese railroad workers and features stops at the Shamrock Cardrooms and the Cozy Rooms Bordello. Learn about the "amethyst" glass in the sidewalks and the mysterious shaking "no parking" sign on Main St. Two different 45-min. tours are offered: Tour I (the underground) continues into Tour II (the Cozy Rooms and jail). Splurge and take both tours ($5 each). Tour times vary widely so call ahead (office hours Mon.-Sat. 8am-5pm).

APPENDIX

■■■ TELEPHONES

Operator: 0
Local Directory Assistance: 411
Long-Distance Directory Assistance: 0 or 1-(area code)-555-1212

■ International Calls

You can place international calls from any telephone. To call direct, dial the universal international access code (011) followed the country code, the city code, and the local number. Country codes and city codes may sometimes be listed with a zero in front (e.g. 033), but when using 011, drop succeeding zeros (e.g., 011-33). In some areas you will have to give the operator the number and he or she will place the call.

Country Codes
   United Kingdom: 44
   Ireland: 353
   Australia: 61
   New Zealand: 64
   South Africa: 27

■■■ TIME

U.S. residents tell time on the Latinate 12-hour, not 24-hour, clock. Hours after noon are *post meridiem* or pm (e.g. 2pm); hours before noon are *ante meridiem* or am (e.g. 2am). Noon is sometimes referred to as 12pm and midnight as 12am (though purists object to these denotations); *Let's Go* uses "noon" and "midnight." The Continental U.S. is divided into four time zones: Eastern, Central, Mountain and Pacific. Hawaii and Alaska claim their own time zones as well. When it's noon Eastern standard time (EST), it's 11am Central, 10am Mountain, 9am Pacific, 8am Alaskan and 7am Hawaiian-Aleutian. Most states advance their clocks by one hour for daylight saving time. In 1994, daylight saving time will begin on Sunday, April 3 at 2am. It will end on Sunday, Oct. 30 at 2am; then, set your clocks back one hour to 1am.

   The four Continental time zones are also found in Canada. Daylight Saving Time exists everywhere in Canada, with the exceptions of Saskatchewan and northeastern British Columbia. Canadians—especially residents of Quebec—use the 24-hour clock much more often than their neighbors to the south.

■■■ HOLIDAYS

As the federal government is not empowered to designate holidays for the nation, the U.S. technically does not have any national holidays. But since states almost invariably adopt the holidays that the feds declare for DC (over which they do, of course, have jurisdiction), holidays in this country are nearly standardized. The legal public holidays appearing in the following list are celebrated in both the U.S. and Canada unless otherwise noted.

New Year's Day: Sat., Jan.1
Martin Luther King, Jr., Day: Mon., Jan.17 (U.S.)
Presidents Day (also called Washington-Lincoln Day and Washington's Birthday): Mon., Feb.21 (U.S.)
Good Friday: Friday, April 1

Easter Monday: Mon., April 4 (Canada)
Victoria Day: Mon., May 23 (Canada)
Memorial Day (also called Decoration Day): Mon., May 30 (U.S.)
Canada Day: Fri., July 1 (Canada)
Independence Day: Mon., July 4 (U.S.)
British Columbia Day: Mon., Aug. 1 (BC)
Provincial Civic Holiday: Mon., Aug. 1 (Ont., Man., NWT)
Discovery Day: Mon., Aug. 15 (YT)
Labor Day: Mon., Sept.5
Columbus Day (observed): Mon., Oct.10 (U.S.)
Thanksgiving: Mon., Oct.10 (Canada)
Election Day: Tues., Nov. 8
Veterans Day: Fri., Nov. 11 (U.S.)
Remembrance Day: Fri., Nov. 11 (Canada)
Thanksgiving: Thurs., Nov. 24 (U.S.)
Christmas Day: Sun., Dec. 25

■■■ MEASUREMENTS

Although the metric system has made considerable inroads into American business and science, the British system of weights and measures continues to prevail in the U.S. The following is a list of U.S. units and their metric equivalents:

1 inch (in.) =25.4 millimeters (mL)
1 foot (ft.) = 0.30 meter (m)
1 yard (yd.) = 0.91 meter (m)
1 mile (mi.) = 1.61 kilometers (km)
1 ounce (oz.; mass) = 28.35 grams (g)
1 pound (lb.) = 0.45 kilogram (kg)
1 liquid quart (qt.) = 0.95 liter (L)

Here are the comparative values of some U.S. units of measurement:

1 foot = 12 inches
1 yard = 3 feet
1 mile = 5280 feet
1 pound = 16 ounces (weight)
1 cup = 8 ounces (volume)
1 pint = 2 cups
1 quart = 2 pints
1 gallon = 4 quarts

It should be noted that gallons in the U.S. are not identical to those across the Atlantic; one U.S. gallon equals 0.83 Imperial gallons. **Electric outlets** throughout the U.S., Canada, and Mexico provide current at 117 volts, 60 cycles (Hertz) and American plugs usually have 2 rectangular prongs; plugs for larger appliances often have a third prong for the purpose of grounding. Appliances designed for the European electrical system (220 volts) will not operate without a transformer and a plug adapter (this includes electric systems for disinfecting contact lenses). Transformers are sold to convert specific wattages (e.g. 0-50 watt transformers for razors and radios; larger watt transformers for hair dryers and other appliances).

The U.S. uses the Fahrenheit **temperature scale.** To convert Fahrenheit to Centigrade temperatures, subtract 32, then multiply by 5/9. To convert from Centigrade to Fahrenheit, multiply by 9/5 and then add 32. Or, just remember that 32° is the freezing point of water, 212° its boiling point, normal human body temperature is 98.6°, and room temperature hovers around 70°.

INDEX